MARKETING
An Introduction

fifth edition

MARKETING

An Introduction

Gary Armstrong
University of North Carolina

Philip Kotler
Northwestern University

Prentice Hall, Upper Saddle River, New Jersey 07458

Acquisitions Editor: Whitney Blake
Assistant Editor: John Larkin
Editorial Assistant: Michele Foresta
Editor-in-Chief: Natalle Anderson
Managing Editor (editorial): Bruce Kaplan
Marketing Manager: Shannon Moore
Production Editor: Michelle Rich
Associate Managing Editor: John Roberts
Manufacturing Buyer: Ken Clinton
Manufacturing Supervisor: Arnold Vila
Manufacturing Manager: Vincent Scelta
Designer: Kevin Kall
Design Manager: Patricia Smythe
Interior Design: Digitext, Inc.
Photo Research Supervisor: Melinda Lee Reo
Image Permission Supervisor: Kay Dellosa
Photo Researcher: Melinda Alexander
Cover Design: Michael J. Frohbeis
Illustrator (Interior): Progressive Information Technologies
Cover Illustration/Photo: Digital Stock
Composition: Progressive Information Technologies

Library of Congress Cataloging-in-Publication Data
Armstrong, Gary.
    Marketing : an introduction / Gary Armstrong, Philip Kotler.—
5th ed.
     p. cm.
    Kotler's name appears first on the earlier ed.
    Includes bibliographical references and indexes.
    ISBN 0-13-012771-X
    1. Marketing.   I. Kotler, Philip.   II. Title.
HF5415.K625   1999
658.8—dc21
                                               99-35215
                                                 CIP

Prentice-Hall International (UK) Limited, London
Prentice-Hall of Australia Pty. Limited, Sydney
Prentice-Hall Canada, Inc., Toronto
Prentice-Hall Hispanoamericana, S.A., Mexico
Prentice-Hall of India Private Limited, New Delhi
Prentice-Hall of Japan, Inc., Tokyo
Pearson Education Asia Pte. Ltd., Singapore
Editora Prentice-Hall do Brasil, Ltda., Rio de Janeiro

Printed in the United States of America

10 9 8 7 6 5

To Kathy, K.C., and Mandy;
Nancy, Amy, Melissa, and Jessica

Brief Contents

Understanding Marketing and the Marketing Management Process

Analyzing Marketing Opportunities

Developing Marketing Strategy and the Marketing Mix

Extending Marketing

Appendices

Contents

Analyzing Marketing Opportunities

Developing Marketing Strategy and the Marketing Mix

PART IV   Extending Marketing

About the Authors

As a team, Gary Armstrong and Philip Kotler provide a blend of skills uniquely suited to writing an introductory marketing text. Professor Armstrong is an award-winning teacher of undergraduate business students. Professor Kotler is one of the world's leading authorities on marketing. Together they make the complex world of marketing practical, approachable, and enjoyable.

Gary Armstrong is Crist W. Blackwell Distinguished Professor of Undergraduate Education in the Kenan-Flagler Business School at the University of North Carolina at Chapel Hill. He holds undergraduate and master's degrees in business from Wayne State University in Detroit, and he received his Ph.D. in marketing from Northwestern University. Dr. Armstrong has contributed numerous articles to leading business journals. As a consultant and researcher, he has worked with many companies on marketing research, sales management, and marketing strategy. But Professor Armstrong's first love is teaching. His Blackwell Distinguished Professorship is the only permanent endowed professorship for distinguished undergraduate teaching at the University of North Carolina at Chapel Hill. He has been very active in the teaching and administration of Kenan-Flagler's undergraduate program. His recent administrative posts include Chair of the Marketing Faculty, Associate Director of the Undergraduate Business Program, Director of the Business Honors Program, and others. He works closely with business student groups and has received several campus-wide and Business School teaching awards. He is the only repeat recipient of the school's highly regarded Award for Excellence in Undergraduate Teaching, which he has received three times.

Philip Kotler is S. C. Johnson & Son Distinguished Professor of International Marketing at the Kellogg Graduate School of Management, Northwestern University. He received his master's degree at the University of Chicago and his Ph.D. at M.I.T., both in economics. Dr. Kotler is author of *Marketing Management: Analysis, Planning, Implementation, and Control* (Prentice-Hall), now in its tenth edition and the world's most widely used marketing textbook in graduate schools of business. He has authored several other successful books and has written over 100 articles for leading journals. He is the only three-time winner of the coveted Alpha Kappa Psi award for the best annual article in the *Journal of Marketing*. Dr. Kotler's numerous major honors include the *Paul D. Converse Award* given by the American Marketing Association to honor "outstanding contributions to science in marketing" and the *Stuart Henderson Britt Award* as Marketer of the Year. He was named the first recipient of two major awards: the *Distinguished Marketing Educator of the Year Award* given by the American Marketing Association and the *Philip Kotler Award for Excellence in Health Care Marketing* presented by the Academy for Health Care Services Marketing. He has also received the *Charles Coolidge Parlin Award*, which each year honors an outstanding leader in the field of marketing. In 1995, he received the *Marketing Educator of the Year Award* from Sales and Marketing Executives International. Dr. Kotler has served as chairman of the College on Marketing of the Institute of Management Sciences (TIMS) and a director of the American Marketing Association. He has received honorary doctorate degrees from DePaul University, the University of Zurich, and the Athens University of Economics and Business. He has consulted with many major U.S. and foreign companies on marketing strategy.

Preface

Marketing: An Introduction, fifth edition, takes an exciting new direction in its quest to guide new marketing students down the intriguing, discovery-laden road to learning marketing. As in previous editions, the goal remains to help students master the basic concepts and practices of modern marketing in an enjoyable and practical way. And, as before, achieving this goal involves a constant search for the best balance among the "three pillars" that support the text—theories and concepts, practices and applications, and pedagogy. In the fifth edition, however, we swing that balance whole-heartedly toward *pedagogy*—toward improving the effectiveness of *Marketing: An Introduction* as a *teaching* and *learning tool.*

This exciting new teaching and learning thrust comes to life through a shorter, livelier design that features a new set of *Road to Marketing* learning aids that help to guide beginning students in their marketing journey. These new "road map" learning tools appear at the beginning, within, and at the end of each chapter, helping students to learn, link, and apply important marketing concepts more effectively. Students are challenged to stop and think at important junctures in their journey, to review and link key chapter concepts, and to apply newly-learned marketing concepts in practical Internet applications and in realistic situations.

Marketing: An Introduction—A New Learning Approach

Our goal with the fifth edition of *Marketing: An Introduction* is to create a more effective teaching and learning environment. Most students learning marketing want a broad picture of marketing's basics. They want to know about important marketing principles and concepts and how these concepts are applied in actual marketing management practice. However, they don't want to drown in a sea of details, or to be overwhelmed by marketing's nuances and complexities. Instead, they want a text that guides them effectively and efficiently down the road to learning marketing in an easy to grasp, lively, and enjoyable way.

Marketing: An Introduction, fifth edition, serves all of these important needs of beginning marketing students. The book is complete, covering all of the important principles and concepts that the marketer and consumer need to know. Moreover, it takes a practical, marketing-management approach—concepts are applied through countless examples of situations in which well-known and little-known companies assess and solve their marketing problems.

Marketing: An Introduction, fifth edition, tells the stories that reveal the drama of modern marketing: Ritz-Carlton's zeal for taking care of customers; Home Depot's penchant for taking care of those who take care of customers; Nike's fight to redefine its relationships by learning how to be both big *and* beautiful; Harley-Davidson's success in selling to "Rubbies" (rich urban bikers) rather than rebels; Pillsbury's use of the Internet to build customer relationships; Caterpillar's and its dealers' promise to customers of "buy the iron, get the company;" the National Basketball Association's global marketing prowess; Ben & Jerry's difficulties in pursuing "caring capitalism" as it aims to do *good* while also doing *well*; Dell Computer's stunning direct selling formula, which has made Michael Dell one of the world's richest people; and Volkswagen's attempt to surf today's massive nostalgia wave by introducing the New Beetle, a car that "represents our romantic past but reinvented for our hectic here-and-now." These and dozens of other examples and illustrations throughout each chapter reinforce key concepts and bring marketing to life.

More than ever before, however, the fifth edition of *Marketing: An Introduction* makes the teaching and learning of marketing easier, more effective, and more enjoyable. The new *Road to Marketing* aids help students to learn, link, and apply important concepts. These new learning aids can be found throughout each chapter and include the following:

- *Road Map: Previewing the Concepts* sections, at the beginning of each chapter, briefly preview chapter concepts, link them with previous chapter concepts, outline chapter learning objectives, and introduce the chapter-opening real-world example.
- *Speed Bump: Linking the Concepts* sections are "concept checks" inserted at key points in each chapter as "speed bumps" to slow students down to make sure they grasp and apply key concepts and linkages. Each speed bump consists of a brief statement and several concept and application questions.
- *Rest Stop: Reviewing the Concepts* sections at the end of each chapter review chapter concepts and summarize each chapter objective.
- *Navigating the Key Terms* sections list the chapter's key terms; an accompanying Web page reviews the meaning and importance of each term.
- *Travel Log* sections include concept checks to test students understanding of basic concepts, and discussion questions to apply chapter ideas.
- *Traveling the Net* application exercises guide students through the fascinating real world of marketing and the Internet.
- *MAP—Marketing Applications* include interesting case histories, real-life situations, or timely descriptions of business situations to put students in the role of a marketing manager making real marketing decisions.

There is more. The fifth edition's shorter length makes it more manageable for beginning marketing students to cover during a given quarter or semester. Its approachable writing style and level are well suited to the beginning marketing student. A livelier design and the abundant use of illustrations, Marketing at Work exhibits, and video cases help bring life to the marketing journey.

Together, this focus on basic concepts, lively and realistic examples and applications, and innovative learning aids makes *Marketing: An Introduction* the most effective teaching and learning tool available today.

Content Changes in the Fifth Edition

The fifth edition of *Marketing: An Introduction* offers important improvements in content and organization.

The revision further enhances a number of major marketing themes, including:

- *Delivering superior customer value, satisfaction, and quality*—market-centered strategy and "taking care of the customer."
- *Relationship marketing*—keeping customers and capturing *customer lifetime value* by building value-laden customer relationships.

- *Marketing technologies*—the Internet and other information and communications technologies that are revolutionizing the ways companies deliver customer value.
- *Total marketing quality*—the importance of customer-driven, total quality as a means of delivering total customer satisfaction.
- *Value-delivery networks*—cross-functional teamwork within companies and cross-company, supply-chain partnerships to create effective customer value-delivery systems.
- *Global marketing*—chapter-by-chapter, integrated coverage plus a full chapter focusing on international marketing considerations.
- *Marketing ethics, environmentalism, and social responsibility*—chapter-by-chapter integrated coverage plus a full chapter on marketing ethics and social responsibility.

The fifth edition of *Marketing: An Introduction* provides extensive coverage of the *new marketing technologies* that are revolutionizing the way companies bring value to their customers. A new chapter 14, "Direct and On-line Marketing," introduces students to the burgeoning use of Internet, database, and related technologies that promise to change the very nature of buying and selling. People everywhere in the world can access on-line services and the Internet to give and get advice on products, determine the best values, and reap the many benefits of electronic commerce. From the virtual reality displays that test new products to on-line virtual stores that sell them, the technology boom has created exciting new ways to learn about and track customers, create products and services tailored to meet customer needs, distribute products more efficiently and effectively, and communicate with customers in large groups or one-to-one. In this new chapter—and in dozens of new examples, Marketing at Work highlights, and illustrations throughout the text—students will learn about the wonders of new marketing technologies, from the Internet, database marketing, and mass customization to Web-based marketing research and technological advances in marketing logistics. New *Traveling the Net* sections at the end of each chapter provide applications and exercises that guide students through the fascinating world of marketing and the Internet.

The fifth edition contains new material on a wide range of important topics: environmental sustainability and environmental management, diversity, levels of market segmentation, "markets of one" or one-to-one marketing, internal and on-line marketing databases, Internet and on-line marketing research, Internet purchasing, value-added marketing, integrated marketing communications, third-party logistics, integrated direct marketing, international marketing, and socially responsible marketing.

The fifth edition of *Marketing: An Introduction* has been *streamlined* to better fit today's multifaceted classroom. Despite the addition of a new chapter and much new coverage of marketing technologies, the text contains one less chapter than the previous edition—a total of 16 chapters. First, the consumer behavior and business buyer behavior chapters have been merged into a single, integrated buyer behavior chapter. Integrated marketing communications is now presented in three chapters: *IMC: Advertising and Public Relations*; *IMC: Personal Selling and Sales Promotion*; and *Direct and On-line Marketing*. The result is a more streamlined text that still provides complete coverage of marketing basics yet allows instructors the freedom to include more cases, videos, and other materials tailored to their individual classroom preferences.

Finally, the fifth edition has been thoroughly refreshed, with dozens of new and updated Marketing at Work highlights, video cases, ads and illustrations, and in-text examples. Tables, figures, references, and exhibits have been carefully updated. The Careers in Marketing appendix has been reworked and refreshed.

Learning Aids

As well as the innovative *Road to Marketing* learning aids, *Marketing: An Introduction* has the following additional learning aids.

- *Chapter-opening examples.* Each chapter starts with a dramatic marketing story that introduces the chapter material and arouses student interest.
- *Full-color figures, photographs, advertisements, and illustrations.* Throughout each chapter, key concepts and applications are illustrated with strong, full-color visual materials.
- *Marketing at Work exhibits.* Additional examples and important information are highlighted in Marketing at Work exhibits throughout the text.
- *Video cases.* Seventeen written video cases are provided in a section at the end of the text, supported by exciting new case videos. The videos and cases help to bring key marketing concepts and issues to life in the classroom.
- *Appendixes.* Two appendixes, "Marketing Arithmetic" and "Careers in Marketing," provide additional, practical information for students.
- *Glossary.* At the end of the book, an extensive glossary provides quick reference to the key terms found in the book.
- *Indexes.* Subject, company, and author indexes reference all information and examples in the book.

A Total Teaching Package

A successful marketing course requires more than a well-written book. Today's classroom requires a dedicated teacher and a fully-integrated teaching system. A total package of teaching and learning supplements extends this edition's emphasis on effective teaching and learning. The following aids support *Marketing: An Introduction:*

- **On Location—Custom Case Videos for Marketing.** PH is proud to present a new set of custom videos to accompany the fifth edition, together with new video cases. A full description of the videos, together with sample clips and written cases are available on the PH Marketing Spot at www.prenhall.com/phmarketing. New segments include Yahoo!, Nascar, WNBA, Forum Shops, Kodak, New Product Showcase and Museum, and House of Blues as well as a special millennium segment featuring Philip Kotler.
- **Instructor's Resource Manual.** Together with the FACTS books, this manual has chapter by chapter teaching outlines and answers to end-of-chapter problems and applications. A full set of teaching notes for the video cases is also included.
- **F.A.C.T.S..** Faculty Activities and Teaching Strategies—this manual is a unique resource which organizes all of the supplementary material by chapter, with special emphasis on the media supplements such as PowerPoint files and Web resources. This manual also includes additional Internet exercises and class projects.
- **Test Item File.** Acclaimed by adopters, this test bank is carefully revised and tested. The test bank includes up to 75 multiple choice and true/false questions per chapter, together with essay and application questions. All questions are graded for difficulty and include page references.

◻ *IBM Test Manager*. The PH Test Manager offers electronic test generation and answer keys.

◻ *Color Transparencies.* Two sets of transparencies enhance your lecture presentation. The first set includes acetates of the PowerPoint slides and text figures, also available on disk. In addition, a unique set of advertisements transparencies showcase an up-to-date collection of ads with teaching notes.

◻ *PowerPoint Files*. Up to 20 slides per chapter, this set of lecture aids follows the chapter outline and also offers additional material from outside the text. These files are also included on our CW/PHLIP Web site and on the PH Presentation Manager CD-Rom.

◻ *CW/PHLIP 2000*. Our acclaimed Web resource has been greatly improved to include electronic study guides for students, additional Internet exercises and links for students, and a complete array of teaching material (including downloadable versions of the Instructor's Manual, PowerPoint slides and FACTS book) with bi-weekly up-dates during each semester. Try the syllabus builder to plan your course. Go to www.prenhall.com/kotler to preview this fantastic resource!

◻ *Free print supplements*. Order your copies of Armstrong/Kotler with any of the following supplements for your students:

> *Real Marketing CD-Rom*. Available at a nominal charge, this CD contains video clips and written video cases for 16 videos, together with a hot button to link students to the CW/PHLIP site.
>
> *The Internet—A New Marketing Tool 1999 Edition* by Frost/Strauss is a short and exciting booklet which introduces students to the Web and offers individual and group exercises. FREE with the text.
>
> *Hot Topics in Marketing.* FREE with the text, this short booklet contains 6 case studies of four to six pages in length on hot topics such as data mining, nostalgia marketing, on-line brokerages, and much more.
>
> *Marketing Plan Pro CD-Rom.* Available at a nominal charge, this highly acclaimed program enables students to build a marketing plan from scratch. Our most requested supplement, this program has been chosen as the best commercially available marketing plan software. Marketing Plan Pro also includes sample marketing plans.

As the supplement packages grow larger and encompass various technologies, PH is committed to helping adopters of Armstrong/Kotler to evaluate and organize these items. For a preview of these items, visit www.prenhall.com/phmarketing. The Marketing Spot has all the information you might need to evaluate the package.

Acknowledgments

A book is the work of many people, not just its authors. We owe a great deal to the pioneers of marketing who first identified its major issues and developed its concepts and techniques. Our thanks also go to our colleagues at the J. L. Kellogg Graduate School of Management, Northwestern University and the Kenan-Flagler Business School, University of North Carolina at Chapel Hill for ideas and suggestions. We owe special thanks to Martha McEnally of the University of North Carolina, Greensboro for her valuable work in preparing high-quality video cases, together with Linda Carpenter, producer, for her excellent work on the new video segments.

We thank John R. Brooks, Jr. for his innovative and tireless work in preparing end-of-chapter material as well as the FACTS Guide, Instructor's Manual, and Test Bank. We also thank Kellye Brooks for her work in developing the new PowerPoint slides. Finally, we thank Betsey Christian for her able editing assistance.

Dan Cooper at Marist College maintains the PHLIP Web support for this new edition. We thank him for his continuing efforts in updating the Web support every two weeks.

Many reviewers at other colleges provided valuable comments and suggestions. We are indebted to the following colleagues who provided feedback for the fifth edition:

Michael Conard
Teikyo Post University

Herbert Sherman
Long Island University, Southampton

Eileen Keller
Kent State University

Jim Spiers
Arizona State University

Herbert Miller
University of Texas, Austin

Peter Stone
Spartanburg Technical College

We again thank former reviewers who have contributed to the success of this text:

Gemmy Allen
Mountain View College

John de Young
Cumberland County College

Abi Almeer
Nova University

Lee Dickson
Florida International University

Arvid Anderson
University of North Carolina, Wilmington

Mike Dotson
Appalachian State University

Arnold Bornfriend
Worcester State College

Peter Doukas
Westchester Community College

Donald Boyer
Jefferson College

David Forlani
University of North Florida

Alejandro Camacho
University of Georgia

Jack Forrest
Middle Tennessee State University

William J. Carner
University of Texas-Austin

Gerald Cavallo
Fairfield University

Lucette Comer
Florida International University

Ron Cooley
South Suburban College

June Cotte
University of Connecticut

Ronald Coulter
Southwest Missouri State University

James Kennedy
Navarro College

Eric Kulp
Middlesex County College

Ed Laube
Macomb Community College

Gregory Lincoln
Westchester Community College

John Lloyd
Monroe Community College

Dorothy Maas
Delaware County Community College

Ajay Manrai
University of Delaware

Lalita Manrai
University of Delaware

James McAlexander
Oregon State University

Donald McBane
Clemson University

Debbora Meflin-Bullock
California State Polytechnic University

Randall Mertz
Mesa Community College

Veronica Miller
Mt. St. Mary's College

Joan Mizis
St. Louis Community College

John Gauthier
Gateway Technical Institute

Eugene Gilbert
California State University, Sacramento

Diana Grewal
University of Miami

Esther Headley
The Wichita State University

Sandra Heusinkveld
Normandale Community College

James Jeck
North Carolina State University

George Palz
Erie Community College

Tammy Pappas
Eastern Michigan University

Alison Pittman
Brevard Community College

Lana Podolak
Community College of Beaver County

Joel Porrish
Springfield College

Robert L. Powell
Gloucester County College

Eric Pratt
New Mexico State University

Robert Ross
The Wichita State University

Andre San Augustine
The University of Arizona

Dwight Scherban
Central Connecticut State College

Eberhard Scheuing
St. John's University

Pamela Schindler
Wittenberg University

Raymond Schwartz
Montclair State College

Raj Sethuraman
University of Iowa

Melissa Moore
University of Connecticut

Robert Moore
University of Connecticut

William Morgenroth
University of South Carolina, Columbia

Linda Moroble
Dallas County Community College

Sandra Moulton
Technical College of Alamance

Jim Muncy
Valdosta State

Lee Neumann
Bucks County Community College

Dave Olsen
North Hennepin Community College

Thomas Packzkowski
Cayuga Community College

Reshma H. Shah
University of Pittsburgh

Jack Sheeks
Broward Community College

Dee Smith
Lansing Community College

Ira Teich
Long Island University

Donna Tillman
California State Polytechnic University

Andrea Weeks
Fashion Institute of Design & Merchandising

Sumner White
Massachusetts Bay Community College

Steve Winter
Orange County Community College

Bill Worley
Allan Hancock College

We also owe a great deal to the people at Prentice Hall who helped develop this book. Marketing editor Whitney Blake supplied many good ideas, substantial support, and encouragement (even prodding). We also owe many thanks to Bruce Kaplan for his caring, valuable advice and assistance through several phases of this revision and to Michelle Rich, who helped shepherd the project smoothly through production.

Michele Foresta, editorial assistant for marketing, consistently helped prepare materials for timely publication. We also thank John Larkin for his management of the teaching package for this new edition. Shannon Moore developed imaginative marketing and advertising materials as well as the new Marketing Spot Web site. Janet Ferruggia directed the promotional campaign with Shannon. We thank all members at PH who contributed to the book's success, including the PH sales force.

Finally, we owe many thanks to our families—Kathy, KC, and Mandy Armstrong, and Nancy, Amy, Melissa, and Jessica Kotler—for their constant support and encouragement. To them, we dedicate this book.

GARY ARMSTRONG

PHILIP KOTLER

Marketing in a Changing World: Creating Customer Value and Satisfaction

ROAD MAP:
Previewing the Concepts

Fasten your seat belt! You're about to begin an exciting journey toward learning about marketing. To start you off in the right direction, we'll first define marketing and its key concepts. Then, you'll visit the various philosophies that guide marketing management and the challenges marketing faces as we move into the new millennium. The goal of marketing is to create profitable customer relationships by delivering superior value to customers. Understanding these basic concepts, and forming your own ideas about what they really mean to you, will give you a solid foundation for all that follows.

▶ **After studying this chapter, you should be able to**

1. **define what marketing is and discuss its core concepts**
2. **explain the relationships between customer value, satisfaction, and quality**
3. **define marketing management and understand how marketers manage demand and build profitable customer relationships**
4. **compare the five marketing management philosophies**
5. **analyze the major challenges facing marketers heading into the next century**

Our first stop: Nike. This superb marketer has built one of the world's most dominant brands. The Nike example shows the importance of—and the difficulties in—building lasting, value-laden customer relationships. Even highly successful Nike can't rest on past successes. Facing "big-brand backlash," it must now learn how to be both big and beautiful. Ready? Here we go.

The "Swoosh"—it's everywhere! Just for fun, try counting the swooshes whenever you pick up the sports pages, or watch a pickup basketball game, or tune into a televised golf match. Nike has built the ubiquitous swoosh (which represents the wing of Nike, the Greek goddess of victory) into one of the best-known brand symbols on the planet.

The power of its brand and logo speaks loudly of Nike's superb marketing skills. The company's strategy of building superior products around popular athletes has forever changed the face of sports marketing. Nike spends hundreds of millions of dollars each year on big-name endorsements, splashy promotional events, and lots of attention-getting ads. Over the years, Nike has associated itself with some of the biggest names in sports. No matter what your sport, chances are good that one of your favorite athletes wears the Nike Swoosh.

Nike knows, however, that good marketing is more than promotional hype and promises—it means consistently delivering real value to customers. Nike's initial success resulted from the technical superiority of its running and basketball shoes, pitched to serious athletes who were frustrated by the lack of innovation in athletic equipment. To this day, Nike leads the industry in product development and innovation.

Nike gives its customers more than just good athletic gear. As the company notes on its Web page (www.nike.com), "Nike has always known the truth—it's not so much the shoes but where they take you." Beyond shoes, apparel, and equipment, Nike markets a way of life, a sports culture, a "Just Do It" attitude. Says Phil Knight, Nike's Co-founder and chief executive, "Basically, our culture and our style is to be a rebel." The company was built on a genuine passion for sports and maverick disregard for convention, hard work, serious sports, and performance. When you wear Nike gear, you share a little of Michael Jordan's intense competitiveness, Tiger Woods' cool confidence, Jackie Joyner-Kersee's gritty endurance, Ken Griffey Jr.'s selfless consistency, or Michael Johnson's blurring speed. Nike is athletes, athletes are sports, *Nike is sports*.

Nike seems to care as much about its customers' lives as their bodies. It doesn't just promote sales, it promotes *sports* for the benefit of all. For example, its "If you let me play" campaign lends strong support to women's sports and the many benefits of sports participation for girls and young women. Nike also invests in a wide range of lesser-known sports, even though they provide less-lucrative marketing opportunities. Such actions establish Nike not just as a producer of good athletic gear but also as a good and caring *company*.

Taking care of customers has paid off handsomely for Nike. Over the decade preceding 1997, Nike's revenues grew at an incredible annual rate of 21 percent; annual return to investors averaged 47 percent. Nike flat-out dominates the world's athletic footwear market. It captures an eye-popping 47 percent share of the U.S. market—twice that of its nearest competitor Reebok—and a 27 percent share internationally. Nike has moved aggressively into new product categories, sports, and regions of the world. In only a few years, Nike's sports apparel business has grown explosively to account for nearly a quarter of Nike's $9 billion in yearly sales. Nike's familiar swoosh logo now appears on everything from sunglasses and soccer balls to batting gloves and hockey sticks. It has invaded a dozen new sports, including baseball, golf, ice and street hockey, in-line skating, wall climbing, and hiking.

In 1998, however, Nike stumbled and its sales slipped. Many factors contributed to the company's sales woes. The "brown shoe" craze for hiking and outdoor styles such as Timberland's ate into the athletic sneaker business. Competition improved: A revitalized Adidas saw its U.S. sales surge as Nike's sales declined. But Nike's biggest obstacle may be its own incredible success—it may have overswooshed America. The brand now appears to be suffering from big-brand backlash, and the swoosh is becoming too common to be cool. According to one analyst, "When Tiger Woods made his debut in Nike gear, there were so many logos on him that he looked as if he'd got caught in an embroidering machine." A Nike executive admits, "There has been a little bit of backlash about the number of swooshes that are out there." Moreover, with sales of more than $9 billion, Nike has moved from maverick to mainstream. Today, rooting for Nike is like rooting for Microsoft.

To address these problems, Nike is returning to the basics—focusing on innovation, developing new product lines, creating subbrands (such as the Michael Jordan brand with its "Jumping Man" logo), and deemphasizing the Swoosh.

Nike is also entering new markets aggressively, especially overseas markets. During 1998, Nike sales outside the United States increased 49 percent and now represent about 38 percent of total sales. However, to dominate globally as it does in the United States, Nike must dominate in soccer, the world's most popular sport. The multibillion-dollar world soccer market currently accounts for only 3 percent of its sales. Now, soccer is one of Nike's top priorities.

World soccer has long been dominated by Adidas, which claims an 80 percent global market share in soccer gear. Nike is building its soccer business by applying the philosophy it has attached to other leading categories—listen to the athletes and give them what they want. Nike does not have Adidas' tradition but it has a younger vision which is what the company feels will carry them into the new millenium as a serious challenger to the Adidas foothold.

Competitors can hope that Nike's slump will continue, but few are counting on it. Most can only sit back and marvel at Nike's marketing prowess. Says Fila's advertising vice-president, "They are so formidable, no matter how well we may execute something, our voice will never be as loud as theirs." As for soccer, the president of Puma North America sees Nike's tactics as heavy handed but has little doubt that Nike's superb marketing will prevail. He states flatly, "Nike will control the soccer world."

Still, winning in worldwide soccer, or in anything else Nike does, will take more than just writing fat checks. To stay on top, Nike will have to deliver worldwide the same kind of quality, innovation, and value that built the brand so powerfully in the United States. It will have to earn respect on a country-by-country basis and become a part of the cultural fabric of each new market. No longer the rebellious, antiestablishment upstart, huge Nike must continually reassess its relationships with customers. Says Knight, "Now that we've [grown so large], there's a fine line between being a rebel and being a bully. . . . [To our customers,] we have to be beautiful as well as big."[1]

Today's successful companies at all levels have one thing in common: Like Nike, they are strongly customer focused and heavily committed to marketing. These companies share an absolute dedication to understanding and satisfying the needs of customers in well-defined target markets. They motivate everyone in the organization to produce superior value for their customers, leading to high levels of customer satisfaction. As Bernie Marcus of Home Depot asserts, "All of our people understand what the Holy Grail is. It's not the bottom line. It's an almost blind, passionate commitment to taking care of customers."

What Is Marketing?

More than any other business function, marketing deals with customers. Creating customer value and satisfaction are at the very heart of modern marketing thinking and practice. Although we will explore more detailed definitions of marketing later in this chapter, perhaps the simplest definition is this one: Marketing is the delivery of customer satisfaction at a profit. The twofold goal of marketing is to attract new customers by promising superior value and to keep current customers by delivering satisfaction.

Wal-Mart has become the world's largest retailer by delivering on its promise, "Always low prices—always." FedEx dominates the U.S. small-package freight industry by consistently making good on its promise of fast, reliable small-package delivery. Ritz-Carlton promises—and delivers—truly "memorable experiences" for its hotel guests. And Coca-Cola, long the world's leading soft drink, delivers on the simple but enduring promise, "Always Coca-Cola"—always thirst-quenching, always good with food, always cool, always a part of your life. These and other highly successful companies know that if they take care of their customers, market share and profits will follow.

Sound marketing is critical to the success of every organization—large or small, for-profit or not-for-profit, domestic or global. Large for-profit firms such as McDonald's, Sony, FedEx, Wal-Mart, and Marriott use marketing. But so do not-for-profit organizations such as colleges, hospitals, museums, symphony orchestras, and even churches. Moreover, marketing is practiced not only in the United States but also in the rest of the world. Most countries in North and South America, Western Europe, and Asia have well-developed marketing systems. Even in Eastern Europe and other parts of the world where marketing has long had a bad name, dramatic political and social changes have created new opportunities for marketing. Business and government leaders in most of these nations are eager to learn everything they can about modern marketing practices.

You already know a lot about marketing—it's all around you. You see the results of marketing in the abundance of products in your nearby shopping mall. You see marketing in the advertisements that fill your TV screen, magazines, and mailbox. At home, at school, where you work, where you play—you are exposed to marketing in almost everything you do. Yet there is much more to marketing than meets the consumer's casual eye. Behind it all is a massive network of people and activities competing for your attention and purchasing dollars.

This book will give you a more complete and formal introduction to the basic concepts and practices of today's marketing. In this chapter, we begin by defining marketing and its core concepts, describing the major philosophies of marketing thinking and practice, and discussing some of the major new challenges that marketers now face.

Marketing Defined

What does the term *marketing* mean? Many people think of marketing only as selling and advertising. And no wonder—every day we are bombarded with television commercials, newspaper ads, direct-mail campaigns, and sales calls. However, selling and advertising are only the tip of the marketing iceberg. Although they are important, they are only two of many marketing functions and are often not the most important ones.

Today, marketing must be understood not in the old sense of making a sale— "telling and selling"—but in the new sense of *satisfying customer needs*. If the marketer does a good job of understanding consumer needs; develops products that provide superior value; and prices, distributes, and promotes them effectively, these products

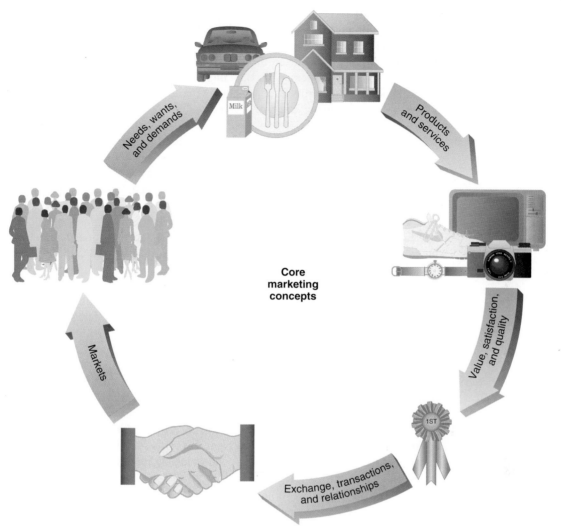

Figure 1-1
Core marketing concepts

will sell very easily. Thus, selling and advertising are only part of a larger "marketing mix"—a set of marketing tools that work together to affect the marketplace.

We define **marketing** as a social and managerial process by which individuals and groups obtain what they need and want through creating and exchanging products and value with others. To explain this definition, we will examine the following important terms: *needs, wants, and demands; products and services; value, satisfaction, and quality; exchange, transactions, and relationships;* and *markets.* Figure 1-1 shows that these core marketing concepts are linked, with each concept building on the one before it.

Marketing
A social and managerial process by which individuals and groups obtain what they need and want through creating and exchanging products and value with others.

Needs, Wants, and Demands

The most basic concept underlying marketing is that of human needs. Human **needs** are states of felt deprivation. They include basic *physical* needs for food, clothing, warmth, and safety; *social* needs for belonging and affection; and *individual* needs for knowledge

Need
A state of felt deprivation.

and self-expression. These needs were not invented by marketers; they are a basic part of the human makeup.

Want
The form taken by a human need as shaped by culture and individual personality.

Wants are the form human needs take as they are shaped by culture and individual personality. A hungry person in the United States might want a Big Mac, French fries, and a Coke. A hungry person in Bali might want mangoes, suckling pig, and beans. Wants are described in terms of objects that will satisfy needs.

Demands
Human wants that are backed by buying power.

People have almost unlimited wants but limited resources. Thus, they want to choose products that provide the most value and satisfaction for their money. When backed by buying power, wants become **demands**. Consumers view products as bundles of benefits and choose products that give them the best bundle for their money. A Honda Civic means basic transportation, low price, and fuel economy; a Lexus means comfort, luxury, and status. Given their wants and resources, people demand products with the benefits that add up to the most satisfaction.

Outstanding marketing companies go to great lengths to learn about and understand their customers' needs, wants, and demands. They conduct consumer research about consumer likes and dislikes. They analyze customer inquiry, warranty, and service data. They observe customers using their own and competing products and train salespeople to be on the lookout for unfulfilled customer needs.

In these outstanding companies, people at all levels—including top management—stay close to customers. For example, top executives from Wal-Mart spend two days each week visiting stores and mingling with customers. At Disney World, at least once in his or her career, each manager spends a day touring the park in a Mickey, Minnie, Goofy, or other character costume. Moreover, all Disney World managers spend a week each year on the front line—taking tickets, selling popcorn, or loading and unloading rides. At Motorola, top executives routinely visit corporate customers at their offices to gain better insights into their needs. And at Marriott, to stay in touch with customers, Chairman of the Board and President Bill Marriott personally reads some 10 percent of the 8,000 letters and 2 percent of the 750,000 guest comment cards submitted by customers each year. Understanding customer needs, wants, and demands in detail provides important input for designing marketing strategies.

Products and Services

Product
Anything that can be offered to a market for attention, acquisition, use, or consumption that might satisfy a want or need. It includes physical objects, services, persons, places, organizations, and ideas.

People satisfy their needs and wants with products and services. A **product** is anything that can be offered to a market to satisfy a need or want. The concept of *product* is not limited to physical objects—anything capable of satisfying a need can be called a product. In addition to tangible goods, products include **services**, which are activities or benefits offered for sale that are essentially intangible and do not result in the ownership of anything. Examples include banking, airline, hotel, tax preparation, and home repair services. Broadly defined, products also include other entities such as *persons*, *places*, *organizations*, *activities*, and *ideas*. Consumers decide which entertainers to watch on television, which places to visit on vacation, which organizations to support through contributions, and which ideas to adopt. To the consumer, these are all products. If at times the term *product* does not seem to fit, we could substitute other terms such as *satisfier*, *resource*, or *offer*.

Service
Any activity or benefit that one party can offer to another that is essentially intangible and does not result in the ownership of anything.

Many sellers make the mistake of paying more attention to the specific products they offer than to the benefits produced by these products. They see themselves as selling a product rather than providing a solution to a need. A manufacturer of drill bits may think that the customer needs a drill bit, but what the customer *really* needs is a hole. These sellers may suffer from "marketing myopia"—they are so taken with their products that they focus only on existing wants and lose sight of underlying customer needs.[2]

Products do not have to be physical objects. Here, the "product" is an idea: "Smoking bothers others."

They forget that a product is only a tool to solve a consumer problem. These sellers will have trouble if a new product comes along that serves the customer's need better or less expensively. The customer with the same *need* will *want* the new product.

Value, Satisfaction, and Quality

Consumers usually face a broad array of products and services that might satisfy a given need. How do they choose among these many products and services? Consumers make buying choices based on their perceptions of the value that various products and services deliver.

Customer Value **Customer value** is the difference between the values the customer gains from owning and using a product and the costs of obtaining the product. For example, FedEx customers gain a number of benefits. The most obvious is fast and reliable package delivery. However, when using FedEx, customers also may receive some status

Customer value
The difference between the values the customer gains from owning and using a product and the costs of obtaining the product.

and image values. Using FedEx usually makes both the package sender and the receiver feel more important. When deciding whether to send a package via FedEx, customers will weigh these and other values against the money, effort, and psychic costs of using the service. Moreover, they will compare the value of using FedEx against the value of using other shippers—UPS, Airborne Express, the U.S. Postal Service—and select the one that gives them the greatest delivered value.

Customers often do not judge product values and costs accurately or objectively. They act on *perceived* value. For example, does FedEx really provide faster, more reliable delivery? If so, is this better service worth the higher prices FedEx charges? The U.S. Postal Service argues that its express service is comparable, and its prices are much lower. However, judging by market share, most consumers perceive otherwise. FedEx dominates with more than a 45 percent share of the U.S. express-delivery market, compared with the U.S. Postal Service's 8 percent. The Postal Service's challenge is to change these customer value perceptions.[3]

Customer satisfaction
The extent to which a product's perceived performance matches a buyer's expectations.

Customer Satisfaction **Customer satisfaction** depends on a product's perceived performance in delivering value relative to a buyer's expectations. If the product's performance falls short of the customer's expectations, the buyer is dissatisfied. If performance matches expectations, the buyer is satisfied. If performance exceeds expectations, the buyer is delighted. Outstanding marketing companies go out of their way to keep their customers satisfied. Satisfied customers make repeat purchases, and they tell others about their good experiences with the product. The key is to match customer expectations with company performance. Smart companies aim to *delight* customers by promising only what they can deliver, then delivering *more* than they promise.[4]

Customer expectations are based on past buying experiences, the opinions of friends, and marketer and competitor information and promises. Marketers must be careful to set the right level of expectations. If they set expectations too low, they may satisfy those who buy but fail to attract enough buyers. If they raise expectations too high, buyers will be disappointed.

The American Customer Satisfaction Index, which tracks customer satisfaction in more than two dozen U.S. manufacturing and service industries, shows that overall customer satisfaction has been declining slightly in recent years.[5] It is unclear whether this has resulted from a decrease in product and service quality or from an increase in customer expectations. In either case, it presents an opportunity for companies that can deliver superior customer value and satisfaction.

Today's most successful companies are raising expectations—and delivering performance to match. These companies embrace *total customer satisfaction*. They aim high because they know that customers who are merely satisfied will find it easy to switch suppliers when a better offer comes along. For example, one study showed that completely satisfied customers are nearly 42 percent more likely to be loyal than merely satisfied customers. Another study by AT&T showed that 70 percent of customers who say they are satisfied with a product or service are still willing to switch to a competitor; customers who are *highly* satisfied are much more loyal. Xerox found that its totally satisfied customers are six times more likely to repurchase Xerox products over the next 18 months than its satisfied customers.[6] Customer *delight* creates an emotional affinity for a product or service, not just a rational preference, and this creates high customer loyalty. Highly satisfied customers are less price sensitive, remain customers longer, and talk favorably to others about the company and its products.

Although the customer-centered firm seeks to deliver high customer satisfaction relative to competitors, it does not attempt to *maximize* customer satisfaction. A company can always increase customer satisfaction by lowering its price or increasing its services, but this may result in lower profits. Thus, the purpose of marketing is to generate customer value profitably. This requires a very delicate balance: The marketer must continue to generate more customer value and satisfaction but not "give away the house."[7]

Quality Quality has a direct impact on product or service performance. Thus, it is closely linked to customer value and satisfaction. In the narrowest sense, quality can be defined as "freedom from defects." But most customer-centered companies go beyond this narrow definition of quality. Instead, they define quality in terms of customer satisfaction. For example, the vice-president of quality at Motorola, a company that pioneered total quality efforts in the United States, says that "quality has to do something for the customer. . . . Our definition of a defect is 'if the customer doesn't like it, it's a defect.'"[8] Similarly, the American Society for Quality Control defines quality as the totality of features and characteristics of a product or service that bear on its ability to *satisfy customer needs*. These customer-focused definitions suggest that quality begins with customer needs and ends with customer satisfaction. The fundamental aim of today's *total quality* movement has become *total customer satisfaction*.

Total quality management (TQM) is an approach in which all the company's people are involved in constantly improving the quality of products, services, and business processes. TQM swept the corporate boardrooms of the 1980s. Companies ranging from giants such as AT&T, Xerox, and FedEx to smaller businesses such as the Granite Rock Company of Watsonville, California, have credited TQM with greatly improving their market shares and profits.

> **Total quality management (TQM)**
> Programs designed to constantly improve the quality of products, services, and marketing processes.

However, many companies adopted the language of TQM but not the substance, or viewed TQM as a cure-all for all the company's problems. Still others became obsessed with narrowly defined TQM principles and lost sight of broader concerns for customer value and satisfaction. As a result, many TQM programs begun in the 1980s failed, causing a backlash against TQM.

When applied in the context of creating customer satisfaction, however, total quality principles remain a requirement for success. Although many firms don't use the TQM label anymore, for most top companies customer-driven quality has become a way of doing business. Most customers will no longer tolerate even average quality. Companies today have no choice but to adopt quality concepts if they want to stay in the race, let alone be profitable. Thus, the task of improving product and service quality should be a company's top priority. However, quality programs must be designed to produce measurable results. Many companies now apply the notion of "return on quality (ROQ)." They make certain that the quality they offer is the quality that customers want. This quality, in turn, yields returns in the form of improved sales and profits.[9]

Marketers have two major responsibilities in a quality-centered company. First, they must participate in forming strategies that will help the company win through total quality excellence. They must be the customer's watchdog or guardian, complaining loudly for the customer when the product or the service is not right. Second, marketers must deliver marketing quality as well as production quality. They must perform each marketing activity—marketing research, sales training, advertising, customer service, and others—to high standards. Marketing at Work 1-1 presents some important conclusions about total marketing quality strategy.

Exchange, Transactions, and Relationships

Marketing occurs when people decide to satisfy needs and wants through exchange. **Exchange** is the act of obtaining a desired object from someone by offering something in return. Exchange is only one of many ways that people can obtain a desired object. For

> **Exchange**
> The act of obtaining a desired object from someone by offering something in return.

Marketing at Work 1-1

Pursuing a Total Quality Marketing Strategy

The Japanese have long taken to heart lessons about winning through *total quality management* (TQM). Their quest for quality paid off handsomely. Consumers around the world flocked to buy high-quality Japanese products, leaving many American and European firms playing catch-up. Japan was the first country to award a national quality prize, the Deming prize, named after the American statistician who taught the importance of quality to postwar Japan.

In recent years, however, Western firms have closed the quality gap. Many have started their own quality programs in an effort to compete both globally and at home with the Japanese. In the mid-1980s, the United States established the Malcolm Baldrige National Quality Award, which encourages U.S. firms to implement quality practices. Not wanting to be left out of the quality race, Europe developed the European Quality Award in 1993. It also initiated an exacting set of quality standards called ISO 9000.

Whereas the Baldrige and other quality awards measure less-tangible aspects of quality, such as customer satisfaction and continuous improvement, ISO 9000 is a set of generally accepted accounting principles for documenting quality. As of 1994, 74 countries had officially recognized ISO 9000 as an international standard for quality systems. Many customers in these countries are now demanding ISO certification as a prerequisite for doing business with a seller. To earn ISO 9000 certification, sellers must undergo a quality audit every six months by a registered ISO (International Standards Organization) assessor.

Thus, total quality has become a truly global concern. Total quality stems from the following premises about quality improvement:

1. *Quality is in the eyes of the customer:* Quality must begin with customer needs and end with customer perceptions. As Motorola's vice-president of quality suggests, "Beauty is in the eye of the beholder. If [a product] does not work the way that the user needs it to work, the defect is as big to the user as if it doesn't work the way the designer planned it." Thus, the fundamental aim of today's quality movement has become "total customer satisfaction."

2. *Quality must be reflected not just in the company's products but in every company activity:* Leonard A. Morgan of General Electric says, "We are not just concerned with the quality of the product, but with the quality of our advertising, service, product literature, delivery, and after-sales support."

3. *Quality requires total employee commitment:* Quality can be delivered only by companies in which all employees are committed to quality and motivated and trained to deliver it. Successful companies remove the barriers between departments. Their employees work as teams to carry out core business processes and to create desired outcomes. Employees work to satisfy their internal customers as well as external customers.

---

example, hungry people could find food by hunting, fishing, or gathering fruit. They could beg for food or take food from someone else. Or they could offer money, another good, or a service in return for food.

As a means of satisfying needs, exchange has much in its favor. People do not have to prey on others or depend on donations, nor must they possess the skills to produce every necessity for themselves. They can concentrate on making things that they are good at making and trade them for needed items made by others. Thus, exchange allows a society to produce much more than it would with any alternative system.

Transaction
A trade between two parties that involves at least two things of value, agreed-upon conditions, a time of agreement, and a place of agreement.

Whereas exchange is the core concept of marketing, a transaction, in turn, is marketing's unit of measurement. A **transaction** consists of a trade of values between two parties: One party gives X to another party and gets Y in return. For example, you pay Sears $350 for a television set. This is a classic *monetary transaction*, but not all transactions involve money. In a *barter transaction*, you might trade your old refrigerator in return for a neighbor's secondhand television set.

In the broadest sense, the marketer tries to bring about a response to some offer. The response may be more than simply buying or trading goods and services. A political candidate, for instance, wants votes, a church wants membership, and a social

4. *Quality requires high-quality partners:* Quality can be delivered only by companies whose marketing system partners also deliver quality. Therefore, a quality-driven company must find and align itself with high-quality suppliers and distributors.

5. *A quality program cannot save a poor product:* The Pontiac Fiero launched a quality program, but because the car didn't have a performance engine to support its performance image, the quality program did not save the car. A quality program cannot compensate for product deficiencies.

6. *Quality can always be improved:* The best companies believe in "continuous improvement of everything by everyone." The best way to improve quality is to benchmark the company's performance against the "best-of-class" competitors or the best performers in other industries, striving to equal or surpass them.

7. *Quality improvement sometimes requires quantum leaps:* Although the company should strive for continuous quality improvement, it must at times seek a quan-

tum quality improvement. Companies can sometimes obtain small improvements by working harder. But large improvements call for fresh solutions and for working smarter. For example, Hewlett-Packard did not target a 10 percent reduction in defects, it targeted a *tenfold* reduction and got it.

8. *Quality does not cost more:* Managers once argued that achieving more quality would cost more and slow down production. But improving quality involves learning ways to do things right the first time. Quality is not *inspected* in; it must be *designed* in. Doing things right the first time reduces the costs of salvage, repair, and redesign, not to mention losses in customer goodwill. Motorola claims that its quality drive has saved $9 billion in manufacturing costs during the last eight years. And a recent study found that quality programs usually pay off. The 16 Baldrige Award winners since 1988 have outperformed the Standard & Poor's 500-stock index by 3 to 1 in terms of return on investment. Even the 48 companies that didn't win a Baldrige Award but made it to the final

round of judging bested the S&P 500 by 2 to 1.

9. *Quality is necessary but may not be sufficient:* Improving a company's quality is absolutely necessary to meet the needs of more-demanding buyers. At the same time, higher quality may not ensure a winning advantage, especially as all competitors increase their quality to more or less the same extent. For example, Singapore Airlines enjoyed a reputation as the world's best airline. However, competing airlines have attracted larger shares of passengers recently by narrowing the perceived gap between their service quality and Singapore's service quality.

Sources: Quotes from Lois Therrien, "Motorola and NEC: Going for Glory," *Business Week*, special issue on quality, 1991, pp. 60–61. Also see Cyndee Miller, "TQM Out; 'Continuous Process Improvement' In," *Marketing News*, May 9, 1994, pp. 5, 10; George Thorne, "TQM Connects All Segments of Marketing," *Advertising Age's Business Marketing*, March 1998, p. 34; Otis Port, "Baldrige's Other Reward," *Business Week*, March 10, 1997, p. 75; Mary Litsikas, "Companies Choose ISO Certification for Internal Benefits," *Quality*, January 1997, pp. 20–26; "ISO 9000 and Quality: A World Class Advantage," special section, *Industrial Distribution*, January 1998, p. 61; "ISO 9000: Leverage ISO 9000 for Added Value and Bottom-Line Benefits," *Fortune*, May 11, 1998, pp. S1–S4; and Nancy Chase, "Beyond Compliance," *Quality*, December 1998, pp. 62–66.

action group wants idea acceptance. Marketing consists of actions taken to obtain a desired response from a target audience toward some product, service, idea, or other object.

Transaction marketing is part of the larger idea of **relationship marketing**. Beyond creating short-term transactions, marketers need to build long-term relationships with valued customers, distributors, dealers, and suppliers. They want to build strong economic and social ties by promising and consistently delivering high-quality products, good service, and fair prices. Increasingly, marketing is shifting from trying to maximize the profit on each individual transaction to building mutually beneficial relationships with consumers and other parties. In fact, ultimately a company wants to build a unique company asset called a *marketing network*. A marketing network consists of the company and all its supporting stakeholders: customers, employees, suppliers, distributors, retailers, ad agencies, and others with whom it has built mutually profitable business relationships. Increasingly, competition is not between companies but rather between whole networks, with the prize going to the company that has built the better network. The operating principle is simple: Build a good network of relationships with key stakeholders and profits will follow.[10]

Relationship marketing
The process of creating, maintaining, and enhancing strong, value-laden relationships with customers and other stakeholders.

Relationship marketing: To get to know them better, Ford invites customers to brainstorming sessions. "We talk about cars, sure. But we often talk about non-car things: computers, the environment, and quality in very general terms."

Relationship marketing is oriented more toward the long term. The goal is to deliver long-term value to customers, and the measures of success are long-term customer satisfaction and retention. Beyond offering consistently high value and satisfaction, marketers can use a number of specific marketing tools to develop stronger bonds with consumers. First, a company might build value and satisfaction by adding *financial benefits* to the customer relationship. For example, airlines offer frequent-flyer programs, hotels give room upgrades to their frequent guests, and supermarkets give patronage refunds.

A second approach is to add *social benefits* as well as financial benefits. Here, the company works to increase its social bonds with customers by learning individual customers' needs and wants and then personalizing its products and services. For example, Ritz-Carlton Hotels employees treat customers as individuals, not as nameless, faceless members of a mass market. Whenever possible, they refer to guests by name and give each guest a warm welcome every day. They record specific guest preferences in the company's customer database, which holds more than 500,000 individual customer preferences, accessible by all hotels in the worldwide Ritz chain. A guest who requests a foam pillow at the Ritz in Montreal will be delighted to find one waiting in the room when he or she checks into the Atlanta Ritz months later.[11]

To build better relationships with its customers, during the summer of 1994 Saturn invited all of its almost 700,000 owners to a "Saturn Homecoming" at its manufacturing facility in Spring Hill, Tennessee. The two-day affair included family events, plant tours, and physical challenge activities designed to build trust and a team spirit. Says Saturn's manager of corporate communications, "The Homecoming party is another way of building . . . relationships, and it shows that we treat our customers differently than any other car company." More than 40,000 guests attended, coming from as far as Alaska and Taiwan.[12]

A third approach to building customer relationships is to add *structural ties* as well as financial and social benefits. For example, a business marketer might supply customers with special equipment or computer linkages that help them manage their orders, payroll, or inventory. FedEx, for instance, offers its FedEx Ship program to thousands of its best corporate and individual customers to keep them from defecting to competitors like UPS. The program provides free computer software that allows customers to link with FedEx's computers. Customers can use the software to arrange shipments and to check the status of their FedEx packages. For customers who are connected to the Internet, FedEx offers these same services through its Web site.

Relationship marketing means that marketers must focus on managing their customers as well as their products. At the same time, they don't want relationships with every customer. In fact, there are undesirable customers for every company. The objective is to determine which customers the company can serve most effectively relative to competitors. In some cases, companies may even want to "fire" customers that are too unreasonable or that cost more to serve than they are worth. Ultimately, marketing is the art of attracting and keeping *profitable customers.*[13]

Markets

The concepts of exchange and relationships lead to the concept of a market. A **market** is the set of actual and potential buyers of a product. These buyers share a particular need or want that can be satisfied through exchanges and relationships. Thus, the size of a market depends on the number of people who exhibit the need, have resources to engage in exchange, and are willing to offer these resources in exchange for what they want.

Market
The set of all actual and potential buyers of a product or service.

Originally the term *market* stood for the place where buyers and sellers gathered to exchange their goods, such as a village square. Economists use the term *market* to refer to a collection of buyers and sellers who transact in a particular product class, as in the housing market or the grain market. Marketers, however, see the sellers as constituting an industry and the buyers as constituting a market.

Modern economies operate on the principle of division of labor, whereby each person specializes in producing something, receives payment, and buys needed things with this money. Thus, modern economies abound in markets. Producers go to resource markets (raw material markets, labor markets, money markets), buy resources, turn them into goods and services, and sell them to intermediaries, who sell them to consumers. The consumers sell their labor, for which they receive income to pay for the goods and services that they buy. The government is another market that plays several roles. It buys goods from resource, producer, and intermediary markets; it pays them; it taxes these markets (including consumer markets); and it returns needed public services. Thus, each nation's economy and the whole world economy consist of complex, interacting sets of markets that are linked through exchange processes.

Marketers are keenly interested in markets. Their goal is to understand the needs and wants of specific markets and to select the markets that they can serve best. In turn, they can develop products and services that will create value and satisfaction for customers in these markets, resulting in sales and profits for the company.

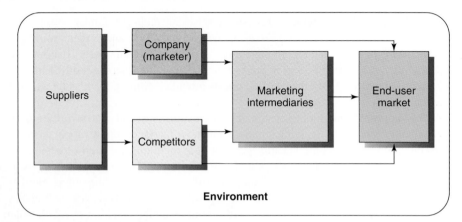

Figure 1-2
Main actors and forces in a modern marketing system

Marketing

The concept of markets finally brings us full circle to the concept of marketing. Marketing means managing markets to bring about exchanges and relationships for the purpose of creating value and satisfying needs and wants. Thus, we return to our definition of marketing as a process by which individuals and groups obtain what they need and want by creating and exchanging products and value with others.

Exchange processes involve work. Sellers must search for buyers, identify their needs, design good products and services, set prices for them, promote them, and store and deliver them. Activities such as product development, research, communication, distribution, pricing, and service are core marketing activities. Although we normally think of marketing as being carried on by sellers, buyers also carry on marketing activities. Consumers do marketing when they search for the goods they need at prices they can afford. Company purchasing agents do marketing when they track down sellers and bargain for good terms.

Figure 1-2 shows the main elements in a modern marketing system. In the usual situation, marketing involves serving a market of end users in the face of competitors. The company and the competitors send their respective products and messages to consumers either directly or through marketing intermediaries to the end users. All of the actors in the system are affected by major environmental forces (demographic, economic, physical, technological, political–legal, social–cultural).

Each party in the system adds value for the next level. Thus, a company's success depends not only on its own actions but also on how well the entire system serves the needs of final consumers. Wal-Mart cannot fulfill its promise of low prices unless its suppliers provide merchandise at low costs. And Ford cannot deliver high quality to car buyers unless its dealers provide outstanding service.

Linking the Concepts

Stop here for a moment and stretch your legs. What have you learned so far about marketing? For the moment, set aside the more formal definitions we've examined and try to develop your own understanding of marketing.

- In *your own words*, what *is* marketing? Write down *your* definition. Does your definition include such key concepts as customer value and relationships?
- What does marketing *mean* to you? How does it affect your life on a daily basis?
- What brand of athletic shoes did you purchase last? Describe your relationship with Nike, Reebok, Adidas, or whatever company made the shoes you purchased.

Marketing Management

We define **marketing management** as the analysis, planning, implementation, and control of programs designed to create, build, and maintain beneficial exchanges with target buyers for the purpose of achieving organizational objectives. Thus, marketing management involves managing demand, which in turn involves managing customer relationships.

Marketing management
The analysis, planning, implementation, and control of programs designed to create, build, and maintain beneficial exchanges with target buyers for the purpose of achieving organizational objectives.

Demand Management

Some people think of marketing management as finding enough customers for the company's current output, but this view is too limited. The organization has a desired level of demand for its products. At any point in time, there may be no demand, adequate demand, irregular demand, or too much demand, and marketing management must find ways to deal with these different demand states. Marketing management is concerned not only with finding and increasing demand but also with changing or even reducing it.

For example, the Golden Gate Bridge sometimes carries an unsafe level of traffic, and Yosemite National Park is badly overcrowded in the summer. Power companies sometimes have trouble meeting demand during peak usage periods. In these and other cases of excess demand, **demarketing** may be required to reduce demand temporarily or permanently. The aim of demarketing is not to destroy demand but only to reduce or shift it.[14] Thus, marketing management seeks to affect the level, timing, and nature of demand in a way that helps the organization achieve its objectives. Simply put, marketing management is *demand management.*

Demarketing
Marketing to reduce demand temporarily or permanently—the aim is not to destroy demand but only to reduce or shift it.

Building Profitable Customer Relationships

Managing demand means managing customers. A company's demand comes from two groups: new customers and repeat customers. Traditional marketing theory and practice have focused on attracting new customers and making the sale. Today, however, the emphasis is shifting. Beyond designing strategies to *attract* new customers and create *transactions* with them, companies now are going all out to *retain* current customers and build lasting customer *relationships.*

Why the new emphasis on keeping customers? In the past, companies facing an expanding economy and rapidly growing markets could practice the "leaky-bucket" approach to marketing. Growing markets meant a plentiful supply of new customers. Companies could keep filling the marketing bucket with new customers without worrying about losing old customers through holes in the bottom of the bucket. However, companies today are facing some new marketing realities. Changing demographics, a slow-growth economy, more sophisticated competitors, and overcapacity in many industries—all of these factors mean that there are fewer new customers to go around. Many companies now are fighting for shares of flat or fading markets. Thus, the costs of attracting new customers are rising. In fact, it costs five times as much to attract a new customer as it does to keep a current customer satisfied.[15]

Companies are also realizing that losing a customer means more than losing a single sale—it means losing the entire stream of purchases that the customer would make over a lifetime of patronage. For example, the *customer lifetime value* of a Taco Bell customer exceeds $12,000. For General Motors or Ford, the customer lifetime value of a customer might well exceed $340,000. Thus, working to retain customers makes good

Marketing at Work 1-2

Customer Relationships: Keeping Customers Satisfied

Some companies go to extremes to coddle their customers. Consider the following examples:

- An L.L. Bean customer says he lost all his fishing equipment—and nearly his life—when a raft he bought from the company leaked and forced him to swim to shore. He recovered the raft and sent it to the company along with a letter asking for a new raft and $700 to cover the fishing equipment he says he lost. He gets both.

- An American Express cardholder fails to pay more than $5,000 of his September bill. He explains that during the summer he'd purchased expensive rugs in Turkey. When he got home, appraisals showed that the rugs were worth half of what he'd paid. Rather than asking suspicious questions or demanding payment, the American Express representative notes the dispute, asks for a letter summarizing the appraisers' estimates, and offers to help solve the problem. And until the

conflict is resolved, American Express doesn't ask for payment.

- Under the sultry summer sun, a Southwest Airlines flight attendant pulls shut the door and the Boeing 737 pushes away. Meanwhile, a ticketholder, sweat streaming from her face, races down the jetway, only to find that she's arrived too late. However, the Southwest pilot spies the anguished passenger and returns to the gate to pick her up. Says Southwest's executive vice-president for customers,

Satisfied customers come back again and again. The customer lifetime value of a Taco Bell customer exceeds $12,000.

economic sense. A company can lose money on a specific transaction but still benefit greatly from a long-term relationship.[16]

Attracting new customers remains an important marketing management task. However, today's companies must also focus on retaining current customers and building profitable, long-term relationships with them. The key to customer retention is superior customer value and satisfaction. With this in mind, many companies are going to extremes to keep their customers satisfied. (See Marketing at Work 1-2.)

"It broke every rule in the book, but we congratulated the pilot on a job well done."

- A frustrated homeowner faces a difficult and potentially costly home plumbing repair. He visits the nearby Home Depot store, prowls the aisles, and picks up an armful of parts and supplies—$67 worth in all—that he thinks he'll need to do the job. However, before he gets to the checkout counter, a Home Depot salesperson heads him off. After some coaxing, the salesperson finally convinces the do-it-your-selfer that there's a simpler solution to his repair problem. The cost: $5.99 and a lot less trouble.

- A Nordstrom salesclerk stops a customer in the store and asks if the shoes she's wearing had been bought there. When the customer says yes, the clerk insists on replacing them on the spot "they have not worn as well as they should." In another case, a salesclerk gives a customer a refund on a tire—Nordstrom doesn't carry tires, but the store prides itself on a no-questions-asked return policy.

From a dollars-and-cents point of view, these examples sound like a crazy way to do business. How can you make money by giving away your products, providing free extra services, talking your customers into paying less, or letting customers get away without paying their bills on time? Yet studies show that going to such extremes to keep customers happy, although costly, goes hand in hand with good financial performance. Satisfied customers come back again and again. Thus, in today's highly competitive marketplace, companies can well afford to lose money on one transaction if it helps to cement a profitable long-term customer relationship.

Keeping customers satisfied involves more than simply opening a complaint department, smiling a lot, and being nice. Companies that do the best job of taking care of customers set high customer service standards and often make seemingly outlandish efforts to achieve them. At these companies, exceptional value and service are more than a set of policies or actions—they are a companywide attitude, an important part of the overall company culture.

American Express loves to tell stories about how its people have rescued customers from disasters ranging from civil wars to earthquakes, no matter what the cost. The company gives cash rewards of up to $1,000 to "Great Performers," such as Barbara Weber, who moved mountains of U.S. State Department and Treasury Department bureaucracy to refund $980 in stolen traveler's checks to a customer stranded in Cuba. Four Seasons Hotels, long known for its outstanding service, tells its employees the story of Ron Dyment, a doorman in Toronto, who forgot to load a departing guest's briefcase into his taxi. The doorman called the guest, a lawyer in Washington, D.C., and learned that he desperately needed the briefcase for a meeting the following morning. Without first asking for approval from management, Dyment hopped on a plane and returned the briefcase. The company named Dyment Employee of the Year. Similarly, the Nordstrom department store chain thrives on stories about its service heroics, such as employees dropping off orders at customers' homes or warming up cars while customers spend a little more time shopping. There's even a story about a man whose wife, a loyal Nordstrom customer, died with her Nordstrom account $1,000 in arrears. Not only did Nordstrom settle the account, it also sent flowers to the funeral.

There's no simple formula for taking care of customers, but neither is it a mystery. According to the president of L.L. Bean, "A lot of people have fancy things to say about customer service . . . but it's just a day-in, day-out, ongoing, never-ending, unremitting, persevering, compassionate type of activity." For the companies that do it well, it's also very rewarding.

Sources: Bill Kelley, "Five Companies that Do It Right—and Make It Pay," *Sales & Marketing Management*, April 1988, pp. 57–64; Patricia Sellers, "Companies That Serve You Best," *Fortune*, May 31, 1993, pp. 74–88; Rahul Jacob, "Why Some Customers Are More Equal Than Others," *Fortune*, September 19, 1994, pp. 215–224; Brian Silverman, "Shopping for Loyal Customers," *Sales & Marketing Management*, March 1995, pp. 96–97; and Howard E. Butz Jr. and Leonard Goodstein, "Measuring Customer Value: Gaining the Strategic Advantage," *Organizational Dynamics*, Winter 1996, pp. 63–77.

Marketing Management Philosophies

We describe marketing management as carrying out tasks to achieve desired exchanges with target markets. What *philosophy* should guide these marketing efforts? What weight should be given to the interests of the organization, customers, and society? Very often these interests conflict.

There are five alternative concepts under which organizations conduct their marketing activities: the *production*, *product*, *selling*, *marketing*, and *societal marketing* concepts.

The Production Concept

Production concept
The philosophy that consumers will favor products that are available and highly affordable and that management should therefore focus on improving production and distribution efficiency.

The **production concept** holds that consumers will favor products that are available and highly affordable. Therefore, management should focus on improving production and distribution efficiency. This concept is one of the oldest philosophies that guides sellers.

The production concept is still a useful philosophy in two types of situations. The first occurs when the demand for a product exceeds the supply. Here, management should look for ways to increase production. The second situation occurs when the product's cost is too high and improved productivity is needed to bring it down. For example, Henry Ford's whole philosophy was to perfect the production of the Model T so that its cost could be reduced and more people could afford it. He joked about offering people a car of any color as long as it was black.

For many years, Texas Instruments (TI) followed a philosophy of increased production and lower costs in order to bring down prices. It won a major share of the American handheld calculator market using this approach. However, companies operating under a production philosophy run a major risk of focusing too narrowly on their own operations. For example, when TI used this strategy in the digital watch market, it failed. Although TI's watches were priced low, customers did not find them very attractive. In its drive to bring down prices, TI lost sight of something else that its customers wanted—namely, affordable, *attractive* digital watches.

The Product Concept

Product concept
The idea that consumers will favor products that offer the most quality, performance, and features and that the organization should therefore devote its energy to making continuous product improvements.

Another major concept guiding sellers, the **product concept**, holds that consumers will favor products that offer the most in quality, performance, and innovative features. Thus, an organization should devote energy to making continuous product improvements. Some manufacturers believe that if they can build a better mousetrap, the world will beat a path to their door.[17] But they are often rudely shocked. Buyers may well be looking for a better solution to a mouse problem but not necessarily for a better mousetrap. The solution might be a chemical spray, an exterminating service, or something that works better than a mousetrap. Furthermore, a better mousetrap will not sell unless the manufacturer designs, packages, and prices it attractively; places it in convenient distribution channels; brings it to the attention of people who need it; and convinces buyers that it is a better product.

The product concept also can lead to marketing myopia. For instance, railroad management once thought that users wanted *trains* rather than *transportation* and overlooked the growing challenge of airlines, buses, trucks, and automobiles. Many colleges have assumed that high school graduates want a liberal arts education and have thus overlooked the increasing challenge of vocational schools.

The Selling Concept

Selling concept
The idea that consumers will not buy enough of the organization's products unless the organization undertakes a large-scale selling and promotion effort.

Many organizations follow the **selling concept**, which holds that consumers will not buy enough of the organization's products unless it undertakes a large-scale selling and promotion effort. The concept is typically practiced with unsought goods—those that buyers do not normally think of buying, such as encyclopedias or insurance. These industries must be good at tracking down prospects and selling them on product benefits.

Most firms practice the selling concept when they have overcapacity. Their aim is to sell what they make rather than make what the market wants. Such marketing carries high risks. It focuses on creating sales transactions rather than on building long-term, profitable relationships with customers. It assumes that customers who are coaxed into buying the product will like it. Or, if they don't like it, they will possibly forget their disappointment and buy it again later. These are usually poor assumptions to make about buyers. Most studies show that dissatisfied customers do not buy again. Worse yet, while the average satisfied customer tells three others about good experiences, the average dissatisfied customer tells ten others about his or her bad experiences.[18]

The Marketing Concept

The **marketing concept** holds that achieving organizational goals depends on determining the needs and wants of target markets and delivering the desired satisfactions more effectively and efficiently than competitors do. The marketing concept has been stated in colorful ways, such as "We make it happen for you" (Marriott); "To fly, to serve" (British Airways); "We're not satisfied until you are" (GE); and "Let us exceed your expectations" (Celebrity Cruise Lines). JCPenney's motto also summarizes the marketing concept: "To do all in our power to pack the customer's dollar full of value, quality, and satisfaction."

The selling concept and the marketing concept are sometimes confused. Figure 1-3 compares the two concepts. The selling concept takes an *inside-out* perspective. It starts with the factory, focuses on the company's existing products, and calls for heavy selling and promotion to obtain profitable sales. It focuses heavily on customer conquest—getting short-term sales with little concern about who buys or why. In contrast, the marketing concept takes an *outside-in* perspective. It starts with a well-defined market, focuses on customer needs, coordinates all the marketing activities affecting customers, and makes profits by creating long-term customer relationships based on customer value and satisfaction. Under the marketing concept, companies produce what consumers want, thereby satisfying consumers and making profits.[19]

Many successful and well-known companies have adopted the marketing concept. Procter & Gamble, Disney, Wal-Mart, Marriott, Nordstrom, and McDonald's follow it faithfully. L.L. Bean, the highly successful catalog retailer of clothing and outdoor sporting equipment, was founded on the marketing concept. In 1912, in his first circulars, L.L. Bean included the following notice: "I do not consider a sale complete until goods are worn out and the customer still is satisfied. We will thank anyone to return goods that are not perfectly satisfactory. . . . Above all things we wish to avoid having a dissatisfied customer."

Marketing concept
The marketing management philosophy that holds that achieving organizational goals depends on determining the needs and wants of target markets and delivering the desired satisfactions more effectively and efficiently than competitors do.

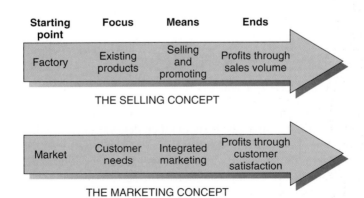

Starting point	Focus	Means	Ends
Factory	Existing products	Selling and promoting	Profits through sales volume

THE SELLING CONCEPT

Market	Customer needs	Integrated marketing	Profits through customer satisfaction

THE MARKETING CONCEPT

Figure 1-3
The selling and marketing concepts contrasted

L.L. Bean dedicates itself to high customer satisfaction. The orange poster at this customer rep's station pledges: "Our products are guaranteed to give 100% satisfaction in every way."

Today, L.L. Bean dedicates itself to giving "perfect satisfaction in every way." To inspire its employees to practice the marketing concept, L.L. Bean has for decades displayed posters around its offices that proclaim the following:

> What is a customer? A customer is the most important person ever in this company—in person or by mail. A customer is not dependent on us, we are dependent on him. A customer is not an interruption of our work, he is the purpose of it. We are not doing a favor by serving him, he is doing us a favor by giving us the opportunity to do so. A customer is not someone to argue or match wits with—nobody ever won an argument with a customer. A customer is a person who brings us his wants—it is our job to handle them profitably to him and to ourselves.

In contrast, many companies claim to practice the marketing concept but do not. They have the *forms* of marketing, such as a marketing vice-president, product managers, marketing plans, and marketing research, but this does not mean that they are *market-focused* and *customer-driven* companies. The question is whether they are finely tuned to changing customer needs and competitor strategies. Formerly great companies—General Motors, IBM, Sears, Zenith—all lost substantial market share because they failed to adjust their marketing strategies to the changing marketplace.

Several years of hard work are needed to turn a sales-oriented company into a marketing-oriented company. The goal is to build customer satisfaction into the very fabric of the firm. Customer satisfaction is no longer a fad. As one marketing analyst notes, "It's becoming a way of life in corporate America. . . . as embedded into corporate cultures as information technology and strategic planning."[20]

The Societal Marketing Concept

Societal marketing concept
The idea that the organization should determine the needs, wants, and interests of target markets and deliver the desired satisfactions more effectively and efficiently than do competitors in a way that maintains or improves the consumer's and society's well-being.

The **societal marketing concept** holds that the organization should determine the needs, wants, and interests of target markets. It should then deliver superior value to customers in a way that maintains or improves the consumer's *and the society's* well-being. The societal marketing concept is the newest of the five marketing management philosophies.

The societal marketing concept questions whether the pure marketing concept is adequate in an age of environmental problems, resource shortages, rapid population

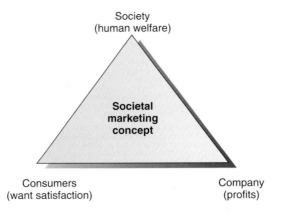

Society
(human welfare)

Societal
marketing
concept

Consumers
(want satisfaction)

Company
(profits)

Figure 1-4
Three considerations
underlying the societal
marketing concept

growth, worldwide economic problems, and neglected social services. It asks if the firm that senses, serves, and satisfies individual wants is always doing what's best for consumers and society in the long run. According to the societal marketing concept, the pure marketing concept overlooks possible conflicts between consumer *short-run wants* and consumer *long-run welfare.*

Consider the fast-food industry. Most people see today's giant fast-food chains as offering tasty and convenient food at reasonable prices. Yet many consumer and environmental groups have voiced concerns. Critics point out that hamburgers, fried chicken, French fries, and most other foods sold by fast-food restaurants are high in fat and salt. The products are wrapped in convenient packaging, but this leads to waste and pollution. Thus, in satisfying consumer wants, the highly successful fast-food chains may be harming consumer health and causing environmental problems.

Such concerns and conflicts led to the societal marketing concept. As Figure 1-4 shows, the societal marketing concept calls on marketers to balance three considerations in setting their marketing policies: company profits, consumer wants, *and* society's interests. Originally, most companies based their marketing decisions largely on short-run company profit. Eventually, they began to recognize the long-run importance of satisfying consumer wants, and the marketing concept emerged. Now many companies are beginning to think of society's interests when making their marketing decisions.

One such company is Johnson & Johnson, rated each year in a *Fortune* magazine poll as one of America's most-admired companies, especially for its community and environmental responsibility. Johnson & Johnson's concern for societal interests is summarized in a company document called "Our Credo," which stresses honesty, integrity, and putting people before profits. Under this credo, Johnson & Johnson would rather take a big loss than ship a bad batch of one of its products. And the company supports many community and employee programs that benefit its consumers and workers and the environment. Johnson & Johnson's chief executive puts it this way: "If we keep trying to do what's right, at the end of the day we believe the marketplace will reward us."[21]

The company backs these words with actions. Consider the tragic tampering case in which eight people died from swallowing cyanide-laced capsules of Tylenol, a Johnson & Johnson brand. Although Johnson & Johnson believed that the pills had been altered in only a few stores, not in the factory, it quickly recalled all of its product. The recall cost the company $240 million in earnings. In the long run, however, the company's swift recall of Tylenol strengthened consumer confidence and loyalty, and Tylenol remains the nation's leading brand of pain reliever. In this and other cases, Johnson & Johnson management has found that doing what's right benefits both consumers and the company. Says the chief executive, "The Credo should not be viewed as some kind of social welfare

Our Credo

We believe our first responsibility is to the doctors, nurses and patients,
to mothers and fathers and all others who use our products and services.
In meeting their needs everything we do must be of high quality.
We must constantly strive to reduce our costs
in order to maintain reasonable prices.
Customers' orders must be serviced promptly and accurately.
Our suppliers and distributors must have an opportunity
to make a fair profit.

We are responsible to our employees,
the men and women who work with us throughout the world.
Everyone must be considered as an individual.
We must respect their dignity and recognize their merit.
They must have a sense of security in their jobs.
Compensation must be fair and adequate,
and working conditions clean, orderly and safe.
We must be mindful of ways to help our employees fulfill
their family responsibilities.
Employees must feel free to make suggestions and complaints.
There must be equal opportunity for employment, development
and advancement for those qualified.
We must provide competent management,
and their actions must be just and ethical.

We are responsible to the communities in which we live and work
and to the world community as well.
We must be good citizens — support good works and charities
and bear our fair share of taxes.
We must encourage civic improvements and better health and education.
We must maintain in good order
the property we are privileged to use,
protecting the environment and natural resources.

Our final responsibility is to our stockholders.
Business must make a sound profit.
We must experiment with new ideas.
Research must be carried on, innovative programs developed
and mistakes paid for.
New equipment must be purchased, new facilities provided
and new products launched.
Reserves must be created to provide for adverse times.
When we operate according to these principles,
the stockholders should realize a fair return.

Johnson & Johnson

Johnson & Johnson's concern for society is summarized in its credo and in the company's actions over the years. Says one J&J executive, "It's just plain good business."

program . . . it's just plain good business."[22] Thus, over the years, Johnson & Johnson's dedication to consumers and community service has made it one of America's most-admired companies *and* one of the most profitable.

Linking the Concepts

We've covered a lot of territory. Again, slow down for a moment and develop *your own* thoughts about marketing and marketing management.

- In *your own words*, what *is* marketing management and what does it seek to accomplish?
- What marketing management philosophy appears to guide Nike? How does this compare with the marketing philosophy that guides Johnson & Johnson? Can you think of another company guided by a very different philosophy? Is there one marketing management philosophy that's best for all companies?

Marketing Challenges in the New Millennium

Marketing operates within a dynamic global environment. Every decade calls upon marketing managers to think freshly about their marketing objectives and practices. Rapid changes can quickly make yesterday's winning strategies out of date. As management thought-leader Peter Drucker once observed, a company's winning formula for the last decade will probably be its undoing in the next decade.

What are the marketing challenges as we move into the twenty-first century? Today's companies are wrestling with changing customer values and orientations; economic stagnation; environmental decline; increased global competition; and a host of other economic, political, and social problems. However, these problems also provide marketing opportunities. We now look more deeply into several key trends and forces that are changing the marketing landscape and challenging marketing strategy: the growth of nonprofit marketing, the information technology boom, rapid globalization, the changing world economy, and the call for more socially responsible actions.

Growth of Nonprofit Marketing

In the past, marketing has been most widely applied in the business sector. In recent years, however, marketing also has become a major component in the strategies of many nonprofit organizations, such as colleges, hospitals, museums, symphony orchestras, and even churches. Consider the following examples:

◇ As hospital costs and room rates soar, many hospitals face underutilization, especially in their maternity and pediatrics sections. Many have taken steps toward marketing. One Philadelphia hospital, competing for maternity patients, offers a room with a Jacuzzi and a steak-and-champagne dinner with candlelight for new parents. St. Mary's Medical Center in Evanston, Indiana, uses innovative billboards to promote its emergency care service. Other hospitals, in an effort to attract physicians, have installed services such as saunas, chauffeurs, and private tennis courts.[23]

◇ Even before opening its doors, one church hired a research firm to find out what its customers would want. The research showed that the "unchurched"—people with no current church connection—found church boring and church services irrelevant to their everyday lives. They complained churches were always hitting them up for money. So the church added contemporary music and skits, loosened its dress codes, and presented sermons on topics such as money management and parenting. Its direct-mail piece read: "Given up on the church? We don't blame you. Lots of people have. They're fed up with boring sermons, ritual that doesn't mean anything . . . music that nobody likes . . . [and] preachers who seem to be more interested in your wallet than you. . . . Church can be different. Give us a shot." The results have been impressive. Within a year of opening, the church had attracted nearly 400 members, 80 percent of whom were not previously attending church.[24]

◇ Many nonprofit organizations are now licensing their names and symbols to what they deem appropriate products and making royalties off sales. Two recent examples include the Arthritis Foundation Pain Reliever, marketed by McNeil Consumer Products, and VFW Coffee, marketed by Tetley. The VFW name may soon be associated with a product marketed by Adolph Coors. Royalties from such products can provide a significant boost to the budgets of nonprofits previously dependent on donations for survival.[25]

Similarly, many private colleges, facing declining enrollments and rising costs, are using marketing to compete for students and funds. They are defining target markets, improving their communication and promotion, and responding better to student needs and wants. Many performing arts groups—even the Lyric Opera Company of Chicago, which has seasonal sellouts—face huge operating deficits that they must cover by more aggressive donor marketing. Finally, many long-standing nonprofit organizations—the

YMCA, the Salvation Army, the Girl Scouts—have lost members and are now moderniz-ing their missions and "products" to attract more members and donors.[26]

Even government agencies have shown an increased interest in marketing. For example, the U.S. Army has a marketing plan to attract recruits, and various government agencies are now designing *social marketing campaigns* to encourage energy conserva-tion and concern for the environment or to discourage smoking, excessive drinking, and drug use. Even the once-stodgy U.S. Postal Service has developed innovative marketing plans to sell commemorative stamps, promote its priority mail services against those of FedEx and UPS, and lift its image through sponsorships of the U.S. Olympics and other causes.[27] The continued growth of nonprofit and public-sector marketing presents new and exciting challenges for marketing managers.

The Information Technology Boom

The explosive growth in computer, telecommunications, and information technology has had a major impact on the way companies bring value to their customers. The technology boom has created exciting new ways to learn about and track customers, create products and services tailored to meet customer needs, distribute products more efficiently and effectively, and communicate with customers in large groups or one-to-one. For example, through videoconferencing, marketing researchers at a company's headquarters in New York can look in on focus groups in Chicago or Paris without ever stepping onto a plane. With only a few clicks of a mouse button, a direct marketer can tap into on-line data services to learn anything from what car you drive to what you read to what flavor of ice cream you prefer.

Every 20 years since 1960, the amount of computer power that can be bought for one dollar has increased a thousandfold. That's a millionfold increase in just the last 35 years.[28] Using today's vastly more powerful computers, marketers create detailed databases and use them to target individual customers with offers designed to meet their specific needs and buying patterns. With a new wave of communication and advertising tools—ranging from cell phones, fax machines, and CD-ROMs to interactive TV and video kiosks at airports and shopping malls—marketers can zero in on selected customers with carefully targeted messages. Through electronic commerce, customers can design, order, and pay for products and services—all without ever leaving home. From virtual reality displays that test new products to on-line virtual stores that sell them, the boom in computer, telecommunication, and information technology is affecting every aspect of marketing.

Internet (or the Net)
The vast and burgeoning global web of computer net-works that links computers around the world.

The Internet Perhaps the most dramatic new technology surrounds the development of the "information superhighway" and its foundation, the **Internet**. The Internet is a vast and burgeoning global web of computer networks with no central management or own-ership. It was created during the late 1960s by the U.S. Department of Defense initially to link government labs, contractors, and military installations. Today, the Internet links computer users of all types around the world. Anyone with a PC and a modem—or a TV with a set-top "Web box"—and the right software can browse the Internet to obtain or share information on almost any subject and to interact with other users.[29] Companies are using the Internet to link employees in remote offices, distribute sales information more quickly, build closer relationships with customers and suppliers, and sell and distribute their products more efficiently and effectively.

Internet usage surged in the early 1990s with the development of the user-friendly World Wide Web. The U.S. Internet population grew from only 1 million people in 1994 to more than 60 million in 1998; it will grow to a projected 133 million by the year 2000.

The Internet is truly a worldwide phenomenon. One study projects that worldwide Internet purchasing will grow from only $296 million in 1995 to nearly $426 billion in 2002.[30] Notes one analyst, "In just three years, the Net has gone from a playground for nerds into a vast communications and trading center where some 90 million people swap information and do deals around the world. . . . More than 400,000 companies have hung www.single.com atop their digital doorways with the notion that being anywhere on the Net means selling virtually everywhere."[31] The World Wide Web has given companies access to millions of new customers at a fraction of the cost of print and television advertising. Companies of all types are now attempting to snare new customers in the Web. For example:

- ✧ Car makers such as Toyota (www.Toyota.com) use the Internet to develop relationships with owners as well as to sell cars. Its site offers product information, dealer services and locations, leasing information, and much more. For example, visitors to the site can view any of seven lifestyle magazines—*alt.Terrain*, *A Man's Life*, *Women's Web Weekly*, *Sportzine*, *Living Arts*, *Living Home*, and *Car Culture*—designed to appeal to Toyota's well-educated, above-average-income target audience.
- ✧ Sports fans can cozy up with Nike by logging onto www.nike.com, where they can check out the latest Nike products, explore the company's history, download Michael Jordan's latest stats, or keep up with Tiger Woods's latest movements. Through its Web page, in addition to its mass-media presence, Nike relates with customers in a more personal, one-to-one way.
- ✧ The Ty Web site (www.ty.com) builds relationships with children who collect Beanie Babies by offering extra information, including the "birth date" of the 50-plus toys, highlights on special Beanie Babies each month, promotion of newly developed Beanie Babies, and even an honor-role section that includes a child's photo and grades. Is it effective? By mid-1998, based on the counter on the site, Ty.com had received almost 2 billion visitors.

It seems that almost every business—from garage-based start-ups to established giants such as IBM, GE, Marriott Hotels, JCPenney, and American Airlines—is setting up shop on the Internet. All are racing to explore and exploit the Web's possibilities for marketing, shopping, and browsing for information. However, for all its potential, the Internet does have drawbacks. It's yet to be seen how many of the millions of Web browsers will become actual buyers. Despite growing use of the Web for shopping, in a recent survey 54 percent of Web users said that they were not likely to use the Internet for on-line purchases ever in the future. And although the value of a Web site is difficult to measure, the actuality is that few companies have made any money from their Internet efforts.[32]

However, given the lightning speed at which Internet technology and applications are developing, it's unlikely that these drawbacks will deter the millions of businesses and consumers who are logging onto the Internet each day. "Marketers aren't going to have a choice about being on the Internet," says Midori Chan, vice-president of creative services at Interse, which helped put Windham Hill Records and Digital Equipment Corp. on the Internet, "To not be on the Internet . . . is going to be like not having a phone."[33] We will examine these on-line marketing developments more fully in chapter 14.

Rapid Globalization

The world economy has undergone radical change during the past two decades. Geographical and cultural distances have shrunk with the advent of jet planes, fax machines, global computer and telephone hookups, world television satellite broadcasts, and other technical advances. This has allowed companies to greatly expand their geographical market coverage, purchasing, and manufacturing. The result is a vastly more complex marketing environment for both companies and consumers.

Today, almost every company, large or small, is touched in some way by global competition—from the neighborhood florist that buys its flowers from Mexican nurseries, to the small New York clothing retailer that imports its merchandise from Asia, to the U.S. electronics manufacturer that competes in its home markets with giant Japanese rivals, to the large American consumer goods producer that introduces new products into emerging markets abroad.

American firms have been challenged at home by the skillful marketing of European and Asian multinationals. Companies such as Toyota, Siemens, Nestlé, Sony, and

Marketing at Work 1-3
Going Global: Coca-Cola Dominates

Coca-Cola is certainly no stranger to global marketing. Long the world's leading soft-drink maker, the company now sells its brands in more than 200 countries. In fact, in recent years, as its domestic markets have lost their fizz, Coca-Cola has revved up every aspect of its global marketing. The result: near world dominance of the soft-drink market.

The great "global cola wars" between Coca-Cola and rival Pepsi have become decidedly one-sided. Whereas in the United States Coca-Cola captures a 44 percent market share versus Pepsi's 31 percent, it outsells Pepsi three to one overseas and boasts four of the world's five leading soft-drink brands: Coca-Cola, Diet Coke, Sprite, and Fanta. Coca-Cola has handed Pepsi a number of

crushing international setbacks. As a result, Pepsi has recently experienced flat or declining international soda sales. During the same period, Coca-Cola has reported strong growth in Latin America and grew a stunning 29 percent in China, 17 percent in India, and 16 percent in the Philippines.

Pepsi is now retrenching its efforts abroad by focusing on emerg-

Coca-Cola dominates the global soft-drink market, selling its products in more than 200 countries.

Samsung have often outperformed their U.S. competitors in American markets. Similarly, U.S. companies in a wide range of industries have found new opportunities abroad. General Motors, Exxon, IBM, General Electric, DuPont, Motorola, Coca-Cola, and dozens of other American companies have developed truly global operations, making and selling their products worldwide. Marketing at Work 1-3 provides just one of countless examples of U.S. companies taking advantage of international marketing opportunities.

Today, companies are not only trying to sell more of their locally produced goods in international markets, they also are buying more components and supplies abroad. For example, Bill Blass, one of America's top fashion designers, may choose cloth woven from Australian wool with designs printed in Italy. He will design a dress and fax the drawing to a Hong Kong agent, who will place the order with a Chinese factory. Finished dresses

ing markets—China, India, and Indonesia—where Coke is growing but does not yet dominate. Together, these three emerging markets boast 2.4 billion people, nearly half the world's total population. With their young populations, exploding incomes, and underdeveloped soft-drink demand, they represent prime potential for Coca-Cola and Pepsi. For example, China's 1.2 billion consumers drink an average of only five servings of soda per year, compared with 343 in the United States, creating heady opportunities for growth. And Indonesia, with 200 million people, nearly all of them Muslims forbidden to consume alcohol, is what one top Coca-Cola executive calls a "soft-drink paradise."

But even in these emerging markets, Pepsi will find the going rough in the face of Coca-Cola's international marketing savvy and heavy investment. For instance, by the turn of the century, Coca-Cola will have spent almost $2 billion building state-of-the-art Asian bottling plants and distribution systems. And Coca-Cola possesses proven marketing prowess. It carefully tailors its ads and other marketing efforts for each local market. For example, its Chinese New Year television ad featured a dragon in a holiday parade, adorned from head to tail with red Coke cans. The spot concluded, "For

many centuries, the color red has been the color for good luck and prosperity. Who are we to argue with ancient wisdom?" In India, Coca-Cola aggressively cultivates a local image. It claimed official sponsorship for World Cup cricket, a favorite national sport, and used Indian cricket fans rather than actors to promote Coke products. Coca-Cola markets effectively to both retailers and imbibers. Observes one Coke watcher, "The company hosts massive gatherings of up to 15,000 retailers to showcase everything from the latest coolers and refrigerators, which Coke has for loan, to advertising displays. And its salespeople go house-to-house in their quest for new customers. In New Delhi alone, workers handed out more than 100,000 free bottles of Coke and Fanta last year."

Nothing better illustrates Coca-Cola's surging global power than the explosive growth of Sprite. Sprite's advertising uniformly targets the world's young people with the tag line "Image is nothing. Thirst is everything. Obey your thirst." The campaign taps into the rebellious side of teenagers and into their need to form individual identities. According to Sprite's director of brand marketing, "The meaning of [Sprite] and what we stand for is exactly the same globally. Teens tells us it's incredibly

relevant in nearly every market we go into." However, as always, Coca-Cola tailors its message to local consumers. In China, for example, the campaign has a softer edge: "You can't be irreverent in China, because it's not acceptable in that society. It's all about being relevant [to the specific audience]," notes the marketer. As a result of such smart targeting and powerful positioning, Sprite's worldwide sales have surged 35 percent in the past three years, making it the world's number-four soft-drink brand.

Coca-Cola's success as a global power has made it one of the most enduringly profitable companies in history. And, as one observer states, "Coke will remain the 800 pound gorilla in the soft drink business for the foreseeable future." How profitable has Coca-Cola been over the decades? Incredibly, a single share of Coca-Cola stock purchased for $40 in 1919 would be worth $4,847,000 today.

Sources: Quotes from Mark L. Clifford and Nicole Harris, "Coke Pours into Asia," *Business Week*, October 28, 1996, pp. 72–77; Mark Gleason, "Sprite Is Riding Global Ad Effort to No. 4 Status," *Advertising Age*, November 18, 1996, p. 30; and Scott Reeves, "Pepsi's Fizz," *Barron's*, January 12, 1998, p. 15. Also see, Lori Bongiorno, "Fiddling with the Formula at Pepsi," *Business Week*, October 14, 1996, p. 42; Nicole Harris, "If You Can't Beat 'Em, Copy 'Em," *Business Week*, November 17, 1997, p. 50; Larry Light and David Greising, "Litigation: The Choice of a New Generation," *Business Week*, May 25, 1998, p. 42; Ed Marso, "Cola Wars," *Asian Business*, December 1998, pp. 10–12; and Larry Light, "The Pepsi Regeneration," *Business Week*, March 22, 1999, p. 44.

will be airfreighted to New York, where they will be redistributed to department and specialty stores around the country.

Many domestically purchased goods and services are hybrids, with design, materials purchases, manufacturing, and marketing taking place in several countries. Americans who decide to "buy American" might be surprised to learn that a Dodge Colt was actually made in Japan and a Honda was primarily assembled in the United States from American-made parts.

Thus, managers in countries around the world are asking: What is global marketing? How does it differ from domestic marketing? How do global competitors and forces affect our business? To what extent should we "go global"? Many companies are forming strategic alliances with foreign companies, even competitors, who serve as suppliers or marketing partners. The past few years have produced some surprising alliances between such competitors as Ford and Mazda, General Electric and Matsushita, and AT&T and Olivetti. Winning companies in the next century may well be those that have built the best global networks.

The Changing World Economy

A large part of the world has grown poorer during the past few decades. A sluggish world economy has resulted in more difficult times for both consumers and marketers. Around the world, people's needs are greater than ever, but in many areas, people lack the means to pay for needed goods. Markets, after all, consist of people with needs *and* purchasing power. In many cases, the latter is currently lacking. In the United States, although wages have risen, real buying power has declined, especially for the less-skilled members of the workforce. Many U.S. households have managed to maintain their buying power only because both spouses work. Furthermore, many workers have lost their jobs as manufacturers have "downsized" to cut costs.

Current economic conditions create both problems and opportunities for marketers. Some companies are facing declining demand and see few opportunities for growth. Others, however, are developing new solutions to changing consumer problems. Many are finding ways to offer consumers "more for less." Wal-Mart rose to market leadership on two principles, emblazoned on every Wal-Mart store: "Satisfaction Guaranteed" and "We Sell for Less—Always." When consumers enter a Wal-Mart store, they are welcomed by a friendly greeter and find a huge assortment of good-quality merchandise at everyday low prices. The same principle explains the explosive growth of factory outlet malls and discount chains—these days, customers want value. This even applies to luxury products: Toyota introduced its successful Lexus luxury automobile with the headline, "Perhaps the First Time in History that Trading a $72,000 Car for a $36,000 Car Could Be Considered Trading Up."

The Call for More Ethics and Social Responsibility

Today's marketers must also take responsibility for the social and environmental impact of their actions. Corporate ethics has become a hot topic in almost every business arena, from the corporate boardroom to the business school classroom. And few companies can ignore the renewed and very demanding environmental movement.

The ethics and environmental movements will place even stricter demands on companies in the future. Consider recent environmental developments. After the fall of communism, the West was shocked to find out about the massive environmental negligence of the former Eastern bloc governments. In many Eastern European countries, the air is fouled, the water is polluted, and the soil is poisoned by chemical dumping. In June

"During the week I design pumps and mixers that protect rivers and lakes from pollution.

On weekends I get to enjoy my work."

HJALMAR FRIES
ITT FLYGT STOCKHOLM

Today's forward-thinking companies are responding strongly to the ethics and environmental movements. Here, ITT states "All of our companies share a common goal: To improve the quality of life. Because It's not just how you make a living that's important, it's how you live."

1992, representatives from more than 100 countries attended the Earth Summit in Rio de Janeiro to consider how to handle problems such as the destruction of rain forests, global warming, endangered species, and other environmental threats. Clearly, in the future companies will be held to an increasingly higher standard of environmental responsibility in their marketing and manufacturing activities.[34]

The New Marketing Landscape

The past decade taught business firms everywhere a humbling lesson. Domestic companies learned that they can no longer ignore global markets and competitors. Successful firms in mature industries learned that they cannot overlook emerging markets, technologies, and management approaches. Companies of every sort learned that they cannot remain inwardly focused, ignoring the needs of customers and their environment.

The most powerful U.S. companies of the 1970s included companies such as General Motors and Sears. But both of these giant companies failed at marketing, and today both are struggling. Each failed to understand its changing marketplace, its customers, and the need to provide value. Today, General Motors is still trying to figure out why so many consumers around the world switched to Japanese and European cars. Mighty Sears has lost its way, losing share both to fashionable department and specialty stores on the one hand and to discount mass merchandisers on the other.

As we move into the next century, companies will have to become customer oriented and market driven in all that they do. It's not enough to be product or technology driven—too many companies still design their products without customer input, only to find them rejected in the marketplace. It is not enough to be good at winning new customers—too many companies forget about customers after the sale, only to lose their future business. Not surprisingly, we are now seeing a flood of books with titles such as *The Customer-Driven Company, Customers for Life, Turning Lost Customers Into Gold, Customer Bonding, Sustaining Knock Your Socks Off Service*, and *The Loyalty Effect*.[35] These books emphasize that the key to success in the rapidly changing marketing environment will be a strong focus on the marketplace and a total marketing commitment to providing value to customers.

REST STOP Reviewing the Concepts

Now that you've completed the first leg of your marketing journey, let's review what you've seen. So far, we've examined the basics of what marketing is, the philosophies that guide it, and the challenges it faces in the new millennium.

Today's successful companies—whether large or small, for-profit or nonprofit, domestic or global—share a strong customer focus and a heavy commitment to marketing. Many people think of marketing as only selling or advertising. But marketing combines many activities—marketing research, product development, distribution, pricing, advertising, personal selling, and others—designed to sense, serve, and satisfy consumer needs while meeting the organization's goals. Marketing seeks to attract new customers by promising superior value and to keep current customers by delivering satisfaction.

Marketing operates within a dynamic global environment. Rapid changes can quickly make yesterday's winning strategies obsolete. In the next century marketers will face many new challenges and opportunities. To be successful, companies will have to be strongly market focused.

1. Define what marketing is and discuss its core concepts.

Marketing is a social and managerial process by which individuals and groups obtain what they need and want through creating and exchanging products and value with others. The core concepts of marketing are *needs, wants*, and *demands*; *products and services*; *value, satisfaction*, and *quality*; *exchange, transactions*, and *relationships*; and *markets*. *Wants* are the form assumed by human needs when shaped by culture and individual personality. When backed by buying power, wants become *demands*. People satisfy their needs, wants, and demands with products and services. A *product* is anything that can be offered to a market to satisfy a need, want, or demand. Products also include *services* and other entities such as *persons, places, organizations, activities*, and *ideas*.

2. Explain the relationships between customer value, satisfaction, and quality.

In deciding which products and services to buy, consumers rely on their perception of relative value. *Customer value* is the difference between the values the customer gains from owning and using a product and the costs of obtaining and using the product. *Customer satisfaction* depends on a product's perceived performance in delivering value relative to a buyer's expectations. Customer satisfaction is closely linked to *quality*, leading many companies to adopt *total quality management* (TQM) practices. Marketing occurs when people satisfy their needs, wants, and demands through *exchange*. Beyond creating short-term exchanges, marketers need to build long-term relationships with valued customers, distributors, dealers, and suppliers.

3. Define marketing management and examine how marketers manage demand and build profitable customer relationships.

Marketing management is the analysis, planning, implementation, and control of programs designed to create, build, and maintain beneficial exchanges with target buyers for the purpose of achieving organizational objectives. It involves more than simply finding enough customers for the company's current output. Marketing is at times also concerned with changing or even reducing demand. Managing demand means managing customers. Beyond designing strategies to *attract* new customers and create *transactions* with them, today's companies are focusing on *retaining* current customers and building lasting relationships through offering superior customer value and satisfaction.

4. Compare the five marketing management philosophies.

Marketing management can be guided by five different philosophies. The *production concept* holds that consumers favor products that are available and highly affordable; management's task is to improve production efficiency and bring down prices. The *product concept* holds that consumers favor products that offer the most quality, performance, and innovative features; thus, little promotional effort is required. The *selling concept* holds that consumers will not buy enough of the organization's products unless it undertakes a large-scale selling and promotion effort. The *marketing concept* holds that achieving organizational goals depends on determining the needs and wants of target markets and delivering the desired satisfactions more effectively and efficiently than competitors do. The *societal marketing* concept holds that generating customer satisfaction *and* long-run societal well-being are the keys to achieving both the company's goals and its responsibilities

5. Analyze the major challenges facing marketers heading into the next century.

As they head into the next century, companies are wrestling with changing customer values and orientations; a sluggish world economy; the growth of nonprofit marketing; the information technology boom, including the Internet; rapid globalization, including increased global competition; a call for greater ethical and social responsibility; and a host of other economic, political, and social challenges.

Navigating the Key Terms

For a detailed analysis of the meaning and importance of each of the following key terms, visit our Web page at **www.prenhall.com/kotler**

Customer satisfaction
Customer value
Demands
Demarketing

Exchange
Internet
Market
Marketing
Marketing concept
Marketing management
Needs
Product
Product concept

Production concept
Relationship marketing
Selling concept
Service
Societal marketing concept
Total quality management (TQM)
Transaction
Wants

Travel Log

The following concept checks and discussion questions will help you to keep track of and apply the concepts you've studied in this chapter.

Concept Checks

Fill in the blanks, then look below for the correct answers.

1. _____ is the delivery of customer satisfaction at a profit.
2. Today, marketing must be understood not in the old sense of making a sale—"telling and selling"—but in the new sense of _____.
3. The concept of _____ is not limited to physical objects—anything capable of satisfying a need can be called a _____.
4. _____ is the difference between the values the customer gains from owning and using a product and the costs of obtaining the product.
5. Smart companies aim to _____ customers by promising only what they can deliver, then delivering more than they promise. Customer _____ creates an emotional affinity for a product or service, not just a rational preference, and this creates high customer loyalty.

6. The fundamental aim of today's total quality movement has become _____.

7. The goal of _____ is to deliver long-term value to customers, and the measures of success are long-term customer satisfaction and retention.

8. A _____ is the set of actual and potential buyers of a product.

9. There are five alternative concepts under which organizations conduct their marketing activities: They are the _____, _____, _____, _____, and _____ concepts.

10. "We make it happen for you," "To fly, to serve," "We're not satisfied until you are," and "Let us exceed your expectations" are all colorful illustrations of the _____ concept.*

Discussing the Issues

1. Answer the question, "What is marketing?"

2. Discuss the concept of customer value and its importance to successful marketing. How are the concepts of customer value and relationship marketing linked?

3. Identify the single biggest difference between the marketing concept and the production, product, and selling concepts. Discuss which concepts are easier to apply in the short run. Which concept offers the best long-run success? Why?

4. According to economist Milton Friedman, "Few trends could so thoroughly undermine the very foundations of our free society as the acceptance by corporate officials of a social responsibility other than to make as much money for their stockholders as possible." Do you agree or disagree with Friedman's statement? What are some of the drawbacks of the societal marketing concept?

5. As indicated in the text, "The explosive growth in computer, telecommunications, and information technology has had a major impact on the way companies bring value to their customers." List and briefly explain five ways this trend has affected average consumers and their purchasing habits. Be sure to include in your discussion the impact of the Internet on marketing practices.

* *Concept check answers:* 1. marketing; 2. satisfying customer needs; 3. product, product; 4. customer value; 5. delight, delight; 6. total customer satisfaction; 7. relationship marketing; 8. market; 9. production, product, selling, marketing, and societal marketing concepts; 10. marketing concept

Traveling the Net

Point of Interest: The Marketing Concept

Companies can demonstrate the marketing concept on their Web sites by including features that are important to customers and prospects. Web users want to know about product benefits and where they can purchase the firm's products. However, sites that give users something of interest beyond product descriptions create additional value for the customer. Many sites attempt to target customer segments by language, gender, degree of technical understanding, and age. Finally, an important sign of customer orientation is having an e-mail address that is easy to remember, use, and communicate to the consumer. Evaluate the following Web site based on its perceived attention to the marketing concept: www.apple.com

For Discussion

1. What do you think is the most important customer benefit stressed on this site?

2. What new products did you find?

3. To what extent does this site employ the marketing concept? Support your judgment.

4. Is there anything missing from the site? How could Apple improve the site to enhance the marketing of its products?

Application Thinking

Go to www.compaq.com, www.dell.com, and www.ibm.com and compare these sites to the www.apple.com site in terms of how well they apply the marketing concept. Develop a list of important site characteristics and construct a grid in which you compare the sites on these characteristics. Present your findings in class.

MAP—Marketing Applications

Using the MAP Feature

The best way to become a good marketing decision maker is to practice marketing decision making. In MAP (marketing application) stops at the end of each chapter, you will find interesting case histories, real-life situations, or timely descriptions from business articles that illustrate specific chapter subjects. At each MAP stop, you will be asked to make marketing decisions as though you are the marketing manager of the company in question. Here's your first MAP Stop—have fun on your journey!

MAP Stop 1

For many years, Apple Computer's share of market has dwindled, stock prices have fallen, and consumers have lost confidence in what was once one of the computer industry's most dynamic and fun companies. Now, things may be changing. The company recently introduced its first really exciting new product in many years—the iMac. The iMac appears to be a throwback to the original Macintosh. It has a price tag of $1,299, an all-in-one design (with no provision for expansion), and a flashy metallic blue color and space-age-looking monitor that really catch the eye. The main virtue of the iMac is its simplicity (you can get it set up and running in about five minutes). With the iMac, Apple appears to be targeting first-time users who want a computer that is easy to understand, uses one system, has a hookup to the Internet, and will fit easily on a desk or in a dorm room. The iMac seems to have it all. However, critics point out that it only has a CD drive, a small 15″ monitor, and a 4-GB hard drive.

Thinking Like a Marketing Manager

1. What elements of the marketing concept does Apple appear to be applying with the iMac?
2. Go to a retail outlet that carries the iMac, or go online to www.apple.com, and review the new product for yourself. What seem to be the advantages and the disadvantages of the product? What do you think will be the primary target market(s) for the product?
3. Keeping in mind the marketing concept, relationship marketing, and customer value, design a strategy to overcome criticisms of the iMac and help it maintain profitable sales past its introductory period. Present your strategy to the class.

Strategic Planning and the Marketing Process

ROAD MAP:

Previewing the Concepts

Ready to travel on? In the first chapter, you learned the core concepts and philosophies of marketing. In this leg of your journey, we'll dig more deeply into marketing's role in the broader organization and into the specifics of the marketing process. First, marketing urges a whole-company philosophy that puts customers at the center. Then, marketers work with other company functions to design strategies for delivering value to carefully targeted customers and to develop "marketing mixes"—consisting of product, price, distribution, and promotion tactics—to carry out these strategies profitably. These first two chapters will give you a full introduction to the basics of marketing, the decisions marketing managers make, and where marketing fits into an organization.

▶ After studying this chapter, you should be able to

1. explain companywide strategic planning and its four steps
2. discuss how to design business portfolios and growth strategies
3. explain functional planning strategies and assess marketing's role in strategic planning
4. describe the marketing process and the forces that influence it
5. list the marketing management functions, including the elements of a marketing plan

First stop: Intel, another company which flat-out dominates its industry. As you read about Intel, ask yourself: Just what *is* it about this company's marketing strategy that has given it a 90 percent market share and left competitors in the dust? What is Intel doing so right?

For more than 25 years, Intel has dominated the microprocessor market for personal computers. Its sales and profits have soared accordingly. In the little more than a dozen years since IBM introduced its first PCs based on Intel's 8088 microprocessor, the chip giant's sales have jumped more than twentyfold to more than $25 billion. Its share of the microprocessor market now tops 90 percent, turning competitors such as Advanced Micro Devices (AMD) and Cyrix into little more than also-rans. During the past 10 years, with gross margins hovering at around 60 percent, Intel's average annual return has been an astounding 36 percent.

Intel's stunning success results from strong strategic planning and its relentless dedication to a simple marketing strategy: Provide the most value and satisfaction to customers through product leadership. Some companies deliver superior value through convenience and low prices; others by coddling their customers and tailoring products to meet the special needs of precisely defined market niches. In contrast, Intel's marketing strategy rests on delivering superior value by creating a continuous stream of leading-edge

products. Then, it communicates its superior value directly to final buyers. The result is intense customer loyalty and preference, both from the computer and software producers who add ever-more features that require increasingly brawny microprocessors and from final PC buyers who want their PCs to do ever-more cool things.

Intel's microprocessors are true wonders of modern technology. Intel invests heavily to develop state-of-the-art products and bring them quickly to market—last year alone it spent a whopping $5 billion on R&D and capital spending. The result is a rapid succession of ever-better chips that no competitor can match. For example, less than a decade ago, we marveled at Intel's i386 microprocessors, which contained one-quarter million transistors and ran at clock speeds approaching 20 megahertz. However, Intel's next generation Pentium II series microprocessors contained more than 5 million transistors and ran at speeds exceeding 450 megahertz. Incredibly, the Intel microprocessors of 2011 will pack a cool *billion* transistors and will blaze along at clock speeds of 10 gigahertz (or 10,000 megahertz).

In fact, Intel has innovated at such a torrid pace that its microprocessors have at times outpaced market needs and capabilities. For example, in the early 1990s, the industry's existing bus system—the internal network that directs the flow of electrons within a computer—served up data at a far slower rate than Intel's new Pentium could handle. Why should producers buy the faster chips if existing PC architecture couldn't take advantage of it? Instead of waiting for PC makers to act, Intel quickly designed a new bus called PCI and shared it with computer makers. The PCI became the standard bus on PCs, paving the way for Intel's faster chips.

Intel's growth depends on increasing the demand for microprocessors, which in turn depends on growth in PC applications and sales. Thus, Intel has taken its marketing strategy a step further. Rather than sitting back and relying on others to create new market applications requiring its increasingly powerful microprocessors, it now develops such applications itself. According to one account, to ensure continued growth in the demand for its microprocessors, Intel has set out "to make the PC the central appliance in our lives. In [Intel's] vision, we will use PCs to watch TV, to play complex games on the Internet, to store and edit family photos, to manage the appliances in our homes, and to stay in regular video contact with our family, friends, and co-workers." Of course, at the heart of all of these applications will be the latest Intel-powered PC.

To realize this vision, Intel has invested heavily in market development. For example, it set up the Intel Architecture Labs (IAL), where 600 employees work to expand the market for all PC-related products, not just Intel products. One IAL project involves finding ways to help popularize Internet telephony, through which PC owners can make long-distance voice phone calls over the Net. IAL helped develop better technology for making such calls, worked with the Internet industry to develop telephony standards, and gave away Intel software supporting the standard. Next, Intel will promote technologies and software for Internet videophones. It expects that PC makers will soon build these telephony functions into their products. The result: More people will buy new PCs containing powerful Intel microprocessors.

In recent years, Intel has also invested in dozens of small companies working on projects that might spark demand for the processing power that only Intel can supply. The company's widely varied investments include the Palace, which creates virtual Web communities; Citrix Systems, which makes software to link Internet users; Biztravel.com, an on-line travel service; and CyberCash, which is developing an on-line payment system. Another Intel acquisition, OnLive! Technologies, is an Internet chat room program that offers on-line interactions through 3-D characters. "The next killer app," says the former head of Intel's Internet and Communications Group, "is use of the Internet for on-line [socializing]." He sees the day when individuals can use computers in their own homes to watch a ball game or movie as a group, making comments through their on-line 3-D characters as they watch. Again, such applications will require far more computing power than today's PCs afford. And new Intel chips will provide the needed power.

Intel's marketing strategy goes far beyond superior products and market development. In mid-1991, Intel launched its "Intel Inside" advertising campaign. Traditionally, chip companies like Intel had marketed only to the manufacturers who buy chips directly. But as long as microprocessors remained anonymous little lumps hidden inside a user's computer, Intel remained at the mercy of the clone makers and other competitors. The groundbreaking "Intel Inside" campaign appeals directly to final computer buyers — Intel's customers' customers. Brand-awareness ads — such as those in the current "Bunny People" campaign — create brand personality and convince PC buyers that Intel microprocessors really are superior. Intel also subsidizes ads by PC manufacturers that include the "Intel Inside" logo. Over the years, the hundreds of millions of dollars invested in the "Intel Inside" campaign have created strong brand preference for Intel chips among final buyers. This, in turn, has made Intel's chips more attractive to computer manufacturers.

Looking ahead, Intel must plan its strategy carefully. Its continued torrid growth and industry dominance will depend on its ability to produce a steady flow of state-of-the-art chips for markets ranging from inexpensive home computers to high-end servers. It will have to create irresistible new applications that will lure new consumers into PC ownership and encourage current owners to trade up their machines. Intel's top executives don't foresee any slowing of the pace. Says Intel President Craig Barrett, "We picture ourselves going down the road at 120 miles an hour. Somewhere there's going to be a brick wall, . . . but our view is that it's better to run into the wall than to anticipate it and fall short."[1]

All companies must look ahead and develop long-term strategies to meet the changing conditions in their industries. Each company must find the game plan that makes the most sense given its specific situation, opportunities, objectives, and resources. The hard task of selecting an overall company strategy for long-run survival and growth is called *strategic planning*.

In this chapter, we look first at the organization's overall strategic planning. Next, we discuss marketing's role in the organization as it is defined by the overall strategic plan. Finally, we explain the marketing management process—the process that marketers undertake to carry out their role in the organization.

Strategic Planning

Many companies operate without formal plans. In new companies, managers are some-times so busy they have no time for planning. In small companies, managers sometimes think that only large corporations need formal planning. In mature companies, many managers argue that they have done well without formal planning and that therefore it cannot be too important. They may resist taking the time to prepare a written plan. They may argue that the marketplace changes too quickly for a plan to be useful, that it would end up collecting dust.

Yet formal planning can yield many benefits for all types of companies, large and small, new and mature. It encourages management to think ahead systematically. It forces the company to sharpen its objectives and policies, leads to better coordination of com-pany efforts, and provides clearer performance standards for control. The argument that planning is less useful in a fast-changing environment makes little sense. In fact, the opposite is true: Sound planning helps the company to anticipate and respond quickly to environmental changes and to prepare better for sudden developments.

Companies usually prepare annual plans, long-range plans, and strategic plans. The annual and long-range plans deal with the company's current businesses and how to keep them going. In contrast, the strategic plan involves adapting the firm to take advantage of opportunities in its constantly changing environment. We define **strategic planning** as the process of developing and maintaining a strategic fit between the organization's goals and capabilities and its changing marketing opportunities.

Strategic planning sets the stage for the rest of the planning in the firm. It relies on defining a clear company mission, setting supporting company objectives, designing a sound business portfolio, and coordinating functional strategies (see Figure 2-1). At the corporate level, the company first defines its overall purpose and mission. This mission then is turned into detailed supporting objectives that guide the whole company. Next, headquarters decides what portfolio of businesses and products is best for the company and how much support to give each one. In turn, each business and product unit must develop detailed marketing and other departmental plans that support the companywide plan. Thus, marketing planning occurs at the business unit, product, and market levels. It supports company strategic planning with more detailed planning for specific marketing opportunities.[2]

Strategic planning
The process of developing and maintaining a strategic fit between the organization's goals and capabilities and its changing marketing opportu-nities. It involves defining a clear company mission, set-ting supporting objectives, designing a sound business portfolio, and coordinating functional strategies.

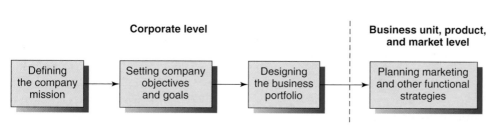

Figure 2-1
Steps in strategic planning

Defining the Company Mission

An organization exists to accomplish something. At first, it has a clear purpose or mission, but over time its mission may become unclear as the organization grows, adds new products and markets, or faces new conditions in the environment. When management senses that the organization is drifting, it must renew its search for purpose. It is time to ask: What is our business? Who is the customer? What do consumers value? What should our business be? These simple-sounding questions are among the most difficult the company will ever have to answer. Successful companies continuously raise these questions and answer them carefully and completely.

Many organizations develop formal mission statements that answer these questions. A **mission statement** is a statement of the organization's purpose—what it wants to accomplish in the larger environment. A clear mission statement acts as an "invisible hand" that guides people in the organization.

Traditionally, companies have defined their businesses in product terms ("We manufacture furniture") or in technological terms ("We are a chemical-processing firm"). But mission statements should be *market oriented*. Products and technologies eventually become outdated, but basic market needs may last forever. A market-oriented mission statement defines the business in terms of satisfying basic customer needs. For example, AT&T is in the communications business, not the telephone business. 3M does more than just make adhesives, scientific equipment, and health care products. It solves people's problems by putting innovation to work for them. Chrysler does more than simply make cars; it produces driving satisfaction. Its mission is to "produce cars and trucks that people will want to drive, will enjoy driving, and will want to buy again." Likewise,

Mission statement
A statement of the organization's purpose—what it wants to accomplish in the larger environment.

Company mission: 3M does more than just make adhesives, scientific equipment, health care, and communications products. It solves customers' problems by putting innovation to work for them.

Table 2-1 Market-Oriented Business Definitions

Company	Product-Oriented Definition	Market-Oriented Definition
Revlon	We make cosmetics.	We sell lifestyle and self-expression; success and status; memories, hopes, and dreams.
Disney	We run theme parks.	We provide fantasies and entertainment—a place where America still works the way it's supposed to.
Wal-Mart	We run discount stores.	We offer products and services that deliver value to Middle Americans.
Xerox	We make copying, fax, and other office machines.	We make businesses more productive by helping them scan, store, retrieve, revise, distribute, print, and publish documents.
O. M. Scott	We sell grass seed and fertilizer.	We deliver green, healthy-looking yards.
Home Depot	We sell tools and home repair/improvement items.	We provide advice and solutions that transform ham-handed homeowners into Mr. and Ms. Fixits.
Ritz-Carlton	We rent rooms.	We create memorable experiences.

Southwest Airlines sees itself as providing not just air travel, but total customer service. Its mission: "The mission of Southwest Airlines is dedication to the highest quality of Customer Service delivered with a sense of warmth, friendliness, individual pride, and Company spirit."[3] Table 2-1 provides several other examples of product-oriented versus market-oriented business definitions.

Management should avoid making its mission too narrow or too broad. A pencil manufacturer who says it is in the communication equipment business is stating its mission too broadly. Missions should be *realistic*. Singapore Airlines would be deluding itself if it adopted the mission to become the world's largest airline. Missions should also be *specific*. Many mission statements are written for public relations purposes and lack specific, workable guidelines. The statement, "We want to become the leading company in this industry by producing the highest-quality products with the best service at the lowest prices" sounds good, but it is full of generalities and contradictions. Celestial Seasonings' mission statement is very specific: "Our mission is to grow and dominate the U.S. specialty tea market by exceeding consumer expectations with: The best tasting, 100 percent natural hot and iced teas, packaged with Celestial art and philosophy, creating the most valued tea experience. . . ."[4]

Missions should fit the *market environment*. The Girl Scouts of America would not recruit successfully in today's environment with their former mission: "to prepare young girls for motherhood and wifely duties." The organization should base its mission on its *distinctive competencies*. McDonald's could probably enter the solar energy business, but that would not take advantage of its core competence—providing low-cost food and fast service to large groups of customers.

Finally, mission statements should be *motivating*. A company's mission should not be stated as making more sales or profits—profits are only a reward for undertaking a useful activity. A company's employees need to feel that their work is significant and that it contributes to people's lives. Contrast the missions of IBM and Microsoft. When IBM sales were $50 billion, President John Akers said that IBM's goal was to become a $100 billion company by the end of the century. Meanwhile, Microsoft's long-term goal has been IAYF—"information at your fingertips"—to put information at the fingertips of every person. Microsoft's mission is much more motivating than is IBM's.[5]

One study found that "visionary companies" set a purpose beyond making money. For example, Walt Disney Company's aim is "making people happy." But even though profits may not be part of these companies' mission statements, they are the inevitable result. The study showed that 18 visionary companies outperformed other companies in the stock market by more than six to one over the period from 1926 to 1990.[6]

Setting Company Objectives and Goals

The company's mission needs to be turned into detailed supporting objectives for each level of management. Each manager should have objectives and be responsible for reaching them. For example, Monsanto operates in many businesses, including agriculture, pharmaceuticals, and food products. The company defines its mission as one of helping to feed the world's exploding population while at the same time sustaining the environment. This mission leads to a hierarchy of objectives, including business objectives and marketing objectives. Monsanto's overall objective is to create environmentally better products and get them to market faster at lower costs. For its part, the agricultural division's objective is to increase agricultural productivity and reduce chemical pollution by researching new pest- and disease-resistant crops that produce higher yields without chemical spraying. But research is expensive and requires improved profits to plow back into research programs. So improving profits becomes another major business objective. Profits can be improved by increasing sales or reducing costs. Sales can be increased by improving the company's share of the U.S. market, by entering new foreign markets, or both. These goals then become the company's current marketing objectives.[7]

Monsanto defines its mission as one of "food, hope, health"—of helping to feed the world's exploding population while at the same time sustaining the environment. This mission leads to specific business and marketing objectives.

Marketing strategies must be developed to support these marketing objectives. To increase its U.S. market share, Monsanto might increase its product's availability and promotion. To enter new foreign markets, the company may cut prices and target large farms abroad. These are its broad marketing strategies. Each broad marketing strategy must then be defined in greater detail. For example, increasing the product's promotion may require more salespeople and more advertising; if so, both requirements will have to be spelled out. In this way, the firm's mission is translated into a set of objectives for the current period. The objectives should be as specific as possible. The objective to "increase our market share" is not as useful as the objective to "increase our market share to 15 percent by the end of the second year."

Designing the Business Portfolio

Guided by the company's mission statement and objectives, management now must plan its **business portfolio**, the collection of businesses and products that make up the company. The best business portfolio is the one that best fits the company's strengths and weaknesses to opportunities in the environment. The company must (1) analyze its *current* business portfolio and decide which businesses should receive more, less, or no investment, and (2) develop growth strategies for adding *new* products or businesses to the portfolio.[8]

Business portfolio
The collection of businesses and products that make up the company.

Analyzing the Current Business Portfolio

The major activity in strategic planning is business **portfolio analysis**, whereby management evaluates the businesses making up the company. The company will want to put strong resources into its more profitable businesses and phase down or drop its weaker ones. For example, in recent years, Dial Corp has strengthened its portfolio by selling off its less-attractive businesses: bus line (Greyhound), knitting supplies, meatpacking, and computer leasing businesses. At the same time, it invested more heavily in its consumer products (Dial soap, Armour Star meats, Purex laundry products, and others) and services (Premier Cruise Lines, Dobbs airport services).

Portfolio analysis
A tool by which management identifies and evaluates the various businesses that make up the company.

Management's first step is to identify the key businesses making up the company. These can be called the strategic business units. A **strategic business unit (SBU)** is a unit of the company that has a separate mission and objectives and that can be planned independently from other company businesses. An SBU can be a company division, a product line within a division, or sometimes a single product or brand.

The next step in business portfolio analysis calls for management to assess the attractiveness of its various SBUs and decide how much support each deserves. In some companies, this is done informally. Management looks at the company's collection of businesses or products and uses judgment to decide how much each SBU should contribute and receive. Other companies use formal portfolio-planning methods.

The purpose of strategic planning is to find ways in which the company can best use its strengths to take advantage of attractive opportunities in the environment. So most standard portfolio-analysis methods evaluate SBUs on two important dimensions—the attractiveness of the SBU's market or industry and the strength of the SBU's position in that market or industry. The best-known portfolio-planning method was developed by the Boston Consulting Group, a leading management consulting firm.

Strategic business unit (SBU)
A unit of the company that has a separate mission and objectives and that can be planned independently from other company businesses. An SBU can be a company division, a product line within a division, or sometimes a single product or brand.

Growth–share matrix
A portfolio-planning method that evaluates a company's strategic business units in terms of their market growth rate and relative market share. SBUs are classified as stars, cash cows, question marks, or dogs.

The Boston Consulting Group Approach Using the Boston Consulting Group (BCG) approach, a company classifies all its SBUs according to the **growth–share matrix** shown in Figure 2-2. On the vertical axis, *market growth rate* provides a measure of market attractiveness. On the horizontal axis, *relative market share* serves as a measure of company strength in the market. By dividing the growth–share matrix as indicated, four types of SBUs can be distinguished:

Stars. Stars are high-growth, high-share businesses or products. They often need heavy investment to finance their rapid growth. Eventually their growth will slow down, and they will turn into cash cows.

Cash cows. Cash cows are low-growth, high-share businesses or products. These established and successful SBUs need less investment to hold their market share. Thus, they produce a lot of cash that the company uses to pay its bills and to support other SBUs that need investment.

Question marks. Question marks are low-share business units in high-growth markets. They require a lot of cash to hold their share, let alone increase it. Management has to think hard about which question marks it should try to build into stars and which should be phased out.

Dogs. Dogs are low-growth, low-share businesses and products. They may generate enough cash to maintain themselves but do not promise to be large sources of cash.

The 10 circles in the growth–share matrix represent a company's 10 current SBUs. The company has two stars, two cash cows, three question marks, and three dogs. The areas of the circles are proportional to the SBU's dollar sales. This company is in fair shape, although not in good shape. It wants to invest in the more promising question marks to make them stars and to maintain the stars so that they will become cash cows as their markets mature. Fortunately, it has two good-sized cash cows whose income helps finance the company's question marks, stars, and dogs. The company should take some decisive action concerning its dogs and its question marks. The picture would be worse if the company had no stars, if it had too many dogs, or if it had only one weak cash cow.

Once it has classified its SBUs, the company must determine what role each will play in the future. One of four strategies can be pursued for each SBU. The company can invest more in the business unit in order to *build* its share. Or it can invest just enough to

Figure 2-2
The BCG growth-share matrix

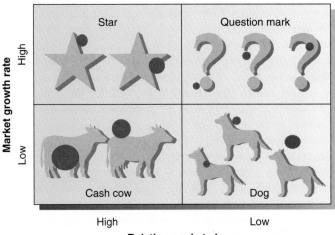

hold the SBU's share at the current level. It can *harvest* the SBU, milking its short-term cash flow regardless of the long-term effect. Finally, the company can *divest* the SBU by selling it or phasing it out and using the resources elsewhere.

As time passes, SBUs change their positions in the growth–share matrix. Each SBU has a life cycle. Many SBUs start out as question marks and move into the star category if they succeed. They later become cash cows as market growth falls, then finally die off or turn into dogs toward the end of their life cycle. The company needs to add new products and units continuously so that some of them will become stars and, eventually, cash cows that will help finance other SBUs.

Problems with Matrix Approaches The BCG and other formal methods revolutionized strategic planning. However, such approaches have limitations. They can be difficult, time-consuming, and costly to implement. Management may find it difficult to define SBUs and measure market share and growth. In addition, these approaches focus on classifying *current* businesses but provide little advice for *future* planning. Management must still rely on its own judgment to set the business objectives for each SBU, to determine what resources each will be given, and to figure out which new businesses should be added.

Formal planning approaches can also lead the company to place too much emphasis on market-share growth or growth through entry into attractive new markets. Using these approaches, many companies plunged into unrelated and new high-growth businesses that they did not know how to manage—with very bad results. At the same time, these companies were often too quick to abandon, sell, or milk to death their healthy mature businesses. As a result, many companies that diversified too broadly in the past now are narrowing their focus and getting back to the basics of serving one or a few industries that they know best.

Despite such problems, and although many companies have dropped formal matrix methods in favor of more customized approaches that are better suited to their situations, most companies remain firmly committed to strategic planning. During the 1970s, many companies embraced high-level corporate strategy planning as a kind of magical path to growth and profits. By the early 1980s, however, such strategic planning took a back seat to cost and efficiency concerns, as companies struggled to become more competitive through improved quality, restructuring, downsizing, and reengineering. Recently, strategic planning has made a strong comeback. However, unlike former strategic-planning efforts, which rested mostly in the hands of senior managers, today's strategic planning has been decentralized. Increasingly, companies are moving responsibility for strategic planning out of company headquarters and placing it in the hands of cross-functional teams of line and staff managers who are close to their markets. Some teams even include customers and suppliers in their strategic planning processes.[9]

Such analysis is no cure-all for finding the best strategy. But it can help management to understand the company's overall situation, to see how each business or product contributes, to assign resources to its businesses, and to orient the company for future success. When used properly, strategic planning is just one important aspect of overall strategic management, a way of thinking about how to manage a business.

Developing Growth Strategies

Beyond evaluating current businesses, designing the business portfolio involves finding businesses and products the company should consider in the future. One useful device for identifying growth opportunities is the **product/market expansion grid**,[10] shown in Figure 2-3. We apply it here to Levi Strauss & Co. (see Marketing at Work 2-1).

Product/market expansion grid
A portfolio-planning tool for identifying company growth opportunities through market penetration, market development, product development, or diversification.

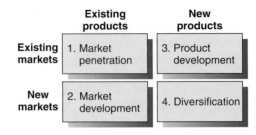

Figure 2-3
Market opportunity
identification through
the product/market
expansion grid

Marketing at Work 2-1

Levi Strauss and Co.: Breaking in New Products and Markets

Invented in 1850 by Levi Strauss, a Bavarian immigrant who sold canvas pants to California gold seekers, blue jeans have long been an institution in American life. And Levi Strauss & Co. has long dominated the jeans industry. From the 1950s through the 1970s, as the baby boom caused an explosion in the number of young people, growth in jeans sales came easily. Levi Strauss & Co. concentrated on simply trying to make enough jeans to satisfy a seemingly insatiable young baby-boomer market. However, by the early 1980s, the baby boomers were aging and their tastes were changing along with their waistlines—they bought fewer jeans and wore them longer. Meanwhile, the 18- to 24-year-old segment, the group traditionally most likely to buy jeans, was shrinking. Thus, Levi found itself fighting for share in a fading jeans market and looking for new strategies for growth.

At first, despite the declining market, Levi Strauss & Co. stuck closely to its basic jeans business. It sought growth by substantially increasing its advertising and selling through national retailers like Sears and JCPenney. When these tactics failed, Levi looked for growth through diversification into faster-growing fashion and specialty apparel businesses. It hastily added more than 75 new lines, including high fashions, sportswear, and athletic wear. By 1984, Levi had diversified into a muddled array of businesses ranging from blue jeans to men's hats, skiwear, rainwear, and even women's polyester pants and denim maternity wear. The results were disastrous: Profits plunged by 79 percent in just one year.

In 1985, in an effort to turn around an ailing Levi Strauss & Co., new management implemented a bold new strategic plan. It sold most of the ill-fated fashion and specialty apparel businesses and took the company back to what it had always done best—making and selling jeans. For starters, Levi rejuvenated its flagship product, the basic button-fly, shrink-to-fit 501 jeans. It invested $38 million in the now-classic "501 blues" advertising campaign, a series of hip, documentary-style "reality ads." Never before had a company spent so much on a single item of clothing. The 501 blues campaign reminded consumers of Levi's strong tradition and refocused the company on its basic, blue jeans heritage. During the next four years, the campaign would more than double the sales of 501s.

Building on this solid-blue base, Levi began to add new products. In late 1986, Levi introduced Dockers, casual and comfortable cotton pants targeted toward the aging male baby boomers. A natural extension of the jeans business, the new line had even broader appeal than anticipated. Not only did adults buy Dockers, so did their children. It seems that every American adolescent boy needed at least one pair of casual cotton pants dressy enough to wear when meeting his girlfriend's parents. The Dockers line has now become America's best-selling trousers—a 1 billion-dollar-a-year success. Seventy-five percent of all U.S. men ages 18 to 45 own at least one pair. Levi has continued to develop new products for the aging, conservative boomers. For example, in 1997 the company introduced Slates, a line of men's dress slacks sold through high-end department stores.

In addition to introducing new products, Levi Strauss & Co. also stepped up its efforts to develop new markets. In 1991, for example, it launched an innovative three-year "Jeans for Women" advertising campaign featuring renderings of the female form in blue jeans by female artists. It also aired a national Spanish-language TV advertising campaign aimed at increasing its appeal to the young, fast-growing, and brand-loyal Hispanic market.

First, Levi Strauss management might consider whether the company's major brands can achieve deeper **market penetration**—making more sales to current customers without changing products. For example, to increase its jeans sales, Levi Strauss & Co. might cut prices, increase advertising, get its products into more stores, or obtain better store displays and point-of-purchase merchandising from its retailers. Basically, Levi's management would like to increase usage by current customers and attract customers of other clothing brands to Levi's.

Market penetration
A strategy for company growth by increasing sales of current products to current market segments without changing the product.

Despite these growth efforts, Levi's U.S. sales have grown only slowly throughout the 1990s. However, although domestic sales have languished, consumers overseas can't get enough of Levi's. Levi's most dramatic growth has been in its international markets. Levi now has become the only truly global U.S. apparel maker. Its strategy is to "think globally, act locally." It operates a closely coordinated worldwide marketing, manufacturing, and distribution system encompassing more than 40 countries. Twice each year, Levi brings together managers from around the world to share product and advertising ideas and to search for those that have global appeal. For example, the Dockers line originated in Argentina but quickly became a worldwide bestseller. The red-and-white store logo containing Levi's trademark stitch pattern, which now adorns each of its 1,000 Original Levi's stores around the globe, was designed in Europe and adopted worldwide. However, within its global strategy, Levi encourages local units to tailor products and programs to their home markets. For example, in Brazil, it developed the Feminina line of curvaceously cut jeans that provide the ultratight fit that Brazilian women favor.

In most markets abroad, Levi Strauss & Co. boldly plays up its deep American roots. For example, James Dean is a central figure in almost all Levi advertising in Japan.

Indonesian ads show Levi-clad teenagers driving around Dubuque, Iowa in 1960s convertibles. And almost all foreign ads feature English-language music. Whereas Americans usually think of their Levi's as basic knockaround wear, most European and Asian consumers view them as upscale fashion statements. The prices match the snob appeal—a pair of Levi 501 jeans selling for $30 in the United States goes for about $63 in Tokyo and $88 in Paris.

To reach around the world more effectively, Levi's operates two Web sites (www.levi.com and www.dockers.com) that feature everything from the history of the brand to fashion tips, games, and youth trends. It has also begun peddling its jeans through on-line stores, which stock more than 120 items in 3,000 variations. Consumers worldwide can log on, use a "Fit Calculator" to find the best size, visit the "Changing Room" to see how mixes and matches of various tops and bottoms look together, and try out the "Style Finder," which recommends styles based on their tastes for music, fashion, and lifestyle. According to the company's vice-president of global marketing, reaction to the Web sites has "exceeded our wildest expectations."

Levi's aggressive and innovative global marketing efforts have produced stunning results. As the domestic market continues to shrink, foreign sales now yield more

than half of the company's total sales. Levi's foreign business is growing at a 50 percent greater rate than its domestic business, and the company continues to look for new international growth opportunities. For example, Levi's is now selling to jeans-starved consumers in India, Eastern Europe, and Russia (but not China, which Levi's exited in a human rights protest).

Thus, by building a strong base in its core jeans business, coupled with well-planned growth through product and market development, Levi Strauss & Co. has found ways to grow profitably despite the decline in the domestic jeans market. Since the 1985 turnaround, the company has more than tripled its revenues and increased its total market value almost fourteenfold. As one company observer suggests, Levi's has learned that "with the right mix of persistence and smarts, [planning new products and] cracking new markets can seem as effortless as breaking in a new pair of Levi's stone-washed jeans."

Sources: "Levi's: The Jeans Giant Slipped as the Market Shifted," *Business Week*, November 5, 1984, pp. 79–80; Joshua Hyatt, "Levi Strauss Learns a Fitting Lesson," *Inc.*, August 1985, p. 17; Maria Shao, "For Levi's, A Flattering Fit Overseas," *Business Week*, November 5, 1990, pp. 76–77; Rebecca A. Fannin, "Levi's Global Guru Shakes Up Culture," *Advertising Age International*, November 1996, pp. i20, i23; Linda Himelstein, "Levi's Is Hiking Up Its Pants," *Business Week*, December 1, 1997, pp. 70–75; Suzette Hill, "Levi Strauss Shrinks to Fit the U.S. Market," *Apparel Industry Magazine*, January 1998, pp. 32–44; Steve Casimiro, "The Khakiest Place on Earth," *Fortune*, March 30, 1998, p. 40; Luisa Kroll, "Digital Denim," *Forbes*, December 28, 1998, pp. 102–103; and "Levi's Ongoing Quest for Street Cred," *Fortune*, February 1, 1999, p. 40.

Market penetration: Clorox increases market penetration by suggesting new household uses for its bleach.

Market development
A strategy for company growth by identifying and developing new market segments for current company products.

Product development
A strategy for company growth by offering modified or new products to current market segments. Developing the product concept into a physical product in order to ensure that the product idea can be turned into a workable product.

Diversification
A strategy for company growth by starting up or acquiring businesses outside the company's current products and markets.

Second, Levi Strauss management might consider possibilities for **market development**—identifying and developing new markets for its current products. For instance, managers could review new *demographic markets*—children, senior consumers, women, ethnic groups—to see if any new groups could be encouraged to buy Levi's products for the first time or to buy more of them. For example, Levi Strauss & Co. launched new advertising campaigns to boost its jeans sales in female and Hispanic markets. Managers also could review new *geographical markets*. During the past few years, Levi Strauss & Co. has substantially increased its marketing efforts and sales to Western Europe, Asia, and Latin America. It is now targeting newly opened markets in Eastern Europe, Russia, India, and China.

Third, management could consider **product development**—offering modified or new products to current markets. Current Levi's products could be offered in new styles, sizes, and colors. Or Levi's could offer new lines and launch new brands of casual clothing to appeal to different users or to obtain more business from current customers. This occurred when Levi's introduced its Dockers and Slate lines.

Fourth, Levi Strauss might consider **diversification**. It could start up or buy businesses outside of its current products and markets. For example, the company could move into industries such as men's fashions, recreational and exercise apparel, or other related businesses. Some companies try to identify the most attractive emerging industries. They feel that half the secret of success is to enter attractive industries instead of trying to be efficient in unattractive ones. However, a company that diversifies too broadly into unfamiliar products or industries can lose its market focus — exactly what happened to Levi Strauss & Company.

Planning Functional Strategies

The company's strategic plan establishes what kinds of businesses the company will be in and its objectives for each. Then, within each business unit more detailed planning must take place. The major functional departments in each unit — marketing, finance, accounting, purchasing, manufacturing, information systems, human resources, and others — must work together to accomplish strategic objectives.

Marketing's Role in Strategic Planning There is much overlap between overall company strategy and marketing strategy. Marketing looks at consumer needs and the company's ability to satisfy them; these same factors guide the company's overall mission and objectives.

Marketing plays a key role in the company's strategic planning in several ways. First, marketing provides a guiding *philosophy* — the marketing concept — that suggests company strategy should revolve around serving the needs of important consumer groups. Second, marketing provides *inputs* to strategic planners by helping to identify attractive market opportunities and by assessing the firm's potential to take advantage of them. Finally, within individual business units, marketing designs *strategies* for reaching the unit's objectives. Once the unit's objectives are set, marketing's task is to carry them out profitably.

Marketing and the Other Business Functions Customer value and satisfaction are important ingredients in the marketer's formula for success. However, marketing alone cannot produce superior value for customers. *All* departments must work together in this important task. Each company department can be thought of as a link in the company's **value chain**.[11] That is, each department carries out value-creating activities to design, produce, market, deliver, and support the firm's products. The firm's success depends not only on how well each department performs its work but also on how well the activities of various departments are coordinated.

Value chain
A major tool for identifying ways to create more customer value.

For example, Wal-Mart's goal is to create customer value and satisfaction by providing shoppers with the products they want at the lowest possible prices. Marketers at Wal-Mart play an important role. They learn what customers need and want and stock the store's shelves with the desired products at unbeatable low prices. They prepare advertising and merchandising programs and assist shoppers with customer service. Through these and other activities, Wal-Mart's marketers help deliver value to customers. However, the marketing department needs help from the company's other departments. For example, Wal-Mart's ability to offer the right products at low prices depends on the purchasing department's skill in tracking down the needed suppliers and buying from them at low cost. Similarly, Wal-Mart's information systems department must provide fast and accurate information about which products are selling in each store. And its operations people must provide effective, low-cost merchandise handling.

A company's value chain is only as strong as its weakest link. Thus, success depends on how well each department performs its work of adding value for customers and on how well the activities of various departments are coordinated. At Wal-Mart, if purchasing can't bring the lowest prices from suppliers or if operations can't distribute merchandise at the lowest costs, then marketing can't deliver on its promise of lowest prices.

Ideally, then, a company's different functions should work in harmony to produce value for consumers. But, in practice, departmental relations are full of conflicts and misunderstandings. The marketing department takes the consumer's point of view. But when marketing tries to develop customer satisfaction, it can cause other departments to do a poorer job *in their terms*. Marketing department actions can increase purchasing costs, disrupt production schedules, increase inventories, and create budget headaches. Thus, the other departments may resist the marketing department's efforts.

Yet marketers must find ways to get all departments to "think consumer" and to develop a smoothly functioning value chain.

> Creating value for buyers is much more than a "marketing function"; rather, [it's] analogous to a symphony orchestra in which the contribution of each subgroup is tailored and integrated by a conductor—with a synergistic effect. A seller must draw upon and integrate effectively . . . its entire human and other capital resources. . . . [Creating superior value for buyers] is the proper focus of the entire business and not merely of a single department in it.[12]

Marketing management can best gain support for its goal of customer satisfaction by working to understand the company's other departments. Marketing managers need to work closely with managers of other functions to develop a system of functional plans under which the different departments can work together to accomplish the company's overall strategic objectives.

Value delivery network
The network made up of the company, suppliers, distributors, and ultimately customers who "partner" with each other to improve the performance of the entire system.

Marketing and Its Partners in the Marketing System In its search for competitive advantage, the firm needs to look beyond its own value chain and into the value chains of its suppliers, distributors, and, ultimately, customers. More companies today are "partnering" with the other members of the marketing system to improve the performance of the entire customer **value delivery network**. For example, Campbell Soup operates a qualified supplier program in which it sets high standards for suppliers and chooses only the

Customer value delivery system: Campbell operates a qualified supplier program in which it chooses only the few suppliers who can meet its demanding quality requirements. Campbell's experts then work with suppliers to constantly improve their joint performance.

few who are willing to meet its demanding requirements for quality, on-time delivery, and continuous improvement. Campbell then assigns its own experts to work with suppliers to constantly improve their joint performance.

Similarly, Honda has designed a program for working closely with its suppliers to help them reduce their costs and improve quality. For example, when Honda chose Donnelly Corporation to supply all of the mirrors for its U.S.-made cars, it sent engineers swarming over Donnelly's plants, looking for ways to improve its products and operations. This helped Donnelly reduce its costs by 2 percent in the first year. As a result of its improved performance, Donnelly's sales to Honda have grown from $5 million annually to more than $60 million in less than 10 years. In turn, Honda has gained an efficient, low-cost supplier of quality components. And as a result of its partnerships with Donnelly and other suppliers, Honda can offer greater value to customers in the form of lower-cost, higher-quality cars.[13]

Today, companies are selecting partners carefully and working out mutually profitable strategies. In today's marketplace, competition no longer takes place between individual competitors. Rather, it takes place between the entire value delivery networks created by these competitors. Thus, if Honda has built a more potent value delivery network than Ford or another competitor, it will win more market share and profit.

Strategic Planning and Small Businesses

Many discussions of strategic planning focus on large corporations with many divisions and products. However, small businesses can also benefit from sound strategic planning. Whereas most small ventures start out with extensive business and marketing plans used to attract potential investors, strategic planning often falls by the wayside once the business gets going. Entrepreneurs and presidents of small companies are more likely to spend their time "putting out fires" than planning. But what does a small firm do when it finds that it has taken on too much debt, when its growth is exceeding production capacity, or when it's losing market share to a competitor with lower prices? Strategic planning can help small business managers to anticipate such situations and determine how to prevent or handle them.

King's Medical Company, of Hudson, Ohio provides an example of how one small company uses very simple strategic planning tools to chart its course every three years. King's Medical owns and manages magnetic-resonance-imaging (MRI) equipment— million-dollar-plus machines that produce X-ray-type pictures. William Patton, the company's chief executive and "planning guru," points to strategic planning as the key to his small company's very rapid growth and high profit margins. Patton claims, "A lot of literature says there are three critical issues to a small company: cash flow, cash flow, cash flow. I agree those issues are critical, but so are three more: planning, planning, planning." King's Medical's planning process, which hinges on an assessment of the company, its place in the market, and its goals, includes the following steps.[14]

1. Identify the major elements of the business environment in which the organization has operated over the past few years.
2. Describe the mission of the organization in terms of its nature and function for the next two years.
3. Explain the internal and external forces that will impact the mission of the organization.
4. Identify the basic driving force that will direct the organization in the future.

5. Develop a set of long-term objectives that will identify what the organization will become in the future.
6. Outline a general plan of action that defines the logistical, financial, and personnel factors needed to integrate the long-term objectives into the total organization.

Clearly, strategic planning is crucial to a small company's future. Thom Wellington, president of Wellington Environmental Consulting and Construction, Inc., says that it's important to do strategic planning at a site away from the office. An off-site location offers psychologically neutral ground where employees can be "much more candid," and it takes entrepreneurs away from the scene of the fires they spend so much time stamping out.[15]

Linking the Concepts

Here's a good place to pause for a moment to think about and apply what you've read in the first part of this chapter.

- Why are we talking about companywide strategic planning so early in a marketing text? What *does* strategic planning have to do with marketing?
- What are Levi Strauss & Co.'s mission and strategy? What role does marketing play in helping Levi Strauss to accomplish this mission and strategy?
- What roles do other functional departments play, and how can Levi Strauss's marketers work more effectively with these other functions to maximize overall customer value?

The Marketing Process

Marketing process
The process of (1) analyzing marketing opportunities; (2) selecting target markets; (3) developing the marketing mix; and (4) managing the marketing effort.

The strategic plan defines the company's overall mission and objectives. Within each business unit, marketing plays a role in helping to accomplish the overall strategic objectives. Marketing's role and activities in the organization are shown in Figure 2-4, which summarizes the entire **marketing process** and the forces influencing company marketing strategy.

Target consumers stand in the center. The company identifies the total market, divides it into smaller segments, selects the most promising segments, and focuses on serving and satisfying these segments. It designs a marketing mix made up of factors under its control—product, price, place, and promotion. To find the best marketing mix and put it into action, the company engages in marketing analysis, planning, implementation, and control. Through these activities, the company watches and adapts to the marketing environment. We will now look briefly at each element in the marketing process. In later chapters, we will discuss each element in more depth.

Targeting Consumers

To succeed in today's competitive marketplace, companies must be customer centered, winning customers from competitors and keeping them by delivering greater value. But before it can satisfy consumers, a company must first understand their needs and wants. Thus, sound marketing requires a careful analysis of consumers. Companies know that they cannot satisfy all consumers in a given market—at least not all consumers in the same way. There are too many different kinds of consumers with too many different kinds of needs. And some companies are in a better position to serve certain segments of the market. Thus, each company must divide up the total market, choose the best segments,

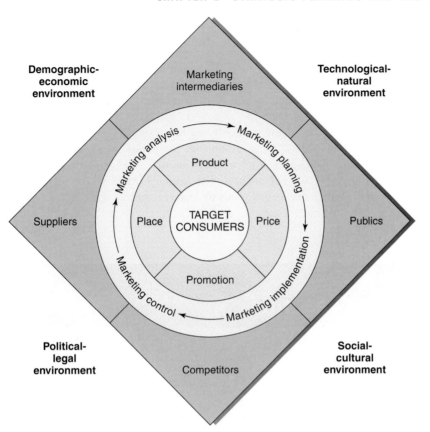

Figure 2-4
Factors influencing
company marketing
strategy

and design strategies for profitably serving chosen segments better than its competitors do. This process involves three steps: *market segmentation, market targeting*, and *market positioning*.

Market Segmentation The market consists of many types of customers, products, and needs, and the marketer has to determine which segments offer the best opportunity for achieving company objectives. Consumers can be grouped and served in various ways based on geographic, demographic, psychographic, and behavioral factors. The process of dividing a market into distinct groups of buyers with different needs, characteristics, or behavior who might require separate products or marketing mixes is called **market segmentation**.

Every market has segments, but not all ways of segmenting a market are equally useful. For example, Tylenol would gain little by distinguishing between male and female users of pain relievers if both respond the same way to marketing efforts. A **market segment** consists of consumers who respond in a similar way to a given set of marketing efforts. In the car market, for example, consumers who choose the biggest, most comfortable car regardless of price make up one market segment. Another segment would be customers who care mainly about price and operating economy. It would be difficult to make one model of car that was the first choice of every consumer. Companies are wise to focus their efforts on meeting the distinct needs of one or more market segments.

Market Targeting After a company has defined market segments, it can enter one or many segments of a given market. **Market targeting** involves evaluating each market segment's attractiveness and selecting one or more segments to enter. A company should

Market segmentation
Dividing a market into distinct groups of buyers on the basis of needs, characteristics, or behavior who might require separate products or marketing mixes.

Market segment
A group of consumers who respond in a similar way to a given set of marketing efforts.

Market targeting
The process of evaluating each market segment's attractiveness and selecting one or more segments to enter.

target segments in which it can generate the greatest customer value and sustain it over time. A company with limited resources might decide to serve only one or a few special segments or "market niches." This strategy limits sales but can be very profitable (see Marketing at Work 2-2). Or a company might choose to serve several related segments—perhaps those with different kinds of customers but with the same basic wants. Or a large company might decide to offer a complete range of products to serve all market segments.

Most companies enter a new market by serving a single segment, and if this proves successful, they add segments. Large companies eventually seek full market coverage. They want to be the General Motors of their industry. GM says that it makes a car for every "person, purse, and personality." The leading company normally has different products designed to meet the special needs of each segment.

Marketing at Work 2-2
Jollibee: Small Can Be Beautiful

When someone says "fast-food restaurant," what's the first name that comes to mind? Chances are good that it's McDonald's, the world's largest food-service organization. McDonald's holds a 42 percent share of the U.S. fast-food burger market, many times the share of its nearest competitor Burger King, and is rapidly expanding its worldwide presence. Ask the same question in the Philippines, however, and the first name uttered likely will be Jollibee. That's right, Jollibee. In the grand scheme of global commerce, Jollibee Foods Corporation isn't exactly a household name. But in its niche, the Philippines, it's king of the burger market.

At first glance, the rivalry between Jollibee and McDonald's looks like no contest. McDonald's has more than 21,000 outlets in 96 countries, 2,735 of them in Asia alone, and nearly $30 billion in annual systemwide sales. By comparison, Jollibee has fewer than 225 restaurants contributing just $313 million in annual revenues. Its sales equal only a fraction of the $1 billion that McDonald's spends annually just on U.S. advertising. Despite these lopsided numbers, in the Philippines, small Jollibee is giving giant McDonald's more than it can handle. Jollibee captures a 75 percent share of the Philippines' hamburger chain market and 55 percent of the fast-food market as a whole. And its sales are growing rapidly and profitably.

Market nicher Jollibee is king of the burger market in the Philippines. The Jollibee burger is similar to "what a Filipino mother would cook at home."

Market Positioning After a company has decided which market segments to enter, it must decide what positions it wants to occupy in those segments. A product's *position* is the place the product occupies relative to competitors in consumers' minds. If a product is perceived to be exactly like another product on the market, consumers would have no reason to buy it.

Market positioning is arranging for a product to occupy a clear, distinctive, and desirable place relative to competing products in the minds of target consumers. Thus, marketers plan positions that distinguish their products from competing brands and give them the greatest strategic advantage in their target markets. For example, at Ford "quality is job 1," and Buick has "the power of understatement." Saturn is "a different kind of company, different kind of car." Mazda has "a passion for the road," and Toyota consumers say, "I love what you do for me." Jaguar is positioned as "a blending of art and machine," whereas Mercedes is "engineered like no other car in the world." The luxurious

Market positioning
Arranging for a product to occupy a clear, distinctive, and desirable place relative to competing products in the minds of target consumers. Formulating competitive positioning for a product and a detailed marketing mix.

What's Jollibee's secret? Smart niching. Whereas McDonald's exports largely standardized fare to consumers around the world, Jollibee is relentlessly local—it concentrates on serving the unique tastes of Filipino consumers. In many ways, Jollibee's operations mirror those of McDonald's: Both offer cleanliness, fast service, and convenient locations. Jollibee's Champ burger competes with the Big Mac and its peach-mango pie replicates McDonald's apple version. However, in contrast to the fairly bland fare that McDonald's serves so successfully worldwide, Jollibee's menu and flavors are specially suited to Filipino tastes. The local chain cooks up sweet, spicy burgers and serves seasoned chicken and spaghetti with sweet sauce, the way Filipinos like it. It serves these meals with rice or noodles, not french fries. "We've designed these products, which are really all-American delights, to suit the Filipino palate," says Jollibee's marketing vice-president. Some items, however, are uniquely Filipino. For example, Jollibee's Palabok Fiesta meal, featuring noodles with fish and shrimp, is very popular in the Philippines. Most Americans wouldn't like it because it smells of fish.

Beyond its special understanding of the Filipino palate, Jollibee has also mastered the country's culture and lifestyle. "What happens in the normal Filipino family is that weekends are especially for children," notes a Philippines business analyst, "and parents try to ask their children where they want to eat." Jollibee lures kids with in-store play activities and a cast of captivating characters. Its hamburger-headed Champ, complete with boxing gloves, goes head-to-head with McDonald's Hamburglar. And its massive orange-jacketed bee and a blond spaghetti-haired girl named Hetti are better known and loved in the Philippines than Ronald McDonald.

Jollibee has some additional advantages in this seemingly unfair rivalry. Although much smaller in global terms than McDonald's, Jollibee concentrates its limited resources within the Philippines, where its restaurants outnumber McDonald's two to one. It also receives a measure of protection through government regulations that limit McDonald's and other foreign competitors. But its primary advantage comes from simply doing a better job of giving Filipino consumers what they want. Small

can be beautiful, and Jollibee has shown that through smart niching small players can compete effectively against industry giants.

In an effort to conquer Jollibee's niche, McDonald's is launching a comeback. It's rapidly adding new locations and introducing its own Filipino-style dishes—spicy fried chicken with rice, sweet-tasting spaghetti, and a heavily seasoned burger called the McDo. However, Jollibee managers don't seem overly worried about their rival's new moves. McDonald's may have greater universal appeal, but Jollibee knows its niche. "Maybe they'll gain market share," says Jollibee's chief executive, "but I don't think anybody can beat us out because, in the final analysis, the customer is the one deciding." And for most Filipinos, the choice is clear. Notes the business analyst, "The Jollibee burger is similar to what a Filipino mother would cook at home."

Sources: Quotes from Hugh Filman, "Happy Meals for McDonald's Rival," *Business Week*, July 29, 1996, p. 77; and Cris Prystay and Sanjay Kumar, "Asia Bites Back," *Asian Business*, January 1997, pp. 58–60. Also see John H. Christy and Gustavo Lombo, "Foreign Gems," *Forbes*, November 4, 1996, pp. 258–262; Andrew Tanzer, "Bee Bites Clown," *Forbes*, October 20, 1997, pp. 182–183; David Leonhardt, "McDonald's: Can It Regain Its Golden Touch?" *Business Week*, March 9, 1998, pp. 70–77; and Robert Klara, "Coming to America," *Restaurant Business*, November 15, 1998, pp. 28–39.

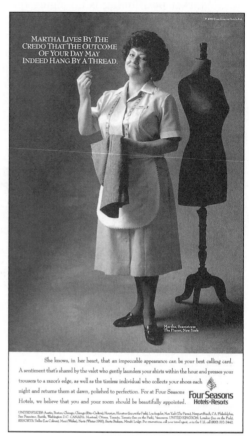

Market positioning: Red Roof Inns positions on value—it doesn't "add frills that only add to your bill." In contrast, Four Seasons Hotels positions on luxury. For those who can afford it, Four Seasons offers endless amenities—such as a seamstress, a valet, and a "tireless individual who collects your shoes each night and returns them at dawn, polished to perfection."

Bentley: "You don't park it. You position it." Such deceptively simple statements form the backbone of a product's marketing strategy.

In positioning its product, the company first identifies possible competitive advantages on which to build the position. To gain competitive advantage, the company must offer greater value to chosen target segments, either by charging lower prices than competitors do or by offering more benefits to justify higher prices. But if the company positions the product as *offering* greater value, it must then *deliver* that greater value. Thus, effective positioning begins with actually *differentiating* the company's marketing offer so that it gives consumers more value than they are offered by the competition. Once the company has chosen a desired position, it must take strong steps to deliver and communicate that position to target consumers. The company's entire marketing program should support the chosen positioning strategy.

Developing the Marketing Mix

Once the company has decided on its overall competitive marketing strategy, it is ready to begin planning the details of the marketing mix, one of the major concepts in modern marketing. We define **marketing mix** as the set of controllable, tactical marketing tools that the firm blends to produce the response it wants in the target market. The marketing mix consists of everything the firm can do to influence the demand for its product. The many possibilities can be collected into four groups of variables known as the "four Ps": *product*, *price*, *place*, and *promotion*.[16] Figure 2-5 shows the particular marketing tools under each P.

Marketing mix
The set of controllable tactical marketing tools—product, price, place, and promotion—that the firm blends to produce the response it wants in the target market.

Product means the goods-and-service combination the company offers to the target market. Thus, a Ford Taurus product consists of nuts and bolts, spark plugs, pistons, headlights, and thousands of other parts. Ford offers several Taurus styles and dozens of optional features. The car comes fully serviced and with a comprehensive warranty that is as much a part of the product as the tailpipe.

Price is the amount of money customers have to pay to obtain the product. Ford calculates suggested retail prices that its dealers might charge for each Taurus. But Ford dealers rarely charge the full sticker price. Instead, they negotiate the price with each customer, offering discounts, trade-in allowances, and credit terms to adjust for the current competitive situation and to bring the price into line with the buyer's perception of the car's value.

Place includes company activities that make the product available to target consumers. Ford maintains a large body of independently owned dealerships that sell the company's many different models. Ford selects its dealers carefully and supports them

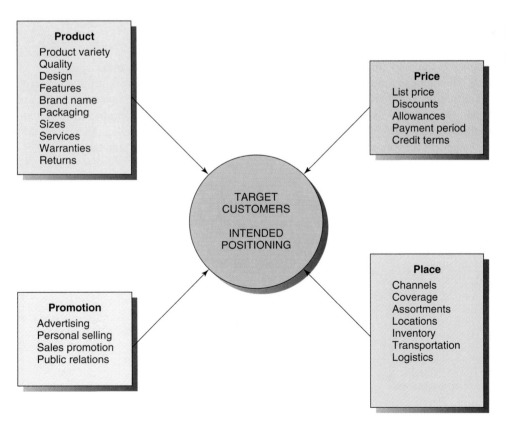

Figure 2-5
The four Ps of the marketing mix

strongly. The dealers keep an inventory of Ford automobiles, demonstrate them to potential buyers, negotiate prices, close sales, and service the cars after the sale.

Promotion means activities that communicate the merits of the product and persuade target customers to buy it. Ford spends more than $1.1 billion each year on advertising to tell consumers about the company and its products. Dealership salespeople assist potential buyers and persuade them that Ford is the best car for them. Ford and its dealers offer special promotions—sales, cash rebates, low financing rates—as added purchase incentives.

An effective marketing program blends all of the marketing mix elements into a coordinated program designed to achieve the company's marketing objectives by delivering value to consumers. The marketing mix constitutes the company's tactical toolkit for establishing strong positioning in target markets.

Managing the Marketing Effort

The company wants to design and put into action the marketing mix that will best achieve its objectives in its target markets. Figure 2-6 shows the relationship between the four marketing management functions—*analysis*, *planning*, *implementation*, and *control*. The company first develops overall strategic plans, then translates these companywide strategic plans into marketing and other plans for each division, product, and brand. Through implementation, the company turns the plans into actions. Control consists of measuring and evaluating the results of marketing activities and taking corrective action where needed. Finally, marketing analysis provides information and evaluations needed for all of the other marketing activities.

Marketing Analysis

Managing the marketing function begins with a complete analysis of the company's situation. The company must analyze its markets and marketing environment to find attractive opportunities and to avoid environmental threats. It must analyze company strengths and weaknesses as well as current and possible marketing actions to determine which opportunities it can best pursue. Marketing provides input to each of the other marketing management functions. We discuss marketing analysis more fully in chapter 4.

Figure 2-6
The relationship between analysis, planning, implementation, and control

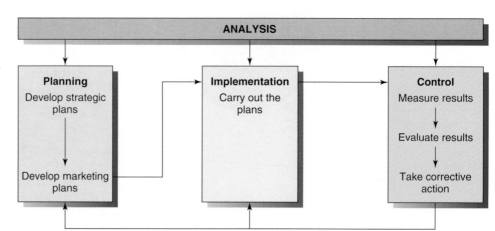

Marketers must continually plan their analysis, implementation, and control activities.

Marketing Planning

Through strategic planning, the company decides what it wants to do with each business unit. Marketing planning involves deciding on marketing strategies that will help the company attain its overall strategic objectives. A detailed marketing plan is needed for each business, product, or brand. What does a marketing plan look like? Our discussion focuses on product or brand plans.

Table 2-2 outlines the major sections of a typical product or brand plan. The plan begins with an executive summary, which quickly overviews major assessments, goals, and recommendations. The main section of the plan presents a detailed analysis of the current marketing situation as well as potential threats and opportunities. It next states major objectives for the brand and outlines the specifics of a marketing strategy for achieving them. A **marketing strategy** is the marketing logic by which the company hopes to achieve its marketing objectives. It consists of specific strategies for target markets, positioning, the marketing mix, and marketing expenditure levels. In this section, the planner explains how each strategy responds to the threats, opportunities, and critical issues spelled out earlier in the plan. Additional sections of the marketing plan lay out an action program for implementing the marketing strategy along with the details of a supporting *marketing budget*. The last section outlines the controls that will be used to monitor progress and take corrective action.[17]

Marketing strategy
The marketing logic by which the business unit hopes to achieve its marketing objectives.

Marketing Implementation

Planning good strategies is only a start toward successful marketing. A brilliant marketing strategy counts for little if the company fails to implement it properly. **Marketing implementation** is the process that turns marketing *plans* into marketing *actions* in order to accomplish strategic marketing objectives. Implementation involves day-to-day, month-to-month activities that effectively put the marketing plan to work. Whereas marketing

Marketing implementation
The process that turns marketing strategies and plans into marketing actions in order to accomplish strategic marketing objectives.

Table 2-2   Contents of a Marketing Plan

Section	Purpose
Executive summary	Presents a brief summary of the main goals and recommendations of the plan for management review, helping top management to find the plan's major points quickly. A table of contents should follow the executive summary.
Current marketing situation	Describes the target market and the company's position in it, including information about the market, product performance, competition, and distribution. This section includes: ▢ A *market description* that defines the market and major segments, then reviews customer needs and factors in the marketing environment that may affect customer purchasing. ▢ A *product review* that shows sales, prices, and gross margins of the major products in the product line. ▢ A review of *competition*, which identifies major competitors and assesses their market positions and strategies for product quality, pricing, distribution, and promotion. ▢ A review of *distribution* which evaluates recent sales trends and other developments in major distribution channels.
Threats and opportunity analysis	Assesses major threats and opportunities that the product might face, helping management to anticipate important positive or negative developments that might have an impact on the firm and its strategies.
Objectives and issues	States the marketing objectives that the company would like to attain during the plan's term and discusses key issues that will affect their attainment. For example, if the goal is to achieve a 15 percent market share, this poses a key issue: How can market share be increased?
Marketing strategy	Outlines the broad marketing logic by which the business unit hopes to achieve its marketing objectives and the specifics of target markets, positioning, and marketing expenditure levels. It outlines specific strategies for each marketing-mix element and explains how each responds to the threats, opportunities, and critical issues spelled out earlier in the plan.
Action programs	Spells out how marketing strategies will be turned into specific action programs that answer the following questions: *What* will be done? *When* will it be done? *Who* is responsible for doing it? And *how much* will it cost?
Budgets	Details a supporting marketing budget that is essentially a projected profit-and-loss statement. It shows expected revenues (forecasted number of units sold and the average net price) and expected costs (of production, distribution, and marketing). The difference is the projected profit. Once approved by higher management, the budget is the basis for materials buying, production scheduling, personnel planning, and marketing operations.
Controls	Outlines the controls that will be used to monitor progress and allow higher management to review implementation results and spot products that are not meeting their goals.

planning addresses the *what* and *why* of marketing activities, implementation addresses the *who*, *where*, *when*, and *how*.

Many managers think that "doing things right" (implementation) is as important, or even more important, than "doing the right things" (strategy). The fact is that both are critical to success.[18] However, companies can gain competitive advantages through effective implementation. One firm can have essentially the same strategy as another yet win in the marketplace through faster or better execution. Still, implementation is difficult—it is often easier to think up good marketing strategies than it is to carry them out.

People at all levels of the marketing system must work together to implement marketing plans and strategies. At Procter & Gamble, for example, marketing implementation requires day-to-day decisions and actions by thousands of people both inside and outside the organization. Marketing managers make decisions about target segments, branding, packaging, pricing, promoting, and distributing. They work with people elsewhere in the company to get support for their products and programs. They talk with engineering about product design, with manufacturing about production and inventory levels, and with finance about funding and cash flows. They also work with outside people, such as advertising agencies to plan ad campaigns and the media to obtain publicity support. The sales force urges retailers to advertise P&G products, provide ample shelf space, and use company displays.

Successful marketing implementation depends on how well the company blends its people, organizational structure, decision and reward systems, and company culture into a cohesive action program that supports its strategies. At all levels, the company must be staffed by people who have the needed skills, motivation, and personal characteristics. The company's formal organization structure plays an important role in implementing marketing strategy; so do its decision and reward systems. For example, if a company's compensation system rewards managers for short-run profit results, they will have little incentive to work toward long-run market-building objectives.

Finally, to be successfully implemented, the firm's marketing strategies must fit with its company culture, the system of values and beliefs shared by people in the organization. A study of America's most successful companies found that these companies have almost cultlike cultures built around strong, market-oriented missions. At companies such as Wal-Mart, Microsoft, Nordstrom, Citicorp, Procter & Gamble, Walt Disney, and Hewlett-Packard, "employees share such a strong vision that they know in their hearts what's right for their company."[19]

Marketing Department Organization

The company must design a marketing department that can carry out marketing strategies and plans. If the company is very small, one person might do all of the marketing work—research, selling, advertising, customer service, and other activities. As the company expands, a marketing department organization emerges to plan and carry out marketing activities. In large companies, this department contains many specialists. Thus, Kraft has product managers, sales managers and salespeople, market researchers, advertising experts, and other specialists.

Modern marketing departments can be arranged in several ways. The most common form of marketing organization is the *functional organization* in which different marketing activities are headed by a functional specialist—a sales manager, advertising manager, marketing research manager, customer-service manager, new-product manager. A company that sells across the country or internationally often uses a *geographic organization* in which its sales and marketing people are assigned to specific countries, regions, and districts. Geographic organization allows salespeople to settle into a territory, get to know their customers, and work with a minimum of travel time and cost.

Companies with many, very different products or brands often create a *product management organization*. Using this approach, a product manager develops and implements a complete strategy and marketing program for a specific product or brand. Product management first appeared at Procter & Gamble in 1929. A new company soap, Camay, was not doing well, and a young Procter & Gamble executive was assigned to give his exclusive attention to developing and promoting this product. He was successful, and the company soon added other product managers.[20] Since then, many firms, especially consumer products companies, have set up product management organizations. However, recent dramatic changes in the marketing environment have caused many companies to rethink the role of the product manager (see Marketing at Work 2-3).

Marketing at Work 2-3
Rethinking Brand Management

Brand management has become a fixture in most consumer packaged-goods companies. Brand managers plan brand strategy and watch over their brands' profits. Working closely with advertising agencies, they create national advertising campaigns to build market share and consumer brand loyalty. The brand management system made sense in its earlier days, when the food companies were all-powerful, consumers were brand loyal, and national media could reach mass markets effectively. Recently, however, many companies have begun to question whether this system fits well with today's marketing realities.

Two major environmental forces are causing companies to rethink brand management. First, consumers, markets, and marketing strategies have changed dramatically. Today's consumers face an ever-growing set of acceptable brands and are exposed to never-ending price promotions. As a result, they are becoming less brand loyal. Also, whereas brand managers have traditionally focused on longer-term, national brand-building strategies targeting mass audiences, today's marketplace realities demand shorter-term, sales-building strategies designed for local markets.

A second major force affecting brand management is the growing power of retailers. Larger, more powerful, and better-informed retailers are now demanding more

Rethinking the role of the product manager: Campbell set up "brand sales managers."

trade promotions in exchange for scarce shelf space. The increase in trade promotion spending leaves fewer dollars for national advertis-

ing, the brand manager's primary marketing tool. Retailers also want more customized "multibrand" promotions that span many of the

For companies that sell one product line to many different types of markets that have different needs and preferences, a *market management organization* might be best. A market management organization is similar to the product management organization. Market managers are responsible for developing marketing strategies and plans for their specific markets. This system's main advantage is that the company is organized around the needs of specific customer segments.

producer's brands and help retailers to compete better. Such promotions are beyond the scope of any single brand manager and must be designed at higher levels of the company.

These and other events have significantly changed the way companies market their products, causing marketers to rethink the brand management system that has served them so well for many years. Although it is unlikely that brand managers will soon be extinct, many companies have been groping for alternative ways to manage their brands.

One alternative is to change the nature of the brand manager's job. For example, some companies are asking their brand managers to spend more time in the field working with salespeople, learning what is happening in stores and getting closer to the customer. Campbell Soup created brand sales managers, combination product managers and salespeople charged with handling brands in the field, working with the trade, and designing more localized brand strategies.

As another alternative, Procter & Gamble, Colgate-Palmolive, Kraft, RJR Nabisco, and other companies adopted *category management* systems. Under this system, brand managers report to a category manager, who has total responsibility for an entire product line. For example, at Procter & Gamble, the brand manager for Dawn liquid dishwashing detergent reports to a manager who is responsible for

Dawn, Ivory, Joy, and all other liquid detergents. The liquids manager, in turn, reports to a manager who is responsible for all of Procter & Gamble's packaged soaps and detergents, including dishwashing detergents and liquid and dry laundry detergents.

Category management offers many advantages. First, rather than focusing on specific brands, category managers shape the company's entire category offering. This results in a more complete and coordinated category offer. Perhaps the most important benefit of category management is that it links up better with retailer category-buying systems, in which retailers have begun making their individual buyers responsible for working with all suppliers of a specific product category.

Some companies are combining category management with another concept: *brand teams* or *category teams*. For example, instead of having several cookie brand managers, Nabisco has three cookie category-management teams—one each for adult rich cookies, nutritional cookies, and children's cookies. Headed by a category manager, each category team includes several marketing people—brand managers, a sales-planning manager, and a marketing information specialist—who handle brand strategy, advertising, and sales promotion. Each team also includes specialists from finance, research and development, manufacturing, engineering, and distribution. Thus, category managers act as small businesspeo-

ple, with complete responsibility for an entire category and with a full complement of people to help them plan and implement category marketing strategies.

Thus, brand managers' jobs are changing, and these changes are much needed. The traditional brand management system is product driven, not customer driven. Brand managers focus on pushing their brands out to anyone and everyone, and they often concentrate so heavily on a single brand that they lose sight of the marketplace. Even category management focuses on products, for example, "cookies" as opposed to "Oreos." But today, more than ever, companies must start not with brands, but with the needs of the consumers and retailers that these brands serve. Colgate recently took a step in this direction. It moved from *brand management* (Colgate brand toothpaste) to *category management* (all Colgate-Palmolive toothpaste brands) to a new stage, *customer need management* (customers' oral health needs). This last stage finally gets the entire organization to focus on building long-term customer relationships based on fulfilling customer needs.

Sources: See Robert Dewar and Don Schultz, "The Product Manager: An Idea Whose Time Has Gone," *Marketing Communications*, May 1989, pp. 28–35; "Death of the Brand Manager," *The Economist*, April 9, 1994, pp. 67–68; George S. Low and Ronald A. Fullerton, "Brands, Brand Management, and the Brand Manager System: A Critical-Historical Evaluation," *Journal of Marketing Research*, May 1994, pp. 173–90; Alan J. Bergstrom, "Brand Management Poised for Change," *Marketing News*, July 7, 1997, p. 5; James Bell, "Brand Management for the Next Millennium," *The Journal of Business Strategy*, March–April 1998, p. 7; Doug Baron, "Customer vs. Brand management," *Brandweek*, November 2, 1998, pp. 32–34.

Large companies that produce many different products flowing into many different geographic and customer markets usually employ some *combination* of the functional, geographic, product, and market organization forms. This ensures that each function, product, and market receives its share of management attention. However, it can also add costly layers of management and reduce organizational flexibility. Still, the benefits of organizational specialization usually outweigh the drawbacks.[21]

Marketing Control

Marketing control
The process of measuring and evaluating the results of marketing strategies and plans and taking corrective action to ensure that marketing objectives are achieved.

Because many surprises occur during the implementation of marketing plans, the marketing department must practice constant marketing control. **Marketing control** involves evaluating the results of marketing strategies and plans and taking corrective action to ensure that objectives are attained. Figure 2-7 shows that implementation involves four steps. Management first sets specific marketing goals. It then measures its performance in the marketplace and evaluates the causes of any differences between expected and actual performance. Finally, management takes corrective action to close the gaps between its goals and its performance. This may require changing the action programs or even changing the goals.

Operating control involves checking ongoing performance against the annual plan and taking corrective action when necessary. Its purpose is to ensure that the company achieves the sales, profits, and other goals set out in its annual plan. It also involves determining the profitability of different products, territories, markets, and channels.

Marketing audit
A comprehensive, systematic, independent, and periodic examination of a company's environment, objectives, strategies, and activities to determine problem areas and opportunities and to recommend a plan of action to improve the company's marketing performance.

Strategic control involves looking at whether the company's basic strategies are well matched to its opportunities. Marketing strategies and programs can quickly become outdated, and each company should periodically reassess its overall approach to the marketplace. A major tool for such strategic control is a **marketing audit**. The marketing audit is a comprehensive, systematic, independent, and periodic examination of a company's environment, objectives, strategies, and activities to determine problem areas and opportunities. The audit provides good input for a plan of action to improve the company's marketing performance.[22]

The marketing audit covers *all* major marketing areas of a business, not just a few trouble spots. It assesses the marketing environment, marketing strategy, marketing organization, marketing systems, marketing mix, and marketing productivity and profitability. The audit is normally conducted by an objective and experienced outside party. The findings may come as a surprise—and sometimes as a shock—to management. Management then decides which actions make sense and how and when to implement them.

The Marketing Environment

Managing the marketing function would be hard enough if the marketer had to deal only with the controllable marketing mix variables. But the company operates in a complex marketing environment, consisting of uncontrollable forces to which the company

Figure 2-7
The control process

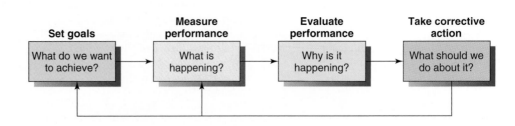

must adapt. The environment produces both threats and opportunities. The company must carefully analyze its environment so that it can avoid the threats and take advantage of the opportunities.

The company's marketing environment includes forces close to the company that affect its ability to serve consumers, such as other company departments, channel members, suppliers, competitors, and publics. It also includes broader demographic and economic forces, political and legal forces, technological and ecological forces, and social and cultural forces. The company needs to consider all of these forces when developing and positioning its offer to the target market. The marketing environment is discussed more fully in chapter 3.

REST STOP   Reviewing the Concepts

What have you learned so far on your journey through marketing? So far, we've defined marketing and its core concepts and philosophies, examined marketing's role under overall company strategy, overviewed the key elements of the marketing process, and outlined the major marketing management functions. So you've had a pretty good overview of the fundamentals of marketing. In future chapters, we'll expand on these fundamentals.

Strategic planning sets the stage for the rest of the company's planning. Marketing contributes to strategic planning, and the overall plan defines marketing's role in the company. Although formal planning offers a variety of benefits to companies, not all companies use it or use it well. Although many discussions of strategic planning focus on large corporations, small business also can benefit greatly from sound strategic planning.

1. Explain companywide strategic planning and its four steps.

Strategic planning involves developing a strategy for long-run survival and growth. It consists of four steps: defining the company's mission, setting objectives and goals, designing a business portfolio, and developing functional plans. *Defining a clear company mission* begins with drafting a formal mission statement, which should be market oriented, realistic, motivating, and consistent with the market environment. The mission is then transformed into detailed *supporting goals and objectives* to guide the entire company. Based on those goals and objectives, headquarters designs a *business portfolio*, deciding which businesses and products should receive more or fewer resources. In turn, each business and product unit must develop detailed marketing plans in line with the companywide plan. Comprehensive and

sound marketing plans support company strategic planning by detailing specific opportunities.

2. Discuss how to design business portfolios and develop growth strategies.

Guided by the company's mission statement and objectives, management plans its *business portfolio*, or the collection of businesses and products that make up the company. To produce a business portfolio that best fits the company's strengths and weaknesses to opportunities in the environment, the company must analyze and adjust its *current* business portfolio and develop growth strategies for adding *new* products or businesses to the portfolio. The company might use a formal portfolio-planning method like the *BCG growth–share matrix*. But many companies are now designing more customized portfolio-planning approaches that better suit their unique situations. The *product/market expansion grid* suggests four possible growth paths: market penetration, market development, product development, and diversification.

3. Explain functional planning strategies and marketing's role in strategic planning.

Once strategic objectives have been defined, management within each business must prepare a set of *functional plans* that coordinates the activities of the marketing, finance, operations, and other departments. A company's success depends on how well each department performs its customer value-adding activities, and on how well the departments work together to serve the customer. Each department has a different idea about which objectives and activities are most important. The marketing department stresses the consumer's point of view, whereas the operations department may be more concerned with reducing production costs. In order to best accomplish the firm's overall strategic objectives, marketing managers must understand other functional managers' points of view.

Marketing plays an important role throughout the strategic planning process. It provides *inputs* to strategic planning concerning attractive market possibilities, and marketing's customer focus serves as a *guiding philosophy* for planning. Marketers design *strategies* to help meet strategic objectives and prepare programs to carry them out profitably. Marketing also plays an integrative role to help ensure that departments work together toward the goal of delivering superior customer value and satisfaction.

4. Describe the marketing process and the forces that influence it.

The *marketing process* matches consumer needs with the company's capabilities and objectives. Consumers are at the center of the marketing process. The company divides the total market into smaller segments, selecting the segments it can best serve. It then designs a *marketing mix* to differentiate its marketing offer and position this offer in selected target segments. The marketing mix consists of product, price, place, and promotion decisions.

5. List the marketing management functions, including the elements of a marketing plan.

To find the best mix and put it into action, the company engages in marketing analysis, planning, implementation, and control. The main components of a *marketing plan* are the executive summary, current marketing situation, threats and opportunities, objectives and issues, marketing strategies, action programs, budgets, and controls. To plan good strategies is often easier than to carry them out. To be successful, companies must also be effective at *implementation*—turning marketing strategies into marketing actions.

Much of the responsibility for implementation goes to the company's marketing department. Modern marketing departments can be organized in one or a combination of ways: *functional marketing organization, geographic organization, product management organization,* or *market management organization.* Marketing organizations carry out *marketing control,* both operating control and strategic control. They use *marketing audits* to determine marketing opportunities and problems and to recommend short-run and long-run actions to improve overall marketing performance. Through these activities, the company watches and adapts to the marketing environment.

Navigating the Key Terms

For a detailed analysis of the meaning and importance of each of the following key terms, visit our Web page at **www.prenhall.com/kotler**

Business portfolio
Diversification
Growth–share matrix
Market development
Market penetration

Market positioning
Market segment
Market segmentation
Market targeting
Marketing audit
Marketing control
Marketing implementation
Marketing process
Marketing mix
Marketing strategy

Mission statement
Portfolio analysis
Product development
Product/market expansion grid
Strategic business unit (SBU)
Strategic planning
Value chain
Value delivery network

Travel Log

The following concept checks and discussion questions will help you to keep track of and apply the concepts you've studied in this chapter.

Concept Checks

1. _____ is the process of developing and maintaining a strategic fit between the organization's

goals and capabilities and its changing marketing opportunities.

2. A _____ is a statement of the organization's purpose — what it wants to accomplish in the larger environment.

3. Management should avoid making its mission too narrow or too broad. According to the text, missions should be _____ and _____, fit the _____, be based on _____, and be _____.

4. A business portfolio is the collection of businesses and products that make up the company. The best business portfolio is the one that _____.

5. A company can classify all its SBUs into one of four types according to the BCG growth–share matrix. _____ are low-growth, high-share businesses or products that produce a lot of cash that is used to support other SBUs.

6. A company can pursue one of four strategies for each SBU. It can _____, _____, _____, or _____ the SBU.

7. Using a _____ growth strategy, the marketing manager attempts to make more sales to current customers without changing products.

8. When each department within a firm carries out value-creating activities to design, produce, market, deliver, and support the firm's products, the department can be thought of as a link in the company's _____.

9. _____ is the process of dividing a market into distinct groups of buyers with different needs, characteristics, or behavior who might require separate products or marketing mixes.

10. The "four Ps" of the marketing mix are _____, _____, _____, and _____.*

Discussing the Issues

1. Define strategic planning. List and briefly describe the four steps of the strategic-planning process.

2. In a series of job interviews, you ask three recruiters to describe the missions of their companies. One says, "To make profits." Another says, "To create customers." The third says, "To fight world hunger." Analyze and discuss what these mission statements tell you about each of the companies.

3. An electronics manufacturer obtains the semiconductors it uses in production from a company-owned subsidiary that also sells to other manufacturers. The subsidiary is smaller and less profitable than are competing producers, and its growth rate has been below the industry average during the past five years. Into which cell of the BCG growth–share matrix does this strategic business unit fall? What should the parent company do with this SBU?

4. Beyond evaluating current businesses, designing the business portfolio involves finding businesses and products the company should consider in the future. Use the product/market expansion grid to explore growth opportunities for a company different from the one used in the text. Be sure that your example covers all four cells.

5. Overall, which is the most important part of the marketing management process: analysis, planning, implementation, or control? Discuss whether a company that "does things right" is more or less likely to succeed than a company that "does the right things."

* Concept check answers: 1. strategic planning; 2. mission statement; 3. realistic, specific, market environment, distinctive competencies, and motivating; 4. best fits the company's strengths and weaknesses to opportunities in the environment; 5. cash cows; 6. build, hold, harvest, or divest; 7. market penetration; 8. value chain; 9. market segmentation; 10. product, price, place, and promotion.

Traveling the Net

Point of Interest: Strategic Planning

Selling computers via the Internet is big business. Gateway 2000, Inc. has proven that selling via the mail, telephone, or the Internet can be very profitable. This computer company has succeeded through careful strategic planning and substantial marketing skill. As a future marketing manager, you can learn some of Gateway's secrets by going to its Web site (www.gateway.com). By reading the company's very interesting history, you can trace the decisions that have enabled it to grow at a fantastic rate. Evaluate the Gateway 2000 Web site.

For Discussion

1. What appears to be the company's mission statement?

2. What customer group(s) does Gateway appear to be targeting? What marketing position does it appear to be seeking? What leads you to believe this?

3. What can you determine about Gateway's marketing mix? What are its product, pricing, distribution, and promotion strategies? What new distribution tactics seem to be on the company's horizon?

4. What is Gateway's chief strategic advantage? Its chief disadvantage?

Application Thinking

Assume that you are one of Gateway's direct marketing competitors. Assess the major strengths and weaknesses of Gateway's strategy. Design a strategic plan by which your company can compete effectively against Gateway in the future. Be sure to consider which target market you wish to pursue and how you might build a Web site that would rival Gateway's. In developing your strategy, you may find the following Web sites helpful: (a) American Demographics and Marketing Tools (www.demographics.com)—provides information for strategic planners seeking to refine their demographic segments; (b) Mouse Tracks (nsns.com/Mouse Tracks)—provides information about building successful marketing Web sites; and Dell Computers (www.dell.com)—shows how a competitor uses the Internet to market its products.

 MAP—Marketing Applications

MAP Stop 2

At one time, Gateway 2000 was known as the company to choose if you wanted to buy a cheaper computer with design-it-yourself features by phone or mail order. Although initially successful, this one-dimensional strategy could take the company only so far. Competitors were rapidly expanding their offerings, developing new channels, forming alliances, and moving into cyberspace commerce. As a result, two years ago Gateway began to change its direction and marketing emphasis. For example, it began opening retail stores that sell and service Gateway products (it currently operates more than 400 retail outlets). The familiar black and white Holstein cowhide-looking boxes used for shipping Gateway products appear now to be giving way to stylish new retail stores placed in the heart of the territories of larger computer retailers (such as CompUSA, Circuit City, and Best Buy). In addition, in order to attract new sales and computer talent, Gateway is moving its administrative headquarters from the cornfields of South Dakota to sunny San Diego, California. It also appears to be redirecting some of its target marketing efforts toward small businesses and away from the large-company market that is heavily targeted by competitors. Gateway is betting that its new strategy will help it to dent rival Dell Computer's sizable market share.

Thinking Like a Marketing Manager

1. How do you think the mission for Gateway 2000, Inc. might have changed in the last few years? What would be an appropriate mission for the company today?

2. Considering the product/market expansion grid, what strategy does Gateway appear to be following?

3. See if there is a new Gateway store in your area. If so, visit the store and compare it to stores in the area that sell competing products. If there are no stores in your area, go to the Gateway Web site for information on the stores and then visit competing stores in your area for comparison.

4. Write a marketing strategy for Gateway 2000, Inc. that will carry the firm into the next century. Be sure to use the steps found in Figure 2-1 in constructing your strategy. Report your ideas to the class.

The Global Marketing Environment

ROAD MAP:

Previewing the Concepts

Now that you understand marketing's fundamentals, your marketing journey continues with the first of three chapters that look into analyzing marketing opportunities. In this chapter, you'll discover that marketing does not operate in a vacuum, but rather in a complex and changing environment. Other *actors* in this environment—suppliers, intermediaries, customers, competitors, publics, and others—may work with or against the company. Major environmental *forces*—demographic, economic, natural, technological, political, and cultural—shape marketing opportunities, pose threats, and affect the company's ability to serve customers and develop lasting relationships with them. To understand marketing, and to develop effective marketing strategies, you must first understand the context in which marketing operates.

▶ **After studying this chapter, you should be able to**

1. **describe the environmental forces that affect the company's ability to serve its customers**
2. **explain how changes in the demographic and economic environments affect marketing decisions**
3. **identify the major trends in the firm's natural and technological environments**
4. **explain the key changes in the political and cultural environments**
5. **discuss how companies can react to the marketing environment**

   At our first stop, we'll check out a major development in the marketing environment, millennial fever, and the nostalgia boom that it has produced. Volkswagen has responded with the recent introduction of a born-again Beetle. As you read on, ask yourself: Is this New Beetle really the right car for the times? Will it succeed in the long run or is it just a passing fad?

As we hurtle into the new millennium, social experts are busier than ever assessing the impact of a host of environmental forces on consumers and the marketers who serve them. "An old year turns into a new one," observes one such expert, "and the world itself, at least for a moment, seems to turn also. Images of death and rebirth, things ending and beginning, populate . . . and haunt the mind. Multiply this a thousand-fold, and you get 'millennial fever' . . . driving consumer behavior in all sorts of interesting ways."

Such millennial fever has hit the nation's baby boomers, the most commercially influential demographic group in history, especially hard. The oldest boomers, now in their fifties, are resisting the aging process with the vigor they once reserved for antiwar protests. Other factors are also at work. Today, people of all ages seem to feel a bit overworked, overstimulated, and overloaded. "Americans are overwhelmed . . . by the breathtaking onrush of the Information Age, with its high-speed modems, cell phones, and pagers," suggests the expert. "While we hail the benefits of the wired '90s, at the same time we are buffeted by the rapid pace of change."

The result of this "millennial fever": a yearning to turn back the clock, to return to simpler times. This yearning has in turn produced a massive nostalgia wave. "We are creating a new culture, and we don't know what's going to happen," explains a noted futurist. "So we need some warm fuzzies from our past." Marketers of all kinds have responded to these nostalgia pangs by recreating products and images that help take consumers back to "the good old days." Examples are plentiful: Kellogg has revived old Corn Flakes packaging, and car makers have created retro roadsters such as the Porsche Boxter. A Pepsi commercial rocks to the Rolling Stones' "Brown Sugar," while James Brown's "I Feel Good" helps sell Senokot laxatives. Disney developed an entire town — Celebration, Florida — to recreate the look and feel of 1940s neighborhoods. And master marketer Coca-Cola resurrected the old red button logo and its heritage contour bottle. The current ad theme, "Always Coca-Cola," encapsulates both the past and the future. According to a Coca-Cola marketing executive, when the company introduced a plastic version of its famous contour bottle in 1994, sales grew by double digits in some markets.

Perhaps no company has more riding on the nostalgia wave than Volkswagen. The original Volkswagen Beetle first sputtered into America in 1949. With its simple, buglike design, no-frills engineering, and economical operation, the Beetle was the antithesis of Detroit's chrome-laden gas guzzlers. Although most owners would readily admit that their Beetles were underpowered, noisy, cramped, and freezing in the winter, they saw these as endearing qualities. Overriding these minor inconveniences, the Beetle was cheap to buy and own, dependable, easy to fix, fun to drive, and anything but flashy.

During the 1960s, as young baby boomers by the thousands were buying their first cars, demand exploded and the Beetle blossomed into an unlikely icon. Bursting with personality, the understated Bug came to personify an era of rebellion against conventions. It became the most popular car in American history, with sales peaking at 423,000 in 1968. By the late 1970s, however, the boomers had moved on, Bug mania had faded, and Volkswagen had dropped Beetle production for the United States. Still, more than 20 years later, the mere mention of these chugging oddities evokes smiles and strong emotions. Almost everyone over the age of 23, it seems, has a "feel-good" Beetle story to tell.

Now, in an attempt to surf the nostalgia wave, Volkswagen has introduced a New Beetle. Outwardly, the reborn Beetle resembles the original, tapping the strong emotions and memories of times gone by. Beneath the skin, however, the New Beetle is packed

with modern features. According to an industry expert, "The Beetle comeback is . . . based on a combination of romance and reason—wrapping up modern conveniences in an old-style package. Built into the dashboard is a bud vase perfect for a daisy plucked straight from the 1960s. But right next to it is a high-tech multi-speaker stereo—and options like power windows, cruise control, and a power sunroof make it a very different car than the rattly old Bug. The new version . . . comes with all the modern features car buyers demand, such as four air bags and power outlets for cell phones. But that's not why VW expects folks to buy it. With a familiar bubble shape that still makes people smile as it skitters by, the new Beetle offers a pull that is purely emotional."

Advertising for the New Beetle plays strongly on the nostalgia theme, while at the same time refreshing the old Beetle heritage. "If you sold your soul in the '80s," tweaks one ad, "here's your chance to buy it back." Other ads read, "Less flower, more power," and "Comes with wonderful new features. Like heat." Still another ad declares "0 to 60? Yes." The car's Web page (www3.vw.com/cars/newbeetle/main.html) summarizes: "The New Beetle has what any Beetle always had. Originality. Honesty. A point of view. It's an exhaustive and zealous rejection of banality. Isn't the world ready for that kind of car again?"

Volkswagen invested $560 million to bring the New Beetle to market. However, this investment appears to be paying big dividends. Demand quickly outstripped supply. Even before the first cars reached VW showrooms, dealers across the country had long waiting lists of people who'd paid for the car without ever seeing it, let alone driving it. One California dealer claimed that the New Beetle was such a traffic magnet that he had to remove it from his showroom floor every afternoon at 2 P.M. to discourage gawkers and let his salespeople work with serious prospects. The dealer encountered similar problems when he took to the streets in the new car. "You can't change lanes," said the dealer. "People drive up beside you to look."

Volkswagen's initial first-year sales projections of 50,000 New Beetles in North America proved pessimistic. After only nine months, the company had sold more than 64,000 of the new bugs in the United States and Canada. The smart little car also garnered numerous distinguished awards, including *Motor Trend's* 1999 Import Car of the Year, *Time Magazine's* The Best of 1998 Design, *Business Week's* Best New Products, and 1999 North American Car of the Year, awarded by an independent panel of top journalists who cover the auto industry.

The New Beetle appears to be a cross-generational hit, appealing to more than the stereotyped core demographic target of Woodstock-recovered baby boomers. Even kids too young to remember the original Bug appear to love this new one. "It's like you have a rock star here and everybody wants an autograph," states a VW sales manager. "I've never seen a car that had such a wide range of interest, from 16-year-olds to 65-year-olds." One wait-listed customer confirms the car's broad appeal. "In 1967, my Dad got me a VW. I loved it. I'm sure the new one will take me back," says the customer. "I'm getting the New Beetle as a surprise for my daughter, but I'm sure I'm going to be stealing it from her all the time."

"Millennial fever" results from the convergence of a wide range of forces in the marketing environment—from technological, economic, and demographic forces to cultural, social, and political ones. Most trend analysts believe that the nostalgia craze will only grow as the baby boomers continue to age. If so, the New Beetle, so full of the past, has a very bright future. "The Beetle is not just empty nostalgia," says Gerald Celente, publisher of *Trend Journal*. "It is a practical car that is also tied closely to the emotions of a generation." Says another trend analyst, the New Beetle "is our romantic past, reinvented for our hectic here-and-now. Different, yet deeply familiar—a car for the times."[1]

Marketing environment
The actors and forces outside marketing that affect marketing management's ability to develop and maintain successful transactions with its target customers.

A company's **marketing environment** consists of the actors and forces outside marketing that affect marketing management's ability to develop and maintain successful relationships with its target customers. The marketing environment offers both opportunities and threats. Successful companies know the vital importance of constantly watching and adapting to the changing environment.

A company's marketers take the major responsibility for identifying significant changes in the environment. More than any other group in the company, marketers must be the trend trackers and opportunity seekers. Although every manager in an organization needs to observe the outside environment, marketers have two special aptitudes. They have disciplined methods—marketing intelligence and marketing research—for collecting information about the marketing environment. They also spend more time in the customer and competitor environment. By conducting systematic environmental scanning, marketers are able to revise and adapt marketing strategies to meet new challenges and opportunities in the marketplace.

Microenvironment
The forces close to the company that affect its ability to serve its customers—the company, suppliers, marketing channel firms, customer markets, competitors, and publics.

Macroenvironment
The larger societal forces that affect the microenvironment—demographic, economic, natural, technological, political, and cultural forces.

The marketing environment is made up of a *microenvironment* and a *macroenvironment*. The **microenvironment** consists of the forces close to the company that affect its ability to serve its customers—the company, suppliers, marketing channel firms, customer markets, competitors, and publics. The **macroenvironment** consists of the larger societal forces that affect the microenvironment—demographic, economic, natural, technological, political, and cultural forces. We look first at the company's microenvironment.

The Company's Microenvironment

Marketing management's job is to attract and build relationships with customers by creating customer value and satisfaction. However, marketing managers cannot accomplish this task alone. Their success will depend on other actors in the company's microenvironment—other company departments, suppliers, marketing intermediaries, customers, competitors, and various publics, which combine to make up the company's value delivery system.

The Company

In designing marketing plans, marketing management takes other company groups into account—groups such as top management, finance, research and development (R&D), purchasing, manufacturing, and accounting. All these interrelated groups form the internal environment (see Figure 3-1). Top management sets the company's mission, objectives,

Figure 3-1
The company's internal environment

broad strategies, and policies. Marketing managers make decisions within the plans made by top management, and marketing plans must be approved by top management before they can be implemented.

Marketing managers must also work closely with other company departments. Finance is concerned with finding and using funds to carry out the marketing plan. The R&D department focuses on designing safe and attractive products. Purchasing worries about getting supplies and materials, whereas manufacturing is responsible for producing the desired quality and quantity of products. Accounting has to measure revenues and costs to help marketing know how well it is achieving its objectives. Together, all of these departments have an impact on the marketing department's plans and actions. Under the marketing concept, all of these functions must "think consumer," and they should work in harmony to provide superior customer value and satisfaction.

Suppliers

Suppliers are an important link in the company's overall customer value delivery system. They provide the resources needed by the company to produce its goods and services. Supplier problems can seriously affect marketing. Marketing managers must watch supply availability—supply shortages or delays, labor strikes, and other events can cost sales in the short run and damage customer satisfaction in the long run. Marketing managers also monitor the price trends of their key inputs. Rising supply costs may force price increases that can harm the company's sales volume.

Marketing Intermediaries

Marketing intermediaries help the company to promote, sell, and distribute its goods to final buyers. They include *resellers, physical distribution firms, marketing services agencies*, and *financial intermediaries*. *Resellers* are distribution channel firms that help the company find customers or make sales to them. These include wholesalers and retailers, who buy and resell merchandise. Selecting and working with resellers is not easy. No longer do manufacturers have many small, independent resellers from which to choose. They now face large and growing reseller organizations. These organizations frequently have enough power to dictate terms or even shut the manufacturer out of large markets.

Physical distribution firms help the company to stock and move goods from their points of origin to their destinations. Working with warehouse and transportation firms, a company must determine the best ways to store and ship goods, balancing factors such as cost, delivery, speed, and safety. *Marketing services agencies* are the marketing research firms, advertising agencies, media firms, and marketing consulting firms that help the company target and promote its products to the right markets. When the company decides to use one of these agencies, it must choose carefully because these firms vary in creativity, quality, service, and price. *Financial intermediaries* include banks, credit companies, insurance companies, and other businesses that help finance transactions or insure against the risks associated with the buying and selling of goods. Most firms and customers depend on financial intermediaries to finance their transactions.

Like suppliers, marketing intermediaries form an important component of the company's overall value delivery system. In its quest to create satisfying customer relationships, the company must do more than just optimize its own performance. It must partner effectively with suppliers and marketing intermediaries to optimize the performance of the entire system.

Marketing intermediaries
Firms that help the company to promote, sell, and distribute its goods to final buyers; they include resellers, physical distribution firms, marketing service agencies, and financial intermediaries.

Financial intermediaries: Firms like Credit Suisse offer a wide range of international financial services, from Atlanta and Abu Dhabi to Barcelona and Beijing.

Customers

The company needs to study its customer markets closely. Figure 3-2 shows five types of customer markets. *Consumer markets* consist of individuals and households that buy goods and services for personal consumption. *Business markets* buy goods and services for further processing or for use in their production process, whereas *reseller markets* buy goods and services to resell at a profit. *Government markets* are made up of government

Figure 3-2
Types of customer markets

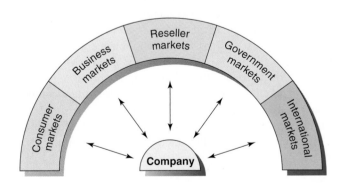

agencies that buy goods and services to produce public services or transfer the goods and services to others who need them. Finally, *international markets* consist of these buyers in other countries, including consumers, producers, resellers, and governments. Each market type has special characteristics that call for careful study by the seller.

Competitors

The marketing concept states that to be successful, a company must provide greater customer value and satisfaction than its competitors. Thus, marketers must do more than simply adapt to the needs of target consumers. They also must gain strategic advantage by positioning their offerings strongly against competitors' offerings in the minds of consumers.

No single competitive marketing strategy is best for all companies. Each firm should consider its own size and industry position compared to those of its competitors. Large firms with dominant positions in an industry can use certain strategies that smaller firms cannot afford. But being large is not enough. There are winning strategies for large firms, but there are also losing ones. And small firms can develop strategies that give them better rates of return than large firms enjoy.

Publics

The company's marketing environment also includes various publics. A **public** is any group that has an actual or potential interest in or impact on an organization's ability to achieve its objectives. Figure 3-3 shows seven types of publics.

Public
Any group that has an actual or potential interest in or impact on an organization's ability to achieve its objectives.

- *Financial publics* influence the company's ability to obtain funds. Banks, investment houses, and stockholders are the major financial publics.
- *Media publics* carry news, features, and editorial opinion. They include newspapers, magazines, and radio and television stations.
- *Government publics.* Management must take government developments into account. Marketers must often consult the company's lawyers on issues of product safety, truth in advertising, and other matters.
- *Citizen-action publics.* A company's marketing decisions may be questioned by consumer organizations, environmental groups, minority groups, and others. Its public relations department can help it stay in touch with consumer and citizen groups.
- *Local publics* include neighborhood residents and community organizations. Large companies usually appoint a community relations officer to deal with the community, attend meetings, answer questions, and contribute to worthwhile causes.

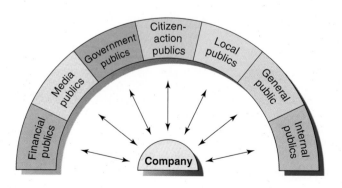

Figure 3-3
Types of publics

Companies market to internal publics as well as to customers: Wal-Mart includes employees as models in its advertising, making them feel good about working for the company.

◌ *General public.* A company needs to be concerned about the general public's attitude toward its products and activities. The public's image of the company affects its buying behavior.

◌ *Internal publics* include workers, managers, volunteers, and the board of directors. Large companies use newsletters and other means to inform and motivate their internal publics. When employees feel good about their company, this positive attitude spills over to external publics.

A company can prepare marketing plans for these major publics as well as for its customer markets. Suppose the company wants a specific response from a particular public, such as goodwill, favorable word of mouth, or donations of time or money. The company would have to design an offer to this public that is attractive enough to produce the desired response.

The Company's Macroenvironment

The company and all of the other actors operate in a larger macroenvironment of forces that shape opportunities and pose threats to the company. Figure 3-4 shows the six major forces in the company's macroenvironment. In the remaining sections of this chapter, we examine these forces and show how they affect marketing plans.

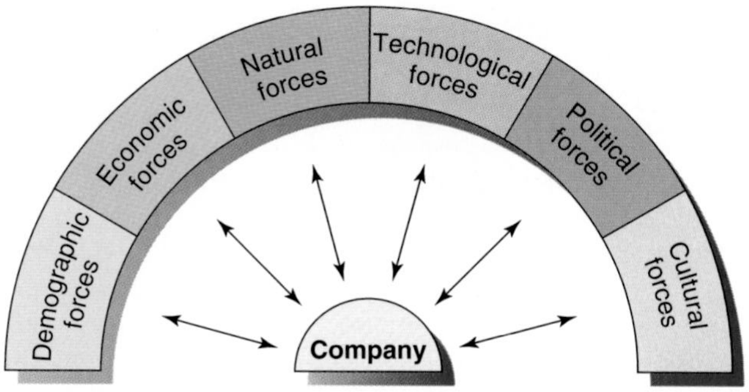

Figure 3-4
Major forces in the company's macroenvironment

Demographic Environment

Demography is the study of human populations in terms of size, density, location, age, gender, race, occupation, and other statistics. The demographic environment is of major interest to marketers because it involves people, and people make up markets.

The world population is growing at an explosive rate. It now totals more than 5.9 billion and will exceed 7.9 billion by the year 2025.[2] The explosive world population growth has major implications for business. A growing population means growing human needs to satisfy. Depending on purchasing power, it may also mean growing market opportunities. For example, to curb its skyrocketing population, the Chinese government has passed regulations limiting families to one child each. As a result, Chinese children are spoiled and fussed over as never before. Known in China as "little emperors," Chinese children are being showered with everything from candy to computers as a result of what's known as the "six-pocket syndrome." As many as six adults—including parents, grandparents, great-grandparents, and aunts and uncles—may be indulging the whims of each child. This trend has encouraged toy companies such as Japan's Bandai Company (known for its Mighty Morphin Power Rangers), Denmark's Lego Group, and Mattel to enter the Chinese market.[3]

The world's large and highly diverse population poses both opportunities and challenges (see Marketing at Work 3-1). Thus, marketers keep close track of demographic trends and developments in their markets, both at home and abroad. They track changing age and family structures, geographic population shifts, educational characteristics, and population diversity. Here, we discuss the most important demographic trends in the United States.

Changing Age Structure of the U.S. Population The U.S. population stood at more than 270 million in 1998 and may reach 300 million by the year 2020.[4] The single most important demographic trend in the United States is the changing age structure of the population. The U.S. population is getting *older*, for two reasons. First, there is a long-term slowdown in the birthrate, so there are fewer young people to pull the population's average age down. Second, life expectancy is increasing, so there are more older people to pull the average age up.

During the **baby boom** that followed World War II and lasted until the early 1960s, the annual birthrate reached an all-time high. The baby boom created a huge "bulge" in the U.S. age distribution—the 78 million baby boomers now account for almost one-third of the nation's population. And as the baby boom generation ages, the nation's average age climbs with it. Because of its sheer size, the baby boom generation

Demography
The study of human populations in terms of size, density, location, age, gender, race, occupation, and other statistics.

Baby boom
The major increase in the annual birthrate following World War II and lasting until the early 1960s. The "baby boomers," now moving into middle age, are a prime target for marketers.

Marketing at Work 3-1
If the World Were a Village

Think for a few minutes about the world and your place in it. If we reduced the world to a village of 1,000 people representative of the world's population, this would be our reality:

- Our village would have 520 women and 480 men; 330 children and 60 people over age 65; 10 college graduates and 335 illiterate adults.
- We'd have 52 North Americans, 55 Russians, 84 Latin Americans, 95 Europeans, 124 Africans, and 584 Asians.
- Communication would be difficult: 165 of us would speak Mandarin, 86 English, 83 Hindi, 64 Spanish, 58 Russian, and 37

Arabic. The other half of us would speak one of more than 200 other languages.
- Among us we'd have 329 Christians, 178 Moslems, 132 Hindus, 62 Buddhists, 3 Jews, 167 nonreligious, 45 atheists, and 84 others.
- About one-third of our people would have access to clean, safe drinking water. About half of our children would be immunized against infections.
- The woodlands in our village would be decreasing rapidly and wasteland would be growing. Forty percent of the village's crop land, nourished by 83 percent of our fertilizer, would produce 72 percent of the food to feed its 270 well-fed owners. The

remaining 60 percent of the land and 17 percent of the fertilizer would produce 28 percent of the food to feed the other 730 people. Five hundred people in the village would suffer from malnutrition.
- Only 200 of the 1,000 people would control 75 percent of our village's wealth. Another 200 would receive only 2 percent of the wealth. Seventy people would own cars. One would have a computer, and that computer probably would not be connected to the Internet.

Source: Taken from The World Village Project Web site, www.WorldVillage.org, April 1999.

---

accounts for many major demographic and socioeconomic changes in the United States.

The baby boom was followed by a "birth dearth," and by the mid 1970s the birthrate had fallen sharply. This decrease was caused by smaller family sizes resulting from Americans' desire to improve their personal living standards, the increasing desire of women to work outside the home, and improved birth control. Although family sizes are expected to remain smaller, the birthrate has climbed again as the baby boom generation moves through the childbearing years, creating a second and almost-as-large "baby boomlet." However, following this boomlet, the birthrate will again decline as we move into the twenty-first century.[5] Table 3-1 shows estimates of the changing age distribution of the U.S. population through 2050. The differing growth rates for various age groups will strongly affect marketers' targeting strategies (see Marketing at Work 3-2).

The Changing American Family The American ideal of the two-child, two-car suburban family has lately been losing some of its luster. People are marrying later and having fewer children. Despite the recent "baby boomlet," the number of married couples with children will continue to decline through the end of the twentieth century. In fact, couples with children under 18 now make up only about 35 percent of all families.[6]

Also, the number of working women has increased greatly. Currently, in the United States, 58 percent of all women 16 and older are working or looking for a job. It is expected that 65 percent of women will be in the labor force by 2005.[7] Marketers of tires, automobiles, insurance, travel, and financial services are increasingly directing their advertising to working women. As a result of the shift in the traditional roles and values of husbands and wives, with husbands assuming more domestic functions such as shopping and child care, more food and household appliance marketers are targeting husbands.

Table 3-1 Percent Distribution of U.S. Population by Age

Age Group	1998	2000	2005	2010	2020	2030	2040	2050
Under 5	7.1	6.9	6.7	6.7	6.8	6.6	6.8	6.9
5 to 13	13.2	13.1	12.5	12.0	12.0	12.0	11.9	12.1
14 to 17	5.7	5.7	5.9	5.7	5.3	5.4	5.4	5.4
18 to 24	9.3	9.6	9.9	10.1	9.3	9.2	9.3	9.2
25 to 34	14.4	13.6	12.7	12.9	13.3	12.3	12.4	12.5
35 to 44	16.4	16.3	14.7	12.9	12.3	12.8	11.9	12.0
45 to 54	12.8	13.5	14.5	14.6	11.7	11.2	11.8	11.0
55 to 64	8.4	8.7	10.4	11.9	12.9	10.5	10.2	10.8
65 to 74	6.8	6.6	6.4	7.1	9.7	10.8	8.9	8.8
75 to 84	4.4	4.5	4.5	4.3	4.8	6.8	7.7	6.6
85 years and over	1.5	1.6	1.7	1.9	2.0	2.4	3.7	4.6

Source: Based on information from the U.S. Census Web site, www.census.gov/statab/freq/96s0017.txt, June 27, 1998.

Finally, the number of nonfamily households is increasing. Many young adults leave home and move into apartments. Other adults choose to remain single. Still others are divorced or widowed people living alone. By the year 2000, 46 percent of all households will be nonfamily or single-parent households—the fastest-growing categories of households. These groups have their own special needs. For example, they need smaller apartments; inexpensive and smaller appliances, furniture, and furnishings; and food that is packaged in smaller sizes.

As the number of working moms increases, more marketers are targeting this segment for products such as automobiles, insurance, travel, and financial services.

Marketing at Work 3-2

The Baby Boomers, the Generation Xers, and the Baby Boomlet

Demographics involve people, and people make up markets. Thus, marketers track demographic groups carefully. Three of today's most important demographic groups are the so-called *baby boomers*, the *Generation Xers*, and the *baby boomlet* generation.

The Baby Boomers

The postwar baby boom, which began in 1946 and ran through 1964, produced 78 million babies. Since then, the baby boomers have become one of the biggest forces shaping the marketing environment. The boomers have presented a moving target, creating new markets as they grew from infancy to their preadolescent, teenage, young-adult, and now middle-age years. Today's baby boomers account for almost a third of the population but make up 40 percent of the workforce and earn more than half of all personal income.

Baby boomers cut across all walks of life. But marketers typically have paid the most attention to the small upper crust of the boomer generation—its more educated, mobile, and wealthy segments. These segments have gone by many names. In the 1980s, they were called "yuppies" (young urban professionals); "bumpies" (black upwardly mobile professionals); "yummies" (young upwardly mobile mommies), and "DINKs" (dual-income, no-kids couples). In the 1990s, however, yuppies and DINKs have given way to a new breed, with names such as DEWKs (dual earners with kids); MOBYs (mother older, baby younger); WOOFs (well-off older folks); or

SPORTS ILLUSTRATED FOR KIDS magazine inspires kids who love sports to love reading.

SAVE OVER 23%* *OFF THE COVER PRICE

EVERY ISSUE IS PACKED WITH GREAT STUFF KIDS WANT:
• Stories and sports tips from their favorite athletes & teams
• Spectacular action photos
• Challenging games, fun contests

See for yourself why millions of boys and girls ages 7 and up cheer for SPORTS ILLUSTRATED FOR KIDS. Call now for your FREE PREVIEW ISSUE. Try it—risk free! If your child likes it, pay only $29.95 for 12 monthly issues plus our annual sports almanac. Or return the bill marked "cancel" and owe absolutely nothing.

Sports Illustrated FOR KIDS

SEND THE PERFECT GIFT TODAY!

TO GET YOUR FREE PREVIEW ISSUE
Call Toll Free:
1-800-628-3688
CHECK US OUT ON THE WEB AT WWW.SIKIDS.COM

just plain GRUMPIES (just what the name suggests).

The older boomers are now in their fifties; the youngest are in their mid-to-late thirties. Thus, the boomers have evolved from the "youthquake generation" to the "backache generation." They have slowed up, settled down, and are raising children. They are also reaching their peak earning and spending years. Thus, they constitute a lucrative market for housing, furniture and appliances, children's products, low-calorie foods and beverages, physical fitness products, high-priced cars, convenience products, and travel and financial services.

The maturing boomers are experiencing the pangs of midlife and rethinking the purpose and value of their work, responsibilities, and relationships. They are approaching life with a new stability and reasonableness in the way they live, think, eat, and spend. Community and family values have become more important, and staying home with the family has become their favorite way to spend an evening.

The Generation Xers

Some marketers think that focusing on the boomers has caused companies to overlook other important segments, especially younger consumers. Focus has increasingly shifted in recent years to a new group, those born between 1965 and 1976. Author Douglas Coupland calls them "Generation X," because they lie in the shadow of the boomers and lack obvious distinguishing characteristics. Others call them the "baby busters," "shadow generation," "twentysomethings," or "yiffies"—young, individualistic, freedom-minded few.

The GenXers are defined as much by their shared experiences as by their age. Increasing divorce rates and higher employment for their mothers made them the first generation of latchkey kids. Whereas the boomers created a sexual revolution, the GenXers have lived in the age of AIDS. Having grown up during times of recession and corporate downsizing, they have developed a more cautious economic outlook. As a result, the GenXers are a more skeptical bunch, cynical of frivolous marketing pitches that promise easy success. They buy lots of products, such as sweaters, boots, cosmetics, electronics, cars, fast food, beer, computers, and mountain bikes. However, their cynicism makes them more savvy shoppers, and their financial pressures make them more value conscious. They like lower prices and a more functional look. The GenXers respond to honesty in advertising, and they like irreverence and sass and ads that mock the traditional advertising approach.

GenXers share new cultural concerns. They care about the environment and respond favorably to socially responsible companies. Although they seek success, they are less materialistic; they prize experience, not acquisition. They are cautious romantics who want a better quality of life and are more interested in job satisfaction than in sacrificing personal happiness and growth for promotion.

Once labeled as "The MTV generation: Net surfing, nihilistic [body-piercing slackers] whining about McJobs," the GenXers are now growing up and beginning to take over. They do surf the Net more than other groups, but with serious intent. The 45 million GenXers are poised to displace the lifestyles, culture, and materialistic values of the baby boomers. And they represent $125 billion in annual purchasing power. By the year 2010, they will have overtaken the baby boomers as a primary market for almost every product category. According to one analyst, "They are flocking to technology startups, founding small businesses, and even taking up causes—all in their own way. They're the next big thing. Boomers, beware!"

The Baby Boomlet

Both the baby boomers and Gen-Xers will one day be passing the reins to the latest demographic group, the baby boomlet generation. Born between 1977 and 1994, these children of the baby boomers now number 72 million, dwarfing the GenXers and almost equal in size to the baby boomer segment. Ranging from preteens to twenties, the boomlet generation is still forming its buying preferences and behaviors.

The baby boomlet has created a large and growing kid market.

Children under 17 years of age influence an estimated $295 billion worth of purchases each year. After years of bust, markets for children's toys and games, clothes, furniture, and food are enjoying a boom. For instance, Sony and other electronics firms are now offering products designed especially for children. Many retailers are opening separate children's clothing chains, such as GapKids and Kids 'R' Us. And a number of new media have appeared that cater specifically to this market: *Time*, *Sports Illustrated*, and *People* have all started new editions for kids and teens. Banks offer banking and investment services for kids, including investment camps. Major advertising agencies have even opened new divisions—such as Saatchi & Saatchi Advertising's Kid Connection division and Grey Advertising's 18 & Under division—that specialize in helping their clients shape their appeals for young audiences. Boomers and GenXers, prepare to step aside!

Sources: Quotes from Margot Hornblower, "Great X," *Time*, June 9, 1997, pp. 58–69. Also see Bruce Horowitz, "Gen X in a Class By Itself," *USA Today*, September 23, 1996, p. B1; Jeff Minerd, "Bringing Out the Best in Generation X," *Futurist*, January 1999, p. 6; Laura Brad Edmondson, "Children in 2001," *American Demographics*, March 1997, pp. 14–15; David Leonhardt, "Hey Kid, Buy This," *Business Week*, June 30, 1997, pp. 62–67; James U. McNeal, "Tapping the Three Kids' Markets," *American Demographics*, April 1998, pp. 37–40; Walker Smith and Ann Clurman, *Rocking the Ages* (New York: HarperBusiness, 1998); and Geoffrey E. Meredith and Charles D. Schewe, "Market by Cohorts, Not Generations," *Marketing News*, February 1, 1999, p. 22.

Geographic Shifts in Population Americans are a mobile people with about 12 million U.S. households moving each year, more than one out of every ten.[8] Such population shifts interest marketers because people in different regions buy differently. Over the past two decades, the U.S. population has shifted toward the Sunbelt states. The West and South have grown while the Midwest and Northeast states lost population. Also, for more than a century, Americans have been moving from rural to metropolitan areas. In the 1950s, they made a massive exit from the cities to the suburbs. Today, the migration to the suburbs continues, and the suburbs are spilling over into rural areas. More and more Americans are also moving to "micropolitan areas," small cities located beyond congested metropolitan areas. These smaller micros offer many of the advantages of metro areas—jobs, restaurants, diversions, community organizations—but without the population crush, traffic jams, high crime rates, and high property taxes often associated with heavily urbanized areas. The U.S. Census Bureau calls sprawling urban areas MSAs (Metropolitan Statistical Areas).[9] Companies use MSAs in researching the best geographical segments for their products and in deciding where to buy advertising time. MSA research shows, for example, that people in Seattle buy more toothbrushes per capita than any other U.S. city, people in Salt Lake City eat more candy bars, folks from New Orleans use more ketchup, and those in Miami drink more prune juice.[10]

A Better-Educated and More White-Collar Population The U.S. population is becoming better educated. For example, in 1996, 82 percent of the U.S. population over age 25 had completed high school and 24 percent had completed college, compared with 69 percent and 17 percent in 1980. The rising number of educated people will increase the demand for quality products, books, magazines, and travel. It suggests a decline in television viewing because college-educated consumers watch less TV than does the population at large. The workforce also is becoming more white collar. Between 1950 and 1985, the proportion of white-collar workers rose from 41 percent to 54 percent, that of blue-collar workers declined from 47 percent to 33 percent, and that of service workers increased from 12 percent to 14 percent. These trends have continued through the 1990s.[11]

Increasing Diversity Countries vary in their ethnic and racial makeup. At one extreme is Japan, where almost everyone is Japanese. At the other extreme is the United States, with people from virtually all nations. The United States has often been called a melting pot in which diverse groups from many nations and cultures have melted into a single, more homogenous whole. Instead, the United States seems to have become more of a "salad bowl" in which various groups have mixed together but have maintained their diversity by retaining and valuing important ethnic and cultural differences.

Marketers are facing increasingly diverse markets, both at home and abroad as their operations become more international in scope. In the United States alone, ethnic population growth is six times greater than the Caucasian growth rate, and ethnic consumers buy more than $600 billion of goods and services each year. The U.S. population is 72 percent white, with African Americans making up another 13 percent. The Hispanic population has grown rapidly and now stands at about 11 percent of the U.S. population. The U.S. Asian population also has grown rapidly in recent years and now totals about 3 percent of the population. The remaining 1 percent of the population is made up of American Indian, Eskimo, and Aleut. During the next half century, the proportions of both Hispanics and Asians will more than double. Moreover, there are nearly 25 million people living in the United States—more that 9 percent of the population—who were born in another country.[12]

Many large companies, ranging from large retailers such as Sears and Wal-Mart to consumers products companies such as Levi Strauss & Co. and Procter & Gamble, now target specially designed products and promotions to one or more of these groups. Miller beer, for example, created television ads for the Hispanic market shown exclusively on Spanish-speaking channels. Even within the Hispanic market, however, different consumers have diverse interests and beliefs depending on country of origin, length of time in the United States, geographic placement, and other factors. Thus, although Miller employs the same visual elements across the country, it alters background music and voice-overs to reflect differences between, for example, Cubans in New York City and Mexican Americans in Los Angeles.

WHEN YOU'RE BUILDING CARS AND TRUCKS FOR EVERYONE IN THE COUNTRY, YOU COUNT ON EVERYONE'S POINT OF VIEW.

The world isn't populated by a single type of person. That's why General Motors builds so many different kinds of cars and trucks. And it's why we have so many different kinds of people building them. They supply the fresh ideas and new perspectives that keep us vital. At GM, we've discovered that to satisfy a whole world of customers, you need people of every make and model.

General Motors
CHEVROLET PONTIAC OLDSMOBILE BUICK CADILLAC GMC

PEOPLE IN MOTION

General Motors employees who influence how we build our cars and trucks:

All of them.

www.gm.com

GM celebrates diversity: "The world isn't populated by a single type person. . . . To satisfy a whole world of consumers, you need people of every make and model."

Diversity goes beyond ethnic heritage. For example, there are more than 52 million disabled people in the United States—a market larger than African Americans or Hispanics—representing almost $800 million in annual spending power. People with mobility challenges are an ideal target market for companies such as Peapod (www.peapod.com), which teams up with large supermarket chains in many heavily populated areas to offer on-line grocery shopping and home delivery. They also represent a growing market for travel, sports, and other leisure-oriented products and services.[13]

Linking the Concepts

Pull over here for a moment and think about how deeply all of these demographic factors impact all of us and, as a result, marketers' strategies.

- Apply these demographic developments to your own life. Think of some specific examples of how the changing demographic factors affect you and your buying behavior
- Identify a specific company that has done a good job of reacting to the shifting demographic environment—generational segments (baby boomers, GenXers, or the baby boomlet group), the changing American family, increased diversity. Compare this company to one that's done a poor job.

Economic Environment

Economic environment
Factors that affect consumer buying power and spending patterns.

Markets require buying power as well as people. The **economic environment** consists of factors that affect consumer purchasing power and spending patterns. Nations vary greatly in their levels and distribution of income. Some countries have *subsistence economies*—they consume most of their own agricultural and industrial output. These countries offer few market opportunities. At the other extreme are *industrial economies*, which constitute rich markets for many different kinds of goods. Marketers must pay close attention to major trends and consumer spending patterns both across and within their world markets. Following are some of the major economic trends in the United States.

Changes in Income In the early 1980s, the U.S. economy entered its longest peacetime boom. During the "roaring eighties," American consumers fell into a consumption frenzy, fueled by income growth, federal tax reductions, rapid increases in housing values, and a boom in borrowing. They bought and bought, seemingly without caution, amassing record levels of debt. "It was fashionable to describe yourself as 'born to shop.' When the going gets tough, it was said, the tough go shopping."[14]

In the 1990s, the baby boom generation has moved into its prime wage-earning years, and the number of small families headed by dual-career couples continues to increase. Thus, many consumers continue to demand quality products and better service, and they are able to pay for them. They are spending more on time-saving products and services, travel and entertainment, physical fitness products, cultural activities, and continuing education.

However, the free spending and high expectations of the 1980s were dashed by the recession in the early 1990s. In fact, the 1990s has become the decade of the "squeezed consumer." Along with rising incomes in some segments have come increased financial burdens—repaying debts acquired during earlier spending splurges, facing increased household and family expenses, and saving ahead for college tuition payments and retirement. These financially squeezed consumers have sobered up, pulled back, and adjusted to their changing financial situations. They are spending more carefully and seeking greater value in the products and services they buy.

Value marketing has become the watchword for many marketers during this economic downturn. Rather than offering high quality at a high price, or lesser quality at very low prices, marketers are looking for ways to offer today's more financially cautious buyers greater value—just the right combination of product quality and good service at a fair price.

Marketers should pay attention to *income distribution* as well as average income. Income distribution in the United States is still very skewed. At the top are *upper-class* consumers, whose spending patterns are not affected by current economic events and who are a major market for luxury goods. There is a comfortable *middle class* that is somewhat careful about its spending but can still afford the good life some of the time. The *working class* must stick close to the basics of food, clothing, and shelter and must try hard to save. Finally, the *under class* (persons on welfare and many retirees) must count their pennies when making even the most basic purchases. Over the past three decades, the rich have grown richer, the middle class has shrunk, and the poor have remained poor. In 1994, the top 5 percent of income-earning households in the United States captured more than 21 percent of aggregate income, up from 16.6 percent in 1970. Meanwhile, the share of income captured by the bottom 20 percent of income-earning households decreased from 4.1 percent to 3.6 percent.[15]

This distribution of income has created a two-tiered market. Many companies are now tailoring their marketing offers to two different markets—the affluent and the

As highlighted in this *BusinessWeek* cover, Walt Disney markets two distinct Pooh bears to match its two-tiered market.

less affluent. For example, Walt Disney Company markets two distinct Winnie-the-Pooh bears:

> The original line-drawn figure appears on fine china, pewter spoons, and pricey kids' stationery found in upscale specialty and department stores such as Nordstrom and Bloomingdale's. The plump, cartoonlike Pooh, clad in a red shirt and a goofy smile, adorns plastic key chains, polyester bed sheets, and animated videos. It sells in Wal-Mart stores and five-and-dime shops. Except at Disney's own stores, the two Poohs do not share the same retail shelf. [Thus, Disney offers both] upstairs and downstairs Poohs, hoping to land customers on both sides of the [income] divide.[16]

Changing Consumer Spending Patterns Table 3-2 shows the proportion of total expenditures made by U.S. households at different income levels for major categories of goods and services. Food, housing, and transportation use up most household income. However, consumers at different income levels have different spending patterns. Some of these differences were noted over a century ago by Ernst Engel, who studied how people

Table 3-2 Consumer Spending at Different Income Levels

Expenditure	% of Spending at Different Income Levels		
	$10,000–$15,000	$20,000–$30,000	$70,000 and Over
Food	16.4%	15.6%	11.6 %
Housing	35.9	31.3	29.5
Utilities	9.4	7.9	4.7
Clothing	5.4	5.5	5.2
Transportation	15.6	17.8	17.0
Health Care	6.5	6.8	5.9
Entertainment	4.9	4.7	5.7
Tobacco	1.3	1.3	.37
Contributions	2.1	3.2	4.7
Insurance	3.4	7.6	15.6

Source: Consumer Expenditure Survey, U.S. Department of Labor, Bureau of Labor Statistics, Bulletin 2462, September 1995, pp. 15–17. Also see Paula Mergenhagan, "What Can Minimum Wage Buy," *American Demographics*, January 1996, pp. 18–21.

shifted their spending as their income rose. He found that as family income rises, the percentage spent on food declines, the percentage spent on housing remains about constant (except for such utilities as gas, electricity, and public services, which decrease), and both the percentage spent on most other categories and that devoted to savings increase. **Engel's laws** generally have been supported by later studies.

Changes in major economic variables such as income, cost of living, interest rates, and savings and borrowing patterns have a large impact on the marketplace. Companies watch these variables by using economic forecasting. Businesses do not have to be wiped out by an economic downturn or caught short in a boom. With adequate warning, they can take advantage of changes in the economic environment.

Natural Environment

The **natural environment** involves the natural resources that are needed as inputs by marketers or that are affected by marketing activities. Environmental concerns have grown steadily during the past two decades. Some trend analysts labeled the 1990s as the "Earth Decade," claiming that the natural environment is the major worldwide issue facing business and the public. In many cities around the world, air and water pollution have reached dangerous levels. World concern continues to mount about the depletion of the earth's ozone layer and the resulting "greenhouse effect," a dangerous warming of the earth. And many environmentalists fear that we soon will be buried in our own trash.

Marketers should be aware of several trends in the natural environment. The first involves growing *shortages of raw materials*. Air and water may seem to be infinite resources, but some groups see long-run dangers. Air pollution chokes many of the world's large cities and water shortages are already a big problem in some parts of the United States and the world. Renewable resources, such as forests and food, also have to be used wisely. Nonrenewable resources, such as oil, coal, and various minerals, pose a serious problem. Firms making products that require these scarce resources face large cost increases, even if the materials do remain available.

A second environmental trend is *increased pollution*. Industry will almost always damage the quality of the natural environment. Consider the disposal of chemical and nuclear wastes; the dangerous mercury levels in the ocean; the quantity of chemical

Engel's laws
Differences noted over a century ago by Ernst Engel in how people shift their spending across food, housing, transportation, health care, and other goods and services categories as family income rises.

Natural environment
Natural resources that are needed as inputs by marketers or that are affected by marketing activities.

pollutants in the soil and food supply; and the littering of the environment with non-biodegradable bottles, plastics, and other packaging materials.

A third trend is *increased government intervention* in natural resource management. The governments of different countries vary in their concern and efforts to promote a clean environment. Some, like the German government, vigorously pursue environmental quality. Others, especially many poorer nations, do little about pollution, largely because they lack the needed funds or political will. Even the richer nations lack the vast funds and political accord needed to mount a worldwide environmental effort. The general hope is that companies around the world will accept more social responsibility, and that less-expensive devices can be found to control and reduce pollution.

In the United States, the Environmental Protection Agency (EPA) was created in 1970 to set and enforce pollution standards and to conduct pollution research. In the future, companies doing business in the United States can expect strong controls from government and pressure groups. Instead of opposing regulation, marketers should help develop solutions to the material and energy problems facing the world.

Concern for the natural environment has spawned the so-called green movement. Today, enlightened companies go beyond what government regulations dictate. They are developing environmentally sustainable strategies and practices in an effort to create a world economy that the planet can support indefinitely. They are responding to consumer

THE OZONE LAYER HAS PROTECTED US FOR 1.5 BILLION YEARS. **IT'S TIME WE** RETURNED THE FAVOR.

All Chrysler Corporation vehicles made since January, 1994 have air conditioners that use CFC-free refrigerants. Thanks to safer substitutes and system redesigns, we are years ahead of government guidelines. It's just one small step to solving a problem that's been hanging over all our heads.

C H R Y S L E R
C O R P O R A T I O N
Chrysler · Plymouth · Dodge · Dodge Trucks · Jeep® · Eagle

Many companies are responding to consumer demands for more environmentally responsible products. Here, Chrysler notes "we are years ahead of government guidelines."

demands with ecologically safer products, recyclable or biodegradable packaging, better pollution controls, and more energy-efficient operations. 3M runs a Pollution Prevention Pays program that has led to a substantial reduction in pollution and costs. AT&T uses a special software package to choose the least harmful materials, cut hazardous waste, reduce energy use, and improve product recycling in its operations. McDonald's eliminated polystyrene cartons and now uses smaller, recyclable paper wrappings and napkins. IBM's AS/400e series of midrange business computers is more energy efficient, contains recycled content, and is designed to be disassembled for recycling. And Dixon-Ticonderoga, the folks who developed the first pencil made in the United States, developed a crayon made from soybeans rather than paraffin wax, a byproduct of oil drilling. Soybeans are a renewable resource and produce brighter, richer colors and a smoother texture. More and more, companies are recognizing the link between a healthy economy and a healthy ecology.[17]

Technological Environment

Technological environment
Forces that create new technologies, creating new product and market opportunities.

The **technological environment** is perhaps the most dramatic force now shaping our destiny. Technology has released such wonders as antibiotics, organ transplants, notebook computers, and the Internet. It also has released such horrors as nuclear missiles, chemical weapons, and assault rifles. It has released such mixed blessings as the automobile, television, and credit cards. Our attitude toward technology depends on whether we are more impressed with its wonders or its blunders.

The technological environment changes rapidly. Think of all of today's common products that were not available 100 years ago, or even 30 years ago. Abraham Lincoln did not know about automobiles, airplanes, phonographs, radios, or the electric light. Woodrow Wilson did not know about television, aerosol cans, automatic dishwashers, room air conditioners, antibiotics, or computers. Franklin Delano Roosevelt did not know about xerography, synthetic detergents, tape recorders, birth control pills, or earth satellites. And John F. Kennedy did not know about personal computers, compact disk players, VCRs, or the World Wide Web.

Technological environment: Technology is perhaps the most dramatic force shaping the marketing environment. Here, a Samburu warrior in northern Kenya makes a call on a cellular telephone.

New technologies create new markets and opportunities. However, every new technology replaces an older technology. Transistors hurt the vacuum-tube industry, xerography hurt the carbon-paper business, the auto hurt the railroads, and compact disks hurt phonograph records. When old industries fought or ignored new technologies, their businesses declined. Thus, marketers should watch the technological environment closely. Companies that do not keep up with technological change soon will find their products outdated. And they will miss new product and market opportunities.

The United States leads the world in research and development spending.[18] Scientists today are researching a wide range of promising new products and services, ranging from practical solar energy, electric cars, and cancer cures to voice-controlled computers and genetically engineered food crops. Today's research usually is carried out by research teams rather than by lone inventors like Thomas Edison, Samuel Morse, or Alexander Graham Bell. Many companies are adding marketing people to R&D teams to try to obtain a stronger marketing orientation. Scientists also speculate on fantasy products, such as flying cars, three-dimensional televisions, and space colonies. The challenge in each case is not only technical but also commercial—to make *practical, affordable* versions of these products.

As products and technology become more complex, the public needs to know that they are safe. Thus, government agencies investigate and ban potentially unsafe products. In the United States, the Federal Food and Drug Administration has set up complex regulations for testing new drugs. The Consumer Product Safety Commission sets safety standards for consumer products and penalizes companies that fail to meet them. Such regulations have resulted in much higher research costs and in longer times between new-product ideas and their introduction. Marketers should be aware of these regulations when applying new technologies and developing new products.

Political Environment

Marketing decisions are strongly affected by developments in the political environment. The **political environment** consists of laws, government agencies, and pressure groups that influence and limit various organizations and individuals in a given society.

Political environment
Laws, government agencies, and pressure groups that influence and limit various organizations and individuals in a given society.

Legislation Regulating Business Even the most liberal advocates of free-market economies agree that the system works best with at least some regulation. Well-conceived regulation can encourage competition and ensure fair markets for goods and services. Thus, governments develop *public policy* to guide commerce—sets of laws and regulations that limit business for the good of society as a whole. Almost every marketing activity is subject to a wide range of laws and regulations.

INCREASING LEGISLATION Legislation affecting business around the world has increased steadily over the years. The United States has many laws covering issues such as competition, fair trade practices, environmental protection, product safety, truth in advertising, packaging and labeling, pricing, and other important areas (see Table 3-3). The European Commission has been active in establishing a new framework of laws covering competitive behavior, product standards, product liability, and commercial transactions for the nations of the European Union. Several countries have gone farther than the United States in passing strong consumerism legislation. For example, Norway bans several forms of sales promotion—trading stamps, contests, premiums—as being inappropriate or unfair ways of promoting products. Thailand requires food processors selling national brands to market low-price brands also, so that low-income consumers can find economy brands on the shelves. In India, food companies must obtain special approval to launch brands that

Table 3-3   Major U.S. Legislation Affecting Marketing

Legislation	Purpose
Sherman Antitrust Act (1890)	Prohibits monopolies and activities (price fixing, predatory pricing) that restrain trade or competition in interstate commerce.
Federal Food and Drug Act (1906)	Forbids the manufacture or sale of adulterated or fraudulently labeled foods and drugs. Created the Food and Drug Administration.
Clayton Act (1914)	Supplements the Sherman Act by prohibiting certain types of price discrimination, exclusive dealing, and tying clauses (which require a dealer to take additional products in a seller's line).
Federal Trade Commission Act (1914)	Establishes a commission to monitor and remedy unfair trade methods.
Robinson-Patman Act (1936)	Amends Clayton Act to define price discrimination as unlawful. Empowers FTC to establish limits on quantity discounts, forbid some brokerage allowances, and prohibit promotional allowances except when made available on proportionately equal terms.
Wheeler-Lea Act (1938)	Makes deceptive, misleading, and unfair practices illegal regardless of injury to competition. Places advertising of food and drugs under FTC jurisdiction.
Lanham Trademark Act (1946)	Protects and regulates distinctive brand names and trademarks.
National Traffic and Safety Act (1958)	Provides for the creation of compulsory safety standards for automobiles and tires.
Fair Packaging and Labeling Act (1966)	Provides for the regulation of packaging and labeling of consumer goods. Requires that manufacturers state what the package contains, who made it, and how much it contains.
Child Protection Act (1966)	Bans sale of hazardous toys and articles. Sets standards for child-resistant packaging.
Federal Cigarette Labeling and Advertising Act (1967)	Requires that cigarette packages contain the following statement: "Warning: The Surgeon General Has Determined That Cigarette Smoking Is Dangerous To Your Health."
National Environmental Policy Act (1969)	Establishes a national policy on the environment. The 1970 Reorganization Plan established the Environmental Protection Agency.
Consumer Product Safety Act (1972)	Establishes the Consumer Product Safety Commission and authorizes it to set safety standards for consumer products as well as exact penalties for failure to uphold those standards.
Magnuson-Moss Warranty Act (1975)	Authorizes the FTC to determine rules and regulations for consumer warranties and provides consumer access to redress, such as the class-action suit.
Children's Television Act (1990)	Limits number of commercials aired during children's programs.
Nutrition Labeling and Education Act (1990)	Requires that food product labels provide detailed nutritional information.
Telephone Consumer Protection Act (1991)	Establishes procedures to avoid unwanted telephone solicitations. Limits marketers' use of automatic telephone dialing systems and artificial or prerecorded voices.

duplicate those already existing on the market, such as additional cola drinks or new brands of rice.

Understanding the public policy implications of a particular marketing activity is not a simple matter. For example, in the United States, there are many laws created at the national, state, and local levels, and these regulations often overlap. Aspirins sold in

Dallas are governed both by federal labeling laws and by Texas state advertising laws. Moreover, regulations are constantly changing—what was allowed last year may now be prohibited, and what was prohibited may now be allowed. For example, with the demise of the Soviet bloc, ex-Soviet nations are rapidly passing laws to both regulate and promote an open-market economy. Marketers must work hard to keep up with changes in regulations and their interpretations.

Business legislation has been enacted for a number of reasons. The first is to *protect companies* from each other. Although business executives may praise competition, they sometimes try to neutralize it when it threatens them. So laws are passed to define and prevent unfair competition. In the United States, such laws are enforced by the Federal Trade Commission and the Antitrust Division of the Attorney General's office.

The second purpose of government regulation is to *protect consumers* from unfair business practices. Some firms, if left alone, would make shoddy products, tell lies in their advertising, and deceive consumers through their packaging and pricing. Unfair business practices have been defined and are enforced by various agencies.

The third purpose of government regulation is to *protect the interests of society* against unrestrained business behavior. Profitable business activity does not always create a better quality of life. Regulation arises to ensure that firms take responsibility for the social costs of their production or products.

CHANGING GOVERNMENT AGENCY ENFORCEMENT International marketers will encounter dozens, or even hundreds, of agencies set up to enforce trade policies and regulations. In the United States, Congress has established federal regulatory agencies such as the Federal Trade Commission, the Food and Drug Administration, the Interstate Commerce Commission, the Federal Communications Commission, the Federal Power Commission, the Civil Aeronautics Board, the Consumer Products Safety Commission, the Environmental Protection Agency, and the Office of Consumer Affairs. Because such government agencies have some discretion in enforcing the laws, they can have a major impact on a company's marketing performance. At times, the staffs of these agencies have appeared to be overly eager and unpredictable. Some of the agencies sometimes have been dominated by lawyers and economists who lacked a practical sense of how business and marketing work. In recent years, the Federal Trade Commission has added staff marketing experts, who can better understand complex business issues.

New laws and their enforcement will continue or increase. Business executives must watch these developments when planning their products and marketing programs. Marketers need to know about the major laws protecting competition, consumers, and society. They need to understand these laws at the local, state, national, and international levels.[19]

Increased Emphasis on Ethics and Socially Responsible Actions
Written regulations cannot possibly cover all potential marketing abuses, and existing laws are often difficult to enforce. However, beyond written laws and regulations, business is also governed by social codes and rules of professional ethics. Enlightened companies encourage their managers to look beyond what the regulatory system allows and simply "do the right thing." These socially responsible firms actively seek out ways to protect the long-run interests of their consumers and the environment.

The recent rash of business scandals and increased concerns about the environment have created fresh interest in the issues of ethics and social responsibility. Almost every aspect of marketing involves such issues. Unfortunately, because these issues usually involve conflicting interests, well-meaning people can honestly disagree about the right course of action in a given situation. Thus, many industrial and professional trade associations have suggested codes of ethics, and many companies now are developing policies and guidelines to deal with complex social responsibility issues.

Throughout the text, we present Marketing at Work exhibits that summarize the main public policy and social responsibility issues surrounding major marketing decisions. These exhibits discuss the legal issues that marketers should understand and the common ethical and societal concerns that marketers face. In chapter 16, we discuss a broad range of societal marketing issues in greater depth.

Cultural Environment

Cultural environment
Institutions and other forces that affect society's basic values, perceptions, preferences, and behaviors.

The **cultural environment** is made up of institutions and other forces that affect a society's basic values, perceptions, preferences, and behaviors. People grow up in a particular society that shapes their basic beliefs and values. They absorb a world view that defines their relationships with others. The following cultural characteristics can affect marketing decision making.

Persistence of Cultural Values

People in a given society hold many beliefs and values. Their *core* beliefs and values have a high degree of persistence. For example, most Americans believe in working, getting married, giving to charity, and being honest. These beliefs shape more-specific attitudes and behaviors found in everyday life. Core beliefs and values are passed on from parents to children and are reinforced by schools, churches, business, and government.

Secondary beliefs and values are more open to change. Believing in marriage is a core belief; believing that people should get married early in life is a secondary belief. Marketers have some chance of changing secondary values, but little chance of changing core values. For example, family-planning marketers could argue more effectively that people should get married later than that they should not get married at all.

Shifts in Secondary Cultural Values

Although core values are fairly persistent, cultural swings do take place. Consider the impact of popular music groups, movie personalities, and other celebrities on young people's hairstyling, clothing, and sexual norms. Marketers want to predict cultural shifts in order to spot new opportunities or threats. Several firms offer "futures" forecasts in this connection, such as Yankelovich's Monitor, Market Facts' BrainWaves Group, and the Trends Research Institute. The Yankelovich Monitor tracks 41 U.S. cultural values, such as "antibigness," "mysticism," "living for today," "away from possessions," and "sensuousness." Monitor describes the percentage of the population that shares the attitude as well as the percentage that goes against the trend.[20] For instance, the percentage of people who value physical fitness and well-being has risen steadily over the years. Such information helps marketers cater to trends with appropriate products and communication appeals. (See Marketing at Work 3-3 for a summary of today's cultural trends.)

The major cultural values of a society are expressed in people's views of themselves and others, as well as in their views of organizations, society, nature, and the universe.

PEOPLE'S VIEWS OF THEMSELVES. People vary in their emphasis on serving themselves versus serving others. Some people seek personal pleasure, wanting fun, change, and escape. Others seek self-realization through religion, recreation, or the avid pursuit of careers or other life goals. People use products, brands, and services as a means of self-expression, and they buy products and services that match their views of themselves.

In the 1980s, personal ambition and materialism increased dramatically, with significant marketing implications. In a "me-society," people buy their "dream cars" and take their "dream vacations." They spend more time in outdoor health activities (jogging, tennis), in thought, and on arts and crafts. The leisure industry (camping, boating, arts and crafts, and sports) faces good growth prospects in a society in which people seek self-fulfillment.

PEOPLE'S VIEWS OF OTHERS More recently, observers have noted a shift from a "me-society" to a "we-society" in which more people want to be with and serve others. Notes one trend tracker, "People want to get out, especially those 48 million people working out of their home and feeling a little cooped-up [and] all those shut-ins who feel unfulfilled by the cyberstuff that was supposed to make them feel like never leaving home."[21] Moreover, moving into the new millennium, materialism, flashy spending, and self-indulgence have been replaced by more sensible spending, saving, family concerns, and helping others. The aging baby boomers are limiting their spending to products and services that improve their lives instead of boosting their images. This suggests a bright future for products and services that serve basic needs and provide real value rather than those relying on glitz and hype. It also suggests a greater demand for "social support" products and services that improve direct communication between people, such as health clubs and family vacations.

PEOPLE'S VIEWS OF ORGANIZATIONS People vary in their attitudes toward corporations, government agencies, trade unions, universities, and other organizations. By and large, people are willing to work for major organizations and expect them, in turn, to carry out society's work. The late 1980s saw a sharp decrease in confidence in and loyalty toward America's business and political organizations and institutions. People were giving a little less to their organizations and were trusting them less. However, by the mid-1990s, these attitudes appeared to be turning around, with people showing signs of "cautious trust" of institutions.[22]

This trend suggests that organizations need to find new ways to win consumer confidence. They need to review their advertising communications to make sure their messages are honest. Also, they need to review their various activities to make sure that they are being good corporate citizens. More companies are linking themselves to worthwhile causes, measuring their images with important publics, and using public relations to build more positive images (see Marketing at Work 3-4).[23]

PEOPLE'S VIEWS OF SOCIETY People vary in their attitudes toward their society; patriots defend it, reformers want to change it, malcontents want to leave it. People's orientation to their society influences their consumption patterns, levels of savings, and attitudes toward the marketplace.

The 1980s and 1990s have seen an increase in consumer patriotism. For example, one study showed that more than 80 percent of those surveyed say, "Americans should always try to buy American"—up from 72 percent in 1972.[24] Many U.S. companies have responded with "made in America" themes and flag-waving promotions. For example, Black & Decker added a flaglike symbol to its tools. And for the past several years, the American textile industry has blitzed consumers with its "Crafted with Pride in the USA" advertising campaign, insisting that "made in the USA" matters. In 1991, many companies used patriotic appeals and promotions to express their support of American troops in the Gulf War and to ride the wave of national pride and patriotism that followed.

PEOPLE'S VIEWS OF NATURE People vary in their attitudes toward the natural world. Some feel ruled by it, others feel in harmony with it, and still others seek to master it. A long-term trend has been people's growing mastery over nature through technology

Marketing at Work 3-3

Popcorn's Cultural Trends

Futurist Faith Popcorn runs BrainReserve, a marketing consulting firm that monitors cultural trends and advises companies such as AT&T, Citibank, Black & Decker, Hoffman-La Roche, Nissan, Rubbermaid, and many others on how these trends will affect their marketing and other decisions. Using its trend predictions, BrainReserve generates new product ideas for clients, breathes new life into fading brands, and develops marketing strategies and concepts that create long-term competitive advantage. Popcorn and her associates have identified 16 major cultural trends affecting U.S. consumers:

1. *Cocooning:* Many Americans have the impulse to stay inside when the outside gets too tough and scary. Self-preservation is the underlying theme. More people are turning their homes into nests: redecorating their houses, watching TV movies, ordering from catalogs, and using answering machines to filter out the outside world. Another breed of cocooner is Wandering Cocoons, people who eat in their cars and communicate through their car phones.

2. *99 Lives:* This is also called the "hurry-up" trend. People today feel time poor and must juggle many roles and responsibilities. An example is the "SuperMom" who must handle a full-time career while also managing her home and children. They attempt to relieve time pressures by using fax machines and car phones, eating at fast-food restaurants, and buying convenience services. Marketers can meet this need by creating *cluster marketing* enterprises—all-in-one service stops, such as Video Town Launderette, which, in addition to its laundry facilities, includes a tanning room, an exercise bike,

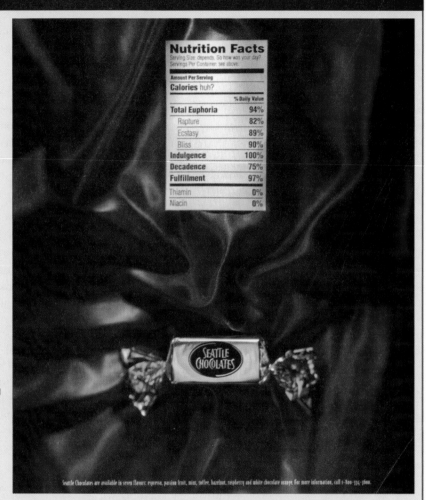

Seattle Chocolates takes advantage of the trend toward small consumer indulgences: "Total Euphoria 94%, Decadence 75%, Indulgence 100%!"

copying and fax machines, and 6,000 video titles for rent.

3. *Cashing Out:* More and more people are opting for a simpler, less-stressed lifestyle. An executive suddenly quits his or her career, escapes the hassles of big-city life, and turns up in Vermont or Montana running a small newspaper, managing a bed-and-breakfast establishment, or starting a band. People cash out because they

don't think the stress is worth it. They nostalgically try to return to small-town values, seeking clean air, safe schools, and plain-speaking neighbors.

4. *Clanning:* As the world grows more chaotic, people are feeling a growing need to join up with and belong to groups of like kind. Marketers are responding with products, services, and programs that help make consumers feel a part of something. For example, Sears launched a Best Customer Program and Harley-Davidson sponsors its Harley Owners Group (HOG).

5. *Anchoring:* People are looking to ancient practices to provide anchors or support for their modern lifestyles. This trend explains the widespread popularity of astrology, meditation, angels, yoga, aromatherapy, and Eastern religions. Marketers should find ways to make their products and services more meaningful to customers.

6. *Egonomics:* People want to develop individuality in order to be seen and treated as different from others. This is not an ego trip, but simply the wish to individualize oneself through possessions and experiences. Egonomics gives marketers an opportunity to succeed by offering customized goods, services, and experiences.

7. *Female Think:* People are recognizing that men and women act and think differently. A strong indicator of female think is the popularity of books such as *Men Are From Mars, Women Are From Venus*. "Creating relationships is the motor that drives women," Popcorn explains. "Consequently, you have to market differently to women." An example is Saturn Car Company, which has created strong relationships with its customers, many of whom are women.

8. *Mancipation:* In contrast to female think, *mancipation* refers to the emancipation of men. Men are no longer required to be macho, distant, and strong. Rather, they are encouraged to publicly share more traditionally feminine emotions and characteristics. This trend is revealed in ads featuring men as nurturing dads and concerned husbands. Politically, the trend is surfacing as paternity and family

leave policies become more detailed and flexible.

9. *Being Alive:* People are motivated to lead longer and more enjoyable lives. They are moving toward vegetarianism, low-tech medicine, meditation, and other life extenders and enhancers. Marketers can meet these needs by designing healthier products and services for consumers.

10. *Down-aging:* Older people are tending to act and feel younger than their age. They spend more on youthful clothes, hair coloring, and facial plastic surgery. They engage in more playful behavior and act in ways previously thought not to be appropriate for their age group. They buy adult toys, attend adult camps, and sign up for adventure vacations.

11. *Small Indulgences:* Stressed-out consumers need occasional emotional fixes. A consumer might not be able to afford a two-week trip to Europe but might spend a weekend in New Orleans instead. He or she might eat healthily all week, then splurge with a pint of superpremium Häagen-Dazs ice cream over the weekend. Marketers should be aware of the ways in which consumers feel deprived and look for opportunities to offer small indulgences that provide an emotional lift.

12. *Pleasure Revenge:* Increasing numbers of consumers are turning back to "deviant" behavior. Rather than self-control and deprivation in the name of good health and acceptable behavior, people are proudly and publicly in pursuit of pleasure. They're fed up with following the health kick of the early 1990s. The result of this trend, among other things, is an increase in the consumption of red meat, fats, and sugars coupled with decreasing sales of typical health food alternatives.

13. *Fantasy Adventure:* Many people feel the need to find emotional escapes to offset their daily routines. People might seek vacations, eat exotic foods, or go to Disneyland. For marketers, this is an opportunity to create new fantasy products and services, or to add fantasy touches to their current products and services. This trend will feed the growth of virtual reality throughout the coming decade.

14. *Icon Toppling:* This trend translates into "if it's big, it's bad." Marketers are responding by finding ways to think, act, and look smaller. And example is Miller's Plank Road Brewery beer, which has the look and feel of today's popular microbrewery beverages.

15. *The Vigilante Consumer:* Vigilante consumers are those who will no longer tolerate shoddy products and poor service. They want companies to be more aware and responsive. So they act up, boycott, write letters, and buy "green products." Marketers must serve as the consciences of their companies to bring these consumers better, more responsible products and services.

16. *S.O.S. (Save Our Society):* A growing number of people want to make society more socially responsible with respect to education, ethics, and the environment. People join groups to promote more social responsibility on the part of companies and other citizens. The best response for marketers is to urge their own companies to practice more socially responsible marketing.

Source: See Faith Popcorn, *The Popcorn Report* (New York: Harper Business, 1992); Faith Popcorn and Lys Marigold, *Clicking* (New York: HarperCollins, 1997); Sacha Cohen, "Clicking," *Training & Development*, October 1996, pp. 65–66; and "Books in Review," *Marketing News*, February 2, 1998, p. 18.

Marketing at Work 3-4

Cause-Related Marketing: Doing Well by Doing Good

These days, every product seems to be tied to some cause. Buy Purina cat food and help the American Association of Zoological Parks and Aquariums save endangered big cat species. Drink Tang and earn money for Mothers Against Drunk Driving. Drive a Dollar rental car and help support the Special Olympics. Or if you want to help the Leukemia Society of America, buy Helping Hand trash bags or toilet paper. Pay for these purchases with the right charge card and you can support a local cultural arts group or help fight cancer or heart disease.

Cause-related marketing has become one of the hottest forms of corporate giving. It lets companies "do well by doing good" by linking purchases of the company's products or services with fund-raising for worthwhile causes or charitable organizations. Cause-related marketing has grown rapidly since the early 1980s, when American Express offered to donate 1 cent to the restoration of the Statue of Liberty for each use of its charge card. American Express ended up having to contribute $1.7 million, but the cause-related campaign produced a 28 percent increase in card usage.

Companies now sponsor dozens of cause-related marketing campaigns each year. Many are backed by large budgets and a full complement of marketing activities. Here are other examples:

Johnson & Johnson teamed with the Children's Hospital Medical Center and the National Safety Council to sponsor a five-year, cause-related marketing campaign to reduce preventable children's injuries, the leading killer of children. Some 43 other nonprofit groups, including the American Red Cross, National Parent Teachers Association, and the Boy and Girl Scouts of America, helped to promote the campaign. The campaign offered consumers a free Safe Kids safety kit for children in exchange for proofs of purchase. Consumers could also buy a Child's Safety Video for $9.95. The video featured a game show format that made learning about safety entertaining as well as educational. To promote the campaign, Johnson & Johnson distributed almost 50 million advertising inserts in daily newspapers and developed a special information kit for retailers

Cause-related marketing: Johnson & Johnson teams with the National Safety Council to sponsor its Safe Kids program to reduce children's injuries.

and the belief that nature is bountiful. More recently, however, people have recognized that nature is finite and fragile, that it can be destroyed or spoiled by human activities.

Love of nature is leading to more camping, hiking, boating, fishing, and other outdoor activities. Business has responded by offering more products and services

containing posters, floor displays, and other in-store promotion materials. Safe Kids Safety Tip Sheets and emergency phone stickers were also available as free consumer handouts.

Procter & Gamble has sponsored many cause-related marketing campaigns. For example, during the past many years, Procter & Gamble has mailed out billions of coupons on behalf of the Special Olympics for retarded children, helping make the event a household word. Procter & Gamble supports its Special Olympics efforts with national advertising and public relations, and its salespeople work with local volunteers to encourage retailers to build point-of-purchase displays. In another recent cause-related marketing effort, Procter & Gamble has set up the Jif Children's Education Fund. For every pound of Jif peanut butter sold during the three-month promotion, Procter & Gamble donates 10 cents to the fund, which will be distributed to parent-teacher groups at registered elementary schools in America. The program is designed to raise more than $4 million for U.S. elementary education.

Since 1993, American Express has joined with Share Our Strength (SOS), a hunger-relief organization, to sponsor its Charge Against Hunger program. Every time someone uses an American Express card between November 1 and December 31, the company donates 3 cents to SOS, up to a total of $5 million per year. In recent years, other corporations

have "joined the charge," including Kmart, Melville Corporation, Calphalon, and the National Football League. For example, in 1994, Kmart donated 10 cents for every American Express card transaction at its stores between November 27 and the end of the year. The program has been highly successful. Over the past three years, American Express and its partners have donated more than $16 million to SOS. And American Express has found that the program has increased card transactions, merchant card acceptance, and cardholder support.

Cause-related marketing has stirred some controversy. Critics are concerned that cause-related marketing might eventually undercut traditional "no-strings" corporate giving, as more and more companies grow to expect marketing benefits from their contributions. Critics also worry that cause-related marketing will cause a shift in corporate charitable support toward more visible, popular, and low-risk charities—those with more certain and substantial marketing appeal. For example, MasterCard's "Choose to Make a Difference" campaign raises money for six charities, each selected in part because of its popularity in a consumer poll. Finally, critics worry that cause-related marketing is more a strategy for selling than a strategy for giving, that "cause-related" marketing is really "cause-exploitative" marketing. Thus, companies using cause-related marketing might find themselves walking a fine line

between increased sales and an improved image, and facing charges of exploitation.

However, if handled well, cause-related marketing can greatly benefit both the company and the charitable organization. The company gains an effective marketing tool while building a more positive public image. One recent study found that 78 percent of consumers would be more likely to buy a product associated with a cause that they care about. In another study, 54 percent of consumers said they would pay a premium price for a product that supports such a cause. Similarly, the charitable organization gains greater visibility and important new sources of funding. This additional funding can be substantial. In total, such campaigns now contribute some $100 million annually to the coffers of charitable organizations, and surveys show that these cause-related contributions usually add to, rather than undercut, direct company contributions. Thus, when cause marketing works, everyone wins.

Sources: See Nancy Arnott, "Marketing with a Passion," *Sales & Marketing Management*, January 1994, pp. 64–71; Minette E. Drumwright, "Company Advertising with a Social Dimension: The Role of Noneconomic Criteria," *Journal of Marketing*, October 1996, pp. 71–87; Alan R. Andreason, "Profits of Nonprofits," *Harvard Business Review*, November–December 1996, pp. 47–59; Julie Garrett and Lisa Rochlin, "Cause Marketers Must Learn to Play by Rules," *Marketing News*, May 12, 1997, p. 4; and Sarah Lorge, "Is Cause-Related Marketing Worth It?" *Sales & Marketing Management*, June 1998, p. 72; Deborah J. Webb and Lois A. Mohr, "A Typology of Consumer Responses to Cause-Related Marketing: From Skeptics to Socially Concerned," *Journal of Marketing & Public Policy*, Fall 1998, p. 226–238; and Michelle Wirth Fellman, "Cause Marketing Takes a Strategic Turn," *Marketing News*, April 26, 1999, p. 4.

catering to these interests. Tour operators are offering more wilderness adventures, and retailers are offering more fitness gear and apparel. Food producers have found growing markets for "natural" products such as natural cereal, natural ice cream, and health foods. Marketing communicators are using appealing natural backgrounds in advertising their products.

PEOPLE'S VIEWS OF THE UNIVERSE Finally, people vary in their beliefs about the origin of the universe and their place in it. Although most Americans practice religion, religious conviction and practice have been dropping off gradually through the years. As people lose their religious orientation, they seek goods and experiences with more immediate satisfactions. During the 1980s, people increasingly measured success in terms of career achievement, wealth, and worldly possessions.

Some futurists, however, have noted an emerging renewal of interest in religion and a new spiritualism, perhaps as a part of a broader search for a new inner purpose. People have been moving away from materialism and dog-eat-dog ambition to seek more permanent values—family, community, earth, faith—and a more certain grasp of right and wrong. "Spirituality is in," notes one expert, and this trend is reflected in many companies' marketing efforts: "IBM's Solutions for a Small Planet campaign features several ads using religious themes. Catholic nuns walk to vespers while speaking OS/2 networks and surfing the Net. Eastern monks 'meditate' telepathically about Lotus Notes on a rocky hillside. Gatorade has Michael Jordan running through Tibetan mountains where he meets an Eastern holy man who imparts this stirring wisdom: 'Life is a sport; drink it up.' [Nissan offers similar advice:] 'Life is a Journey, Enjoy the Ride.' "[25]

Linking the Concepts

Slow down and cool your engine. You've now read about a large number of environmental forces. How are all of these environments *linked* with each other? With company marketing strategy?

- How are major demographic forces linked with economic changes? With major cultural trends? How are the natural and technological environments linked? Think of an example of a company that has recognized one of these links and turned it into a marketing opportunity.
- Is the marketing environment uncontrollable—something that the company can only prepare for and react to? Or can companies be proactive in changing environmental factors? Think of a good example that makes your point, then read on.

Responding to the Marketing Environment

Environmental management perspective
A management perspective in which the firm takes aggressive actions to affect the publics and forces in its marketing environment rather than simply watching and reacting to them.

Many companies view the marketing environment as an uncontrollable element to which they must adapt. They passively accept the marketing environment and do not try to change it. They analyze the environmental forces and design strategies that will help the company avoid the threats and take advantage of the opportunities the environment provides.

Other companies take an **environmental management perspective**.[26] Rather than simply watching and reacting, these firms take aggressive actions to affect the publics and forces in their marketing environment. Such companies hire lobbyists to influence legislation affecting their industries and stage media events to gain favorable press coverage. They run advertorials (ads expressing editorial points of view) to shape public opinion. They press lawsuits and file complaints with regulators to keep competitors in line, and they form contractual agreements to better control their distribution channels.

Often, companies can find positive ways to overcome seemingly uncontrollable environmental constraints. For example:

Cathay Pacific Airlines . . . determined that many travelers were avoiding Hong Kong because of lengthy delays at immigration. Rather than assuming that this was a problem they could not solve, Cathay's senior staff asked the Hong Kong government how to avoid these immigration delays. After lengthy discussions, the airline agreed to make an annual grant-in-aid to the government to hire more immigration inspectors—but these reinforcements would service primarily the Cathay Pacific gates. The reduced waiting period increased customer value and thus strengthened [Cathay's competitive advantage].[27]

Marketing management cannot always control environmental forces. In many cases, it must settle for simply watching and reacting to the environment. For example, a company would have little success trying to influence geographic population shifts, the economic environment, or major cultural values. But whenever possible, smart marketing managers will take a *proactive* rather than *reactive* approach to the marketing environment.

REST STOP   Reviewing the Concepts

In this and the next two chapters, you'll examine the environments of marketing and how companies analyze these environments to discover opportunities and create effective marketing strategies. Companies must constantly watch and adapt to the *marketing environment* in order to seek opportunities and ward off threats. The marketing environment comprises all the actors and forces influencing the company's ability to transact business effectively with its target market.

1. Describe the environmental forces that affect the company's ability to serve its customers.

The company's *microenvironment* consists of other actors close to the company that combine to form the company's value delivery system or which affect its ability to serve its customers. It includes the company's *internal environment*—its several departments and management levels—as it influences marketing decision making. *Marketing channel firms*—suppliers and marketing intermediaries, including resellers, physical distribution firms, marketing services agencies, and financial intermediaries—cooperate to create customer value. Five types of customer *markets* include consumer, producer, reseller, government, and international markets. *Competitors* vie with the company in an effort to serve customers better. Finally, various *publics* have an actual or potential interest in or impact on the company's ability to meet its objectives.

The *macroenvironment* consists of larger societal forces that affect the entire microenvironment. The six forces making up the company's macroenvironment include demographic, economic, natural, technological, political, and cultural forces. These forces shape opportunities and pose threats to the company.

2. Explain how changes in the demographic and economic environments affect marketing decisions.

Demography is the study of the characteristics of human populations. Today's *demographic environment* shows a changing age structure, shifting family profiles, geographic population shifts, a more-educated and more white-collar population, and increasing diversity. The *economic environment* consists of factors that affect buying power and patterns. The economic environment is characterized by lower real income and shifting consumer spending patterns. Today's squeezed consumers are seeking greater value—just the right combination of good quality and service at a fair price. The distribution of income also is shifting. The rich have grown richer, the middle class has shrunk, and the poor have remained poor, leading to a two-tiered market. Many companies now tailor their marketing offers to two different markets—the affluent and the less affluent.

3. Identify the major trends in the firm's natural and technological environments.

The *natural environment* shows four major trends: shortages of certain raw materials, increased costs of energy, higher pollution levels, and more government intervention in natural resource management. Environmental concerns create marketing opportunities for alert companies. The marketer should watch for four major trends in the *technological environment*: the rapid pace of technological change, high R&D budgets, the concentration by companies on minor product improvements, and increased government regulation. Companies that fail to keep up with technological change will miss out on new product and marketing opportunities.

4. Explain the key changes in the political and cultural environments.

The *political environment* consists of laws, agencies, and groups that influence or limit marketing actions. The political environment has undergone three changes that affect marketing worldwide: increasing legislation regulating business, strong government agency enforcement, and greater emphasis on ethics and socially responsible actions. The *cultural environment* is made up of institutions and forces that affect a society's values, perceptions, preferences, and behaviors. The environment shows long-term trends toward a "we-society," a return to cautious trust of institutions, increasing patriotism, greater appreciation for nature, a new spiritualism, and search for more meaningful and enduring values.

5. Discuss how companies can react to the marketing environment.

Companies can passively accept the marketing environment as an uncontrollable element to which they must adapt, avoiding threats and taking advantage of opportunities as they arise. Or they can take an *environmental management perspective*, proactively working to change the environment rather than simply reacting to it. Whenever possible, companies should try to be proactive rather than reactive.

Navigating the Key Terms

For a detailed analysis of the meaning and importance of each of the following key terms. visit our Web page at **www. prenhall.com/kotler**

Baby boom
Cultural environment

Demography
Economic environment
Engel's laws
Environmental management perspective
Macroenvironment
Marketing environment

Marketing intermediaries
Microenvironment
Natural environment
Political environment
Public
Technological environment

Travel Log

The following concept checks and discussion questions will help you to keep track of and apply the concepts you've studied in this chapter.

Concept Checks

1. A company's _____ consists of the actors and forces outside marketing that affect marketing management's ability to develop and maintain successful relationships with its target customers.

2. The _____ consists of the forces close to the company that affect its ability to serve its customers—the company, marketing channel firms, customer markets, competitors, and publics.

3. _____ (such as resellers, physical distribution firms, marketing services agencies, and financial intermediaries) help the company to promote, sell, and distribute its goods to final buyers.

4. If a company's marketing decisions were to be questioned by consumer organizations, environmental groups, and minority groups, then the company would need to develop strategies to respond to these _____ publics.

5. Americans are a mobile population. Today, there is an increasing trend toward population movement toward _____ areas, small cities located beyond congested metropolitan areas.

6. Marketers are increasingly seeking ways to offer financially cautious buyers greater value—just the right combination of product quality and good service at a fair price. This is called _____ marketing.

7. According to one of _____ laws, as family income rises, the percentage spent on food declines.

8. Marketers should be aware of several trends in the natural environment. Chief among these are

the _____, _____, and
_____.

9. Business legislation has been enacted for a number of reasons. Chief among these are to protect _____, to protect _____, and to protect _____.

10. Recent studies suggest that consumers are interested in getting out more, family concerns, and helping others. This is evidence that our society is moving more towards a "_____- society."*

Discussing the Issues

1. In the 1930s, President Franklin Roosevelt used his cigarette holder as a personal trademark. Would a president be seen smoking today? What changes in the cultural environment are affecting smoking behavior and cigarette marketing? Considering the recent rash of court rulings and settlements concerning the tobacco industry, how might a cigarette manufacturer market its products differently to meet this new environment? What are the long-term prospects for the industry?

2. Define millennial fever and cite several examples. How can marketers use this phenomenon in designing their marketing strategies?

3. It has been said that the single most important demographic trend in the United States is the changing age structure of the population. Suggest specific strategies that would help companies in each of the following industries adjust to these changing age patterns: automobiles, computers and computer software, and toys and games.

4. Americans are becoming more concerned about the natural environment. Explain how this trend would affect a company that markets plastic sandwich bags. List and explain some effective responses to this trend.

5. Hardly a day passes without mention of the difficulties that our economy will face with the Y2K bug (year 2000 bug—the inability of many computers to distinguish between the year 2000 and the year 1900). Experts disagree on how much confusion and harm that this phenomenon will cause for our government, economy, and business practices. Does this problem concern you? Why or why not? What actions should marketers be taking with respect to this potential danger? How could the solution to this problem be approached using proactive rather than reactive measures?

* *Concept check answers:* 1. marketing environment; 2. microenvironment; 3. marketing intermediaries; 4. citizen-action; 5. micropolitan; 6. value; 7. Engel's; 8. growing shortages of raw materials, increased pollution, and increased government intervention in natural resource management; 9. companies from each other, consumers from unfair business practices, and the interests of society against unrestrained business behavior; 10. we.

Traveling the Net

Point of Interest: The Technological Environment

One of the essential tools for effectively using the Internet for marketing purposes is the ability to have access to high-powered search engines. Although many engines are available, it is difficult to determine which is best. Marketers must develop an effective way of determining which search engines to use. Additionally, the marketer must determine which search engines customers are using. Often the marketer will place advertising on a search engine or will otherwise support the search engine. Consider the users of the following search engines: (a) ALTAVISTA (www.altavista.digital.com)— 7 million monthly visitors, 30 million sites indexed; (b) EXCITE (www.excite.com)—17 million monthly visitors, 50 million sites indexed; (c) HOTBOT (www.hotbot.com)—unknown number of monthly visitors, 54 million sites indexed; (d) LYCOS (www.lycos.com)—11 million monthly visitors; 66 million sites indexed; and (e) YAHOO (www.yahoo.com)— 32 million monthly visitors; 370,000 sites indexed. Evaluate the above search engines, paying special attention to each site's usefulness to marketing.

For Discussion

1. Assess the strengths and weaknesses of each of the preceding search engines.

2. Why is it important for a company to know which search engines are being used by its customers?

3. Which search engines seem to be the most user friendly?

4. Which sites will roll the viewer to another search engine site automatically?

5. What do you think of the design of the search engines?

Application Thinking

Go to the search engine sites mentioned above and compare them based on their ability to research the following topic: purchasing a digital camera. Construct an evaluation grid in which you assess which of the search engines has been most useful in your purchase quest. Present your findings to the class.

MAP — Marketing Applications

MAP Stop 3

When Stanford University graduate students Jerry Yang and David Filo developed Yahoo, they had little idea how far their revolutionary concept would go. Their original concept was to make "wasting time on the Internet" easier. Commercial applications came later. Today, more Internet users recognize the name Yahoo than Microsoft. One of the reasons for the search engine's popularity is its ability to focus on people's tastes rather than just delivering information or access to every Web site possible. Yahoo has become a full-blown package of information and services, specifically focusing on subtopics such as health, real estate, health search, news, personalization, travel, and shopping. The challenge facing Yahoo today is how to convince corporate America that it can get a big bang for its buck by advertising on-line on the Yahoo site. Strong future challenges are expected from large competitors such as America Online and Microsoft.

Thinking Like a Marketing Manager

1. How will a search engine like Yahoo affect a marketing company's technological environment? What are the unique aspects of Yahoo?

2. Select one of your favorite products. Go to Yahoo at www.yahoo.com and search for your product's Web site and for sites of competing products. What could Yahoo do to enhance the ability of your product's site to be an "instant" success? What type of ads would you consider running on the Yahoo site?

3. Given the rapidly changing Internet environment, how do you think Yahoo will fare in the future? What critical issues will the company face and what strategic changes will be called for? If you were the marketing manager at Yahoo, what strategic alliances would you begin to investigate?

Marketing Research and Information Systems

ROAD MAP:
Previewing the Concepts

In the last chapter, you learned about the complex and changing marketing environment. In this chapter, we'll look at the research and analysis tools that companies use to assess the environment and the impact of their products and marketing programs. First, we'll examine marketing information systems designed to give managers the right information, in the right form, at the right time to help them make better marketing decisions. Then, we'll take a closer look at the marketing research process and at some special marketing research considerations. To succeed in today's marketplace, companies must know how to manage mountains of information effectively.

▶ **After reading this chapter, you should be able to**

1. **explain the importance of information to the company**
2. **define the marketing information system and discuss its parts**
3. **outline the steps in the marketing research process**
4. **compare the advantages and disadvantages of various methods of collecting information**
5. **discuss the special issues some marketing researchers face, including public policy and ethics issues**

We'll start the chapter with Black & Decker, whose skillful use of marketing research has made the company "very good at taking market share away from competitors." In reading this story, you'll learn how listening to customers can result in highly successful products and marketing programs.

When Duncan Black and Alonzo Decker opened their first machine shop in 1910, portable power tools had yet to be invented. The typical industrial electric drill was a cumbersome, 50-pound unit; two people were required to operate it, with a third controlling the power source. Black and Decker saw the need for a smaller, easier-to-use tool and designed a revolutionary new model—one with a smaller motor, a pistol grip, and a trigger switch. The rest is history. The original Black & Decker portable drill now resides in the Smithsonian Institution's National Museum of American History, and Black & Decker is now a leading marketer of portable power tools.

Black & Decker owes much of its success to its relentless efforts to learn all it can about customers. In 1991, market research revealed a growing but underserved power tool segment—serious do-it-yourselfers (SDIYers)—those who take on large, complex home improvement projects by themselves. Some 22 million strong, these serious handymen need more than the run-of-the-mill, entry-level tools used by occasional do-it-yourselfers but less than the expensive, high-quality tools used by professionals. Black & Decker set out to develop a midrange line, Quantum, that would bridge the gap between entry-level and professional tools.

The Quantum quest began with exhaustive consumer research to find out exactly what these serious do-it-yourselfers wanted in their power tools. Black & Decker first enlisted the services of 50 typical SDIYers—male homeowners, aged 25 to 54, who own more than six power tools and who undertake one or more major home improvement projects every year. For more than four months, these 50 people were subjected to intense scrutiny, serving like mice in a cage as a kind of living laboratory. According to *Fortune* magazine, "They were questioned about the tools they use and why they had picked particular brands. B&D executives hung out with them in their homes and around their workshops. They watched how the 50 used their tools and asked why they liked or disliked certain ones, how the tools felt in their hands, and even how they cleaned up their workspace when they finished. The B&D people tagged along on shopping trips too, monitoring what the SDIYers bought and how much they spent. On occasion executives even took an industrial psychologist with them on home visits, hoping this would tell even more about what the customer wanted." Black & Decker followed up this initial market research by interviewing hundreds of tool customers who had mailed in warranty cards, asking similar questions about tool preferences and buying behavior.

Once it understood their needs and preferences, Black & Decker set out to create a line of tools that would give the SDIYers what they wanted. It created a "fusion team"— 85 Black & Decker employees from around the world, including marketers, engineers, designers, finance people, and others. Poring over the research findings, Team Quantum addressed consumers' concerns one by one. SDIYers wanted cordless tools that held their power long enough to complete long jobs; the team created a more powerful drill with a battery pack that recharged in only an hour instead of 24 hours. The handymen wanted tools that required less cleanup after the day's work was done. So the new Quantum circular saws and sanders came equipped with a bag attachment that sucked up sawdust and eliminated cleanup. Finally, although confident about their own abilities, SDIYers sometimes wanted access to expert advice on their tools and projects. To satisfy this requirement, Black & Decker set up *Powersource: The Information Network for Serious Do-It-Yourselfers*. This innovative program provided a toll-free hotline staffed by experienced advisers ready to answer home repair questions from 7 A.M to 10 P.M., seven days a week. *Powersource* also offered customers an assortment of detailed plans for building furniture and other home improvement projects and a subscription to *Shop Talk*, a newsletter containing workshop tips and project guides.

Black & Decker relied on additional consumer research to guide other important decisions. Quantum tools were colored a deep green because consumers associated this color with quality and reliability. Even the Quantum name was based on research—consumers could pronounce it easily, and they felt that the name suggested a product that was a step above others.

The new Quantum line, introduced in mid-1993 as "Serious Tools for Serious Projects," became an immediate success. Sales were brisk, and the line won a number of retailing awards, including the highly regarded Retailers' Choice Award from *Do-It-Yourself Retailing* magazine. And based on the new tool line and on its strong commitment to customer service, Black & Decker earned Vendor of the Year Awards from Wal-Mart, Builders Square, Channel Home Centers, and a number of other retailers.

Despite this early success, Black & Decker continued to listen to its customers. Within a few months of the Quantum introduction, the company held a three-day phoneathon to gather the thoughts of 2,500 customers concerning their new Quantum tools. As *Fortune* reported: "Nearly 200 employees—assembly-line workers, marketing executives, and everyone in between—flew from around the world to company headquarters in Towson, Maryland, where the cafeteria had been set up with phone banks, computers, and, in the words of Quantum program manager Clifford Hall, 'lots of pizza.' Says he: 'We want everyone associated with Quantum to hear what the consumer has to say.'" All of this marketing research appears to be paying off handsomely. According to one industry analyst, "Black & Decker has become very good at taking market share away from rival companies. They just know their customer."[1]

In order to produce superior value and satisfaction for customers, companies need information at almost every turn. As the Black & Decker story highlights, good products and marketing programs begin with a thorough understanding of consumer needs and wants. Companies also need an abundance of information on competitors, resellers, and other actors and forces in the marketplace. Increasingly, marketers are viewing information not just as an input for making better decisions but also as an important strategic asset and marketing tool.

During the past century, most companies were small and knew their customers firsthand. Managers picked up marketing information by being around people, observing them, and asking questions. During this century, however, many factors have increased the need for more and better information. As companies become national or international in scope, they need more information on larger, more distant markets. As incomes increase and buyers become more selective, sellers need better information about how buyers respond to different products and appeals. As sellers use more complex marketing approaches and face more competition, they need information on the effectiveness of their marketing tools. Finally, in today's more rapidly changing environments, managers need more up-to-date information to make timely decisions.

Fortunately, increasing information requirements have been met by an explosion of information technologies. The past 30 years have witnessed the emergence of small but powerful computers, fax machines, CD-ROM drives, videoconferencing, the Internet, and a host of other advances that have revolutionized information handling. Using improved information systems, companies can now generate information in great quantities. In fact, today's managers often receive too much information. For example, one study found that with all the companies offering data, and with all the information now available through supermarket scanners, a packaged-goods brand manager is bombarded with one million to one *billion* new numbers each week. Another study found that, on average, American office workers spend 60 percent of their time processing documents; a typical manager reads about a million words a week. The typical business Internet user receives 25 e-mails a day; 15 percent of users receive between 50 and 100 e-mails per day. Thus, the running out of information is not a problem, but seeing through the "data smog" is.[2]

Despite this data glut, marketers frequently complain that they lack enough information of the *right* kind. For example, a recent survey of managers found that although half the respondents said they couldn't cope with the volume of information coming at them, two-thirds wanted even more. The researcher concluded that, "despite the volume, they're still not getting what they want."[3] Thus, most marketing managers don't need *more* information, they need *better* information. Companies have greater capacity to provide managers with good information but often have not made good use of it. Many companies are now studying their managers' information needs and designing information systems to meet those needs.

The Marketing Information System

Marketing information system (MIS)
People, equipment, and procedures to gather, sort, analyze, evaluate, and distribute needed, timely, and accurate information to marketing decision makers.

A **marketing information system (MIS)** consists of people, equipment, and procedures to gather, sort, analyze, evaluate, and distribute needed, timely, and accurate information to marketing decision makers. Figure 4-1 shows that the MIS begins and ends with marketing managers. First, it interacts with these managers to *assess information needs*. Next, it *develops needed information* from internal company data, marketing intelligence activities, marketing research, and information analysis. Finally, the MIS *distributes information* to managers in the right form at the right time to help them make better marketing decisions.

Assessing Information Needs

A good marketing information system balances the information managers would *like* to have against what they really *need* and what is *feasible* to offer. The company begins by interviewing managers to find out what information they would like. Some managers will ask for whatever information they can get without thinking carefully about what they really need. Too much information can be as harmful as too little. Other managers may omit things they ought to know or may not know to ask for some types of information they should have. For example, managers might need to know that a competitor plans to introduce a new product during the coming year. Because they do not know about the new product, they do not think to ask about it. The MIS must watch the marketing environment in order to provide decision makers with information they should have to make key marketing decisions.

Sometimes the company cannot provide the needed information, either because it is not available or because of MIS limitations. For example, a brand manager might want to

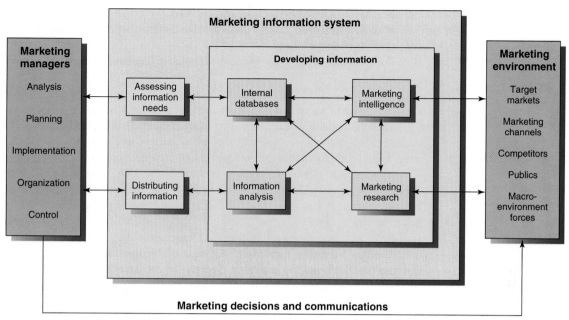

Figure 4-1
The marketing information system

know how competitors will change their advertising budgets next year and how these changes will affect industry market shares. The information on planned budgets probably is not available. Even if it is, the company's MIS may not be advanced enough to forecast resulting changes in market shares.

Finally, the costs of obtaining, processing, storing, and delivering information can mount quickly. The company must decide whether the benefits of having additional information are worth the costs of providing it, and both value and cost are often hard to assess. By itself, information has no worth; its value comes from its *use*. In many cases, additional information will do little to change or improve a manager's decision, or the costs of the information may exceed the returns from the improved decision. Marketers should not assume that additional information will always be worth obtaining. Rather, they should weigh carefully the costs of additional information against the benefits resulting from it.[4]

Developing Information

The information needed by marketing managers can be obtained from *internal data, marketing intelligence*, and *marketing research*. The information analysis system then processes this information to make it more useful for managers.

Internal Data Many companies build extensive **internal databases**, computerized collections of information obtained from data sources within the company. Marketing managers can readily access and work with information in the database to identify marketing opportunities and problems, plan programs, and evaluate performance.

Information in the database can come from many sources. The accounting department prepares financial statements and keeps detailed records of sales, costs, and cash flows. Manufacturing reports on production schedules, shipments, and inventories. The sales force reports on reseller reactions and competitor activities. The marketing department furnishes information on customer demographics, psychographics, and buying

Internal databases
Computerized collections of information obtained from data sources within the company.

behavior, and the customer service department keeps records of customer satisfaction or service problems. Research studies done for one department may provide useful information for several others.

Here are examples of how companies use internal databases to make better marketing decisions:[5]

❖ *Frito-Lay:* Frito-Lay uses its sophisticated internal information system to analyze daily sales performance. Each day, Frito-Lay's salespeople report their day's efforts via handheld computers into Frito-Lay headquarters in Dallas. Twenty-four hours later, Frito-Lay's marketing managers have a complete report analyzing the previous day's sales of Fritos, Doritos, and other brands. The system helps marketing managers make better decisions and makes the salespeople more effective. It greatly reduces the number of hours spent filling out reports, giving salespeople extra time for selling.

❖ *USAA:* USAA, which provides financial services to U.S. military personnel and their families, maintains a customer database built from customer purchasing histories and from information collected directly from customers. To keep the database fresh, the organization regularly surveys its three million customers worldwide to learn such things as whether they have children (and if so, how old they are), if they have moved recently, and when they plan to retire. USAA uses the database to tailor marketing offers to the specific needs of individual customers. For example, if the family has college-age children, the USAA sends those children information on how to manage their credit cards. If the family has younger children, it sends booklets on things like financing a child's education. Or, for customers looking toward retirement, it sends information on estate planning. Through skillful use of its database, USAA serves each customer uniquely, resulting in high levels of customer loyalty—the roughly $7 billion company retains 97 percent of its customers. Says USAA's chief marketing executive, "We make it a point, in all of our materials, to let [customers] know that we're there for them as they make transactions."

Internal databases usually can be accessed more quickly and cheaply than other information sources, but they also present some problems. Because internal information was collected for other purposes, it may be incomplete or in the wrong form for making marketing decisions. For example, sales and cost data used by the accounting department for preparing financial statements must be adapted for use in evaluating product, sales force, or channel performance. Data ages quickly; keeping the database current requires a major effort. In addition, a large company produces mountains of information, and keeping track of it all is difficult. The database information must be well integrated and readily accessible through user-friendly interfaces so that managers can find it easily and use it effectively.

Marketing intelligence
Everyday information about developments in the marketing environment that helps managers prepare and adjust marketing plans.

Marketing Intelligence **Marketing intelligence** is systematic collection and analysis of publicly available information about competitors and developments in the marketing environment. A marketing intelligence system gathers, analyzes, and distributes information about the company's competitive, technological, customer, economic, social, and political and regulatory environments. Its goal is to improve strategic decision making, assess and track competitors' actions, and provide early warning of opportunities and threats. The marketing intelligence system determines what intelligence is needed, collects it by searching the environment, and delivers it to marketing managers.[6]

Marketing intelligence can be gathered from many sources (see Marketing at Work 4-1). Much intelligence can be collected from the company's own personnel—executives, engineers and scientists, purchasing agents, and the sales force. But company people are often busy and fail to pass on important information. The company must sell its people on their importance as intelligence gatherers, train them to spot new developments, interact with them on an ongoing basis, and urge them to report intelligence back to the company.

The company can get suppliers, resellers, and customers to pass along important intelligence. Or competitors themselves may reveal information through their annual reports, business publications, trade show exhibits, press releases, advertisements, and Web pages. The company can buy and analyze competitors' products, monitor their sales, and check for new patents.

Finally, companies buy intelligence information from outside suppliers, ranging from marketing research firms to consultants who specialize in competitive intelligence. Increasingly, marketing intelligence activities have gone high-tech. Many companies now routinely use the Internet to search for information about competitors and environmental events. And for a fee, companies can subscribe to any of more than 3,000 *on-line data-bases* and information search services such as Dialog, DataStar, Lexis-Nexis, Dow Jones News Retrieval, UMI ProQuest, and Dun & Bradstreet's Online Access. We discuss these and other well-known on-line data services in more detail later in the chapter.

Some companies set up an office to collect and circulate marketing intelligence. The staff scans major publications, surfs the Internet, summarizes important news, and sends bulletins to marketing managers. It develops a file of intelligence information and helps managers evaluate new information. These services greatly improve the quality of information available to marketing managers.

Marketing Research In addition to information about competitors and environmental happenings, marketers often need formal studies of specific situations. For example, Toshiba wants to know how many and what kinds of people or companies will buy its new superfast notebook computer. Or Barat College in Lake Forest, Illinois, needs to know what percentage of its target market has heard of Barat, how they heard, what they know, and how they feel about Barat. In such situations, the marketing intelligence system will not provide the detailed information needed. Managers will need marketing research.

We define **marketing research** as the systematic design, collection, analysis, and reporting of data relevant to a specific marketing situation facing an organization. Every marketer needs research. Marketing researchers engage in a wide variety of activities, ranging from market potential and market share studies, to assessments of customer satisfaction and purchase behavior, to studies of pricing, product, distribution, and promotion activities.

Marketing research
The systematic design, collection, analysis, and reporting of data relevant to a specific marketing situation facing an organization.

A company can conduct marketing research in its own research department or have some or all of it done outside, depending on its own research skills and resources. Although most large companies have their own marketing research departments, they often use outside firms to do special research tasks or special studies. A company with no research department has to buy the services of research firms.

Information Analysis Information gathered by the company's marketing intelligence and marketing research systems often requires more analysis, and sometimes managers may need more help to apply the information to their marketing problems and decisions. This help may include advanced statistical analysis to learn more about both the relationships within a set of data and their statistical reliability. Such analysis allows managers to go beyond means and standard deviations in the data and to answer questions about markets, marketing activities, and outcomes.

Information analysis might also involve a collection of analytical models that will help marketers make better decisions. Each model represents some real system, process,

Marketing at Work 4-1

Marketing Intelligence: Snooping to Conquer

Competitive intelligence gathering has grown dramatically as more and more companies are now busily snooping on their competitors. Techniques range from quizzing the company's own employees and benchmarking competitors' products to surfing the Internet, lurking around industry trade shows, and rooting through rival's trash bins.

Collecting Information Internally

According to the chief of corporate intelligence for Ryder System, Inc., "Eighty percent of what you need to know can be found by talking to your own employees." Here's an example of how listening to its own people paid off for Xerox:

In early 1995, a Kodak copier salesman told a Xerox technician that he was being trained to service Xerox products. The Xerox employee told his boss, who passed the news to the intelligence unit. Using such clues as a classified ad Kodak placed seeking new people with Xerox product experience, they verified Kodak's plan—code-named Ulysses—to service Xerox copiers. . . . The warning allowed Xerox to devise a scheme to [protect its profitable service business through its] Total Satisfaction Guarantee, which allowed copier returns for any reason as long as *Xerox* did the servicing. By [the time] Kodak launched its plan, Xerox had been trumpeting its [program] for three months.

Four other car companies have already bought one. Whatever do you suppose they want them for?

Porsche 968: The next evolution.

Collecting intelligence: Porsche notes that "it's not unusual for car companies to check out each other's creations . . . A new Porsche gets an inordinate amount of attention."

Getting Information from Recruits and Competitors' Employees

Companies can obtain intelligence through job interviews or from conversations with competitors' employees. When holding interviews, some companies pay special attention to those who have worked for competitors. Job seekers are eager to impress and often have not been warned about divulging sensitive information. Companies also send engineers to trade shows to talk with competitors' technical people. According to *Fortune*: "Often conversations start innocently—just a few fellow technicians discussing processes and problems . . . [yet competitors'] engineers and scientists often brag about surmounting technical challenges, in the process divulging sensitive information."

Getting Information from People Who Do Business with Competitors

Key customers can keep the company informed about competitors and their products, and intelligence can be gathered by infiltrating customers' business operations. For example, prior to introducing its Good News razor in the United States, Gillette told a large Canadian account the planned U.S. introduction date. The Canadian distributor promptly called Bic and told it about the impending product launch. By putting on a crash program, Bic was

or outcome. These models can help answer the questions of *what if* and *which is best*. During the past 20 years, marketing scientists have developed numerous models to help marketing managers make better marketing mix decisions, design sales territories and sales-call plans, select sites for retail outlets, develop optimal advertising mixes, and forecast new-product sales.[7]

able to start selling its razor shortly after Gillette did.

Getting Information from Published Materials and Public Documents

Keeping track of seemingly meaningless published information can provide competitor intelligence. For instance, as Xerox learned, the types of people sought in help-wanted ads can indicate something about a competitor's new strategies and products. Government agencies are another good source. For example, a company can't legally photograph a competitor's plant from the air. However, publicly available aerial photos are often on file with the U.S. Geological Survey or Environmental Protection Agency. In another instance, a company attempting to assess the capacity of a competitor's plant struck gold when it found that a publicly available Uniform Commercial Code filing the competitor had submitted to the state contained a detailed list of all the equipment in the competitor's plant.

Getting Information by Observing Competitors or Analyzing Physical Evidence

Companies can get to know competitors better by buying their products or examining other physical evidence. For example, to design the first Taurus models, Ford compiled a list of more than 400 features its customers said they liked best about competing cars. Then it matched or topped the best of the competition. The result: Taurus soon became America's best-selling car.

Companies can also examine many other types of physical evidence. For example, to gauge competitor shipping volumes, companies have measured the rust on rails of railroad sidings to their competitors' plants or have counted the trucks leaving loading bays. Some companies even rifle their competitors' garbage, which is legally considered abandoned property once it leaves the premises. Although some companies now shred technical documents, they may overlook the almost-as-revealing refuse from the marketing or public relations departments. In one example of garbage snatching, Avon admitted that it had hired private detectives to paw through the dumpster of rival Mary Kay Cosmetics. An outraged Mary Kay sued to get its garbage back, but Avon claimed that it had done nothing illegal. The dumpster had been located in a public parking lot, and Avon had videotapes to prove it.

Surfing the Internet and On-line Databases

The Internet provides quick and inexpensive access to a rich assortment of intelligence information. By simply checking competitors' Web sites, a company can glean important details concerning rivals' products, prices, promotional campaigns, and overall marketing strategies. Using Internet search engines such as Yahoo or Infoseek, marketers can search specific competitor names, events, or trends and see what turns up. One Web site (www.fuld.com) even provides a

Competitive Intelligence Guide offering sleuthing tips.

Intelligence seekers also pore through any of thousands of on-line databases. Some are free. For example, the U.S. Security and Exchange Commission's Edgar database (www.sec.gov/) provides access to a huge stockpile of financial and other information on public companies. Other on-line data sources provide information and searches for a fee. Using the Dialog or Lexis-Nexis databases, companies can conduct complex information searches in a flash from the comfort of their keyboards.

The growing use of marketing intelligence raises a number of ethical issues. Although most of the preceding techniques are legal, and some are considered to be shrewdly competitive, many involve questionable ethics. Clearly, companies should take advantage of publicly available information. However, they should not stoop to snoop. With all the legitimate intelligence sources now available, a company does not have to break the law or accepted codes of ethics to get good intelligence.

Sources: Excerpts and quotes from Jeremy Main, "How to Steal the Best Ideas Around," *Fortune*, October 19, 1992, pp. 102–6; Steven Flax, "How to Snoop on Your Competitors," *Fortune*, May 14, 1984, pp. 29–33; Stan Crock, "They Snoop to Conquer," *Business Week*, October 28, 1996; and Melinda Jensen Ligos, "Spy Games," *Sales & Marketing Management*, June 1997, p. 13. Also see Wendy Zellner and Bruce Hager, "Dumpster Raids? That's Not Very Ladylike, Avon," *Business Week*, April 1, 1991, p. 32; David B. Montgomery and Charles Weinberg, "Toward Strategic Intelligence Systems," *Marketing Management*, Winter 1998, pp. 44–52; Bill Fiora, "Ethical Business Intelligence is NOT Mission Impossible," *Strategy & Leadership*, January–February 1998, pp. 40–41; and Kirk W.M. Tyson, *The Complete Guide to Competitive Intelligence* (Kirk Tyson International, 1998); and Charles Bowen, "Business Sleuthing: The Web Has the Dirt," *Editor & Publisher*, December 19, 1998, p. 23.

Distributing Information

Marketing information has no value until managers use it to make better marketing decisions. The information gathered through marketing intelligence and marketing research must be distributed to the right marketing managers at the right time. Most companies have centralized marketing information systems that provide managers with regular performance reports, intelligence updates, and reports on the results of studies. Managers need these routine reports for making regular planning, implementation, and control decisions. But marketing managers may also need nonroutine information for special situations and on-the-spot decisions. For example, a sales manager having trouble with a large customer may want a summary of the account's sales and profitability over the past year. Or a retail store manager who has run out of a best-selling product may want to know the current inventory levels in the chain's other stores. In companies with only centralized information systems, these managers must request the information from the MIS staff and wait. Often, the information arrives too late to be useful.

Developments in information technology have caused a revolution in information distribution. With recent advances in computers, software, and telecommunication, most companies have decentralized their marketing information systems. In many companies, marketing managers have direct access to the information network through personal computers and other means. From any location, they can obtain information from company databases or outside information services, analyze the information using statistical packages and models, prepare reports using word processing and presentation software, and communicate with others in the network through electronic communications.

Such systems offer exciting prospects. They allow managers to get the information they need directly and quickly and to tailor it to their own needs. As more managers develop the skills needed to use such systems, and as improvements in the technology make them more economical, more marketing companies will use decentralized marketing information systems.

Linking the Concepts

Before we dig more deeply into the marketing research process, be certain that you've got the "big picture" concerning marketing information systems.

- What's the overall goal of an MIS? How are the individual components linked and what does each contribute? Take another look at Figure 4-1—it provides a good organizing framework for the entire chapter.
- Apply the MIS framework to Black & Decker. What does this company appear to be doing well? Poorly?

The Marketing Research Process

The marketing research process (see Figure 4-2) has four steps: *defining the problem and research objectives*, *developing the research plan*, *implementing the research plan*, and *interpreting and reporting the findings*.

Figure 4-2
The marketing
research process

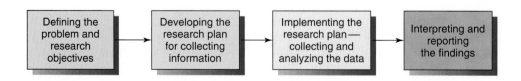

Defining the Problem and Research Objectives

The marketing manager and the researcher must work closely together to define the problem carefully, and they must agree on the research objectives. The manager best understands the decision for which information is needed; the researcher best understands marketing research and how to obtain the information.

Managers should know enough about marketing research to help in the planning and the interpretation of research results. If they know little about marketing research, they may obtain the wrong information, accept wrong conclusions, or ask for information that costs too much. Experienced marketing researchers who understand the manager's problem should also be involved at this stage. The researcher must be able to help the manager define the problem and suggest ways that research can help the manager make better decisions.

Defining the problem and research objectives is often the hardest step in the research process. The manager may know that something is wrong, without knowing the specific causes. For example, managers of a large discount retail store chain hastily decided that falling sales were caused by poor advertising, and they ordered research to test the company's advertising. When this research showed that current advertising was reaching the right people with the right message, the managers were puzzled. It turned out that the real problem was that the chain was not delivering the prices, products, and service promised in the advertising. Careful problem definition would have avoided the cost and delay of doing advertising research. In the classic New Coke case, the Coca-Cola Company defined its research problem too narrowly, with disastrous results (see Marketing at Work 4-2).

After the problem has been defined carefully, the manager and researcher must set the research objectives. A marketing research project might have one of three types of objectives. The objective of **exploratory research** is to gather preliminary information that will help define the problem and suggest hypotheses. The objective of **descriptive research** is to describe things such as the market potential for a product or the demographics and attitudes of consumers who buy the product. The objective of **causal research** is to test hypotheses about cause-and-effect relationships. For example, would a 10 percent decrease in tuition at a private college result in an enrollment increase sufficient to offset the reduced tuition? Managers often start with exploratory research and later follow with descriptive or causal research.

The statement of the problem and research objectives guides the entire research process. The manager and researcher should put the statement in writing to be certain that they agree on the purpose and expected results of the research.

Exploratory research
Marketing research to gather preliminary information that will help define problems and suggest hypotheses.

Descriptive research
Marketing research to better describe marketing problems, situations, or markets, such as the market potential for a product or the demographics and attitudes of consumers.

Causal research
Marketing research to test hypotheses about cause-and-effect relationships.

Developing the Research Plan

The second step of the marketing research process calls for determining the information needed, developing a plan for gathering it efficiently, and presenting the plan to marketing management. The plan outlines sources of existing data and spells out the specific research approaches, contact methods, sampling plans, and instruments that researchers will use to gather new data.

Determining Specific Information Needs Research objectives must be translated into specific information needs. For example, suppose Campbell decides to conduct research on how consumers would react to the company replacing its familiar red-and-white soup can with new bowl-shaped plastic containers that it has used successfully for

Marketing at Work 4-2
The Rise and Fall of New Coke: What's the Problem?

In 1985, the Coca-Cola Company made a classic marketing blunder. After 99 successful years, it set aside its long-standing rule—"Don't mess with Mother Coke"—and dropped its original-formula Coke! In its place came *New* Coke with a sweeter, smoother taste.

At first, amid the introductory flurry of advertising and publicity, New Coke sold well. But sales soon went flat, as a stunned public reacted. Coke began receiving sacks of mail and more than 1,500 phone calls each day from angry consumers. A group called "Old

Cola Drinkers" staged protests, handed out T-shirts, and threatened a class-action suit unless Coca-Cola brought back the old formula. Most marketing experts predicted that New Coke would be the "Edsel of the Eighties." After only three months, the Coca-Cola Company

When Coca-Cola introduced New Coke, consumers reacted angrily—they staged protests, handed out T-shirts, and threatened class action suits to get the old formula back.

a number of its other products. The containers would cost more, but would allow consumers to heat the soup in a microwave oven and eat it without using dishes. This research might call for the following specific information:

- The demographic, economic, and lifestyle characteristics of current soup users. (Busy working couples might find the convenience of the new packaging worth the price; families with children might want to pay less and wash the pan and bowls.)

brought old Coke back. Now called "Coke Classic," it sold side-by-side with New Coke on supermarket shelves. The company said that New Coke would remain its flagship brand, but consumers had a different idea. By the end of 1985, Classic was outselling New Coke in supermarkets by two to one.

Quick reaction saved the company from potential disaster. It stepped up efforts for Coke Classic and slotted New Coke into a supporting role. Coke Classic again became the company's main brand, and the country's leading soft drink. New Coke became the company's "attack brand"—its Pepsi stopper—and ads boldly compared New Coke's taste with Pepsi's. Still, New Coke managed only a 2 percent market share. In the spring of 1990, the company repackaged New Coke and relaunched it as a brand extension with a new name, Coke II. Today, Coke Classic captures more than 20 percent of the U.S. soft-drink market; Coke II holds a miniscule 0.1 percent.

Why was New Coke introduced in the first place? What went wrong? Many analysts blame the blunder on poor marketing research.

In the early 1980s, although Coke was still the leading soft drink, it was slowly losing market share to Pepsi. For years, Pepsi had successfully mounted the "Pepsi Challenge," a series of televised taste tests showing that consumers preferred the sweeter taste of Pepsi. By early 1985, although Coke led in the overall market, Pepsi led in share of supermarket sales by 2 percent. (That doesn't sound like much, but 2 percent of the huge soft-drink market amounts to more than $1 billion in retail sales!) Coca-Cola had to do something to stop the loss of its market share, and the solution appeared to be a change in Coke's taste.

Coca-Cola began the largest new-product research project in the company's history. It spent more than two years and $4 million on research before settling on a new formula. It conducted some 200,000 taste tests—30,000 on the final formula alone. In blind tests, 60 percent of consumers chose the new Coke over the old, and 52 percent chose it over Pepsi. Research showed that New Coke would be a winner, and the company introduced it with confidence. So what happened?

Looking back, we can see that Coke defined its marketing research problem too narrowly. The research looked only at taste; it did not explore consumers' feelings about dropping the old Coke and replacing it with a new version. It took no account of the *intangibles*—Coke's name, history, packaging, cultural heritage, and image. However, to many people, Coke stands alongside baseball, hot dogs, and apple pie as an American institution; it represents the very fabric of America. Coke's symbolic meaning turned out to be more important to many consumers than its taste. Research addressing a broader set of issues would have detected these strong emotions.

Coke's managers may also have used poor judgment in interpreting the research and planning strategies around it. For example, they took the finding that 60 percent of consumers preferred New Coke's taste to mean that the new product would win in the marketplace, as when a political candidate wins with 60 percent of the vote. But it also meant that 40 percent still liked the original formula. By dropping the old Coke, the company trampled the taste buds of the large core of loyal Coke drinkers who didn't want a change. The company might have been wiser to leave the old Coke alone and introduce New Coke as a brand extension, as it later did successfully with Cherry Coke.

The Coca-Cola Company has one of the largest, best-managed, and most advanced marketing research operations in America. Good marketing research has kept the company atop the rough-and-tumble soft-drink market for decades. But marketing research is far from an exact science. Consumers are full of surprises and figuring them out can be awfully tough. If Coca-Cola can make a large marketing research mistake, any company can.

Sources: See "Coke 'Family' Sales Fly as New Coke Stumbles," *Advertising Age*, January 17, 1986, p. 1; Jack Honomichl, "Missing Ingredients in 'New' Coke's Research," *Advertising Age*, July 22, 1985, p. 1; Leah Rickard, "Remembering New Coke," *Advertising Age*, April 17, 1995, p. 6; Debra Goldman, "Power to the People," *Adweek*, October 6, 1997, p. 74; and Kent Steinreide and Sarah Theodore, "1997 Soft Drink Wrap-Up," *Beverage Industry*, March 1998, pp. 36–42.

- Consumer-usage patterns for soup: how much soup they eat, where, and when. (The new packaging might be ideal for adults eating lunch on the go but less convenient for parents feeding lunch to several children.)
- Retailer reactions to the new packaging. (Failure to get retailer support could hurt sales of the new package.)
- Consumer attitudes toward the new packaging. (The red-and-white Campbell can has become an American institution—will consumers accept the new packaging?)

⏱ Forecasts of sales of both new and current packages. (Will the new packaging increase Campbell's profits?)

Campbell managers will need these and many other types of information to decide whether to introduce the new packaging.

Gathering Secondary Information To meet the manager's information needs, the researcher can gather secondary data, primary data, or both. **Secondary data** consist of information that already exists somewhere, having been collected for another purpose. **Primary data** consist of information collected for the specific purpose at hand.

Researchers usually start by gathering secondary data. The company's internal database provides a good starting point. However, the company can also tap a wide assortment of external information sources, ranging from company, public, and university libraries to government and business publications. Table 4-1 describes a number of other important sources of secondary data, including commercial data services, on-line database services, and Internet data sources.

COMMERCIAL DATA SOURCES Companies can buy secondary data reports from outside suppliers. For example, Nielsen Marketing Research sells data on brand shares, retail prices, and percentages of stores stocking different brands. Information Resources, Inc., sells supermarket scanner purchase data from a panel of 60,000 households nationally, with measures of trial and repeat purchasing, brand loyalty, and buyer demographics. The *Monitor* service by Yankelovich and Partners sells information on important social and lifestyle trends.[8] These and other firms supply high-quality data to suit a wide variety of marketing information needs.

ON-LINE DATABASES AND INTERNET DATA SOURCES Using commercial **on-line databases**, marketing researchers can conduct their own searches of secondary data sources. A recent survey of marketing researchers found that 81 percent use such on-line services for

Secondary data
Information that already exists somewhere, having been collected for another purpose.

Primary data
Information collected for the specific purpose at hand.

On-line databases
Computerized collections of information available from on-line commercial sources or via the Internet.

Table 4-1   Commercial, On-line Database, and Internet Data Sources

Commercial Data Services

Here are just a few of the dozens of commercial research houses selling data to subscribers:

A.C. Nielsen Corporation provides supermarket scanner data on sales, market share, and retail prices (ScanTrack), data on household purchasing (ScanTrack National Electronic Household Panel), data on television audiences (Nielsen National Television Index), and others.

Information Resources, Inc. provides supermarket scanner data for tracking grocery product movement (InfoScan) and single-source data collection (BehaviorScan).

The Arbitron Company provides local-market radio audience and advertising expenditure information, along with a wealth of other media and ad spending data.

PMSI/Source Infomatics provides reports on the movement of pharmaceuticals, hospital laboratory supplies, animal health products, and personal care products.

MMRI (Simmons Market Research Bureau) provides reports covering television markets, sporting goods, and proprietary drugs, giving lifestyle and geodemographic data by sex, income, age, and brand preferences (selective markets and media reaching them).

Table 4-1 (*continued*)

On-line Database Services

Here are only a few of the many on-line database services:

DIALOG offers several services, including ABI/INFORM, which provides information on business management and administration from over 800 publications. The site also provides access to full text reports and newsletters from 50 industries and a collection of U.S. public opinion surveys. In addition, subscribers can view Dun & Bradstreet data, such as census statistics and business directories, by searching through Donnelly Demographics and Dun's Electronic Business Directory.

LEXIS-NEXIS, in addition to providing access to articles from a wide range of business magazines and journals, features in-depth research reports from research firms, SEC filings, Standard & Poor's, and worldwide investment banks. Users can also access information from consumer goods and marketing trade publications. The service also includes PROMT/PLUS, which tracks competitors and industries, identifies trends, and evaluates advertising and promotion techniques.

CompuServe provides a variety of on-line database services. For example, its *Business Demographics* files summarize statistics on state employees by industry codes and categorizes retail trade businesses by employee counts. By mining the *Neighborhood Report*, a user can access summaries of the demographics of any zip code in the U.S. Other CompuServe databases offer full-text articles, news releases, and market and industry research report indices. The service also provides access to an additional 850 databases, ranging from newspapers and newsletters to government reports and patent records.

Dow Jones News Retrieval specializes in providing in-depth financial, historical, and operational information on public and private companies. The site offers Standard & Poor's profiles as well as Dun & Bradstreet profiles and company reports. In addition, the service compares stock price, volume, and data on companies and industries and summarizes same-day business and financial stories from both the United States and Japan.

Internet Data Sources

Most of the above on-line information services also provide Web-based versions. Literally thousands of other Web sites also offer data, often at little or no cost. The best way to locate such sources is by using Internet search engines to search specific topics. Here is just a tiny sampling of sites offering specialized information on a variety of business related topics. The *U.S. Securities and Exchange Commission* Edgar database (www.sec.gov/) provides financial information on public companies. The *Small Business Administration* (www.sbaonline.gov/) site provides a rich variety of information for small business managers, along with links to dozens of other relevant sites. *Avenue Technologies* (www.com.avetech/avenue) presents summaries and full reports on over 25,000 public, private, and international companies. Similarly, *Dun & Bradstreet's Online Access* (www.dbisna.com/dbis/product/secure.html) offers short financial reports on 10 million U.S. companies. In addition to garnering financial information on companies and industries, Internet users can do real-time research. *Ecola's 24-Hour Newsstand* (www.ecola.com/news) links users to the Web sites of over 2,000 newspapers, journals, and computer publications. Researchers can view recent new articles on-line through *CNN Interactive* (www.cnn.com). Market researchers can visit the *American Demographics* site (www.demographics.com) and browse a directory of marketing experts.

Sources: See Christel Beard and Betsey Wiesendanger, "The Marketer's Guide to Online Databases," *Sales & Marketing Management*, January 1993, pp. 37–41; Susan Greco, "The Online Sleuth," *Inc.*, October 1996, pp. 88–89; Marydee Ojala, "The Daze of Future Business Research," *Online*, January–February 1998, pp. 78–80; Guy Kawasaki, "Get Your Facts Here," *Forbes*, March 23, 1998, p. 156; and "Online Services Offering Intranet Toolkits," *Database*, April–May 1999, p. 9.

On-line database services such as Compu-Serve, Dialog, and Lexis-Nexis put an incredible wealth of information at the keyboards of marketing decision makers.

conducting research.[9] A readily available on-line database exists to fill almost any marketing information need. General database services such as CompuServe, Dialog, and Lexis-Nexis put an incredible wealth of information at the keyboards of marketing decision makers. For example, a company doing business in Germany can check out CompuServe's German Company Library of financial and product information on over 48,000 German-owned firms. A U.S. auto parts manufacturer can punch up Dun & Bradstreet Financial Profiles and Company Reports to develop biographical sketches of key General Motors, Ford, and Chrysler executives. Just about any information a marketer might need—demographic data, today's Associated Press news wire reports, a list of active U.S. trademarks in the United States—is available from on-line databases.[10]

The Internet offers a mind-boggling array of databases and other secondary information sources, many free to the user. Beyond commercial Web sites offering information for a fee, almost every industry association, government agency, business publication, and news medium offers free information to those tenacious enough to find their Web sites. In fact, there are so many Web sites offering data that finding the right ones can become an almost overwhelming task.

ADVANTAGES AND DISADVANTAGES OF SECONDARY DATA. Secondary data can usually be obtained more quickly and at a lower cost than primary data. For example, an Internet or on-line database search might provide all the information Campbell needs on microwave oven usage, quickly and at almost no cost. A study to collect primary information might take weeks or months and cost thousands of dollars. Also, secondary sources sometimes can provide data an individual company cannot collect on its own — information that either is not directly available or would be too expensive to collect. For example, it would be too expensive for Campbell to conduct a continuing retail store audit to find out about the market shares, prices, and displays of competitors' brands. But it can buy the InfoScan service from Information Resources, Inc., which provides this information from thousands of scanner-equipped supermarkets in dozens of U.S. markets.

Secondary data can also present problems. The needed information may not exist — researchers can rarely obtain all the data they need from secondary sources. For example, Campbell will not find existing information about consumer reactions to new packaging that it has not yet placed on the market. Even when data can be found, they might not be very usable. The researcher must evaluate secondary information carefully to make certain it is *relevant* (fits research project needs), *accurate* (reliably collected and reported), *current* (up-to-date enough for current decisions), and *impartial* (objectively collected and reported).

Secondary data provide a good starting point for research and often help to define problems and research objectives. In most cases, however, the company must also collect primary data.

Planning Primary Data Collection Good decisions require good data. Just as researchers must carefully evaluate the quality of secondary information, they also must take great care when collecting primary data to make sure that it will be relevant, accurate, current, and unbiased. Table 4-2 shows that designing a plan for primary data collection calls for a number of decisions on *research approaches, contact methods, sampling plan*, and *research instruments*.

RESEARCH APPROACHES. **Observational research** is the gathering of primary data by observing relevant people, actions, and situations. For example, a maker of personal care products might pretest its ads by showing them to people and measuring eye movements, pulse rates, and other physical reactions. Or a bank might evaluate possible new branch locations by checking traffic patterns, neighborhood conditions, and the location of competing branches. Steelcase used observation to help design new office furniture for use by work teams.

Observational research
The gathering of primary data by observing relevant people, actions, and situations.

To learn firsthand how teams actually operate, it set up video cameras at various companies and studied the tapes, looking for motions and behavior patterns that customers themselves might not even notice. It found that teams work best when they can do some work together and some privately. So Steelcase designed highly

Table 4-2 Planning Primary Data Collection

Research Approaches	Contact Method	Sampling Plan	Research Instruments
Observation	Mail	Sampling unit	Questionnaire
Survey	Telephone	Sample size	Mechanical instruments
Experiment	Personal computer	Sampling procedure	

Observational research: In designing its highly successful Personal Harbor modular office units, Steelcase set up video cameras at various companies to study motions and behavior patterns that customers themselves might not even notice.

successful modular office units called Personal Harbor. These units are "rather like telephone booths in size and shape." They can be arranged around a common space where a team works, letting people work together but also alone when necessary. Says a Steelcase executive, "Market data wouldn't necessarily have pointed us that way. It was more important to know how people actually work."[11]

Urban Outfitters, the fast-growing specialty clothing chain, prefers observation to other types of market research. "We're not after people's statements," notes the chain's president, "we're after their actions." The company develops customer profiles by video-taping and taking photographs of customers in its stores. This helps managers determine what people are actually wearing and allows them to make quick decisions on merchandise.[12]

Several companies sell information collected through *mechanical* observation. For example, the Nielsen Media Research attaches *people meters* to television sets in selected homes to record who watches which programs. It then rates the size and demographic makeup of audiences for different television programs.[13] The television networks use these ratings to judge program popularity and to set charges for advertising time. Advertisers use the ratings when selecting programs for their commercials. *Checkout scanners* in retail stores record consumer purchases in detail. Consumer products companies and retailers use scanner information to assess and improve product sales and store performance. Some marketing research firms now offer **single-source data systems** that electronically monitor both consumers' purchases and consumers' exposure to various marketing activities in an effort to better evaluate the link between the two (see Marketing at Work 4-3).

Observational research can be used to obtain information that people are unwilling or unable to provide. In some cases, observation may be the only way to obtain the needed information. In contrast, some things simply cannot be observed, such as feelings, attitudes and motives, or private behavior. Long-term or infrequent behavior is also difficult to observe. Because of these limitations, researchers often use observation along with other data collection methods.

Survey research is the approach best suited for gathering *descriptive* information. A company that wants to know about people's knowledge, attitudes, preferences, or buying behavior can often find out by asking individuals directly.

Single-source data systems Electronic monitoring systems that link consumers' exposure to television advertising and promotion with what they buy in stores.

Survey research The gathering of primary data by asking people questions about their knowledge, attitudes, preferences, and buying behavior.

Survey research is the most widely used method for primary data collection, and it is often the only method used in a research study. Researchers interview tens of millions of Americans each year in surveys. The major advantage of survey research is its flexibility. It can be used to obtain many different kinds of information in many different situations. Depending on the survey design, it also may provide information more quickly and at lower cost than observational or experimental research.

However, survey research also presents some problems. Sometimes people are unable to answer survey questions because they cannot remember or have never thought about what they do and why. Or people may be unwilling to respond to unknown interviewers or about things they consider private. Respondents may answer survey questions even when they do not know the answer in order to appear smarter or more informed. Or they may try to help the interviewer by giving pleasing answers. Finally, busy people may not take the time, or they might resent the intrusion into their privacy.

Whereas observation is best suited for exploratory research and surveys for descriptive research, **experimental research** is best suited for gathering *causal* information. Experiments involve selecting matched groups of subjects, giving them different treatments, controlling unrelated factors, and checking for differences in group responses. Thus, experimental research tries to explain cause-and-effect relationships. Observation and surveys may be used to collect information in experimental research.

Experimental research
The gathering of primary data by selecting matched groups of subjects, giving them different treatments, controlling related factors, and checking for differences in group responses.

Before adding a new sandwich to the menu, researchers at McDonald's might use experiments to answer questions such as the following:

- How much will the new sandwich increase McDonald's sales?
- How will the new sandwich affect the sales of other menu items?
- Which advertising approach would have the greatest effect on sales of the sandwich?
- How would different prices affect the sales of the product?
- Should the new item be targeted toward adults, children, or both?

To test the effects of two different prices, McDonald's could set up a simple experiment: It could introduce the new sandwich at one price in its restaurants in one city and at another price in restaurants in another city. If the cities are similar, and if all other marketing efforts for the sandwich are the same, then differences in sales in the two cities could be related to the price charged. More complex experiments could be designed to include other variables and other locations.

CONTACT METHODS Information can be collected by mail, telephone, personal interview, or computer. Table 4-3 shows the strengths and weaknesses of each of these contact methods.

Mail questionnaires can be used to collect large amounts of information at a low cost per respondent. Respondents may give more honest answers to more personal questions on a mail questionnaire than to an unknown interviewer in person or over the phone. Also, no interviewer is involved to bias the respondent's answers. However, mail questionnaires are not very flexible—all respondents answer the same questions in a fixed order, and the researcher cannot adapt the questionnaire based on earlier answers. Mail surveys usually take longer to complete, and the response rate—the number of people returning completed questionnaires—is often very low. Finally, the researcher often has little control over the mail questionnaire sample. Even with a good mailing list, it is hard to control *who* at the mailing address fills out the questionnaire.

Telephone interviewing is the best method for gathering information quickly, and it provides greater flexibility than mail questionnaires. Interviewers can explain difficult questions, and they can skip some questions or probe on others depending on the answers

Marketing at Work 4-3

Single-Source Data Systems: A Powerful Way to Measure Marketing Impact

Information Resources, Inc. knows all there is to know about the members of its panel households—what they eat for lunch; what they put in their coffee; and what they use to wash their hair, quench their thirsts, or make up their faces. The research company electronically monitors the television programs these people watch and tracks the brands they buy, the coupons they use, where they shop, and what newspapers and magazines they read. These households are a part of IRI's BehaviorScan service, a *single-source data system* that links consumers' exposure to television advertising, sales promotion, and other marketing efforts with their store purchases. BehaviorScan and other single-source data systems have revolutionized the way consumer products companies measure the impact of their marketing activities.

The basics of single-source research are straightforward, and the IRI BehaviorScan system provides a good example. IRI maintains a

Single-source data systems link marketing efforts directly with consumer buying behavior. Here, a BehaviorScan panel member makes a purchase.

Table 4-3 Strengths and Weaknesses of Contact Methods

	Mail	Telephone	Personal	On-line
Flexibility	Poor	Good	Excellent	Good
Quantity of data that can be collected	Good	Fair	Excellent	Good
Control of interviewer effects	Excellent	Fair	Poor	Fair
Control of sample	Fair	Excellent	Fair	Poor
Speed of data collection	Poor	Excellent	Good	Excellent
Response rate	Fair	Good	Good	Good
Cost	Good	Fair	Poor	Excellent

Source: Adapted with permission of Macmillian Publishing Company from *Marketing Research: Measurement and Method,* 7th ed., by Donald S. Tull and Del I. Hawkins. Copyright 1993 by Macmillan Publishing Company.

panel of 60,000 households in 27 markets. The company meters each home's television set to track who watches what and when, and it quizzes family members to find out what they read. It carefully records important facts about each household, such as family income, age of children, lifestyle, and product and store buying history.

IRI also employs a panel of retail stores in each of its markets. For a fee, these stores agree to carry the new products that IRI wishes to test, and they allow IRI to control factors such as shelf location, stocking, point-of-purchase displays, and pricing for these products.

Each BehaviorScan household receives an identification number. When household members shop for groceries in IRI panel stores, they give their identification number to the store checkout clerk. All the information about the family's purchases—brands bought, package sizes, prices paid—is recorded by the store's electronic scanner and immediately entered by computer into the family's purchase file. The system also records any other in-store factors that might affect purchase decisions, such as special competitor price promotions or shelf displays.

Thus, IRI builds a complete record of each household's demographic and psychographic makeup, purchasing behavior, media habits, and the conditions surrounding purchase. But IRI takes the process a step farther. Through cable television, IRI controls the advertisements being sent to each household. It can beam different ads and promotions to different panel households and then use the purchasing information obtained from scanners to assess which ads had more or less impact and how various promotions affected different kinds of consumers. In short, from a single source, companies can obtain information that links their marketing efforts directly with consumer buying behavior.

BehaviorScan and other single-source systems have their drawbacks, and some researchers are skeptical. One hitch is that such systems produce truckloads of data, more than most companies can handle. Another problem is cost: Single-source data can cost marketers hundreds of thousands of dollars a year per brand. Also, because such systems are set up in only a few market areas, usually small cities, the marketer often finds it difficult to generalize from the measures and results. Finally, although single-source systems provide important information for assessing the impact of promotion and advertising, they shed little light on the effects of other key marketing actions.

Despite these drawbacks, many companies rely on single-source data systems to test new products and new marketing strategies. And consumer researchers rely heavily on the data supplied by such systems in studies evaluating product performance and consumer buying behavior. When properly used, such systems can provide marketers with fast and detailed information about how their products are selling, who is buying them, and what factors affect purchase.

Sources: See Joanne Lipman, "Single-Source Ad Research Heralds Detailed Look at Household Habits," *Wall Street Journal,* February 16, 1988, p. 39; Magid H. Abraham and Leonard M. Lodish, "Getting the Most out of Advertising and Promotion," *Harvard Business Review,* May–June 1990, pp. 50–60; "Long-Term Effect of TV Advertising: Estimates from In-Market Experiments," *Stores,* January 1996, pp. RR1–RR3; Jack Honomichl, "The Honomichl 50," *Marketing News,* June 9, 1997, p. H1–H6; and www.infores.com/public/prodserv/AB/bscan.html, April 1999.

they receive. Response rates tend to be higher than with mail questionnaires, and telephone interviewing also allows greater sample control. Interviewers can ask to speak to respondents with the desired characteristics, or even by name.

However, with telephone interviewing, the cost per respondent is higher than with mail questionnaires. Also, people may not want to discuss personal questions with an interviewer. Using an interviewer also introduces interviewer bias—the way interviewers talk, how they ask questions, and other differences may affect respondents' answers. Finally, different interviewers may interpret and record responses differently, and under time pressures some interviewers might even cheat by recording answers without asking questions.

Personal interviewing takes two forms—individual and group interviewing. *Individual interviewing* involves talking with people in their homes or offices, on the street, or in shopping malls. Such interviewing is flexible. Trained interviewers can hold a respondent's attention for a long time and can explain difficult questions. They can guide interviews, explore issues, and probe as the situation requires. They can show subjects actual products, advertisements, or packages and observe reactions and behavior. In most cases, personal interviews can be conducted fairly quickly. However, individual personal interviews may cost three to four times as much as telephone interviews.

Group interviewing consists of inviting six to ten people to gather for a few hours with a trained moderator to talk about a product, service, or organization. The participants normally are paid a small sum for attending. The meeting is held in a pleasant place and refreshments are served to foster an informal setting. The moderator encourages free and easy discussion, hoping that group interactions will bring out actual feelings and thoughts. At the same time, the moderator "focuses" the discussion—hence the name **focus group interviewing**. The comments are recorded through written notes or on videotapes that are studied later.

Today, modern communications technology is changing the way that focus groups are conducted:

> In the old days, advertisers and agencies flew their staff to Atlanta or Little Rock to watch focus groups from behind one-way mirrors. The staff usually spent more time in hotels and taxis than they did doing research. Today, they are staying home. Videoconferencing links, television monitors, remote-control cameras, and digital transmission are boosting the amount of focus group research done over long-distance lines. [In a typical videoconferencing system], two cameras focused on the group are controlled by clients who hold a remote keypad. Executives in a far-off boardroom can zoom in on faces and pan the focus group at will. . . . A two-way sound system connects remote viewers to the backroom, focus group room, and directly to the monitor's earpiece. [Recently], while testing new product names in one focus group, the [client's] creative director . . . had an idea and contacted the moderator, who tested the new name on the spot.[14]

Focus group interviewing has become one of the major marketing research tools for gaining insight into consumer thoughts and feelings. However, focus group studies usually employ small sample sizes to keep time and costs down, and it may be hard to generalize from the results. Because interviewers have more freedom in personal interviews, the problem of interviewer bias is greater.

Whichever contact method is best depends on what information the researcher wants, as well as the number and types of respondents to be contacted. Advances in computers and communications have had a large impact on methods of obtaining information.

Focus group interviewing Personal interviewing that involves inviting six to ten people to gather for a few hours with a trained interviewer to talk about a product, service, or organization. The interviewer "focuses" the group discussion on important issues.

Video-conferenced focus groups: Executives in a far-off boardroom can "sit in" on focus group sessions.

For example, most research firms now do Computer Assisted Telephone Interviewing (CATI). Professional interviewers call respondents around the country, often using phone numbers drawn at random. When the respondent answers, the interviewer reads a set of questions from a video screen and types the respondent's answers directly into the computer.

Other firms use *computer interviewing* in which respondents sit down at a computer, read questions from a screen, and type their own answers into the computer. The computers might be located at a research center, trade show, shopping mall, or retail location. For example, Boston Market uses touch-screen computers in its restaurants to obtain instant feedback from customers. Other researchers are conducting interactive focus groups using computers. Some researchers are even using Completely Automated Telephone Surveys (CATS), which employ voice response technology to conduct interviews. The recorded voice of an interviewer asks the questions, and respondents answer by pressing numbers on their pushbutton phones.[15]

The latest technology to hit marketing research is the fast-growing Internet. Increasingly, marketing researchers are collecting primary data through **on-line (Internet) marketing research**—*Internet surveys* and *on-line focus groups*. Although on-line research offers much promise, and some analysts predict that the Internet will soon be the primary marketing research tool, others are more cautious. Marketing at Work 4-4 summarizes the advantages, drawbacks, and prospects for conducting marketing research on the Net.

On-line (Internet) marketing research
Collecting primary data through Internet surveys and on-line focus groups.

SAMPLING PLANS Marketing researchers usually draw conclusions about large groups of consumers by studying a small sample of the total consumer population. A **sample** is a segment of the population selected to represent the population as a whole. Ideally, the sample should be representative so that the researcher can make accurate estimates of the thoughts and behaviors of the larger population.

Sample
A segment of the population selected for marketing research to represent the population as a whole.

Designing the sample requires three decisions. First, *who* is to be surveyed (what *sampling unit*)? The answer to this question is not always obvious. For example, to study the decision-making process for a family automobile purchase, should the researcher interview the husband, wife, other family members, dealership salespeople, or all of these? The researcher must determine what information is needed and who is most likely to have it.

Second, *how many* people should be surveyed (what *sample size*)? Large samples give more reliable results than small samples. It is not necessary to sample the entire target market or even a large portion to get reliable results, however. If well chosen, samples of less than 1 percent of a population can often give good reliability.

Third, *how* should the people in the sample be *chosen* (what *sampling procedure*)? Table 4-4 describes different kinds of samples. Using *probability samples*, each population member has a known chance of being included in the sample, and researchers can calculate confidence limits for sampling error. But when probability sampling costs too much or takes too much time, marketing researchers often take *nonprobability samples*, even though their sampling error cannot be measured. These varied ways of drawing samples have different costs and time limitations as well as different accuracy and statistical properties. Which method is best depends on the needs of the research project.

RESEARCH INSTRUMENTS In collecting primary data, marketing researchers have a choice of two main research instruments—the *questionnaire* and *mechanical devices*. The *questionnaire* is by far the most common instrument, whether administered in person, by phone, or online. Questionnaires are very flexible—there are many ways to ask questions. However, they must be developed carefully and tested before they can be used

Marketing at Work 4-4

Marketing Research on the Internet

Like the Internet itself, performing marketing research on the Net is still in its infancy. But as the use of the World Wide Web and on-line services becomes more habit than hype for a small but desirable fraction of U.S. consumers, on-line research is becoming a quick, easy, and inexpensive way to tap into their opinions. "Only 20 percent of the country is on the Internet," says Paul Jacobson, an executive of Greenfield Online, an on-line research company. "But there are a great number of companies which want to reach that group because they're early adopters and leading-edge consumers."

On-line researchers don't pretend that Web surfers are representative of the U.S. population. On-line users tend to be better educated, more affluent, and younger than the average consumer, and a higher proportion are male. However, these are highly important consumers to companies offering products and services on-line. They are also some of the hardest to reach when conducting research. On-line surveys and chat sessions (or on-line focus groups)

often prove effective in getting elusive teen, single, affluent, and well-educated audiences to participate.

"It's very solid for reaching hard-to-get segments," says Jacobson. "Doctors, lawyers, professionals—people you might have difficulty reaching because they are not interested in taking part in surveys. It's also a good medium for reaching working mothers and others who lead busy lives. They can do it in their own space and at their own convenience."

On-line research isn't right for every company or product. For example, mass marketers who need to survey a representative cross section of the population will find on-line research methodologies less useful. "If the target for the product or service you're testing is inconsistent with the Internet user profile, then it's not the medium to use," Jacobson points out. "Is it the right medium to test Campbell's Chunky Soup? Probably not. But if you want to test how people feel about Campbell's Web site, yes."

When appropriate, on-line research offers marketers two distinct

advantages over traditional surveys and focus groups: speed and cost-effectiveness. On-line researchers routinely field quantitative studies and fill response quotas in only a matter of days. On-line focus groups require some advance scheduling, but results are practically instantaneous. Notes an on-line researcher, "On-line research is very fast, and time is what everybody wants now. Clients want the information yesterday."

Research on the Internet is also relatively inexpensive. Participants can dial in for a focus group from anywhere in the world, eliminating travel, lodging, and facility costs, making online chats cheaper than traditional focus groups. And for surveys, the Internet eliminates most of the postage, phone, labor, and printing costs associated with other survey approaches. Moreover, sample size has little influence on costs. "There's not a huge difference between 10 and 10,000 on the Web," said Tod Johnson, head of NPD Group, a firm which conducts on-line research. "The cost [of research on the Web] can be anywhere from 10 percent to

Table 4-4 Types of Samples

Probability Sample	
Sample random sample	Every member of the population has a known and equal chance of selection.
Stratified random sample	The population is divided into mutually exclusive groups (such as age groups), and random samples are drawn from each group.
Cluster (area) sample	The population is divided into mutually exclusive groups (such as blocks), and the researcher draws a sample of the groups to interview.
Nonprobability Sample	
Convenience sample	The researcher selects the easiest population members from which to obtain information.
Judgment sample	The researcher uses his or her judgment to select population members who are good prospects for accurate information.
Quota sample	The researcher finds and interviews a prescribed number of people in each of several categories.

80 percent less, especially when you talk about big samples."

However, using the Internet to conduct marketing research does have some drawbacks. One major problem is knowing who's in the sample. Tom Greenbaum, president of Groups Plus, recalls a cartoon in *The New Yorker* in which two dogs are seated at a computer: "On the Internet, nobody knows you are a dog," one says to the other. "If you can't see a person with whom you are communicating, how do know who they really are?" he says. Moreover, trying to draw conclusions from a "self-selected" sample of on-line users, those who clicked through to a questionnaire or accidentally landed in a chat room, can be troublesome. "Using a convenient sample is a way to do research quickly, but when you're done, you kind of scratch your head and ask what it means."

To overcome such sample and response problems, NPD and many other firms that offer on-line services construct panels of qualified Web regulars to respond to surveys and participate in on-line focus groups. NPD's panel consists of 15,000 consumers recruited on-line and verified by telephone; Green-

field Online picks users from its own database, then calls them periodically to verify that they are who they say they are. Another on-line research firm, Research Connections, recruits in advance by telephone, taking time to help new users connect to the Internet, if necessary.

Even when using qualified respondents, focus group responses can lose something in the translation. "You're missing all of the key things that make a focus group a viable method," says Greenbaum. "You may get people on-line to talk to each other and play off each other, but it's very different to watch people get excited about a concept." Eye contact and body language are two direct, personal interactions of traditional focus group research that are lost in the on-line world. And while researchers can offer seasoned moderators, the Internet format— running, typed commentary and on-line "emoticons" (punctuation marks that express emotion, such as :-) to signify happiness)—greatly restricts respondent expressiveness. Similarly, technology limits researchers' capability to show visual cues to research subjects. But just

as it hinders the two-way assessment of visual cues, Web research can actually permit some participants the anonymity necessary to elicit an unguarded response. "There are reduced social effects on-line," Jacobson says. "People are much more honest in this medium."

Some researchers are wildly optimistic about the prospects for marketing research on the Internet; others are more cautious. One expert predicts that in the next few years, 50 percent of all research will be done on the Internet. "Ten years from now, national telephone surveys will be the subject of research methodology folklore," he proclaims. "That's a little too soon," cautions another expert. "But in 20 years, yes."

Source: Portions adapted from Ian P. Murphy, "Interactive Research," *Marketing News*, January 20, 1997, pp. 1, 17. Selected quotes from "NFO Executive Sees Most Research Going to Internet," *Advertising Age*, May 19, 1997, p. 50; and Kate Maddox, "Virtual Panels Add Real Insight for Marketers," *Advertising Age*, June 29, 1998, pp. 34, 40. Also see Brad Edmondson, "The Wired Bunch," *American Demographics*, June 1997, pp. 10–15; Charlie Hamlin, "Market Research and the Wired Consumer," *Marketing News*, June 9, 1997, p. 6; P. K. Kannan, "Marketing Information on the I-Way," *Communications of the ICM*, March 1998, pp. 35–40, Dick McCullough, "Web-Based Market Research Ushers in New Age," *Marketing News*, September 14, 1998, pp. 27–28; and Timothy K. Maloy, *The Internet Research Guide* (Watson-Guptell Publications: 1999).

on a large scale. A carelessly prepared questionnaire usually contains several errors (see Table 4-5).

In preparing a questionnaire, the marketing researcher must first decide what questions to ask. Questionnaires frequently leave out questions that should be answered and include questions that cannot be answered, will not be answered, or need not be answered. Each question should be checked to see that it contributes to the research objectives.

The *form* of each question can influence the response. Marketing researchers distinguish between closed-end questions and open-end questions. *Closed-end questions* include all the possible answers, and subjects make choices among them. Examples include multiple-choice questions and scale questions. *Open-end questions* allow respondents to answer in their own words. In a survey of airline users, Delta might simply ask, "What is your opinion of Delta Airlines?" Or it might ask people to complete a sentence: "When I choose an airline, the most important consideration is . . . ." These and other kinds of open-end questions often reveal more than closed-end questions because respondents are not limited in their answers. Open-end questions are especially useful in exploratory

Table 4-5   A "Questionable Questionnaire"

Suppose that a summer camp director had prepared the following questionnaire to use in interviewing the parents of prospective campers. How would you assess each question?

1. What is your income to the nearest hundred dollars? *People don't usually know their income to the nearest hundred dollars nor do they want to reveal their income that closely. Moreover, a researcher should never open a questionnaire with such a personal question.*

2. Are you a strong or weak supporter of overnight summer camping for your children? *What do "strong" and "weak" mean?*

3. Do your children behave themselves well at a summer camp? Yes ( ) No ( ) *"Behave" is a relative term. Furthermore, are "yes" and "no" the best response options for this question? Besides, will people answer this honestly and objectively? Why ask the question in the first place?*

4. How many camps mailed literature to you last year? This year? *Who can remember this?*

5. What are the most salient and determinant attributes in your evaluation of summer camps? *What are "salient" and "determinant" attributes? Don't use big words on me!*

6. Do you think it is right to deprive your child of the opportunity to grow into a mature person through the experience of summer camping?
A loaded question. Given the bias, how can any parent answer "yes"?

research, when the researcher is trying to find out *what* people think but not measuring *how many* people think in a certain way. Closed-end questions, on the other hand, provide answers that are easier to interpret and tabulate.

Researchers should also use care in the *wording* and *ordering* of questions. They should use simple, direct, unbiased wording. Questions should be arranged in a logical order. The first question should create interest if possible, and difficult or personal questions should be asked last so that respondents do not become defensive.

Although questionnaires are the most common research instrument, *mechanical instruments* also are used. We discussed two mechanical instruments, people meters and supermarket scanners, earlier in the chapter. Another group of mechanical devices measures subjects' physical responses. For example, a galvanometer measures the strength of interest or emotions aroused by a subject's exposure to different stimuli, such as an ad or picture. The galvanometer detects the minute degree of sweating that accompanies emotional arousal. The tachistoscope flashes an ad to a subject at an exposure range from less than one-hundredth of a second to several seconds. After each exposure, respondents describe everything they recall. Eye cameras are used to study respondents' eye movements to determine at what points their eyes focus first and how long they linger on a given item.

Presenting the Research Plan At this stage, the marketing researcher should summarize the plan in a *written proposal*. A written proposal is especially important when the research project is large and complex or when an outside firm is to carry it out. The proposal should cover the management problems addressed and the research objectives, the information to be obtained, the sources of secondary information or methods for collecting primary data, and the way the results will help management decision making. The proposal also should include research costs. A written research plan or proposal ensures that the marketing manager and researchers have considered all the important aspects of the research, and that they agree on why and how the research will be done.

Implementing the Research Plan

The researcher next puts the marketing research plan into action. This involves collecting, processing, and analyzing the information. Data collection can be carried out by the company's marketing research staff or by outside firms. The company keeps more control over the collection process and data quality by using its own staff. However, outside firms that specialize in data collection often can do the job more quickly and at lower cost.

The data collection phase of the marketing research process is generally the most expensive and the most subject to error. The researcher should watch fieldwork closely to make sure that the plan is implemented correctly and to guard against problems with contacting respondents, with respondents who refuse to cooperate or who give biased or dishonest answers, and with interviewers who make mistakes or take shortcuts.

Researchers must process and analyze the collected data to isolate important information and findings. They need to check data from questionnaires for accuracy and completeness and code it for computer analysis. The researchers then tabulate the results and compute averages and other statistical measures.

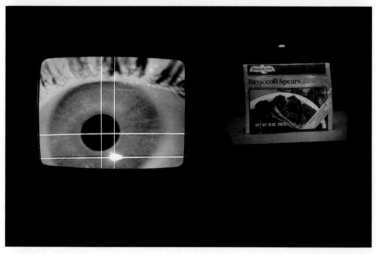

Mechanical research instruments: Eye cameras determine where eyes land and how long they linger on a given item.

Interpreting and Reporting the Findings

The researcher must now interpret the findings, draw conclusions, and report them to management. The researcher should not try to overwhelm managers with numbers and fancy statistical techniques. Rather, the researcher should present important findings that are useful in the major decisions faced by management.

However, interpretation should not be left only to the researchers. They are often experts in research design and statistics, but the marketing manager knows more about the problem and the decisions that must be made. In many cases, findings can be interpreted in different ways, and discussions between researchers and managers will help point to the best interpretations. The manager will also want to check that the research project was carried out properly and that all the necessary analysis was completed. Or, after seeing the findings, the manager may have additional questions that can be answered through further sifting of the data. Finally, the manager is the one who ultimately must decide what action the research suggests. The researchers may even make the data directly available to marketing managers so that they can perform new analyses and test new relationships on their own.

Interpretation is an important phase of the marketing process. The best research is meaningless if the manager blindly accepts faulty interpretations from the researcher. Similarly, managers may be biased—they might tend to accept research results that show what they expected and to reject those that they did not expect or hope for. Thus, managers and researchers must work together closely when interpreting research results, and both must share responsibility for the research process and resulting decisions.[16]

Linking the Concepts

Whew! We've covered a lot of territory. Hold up a minute, take a breather, and see if you can *apply* the marketing research process you've just studied.

- Looking back, how *should* Coca-Cola have designed its New Coke research? Sketch out a brief research plan.
- Could you use this marketing research process to analyze career opportunities and job possibilities? (Think of yourself as a "product" and employers as potential "customers.") What would your research plan look like?

Other Marketing Research Considerations

This section discusses marketing research in two special contexts: marketing research by small businesses and nonprofit organizations, and international marketing research. Finally, we look at public policy and ethics issues in marketing research.

Marketing Research in Small Businesses and Nonprofit Organizations

Managers of small businesses and nonprofit organizations often think that marketing research can be done only by experts in large companies with big research budgets. But many of the marketing research techniques discussed in this chapter also can be used by smaller organizations in a less formal manner and at little or no expense.

Managers of small businesses and nonprofit organizations can obtain good marketing information simply by *observing* things around them. For example, retailers can

Many associations, media, and government agencies provide special help to small organizations. Here, the U.S. Small Business Administration offers a Web site that gives advice on topics ranging from starting, financing, and expanding a small business to ordering business cards.

evaluate new locations by observing vehicle and pedestrian traffic. They can visit competing stores to check on facilities and prices. They can evaluate their customer mix by recording how many and what kinds of customers shop in the store at different times. Competitor advertising can be monitored by collecting advertisements from local media.

Managers can conduct informal *surveys* using small convenience samples. The director of an art museum can learn what patrons think about new exhibits by conducting informal focus groups—inviting small groups to lunch and having discussions on topics of interest. Retail salespeople can talk with customers visiting the store; hospital officials can interview patients. Restaurant managers might make random phone calls during slack hours to interview consumers about where they eat out and what they think of various restaurants in the area.

Managers also can conduct their own simple *experiments*. For example, by changing the themes in regular fund-raising mailings and watching the results, a nonprofit manager can find out much about which marketing strategies work best. By varying newspaper advertisements, a store manager can learn the effects of things such as ad size and position, price coupons, and media used.

Small organizations can obtain most of the secondary data available to large businesses. In addition, many associations, local media, chambers of commerce, and government agencies provide special help to small organizations. The U.S. Small Business Administration offers dozens of free publications and a Web site (www.sbaonline.sba.gov/) that give advice on topics ranging from starting, financing, and expanding a small business to ordering business cards. Local newspapers often provide information on local shoppers and their buying patterns.

In summary, secondary data collection, observation, surveys, and experiments can all be used effectively by small organizations with small budgets. Although these informal research methods are less complex and less costly, they still must be conducted carefully.

Managers must think carefully about the objectives of the research, formulate questions in advance, recognize the biases introduced by smaller samples and less-skilled researchers, and conduct the research systematically.[17]

International Marketing Research

International marketing researchers follow the same steps as domestic researchers, from defining the research problem and developing a research plan to interpreting and reporting the results. However, these researchers often face more and different problems. Whereas domestic researchers deal with fairly homogenous markets within a single country, international researchers deal with differing markets in many different countries. These markets often vary greatly in their levels of economic development, cultures and customs, and buying patterns.

In many foreign markets, the international researcher has a difficult time finding good *secondary data*. Whereas U.S. marketing researchers can obtain reliable secondary data from dozens of domestic research services, many countries have almost no research services at all. Some of the largest international research services operate in many countries. For example, A.C. Nielsen Company, the world's largest marketing research company, has offices in more than 90 countries outside the United States. And 45 percent of the revenues of the world's 25 largest marketing research firms comes from outside their own countries.[18] However, most research firms operate in only a relative handful of countries. Thus, even when secondary information is available, it usually must be obtained from many different sources on a country-by-country basis, making the information difficult to combine or compare.

Because of the scarcity of good secondary data, international researchers often must collect their own primary data. Here again, researchers face problems not found domestically. For example, they may find it difficult simply to develop good samples. U.S. researchers can use current telephone directories, census tract data, and any of several sources of socioeconomic data to construct samples. However, such information is largely lacking in many countries.

Once the sample is drawn, the U.S. researcher usually can reach most respondents easily by telephone, by mail, or in person. Reaching respondents is often not so easy in other parts of the world. Researchers in Mexico cannot rely on telephone and mail data collection, most data collection is door to door and concentrated in three or four of the largest cities. And most surveys in Mexico bypass the large segment of the population in which native tribes speak languages other than Spanish. In some countries, few people have phones; there are only four phones per thousand people in Egypt, six per thousand in Turkey, and thirty-two per thousand in Argentina. In other countries, the postal system is notoriously unreliable. In Brazil, for instance, an estimated 30 percent of the mail is never delivered. In many developing countries, poor roads and transportation systems make certain areas hard to reach, making personal interviews difficult and expensive.[19]

Cultural differences from country to country cause additional problems for international researchers. Language is the most obvious obstacle. For example, questionnaires must be prepared in one language and then translated into the languages of each country researched. Responses then must be translated back into the original language for analysis and interpretation. This adds to research costs and increases the risks of error.

Translating a questionnaire from one language to another is anything but easy. Many idioms, phrases, and statements mean different things in different cultures. For example, a Danish executive noted, "Check this out by having a different translator put back into English what you've translated from English. You'll get the shock of your life. I remember [an example in which] 'out of sight, out of mind' had become 'invisible things are insane.'"[20]

Customs in some countries prohibit people from talking with strangers—a researcher simply may not be allowed to speak with people about brand attitudes or buying behavior.

Buying roles and consumer decision processes vary greatly from country to country, further complicating international marketing research. Consumers in different countries also vary in their attitudes toward marketing research. People in one country may be very willing to respond; in other countries, nonresponse can be a major problem. For example, customs in some Islamic countries prohibit people from talking with strangers; a researcher simply may not be allowed to speak by phone with women about brand attitudes or buying behavior. In certain cultures, research questions often are considered too personal. For example, in many Latin American countries, people may feel embarrassed to talk with researchers about their choices of shampoo, deodorant, or other personal care products. Even when respondents are *willing* to respond, they may not be *able* to because of high functional illiteracy rates. And middle-class people in developing countries often make false claims in order to appear well-off. For example, in a study of tea consumption in India, over 70 percent of middle-income respondents claimed that they used one of several national brands. However, the researchers had good reason to doubt these results—more than 60 percent of the tea sold in India is unbranded generic tea.

Despite these problems, the recent growth of international marketing has resulted in a rapid increase in the use of international marketing research. Global companies have little choice but to conduct such research. Although the costs and problems associated with international research may be high, the costs of not doing it—in terms of missed opportunities and mistakes—might be even higher. Once recognized, many of the problems associated with international marketing research can be overcome or avoided.

Public Policy and Ethics in Marketing Research

Most marketing research benefits both the sponsoring company and its consumers. Through marketing research, companies learn more about consumers' needs, resulting in more satisfying products and services. However, the misuse of marketing research can also harm or annoy consumers. Two major public policy and ethics issues in marketing research are intrusions on consumer privacy and the misuse of research findings.

Intrusions on Consumer Privacy Many consumers feel positively about marketing research and believe that it serves a useful purpose. Some actually enjoy being interviewed and giving their opinions. However, others strongly resent or even mistrust marketing research. A few consumers fear that researchers might use sophisticated techniques to probe our deepest feelings and then use this knowledge to manipulate our buying. Others may have been taken in by previous "research surveys" that actually turned out to be attempts to sell them something. Still other consumers confuse legitimate marketing research studies with telemarketing or database development efforts and say "no" before the interviewer can even begin. Most, however, simply resent the intrusion. They dislike mail or telephone surveys that are too long or too personal or that interrupt them at inconvenient times.

Increasing consumer resentment has become a major problem for the research industry. This resentment has led to lower survey response rates in recent years. One study found that 38 percent of Americans now refuse to be interviewed in an average survey, up dramatically from a decade ago. Another study found that 59 percent of consumers had refused to give information to a company because they thought it was not really needed or too personal, up from 42 percent just five years earlier.[21]

The research industry is considering several options for responding to this problem. One is to expand its "Your Opinion Counts" program to educate consumers about the benefits of marketing research and to distinguish it from telephone selling and database building. Another option is to provide a toll-free number that people can call to verify that a survey is legitimate. The industry also has considered adopting broad standards, perhaps based on Europe's International Code of Marketing and Social Research Practice. This code outlines researchers' responsibilities to respondents and to the general public. For example, it says that researchers should make their names and addresses available to participants, and it bans companies from representing activities such as database compilation or sales and promotional pitches as research.

Misuse of Research Findings Research studies can be powerful persuasion tools; companies often use study results as claims in their advertising and promotion. Today, however, many research studies appear to be little more than vehicles for pitching the sponsor's products. In fact, in some cases, the research surveys appear to have been designed just to produce the intended effect. Few advertisers openly rig their research designs or blatantly misrepresent the findings; most abuses tend to be subtle "stretches." Consider the following examples:[22]

- ✦ A study by Chrysler contends that Americans overwhelmingly prefer Chrysler to Toyota after test driving both. However, the study included just 100 people in each of two tests. More importantly, none of the people surveyed owned a foreign car, so they appear to be favorably predisposed to U.S. cars.

✧   A Black Flag survey asked: "A roach disk . . . poisons a roach slowly. The dying roach returns to the nest and after it dies is eaten by other roaches. In turn these roaches become poisoned and die. How effective do you think this type of product would be in killing roaches?" Not surprisingly, 79 percent said effective.

✧   A poll sponsored by the disposable diaper industry asked: "It is estimated that disposable diapers account for less than 2 percent of the trash in today's landfills. In contrast, beverage containers, third-class mail, and yard waste are estimated to account for about 21 percent of the trash in landfills. Given this, in your opinion, would it be fair to ban disposable diapers?" Again, not surprisingly, 84 percent said no.

Thus, subtle manipulations of the study's sample, or the choice or wording of questions, can greatly affect the conclusions reached.

In others cases, so-called independent research studies actually are paid for by companies with an interest in the outcome. Small changes in study assumptions or in how results are interpreted can subtly affect the direction of the results. For example, at least four widely quoted studies compare the environmental effects of using disposable diapers to those of using cloth diapers. The two studies sponsored by the cloth diaper industry conclude that cloth diapers are more environmentally friendly. Not surprisingly, the other two studies, sponsored by the paper diaper industry, conclude just the opposite. Yet both appear to be correct *given* the underlying assumptions used.

Recognizing that surveys can be abused, several associations—including the American Marketing Association, the Council of American Survey Research Organizations, and the Marketing Research Association—have developed codes of research ethics and standards of conduct.[23] In the end, however, unethical or inappropriate actions cannot simply be regulated away. Each company must accept responsibility for policing the conduct and reporting of its own marketing research to protect consumers' best interests and its own.

REST STOP   Reviewing the Concepts

In the previous chapter, we discussed the marketing environment. In this chapter, you've studied tools used to gather and manage information that managers can use to assess opportunities in the environment and the impact of a firm's marketing efforts. After this brief pause for rest and reflection, we'll head out again in the next chapter to take a closer look at the object of all of this activity—consumers and their buying behavior.

In today's complex and rapidly changing environment, marketing managers need more and better information to make effective and timely decisions. This greater need for information has been matched by the explosion of information technologies for supplying information. Using today's new technologies, companies can now handle great quantities of information, sometimes even too much. Yet marketers often complain that they lack enough of the *right* kind of information or have an excess of the *wrong* kind. In response, many companies are now studying their mangers' information needs and designing information systems to satisfy those needs.

1. Explain the importance of information to the company.

Good products and marketing programs start with a complete understanding of consumer needs and wants. Thus, the company needs sound information in order to produce superior value and satisfaction for customers. The company also requires information on competitors, resellers, and other actors and forces in the marketplace.

2. Define the marketing information system and discuss its parts.

The *marketing information system* (MIS) consists of people, equipment, and procedures to gather, sort, analyze, evaluate, and distribute needed, timely, and accurate information to marketing decision makers. A well-designed information system begins and ends with users. The MIS first *assesses information needs*, then *develops information* from internal databases, marketing intelligence activities, and marketing research. *Internal databases* provide information on the company's own sales, costs, inventories, cash flows, and accounts receivable and payable. Such data can be obtained quickly and cheaply but often needs to be adapted for marketing decisions. *Marketing intelligence* activities supply everyday information about developments in the external marketing environment. *Market research* consists of collecting information relevant to a specific marketing problem faced by the company. Lastly, the MIS *distributes information* gathered from these sources to the right managers in the right form and at the right time to help them make better marketing decisions.

3. Outline the four steps in the marketing research process.

The first step in the marketing research process involves *defining the problem and setting the research objectives*, which may be exploratory, descriptive, or causal. The second step consists of *developing a research plan* for collecting data from primary and secondary sources. The third step calls for *implementing the marketing research plan* by gathering, processing, and analyzing the information. The fourth step consists of *interpreting and reporting the findings*. Additional information analysis helps marketing managers apply the information and provides them with sophisticated statistical procedures and models from which to develop more rigorous findings.

4. Compare the advantages and disadvantages of various methods of collecting information.

Both *internal* and *external* secondary data sources often provide information more quickly and at a lower cost than primary data sources, and they can sometimes yield information that a company cannot collect by itself. However, needed information might not exist in secondary sources, and even if data can be found, it might be largely unusable. Researchers must also evaluate secondary information to ensure that it is *relevant*, *accurate*, *current*, and *impartial*. Primary research must also be evaluated for these features. Each primary data collection method—*observational, survey,* and *experimental*—has its own advantages and disadvantages. Each of the various primary research contact methods—mail, telephone, personal interview, or computer—also has its own advantages and drawbacks. Similarly, each contact method has its plusses and minuses.

5. Discuss the special issues some market researchers face, including public policy and ethics issues.

Some marketers face special marketing research situations, such as those conducting research in small business, nonprofit, or international situations. Marketing research can be conducted effectively by small businesses and nonprofit organizations with limited budgets. International marketing researchers follow the same steps as domestic researchers but often face more and different problems. All organizations need to respond responsibly to major public policy and ethical issues surrounding marketing research, including issues of intrusions on consumer privacy and misuse of research findings.

Navigating the Key Terms

For a detailed analysis of the meaning and importance of each of the following key terms, visit our Web page at **www.prenhall.com/kotler**

Causal research
Descriptive research
Experimental research

Exploratory research
Focus group interviewing
Internal databases
Marketing information system (MIS)
Marketing intelligence
Marketing research
On-line databases
On-line (Internet) marketing research

Observational research
Primary data
Sample
Secondary data
Single-source data systems
Survey research

Travel Log

The following concept checks and discussion questions will help you to keep track of and apply the concepts you've studied in this chapter.

Concept Checks

1. A _____ consists of people, equipment, and procedures to gather, sort, analyze, evaluate, and distribute needed, timely, and accurate information to marketing decision makers.

2. The information needed by marketing managers can be obtained from _____, _____, and _____.

3. _____ is a systematic collection and analysis of publicly available information about competitors and developments in the marketing environment.

4. _____ can be defined as the systematic design, collection, analysis, and reporting of data relevant to a specific marketing situation facing an organization.

5. The marketing research process has four steps: _____, _____, _____, and _____.

6. A marketing research project might have any one of three types of objectives: _____ research, _____ research, or _____ research.

7. The objective of _____ research is to test hypotheses about cause-and-effect relationships.

8. _____ data consist of information collected for the specific purpose at hand.

9. _____ research is the approach best suited for gathering descriptive information.

10. Of the four research contact methods discussed, _____ is the only one rated as "excellent" with respect to low cost.*

Discussing the Issues

1. Many companies build extensive internal databases that marketing managers can access to identify marketing opportunities and problems, plan programs, and evaluate performance. If you were the marketing manager for a large computer software manufacturer, what types of information would you like to have available in your internal database? Explain.

2. A recent survey confirmed that at least three-fourths of marketing researchers use commercial on-line database services for conducting research. Go on-line, find a marketing research database, describe the database, and evaluate the services offered. Was the database free or fee-based?

3. Name the type of research that would be appropriate in the following situations, and explain why:
   a. Kellogg wants to investigate the impact of young children on their parents' decisions to buy breakfast foods.
   b. Your college bookstore wants to get some insights into how students feel about the store's merchandise, prices, and service.
   c. McDonald's is considering where to locate a new outlet in a fast-growing suburb.
   d. Gillette wants to determine whether a new line of deodorant for children will be profitable.

4. Retail toy giants are forecasting a down year for the upcoming Christmas season, based largely on an expected 15 percent decline in the action-hero business. Keeping in mind the Marketing at Work 4-2 example, in which Coca-Cola blundered by defining its New Coke research problem too narrowly, what advice could you give to toy manufacturers and retailers on how to do research for the Christmas season? What factors will be critical to their success? What form of research would you suggest? To whom should the research be directed?

5. Focus group interviewing is both a widely used and widely criticized research technique in marketing. List the advantages and disadvantages of focus groups. Suggest some kinds of questions that are suitable for exploration through focus groups.

---

* Concept check answers: 1. marketing information system (MIS); 2. internal data, marketing intelligence, and marketing research; 3. marketing intelligence; 4. marketing research; 5. defining the problem and research objectives, developing the research plan, implementing the research plan, and interpreting and reporting the findings; 6. exploratory, descriptive, and causal; 7. causal; 8. primary; 9. survey; 10. on-line.

Traveling the Net

Point of Interest: Researching Minorities

All marketers want to know more about their customers. This is especially true for the potentially profitable ethnic minority markets. The Internet has provided a means of gaining more information about these markets and their preferences. In addition, the Internet is color-blind. Therefore, marketing efforts and data gathering for research projects are much easier than might be expected. The Internet's anonymity and low cost has helped many minority businesses begin operation and has helped those seeking to explore preferences of minority customers in ways that might have been difficult in the past. All of the following sites are available for assistance in minority marketing and research: (a) www.minority.net—a large business-to-business E-commerce mall; (b) www.twmall.com—a large Asian-American mall that does business in several languages; (c) www.collard-cards.com—a site that sells greeting cards and cookbooks featuring upbeat black images; (d) www.demographics.com—a site that explores various demographic segments and trends that affect them.

For Discussion

1. What is the potential for marketing to minorities via the Internet?
2. What are the primary advantages and disadvantages afforded by the Web sites mentioned above?

3. What unique features are offered by these sites that might assist a marketer wishing to reach minority markets?
4. Using the *American Demographics* Web site (www.demographics.com), determine the potential (size) of the African American, Hispanic American, and Asian American Web segments. What other information about these minorities can you find?
5. Which minority segments appear to be growing the most rapidly? Where did you find this information?

Application Thinking

Using information that you obtained by exploring the preceding Web sites, find and evaluate three minority-related Web sites (one place to start might be www.bnl.com/cityboxers—an African American online retailer of hand-tailored boxer shorts). Build an evaluation grid to aid in your assessment. Some factors that you might consider include: (a) How do your chosen sites express ethnicity? (b) How broad-based is the appeal expressed in the site? (c) Do language or graphics express ethnicity? (d) Does ethnicity help or hurt the Web site? Be sure to consider what form of research might help the chosen sites to do a more effective job of marketing. Present your findings to the class.

MAP—Marketing Applications

MAP Stop 4

When you do business from a home office, it's just you and your personal support devices (such as a telephone, cell phone, fax machine, computer, and e-mail) against the daily deadlines that never seem to go away. For many who are saying "adios" to the company office, communication contact is essential for maintaining productivity and independence. The home office trend is projected to be huge. This fact has not escaped the notice of personal support equipment manufacturers such as Sony, Nokia, Samsung, and Motorola. Equipment used by today's home office telecommuter is no

longer clunky, oversized, or devoid of style. Equipment has been redesigned to fit into small rooms, personal automobiles, or even briefcases. Much of the equipment being demanded from these markets revolves around the all-in-one concept (for example, an all-in-one copier, printer, scanner, fax machine, and computer). According to most analysts, equipment efficiency, productivity, accuracy, attractiveness, and dependability outweigh cost considerations. Lastly, since this personal support equipment is being bought by individuals, marketing strategies are being designed to impress individuals rather than purchasing agents.

Thinking Like a Marketing Manager

1. If you were a marketing manager for a personal equipment firm, how would you propose to research the growing home office and telecommuting market? Design a research plan that would yield the needed information.

2. What subsegments within these markets might be important? For example, would males and females from this segment have different needs? If so, explain why.

3. Think of a "homeware" or "commuteware" product or service that would be of benefit to the markets described. Formulate a research plan that would demonstrate the potential for your proposed product or service.

4. List four benefits of "home officing." List four difficulties. As a marketing manager, how would you help customers deal with the difficulties?

Consumer and Business Buyer Behavior

N
W E
S

ROAD MAP:
Previewing the Concepts

In the previous chapter, you studied how marketers obtain, analyze, and use information to identify marketing opportunities and to assess marketing programs. In this chapter, you'll continue your marketing journey with a closer look at the most important element of the marketing environment—customers. The aim of marketing is to somehow affect how consumers think about and behave toward the organization and its marketing offers. To affect the whats, whens, and hows of buying behavior, marketers must first understand the *whys*. We look first at *final consumer* buying influences and processes and then at the buying behavior of *business customers*. You'll see that understanding buying behavior is an essential but very difficult task.

▶ **After studying this chapter, you should be able to**

1. **understand the consumer market and the major factors that influence consumer buyer behavior**
2. **identify and discuss the stages in the buyer decision process**
3. **describe the adoption and diffusion process for new products**
4. **define the business market and identify the major factors that influence business buyer behavior**
5. **list and define the steps in the business buying decision process**

Our first point of interest: Harley Davidson, maker of the nation's top-selling heavyweight motorcycles. Who rides these big Harley "Hogs"? What moves them to tattoo their bodies with the Harley emblem, abandon home and hearth for the open road, and flock to Harley rallies by the hundreds of thousands? *You* might be surprised, but Harley Davidson knows *very* well.

ew brands engender such intense loyalty as that found in the hearts of Harley-Davidson owners. "The Harley audience is granitelike" in its devotion, laments the vice-president of sales for competitor Yamaha. Observes the publisher of *American Iron*, an industry publication, "You don't see people tattooing Yamaha on their bodies." Each year, in early March, more than 400,000 Harley bikers rumble through the streets of Daytona Beach, Florida, to attend Harley-Davidson's Bike Week celebration. Bikers from across the nation lounge on their low-slung Harleys, swap biker tales, and sport T-shirts proclaiming "I'd rather push a Harley than drive a Honda."

Riding such intense emotions, Harley-Davidson has rumbled its way to the top of the fast-growing heavyweight motorcycle market. Harley's "Hogs" capture more than one-fifth of all U.S. bike sales and more than half of the heavyweight segment. Both the segment and Harley's sales are growing rapidly, and Harley-Davidson recently announced its twelfth consecutive year of record profits. In fact, for several years running, sales have far outstripped supply, with customer waiting lists of up to three years for popular models and street prices running well above suggested list prices. "We've seen people buy a new Harley and then sell it in the parking lot for $4,000 to $5,000 more," says one dealer.

Harley-Davidson's marketers spend a great deal of time thinking about customers and their buying behavior. They want to know who their customers are, what they think and how they feel, and why they buy a Harley rather than a Yamaha, or a Suzuki, or a big Honda American Classic. What is it that makes Harley buyers so fiercely loyal? These are difficult questions; even Harley owners themselves don't know exactly what motivates their buying. But Harley management puts top priority on understanding customers and what makes them tick.

Who rides a Harley? You might be surprised. It's no longer the Hell's Angels crowd—the burly, black-leather-jacketed rebels and biker chicks that once made up Harley's core clientele. Motorcycles are attracting a new breed of riders—older, more affluent, and better educated. Harley now appeals more to "Rubbies" (rich urban bikers) than to rebels. The average Harley customer is a 43-year-old husband with a median household income of $66,400. Harley's big, comfortable cruisers give these new consumers the easy ride, prestige, and twist-of-the-wrist power they want and can afford.

Harley-Davidson makes good bikes, and to keep up with its shifting market, the company has upgraded its showrooms and sales approaches. But Harley customers are buying a lot more than just a quality bike and a smooth sales pitch. To gain a better understanding of customers' deeper motivations, Harley-Davidson conducted focus groups in which it invited bikers to make cut-and-paste collages of pictures that expressed their feelings about Harley-Davidsons. (Can't you just see a bunch of hard-core bikers doing this?) It then mailed out 16,000 surveys containing a typical battery of psychological, sociological, and demographic questions as well as subjective questions such as "Is Harley more typified by a brown bear or a lion?" The research revealed seven core customer types: adventure-loving traditionalists, sensitive pragmatists, stylish status seekers, laid-back campers, classy capitalists, cool-headed loners, and cocky misfits. However, all owners appreciated their Harleys for the same basic reasons. "It didn't matter if you were the guy who swept the floors of the factory or if you were the CEO at that factory, the

When Was The Last Time You Felt This Strongly About Anything?

attraction to Harley was very similar," says a Harley executive. "Independence, freedom, and power were the universal Harley appeals."

These studies confirm that Harley customers are doing more than just buying motorcycles. They're making a lifestyle statement and displaying an attitude. As one analyst suggests, owning a Harley makes you "the toughest, baddest guy on the block. Never mind that [you're] a dentist or an accountant. You [feel] wicked astride all that power." Your Harley renews your spirits and announces your independence. As the Harley Web home page announces, "Thumbing the starter of a Harley-Davidson does a lot more than fire the engine. It fires the imagination." The classic look, the throaty sound, the very idea of a Harley—all contribute to its mystique. Owning this "American legend" makes you a part of something bigger, a member of the Harley family. The fact that you have to wait to get a Harley makes it all that much more satisfying to have one. In fact, the company deliberately restricts its output. "Our goal is to eventually run production at a level that's always one motorcycle short of demand," says Harley-Davidson's chief executive.

Such strong emotions and motivations are captured in a recent Harley-Davidson advertisement. The ad shows a close-up of an arm, the bicep adorned with a Harley-Davidson tattoo. The headline asks, "When was the last time you felt this strongly about anything?" The ad copy outlines the problem and suggests a solution:

> "Wake up in the morning and life picks up where it left off. You do what has to be done. Use what it takes to get there. And what once seemed exciting has now become part of the numbing routine. It all begins to feel the same. Except when you've got a Harley-Davidson. Something strikes a nerve. The heartfelt thunder rises up, refusing to become part of the background. Suddenly things are different. Clearer. More real. As they should have been all along. The feeling is personal. For some, owning a Harley is a statement of individuality. For others, owning a Harley means being a part of a home-grown legacy that was born in a tiny Milwaukee shed in 1903. . . . To the uninitiated, a Harley-Davidson motorcycle is associated with a certain look, a certain sound. Anyone who owns one will tell you it's much more than that. Riding a Harley changes you from within. The effect is permanent. Maybe it's time you started feeling this strongly. Things are different on a Harley."[1]

The Harley-Davidson example shows that many different factors affect consumer buying behavior. Buying behavior is never simple, yet understanding it is the essential task of marketing management. First, we explore the dynamics of final-consumer markets and consumer buyer behavior. We then examine business markets and the business buying process.

Consumer Markets and Consumer Buyer Behavior

Consumer buyer behavior
The buying behavior of final consumers—individuals and households who buy goods and services for personal consumption.

Consumer market
All the individuals and households who buy or acquire goods and services for personal consumption.

Consumer buyer behavior refers to the buying behavior of final consumers, individuals and households who buy goods and services for personal consumption. All of these final consumers combined make up the **consumer market**. The American consumer market consists of more than 270 million people who consume many trillions of dollars worth of goods and services each year, making it one of the most attractive consumer markets in the world. The world consumer market consists of more than 5.9 *billion* people.[2]

Consumers around the world vary tremendously in age, income, education level, and tastes. They also buy an incredible variety of goods and services. How these diverse consumers make their choices among various products embraces a fascinating array of factors.

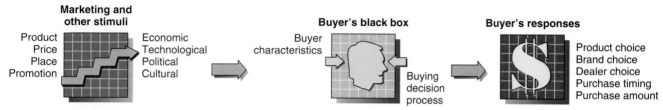

Figure 5-1
Model of buyer behavior

Model of Consumer Behavior

Consumers make many buying decisions every day. Most large companies research consumer buying decisions in great detail to answer questions about what consumers buy, where they buy, how and how much they buy, when they buy, and why they buy. Marketers can study actual consumer purchases to find out what they buy, where, and how much. But learning about the *whys* of consumer buying behavior is not so easy; the answers are often locked deep within the consumer's head.

The central question for marketers is: How do consumers respond to various marketing efforts the company might use? The starting point is the stimulus-response model of buyer behavior shown in Figure 5-1. This figure shows that marketing and other stimuli enter the consumer's "black box" and produce certain responses.[3] Marketing stimuli consist of the four *P*s: product, price, place, and promotion. Other stimuli include major forces and events in the buyer's environment: economic, technological, political, and cultural. All these inputs enter the buyer's black box, where they are turned into a set of observable buyer responses: product choice, brand choice, dealer choice, purchase timing, and purchase amount.

The marketer wants to understand how the stimuli are changed into responses inside the consumer's black box, which has two parts. First, the buyer's characteristics influence how he or she perceives and reacts to the stimuli. Second, the buyer's decision process itself affects the buyer's behavior. We look first at buyer characteristics as they affect buying behavior and then at the buyer decision process.

Characteristics Affecting Consumer Behavior

Consumer purchases are influenced strongly by cultural, social, personal, and psychological characteristics, shown in Figure 5-2. For the most part, marketers cannot control such factors, but they must take them into account. We illustrate these characteristics for the

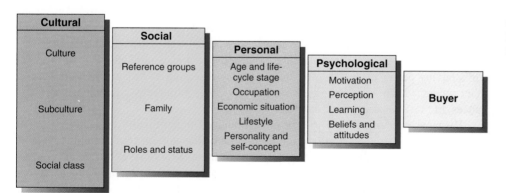

Figure 5-2
Factors influencing
consumer behavior

case of a hypothetical consumer named Anna Flores. Anna is a married college graduate who works as a brand manager in a leading consumer packaged-goods company. She wants to find a new leisure-time activity that will provide some contrast to her working day. This need has led her to consider buying a camera and taking up photography. Many characteristics in her background will affect the way she evaluates cameras and chooses a brand.

Cultural Factors Cultural factors exert the broadest and deepest influence on consumer behavior. The marketer needs to understand the role played by the buyer's *culture*, *subculture*, and *social class*.

Culture

The set of basic values, perceptions, wants, and behaviors learned by a member of society from family and other important institutions.

CULTURE **Culture** is the most basic cause of a person's wants and behavior. Human behavior is largely learned. Growing up in a society, a child learns basic values, perceptions, wants, and behaviors from the family and other important institutions. A child in the United States normally learns or is exposed to the following values: achievement and success, activity and involvement, efficiency and practicality, progress, material comfort, individualism, freedom, humanitarianism, youthfulness, and fitness and health. Every group or society has a culture, and cultural influences on buying behavior may vary greatly from country to country. Failure to adjust to these differences can result in ineffective marketing or embarrassing mistakes.

Anna Flores's cultural background will affect her camera-buying decision. Anna's desire to own a camera may result from her being raised in a modern society that has developed camera technology and a whole set of consumer learnings and values. Anna knows what cameras are, she knows how to read instructions, and her society has accepted the idea of women photographers.

Marketers are always trying to spot *cultural shifts* in order to discover new products that might be wanted. For example, the cultural shift toward greater concern about health and fitness has created a huge industry for exercise equipment and clothing, lower-fat and more natural foods, and health and fitness services. The shift toward informality has resulted in more demand for casual clothing and simpler home furnishings. And the increased desire for leisure time has resulted in more demand for convenience products and services, such as microwave ovens and fast food.

Subculture

A group of people with shared value systems based on common life experiences and situations.

SUBCULTURE Each culture contains smaller **subcultures**, or groups of people with shared value systems based on common life experiences and situations. Subcultures include nationalities, religions, racial groups, and geographic regions. Many subcultures make up important market segments, and marketers often design products and marketing programs tailored to their needs. Examples of four such important subculture groups include Hispanic, African American, Asian, and mature consumers.

The U.S. *Hispanic market*—Americans of Cuban, Mexican, Central American, South American, and Puerto Rican descent—consists of 29 million consumers who buy more than $348 billion worth of goods and services each year.[4] Hispanics have long been a target for marketers of food, beverages, and household care products. But as the segment's buying power increases, Hispanics are now emerging as an attractive market for pricier products such as computers, financial services, photography equipment, large appliances, life insurance, and automobiles.

Hispanic consumers tend to buy more branded, higher-quality products; generics don't sell well to Hispanics. Perhaps more important, Hispanics are very brand loyal, and they favor companies who show special interest in them. Sears makes a special effort to target Hispanic consumers. The retail chain has designated more than 130 of its stores with customer bases exceeding 20 percent Latino as special Hispanic stores. "We make a

McDonald's targets important subcultures, such as Hispanics and African Americans.

special effort to staff those stores with bilingual sales personnel, to use bilingual signage, and to support community programs," says a Sears spokesperson.[5]

If the U.S. population of *African Americans* were a separate nation, its buying power of $469 billion annually would rank twelfth in the free world.[6] The black population in the United States is growing in affluence and sophistication. Although more price-conscious than other segments, blacks are also strongly motivated by quality and selection. They place more importance on brand names, are more brand loyal, do less "shopping around." In recent years, many large companies have developed special products and services, packaging, and appeals for the black consumer market. For example, JC Penney revamped about 170 stores to target African Americans, changing its merchandise and store layout, and used black models in its ads. And Sears recently introduced its Mosaic by Alvin Bell fashion line for African American women, supported by TV ads featuring a jazz version of its "softer side" theme and magazine ads in *Black Elegance*, *Ebony*, *Essence*, and *Heart & Soul*.[7]

Asian Americans, the fastest-growing and most affluent U.S. demographic segment, now number more than 10 million, with spending power of $110 billion annually. Chinese constitute the largest group, followed by Filipinos, Japanese, Asian Indians, and Koreans. Asian American family income exceeds the national average by 19 percent.[8] Long-distance telephone companies and financial services marketers have long targeted Asian American consumers, but until recently, packaged-goods firms, automobile companies, retailers, and fast-food chains have lagged in this segment. Language and cultural traditions appear to be the biggest barriers. For example, 66 percent of Asian Americans are foreign-born, and 56 percent of those five years and older do not speak English fluently.

Still, because of the segment's rapidly growing buying power, many firms are now looking seriously at this market.[9]

As the U.S. population ages, *mature consumers*—those 65 and older—are becoming a very attractive market. Now 32 million strong, seniors are better off financially; they average twice the disposable income of consumers in the under-35 group. Because seniors have more time and money, they are an ideal market for exotic travel, restaurants, high-tech home entertainment products, leisure goods and services, designer furniture and fashions, financial services, and health care services. Their desire to look as young as they feel makes seniors good candidates for cosmetics and personal care products, health foods, fitness products, and other items that combat the effects of aging. The best strategy is to appeal to seniors' active, multidimensional lives. For example, a recent Nike commercial features a senior weight lifter who proudly proclaims, "I'm not strong for my age. I'm strong!" Similarly, Kellogg aired a TV spot for All-Bran cereal in which individuals ranging in age from 53 to 81 are featured playing ice hockey, water skiing, running hurdles, and playing baseball, all to the tune of "Wild Thing." And an Aetna commercial portrays a senior who, after retiring from a career as a lawyer, fulfills a lifelong dream to become an archeologist.[10]

Social classes
Relatively permanent and ordered divisions in a society whose members share similar values, interests, and behaviors.

SOCIAL CLASS Almost every society has some form of social class structure. **Social classes** are society's relatively permanent and ordered divisions whose members share similar values, interests, and behaviors. Social scientists have identified the seven American social classes (see Table 5-1).

Social class is not determined by a single factor, such as income, but is measured as a combination of occupation, income, education, wealth, and other variables. In some social systems, members of different classes are reared for certain roles and cannot change their social positions. In the United States, however, the lines between social classes are not fixed and rigid; people can move to a higher social class or drop into a lower one. Marketers are interested in social class because people within a given social class tend to exhibit similar buying behavior.[11] Social classes show distinct product and brand preferences in areas such as clothing, home furnishings, leisure activity, and automobiles. Anna Flores's social class may affect her camera decision. If she comes from a higher social class background, her family probably owned an expensive camera and she may have dabbled in photography.

Social Factors A consumer's behavior also is influenced by social factors, such as the consumer's *small groups*, *family*, and *social roles and status*.

Group
Two or more people who interact to accomplish individual or mutual goals.

GROUPS A person's behavior is influenced by many small **groups**. Groups that have a direct influence and to which a person belongs are called *membership groups*. In contrast, *reference groups* serve as direct (face-to-face) or indirect points of comparison or reference in forming a person's attitudes or behavior. People often are influenced by reference groups to which they do not belong. For example, an *aspirational group* is one to which the individual wishes to belong, as when a teenage basketball player hopes to play someday for the Chicago Bulls. Marketers try to identify the reference groups of their target markets. Reference groups expose a person to new behaviors and lifestyles, influence the person's attitudes and self-concept, and create pressures to conform that may affect the person's product and brand choices.

Opinion leader
Person within a reference group who, because of special skills, knowledge, personality, or other characteristics, exerts influence on others.

The importance of group influence varies across products and brands. It tends to be strongest when the product is visible to others whom the buyer respects. Manufacturers of products and brands subjected to strong group influence must figure out how to reach **opinion leaders**—people within a reference group who, because of special skills,

Table 5-1 Characteristics of Seven Major American Social Classes

Upper uppers (less than 1 percent)

Upper uppers are the social elite who live on inherited wealth and have well-known family backgrounds. They give large sums to charity, own more than one home, and send their children to the finest schools. They often buy and dress conservatively rather than showing off their wealth.

Lower uppers (about 2 percent)

Lower uppers have earned high income or wealth through exceptional ability in the professions or business. They usually begin in the middle class. They tend to be active in social and civic affairs and buy for themselves and their children the symbols of status, such as expensive homes, educations, swimming pools, and automobiles. They want to be accepted in the upper-upper stratum, a status more likely to be achieved by their children than by themselves.

Upper middles (12 percent)

Upper middles possess neither family status nor unusual wealth. They have attained positions as professionals, independent businesspersons, and corporate managers. They believe in education and want their children to develop professional or administrative skills. They are joiners and highly civic-minded.

Middle class (32 percent)

The middle class is made up of average-pay white- and blue-collar workers who live on the "the better side of town" and try to "do the proper things." To keep up with the trends, they often buy products that are popular. Most are concerned with fashion, seeking the better brand names. Better living means owning a nice home in a nice neighborhood with good schools.

Working class (38 percent)

The working class consists of those who lead a "working-class lifestyle," whatever their income, school background, or job. They depend heavily on relatives for economic and emotional support, for advice on purchases, and for assistance in times of trouble.

Upper lowers (9 percent)

Upper lowers are working (are not on welfare), although their living standard is just above poverty. Although they strive toward a higher class, they often lack education and perform unskilled work for poor pay.

Lower lowers (7 percent)

Lower lowers are on welfare, visibly poverty stricken, and usually out of work or have "the dirtiest jobs." Often, they are not interested in finding a job and are permanently dependent on public aid or charity for income. Their homes, clothes, and possessions are "dirty," "raggedy," and "broken-down."

Source: See Richard P. Coleman, "The Continuing Significance of Social Class to Marketing," *Journal of Consumer Research*, December 1983, pp. 265–80. © Journal of Consumer Research, Inc., 1983. Also see Leon G. Schiffman and Leslie Lazar Kanuk, *Consumer Behavior*, 6th ed. (Upper Saddle River, NJ: Prentice Hall, 1997), p. 388.

knowledge, personality, or other characteristics, exert influence on others. Many marketers try to identify opinion leaders for their products and direct marketing efforts toward them. Chrysler used opinion leaders to launch its LH-series cars—the Concorde, Dodge Intrepid, and Eagle Vision. It lent cars on weekends to 6,000 influential community and business leaders in 25 cities. In surveys, 98 percent of the test drivers said that they would recommend the models to friends. And it appears that they did—Chrysler sold out production the first year.[12] In other cases, advertisements can simulate opinion leadership, showing informal discussions between people and thereby reducing the need for consumers to seek advice from others. For example, in a recent ad for Herrera for Men cologne, two women discuss the question, "Did you ever notice how good he smells." The reason? "He wears the most wonderful cologne."[13]

Family Family members can strongly influence buyer behavior. The family is the most important consumer buying organization in society, and it has been researched extensively. Marketers are interested in the roles and influence of the husband, wife, and children on the purchase of different products and services.

Husband-wife involvement varies widely by product category and by stage in the buying process. Buying roles change with evolving consumer lifestyles. In the United States, the wife traditionally has been the main purchasing agent for the family, especially in the areas of food, household products, and clothing. But with 70 percent of women holding jobs outside the home and the willingness of husbands to do more of the family's purchasing, all this is changing. For example, women now buy about 45 percent of all cars and men account for about 40 percent of food-shopping dollars.[14]

Such changes suggest that marketers who've typically sold their products to only women or only men are now courting the opposite sex. For example, after research revealed that women now account for nearly half of all hardware store purchases, home improvement retailer Builders Square turned what had been an intimidating warehouse into a female-friendly retail outlet. The new Builders Square II outlets feature decorator design centers at the front of the store. To attract more women, Builders Square runs ads targeting women in *Home, House Beautiful, Woman's Day,* and *Better Homes and Gardens.* It even offers bridal registries.[15]

Children may also have a strong influence on family buying decisions. Chevrolet recognizes these influences in marketing its Chevy Venture minivan. For example, it ran ads to woo these "back-seat consumers" in *Sports Illustrated for Kids,* which attracts mostly 8- to 14-year old boys. "We're kidding ourselves when we think kids aren't aware of brands," says Venture's brand manager, adding that even she was surprised at how often parents told her that kids played a tie-breaking role in deciding which car to buy.[16]

Family members exert strong influence on buying decisions. This Chevy Venture minivan ad appeals to the entire family.

ROLES AND STATUS A person belongs to many groups—family, clubs, organizations. The person's position in each group can be defined in terms of both role and status. A *role* consists of the activities people are expected to perform according to the persons around them. With her parents, Anna Flores plays the role of daughter; in her family, she plays the role of wife; in her company, she plays the role of brand manager. Each role carries a *status* reflecting the general esteem given to it by society. People often choose products that reflect their roles and status in society. For example, the role of brand manager has more status in our society than the role of daughter. As a brand manager, Anna will buy the kind of clothing that reflects this role and status.

Personal Factors A buyer's decisions also are influenced by personal characteristics such as the buyer's *age and life-cycle stage*, *occupation*, *economic situation*, *lifestyle*, and *personality and self-concept*.

AGE AND LIFE-CYCLE STAGE People change the goods and services they buy over their lifetimes. Buying is also shaped by the stage of the *family life cycle*, the stages through which families might pass as they mature over time. Marketers often define their target markets in terms of life-cycle stage and develop appropriate products and marketing plans for each stage. Traditional family life-cycle stages include young singles and married couples with children. Today, however, marketers are increasingly catering to a growing number of alternative, nontraditional stages such as unmarried couples, couples marrying later in life, childless couples, single parents, extended parents (those with young adult children returning home), and others.

OCCUPATION A person's occupation affects the goods and services bought. Blue-collar workers tend to buy more rugged work clothes, whereas white-collar workers buy more business suits. Marketers try to identify the occupational groups that have an above-average interest in their products and services. A company can even specialize in making products needed by a given occupational group. Thus, computer software companies will design different products for brand managers, accountants, engineers, lawyers, and doctors.

ECONOMIC SITUATION A person's economic situation will affect product choice. Anna Flores can consider buying an expensive Nikon if she has enough spendable income, savings, or borrowing power. Marketers of income-sensitive goods watch trends in personal income, savings, and interest rates. If economic indicators point to a recession, marketers can take steps to redesign, reposition, and reprice their products accordingly.

LIFESTYLE People coming from the same subculture, social class, and occupation may have quite different lifestyles. **Lifestyle** is a person's pattern of living. It involves measuring consumers' major *AIO dimensions*: *activities* (work, hobbies, shopping, sports, social events), *interests* (food, fashion, family, recreation), and *opinions* (about themselves, social issues, business, products). Lifestyle captures something more than the person's social class or personality; it profiles a person's whole pattern of acting and interacting in the world.

Lifestyle
A person's pattern of living as expressed in his or her activities, interests, and opinions.

Several research firms have developed lifestyle classifications. The most widely used is the SRI *Values and Lifestyles* (*VALS*) typology. VALS 2 classifies people according to how they spend their time and money. It divides consumers into eight groups based on two major dimensions: self-orientation and resources. *Self-orientation* groups include *principle-oriented* consumers who buy based on their views of the world; *status-oriented* buyers who base their purchases on the actions and opinions of others; and *action-oriented* buyers who are driven by their desire for activity, variety, and risk taking. Consumers

Dig in the garden. Wash the car. Go to a movie.
Walk the dog. Burp the kid.

Lee Relaxed Rider™ jeans are designed to fit the natural curves of a woman's body. But most importantly, they're designed to fit the natural curves of a woman's life. Dress them up. Or dress them down. When you're ready to go. Or when it's time to relax. Nobody fits your body...or the way you live...better than Lee.
R E L A X E D · R I D E R S

Lee
The brand that fits.

Lifestyles: Lee Relaxed Riders fit the lifestyle of the modern woman on the go. "Nobody fits your body . . . or the way you live . . . better than Lee."

within each orientation are further classified into those with *abundant resources* and those with *minimal resources*, depending on whether they have high or low levels of income, education, health, self-confidence, energy, and other factors. Consumers with either very high or very low levels of resources are classified without regard to their self-orientations (actualizers, strugglers). Actualizers are people with so many resources that they can indulge in any or all self-orientations. In contrast, strugglers are people with too few resources to be included in any consumer orientation. SRI is now developing an iVALS typology, which focuses on the lifestyles and behaviors of on-line service and Internet users. SRI's Web site (future.sri.com) allows visitors to complete the VALS 2 questionnaire to determine their VALS 2 type.[17]

Iron City beer, a well-known brand in Pittsburgh, used VALS 2 to update its image and improve sales. Iron City was losing sales; its aging core users were drinking less beer, and younger men weren't buying the brand. According to VALS research, experiencers drink the most beer, followed by strivers. To assess Iron City's image problems, the company gave the men in these groups stacks of pictures of different kinds of people and asked them to identify first Iron City brand users and then people most like themselves. The men pictured Iron City drinkers as blue-collar steelworkers stopping off at the local bar. However, they saw themselves as more modern, hard-working, and fun-loving. They strongly rejected the outmoded, heavy-industry image of Pittsburgh. Based on this research, Iron City created ads linking its beer to the new self-image of target consumers. The ads mingled images of the old Pittsburgh with those of the new, dynamic city and scenes of young experiencers and strivers having fun and working hard. Within just one month of the start of the campaign, Iron City sales shot up by 26 percent.[18]

When used carefully, the lifestyle concept can help the marketer understand changing consumer values and how they affect buying behavior. Anna Flores, for example, can choose to live the role of a capable homemaker, a career woman, or a free spirit—or all three. She plays several roles, and the way she blends them expresses her lifestyle. If she becomes a professional photographer, this would change her lifestyle, in turn changing what and how she buys.

Heavy coffee drinkers tend to be high on sociability, so to attract customers, Starbucks and other coffee houses create environments in which people can relax and socialize over a cup of steaming coffee.

PERSONALITY AND SELF-CONCEPT Each person's distinct personality influences his or her buying behavior. *Personality* refers to the unique psychological characteristics that lead to relatively consistent and lasting responses to one's own environment. Personality is usually described in terms of traits such as self-confidence, dominance, sociability, autonomy, defensiveness, adaptability, and aggressiveness. Personality can be useful in analyzing consumer behavior for certain product or brand choices. For example, coffee marketers have discovered that heavy coffee drinkers tend to be high on sociability. Thus, to attract customers, Starbucks and other coffee houses create environments in which people can relax and socialize over a cup of steaming coffee.

Many marketers use a concept related to personality—a person's *self-concept* (also called *self-image*). The basic self-concept premise is that people's possessions contribute to and reflect their identities; that is, "we are what we have." Thus, in order to understand consumer behavior, the marketer must first understand the relationship between consumer self-concept and possessions. For example, the founder and chief executive of Barnes & Noble, the nation's leading bookseller, notes that people buy books to support their self-images:

> People have the mistaken notion that the thing you do with books is read them. Wrong. . . . People buy books for what the purchase says about them—their taste, their cultivation, their trendiness. Their aim . . . is to connect themselves, or those to whom they give the books as gifts, with all the other refined owners of Edgar Allen Poe collections or sensitive owners of Virginia Woolf collections. . . . [The result is that] you can sell books as consumer products, with seductive displays, flashy posters, an emphasis on the glamour of the book, and the fashionableness of the bestseller and the trendy author.[19]

Psychological Factors

A person's buying choices are further influenced by four major psychological factors: *motivation*, *perception*, *learning*, and *beliefs and attitudes*.

MOTIVATION We know that Anna Flores became interested in buying a camera. Why? What is she *really* seeking? What *needs* is she trying to satisfy? A person has many needs at any given time. Some are *biological*, arising from states of tension such as hunger, thirst, or discomfort. Others are *psychological*, arising from the need for recognition, esteem, or belonging. A **motive** (or *drive*) is a need that is sufficiently pressing to direct the person

Motive (drive)
A need that is sufficiently pressing to direct the person to seek satisfaction of the need.

Marketing at Work 5-1
"Touchy-Feely" Research into Consumer Motivations

The term *motivation research* refers to qualitative research designed to probe consumers' hidden, subconscious motivations. Because consumers often don't know or can't describe just why they act as they do, motivation researchers use a variety of nondirective and projective techniques to uncover underlying emotions and attitudes toward brands and buying situations. The techniques range from sentence completion, word association, and inkblot or cartoon interpretation tests, to having consumers describe typical brand users or form daydreams and fantasies about brands or buying situations. Some of these techniques verge on the bizarre. One writer offers the following tongue-in-cheek summary of a motivation research session:

Good morning, ladies and gentlemen. We've called you here today for a little consumer research. Now, lie down on the couch, toss your inhibitions out the window, and let's try a little free association. First, think about brands as if they were your *friends*. Imagine you could talk to your TV dinner. What would he say? And what would you say to him? . . . Now, think of your shampoo as an animal. Go on, don't be shy. Would

it be a panda or a lion? A snake or a wooly worm? For our final exercise, let's all sit up and pull out our magic markers. Draw a picture of a typical cake-mix user. Would she wear an apron or a negligee? A business suit or a can-can dress?

Such projective techniques seem pretty goofy. But more and more, marketers are turning to these touchy-feely approaches to probe consumer psyches and develop better marketing strategies.

Many advertising agencies employ teams of psychologists, anthropologists, and other social scientists to carry out motivation research. One agency routinely conducts one-on-one, therapylike interviews to delve into the inner workings of consumers. Another agency asks consumers to describe their favorite brands as animals or cars (say, Cadillacs versus Chevrolets) in order to assess the prestige associated with various brands. Still another agency has consumers draw figures of typical brand users:

In one instance, the agency asked 50 interviewees to sketch likely buyers of two different brands of cake mixes. Consistently, the group portrayed Pillsbury customers as apron-clad, grandmotherly types, while they pictured Duncan Hines purchasers as svelte, contemporary women.

Motivation research: When asked to sketch figures of typical cake-mix users, subjects portrayed Pillsbury customers as grandmotherly types and Duncan Hines buyers as svelte and contemporary.

to seek satisfaction. Psychologists have developed theories of human motivation. Two of the most popular—the theories of Sigmund Freud and Abraham Maslow—have quite different meanings for consumer analysis and marketing.

Sigmund Freud assumed that people are largely unconscious about the real psychological forces shaping their behavior. He saw the person as growing up and repressing many urges. These urges are never eliminated or under perfect control; they emerge in dreams, in slips of the tongue, in neurotic and obsessive behavior, or ultimately in psychoses. Thus, Freud suggested that a person does not fully understand his or her motivation. If Anna Flores wants to purchase an expensive camera, she may describe her motive as wanting a hobby or career. At a deeper level, she may be purchasing the camera to impress others with her creative talent. At a still deeper level, she may be buying the camera to feel young and independent again. Motivation researchers collect in-depth

In a similar study, American Express had people sketch likely users of its gold-card versus its green card. Respondents depicted gold-card holders as active, broad-shouldered men; green-card holders were perceived as "couch potatoes" lounging in front of television sets. Based on these results, the company positioned its gold card as a symbol of responsibility for people capable of controlling their lives and finances.

Some motivation research studies employ more basic techniques, such as simply mingling with or watching consumers to find out what makes them tick. In an effort to understand the teenage consumer market better, ad agency BSB Worldwide videotaped teenagers' rooms in 25 countries. It found surprising similarities across countries and cultures:

> From the steamy playgrounds of Los Angeles to the stately boulevards of Singapore, kids show amazing similarities in taste, language, and attitude. . . . From the gear and posters on display, it's hard to tell whether the rooms are in Los Angeles, Mexico City, or Tokyo. Basketballs sit alongside soccer balls. Closets overflow with staples from an international, unisex uniform: baggy Levi's or

> Deisel jeans, NBA jackets, and rugged shoes from Timberland or Doc Martens.

Bugle Boy found that traditional focus groups fail miserably in getting the scoop on teens and GenXers. These often-cynical young people are skeptical of sales pitches and just won't speak up in a conference room with two-way mirrors. Working with Chilton Research, Bugle Boy found an innovative solution. It plucked four young men out of obscurity, handed each of them an 8-mm video camera, and told them to document their lives. The young amateurs were given only broad categories to work with: school, home, closet, and shopping. Bugle Boy then used the videos to prompt discussions of product and lifestyle issues in "free-form" focus groups held in unconventional locations, such as restaurants. Says one Bugle Boy ad manager, "I think this really helped us to get a handle on what these kids do. It let us see what their lives are all about, their awareness of the Bugle Boy brand, and how they perceive the brand."

Similarly, researchers at Sega of America's ad agency have learned a lot about video game buying behavior by hanging around with 150 kids in their bedrooms and by shopping with them in malls. Above all

else, they learned, do everything fast. As a result, in Sega's most recent 15-second commercials, some images fly by so quickly that adults cannot recall seeing them, even after repeated showings. The kids, weaned on MTV, recollect them keenly.

Some marketers dismiss such motivation research as mumbo jumbo. And these approaches do present some problems: They use small samples and researcher interpretations of results are often highly subjective, sometimes leading to rather exotic explanations of otherwise ordinary buying behavior. However, others believe strongly that these approaches can provide interesting nuggets of insight into the relationships between consumers and the brands they buy. To marketers who use them, motivation research techniques provide a flexible and varied means of gaining insights into deeply held and often mysterious motivations behind consumer buying behavior.

Sources: Excerpts from Annetta Miller and Dody Tsiantar, "Psyching Out Consumers," *Newsweek*, February 27, 1989, pp. 46–47; and Shawn Tully, "Teens: The Most Global Market of All," *Fortune*, May 6, 1994, pp. 90–97. Also see Rebecca Piirto, "Words that Sell," *American Demographics*, January 1992, p. 6; "They Understand Your Kids," *Fortune*, special issue, Autumn/Winter 1993, pp. 29–30; Cyndee Miller, "Sometimes a Researcher Has No Alternative But to Hang Out in a Bar," *Marketing News*, January 3, 1994, pp. 16, 26; and Ronald B. Lieber, "Storytelling: A New Way to Get Close to Your Customer," *Fortune*, February 3, 1997, pp. 102–8.

information from small samples of consumers to uncover the deeper motives for their product choices (see Marketing at Work 5-1).

Abraham Maslow sought to explain why people are driven by particular needs at particular times. Why does one person spend much time and energy on personal safety and another on gaining the esteem of others? Maslow's answer is that human needs are arranged in a hierarchy, as shown in Figure 5-3, from the most pressing to the least pressing. They include *physiological* needs, *safety* needs, *social* needs, *esteem* needs, and *self-actualization* needs. A person tries to satisfy the most important need first. When that need is satisfied, it will stop being a motivator and the person will then try to satisfy the next most important need. For example, starving people (physiological need) will not take an interest in the latest happenings in the art world (self-actualization needs), nor in how they are seen or esteemed by others (social or esteem needs), nor even in whether they are

Figure 5-3

Maslow's hierarchy of needs

Source: From *Motivation and Personality* by Abraham H. Maslow. Copyright © 1970 by Abraham H. Maslow. Copyright 1954, 1987 by Harper & Row Publishers, Inc. Reprinted by permission of Addison Wesley Educational Publishers Inc. Also see Barbara Marx Hubbard, "Seeking Our Future Potentials," *The Futurist*, May 1998, pp. 29–32.

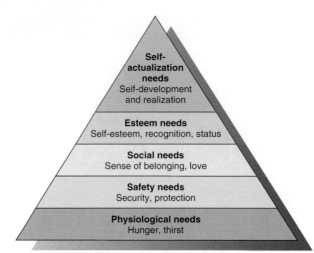

Self-actualization needs
Self-development and realization

Esteem needs
Self-esteem, recognition, status

Social needs
Sense of belonging, love

Safety needs
Security, protection

Physiological needs
Hunger, thirst

breathing clean air (safety needs). But as each important need is satisfied, the next most important need will come into play.

What light does Maslow's theory throw on Anna Flores's interest in buying a camera? We can guess that Anna has satisfied her physiological, safety, and social needs; they do not motivate her interest in cameras. Her camera interest might come from a strong need for more esteem. Or it might come from a need for self-actualization—she might want to be a creative person and express herself through photography.[20]

Perception

The process by which people select, organize, and interpret information to form a meaningful picture of the world.

PERCEPTION A motivated person is ready to act. How the person acts is influenced by his or her own perception of the situation. All of us learn by the flow of information through our five senses: sight, hearing, smell, touch, and taste. However, each of us receives, organizes, and interprets this sensory information in an individual way. **Perception** is the process by which people select, organize, and interpret information to form a meaningful picture of the world.

People can form different perceptions of the same stimulus because of three perceptual processes: selective attention, selective distortion, and selective retention. People are exposed to a great amount of stimuli every day. For example, the average person may be exposed to more than 1,500 ads in a single day. It is impossible for a person to pay attention to all these stimuli. *Selective attention*—the tendency for people to screen out most of the information to which they are exposed—means that marketers have to work especially hard to attract the consumer's attention.

Even noted stimuli do not always come across in the intended way. Each person fits incoming information into an existing mind-set. *Selective distortion* describes the tendency of people to interpret information in a way that will support what they already believe. Anna Flores may hear a salesperson mention some good and bad points about a competing camera brand. Because she already has a strong leaning toward Nikon, she is likely to distort those points in order to conclude that Nikon is the better camera. Selective distortion means that marketers must try to understand the mind-sets of consumers and how these will affect interpretations of advertising and sales information.

People also will forget much that they learn. They tend to retain information that supports their attitudes and beliefs. Because of *selective retention*, Anna is likely to remember good points made about the Nikon and to forget good points made about competing cameras. Because of selective exposure, distortion, and retention, marketers have to work hard to get their messages through. This fact explains why marketers use so much drama and repetition in sending messages to their market.

Interestingly, although most marketers worry about whether their offers will be perceived at all, some consumers worry that they will be affected by marketing messages without even knowing it—through *subliminal advertising*. In 1957, a researcher announced that he had flashed the phrases "Eat popcorn" and "Drink Coca-Cola" on a screen in a New Jersey movie theater every five seconds for 1/300th of a second. He reported that although viewers did not consciously recognize these messages, they absorbed them subconsciously and bought 58 percent more popcorn and 18 percent more Coke. Suddenly advertisers and consumer-protection groups became intensely interested in subliminal perception. People voiced fears of being brainwashed, and California and Canada declared the practice illegal. Although the researcher later admitted to making up the data, the issue has not died. Some consumers still fear that they are being manipulated by subliminal messages.

Numerous studies by psychologists and consumer researchers have found no link between subliminal messages and consumer behavior. It appears that subliminal advertising simply doesn't have the power attributed to it by its critics. And most advertisers scoff at the notion of an industry conspiracy to manipulate consumers through "invisible" messages.

LEARNING When people act, they learn. **Learning** describes changes in an individual's behavior arising from experience. Learning theorists say that most human behavior is learned. Learning occurs through the interplay of *drives*, *stimuli*, *cues*, *responses*, and *reinforcement*.

> **Learning**
> Changes in an individual's behavior arising from experience.

We saw that Anna Flores has a drive for self-actualization. A *drive* is a strong internal stimulus that calls for action. Her drive becomes a motive when it is directed toward a particular *stimulus object*, in this case a camera. Anna's response to the idea of buying a camera is conditioned by the surrounding cues. *Cues* are minor stimuli that determine when, where, and how the person responds. Seeing cameras in a shop window, hearing of a special sale price, and receiving her husband's support are all cues that can influence Anna's *response* to her interest in buying a camera.

Suppose Anna buys the Nikon. If the experience is rewarding, she will probably use the camera more and more. Her response to cameras will be *reinforced*. Then the next time she shops for a camera, binoculars, or some similar product, the probability is greater that she will buy a Nikon product. The practical significance of learning theory for marketers is that they can build up demand for a product by associating it with strong drives, using motivating cues, and providing positive reinforcement.

BELIEFS AND ATTITUDES Through doing and learning, people acquire beliefs and attitudes. These, in turn, influence their buying behavior. A **belief** is a descriptive thought that a person has about something. Anna Flores may believe that a Nikon camera takes great pictures, stands up well under hard use, and costs $450. These beliefs may be based on real knowledge, opinion, or faith and may or may not carry an emotional charge. For example, Anna Flores's belief that a Nikon camera is heavy may or may not matter to her decision.

> **Belief**
> A descriptive thought that a person holds about something.

Marketers are interested in the beliefs that people formulate about specific products and services because these beliefs make up product and brand images that affect buying behavior. If some of the beliefs are wrong and prevent purchase, the marketer will want to launch a campaign to correct them.

People have attitudes regarding religion, politics, clothes, music, food, and almost everything else. **Attitude** describes a person's relatively consistent evaluations, feelings, and tendencies toward an object or idea. Attitudes put people into a frame of mind of liking or disliking things, of moving toward or away from them. Thus, Anna Flores may

> **Attitude**
> A person's consistently favorable or unfavorable evaluations, feelings, and tendencies toward an object or idea.

Figure 5-4
Buyer decision process

| Need recognition | → | Information search | → | Evaluation of alternatives | → | Purchase decision | → | Postpurchase behavior |

hold attitudes such as "buy the best," "the Japanese make the best electronics products in the world," and "creativity and self-expression are among the most important things in life." If so, the Nikon camera would fit well into Anna's existing attitudes.

Attitudes are difficult to change. A person's attitudes fit into a pattern, and to change one attitude may require difficult adjustments in many others. Thus, a company should usually try to fit its products into existing attitudes rather than attempt to change attitudes.

We can now appreciate the many forces acting on consumer behavior. The consumer's choice results from the complex interplay of cultural, social, personal, and psychological factors.

The Buyer Decision Process

Now that we have looked at the influences that affect buyers, we are ready to look at how final consumers make buying decisions. Figure 5-4 shows that the buyer decision process consists of five stages: *need recognition, information search, evaluation of alternatives, purchase decision,* and *postpurchase behavior*

The figure implies that consumers pass through all five stages with every purchase. But in more routine purchases, consumers often skip or reverse some of these stages. A person buying his or her regular brand of toothpaste would recognize the need and go right to the purchase decision, skipping information search and evaluation. However, we use the model in Figure 5-4 because it shows all the considerations that arise when a consumer faces a new and complex purchase situation.

Need Recognition The buying process starts with need recognition—the buyer recognizes a problem or need. The need may be triggered by *internal stimuli*—hunger, thirst, sex—or it can be triggered by *external stimuli*. For example, Anna Flores might feel the need for a new hobby when her busy season at work slowed down, and she thought of

Need recognition can be triggered by advertising. This ad asks an arresting question that alerts parents to the need for a high-quality bike helmet.

cameras after talking to a friend about photography or seeing a camera ad. At this stage, the marketer should research consumers to find out what kinds of needs or problems arise, what factors brought them about, and how they led the consumer to this particular product.

Information Search. An aroused consumer may or may not search for more information. If the consumer's drive is strong and a satisfying product is near at hand, the consumer is likely to buy it then. If not, the consumer may store the need in memory or undertake an information search related to the need. At the least, Anna Flores will probably pay more attention to camera ads, cameras used by friends, and camera conversations. Or Anna may actively look for reading material, phone friends, and gather information in other ways. The amount of searching she does will depend on the strength of her drive, the amount of information she starts with, the ease of obtaining more information, the value she places on additional information, and the satisfaction she gets from searching.

The consumer can obtain information from any of several sources. These include *personal sources* (family, friends, neighbors, acquaintances), *commercial sources* (advertising, salespeople, dealers, packaging, displays), *public sources* (mass media, consumer-rating organizations), and *experiential sources* (handling, examining, using the product). The relative influence of these information sources varies with the product and the buyer. Generally, the consumer receives the most information about a product from commercial sources—those controlled by the marketer. The most effective sources, however, tend to be personal. Commercial sources normally *inform* the buyer, but personal sources *legitimize* or *evaluate* products for the buyer.

As more information is obtained, the consumer's awareness and knowledge of the available brands and features increases. In her information search, Anna Flores learned about the many camera brands available. The information also helped her drop certain brands from consideration. A company must design its marketing mix to make prospects aware of and knowledgeable about its brand. It should carefully identify consumers' sources of information and the importance of each source.

Evaluation of Alternatives We have seen how the consumer uses information to arrive at a set of final brand choices. How does the consumer choose among the alternative brands? The marketer needs to know about alternative evaluation—that is, how the consumer processes information to arrive at brand choices. Unfortunately, consumers do not use a simple and single evaluation process in all buying situations. Instead, several evaluation processes are at work.

The consumer arrives at attitudes toward different brands through some evaluation procedure. How consumers go about evaluating purchase alternatives depends on the individual consumer and the specific buying situation. In some cases, consumers use careful calculations and logical thinking. At other times, the same consumers do little or no evaluating; instead, they buy on impulse and rely on intuition. Sometimes consumers make buying decisions on their own; sometimes they turn to friends, consumer guides, or salespeople for buying advice.

Suppose Anna Flores has narrowed her choices to four cameras. And suppose that she is primarily interested in four attributes—picture quality, ease of use, camera size, and price. Anna has formed beliefs about how each brand rates on each attribute. Clearly, if one camera rated best on all the attributes, we could predict that Anna would choose it. However, the brands vary in appeal. Anna might base her buying decision on only one attribute, and her choice would be easy to predict. If she wants picture quality above everything, she will buy the camera that she thinks has the best picture quality. But most buyers consider several attributes, each with different importance. If we knew the importance weights that Anna assigns to each of the four attributes, we could predict her camera choice more reliably.

Marketers should study buyers to find out how they actually evaluate brand alternatives. If they know what evaluative processes go on, marketers can take steps to influence the buyer's decision.

Purchase Decision In the evaluation stage, the consumer ranks brands and forms purchase intentions. Generally, the consumer's purchase decision will be to buy the most preferred brand, but two factors can come between the purchase *intention* and the purchase *decision*. The first factor is the *attitudes of others*. If Anna Flores's husband feels strongly that Anna should buy the lowest-priced camera, then the chances of Anna's buying a more expensive camera will be reduced.

The second factor is *unexpected situational factors*. The consumer may form a purchase intention based on factors such as expected income, expected price, and expected product benefits. However, unexpected events may change the purchase intention. Anna Flores may lose her job, some other purchase may become more urgent, or a friend may report being disappointed in her preferred camera. Or a close competitor may drop its price. Thus, preferences and even purchase intentions do not always result in actual purchase choice.

Postpurchase Behavior The marketer's job does not end when the product is bought. After purchasing the product, the consumer will be satisfied or dissatisfied and will engage in postpurchase behavior of interest to the marketer. What determines whether the buyer is satisfied or dissatisfied with a purchase? The answer lies in the relationship between the *consumer's expectations* and the product's *perceived performance*. If the product falls short of expectations, the consumer is disappointed; if it meets expectations, the consumer is satisfied; if it exceeds expectations, the consumer is delighted.

The larger the gap between expectations and performance, the greater the consumer's dissatisfaction. This suggests that sellers should make product claims that faithfully represent the product's performance so that buyers are satisfied. Some sellers might even understate performance levels to boost consumer satisfaction with the product. For example, Boeing's salespeople tend to be conservative when they estimate the potential benefits of their aircraft. They almost always underestimate fuel efficiency—they promise a 5 percent savings that turns out to be 8 percent. Customers are delighted with better-than-expected performance; they buy again and tell other potential customers that Boeing lives up to its promises.

Cognitive dissonance
Buyer discomfort caused by postpurchase conflict.

Almost all major purchases result in **cognitive dissonance**, or discomfort caused by postpurchase conflict. After the purchase, consumers are satisfied with the benefits of the chosen brand and are glad to avoid the drawbacks of the brands not bought. However, every purchase involves compromise. Consumers feel uneasy about acquiring the drawbacks of the chosen brand and about losing the benefits of the brands not purchased. Thus, consumers feel at least some postpurchase dissonance for every purchase.[21]

Why is it so important to satisfy the customer? Such satisfaction is important because a company's sales come from two basic groups—*new customers* and *retained customers*. It usually costs more to attract new customers than to retain current ones, and the best way to retain current customers is to keep them satisfied. Satisfied customers buy a product again, talk favorably to others about the product, pay less attention to competing brands and advertising, and buy other products from the company. Many marketers go beyond merely *meeting* the expectations of customers—they aim to *delight* the customer.

A dissatisfied consumer responds differently. Whereas, on average, a satisfied customer tells 3 people about a good product experience, a dissatisfied customer gripes to 11 people. In fact, one study showed that 13 percent of the people who had a problem with an organization complained about the company to more than 20 people.[22] Clearly, bad word of mouth travels farther and faster than good word of mouth and can quickly damage consumer attitudes about a company and its products.

Therefore, a company would be wise to measure customer satisfaction regularly. It cannot simply rely on dissatisfied customers to volunteer their complaints when they are dissatisfied. Some 96 percent of unhappy customers never tell the company about their problem. Companies should set up systems that *encourage* customers to complain (see Marketing at Work 5-2). In this way, the company can learn how well it is doing and how it can improve. But listening is not enough—the company also must respond constructively to the complaints it receives.

The Buyer Decision Process for New Products

We have looked at the stages buyers go through in trying to satisfy a need. Buyers may pass quickly or slowly through these stages, and some of the stages may even be reversed. Much depends on the nature of the buyer, the product, and the buying situation.

We now look at how buyers approach the purchase of new products. A **new product** is a good, service, or idea that is perceived by some potential customers as new. It may have been around for a while, but our interest is in how consumers learn about products for the first time and make decisions on whether to adopt them. We define the **adoption process** as "the mental process through which an individual passes from first learning about an innovation to final adoption,"[23] and *adoption* as the decision by an individual to become a regular user of the product.

New product
A good, service, or idea that is perceived by some potential customers as new.

Adoption process
The mental process through which an individual passes from first hearing about an innovation to final adoption.

Stages in the Adoption Process Consumers go through five stages in the process of adopting a new product:

- *Awareness:* The consumer becomes aware of the new product but lacks information about it.
- *Interest:* The consumer seeks information about the new product.
- *Evaluation:* The consumer considers whether trying the new product makes sense.
- *Trial:* The consumer tries the new product on a small scale to improve his or her estimate of its value.
- *Adoption:* The consumer decides to make full and regular use of the new product.

This model suggests that the new-product marketer should think about how to help consumers move through these stages. A manufacturer of large-screen televisions may discover that many consumers in the interest stage do not move to the trial stage because of uncertainty and the large investment. If these same consumers were willing to use a large-screen television on a trial basis for a small fee, the manufacturer should consider offering a trial-use plan with an option to buy.

Individual Differences in Innovativeness People differ greatly in their readiness to try new products. In each product area, there are "consumption pioneers" and early adopters. Other individuals adopt new products much later. People can be classified into the adopter categories shown in Figure 5-5. After a slow start, an increasing number of

Marketing at Work 5-2

Postpurchase Satisfaction: Turning Company Critics Into Loyal Customers

What should companies do with dissatisfied customers? Everything they can! Unhappy customers not only stop buying but also can quickly damage the company's image. Studies show that customers tell four times as many other people about bad experiences as they do about good ones. In contrast, dealing effectively with gripes can actually boost customer loyalty and the company's image. Thus, enlightened companies don't try to hide from dissatisfied customers. To the contrary, they go out of their way to *encourage* customers to complain, then bend over backwards to make disgruntled buyers happy.

The first opportunity to handle gripes often comes at the point of purchase. Many service firms teach their customer-contact people how to resolve problems and diffuse customer anger. Some companies go to extremes to see things the customer's way and to reward complaining, seemingly without regard for profit impact. For example, retailer Neiman Marcus is incredibly gracious with complainers. "We're not just looking for today's sale. We want a long-term relationship with our customers," says Gwen Baum, the chain's director of customer satisfaction. "If that means taking

back a piece of Baccarat crystal that isn't from one of our stores, we'll do it." Such actions create tremendous buyer loyalty and goodwill, and for most retailers, customers who return items that they bought elsewhere or have already used account for less than 5 percent of all returns.

Many companies have also set up toll-free 800-number systems to coax out and deal with consumer problems. Today, more than two-thirds of all U.S. manufacturers offer toll-free numbers to handle complaints, inquiries, and orders. For example, Coca-Cola set up its 1-800-GET-COKE lines in late 1983 after studies showed that only 1 unhappy person in 50 bothers to complain. "The other 49 simply switch brands," explains the company's director of consumer affairs, "so it just makes good sense to seek them out."

Every weekday, Pillsbury handles more than 2,000 people who call its 800 number with complaints, compliments, and questions. On the day before Thanksgiving, the busiest day, Pillsbury's customer service reps, mostly women with college degrees and training in nutrition and home economics, assist 3,000 callers with their holiday dinners.

For callers who speak little or no English, Pillsbury can dial an AT&T number that hooks up interpreters for any of 140 languages in a three-way call with the customer and company.

Now in its tenth year, the Gerber Helpline (1-800-GERBER) has received more than 4 million calls. Helpline staffers, most of them mothers or grandmothers themselves, provide baby care advice 24-hours a day, 365 days a year to more than 2,400 callers a day. In 1994, the helpline received 647,875 calls. The helpline is staffed by English, French, and Spanish-speaking operators, and interpreters are available for most other languages. Callers include new parents, day care providers, and even health professionals. One in five of all calls to the helpline come from men. Callers ask a wide variety of questions, from when to feed a baby specific foods to how to babyproof a home. "It used to be that mom or grandmom was right around the corner to answer your baby questions," notes the manager of the Gerber helpline. "But more and more, that's not the case. For new or expectant parents, it's nice to know that they can pick up the phone any time of day and talk to

people adopt the new product. The number of adopters reaches a peak and then drops off as fewer nonadopters remain. Innovators are defined as the first 2.5 percent of the buyers to adopt a new idea (those beyond two standard deviations from mean adoption time); the early adopters are the next 13.5 percent (between one and two standard deviations); and so forth.

The five adopter groups have differing values. *Innovators* are venturesome—they try new ideas at some risk. *Early adopters* are guided by respect—they are opinion leaders in their communities and adopt new ideas early but carefully. The *early majority* are deliberate—although they rarely are leaders, they adopt new ideas before the average person. The *late majority* are skeptical—they adopt an innovation only after a majority

Keeping customers happy: the Gerber Helpline has fielded more than 4 million calls providing baby care advice 24-hours a day, 365 days a year to more than 2,400 callers a day.

someone that understands and can help."

General Electric's Answer Center may be the most extensive 800-number system in the nation. It handles more than 3 million calls a year, only 5 percent of them complaints. At the heart of the system is a giant database that provides the center's service reps with instant access to more than 1 million answers concerning 8,500 models in 120 product lines. The center receives some unusual calls, as when a submarine off the Connecticut coast requested help fixing a motor, or when technicians on a James Bond film couldn't get their underwater lights working. Still, according to GE, its people resolve 90 percent of

complaints or inquiries on the first call, and complainers often become even more loyal customers. Although the company spends an average of $3.50 per call, it reaps two to three times that much in new sales and warranty savings.

The best way to keep customers happy is to provide good products and services in the first place. Short of that, however, a company must develop a good system for ferreting out and handling consumer problems. Such a system can be much more than a necessary evil—customer happiness usually shows up on the company's bottom line. One recent study found that dollars invested in complaint-handling and inquiry systems yield an average

return of between 100 percent and 200 percent. Maryanne Rasmussen, vice-president of worldwide quality at American Express, offers this formula: "Better complaint handling equals higher customer satisfaction equals higher brand loyalty equals higher performance."

Sources: Quotes from Patricia Sellers, "How to Handle Consumer Gripes," *Fortune*, October 24, 1988, pp. 88–100; and "On Mother's Day, Advice Goes a Long Way," *PR Newswire*, Ziff Communications, May 2, 1995. Also see Roland T. Rust, Bala Subramanian, and Mark Wells, "Making Complaints a Management Tool," *Marketing Management*, Fall 1992, pp. 41–45; Tibbett L. Speer, "They Complain Because They Care," *American Demographics*, May 1966, pp. 13–14; Thomas A. Stewart, "A Satisfied Customer Isn't Enough," *Fortune*, July 21, 1997, pp. 112–3; Stephen S. Tax, Stephen W. Brown, and Murali Chandrashekaran, "Customer Evaluations of Service Complaint Experiences: Implications for Relationship Marketing," *Journal of Marketing*, April 1998, pp. 60–76; and Marcia Stepanek, "You'll Wanna Hold Their Hands," *Business Week*, March 22, 1999, pp. EB30–EB31.

of people have tried it. Finally, *laggards* are tradition-bound—they are suspicious of changes and adopt the innovation only when it has become something of a tradition itself.

This adopter classification suggests that an innovating firm should research the characteristics of innovators and early adopters and should direct marketing efforts toward them. In general, innovators tend to be relatively younger, better educated, and higher in income than later adopters and nonadopters. They are more receptive to unfamiliar things, rely more on their own values and judgment, and are more willing to take risks. They are less brand loyal and more likely to take advantage of special promotions such as discounts, coupons, and samples.

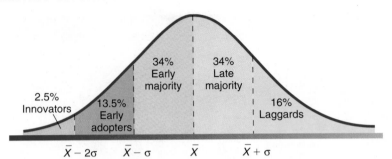

Figure 5-5

Adopter categorization on the basis of relative time of adoptions of innovations

Source: Reprinted with the permission of The Free Press, a Division of Simon & Schuster, from *Diffusion of Innovations*, Fourth Edition, by Everett M. Rogers. Copyright © 1962, 1971, 1983 by The Free Press.

Influence of Product Characteristics on Rate of Adoption The characteristics of the new product affect its rate of adoption. Some products catch on almost overnight (Beanie Babies), whereas others take a long time to gain acceptance (personal computers). Five characteristics are especially important in influencing an innovation's rate of adoption. For example, consider the characteristics of large-screen televisions in relation to the rate of adoption:

- *Relative advantage:* the degree to which the innovation appears superior to existing products. The greater the perceived relative advantage of using a large-screen TV — say, in picture quality and ease of viewing — the sooner such TVs will be adopted.
- *Compatibility:* the degree to which the innovation fits the values and experiences of potential consumers. Large-screen TVs, for example, are highly compatible with the lifestyles found in upper-middle-class homes.
- *Complexity:* the degree to which the innovation is difficult to understand or use. Large-screen TVs are not very complex and will therefore take less time to penetrate U.S. homes than more complex innovations.
- *Divisibility:* the degree to which the innovation may be tried on a limited basis. Large-screen TVs are still expensive. To the extent that people can lease them with an option to buy, their rate of adoption will increase.
- *Communicability:* the degree to which the results of using the innovation can be observed or described to others. Because large-screen TVs lend themselves to demonstration and description, their use will spread faster among consumers.

Other characteristics influence the rate of adoption, such as initial and ongoing costs, risk and uncertainty, and social approval. The new-product marketer has to research all these factors when developing the new product and its marketing program.

Consumer Behavior Across International Borders

Understanding consumer behavior is difficult enough for companies marketing within the borders of a single country. For companies operating in many countries, however, understanding and serving the needs of consumers can be daunting. Although consumers in different countries may have some things in common, their values, attitudes, and behaviors often vary greatly. International marketers must understand such differences and adjust their products and marketing programs accordingly.

Sometimes the differences are obvious. For example, in the United States, where most people eat cereal regularly for breakfast, Kellogg focuses its marketing on persuading consumers to select a Kellogg brand rather than a competitor's brand. In France, however, where most people prefer croissants and coffee or no breakfast at all, Kellogg advertising simply attempts to convince people that they should eat cereal for breakfast. Its packaging includes step-by-step instructions on how to prepare cereal. In India, where many consumers eat heavy, fried breakfasts and 22 percent of consumers skip the meal altogether, Kellogg's advertising attempts to convince buyers to switch to a lighter, more nutritious breakfast diet.[24]

Often, differences across international markets are more subtle. They may result from physical differences in consumers and their environments. For example, Remington makes smaller electric shavers to fit the smaller hands of Japanese consumers and battery-powered shavers for the British market, where few bathrooms have electrical outlets. Other differences result from varying customs. In Japan, for example, where humility and deference are considered great virtues, pushy, hard-hitting sales approaches are considered offensive. Failing to understand such differences in customs and behaviors from one country to another can spell disaster for a marketer's international products and programs.

Marketers must decide on the degree to which they will adapt their products and marketing programs to meet the unique cultures and needs of consumers in various markets. On the one hand, they want to standardize their offerings in order to simplify operations and take advantage of cost economies. On the other hand, adapting marketing efforts within each country results in products and programs that better satisfy the needs of local consumers.

Linking the Concepts

Here's a good place to pull over and apply the concepts you've examined in the first part of this chapter.

- Think about a specific major purchase you've made recently. What buying process did you follow? What major factors influenced your decision?
- Pick a company that we've discussed in a previous chapter—Nike, Coca-Cola, Black & Decker, Wal-Mart, Volkswagen, or another. Does the company you chose understand its customers and their buying behavior?
- Think about Intel (from chapter 2), which sells its products to computer makers and other businesses rather than to final consumers. How would Intel's marketing to business customers differ from Nike's marketing to final consumers? The second part of the chapter deals with this issue.

Business Markets and Business Buyer Behavior

In one way or another, most large companies sell to other organizations. Many companies, such as DuPont, Xerox, Boeing, Motorola, and countless other firms, sell *most* of their products to other businesses. Even large consumer products companies, which make products used by final consumers, must first sell their products to other businesses. For example, before General Mills can sell its many familiar brands—Cheerios, Betty Crocker cake mixes, Gold Medal flour, and others—to final consumers, it must first sell them to the wholesalers and retailers that serve the consumer market.

Business buyer behavior refers to the buying behavior of all the organizations that buy goods and services for use in the production of other products and services that are

> **Business buyer behavior**
> The buying behavior of organizations that buy goods and services for use in the production of other products and services that are sold, rented, or supplied to others. It also includes buying of goods by retailers and wholesalers for the purpose of reselling or renting them.

sold, rented, or supplied to others. It also includes retailing and wholesaling firms that acquire goods for the purpose of reselling or renting them to others at a profit.

Business Markets

The business market is *huge*. In fact, business markets involve far more dollars and items than do consumer markets. For example, think about the large number of business transactions involved in the production and sale of a single set of Goodyear tires. Various suppliers sell Goodyear the rubber, steel, equipment, and other goods that it needs to produce the tires. Goodyear then sells the finished tires to retailers, who in turn sell them to consumers. Thus, many sets of *business* purchases were made for only one set of *consumer* purchases. In addition, Goodyear sells tires as original equipment to manufacturers who install them on new vehicles and as replacement tires to companies that maintain their own fleets of company cars, trucks, buses, or other vehicles.

In some ways, business markets are similar to consumer markets. Both involve people who assume buying roles and make purchase decisions to satisfy needs. However, business markets differ in many ways from consumer markets. The main differences are in *market structure and demand*, the *nature of the buying unit*, and the *types of decisions and the decision process* involved.

Market Structure and Demand The business marketer normally deals with *far fewer but far larger buyers* than the consumer marketer does. For example, when Goodyear sells replacement tires to final consumers, its potential market includes the owners of the millions of cars currently in use in the United States. But Goodyear's fate in the business market depends on getting orders from one of only a few large automakers. Even in large business markets, a few buyers normally account for most of the purchasing.

Business markets are also more *geographically concentrated*. More than half the nation's business buyers are concentrated in eight states: California, New York, Ohio, Illinois, Michigan, Texas, Pennsylvania, and New Jersey. Further, business demand is **derived demand**—it ultimately derives from the demand for consumer goods. General Motors buys steel because consumers buy cars. If consumer demand for cars drops, so will the demand for steel and all the other products used to make cars. Therefore, business marketers sometimes promote their products directly to final consumers to increase

Derived demand
Business demand that ultimately comes from (derives from) the demand for consumer goods.

Intel launched its highly successful "Intel Inside" logo advertising campaign to convince computer buyers that it really does matter what chip comes inside their computers. Now, Compaq and most other computer makers feature the logo in ads like this one.

business demand. For example, Intel's long-running "Intel Inside" advertising campaign sells personal computer buyers on the virtues of Intel microprocessors. The increased demand for Intel chips boosts demand for the PCs containing them, and both Intel and its business partners benefit.

Nature of the Buying Unit Compared with consumer purchases, a business purchase usually involves *more buyers* and a *more professional purchasing effort*. Often, business buying is done by trained purchasing agents who spend their working lives learning how to buy better. The more complex the purchase, the more likely that several people will participate in the decision-making process. Buying committees made up of technical experts and top management are common in the buying of major goods. As one observer notes, "It's a scary thought: Your customers may know more about your company and products than you do. . . . Companies are putting their best and brightest people on procurement patrol."[25] Therefore, business marketers must have well-trained salespeople to deal with well-trained buyers.

Types of Decisions and the Decision Process Business buyers usually face *more complex* buying decisions than do consumer buyers. Purchases often involve large sums of money, complex technical and economic considerations, and interactions among many people at many levels of the buyer's organization. Because the purchases are more complex, business buyers may take longer to make their decisions.

The business buying process tends to be *more formalized* than the consumer buying process. Large business purchases usually call for detailed product specifications, written purchase orders, careful supplier searches, and formal approval. Finally, in the business buying process, buyer and seller are often much *more dependent* on each other. Consumer marketers are usually at a distance from their customers. In contrast, business marketers may roll up their sleeves and work closely with their customers during all stages of the buying process — from helping customers define problems, to finding solutions, to supporting after-sale operation. In the long run, business marketers keep a customer's sales by meeting current needs *and* by working with customers to help them succeed with their own customers.

Business Buyer Behavior

At the most basic level, marketers want to know how business buyers will respond to various marketing stimuli. Figure 5-6 shows a model of business buyer behavior. In this model, marketing and other stimuli affect the buying organization and produce certain buyer responses. As with consumer buying, the marketing stimuli for business buying consist of the four Ps: product, price, place, and promotion. Other stimuli include major forces in the environment: economic, technological, political, cultural, and competitive. These stimuli enter the organization and are turned into buyer responses: product or service choice; supplier choice; order quantities; and delivery, service, and payment terms. In order to design good marketing mix strategies, the marketer must understand what happens within the organization to turn stimuli into purchase responses.

Within the organization, buying activity consists of two major parts: the *buying center*, made up of all the people involved in the buying decision, and the *buying decision process*. The model shows that the buying center and the buying decision process are influenced by internal organizational, interpersonal, and individual factors as well as by external environmental factors.

The model in Figure 5-6 suggests four questions about business buyer behavior: What buying decisions do business buyers make? Who participates in the buying process?

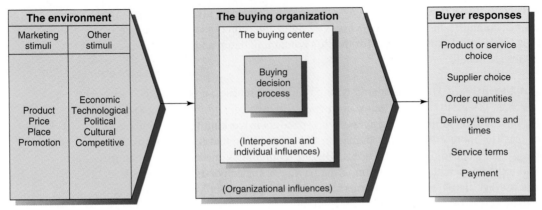

Figure 5-6
A model of business buyer behavior

What are the major influences on buyers? How do business buyers make their buying decisions?

Major Types of Buying Situations There are three major types of buying situations.[26] At one extreme is the **straight rebuy**, which is a fairly routine decision. Based on past buying satisfaction, the buyer's purchasing department simply chooses from the various suppliers on its list and reorders something without any modifications. "In" suppliers try to maintain product and service quality. They often propose automatic reordering systems so that the purchasing agent will save reordering time. "Out" suppliers try to offer something new or exploit dissatisfaction so that the buyer will consider them.

In the middle is a **modified rebuy**, in which the buyer wants to modify product specifications, prices, terms, or suppliers. The modified rebuy usually involves more research and decision participants than the straight rebuy. "In" suppliers may become nervous and feel pressured to put their best foot forward to protect an account. "Out" suppliers may see the modified rebuy situation as an opportunity to make a better offer and gain new business.

At the other extreme is the **new task**, which may call for thorough research. A company buying a product or service for the first time faces a new-task situation. In such cases, the greater the cost or risk, the larger the number of decision participants and the greater their efforts to collect information. The new-task situation is the marketer's greatest opportunity and challenge. The marketer not only tries to reach as many key buying influences as possible but also provides help and information.

Many business buyers prefer to buy a packaged solution to a problem from a single seller. Instead of buying and putting all the components together, the buyer may ask sellers to supply the components *and* assemble the package or system. The sale often goes to the firm that provides the most complete system meeting the customer's needs. Thus, **systems selling** is often a key business marketing strategy for winning and holding accounts.

For example, the Indonesian government requested bids to build a cement factory near Jakarta. An American firm's proposal included choosing the site, designing the cement factory, hiring the construction crews, assembling the materials and equipment, and turning the finished factory over to the Indonesian government. A Japanese firm's proposal included all of these services, plus hiring and training workers to run the factory, exporting the cement through their trading companies, and using the cement to build

Straight rebuy
A business buying situation in which the buyer routinely reorders something without any modifications.

Modified rebuy
A business buying situation in which the buyer wants to modify product specifications, prices, terms, or suppliers.

New task
A business buying situation in which the buyer purchases a product or service for the first time.

Systems selling
Buying a packaged solution to a problem from a single seller thus avoiding all the separate decisions involved in a complex buying situation.

some needed roads and new office buildings in Jakarta. Although the Japanese firm's proposal cost more, it won the contract. Clearly, the Japanese viewed the problem not as just building a cement factory (the narrow view of systems selling) but of running it in a way that would contribute to the country's economy. They took the broadest view of the customer's needs. This is true systems selling.[27]

Participants in the Business Buying Process Who does the buying of the trillions of dollars worth of goods and services needed by business organizations? The decision-making unit of a buying organization is called its **buying center**: all the individuals and units that participate in the business decision-making process. The buying center includes all members of the organization who play a role in the purchase decision process. This group includes the actual users of the product or service, those who make the buying decision, those who influence the buying decision, those who do the actual buying, and those who control buying information.

> **Buying center**
> All the individuals and units that participate in the business buying decision process.

The buying center is not a fixed and formally identified unit within the buying organization. It is a set of buying roles assumed by different people for different purchases. Within the organization, the size and makeup of the buying center will vary for different products and for different buying situations. For some routine purchases, one person—say, a purchasing agent—may assume all the buying center roles. For more complex purchases, the buying center may include 20 or 30 people from different levels and departments in the organization.

The buying center concept presents a major marketing challenge. The business marketer must learn who participates in the decision, each participant's relative influence, and what evaluation criteria each decision participant uses. For example, Baxter International, the large health care products and services company, sells disposable surgical gowns to hospitals. It identifies the hospital personnel involved in this buying decision as the vice-president of purchasing, the operating room administrator, and the surgeons. Each participant plays a different role. The vice-president of purchasing analyzes whether the hospital should buy disposable gowns or reusable gowns. If analysis favors disposable gowns, then the operating room administrator compares competing products and prices and makes a choice. This administrator considers the gown's absorbency, antiseptic quality, design, and cost, and normally buys the brand that meets requirements at the lowest cost. Finally, surgeons affect the decision later by reporting their satisfaction or dissatisfaction with the brand.

The buying center usually includes some obvious participants who are involved formally in the buying decision. For example, the decision to buy a corporate jet will probably involve the company's CEO, chief pilot, a purchasing agent, some legal staff, a member of top management, and others formally charged with the buying decision. It may also involve less obvious, informal participants, some of whom may actually make or strongly affect the buying decision. Sometimes, even the people in the buying center are not aware of all the buying participants. For example, Gulfstream has found that the decision about which corporate jet to buy may be influenced by some not-so-obvious participants:

> Although many people inside the customer company can be influential, the most important influence may turn out to be the CEO's spouse. The typical buyer spends about $4 million to outfit the plane's interior. This covers top-of-the-line stereo sound and video systems, a lavish galley, and a bewildering array of custom-made furnishings. To help with such decisions, many CEOs hire designers and bring their spouses along to planning sessions. As one salesperson notes, "Wives are behind the CEO's decisions on a lot of things, not just airplanes. . . . A crucial

One of the most successful business ads of all time, IBM's "pillow" ad focused not on "objective" buying factors but on the peace of mind that results from doing business with IBM.

moment in a deal comes when the CEO's wife takes off her shoes and starts decorating the plane."[28]

Major Influences on Business Buyers Business buyers are subject to many influences when they make their buying decisions. Some marketers assume that the major influences are economic. They think buyers will favor the supplier who offers the lowest price, or the best product, or the most service. They concentrate on offering strong economic benefits to buyers. However, business buyers actually respond to both economic and personal factors. Far from being cold, calculating, and impersonal, business buyers are human and social as well. They react to both reason and emotion.

Today, most business-to-business marketers recognize that emotion plays an important role in business buying decisions. For example, one of the most successful business ads of all time is IBM's "pillow" ad. The ad's illustration showed only a large pillow with IBM's blue logo imprinted on the pillow cover. "What most people want from a computer service company is a good night's sleep," read the headline. The ad message focused on the peace of mind that results from doing business with IBM in a way that touched readers emotionally.[29]

Figure 5-7 lists various groups of influences on business buyers: environmental, organizational, interpersonal, and individual.[30] *Environmental factors* play a major role. For example, buyer behavior can be heavily influenced by factors in the current and expected

Figure 5-7
Major influences on business buyer behavior

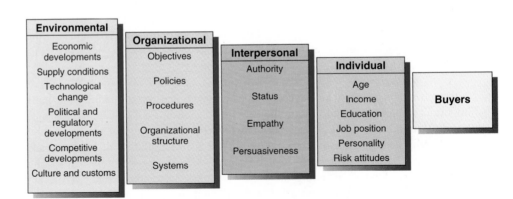

economic environment, such as the level of primary demand, the economic outlook, and the cost of money. Another environmental factor is shortages in key materials. Many companies now are more willing to buy and hold larger inventories of scarce materials to ensure adequate supply. Business buyers also are affected by technological, political, and competitive developments in the environment. Finally, culture and customs can strongly influence business buyer reactions to the marketer's behavior and strategies, especially in the international marketing environment (see Marketing at Work 5-3).

Business buyer behavior is also influenced strongly by *organization factors*. Each buying organization has its own objectives, policies, procedures, structure, and systems, and the business marketer must understand these factors well. Questions such as these arise: How many people are involved in the buying decision? Who are they? What are their evaluative criteria? What are the company's policies and limits on its buyers?

The buying center usually includes many participants who influence each other, so *interpersonal factors* also influence the business buying process. However, it is often difficult to assess such interpersonal factors and group dynamics. As one writer notes, "Managers do not wear tags that say 'decision maker' or 'unimportant person.' The powerful are often invisible, at least to vendor representatives."[31] Nor does the buying center participant with the highest rank always have the most influence. Participants may influence the buying decision because they control rewards and punishments, are well liked, have special expertise, or have a special relationship with other important participants. Interpersonal factors are often very subtle. Whenever possible, business marketers must try to understand these factors and design strategies that take them into account.

Finally, business buyers are influenced by *personal factors*. Each participant in the business buying decision process brings in personal motives, perceptions, and preferences. These individual factors are affected by personal characteristics such as age, income, education, professional identification, personality, and attitudes toward risk. Also, buyers have different buying styles. Some may be technical types who make in-depth analyses of competitive proposals before choosing a supplier. Other buyers may be intuitive negotiators who are adept at pitting the sellers against one another for the best deal.

The Business Buying Process Figure 5-8 shows the eight stages of the business buying process.[32] Buyers who face a new-task buying situation usually go through all stages of the buying process. Buyers making modified or straight rebuys may skip some of the stages. We will examine these steps for the typical new-task buying situation.

PROBLEM RECOGNITION The buying process begins when someone in the company recognizes a problem or need that can be met by acquiring a specific product or service. Problem recognition can result from internal or external stimuli. Internally, the company may decide to launch a new product that requires new production equipment and materials.

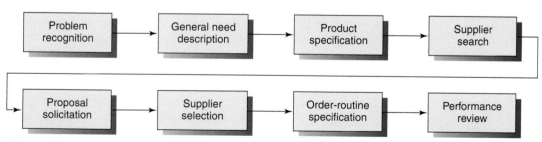

Figure 5-8
Stages of the business buying process

Marketing at Work 5-3

International Marketing Manners: When in Rome, Do as the Romans Do

Picture this: Consolidated Amalgamation, Inc. thinks it's time that the rest of the world enjoyed the same fine products it has offered American consumers for two generations. It dispatches Vice-President Harry E. Slicksmile to Europe to explore the territory. Mr. Slicksmile stops first in London, where he makes short work of some bankers—he rings them up on the phone. He handles Parisians with similar ease: After securing a table at La Tour d'Argent, he greets his luncheon guest, the director of an industrial engineering firm, with the words, "Just call me Harry, Jacques."

In Germany, Mr. Slicksmile is a powerhouse. Whisking through a lavish, state-of-the-art marketing presentation, complete with flip charts and audiovisuals, he shows 'em that this Georgia boy *knows* how to make a buck. Heading on to Milan, Harry strikes up a conversation with the Japanese businessman sitting next to him on the plane. He flips his card onto the guy's tray and, when the two say good-bye, shakes hands warmly and clasps the man's right arm. Later, for his appointment with the owner of an Italian packaging design firm, our hero wears his comfy corduroy sport coat, khaki pants, and Topsiders. Everybody knows Italians are zany and laid back, right?

Wrong. Six months later, Consolidated Amalgamation has nothing to show for the trip but a pile of bills. In Europe, they weren't wild about Harry.

This hypothetical case has been exaggerated for emphasis. Americans are seldom such dolts. But experts say success in international business has a lot to do with knowing the territory and its people. By learning English and extending themselves in other ways, the world's business leaders have met Americans more than halfway. In contrast, Americans too often do little except assume that others will march to their music. "We want things to be 'American' when we travel. Fast. Convenient. Easy. So we become 'ugly Americans' by demanding that others change," says one American world trade expert. "I think more business would be done if we tried harder."

Poor Harry tried, all right, but in all the wrong ways. The British do not, as a rule, make deals over the phone as much as Americans do. It's not so much a "cultural" difference as a difference in approach. A proper Frenchman neither likes instant familiarity—questions about family, church, or alma mater—nor refers to strangers by

---

Or a machine may break down and need new parts. Perhaps a purchasing manager is unhappy with a current supplier's product quality, service, or prices. Externally, the buyer may get some new ideas at a trade show, see an ad, or receive a call from a salesperson who offers a better product or a lower price. In fact, in their advertising, business marketers often alert customers to potential problems and then show how their products provide solutions.

GENERAL NEED DESCRIPTION Having recognized a need, the buyer next prepares a general need description that describes the characteristics and quantity of the needed item. For standard items, this process presents few problems. For complex items, however, the buyer may have to work with others—engineers, users, consultants—to define the item. The team may want to rank the importance of reliability, durability, price, and other attributes desired in the item. In this phase, the alert business marketer can help the buyers define their needs and provide information about the value of different product characteristics.

Value analysis
An approach to cost reduction in which components are studied carefully to determine if they can be redesigned, standardized, or made by less costly methods of production.

PRODUCT SPECIFICATION The buying organization next develops the item's technical product specifications, often with the help of a value analysis engineering team. **Value analysis** is an approach to cost reduction in which components are studied carefully to determine if they can be redesigned, standardized, or made by less costly methods of production. The team decides on the best product characteristics and specifies

their first names. "That poor fellow, Jacques, probably wouldn't show anything, but he'd recoil. He'd *not* be pleased," explains an expert on French business practices. "It's considered poor taste," he continues. "Even after months of business dealings, I'd wait for him or her to make the invitation [to use first names] . . . You are always right, in Europe, to say 'Mister.'"

Harry's flashy presentation would likely have been a flop with the Germans, who dislike overstatement and ostentatiousness. According to one German expert, however, German businessmen have become accustomed to dealing with Americans. Although differences in body language and customs remain, the past 20 years have softened them. "I hugged an American woman at a business meeting last night," he said. "That would be normal in France, but [older] Germans still have difficulty [with the custom]." He says that calling secretaries by their first names would still be

considered rude: "They have a right to be called by the surname. You'd certainly ask—and get—permission first." In Germany, people address each other formally and correctly—someone with two doctorates (which is fairly common) must be referred to as "Herr Doktor Doktor."

When Harry Slicksmile grabbed his new Japanese acquaintance by the arm, the executive probably considered him disrespectful and presumptuous. Japan, like many Asian countries, is a "no-contact culture" in which even shaking hands is a strange experience. Harry made matters worse by tossing his business card. Japanese people revere the business card as an extension of self and as an indicator of rank. They do not *hand* it to people, they *present* it—with both hands. In addition, the Japanese are sticklers about rank. Unlike Americans, they don't heap praise on subordinates in a room; they will praise only the highest-ranking official present.

Hapless Harry's last gaffe was assuming that Italians are like Hollywood's stereotypes of them. The flair for design and style that has characterized Italian culture for centuries is embodied in the businesspeople of Milan and Rome. They dress beautifully and admire flair, but they blanch at garishness or impropriety in others' attire.

Thus, to compete successfully in global markets, or even to deal effectively with international firms in their home markets, companies must help their managers to understand the needs, customs, and cultures of international business buyers. The old advice is still good advice: When in Rome, do as the Romans do.

Sources: Adapted from Susan Harte, "When in Rome, You Should Learn to Do What the Romans Do," *The Atlanta Journal-Constitution*, January 22, 1990, pp. D1, D6. Also see Lufthansa's *Business Travel Guide/Europe*; Sergey Frank, "Global Negotiating," *Sales & Marketing Management*, May 1992, pp. 64–69; Andrea L. Simpson, "Doing Business in Asia Pacific Requires New Skills," *Marketing News*, August 4, 1995, p. 4; and Cynthia Kemper, "Global Sales Success Depends on Cultural Insight," *World Trade*, May 1998, pp. S2–S4.

them accordingly. Sellers, too, can use value analysis as a tool to help secure a new account. By showing buyers a better way to make an object, outside sellers can turn straight rebuy situations into new-task situations that give them a chance to obtain new business.

SUPPLIER SEARCH The buyer now conducts a supplier search to find the best vendors. The buyer can compile a small list of qualified suppliers by reviewing trade directories, doing a computer search, or phoning other companies for recommendations. The newer the buying task, and the more complex and costly the item, the greater the amount of time the buyer will spend searching for suppliers. The supplier's task is to get listed in major directories and build a good reputation in the marketplace. Salespeople should watch for companies in the process of searching for suppliers and make certain that their firm is considered.

Many business buyers go to extremes in searching for and qualifying suppliers. Consider the hurdles that Xerox has set up in qualifying suppliers:

✧ Xerox qualifies only suppliers who meet ISO 9000 international quality standards (see chapter 2). But to win the company's top award—certification status—a supplier must first complete the Xerox Multinational Supplier Quality Survey. The survey requires the supplier to issue a quality assurance manual, adhere to continuous improvement principles, and demonstrate effective systems implementation. Once a supplier has been qualified, it must participate in Xerox's Continuous Supplier Involvement process, in which the two companies work together to create specifications for quality, cost, delivery times, and process capability. The final step toward certification requires a supplier to undergo additional quality training and an evaluation based on the same criteria as the Malcolm Baldrige National Quality

Marketing at Work 5-4
Business-to-Business Buying and the Internet

To most consumers, excitement about Internet buying has focused on Web sites selling computers, software, clothing, books, flowers, or other retail goods. However, consumer goods sales via the Web are dwarfed by the Internet sales of business goods. In fact, some experts predict U.S. business-to-business Internet trade in the hundreds of billions of dollars a year by the turn of the century.

General Electric is among the pioneers in Internet purchasing. In early 1995, GE's Information Services division (GEIS) launched a Web site that allowed buyers in GE's many divisions to purchase industrial products electronically. This Web site let GE buyers snap out requests for bids to thousands of suppliers, who could then respond over the Internet. Such electronic purchasing has saved GE's many divisions money, time, and piles of paperwork. According to a *Forbes* account, here's how it works:

Last month the machinery at a GE Lighting factory in Cleveland broke down. GE Lighting needed custom replacement parts, fast. In the past GE would have asked for bids from just four domestic suppliers. There was just too much hassle getting the paperwork and production-line blueprints together and sent out to [a long list of] suppliers. But this time they posted the specifications and "requests for quotes" on GE's Web site—and drew seven other bidders. The winner was a Hungarian [vendor] . . . that would not

[even] have been contacted in the days of paper purchasing forms. The Hungarian firm's replacement parts arrived quicker, and GE Lighting paid just $320,000, a 20 percent savings.

Within little more than a year, GE's Internet purchasing system had logged more than $350 million worth of purchases by GE divisions, at a 10 percent to 15 percent savings in costs and a five-day reduction in average order time. In 1997, GE purchased $1 billion worth of materials via the Net and by 2000 expects to be buying $5 billion worth, at 20 percent savings over the old way.

Based on its own success, GE opened its on-line procurement services to other companies in the form of the Trading Process Network (TPN) (www.tpn.geis.com). TPN is an on-line purchasing service that lets buyers prepare bids, select suppliers, and post orders to its Web site. Users can select items they wish to buy and use a purchasing card for payment. Once the order is placed, TPN sends a purchase order to a selected supplier or asks for bids from several qualified suppliers. Users of the TPN service have experienced up to a 50 percent reduction in order cycle times, 30 percent reduction in procurement costs, and 20 percent reduction in material costs.

Despite its head start in providing Internet purchasing services, GE will face formidable competition. As noted in *Forbes*:

GEIS has jumped ahead of such companies as IBM, Microsoft, and Netscape to lead the race into business-to-business Internet commerce. The tough part of establishing such a system, says Orville Bailey, who manages GEIS' Internet project, is just getting it started. Buyers don't want to invest in a system unless suppliers are already on board, and vice versa. "It's the classic chicken-or-the-egg problem," says Bailey. [Here, GE's tremendous size gives it] a crucial advantage. GE divisions spend more than $30 billion a year on other companies' goods and services. So when GE announced that it would be soliciting bids over the Internet, even the smallest, most technophobic of its suppliers listened up. Smiles Bailey: "We could build the critical mass" [needed to get the Internet commerce network up and running].

Now, with its own network of industrial goods suppliers already hooked into the system, GE is finding it easy to resell the Internet purchasing technology to other companies that want to handle their purchasing just like GE. For access to its Web [TPN] site, GE Information Services charges buyers an initial fee of $70,000 and an undisclosed annual fee based on volume. Suppliers get to sign on to the system for free.

The first [outside firm] to sign on was Textron Automotive, a subsidiary of the $9.3 billion Textron, Inc. Like GE, Textron Automotive

Award. Not surprisingly, only 176 suppliers worldwide have achieved the 95 percent rating required for certification as a Xerox supplier.[33]

PROPOSAL SOLICITATION In the proposal solicitation stage of the business buying process, the buyer invites qualified suppliers to submit proposals. In response, some suppliers will send only a catalog or a salesperson. However, when the item is complex or expensive,

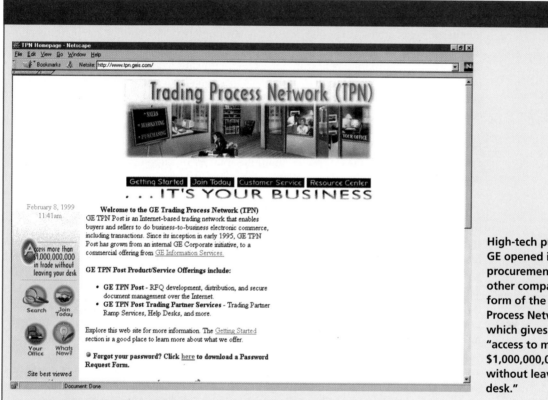

High-tech purchasing: GE opened its on-line procurement services to other companies in the form of the Trading Process Network (TPN), which gives users "access to more than $1,000,000,000 in trade without leaving your desk."

buys a lot of raw materials and components: resin, ashtrays, metal clips, and other parts used in auto dashboards and paneling. By year end, Textron Automotive hopes to place all its orders—more than $500 million a year—over the GE Information Services Web site.

GEIS' Bailey expects various GE units to be buying goods at the rate of $2 billion a year by next year and outside firms like Textron Automotive to be doing another $3 billion or so. If a $134 billion market for business-to-business Internet commerce by the year 2000 does materialize, . . . [GE

estimates that] up to $50 billion of that will move over GE's Internet purchasing system. What of the much-ballyhooed retail Web sites? . . . Those sites will do about $10 billion in 2000. That's one-fifth the potential volume of GE's business goods Web site alone.

Thus, the Internet promises to change dramatically the face of business buying and hence the face of business-to-business marketing. As one expert suggests, "Internet presence is becoming as common as business cards and faxes." To stay

in the game, business-to-business marketers will need a well-thought-out Internet marketing strategy to support their other business marketing efforts.

Sources: Extracts from Scott Woolley, "Double Click for Resin," *Forbes*, March 10, 1997, pp. 132. Also see Kenneth Leung, "Keep This in Mind about Internet Marketing," *Marketing News*, June 23, 1997, p. 7; Clinton Wilder, "Web-Based Purchasing," *Informationweek*, March 24, 1997, pp. 83–84; Dana Blankenhorn, "GE's E-commerce Network Opens Up to Other Marketers," *Advertising Age's Business Marketing*, May 1997, pp. M4, M11; "Consolidated Edison of New York Selects GE's Trading Process Network to Facilitate Internet Sourcing," press release, www.tpn.geis.com, February 10, 1998; Robert D. Hof, "The 'Click Here' Economy," *Business Week*, June 22, 1998, pp. 122–8; and Richard Waugh and Scott Elliff, "Using the Internet of Achieve Improvements at General Electric," *Hospital Material Management Quarterly*, November 1998, pp. 81–83.

the buyer will usually require detailed written proposals or formal presentations from each potential supplier. Business marketers must be skilled in researching, writing, and presenting proposals in response to buyer proposal solicitations. Proposals should be marketing documents, not just technical documents. Presentations should inspire confidence and should make the marketer's company stand out from the competition.

SUPPLIER SELECTION The members of the buying center now review the proposals and select a supplier or suppliers. During supplier selection, the buying center often will draw up a list of the desired supplier attributes and their relative importance. In one survey, purchasing executives listed the following attributes as most important in influencing the relationship between supplier and customer: quality products and services, on-time delivery, ethical corporate behavior, honest communication, and competitive prices. Other important factors include repair and servicing capabilities, technical aid and advice, geographic location, performance history, and reputation.[34] The members of the buying center will rate suppliers against these attributes and identify the best suppliers.

Buyers may attempt to negotiate with preferred suppliers for better prices and terms before making the final selections. In the end, they may select a single supplier or a few suppliers. Many buyers prefer multiple sources of supplies to avoid being totally dependent on one supplier and to allow comparisons of prices and performance of several suppliers over time.

ORDER-ROUTINE SPECIFICATION The buyer now prepares an order-routine specification. It includes the final order with the chosen supplier or suppliers and lists items such as technical specifications, quantity needed, expected time of delivery, return policies, and warranties. In the case of maintenance, repair, and operating items, buyers may use *blanket contracts* rather than periodic purchase orders. A blanket contract creates a long-term relationship in which the supplier promises to resupply the buyer as needed at agreed prices for a set time period. A blanket order eliminates the expensive process of renegotiating a purchase each time that stock is required. It also allows buyers to write more, but smaller, purchase orders, resulting in lower inventory levels and carrying costs. Blanket contracting leads to more single-source buying and to buying more items from that source. This practice locks the supplier in tighter with the buyer and makes it difficult for other suppliers to break in unless the buyer becomes dissatisfied with prices or service.

PERFORMANCE REVIEW In this stage, the buyer reviews supplier performance. The buyer may contact users and ask them to rate their satisfaction. The performance review may lead the buyer to continue, modify, or drop the arrangement. The seller's job is to monitor the same factors used by the buyer to make sure that the seller is giving the expected satisfaction.

We have described the stages that typically would occur in a new-task buying situation. The eight-stage model provides a simple view of the business buying decision process. The actual process is usually much more complex. In the modified rebuy or straight rebuy situation, some of these stages would be compressed or bypassed. Each organization buys in its own way, and each buying situation has unique requirements. Different buying center participants may be involved at different stages of the process. Although certain buying process steps usually do occur, buyers do not always follow them in the same order, and they may add other steps. Often, buyers will repeat certain stages of the process.

During the past few years, advances in technology have had a dramatic impact on the business-to-business marketing process. Increasingly, business buyers are purchasing all kinds of products and services electronically, through electronic data interchange links or on the Internet. Such high-tech purchasing gives buyers access to new suppliers, lowers purchasing costs, and hastens order processing and delivery (see Marketing at Work 5-4). In turn, business marketers are connecting with customers on-line to share marketing information, sell products and services, provide customer-support services, and maintain ongoing customer relationships.

REST STOP Reviewing the Concepts

This chapter is the last of three chapters on analyzing marketing opportunities by looking closely at consumers and their buying behavior. The American consumer market consists of more than 270 million people who consume many trillions of dollars worth of goods and services each year. The business market involves far more dollars and items than the consumer market. Final consumers and business buyers vary greatly in their characteristics and circumstances. Understanding *consumer* and *business buyer behavior* is one of the biggest challenges marketers face.

1. Understand the consumer market and the major factors that influence consumer buyer behavior.

The *consumer market* consists of all the individuals and households who buy or acquire goods and services for personal consumption. A simple stimulus-response model of consumer behavior suggests that marketing stimuli and other major forces enter the consumer's "black box." This black box has two parts: buyer characteristics and the buyer's decision process. Once in the black box, the inputs result in observable buyer responses, such as product choice, brand choice, purchase timing, and purchase amount.

Consumer buyer behavior is influenced by four key sets of buyer characteristics: cultural, social, personal, and psychological. Understanding these factors can help marketers to identify interested buyers and to shape products and appeals to serve consumer needs better. *Culture* is the most basic determinant of a person's wants and behavior. People in different cultural, subcultural, and social class groups have different product and brand preferences. *Social factors,* such as small group and family influences, strongly affect product and brand choices, as do *personal characteristics,* such as age, life-cycle stage, occupation, economic circumstances, lifestyle, and personality. Finally, consumer buying behavior is influenced by four major sets of *psychological factors*: motivation, perception, learning, and beliefs and attitudes. Each of these factors provides a different perspective for understanding the workings of the buyer's black box.

2. Identify and discuss the stages in the buyer decision process.

When making a purchase, the buyer goes through a decision process consisting of need recognition, information search, evaluation of alternatives, purchase decision, and postpurchase behavior. During *need recognition,* the consumer recognizes a problem or need that could be satisfied by a product or service. Once the need is recognized, the consumer moves into the *information search* stage. With information in hand the consumer proceeds to *alternative evaluation* and assesses brands in the choice set. From there, the consumer makes a *purchase decision* and actually buys the product. In the final stage of the buyer decision process, *postpurchase behavior,* the consumer takes action based on satisfaction or dissatisfaction. The marketer's job is to understand the buyer's behavior at each stage and the influences that are operating.

3. Describe the adoption and diffusion process for new products.

The product *adoption process* is comprised of five stages: awareness, interest, evaluation, trial, and adoption. New-product marketers must think about how to help consumers move through these stages. With regard to the *diffusion process* for new products, consumers respond at different rates, depending on consumer and product characteristics. Consumers may be innovators, early adopters, early majority, late majority, or laggards. Each group may require different marketing approaches. Marketers often try to bring their new products to the attention of potential early adopters, especially those who are opinion leaders.

4. Define the business market and identify the major factors that influence business buyer behavior.

The *business market* comprises all organizations that buy goods and services for use in the production of other products and services or for the purpose of reselling or renting them to others at a profit. As compared to consumer markets, business markets usually have fewer, larger buyers who are more geographically concentrated. Business demand is derived demand, and the business buying decision usually involves more, and more professional, buyers.

Business buyers make decisions that vary with the three types of *buying situations*: straight rebuys, modified rebuys, and new tasks. The decision-making unit of a buying organization—the *buying center*—can consist of many different persons playing many different roles. The business marketer needs to know the following: Who are the major buying center participants? In what decisions do they exercise influence and to what degree? What evaluation criteria does each decision participant use? The business marketer also needs to understand the major environmental, organizational, interpersonal, and individual influences on the buying process.

5. List and define the steps in the business buying decision process.

The *business buying decision process* itself can be quite involved, with eight basic stages: problem recognition, general need description, product specification, supplier search, proposal solicitation, supplier selection, order-routine specification, and performance review. Buyers who face a new-task buying situation usually go through all stages of the buying process. Buyers making modified or straight rebuys may skip some of the stages.

Navigating the Key Terms

For a detailed analysis of the meaning and importance of each of the following key terms, visit our Web page at **www.prenhall.com/kotler**.

Adoption process
Attitude
Belief
Business buyer behavior
Buying center

Cognitive dissonance
Consumer buyer behavior
Consumer market
Culture
Derived demand
Groups
Learning
Lifestyle
Modified rebuy
Motive (or drive)

New product
New task
Opinion leaders
Perception
Social class
Straight rebuy
Subculture
Systems selling
Value analysis

Travel Log

The following concept checks and discussion questions will help you to keep track of and apply the concepts you've studied in this chapter.

Concept Checks

1. _____ refers to the buying behavior of final consumers—individuals and households who buy goods and services for personal consumption.

2. _____ are society's relatively permanent and ordered divisions whose members share similar values, interests, and behaviors.

3. People within a reference group who, because of special skills, knowledge, personality, or other characteristics, exert influence on others are called _____ .

4. Lifestyle is a person's pattern of living. It involves measuring a consumer's major *AIO* dimensions

where $A =$ _____ , $I =$ _____ , and $O =$ _____ .

5. Abraham Maslow sought to explain why people are driven by particular needs at particular times. He identified five primary need categories which include _____ needs, _____ needs, _____ needs, _____ needs, and _____ needs.

6. The buyer decision process consists of five stages: _____ , _____ , _____ , _____ , and _____ .

7. Consumers go through five stages in the process of adopting a new product: _____ , _____ , _____ , _____ , and _____ .

8. Five characteristics are especially important in influencing an innovation's rate of adoption.

_____ is the degree to which the innovation appears superior to existing products.

9. There are three major types of business buying situations: _____, _____, and _____.

10. The _____ includes all members of the organization who play a role in the purchase decision process.*

Discussing the Issues

1. List several factors that you could add to the model shown in Figure 5-1 to make it a more complete description of consumer behavior. Explain your ideas and reasoning.

2. In designing the advertising for a soft drink, which would you find more helpful: information about consumer demographics or information about consumer lifestyles? Give examples of how you would use each type of information.

3. For many Americans, changing to a healthier lifestyle might be thought of as an innovation. This might require changes in diet, exercise, smoking, and drinking habits. Discuss this innovation in terms of its relative advantage, compatibility, complexity, divisibility, and communicability. Is a healthy lifestyle likely to be adopted quickly by most Americans? Provide examples of the different adopter groups for acceptance of a healthy lifestyle (see Figure 5-5).

4. Which types of buying situations are represented by the following: (a) Chrysler's purchase of computers that go into cars and adjust engine performance to changing driving conditions, (b) Volkswagen's purchase of spark plugs for its line of vans, and (c) Honda's purchase of light bulbs for a new Acura model.

5. Assume that you are selling fleet cars to be used by a company's sales force. The salespeople want larger, more comfortable cars, which are more profitable for you, but the fleet buyer wants to buy smaller, more economical cars. List who might be in the buying center. Outline how you could meet the varying needs of these participants.

* *Concept check answers:* 1. consumer buyer behavior; 2. social classes; 3. opinion leaders; 4. activities, interests, opinions; 5. physiological, safety, social, esteem, self-actualization; 6. need recognition, information search, evaluation of alternatives, purchase decision, postpurchase behavior; 7. awareness, interest, evaluation, trial, adoption; 8. relative advantage; 9. straight rebuy, modified rebuy, and new-task; 10. buying center.

Traveling the Net

Point of Interest: Values and Lifestyles of Consumers

SRI's Values and Lifestyles Program (VALS) is used by many marketers who wish to understand the psychographics, values, and lifestyles of both existing and potential customers. SRI has categorized Internet users according to iVALS segments, a VALS typology designed for Net users. Companies and advertisers on the Web can use this information to develop their appeals, strategies, and promotions. The philosophy is that consumers purchase products that shape their identities using psychological, physical, demographic, and material resources. Visit SRI at www.future.sri.com and follow the links to the iVALS questionnaire. Take the iVALS survey to determine your type.

For Discussion

1. Into what iVALS were you classified? Do you agree with the assessment? Why or why not?

2. How do the iVALS segments differ from VALS2 segments discussed in this chapter?

3. How can marketers use iVALS information to better serve their consumers? Name five types of products or services for which iVALS information would be particularly useful. Explain your choices.

4. How could advertisers use iVALS or VALS2 information to better communicate with consumers. Find three advertising examples from Web sites or current magazines that you believe are targeted toward specific iVALS or VALS2 segments. Explain your reasoning.

Application Thinking

Are iVALS and VALS2 segments really useful? Most motorcycle companies seem to think so. Over the years, these companies have found that consumers buy motorcycles for many reasons other than just engine performance. Styling, uniqueness, design, prestige, brand loyalty, and ego-enhancement are but a few of the factors considered by would-be buyers. Visit www.honda.com, www.yamaha.com, and www.suzuki.com and develop a grid profiling the iVALS or VALS2 segments that these companies appear to be targeting. How might these segments differ from those targeted by Harley-Davidson (see the chapter-opening example)? Using the profiles you have constructed, discuss how Harley-Davidson (www.harleydavidson.com) might use these classifications to gain market share from its foreign competitors. See if you can find advertisements used by the various companies that might support your thinking. Present your findings to the class.

MAP — Marketing Applications

MAP Stop 5

A woman consumer exclaims, "Wow, it's phenomenal!" The object of her attention is a high-definition TV (HDTV), which is being touted as the biggest break-through in television technology in the past 45 years. The product of a decade's worth of research, HDTV offers more than twice the resolution of today's televisions, a difference as striking as that between black-and-white television and color. However, although HDTV shows vast promise, the revolution looks like it will be a complicated and awkward one. There are several reasons: (a) terribly high initial prices (projected to be $5,500 to $10,000 for the typical set), (b) a lack of initial HDTV programming, (c) uncertainty of mandated "must-carry" Federal legislation concerning networks and local affiliates, and (d) the reluctance of certain market segments to accept change and new technology. However, many consumers may be willing to spend whatever is necessary to have this superior new technology (note the popularity of other forms of digital technology). The challenge facing the industry is how to find and motivate early adopters to accept the new technology and the products that will come from it.

Thinking Like a Marketing Manager

1. If you were the marketing manager for an HDTV manufacturer, how would you find the early adopter market segment? What would you anticipate their demographic characteristics to be?
2. What would be the best way to reach this segment with information about your new generation of televisions? Devise a strategy to get them into retail stores to see your line of new televisions.
3. Once customers visit stores to see the new HDTVs, they are bound to have objections that must be overcome. What might these objections be? Considering the consumer behavior model presented in the chapter, design a strategy for helping retail salespeople to overcome these objections.
4. What do you think will be the future of HDTV? What other products and industries will HDTV technology impact?

Market Segmentation, Targeting, and Positioning for Competitive Advantage

chapter 6

ROAD MAP:
Previewing the Concepts

So far in your marketing journey, you've learned what marketing is and about the complex environments in which it operates. With that as background, you're now ready to travel more deeply into marketing strategy and tactics. This chapter looks further into key marketing strategy decisions: how to divide up markets in meaningful customer groups (market segmentation), choose which customer groups to serve (market targeting), and create marketing offers that best serve targeted customers (positioning). Then, the next eight chapters explore in depth the tactical marketing tools—the four *P*s, —through which marketers bring these strategies to life.

▶ After studying this chapter, you should be able to

1. define the three steps of target marketing: market segmentation, market targeting, and market positioning
2. list and discuss the major levels of market segmentation and bases for segmenting consumer and business markets
3. explain how companies identify attractive market segments and choose a market coverage strategy
4. discuss how companies position their products for maximum competitive advantage in the marketplace

Next stop: Procter & Gamble, one of the world's premier consumer goods companies. Some 99 percent of all U.S. households use at least one P&G brand, and the typical household regularly buys and uses from one to two *dozen* P&G brands. How many P&G products can you name? Why does this superb marketer compete with itself on supermarket shelves by marketing eleven different brands of laundry detergent? The P&G story provides a great example of how smart marketers use segmentation, targeting, and positioning.

Procter & Gamble makes eleven brands of laundry detergent (Tide, Cheer, Bold, Gain, Era, Dash, Oxydol, Solo, Dreft, Ivory Snow, and Ariel). It also sells eight brands of hand soap (Zest, Coast, Ivory, Safeguard, Camay, Oil of Olay, Kirk's and Lava); six shampoos (Prell, Head & Shoulders, Ivory, Pert, Pantene, and Vidal Sassoon); four brands each of liquid dishwashing detergents (Joy, Ivory, Dawn, and Liquid Cascade), toothpaste (Crest, Gleam, Complete, and Denquel), and coffee (Folger's, High Point, Butternut, and Maryland Club); three brands each of floor cleaner (Spic & Span, Top Job, and Mr. Clean) and toilet tissue (Charmin, Banner, and Summit); and two brands each of deodorant (Secret and Sure), cooking oil (Crisco and Puritan), fabric softener (Downy and Bounce), and disposable diapers (Pampers and Luvs). Moreover, many of the brands are offered in several sizes and formulations (for example, you can buy large or small

packages of powdered or liquid Tide in any of three forms—regular, unscented, or with bleach).

These P&G brands compete with one another on the same supermarket shelves. But why would P&G introduce several brands in one category instead of concentrating its resources on a single leading brand? The answer lies in the fact that different people want different *mixes of benefits* from the products they buy. Take laundry detergents as an example. People use laundry detergents to get their clothes clean. But they also want other things from their detergents such as economy, bleaching power, fabric softening, fresh smell, strength or mildness, and lots of suds. We all want *some* of every one of these benefits from our detergent, but we may have different *priorities* for each benefit. To some people, cleaning and bleaching power are most important; to others, fabric softening matters most; still others want a mild, fresh-scented detergent. Thus, there are groups, or segments, of laundry detergent buyers, and each segment seeks a special combination of benefits.

Procter & Gamble has identified at least eleven important laundry detergent segments, along with numerous subsegments, and has developed a different brand designed to meet the special needs of each. The eleven P&G brands are positioned for different segments as follows:

- Tide "helps keep clothes looking like new." It's the all-purpose family detergent that is "tough on greasy stains." Tide with Bleach is "so powerful, it whitens down to the fiber."
- Cheer with Triple Color Guard is the "color expert." It guards against fading, color transfer, and fuzzy build-up. Cheer Free is "dermatologist tested . . . contains no irritating perfume or dye."
- Bold is the detergent with built-in fabric softener. It's "for clean, soft, fresh-smelling clothes." Bold liquid adds "the fresh fabric softener scent."
- Gain, originally P&G's "enzyme" detergent, was repositioned as the detergent that gives you clean, fresh-smelling clothes. It "cleans and freshens like sunshine. It's not just plain clean, it's Gain clean."
- Era has "built-in stain removers." It's "the power tool for stains."
- Dash is P&G's value entry. It "attacks tough dirt," but "Dash does it for a great low price."
- Oxydol contains "stain-seeking bleach." It "combines the cleaning power of detergents with the whitening power of nonchlorine bleach, so your whites sparkle and your clothes look bright." So "don't reach for the bleach — grab a box of Ox!"
- Solo contains detergent and fabric softener in a liquid form. It's targeted heavily toward the Northeast, a strong liquid detergent market.
- Ivory Snow is "Ninety-nine and forty-four one hundredths percent pure." It "gently cleans fine washable and baby clothes . . . leaving them feeling soft." It's "clinically proven to be mild to skin."
- Dreft also "helps remove tough baby stains . . . for a clean you can trust." And, it "doesn't remove the flame resistance of children's sleepware."
- Ariel is a tough cleaner targeted to the Hispanic market. It's also the No. 1 brand in Mexico and P&G's major brand in Europe.

By segmenting the market and having several detergent brands, P&G has an attractive offering for consumers in all important preference groups. All its brands combined capture a nearly 60 percent share of the $4.3 billion U.S. laundry detergent market — two and one-half times that of nearest rival Unilever and much more than any single brand could obtain by itself.[1]

The term *market* has acquired many meanings over the years. In its original meaning, a market is a physical place where buyers and sellers gather to exchange goods and services. Medieval towns had market squares where sellers brought their goods and buyers shopped for goods. In today's cities, buying and selling occur in shopping areas rather than markets. To an economist, a market describes all the buyers and sellers who transact over some good or service. Thus, the soft-drink market consists of sellers such as Coca-Cola and PepsiCo and of all the consumers who buy soft drinks. To a marketer, a **market** is the set of all actual and potential buyers of a product or service.

Market
The set of all actual and potential buyers of a product or service.

Organizations that sell to consumer and business markets recognize that they cannot appeal to all buyers in those markets, or at least not to all buyers in the same way. Buyers are too numerous, too widely scattered, and too varied in their needs and buying practices. Moreover, different companies vary widely in their abilities to serve different segments of the market. Rather than trying to compete in an entire market, sometimes against superior competitors, each company must identify the parts of the market that it can serve best.

Today, most companies are moving from mass marketing. Instead, they practice *market segmentation and targeting* — identifying market segments, selecting one or more

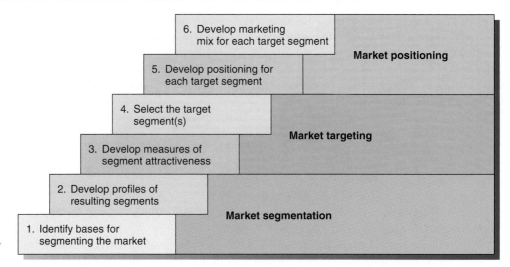

Figure 6-1
Steps in market segmentation, targeting, and positioning

Market segmentation
Dividing a market into distinct groups of buyers on the basis of needs, characteristics, or behavior who might require separate products or marketing mixes.

Market targeting
The process of evaluating each market segment's attractiveness and selecting one or more segments to enter.

Market positioning
Arranging for a product to occupy a clear, distinctive, and desirable place relative to competing products in the minds of target consumers.

of them, and developing products and marketing mixes tailored to each. In this way, sellers can develop the right product for each target market and adjust their prices, distribution channels, and advertising to reach the target market efficiently. Instead of scattering their marketing efforts (the "shotgun" approach), they can focus on the buyers who have greater purchase interest (the "rifle" approach).

Figure 6-1 shows the three major steps in target marketing. The first is **market segmentation**—dividing a market into distinct groups of buyers with different needs, characteristics, or behaviors who might require separate products or marketing mixes. The company identifies different ways to segment the market and develops profiles of the resulting market segments. The second step is **market targeting**—evaluating each market segment's attractiveness and selecting one or more of the market segments to enter. The third step is **market positioning**—setting the competitive positioning for the product and creating a detailed marketing mix. We discuss each of these steps in turn.

Market Segmentation

Markets consist of buyers, and buyers differ in one or more ways. They may differ in their wants, resources, locations, buying attitudes, and buying practices. Through market segmentation, companies divide large, heterogeneous markets into smaller segments that can be reached more efficiently with products and services that match their unique needs. In this section, we discuss five important segmentation topics: levels of market segmentation, segmenting consumer markets, segmenting business markets, segmenting international markets, and requirements for effective segmentation.

Levels of Market Segmentation

Because buyers have unique needs and wants, each buyer is potentially a separate market. Ideally, then, a seller might design a separate marketing program for each buyer. However, although some companies attempt to serve buyers individually, many others face larger numbers of smaller buyers and do not find complete segmentation worthwhile. Instead, they look for broader classes of buyers who differ in their product needs or buying responses. Thus, market segmentation can be carried out at several different levels. Figure 6-2 shows that companies can practice no segmentation (mass marketing), complete segmentation (micromarketing), or something in between (segment marketing or niche marketing).

Mass Marketing Companies have not always practiced target marketing. In fact, for most of this century, major consumer products companies held fast to *mass marketing*— mass producing, mass distributing, and mass promoting about the same product in about the same way to all consumers. Henry Ford epitomized this marketing strategy when he offered the Model T Ford to all buyers; they could have the car "in any color as long as it is black." Similarly, Coca-Cola at one time produced only one drink for the whole market, hoping it would appeal to everyone.

   The traditional argument for mass marketing is that it creates the largest potential market, which leads to the lowest costs, which in turn can translate into either lower prices or higher margins. However, many factors now make mass marketing more difficult. For example, the world's mass markets have slowly splintered into a profusion of smaller segments—the baby boomer segment here, the GenXers there; here the Hispanic market, there the black market; here working women, there single parents; here the Sun Belt, there the Rust Belt. Today, marketers find it very hard to create a single product or program that appeals to all of these diverse groups. The proliferation of advertising media and distribution channels has also made it difficult to practice "one-size-fits-all" marketing:

> [Consumers] . . . have more ways to shop: at giant malls, specialty shops, and superstores; through mail-order catalogs, home shopping networks, and virtual stores on the Internet. And they are bombarded with messages pitched through a growing number of channels: broadcast and narrow-cast television, radio, on-line computer networks, the Internet, telephone services such as fax and telemarketing, and niche magazines and other print media.[2]

   No wonder some have claimed that mass marketing is dying. Not surprisingly, many companies are retreating from mass marketing and turning to segmented marketing.

Segment Marketing A company that practices **segment marketing** recognizes that buyers differ in their needs, perceptions, and buying behaviors. The company tries to isolate broad segments that make up a market and adapts its offers to more closely match the needs of one or more segments. Thus, Marriott markets to a variety of segments— business travelers, families, and others—with packages adapted to their varying needs. GM has designed specific models for different income and age groups. In facts, it sells models for segments with varied *combinations* of age and income. For instance, GM designed its Buick Park Avenue for older, higher-income consumers.

Segment marketing
Isolating broad segments that make up a market and adapting the marketing to match the needs of one or more segments.

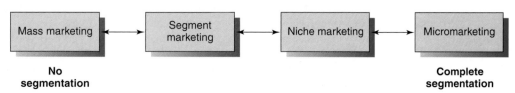

Figure 6-2
Levels of marketing segmentation

Segment Marketing: Marriott markets to a variety of segments with packages adapted to their varying needs. Here it offers the business traveler a "king-sized desk, an ergonomic chair, and outlets and dataports at eye level." For the family traveler, "Together time from Marriott: kids eat and stay free."

Segment marketing offers several benefits over mass marketing. The company can market more efficiently, targeting its products or services, channels, and communications programs toward only consumers that it can serve best. The company can also market more effectively by fine-tuning its products, prices, and programs to the needs of carefully defined segments. And the company may face fewer competitors if fewer competitors are focusing on this market segment.

Niche marketing

Focusing on subsegments or niches with distinctive traits that may seek a special combination of benefits.

Niche Marketing Market segments are normally large, identifiable groups within a market—for example, luxury car buyers, performance car buyers, utility car buyers, and economy car buyers. **Niche marketing** focuses on subgroups within these segments. A *niche* is a more narrowly defined group, usually identified by dividing a segment into subsegments or by defining a group with a distinctive set of traits who may seek a special combination of benefits. For example, the utility vehicles segment might include light-duty pickup trucks and sport utility vehicles (SUVs). And the sport utility vehicles subsegment might be further divided into standard SUV (as served by Ford and Chevrolet) and luxury SUV (as served by Lexus) niches.

Whereas segments are fairly large and normally attract several competitors, niches are smaller and normally attract only one or a few competitors. Niche marketers presumably understand their niches' needs so well that their customers willingly pay a price premium. For example, Ferrari gets a high price for its cars because its loyal buyers feel that no other automobile comes close to offering the product-service-membership benefits that Ferrari does.

Niching offers smaller companies an opportunity to compete by focusing their limited resources on serving niches that may be unimportant to or overlooked by larger competitors. For example, Progressive Corporation, a Cleveland auto insurer, grew rapidly as a result of filling a niche: The company sells "nonstandard" auto insurance to high-risk drivers with a record of auto accidents or drunkenness. Progressive charges a high price for coverage, has made a lot of money, and had the field to itself for several years. However, large companies also practice niche marketing. For example, American Express offers not only its traditional green cards but also gold cards, corporate cards, and even platinum cards aimed at a niche consisting of the top-spending 1 percent of its 36 million cardholders.[3] And Nike makes athletic gear for basketball, running, and soccer but also for smaller niches such as biking and street hockey.

In many markets today, niches are the norm. As an advertising agency executive observed, "There will be no market for products that everybody likes a little, only for products that somebody likes a lot."[4] Other experts assert that companies will have to "niche or be niched."[5]

Micromarketing Segment and niche marketers tailor their offers and marketing programs to meet the needs of various market segments. At the same time, however, they do not customize their offers to each individual customer. Thus, segment marketing and niche marketing fall between the extremes of mass marketing and micromarketing. **Micromarketing** is the practice of tailoring products and marketing programs to suit the tastes of specific individuals and locations. Micromarketing includes *local marketing* and *individual marketing*.

LOCAL MARKETING **Local marketing** involves tailoring brands and promotions to the needs and wants of local customer groups—cities, neighborhoods, and even specific stores. Thus, retailers such as Sears and Wal-Mart routinely customize each store's merchandise and promotions to match its specific clientele, and Citibank provides different mixes of banking services in its branches depending on neighborhood demographics. Kraft helps supermarket chains identify the specific cheese assortments and shelf positioning that will optimize cheese sales in low-income, middle-income, and high-income stores and in different ethnic communities.

Local marketing has some drawbacks. It can drive up manufacturing and marketing costs by reducing economics of scale. It can also create logistical problems as companies try to meet the varied requirements of different regional and local markets. And a brand's overall image might be diluted if the product and message vary in different localities. Still, as companies face increasingly fragmented markets, and as new supporting technologies develop, the advantages of local marketing often outweigh the drawbacks. Local marketing helps a company to market more effectively in the face of pronounced regional and local differences in community demographics and lifestyles. It also meets the needs of the company's first-line customers—retailers—who prefer more fine-tuned product assortments for their neighborhoods.

INDIVIDUAL MARKETING In the extreme, micromarketing becomes **individual marketing**—tailoring products and marketing programs to the needs and preferences of individual customers. Individual marketing has also been labeled "markets-of-one marketing," "customized marketing," and "one-to-one marketing" (see Marketing at Work 6-1).[6] The prevalence of mass marketing has obscured the fact that for centuries consumers were served as individuals: The tailor custom-made the suit, the cobbler designed shoes for the individual, the cabinetmaker made furniture to order. Today, however, new technologies are permitting many companies to return to customized marketing. More powerful

---

Micromarketing
The practice of tailoring products and marketing programs to suit the tastes of specific individuals and locations; includes *local marketing* and *individual marketing*.

Local marketing
Tailoring brands and promotions to the needs and wants of local customer groups—cities, neighborhoods, and even specific stores.

Individual marketing
Tailoring products and marketing programs to the needs and preferences of individual customers—also labeled "markets-of-one marketing," "customized marketing," and "one-to-one marketing."

Marketing at Work 6-1
Markets of One: Customizing the Marketing Offer

Several technologies have converged in recent years to allow companies in a wide range of industries to treat large numbers of customers as unique "markets of one." Advances in computer design, database, interactive communication, and manufacturing technologies have given birth to "mass customization," the process through which firms interact one-to-one with masses of customers to design products and services tailor-made to individual needs. Here are some examples:

Check into any Ritz-Carlton hotel around the world, and you'll be amazed at how well the hotel's employees manage to anticipate your slightest need. Without ever asking, they seem to know that you want a nonsmoking room with a king-size bed, a nonallergenic pillow, and breakfast with decaffeinated coffee in your room. How does the Ritz-Carlton work this magic? Starting with a fervent dedication to satisfying the unique needs of each of its thousands of guests, the hotel employs a system that combines information technology and flexible operations to customize the hotel experience. At the heart of the system is a huge customer database, which contains information about guests gathered through the observations of hotel employees. Each day, hotel staffers—from those at the front desk to those in maintenance and housekeeping—discreetly record the unique habits, likes, and

dislikes of each guest on small "guest preference pads." These observations are then transferred to a corporatewide "guest history database." Every morning, a "guest historian" at each hotel reviews the files of all new arrivals who have previously stayed at a Ritz-Carlton and prepares a list of suggested extra touches that might delight each guest. Guests have responded strongly to such markets-of-one service. Since inaugurating the guest-history system in 1992, the Ritz-Carlton has boosted guest retention by 23 percent. An amazing 95 percent of departing guests report that their stay has been a truly memorable experience.

Peapod, the Chicago-based grocery shopping and delivery service, takes advantage of interactive on-line technology to let customers create the virtual supermarket that best fits their individual needs. Using a personal computer, they can request products by category (baked goods), by item (bread), by brand (Pepperidge Farm), or even by what is on sale that day. Within categories, customers can choose to have items arranged by brand, unit price, package size, or alphabetically. They can also create and save standard and special shopping lists for repeated use, say for breakfast cereals or snack foods. Peapod teaches its customers to shop more efficiently. As

a result, despite paying a monthly service fee, most customers discover that they save money because they do better comparison shopping, use more coupons, and purchase fewer impulse items than if they shopped in a real supermarket. In addition, virtual shopping saves time and is more flexible—consumers can shop from home or work. How much do consumers like shopping in a virtual supermarket? The nation's largest on-line shopping service, Peapod has attracted 75,000 members in seven cities—Atlanta, Boston, Chicago, Dallas, Houston, San Francisco, and Columbus, Ohio. Peapod accounts for 15 percent of the sales volume of the Jewel and Safeway stores in these market areas and has an amazingly high customer retention rate of 80 percent. Andersen Consulting predicts that 15 to 20 million U.S. households will "trade carts for clicks" by the year 2007, creating a $60 billion on-line grocery market.

At Andersen Windows, customers now help design their own windows, whether they're complex, lofty Gothic windows or inches-high miniatures. Previously, as the number of different products offered by Andersen grew from 28,000 in 1985 to 86,000 in 1991, the company's customers—mainly homeowners and building contractors—faced a mind-numbing array of standard win-

computers, detailed databases, robotic production, and immediate and interactive communication media such as e-mail, fax, and the Internet—all have combined to foster "mass customization."[7] *Mass customization* is the ability to prepare on a mass scale individually designed products and communications to meet each customer's requirements.

An example is the National Industrial Bicycle Company in Japan (the Panasonic brand in the United States), which uses flexible manufacturing to turn out large numbers of bikes specially fitted to the needs of individual buyers. Customers visit their local bike

Mass customization: At Andersen Windows, customers now help design their own unique windows, whether complex, lofty Gothic windows, or inches-high miniatures.

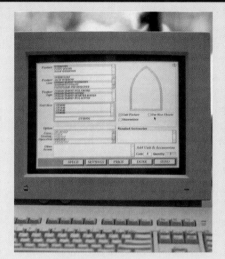

dow choices, displayed in rows of hefty catalogs. Designing a complicated custom treatment—such as an arched window—required advanced design skills and a working knowledge of trigonometry. Preparing a price quote for windows could take several hours, and the quote itself could run as long as 15 pages. One alarming result of this complexity was a rising error rate. By 1991, 20 percent of truckloads of Andersen windows contained at least one discrepancy. Andersen responded by supplying its distributors and retailers with what is essentially an interactive, computerized catalog system called Windows of Knowledge. An industry analyst describes the system: "Using this tool, a salesperson can help customers [select from 50,000 possible window components] and add, change, and strip away features until they've designed a window

they're pleased with. It's akin to playing with building blocks. The computer automatically checks the window specs for structural soundness and then generates a price quote. . . . The retailer's computer transmits each order to [the factory] where it's assigned a unique 'license plate number,' which can be tracked . . . using bar-code technology from the assembly line through to the warehouse." Such "batch-of-one" manufacturing has greatly increased the customer's product selection while at the same time reducing errors. Last year, Andersen offered a whopping 188,000 different products, yet fewer than one in 200 truckloads contained an order problem. Moreover, by making almost everything to order, Andersen has greatly reduced its inventory requirements. Distributors are delighted with the Windows of Knowledge

system. Says one retailer, "It's a terrific tool. It does things that would drive me crazy when I used to have to do them by hand." But the real winners are the homeowners and contractors who get just the windows they want with a minimum of hassle. All this has made Andersen a real markets-of-one advocate. Sums up one executive, "We're on a journey toward purer and purer mass customization."

Sources: B. Joseph Pine II, Don Peppers, and Martha Rogers, "Do You Want to Keep Your Customers Forever?" Harvard Business Review, March–April 1995, pp. 103–14; Christopher W. Hart, "Made to Order," Marketing Management, Summer 1996, pp. 11–22; Justin Martin, "Are You as Good as You Think You Are?" Fortune, September 30, 1996; James H. Gilmore and B. Joseph Pine II, "The Four Faces of Mass Customization," Harvard Business Review, January–February 1997, pp. 91–101; Kim Cleland, "Peapod, Shoppers Express Vie for Online Grocery Business," Advertising Age, June 9, 1997, p. 40; Jennifer Tanaka, "From Soup to Nuts," Newsweek, March 16, 1998, pp. 77–79; Don Peppers, Martha Rogers, and Bob Dorf, "Is Your Company Ready for One-to-One Marketing?" Harvard Business Review, January–February 1999, pp. 151–160; and Don Peppers and Martha Rogers, "The Short Way to Long-Term Relationships," Sales & Marketing Management, May 1999, pp. 24–25.

shop where the shopkeeper measures them on a special frame and faxes the specifications to the factory. At the factory, the measurements are punched into a computer, which creates blueprints in three minutes that would take a draftsman 60 times that long. The computer then guides robots and workers through the production process. The factory is ready to produce any of 18 million variations on 18 bicycle models in 199 color patterns and about as many sizes as there are people. The price is steep—between $545 and $3,200— but within two weeks the buyer is riding a custom-made, one-of-a-kind machine.

Business-to-business marketers are also finding new ways to customize their offerings. For example, ChemStation, a $25 million industrial-detergent company, formulates its cleaning products one by one for customers. It all began when company founder and CEO George Homan realized that, because of varying environments, similar detergents weren't working equally well even for customers in the same industries. To provide the best customer value, he set out to tailor detergents to each customer's specific circumstances. The mass-customization process starts when ChemStation salespeople collect information about a specific customer's cleaning needs, which is then fed into a customer database called the Tank Management System (TMS). Next, a company chemist develops a special "detergent recipe" for the customer, assigns it a number, and enters the formula into the TMS. Then, workers at far-flung plants can simply enter the customer's recipe number into a computer-controlled machine, which mixes up a batch of the special brew. A ChemStation employee delivers the custom-made mixture to a reusable tank that has been installed at the customer's site. The company monitors usage and automatically refills the tank when supplies run low.

The customer knows little about the process; it knows only that ChemStation gives it exactly what it needs. At the same time that the mass-customization system improves customer value and satisfaction, it also reduces costs, resulting in higher margins. Since ChemStation began mass customizing in 1985, cost per customer has fallen nearly 25 percent while gross margins per customer have jumped to nearly 50 percent. Mass customization also helps ChemStation to lock out competitors. The fact that no one—not even the customer—knows what goes into each formula makes it hard for a customer to jump to competitors. "We tell [customers] it's a secret," says Homan. "We're not as protective [about our formulas] as Coca-Cola, but we're close."[8]

The move toward individual marketing mirrors the trend in consumer *self-marketing*. Increasingly, individual customers are taking more responsibility for determining which products and brands to buy. Consider two business buyers with two different purchasing styles. The first sees several salespeople, each trying to persuade him to buy their product. The second sees no salespeople but rather logs onto the Internet; searches for information on and evaluations of available products; interacts electronically with various suppliers, users, and product analysts; and then makes up her own mind about the best offer. The second purchasing agent has taken more responsibility for the buying process, and the marketer has had less influence over her buying decision.

As the trend toward more interactive dialogue and less advertising monologue continues, self-marketing will grow in importance. As more buyers look up consumer reports, join Internet product discussion forums, and place orders via phone or on-line, marketers will have to influence the buying process in new ways. They will need to involve customers more in all phases of the product development and buying processes, increasing opportunities for buyers to practice self-marketing.

According to the chief designer for Mazda, "Customers will want to express their individuality with the products they buy." The opportunities offered by these technologies promise to turn marketing from "a broadcast medium to a dialogue medium," in which the customer participates actively in the design of the product and offer.[9] We will examine the trends toward one-to-one marketing and self-marketing further in chapter 14.

Bases for Segmenting Consumer Markets

There is no single way to segment a market. A marketer has to try different segmentation variables, alone and in combination, to find the best way to view the market structure. Table 6-1 outlines the major variables that might be used in segmenting consumer markets. Here we look at the major *geographic*, *demographic*, *psychographic*, and *behavioral variables*.

Table 6-1   Major Segmentation Variables for Consumer Markets

Geographic	
World region or country	North America, Western Europe, Middle East, Pacific Rim, China, India, Canada, Mexico
Country region	Pacific, Mountain, West North Central, West South Central, East North Central, East South Central, South Atlantic, Middle Atlantic, New England
City or metro size	Under 5,000; 5,000–20,000; 20,000–50,000; 50,000–100,000; 100,000–250,000; 250,000–500,000; 500,000–1,000,000; 1,000,000–4,000,000; 4,000,000 or over
Density	Urban, suburban, rural
Climate	Northern, southern
Demographic	
Age	Under 6, 6–11, 12–19, 20–34, 35–49, 50–64, 65+
Gender	Male, female
Family size	1–2, 3–4, 5+
Family life cycle	Young, single; young married, no children; young, married with children; older, married with children; older, married, no children under 18; older, single; other
Income	Under $10,000; $10,000–$20,000; $20,000–$30,000; $30,000–$50,000; $50,000–$100,000; $100,000 and over
Occupation	Professional and technical; managers, officials, and proprietors; clerical, sales; craftspeople; foremen; operatives; farmers; retired; students; homemakers; unemployed
Education	Grade school or less; some high school; high school graduate; some college; college graduate
Religion	Catholic, Protestant, Jewish, Muslim, Hindu, other
Race	Asian, Hispanic, black, white
Nationality	North American, South American, British, French, German, Italian, Japanese
Psychographic	
Social class	Lower lowers, upper lowers, working class, middle class, upper middles, lower uppers, upper uppers
Lifestyle	Achievers, strivers, strugglers
Personality	Compulsive, gregarious, authoritarian, ambitious
Behavioral	
Occasions	Regular occasion, special occasion
Benefits	Quality, service, economy, convenience, speed
User status	Nonuser, ex-user, potential user, first-time user, regular user
Usage rate	Light user, medium user, heavy user
Loyalty status	None, medium, strong, absolute
Readiness stage	Unaware, aware, informed, interested, desirous, intending to buy
Attitude toward product	Enthusiastic, positive, indifferent, negative, hostile

Geographic Segmentation **Geographic segmentation** calls for dividing the market into different geographical units such as nations, regions, states, counties, cities, or neighborhoods. A company may decide to operate in one or a few geographical areas, or to operate in all areas but pay attention to geographical differences in needs and wants.

Geographic segmentation
Dividing a market into different geographical units such as nations, states, regions, counties, cities, or neighborhoods.

Many companies today are localizing their products, advertising, promotion, and sales efforts to fit the needs of individual regions, cities, and even neighborhoods. For example, Campbell sells Cajun gumbo soup in Louisiana and Mississippi and makes its nacho cheese soup spicier in Texas and California. P&G sells Ariel laundry detergent primarily in Los Angeles, San Diego, San Francisco, Miami, and south Texas—areas with larger concentrations of Hispanic consumers.[10]

Other companies are seeking to cultivate as-yet untapped territory. For example, many large companies are fleeing the fiercely competitive major cities and suburbs to set up shop in small-town America. Hampton Inns has opened a chain of smaller-format motels in towns too small for its standard-sized units. For example, Townsend, Tennessee, with a population of only 329, is small even by small-town standards. But looks can be deceiving. Situated on a heavily traveled and picturesque route between Knoxville and the Smoky Mountains, the village serves both business and vacation travelers. Hampton Inns opened a unit in Townsend and plans to open 100 more in small towns. It costs less to operate in these towns, and the company builds smaller units to match lower volume. The Townsend Hampton Inn, for example has 54 rooms instead of the usual 135.[11] Retailers from Sears to Saks Fifth Avenue are following suit. For example, Saks is implementing a new "Main Street" strategy, opening smaller stores in affluent suburbs and small towns that cannot support full-line Saks stores. Its new store in Greenwich, Connecticut, is less than one-third the size of regular stores found in malls and big cities.[12]

Demographic segmentation
Dividing the market into groups based on demographic variables such as age, sex, family size, family life cycle, income, occupation, education, religion, race, and nationality.

Demographic Segmentation **Demographic segmentation** divides the market into groups based on variables such as age, gender, family size, family life cycle, income, occupation, education, religion, race, and nationality. Demographic factors are the most popular bases for segmenting customer groups. One reason is that consumer needs, wants, and usage rates often vary closely with demographic variables. Another is that demographic variables are easier to measure than most other types of variables. Even when market segments are first defined using other bases, such as personality or behavior, their demographic characteristics must be known in order to assess the size of the target market and to reach it efficiently.

Age and life-cycle segmentation
Dividing a market into different age and life-cycle groups.

AGE AND LIFE-CYCLE STAGE Consumer needs and wants change with age. Some companies use **age and life-cycle segmentation**, offering different products or using different marketing approaches for different age and life-cycle groups. For example, many companies now use different products and appeals to target kids, teens, GenXers, baby boomers, or mature consumers. McDonald's targets children, teens, adults, and seniors with different ads and media. Its ads to teens feature dance-beat music, adventure, and fast-paced cutting from scene to scene; ads to seniors are softer and more sentimental. Procter & Gamble boldly targets its Oil of Olay ProVital subbrand at women over 50 years of age. With the aging of the baby boomers, the 50-plus segment is the fastest growing consumer segment in the United States.

Marketers must be careful to guard against stereotypes when using age and life-cycle segmentation. Although some 70-year-olds require wheelchairs, others play tennis. Similarly, whereas some 40-year-old couples are sending their children off to college, others are just beginning new families. Thus, age is often a poor predictor of a person's life cycle, health, work or family status, needs, and buying power. Companies marketing to mature consumers usually employ positive images and appeals. For example, ads for Oil of Olay ProVital feature attractive older spokeswomen and uplifting messages. "Many women 50 and older have told us that as they age, they feel more confident, wiser, and freer than ever before," observes Olay's marketing director. "These women are redefining beauty." ProVital advertising reflects this positive attitude.[13]

GENDER **Gender segmentation** has long been used in clothing, cosmetics, toiletries, and magazines. For example, although early deodorants were used by both sexes, many producers are now featuring brands for a single sex. Procter & Gamble was among the first with Secret, a brand specially formulated for a woman's chemistry, packaged and advertised to reinforce the female image. Recently, other marketers have noticed opportunities for gender segmentation. For example, Merrill Lynch offers a *Financial Handbook for Women Investors* who want to "shape up their finances." Owens-Corning consciously aimed a major advertising campaign for home insulation at women after its study on women's role in home improvement showed that two-thirds were involved in materials installation, with 13 percent doing it themselves. Half the women surveyed compared themselves to Bob Vila and Tim Allen, while less than half compared themselves to Martha Stewart.[14]

Gender segmentation Dividing a market into different groups based on sex.

The automobile industry also uses gender segmentation extensively. Women buy half of all new cars sold in the United States and influence 80 percent of all new-car purchasing decisions. By the year 2000, women will purchase an estimated 60 percent of all new cars. Thus, women have become a valued target market for the auto companies. "Selling to women should be no different than selling to men," notes one analyst. "But there are subtleties that make a difference."[15] Women have different frames, less upper-body strength, and greater safety concerns. To address these issues, automakers are designing cars with hoods and trunks that are easier to open, seats that are easier to adjust, and seat belts that fit women better. They've also increased their safety focus, emphasizing features such as air bags and remote door locks.

In advertising, more and more car manufacturers are targeting women directly. In contrast to the car advertising of past decades, these ads portray women as competent and knowledgeable consumers who are interested in what a car is all about, not just the color. For example, in one Pontiac ad a savvy young woman brings her brother to a dealership to help her pick a color for her new car. In another, "a woman daydreams about a romantic ride with an attractive male, winding along a coastal highway that brings them to an elegant restaurant. She's driving."[16]

INCOME **Income segmentation** has long been used by the marketers of products and services such as automobiles, boats, clothing, cosmetics, financial services, and travel. Many companies target affluent consumers with luxury goods and convenience services. Stores such as Neiman Marcus pitch everything from expensive jewelry and fine fashions to glazed Australian apricots priced at $20 a pound. Prada's hot-selling black vinyl backpack sells for $450, and a front-row seat at a New York Knicks game at Madison Square Garden goes for $1,000.[17]

Income segmentation Dividing a market into different income groups.

However, not all companies that use income segmentation target the affluent. Despite their lower spending power, the nation's 40 million lower-income households offer an attractive market to many marketers. Many companies, such as Family Dollar stores, profitably target lower-income consumers. When Family Dollar real estate experts scout locations for new stores, they look for lower-middle-class neighborhoods where people wear less-expensive shoes and drive old cars that drip a lot of oil. The typical Family Dollar customer's household earns about $25,000 a year, and the average customer spends only about $8 per trip to the store. Yet the store's low-income strategy has made it one of the most profitable discount chains in the country. Greyhound Lines, with its inexpensive nationwide bus network, also targets lower-income consumers. Almost half of its revenues come from people with annual incomes under $15,000. Chase Manhattan Bank is even opening up accounts for and issuing credit cards to homeless war veterans who live in New York. Some 350 vets have opened accounts with a combined balance of more than $2 million (largely because of lump-sum benefits they receive for injuries).[18]

Psychographic segmentation
Dividing a market into different groups based on social class, lifestyle, or personality characteristics.

Psychographic Segmentation **Psychographic segmentation** divides buyers into different groups based on social class, lifestyle, or personality characteristics. People in the same demographic group can have very different psychographic makeups.

In chapter 5, we described American social classes and showed that social class has a strong effect on preferences in cars, clothes, home furnishings, leisure activities, reading habits, and retailers. Many companies design products or services for specific social classes, building in features that appeal to these classes.

In chapter 5, we also discussed how the products people buy reflect their lifestyles. Marketers are increasingly segmenting their markets by consumer lifestyles. For example, Duck Head apparel targets a casual student lifestyle claiming, "You can't get them old until you get them new." *Redbook* magazine targets a lifestyle segment it calls "*Redbook* Jugglers," defined as 25– to 44–year–old women who must juggle husband, family, home, and job. According to a *Redbook* ad, "She's a product of the 'me generation,' the thirty-something woman who balances home, family, and career–more than any generation before her, she refuses to put her own pleasures aside. She's old enough to know what she wants. And young enough to go after it." According to *Redbook*, this consumer makes an ideal target for marketers of health food and fitness products. She wears out more exercise shoes, swallows more vitamins, drinks more diet soda, and works out more often than do other consumer groups.

Marketers also have used personality variables to segment markets, giving their products personalities that correspond to consumer personalities. Successful market segmentation strategies based on personality have been used for products such as cosmetics, cigarettes, insurance, and liquor.[19]

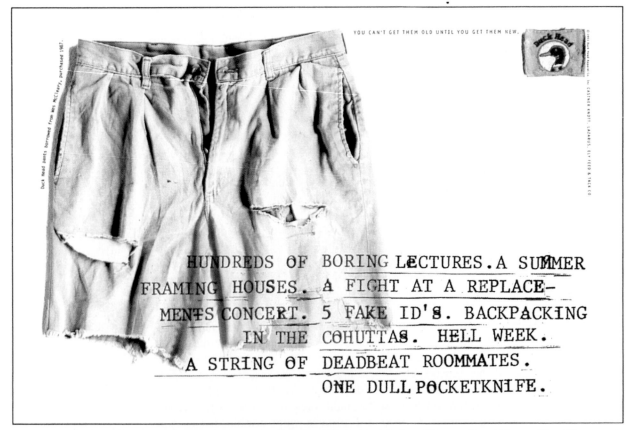

Lifestyle segmentation: Duck Head targets a casual student lifestyle, claiming, "You can't get them old until you get them new."

Honda's marketing campaign for its motor scooters provides a good example of personality segmentation. Honda *appears* to target its Spree, Elite, and Aero motor scooters at hip and trendy 22-year-olds. But it *actually* designs ads geared to a much broader personality group. One ad, for example, shows a delighted child bouncing up and down on his bed while the announcer says, "You've been trying to get there all your life." The ad reminds viewers of the euphoric feelings they got when they broke away from authority and did things their parents told them not to do. It suggests that they can feel that way again by riding a Honda scooter. So even though Honda seems to be targeting young consumers, the ads appeal to trendsetters and independent personalities in all age groups. In fact, more than half of Honda's scooter sales are to young professionals and older buyers—15 percent are purchased by the over-50 group. Honda is appealing to the rebellious, independent kid in all of us. Honda notes on its Web page, "On a Honda scooter, every day is independence day!"[20]

Behavioral Segmentation **Behavioral segmentation** divides buyers into groups based on their knowledge, attitudes, uses, or responses to a product. Many marketers believe that behavior variables are the best starting point for building market segments.

Behavioral segmentation
Dividing a market into groups based on consumer knowledge, attitude, use, or response to a product.

OCCASIONS Buyers can be grouped according to occasions when they get the idea to buy, actually make their purchase, or use the purchased item. **Occasion segmentation** can help firms build up product usage. For example, orange juice is most often consumed at breakfast, but orange growers have promoted drinking orange juice as a cool and refreshing drink at other times of the day. In contrast, Coca-Cola's "Coke in the Morning" advertising campaign attempts to increase Coke consumption by promoting the beverage as an early morning pick-me-up. Some holidays, such as Mother's Day and Father's Day, were originally promoted partly to increase the sale of candy, flowers, cards, and other gifts. And many food marketers prepare special offers and ads for holiday occasions. For example, Beatrice Foods runs special Thanksgiving and Christmas ads for Reddi-wip during November and December, months which account for 30 percent of all whipped cream sales.

Occasion segmentation
Dividing the market into groups according to occasions when buyers get the idea to buy, actually make their purchase, or use the purchased item.

Kodak uses occasion segmentation in designing and marketing its single-use cameras. The customers simply snaps off the roll of pictures and returns the film, camera and all, to be processed. By mixing lenses, film speeds, and accessories, Kodak has developed special versions of the camera for about any picture-taking occasion, from underwater photography to taking baby pictures:

Standing on the edge of the Grand Canyon? [Single-use cameras] can take panoramic, wide-angle shots. Snorkeling? Focus on that flounder with a [different single-use camera]. Sports fans are another target: Kodak now markets a telephoto version with ultrafast . . . film for the stadium set. . . . Planners are looking at a model equipped with a short focal-length lens and fast film requiring less light . . . they figure parents would like . . . to take snapshots of their babies without the disturbing flash. . . . In one Japanese catalog aimed at young women, Kodak sells a package of five pastel-colored cameras . . . including a version with a fish-eye lens to create a rosy, romantic glow.[21]

BENEFITS SOUGHT A powerful form of segmentation is to group buyers according to the different *benefits* that they seek from the product. **Benefit segmentation** requires finding the major benefits people look for in the product class, the kinds of people who look for each benefit, and the major brands that deliver each benefit. For example, one study of the

Benefit segmentation
Dividing the market into groups according to the different benefits that consumers seek from the product.

Occasion segmentation: Beatrice Foods runs special Thanksgiving and Christmas ads for Reddi-wip during November and December, months which account for 30 percent of all whipped cream sales.

Nothing dresses up your traditional holiday desserts like the original taste of Reddi-wip whipped cream.

benefits derived from travel uncovered three major market segments: those who traveled to get away and be with family, those who travel for adventure or educational purposes, and people who enjoy the "gambling" and "fun" aspects of travel.[22]

One of the best examples of benefit segmentation was conducted in the toothpaste market (see Table 6-2). Research found four benefit segments: economic, medicinal, cosmetic, and taste. Each benefit group had special demographic, behavioral and psychographic characteristics. For example, the people seeking to prevent decay tended to have large families, were heavy toothpaste users, and were conservative. Each segment also favored certain brands. Most current brands appeal to one of these segments. For example, Crest toothpaste stresses protection and appeals to the family segment, whereas Aim looks and tastes good and appeals to children.

Companies can use benefit segmentation to clarify the benefit segment to which they are appealing, its characteristics, and the major competing brands. They can also search for new benefits and launch brands that deliver them.

Table 6-2 Benefit Segmentation of the Toothpaste Market

Benefit Segments	Demographics	Behavior	Psychographics	Favored Brands
Economy (low price)	Men	Heavy users	High autonomy, value oriented	Brands on sale
Medicinal (decay prevention)	Large families	Heavy users	Hypochondriac, conservative	Crest
Cosmetic (bright teeth)	Teens, young adults	Smokers	High sociability, active	Aqua-Fresh, Ultra Brite
Taste (good tasting)	Children	Spearmint lovers	High self-involvement, hedonistic	Colgate, Aim

Source: Adapted from Russell I. Haley, "Benefit Segmentation: A Decision Oriented Research Tool," *Journal of Marketing*, July 1963, pp. 30–35. See also Russell I. Haley, "Benefit Segmentation: Backwards and Forwards," *Journal of Advertising Research*, February–March 1984, pp. 19–25.

USER STATUS Markets can be segmented into groups of nonusers, ex-users, potential users, first-time users, and regular users of a product. For example, one study found that blood donors are low in self-esteem, low risk takers, and more highly concerned about their health; nondonors tend to be the opposite on all three dimensions. This suggests that social agencies should use different marketing approaches for keeping current donors and attracting new ones. A company's market position also influences its focus. Market share leaders focus on attracting potential users, whereas smaller firms focus on attracting current users away from the market leader.

USAGE RATE Markets can also be segmented into light, medium, and heavy product users. Heavy users are often a small percentage of the market but account for a high percentage of total consumption. Marketers usually prefer to attract one heavy user to their product or service rather than several light users. For example, a recent study of U.S.-branded ice cream buyers showed that heavy users make up only 18 percent of all buyers but consume 55 percent of all the ice cream sold. On average, these heavy users pack away 13 gallons of ice cream per year versus only 2.4 gallons for light users. Similarly, a travel industry study showed that frequent users of travel agents for vacation travel are more involved, more innovative, more knowledgeable, and more likely to be opinion leaders than less frequent users. Heavy users take more trips and gather more information about vacation travel from newspapers, magazines, books, and travel shows. Clearly, a travel agency would benefit by directing its marketing efforts toward heavy users, perhaps using telemarketing and special promotions.[23]

LOYALTY STATUS A market can also be segmented by consumer loyalty. Consumers can be loyal to brands (Tide), stores (Wal-Mart), and companies (Ford). Buyers can be divided into groups according to their degree of loyalty. Some consumers are completely loyal—they buy one brand all the time. Others are somewhat loyal—they are loyal to two or three brands of a given product or favor one brand while sometimes buying others. Still other buyers show no loyalty to any brand. They either want something different each time they buy or they buy whatever's on sale.

A company can learn a lot by analyzing loyalty patterns in its market. It should start by studying its own loyal customers. Colgate finds that its loyal buyers are more middle class, have larger families, and are more health conscious. These characteristics pinpoint the target market for Colgate. By studying its less-loyal buyers, the company can detect which brands are most competitive with its own. If many Colgate buyers also buy Crest,

Colgate can attempt to improve its positioning against Crest, possibly by using direct-comparison advertising. By looking at customers who are shifting away from its brand, the company can learn about its marketing weaknesses. As for nonloyals, the company may attract them by putting its brand on sale.

Using Multiple Segmentation Bases Marketers rarely limit their segmentation analysis to only one or a few variables. Rather, they are increasingly using multiple segmentation bases in an effort to identify smaller, better-defined target groups. Thus, a bank may not only identify a group of wealthy retired adults but, within that group, distinguish several segments depending on their current income, assets, savings and risk preferences, and lifestyles.

Companies often begin by segmenting their markets using a single base, then expand using other bases. Consider the experiences of Paging Network, Inc. (PageNet), a small paging services provider. PageNet found itself competing with the giant communications companies for the pager market of more than 40 million Americans who now carry the pocket-size gizmos. PageNet couldn't differentiate itself from competitors such as Southwestern Bell and Pacific Telesis by boasting unique technology. Moreover, the company was already competing on price, setting its prices about 20 percent below those of competitors. Thus, PageNet used smart segmentation to boost its competitive advantage.

At first, PageNet used geographic segmentation, targeting easily accessible markets in Ohio and its home state of Texas. In both areas, local competitors were vulnerable to PageNet's aggressive pricing. Once these markets were secure, the company introduced its products into 13 additional geographically dispersed market segments that represented the most growth potential. But PageNet's segmenting strategy didn't end with geography. The small company next developed profiles of major users of paging services and targeted the most promising user groups. Among the primary user groups targeted were salespeople, messengers, and service people.

Flush with success, PageNet set out to capture the largest possible percentage of the total market for pagers. To reach its objective of 75 percent market penetration, PageNet next used lifestyle segmentation to target additional consumer groups, such as parents who leave their babies with sitters, commuters who are out of reach while traveling to and from work, and elderly people living alone whose families want to keep an eye on them.

Looking to broaden its segments even further by reaching larger audiences, PageNet began to distribute its products through the electronics departments of Kmart, Wal-Mart, and Home Depot. It gave these outlets very attractive discounts in return for the right to keep the revenue from the monthly service charges on any pagers sold. With a sales forecast of 80,000 new users, PageNet's managers calculated that the enormous potential revenue from service charges would more than make up for the smaller up-front profits from the discounted products.

The results of this multiple segmentation strategy: PageNet's subscriber base has expanded at a rate of 50 percent annually over the past 10 years. With sales exceeding $800 million, PageNet is now the largest and fastest-growing paging systems and services company in the nation. The company is now expanding its target once again with a service called VoiceNow, which transmits voice messages directly to customers' pagers, turning them into portable answering machines. Explains George Perrin, PageNet's founder and chairman, "We are going after the consumer who wants short bursts of information."[24]

One of the most promising developments in multivariable segmentation is "geo-demographic" segmentation. Several business information services have arisen to help marketing planners link U.S. Census data with lifestyle patterns to better segment their markets down to Zip codes, neighborhoods, and even blocks. Among the leading services are PRIZM by Claritas and ClusterPLUS by Donnelley Marketing Information Services (see Marketing at Work 6-2).

Segmenting Business Markets

Consumer and business marketers use many of the same variables to segment their markets. Business buyers can be segmented geographically or by benefits sought, user status, usage rate, and loyalty status. Yet, business marketers also use some additional variables, such as customer *demographics* (industry, company size), *operating characteristics*, *purchasing approaches*, *situational factors*, and *personal characteristics*.

By going after segments instead of the whole market, companies have a much better chance to deliver value to consumers and to receive maximum rewards for close attention to consumer needs. Thus, Hewlett-Packard's Computer Systems Division targets specific industries that promise the best growth prospects, such as telecommunications and financial services. Its "red team" sales force specializes in developing and serving major customers in these targeted industries.[25]

Within the chosen industry, a company can further segment by *customer size* or *geographic location*. For example, Hewlett-Packard's "blue team" telemarkets to smaller accounts and to those that don't fit neatly into the strategically targeted industries on which H-P focuses. A company might also set up separate systems for dealing with larger or multiple-location customers. For example, Steelcase, a major producer of office furniture, first segments customers into 10 industries, including banking, insurance, and electronics. Next, company salespeople work with independent Steelcase dealers to handle smaller, local, or regional Steelcase customers in each segment. But many national, multiple-location customers, such as Exxon or IBM, have special needs that may reach beyond the scope of individual dealers. So Steelcase uses national accounts managers to help its dealer networks handle its national accounts.

Within a given target industry and customer size, the company can segment by purchase approaches and criteria. As in consumer segmentation, many marketers believe that *buying behavior* and *benefits* provide the best basis for segmenting business markets. For example, a study of the customers of Signode Corporation's industrial packaging division revealed four segments, each seeking a different mix of price and service benefits.[26]

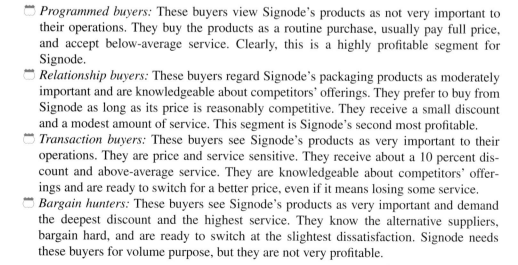

- *Programmed buyers:* These buyers view Signode's products as not very important to their operations. They buy the products as a routine purchase, usually pay full price, and accept below-average service. Clearly, this is a highly profitable segment for Signode.
- *Relationship buyers:* These buyers regard Signode's packaging products as moderately important and are knowledgeable about competitors' offerings. They prefer to buy from Signode as long as its price is reasonably competitive. They receive a small discount and a modest amount of service. This segment is Signode's second most profitable.
- *Transaction buyers:* These buyers see Signode's products as very important to their operations. They are price and service sensitive. They receive about a 10 percent discount and above-average service. They are knowledgeable about competitors' offerings and are ready to switch for a better price, even if it means losing some service.
- *Bargain hunters:* These buyers see Signode's products as very important and demand the deepest discount and the highest service. They know the alternative suppliers, bargain hard, and are ready to switch at the slightest dissatisfaction. Signode needs these buyers for volume purpose, but they are not very profitable.

This segmentation scheme has helped Signode to do a better job of designing marketing strategies that take into account each segment's unique reactions to varying levels of price and service.[27]

Marketing at Work 6-2

Blue Blood Estates to Shotguns & Pickups: Segmenting America's Neighborhoods

Using a host of demographic and socioeconomic factors drawn from the U.S. Census data, the Claritas' PRIZM systems has classified every one of the over 500,000 U.S. neighborhood markets into one of 62 clusters.

You're 35 years old. The price tag on your suits shows that you're a success. You drive a Volvo. You know your way around the olive oil section of the store, buy fresh-ground coffee, and go on scuba-diving trips. You're living out your own, individual version of the good life in the suburbs. You're unique—not some demographic cliche. Wrong. You're a prime example of [PRIZM's] "Kids & Cul-de-Sacs". . . . If you consume, you can't hide from from Zip Code seer Claritas.

The "Kids & Cul-de-Sacs" cluster points to a new migration to the suburbs. Other PRIZM clusters include "Blue Blood Estates," "Money & Brains," "Young Literati," "Shotguns & Pickups," "American Dreams," and "Gray Power." The clusters were formed by manipulating characteristics such as education, income, occupation, family life cycle, housing, ethnicity, and urbanization. For example, "Blue Blood Estates" neighborhoods are suburban areas populated mostly by active, college-educated, successful managers and professionals. They include some of America's wealthiest neighborhoods, areas characterized by low household density, highly homogenous residents, a heavy family orientation, and mostly single-unit housing. In contrast, the "Shotgun & Pickups" cluster includes the hundreds of small villages and four-corners towns that dot America's rural areas. "American Dreams" reflects new waves of American immigrants; "Young Literati" taps Generation X. Each of the other clusters has a unique combination of characteristics.

Companies can combine these geodemographic PRIZM clusters with other data on product and service usage, media usage, and lifestyles to get a better picture of specific market areas. For example, the "Shotguns & Pickups" cluster is populated by lower-middle-class, blue-collar consumers who use chain saws and snuff and buy more canning jars, dried soups, and powdered soft drinks. The "Hispanic Mix" cluster prefers high-quality dresses, nonfilter cigarettes, and lip gloss. People in this cluster are highly brand conscious, quality conscious, and brand loyal. They have a strong family and home orientation.

Such geodemographic segmentation provides a powerful tool for segmenting markets, refining demand estimates, selecting target markets, and shaping promotion messages. For example, one large packaged-goods company used a similar system, Donnelley's Cluster-PLUS, in combination with Nielsen television ratings and data from Simmons Market Research Bureau to more effectively market an ingredient used in baking cakes and cookies. The company first identified the clusters most likely to contain consumers who regularly bake from scratch. According to Simmons data, the top-ranking cluster is "Low-Mobility Rural Families"; 39 percent of this group bake heavily from scratch, far greater than the 17 percent national average. Merging the 10 highest-ranking clusters, the company identified the best prospects as older, rural, and blue-collar consumers in the South and Midwest.

Segmenting International Markets

Few companies have either the resources or the will to operate in all, or even most, of the countries that dot the globe. Although some large companies, such as Coca-Cola or Sony, sell products in as many as 200 countries, most international firms focus on a smaller set. Operating in many countries presents new challenges. The different countries of the world, even those that are close together, can vary dramatically in their economic, cultural, and political makeup. Thus, just as they do within their domestic markets, international firms need to group their world markets into segments with distinct buying needs and behaviors.

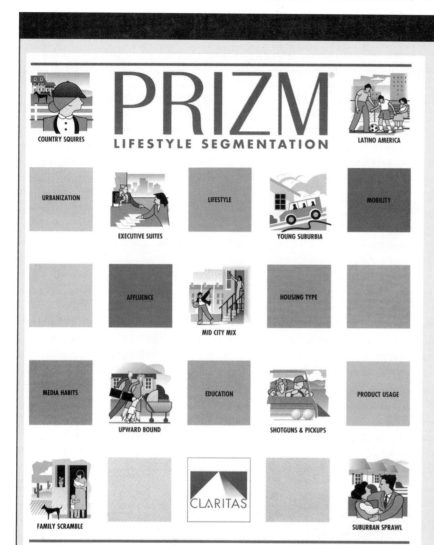

COUNTRY SQUIRES

PRIZM®
LIFESTYLE SEGMENTATION

LATINO AMERICA

URBANIZATION

EXECUTIVE SUITES

LIFESTYLE

YOUNG SUBURBIA

MOBILITY

AFFLUENCE

MID CITY MIX

HOUSING TYPE

MEDIA HABITS

UPWARD BOUND

EDUCATION

SHOTGUNS & PICKUPS

PRODUCT USAGE

FAMILY SCRAMBLE

CLARITAS

SUBURBAN SPRAWL

Using a host of demographic and socioeconomic factors drawn from the U.S. Census data, the PRIZM system has classified every one of the over 500,000 U.S. neighborhood markets into one of 62 clusters.

Next, using Nielsen ratings, the company examined the television viewing habits of the 10 best clusters. It turns out that the from-scratch bakers watch many highly rated programs, but some generally less-popular programs are also popular with this group. The packaged-goods company improved its efficiency by running ads only on programs reaching large concentrations of from-scratch bakers, regardless of the size of the total audience. Thus, the ClusterPLUS–Simmons-Nielsen connection resulted in a basic shift in the company's television advertising, from a mass-media, "shotgun" approach to a more highly targeted one.

Sources: Quote from Christina Del Valle, "They Know Where You Live—And How You Buy," *Business Week,* February 7, 1994, p. 89. Also see Jonathon Marks, "Clusters Plus Nielsen Equals Efficient Marketing," *American Demographics,* September 1991, p. 16; Karen Dempsey, "Up Close and Personal," *Marketing,* direct marketing supplement, July, 11, 1996, pp. III–IV; and Leon G. Schiffman and Leslie Lazar Kanuk, *Consumer Behavior,* 6th ed. (Upper Saddle River, NJ: Prentice Hall, 1997), pp. 66–67 and pp. 392–5.

Companies can segment international markets using one or a combination of several variables. They can segment by *geographic location,* grouping countries by regions such as Western Europe, the Pacific Rim, the Middle East, or Africa. In fact, countries in many regions already have organized geographically into market groups or "free trade zones," such as the European Union, the European Free Trade Association, and the North American Free Trade Association. These associations reduce trade barriers between member countries, creating larger and more homogeneous markets.

Geographic segmentation assumes that nations close to one another will have many common traits and behaviors. Although this is often the case, there are many exceptions. For example, although the United States and Canada have much in common, both differ culturally and economically from neighboring Mexico. Even within a region, consumers can differ widely. For example, many U.S. marketers think that all Central and South American countries are the same, including their 400 million inhabitants. However, the Dominican Republic is no more like Brazil than Italy is like Sweden. Many Latin Americans don't speak Spanish, including 140 million Portuguese-speaking Brazilians and the millions in other countries who speak a variety of Indian dialects.[28]

World markets can be segmented on the basis of *economic factors*. For example, countries might be grouped by population income levels or by their overall level of economic development.[29] Some countries, such as the United States, Britain, France, Germany, Japan, Canada, Italy, and Russia have established, highly industrialized economies. Other countries have newly industrialized or developing economies (Singapore, Taiwan, Korea, Brazil, Mexico). Still others are less developed (China, India). A company's economic structure shapes its population's product and service needs and, therefore, the marketing opportunities it offers.

Countries can be segmented by *political and legal factors* such as the type and stability of government, receptivity to foreign firms, monetary regulations, and the amount of bureaucracy. Such factors can play a crucial role in a company's choice of which countries to enter and how. *Cultural factors* can also be used, grouping markets according to common languages, religions, values and attitudes, customs, and behavioral patterns.

Segmenting international markets on the basis of geographic, economic, political, cultural, and other factors assumes that segments should consist of clusters of countries. However, many companies use a different approach called **intermarket segmentation**. Using this approach, they form segments of consumers who have similar needs and buying behavior even though they are located in different countries. For example, Mercedes-Benz targets the world's well-to-do, regardless of their country. And Pepsi uses ads filled with kids, sports, and rock music to target the world's teenagers. A recent study of more than 6,500 teenagers from 26 countries showed that teens around the world live surprisingly parallel lives. As one expert notes, "From Rio to Rochester, teens can be found enmeshed in much the same regimen: . . . drinking Coke, . . . dining on Big

Intermarket segmentation Forming segments of consumers who have similar needs and buying behavior even though they are located in different countries.

Intermarket segmentation: Teens show surprising similarity no matter where in the world they live. For instance, this young woman could live almost anywhere. Thus, many companies target teenagers with worldwide marketing campaigns.

Macs, surfin' the 'Net on their Macintosh computers. . . . And then there's the international teen uniform: baggy Levi's or Diesel Jeans, T-shirt, Nikes or Doc Martens, and leather jacket."[30] Many companies are targeting teens with globally standardized products and advertisements. For example, Pepsi introduced sugar-free Pepsi Max in 16 countries, including Britain, Australia, and Japan, with a single set of ads aimed at teens who like to live on the wild side.[31]

Requirements for Effective Segmentation

Clearly, there are many ways to segment a market, but not all segmentations are effective. For example, buyers of table salt could be divided into blond and brunette customers. But hair color obviously does not affect the purchase of salt. Furthermore, if all salt buyers bought the same amount of salt each month, believed that all salt is the same, and wanted to pay the same price, the company would not benefit from segmenting this market.

To be useful, market segments must be:

- *Measurable:* The size, purchasing power, and profiles of the segments can be measured. Certain segmentation variables are difficult to measure. For example, there are 32.5 million left-handed people in the United States—almost equaling the entire population of Canada. Yet few products are targeted toward this left-handed segment. The major problem may be that the segment is hard to identity and measure. There are no data on the demographics of lefties, and the U.S. Census Bureau does not keep track of left-handedness in its surveys. Private data companies keep reams of statistics on other demographic segments, but not on left-handers.[32]
- *Accessible:* The market segments can be effectively reached and served. Suppose a fragrance company finds that heavy users of its brand are single men and women who stay out late and socialize a lot. Unless this group lives or shops at certain places and is exposed to certain media, its members will be difficult to reach.
- *Substantial:* The market segments are large or profitable enough to serve. A segment should be the largest possible homogenous group worth pursuing with a tailored marketing program. It would not pay, for example, for an automobile manufacturer to develop cars for persons whose height is less than four feet.
- *Differentiable:* The segments are conceptually distinguishable and respond differently to different marketing mix elements and programs. If married and unmarried women respond similarly to a sale on perfume, they do not constitute separate segments.
- *Actionable:* Effective programs can be designed for attracting and serving the segments. For example, although one small airline identified seven market segments, its staff was too small to develop separate marketing programs for each segment.

Linking the Concepts

Slow down a bit and smell the roses. How do the companies you do business with employ the segmentation concepts you're reading about here?

- Take another look at Figure 6-2. Can you identify specific companies, other than the examples already discussed, that practice each level of segmentation?
- Using the segmentation bases you've just read about, segment the U.S. footwear market. Describe each of the major segments and subsegments. Keep these segments in mind as you read the next section on market targeting.

Market Targeting

Market segmentation reveals the firm's market segment opportunities. The firm now has to evaluate the various segments and decide how many and which ones to target. We now look at how companies evaluate and select target segments.

Evaluating Market Segments

In evaluating different market segments, a firm must look at three factors: segment size and growth, segment structural attractiveness, and company objectives and resources. The company must first collect and analyze data on current segment sales, growth rates, and expected profitability for various segments. It will be interested in segments that have the right size and growth characteristics. But "right size and growth" is a relative matter. The largest, fastest-growing segments are not always the most attractive ones for every company. Smaller companies may lack the skills and resources needed to serve the larger segments or may find these segments too competitive. Such companies may select segments that are smaller and less attractive, in an absolute sense, but that are potentially more profitable for them.

The company also needs to examine major structural factors that affect long-run segment attractiveness.[33] For example, a segment is less attractive if it already contains many strong and aggressive *competitors*. The existence of many actual or potential *substitute products* may limit prices and the profits that can be earned in a segment. The relative *power of buyers* also affects segment attractiveness. Buyers with strong bargaining power relative to sellers will try to force prices down, demand more services, and set competitors against one another—all at the expense of seller profitability. Finally, a segment may be less attractive if it contains *powerful suppliers* who can control prices or reduce the quality or quantity of ordered goods and services.

Even if a segment has the right size and growth and is structurally attractive, the company must consider its own objectives and resources in relation to that segment. Some attractive segments could be dismissed quickly because they do not mesh with the company's long-run objectives. Even if a segment fits the company's objectives, the company must consider whether it possesses the skills and resources it needs to succeed in that segment. Companies should only enter segments in which they can develop competitive advantages. Finally, a segment might be a poor choice from an environmental, political, or social-responsibility viewpoint. For example, in recent years, several companies and industries have been criticized for unfairly targeting vulnerable segments—children, the elderly, low-income minorities, and others—with questionable products or tactics (see Marketing at Work 6-3).

If a segment fits the company's objectives, the company then must decide whether it possesses the skills and resources needed to succeed in that segment. If the company lacks the strengths needed to compete successfully in a segment and cannot readily obtain them, it should not enter the segment. Even if the company possesses the *required* strengths, it needs to employ skills and resources *superior* to those of the competition in order to really win in a market segment. The company should enter segments only in which it can offer superior value and gain advantages over competitors.

Target market
A set of buyers sharing common needs or characteristics that the company decides to serve.

Selecting Market Segments

After evaluating different segments, the company must now decide which and how many segments to serve. This is the problem of *target market selection*. A **target market** consists of a set of buyers who share common needs or characteristics that the company decides to serve. Figure 6-3 shows that the firm can adopt one of three market-coverage strategies: *undifferentiated marketing*, *differentiated marketing*, and *concentrated marketing*.

Undifferentiated Marketing Using an **undifferentiated marketing** strategy, a firm might decide to ignore market segment differences and go after the whole market with one offer. This mass-marketing strategy focuses on what is *common* in the needs of consumers rather than on what is *different*. The company designs a product and a marketing program that will appeal to the largest number of buyers. It relies on mass distribution and mass advertising, and it aims to give the product a superior image in people's minds. An example of undifferentiated marketing is the Hershey Company's marketing some years ago of only one chocolate candy bar for everyone.

> Undifferentiated marketing provides cost economies. The narrow product line keeps down production, inventory, and transportation costs. The undifferentiated advertising program keeps down advertising costs. The absence of segment marketing research and planning lowers the costs of marketing research and product management.

> Most modern marketers, however, have strong doubts about this strategy. Difficulties arise in developing a product or brand that will satisfy all consumers. Firms using undifferentiated marketing typically develop an offer aimed at the largest segments in the market. When several firms do this, heavy competition develops in the largest segments, and less satisfaction results in the smaller ones. The final result is that the larger segments may be less profitable because they attract heavy competition. Recognition of this problem has led firms to be more interested in smaller market segments.

Undifferentiated marketing
A market-coverage strategy in which a firm decides to ignore market segment differences and go after the whole market with one offer.

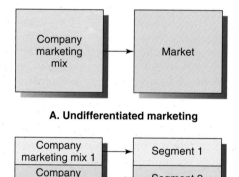

A. Undifferentiated marketing

B. Differentiated marketing

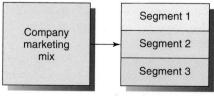

C. Concentrated marketing

Figure 6-3
Three alternative market-coverage strategies

Marketing at Work 6-3
Socially Responsible Market Targeting

Market segmentation and targeting form the core of modern marketing strategy. Smart targeting helps companies to be more efficient and effective by focusing on the segments that they can satisfy best. Targeting also benefits consumers— companies reach specific groups of consumers with offers carefully tailored to satisfy their needs. However, market targeting sometimes generates controversy and concern. Issues usually involve the targeting of vulnerable or disadvantaged consumers with controversial or potentially harmful products.

For example, over the years, the cereal industry has been heavily criticized for its marketing efforts directed toward children. Critics worry that sophisticated advertising, in which high-powered appeals are presented through the mouths of lovable animated characters will overwhelm children's defenses. They claim that toys and other premiums offered with cereals will distract children and make them want a particular cereal for the wrong reasons. All of this, critics fear, will entice children to gobble too much sugared cereal or to eat poorly balanced breakfasts. The marketers of toys and other children's products have been similarly battered, often with good justification. Some critics have even called for a complete ban on advertising to children. Children cannot understand the selling intent of the advertiser, critics reason, so any advertising targeted toward children is inherently unfair. To encourage responsible advertising to children, the Children's Advertising Review Unit, the advertising industry's self-regulatory agency, has published extensive children's advertising guidelines that recognize the special needs of child audiences.

Cigarette, beer, and fast-food marketers also have generated much controversy in recent years by their attempts to target inner-city minority consumers. For example, McDonald's and other chains have drawn criticism for pitching their high-fat, salt-laden fare to low-income, inner-city residents who are much more likely than suburbanites to be heavy consumers. R.J. Reynolds took heavy flak in 1990 when it announced plans to market Uptown, a menthol cigarette targeted toward low-income blacks. It quickly dropped the brand in the face of a loud public outcry and heavy pressure from black leaders. G. Heileman Brewing made a similar mistake with PowerMaster, a potent malt liquor targeted toward the black community. Although the brand seemed to make sense initially, it was ill-fated from the start:

Sales of ordinary beer (3.5 percent alcohol) have slowly been going pfffft for years now, while sales of some higher-proof beers have risen 25 to 30 percent annually. So the decision by G. Heileman Brewing to extend its Colt 45 malt liquor line with PowerMaster, a new high-test malt (5.9 percent alcohol), wasn't [at first glance] dumb.

However, since malt liquor had become the drink of choice among many in the inner city, Heileman focused its marketing efforts for PowerMaster on inner-city blacks. However, this group suffers disproportionately from liver diseases

---

Differentiated marketing
A market-coverage strategy in which a firm decides to target several market segments and designs separate offers for each.

Differentiated Marketing Using a **differentiated marketing** strategy, a firm decides to target several market segments or niches and designs separate offers for each. General Motors tries to produce a car for every "purse, purpose, and personality." Nike offers athletic shoes for a dozen or more different sports, from running, fencing, and aerobics to bicycling and baseball. And Wal-Mart appeals to the needs of different shopper segments with Wal-Mart discount stores, Wal-Mart Supercenters, and Sam's Warehouse stores. By offering product and marketing variations, these companies hope for higher sales and a stronger position within each segment. They hope that a stronger position in several segments will strengthen consumers' overall identification of the company with the product category. They also hope for more loyal purchasing, because the firm's offer better matches each segment's desires.

A growing number of firms have adopted differentiated marketing. Differentiated marketing typically creates more total sales than does undifferentiated marketing. Procter & Gamble gets a higher total market share with 11 brands of laundry detergent than it could with only 1. But differentiated marketing also increases the costs of doing business.

brought on by alcohol, and the inner-city is already plagued by alcohol-related problems such as crime and violence. Thus, Heileman's targeting decision drew substantial criticism.

PowerMaster became a magnet of controversy from the moment it raised its alcohol-enhanced head. Federal officials, industry leaders, black activists, and media types weighed in with protests that PowerMaster . . . was an example of a bad product, bad marketing, and, essentially, a bad idea. . . . [Only] weeks after its planned debut, [PowerMaster] was just a malty memory.

Even some industry insiders objected to the Heileman's targeting tactics. For example, when the PowerMaster controversy erupted, the president of Anheuser-Busch wrote to Heileman's chairman, suggesting that the planned product might indicate "that we put profits before the consideration of the communities we serve."

The meteoric growth of the Internet and other carefully targeted direct media has raised fresh concerns about potential targeting abuses. The Internet allows increasing refinement of audiences and, in turn, more precise targeting. This might help makers of questionable products or deceptive advertisers to more readily victimize the most vulnerable audiences. As one expert observes, "In theory, an audience member could have tailor-made deceptive messages sent directly to his or her computer screen."

Not all attempts to target children, minorities, or other special segments draw such criticism. In fact, most provide benefits to targeted consumers. For example, Colgate-Palmolive's Colgate Junior toothpaste has special features designed to get children to brush longer and more often—it's less foamy, has a milder taste, and contains sparkles, and it exits the tube in a star-shaped column. Golden Ribbon Playthings has developed a highly acclaimed and very successful black character doll named "Huggy Bean" targeted toward minority consumers. Huggy comes with books and toys that connect her with her African heritage. Many cosmetics companies have responded to the special needs of minority segments by adding products specifically designed for black, Hispanic, or Asian women. For example, Maybelline introduced a highly successful line called "Shades of You" targeted to black women, and other companies have followed with their own lines of multicultural products.

Thus, in market targeting, the issue is not really *who* is targeted but rather *how* and for *what*. Controversies arise when marketers attempt to profit at the expense of targeted segments—when they unfairly target vulnerable segments or target them with questionable products or tactics. Socially responsible marketing calls for segmentation and targeting that serve not just the interests of the company but also the interests of those targeted.

Sources: Quotes from "PowerMaster," *Fortune*, January 13, 1992, p. 82, and Herbert Rotfeld, "The FTC and Marketing Abuse," *Marketing News*, March 17, 1997, p. 4. Also see "Selling Sin to Blacks," *Fortune*, October 21, 1991, p. 100; Dorothy J. Gaiter, "Black-Owned Firms Are Catching an Afrocentric Wave," *Wall Street Journal*, January 8, 1992, p. B2; N. Craig Smith and Elizabeth Cooper-Martin, "Ethics and Target Marketing: The Role of Product Harm and Consumer Vulnerability," *Journal of Marketing*, July 1997, pp. 1–20; Joseph Turow, "Breaking Up America: The Dark Side of Target Marketing," *American Demographics*, November 1997, pp. 51–54; Rodman Sims, "When Does Target Marketing Become Exploitation?" *Marketing News*, November 24, 1997, p. 10; and George G. Brenkert, "Marketing to Inner-City Blacks: PowerMaster and Moral Responsibility," *Business Ethics Quarterly*, January 1998, pp. 1–18.

A firm usually finds it more expensive to develop and produce, say 10 units of 10 different products than 100 units of one product. Developing separate marketing plans for the separate segments requires extra marketing research, forecasting, sales analysis, promotion planning, and channel management. And trying to reach different market segments with different advertising increases promotion costs. Thus, the company must weigh increased sales against increased costs when deciding on a differentiated marketing strategy.

Concentrated Marketing A third market-coverage strategy, **concentrated marketing**, is especially appealing when company resources are limited. Instead of going after a small share of a large market, the firm goes after a larger share of one or a few submarkets. For example, Oshkosh Truck is the world's largest producer of airport rescue trucks and front-loading concrete mixers. Recycled Paper Products concentrates on the market for alternative greeting cards. And Soho Natural Sodas concentrates on a narrow segment of the soft-drink market. Here's another example of a highly successful market nicher:

Concentrated marketing
A market-coverage strategy in which a firm goes after a large share of one or a few submarkets.

When the mighty U.S. Fleet edged its way up the Persian Gulf during Operation Desert Storm it was lead by five little plastic boats. The little British Royal Navy Hunt Class MCMVs (Mine Counter-Measure Vessels) were in a league of their own at the dangerous job of clearing a path for the main fleet. They were made by Vosper Thornycroft, a small British company that has mastered the art of niching. Vosper sells specially designed vessels to governments around the world. It now dominates the niche for glass-reinforced plastic (GRP) mine hunters, corvettes, and patrol craft—just the sorts of ships that today's smaller navies want. Vosper's strength extends beyond the vessels it makes. Along with the vessels, Vosper offers maritime training and support services, where they have pioneered computer-based learning. Many clients come from the Middle East and travel with their families, so Vosper has built an Arabic school for 70 students next to its maritime training center. As a result of its successful niching, Vosper's value has increased more than twelvefold during the past ten years.[34]

Concentrated marketing provides an excellent way for small new businesses to get a foothold against larger, more resourceful competitors. For example, Southwest Airlines began by concentrating on serving intrastate, no-frills commuters. PageNet got off to a successful start by concentrating on limited geographic areas. Through concentrated marketing, the firm achieves a strong market position in the segments or niches it serves because of its greater knowledge of the segment's needs and the special reputation it acquires. It also enjoys many operating economies because of specialization in production, distribution, and promotion. If the segment is well chosen, the firm can earn a high rate of return on its investment.

Vosper Thornycroft has mastered the art of niching—it sells specially designed vessels to governments around the world.

At the same time, concentrated marketing involves higher-than-normal risks. The particular market segment can turn sour. Or larger competitors may decide to enter the same segment. For example, California Cooler's success in the wine cooler segment attracted many large competitors, causing the original owners to sell to a larger company that had more marketing resources. For these reasons, many companies prefer to diversify in several market segments.

Rapid advances in computer and communications technology are allowing many large, mass marketers to act more like concentrated marketers. Using detailed customer databases, these marketers segment their mass markets into small groups of like-minded buyers. For example, using home delivery information, Pizza Hut has developed a database containing electronic profiles of the pizza-eating habits of some 9 million customers across the country. It uses this database to develop carefully targeted promotions. In one summer promotion, "Lovers of Neapolitan-style pizza got offers for those, not for thin-crust pizza. Consumers who had been willing to try new foods got a mailing for Bigfoot, a giant-pizza innovation. Customers who had not ordered in a while got deeper discounts than others. [These targeted promotions were] very precise—and very successful."[35]

Choosing a Market-Coverage Strategy Many factors need to be considered when choosing a market-coverage strategy. Which strategy is best depends on *company resources*. When the firm's resources are limited, concentrated marketing makes the most sense. The best strategy also depends on the degree of *product variability*. Undifferentiated marketing is more suited for uniform products such as grapefruit or steel. Products that can vary in design, such as cameras and automobiles, are more suited to differentiation or concentration. The *product's life-cycle stage* also must be considered. When a firm introduces a new product, it is practical to launch only one version, and undifferentiated marketing or concentrated marketing makes the most sense. In the mature stage of the product life cycle, however, differentiated marketing begins to make more sense. Another factor is *market variability*. If most buyers have the same tastes, buy the same amounts, and react the same way to marketing efforts, undifferentiated marketing is appropriate. Finally, *competitors' marketing strategies* are important. When competitors use segmentation, undifferentiated marketing can be suicidal. Conversely, when competitors use undifferentiated marketing, a firm can gain an advantage by using differentiated or concentrated marketing.

Linking the Concepts

Time to coast for a bit and take stock.

- At the last speed bump, you segmented the U.S. footwear market. Now, pick two companies that serve this market and describe their segmentation and targeting strategies. Can you come up with one that targets many different segments versus another that focuses on only one or a few segments?
- How does each company you chose differentiate its marketing offer and image? Has each done a good job of establishing this differentiation in the minds of targeted consumers? The final section in the chapter deals with such positioning issues.

Positioning for Competitive Advantage

Product position
The way the product is defined by consumers on important attributes; the place the product occupies in consumers' minds relative to competing products.

Once a company has decided which segments of the market it will enter, it must decide what positions it wants to occupy in those segments. A **product's position** is the way the product is *defined by consumers* on important attributes—the place the product occupies in consumers' minds relative to competing products. Thus, Tide is positioned as a powerful, all-purpose family detergent; Solo is positioned as a liquid detergent with fabric softener; Ivory Snow is positioned as the gentle detergent for fine washables and baby clothes. In the automobile market, Toyota Tercel and Suburu are positioned on economy, Mercedes and Cadillac on luxury, and Porsche and BMW on performance. Volvo positions powerfully on safety.

Consumers are overloaded with information about products and services. They cannot reevaluate products every time they make a buying decision. To simplify the buying process, consumers organize products into categories—they "position" products, services, and companies in their minds. A product's position is the complex set of perceptions, impressions, and feelings that consumers have for the product compared with competing products. Consumers position products with or without the help of marketers. But marketers do not want to leave their product's positions to chance. They must *plan* positions that will give their products the greatest advantage in selected target markets, and they must design marketing mixes to create these planned positions.

Positioning Strategies

Marketers can follow several positioning strategies. They can position their products on specific *product attributes*—Honda Civic advertises its low price; BMW promotes performance. Products can be positioned on the needs they fill or the *benefits* they offer—Crest reduces cavities; Aim tastes good. Or products can be positioned according to *usage occasions*—in the summer, Gatorade can be positioned as a beverage for replacing athletes' body fluids; in the winter, it can be positioned as the drink to use when the doctor recommends plenty of liquids. Another approach is to position the product for certain classes of *users*—Johnson & Johnson improved the market share for its baby shampoo from 3 percent to 14 percent by repositioning the product as one for adults who wash their hair frequently and need a gentle shampoo.

A product can also be positioned directly *against a competitor*. For example, in its ads, Citibank VISA compares itself directly with American Express by saying, "You'd better take your VISA card, because they don't take American Express." In its famous "We're number two, so we try harder" campaign, Avis successfully positioned itself against the larger Hertz. A product may also be positioned *away from competitors*—for many years, 7-Up has positioned itself as the "un-cola," the fresh and thirst-quenching alternative to Coke and Pepsi. And Barbasol television ads position the company's shaving cream and other products as "great toiletries for a lot less money."

Finally, the product can be positioned for different *product classes*. For example, some margarines are positioned against butter, others against cooking oils. Camay hand soap is positioned with bath oils rather than with soap. Marketers often use a *combination* of these positioning strategies. Arm & Hammer baking soda has been positioned as a deodorizer for refrigerators and garbage disposals (product class *and* usage situation).

Choosing and Implementing a Positioning Strategy

Some firms find it easy to choose their positioning strategy. For example, a firm well known for quality in certain segments will go for this position in a new segment if there

Gas. Food. Lodging. (Last two optional.)

Porche positions on performance: its Boxter "leaves everything else behind. Including primitive urges involving sustenance or shelter."

are enough buyers seeking quality. But in many cases, two or more firms will go after the same position. Then, each will have to find other ways to set itself apart, such as promising "high quality for a lower cost" or "high quality with more technical service." Each firm must differentiate its offer by building a unique bundle of competitive advantages that appeals to a substantial group within the segment.

The positioning task consists of three steps: identifying a set of possible competitive advantages upon which to build a position, selecting the right competitive advantages, and effectively communicating and delivering the chosen position to the market.

Identifying Possible Competitive Advantages Consumers typically choose products and services that give them the greatest value. Thus, the key to winning and keeping customers is to understand their needs and buying processes better than competitors do and to deliver more value. To the extent that a company can position itself as providing superior value to selected target markets, either by offering lower prices or by providing more benefits to justify higher prices, it gains **competitive advantage**. But solid positions cannot be built on empty promises. If a company positions its product as *offering* the best quality and service, it must then *deliver* the promised quality and service. Thus, positioning begins with actually *differentiating* the company's marketing offer so that it will give consumers more value than competitors' offers do. To find points of differentiation, marketers must think through the customer's entire experience with the company's product or service. An alert company can find ways to differentiate itself at every point where it comes in contact with customers.[36]

Competitive advantage An advantage over competitors gained by offering consumers greater value, either through lower prices or by providing more benefits that justify higher prices.

In what specific ways can a company differentiate its offer from those of competitors? A company or market offer can be differentiated along the lines of *product*, *services*, *people*, or *image*.

PRODUCT DIFFERENTIATION Differentiation of physical products takes place along a continuum. At one extreme we find products that allow little variation: chicken, steel, aspirin. Yet even here some meaningful differentiation is possible. For example, Perdue claims that its branded chickens are better—fresher and more tender—and gets a 10 percent price premium based on this differentiation.

At the other extreme are products that can be highly differentiated, such as automobiles, commercial machinery, and furniture. Here the company faces an abundance of design parameters. It can offer a variety of standard or optional *features* not provided by competitors. Thus, Volvo provides new and better safety features; Delta Airlines offers wider seating and free in-flight telephone use. Companies can also differentiate their products on *performance*. Whirlpool designs its dishwasher to run more quietly; Procter & Gamble formulates Liquid Tide to get clothes cleaner. *Style* and *design* can also be important differentiating factors. Thus, many car buyers pay a premium for Jaguar automobiles because of their unique look, even though Jaguar has sometimes had a poor reliability record. Similarly, companies can differentiate their products on such attributes as *consistency*, *durability*, *reliability*, or *repairability*.

SERVICES DIFFERENTIATION In addition to differentiating its physical product, the firm can also differentiate the services that accompany the product. Some companies gain competitive advantage through speedy, convenient, or careful *delivery*. Deluxe, the check supply company, has built an impressive reputation for shipping out replacement checks one day after receiving an order—without being late once in 12 years. And Bank One has opened full-service branches in supermarkets to provide location convenience along with Saturday, Sunday, and weekday-evening hours.

Installation can also differentiate one company from another, as can *repair* services. Many an automobile buyer will gladly pay a little more and travel a little farther to buy a car from a dealer that provides top-notch repair service. Some companies differentiate their offers by providing *customer training* service or *consulting services*—data, information systems, and advising services that buyers need. For example, McKesson Corporation, a major drug wholesaler, consults with its 12,000 independent pharmacists to help them set up accounting, inventory, and computerized ordering systems. By helping its customers compete better, McKesson gains greater customer loyalty and sales.

Companies can find many other ways to add value through differentiated services. Milliken & Company provides a good example. The company sells shop towels to industrial launderers who rent them to factories. These towels are physically similar to competitors' towels, yet Milliken charges a higher price and enjoys the leading market share. How can it charge more for what is essentially a commodity? The answer is that Milliken continuously "decommoditizes" this product through continuous service enhancements. It trains its customers' salespeople, supplies them with prospect leads and sales promotional material, and lends its own salespeople to work on Customer Action Teams. It provides computer order-entry and freight-optimization systems, carries out marketing research for customers, and sponsors quality improvement workshops. Launderers are more than willing to buy Milliken shop towels and pay a premium price because the extra services improve their profitability.[37]

PEOPLE DIFFERENTIATION Companies can gain a strong competitive advantage through hiring and training better people than their competitors do. Thus, Singapore Airlines enjoys an excellent reputation largely because of the grace of its flight attendants. McDonald's people are courteous, IBM people are professional and knowledgeable, and Disney people are friendly and upbeat. The sales forces of such companies as Connecticut General Life and Merck enjoy excellent reputations, which set their companies apart from competitors. Wal-Mart has differentiated its superstores by employing "people greeters" who welcome shoppers, give advice on where to find items, mark merchandise brought for returns or exchanges, and give gifts to children.

People differentiation requires that a company select its customer-contact people carefully and train them well. For example, guests at a Disney theme park quickly learn that every Disney employee is competent, courteous, and friendly. From the hotel check-in agents, to the monorail drivers, to the ride attendants, to the people who sweep Main Street USA, each employee understands the importance of understanding customers, communicating with them clearly and cheerfully, and responding quickly to their requests and problems. Each is carefully trained to "make a dream come true."

IMAGE DIFFERENTIATION Even when competing offers look the same, buyers may perceive a difference based on company or brand images. Thus, companies work to establish *images* that differentiate them from competitors. A company or brand image should convey the product's distinctive benefits and positioning. Developing a strong and distinctive image calls for creativity and hard work. A company cannot plant an image in the public's mind overnight using only a few advertisements. If *Motorola* means *quality*, this image must be supported by everything the company says and does.

Symbols can provide strong company or brand recognition and image differentiation. Companies design signs and logos that provide instant recognition. They associate themselves with objects or characters that symbolize quality or other attributes, such as the McDonald's golden arches, the Prudential rock, or the Pillsbury doughboy. The company might build a brand around a famous person, as Nike did with its Air Jordan basketball shoes. Some companies even become associated with colors, such as IBM (blue), Campbell (red and white), or Kodak (red and yellow).

The chosen symbols must be communicated through advertising that conveys the company's or brand's personality. The ads attempt to establish a storyline, a mood, a performance level—something distinctive about the company or brand. The atmosphere of the physical space in which the organization produces or delivers its products and services can be another powerful image generator. Hyatt hotels have become known for their atrium lobbies and Victoria Station restaurants for their boxcar locations. Thus, a bank that wants to distinguish itself as the "friendly bank" must choose the right building and interior design, layout, colors, materials, and furnishings to reflect these qualities.

Selecting the Right Competitive Advantages
Suppose a company is fortunate enough to discover several potential competitive advantages. It now must choose the ones on which it will build its positioning strategy. It must decide *how many* differences to promote and *which ones.*

HOW MANY DIFFERENCES TO PROMOTE? Many marketers think that companies should aggressively promote only one benefit to the target market. Ad man Rosser Reeves, for example, said a company should develop a *unique selling proposition* (USP) for each brand and stick to it. Each brand should pick an attribute and tout itself as "number one" on that attribute. Buyers tend to remember "number one" better, especially in an overcommunicated society. Thus, Crest toothpaste consistently promotes its anticavity protection, and Volvo promotes safety. What are some of the number-one positions to promote? The major ones are "best quality," "best service," "lowest price," "best value," and "most advanced technology." A company that hammers away at one of these positions and consistently delivers on it probably will become best known and remembered for it.

Other marketers think that companies should position themselves on more than one differentiating factor. This may be necessary if two or more firms are claiming to be best on the same attribute. Steelcase, an office furniture systems company, differentiates itself from competitors on two benefits: best on-time delivery and best installation support.

Today, in a time when the mass market is fragmenting into many small segments, companies are trying to broaden their positioning strategies to appeal to more segments. For example, Lever Brothers introduced the first 3-in-1 bar soap—Lever 2000—offering cleansing, deodorizing, *and* moisturizing benefits. Clearly, many buyers want all three benefits, and the challenge was to convince them that one brand can deliver all three. Judging from Lever 2000's outstanding success, Lever Brothers easily met the challenge. However, as companies increase the number of claims for their brands, they risk disbelief and a loss of clear positioning.

In general, a company needs to avoid three major positioning errors. The first is *underpositioning*—failing to ever really position the company at all. Some companies discover that buyers have only a vague idea of the company or that they do not really know anything special about it. The second error is *overpositioning*—giving buyers too narrow a picture of the company. Thus, a consumer might think that the Steuben glass company makes only fine art glass costing $1,000 and up, when in fact it makes affordable fine glass starting at around $50. Finally, companies must avoid *confused positioning*—leaving buyers with a confused image of a company. For example, Burger King has struggled without success for years to establish a profitable and consistent position. Over the past decade, it has fielded six separate advertising campaigns, with themes ranging

Marketing at Work 6-4
Schott: Positioning for Success

Schott, the German manufacturer of glass for industrial and consumer products, had a problem deciding how to position its innovative product Ceran in the American market. The product, a glass–ceramic material made to cover the cooking surface of electric ranges, seemed to have everything going for it. It was completely nonporous (and thus stain resistant), easy to clean, and long-lasting. Best of all, when one burner was lit, the heat didn't spread; it stayed confined to the circle directly above the burner. And after 10 years, cooktops made of Ceran still looked and performed like new.

Schott anticipated some difficulty igniting demand for Ceran in U.S. markets. First it would have to win over American range manufacturers, who would then have to promote Ceran to middle markets—dealers, designers, architects, and builders. These middle-market customers would, in turn, need to influence final consumers. Thus, Schott's U.S. subsidiary set out to sell Ceran aggressively to its target of 14 North American appliance manufacturers. The subsidiary positioned Ceran on its impressive technical and engineering attributes—showing cross sections of stoves and using plenty of high-tech

talk—then waited optimistically for the orders to roll in. The appliance companies listened politely to the rep's pitch, ordered sample quantities—25 or so of each available color—and then . . . nothing. Absolutely nothing.

Research by Schott's advertising agency revealed two problems. First, Schott had failed to position Ceran at all among the manufacturers' customers. The material was still virtually unknown, not only among final consumers but also among dealers, designers, architects, and builders. Second, the company was attempting to position the product on the wrong benefits. When selecting a rangetop to buy, customers seemed to care less about the sophisticated engineering that went into it and more about its appearance and cleanability. Their biggest questions were, "How does it look?" and "How easy is it to use?"

Based on these findings, Schott repositioned Ceran, shifting emphasis toward the material's inherent beauty and design versatility. And it launched an extensive promotion campaign to communicate the new position to middle-market and final buyers. Advertising to designers and remodelers revolved around lines such as "Formalware for your kitchen," which presented the

black rangetop as streamlined and elegant as a tuxedo. As a follow-up, to persuade designers and remodelers to add Ceran to their palette of materials, Schott positioned Ceran as "More than a rangetop, a means of expression." To reinforce this beauty and design positioning, ads featured visuals, including a geometric grid of a rangetop with one glowing red burner.

In addition to advertising, Schott's agency launched a massive public relations effort that resulted in substantial coverage in home design and remodeling publications. It also produced a video news release featuring Ceran that was picked up by 150 local TV stations nationwide. To reinforce a weak link in the selling chain—appliance salespeople who were poorly equipped to answer customer questions about Ceran—the agency created a video that the salespeople could show customers on the TVs in their own appliance stores.

The now properly and strongly positioned Ceran is selling well. All 14 North American appliance makers are buying production quantities of Ceran and using it in their rangetops. All offer not one, but several smooth-top models. Schott is the major smooth-top supplier in the United States, and smooth tops now account for more

from "Herb the nerd doesn't eat here," and "This is a Burger King town," to "The right food for the right times," to "Sometimes you've got to break the rules" and "BK Tee Vee." This barrage of positioning statements has left consumers confused and Burger King with poor sales and profits. "None of the campaigns dealt with the issue of why a consumer should go to Burger King rather than McDonalds," says one marketing expert.[38]

WHICH DIFFERENCES TO PROMOTE? Not all brand differences are meaningful or worthwhile, not every difference makes a good differentiator. Each difference has the potential to create company costs as well as customer benefits. Therefore, the company must carefully select the ways in which it will distinguish itself from competitors. A difference is worth establishing to the extent that it satisfies the following criteria:

Now properly positioned on their inherent beauty and design versatility, Schott's Ceran cooktops are selling very well.

than 15 percent of the electric stove market. And at a recent Kitchen & Bath Show, 69 percent of all range models on display had smooth tops. Schott recently introduced Ceran-topped portable units as an interesting design alternative to traditional hot plates. Also positioned on aesthetics and ease of cleaning, the tabletop units are rapidly gaining popularity in both residential and commercial markets. To keep up with increasing demand, Schott has built a U.S. plant just to produce Ceran for the North American market.

Source: Adapted from Nancy Arnott, "Heating up Sales: Formalware for Your Kitchen," *Sales & Marketing Management,* June 1994, pp. 77–78. Also see Richard J. Babyak, "Tabletop Cooking," *Appliance Manufacturer,* February 1997, pp. 65–67; and Babyyak, "Different Looks," *Appliance Manufacturer,* January 1998, p. 64.

- *Important:* The difference delivers a highly valued benefit to target buyers.
- *Distinctive:* Competitors do not offer the difference, or the company can offer it in a more distinctive way.
- *Superior:* The difference is superior to other ways that customers might obtain the same benefit.
- *Communicable:* The difference is communicable and visible to buyers.
- *Preemptive:* Competitors cannot easily copy the difference.
- *Affordable:* Buyers can afford to pay for the difference.
- *Profitable:* The company can introduce the difference profitably.

Many companies have introduced differentiations that failed one or more of these tests. The Westin Stamford hotel in Singapore advertises that it is the world's tallest hotel, a distinction that is not important to many tourists—in fact, it turns many off. Polaroid's Polarvision, which produced instantly developed home movies, bombed too. Although Polarvision was distinctive and even preemptive, it was inferior to another way of capturing motion, namely, camcorders. And when Pepsi introduced its clear Crystal Pepsi in 1993, customers were unimpressed. Although the new drink was distinctive, consumers didn't see "clarity" as an important benefit in a soft drink.[39] Thus, choosing competitive advantages upon which to position a product or service can be difficult, yet such choices may be crucial to success (see Marketing at Work 6-4).

Communicating and Delivering the Chosen Position Once it has chosen a position, the company must take strong steps to deliver and communicate the desired position to target consumers. All the company's marketing mix efforts must support the positioning strategy. Positioning the company calls for concrete action, not just talk. If the company decides to build a position on better quality and service, it must first *deliver* that position. Designing the marketing mix—product, price, place, and promotion—essentially involves working out the tactical details of the positioning strategy. Thus, a firm that seizes on a high-quality position knows that it must produce high-quality products, charge a high price, distribute through high-quality dealers, and advertise in high-quality media. It must hire and train more service people, find retailers who have a good reputation for service, and develop sales and advertising messages that broadcast its superior service. This is the only way to build a consistent and believable high-quality, high-service position.

Companies often find it easier to come up with a good positioning strategy than to implement it. Establishing a position or changing one usually takes a long time. In contrast, positions that have taken years to build can quickly be lost. Once a company has built the desired position, it must take care to maintain the position through consistent performance and communication. It must closely monitor and adapt the position over time to match changes in consumer needs and competitors' strategies. However, the company should avoid abrupt changes that might confuse consumers. Instead, a product's position should evolve gradually as it adapts to the ever-changing marketing environment.

REST STOP   Reviewing the Concepts

Time to stop and stretch your legs. In this chapter, you've learned about the major elements of marketing strategy: segmentation, targeting, and posi-tioning. Marketers know that they cannot appeal to all buyers in their markets, or at least not to all buyers in the same way. Buyers are too numerous, too widely scattered, and too varied in their needs and buying practices. Therefore, most companies today are moving away from mass marketing. Instead, they practice *target marketing*—identifying market segments, selecting one or more of them, and developing products and marketing mixes tailored to each. In this way, sellers can develop the right product for each target market and adjust their prices, distribution channels, and advertising to reach the target market efficiently.

1. Define the three steps of target marketing: market segmentation, market targeting, and market positioning.

Market segmentation is the act of dividing a market into distinct groups of buyers with different needs, characteristics, or behavior who might require separate products or marketing mixes. Once the groups have been identified, *market targeting* evaluates each market segment's attractiveness and suggests one or more segments to enter. *Market positioning* consists of setting the competitive positioning for the product and creating a detailed marketing plan.

2. List and discuss the major levels of market segmentation and bases for segmenting consumer and business markets.

Market segmentation can be carried out at several different levels, including no segmentation (mass marketing), complete segmentation (micromarketing), or something in between (segment marketing or niche marketing). *Mass marketing* involves mass producing, mass distributing, and mass promoting about the same product in about the same way to all consumers. Using *segmented marketing*, the company tries to isolate broad segments that make up a market and adapts its offers to more closely match the needs of one or more segments. *Niche marketing* focuses on more narrowly defined subgroups within these segments, groups with distinctive sets of traits that may seek a special combination of benefits. *Micromarketing* is the practice of tailoring products and marketing programs to suit the tastes of specific individuals and locations. Micromarketing includes *local marketing* and *individual marketing*.

There is no single way to segment a market. Therefore, the marketer tries different variables to see which give the best segmentation opportunities. For consumer marketing, the major segmentation variables are geographic, demographic, psychographic, and behavioral. In *geographic segmentation*, the market is divided into different geographical units such as nations, states, re-

gions, counties, cities, or neighborhoods. In *demographic segmentation*, the market is divided into groups based on demographic variables, including age, sex, family size, family life cycle, income, occupation, education, religion, race, and nationality. In *psychographic segmentation*, the market is divided into different groups based on social class, lifestyle, or personality characteristics. In *behavioral segmentation*, the market is divided into groups based on consumers' knowledge, attitudes, uses, or responses to a product.

Business marketers use many of the same variables to segment their markets. But business markets also can be segmented by business consumer *demographics* (industry, company size), *operating characteristics*, *purchasing approaches*, and *personal characteristics*. The effectiveness of segmentation analysis depends on finding segments that are *measurable*, *accessible*, *substantial*, and *actionable*.

3. Explain how companies identify attractive market segments and choose a market-coverage strategy.

To target the best market segments, the company first evaluates each segment's size and growth characteristics, structural attractiveness, and compatibility with company resources and objectives. It then chooses one of three market-coverage strategies. The seller can ignore segment differences (*undifferentiated marketing*), develop different market offers for several segments (*differentiated marketing*), or go after one or a few market segments (*concentrated marketing*). Much depends on company resources, product variability, product life-cycle stage, and competitive marketing strategies.

4. Discuss how companies can position their products for maximum competitive advantage in the marketplace.

Once a company has decided which segments to enter, it must decide on its *market positioning strategy*—on which positions to occupy in its chosen segments. It can position its products on specific *product attributes*, according to *usage occasion*, for certain *classes of users*, or by *product class*. It can position either against or away from competitors. The positioning task consists of three steps: identifying a set of possible competitive advantages upon which to build a position, selecting the right competitive advantages, and effectively communicating and delivering the chosen position to the market.

Navigating the Key Terms

For a detailed analysis of the meaning and importance of each of the following key terms, visit our Web page at **www.prenhall.com/kotler**

Age and life-cycle segmentation
Behavioral segmentation
Benefit segmentation
Competitive advantage
Concentrated marketing

Demographic segmentation
Differentiated marketing
Gender segmentation
Geographic segmentation
Income segmentation
Individual marketing
Intermarket segmentation
Local marketing
Market
Market positioning

Market segmentation
Market targeting
Micromarketing
Niche marketing
Occasion segmentation
Product position
Psychographic segmentation
Segment marketing
Target market
Undifferentiated marketing

Travel Log

The following concept checks and discussion questions will help you to keep track of and apply the concepts you've studied in this chapter.

Concept Checks

1. To a marketer, a _____ is the set of all actual and potential buyers of a product or service.
2. According to the chapter, the three major steps in target marketing are _____, _____, and _____.
3. The following statements symbolize which levels of market segmentation: (a) Henry Ford offered Model Ts to customers "in any color as long as it was black": _____; (b) GM has designed specific models of cars for different income and age groups: _____; (c) An auto insurance company sells nonstandard auto insurance to high-risk drivers with a record of auto accidents or drunkenness: _____; (d) A microbrewery tailors its products and marketing programs to suit the tastes of specific locations: _____.
4. The major variables that might be used in segmenting consumer markets include _____, _____, _____, and _____ variables.
5. _____ segmentation divides the market into groups based on variables such as age, gender,

family size, family life cycle, income, occupation, education, religion, race, and nationality.
6. _____ segmentation has long been used in clothing, cosmetics, toiletries, and magazines.
7. For market segmentation to be useful, market segments must be _____, _____, _____, _____, and _____.
8. A _____ consists of a set of buyers who share common needs or characteristics that the company decides to serve.
9. Using a _____ marketing strategy, a firm decides to target several market segments or niches and designs separate offers for each.
10. A company can differentiate its offer from those of competitors along the lines of _____, _____, _____, or _____.*

Discussing the Issues

1. Describe how the Ford Motor Company has moved from mass marketing to segment marketing. Do you think the company will be able to move toward niche marketing or micromarketing? If so, how? How is the company using the Internet (see www.ford.com) to change its marketing segmentation approach.
2. Several years ago, Samuel Adams Brewery led a charge of "microbreweries" in an attack on the

established brewers' domestic beers. What is micromarketing and how might it have been used by these "microbreweries"? Evaluate the strategy.

3. There are many ways to segment a market. However, not all segmentations are effective. Using the five factors necessary for segment usefulness or effectiveness (as mentioned in the text), determine the attractiveness of (a) Internet users, (b) pager owners, and (c) the adult student who returns to college to get an undergraduate degree. Explain how you determined the attractiveness of each potential segment.

4. In 1994, before the Internet became "the master of a generation's universe," Netscape was just another Silicon Valley start-up. However, as the Internet has grown, Netscape's position has changed dramatically. Which of the market-coverage strategies described in the chapter would you choose for Netscape? What is the market-coverage strategy of archrival Microsoft? Explain why you think your market-coverage strategy is the best for Netscape.

5. Collect advertisements that demonstrate the positioning of different automobile brands. Sort the various brands into categories of brands with similar positions. Do the advertised positions match your perceptions of where each brand belongs?

* Concept check answers: 1. market; 2. market segmentation, market targeting, and market positioning; 3. mass marketing, segment marketing, niche marketing, and micromarketing; 4. geographic, demographic, psychographic, and behavioral; 5. demographic; 6. gender; 7. measurable, accessible, substantial, differentiable, actionable; 8. target market; 9. differentiated; 10. product, services, people, or image.

Traveling the Net

Point of Interest: Gender- and Age-Based Market Segments

Marketers often use gender and age as a two-pronged basis for demographic segmentation. With respect to gender, the obvious division is between males and females. Age can be used to further subdivide a specific gender group into either generations (such as Generation Xers) or specific age categories (such as kids, teens, young adults, and seniors). Many companies use specific marketing mixes to appeal directly to either of the gender divisions and then specifically to an age category within the gender classification. One company that seems to specialize in gender- and age-based marketing is Mattel, a $4.8 billion toy powerhouse. Within the company's numerous product lines, one product line dominates—Barbie dolls. On average, the company sells three Barbie dolls every second. Mattel has bet its financial future on Barbie. Go to the Barbie Web site at www.barbie.com and examine the extensive line of products and the marketing strategies used by the company to appeal to young female consumers.

For Discussion

1. What other demographic segmentation approaches did you find in the strategy presented on Mattel's Barbie Web site? Does the company seem to be doing anything to move away from a strictly young-female gender segmentation approach?

2. Is there any evidence on the Web site of psychographic or behavioral market segmentation? Support your conclusions.

3. Click on the "New Friends" icon. Comment on how the company is using micromarketing techniques. Do you think the "New Friends" category gives Mattel a competitive advantage over competitors?

4. Put yourself into the role of being a young female with an interest in collecting dolls. What do you think are the strongest visual strengths of this Web site? What appear to be the primary weaknesses (if any)?

Application Thinking

Many marketers have found the leap from gender and age segmentation to more complex categories of psychographic and behavioral segmentation challenging and difficult. However, Mattel's CEO Jill Barad believes that refined segmentation is worth the effort. She once commented (with respect to little girls' feelings about Barbie dolls) that a Barbie doll was for dreaming and imagining what life can be. Go to the Barbie Web site and assess how Mattel has matched psychographic and behavioral segmentation to gender- and age-based segmentation. Describe and construct profiles for the several market segments that the company is attempting to penetrate. Try to incorporate psychographic and behavioral variables in your profiles. (For additional information on the toy industry, see the Hasbro, Kenner, and Tyco Web sites.)

MAP — Marketing Applications

MAP Stop 6

Recent events suggest that marketers are increasingly moving beyond demographics in their segmentation efforts. Demographics have not been replaced but have instead been merged with psychographic and behavioral variables. For example, companies today appear to be tailoring their strategies, products, and promotions to two tiers of American consumers. Some call this the "Tiffany/Wal-Mart" approach. In automobiles, several General Motors divisions are selling record numbers of new SUVs to "upscale" consumers (those seeking more features at higher prices). At the same time, GM's Saturn division is selling record numbers of pre-owned cars to "downscale" consumers (those seeking value at low cost). In clothing, Gap's Banana Republic stores sell "upscale" jeans for $50 or more, whereas its Old Navy stores sell "value" jeans for $20 or less. Other examples of a two-tier standard include growth of both "used" and "new" clothing stores and growth in the numbers of both public telephones and more "upscale" cell phones. During the past decade, marketers have seen the wealthiest 5 percent of consumers grow richer while the average American's income has remained relatively stagnant.

Thinking Like a Marketing Manager

1. What other examples of two-tier marketing can you find?
2. How does a two-tier (upscale versus downscale) consumer economy affect a marketing manager's marketing strategy?
3. What geographic, demographic, psychographic, or behavioral variables would be most important in designing appeals for the "upscale" and "downscale" markets found in a two-tier economy?
4. Assume that you are the marketing manager for a (a) Wal-Mart store, (b) Barnes and Noble bookstore, and (c) a Sears. For each store, design a marketing strategy for bringing (a) "upscale" consumers, (b) "downscale" consumers, (c) or both into your store. Can strategies for these two distinctly different markets coexist for each of these stores? Explain.

chapter 7

Product and Services Strategy

ROAD MAP:
Previewing the Concepts

Now that you've had a good look at marketing strategy, we'll journey on into the marketing mix—the tactical tools that marketers use to implement their strategies. In this and the next chapter, we'll study how companies develop and manage products. Then, in the chapters that follow, we'll look at pricing, distribution, and marketing communication tools. The product is usually the first and most basic marketing consideration. How well firms manage their individual brands and their overall product and service offerings has a major impact on their success in the marketplace. We'll start with a seemingly simple question: What *is* a product? As it turns out, however, the answer is not so simple.

▶ **After studying this chapter, you should be able to**

1. define *product* and the major classifications of products and services
2. describe the roles of product and service branding, packaging, labeling, and product support services
3. explain the decisions companies make when developing product lines and mixes
4. identify the four characteristics that affect the marketing of a service
5. discuss the additional marketing considerations for services

First stop on this leg of the journey: Revlon fragrances. Remember that seemingly simple question—what is a product? The Revlon example shows why there is no easy answer. What, really, *is* perfume? Revlon knows that when a woman buys perfume, she buys much, much more than a scented liquid in a fancy bottle.

Each year, Revlon sells more than $2.4 billion worth of cosmetics, toiletries, and fragrances to consumers around the world. In one sense, Revlon's perfumes are no more than careful mixtures of oils and chemicals that have nice scents. But Revlon knows that when it sells perfume, it sells much more than fragrant fluids—it sells what the fragrances can do for the women who use them.

Of course, a perfume's scent contributes to its success or failure. Fragrance marketers agree, "No smell; no sell." Most new aromas are developed by elite perfumers at one of many select fragrance houses. Perfume is shipped from the fragrance houses in big, ugly drums—hardly the stuff of which dreams are made! Although a $180-an-ounce perfume may cost no more than $10 to produce, to perfume consumers the product is much more than a few dollars worth of ingredients and a pleasing smell.

Many things beyond the ingredients and scent add to a perfume's allure. In fact, when Revlon designs a new perfume, the scent may be the *last* element developed. Revlon first researches women's feelings about themselves and their relationships with others. It then develops and tests new perfume concepts that match women's changing

values, desires, and lifestyles. When Revlon finds a promising new concept, it creates and names a scent to fit the idea. Revlon's research in the early 1970s showed that women were feeling more competitive with men and that they were striving to find individual identities. For this new woman of the 1970s, Revlon created Charlie, the first of the "lifestyle" perfumes. Thousands of women adopted Charlie as a bold statement of independence, and it quickly became the world's best-selling perfume.

In the late 1970s, Revlon research showed a shift in women's attitudes—"women had made the equality point, which Charlie addressed. Now women were hungering for an expression of femininity." The Charlie girls had grown up; they now wanted perfumes that were subtle rather than shocking. Thus, Revlon subtly shifted Charlie's position: The perfume still made its "independent lifestyle" statement but with an added tinge of "femininity and romance." For the woman of the 1990s, Revlon again refined Charlie's positioning, targeting the woman who was "able to do it all, but smart enough to know what she wants to do."

Going into the new millennium, Revlon now offers Charlie in four versions, each positioned for a specific mood or moment. The original Charlie is "the original rebel—a fragrance that makes you want to go out and change the world." Three brand extensions build on Charlie's seemingly ageless heritage. Charlie White is "the romantic

Charlie—wear it and guys worship the ground you walk on." Charlie Red is "a couple of degrees hotter—when you want to get their attention, wear red." Charlie Sunshine broadens the brand's appeal with a perky positioning targeting younger consumers— "Have fun. Believe in yourself. And feel the sunshine every day!" After 25 years, aided by continuous but subtle repositioning, Charlie remains a best-selling mass-market perfume.

A perfume's *name* is an important product attribute. Revlon uses names such as Charlie, Fleurs de Jontue, Ciara, Scoundrel, Fire and Ice, Cherish, and She to create images that support each perfume's positioning. Competitors offer perfumes with names such as Obsession, Passion, Gossip, Wildheart, Opium, Joy, White Linen, Youth Dew, and Eternity. These names suggest that the perfumes will do something more than just make you smell better. Oscar de la Renta's Ruffles perfume *began* as a name, one chosen because it created images of whimsy, youth, glamour, and femininity—all well suited to the target market of young, stylish women. Only later was a scent selected to go with the product's name and positioning.

Revlon must also carefully *package* its perfumes. To consumers, the bottle and package are the most real symbols of the perfume and its image. Bottles must feel comfortable and be easy to handle, and they must look impressive when displayed in stores. Most important, they must support the perfume's concept and image.

So when a woman buys perfume, she buys much, much more than simply fragrant fluids. The perfume's image, its promises, its scent, its name and package, the company that makes it, the stores that sell it—all become a part of the total perfume product. When Revlon sells perfume, it sells more than just the tangible product. It sells lifestyle, self-expression, and exclusivity; achievement, success, and status; femininity, romance, passion, and fantasy; memories, hopes, and dreams.[1]

Clearly, perfume is more than just perfume when Revlon sells it. This chapter begins with a deceptively simple question: *What is a product?* After answering this question, we look at ways to classify products in consumer and business markets. Then we discuss the important decisions that marketers make regarding individual products, product lines, and product mixes. Finally, we examine the special characteristics and marketing requirements of a special form of product—services.

What Is a Product?

A Sony CD player, a Supercuts haircut, a Bahamas vacation, a GMC truck, H&R Block tax preparation services, and advice from an attorney are all products. We define a **product** as anything that can be offered to a market for attention, acquisition, use, or consumption and that might satisfy a want or need. Products include more than just tangible goods. Broadly defined, products include physical objects, services, persons, places, organizations, ideas, or mixes of these entities. Thus, throughout this text, we use the term *product* broadly to include any or all of these entities. Because of their importance in the world economy, we give special attention to services. **Services** are a form of product that consist of activities, benefits, or satisfactions offered for sale that are essentially intangible and do not result in the ownership of anything. Examples are banking, hotel, tax preparation, and home repair services. We will look at services more closely in a section at the end of this chapter.

Product
Anything that can be offered to a market for attention, acquisition, use, or consumption that might satisfy a want or need. It includes physical objects, services, persons, places, organizations, and ideas.

Service
Any activity or benefit that one party can offer to another that is essentially intangible and does not result in the ownership of anything.

The Product–Service Continuum

A company's offer to the marketplace often includes both tangible goods and services. Each component can be a minor or a major part of the total offer. At one extreme, the offer may consist of a *pure tangible good*, such as soap, toothpaste, or salt—no services accompany the product. At the other extreme are *pure services*, for which the offer consists primarily of a service. Examples include a doctor's exam or financial services. Between these two extremes, however, many goods and services combinations are possible.

For example, a company's offer may consist of a *tangible good with accompanying services*. For example, Ford offers more than just automobiles. Its offer also includes repair and maintenance services, warranty fulfillment, showrooms and waiting areas, and a host of other support services. A *hybrid offer* consists of equal parts of goods and services. For instance, people patronize restaurants both for their food and their service. A *service with accompanying minor goods* consists of a major service along with supporting goods. For example, American Airline passengers primarily buy transportation service, but the trip also includes some tangibles, such as food, drinks, and an airline magazine. The service also requires a capital-intensive good—an airplane—for its delivery, but the primary offer is a service.

Levels of Product

Product planners need to think about products and services on three levels. The most basic level is the *core product*, which addresses the question *What is the buyer really buying*? As Figure 7-1 illustrates, the core product stands at the center of the total product. It consists of the core, problem-solving benefits that consumers seek when they buy a product or service. A woman buying lipstick buys more than lip color. Charles Revson of Revlon saw this early: "In the factory, we make cosmetics; in the store, we sell hope." And Ritz-Carlton Hotels knows that it offers its guests more than simply rooms for rent—it provides "memorable travel experiences." Thus, when designing products, marketers must first define the core of *benefits* the product will provide to consumers.

The product planner must next build an *actual product* around the core product. Actual products may have as many as five characteristics: a quality level, features, design, a brand name, and packaging. For example, a Sony camcorder is an actual product. Its

Figure 7-1
Three levels
of product

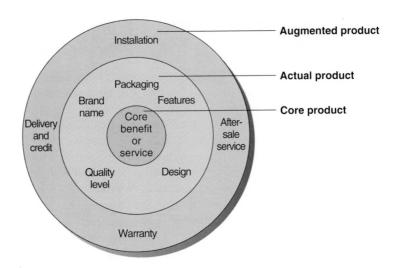

Core, actual, and augmented product: Consumers perceive this Sony camcorder as a complex bundle of tangible and intangible features and services that deliver a core benefit—a convenient, high-quality way to capture important moments.

name, parts, styling, features, packaging, and other attributes have all been combined carefully to deliver the core benefit—a convenient, high-quality way to capture important moments.

Finally, the product planner must build an *augmented product* around the core and actual products by offering additional consumer services and benefits. Sony must offer more than just a camcorder. It must provide consumers with a complete solution to their picture-taking problems. Thus, when consumers buy a Sony camcorder, Sony and its dealers also might give buyers a warranty on parts and workmanship, instructions on how to use the camcorder, quick repair services when needed, and a toll-free telephone number to call if they have problems or questions.

Therefore, a product is more than a simple set of tangible features. Consumers tend to see products as complex bundles of benefits that satisfy their needs. When developing products, marketers first must identify the *core* consumer needs the product will satisfy. They must then design the *actual* product and find ways to *augment* it in order to create the bundle of benefits that will best satisfy consumers.

Product Classifications

Products and services fall into two broad classes based on the types of consumers that use them: *consumer products* and *industrial products*. Broadly defined, products also include other marketable entities such as organizations, persons, places, and ideas.

Consumer Products

Consumer products are those bought by final consumers for personal consumption. Marketers usually classify these goods further based on how consumers go about buying them. Consumer products include *convenience products*, *shopping products*, *specialty*

Consumer product
Product bought by final consumer for personal consumption.

Table 7-1   Marketing Considerations for Consumer Products

Marketing Considerations	Type of Consumer Product			
	Convenience	Shopping	Specialty	Unsought
Customer buying behavior	Frequent purchase, little planning, little comparison or shopping effort, low customer involvement	Less frequent purchase, much planning and shopping effort, comparison of brands on price, quality, style	Strong brand preference and loyalty, special purchase effort, little comparison of brands, low price sensitivity	Little product awareness, knowledge, or, if aware, little interest (or negative interest)
Price	Low price	Higher price	High price	Varies
Distribution	Widespread distribution, convenient locations	Selective distribution in fewer outlets	Exclusive distribution in only one or a few outlets per market area	Varies
Promotion	Mass advertising and sales promotion by the producer	Advertising and personal selling by producer and resellers	More carefully targeted promotion by producer and resellers	Aggressive advertising and personal selling by producer and resellers
Examples	Toothpaste, magazines, laundry detergent	Major appliances, televisions, furniture, clothing	Luxury goods, such as Rolex watches or fine crystal	Life insurance, Red Cross blood donations

products, and *unsought products*. These products differ in the ways consumers buy them and therefore in how they are marketed (see Table 7-1).

Convenience products are consumer products and services that the customer usually buys frequently, immediately, and with a minimum of comparison and buying effort. Examples include soap, candy, newspapers, and fast food. Convenience products are usually low priced, and marketers place them in many locations to make them readily available when customers need them.

Shopping products are less frequently purchased consumer products and services that customers compare carefully on suitability, quality, price, and style. When buying shopping products and services, consumers spend much time and effort in gathering information and making comparisons. Examples include furniture, clothing, used cars, major appliances, and hotel and motel services. Shopping products marketers usually distribute their products through fewer outlets but provide deeper sales support to help customers in their comparison efforts.

Specialty products are consumer products and services with unique characteristics or brand identification for which a significant group of buyers is willing to make a special purchase effort. Examples include specific brands and types of cars, high-priced photographic equipment, designer clothes, and the services of medical or legal specialists. A Lamborghini automobile, for example, is a specialty product because buyers are usually willing to travel great distances to buy one. Buyers normally do not compare specialty products. They invest only the time needed to reach dealers carrying the wanted products.

Unsought products are consumer products that the consumer either does not know about or knows about but does not normally think of buying. Most major new innovations are unsought until the consumer becomes aware of them through advertising. Classic examples of known but unsought products and services are life insurance and blood donations to the Red Cross. By their very nature, unsought products require a lot of advertising, personal selling, and other marketing efforts.

Convenience product
Consumer product that the customer usually buys frequently, immediately, and with a minimum of comparison and buying effort.

Shopping product
Consumer good that the customer, in the process of selection and purchase, characteristically compares on such bases as suitability, quality, price, and style.

Specialty product
Consumer product with unique characteristics or brand identification for which a significant group of buyers is willing to make a special purchase effort.

Unsought product
Consumer product that the consumer either does not know about or knows about but does not normally think of buying.

Industrial Products

Industrial products are those purchased for further processing or for use in conducting a business. Thus, the distinction between a consumer product and an industrial product is based on the *purpose* for which the product is bought. If a consumer buys a lawn mower for use around home, the lawn mower is a consumer product. If the same consumer buys the same lawn mower for use in a landscaping business, the lawn mower is an industrial product.

The three groups of industrial products and services include materials and parts, capital items, and supplies and services. *Materials and parts* include raw materials and manufactured materials and parts. Raw materials consist of farm products (wheat, cotton, livestock, fruits, vegetables) and natural products (fish, lumber, crude petroleum, iron ore). Manufactured materials and parts consist of component materials (iron, yarn, cement, wires) and component parts (small motors, tires, castings). Most manufactured materials and parts are sold directly to industrial users. Price and service are the major marketing factors; branding and advertising tend to be less important.

Capital items are industrial products that aid in the buyer's production or operations, including installations and accessory equipment. Installations consist of major purchases such as buildings (factories, offices) and fixed equipment (generators, drill presses, large computer systems, elevators). Accessory equipment includes portable

Industrial product
Product bought by individuals and organizations for further processing or for use in conducting a business.

Business services: ServiceMaster supplies business services for a wide range of organizations. This advertisement to schools and colleges offers services ranging from custodial, grounds, technology, and energy management services to maintenance and food services.

factory equipment and tools (hand tools, lift trucks) and office equipment (fax machines, desks). They have a shorter life than installations and simply aid in the production process.

The final group of business products is *supplies and services*. Supplies include operating supplies (lubricants, coal, paper, pencils) and repair and maintenance items (paint, nails, brooms). Supplies are the convenience products of the industrial field because they are usually purchased with a minimum of effort or comparison. Business services include maintenance and repair services (window cleaning, computer repair) and business advisory services (legal, management consulting, advertising). Such services are usually supplied under contract.

Organizations, Persons, Places, and Ideas

In addition to tangible products and services, in recent years marketers have broadened the concept of a product to include other marketable entities; namely, organizations, persons, places, and ideas.

Organizations often carry out activities to "sell" the organization itself. *Organization marketing* consists of activities undertaken to create, maintain, or change the attitudes and behavior of target consumers toward an organization. Both profit and nonprofit organizations practice organization marketing. Business firms sponsor public relations or corporate advertising campaigns to polish their images. Nonprofit organizations, such as churches, colleges, charities, museums, and performing arts groups, market their organizations in order to raise funds and attract members or patrons. *Corporate image advertising* is a major tool companies use to market themselves to various publics.

People can also be thought of as products. *Person marketing* consists of activities undertaken to create, maintain, or change attitudes or behavior toward particular people. All kinds of people and organizations practice person marketing. Presidents Reagan and Clinton skillfully marketed themselves, their parties, and their platforms to get needed votes and program support. Entertainers and sports figures like Michael Jordan and Tiger Woods use marketing to promote their careers and improve their impact and incomes. Professionals such as doctors, lawyers, accountants, and architects market themselves in order to build their reputations and increase business. Business leaders use person marketing as a strategic tool to develop their companies' fortunes as well as their own. Businesses, charities, sports teams, fine arts groups, religious groups, and other organizations also use person marketing. Creating or associating with well-known personalities often helps these organizations achieve their goals better.

Place marketing involves activities undertaken to create, maintain, or change attitudes or behavior toward particular places. Examples include business site marketing and tourism marketing. *Business site marketing* involves developing, selling, or renting business sites for factories, stores, offices, warehouses, and conventions. For example, most states operate industrial development offices that try to sell companies on the advantages of locating new plants in their states. Even entire nations, such as Canada, Ireland, Greece, Mexico, and Turkey, have marketed themselves as good locations for business investment. *Tourism marketing* involves attracting vacationers to spas, resorts, cities, states, and nations. The effort is carried out by travel agents, airlines, motor clubs, oil companies, hotels, motels, and governmental agencies. Today, almost every city, state, and country markets its tourist attractions. Texas has advertised, "It's Like a Whole Other Country," Michigan has touted "YES M!CH!GAN—Great Lakes, Great Times" and New York State shouts "I ♥ New York!"[2]

Ideas can also be marketed. In one sense, all marketing is the marketing of an idea, whether it be the general idea of brushing your teeth or the specific idea that Crest

©1997 National Crime Prevention Council

Heroin Addict

Purse Snatcher

Vandal

Car Jacker

...all kicked out
with the help
of kids like me.
–Billy, age 15

Everybody loves to trash teenagers, right?
Maybe they don't realize that we do care.
That we can make a difference.
Get involved in Crime Prevention.
Clean up parks. Teach younger kids.
Start a school or neighborhood watch.
And help make your community
safer and better for everyone.
Together, we can prove them wrong
by doing something right.

Call Toll Free
1-800-722-TEENS
www.weprevent.org

Ad Council

**Social marketing:
The Ad Council has
developed dozens of
social advertising cam-
paigns. This one urges
teenagers to jump in
and help make their
communities better.
"Everyone loves to
trash teenagers,
right? . . . Together,
we can prove them
wrong by doing
something right."**

provides the most effective decay prevention. Here, however, we narrow our focus to the marketing of *social ideas*, such as public health campaigns to reduce smoking, alcoholism, drug abuse, and overeating; environmental campaigns to promote wilderness protection, clean air, and conservation; and other campaigns such as family planning, human rights, and racial equality. This area has been called **social marketing**, and it includes the creation and implementation of programs seeking to increase the acceptability of a social idea, cause, or practice within targeted groups.

Social marketing
The design, implementation, and control of programs seeking to increase the acceptability of a social idea, cause, or practice among a target group.

The Advertising Council of America has developed dozens of social advertising campaigns, including "Smokey the Bear," "Keep America Beautiful," "Join the Peace Corps," "Buy Bonds," "Go to College," "Say No to Drugs," and "Stay Fit." But social marketing involves much more than just advertising. Many public marketing campaigns fail because they assign advertising the primary role and fail to develop and use all the marketing mix tools.[3]

Individual Product Decisions

Figure 7-2 shows the important decisions in the development and marketing of individual products and services. We will focus on decisions about *product attributes*, *branding*, *packaging*, *labeling*, and *product support services*.

Product Attributes

Developing a product or service involves defining the benefits that it will offer. These benefits are communicated and delivered by product attributes such as *quality*, *features*, and *design*.

Product quality

The ability of a product to perform its functions; it includes the product's overall durability, reliability, precision, ease of operation and repair, and other valued attributes.

Product Quality Quality is one of the marketer's major positioning tools. **Product quality** has two dimensions: level and consistency. In developing a product, the marketer must first choose a *quality level* that will support the product's position in the target market. Here, product quality means *performance quality*, the ability of a product to perform its functions. For example, a Rolls-Royce provides higher performance quality than a Chevrolet: It has a smoother ride, handles better, and lasts longer. Companies rarely try to offer the highest possible performance quality level—few customers want or can afford the high levels of quality offered in products such as a Rolls-Royce automobile, a Sub Zero refrigerator, or a Rolex watch. Instead, companies choose a quality level that matches target market needs and the quality levels of competing products.

Beyond quality level, high quality also can mean high levels of quality *consistency*. Here, product quality means *conformance quality*—freedom from defects and *consistency* in delivering a targeted level of performance. All companies should strive for high levels of conformance quality. In this sense, a Chevrolet can have just as much quality as a Rolls-Royce. Although a Chevy doesn't perform as well as a Rolls, it can as consistently deliver the quality that customers pay for and expect.

During the past two decades, a renewed emphasis on quality has spawned a global quality movement. Most firms implemented "Total Quality Management" (TQM) programs, efforts to constantly improve product and process quality in every phase of their operations. Recently, however, the total quality management movement has drawn criticism. Too many companies viewed TQM as a magic cure-all and created token total quality programs that applied quality principles only superficially. Today, companies are taking a "return on quality" approach, viewing quality as an investment and holding quality efforts accountable for bottom-line results.[4]

Beyond simply reducing product defects, the ultimate goal of total quality is to improve customer value. For example, when Motorola first began its total quality program in the early 1980s, its goal was to drastically reduce manufacturing defects. Later,

Figure 7-2
Individual product decisions

however, Motorola's quality concept evolved into one of "customer-defined quality" and "total customer satisfaction." (See Marketing at Work 7-1.) Thus, many companies today have turned quality into a potent strategic weapon. They gain an edge over competitors by consistently and profitably meeting customers' needs and preferences for quality. In fact, quality has now become a competitive necessity—in the twenty-first century, only companies with the best quality will thrive.

Product Features A product can be offered with varying features. A stripped-down model, one without any extras, is the starting point. The company can create higher-level models by adding more features. Features are a competitive tool for differentiating the company's product from competitors' products. Being the first producer to introduce a needed and valued new feature is one of the most effective ways to compete.

How can a company identify new features and decide which ones to add to its product? The company should periodically survey buyers who have used the product and ask these questions: How do you like the product? Which specific features of the product do you like most? Which features could we add to improve the product? The answers provide the company with a rich list of feature ideas. The company can then assess each feature's *value* to customers versus its *cost* to the company. Features that customers value little in relation to costs should be dropped; those that customers value highly in relation to costs should be added.

Product Design Another way to add customer value is through distinctive *product design*. Some companies have reputations for outstanding design, such as Black & Decker in cordless appliances and tools, Steelcase in office furniture and systems, Bose in audio equipment, and Ciba Corning in medical equipment. Design can be one of the most powerful competitive weapons in a company's marketing arsenal.

Design is a larger concept than style. *Style* simply describes the appearance of a product. Styles can be eye-catching or yawn inspiring. A sensational style may grab attention, but it does not necessarily make the product *perform* better. Unlike style, *design* is more than skin deep; it goes to the very heart of a product. Good design contributes to a product's usefulness as well as to its looks.

Good design can attract attention, improve product performance, cut production costs, and give the product a strong competitive advantage in the target market. For example, Braun, a German division of Gillette that has elevated design to a high art, has had outstanding success with its coffee makers, food processors, hair dryers, electric razors, and other small appliances. And Black & Decker has learned that innovative design can be very profitable:

> What could be handier than a flashlight that you don't have to hold while you're probing under the sink for the cause of a leaky faucet? Black & Decker's flexible snakelight looks just like its namesake and attaches itself to almost anything, leaving your hands free. It can also stand up like an illuminated cobra to light your work space. The design won Black & Decker a gold medal in the Industrial Design Excellence Awards competition. More importantly, in a market where the average price is just $6, consumers are paying $30 for this flexible flashlight.[5]

Branding

Perhaps the most distinctive skill of professional marketers is their ability to create, maintain, protect, and enhance brands of their products and services. A **brand** is a name, term, sign, symbol, or design, or a combination of these, that identifies the maker or seller of a product or service. Consumers view a brand as an important part of a product, and branding

Brand
A name, term, sign, symbol, or design, or a combination of these, intended to identify the goods or services of one seller or group of sellers and to differentiate them from those of competitors.

Marketing at Work 7-1

Motorola's Customer-Driven "Six-Sigma" Quality

Founded in 1928, Motorola introduced the first commercially successful car radio—hence the name Motorola, suggesting "sound in motion." During World War II, it developed the first two-way radios ("walkie-talkies"), and by the 1950s, Motorola had become a household name in consumer electronics products. By the 1970s, however, facing intense competition mostly from Japanese firms, Motorola abandoned the radios and televisions that had made it famous. Instead, it focused on advanced telecommunications and electronics products: two-way radios, pagers, wireless telephones, semiconductors, and related technology gizmos. Even so, by the early 1980s, Japanese competitors were still beating Motorola to the market with higher-quality products at lower prices.

During the 1980s, however, Motorola came roaring back. How? The answer was deceptively simple: an obsessive dedication to *quality*. In the early 1980s, Motorola launched an aggressive crusade to improve product quality, first by tenfold, then by a hundredfold. It set the unheard-of goal of "six-sigma" quality. *Six sigma* is a statistical term that means "six standard deviations from a statistical performance average." In plain English, the six-sigma standard means that Motorola set out to slash product defects to fewer than 3.4 per million for every process—99.9997 percent defect-free. "Six sigma" became Motorola's rallying cry. In 1988, it received one of the first annual Malcolm Baldrige National Quality

"Quality means the world to us," claims Motorola. An obsession with customer-driven quality helped the company to achieve worldwide leadership in many product markets.

Awards recognizing "preeminent quality leadership."

Motorola's initial quality efforts focused on manufacturing improvements. The goal was to prevent defects by *designing* products for quality and making things right the *first* time and *every* time. Meeting the six-sigma standard meant that everyone in the organization had to strive for quality improvement. Thus, total quality became an important part of Motorola's basic corporate culture. Motorola spent heavily to educate employees about quality and then rewarded people

can add value to a product. For example, most consumers would perceive a bottle of White Linen perfume as a high-quality, expensive product. But the same perfume in an unmarked bottle would likely be viewed as lower in quality, even if the fragrance were identical.

for making things right. The company also forced its suppliers to meet exacting quality standards. Some suppliers grumbled, but those that survived benefited greatly from their own quality improvements. As an executive from one of Motorola's suppliers put it, "If we can supply Motorola, we can supply God."

As Motorola developed a deeper understanding of the meaning of quality, its initial focus on preventing manufacturing defects evolved into an emphasis on *customer-driven quality* and customer value. "Quality," noted Motorola's vice-president of quality, "has to do something for the customer. If [a product] does not work the way the user needs it to work, the defect is as big to the user as if it doesn't work the way the designer planned it. Our definition of a defect is 'if the customer doesn't like it, it's a defect.'"

Thus, the fundamental aim of Motorola's quality movement became total customer satisfaction. Instead of focusing just on manu-facturing defects, Motorola sur-veyed customers about their quality needs, analyzed customer com-plaints, and studied service records in a constant quest to improve value to the customer. Motorola's executives routinely visited cus-tomers to gain better insights into their needs. As a result, Motorola's total quality management did more than reduce product defects; it helped the company to shift from an inwardly focused, engineering orientation to a market-driven, customer-focused one.

In little more than a decade, Motorola's passion for quality had resulted in stunning success. By 1994, Motorola led all competitors in the global two-way mobile radio market and ranked number one in wireless phones with a 35 percent worldwide market share. Once in danger of being forced out of the pager business altogether, Motorola dominated that market with an astonishing 85 percent global market share. Between 1993 and 1995, revenue growth averaged 27 percent a year and profits soared 53 percent.

The happy ending to another corporate success story? Hold the phone. Following those heady days in the mid-1990s, Motorola's fortunes took a decided turn for the worse. During the next two years, sales growth slowed to only 5 percent and profits fell 33 percent. Customer complaints rose and Motorola's once-dominant 60 per-cent share of the U.S. wireless phone market plunged to only 34 percent. Observes one industry analyst, "One of the world's most admired companies, known for cutting edge technology and gold-plated quality, is coming up stunningly short these days."

What happened? It appears that Motorola's success went to its executives' heads, creating a culture that was "too smug, too engineer-ing driven." The company turned inward and stopped listening to customers. For example, in 1995, customers' pleas for digital wireless phones fell on deaf ears. Instead, Motorola focused myopically on engineering smaller and smaller analog phones. But by 1997, Motorola's customers were already launching digital service—without Motorola phones. Although Motorola finally developed digital technology, it appears only now to have caught up.

The company's hot passion for quality also appeared to have cooled. For example, it lost a $500 million contract with wireless carrier PrimeCo Personal Communi-cations. The problem: Motorola's equipment would sometimes just stop working, leaving PrimeCo's customers unable to make calls. Other large customers encountered similar problems, tarnishing Motorola's once sterling quality reputation.

Despite customer complaints and market-share losses, Motorola is still a major force to be reckoned with. It remains the world leader in mo-bile phones and a top supplier of wireless equipment. And it appears now to be recovering ground quickly in the digital phone market. However, losing some of the pas-sion for customer-focused quality that took Motorola quickly to the top caused the company to stum-ble. "Motorola's tale is a cautionary one," concludes the analyst. "It's a lesson in how a company reaches the pinnacle of its industry—and becomes blinded by its own success. It was [overbearing pride and arrogance that caused Motorola's executives to turn inward and kept them] from recognizing better tech-nologies, changing markets, and customers' needs." Now, he contin-ues, they must "take the starch out of Motorola's culture [and] get back to listening to customers."

Sources: Quotes from "Future Perfect," *The Econo-mist*, January 4, 1992, p. 61; B. G. Yovovich, "Mo-torola's Quest for Quality," *Business Marketing*, September 1991, pp. 14–16; Roger O. Crockett, "How Motorola Lost Its Way," *Business Week*, May 4, 1998, pp. 140–48; and Nikki Tait, "Motorola Tops Fourth-Quarter Expectations," *The Financial Times*, January 14, 1999, p. 18.

Branding has become so strong that today hardly anything goes unbranded. Salt is packaged in branded containers, common nuts and bolts are packaged with a distributor's label, and automobile parts—spark plugs, tires, filters—bear brand names that differ from those of the automakers. Even fruits and vegetables are branded—Sunkist oranges, Dole pineapples, and Chiquita bananas.

Branding helps buyers in many ways. Brand names help consumers identify products that might benefit them. Brands also tell the buyer something about product quality. Buyers who always buy the same brand know that they will get the same features, benefits, and quality each time they buy. Branding also gives the seller several advantages. The brand name becomes the basis on which a whole story can be built about a product's special qualities. The seller's brand name and trademark provide legal protection for unique product features that otherwise might be copied by competitors. And branding helps the seller to segment markets. For example, General Mills can offer Cheerios, Wheaties, Total, Lucky Charms, and many other cereal brands, not just one general product for all consumers.

Brand Equity Brands vary in the amount of power and value they have in the marketplace. A powerful brand has high **brand equity**. Brands have higher brand equity to the extent that they have higher brand loyalty, name awareness, perceived quality, strong brand associations, and other assets such as patents, trademarks, and channel relationships.

Brand equity
The value of a brand, based on the extent to which it has high brand loyalty, name awareness, perceived quality, strong brand associations, and other assets such as patents, trademarks, and channel relationships.

A brand with strong brand equity is a very valuable asset. Measuring the actual equity of a brand name is difficult. However, according to one estimate, the brand equity of Marlboro is $45 billion, Coca-Cola $43 billion, IBM $18 billion, Disney $15 billion, and Kodak $13 billion.[6] The world's top brands include superpowers such as Coca-Cola, Campbell, Disney, Kodak, Sony, Mercedes-Benz, and McDonald's.

High brand equity provides a company with many competitive advantages. A powerful brand enjoys a high level of consumer brand awareness and loyalty. Because consumers expect stores to carry the brand, the company has more leverage in bargaining with resellers. Because the brand name carries high credibility, the company can more easily launch line and brand extensions, as when Coca-Cola leveraged its well-known brand to introduce Diet Coke or when Procter & Gamble introduced Ivory dishwashing detergent. Above all, a powerful brand offers the company some defense against fierce price competition. Some analysts see brands as *the* major enduring asset of a company, outlasting the company's specific products and facilities.

Branding poses challenging decisions to the marketer. Figure 7-3 shows the key branding decisions.

Brand Name Selection A good name can add greatly to a product's success. However, finding the best brand name is a difficult task. It begins with a careful review of the product and its benefits, the target market, and proposed marketing strategies.

Desirable qualities for a brand name include: (1) It should suggest something about the product's benefits and qualities. Examples: DieHard, Easy-Off, Craftsman, Sunkist, Spic and Span, Snuggles, Merrie Maids, and OFF! bug spray. (2) It should be easy to pronounce, recognize, and remember. Short names help. Examples: Tide, Aim, Puffs. But longer ones are sometimes effective. Examples: "Love My Carpet" carpet cleaner, "I Can't Believe It's Not Butter" margarine, Better Business Bureau. (3) The brand name should be distinctive. Examples: Taurus, Kodak, Exxon. (4) The name should translate

Figure 7-3
Major branding
decisions

Brand equity: The Coca-Cola brand is valued at $43 billion, the IBM brand at $18 billion, and the Kodak brand at $12 billion.

easily into foreign languages. Before spending $100 million to change its name to Exxon, Standard Oil of New Jersey tested several names in 54 languages in more than 150 foreign markets. It found that the name Enco referred to a stalled engine when pronounced in Japanese. (5) It should be capable of registration and legal protection. A brand name cannot be registered if it infringes on existing brand names.

Once chosen, the brand name must be protected. Many firms try to build a brand name that will eventually become identified with the product category. Brand names such as Kleenex, Levi's, Jell-O, Scotch Tape, Formica, and Fiberglas have succeeded in this way. However, their very success may threaten the company's rights to the name. Many originally protected brand names, such as cellophane, aspirin, nylon, kerosene, linoleum, yo-yo, trampoline, escalator, thermos, and shredded wheat, are now generic names that any seller can use.

Brand Sponsor A manufacturer has four sponsorship options. The product may be launched as a *manufacturer's brand* (or national brand), as when Kellogg and IBM sell their output under their own manufacturer's brand names. Or the manufacturer may sell to resellers who give it a *private brand* (also called a *store brand* or *distributor brand*). Although most manufacturers create their own brand names, others market *licensed brands*. Finally, two companies can join forces and *co-brand* a product.

MANUFACTURER'S BRANDS VERSUS PRIVATE BRANDS Manufacturers' brands have long dominated the retail scene. In recent times, however, an increasing number of retailers and wholesalers have created their own **private brands**. For example, Sears has created several names: DieHard batteries, Craftsman tools, Kenmore appliances, Weatherbeater paints. Wal-Mart offers its own Sam's American Choice and Great Value brands of beverages and food products to compete against major national brands. And BASF Wyandotte, the world's second-largest antifreeze maker, sells its Alugard antifreeze through intermediaries who market the product under about 80 private brands, including Kmart, True Value, Pathmark, and Rite Aid. Private brands can be hard to establish and costly to stock and promote. However, they also yield higher profit margins for the reseller, and they give resellers exclusive products that cannot be bought from competitors, resulting in greater store traffic and loyalty.

In the so-called *battle of the brands* between manufacturers' and private brands, retailers have many advantages. They control what products they stock, where they go on the shelf, and which ones they will feature in local circulars. They charge manufacturers **slotting fees**, payments demanded by retailers before they will accept new products and find "slots" for them on the shelves. Retailers price their store brands lower than comparable manufacturers' brands, thereby appealing to budget-conscious shoppers, especially in difficult economic times. And most shoppers believe that store brands are often made by one of the larger manufacturers anyway.

As store brands improve in quality and as consumers gain confidence in their store chains, store brands are posing a strong challenge to manufacturers' brands. Consider the case of Loblaw, the Canadian supermarket chain. Its President's Choice Decadent Chocolate Chip Cookies brand is now the leading cookie brand in Canada. Loblaw's private label President's Choice cola racks up 50 percent of Loblaw's canned cola sales. Loblaw even sells its brand through other retailers. For example, President's Choice Decadent Chocolate Chip Cookies are now sold by Jewel Food Stores in Chicago, where they are the number-one seller, beating out even Nabisco's Chips Ahoy brand. Based on such success, the private label powerhouse has expanded into a wide range of food categories. For example, it now offers more than 500 frozen food items under the President's Choice label, ranging from frozen desserts to frozen prepared foods and boxed meats.[7]

In U.S. supermarkets, taken as a single brand, private-label products are the number-one, -two, or -three brand in over 40 percent of all grocery product categories. In all, they capture more than a 20 percent share of U.S. supermarket sales. Private labels are even more prominent in Europe, accounting for as much as 36 percent of supermarket sales in Britain and 24 percent in France. French retail giant Carrefour sells more than 3,000 in-house brands, ranging from cooking oil to car batteries. To fend off private brands, leading brand marketers will have to invest in R&D to bring out new brands, new features, and continuous quality improvements. They must design strong advertising programs to maintain high awareness and preference. And they must find ways to "partner" with major distributors in a search for distribution economies and improved joint performance.[8]

Private brand (or store brand)
A brand created and owned by a reseller of a product or service.

Slotting fees
Payments demanded by retailers before they will accept new products and find "slots" for them on the shelves.

LICENSING Most manufacturers take years and spend millions to create their own brand names. However, some companies license names or symbols previously created by other manufacturers, names of well-known celebrities, characters from popular movies and books—for a fee, any of these can provide an instant and proven brand name. Apparel and accessories sellers pay large royalties to adorn their products—from blouses to ties, and linens to luggage—with the names or initials of fashion innovators such as Bill Blass, Calvin Klein, Pierre Cardin, Gucci, and Halston. Sellers of children's products attach an almost endless list of character names to clothing, toys, school supplies, linens, dolls, lunch boxes, cereals, and other items. The character names range from classics such as Disney, Peanuts, Barbie, and the Muppets to Dr. Seuss characters and Batman.

Name and character licensing has become a big business in recent years. Retail sales of licensed products total more than $73 billion dollars annually. Almost half of all retail toy sales come from products based on movies and TV shows such as *Barney the Dinosaur*, *The Lion King*, or *Star Wars*. Even the Vatican engages in licensing: heavenly images from its art collection, architecture, frescoes, and manuscripts are now imprinted on such earthy objects as T-shirts, ties, glassware, candles, and ornaments.[9]

Many companies have mastered the art of peddling their established brands and characters. For example, through savvy marketing, Warner Brothers has turned Bugs Bunny, Daffy Duck, Foghorn Leghorn, and its more than 100 other *Looney Tunes* characters into the world's favorite cartoon brand. The *Looney Tunes* license, arguably the most sought-after nonsports license in the industry, generates $4 billion in annual retail sales by more than 225 licensees. And Warner Brothers has yet to tap the full potential of many of its secondary characters. The Tazmanian Devil, for example, initially appeared in only five cartoons. But through cross-licensing agreements with organizations such as Harley-Davidson and the NFL, Taz has become something of a pop icon. Warner Brothers sees similar potential for Michigan Frog or Speedy Gonzales for the Hispanic market.[10]

LOONEY TUNES, characters, names, and all related indicia are trademarks of Warner Bros. ©1998.

Warner Brothers has mastered the art of licensing. Its merchandise emblazoned with Looney Tunes characters generates more than $3 billion in annual retail sales for more than 225 licensees.

Co-branding
The practice of using the established brand names of two different companies on the same product.

CO-BRANDING Although companies have been **co-branding** products for many years, there has been a recent resurgence in co-branded products. Co-branding occurs when two established brand names of different companies are used on the same product. For example, Nabisco joined with Pillsbury to create Pillsbury Oreo Bars Baking Mix and with Kraft Foods' Post cereal division to create Oreo O's cereal. Kellogg joined forces with ConAgra to co-brand Healthy Choice from Kellogg's cereals. Ford and Eddie Bauer co-branded a sport utility vehicle—the Ford Explorer, Eddie Bauer edition. General Electric worked with Culligan to develop its Water by Culligan Profile Performance refrigerator with a built-in Culligan water filtration system. And Mattel teamed with Coca-Cola to market Soda Fountain Sweetheart Barbie. In most co-branding situations, one company licenses another company's well-known brand to use in combination with its own.

Co-branding offers many advantages. Because each brand dominates in a different category, the combined brands create broader consumer appeal and greater brand equity. Co-branding also allows a company to expand its existing brand into a category it might otherwise have difficulty entering alone. For example, by licensing its Healthy Choice brand to Kellogg, ConAgra entered the breakfast segment with a solid product. In return, Kellogg could leverage the broad awareness of the Healthy Choice name in the cereal category.

Co-branding also has limitations. Such relationships usually involve complex legal contracts and licenses. Co-branding partners must carefully coordinate their advertising, sales promotion, and other marketing efforts. Finally, when co-branding, each partner must trust the other will take good care of its brand. As one Nabisco manager puts it, "Giving away your brand is a lot like giving away your child—you want to make sure everything is perfect."[11]

Brand Strategy A company has four choices when it comes to brand strategy (see Figure 7-4). It can introduce *line extensions* (existing brand names extended to new forms, sizes, and flavors of an existing product category), *brand extensions* (existing brand names extended to new product categories), *multibrands* (new brand names introduced in the same product category), or *new brands* (new brand names in new product categories).

Line extension
Using a successful brand name to introduce additional items in a given product category under the same brand name, such as new flavors, forms, colors, added ingredients, or package sizes.

LINE EXTENSIONS **Line extensions** occur when a company introduces additional items in a given product category under the same brand name, such as new flavors, forms, colors, ingredients, or package sizes. Thus, Dannon introduced several line extensions, including seven new yogurt flavors, a fat-free yogurt, and a large, economy-size yogurt. The vast majority of new-product activity consists of line extensions.

A company might introduce line extensions as a low-cost, low-risk way to introduce new products in order to meet consumer desires for variety, to utilize excess capacity, or simply to command more shelf space from resellers. However, line extensions involve

Figure 7-4
Four brand strategies

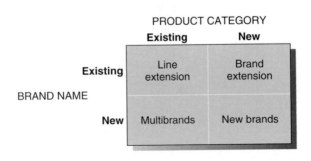

Line extensions: Heavily extended brands can also cause consumer confusion or frustration. A consumer buying cereal at the local supermarket will be confronted by up to 30 different brands, flavors, and sizes of oatmeal alone.

some risks. An overextended brand name might lose its specific meaning. In the past, when consumers asked for a Coke, they received a 6-ounce bottle of the classic beverage. Today, the vendor has to ask: Classic or Cherry Coke? Regular or diet? Caffeine or caffeine-free? Bottle or can? This may leave some consumers wondering what Coke really is. Heavily extended brands can also cause consumer confusion or frustration. A consumer buying cereal at the local supermarket will be confronted by more than 150 brands—up to 30 different brands, flavors, and sizes of oatmeal alone. By itself, Quaker offers its original Quaker Oats, several flavors of Quaker instant oatmeal, and several dry cereals such as Oatmeal Squares, Toasted Oatmeal, and Toasted Oatmeal—Honey Nut. Another risk is that sales of an extension may come at the expense of other items in the line. A line extension works best when it takes sales away from competing brands, not when it "cannibalizes" the company's other items.

BRAND EXTENSIONS A **brand extension** involves the use of a successful brand name to launch new or modified products in a new category. Fruit of the Loom took advantage of its very high name recognition to launch new lines of socks, men's fashion underwear, women's underwear, athletic apparel, and even baby clothes. Honda uses its company name to cover different products such as its automobiles, motorcycles, snowblowers, lawn mowers, marine engines, and snowmobiles. This allows Honda to advertise that it can fit "six Hondas in a two-car garage." Swiss Army Brand sunglasses, Disney cruise lines, Snackwell's snackbars, and Century 21 home improvements, Brinks home security systems—all are brand extensions.

> **Brand extension**
> Using a successful brand name to launch a new or modified product in a new category.

A brand extension gives a new product instant recognition and faster acceptance. It also saves the high advertising costs usually required to build a new brand name. At the same time, a brand extension strategy involves some risk. Brand extensions such as Bic pantyhose, Heinz pet food, Life Savers gum, and Clorox laundry detergent met early deaths. The extension may confuse the image of the main brand. For example, when clothing retailer The Gap saw competitors targeting its value-conscious customers with Gap-like fashions at lower prices, it began testing Gap Warehouse, which sold merchandise at a cut below Gap quality and price. However, the connection confused customers and eroded the Gap image. As a result, the company renamed the stores Old Navy Clothing Company, a brand that has become enormously successful.[12]

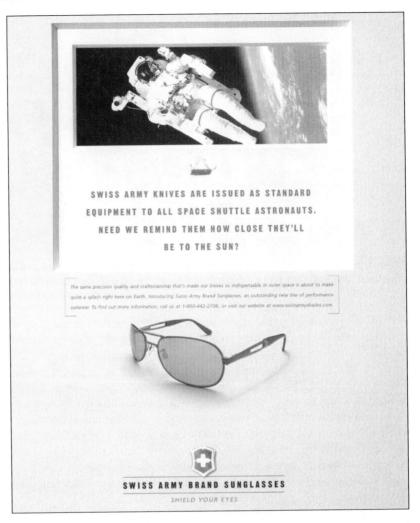

Brand extensions: Swiss Army extends its well-known brand name to a new category—sunglasses.

If a brand extension fails, it may harm consumer attitudes toward the other products carrying the same brand name. Further, a brand name may not be appropriate to a particular new product, even if it is well made and satisfying—would you consider buying Texaco milk or Alpo chili? And a brand name may lose its special positioning in the consumer's mind through overuse. Companies that are tempted to transfer a brand name must research how well the brand's associations fit the new product.[13]

MULTIBRANDS Companies often introduce additional brands in the same category. Thus, P&G markets many different brands in each of its product categories. *Multibranding* offers a way to establish different features and appeal to different buying motives. It also allows a company to lock up more reseller shelf space. Or the company may want to protect its major brand by setting up *flanker* or *fighter brands*. For example, Seiko uses different brand names for its higher-priced watches (Seiko Lasalle) and lower-priced watches (Pulsar) to protect the flanks of its mainstream Seiko brand. Finally, companies may develop separate brand names for different regions or countries, perhaps to suit different cultures or languages. For example, Procter & Gamble dominates the U.S. laundry detergent market with Tide, which in all its forms captures more than a 40 percent market share. Outside North America, however, P&G leads the detergent category with its Ariel brand, now Europe's number-two packaged-goods brand behind Coca-Cola. In the United States, P&G targets Ariel to Hispanic markets.

A major drawback of multibranding is that each brand might obtain only a small market share, and none may be very profitable. The company may end up spreading its resources over many brands instead of building a few brands to a highly profitable level. These companies should reduce the number of brands they sell in a given category and set up tighter screening procedures for new brands.

NEW BRANDS A company may create a new brand name when it enters a new product category for which none of the company's current brand names are appropriate. For example, Japan's Matsushita uses separate names for its different families of products: Technics, Panasonic, National, and Quasar. Or, a company might believe that the power of its existing brand name is waning and a new brand name is needed. Finally, the company may obtain new brands in new categories through acquisitions. For example, S.C. Johnson & Son, marketer of Pledge furniture polish, Glade air freshener, Raid insect spray, Edge shaving gel, and many other well-known brands, added several new power-house brands through its acquisition of Drackett Company, including Windex, Drano, and Vanish toilet bowl cleaner.

As with multibranding, offering too many new brands can result in a company spreading its resources too thin. And in some industries, such as consumer packaged goods, consumers and retailers have become concerned that there are already too many brands, with too few differences between them. Thus, Procter & Gamble, Frito-Lay, and other large consumer product marketers are now pursuing *megabrand* strategies— weeding out weaker brands and focusing their marketing dollars only on brands that can achieve the number-one or -two market-share positions in their categories.

Linking the Concepts

Building and maintaining strong brands is at the heart of successful marketing. Stop and think about all the familiar brands you encounter daily.

- List as many specific examples as you can find of each of the following: (1) brand licensing, (2) co-branding, (3) line extensions, and (4) brand extensions. Can you find a single brand that has done all of these?
- Pick and describe a familiar brand that has been widely extended. What are the benefits and dangers for this specific brand? Can you find some inappropriate brand extensions?

Packaging

Packaging involves designing and producing the container or wrapper for a product. The package may include the product's primary container (the tube holding Colgate toothpaste); a secondary package that is thrown away when the product is about to be used (the cardboard box containing the tube of Colgate); and the shipping package necessary to store, identify, and ship the product (a corrugated box carrying six dozen tubes of Colgate toothpaste). Labeling, printed information appearing on or with the package, is also part of packaging.

Traditionally, the primary function of the package was to contain and protect the product. In recent times, however, numerous factors have made packaging an important marketing tool. Increased competition and clutter on retail store shelves means that packages must now perform many sales tasks—from attracting attention, to describing the product, to making the sale. Companies are realizing the power of good packaging to create instant consumer recognition of the company or brand. For example, in an average

Packaging
The activities of designing and producing the container or wrapper for a product.

supermarket, which stocks 15,000 to 17,000 items, the typical shopper passes by some 300 items per minute, and 53 percent of all purchases are made on impulse. In this highly competitive environment, the package may be the seller's last chance to influence buyers. It becomes a "five-second commercial." The Campbell Soup Company estimates that the average shopper sees its familiar red-and-white can 76 times a year, creating the equivalent of $26 million worth of advertising. The package can also reinforce the product's positioning. Coca-Cola's familiar contour bottle speaks volumes about the product inside. "Even in a shadow, people know it's a Coke," observes a packaging expert. "It's a beautiful definition of how a package can influence the way a consumer perceives a product. People taste Coke differently from a contour bottle versus a generic package."[14]

Innovative packaging can give a company an advantage over competitors. Liquid Tide quickly attained a 10 percent share of the heavy-duty detergent market, partly because of the popularity of its container's innovative drip-proof spout and cap. In

Marketing at Work 7-2
Those Frustrating, Not-So-Easy-To-Open Packages

Some things, it seems, will never change. This classic letter from an angry consumer to Robert D. Stuart, then chairman of Quaker Oats, beautifully expresses the utter frustration all of us have experienced in dealing with so-called easy-opening packages.

Dear Mr. Stuart:

I am an 86-year-old widow in fairly good health. (You may think of this as advanced age, but for me that description pertains to the years ahead. Nevertheless, if you decide to reply to this letter I wouldn't dawdle, actuarial tables being what they are.)

As I said, my health is fairly good. Feeble and elderly, as one understands these terms, I am not. My two Doberman Pinschers and I take a brisk 3-mile walk every day. They are two strong and energetic animals and it takes a bit of doing to keep "brisk" closer to a stroll than a mad dash. But I manage because as yet I don't lack the strength. You will shortly see why this fact is relevant.

I am writing to call your attention to the cruel, deceptive, and utterly [false] copy on your Aunt Jemima buttermilk complete pancake and waffle mix. The words on your package read, "to open—press here and pull back."

Mr. Stuart, though I push and press and groan and strive and writhe and curse and sweat and jab and push, poke and ram . . . whew!—I have never once been able to do what the package instructs—to "press here and pull back" the [blankety-blank]. It can't be done! Talk about failing strength! Have you ever tried and succeeded?

My late husband was a gun collector who among other lethal weapons kept a Thompson machine gun in a locked cabinet. It was a good thing that the cabinet was locked. Oh, the number of times I was tempted to give your package a few short bursts.

That lock and a sense of lady-like delicacy kept me from pursuing that vengeful fantasy. Instead, I keep a small cleaver in my pantry for those occasions when I need to open a package of your delicious Aunt Jemima pancakes.

For many years that whacking away with my cleaver served a dual purpose. Not only to open the [blankety-blank] package but also to vent my fury at your sadists who willfully and maliciously did design that torture apparatus that passes for a package.

Sometimes just for the [blank] of it I let myself get carried away. I don't stop after I've lopped off the top. I whack away until the package is utterly destroyed in an outburst of rage, frustration, and vindictiveness. I wind up with a floorful of your delicious Aunt Jemima pancake mix. But that's a small price to pay for blessed release. (Anyway, the Pinschers lap up the mess.)

So many ingenious, considerate (even compassionate) innovations in package closures have been designed since Aunt Jemima first donned her red bandana. Wouldn't you consider the introduction of a more humane package to replace the example of marketing malevolence to which you resolutely cling? Don't you care, Mr. Stuart?

I'm really writing this to be helpful and in that spirit I am sending a copy to Mr. Tucker, president of Container Corp. I'm sure their clever young designers could be of immeasurable help to you in this matter. At least I feel it's worth a try.

Really, Mr. Stuart, I hope you will not regard me as just another cranky old biddy. I am The Public, the source of your fortunes.

Ms. Roberta Pavloff
Malvern, Pa.

Source: This letter was reprinted in "Some Designs Should Just Be Torn Asunder," *Advertising Age,* January 17, 1983, p. M54.

contrast, poorly designed packages can cause headaches for consumers and lost sales for the company (see Marketing at Work 7-2). For example, Planters Lifesavers Company recently attempted to use innovative packaging to create an association between fresh-roasted peanuts and fresh-roasted coffee. It packaged its Fresh Roast Salted Peanuts in vacuum-packed "Brik-Pacs," similar to those used for ground coffee. Unfortunately, the coffeelike packaging worked too well: Consumers mistook the peanuts for a new brand of flavored coffee and ran them through supermarket coffee-grinding machines, creating a gooey mess, disappointed customers, and lots of irate store managers.[15]

Developing a good package for a new product requires making many decisions. First, the company must establish the *packaging concept*, which states what the package should *be* or *do* for the product. Should it mainly offer product protection, introduce a new dispensing method, suggest certain qualities about the product, or something else? Decisions then must be made on specific elements of the package, such as size, shape, materials, color, text, and brand mark. These elements must work together to support the product's position and marketing strategy. The package must be consistent with the product's advertising, pricing, and distribution.

In recent years, product safety has also become a major packaging concern. We have all learned to deal with hard-to-open "childproof" packages. And after the rash of product tampering scares during the 1980s, most drug producers and food makers are now putting their products in tamper-resistant packages. In making packaging decisions, the company also must heed growing environmental concerns and make decisions that serve society's interests as well as immediate customer and company objectives. Increasingly, companies will be asked to take responsibility for the environmental costs of their products and packaging. For example, consider Germany's packaging ordinance:

> The German Packaging Ordinance (Verpackungsordnung) makes producers and retailers responsible for taking back and recycling packaging waste. Industry has responded with the Duales System (DSD), a nonprofit company set up by German

In Germany, sellers are now responsible for the environmental costs of their products. This widely used "green dot" emblem indicates that a package is acceptable for industry collection systems.

businesses that collects waste directly from consumers. DSD is funded by licensing fees for the now widely used *green dot*: a green arrow emblem indicating that a package is collectible by DSD. Now, rather than tossing their packaging out with the municipal trash, for which they must pay a fee, consumers can take it to a nearby DSD bin to be collected for free. Under the DSD system, stores are no longer required to take back huge mounds of primary sales packaging. To be eligible as DSD trash, however, a sales package must have the green dot. To receive the green dot, packaging must meet strict recycling criteria. So, not surprisingly, retailers are reluctant to carry products without the green dot. Further, German consumers increasingly prefer recyclable packaging materials, and less packaging in general. Thus, the Packaging Ordinance has strongly affected how companies package their products for the German market. Colgate, for example, designed a toothpaste tube that stands on its head on store shelves without a box. Hewlett-Packard redesigned the chassis for its workstations and personal computers, reducing transport packaging by 30 percent. During the first three years under the new system, total household waste production fell more than 10 percent while recycling quantities increased 90 percent. Germany now collects, sorts, and recycles a remarkable 84 percent of targeted sales packaging from homes and small businesses.[16]

Labeling

Labels may range from simple tags attached to products to complex graphics that are part of the package. They perform several functions. At the very least, the label *identifies* the product or brand, such as the name Sunkist stamped on oranges. The label might also *describe* several things about the product: who made it, where it was made, when it was made, its contents, how it is to be used, and how to use it safely. Finally, the label might *promote* the product through attractive graphics.

There has been a long history of legal concerns about packaging and labels. The Federal Trade Commission Act of 1914 held that false, misleading, or deceptive labels or packages constitute unfair competition. Labels can mislead customers, fail to describe important ingredients, or fail to include needed safety warnings. As a result, several federal and state laws regulate labeling. The most prominent is the Fair Packaging and Labeling Act of 1966, which set mandatory labeling requirements, encouraged voluntary industry packaging standards, and allowed federal agencies to set packaging regulations in specific industries.

Labeling has been affected in recent times by *unit pricing* (stating the price per unit of standard measure), *open dating* (stating the expected shelf life of the product), and *nutritional labeling* (stating the nutritional values in the product). The Nutritional Labeling and Educational Act of 1990 requires sellers to provide detailed nutritional information on food products, and recent sweeping actions by the Food and Drug Administration regulate the use of health-related terms such as *low-fat*, *light*, and *high-fiber*. Sellers must ensure that their labels contain all the required information.

Product Support Services

Customer service is another element of product strategy. A company's offer to the marketplace usually includes some services, which can be a minor or a major part of the total offer. Later in the chapter, we will discuss services as products in themselves. Here, we discuss *product support services*, services that augment actual products. More and more companies are using product support services as a major tool in gaining competitive advantage.

A company should design its product and support services to profitably meet the needs of target customers. The first step is to periodically survey customers to assess the value of current services and to obtain ideas for new ones. For example, Cadillac holds regular focus group interviews with owners and carefully watches complaints that come into its dealerships. From this careful monitoring, Cadillac has learned that buyers are very upset by repairs that are not done correctly the first time.

Once the company has assessed the value of various support services to customers, it must next assess the costs of providing these services. It can then develop a package of services that will both delight customers and yield profits to the company. For example, based on its consumer interviews, Cadillac has set up a system directly linking each dealership with a group of 10 engineers who can help walk mechanics through difficult repairs. Such actions helped Cadillac jump, in one year, from fourteenth to seventh in independent rankings of service.[17]

Product Decisions and Social Responsibility

Product decisions have attracted much public attention. When making such decisions, marketers should consider carefully a number of public policy issues and regulations involving acquiring or dropping products, patent protection, product quality and safety, and product warranties.

Regarding the addition of new products, the government may prevent companies from adding products through acquisitions if the effect threatens to lessen competition. Companies dropping products must be aware that they have legal obligations, written or implied, to their suppliers, dealers, and customers who have a stake in the discontinued product. Companies must also must obey U.S. patent laws when developing new products. A company cannot make its product illegally similar to another company's established product.

Manufacturers must comply with specific laws regarding product quality and safety. The Federal Food, Drug, and Cosmetic Act protects consumers from unsafe and adulterated food, drugs, and cosmetics. Various acts provide for the inspection of sanitary conditions in the meat- and poultry-processing industries. Safety legislation has been passed to regulate fabrics, chemical substances, automobiles, toys, and drugs and poisons. The Consumer Product Safety Act of 1972 established a Consumer Product Safety Commission, which has the authority to ban or seize potentially harmful products and set severe penalties for violation of the law.

If consumers have been injured by a product that has been designed defectively, they can sue manufacturers or dealers. Product liability suits are now occurring in federal and state courts at the rate of almost 110,000 per year, with individual awards often running in the millions of dollars.[18] This phenomenon has resulted in huge increases in product-liability insurance premiums, causing big problems in some industries. Some companies pass these higher rates along to consumers by raising prices. Others are forced to discontinue high-risk product lines.

Many manufacturers offer written product warranties to convince customers of their products' quality. To protect consumers, Congress passed the Magnuson-Moss Warranty Act in 1975. The act requires that full warranties meet certain minimum standards, including repair "within a reasonable time and without charge" or a replacement or full refund if the product does not work "after a reasonable number of attempts" at repair. Otherwise, the company must make it clear that it is offering only a limited warranty. The law has led several manufacturers to switch from full to limited warranties and others to drop warranties altogether as a marketing tool.

Product Line Decisions

Product line
A group of products that are closely related because they function in a similar manner, are sold to the same customer groups, are marketed through the same types of outlets, or fall within given price ranges.

We have looked at product strategy decisions such as branding, packaging, labeling, and support services for individual products and services. But product strategy also calls for building a product line. A **product line** is a group of products that are closely related because they function in a similar manner, are sold to the same customer groups, are marketed through the same types of outlets, or fall within given price ranges. For example, Nike produces several lines of athletic shoes, Motorola produces several lines of telecommunications products, and AT&T offers several lines of long-distance telephone services. In developing product line strategies, marketers face a number of tough decisions.

The major product line decision involves *product line length*, the number of items in the product line. The line is too short if the manager can increase profits by adding items; the line is too long if the manager can increase profits by dropping items. Product line length is influenced by company objectives and resources.

Product lines tend to lengthen over time. The sales force and distributors may pressure the product manager for a more complete line to satisfy their customers. Or, the manager may want to add items to the product line to create growth in sales and profits. However, as the manager adds items, several costs rise: design and engineering costs, inventory costs, manufacturing changeover costs, transportation costs, and promotional costs to introduce new items. Eventually top management calls a halt to the mushrooming product line. Unnecessary or unprofitable items will be pruned from the line in a major effort to increase overall profitability. This pattern of uncontrolled product line growth followed by heavy pruning is typical and may repeat itself many times.

The company must manage its product lines carefully. It can systematically increase the length of its product line in two ways: by *stretching* its line and by *filling* its line. *Product line stretching* occurs when a company lengthens its product line beyond its current range. The company can stretch its line downward, upward, or both ways.

Many companies initially locate at the upper end of the market and later stretch their lines *downward*. A company may stretch downward to plug a market hole that otherwise would attract a new competitor or to respond to a competitor's attack on the upper end. Or it may add low-end products because it finds faster growth taking place in the low-end segments. Mercedes stretched downward for all these reasons. Facing a slow-growth luxury car market and attacks by Japanese automakers on its high-end

Product line stretching: Mercedes introduced several smaller, lower-priced models, including the $10,000 Smart micro compact car in a joint venture with Swatch. Affectionately dubbed the "Swatchmobile," the Smart is "designed for two people and a crate of beer."

positioning, Mercedes introduced several smaller, lower-priced models. These included the sporty SLK hard-top convertible (priced at a modest $40,000) and the A-Class line ($20,000). And in a joint venture with Switzerland's Swatch watchmaker, Mercedes will soon launch the $10,000 Smart microcompact car, an environmentally correct second car. Just 7.5 feet long, and affectionately dubbed the "Swatchmobile," the Smart is "designed for two people and a crate of beer."[19]

Companies at the lower end of the market may want to stretch their product lines *upward*. They may be attracted by a faster growth rate or higher margins at the higher end, or they may simply want to position themselves as full-line manufacturers. Sometimes, companies stretch upward in order to add prestige to their current products. General Electric accomplished all of these goals when it added its Monogram line of high-quality built-in kitchen appliances targeted at the select few households earning more than $100,000 a year and living in homes valued at over $400,000.

Companies in the middle range of the market may decide to stretch their lines in *both directions*. Marriott did this with its hotel product line. Along with regular Marriott hotels, it added the Marriott Marquis line to serve the upper end of the market, and the Courtyard and Fairfield Inn lines to serve the lower end. Each branded hotel line is aimed at a different target market. Marriott Marquis aims to attract and please top executives; Marriotts, middle managers; Courtyards, salespeople; and Fairfield Inns, vacationers and others on a tight travel budget. Marriott's Residence Inn provides a home away from home for people who travel for a living, who are relocating, or who are on assignment and need inexpensive temporary lodging. The major risk with this strategy is that some travelers will trade down after finding that the lower-price hotels in the Marriott chain give them pretty much everything they want. However, Marriott would rather capture its customers who move downward than lose them to competitors.

An alternative to product line stretching is *product line filling*, adding more items within the present range of the line. There are several reasons for product line filling: reaching for extra profits, satisfying dealers, using excess capacity, being the leading full-line company, and plugging holes to keep out competitors. Thus, Sony filled its Walkman line by adding solar-powered and waterproof Walkmans and an ultralight model that attaches to a sweatband for joggers, bicyclers, tennis players, and other exercisers. However, line filling is overdone if it results in cannibalization and customer confusion. The company should ensure that new items are noticeably different from existing ones.

Product Mix Decisions

An organization with several product lines has a product mix. A **product mix** (or **product assortment**) consists of all the product lines and items that a particular seller offers for sale. Avon's product mix consists of four major product lines: cosmetics, jewelry, fashions, and household items. Each product line consists of several sublines. For example, cosmetics breaks down into lipstick, eyeliner, powder, and so on. Each line and subline has many individual items. Altogether, Avon's product mix includes 1,300 items. In contrast, a typical Kmart stocks 15,000 items, 3M markets more than 60,000 products, and General Electric manufactures as many as 250,000 items.

A company's product mix has four important dimensions: width, length, depth, and consistency. Product mix *width* refers to the number of different product lines the company carries. For example, Procter & Gamble markets a fairly wide product mix consisting of many product lines, including paper, food, household cleaning, medicinal, cosmetics, and personal care products. Product mix *length* refers to the total number of

Product mix (or product assortment)
The set of all product lines and items that a particular seller offers for sale.

items the company carries within its product lines. P&G typically carries many brands within each line. For example, it sells eleven laundry detergents, eight hand soaps, six shampoos, and four dishwashing detergents.

Product line *depth* refers to the number of versions offered of each product in the line. Thus, P&G's Crest toothpaste comes in three sizes and two formulations (paste and gel). Finally, the *consistency* of the product mix refers to how closely related the various product lines are in end use, production requirements, distribution channels, or some other way. P&G's product lines are consistent insofar as they are consumer products that go through the same distribution channels. The lines are less consistent insofar as they perform different functions for buyers.

These product mix dimensions provide the handles for defining the company's product strategy. The company can increase its business in four ways. It can add new product lines, thus widening its product mix. In this way, its new lines build on the company's reputation in its other lines. The company can lengthen its existing product lines to become a more full-line company. Or it can add more versions of each product and thus deepen its product mix. Finally, the company can pursue more product line consistency—or less—depending on whether it wants to have a strong reputation in a single field or in several fields.

Linking the Concepts

Slow down for a minute. To get a better sense of how large and complex a company's product offering can become, investigate Procter & Gamble's product mix.

- Using P&G's Web site (www.pg.com), its annual report, or other sources, develop a list of all the company's product lines and individual products. What surprises you about this list of products?
- Is P&G's product mix consistent? What overall strategy or logic appears to have guided the development of this product mix?

Services Marketing

One of the major world trends in recent years has been the dramatic growth of services. As a result of rising affluence, more leisure time, and the growing complexity of products that require servicing, the United States has become the world's first service economy. Services now generate 74 percent of U.S. gross domestic product. Whereas service jobs accounted for 55 percent of all U.S. jobs in 1970, by 1993 they accounted for 79 percent of total employment. Services are growing even faster in the world economy, making up a quarter of the value of all international trade. In fact, a variety of service industries—from banking, insurance, and communications to transportation, travel, and entertainment—now accounts for well over 60 percent of the economy in developed countries around the world.[20]

Service industries vary greatly. *Governments* offer services through courts, employment services, hospitals, loan agencies, military services, police and fire departments, postal service, regulatory agencies, and schools. *Private nonprofit organizations* offer services through museums, charities, churches, colleges, foundations, and hospitals. A large number of *business organizations* offer services—airlines, banks, hotels, insurance companies, consulting firms, medical and law practices, entertainment companies, real estate firms, advertising and research agencies, and retailers.

The convenience industry: Services that save you time—for a price.

Not only are there traditional service industries but new types keep popping up to serve a new generation of time-pressed consumers:

> Want someone to fetch a meal from a local restaurant? In Austin, Texas, you can call EatOutIn. Plants need to be watered? In New York, you can call the Busy Body's Helper. Too busy to wrap and mail your packages? Stop by any one of the 72 outlets of Tender Sender, headquartered in Portland, Oregon. "We'll find it, we'll do it, we'll wait for it," chirps Lois Barnett, the founder of Personalized Services in Chicago. She and her crew of six will walk the dog, shuttle the kids to Little League, or wait in line for your theater tickets. Meet the convenience peddlers. They want to save you time. For a price, they'll do just about anything that's legal.[21]

Some service businesses are very large, with total sales and assets in the billions of dollars. There are also tens of thousands of smaller service providers. Selling services presents some special problems calling for special marketing solutions.

Nature and Characteristics of a Service

Activities such as renting a hotel room, depositing money in a bank, traveling on an airplane, getting a haircut, having a car repaired, watching a professional sport, seeing a movie, and getting advice from a lawyer all involve buying a service. A company must consider four special service characteristics when designing marketing programs: *intangibility*, *inseparability*, *variability*, and *perishability*. These characteristics are summarized in Figure 7-5 and discussed in the following sections.

Service intangibility means that services cannot be seen, tasted, felt, heard, or smelled before they are bought. For example, people undergoing cosmetic surgery cannot see the result before the purchase, and airline passengers have nothing but a ticket and the promise of safe delivery to their destinations. To reduce uncertainty, buyers look for "signals" of service quality. They draw conclusions about quality from the place, people, price, equipment, and communications that they can see. Therefore, the service provider's task is to make the service tangible in one or more ways. Whereas product marketers try to add intangibles to their tangible offers, service marketers try to add tangibles to their intangible offers.

Physical goods are produced, then stored, later sold, and still later consumed. In contrast, services are first sold, then produced and consumed at the same time. **Service inseparability** means that services cannot be separated from their providers, whether the

Service intangibility
A major characteristic of services—they cannot be seen, tasted, felt, heard, or smelled before they are bought.

Service inseparability
A major characteristic of services—they are produced and consumed at the same time and cannot be separated from their providers, whether the providers are people or machines.

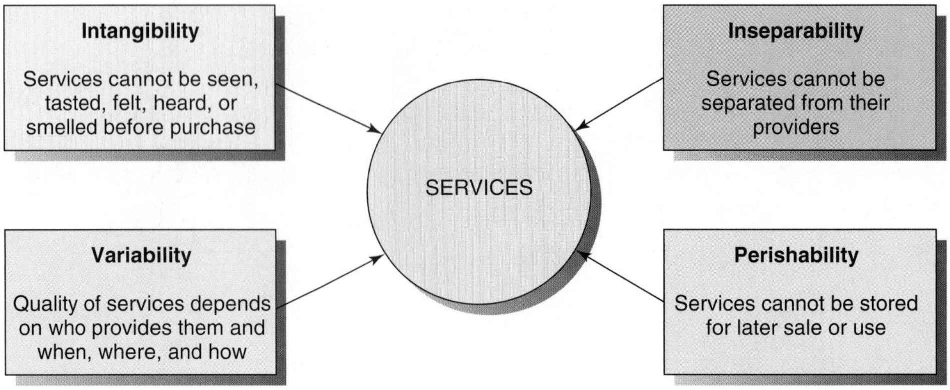

Intangibility		Inseparability
Services cannot be seen, tasted, felt, heard, or smelled before purchase		Services cannot be separated from their providers

SERVICES

Variability		Perishability
Quality of services depends on who provides them and when, where, and how		Services cannot be stored for later sale or use

Figure 7-5
Four service characteristics

providers are people or machines. If a service employee provides the service, then the employee is a part of the service. Because the customer is also present as the service is produced, *provider–customer interaction* is a special feature of services marketing. Both the provider and the customer affect the service outcome.

Service variability
A major characteristic of services—their quality may vary greatly, depending on who provides them and when, where, and how.

Service variability means that the quality of services depends on who provides them as well as when, where, and how they are provided. For example, some hotels—say, Marriott—have reputations for providing better service than others. Still, within a given Marriott hotel, one registration-desk employee may be cheerful and efficient, whereas another standing just a few feet away may be unpleasant and slow. Even the quality of a single Marriott employee's service varies according to his or her energy and frame of mind at the time of each customer encounter.

Service perishability
A major characteristic of services—they cannot be stored for later sale or use.

Service perishability means that services cannot be stored for later sale or use. Some doctors charge patients for missed appointments because the service value existed only at that point and disappeared when the patient did not show up. The perishability of services is not a problem when demand is steady. However, when demand fluctuates, service firms often have difficult problems. For example, because of rush-hour demand, public transportation companies have to own much more equipment than they would if demand were even throughout the day. Thus, service firms often design strategies for producing a better match between demand and supply. For instance, hotels and resorts charge lower prices in the off-season to attract more guests. And restaurants hire part-time employees to serve during peak periods.

Marketing Strategies for Service Firms

Just like manufacturing businesses, good service firms use marketing to position themselves strongly in chosen target markets. Southwest Airlines positions itself as "Just Plane Smart" for commuter flyers—a no-frills, short-haul airline charging very low fares. The Ritz-Carlton Hotel positions itself as offering a memorable experience that "enlivens the senses, instills well-being, and fulfills even the unexpressed wishes and needs of our guests." These and other service firms establish their positions through traditional marketing mix activities.

However, because services differ from tangible products, they often require additional marketing approaches. In a product business, products are fairly standardized and can sit on shelves waiting for customers. But in a service business, the customer and front-line service employee *interact* to create the service. Thus, service providers must interact effectively with customers to create superior value during service encounters.

Effective interaction, in turn, depends on the skills of front-line service employees and on the service production and support processes backing these employees.

The Service–Profit Chain Successful service companies focus their attention on *both* their customers and their employees. They understand the **service–profit chain**, which links service firm profits with employee and customer satisfaction. This chain consists of five links:[22]

- *Internal service quality*—superior employee selection and training, a quality work environment, and strong support for those dealing with customers, which results in . . .
- *Satisfied and productive service employees*—more satisfied, loyal, and hard-working employees, which results in . . .
- *Greater service value*—more effective and efficient customer value creation and service delivery, which results in . . .
- *Satisfied and loyal customers*—satisfied customers who remain loyal, repeat purchase, and refer other customers, which results in . . .
- *Healthy service profits and growth*—superior service firm performance.

Therefore, reaching service profits and growth goals begins with taking care of those who take care of customers (see Marketing at Work 7-3).

All of this suggests that service marketing requires more than just traditional external marketing using the four *P*s. Figure 7-6 shows that service marketing also requires *internal marketing* and *interactive marketing*. **Internal marketing** means that the service firm must effectively train and motivate its customer-contact employees and all the supporting service people to work as a *team* to provide customer satisfaction. For the firm to deliver consistently high service quality, marketers must get everyone in the organization to practice a customer orientation. In fact, internal marketing must *precede* external marketing.

Interactive marketing means that service quality depends heavily on the quality of the buyer–seller interaction during the service encounter. In product marketing, product quality often depends little on how the product is obtained. But in services marketing, service quality depends on both the service deliverer and the quality of the delivery. Thus, service marketers cannot assume that they will satisfy the customer simply by providing good technical service. They have to master interactive marketing skills as well.

Today, as competition and costs increase, and as productivity and quality decrease, more service marketing sophistication is needed. Service companies face three major marketing tasks: They want to increase their *competitive differentiation*, *service quality*, and *productivity*.

Service-profit chain
The chain that links service firm profits with employee and customer satisfaction.

Internal marketing
Marketing by a service firm to train and effectively motivate its customer-contact employees and all the supporting service people to work as a team to provide customer satisfaction.

Interactive marketing
Marketing by a service firm that recognizes that perceived service quality depends heavily on the quality of buyer-seller interaction.

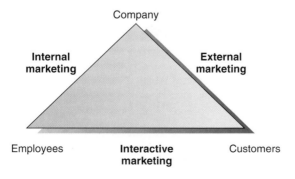

Figure 7-6
Three types of service marketing

Ritz-Carlton: Taking Care of Those Who Take Care of Customers

Ritz-Carlton, a chain of luxury hotels renowned for outstanding service, caters to the top 5 percent of corporate and leisure travelers. The company's Credo sets lofty customer-service goals: "The Ritz-Carlton Hotel is a place where the genuine care and comfort of our guests is our highest mission. We pledge to provide the finest personal service and facilities for our guests who will always enjoy a warm, relaxed yet refined ambience. The Ritz-Carlton experience enlivens the senses, instills well-being, and fulfills even the unexpressed wishes and needs of our guests."

The Credo is more than just words on paper—Ritz-Carlton delivers on its promises. In surveys of departing guests, some 95 percent report that they've had a truly memorable experience. In fact, at Ritz-Carlton, exceptional service encounters have become almost commonplace. Take the experiences of Nancy and Harvey Heffner of Manhattan, who stayed at the Ritz-Carlton Naples, in Naples, Florida. As reported in the *New York Times*:

"The hotel is elegant and beautiful," Mrs. Heffner said, "but more important is the beauty expressed

Ritz-Carlton understands that outstanding service begins with taking care of those who take care of customers.

by the staff. They can't do enough to please you." When the couple's son became sick last year in Naples, the hotel staff brought him hot tea with honey at all hours of the night, she said. When Mr. Heffner had to fly home on business for a day and his return flight was delayed, a driver for the hotel waited in the lobby most of the night.

Such personal, high-quality service has also made the Ritz-Carlton a favorite among conventioneers. Comments one convention planner, "They not only treat us like kings when we hold our top-level meetings in their hotels, but we just never get any complaints."

In 1991, Ritz-Carlton received 121 quality-related awards, along with industry-best rankings by all three hotel-rating organizations. In 1992, it became the first hotel company to win the Malcolm Baldrige National Quality Award. More importantly, service quality has resulted in high customer retention: More than 90 percent of Ritz-Carlton customers return. And despite its hefty $150 average room rate, the chain enjoys a 70 percent occupancy rate, almost nine points above the industry average.

Most of the responsibility for keeping guests satisfied falls to Ritz-Carlton's customer-contact employees. Thus, the hotel chain takes great care in selecting its personnel. "We want only people who care about people," notes Patrick Mene, the company's vice-president of quality. Once selected, employees are given intensive training in the art of coddling customers. New employees attend a two-day orientation, in which top management drums into them the "20 Ritz-Carlton Basics." Basic number one: "The *Credo* will be known, owned, and energized by all employees."

Employees are taught to do everything they can to never lose a guest. "There's no negotiating at Ritz-Carlton when it comes to solving customer problems," says Mene. Staff learn that *anyone* who receives a customer complaint *owns* that complaint until it's resolved. They are trained to drop whatever they're doing to help a customer—no matter what they're doing or what their department. Ritz-Carlton employees are empowered to handle problems on the spot, without consulting higher-ups. Each employee can spend up to $2,000 to redress a guest grievance, and each is allowed to break from his or her routine for as long as needed to make a guest happy. "We master customer satisfaction at the individual level," adds Mene. "This is our most sensitive listening post . . . our early warning system." Thus, while competitors are still reading guest comment cards to learn about customer problems, Ritz-Carlton has already resolved them.

Ritz-Carlton instills a sense of pride in its employees. "You serve," they are told, "but you are not servants." The company motto states, "We are ladies and gentlemen serving ladies and gentlemen." Employees understand their role in Ritz-Carlton's success. "We might not be able to afford a hotel like this," says employee Tammy Patton, "but we can make it so people who can afford it will want to keep coming here."

And so they do. When it comes to customer satisfaction, no detail is too small. Customer-contact people are taught to greet guests warmly and sincerely, using guest names when possible. They learn to use the proper language with guests—words like *good morning*, *certainly*, *I'll be happy to*, and *my pleasure*, never *Hi* or *How's it going?* The Ritz-Carlton Basics urge employees to escort guests to another area of the hotel rather than pointing out directions, to answer the phone within three rings and with a "smile," and to take pride and care in their personal appearance. As Jorge Gonzalez, general manager of the Ritz-Carlton Naples, puts it, "When you invite guests to your house, you want everything to be perfect."

Ritz-Carlton recognizes and rewards employees who perform feats of outstanding service. Under its 5-Star Awards program, outstanding performers are nominated by peers and managers, and winners receive plaques at dinners celebrating their achievements. For on-the-spot recognition, managers award Gold Standard Coupons, redeemable for items in the gift shop and free weekend stays at the hotel. Ritz-Carlton further rewards and motivates its employees with events such as Super Sports Day, an employee talent show, luncheons celebrating employee anniversaries, a family picnic, and special themes in employee dining rooms. As a result, Ritz-Carlton's employees appear to be just as satisfied as its customers. Employee turnover is less than 30 percent a year, compared with 45 percent at other luxury hotels.

Ritz-Carlton's success is based on a simple philosophy: To take care of customers, you must first take care of those who take care of customers. Satisfied employees deliver high service value, which then creates satisfied customers. Satisfied customers, in turn, create sales and profits for the company.

Sources: Quotes from Edwin McDowell, "Ritz-Carlton's Keys to Good Service," *The New York Times,* March 31, 1993, p. D1; Howard Schlossberg, "Measuring Customer Satisfaction Is Easy to Do—Until You Try," *Marketing News,* April 26, 1993, pp. 5, 8; and Ginger Conlon, "True Romance," *Sales & Marketing Management,* May 1996, pp. 85–90. Also see Don Peppers, "Digitizing Desire," *Forbes,* April 10, 1995, p. 76; and Julie Moline, "1997's Winning Hotel Chains," *Global Finance,* February 1998, pp. 20–22.

Managing Service Differentiation In these days of intense price competition, service marketers often complain about the difficulty of differentiating their services from those of competitors. To the extent that customers view the services of different providers as similar, they care less about the provider than the price.

The solution to price competition is to develop a differentiated offer, delivery, and image. The *offer* can include innovative features that set one company's offer apart from competitors' offers. For example, airlines have introduced innovations such as in-flight movies, advance seating, air-to-ground telephone service, and frequent-flyer award programs to differentiate their offers. British Airways even offers international travelers a sleeping compartment, hot showers, and cooked-to-order breakfasts.

Service companies can differentiate their service *delivery* by having more able and reliable customer-contact people, by developing a superior physical environment in which the service product is delivered, or by designing a superior delivery process. For example, a bank might offer its customers electronic home banking as a better way to access banking services than having to drive, park, and wait in line.

Finally, service companies also can work on differentiating their *images* through symbols and branding. For example, the Harris Bank of Chicago adopted the lion as its symbol on its stationery, in its advertising, and even as stuffed animals offered to new depositors. The well-known Harris lion confers an image of strength on the bank. Other

To differentiate its service, British Airways offers international travelers such features as sleeping compartments and hot showers. As the comments in this ad show, customers really appreciate such services.

This ad just writes itself.

well-known service symbols include The Travelers' red umbrella, Merrill Lynch's bull, and Allstate's "good hands."

Managing Service Quality One of the major ways a service firm can differentiate itself is by delivering consistently higher quality than its competitors do. Like manufacturers before them, many service industries have now joined the total quality movement. Customer retention is perhaps the best measure of quality; a service firm's ability to hang onto its customers depends on how consistently it delivers value to them.[23]

Like product marketers, service providers need to identify the expectations of target customers concerning service quality. Unfortunately, service quality is harder to define and judge than is product quality. For instance, it is harder to get agreement on the quality of a haircut than on the quality of a hair dryer. Moreover, although greater service quality results in greater customer satisfaction, it also results in higher costs. Still, investments in service usually pay off through increased customer retention and sales.

Many service companies have invested heavily to develop streamlined and efficient service delivery systems. They want to ensure that customers will receive consistently high-quality service in every service encounter. However, unlike product manufacturers who can adjust their machinery and inputs until everything is perfect, service quality will always vary, depending on the interactions between employees and customers. Problems will inevitably occur. As hard as they try, even the best companies will have an occasional late delivery, burned steak, or grumpy employee. However, although a company cannot always prevent service problems, it can learn to recover from them. And good *service recovery* can turn angry customers into loyal ones. In fact, good recovery can win more customer purchasing and loyalty than if things had gone well in the first place. Therefore, companies should take steps not only to provide good service every time but also to recover from service mistakes when they do occur.[24]

The first step is to *empower* front-line service employees—to give them the authority, responsibility, and incentives they need to recognize, care about, and tend to customer needs. At Marriott, for example, well-trained employees are given the authority to do whatever it takes, on the spot, to keep guests happy. They are also expected to help management ferret out the cause of guests' problems and to inform managers of ways to improve overall hotel service and guests' comfort.[25]

Studies of well-managed service companies show that they share a number of common virtues regarding service quality. Top service companies are *customer obsessed* and set *high service quality standards*. They do not settle merely for good service, they aim for 100 percent defect-free service. A 98 percent performance standard may sound good but, using this standard, 64,000 Federal Express packages would be lost each day, 10 words would be misspelled on each printed page, 400,000 prescriptions would be misfilled daily, and drinking water would be unsafe 8 days a year.[26]

Top service firms also *watch service performance closely*, both their own and that of competitors. They use methods such as comparison shopping, customer surveys, and suggestion and complaint forms. For example, General Electric sends out 700,000 response cards each year to households who rate their service people's performance. Citibank takes regular measures of "ART"—accuracy, responsiveness, and timeliness— and sends out employees who act as customers to check on service quality.

Good service companies also communicate their concerns about service quality to employees and provide performance feedback. At Federal Express, quality measurements are everywhere. When employees walk in the door in the morning, they see the previous week's on-time percentages. Then, the company's in-house television station gives them detailed breakdowns of what happened yesterday and any potential problems for the day ahead.

Managing Service Productivity With their costs rising rapidly, service firms are under great pressure to increase service productivity. They can do so in several ways. The service providers can train current employees better or hire new ones who will work harder or more skillfully. Or the service providers can increase the quantity of their service by giving up some quality. Doctors working for health maintenance organizations (HMOs) have moved toward handling more patients and giving less time to each. The provider can "industrialize the service" by adding equipment and standardizing production, as in McDonald's assembly-line approach to fast-food retailing.

Finally, the service provider can harness the power of technology. Although we often think of technology's power to save time and costs in manufacturing companies, it also has great—and often untapped—potential to make service workers more productive. Consider this example:[27]

✧ Using a help-desk computerized system called Apriori, Storage Dimensions can answer customer-service questions on the spot. When a customer calls Storage Dimensions with a problem, the operator inputs key words. If the customer's question has been asked and answered before by others, as so many have, a solution document "bubbles up" to the top of the PC screen and customer's problems get solved on the spot. Since installing Apriori, SD has reduced problem resolution time from an average of two hours to 20 minutes. As an added bonus, the company has also used information gleaned during the "help" conversations to generate sales leads and product-development ideas.

However, companies must avoid pushing productivity so hard that doing so reduces quality. Attempts to industrialize a service or to cut costs can make a service company more efficient in the short run but reduce its longer-run ability to innovate, maintain service quality, or respond to consumer needs and desires. In some cases, service providers accept reduced productivity in order to create more service differentiation or quality.

International Product and Services Marketing

International product and service marketers face special challenges. First, they must figure out what products and services to introduce and in which countries. Then, they must decide how much to standardize or adapt their products and services for world markets. On the one hand, companies would like to standardize their offerings. Standardization helps a company to develop a consistent worldwide image. It also lowers manufacturing costs and eliminates duplication of research and development, advertising, and product design efforts. On the other hand, consumers around the world differ in their cultures, attitudes, and buying behaviors. And markets vary in their economic conditions, competition, legal requirements, and physical environments. Companies must usually respond to these differences by adapting their product offerings. Something as simple as an electrical outlet can create big product problems:

Those who have traveled across Europe know the frustration of electrical plugs, different voltages, and other annoyances of international travel. . . . Philips, the electrical appliance manufacturer, has to produce 12 kinds of irons to serve just its European market. The problem is that Europe does not have a universal [electrical] standard. The ends of irons bristle with different plugs for different countries. Some have three prongs, others two; prongs protrude straight or angled, round or rectangular, fat, thin, and sometimes sheathed. There are circular plug faces, squares, pentagons, and hexagons. Some are perforated and some are notched. One French plug has a niche like a keyhole; British plugs carry fuses.[28]

Packaging also presents new challenges for international marketers. Packaging issues can be subtle. For example, names, labels, and colors may not translate easily from one country to another. A firm using yellow flowers in its logo might fare well in the United States but meet with disaster in Mexico, where a yellow flower symbolizes death or disrespect. Similarly, although Nature's Gift might be an appealing name for gourmet mushrooms in America, it would be deadly in Germany, where *gift* means "poison." Packaging may also have to be tailored to meet the physical characteristics of consumers in various parts of the world. For instance, soft drinks are sold in smaller cans in Japan to better fit the smaller Japanese hand. Thus, although product and package standardization can produce benefits, companies must usually adapt their offerings to the unique needs of specific international markets.

Service marketers also face special challenges when going global. Some service industries have a long history of international operations. For example, the commercial banking industry was one of the first to grow internationally. Banks had to provide global services in order to meet the foreign exchange and credit needs of their home country clients wanting to sell overseas. In recent years, many banks have become truly global operations. Germany's Deutsche Bank, for example, has branches in 41 countries. Thus, for its clients around the world who wish to take advantage of growth opportunities created by German reunification, Deutsche Bank can raise money not just in Frankfurt but also in Zurich, London, Paris, and Tokyo.

The travel industry also moved naturally into international operations. American hotel and airline companies grew quickly in Europe and Asia during the economic expansion that followed World War II. Credit card companies soon followed—the early worldwide presence of American Express has now been matched by Visa and Master-Card. Business travelers and vacationers like the convenience, and they have now come to expect that their credit cards will be honored wherever they go.

Professional and business services industries such as accounting, management consulting, and advertising have only recently globalized. The international growth of these firms followed the globalization of the manufacturing companies they serve. For example, as their client companies began to employ global marketing and advertising strategies, advertising agencies and other marketing services firms responded by globalizing their own operations.

Retailers are among the latest service businesses to go global. As their home markets become saturated with stores, American retailers such as Wal-Mart, Kmart, Toys 'Я' Us, Office Depot, Saks Fifth Avenue, and Disney are expanding into faster-growing markets abroad. The Japanese retailer Yaohan now operates the largest shopping center in Asia, the 21-story Nextage Shanghai Tower in China, and Carrefour of France is the leading retailer in Brazil and Argentina. Asian shoppers now buy American products in Dutch-owned Makro stores, now Southeast Asia's biggest store group with sales in the region of more than $2 billion.[29]

Service companies wanting to operate in other countries are not always welcomed with open arms. Whereas manufacturers usually face straightforward tariff, quota, or currency restrictions when attempting to sell their products in another country, service providers are likely to face more subtle barriers. In some cases, rules and regulations

Retailers are among the latest service businesses to go global. Here, Asian shoppers buy American products in a Dutch-owned Makro store in Kuala Lumpur.

affecting international service firms reflect the host country's traditions. In others, they appear to protect the country's own fledgling service industries from large global competitors with greater resources. In still other cases, however, the restrictions seem to have little purpose other than to make entry difficult for foreign service firms.

A Turkish law, for example, forbids international accounting firms from bringing capital into the country to set up offices and requires them to use the names of local partners in their marketing rather than their own internationally known company names. To audit the books of a multinational company's branch in Buenos Aires, an accountant must have the equivalent of a high school education in Argentinean geography and history. In New Delhi, India, international insurance companies are not allowed to sell property and casualty policies to the country's fast-growing business community or life insurance to its huge middle class.[30]

Despite such difficulties, the trend toward growth of global service companies will continue, especially in banking, airlines, telecommunications, and professional services. Today, service firms are no longer simply following their manufacturing customers. Instead, they are taking the lead in international expansion.

REST STOP Reviewing the Concepts

Time to kick back and reflect on the key concepts in this first marketing-mix chapter on products and services. A product is more than a simple set of tangible features. In fact, many marketing offers consist of combinations of both tangible goods and services, ranging from *pure tangible goods* at one extreme to *pure services* at the other. Each product or service offered to customers can be viewed on three levels. The *core product* consists of the core problem-solving benefits that consumers seek when they buy a product. The *actual product* exists around the core and includes the quality level, features, design, brand name, and packaging. The *augmented product* is the actual product plus the various services and benefits offered with it, such as warranty, free delivery, installation, and maintenance.

1. Define product and the major classifications of products and services.

Broadly defined, a *product* is anything that can be offered to a market for attention, acquisition, use, or consumption that might satisfy a want or need. Products include physical objects, services, persons, places, organizations, ideas, or mixes of these entities. Services are products that consist of activities, benefits, or satisfactions offered for sale that are essentially intangible, such as banking, hotel, tax preparation, and home repair services.

Products and services fall into two broad classes based on the types of consumers that use them. *Consumer products*, those bought by final consumers, are usually classified according to consumer shopping habits (convenience products, shopping products, specialty products, and unsought products). *Industrial products*, purchased for further processing or use in conducting a business, are classified according to their cost and the way they enter the production process (materials and parts, capital items, and supplies and services). Other marketable entities—such as organizations, persons, places, and ideas—can also be thought of as products.

2. Describe the roles of product and service branding, packaging, labeling, and product support services.

Companies develop strategies for items in their product lines by making decisions about product attributes, branding, packaging, labeling, and product support services. *Product attribute* decisions involve the product quality, features, and design the company will offer. *Branding* decisions include selecting a brand name, garnering brand sponsorship, and developing a brand strategy. *Packaging* provides many key benefits, such as protection, economy, convenience, and promotion. Package decisions often include designing *labels*, which identify, describe, and possibly promote the product. Companies also develop *product support services* that enhance customer service and satisfaction and safeguard against competitors.

3. Explain the decisions that companies make when developing product lines and mixes.

Most companies produce a product line rather than a single product. A *product line* is a group of products that are related in function, customer-purchase needs, or distribution channels. In developing a product line strategy, marketers face a number of tough decisions. *Line stretching* involves extending a line downward, upward, or in both directions to occupy a gap that might otherwise be filled by a competitor. In contrast, *line filling* involves adding items within the present range of the line. The set of product lines and items offered to customers by a particular seller make up the *product mix*. The mix can be described by four dimensions: width, length, depth, and consistency. These dimensions are the tools for developing the company's product strategy.

4. Identify the four characteristics that affect the marketing of a service.

As we move toward a *world service economy*, marketers need to know more about marketing services. *Services* are characterized by four key characteristics. First, services are *intangible*; they cannot be seen, tasted, felt, heard, or smelled. Services are also *inseparable* from their service providers. Services are *variable* because their quality depends on the service provider as well as the environment surrounding the service delivery. Finally, services are *perishable*. As a result, they cannot be inventoried, built up, or back ordered. Each characteristic poses problems and marketing requirements. Marketers work to find ways to make the service more tangible, to increase the productivity of providers who are inseparable from their products, to standardize the quality in the face of variability, and to improve demand movements and supply capacities in the face of service perishability.

5. Discuss the additional marketing considerations that services require.

Good service companies focus attention on *both* customers and employees. They understand the *service–profit chain*, which links service firm profits with employee and customer satisfaction. Services marketing strategy calls not only for external marketing but also for *internal marketing* to motivate employees and *interactive marketing* to create service delivery skills among service providers. To succeed, service marketers must create *competitive differentiation*, offer high *service quality*, and find ways to increase *service productivity*.

Navigating the Key Terms

For a detailed analysis of the meaning and importance of each of the following key terms, visit our Web page at **www.prenhall.com/kotler.**

Brand
Brand equity
Brand extension
Co-branding
Consumer product
Convenience product

Industrial product
Interactive marketing
Internal marketing
Line extension
Packaging
Private brand (or store brand)
Product
Product line
Product mix (or product assortment)
Product quality
Service

Service inseparability
Service intangibility
Service perishability
Service variability
Service–profit chain
Shopping product
Slotting fees
Social marketing
Specialty product
Unsought product

Travel Log

The following concept checks and discussion questions will help you to keep track of and apply the concepts you've studied in this chapter.

Concept Checks

1. The text defines a(n) _____ as anything that can be offered to a market for attention, acquisition, use, or consumption and that might satisfy a want or need.
2. _____ are a form of product that consist of activities, benefits, or satisfactions offered for sale that are essentially intangible and do not result in the ownership of anything.
3. Product planners need to think about products and services on three levels: the _____ product, the _____ product, and the _____ product.
4. _____ products are less frequently purchased consumer products and services that customers carefully compare on suitability, quality, price, and style.
5. "Smokey the Bear," "Keep America Beautiful," and "Join the Peace Corps" are all examples of _____ marketing advertising campaigns created by the Advertising Council of America.

6. A(n) _____ is a name, term, sign, symbol, or design, or a combination of these that identifies the maker or seller of a product or service.
7. A good brand name should: (a) suggest something about the product's _____; (b) be easy to _____; (c) be _____; (d) easily translate into _____; and, (e) be capable of _____.
8. _____ are additional items in a given category under the same brand name, such as new flavors, forms, colors, ingredients, or package sizes.
9. Product mix _____ refers to the number of different product lines the company carries.
10. A company must consider four special service characteristics when designing marketing programs: _____, _____, _____, and _____.*

Discussing the Issues

1. What do you see as the primary differences between products and services? Give illustrations of the differences that you identify. Give an original example of a hybrid offer.
2. List and explain the core, actual, and augmented

---

* *Concept checks answers:* 1. product; 2. service; 3. core, actual, and augmented; 4. shopping; 5. social; 6. brand; 7. (a) benefits and qualities; (b) pronounce, recognize, and remember; (c) distinctive; (d) foreign languages; (e) registration and legal protection; 8. line extensions; 9. width; 10. intangibility, inseparability, variability, and perishability

products for educational experiences that universities offer. How are these different (if there is a difference) from the products offered by junior colleges?

3. In recent years, marketers have broadened marketing efforts into the areas of organizations, persons, places, and ideas. Give an example of recent successful marketing efforts in each of the four areas. Do you think these areas are valid extensions for marketing efforts? Explain your reasoning.

4. For many years there was one type of Coca-Cola, one type of Tide, and one type of Crest (in mint and regular). Now we find Coke in six or more varieties; Ultra, Liquid, and Unscented Tide; and Crest Gel with sparkles for kids. List some of the issues these brand extensions raise for the manufacturers, retailers, and consumers. Is more always better?

5. Illustrate how a theater can deal with the intangibility, inseparability, variability, and perishability of the service it provides. Give specific examples.

 # Traveling the Net

Point of Interest: Service Strategies

The core service strategy in the automobile industry is transportation. The problem-solving benefit is how to get from one place to another quickly and safely. However, most automobile manufacturers attempt to differentiate their products with many additional benefits. The various approaches to service are almost as varied as are the automobile manufacturers themselves. Examine the following Web sites for Ford (www.ford.com), General Motors (www.gm.com), Chrysler (www.chrysler.com), Honda (www.honda.com), Lexus (www.lexus.com), Mercedes-Benz (www.MBUSA.com), and Toyota Motors (www.toyota.com). Rather than just examining the automobiles, look closely for services and service options. Notice the different strategies used by each company.

For Discussion

1. What do you think are the primary services offered by the various automobile manufacturers? List these in a grid format so that you can compare one company against another.

2. What are the common services that seem to be present in the majority of the service strategies? How do the companies seem to differentiate themselves with respect to service?

3. Did you observe any service–profit chains in the Web sites that you examined? If so, describe what you found.

4. Did you observe any attempt by the various automobile manufacturers to do interactive marketing with respect to service? If so, describe what you observed

5. If you were choosing a new car, truck, SUV, or van (based on what you have observed about service on the various Web sites), which manufacturer's product would you choose? Explain your choice.

Application Thinking

Saturn, which for the past several years has been a breath of fresh air to General Motors' product line, has begun to slip recently. In response, GM has revamped Saturn's Web site and service strategies. The Saturn Web site is now all business. Gone is the flashy advertising approach that (while creative) was no longer attracting service-oriented customers. Today, the Web site helps customers select models, calculate payments, and find dealers on-line. Saturn has even made the Web site the star of its recent television advertising campaign. Web site visits have tripled in recent months to an estimated 7,000 per day. The company believes that as much as 80 percent of sales leads are now generated by the revamped Web site. Review the Saturn site (www.saturn.com) and analyze the services that it provides. Put yourself in the shoes of a new car buyer. What additions would you suggest? What weaknesses (if any) do you find? Compare your analysis of Saturn to the grid you prepared previously. Assuming you were the marketing manager for Saturn, recommend a strategy for increasing service to customers and to Internet users.

MAP—Marketing Applications

MAP Stop 7

The explosion in Internet usage has many companies rethinking their brand strategies. Increasing numbers of consumers are turning from one-to-one relationships in stores to one-to-one relationships via their home computers and the Internet. In response, more and more companies are integrating Web marketing efforts into their marketing mixes. Following Web pioneers such as America Online, Yahoo!, and Amazon.com, big spenders such as Coca-Cola, General Motors, and Procter & Gamble are going on-line in a big way. In addition to old-style brand and loyalty building, the Web adds "experiential marketing" components (where consumers experience the brand in different ways). However, using the Web to build new brand loyalties, disseminate information, and form new relationships takes time. Hence, Internet strategies will have to focus on getting Internet surfers to visit frequently and to linger longer, not "hit and run." Companies such as Saturn, Eddie Bauer, and L.L. Bean are all betting that browsing the Web will be easier and more popular in the future than browsing the local car lot or department store. According to many experts, ordering on-line will soon be standard practice.

Thinking Like a Marketing Manager

1. Can brand loyalty be developed or maintained through on-line shopping? Explain.
2. Explain how companies like Saturn, Eddie Bauer, Amazon.com, and L.L. Bean have become successful Internet marketers. Do you see any common strategies?
3. How could a company give a consumer more experiential marketing experiences on a Web site?
4. Assume that you are the marketing manager for (a) Kodak, (b) Budweiser, (c) Revlon, or (d) Pepsi. Design a strategy for bringing Generation Xers to your Web site. What goals would you set for the site? What experiences might you give visitors to the site? How could you get them to stay on your site longer?

New-Product Development and Product Life-Cycle Strategies

ROAD MAP:
Previewing the Concepts

In the previous chapter, you learned about decisions that marketers make in managing individual brands and entire product mixes. In this chapter, we'll cruise on into two additional product topics: developing new products and managing products through their life cycles. New products are the lifeblood of an organization. However, new-product development is risky, and many new products fail. So, the first part of this chapter lays out a process for finding and growing successful new products. Once introduced, marketers want their products to enjoy a long and happy life. In the second part of the chapter, you'll see that every product passes through several life-cycle stages and that each stage poses new challenges requiring different marketing strategies and tactics.

▶ After studying this chapter, you should be able to

1. **explain how companies find and develop new-product ideas**
2. **list and define the steps in the new-product development process**
3. **describe the stages of the product life cycle**
4. **describe how marketing strategies change during the product's life cycle**

First point of interest: Gillette, described by some as "a new-product machine." The chances are good that you use a Gillette shaving product—Gillette owns a mind-boggling 68 percent of the U.S. wet-shave market! As you'll see, it owes much of this success to its passion for innovation and its finely tuned new-product development process.

"**N**ew products!" declares Gillette's Chairman and CEO Alfred M. Zeien, "that's the name of the game." Since its founding in 1901, Gillette's heavy commitment to innovation has kept the company razor sharp. Gillette is best known for its absolute dominance of the razor-and-blades market. However, all of its divisions—Duracell batteries, Gillette toiletries and cosmetics (Right Guard, Soft & Dri), stationery products (Parker, Paper Mate, and Waterman pens), Oral-B toothbrushes, and Braun electrical appliances—share common traits: Each is profitable, fast growing, number-one worldwide in its markets, and anchored by a steady flow of innovative new-product offerings. Zeien predicts that 50 percent of Gillette's new products will soon come from products that didn't exist five years ago—that's twice the level of innovation found at the average consumer products company. "Gillette is a new-product machine," says one Wall Street analyst.

New products don't just happen at Gillette. New-product success starts with a companywide culture that supports innovation. Whereas many companies try to protect their successful current products, Gillette encourages innovations that will cannibalize its established product hits. "They know that if they don't bring out a new zinger, someone else will," observes an industry consultant. Gillette also accepts blunders and dead ends

as a normal part of creativity and innovation. It knows that it must generate dozens of new-product ideas to get just one success in the marketplace. The company scorns what CEO Zeien calls "putting blue dots in the soap powder"—attaching superficial frills to existing products and labeling them innovations. However, Gillette strongly encourages its people to take creative risks in applying cutting-edge technologies to find substantial improvements that make life easier for customers.

New-product development is complex and expensive, but Gillette's mastery of the process has put the company in a class of its own. For example, Gillette spent $275 million on designing and developing its Sensor family of razors, garnering 29 patents along the way. It spent an incredible $1 billion on the development of Sensor's successor, the triple-bladed Mach3, and applied for 35 more patents. Competing brands Bic and Wilkinson have managed to claim significant shares of the disposable-razor market, and Shick, Norelco, and Remington compete effectively in electric razors with Gillette's Braun unit. But Gillette, with its stunning technological superiority, operates with virtually no competition worldwide in the burgeoning cartridge-razor sector. Backed by Gillette's biggest new-product launch ever, the Mach3 promises to strengthen the company's stranglehold on this market. Within only a few months of its introduction, the new razor and blades were number-one sellers.

At Gillette, it seems that almost everyone gets involved in one way or another with new-product development. Even people who don't participate directly in the product design and development are likely to be pressed into service testing prototypes. Every working day at Gillette, 200 volunteers from various departments come to work unshaven, troop to the second floor of the company's gritty South Boston manufacturing and research plant, and enter small booths with a sink and mirror. There they take instructions from technicians on the other side of a small window as to which razor, shaving cream, or aftershave to use. The volunteers evaluate razors for sharpness of blade, smoothness of glide, and ease of handling. When finished, they enter their judgments into a computer. In a nearby shower room, women perform the same ritual on their legs, underarms, and what the company delicately refers to as the "bikini area." "We bleed so you'll get a good shave at home," says one Gillette employee.

Gillette also excels at bringing new products to market. The company understands that, once introduced, fledgling products need generous manufacturing and marketing support to thrive in the hotly competitive consumer products marketplace. To deliver the required support, Gillette has devised a formula that calls for R&D, capital investment, and advertising expenditures—which it refers to collectively as "growth drivers"—to rise in combination at least as fast as sales. Last year, spending on these growth drivers rose 16 percent as compared with a 12 percent rise in sales. The company is spending a staggering $300 million on introductory advertising and marketing for the Mach3 alone.

Thus, over the decades, superior new products have been the cornerstone of Gillette's amazing success. Since 1990, the company's earnings have grown at an annual rate of 17 percent, with an average annual return on equity of 33 percent. Among consumer products companies, Gillette's return on sales is second only to Coca-Cola's. The company commands the loyalty of more than 700 million shavers in 200 countries around the globe. These customers have purchased hundreds of millions of Sensor razors and billions of blades, giving Gillette 68 percent of the wet-shave market in the United States, 73 percent in Europe, and 91 percent in Latin America.

Gillette's new-product prowess is so much a part of its image that it has even become the stuff of jokes. Quips down-home humorist Dave Barry, "One day soon the Gillette Company will announce the development of a razor that, thanks to a computer microchip, can actually travel ahead in time and shave beard hairs that don't even exist yet."[1]

A company has to be good at developing and managing new products. Every product seems to go through a life cycle: it is born, goes through several phases, and eventually dies as newer products come along that better serve consumer needs. This product life cycle presents two major challenges: First, because all products eventually decline, a firm must be good at developing new products to replace aging ones (the problem of *new-product development*). Second, the firm must be good at adapting its marketing strategies in the face of changing tastes, technologies, and competition as products pass through life-cycle stages (the problem of *product life-cycle strategies*). We first look at the problem of finding and developing new products and then at the problem of managing them successfully over their life cycles.

New-Product Development Strategy

Given the rapid changes in consumer tastes, technology, and competition, companies must develop a steady stream of new products and services. A firm can obtain new products in two ways. One is through *acquisition*—by buying a whole company, a patent, or a license to produce someone else's product. The other is through **new-product development** in the company's own research and development department. By *new products* we mean original products, product improvements, product modifications, and new brands that the firm develops through its own research and development efforts. In this chapter, we concentrate on new-product development.

Innovation can be very risky. Ford lost $350 million on its Edsel automobile, RCA lost $580 million on its SelectaVision videodisc player, and Texas Instruments lost a staggering $660 million before withdrawing from the home computer business. Other costly product failures from sophisticated companies include New Coke (Coca-Cola

New-product development
The development of original products, product improvements, product modifications, and new brands through the firm's own R&D efforts.

Company), Eagle Snacks (Anheuser-Busch), Zap Mail electronic mail (Federal Express), Polarvision instant movies (Polaroid), Premier "smokeless" cigarettes (R. J. Reynolds), Clorox detergent (Clorox Company), and Arch Deluxe sandwiches (McDonald's).

New products continue to fail at a disturbing rate. One study estimated that new consumer packaged goods (consisting mostly of line extensions) fail at a rate of 80 percent. Another study suggested that although some 13,000 new products hit the market each year, only 40 percent will be around five years later. Still another study found that about 33 percent of new industrial products fail at launch.[2] Why do so many new products fail? There are several reasons. Although an idea may be good, the market size may have been overestimated. Perhaps the actual product was not designed as well as it should have been. Or maybe it was incorrectly positioned in the market, priced too high, or advertised poorly. A high-level executive might push a favorite idea despite poor marketing research findings. Sometimes the costs of product development are higher than expected, and sometimes competitors fight back harder than expected.

Because so many new products fail, companies are anxious to learn how to improve their odds of new-product success. One way is to identify successful new products and find out what they have in common. Various studies suggest that new-product success depends on developing a *unique superior product*, one with higher quality, new features, and higher value in use. Another key success factor is a *well-defined product concept* prior to development, in which the company carefully defines and assesses the target market, the product requirements, and the benefits before proceeding. Other success factors have also been suggested: senior management commitment, relentless innovation, and a smoothly functioning new-product development process.[3] In all, to create successful new products, a company must understand its consumers, markets, and competitors and develop products that deliver superior value to customers.

So companies face a problem: they must develop new products, but the odds weigh heavily against success. The solution lies in strong new-product planning and in setting up a systematic *new-product development process* for finding and growing new products. Figure 8-1 shows the eight major steps in this process.

Idea Generation

Idea generation
The systematic search for new-product ideas.

New-product development starts with **idea generation**—the systematic search for new-product ideas. A company typically has to generate many ideas in order to find a few good ones. At Gillette, of every 45 carefully developed new-product ideas, 3 make it into

Figure 8-1
Major stages in new-product development

the development stage and only one eventually reaches the marketplace. DuPont has found that it can take as many as 3,000 raw ideas to produce just two winning commercial products, and pharmaceuticals companies may require 6,000 to 8,000 starting ideas for every successful commercial new product.[4]

The search for new-product ideas should be systematic rather than haphazard. Otherwise, although the company may find many ideas, most will not be good ones for its type of business. Top management can avoid this error by carefully defining its new-product development strategy. Major sources of new-product ideas include internal sources, customers, competitors, distributors and suppliers, and others.

Many new-product ideas come from *internal sources* within the company. The company can find new ideas through formal research and development. It can pick the brains of its executives, scientists, engineers, and manufacturing people. The company's salespeople are another good source because they are in daily contact with customers. Toyota claims that its employees submit two million ideas annually—about 35 suggestions per employee—and that more than 85 percent of these ideas are implemented. Some companies have developed successful "intrapreneurial" programs that encourage employees to think up and develop new product ideas. For example, 3M's well-known "15 percent rule" allows employees to spend 15 percent of their time "bootlegging"— working on projects of personal interest whether or not those projects directly benefit the company. The spectacularly successful Post-it notes evolved out of this program. Similarly, Texas Instruments' IDEA program provides funds for employees who pursue their own ideas. Among the successful new products to come out of the IDEA program was TI's Speak 'n' Spell, the first children's toy to contain a microchip. Many other speaking toys followed, ultimately generating several hundred million dollars for TI.[5]

Good new-product ideas also come from watching and listening to *customers*. The company can analyze customer questions and complaints to find new products that better solve consumer problems. Company engineers or salespeople can meet with customers to get suggestions. Or the company can conduct surveys or focus groups to learn about consumer needs and wants. For example, 3M used focus groups to find a way to gain a foothold in the wool soap-scouring-pad market against established rivals SOS and Brillo. Consumers complained that standard wool pads scratched their expensive cookware. In response, 3M developed its highly successful Scotch-Brite Never Scratch soap pad, made from gentler minerals that did not damage cookware.[6]

Companies can learn a great deal from observing and listening to customers. United States Surgical Corporation (USSC) has developed most of its surgical instruments by working closely with surgeons. The company was quick to pick up on early experiments in laparoscopy, surgery performed by inserting a tiny TV camera into the body along with slim, long-handled instruments. In recent years, USSC's focus has changed from marketing individual surgical instruments to offering a total package of products and services aimed at helping hospitals achieve cost-effective surgery. Now, in addition to visiting with surgeons, the company invites representatives from materials management, financial, and other areas of customer hospitals to its corporate offices, listening and sharing information. USSC now captures about 58 percent of the single-use laparoscopy market.[7]

Finally, consumers often create new products and uses on their own, and companies can benefit by finding these products and putting them on the market. Customers can also be a good source of ideas for new product uses that can expand the market for and extend the life of current products. For example, the WD-40 Company, maker of the multipurpose household lubricant and solvent, sponsored annual contests to obtain new uses from customers (see Marketing at Work 8-1). Similarly, Avon capitalized on new uses discovered by consumers for its Skin-So-Soft bath oil and moisturizer. For years, customers have been spreading the word that Skin-So-Soft bath oil is also a terrific bug repellent.

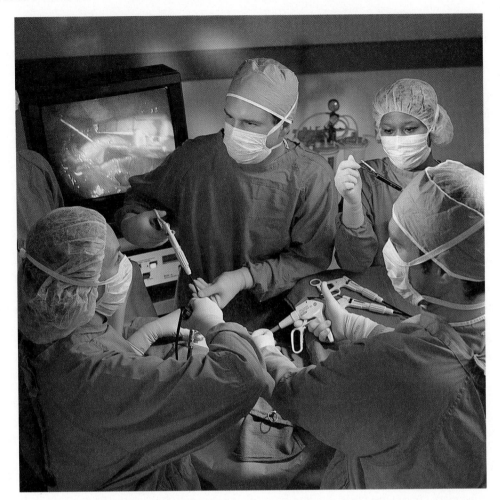

New-product ideas from customers: United States Surgical Corporation became the innovative leader in laparoscopic surgery by watching and listening to surgeons, even gowning up and joining them in the operating room.

Whereas some consumers were content simply to bathe in water scented with the fragrant oil, others carried it in their backpacks to mosquito-infested campsites or kept a bottle on the deck of their beach houses. Now, Avon is offering Skin-So-Soft Moisturizing Suncare Plus, a triple-action product that provides an insect repellent and waterproof SPF 15 sunscreen as well as moisturizers.[8]

Competitors are another good source of new-product ideas. Companies watch competitors' ads and other communications to get clues about their new products. They buy competing new products, take them apart to see how they work, analyze their sales, and decide whether they should bring out a new product of their own. For example, when designing its highly successful Taurus, Ford tore down more than 50 competing models, layer by layer, looking for things to copy or improve on. It copied the Audi's accelerator-pedal "feel," the Toyota Supra fuel gauge, the BMW 528e tire and jack storage system, and 400 other such outstanding features. Ford did this again when it redesigned the Taurus in 1992.[9]

Finally, *distributors and suppliers* contribute many good new-product ideas. Resellers are close to the market and can pass along information about consumer problems and new-product possibilities. Suppliers can tell the company about new concepts, techniques, and materials that can be used to develop new products. Other idea sources include trade magazines, shows, and seminars; government agencies; new-product consultants; advertising agencies; marketing research firms; university and commercial laboratories; and inventors.

Idea Screening

The purpose of idea generation is to create a large number of ideas. The purpose of the succeeding stages is to *reduce* that number. The first idea-reducing stage is **idea screening**, which helps spot good ideas and drop poor ones as soon as possible. Product-development costs rise greatly in later stages, so the company wants to go ahead only with the product ideas that will turn into profitable products. As one marketing executive suggests, "Three executives sitting in a room can get 40 good ideas ricocheting off the wall in minutes. The challenge is getting a steady stream of good ideas out of the labs and creativity campfires, through marketing and manufacturing, and all the way to consumers."[10]

> **Idea screening**
> Screening new-product ideas in order to spot good ideas and drop poor ones as soon as possible.

Many companies require their executives to write up new-product ideas on a standard form that can be reviewed by a new-product committee. The write-up describes the product, the target market, and the competition. It makes some rough estimates of market size, product price, development time and costs, manufacturing costs, and rate of return. The committee then evaluates the idea against a set of general criteria. For example, at Kao Company, the large Japanese consumer products company, the committee asks questions such as these: Is the product truly useful to consumers and society? Is it good for our particular company? Does it mesh well with the company's objectives and strategies? Do we have the people, skills, and resources to make it succeed? Does it deliver more value to customers than competing products? Is it easy to advertise and distribute? Many companies have well-designed systems for rating and screening new-product ideas.

Concept Development and Testing

An attractive idea must be developed into a **product concept**. It is important to distinguish between a product idea, a product concept, and a product image. A *product idea* is an idea for a possible product that the company can see itself offering to the market. A *product concept* is a detailed version of the idea stated in meaningful consumer terms. A *product image* is the way consumers perceive an actual or potential product.

> **Product concept**
> A detailed version of the new-product idea stated in meaningful consumer terms.

Concept Development Suppose Toyota is getting ready to commercialize its experimental fuel-cell-powered electric car. This car creates hydrogen from methanol fuel and converts it to electricity to power the car's engine. The low-polluting fuel-cell system is highly fuel efficient and gives the new car an environmental advantage over standard internal combustion engine cars. Once methanol is widely available, the car would have unlimited

Toyota's task is to develop its new fuel-cell electric car into alternative product concepts, find out how attractive each concept is to customers, and choose the best one.

Marketing at Work 8-1
WD-40: Slick Ways to Create New Uses

Along with duct tape and the trusty hammer, WD-40 has become one of the truly essential survival items in most American homes. Originally developed in 1953 to prevent rust and corrosion on Atlas missiles, it takes its name from the 40th and final attempt at creating a *water* displacement formula. Over the past 40 years, WD-40 has achieved a kind of cult status—it now captures an 80 percent share of the U.S multipurpose spray lubricants market.

The WD-40 Company has shown a real knack for extending the life of WD-40 and for expanding the market by finding new uses for its popular substance. Many fresh concepts come from current users, who entered one of the company's contests. Contest winners received cash prizes, and many have had their ideas featured in the

Bird droppings on hood.

Moth on front grill.

Road tar on hubcaps.

Radioactive spacedust on fender.

Spray WD-40, wait, wipe. Four times a day if possible.
—Everitt

The WD-40 Company has shown a real knack for extending the life of WD-40 and for expanding the market by finding new uses for its popular substance.

range, giving it a huge edge over battery-powered electric cars such as GM's recently introduced EV_1, which travels only about 80 miles before needing 3 to 12 hours of recharging.[11]

Toyota's task is to develop this new product into alternative product concepts, find out how attractive each concept is to customers, and choose the best one. It might create the following product concepts for the fuel-cell electric car:

Concept 1   A moderately priced subcompact designed as a second family car to be used around town. The car is ideal for running errands and visiting friends.

Concept 2   A medium-cost sporty compact appealing to young people.

Concept 3   An inexpensive subcompact "green" car appealing to environmentally conscious people who want practical transportation and low pollution.

company's "There's Always Another Use" advertising campaign.

Some entrants suggest simple and practical uses. One recent winning entry came from a teacher who used WD-40 to clean old chalkboards in her classroom. "Amazingly, the boards started coming to life again," she reports. "Not only were they restored, but years of masking and scotch tape residue came off as well." Other entrants report some pretty unusual uses. First place went one year to a California woman whose parakeet, "Cookie," fell off her shoulder and landed on sticky mousetrap paper. When she tried to free the bird, she got both her hands stuck. The vet used good old WD-40 to free both victims. Still other reported uses seem highly improbable—one entrant claims that after spraying his Frisbee with WD-40, it flew out of sight, never to be seen again.

By now, almost everyone has discovered that WD-40 comes in handy for lubricating machinery, protecting tools from rust, loosening nuts and bolts, quieting squeaky hinges, and freeing stuck doors, drawers, windows, and zippers. And many fans know that you can use WD-40 to remove sticky-back labels from glassware, plastic, and metal items;

bubble gum from hair and carpets; scuff marks from vinyl floors; and crayon marks from just about anywhere. Whether it be crayon or bubble gum on walls or in hair, WD-40 is a lifesaver for the parents of precocious mess-makers. For example, when one user's two-year-old daughter took crayons in hand to create a colorful rainbow on the living room wall, a few squirts of WD-40 took care of the problem.

Such common uses make good sense, but did you hear about the nude burglary suspect who had wedged himself in a vent at a cafe in Denver? The fire department extracted him with a large dose of WD-40. Or how about the Mississippi naval officer who used WD-40 to repel an angry bear? Then there's the college student who wrote to say that a friend's nightly amorous activities in the next room were causing everyone in his dorm to lose sleep—he solved the problem by treating the squeaky bedsprings with WD-40.

Others report using WD-40 to clean paint brushes, renew old printer and typewriter ribbons, keep snow from sticking to snow shovels, and clean hard-water stains and soap scum off shower doors

and bathroom tiles. One inventive cemetery groundskeeper even uses WD-40 to clean and polish headstones. Many a fisherman reports that spraying a little WD-40 on bait helps them catch more fish. Some recreational users claim that spraying their golf clubs, golf balls, or bowling balls has greatly improved their game.

WD-40 has been used to unstick just about everything, including a repairman's finger from a toilet fitting, a little boy's head from his potty-training seat, and a cow's head from a fence. Reports the farmer, "We just sprayed a little WD-40 on his head, and he slipped right out." Ranchers and racehorse trainers say they use WD-40 to untangle manes and tails and to repel mud from hooves. And then there's the Florida man who found an entirely different way to use the product. When modern-day pirates boarded his boat, he hit one of the would-be hijackers over the head with a can of WD-40, which knocked him off the boat and saved the day.

Source: Numerous WD-40 Company press releases created by Phillips-Ramsey Advertising & Public Relations, San Diego, California. Also see Teresa Buyikian, "New Ads from Phillips-Ramsey Promote Alternative Uses for WD-40," *Adweek*, April 13, 1998, p. 4.

Concept Testing **Concept testing** calls for testing new-product concepts with groups of target consumers. The concepts may be presented to consumers symbolically or physically. Here, in words, is concept 3:

> ✧   An efficient, fun-to-drive, fuel-cell-powered electric subcompact car that seats four. This high-tech wonder runs on hydrogen created from methanol fuel, providing practical and reliable transportation with almost no pollution. It goes up to 80 miles per hour, gets 66 miles per gallon of fuel, and unlike battery-powered electric cars, it never needs recharging. It's priced, fully equipped, at $18,000.

For some concept tests, a word or picture description might be sufficient. However, a more concrete and physical presentation of the concept will increase the reliability of the concept test. Today, some marketers are finding innovative ways to make product

Concept testing
Testing new-product concepts with a group of target consumers to find out if the concepts have strong consumer appeal.

Table 8-1   Questions for Electric Car Concept Test

1. Do you understand the concept of a fuel-cell-powered electric car?
2. Do you believe the claims about the car's performance?
3. What are the major benefits of the fuel-cell-powered electric car compared with a conventional car?
4. What are its advantages compared with a battery-powered electric car?
5. What improvements in the car's features would you suggest?
6. For what uses would you prefer a fuel-cell-powered electric car to a conventional car?
7. What would be a reasonable price to charge for the car?
8. Who would be involved in your decision to buy such a car? Who would drive it?
9. Would you buy such a car? (Definitely, probably, probably not, definitely not)

concepts more real to consumer subjects. For example, some are using virtual reality to test product concepts. Virtual reality programs use computers and sensory devices (such as gloves or goggles) to simulate reality. For example, a designer of kitchen cabinets can use a virtual reality program to help a customer "see" how his or her kitchen would look and work if remodeled with the company's products. Although virtual reality is still in its infancy, its applications are increasing daily.[12]

After being exposed to the concept, consumers then may be asked to react to it by answering questions such as those in Table 8-1. The answers will help the company decide which concept has the strongest appeal. For example, the last question asks about the consumer's intention to buy. Suppose 10 percent of the consumers said they "definitely" would buy and another 5 percent said "probably." The company could project these figures to the full population in this target group to estimate sales volume. Even then, the estimate is uncertain because people do not always carry out their stated intentions.

Many firms routinely test new-product concepts with consumers before attempting to turn them into actual new products. For example, each month Richard Saunders, Inc.'s Acu-Poll research system tests 35 new-product concepts in person on 100 nationally representative grocery store shoppers. The poll rates participants' interest in buying a given new product, their perceptions of how new and different the product idea is, and their judgment of the product's value compared with its price. In a recent poll, Nabisco's Oreo Chocolate Cones concept received a rare A+ rating, meaning that consumers think it is an outstanding concept that they would try and buy. Other product concepts didn't fare so well. Nubrush Anti-Bacterial Toothbrush Spray disinfectant, from Applied Microdontics, received an F. Consumers found Nubrush to be overpriced, and most don't think they have a problem with "infected" toothbrushes. Another concept that fared poorly was Chef Williams 5 Minute Marinade, which comes with a syringe customers use to inject the marinade into meats. "I can't see that on grocery shelves," comments an Acu-Poll executive. Some consumers might find the thought of injecting something into meat a bit repulsive, and "it's just so politically incorrect to have this syringe on there."[13]

Marketing Strategy Development

Suppose Toyota finds that concept 3 for the fuel-cell-powered electric car tests best. The next step is **marketing strategy development**, designing an initial marketing strategy for introducing this car to the market.

Marketing strategy development
Designing an initial marketing strategy for a new product based on the product concept.

The *marketing strategy statement* consists of three parts. The first part describes the target market; the planned product positioning; and the sales, market share, and profit goals for the first few years. Thus:

✧ The target market is younger, well-educated, moderate-to-high-income individuals, couples, or small families seeking practical, environmentally responsible transportation. The car will be positioned as more economical to operate, more fun to drive, and less polluting than today's internal combustion engine cars, and as less restricting than battery-powered electric cars, which must be recharged regularly. The company will aim to sell 100,000 cars in the first year, at a loss of not more than $15 million. In the second year, the company will aim for sales of 120,000 cars and a profit of $25 million.

The second part of the marketing strategy statement outlines the product's planned price, distribution, and marketing budget for the first year:

✧ The fuel-cell-powered electric car will be offered in three colors and will have optional air-conditioning and power-drive features. It will sell at a retail price of $18,000—with 15 percent off the list price to dealers. Dealers who sell more than 10 cars per month will get an additional discount of 5 percent on each car sold that month. An advertising budget of $20 million will be split 50-50 between national and local advertising. Advertising will emphasize the car's fun and low emissions. During the first year, $100,000 will be spent on marketing research to find out who is buying the car and their satisfaction levels.

The third part of the marketing strategy statement describes the planned long-run sales, profit goals, and marketing mix strategy:

✧ Toyota intends to capture a 3 percent long-run share of the total auto market and realize an after-tax return on investment of 15 percent. To achieve this, product quality will start high and be improved over time. Price will be raised in the second and third years if competition permits. The total advertising budget will be raised each year by about 10 percent. Marketing research will be reduced to $60,000 per year after the first year.

Business Analysis

Once management has decided on its product concept and marketing strategy, it can evaluate the business attractiveness of the proposal. **Business analysis** involves a review of the sales, costs, and profit projections for a new product to find out whether they satisfy the company's objectives. If they do, the product can move to the product-development stage.

To estimate sales, the company might look at the sales history of similar products and conduct surveys of market opinion. It can then estimate minimum and maximum sales to assess the range of risk. After preparing the sales forecast, management can estimate the expected costs and profits for the product, including marketing, R&D, manufacturing, accounting, and finance costs. The company then uses the sales and costs figures to analyze the new product's financial attractiveness.

Business analysis
A review of the sales, costs, and profit projections for a new product to find out whether these factors satisfy the company's objectives.

Product Development

So far, for many new-product concepts, the product may have existed only as a word description, a drawing, or perhaps a crude mock-up. If the product concept passes the business test, it moves into **product development**. Here, R&D or engineering develops the product concept into a physical product. The product-development step, however, now

Product development
Developing the product concept into a physical product in order to ensure that the product idea can be turned into a workable product.

calls for a large jump in investment. It will show whether the product idea can be turned into a workable product.

The R&D department will develop and test one or more physical versions of the product concept. R&D hopes to design a prototype that will satisfy and excite consumers and that can be produced quickly and at budgeted costs. Developing a successful prototype can take days, weeks, months, or even years. Often, products undergo rigorous functional tests to make sure that they perform safely and effectively. Here are some examples of such functional tests:[14]

✧ A scuba-diving Barbie doll must swim and kick for 15 straight hours to satisfy Mattel that she will last at least one year. But because Barbie may find her feet in small owners' mouths rather than in the bathtub, Mattel has devised another, more tortuous test: Barbie's feet are clamped by two steel jaws to make sure that her skin doesn't crack—and choke—potential owners.

✧ At Shaw Industries, temps are paid $5 an hour to pace up and down five long rows of sample carpets for up to eight hours a day, logging an average of 14 miles each. One regular reads three mysteries a week while pacing and shed 40 pounds in two years. Shaw Industries counts walkers' steps and figures that 20,000 steps equal several years of average carpet wear.

✧ Acting on behalf of manufacturers, the Buyers Laboratory in Hackensack, New Jersey, tests the writing quality of ballpoint, felt-tip, and roller-ball pens. Its 50-pound "pen rig" measures a pen's life span. The range fluctuates, but a medium-tip, made-in-the-U.S.A. ballpoint might last for 7,775 feet. In general, pens that blob, skip, and dot receive low ratings. Which pens fail the test altogether? "Some points are so fine they cut through the paper," says one supervisor, "and some felt-tips wear down long before the ink runs out."

The prototype must have the required functional features and also convey the intended psychological characteristics. The electric car, for example, should strike consumers as being well built, comfortable, and safe. Management must learn what makes

Product testing: Shaw Industries pays temps to pace up and down five long rows of sample carpets for up to eight hours a day, logging an average of 14 miles each.

consumers decide that a car is well built. To some consumers, this means that the car has "solid-sounding" doors. To others, it means that the car is able to withstand heavy impact in crash tests. Consumer tests are conducted, in which consumers test-drive the car and rate its attributes.

Test Marketing

If the product passes functional and consumer tests, the next step is **test marketing**, the stage at which the product and marketing program are introduced into more realistic market settings. Test marketing gives the marketer experience with marketing the product before going to the great expense of full introduction. It lets the company test the product and its entire marketing program—positioning strategy, advertising, distribution, pricing, branding and packaging, and budget levels.

> **Test marketing**
> The stage of new-product development in which the product and marketing program are tested in more realistic market settings.

The amount of test marketing needed varies with each new product. Test marketing costs can be enormous, and it takes time that may allow competitors to gain advantages. When the costs of developing and introducing the product are low, or when management is already confident about the new product, the company may do little or no test marketing. Companies often do not test-market simple line extensions or copies of successful competitor products. For example, Procter & Gamble introduced its Folger's decaffeinated coffee crystals without test marketing, and Pillsbury rolled out Chewy granola bars and chocolate-covered Granola Dipps with no standard test marketing. However, when introducing a new product requires a big investment, or when management is not sure of the product or marketing program, a company may do a lot of test marketing. For instance, Lever USA spent two years testing its highly successful Lever 2000 bar soap in Atlanta before introducing it internationally. And Frito-Lay did 18 months of testing in three markets on at least five formulations before introducing its Baked Lays line of low-fat snacks.[15]

The costs of test marketing can be high, but they are often small when compared with the costs of making a major mistake. For example, London-based Unilever learned a costly lesson when it decided to skip formal test marketing for its new European laundry detergent, Power. It was so excited about Power's patented manganese-based catalyst, the Accelerator, that it skipped testing and forged ahead with a $300-million, Europewide Power introduction. It introduced the product despite a warning from archrival Procter & Gamble that the new stain-annihilating detergent also annihilated customers' clothing. Unilever ignored P&G's warning, and the new Power brand was a disaster. Of course, P&G was not motivated by altruism but by its own hidden agenda: It was secretly preparing to relaunch its flagship European brand Ariel as Ariel Future, a stain-fighting concentrated detergent. P&G ended up bombarding journalists across Europe with color photos of tattered rags washed in Power next to pristine garments laundered with its own Ariel.[16]

Recently, some marketers have begun to use interesting new high-tech approaches to simulated test market research, such as virtual reality and the Internet (see Marketing at Work 8-2).

Commercialization

Test marketing gives management the information needed to make a final decision about whether to launch the new product. If the company goes ahead with **commercialization**—introducing the new product into the market—it will face high costs. The company will have to build or rent a manufacturing facility. And it may have to spend, in the case of a new consumer packaged good, between $10 million and $200 million for advertising, sales promotion, and other marketing efforts in the first year.

> **Commercialization**
> Introducing a new product into the market.

Marketing at Work 8-2
Virtual Reality Test Marketing: The Future Is Now

It's a steamy summer Saturday afternoon. Imagine that you're stopping off at the local supermarket to pick up some icy bottles of your favorite sports drink before heading to the tennis courts. You park the car, cross the parking lot, and walk through the store's automatic doors. You head for aisle 5, passing several displays along the way, and locate your usual sports drink brand. You pick it up, check the price, and take it to the checkout counter. Sounds like a pretty typical shopping experience, doesn't it? But in this case, the entire experience took place on your computer screen, not at the supermarket.

You've just experienced virtual reality—the wave of the future for test marketing and concept-testing research—courtesy of Gadd International Research. Gadd has developed a research tool called Simul-Shop, a CD-ROM virtual reality approach that recreates shopping situations in which researchers can test consumers' reactions to factors such as product positioning, store layouts, and package designs. For example, suppose a cereal marketer wants to test reactions to a new package design and store shelf positioning. Using Simul-Shop on a standard desktop PC, test shoppers begin their shopping spree with a screen showing the outside of a grocery

Virtual reality: The wave of the future for test-marketing and concept-testing research. ARC's Vision Dome allows as many as 40 people at one time to participate in a virtual reality experience.

store. They click to enter the virtual store and are guided to the appropriate store section. Once there, they can scan the shelf, pick up various cereal packages, rotate them, study the labels—even look around to see what is on the shelf behind them. About the only thing they can't do is open the box and taste the cereal. The virtual shopping trip includes full sound and video, along with a guide who directs users through the experience and answers their questions. Explains a

Gadd's research director, "Once [users] move toward the item we want to test, [they] can look at different packaging, shelf layouts, and package colors. Depending on the activity, we can even ask users why they did what they did."

Virtual reality testing can take any of several forms. For example, Alternative Realities Corporation (ARC) has created a virtual reality amphitheater called the Vision-Dome. The Dome offers 360 by 160 degrees of film projection, allowing

The company launching a new product must first decide on introduction *timing*. If Toyota's new electric car will eat into the sales of the company's other cars, its introduction may be delayed. If the car can be improved further, or if the economy is down, the company may wait until the following year to launch it.

Next, the company must decide *where* to launch the new product—in a single location, a region, the national market, or the international market. Few companies have the confidence, capital, and capacity to launch new products into full national or international distribution. They will develop a planned *market rollout* over time. In particular, small

as many as 40 people at one time to participate in a virtual reality experience. The VisionDome is like an IMAX theater, but with one big difference—it's interactive. "When you use a computer to generate an image, . . . you have the advantage of making that image interactive," comments an ARC executive. When conducting research on a car, he suggests, "We can go into a VisionDome, see that car in three dimensions, look at it from every angle, take it out for a test drive, and allow the customer to configure that car exactly the way he wants it." Caterpillar sees enormous potential for the Dome. "We can put one of our tractors in a VisionDome and actually have a customer sit in it and test it under whatever conditions they would use it for," says a Caterpillar design engineer. "The ability to immerse people in the product makes it a phenomenal [research and sales] tool."

Virtual reality as a research tool offers several advantages. For one, it's relatively inexpensive. For example, a firm can conduct a Simul-Shop study for only about $25,000, including initial programming and the actual research on 75 to 100 people. This makes virtual reality research accessible to firms that can't afford full market-testing campaigns or the expense of creating actual mock-ups for each different product color, shape, or size. Another advantage is

flexibility. A virtual reality store can display an almost infinite variety of products, sizes, styles, and flavors in response to consumers' desires and needs. Research can be conducted in almost any simulated surroundings, ranging from food store interiors and new-car showrooms to farm fields or the open road. The technique also offers great interactivity, allowing marketers and consumers to work together via computer on designs of new products and marketing programs.

Finally, virtual reality has great potential for international research, which has often been difficult for marketers to conduct. With virtual reality, researchers can use a single standardized approach to evaluate products and programs worldwide. Consider the following example:

> One multinational company has begun to conduct virtual-shopping studies in North and South America, Europe, Asia, and Australia. Researchers create virtual stores in each country and region using the appropriate local products, shelf layouts, and currencies. Once the stores are on-line, a product concept can be quickly tested across locations. When the studies are completed, the results are communicated to headquarters electronically. The analysis reveals which markets offer the greatest opportunity for a successful launch.

Virtual reality research also has its limitations. The biggest problem: simulated shopping situations never quite match the real thing. Observes one expert, "Just because it's technically [feasible], that doesn't mean that when you put [people] behind a computer you're going to get true responses. Any time you simulate an experience you're not getting the experience itself. It's still a simulation."

So what's ahead for virtual reality in marketing? Some pioneers are extremely enthusiastic about the technology—not just as a research tool, but as a place where even real buying and selling can occur. They predict that the virtual store may become a major channel for personal and direct interactions with consumers, interactions that encompass not only research but sales and service as well. They see great potential for conducting this type of research over the Internet, and virtual stores have become a reality on the Web. As one observer notes, "This is what I read about in science fiction books when I was growing up. It's the thing of the future." For many marketers, that future is already a virtual reality.

Sources: Quotes and extracts from Raymond R. Burke, "Virtual Shopping: Breakthrough in Marketing Research," *Harvard Business Review*, March–April, 1996, pp. 120–31; Tom Dellacave Jr., "Curing Market Research Headaches," *Sales & Marketing Management*, July 1996, pp. 84–85; and Brian Silverman, "Get 'Em While They're Hot," *Sales and Marketing Management*, February 1997, pp. 47–48, p. 52. Also see Tim Studt, "VR Speeds Up Car Designs," *Research & Development*, March 1998, p. 74.

companies may enter attractive cities or regions one at a time. Larger companies, however, may quickly introduce new models into several regions or into the full national market.

Companies with international distribution systems may introduce new products through global rollouts. Colgate-Palmolive uses a "lead-country" strategy. For example, it launched its Palmolive Optims shampoo and conditioner first in Australia, the Philippines, Hong Kong, and Mexico, then rapidly rolled it out into Europe, Asia, Latin America, and Africa. However, international companies are increasingly introducing their new products in swift global assaults. Procter & Gamble did this with its Pampers Phases line of

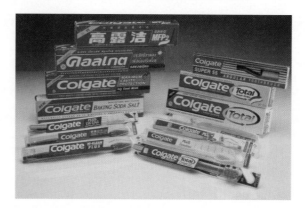

Colgate-Palmolive introduces its new products internationally using a "lead country" strategy, launching the product first in a few important regions, followed by a swift global rollout.

disposable diapers. In the past, P&G typically introduced a new product in the U.S. market. If it was successful, overseas competitors would copy the product in their home markets before P&G could expand distribution globally. With Pampers Phases, however, the company introduced the new product into global markets within one month of introducing it in the United States. It planned to have the product on the shelf in 90 countries within just 12 months of introduction. Such rapid worldwide expansion solidified the brand's market position before foreign competitors could react. P&G has since mounted worldwide introductions of several other new products.[17]

Speeding Up New-Product Development

Sequential product development

A new-product development approach in which one company department works to complete its stage of the process before passing the new product along to the next department and stage.

Many companies organize their new-product development process into an orderly sequence of steps, starting with idea generation and ending with commercialization. Under this **sequential product development** approach, one company department works individually to complete its stage of the process before passing the new product along to the next department and stage. This orderly, step-by-step process can help bring control to complex and risky projects. But it also can be dangerously slow. In today's fast-changing, highly competitive markets, such slow-but-sure product development can result in product failures, lost sales and profits, and crumbling market positions. Speed to market and reducing new-product development cycle time have become pressing concerns to companies in all industries.

Simultaneous (or team-based) product development

An approach to developing new products in which various company departments work closely together, overlapping the steps in the product-development process to save time and increase effectiveness.

Today, in order to get their new products to market more quickly, many companies are adopting a faster, team-oriented approach called **simultaneous (or team-based) product development**. Under this approach, company departments work closely together, overlapping the steps in the product-development process to save time and increase effectiveness. Instead of passing the new product from department to department, the company assembles a team of people from various departments that stays with the new product from start to finish. Such teams usually include people from the marketing, finance, design, manufacturing, and legal departments, and even supplier and customer companies.

Top management gives the product-development team general strategic direction but no clear-cut product idea or work plan. It challenges the team with stiff and seemingly contradictory goals—"turn out carefully planned and superior new products, but do it quickly"—and then gives the team whatever freedom and resources it needs to meet the challenge. In the sequential process, a bottleneck at one phase can seriously slow the entire project. In the simultaneous approach, if one functional area hits snags, it works to resolve them while the team moves on.

The Allen-Bradley Company, a maker of industrial controls, realized tremendous benefits by using simultaneous development. Under its old sequential approach, the company's marketing department handed off a new-product idea to designers, who worked in isolation to prepare concepts that they then passed along to product engineers. The engineers, also working by themselves, developed expensive prototypes and handed them off to manufacturing, which tried to find a way to build the new product. Finally, after many years and dozens of costly design compromises and delays, marketing was asked to sell the new product, which it often found to be too high priced or sadly out of date. Now, all of Allen-Bradley's departments work together to develop new products. The results have been astonishing. For example, the company recently developed a new electrical control in just two years; under the old system, it would have taken six years.

Black & Decker used the simultaneous approach—what it calls "concurrent engineering"—to develop its Quantum line of tools targeted toward serious do-it-yourselfers. B&D assigned a "fusion team," called Team Quantum and consisting of 85 Black & Decker employees from around the world, to get the right product line to customers as quickly as possible. The team included engineers, finance people, marketers, designers, and others from the United States, Britain, Germany, Italy, and Switzerland. From idea to launch, including three months of consumer research, the team developed the highly acclaimed Quantum line in only 12 months.

A Black & Decker "fusion team" developed the highly acclaimed Quantum tool line in only 12 months. The team included 85 marketers, engineers, designers, finance people, and others from the United States, Britain, Germany, Italy, and Switzerland.

The simultaneous approach does have some limitations. Superfast product development can be riskier and more costly than the slower, more orderly sequential approach. Moreover, it often creates increased organizational tension and confusion. And the company must take care that rushing a product to market doesn't adversely affect its quality; the objective is not just to create products faster, but to create them *better* and faster. Despite these drawbacks, in rapidly changing industries facing increasingly shorter product life cycles, the rewards of fast and flexible product development far exceed the risks. Companies that get new and improved products to the market faster than competitors often gain a dramatic competitive edge. They can respond more quickly to emerging consumer tastes and charge higher prices for more advanced designs. As one auto industry executive states, "What we want to do is get the new car approved, built, and in the consumer's hands in the shortest time possible. . . . Whoever gets there first gets all the marbles."[18]

Linking the Concepts

Take a break. Think about new products and how companies find and develop them.

- Suppose that you're on a panel to nominate the "best new products of the year." What products would you nominate and why? See what you can learn about the new-product development process for one of these products.
- Applying the new-product development process you've just studied, develop an idea for an innovative new snack food product and sketch out a brief plan for bringing it to market. Loosen up and have some fun with this.

Product Life-Cycle Strategies

Product life cycle (PLC)
The course of a product's sales and profits over its lifetime. It involves five distinct stages: product development, introduction, growth, maturity, and decline.

After launching the new product, management wants the product to enjoy a long and happy life. Although it does not expect the product to sell forever, the company wants to earn a decent profit to cover all the effort and risk that went into launching it. Management is aware that each product will have a life cycle, although the exact shape and length is not known in advance.

Figure 8-2 shows a typical **product life cycle (PLC)**, the course that a product's sales and profits take over its lifetime. The product life cycle has five distinct stages:

Figure 8-2
Sales and profits over the product's life from inception to demise

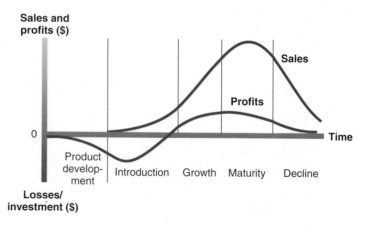

1. *Product development* begins when the company finds and develops a new-product idea. During product development, sales are zero and the company's investment costs mount.
2. *Introduction* is a period of slow sales growth as the product is introduced in the market. Profits are nonexistent in this stage because of the heavy expenses of product introduction.
3. *Growth* is a period of rapid market acceptance and increasing profits.
4. *Maturity* is a period of slowdown in sales growth because the product has achieved acceptance by most potential buyers. Profits level off or decline because of increased marketing outlays to defend the product against competition.
5. *Decline* is the period when sales fall off and profits drop.

Not all products follow this product life cycle. Some products are introduced and die quickly; others stay in the mature stage for a long, long time. Some enter the decline stage and are then cycled back into the growth stage through strong promotion or repositioning.

The PLC concept can describe a *product class* (gasoline-powered automobiles), a *product form* (minivans), or a *brand* (the Ford Taurus). The PLC concept applies differently in each case. Product classes have the longest life cycles—the sales of many product classes stay in the mature stage for a long time. Product forms, in contrast, tend to have the standard PLC shape. Product forms such as "cream deodorants," the "dial telephone," and "phonograph records" passed through a regular history of introduction, rapid growth, maturity, and decline. A specific brand's life cycle can change quickly because of changing competitive attacks and responses. For example, although teeth-cleaning products (product class) and toothpastes (product form) have enjoyed fairly long life cycles, the life cycles of specific brands have tended to be much shorter.

The PLC concept also can be applied to what are known as styles, fashions, and fads. Their special life cycles are shown in Figure 8-3. A **style** is a basic and distinctive mode of expression. For example, styles appear in homes (colonial, ranch); clothing (formal, casual); and art (realist, surrealist, abstract). Once a style is invented, it may last for generations, passing in and out of vogue. A style has a cycle showing several periods of renewed interest. A **fashion** is a currently accepted or popular style in a given field. For example, the "preppie look" in the clothing of the late 1970s and 1980s gave way to the casual and layered look of the 1990s. Fashions tend to grow slowly, remain popular for a while, then decline slowly.

Fads are fashions that enter quickly, are adopted with great zeal, peak early, and decline very quickly. They last only a short time and tend to attract only a limited following. "Pet rocks" have become the classic example of a fad. Upon hearing his friends complain

Style
A basic and distinctive mode of expression.

Fashion
A currently accepted or popular style in a given field.

Fads
Fashions that enter quickly, are adopted with great zeal, peak early, and decline very fast.

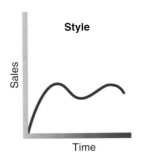

Style

Sales

Time

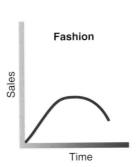

Fashion

Sales

Time

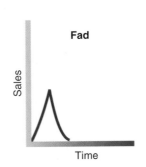

Fad

Sales

Time

Figure 8-3
Styles, fashions, and fads

about how expensive it was to care for their dogs, advertising copywriter Gary Dahl joked about his pet rock and was soon writing a spoof of a dog-training manual for it. Soon Dahl was selling some 1.5 million ordinary beach pebbles at $4 a pop. Yet the fad, which broke in October 1975, had sunk like a stone by the next February. Dahl's advice to those who want to succeed with a fad, "Enjoy it while it lasts." Other examples of fads include Rubik's Cubes, lava lamps, and Beanie Babies. Fads do not survive for long because they normally do not satisfy a strong need or satisfy it well.[19]

The PLC concept can be applied by marketers as a useful framework for describing how products and markets work. But using the PLC concept for forecasting product performance or for developing marketing strategies presents some practical problems.[20] For example, managers may have trouble identifying which stage of the PLC the product is in, pinpointing when the product moves into the next stage, and determining the factors that affect the product's movement through the stages. In practice, it is difficult to forecast the sales level at each PLC stage, the length of each stage, and the shape of the PLC curve.

Using the PLC concept to develop marketing strategy also can be difficult because strategy is both a cause and a result of the product's life cycle. The product's current PLC position suggests the best marketing strategies, and the resulting marketing strategies affect product performance in later life-cycle stages. Yet, when used carefully, the PLC concept can help in developing good marketing strategies for different stages of the product life cycle.

We looked at the product-development stage of the product life cycle in the first part of the chapter. We now look at strategies for each of the other life-cycle stages.

Introduction Stage

Introduction stage
The product life-cycle stage in which the new product is first distributed and made available for purchase.

The **introduction stage** starts when the new product is first launched. Introduction takes time, and sales growth is apt to be slow. Well-known products such as instant coffee, frozen orange juice, and powdered coffee creamers lingered for many years before they entered a stage of rapid growth.

In this stage, as compared to other stages, profits are negative or low because of the low sales and high distribution and promotion expenses. Much money is needed to attract distributors and build their inventories. Promotion spending is relatively high to inform consumers of the new product and get them to try it. Because the market is not generally ready for product refinements at this stage, the company and its few competitors produce basic versions of the product. These firms focus their selling on those buyers who are the readiest to buy.

A company, especially the *market pioneer*, must choose a launch strategy that is consistent with the intended product positioning. It should realize that the initial strategy is just the first step in a grander marketing plan for the product's entire life cycle. If the pioneer chooses its launch strategy to make a "killing," it will be sacrificing long-run revenue for the sake of short-run gain. As the pioneer moves through later stages of the life cycle, it will have to continuously formulate new pricing, promotion, and other marketing strategies. It has the best chance of building and retaining market leadership if it plays its cards correctly from the start.

Growth Stage

Growth stage
The product life-cycle stage in which a product's sales start climbing quickly.

If the new product satisfies the market, it will enter a **growth stage**, in which sales will start climbing quickly. The early adopters will continue to buy, and later buyers will start following their lead, especially if they hear favorable word of mouth. Attracted by the opportunities for profit, new competitors will enter the market. They will introduce new product features, and the market will expand. The increase in competitors leads to an increase in the number of distribution outlets, and sales jump just to build reseller inventories. Prices remain where they are or fall only slightly. Companies keep their promotion spending at the same or a slightly higher level. Educating the market remains a goal, but now the company must also meet the competition.

Profits increase during the growth stage, as promotion costs are spread over a large volume and as unit manufacturing costs fall. The firm uses several strategies to sustain rapid market growth as long as possible. It improves product quality and adds new product features and models. It enters new market segments and new distribution channels. It shifts some advertising from building product awareness to building product conviction and purchase, and it lowers prices at the right time to attract more buyers.

In the growth stage, the firm faces a trade-off between high market share and high current profit. By spending a lot of money on product improvement, promotion, and distribution, the company can capture a dominant position. In doing so, however, it gives up maximum current profit, which it hopes to make up in the next stage.

Maturity Stage

At some point, a product's sales growth will slow down, and the product will enter a **maturity stage**. This maturity stage normally lasts longer than the previous stages, and it poses strong challenges to marketing management. Most products are in the maturity stage of the life cycle, and therefore most of marketing management deals with the mature product.

The slowdown in sales growth results in many producers with many products to sell. In turn, this overcapacity leads to greater competition. Competitors begin marking down prices, increasing their advertising and sales promotions, and upping their R&D budgets to find better versions of the product. These steps lead to a drop in profit. Some of the weaker competitors start dropping out, and the industry eventually contains only well-established competitors.

Although many products in the mature stage appear to remain unchanged for long periods, most successful ones are actually evolving to meet changing consumer needs (see Marketing at Work 8-3). Product managers should do more than simply ride along with or defend their mature products—a good offense is the best defense. They should consider modifying the market, product, and marketing mix.

In *modifying the market*, the company tries to increase the consumption of the current product. It looks for new users and market segments, as when Johnson & Johnson targeted the adult market with its baby powder and shampoo. The manager also looks for ways to increase usage among present customers. Campbell does this by offering recipes and convincing consumers that "soup is good food." Or the company may want to reposition the brand to appeal to a larger or faster-growing segment, as Arrow did when it introduced its new line of casual shirts and announced, "We're loosening our collars."

The company might also try *modifying the product*—changing characteristics such as quality, features, or style to attract new users and to inspire more usage. It might improve the product's quality and performance—its durability, reliability, speed, taste. Or it might add new features that expand the product's usefulness, safety, or convenience. For example, Sony keeps adding new styles and features to its Walkman and Discman lines, and Volvo adds new safety features to its cars. Finally, the company can improve the product's styling and attractiveness. Thus, car manufacturers restyle their cars to attract buyers who want a new look. The makers of consumer food and household

Maturity stage
The stage in the product life cycle in which sales growth slows or levels off.

Marketing at Work 8-3

Crayola Crayons: A Long and Colorful Life Cycle

Binney & Smith Company began making crayons down by Bushkill Creek near Easton, Pennsylvania, in 1903. Partner Edwin Binney's wife, Alice, named them Crayola crayons—after the French *craie*, meaning "stick of color," and *ola*, meaning "oil." In the 90-odd years since, Crayola crayons have become a household staple, not just in the United States, but in more than 60 countries around the world, with boxes printed in 11 languages. The company made its 100 billionth crayon in 1996. If you placed all the Crayola crayons ever made end to end, they would circle the earth four and a half times.

Few people can forget their first pack of "64s"—64 beauties neatly arranged in the familiar green-and-yellow flip-top box with a sharpener on the back. The aroma of a freshly opened Crayola box still drives kids into a frenzy and takes members of the older generation back to some of their fondest childhood memories. In fact, the Crayola smell ranks right up there with those of coffee and peanut butter as one of the 20 most recognized smells in the world. Binney & Smith, now a subsidiary of Hallmark, dominates the crayon market. The average North American wears down 730 crayons by age ten. Sixty-five percent of all American children

Crayola's colorful life cycle: Over the years, Binney & Smith has added a steady stream of new colors, shapes, sizes, and packages.

between the ages of two and seven pick up a crayon at least once a day and color for an average of 28 minutes. Nearly 80 percent of the time, they pick up a Crayola crayon. (For an abundance of additional trivia facts, check out Crayola's Web site at www.crayola.com/.)

In some ways, Crayola crayons haven't changed much since 1903, when they were sold in an eight-pack for a nickel. Crayola has always been the number-one brand, and the crayons are still made by

hand in much the same way as then. But a closer look reveals that Binney & Smith has made many adjustments in order to keep the Crayola brand in the mature stage and out of decline. Over the years, the company has added a steady stream of new colors, shapes, sizes, and packages. It increased the number of colors from the original eight in 1903 (red, yellow, blue, green, orange, black, brown, and white) to 48 in 1949, to 64 in 1958. In 1962, as a result of the civil rights

products introduce new flavors, colors, ingredients, or packages to revitalize consumer buying.

Finally, the company can try *modifying the marketing mix*—improving sales by changing one or more marketing-mix elements. They can cut prices to attract new users and competitors' customers. They can launch a better advertising campaign or use aggressive sales promotions—trade deals, cents-off, premiums, and contests. The company can also move into larger market channels, using mass merchandisers, if these channels are growing. Finally, the company can offer new or improved services to buyers.

movement, it changed its crayon color "flesh" to "peach"; and in 1992, it added multicultural skin tones by which "children are able to build a positive sense of self and respect for cultural diversity." In 1993, it added 16 more colors, with names selected from nearly two million suggestions from consumers, including "razzmatazz," "macaroni & cheese," and "purple mountains majesty." It also created new lines of glow-in-the-dark colors and crayons filled with miniature capsules that burst when rubbed on paper with aromas such as grape, lime, pine, chocolate, licorice, bananas, and bubble gum. Scents considered, but not selected, included leather, hamburger, mildew, and skunk. In all, Crayola crayons now come in 96 colors and a variety of packages, including a 96-crayon attachélike case.

Over the years, the Crayola line has grown to include many new sizes and shapes. Binney & Smith has also extended the Crayola brand to new markets such as Crayola Markers, watercolor paints, themed stamps and stickers, and stencils. The company has licensed the Crayola brand for use on everything from lunch boxes and children's apparel to house paints. Finally, the company has added several programs and services to help strengthen its relationships with Crayola customers. For example, in

1984 it began its Dream Makers art education program, a national elementary-school art program designed to help students capture their dreams on paper and to support art education in schools. In 1986, it set up a toll-free 1-800-CRAYOLA hotline to provide better customer service. In 1994, it launched Crayola Kids magazine, aimed at three- to eight-year-olds, which offers features such as picture books, crafts to make, games, puzzles, and a parents' guide with expert advice on helping develop reading skills and creativity. And it recently added a Web page featuring trivia facts, company history, and games and entertainment for kids of all ages.

Not all of Binney & Smith's life-cycle adjustments have been greeted with open arms by consumers. For example, facing flat sales throughout the 1980s, the company conducted market research that showed that children were ready to break with tradition in favor of some exciting new colors. They were seeing and wearing brighter colors and wanted to be able to color with them as well. So, in 1990, Binney & Smith retired eight colors from the time-honored box of 64—raw umber, lemon yellow, maize, blue grey, orange yellow, orange red, green blue, and violet blue—into the Crayola Hall of Fame. In their place, it

introduced eight more-modern shades—cerulean, vivid tangerine, jungle green, fuchsia, dandelion, teal blue, royal purple, and wild strawberry. The move unleashed a groundswell of protest from loyal Crayola users, who formed such organizations as the RUMPS—the Raw Umber and Maize Preservation Society—and the National Committee to Save Lemon Yellow. Binney & Smith received an average of 334 calls a month from concerned customers. Company executives were flabbergasted—"We were aware of the loyalty and nostalgia surrounding Crayola crayons," a spokesperson says, "but we didn't know we [would] hit such a nerve." Still, fans of the new colors outnumbered the protestors, and the new colors are here to stay. However, the company reissued the old standards in a special collector's tin—it sold all of the 2.5 million tins made. Thus, the Crayola brand continues through its long and colorful life cycle.

Sources: Quotes from "Hue and Cry Over Crayola May Revive Old Colors," *Wall Street Journal,* June 14, 1991, p. B1. Also see Margaret O. Kirk, "Coloring Our Children's World Since '03," *Chicago Tribune,* October 29, 1986, sec. 5, p. 1; Judith D. Schwartz, "Back to School with Binney & Smith's Crayola," *Brandweek,* September 1993, pp. 26, 28; "These Crayons Smell," *Advertising Age,* August 15, 1994, p. 1; Mercedes M. Cardona, "Crayola Breaks Ad Effort to Target Parents' Nostalgia," *Advertising Age,* July 21, 1997, p. 35; Sean Mehegan, "The Color of Money," *Brandweek,* September 15, 1997, pp. 22–23; Ted Allen, "The Endorsement: Crayola Crayons," *Esquire,* January 1999, p. 16; and Crayola's Web site at www.crayola.com/, January 1999.

Linking the Concepts

Pause for a moment and think about some products that, like Crayola Crayons, have been around for a long time.

- Ask a grandparent or someone else who shaved back then to compare a 1940s or 1950s Gillette razor to the most current model. Is Gillette's latest razor really a new product or just a "retread" of the previous version? What do you conclude about product life cycles?
- Mattel's Barbie dolls have been around for decades. How has Mattel protected Barbie from old age and decline?

Decline Stage

The sales of most product forms and brands eventually dip. The decline may be slow, as in the case of oatmeal cereal, or rapid, as in the case of phonograph records. Sales may plunge to zero, or they may drop to a low level where they continue for many years. This is the **decline stage**.

Sales decline for many reasons, including technological advances, shifts in consumer tastes, and increased competition. As sales and profits decline, some firms withdraw from the market. Those remaining may prune their product offerings. They may drop smaller market segments and marginal trade channels, or they may cut the promotion budget and reduce their prices further.

Carrying a weak product can be very costly to a firm, and not just in profit terms. There are many hidden costs. A weak product may take up too much of management's time. It often requires frequent price and inventory adjustments. It requires advertising and sales force attention that might be better used to make "healthy" products more profitable. A product's failing reputation can cause customer concerns about the company and its other products. The biggest cost may well lie in the future. Keeping weak products

Decline stage
The product life-cycle stage in which a product's sales decline.

Table 8-2 Summary of Product Life-Cycle Characteristics, Objectives, and Strategies

	Introduction	Growth	Maturity	Decline
Characteristics				
Sales	Low sales	Rapidly rising sales	Peak sales	Declining sales
Costs	High cost per customer	Average cost per customer	Low cost per customer	Low cost per customer
Profits	Negative	Rising profits	High profits	Declining profits
Customers	Innovators	Early adopters	Middle majority	Laggards
Competitors	Few	Growing number	Stable number beginning to decline	Declining number
Marketing Objectives	Create product and trial	Maximize market share	Maximize profit while defending market share	Reduce expenditure and milk the brand
Strategies				
Product	Offer a basic product	Offer product extensions, service, warranty	Diversify brand and models	Phase out weak items
Price	Use cost-plus formula	Price to penetrate market	Price to match or best competitors	Cut price
Distribution	Build selective distribution	Build intensive distribution	Build more intensive distribution	Go selective: phase out unprofitable outlets
Advertising	Build product awareness among early adopters and dealers	Build awareness and interest in the mass market	Stress brand differences and benefits	Reduce to level needed to retain hard-core loyals
Sales promotion	Use heavy sales promotion to entice trial	Reduce to take advantage of heavy consumer demand	Increase to encourage brand switching	Reduce to minimal level

Source: Philip Kotler, *Marketing Management: Analysis, Planning, Implementation, and Control,* 10th ed. (Upper Saddle River, NJ: Prentice Hall, 2000), chapter 12.

delays the search for replacements, creates a lopsided product mix, hurts current profits, and weakens the company's foothold on the future.

For these reasons, companies need to pay more attention to their aging products. The firm's first task is to identify those products in the decline stage by regularly reviewing sales, market shares, costs, and profit trends. Then, management must decide whether to maintain, harvest, or drop each of these declining products.

Management may decide to *maintain* its brand without change in the hope that competitors will leave the industry. For example, Procter & Gamble made good profits by remaining in the declining liquid soap business as others withdrew. Or management may decide to reposition the brand in hopes of moving it back into the growth stage of the product life cycle. For instance, after watching sales of its Tostitos tortilla chips plunge 50 percent from their mid-1980s high, Frito-Lay reformulated the chips by doubling their size, changing their shape from round to triangular, and using white corn flour instead of yellow. The new Tostitos Restaurant Style Tortilla Chips have ridden the crest of the recent Tex-Mex food craze's record revenues.

Management may decide to *harvest* the product, which means reducing various costs (plant and equipment, maintenance, R&D, advertising, sales force) and hoping that sales hold up. If successful, harvesting will increase the company's profits in the short run. Or management may decide to *drop* the product from the line. It can sell it to another firm or simply liquidate it at salvage value. If the company plans to find a buyer, it will not want to run down the product through harvesting.

Table 8-2 summarizes the key characteristics of each stage of the product life cycle. The table also lists the marketing objectives and strategies for each stage.[21]

REST STOP Reviewing the Concepts

Well, there's one more travel sticker on your marketing bumper. Before we move on to the next marketing-mix destination, let's review the important new product and product life-cycle concepts. A company's current products face limited life spans and must be replaced by newer products. But new products can fail—the risks of innovation are as great as the rewards. The key to successful innovation lies in a total-company effort, strong planning, and a systematic *new-product development* process.

1. Explain how companies find and develop new-product ideas.
Companies find and develop new-product ideas from a variety of sources. Many new-product ideas stem from *internal sources*. Companies conduct formal research and development, pick the brains of their employees, and brainstorm at executive meetings. By conducting surveys and focus groups and analyzing *customer* questions and complaints, companies can generate new-product ideas that will meet specific consumer needs. Companies track *competitors'* offerings and inspect

new products, dismantling them, analyzing their performance, and deciding whether to introduce a similar or improved product. *Distributors and suppliers* are close to the market and can pass along information about consumer problems and new-product possibilities.

2. List and define the steps in the new-product development process.
The new-product development process consists of eight sequential stages. The process starts with *idea generation*. Next comes *idea screening*, which reduces the number of ideas based on the company's own criteria. Ideas that pass the screening stage continue through *product concept development*, in which a detailed version of the new-product idea is stated in meaningful consumer terms. In the next stage, *concept testing*, new-product concepts are tested with a group of target consumers to determine if the concepts have strong consumer appeal. Strong concepts proceed to *marketing strategy development*, in which an initial marketing strategy for the new product is developed from the product concept. In the *business analysis* stage, a review of the sales, costs, and

profit projections for a new product is conducted to determine whether the new product is likely to satisfy the company's objectives. With positive results here, the ideas become more concrete through *test marketing* and finally are launched during *commercialization.*

3. Describe the stages of the product life cycle.

Each product has a *life cycle* marked by a changing set of problems and opportunities. The sales of the typical product follow an S-shaped curve made up of five stages. The cycle begins with the *product-development stage* when the company finds and develops a new-product idea. The *introduction stage* is marked by slow growth and low profits as the product is distributed to the market. If successful, the product enters a *growth stage*, which offers rapid sales growth and increasing profits. Next comes a *maturity stage* when sales growth slows down and profits stabilize. Finally, the product enters a *decline stage* in which sales and profits dwindle. The company's task during this stage is to recognize the decline and to decide whether it should maintain, harvest, or drop the product.

4. Explain how marketing strategies change during the product's life cycle.

In the *introduction stage*, the company must choose a launch strategy consistent with its intended product positioning. Much money is needed to attract distributors and build their inventories and to inform consumers of the new product and achieve trial. In the *growth stage*, companies continue to educate potential consumers and distributors. In addition, the company works to stay ahead of the competition and sustain rapid market growth by improving product quality, adding new product features and models, entering new market segments and distribution channels, shifting some advertising from building product awareness to building product conviction and purchase, and lowering prices at the right time to attract new buyers. In the *maturity stage*, companies continue to invest in maturing products and consider modifying the market, the product, and the marketing mix. When *modifying the market*, the company attempts to increase the consumption of the current product. When *modifying the product*, the company changes some of the product's characteristics—such as quality, features, or style—to attract new users or inspire more usage. When *modifying the marketing mix*, the company works to improve sales by changing one or more of the marketing-mix elements. Once the company recognizes that a product has entered the *decline stage*, management must decide whether to *maintain* the brand without change, hoping that competitors will drop out of the market; *harvest* the product, reducing costs and trying to maintain sales; or *drop* the product, selling it to another firm or liquidating it at salvage value.

Navigating the Key Terms

For a detailed analysis of the meaning and importance of each of the following key terms, visit our Web page at **www.prenhall.com/kotler.**

Business analysis
Commercialization
Concept testing
Decline stage

Fad
Fashion
Growth stage
Idea generation
Idea screening
Introduction stage
Marketing strategy development
Maturity stage
New-product development

Product concept
Product development
Product life cycle (PLC)
Sequential product development
Simultaneous (or team-based) product development
Style
Test marketing

Travel Log

The following concept checks and discussion questions will help you to keep track of and apply the concepts you've studied in this chapter.

Concept Checks

1. Original products, product improvements, product modifications, and new brands that the firm develops

through it own research and development efforts can all be called _____.

2. The eight steps in the new-product development process are idea generation, _____, concept development and testing, _____, business analysis, _____, test marketing, and _____.

3. Major sources of new product ideas include _____, _____, _____, and _____.

4. A _____ is a detailed version of the idea stated in meaningful consumer terms.

5. A marketing strategy statement consists of three parts. Part one describes the target market, the planned product positioning, and the sales, market share, and profit goals for the first few years. Part two outlines the product's planned price, distribution, and marketing budget for the first year. Part three describes _____.

6. The five stages of the product life cycle (PLC) include _____, _____, _____, _____, and _____.

7. The _____ PLC stage is a period of rapid market acceptance and increasing profits.

8. The _____ PLC stage is a period of slow-down in sales growth because the product has achieved acceptance by most potential buyers.

9. As compared with other stages, the _____ PLC stage is characterized as having profits that are negative or low because of low sales and high distribution and promotion expenses.

10. In the maturity stage "the best offense is a good defense." The marketer can consider modifying the _____, _____, or _____.*

Discussing the Issues

1. Pick a familiar company and assume that you are responsible for generating new-product ideas. How would you structure your new-product development process? What sources of new ideas would be most valuable?

2. Less than one third of new-product ideas come from the customer. Does this low percentage conflict with the marketing concept's philosophy of "find a need and fill it"? Why or why not?

3. Vlasic Foods International recently developed a three-inch-wide pickle chip (ten times larger than the traditional pickle chip). This large pickle chip would be for those burger fanatics that want their pickles to stay put and not fall off the bun into their laps. Devise a plan for test marketing Vlasic's new product. What factors would be critical to your test and what type of test subjects would you select? Using the procedures and ideas presented in the text, evaluate the chances for success of this new product. Present your findings to the class.

4. Pick a soft drink, car, fashion, food product, or electronic appliance and trace the product's life cycle. Do appropriate research to make your timeline and application as accurate as possible. Explain how you separated the stages of the product's development. Project when the product might enter a decline stage.

5. Which product life-cycle stage do you think is the most important? Which stage has the highest risk? Which seems to hold the greatest profit potential? Which stage would seem to need the greatest amount of "hands-on" management? Be certain to explain the thinking behind each of your answers.

Concept checks answers: 1. new products; 2. idea screening, marketing strategy, product development, commercialization; 3. internal sources, customers, competitors, distributors and suppliers; 4. product concept; 5. the planned long-run sales, profit goals, and marketing-mix strategy; 6. product development, introduction, growth, maturity, and decline; 7. growth; 8. maturity; 9. introduction; 10. market, product, or marketing mix.

Traveling the Net

Point of Interest: New Products

Lands' End has been a successful catalog retailer for decades. However, as increasing competition begins to erode its profits, the company faces some difficult decisions. As much as 40 percent of Lands' End's sales and 70 percent of its profits come in the last 12 weeks of the calendar year. With mail boxes crammed with other catalogs during the end-of-the-year holiday season, Lands' End has been searching for a break-through strategy that will separate it from the pack. Any new strategy will have far-reaching effects since the company currently mails out some 230 million catalogs. Critics suggest that the Lands' End merchandise has become "tired" and lacks excitement. Relief may be on the way in the form of the company's new Web site. Examine the Lands' End Web site at www.landsend.com.

For Discussion

1. Why do you think that a catalog retailer's merchandise might be viewed as being "tired" by critics? How easy is it for a catalog retailer to integrate new merchandise into its catalog on a continuing basis?
2. Evaluate the Lands' End Web site. Assess the merchandising approach used by the company on its site.
3. Should Land's End consider diversification? If so, what type of diversification would you suggest?
4. Suggest ways that Lands' End can improve its "look" and image.

Application Thinking

In any upscale shopping mall you will find one or more stores that provide cutting-edge new products. These stores carry many products that have never been seen by the general shopping public—expensive products that tend to generate curiosity. One such cutting-edge retailer is The Sharper Image. During gift-giving seasons, The Sharper Image stores are packed with shoppers eager to find "the perfect gift." The company now sells many of its products via its Web site (www.sharperimage.com). Review The Sharper Image and Lands' End Web sites. What similarities do you see? Could any of the strategies used by The Sharper Image Web site be incorporated by Lands' End? Propose a "new image" strategy through which Lands' End could develop a fresh image for itself and its products. Even though these two companies sell different types of products, they can employ similar strategies and attitudes toward new products (especially if effective Web marketing is used).

 # MAP—Marketing Applications

MAP Stop 8

Do you remember 8-track tapes or Betamax VCRs? If you remember and are 21 years of age, you are an exception. The future once seemed bright for both of these product categories. However, advancing technology often overwhelms such "sure bets." One of today's bright stars in the recording and movie industries is the DVD (digital video disk). Experts project that the technology and associated products—disks, players, and others—will enjoy a much longer product life cycle than those of 8-track tapes or Betamax. However, this does not guarantee that spinoff products will have the same bright future. Circuit City Stores recently introduced Divx (short for Digital Video Express), a variant on DVD where consumers buy a movie on a disk for about $4.49 (versus DVD at three times the cost). They then use it for 48 hours (until the viewing privilege ends) and throw it away or rewatch the movie via a permissions and billing phone hookup for $3.25 per viewing. For $15, the consumer can purchase unlimited viewing rights. The advantages of Divx include the ability to build an "on-demand" viewing library, no more midnight trips to the video store to return movies, and no more late fees. Sound interesting? Circuit City is betting on it.

Thinking Like a Marketing Manager

1. Project a product life cycle for the new Divx technology. Describe your conclusions and how you reached them.
2. Give your PLC predictions, what strategies will be essential to the success of this product?
3. What competitors might Divx face? How can it defend against these competitors?
4. Assume that you are the marketing manager for Circuit City. Design a strategy for introducing this new product and for countering potential criticisms. What impact will this new product have on existing movie sales and rentals (on tape, laser disk, and DVD formats)? Evaluate the chances for success of this new product venture. Explain your rationale to the class.

chapter 9

Pricing Products: Pricing Considerations and Strategies

ROAD MAP:
Previewing the Concepts

We continue your marketing journey with a look at a second major marketing-mix tool—pricing. According to one pricing expert, "If effective product development, promotion, and distribution sow the seeds of business success, effective pricing is the harvest."[1] Firms successful at the other marketing-mix activities, he continues, "can still fail unless they can capture some of the value they create in the prices they earn." Yet, despite its importance, many firms do not handle pricing well. In this chapter, we'll examine factors that affect pricing decisions, general pricing approaches, and specific pricing strategies.

▶ **After studying this chapter, you should be able to**

1. **identify and explain the external and internal factors affecting a firm's pricing decisions**
2. **contrast the three general approaches to setting prices**
3. **describe the major strategies for pricing imitative and new products**
4. **explain how companies find a set of prices that maximizes the profits from the total product mix**
5. **discuss how companies adjust their prices to take into account different types of customers and situations**
6. **discuss the key issues related to initiating and responding to price changes**

First stop on the pricing tour: back to Procter & Gamble. This time, we'll look in on P&G's struggle to reshape its industry's distorted, promotion-based pricing system. You'll see that this is no easy task, even for a giant such as Procter & Gamble. This story will help you to appreciate the powerful forces shaping today's pricing decisions.

Procter & Gamble, the huge consumer packaged-goods producer, is part of a complex food-industry distribution channel consisting of producers, wholesale food distributors, and grocery retailers. In early 1992, P&G's relations with many of its resellers took a decided turn for the worse. "We think that [P&G] will end up where most dictators end up—in trouble," fumed the chairman of Stop & Shop, a chain of 119 groceries in the Northeast. Hundreds of miles away, the assistant manager of Paulbeck's SuperValu in International Falls, Minnesota, shared these harsh feelings: "We should drop their top dogs—like half the sizes of Tide—and say 'Now see who put you on the shelf and who'll take you off of it.'"

The cause of the uproar was P&G's new everyday fair-pricing policy, tabbed "value pricing" by the company. Under this sweeping new plan, the company began phasing out most of the large promotional discounts that it had offered resellers in the past. At the same time, it lowered its everyday wholesale list prices for these products by 10 percent

to 25 percent. P&G insists that price fluctuations and promotions had gotten out of hand. During the previous decade, average trade discounts had more than tripled. Some 44 percent of all marketing dollars spent by manufacturers went to trade promotions, up from 24 percent only a decade earlier.

Manufacturers had come to rely on price-oriented trade promotions to differentiate their brands and boost short-term sales. In turn, wholesalers and retail chains were conditioned to wait for manufacturers' "deals." Many perfected "forward buying"—stocking up during manufacturer's price promotions on far more merchandise than they could sell, then reselling it to consumers at higher prices once the promotion was over. Such forward buying created costly production and distribution inefficiencies. P&G's factories had to gear up to meet the resulting huge demand swings. Meanwhile, supermarkets needed more buyers to find the best prices and extra warehouses to store and handle merchandise bought "on deal." The industry's "promotion sickness" also infected consumers. Wildly fluctuating retail prices eroded brand loyalty by teaching consumers to shop for what's on sale, rather than to assess the merits of each brand.

Through value pricing, P&G sought to restore the price integrity of its brands and to begin weaning the industry and consumers from discount pricing. But the strategy came into conflict with the pricing strategies of P&G's distribution channels. Discounts are the bread and butter of many retailers and wholesalers, who had used products purchased from P&G at special low prices for weekly sales to lure value-minded consumers into supermarkets or stores. In other cases, retailers and wholesalers relied on the discounts to pad their profits through forward buying. And although the average costs of products to resellers remained unchanged, resellers lost promotional dollars that they, not P&G, controlled. Thus, the new system gave P&G greater control over how its products were marketed but reduced retailer and wholesaler pricing flexibility.

P&G's new strategy was risky. It alienated some of the very businesses that sell its wares to the public, and it gave competitors an opportunity to take advantage of the ban on promotions by highlighting their own specials. P&G counted on its enormous market clout—retailers could ill afford, the company hoped, to eliminate heavily advertised and immensely popular brands such as Tide detergent, Crest toothpaste, Folger's coffee, Pert shampoo, and Ivory soap. But even P&G's size and power were sorely tested. Some large chains such as A&P, Safeway, and Rite Aid drugstores began pruning out selected P&G sizes or dropping marginal brands such as Prell and Gleem. Certified Grocers, a Midwestern wholesaler, dropped about 50 of the 300 P&G varieties it stocked. And numerous other chains considered moving P&G brands from prime, eye-level space to less-visible shelves, stocking more profitable private-label brands and competitors' products in P&G's place. SuperValu, the nation's largest wholesaler, which also runs retail stores, added surcharges to some P&G products and pared back orders to make up for profits it says it lost.

Despite these strong reactions, P&G stayed the course with its bold new pricing approach, and the strategy appears to be paying off. After an initial drop in sales and market shares, P&G's products in most categories are again growing steadily and producing healthier profits. The company claims that under the new pricing scheme it cut list prices an average of 6 percent across its product portfolio, saving consumers $6 billion. Given this success at home, P&G introduced value pricing to its European markets in 1996. It received the same blistering response from European retailers that it had received from U.S. retailers five years earlier. For example, Germany's largest retailer, Rewe, and its major supermarket chain, Spar, immediately "delisted" several P&G brands, including Ariel, Vizir, and Lenor laundry products, Bess toilet paper, and Tempo tissues. As happened in the United States, initial European sales and market shares dipped as angry retailers responded.

P&G's struggle to reshape the industry's distorted pricing system demonstrates the dynamic forces shaping today's pricing decisions. Ideally, P&G should set its prices at the level that will reflect and enhance the value consumers perceive in its brands. But such value is difficult to assess. Which offers more value: higher regular prices with frequent sales or lower everyday prices? And what impact will each pricing strategy have on consumer perceptions of brand quality? P&G's pricing decisions would be difficult enough if the company had only to set its own prices and gauge customer reactions. However, P&G's pricing decisions affect not just its own sales and profits but those of its marketing partners as well. Thus, P&G must work with resellers to find the pricing structure that is best for all. In the end, customers will judge whether prices accurately reflect the value they receive. Which is the best pricing strategy? Customers will vote with their food-budget dollars.[2]

All profit organizations and many nonprofit organizations must set prices on their products or services. *Price* goes by many names:

> Price is all around us. You pay *rent* for your apartment, *tuition* for your education, and a *fee* to your physician or dentist. The airline, railway, taxi, and bus companies charge you a *fare*; the local utilities call their price a *rate*; and the local bank charges you *interest* for the money you borrow. The price for driving your car on Florida's Sunshine Parkway is a *toll*, and the company that insures your car charges you a *premium*. The guest lecturer charges an *honorarium* to tell you about a government official who took a *bribe* to help a shady character steal *dues* collected by a trade association. Clubs or societies to which you belong may make a special *assessment* to pay unusual expenses. Your regular lawyer may ask for a *retainer* to cover her services. The "price" of an executive is a *salary*, the price of a salesperson may be a *commission*, and the price of a worker is a *wage*. Finally, although economists would disagree, many of us feel that *income taxes* are the price we pay for the privilege of making money.[3]

In the narrowest sense, **price** is the amount of money charged for a product or service. More broadly, price is the sum of all the values that consumers exchange for the benefits of having or using the product or service. Historically, price has been the major factor affecting buyer choice. This is still true in poorer nations, among poorer groups, and with commodity products. However, nonprice factors have become more important in buyer-choice behavior in recent decades.

Price
The amount of money charged for a product or service, or the sum of the values that consumers exchange for the benefits of having or using the product or service.

Price is the only element in the marketing mix that produces revenue; all other elements represent costs. Price is also one of the most flexible elements of the marketing mix. Unlike product features and channel commitments, price can be changed quickly. At the same time, pricing and price competition is the number-one problem facing many marketing executives. Yet, many companies do not handle pricing well. The most common mistakes are pricing that is too cost oriented; prices that are not revised often enough to reflect market changes; pricing that does not take the rest of the marketing mix into account; and prices that are not varied enough for different products, market segments, and purchase occasions.

In this chapter, we focus on the process of setting prices. We look first at the factors marketers must consider when setting prices and at general pricing approaches. Then, we examine pricing strategies for new-product pricing, product-mix pricing, price changes, and price adjustments for buyer and situational factors.

Factors to Consider When Setting Prices

A company's pricing decisions are affected both by internal company factors and external environmental factors (see Figure 9-1).[4]

Internal Factors Affecting Pricing Decision

Internal factors affecting pricing include the company's marketing objectives, marketing-mix strategy, costs, and organization.

Marketing Objectives Before setting price, the company must decide on its strategy for the product. If the company has selected its target market and positioning carefully, then its marketing-mix strategy, including price, will be fairly straightforward. For example, if General Motors decides to produce a new sports car to compete with European sports cars in the high-income segment, this suggests charging a high price. Motel 6, Econo Lodge, and Red Roof Inn have positioned themselves as motels that provide economical rooms for budget-minded travelers; this position requires charging a low price. Thus, pricing strategy is largely determined by decisions on market positioning.

At the same time, the company may seek additional objectives. The clearer a firm is about its objectives, the easier it is to set price. Examples of common objectives are *survival*, *current profit maximization*, *market share leadership*, and *product-quality leadership*.

Companies set *survival* as their major objective if they are troubled by too much capacity, heavy competition, or changing consumer wants. To keep a plant going, a company may set a low price, hoping to increase demand. In this case, profits are less important than survival. As long as their prices cover variable costs and some fixed costs, they can stay in business. However, survival is only a short-term objective. In the long run, the firm must learn how to add value or face extinction.

Figure 9-1
Factors affecting price decisions

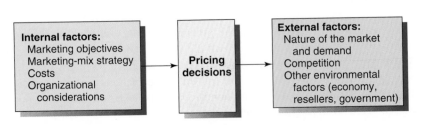

Many companies use *current profit maximization* as their pricing goal. They estimate what demand and costs will be at different prices and choose the price that will produce the maximum current profit, cash flow, or return on investment. In all cases, the company wants current financial results rather than long-run performance. Other companies want to obtain *market share leadership*. They believe that the company with the largest market share will enjoy the lowest costs and highest long-run profit. To become the market share leader, these firms set prices as low as possible.

A company might decide that it wants to achieve *product-quality leadership*. This normally calls for charging a high price to cover higher performance quality and the high cost of R&D. For example, Hewlett-Packard focuses on the high-quality, high-price end of the hand calculator market. Similarly, Pitney Bowes pursues a product-quality leadership strategy for its fax equipment. While Sharp, Canon, and other competitors fight over the low-price fax machine market with machines selling at around $500, Pitney Bowes targets large corporations with machines selling at about $5,000. As a result, it is the leading fax network provider to major corporations, capturing some 45 percent of the large-corporation fax niche.[5]

A company might also use price to attain other, more specific objectives. It can set prices low to prevent competition from entering the market or set prices at competitors'

Hewlett-Packard targets the high-quality, high-price end of the hand calculator market.

levels to stabilize the market. Prices can be set to keep the loyalty and support of resellers or to avoid government intervention. Prices can be reduced temporarily to create excitement for a product or to draw more customers into a retail store. One product may be priced to help the sales of other products in the company's line. Thus, pricing may play an important role in helping to accomplish the company's objectives at many levels.

Marketing-Mix Strategy Price is only one of the marketing-mix tools that a company uses to achieve its marketing objectives. Price decisions must be coordinated with product design, distribution, and promotion decisions to form a consistent and effective marketing program. Decisions made for other marketing-mix variables may affect pricing decisions. For example, producers using many resellers who are expected to support and promote their products may have to build larger reseller margins into their prices. The decision to position the product on high-performance quality will mean that the seller must charge a higher price to cover higher costs.

Companies often position their products on price and then base other marketing-mix decisions on the prices they want to charge. Here, price is a crucial product-positioning factor that defines the product's market, competition, and design. Many firms support such price-positioning strategies with a technique called **target costing**, a potent strategic weapon. Target costing reverses the usual process of first designing a new product, determining its cost, and then asking, "Can we sell it for that?" Instead, it starts with an ideal selling price based on customer considerations, then targets costs that will ensure that the price is met.

The original Swatch watch provides a good example of target costing. Rather than starting with its own costs, Swatch surveyed the market and identified an unserved segment of watch buyers who wanted "a low-cost fashion accessory that also keeps time." Armed with this information about market needs, Swatch set out to give consumers the watch they wanted at a price they were willing to pay, and it managed the new product's costs accordingly. Targeted buyers were concerned about fashion but less concerned about precision, reliability, and durability, so Swatch used less-expensive time-keeping mechanisms. Because the product would be priced cheaply enough to be discarded when the battery died, Swatch used a plastic casing and molded plastic band that might not have held up over the longer life of a traditional watch. By managing costs carefully, Swatch was able to create a watch that offered just the right blend of fashion and function at a price consumers were willing to pay. As a result of its initial major success, consumers have placed increasing value on Swatch products, allowing the company to introduce successively higher-priced designs.[6]

Other companies de-emphasize price and use other marketing-mix tools to create *nonprice* positions. Often, the best strategy is not to charge the lowest price, but rather to differentiate the marketing offer to make it worth a higher price. For example, for years Johnson Controls, a producer of climate-control systems for office buildings, used initial price as its primary competitive tool. However, research showed that customers were more concerned about the total cost of installing and maintaining a system than about its initial price. Repairing broken systems was expensive, time-consuming, and risky. Customers had to shut down the heat or air conditioning in the whole building, disconnect a lot of wires, and face the dangers of electrocution. Johnson decided to change its strategy. It designed an entirely new system called "Metasys." To repair the new system, customers need only pull out an old plastic module and slip in a new one—no tools required. Metasys costs more to make than the old system, and customers pay a higher initial price, but it costs less to install and maintain. Despite its higher asking price, the new Metasys system brought in $500 million in revenues in its first year.[7]

Target costing
Pricing that starts with an ideal selling price, then targets costs that will ensure that the price is met.

Thus, the marketer must consider the total marketing mix when setting prices. If the product is positioned on nonprice factors, then decisions about quality, promotion, and distribution will strongly affect price. If price is a crucial positioning factor, then price will strongly affect decisions made about the other marketing-mix elements. However, even when featuring price, marketers need to remember that customers rarely buy on price alone. Instead, they seek products that give them the best value in terms of benefits received for the price paid. Thus, in most cases, the company will consider price along with all the other marketing-mix elements when developing the marketing program (see Marketing at Work 9-1).

Costs Costs set the floor for the price that the company can charge for its product. The company wants to charge a price that both covers all its costs for producing, distributing, and selling the product and delivers a fair rate of return for its effort and risk. A company's costs may be an important element in its pricing strategy. Many companies work to become the "low-cost producers" in their industries. Companies with lower costs can set lower prices that result in greater sales and profits.

A company's costs take two forms, fixed and variable. *Fixed costs* (also known as *overhead*) are costs that do not vary with production or sales level. For example, a company must pay each month's bills for rent, heat, interest, and executive salaries, whatever the company's output. *Variable costs* vary directly with the level of production. Each personal computer produced by Compaq involves a cost of computer chips, wires, plastic, packaging, and other inputs. These costs tend to be the same for each unit produced. They are called "variable" because their total varies with the number of units produced. *Total costs* are the sum of the fixed and variable costs for any given level of production. Management wants to charge a price that will at least cover the total production costs at a given level of production.

The company must watch its costs carefully. If it costs the company more than competitors to produce and sell its product, the company will have to charge a higher price or make less profit, putting it at a competitive disadvantage.

Organizational Considerations Management must decide who within the organization should set prices. Companies handle pricing in a variety of ways. In small companies, prices are often set by top management rather than by the marketing or sales departments. In large companies, pricing is typically handled by divisional or product-line managers. In industrial markets, salespeople may be allowed to negotiate with customers within certain price ranges. Even so, top management sets the pricing objectives and policies, and it often approves the prices proposed by lower-level management or salespeople. In industries in which pricing is a key factor (aerospace, railroads, oil companies), companies often have a pricing department to set the best prices or help others in setting them. This department reports to the marketing department or top management. Others who have an influence on pricing include sales managers, production managers, finance managers, and accountants.

External Factors Affecting Pricing Decisions

External factors that affect pricing decisions include the nature of the market and demand, competition, and other environmental elements.

The Market and Demand Whereas costs set the lower limit of prices, the market and demand set the upper limit. Both consumer and industrial buyers balance the price of a product or service against the benefits of owning it. Thus, before setting prices, the marketer must understand the relationship between price and demand for its product. In

Marketing at Work 9-1
Carmax: Good Prices and a Whole Lot More

Would you buy a used car from this . . . er, retail store? Circuit City, the nation's leading consumer electronics and appliance retailer, thinks that you will. Its CarMax Auto Superstores are a far cry from the usual, sometimes less-than-reputable, used-car lot. The typical CarMax is located on a sprawling 12- to 15-acre site filled with 500 used but still gleaming cars, trucks, and minivans. As you might expect, given Circuit City's low-price guarantees, price figures prominently into CarMax's positioning—it promises "no-haggle, below-book prices." However, unlike Circuit

City stores, CarMax does not claim to charge the *lowest* prices. Instead, price is only a part—and perhaps not even the most important part—of a broader mix of values that CarMax delivers to its customers.

More than a dozen years ago, when Circuit City first opened, the highly fragmented consumer electronics industry evoked images of sleazy salespeople, bait-and-switch promotions, and high-pressure selling. Although chains like Mad Man Muntz and Crazy Eddie sold at low prices, they left many customers uneasy. Had they gotten the best value? Would the

store stand behind its products? With its large and modern stores, wide selection of goods, knowledgeable salespeople, liberal returns policies, and affordable financing, Circuit City brought new respectability to consumer electronics and appliance retailing.

Now, CarMax faces a similar situation with used cars—a highly fragmented industry and strong consumer concerns about reliability. Research shows that, when buying a used car, 40 percent of consumers question the reputation of the dealer. Circuit City is bringing the same respectability to used-car

At Car Max, price is only part of the formula. Delighted used-car buyers receive a wide mix of values, including selection, convenience, and peace of mind.

this section, we explain how the price–demand relationship varies for different types of markets and how buyer perceptions of price affect the pricing decision. We then discuss methods for measuring the price–demand relationship.

retailing that it brought to consumer electronics. It wants customers to be able to buy used cars from CarMax with the same ease and peace of mind that they purchase television sets, personal computers, camcorders, and refrigerators from Circuit City superstores.

Buying a used car from CarMax is a dramatically different experience. CarMax offers a large selection of cars, without a clunker in the bunch—most are less than five years old and sell for $8,000 to $15,000. Customers walk into a brightly lit showroom, where they are greeted by "sales associates" dressed in polo shirts, khakis, and sneakers. They use computer touch-screens to search the CarMax inventory for cars that meet their specifications and budgets. The computer screen shows color pictures of various choices, and the customer can receive a printout listing any car's specifications, features, mileage, and price, along with what has been done to get the car ready for sale. The sheet even contains a photo of the car and a map showing its location on the lot.

When ready, customers visit the vast lot to see cars, while their children enjoy the latest toys and games in the supervised KidCare Center. If the customer decides to purchase a car, financing can be arranged in less than 15 minutes through Circuit City's finance company. Moreover, CarMax will buy the customer's old car for a set price, whether or not he or she buys a new one. The entire car-buying process, from rumbling in with the old clunker to purring out with a shiny new model, can take less than an hour.

In addition to being quick and convenient, almost everything about CarMax inspires customer confidence. CarMax gives each car a 110-point quality inspection and backs it with a 30-day comprehensive warranty. It even offers a money-back guarantee: a customer who is not 100 percent satisfied can bring the car back within five days for a full refund. CarMax allows no high-pressure selling. Salespeople are carefully selected and trained to help people find the car that's just right for them. They receive commissions based on how many cars they sell, but not on prices. This prevents commission-hungry salespeople from steering customers to more expensive cars.

Finally, at CarMax, a price is a price. Prices are marked right on the car and no haggling is allowed. CarMax prices aren't the lowest around, but they are usually competitive—right around book value. However, these slightly higher prices don't appear to bother customers. Recent studies have shown that many customers willingly pay more to avoid the hassle of negotiating for better deals and to ensure that they get a good car, at a fair price, backed by a reliable seller.

CarMax appears to have started a revolution in used-car retailing. The company now operates seven superstores but will operate a projected 80 to 90 stores by the year 2002. Moreover, CarMax is drawing formidable competitors. Republic Industries has launched two major chains—AutoNation, modeled after CarMax, and ValueStop, featuring older, cheaper models. Republic plans to open 80 to 90 superstores over the next four years. Other competitors such as DriversMart, CarChoice, and CarAmerica are also rolling out bright, technologically sophisticated used-car stores with friendly, no-haggle policies in an effort to grab their chunk of the potential $325 billion used-car market. Still other competitors—Auto-by-Tel, CarSmart, AutoWeb, and others—offer buyers the convenience and privacy of used-car shopping via the Internet.

As one industry expert notes, the used-car industry has typically "ranked from shady to illegal. The public perception [is] horrible, just horrible. People have no confidence." CarMax and its competitors are setting out to change that perception. At CarMax, "You don't feel like you're going to a used-car den where you're about to be taken—you get an above-board, airy feeling." Many customers actually enjoy the used-car buying process at CarMax. "You don't have the high pressure," says one customer. "You get a quality selection, and it's no hassle." Thus, at CarMax, price is important but so are selection and convenience. And it's hard to put a price on peace of mind.

Sources: Quotes from Michael Janofsky, "Circuit City Takes a Spin at Used Car Marketing," *New York Times*, October 25, 1993, p. D1. Also see Jean Halliday, "AutoNation and CarMax Gear Up for Used-Car Clash," *Advertising Age*, October 28, 1996, pp. 3, 50; Bradford Wernie, "Stigma Gone, Used Vehicles Defy the System," *Advertising Age*, April 7, 1997, p. s2; Gail DeGeorge, "Republic Learns Cars Ain't Videos," *Business Week*, February 9, 1998, pp. 82–84; Jean Haliday, "CarMax's Latest Ads Put a 'Face' on Its Brand," *Advertising Age*, October 26, 1998, p. 12; and "The CarMax Story," at www.carmax.com/news/cmstory.html, January, 1999.

PRICING IN DIFFERENT TYPES OF MARKETS The seller's pricing freedom varies with different types of markets. Economists recognize four types of markets, each presenting a different pricing challenge.

Monopolistic competition: Canadian pickle marketer Bick's sets its pickles apart from dozens of other brands using both price and nonprice factors.

Under *pure competition*, the market consists of many buyers and sellers trading in a uniform commodity such as wheat, copper, or financial securities. No single buyer or seller has much effect on the going market price. A seller cannot charge more than the going price because buyers can obtain as much as they need at the going price. Nor would sellers charge less than the market price because they can sell all they want at this price. If price and profits rise, new sellers can easily enter the market. In a purely competitive market, marketing research, product development, pricing, advertising, and sales promotion play little or no role. Thus, sellers in these markets do not spend much time on marketing strategy.

Under *monopolistic competition*, the market consists of many buyers and sellers who trade over a range of prices rather than a single market price. A range of prices occurs because sellers can differentiate their offers to buyers. Either the physical product can be varied in quality, features, or style, or the accompanying services can be varied. Buyers see differences in sellers' products and will pay different prices for them. Sellers try to develop differentiated offers for different customer segments and, in addition to price, freely use branding, advertising, and personal selling to set their offers apart. For example, H.J. Heinz, Vlasic, and several other national brands of pickles compete with dozens of regional and local brands, all differentiated by price and nonprice factors. Because there are many competitors, each firm is less affected by competitors' marketing strategies than in oligopolistic markets.

Under *oligopolistic competition*, the market consists of a few sellers who are highly sensitive to each other's pricing and marketing strategies. The product can be uniform (steel, aluminum) or nonuniform (cars, computers). There are few sellers because it is difficult for new sellers to enter the market. Each seller is alert to competitors' strategies and moves. If a steel company slashes its price by 10 percent, buyers will quickly switch to this supplier. The other steelmakers must respond by lowering their prices or increasing their services. An oligopolist is never sure that it will gain anything permanent through a price cut. In contrast, if an oligopolist raises its price, its competitors might not follow this lead. The oligopolist then would have to retract its price increase or risk losing customers to competitors.

In a *pure monopoly*, the market consists of one seller. The seller may be a government monopoly (the U.S. Postal Service), a private regulated monopoly (a power company), or a private nonregulated monopoly (DuPont when it introduced nylon). Pricing is handled differently in each case. A government monopoly can pursue a variety of pricing objectives. It might set a price below cost because the product is important to buyers who cannot afford to pay full cost. Or the price might be set either to cover costs or to produce good revenue. It can even be set quite high to slow down consumption. In a regulated monopoly, the government permits the company to set rates that will yield a "fair return," one that will let the company maintain and expand its operations as needed. Nonregulated monopolies are free to price at what the market will bear. However, they do not always charge the full price for a number of reasons: a desire to not attract competition, a desire to penetrate the market faster with a low price, or a fear of government regulation.

CONSUMER PERCEPTIONS OF PRICE AND VALUE In the end, the consumer will decide whether a product's price is right. Pricing decisions, like other marketing-mix decisions, must be buyer oriented. When consumers buy a product, they exchange something of value (the price) to get something of value (the benefits of having or using the product). Effective, buyer-oriented pricing involves understanding how much value consumers place on the benefits they receive from the product and setting a price that fits this value.

A company will often find it hard to measure the values customers will attach to its product. For example, calculating the cost of ingredients in a meal at a fancy restaurant is relatively easy. But assigning a value to other satisfactions such as taste, environment, relaxation, conversation, and status is very hard. And these values will vary both for different consumers and different situations. Still, consumers will use these values to evaluate a product's price. If customers perceive that the price is greater than the product's value, they will not buy the product. If consumers perceive that the price is below the product's value, they will buy it, but the seller loses profit opportunities.

ANALYZING THE PRICE–DEMAND RELATIONSHIP Each price the company might charge will lead to a different level of demand. The relationship between the price charged and the resulting demand level is shown in the **demand curve** in Figure 9-2. The demand curve shows the number of units the market will buy in a given time period at different prices that might be charged. In the normal case, demand and price are inversely related; that is, the higher the price, the lower the demand. Thus, the company would sell less if it raised its price from P_1 to P_2. In short, consumers with limited budgets probably will buy less of something if its price is too high.

In the case of prestige goods, the demand curve sometimes slopes upward. For example, Gibson Guitar Corporation recently toyed with the idea of lowering its prices to compete more effectively with Japanese rivals like Yamaha and Ibanez. To its surprise, Gibson found that its instruments didn't sell as well at lower prices. "We had an inverse [price–demand relationship]," noted Gibson's chief executive officer. "The more we

Demand curve
A curve that shows the number of units the market will buy in a given time period at different prices that might be charged.

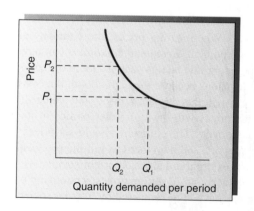

Figure 9-2
Demand Curve

charged, the more product we sold."[8] Consumers thought that higher prices meant more quality. However, if the company charges too high a price, the level of demand will be lower.

Most companies try to measure their demand curves by estimating demand at different prices. The type of market makes a difference. In a monopoly, the demand curve shows the total market demand resulting from different prices. If the company faces competition, its demand at different prices will depend on whether competitors' prices stay constant or change with the company's own prices.

Price elasticity

A measure of the sensitivity of demand to changes in price.

PRICE ELASTICITY OF DEMAND Marketers also need to know **price elasticity**—how responsive demand will be to a change in price. If demand hardly changes with a small change in price, we say the demand is *inelastic*. If demand changes greatly, we say the demand is *elastic*.

What determines the price elasticity of demand? Buyers are less price sensitive when the product they are buying is unique or when it is high in quality, prestige, or exclusiveness. They are also less price sensitive when substitute products are hard to find or when they cannot easily compare the quality of substitutes. Finally, buyers are less price sensitive when the total expenditure for a product is low relative to their income or when the cost is shared by another party.[9]

If demand is elastic rather than inelastic, sellers will consider lowering their price. A lower price will produce more total revenue. This practice makes sense as long as the extra costs of producing and selling more do not exceed the extra revenue.

Competitors' Costs, Prices, and Offers

Another external factor affecting the company's pricing decisions is competitors' costs and prices and possible competitor reactions to the company's own pricing moves. A consumer who is considering the purchase of a Canon camera will evaluate Canon's price and value against the prices and values of comparable products made by Nikon, Minolta, Pentax, and others. In addition, the company's pricing strategy may affect the nature of the competition it faces. If Canon follows a high-price, high-margin strategy, it may attract competition. A low-price, low-margin strategy, however, may stop competitors or drive them out of the market.

Canon needs to benchmark its costs against its competitors' costs to learn whether it is operating at a cost advantage or disadvantage. It also needs to learn the price and quality of each competitor's offer. Once Canon is aware of competitors' prices and offers, it can use them as a starting point for its own pricing. If Canon's cameras are similar to Nikon's, it will have to price close to Nikon or lose sales. If Canon's cameras are not as good as Nikon's, the firm will not be able to charge as much. If Canon's products are better than Nikon's, it can charge more. Basically, Canon will use price to position its offer relative to the competition.

Other External Factors

When setting prices, the company also must consider other factors in its external environment. *Economic conditions* can have a strong impact on the firm's pricing strategies. Economic factors such as boom or recession, inflation, and interest rates affect pricing decisions because they affect both the costs of producing a product and consumer perceptions of the product's price and value. The company must also consider what impact its prices will have on other parties in its environment. How will *resellers* react to various prices? The company should set prices that give resellers a fair profit, encourage their support, and help them to sell the product effectively. The *government* is another important external influence on pricing decisions. Finally, *social concerns* may have to be taken into account. In setting prices, a company's short-term sales, market share, and profit goals may have to be tempered by broader societal considerations.

General Pricing Approaches

The price the company charges will be somewhere between one that is too low to produce a profit and one that is too high to produce any demand. Figure 9-3 summarizes the major considerations in setting price. Product costs set a floor to the price; consumer perceptions of the product's value set the ceiling. The company must consider competitors' prices and other external and internal factors to find the best price between these two extremes.

Companies set prices by selecting a general pricing approach that includes one or more of these three sets of factors. We will examine the following approaches: the *cost-based approach* (cost-plus pricing, break-even analysis, and target-profit pricing); the *buyer-based approach* (value-based pricing); and the *competition-based approach* (going-rate and sealed-bid pricing).

Cost-Based Pricing

The simplest pricing method is **cost-plus pricing**, adding a standard markup to the cost of the product. For example, an appliance retailer might pay a manufacturer $20 for a toaster and mark it up to sell at $30, a 50 percent markup on cost. The retailer's gross margin is $10. If the store's operating costs amount to $8 per toaster sold, the retailer's profit margin will be $2.

> **Cost-plus pricing**
> Adding a standard markup to the cost of the product.

The manufacturer that made the toaster probably used cost-plus pricing. If the manufacturer's standard cost of producing the toaster was $16, it might have added a 25 percent markup, setting the price to the retailers at $20. Similarly, construction companies submit job bids by estimating the total project cost and adding a standard markup for profit. Lawyers, accountants, and other professionals typically price by adding a standard markup to their costs. Some sellers tell their customers they will charge cost plus a specified markup; aerospace companies, for example, price this way to the government.

Does using standard markups to set prices make sense? Generally, no. Any pricing method that ignores demand and competitor prices is not likely to lead to the best price. Steel manufacturer Nucor Corporation successfully uses cost-based pricing. Notes the company's general manager, "We base the price on what it costs to run the mill to capacity twenty-four hours a day."[10] However, Nucor's very low costs allow it to charge very low prices relative to competitors. In contrast, the retail graveyard is full of merchants who insisted on using standard markups after their competitors had gone to discount pricing.

Still, markup pricing remains popular for many reasons. First, sellers are more certain about costs than about demand. By tying the price to cost, sellers simplify pricing—they do not have to make frequent adjustments as demand changes. Second, when all firms in the industry use this pricing method, prices tend to be similar and price competition is thus minimized. Third, many people feel that cost-plus pricing is fairer to both buyers and sellers. Sellers earn a fair return on their investment but do not take advantage of buyers when buyers' demand becomes great.

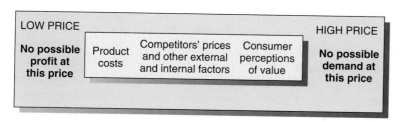

Figure 9-3
Major considerations in setting price

LOW PRICE				HIGH PRICE
No possible profit at this price	Product costs	Competitors' prices and other external and internal factors	Consumer perceptions of value	No possible demand at this price

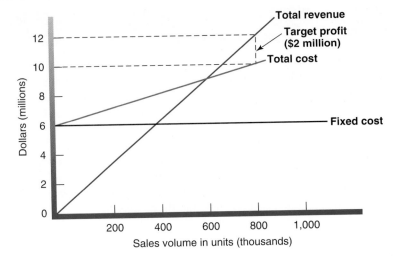

Figure 9-4
Break-even chart for determining target price

Another cost-oriented pricing approach is **break-even pricing**, or a variation called **target-profit pricing**. The firm tries to determine the price at which it will break even or make the target profit it is seeking. Target pricing is used by General Motors, which prices its automobiles to achieve a 15 to 20 percent profit on its investment. This pricing method is also used by public utilities, which are constrained to make a fair return on their investment.

Target pricing uses the concept of a *break-even chart*, which shows the total cost and total revenue expected at different sales volume levels. Figure 9-4 shows a hypothetical break-even chart. Here, fixed costs are $6 million regardless of sales volume, and variable costs are $5 per unit. Variable costs are added to fixed costs to form total costs, which rise with each unit sold. The slope of the total revenue curve reflects the price. Here, the price is $15 (for example, the company's revenue is $12 million on 800,000 units, or $15 per unit).

At the $15 price, the company must sell at least 600,000 units to *break even*; that is, at this level, total revenues will equal total costs of $9 million. If the company wants a target profit of $2 million, it must sell at least 800,000 units to obtain the $12 million of total revenue needed to cover the costs of $10 million plus the $2 million of target profits. In contrast, if the company charges a higher price, say $20 million, it will not need to sell as many units to break even or to achieve its target profit. In fact, the higher the price, the lower the company's break-even point will be.

However, as the *price* increases, *demand* decreases, and the market may not buy even the lower volume needed to break even at the higher price. Much depends on the relationship between price and demand. For example, suppose the company calculates that given its current fixed and variable costs, it must charge a price of $30 for the product in order to earn its desired target profit. But marketing research shows that few consumers will pay more than $25. In this case, the company will have to trim its costs in order to lower the break-even point so that it can charge the lower price consumers expect.

Thus, although break-even analysis and target-profit pricing can help the company to determine minimum prices needed to cover expected costs and profits, they do not take the price–demand relationship into account. When using this method, the company must also consider the impact of price on sales volume needed to realize target profits and the likelihood that the needed volume will be achieved at each possible price.

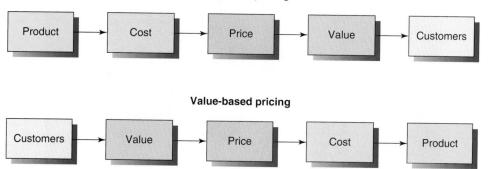

Figure 9-5
Cost-based versus
value-based pricing

Source: Thomas T. Nagle and
Reed K. Holden, *The Strategy
and Tactics of Pricing*, 2d
ed. (Upper Saddle River, NJ:
Prentice Hall, 1995), p.5.

Value-Based Pricing

An increasing number of companies are basing their prices on the product's perceived value. **Value-based pricing** uses buyers' perceptions of value, not the seller's cost, as the key to pricing. Value-based pricing means that the marketer cannot design a product and marketing program and then set the price. Price is considered along with the other marketing-mix variables *before* the marketing program is set.

Value-based pricing
Setting price based on buyers' perceptions of value rather than on the seller's cost.

Figure 9-5 compares cost-based pricing with value-based pricing. Cost-based pricing is product driven. The company designs what it considers to be a good product, totals the costs of making the product, and sets a price that covers costs plus a target profit. Marketing must then convince buyers that the product's value at that price justifies its purchase. If the price turns out to be too high, the company must settle for lower markups or lower sales, both resulting in disappointing profits.

Value-based pricing reverses this process. The company sets its target price based on customer perceptions of the product value. The targeted value and price then drive decisions about product design and what costs can be incurred. As a result, pricing begins with analyzing consumer needs and value perceptions, and price is set to match consumers' perceived value.

A company using value-based pricing must find out what value buyers assign to different competitive offers. However, measuring perceived value can be difficult. Sometimes, consumers are asked how much they would pay for a basic product and for each benefit added to the offer. Or a company might conduct experiments to test the perceived value of different product offers. If the seller charges more than the buyers' perceived value, the company's sales will suffer. Many companies overprice their products, and their products sell poorly. Other companies underprice. Underpriced products sell very well, but they produce less revenue than they would have if price were raised to the perceived-value level.

During the 1990s, marketers have noted a fundamental shift in consumer attitudes toward price and quality. Many companies have changed their pricing approaches to bring them into line with changing economic conditions and consumer price perceptions. More and more, marketers have adopted **value pricing** strategies—offering just the right combination of quality and good service at a fair price. In many cases, this has involved the introduction of less-expensive versions of established, brand-name products. Campbell introduced its Great Starts Budget frozen-food line, Holiday Inn opened several Holiday Express budget hotels, Revlon's Charles of the Ritz offered the Express Bar collection of affordable cosmetics, and fast-food restaurants such as Taco Bell and McDonald's offered "value menus." In other cases, value pricing has involved redesigning existing brands in order to offer more quality for a given price or the same quality for less.

Value pricing
Offering just the right combination of quality and good service at a fair price.

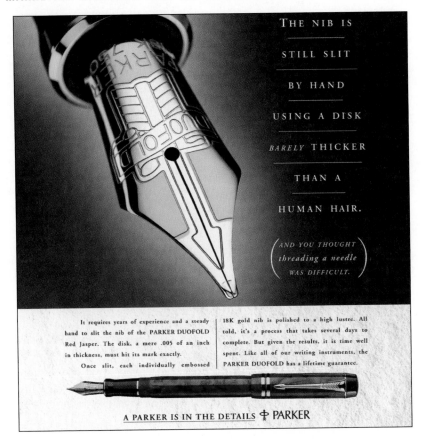

THE NIB IS

STILL SLIT

BY HAND

USING A DISK

BARELY THICKER

THAN A

HUMAN HAIR.

(AND YOU THOUGHT
threading a needle
WAS DIFFICULT.)

It requires years of experience and a steady hand to slit the nib of the PARKER DUOFOLD Red Jasper. The disk, a mere .005 of an inch in thickness, must hit its mark exactly.

Once slit, each individually embossed

18K gold nib is polished to a high lustre. All told, it's a process that takes several days to complete. But given the results, it is time well spent. Like all of our writing instruments, the PARKER DUOFOLD has a lifetime guarantee.

A PARKER IS IN THE DETAILS ✦ PARKER

Perceived value: A less-expensive pen might write as well, but some consumers will pay much more for the intangibles. This Parker model runs $185. Other are priced as high as $3,500.

In many business-to-business marketing situations, the pricing challenge is to find ways to adjust the value of the company's marketing offer in order to escape price competition and to justify higher prices and margins. This is especially true for suppliers of commodity products, which are characterized by little differentiation and intense price competition. In such cases, many companies adopt *value-added* strategies. Rather than cutting prices to match competitors, they attach value-added services to differentiate their offers and thus support higher margins (see Marketing at Work 9-2).

An important type of value pricing at the retail level is *everyday low pricing (EDLP)*. EDLP involves charging a constant, everyday low price with few or no temporary price discounts. In contrast, *high-low pricing* involves charging higher prices on an everyday basis but running frequent promotions to temporarily lower prices on selected items below the EDLP level.[11]

In recent years, high-low pricing has given way to EDLP in retail settings ranging from General Motors car dealerships to upscale department stores such as Nordstrom. Retailers adopt EDLP for many reasons, the most important of which is that constant sales and promotions are costly and have eroded consumer confidence in the credibility of everyday shelf prices. Consumers also have less time and patience for such time-honored traditions as watching for supermarket specials and clipping coupons.

The king of EDLP is Wal-Mart, which practically defined the concept. Except for a few sale items every month, Wal-Mart promises everyday low prices on everything it sells. In contrast, Sears's attempts at EDLP in 1989 failed. To offer everyday low prices, a company must first have everyday low costs. Wal-Mart's EDLP strategy works well

Marketing at Work 9-2

The Value of Value-Added

When a company finds its major competitors offering a similar product at a lower price, the natural tendency is to try to match or beat that price. Although the idea of undercutting competitor's prices and watching customers flock to you is tempting, there are dangers. Successive rounds of price cutting can lead to price wars that erode the profit margins of all competitors in an industry. Or worse, discounting a product can cheapen it in the minds of customers. "It ends up being a losing battle," notes one marketing executive. "You focus away from quality, service, prestige—the things brands are all about."

So, what can a company do when a competitor undercuts its price? Often, the best strategy is not to price below the competitor, but rather to price above and convince customers that the product is worth it. In this way, the company differentiates its offer and shifts the focus from price to value. But what if the company is operating as a supplier in a "commodity" business, in which the products of all competitors seem pretty much alike? In such cases, the company must find ways to "decommoditize" its products. It can do this by developing value-added services that differentiate its offer and justify higher prices and margins.

Increasingly, today's winning suppliers are those who can provide value-added services for their customers. Here are some examples of how suppliers, both small and large, are using value-added services to give them a competitive edge:

☐ *Thomas Industrial Products Co.:* Recently voted #1 in *Industrial Distribution's* list of the Top 25 small distributors, Thomas Industrial Products Company credits the lion's share of its success to its value-added services, which make up 50 percent of its business. The hose and accessory distributor has beat out larger competitors in the mid-Atlantic area by offering customers services such as application assistance, technical engineering, product testing, and custom crimping, coupling, and cutting. Today, Thomas is one of the few companies in the area that performs these services. The company's employees even passed a stringent examination so that Thomas could become a "certified coupler" for several types of hose. Thus, Thomas sells more than just hoses and accessories, considered commodities to most customers. Instead, it sells customer productivity and peace of mind in using these products, which are anything but commodities.

☐ *Jefferson Smurfit Corp.:* When General Electric expanded a no-frost refrigerator line in 1990, it needed more shipping boxes, and fast. Jefferson Smurfit Corporation, a $4.5 billion packaging supplier, assigned a coordinator to juggle production from three of its plants—and sometimes even divert product intended for other customers—to keep GE's Decatur plant humming. This kind of value-added hustling helped Jefferson Smurfit win the GE appliance unit's "Distinguished Supplier Award." It has also sheltered Smurfit from the bruising struggle of competing

only on price. "Today, it's not just getting the best price but getting the best value—and there are a lot of pieces to value," says a vice-president for procurement at Emerson Electric Company, a major Smurfit customer that has cut its supplier count by 65 percent.

☐ *Microsystems Engineering Company:* "The way we sell on value is by differentiating ourselves," says Mark Beckman, director of sales for Microsystems, a software company. "My product is twice as much as my nearest competitor, but we sell as much—if not more than—our competition." Rather than getting into price wars, Microsystems adds value to its products by adding new components and services. "[Customers] get more for their money," says Beckman. "We get the price because we understand what people want." When customers see the extra value, price becomes secondary. Ultimately, Beckman asserts, "Let the customer decide whether the price you're charging is worth all the things they're getting." What if the answer is no? Beckman would suggest that dropping price is the last thing you want to do. Instead, look to the value of value added.

Sources: Jim Morgan, "Value Added: From Cliché to the Real Thing," *Purchasing,* April 3, 1997, pp. 59–61; Richard A. Melcher, "The Middlemen Stay on the March," *Business Week,* January 9, 1995, p. 87; Christine Forbes, "Top 25 Small Distributors," *Industrial Distribution,* January 15, 1992, pp. 30–36; James E. Ellis, "There's Even a Science to Selling Boxes," *Business Week,* August 3, 1992, pp. 51-52; Erika Rasmusson, "The Pitfalls of Price Cutting," *Sales & Marketing Management,* May 1997, p. 17; Kevin J. Clancy, "At What Profit Price?" *Brandweek,* June 23 1997, pp. 24–28; and James C. Anderson and James A. Narus, "Business Marketing: Understand What Customers Value," *Harvard Business Review,* November-December 1998, pp. 53–65.

because its expenses are only 15 percent of sales. Sears, however, was spending 29 percent of sales to cover administrative and other overhead costs. As a result, Sears now offers what the industry calls everyday *fair* pricing, under which it tries to offer customers differentiated products at a consistent, fair price with fewer markdowns.

Linking the Concepts

This concept of value is critical to good pricing and to successful marketing in general. Slow down for a minute and be certain that you appreciate what value really means.

- A few years ago, Buick pitched its top-of-the-line Park Avenue model as "America's best car value." Does this fit with your idea of value?
- Pick two competing brands from a familiar product category (watches, perfume, consumer electronics, restaurants)—one low priced and the other high priced. Which, if either, offers the greatest value?
- Does "value" mean the same thing as "low price"? How do these concepts differ?

Competition-Based Pricing

Competition-base pricing
Setting prices based on the prices that competitors charge for similar products

Consumers will base their judgments of a product's value on the prices that competitors charge for similar products. One form of **competition-based pricing** is *going-rate pricing*, in which a firm bases its price largely on competitors' prices, with less attention paid to its own costs or to demand. The firm might charge the same, more, or less than its major competitors. In oligopolistic industries that sell a commodity such as steel, paper, or fertilizer, firms normally charge the same price. The smaller firms follow the leader: They change their prices when the market leader's prices change, rather than when their own demand or costs change. Some firms may charge a bit more or less, but they hold the amount of difference constant. Thus, minor gasoline retailers usually charge a few cents less than the major oil companies, without letting the difference increase or decrease.

Going-rate pricing is quite popular. When demand elasticity is hard to measure, firms feel that the going price represents the collective wisdom of the industry concerning the price that will yield a fair return. They also feel that holding to the going price will prevent harmful price wars.

Competition-based pricing is also used when firms *bid* for jobs. Using *sealed-bid pricing*, a firm bases its price on how it thinks competitors will price rather than on its own costs or on the demand. The firm wants to win a contract, and winning the contract requires pricing less than other firms. Yet the firm cannot set its price below a certain level. It cannot price below cost without harming its position. In contrast, the higher the company sets its price above its costs, the lower its chance of getting the contract.

New-Product Pricing Strategies

Pricing decisions are subject to an incredibly complex array of environmental and competitive forces. A company sets not a single price, but rather a *pricing structure* that covers different items in its line. This pricing structure changes over time as products move through their life cycles. The company adjusts product prices to reflect changes in costs and demand and to account for variations in buyers and situations. As the competitive environment changes, the company considers when to initiate price changes and when to respond to them.

PRICE

	Higher	Lower
Higher QUALITY	Premium strategy	Good-value strategy
Lower	Overcharging strategy	Economy strategy

Figure 9-6
Price–quality
strategies

We now examine the major dynamic pricing strategies available to management. In turn, we look at *new-product pricing strategies* for products in the introductory stage of the product life cycle, *product-mix pricing strategies* for related products in the product mix, *price-adjustment strategies* that account for customer differences and changing situations, and strategies for initiating and responding to *price changes.*[12]

Pricing strategies usually change as the product passes through its life cycle. The introductory stage is especially challenging. We can distinguish between pricing a product that imitates existing products and pricing an innovative product that is patent protected.

A company that plans to develop an imitative new product faces a product-positioning problem. It must decide where to position the product versus competing products in terms of quality and price. Figure 9-6 shows four possible positioning strategies. First, the

Rolex pursues a premium pricing strategy, selling very high quality watches at a high price. In contrast, Timex uses a good-value strategy, offering good quality watches at more affordable prices.

company might decide to use a *premium pricing* strategy—producing a high-quality product and charging the highest price. At the other extreme, it might decide on an *economy pricing* strategy—producing a lower-quality product but charging a low price. These strategies can coexist in the same market as long as the market consists of at least two groups of buyers, those who seek quality and those who seek price. Thus, Rolex offers very high-quality watches at very high prices, and Timex offers good-quality watches at more affordable prices.

The *good-value* strategy represents a way to attack the premium price. Its says, "We have high quality but at a lower price." If this really is true, and quality-sensitive buyers believe the good-value pricer, they will sensibly buy the product and save money—unless the premium product offers more status or snob appeal. Using an o*vercharging* strategy, the company overprices the product in relation to its quality. In the long run, however, customers will likely feel "taken." They will stop buying the product and will complain to others about it. Thus, this strategy should be avoided.

Companies bringing out an innovative, patent-protected product face the challenge of setting prices for the first time. They can choose between two strategies: *market-skimming pricing* and *market-penetration pricing*.

Market-Skimming Pricing

Market-skimming pricing
Setting a high price for a new product to skim maximum revenues layer by layer from the segments willing to pay the high price; the company makes fewer but more profitable sales.

Many companies that invent new products initially set high prices to "skim" revenues layer by layer from the market. Intel is a prime user of this strategy, called **market-skimming pricing**. One analyst describes Intel's pricing strategy this way: "The chip giant introduces a new, higher-margin microprocessor every 12 months and sends older models down the food chain to feed demand at lower price points."[13] When Intel first introduces a new computer chip, it charges as much as $1,000 for each chip, a price that makes it *just* worthwhile for some segments of the market to adopt computers containing the chip. The new chips power top-of-the-line PCs and servers purchased by customers who just can't wait. As initial sales slow down, and as competitors threaten to introduce similar chips, Intel lowers the price to draw in the next price-sensitive layer of customers. Prices eventually bottom out at close to $200 per chip, making the chip a hot mass-market processor. In this way, Intel skims a maximum amount of revenue from the various segments of the market.[14]

Market skimming makes sense only under certain conditions. First, the product's quality and image must support its higher price, and enough buyers must want the product at that price. Second, the costs of producing a smaller volume cannot be so high that they cancel the advantage of charging more. Finally, competitors should not be able to enter the market easily and undercut the high price.

Market-Penetration Pricing

Market-penetration pricing
Setting a low price for a new product in order to attract a large number of buyers and a large market share.

Rather than setting a high initial price to *skim off* small but profitable market segments, some companies use **market-penetration pricing**. They set a low initial price in order to *penetrate* the market quickly and deeply—to attract a large number of buyers quickly and win a large market share. The high sales volume results in falling costs, allowing the company to cut its price even further. For example, Dell used penetration pricing to enter the personal computer market, selling high-quality computer products through lower-cost direct channels. Its sales soared when IBM, Compaq, Apple, and other competitors selling through retail stores could not match their prices. Wal-Mart and other discount retailers also use penetration pricing. Dell charged low prices to attract high volume. The high volume resulted in lower costs which, in turn, let Dell keep prices low.

Several conditions favor setting a low price. First, the market must be highly price sensitive so that a low price produces more market growth. Second, production and distribution costs must fall as sales volume increases. Finally, the low price must help keep out the competition, and the penetration pricer must maintain its low-price position—otherwise, the price advantage may be only temporary. For example, Dell faced difficult times when IBM and Compaq established their own direct distribution channels. However, through its dedication to low production and distribution costs, Dell has retained its price advantage and established itself as the industry's fastest-growing computer maker.[15]

Product-Mix Pricing Strategies

The strategy for setting a product's price often has to be changed when the product is part of a product mix. In this case, the firm looks for a set of prices that maximizes the profits on the total product mix. Pricing is difficult because the various products have related demand and costs and face different degrees of competition. We now take a closer look at five product-mix pricing situations: *product-line pricing*, *optional-product pricing*, *captive-product pricing*, *byproduct pricing*, and *product-bundle pricing*.

Product-Line Pricing

Companies usually develop product lines rather than single products. For example, Snapper makes many different lawn mowers, ranging from simple walk-behind versions priced at $259.95, $299.95, and $399.95, to elaborate riding mowers priced at $1,000 or more. Each successive lawn mower in the line offers more features. Kodak offers not just one type of film but an assortment, including regular Kodak film, higher-priced Kodak Royal Gold film for special occasions, and a lower-priced, seasonal film called Funtime that

Product-line pricing: Infinity offers a line of home stereo speakers at prices ranging from $275 to $50,000 per pair.

Product line pricing
Setting the price steps between various products in a product line based on cost differences between the products, customer evaluations of different features, and competitors' prices.

competes with store brands. It offers each of these brands in a variety of sizes and film speeds. In **product-line pricing**, management must decide on the price steps to set between the various products in a line.

The price steps should take into account cost differences between the products in the line, customer evaluations of their different features, and competitors' prices. In many industries, sellers use well-established *price points* for the products in their line. Thus, men's clothing stores might carry men's suits at three price levels: $185, $325, and $495. The customer will probably associate low- , average- , and high-quality suits with the three price points. Even if the three prices are raised a little, men normally will buy suits at their own preferred price points. The seller's task is to establish perceived quality differences that support the price differences.

Optional-Product Pricing

Optional-product pricing
The pricing of optional or accessory products along with a main product.

Many companies use **optional-product pricing**: offering to sell optional or accessory products along with their main product. For example, a car buyer may choose to order power windows, cruise control, and a radio with a CD player. Pricing these options is a sticky problem. Automobile companies have to decide which items to include in the base price and which to offer as options. Until recent years, General Motors' normal pricing strategy was to advertise a stripped-down model at a base price to pull people into showrooms and then devote most of the showroom space to showing option-loaded cars at higher prices. The economy model was stripped of so many comforts and conveniences that most buyers rejected it. More recently, however, GM and other U.S. car makers have followed the example of the Japanese automakers and included in the sticker price many useful items previously sold only as options. The advertised price now often represents a well-equipped car.

Captive-Product Pricing

Captive-product pricing
Setting a price for products that must be used along with a main product, such as blades for a razor and film for a camera.

Companies that make products that must be used along with a main product are using **captive-product pricing**. Examples of captive products are razor blades, camera film, video games, and computer software. Producers of the main products (razors, cameras, video game consoles, and computers) often price them low and set high markups on the supplies. Thus, Polaroid prices its cameras low because it makes its money on the film it sells. Gillette sells low-priced razors but makes money on the replacement blades. And Nintendo sells its game consoles at low prices and makes money on video game titles. In fact, whereas Nintendo margins on its consoles run a mere 1 percent to 5 percent, margins on its game cartridges run close to 45 percent. Video game sales contribute more than half the company's profits.[16]

In the case of services, this strategy is called *two-part pricing*. The price of the service is broken into a *fixed fee* plus a *variable usage rate*. Thus, a telephone company charges a monthly rate—the fixed fee—plus charges for calls beyond some minimum number—the variable usage rate. Amusement parks charge admission plus fees for food, midway attractions, and rides over a minimum. The service firm must decide how much to charge for the basic service and how much for the variable usage. The fixed amount should be low enough to induce usage of the service; profit can be made on the variable fees.

Byproduct Pricing

Byproduct pricing
Setting a price for byproducts in order to make the main product's price more competitive.

In producing processed meats, petroleum products, chemicals, and other products, there are often byproducts. If the byproducts have no value and if getting rid of them is costly, this will affect the pricing of the main product. Using **byproduct pricing**, the manufacturer will seek a market for these byproducts and should accept any price that covers more than the cost of storing and delivering them. This practice allows the seller to reduce the main product's price to make it more competitive. Byproducts can even turn out to be profitable. For example, many lumber mills have begun to sell bark chips and sawdust profitably as decorative mulch for home and commercial landscaping.

Sometimes, companies don't realize how valuable their byproducts are. For example, most zoos don't realize that one of their byproducts, their occupants' manure, can be an excellent source of additional revenue. But the Zoo Doo Compost Company has helped many zoos understand the costs and opportunities involved with these byproducts. Zoo Doo licenses its name to zoos and receives royalties on manure sales. "Many zoos don't even know how much manure they are producing or the cost of disposing of it," explains president and founder Pierce Ledbetter. Zoos are often so pleased with any savings they can find on disposal that they don't think to move into active byproduct sales. However, sales of the fragrant byproduct can be substantial. So far, novelty sales have been the largest, with tiny containers of Zoo Doo (and even "Love, Love Me Doo" valentines) available in 160 zoo stores and 700 additional retail outlets. For the long-term market, Zoo Doo looks to organic gardeners who buy 15 to 70 pounds of manure at a time. Zoo Doo is already planning a "Dung of the Month" club to reach this lucrative byproducts market.[17]

Byproduct pricing: Zoo Doo sells tiny containers of zoo "byproducts"—even "Love, Love Me Doo" valentines—through 160 zoo stores and 700 additional retail outlets.

Product-Bundle Pricing

Product bundle pricing
Combining several products
and offering the bundle at a
reduced price.

Using **product-bundle pricing**, sellers often combine several of their products and offer the bundle at a reduced price. Thus, theaters and sports teams sell season tickets at less than the cost of single tickets; hotels sell specially priced packages that include room, meals, and entertainment; computer makers include attractive software packages with their personal computers. Price bundling can promote the sales of products consumers might not otherwise buy, but the combined price must be low enough to get them to buy the bundle.[18]

Price-Adjustment Strategies

Companies usually adjust their basic prices to account for various customer differences and changing situations. Here we examine six price-adjustment strategies: *discount and allowance pricing*, *segmented pricing*, *psychological pricing*, *promotional pricing*, *geographical pricing*, and *international pricing*.

Discount and Allowance Pricing

Most companies adjust their basic price to reward customers for certain responses, such as early payment of bills, volume purchases, and off-season buying. These price adjustments, called *discounts* and *allowances*, can take many forms.

Discount
A straight reduction in price
on purchases during a stated
period of time.

The many forms of **discounts** include a *cash discount*, a price reduction to buyers who pay their bills promptly. A typical example is "2/10, net 30," which means that although payment is due within 30 days, the buyer can deduct 2 percent if the bill is paid within 10 days. The discount must be granted to all buyers meeting these terms. Such discounts are customary in many industries and help to improve the sellers' cash situation and reduce bad debts and credit-collection costs.

A *quantity discount* is a price reduction to buyers who buy large volumes. A typical example might be "$10 per unit for less than 100 units, $9 per unit for 100 or more units." By law, quantity discounts must be offered equally to all customers and must not exceed the seller's cost savings associated with selling large quantities. These savings include lower selling, inventory, and transportation expenses. Discounts provide an incentive to the customer to buy more from one given seller, rather than from many different sources.

A *functional discount* (also called a *trade discount*) is offered by the seller to trade channel members who perform certain functions, such as selling, storing, and recordkeeping. Manufacturers may offer different functional discounts to different trade channels because of the varying services they perform, but manufacturers must offer the same functional discounts within each trade channel.

A *seasonal discount* is a price reduction to buyers who buy merchandise or services out of season. For example, lawn and garden equipment manufacturers offer seasonal discounts to retailers during the fall and winter months to encourage early ordering in anticipation of the heavy spring and summer selling seasons. Hotels, motels, and airlines will offer seasonal discounts in their slower selling periods. Seasonal discounts allow the seller to keep production steady during an entire year.

Allowance
Promotional money paid by
manufacturers to retailers in
return for an agreement to
feature the manufacturer's
products in some way.

Allowances are another type of reduction from the list price. For example, *trade-in allowances* are price reductions given for turning in an old item when buying a new one. Trade-in allowances are most common in the automobile industry but are also given for other durable goods. *Promotional allowances* are payments or price reductions to reward dealers for participating in advertising and sales-support programs.

Segmented Pricing

Companies will often adjust their basic prices to allow for differences in customers, products, and locations. In **segmented pricing**, the company sells a product or service at two or more prices, even though the difference in prices is not based on differences in costs (see Marketing at Work 9-3).

Segmented pricing takes several forms. Under *customer-segment* pricing, different customers pay different prices for the same product or service. Museums, for example, will charge a lower admission for students and senior citizens. Under *product-form pricing*, different versions of the product are priced differently but not according to differences in their costs. For instance, Black & Decker prices its most expensive iron at $54.98, which is $12 more than the price of its next-most-expensive iron. The top model has a self-cleaning feature, yet this extra feature costs only a few more dollars to make. Using *location pricing*, a company charges different prices for different locations, even though the cost of offering each location is the same. For instance, theaters vary their seat prices because of audience preferences for certain locations, and state universities charge higher tuition for out-of-state students. Finally, using *time pricing*, a firm varies its price by the season, the month, the day, and even the hour. Public utilities vary their prices to commercial users by time of day and weekend versus weekday. The telephone company offers lower off-peak charges, and resorts give seasonal discounts.

For segmented pricing to be an effective strategy, certain conditions must exist. The market must be segmentable, and the segments must show different degrees of demand. Members of the segment paying the lower price should not be able to turn around and resell the product to the segment paying the higher price. Competitors should not be able to undersell the firm in the segment being charged the higher price. Nor should the costs of segmenting and watching the market exceed the extra revenue obtained from the price difference. And, of course, the segmented pricing must be legal. Most importantly, segmented prices should reflect real differences in customers' perceived value. Otherwise, in the long run, the practice will lead to customer resentment and ill will.

> **Segmented pricing**
> Selling a product or service at two or more prices, where the difference in prices is not based on differences in costs.

Psychological Pricing

Price says something about the product. For example, many consumers use price to judge quality. A $100 bottle of perfume may contain only $3 worth of scent, but some people are willing to pay the $100 because this price indicates something special.

In using **psychological pricing**, sellers consider the psychology of prices and not simply the economics. For example, one study of the relationship between price and quality perceptions of cars found that consumers perceive higher-priced cars as having higher quality.[19] By the same token, higher-quality cars are perceived to be even higher priced than they actually are. When consumers can judge the quality of a product by examining it or by calling on past experience with it, they use price less to judge quality. When consumers cannot judge quality because they lack the information or skill, price becomes an important quality signal.

Another aspect of psychological pricing is **reference prices**, prices that buyers carry in their minds and refer to when looking at a given product. The reference price might be formed by noting current prices, remembering past prices, or assessing the buying situation. Sellers can influence or use these consumers' reference prices when setting price. For example, a company could display its product next to more expensive ones in order to imply that it belongs in the same class. Department stores often sell women's clothing in separate departments differentiated by price: Clothing found in the more-expensive department is assumed to be of better quality. Companies can also influence consumers'

> **Psychological pricing**
> A pricing approach that considers the psychology of prices and not simply the economics; the price is used to say something about the product.

> **Reference prices**
> Prices that buyers carry in their minds and refer to when they look at a given product.

Marketing at Work 9-3

The Right Product to the Right Customer at the Right Time for the Right Price

Many companies would love to raise prices across the board—but fear losing business. When the Washington Opera Company, located in the nation's capital, was considering increasing ticket prices after a difficult season, Ticket-Services Manager Jimmy Legarreta decided there had to be a better way. He found one after carefully reviewing opera economics. Legarreta knew, and his computer system confirmed, that the company routinely turned away people for Friday- and Saturday-night performances, particularly for prime seats. Meanwhile, midweek tickets went begging.

Legarreta also knew that not all seats were equal, even in the sought-after orchestra section. So the ticket manager and his staff sat in every one of the opera house's 2,200 seats and gave each a value according to the view and the acoustics. With his revenue goal in mind, Legarreta played with ticket prices until he arrived at nine levels, up from five. In the end, the opera raised prices for its most coveted seats by as much as 50 percent but also dropped the prices of some 600 seats. The gamble paid off in a 9 percent revenue increase during the next season.

Legarreta didn't have a name for it, but he was practicing "segmented pricing," an approach that also has many other labels. Airlines call it "yield management" and practice it religiously. Robert

Segmented pricing: Not all seats in an opera house are equal. After sitting in every one of the Washington Opera House's 2,200 seats, management arrived at nine pricing levels. The result: a 9 percent revenue increase.

reference prices by stating high manufacturer's suggested prices, by indicating that the product was originally priced much higher, or by pointing to a competitor's higher price.

Even small differences in price can suggest product differences. Consider a stereo priced at $300 compared to one priced at $299.95. The actual price difference is only 5 cents, but the psychological difference can be much greater. For example, some consumers will see the $299.95 as a price in the $200 range rather than the $300 range. The $299.95 will more likely be seen as a bargain price, whereas the $300 price suggests more quality. Some psychologists argue that each digit has symbolic and visual qualities that should be considered in pricing. Thus, 8 is round and even and creates a soothing effect, whereas 7 is angular and creates a jarring effect.[20]

Promotional Pricing

Promotional pricing
Temporarily pricing products below the list price, and sometimes even below cost, to increase short-run sales.

With **promotional pricing**, companies will temporarily price their products below list price and sometimes even below cost. Promotional pricing takes several forms. Super-markets and department stores will price a few products as *loss leaders* to attract

Cross, a longtime consultant to the airlines, calls it "revenue management." In a book by that name, Cross argues that all companies should apply revenue-management concepts, which emphasize an aggressive micromarket approach to maximizing sales. "Revenue management," Cross writes, "assures that companies will sell the right product to the right consumer at the right time for the right price."

Cross's underlying premise: No two customers value a product or service exactly the same way. Furthermore, the perceived value of a product results from many variables that change over time. Some of Cross's clients use sophisticated simulation modeling to predict sales at different price levels, but the technique doesn't have to be rocket science. If you understand your customers' motivation for buying and you keep careful sales records, it's possible to adjust prices to remedy supply-and-demand imbalances. Legarreta, for example, ended his midweek slump by making opera affordable for more people, yet he accurately predicted that the Washington in-crowd

would pay higher prices for the best weekend seats.

Probably the simplest form of segmented pricing is off-peak pricing, common in the entertainment and travel industries. Marc Epstein, owner of the Milk Street Cafe in Boston, discovered that technique more than 10 years ago, when he noticed he had lines out the door at noon but a near-empty restaurant around his 3 P.M. closing time. After some experimentation, Epstein settled on a 20-percent discount for the hours just before noon and after 2 P.M.—and he's pleased with the results. "If we didn't offer this, our overall revenue would be less," he argues. Epstein did not feel he could simultaneously raise prices during the lunch rush; instead, he has expanded the corporate-catering side of his business, where he can charge more per sandwich because "the perceived value of a catered lunch is higher."

Many other companies could conceivably segment their prices to increase revenues and profits. Cross cites examples ranging from a one-chair barbershop, to an accounting firm, to a health center. But there are risks. When you establish a

range of prices, customers who pay the higher ones may feel cheated. "It can't be a secret that you're charging different prices for the same service," Cross advises. "Customers must know, so they can choose when to use a service."

Even so, promotions designed to shift customer traffic to off-peak times can backfire. Rick Johnson, owner of Madison Car Wash in Montgomery, Alabama, describes his experience with a "Wonderful Wednesday" special: "The incentive was too good. It took away from the rest of the week and made Wednesday a monster day; it was a horrible strain on my facility and my people. I played around with the discount, but it was still a problem. So I finally dropped it."

The moral of the story? You can never know too much about your customers and the different values they assign to your product or service. With that customer knowledge comes power—to make the best pricing decisions.

Source: Adapted with permission from Susan Greco, "Are Your Prices Right?" *Inc,* January 1997, pp. 88–89. Copyright 1997 by Goldhirsh Group, Inc., 38 Commercial Wharf, Boston, MA 02110.

customers to the store in the hope that they will buy other items at normal markups. Sellers will also use *special-event pricing* in certain seasons to draw more customers. Thus, linens are promotionally priced every January to attract weary Christmas shoppers back into stores.

Manufacturers will sometimes offer *cash rebates* to consumers who buy the product from dealers within a specified time; the manufacturer sends the rebate directly to the customer. Rebates have been popular with automakers and producers of durable goods and small appliances, but they are also used with consumer packaged goods. Some manufacturers offer *low-interest financing*, *longer warranties*, or *free maintenance* to reduce the consumer's "price." This practice has recently become a favorite of the auto industry. Or, the seller may simply offer *discounts* from normal prices to increase sales and reduce inventories. As the Procter & Gamble example illustrates, promotional pricing can have adverse effects. Used too frequently and copied by competitors, they can create "deal-prone" customers who wait until brands go on sale before buying them. Or, constantly reduced prices can erode a brand's value in the eyes of customers.

Linking the Concepts

Here's a good place to take a brief break. Remember Procter & Gamble's struggle against promotional pricing in its industry?

- Many other industries have created "deal-prone" consumers through the heavy use of promotional pricing—fast food, airlines, tires, furniture, and others. Pick a company in one of these industries and suggest ways that it might deal with this problem.
- How does the concept of value relate to promotional pricing? Does promotional pricing add to or detract from customer value?

Geographical Pricing

A company also must decide how to price its products for customers located in different parts of the country or world. Should the company risk losing the business of more-distant customers by charging them higher prices to cover the higher shipping costs? Or should the company charge all customers the same prices regardless of location? We will look at five geographical pricing strategies for the following hypothetical situation:

✧ The Peerless Paper Company is located in Atlanta, Georgia, and sells paper products to customers all over the United States. The cost of freight is high and affects the companies from whom customers buy their paper. Peerless wants to establish a geographical pricing policy. It is trying to determine how to price a $100 order to three specific customers: Customer A (Atlanta); Customer B (Bloomington, Indiana), and Customer C (Compton, California).

One option is for Peerless to ask each customer to pay the shipping cost from the Atlanta factory to the customer's location. All three customers would pay the same factory price of $100, with Customer A paying, say, $10 for shipping; Customer B, $15; and Customer C, $25. Called *FOB-origin pricing*, this practice means that the goods are placed *free on board* (hence, *FOB*) a carrier. At that point the title and responsibility pass to the customer, who pays the freight from the factory to the destination. Because each customer picks up its own cost, supporters of FOB pricing feel that this is the fairest way to assess freight charges. The disadvantage, however, is that Peerless will be a high-cost firm to distant customers.

Uniform-delivered pricing is the opposite of FOB pricing. Here, the company charges the same price plus freight to all customers, regardless of their location. The freight charge is set at the average freight cost. Suppose this is $15. Uniform-delivered pricing, therefore, results in a higher charge to the Atlanta customer (who pays $15 freight instead of $10) and a lower charge to the Compton customer (who pays $15 instead of $25). Although the Atlanta customer would prefer to buy paper from another local paper company that uses FOB-origin pricing, Peerless has a better chance of winning over the California customer. Other advantages of uniform-delivered pricing are that it is fairly easy to administer and it lets the firm advertise its price nationally.

Zone pricing falls between FOB-origin pricing and uniform-delivered pricing. The company sets up two or more zones. All customers within a given zone pay a single total price; the more distant the zone, the higher the price. For example, Peerless might set up an East Zone and charge $10 freight to all customers in this zone, a Midwest Zone in which it charges $15, and a West Zone in which it charges $25. In this way, the customers within a given price zone receive no price advantage from the company. For example, customers in Atlanta and Boston pay the same total price to Peerless. The complaint, however, is that the Atlanta customer is paying part of the Boston customer's freight cost.

Using *basing-point pricing*, the seller selects a given city as a "basing point" and charges all customers the freight cost from that city to the customer location, regardless of the city from which the goods are actually shipped. For example, Peerless might set Chicago as the basing point and charge all customers $100 plus the freight from Chicago to their locations. This means that an Atlanta customer pays the freight cost from Chicago to Atlanta, even though the goods may be shipped from Atlanta. If all sellers used the same basing-point city, delivered prices would be the same for all customers and price competition would be eliminated. Industries such as sugar, cement, steel, and automobiles used basing-point pricing for years, but this method has become less popular today. Some companies set up multiple basing points to create more flexibility: They quote freight charges from the basing-point city nearest to the customer.

Finally, the seller who is anxious to do business with a certain customer or geographical area might use *freight-absorption pricing*. Using this strategy, the seller absorbs all or part of the actual freight charges in order to get the desired business. The seller might reason that if it can get more business, its average costs will fall and more than compensate for its extra freight cost. Freight-absorption pricing is used for market penetration and to hold on to increasingly competitive markets.

International Pricing

Companies that market their products internationally must decide what prices to charge in the different countries in which they operate. In some cases, a company can set a uniform worldwide price. For example, Boeing sells its jetliners at about the same price everywhere, whether in the United States, Europe, or a third-world country. However, most companies adjust their prices to reflect local market conditions and cost considerations.

The price that a company should charge in a specific country depends on many factors, including economic conditions, competitive situations, laws and regulations, and development of the wholesaling and retailing system. Consumer perceptions and preferences also may vary from country to country, calling for different prices. Or the company may have different marketing objectives in various world markets, which require changes in pricing strategy. For example, Sony might introduce a new product into mature markets in highly developed countries with the goal of quickly gaining mass-market share; this would call for a penetration-pricing strategy. In contrast, it might enter a less-developed market by targeting smaller, less price-sensitive segments; in this case, market-skimming pricing makes sense.

Costs play an important role in setting international prices. Travelers abroad are often surprised to find that goods that are relatively inexpensive at home may carry outrageously higher price tags in other countries. A pair of Levis selling for $30 in the United States goes for about $63 in Tokyo and $88 in Paris. A McDonald's Big Mac selling for a modest $2.25 here costs $5.75 in Moscow, and an Oral-B toothbrush selling for 19 cents at home costs 90 cents in China. Conversely, a Gucci handbag going for only $60 in Milan, Italy, fetches $240 in the United States. In some cases, such *price escalation* may result from differences in selling strategies or market conditions. In most instances, however, it is simply a result of the higher costs of selling in foreign markets: the additional costs of modifying the product, higher shipping and insurance costs, import tariffs and taxes, costs associated with exchange-rate fluctuations, and higher channel and physical distribution costs.

For example, Campbell found that its distribution costs in the United Kingdom were 30 percent higher than in the United States. U.S. retailers typically purchase soup in large quantities—48-can cases of a single soup by the dozens, hundreds, or carloads. In contrast, English grocers purchase soup in small quantities—typically in 24-can cases of *assorted* soups. Each case must be handpacked for shipment. To handle these small orders, Campbell had to add a costly extra wholesale level to its European channel. The smaller orders also mean that English retailers order two or three times as often as their U.S. counterparts, bumping up billing and order costs. These and other factors caused Campbell to charge much higher prices for its soups in the United Kingdom.[21]

Thus, international pricing presents some special problems and complexities. We discuss international pricing issues in more detail in chapter 15.

Price Changes

After developing their pricing structures and strategies, companies often face situations in which they must initiate price changes or respond to price changes by competitors.

Initiating Price Changes

In some cases, the company may find it desirable to initiate either a price cut or a price increase. In both cases, it must anticipate possible buyer and competitor reactions.

Initiating Price Cuts Several situations may lead a firm to consider cutting its price. One such circumstance is excess capacity. In this case, the firm needs more business and cannot get it through increased sales effort, product improvement, or other measures. It may drop its "follow-the-leader pricing"—charging about the same price as its leading competitor—and aggressively cut prices to boost sales. But as the airline, construction equipment, fast-food, and other industries have learned in recent years, cutting prices in an industry loaded with excess capacity may lead to price wars as competitors try to hold on to market share.

Another situation leading to price changes is falling market share in the face of strong price competition. Several American industries—automobiles, consumer electronics, cameras, watches, and steel, for example—lost market share to Japanese competitors whose high-quality products carried lower prices than did their American counterparts. In response, American companies resorted to more aggressive pricing action. General Motors, for example, cut its subcompact car prices by 10 percent on the West Coast, where Japanese competition was strongest.[22]

A company may also cut prices in a drive to dominate the market through lower costs. Either the company starts with lower costs than its competitors or it cuts prices in the hope of gaining market share that will further cut costs through larger volume. Bausch & Lomb used an aggressive low-cost, low-price strategy to become an early leader in the competitive soft contact lens market.

Initiating Price Increases In contrast, many companies have had to *raise* prices in recent years. They do this knowing that the price increases may be resented by customers, dealers, and even their own sales force. Yet a successful price increase can greatly increase profits. For example, if the company's profit margin is 3 percent of sales, a 1 percent price increase will increase profits by 33 percent if sales volume is unaffected.

A major factor in price increases is cost inflation. Rising costs squeeze profit margins and lead companies to regular rounds of price increases. Companies often raise their prices by more than the cost increase in anticipation of further inflation. Another factor leading to price increases is overdemand: When a company cannot supply all its customers' needs, it can raise its prices, ration products to customers, or both.

Companies can increase their prices in a number of ways to keep up with rising costs. Prices can be raised almost invisibly by dropping discounts and adding higher-priced units to the line. Or prices can be pushed up openly. In passing price increases on to customers, the company should avoid the appearance of price gouging. The price increases should be supported with a company communication program telling customers why prices are being increased. The company sales force should help customers find ways to economize.

Where possible, the company should consider ways to meet higher costs or demand without raising prices. For example, it can shrink the product instead of raising the price, as candy bar manufacturers often do. Or it can substitute less-expensive ingredients or remove certain product features, packaging, or services. Or it can "unbundle" its products and services, removing and separately pricing elements that were formerly part of the offer. IBM, for example, now offers training and consulting as separately priced services.

Buyer Reactions to Price Changes Whether the price is raised or lowered, the action will affect buyers, competitors, distributors, and suppliers and may interest government as well. Customers do not always interpret prices in a straightforward way. They may view a price *cut* in several ways. For example, what would you think if Sony were suddenly to cut its VCR prices in half? You might think that these VCRs are about to be replaced by newer models or that they have some fault and are not selling well. You might think that Sony is abandoning the VCR business and may not stay in this business long enough to supply future parts. You might believe that quality has been reduced. Or you might think that the price will come down even further and that it will pay to wait and see.

Similarly, a price *increase*, which would normally lower sales, may have some positive meanings for buyers. What would you think if Sony *raised* the price of its latest VCR model? On the one hand, you might think that the item is very "hot" and may be unobtainable unless you buy it soon. Or you might think that the recorder is an unusually good value. On the other hand, you might think that Sony is greedy and charging what the traffic will bear.

Buyer reactions to price changes? What would you think if the price of Joy was suddenly cut in half?

Competitor Reactions to Price Changes A firm considering a price change has to worry about the reactions of its competitors as well as its customers. Competitors are most likely to react when the number of firms involved is small, when the product is uniform, and when the buyers are well informed.

How can the firm anticipate the likely reactions of its competitors? If the firm faces one large competitor, and if the competitor tends to react in a set way to price changes, that reaction can be easily anticipated. But if the competitor treats each price change as a fresh challenge and reacts according to its self-interest, the company will have to figure out just what makes up the competitor's self-interest at the time.

The problem is complex because, like the customer, the competitor can interpret a company price cut in many ways. It might think the company is trying to grab a larger market share, that the company is doing poorly and trying to boost its sales, or that the company wants the whole industry to cut prices to increase total demand.

When there are several competitors, the company must guess each competitor's likely reaction. If all competitors behave alike, this amounts to analyzing only a typical competitor. In contrast, if the competitors do not behave alike—perhaps because of differences in size, market shares, or policies—then separate analyses are necessary. However, if some competitors will match the price change, there is good reason to expect that the rest will also match it.

Responding to Price Changes

Here we reverse the question and ask how a firm should respond to a price change by a competitor. The firm needs to consider several issues: Why did the competitor change the price? Was it to take more market share, to use excess capacity, to meet changing cost conditions, or to lead an industrywide price change? Is the price change temporary or permanent? What will happen to the company's market share and profits if it does not respond? Are other companies going to respond? And what are the competitor's and other firms' responses to each possible reaction likely to be?

Besides these issues, the company must make a broader analysis. It has to consider its own product's stage in the life cycle, the product's importance in the company's

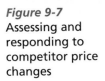

Figure 9-7
Assessing and responding to competitor price changes

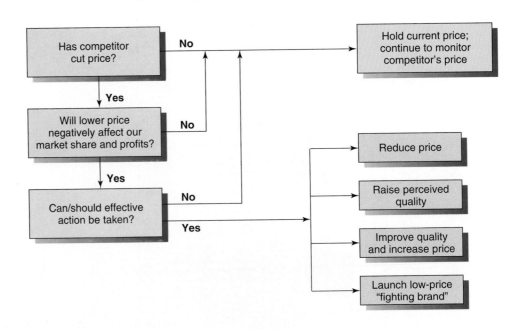

product mix, the intentions and resources of the competitor, and the possible consumer reactions to price changes. The company cannot always make an extended analysis of its alternatives at the time of a price change, however. The competitor may have spent much time preparing this decision, but the company may have to react within hours or days. About the only way to cut down reaction time is to plan ahead both for possible competitor's price changes and possible responses.

Figure 9-7 shows the ways a company might assess and respond to a competitor's price cut. Once the company has determined that the competitor has cut its price and that this price reduction is likely to harm company sales and profits, it might simply decide to hold its current price and profit margin. The company might believe that it will not lose too much market share or that it would lose too much profit if it reduced its own price. It might decide that it should wait and respond when it has more information on the effects of the competitor's price change. For now, it might be willing to hold on to good customers, while giving up the poorer ones to the competitor. The argument against this holding strategy, however, is that the competitor may get stronger and more confident as its sales increase and that the company might wait too long to act.

If the company decides that effective action can and should be taken, it might make any of four responses. First, it could *reduce its price* to match the competitor's price. It may decide that the market is price sensitive and that it would lose too much market share

Fighting brands: When challenged on price by store brands and other low-priced entrants, Procter & Gamble turned a number of its brands into fighting brands, including Luvs disposable diapers.

to the lower-priced competitor. Or it might worry that recapturing lost market share later would be too hard. Cutting the price will reduce the company's profits in the short run. Some companies might also reduce their product quality, services, and marketing communications to retain profit margins, but this will ultimately hurt long-run market share. The company should try to maintain its quality as it cuts prices.

Alternatively, the company might maintain its price but *raise the perceived quality* of its offer. It could improve its communications, stressing the relative quality of its product over that of the lower-price competitor. The firm may find it cheaper to maintain price and spend money to improve its perceived value than to cut price and operate at a lower margin.

Or, the company might *improve quality and increase price*, moving its brand into a higher-price position. The higher quality justifies the higher price, which in turn preserves the company's higher margins. Or the company can hold price on the current product and introduce a new brand at a higher-price position.

Finally, the company might launch a low-price "fighting brand." Often, one of the best responses is to add lower-price items to the line or to create a separate lower-price brand. This is necessary if the particular market segment being lost is price sensitive and will not respond to arguments of higher quality. Thus, when attacked on price by Fuji, Kodak introduced low-price Funtime film. When challenged on price by store brands and other low-price entrants, Procter & Gamble turned a number of its brands into fighting brands, including Luvs disposable diapers, Joy dishwashing detergent, and Camay beauty soap. In response to price pressures, Miller cut the price of its High Life brand by 20 percent in most markets, and sales jumped 9 percent in less than a year.[23]

Public Policy and Pricing

In setting prices, companies are not usually free to charge whatever prices they wish. Many federal and state laws govern the rules of fair play in pricing. The most important pieces of legislation affecting pricing are the Sherman, Clayton, and Robinson-Patman acts, initially adopted to curb the formation of monopolies and to regulate business practices that might unfairly restrain trade. Because these federal statutes can be applied only to interstate commerce, some states have adopted similar provisions for companies that operate locally. Public policy on pricing centers on three potentially damaging pricing practices: price fixing, price discrimination, and deceptive pricing.

Federal legislation on *price fixing* states that sellers must set prices without talking to competitors. Otherwise, price collusion is suspected. Price fixing is illegal per se; that is, the government does not accept any excuses for price fixing. Even a simple conversation between competitors can have serious consequences. For example, during the early 1980s, American Airlines and Braniff were immersed in a price war in the Texas market. In the heat of the battle, American's CEO, Robert Crandall, called the president of Braniff and said, "Raise your . . . fares 20 percent. I'll raise mine the next morning." Fortunately for Crandall, the Braniff president warned him off, saying, "We can't talk about pricing!" As it turns out, the phone conversation had been recorded, and the U.S. Justice Department began action against Crandall and American for price fixing. The charges were eventually dropped—the courts ruled that because Braniff had rejected Crandall's proposal, no actual collusion had occurred and that a proposal to fix prices was not an actual violation of the law. More recently, however, Archer Daniels Midland became mired in scandal when it pleaded guilty to price fixing and paid a $100 million fine. Such cases have made most executives very reluctant to discuss prices in any way with competitors.

The Robinson-Patman Act seeks to prevent unfair *price discrimination* by ensuring that sellers offer the same price terms to a given level of trade. For example, every retailer is entitled to the same price terms, whether the retailer is Sears or the local bicycle shop. However, price discrimination is allowed if the seller can prove that its costs are different when selling to different retailers—for example, that it costs less per unit to sell a large volume of bicycles to Sears than to sell a few bicycles to a local dealer. Or the seller can discriminate in its pricing if the seller manufactures different qualities of the same product for different retailers. The seller has to prove that these differences are proportional. Price differentials may also be used to "match competition" in "good faith," provided the price discrimination is temporary, localized, and defensive rather than offensive.

Deceptive pricing occurs when a seller states prices or price savings that are not actually available to consumers. Some such deceptions are difficult for consumers to discern, as when an airline advertises a low one-way fare that is available only with the purchase of a round-trip ticket or when a retailer sets artificially high "regular" prices then announces "sale" prices close to its previous everyday prices. Many federal and state statutes regulate against deceptive pricing practices. For example, the Automobile Information Disclosure Act requires automakers to attach a statement to new-car windows stating the manufacturer's suggested retail price, the prices of optional equipment, and the dealer's transportation charges. The FTC issues its *Guides Against Deceptive Pricing*, warning sellers not to advertise a price reduction unless it is a saving from the usual retail price, not to advertise "factory" or "wholesale" prices unless such prices are what they are claimed to be, and not to advertise comparable value prices on imperfect goods.

Sellers also are prohibited from using *predatory pricing*, selling below cost with the intention of destroying competition. This protects small sellers from larger ones who might sell items below cost temporarily or in a specific locale to drive them out of business. *Resale price maintenance* is also prohibited; a manufacturer cannot require dealers to charge a specified retail price for its product. Although the seller can propose a manufacturer's *suggested* retail price to dealers, it cannot refuse to sell to a dealer who takes independent pricing action, nor can it punish the dealer by shipping late or denying advertising allowances.[24]

Reviewing the Concepts

REST STOP

Before you put pricing in the rear view mirror, lets review the important concepts. *Price* can be defined as the sum of the values that consumers exchange for the benefits of having and using the product or service. It is the only marketing-mix element that produces revenue; all other elements represent costs. Even so, many companies are not good at handling pricing. Pricing decisions are subject to an incredibly complex array of environmental and competitive forces.

1. Identify and define the external and internal factors affecting a firm's pricing decisions.

External factors that influence pricing decisions include the nature of the *market and demand; competitors' prices and offers*; and factors such as *the economy,*

reseller needs, and *government actions*. The seller's pricing freedom varies with different types of markets. Ultimately, the consumer decides whether the company has set the right price. The consumer weighs the price against the perceived values of using the product; if the price exceeds the sum of the values, consumers will not buy. Therefore, *demand* and *consumer value perceptions* set the ceiling for prices. Consumers also compare a product's price to the prices of *competitors'* products. As a result, a company must learn the price and quality of competitors' offers.

Many *internal factors* influence the company's pricing decisions, including the firm's *marketing objectives, marketing-mix strategy, costs,* and *organization for pricing*. Common pricing objectives include survival, current profit maximization, market share leadership, and product-quality leadership. The pricing strategy is largely determined by the company's *target market* and *positioning objectives*. Pricing decisions affect and are affected by product design, distribution, and promotion decisions and must be carefully coordinated with these other marketing-mix variables. *Costs* set the floor for the company's price; the price must cover all the costs of making and selling the product, plus a fair rate of return. Finally, in order to coordinate pricing goals and decisions, management must decide who within the organization is responsible for setting price.

2. Contrast the three general approaches to setting prices.

A company can select one or a combination of three general pricing approaches: the *cost-based approach* (cost-plus pricing, break-even analysis, and target-profit pricing); the *value-based approach*; and the *competition-based approach*. Cost-based pricing sets prices based on the seller's cost structure, whereas value-based pricing relies on consumer perceptions of value to drive pricing decisions. Competition-based pricing involves setting prices based on what competitors are charging or are expected to charge.

3. Describe the major strategies for pricing imitative and new products.

Pricing is a dynamic process. Companies design a *pricing structure* that covers all their products. They change this structure over time and adjust it to account for different customers and situations. Pricing strategies usually change as a product passes through its life cycle. The company can decide on one of several price-quality strategies for introducing an imitative product, including premium pricing, economy pricing, good-value pricing, or overcharging. In pricing innovative new products, it can follow a *skimming policy* by initially setting high prices to "skim" the maximum amount of revenue from various segments of the market. Or it can use *penetration pricing* by setting a low initial price to penetrate the market deeply and win a large market share.

4. Explain how companies find a set of prices that maximizes the profits from the total product mix.

When the product is part of a product mix, the firm searches for a set of prices that will maximize the profits from the total mix. In *product-line pricing*, the company decides on price steps for the entire set of products it offers. In addition, the company must set prices for

optional products (optional or accessory products included with the main product), *captive products* (products that are required for use of the main product), *byproducts* (waste or residual products produced when making the main product), and *product bundles* (combinations of products at a reduced price).

5. Discuss how companies adjust their prices to take into account different types of customers and situations.

Companies apply a variety of *price-adjustment strategies* to account for differences in consumer segments and situations. One is *discount and allowance pricing*, whereby the company establishes cash, quantity, functional, or seasonal discounts, or varying types of allowances. A second strategy is *segmented pricing*, where the company sells a product at two or more prices to accommodate different customers, product forms, locations, or times. Sometimes companies consider more than economics in their pricing decisions, using *psychological pricing* to better communicate a product's intended position. In *promotional pricing*, a company offers discounts or temporarily sells a product below list price as a special event, sometimes even selling below cost as a loss leader. Another approach is *geographical pricing*, whereby the company decides how to price to near and distant customers. Finally, *international pricing* means that the company adjusts its price to meet conditions and expectations in different world markets.

6. Discuss the key issues related to initiating and responding to price changes.

When a firm considers initiating a *price change*, it must consider customers' and competitors' reactions. There are different implications to *initiating price cuts* and *initiating price increases*. Buyer reactions to price changes are influenced by the meaning customers see in the price change. Competitors' reactions flow from a set reaction policy or a fresh analysis of each situation. There are also many factors to consider in responding to a competitor's price changes. The company that faces a price change initiated by a competitor must try to understand the competitor's intent as well as the likely duration and impact of the change. If a swift reaction is desirable, the firm should preplan its reactions to different possible price actions by competitors. When facing a competitor's price change, the company might sit tight, reduce its own price, raise perceived quality, improve quality and raise price, or launch a fighting brand.

Navigating the Key Terms

For a detailed analysis of the meaning and importance of each of the following key terms, visit our web site at **www.prenhall.com/kotler**.

Allowance
Break-even pricing (target-profit pricing)
Byproduct pricing
Captive-product pricing

Competition-based pricing
Cost-plus pricing
Demand curve
Discount
Market-penetration pricing
Market-skimming pricing
Optional-product pricing
Price
Price elasticity
Product-bundle pricing

Product-line pricing
Promotional pricing
Psychological pricing
Reference prices
Segmented pricing
Target costing
Value pricing
Value-based pricing

Travel Log

The following concept checks and discussion questions will help you to keep track of and apply the concepts you've studied in this chapter.

Concept Checks

1. Rent, tuition, fees, fares, and dues are all examples of the many names of _____.
2. Economists recognize four types of markets, each presenting a different pricing challenge: _____ competition; _____ competition; _____ competition; and _____.
3. Price elasticity is how responsive demand will be to a change in price. If demand changes greatly, we say the demand is _____.
4. The simplest pricing method is _____, under which the marketer adds a standard markup to the cost of the product.
5. _____ pricing means that the marketer cannot design a product and marketing program and then set the price. Price is considered along with the other marketing-mix variables before the marketing program is set.
6. When developing an imitative new product, a company can choose one of four possible positioning strategies with respect to price: a _____ strategy; an _____ strategy; a _____ strategy; or an _____ strategy.
7. If a company chooses to set a low initial price in order to go into the market quickly and deeply (to attract a large number of buyers quickly and win

a large market share), the company would use a _____ pricing strategy.
8. A typical example of a _____ discount is "2/10, net 30," which means that although payment is due within 30 days, the buyer can deduct 2 percent if the bill is paid within 10 days.
9. One study indicates that consumers perceive higher-priced cars as having higher quality and higher-quality cars as being even higher priced than they actually are. This is an example in which _____ pricing might be used.
10. If a customer is asked to pay the entire cost of freight from the factory to the customer's destination (distant customers pay more), the company is most likely using _____ pricing.*

Discussing the Issues

1. An organization must consider many factors when setting prices. Assume the role of the vice-president for financial affairs at a major university. For the past three years, enrollments have been declining by about 10 percent per year. The enrollment decline has produced a similar 10 percent per year decline in revenues. You are under great pressure to raise tuition to compensate for the falling revenues. However, you suspect that raising tuition may only make matters worse. Outline the internal and external pricing factors that you should review before you make your decision.

---

* *Concept check answers:* 1. price; 2. pure, monopolistic, oligopolistic, pure monopoly; 3. elastic; 4. cost-plus pricing; 5. value-based; 6. premium pricing, economy pricing, good-value, overcharging; 7. market-penetration; 8. cash; 9. psychological; 10. FOB-origin.

2. Detergent A is priced at $2.19 for 32 ounces, and detergent B is priced at $1.99 for 26 ounces. Which brand appears most attractive. Assuming equal quality, which is actually the better value? Is there a psychological reason to price this way?

3. Describe which strategy—market skimming or market penetration— the following companies use in pricing their products: (a) McDonald's, (b) Curtis Mathes (television and other home electronics), (c) Bic Corporation (pens, lighters, shavers, and related products), and (d) IBM (personal computers). Are these the right strategies for these companies? Why or why not?

4. The federal government has accused Microsoft of monopolistic practices because it has tied (bundled) the sales of its popular Windows operating systems software to its Web browser product. What pricing strategy does Microsoft seem to be using? Take a side in the monopoly debate and state how you would resolve this ongoing problem.

5. Formulate rules that might govern: (a) initiating price cut, (b) initiating a price increase, (c) reacting to a negative buyer reaction to a price change by your company, (d) your response to a competitor's price change, and (e) a competitor's response to your price change. State any assumptions you are making along with your rules.

Traveling the Net

Point of Interest: Pricing Strategies

America still has its love affair going with the automobile. However, owning this piece of the American dream may not be the answer it once was. Today, you often hear the advice "don't buy a new car—lease it," and more and more consumers are heeding this advice daily. Leasing began with company fleet cars and a few more exotic imports. Today, almost all car brands and models are available through some form of lease plan. If consumers know that new-car prices are holding steady or declining, interest rates are falling, and family incomes are increasing, why would they increasingly view leasing as an attractive option? The answer might lie in prices and pricing strategy. Many buyers are finding that a car that can be purchased outright for $600 a month can be leased for only $490 per month. Now that catches the eye! Consumers are also beginning to understand leasing better than before, debunking many of the myths and taboos associated with leasing. The myths of higher prices, hard-to-understand contracts, hidden costs, early termination fees, and difficulties with mileage overages are all being resolved or put into proper perspective. Examine the following Web sites for more information on leasing: (a) Edmund's (www.edumunds.com), (b) Microsoft's CarPoint (www.carpoint.msn.com), (c) IntelliChoice at (www.intellichoice.com), and (d) Car Wizard at (www.carwizard.com).

For Discussion

1. What are the major advantages and disadvantages of leasing versus owning a car?

2. From the Web sites that you visited, what can you determine about car manufacturers? pricing strategies with respect to owning and leasing?

3. How would leasing impact the used-car business? The rental-car business?

4. With respect to leasing, which of the pricing strategies discussed in the chapter seem to be the most appropriate? Explain.

5. Assuming that you are a car dealer that offers new- and used-car sales and leasing options, construct a pricing strategy for each area. Take into account the internal and external factors that should be considered in developing good strategy decisions. Explain your strategy to the class.

Application Thinking

The lease option is no longer a trend—it is a fact. It has been estimated that as much as one-third of all new cars built will be leased rather than owned. Many consumers are now choosing to put their hard-earned dollars into more permanent assets such as homes. Consumers are more "money-wise" than ever before. The present value of money is a serious consideration for most budget-conscious consumers. To many car shoppers, making huge down payments (often as much as $10,000) to keep monthly payments low no longer seems to make much sense. If car leasing continues to increase in popularity, watch for leasing to expand quickly into other areas (such as computers, home entertainment systems, children's furniture, and major appliances). Assume that you are the marketing manager for a

Cadillac distributorship (see the Cadillac Web site at www.cadillac.com for information on Cadillac and its distributorships). Construct a policy that clearly separates the sale and lease options. What pricing strategies would you choose to apply to the two options? What types of customers would you try to move toward the two options? How would you contact them? How would you separate them once they come to your distributorship? What types of Web site policies would you use to reach customers who shop on-line? Under which option would you have the most local control over pricing? Why?

MAP — Marketing Applications

MAP Stop 9

The computer printer industry is intensely competitive with respect to pricing policies. Only a few years ago, consumers were shocked when they learned that the cost of their printer accounted for as much as 50 percent of the cost of their entire home computer. No more! Printer makers have added speed, color, high definition and quality, expandability options, and links between inkjet and laser technologies. Recently, companies such as Epson, Hewlett-Packard, Canon, Tektronics, and Xerox have introduced more inexpensive, flashier, and more technologically advanced models (see their Web sites for more information). The industry is even producing high-quality portable models that allow executives the capability to move their offices quickly as they travel from one end of the country to the other. This has spurred an increase in true desktop publishing and printing, high-power presentations, and less reliance on the company's home office for support and service. To keep up with the rapid changes in the industry, the major players are rethinking their technology and pricing strategies. Infrared options, battery power, and reduction in size of the primary printing units are now receiving serious consideration as the market becomes more technologically sensitive, more alert to changes, and more demanding of cheaper (yet higher-quality) options.

Thinking Like a Marketing Manager

1. What role does pricing play in selecting a printer for a home computer setup? For a home office setup? A mobile office setup?
2. Describe the pricing strategies used by Epson, Hewlett-Packard, Canon, Tektronics, and Xerox for color printers for personal computers, home offices, and mobile offices.
3. Which of the companies seems to have the most effective pricing strategy? Why? (You might visit each Web site to get additional information.)
4. Assume that you are the marketing manager of a company marketing a new color and seeking quick entry into the small color printer market. Further assume that your company's products are comparable to those of your primary competitors and that you have the capital needed to compete with the industry leaders. Design a pricing strategy that would allow you to compete in the home computer, home office, and mobile office markets. What factors would be critical to your success? How could you combat potential competitive reactions to your new product? What incentives might you offer to distributors to get them to push your new products?

Distribution Channels and Logistics Management

ROAD MAP:

Previewing the Concepts

We now arrive at the third marketing mix tool—distribution. Firms rarely work alone in bringing value to customers. Instead, most are only a single link in a larger supply chain, or distribution channel. As such, an individual firm's success depends not just on how well *it* performs but also on how well its *entire distribution channel* competes with competitors' channels. For example, Ford can make the world's best cars but still not do well if its dealers perform poorly in sales and service against the dealers of Toyota, GM, Chrysler, or Honda. Ford must choose its channel partners carefully and work with them effectively. The first part of this chapter explores the nature of distribution channels and the marketer's channel design and management decisions. We then examine physical distribution, or logistics, an area that is growing dramatically in importance and sophistication. In the next chapter, we'll look more closely at two major channel intermediaries—retailers and wholesalers.

▶ **After studying this chapter, you should be able to**

1. **explain why companies use distribution channels and discuss the functions these channels perform**
2. **discuss how channel members interact and how they organize to perform the work of the channel**
3. **identify the major channel alternatives open to a company**
4. **explain how companies select, motivate, and evaluate channel members**
5. **discuss the nature and importance of physical distribution and integrated logistics management**

While your engine's warming up, we'll take a look at Caterpillar. You might think that Caterpillar's success, and its ability to charge premium prices, rests on the quality of the construction and mining equipment that it produces. But Caterpillar's chairman and CEO sees things differently. The company's dominance, he claims, results from its unparalleled distribution and customer support system—from the strong and caring partnerships that it has built with independent Caterpillar dealers. Read on and see why.

For more than half a century, Caterpillar has dominated the world's markets for heavy construction and mining equipment. Despite market swings and major competitive challenges, the big Cat keeps on purring. Its familiar yellow tractors, crawlers, loaders, and trucks are a common sight at any construction area. With sales of $18.9 billion, Caterpillar is half again as large as its nearest competitor. It now captures more than a 40 percent share of the world's heavy-construction equipment market, and profits and returns stand at record levels. During the past five years, Caterpillar's sales have grown 13 percent per year while its profits have soared 45 percent annually and its stock price has tripled.

Many factors contribute to Caterpillar's enduring success—high-quality products, flexible and efficient manufacturing, a steady stream of innovative new products, and a lean organization that is responsive to customer needs. Although Caterpillar charges premium prices for its equipment, its high-quality and trouble-free operation provide greater long-term value. Yet, according to Donald Fites, Caterpillar's chairman and CEO, these are not the most important reasons for Caterpillar's dominance. Instead, Fites contends, "The biggest reason for Caterpillar's success has been our system of distribution and product support and the close customer relationships it fosters. . . . The backbone of that system is our 186 dealers around the world who sell and service our [equipment]."

Caterpillar's dealers provide a wide range of important services to customers. Fites summarizes:

> After the product leaves our door, the dealers take over. They are the ones on the front line. They're the ones who live with the product for its lifetime. They're the ones customers see. Although we offer financing and insurance, they arrange those deals for customers. They're out there making sure that when a machine is delivered, it's in the condition it's supposed to be in. They're out there training a customer's operators. They service a product frequently throughout its life, carefully monitoring a machine's health and scheduling repairs to prevent costly downtime. The customer . . . knows that there is a $16 billion-plus company called Caterpillar. But the dealers create the image of a company that doesn't just stand *behind* its products but *with* its products, anywhere in the world. Our dealers are the reason that our motto—Buy the Iron, Get the Company—is not an empty slogan.

Caterpillar's dealers build strong customer relationships in their communities. "Our independent dealer in Novi, Michigan, or in Bangkok, Thailand, knows so much more about the requirements of customers in those locations than a huge corporation like Caterpillar could," says Fites. Competitors often bypass their dealers and sell directly to big customers to cut costs or make more profits for themselves. However, Caterpillar wouldn't think of going around its dealers. "The knowledge of the local market and the close relations with customers that our dealers provide are worth every penny," he asserts with passion. "We'd rather cut off our right arm than sell directly to customers and bypass our dealers."

Caterpillar and its dealers work in close harmony to find better ways to bring value to customers. Says Fites, "We genuinely treat our system and theirs as one." The entire system is linked by a single worldwide computer network. For example, working at his desk computer, Fites can check to see how many Cat machines in the world are waiting for parts. Closely linked dealers play a vital role in almost every aspect of Caterpillar's operations, from product design and delivery, to product service and support, to market intelligence and customer feedback.

In the heavy-equipment industry, in which equipment downtime can mean big losses, Caterpillar's exceptional service gives it a huge advantage in winning and keeping customers. For example, consider Freeport-McMoRan, a Cat customer that operates one of the world's largest copper and gold mines, 24 hours a day, 365 days a year. High in the mountains of Indonesia, the mine is accessible only by aerial cableway or helicopter. Freeport-McMoRan relies on more than 500 pieces of Caterpillar mining and construction equipment—worth several hundred million dollars—including loaders, tractors, and mammoth 240-ton, 2,000-plus-horsepower trucks. Many of these machines cost well over $1 million apiece. When equipment breaks down, Freeport-McMoRan loses money fast. Thus, Freeport-McMoRan gladly pays a premium price for machines and service it can count on. It knows that it can count on Caterpillar and its outstanding distribution network for superb support.

The close working relationship between Caterpillar and its dealers comes down to more than just formal contracts and business agreements. According to Fites, the powerful partnership rests on a handful of basic principles and practices:

- *Dealer profitability:* Caterpillar's rule: "Share the gain as well as the pain." When times are good, Caterpillar shares the bounty with its dealers rather than trying to grab all the riches for itself. When times are bad, Caterpillar protects its dealers. For example, in the mid-1980s, facing a depressed global construction-equipment market and cutthroat competition, Caterpillar sheltered its dealers by absorbing much of the economic damage. It lost almost $1 billion dollars in just three years but didn't lose a single dealer. In contrast, competitors' dealers struggled and many failed. As a result, Caterpillar emerged with its distribution system intact and a competitive position stronger than ever.

- *Extraordinary dealer support:* Nowhere is this support more apparent than in the company's parts delivery system, the fastest and most reliable in the industry. Caterpillar maintains 22 parts facilities around the world, which stock 320,000 different parts and ship 84,000 items per day, about one per second every day of the year. In turn, dealers have made huge investments in inventory, warehouses, fleets of trucks, service bays, diagnostic and service equipment, and information technology. Together, Caterpillar and its dealers guarantee parts delivery within 48 hours anywhere in the world. The company ships 80 percent of parts orders immediately and 99 percent on the same day the order is received. In contrast, it's not unusual for competitors' customers to wait four or five days for a part.

- ☐ *Communications:* Caterpillar communicates with its dealers—fully, frequently, and honestly. According to Fites, "There are no secrets between us and our dealers. We have the financial statements and key operating data of every dealer in the world. . . . In addition, virtually all Caterpillar and dealer employees have real-time access to continually updated databases of service information, sales trends and forecasts, customer satisfaction surveys, and other critical data. . . . [Moreover,] virtually everyone from the youngest design engineer to the CEO now has direct contact with somebody in our dealer organizations."

- ☐ *Dealer performance:* Caterpillar does all it can to ensure that its dealerships are run well. It closely monitors each dealership's sales, market position, service capability, financial situation, and other performance measures. It genuinely wants each dealer to succeed, and when it sees a problem, it jumps in to help. As a result, Caterpillar dealerships, many of which are family businesses, tend to be stable and profitable. The average Caterpillar dealership has remained in the hands of the same family for more than 50 years. Some actually predate the 1925 merger that created Caterpillar.

- ☐ *Personal relationships:* In addition to more formal business ties, Cat forms close personal ties with its dealers in a kind of family relationship. Fites relates the following example: "When I see Chappy Chapman, a retired executive vice-president . . . , out on the golf course, he always asks about particular dealers or about their children, who may be running the business now. And every time I see those dealers, they inquire, 'How's Chappy?' That's the sort of relationship we have. . . . I consider the majority of dealers personal friends."

Thus, Caterpillar's superb distribution system serves as a major source of competitive advantage. The system is built on a firm base of mutual trust and shared dreams. Caterpillar and its dealers feel a deep pride in what they are accomplishing together. As Fites puts it, "There's a camaraderie among our dealers around the world that really makes it more than just a financial arrangement. They feel that what they're doing is good for the world because they are part of an organization that makes, sells, and tends to the machines that make the world work."[1]

Marketing channel decisions are among the most important decisions that management faces. A company's channel decisions directly affect every other marketing decision. The company's pricing depends on whether it uses mass merchandisers or high-quality specialty stores. The firm's sales force and advertising decisions depend on how much persuasion, training, motivation, and support the dealers need. Whether a company develops or acquires certain new products may depend on how well those products fit the capabilities of its channel members.

Companies often pay too little attention to their distribution channels, however, sometimes with damaging results. In contrast, many companies have used imaginative distribution systems to *gain* a competitive advantage. Federal Express's creative and imposing distribution system made it the leader in the small-package delivery industry. General Electric gained a strong advantage in selling its major appliances by supporting its dealers with a sophisticated computerized order-processing and delivery system. And Dell Computer revolutionized its industry by selling personal computers directly to consumers rather than through retail stores.

Distribution channel decisions often involve long-term commitments to other firms. For example, companies such as Ford, IBM, or Pizza Hut can easily change their advertising, pricing, or promotion programs. They can scrap old products and introduce new ones as market tastes demand. But when they set up distribution channels through contracts with franchisees, independent dealers, or large retailers, they cannot readily replace these channels with company-owned stores if conditions change. Therefore, management must design its channels carefully, with an eye on tomorrow's likely selling environment as well as today's.

This chapter examines four major questions concerning distribution channels: What is the nature of distribution channels? How do channel firms interact and organize to do the work of the channel? What problems do companies face in designing and managing their channels? What role does physical distribution play in attracting and satisfying customers? In chapter 11, we will look at distribution channel issues from the viewpoint of retailers and wholesalers.

The Nature of Distribution Channels

Distribution channel
A set of interdependent organizations involved in the process of making a product or service available for use or consumption by the consumer or business user.

Most producers use intermediaries to bring their products to market. They try to forge a **distribution channel**—a set of interdependent organizations involved in the process of making a product or service available for use or consumption by the consumer or business user.[2]

Why Are Marketing Intermediaries Used?

Why do producers give some of the selling job to intermediaries? After all, doing so means giving up some control over how and to whom the products are sold. The use of intermediaries results from their greater efficiency in making goods available to target markets. Through their contacts, experience, specialization, and scale of operation, intermediaries usually offer the firm more than it can achieve on its own.

Figure 10-1 shows how using intermediaries can provide economies. Part A shows three manufacturers, each using direct marketing to reach three customers. This system requires nine different contacts. Part B shows the three manufacturers working through one distributor, who contacts the three customers. This system requires only six contacts. In this way, intermediaries reduce the amount of work that must be done by both producers and consumers.

Figure 10-1
How a distributor reduces the number of channel transactions

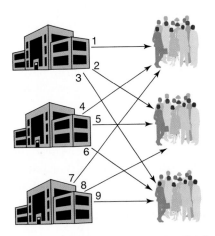 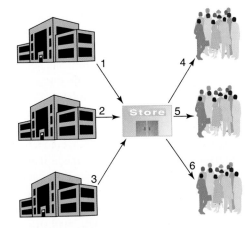

A. Number of contacts without a distributor
M × C = 3 × 3 = 9

B. Number of contacts with a distributor
M + C = 3 + 3 = 6

 = Manufacturer = Customer 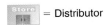 = Distributor

From the economic system's point of view, the role of marketing intermediaries is to transform the assortments of products made by producers into the assortments wanted by consumers. Producers make narrow assortments of products in large quantities, but consumers want broad assortments of products in small quantities. In the distribution channels, intermediaries buy large quantities from many producers and break them down into the smaller quantities and broader assortments wanted by consumers. Thus, intermediaries play an important role in matching supply and demand.

Distribution Channel Functions

The distribution channel moves goods and services from producers to consumers. It overcomes the major time, place, and possession gaps that separate goods and services from those who would use them. Members of the marketing channel perform many key functions. Some help to complete transactions:

- *Information:* gathering and distributing marketing research and intelligence information about actors and forces in the marketing environment needed for planning and aiding exchange.
- *Promotion:* developing and spreading persuasive communications about an offer.
- *Contact:* finding and communicating with prospective buyers.
- *Matching:* shaping and fitting the offer to the buyer's needs, including activities such as manufacturing, grading, assembling, and packaging.
- *Negotiation:* reaching an agreement on price and other terms of the offer so that ownership or possession can be transferred.

Others help to fulfill the completed transactions:

- *Physical distribution:* transporting and storing goods.
- *Financing:* acquiring and using funds to cover the costs of the channel work.
- *Risk taking:* assuming the risks of carrying out the channel work.

The question is not *whether* these functions need to be performed—they must be—but rather *who* will perform them. To the extent that the manufacturer performs these functions, its costs go up and its prices have to be higher. At the same time, when some of these functions are shifted to intermediaries, the producer's costs and prices may be lower, but the intermediaries must charge more to cover the costs of their work. In dividing the work of the channel, the various functions should be assigned to the channel members who can perform them most efficiently and effectively to provide satisfactory assortments of goods to target consumers.

Number of Channel Levels

Distribution channels can be described by the number of channel levels involved. Each layer of marketing intermediaries that performs some work in bringing the product and its ownership closer to the final buyer is a **channel level**. Because the producer and the final consumer both perform some work, they are part of every channel. We use the *number of intermediary levels* to indicate the *length* of a channel. Figure 10-2A shows several consumer distribution channels of different lengths.

Channel 1, called a **direct marketing channel**, has no intermediary levels. It consists of a company selling directly to consumers. For example, Avon, Amway, and Tupperware sell their products door to door or through home and office sales parties; Lands' End sells clothing directly through mail order, telephone, and the Internet; and

Channel level
A layer of intermediaries that performs some work in bringing the product and its ownership closer to the final buyer.

Direct marketing channel
A marketing channel that has no intermediary levels.

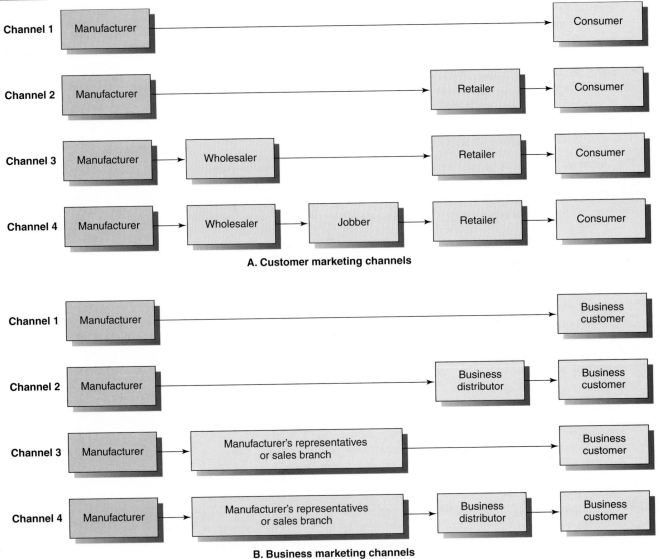

Figure 10-2
Consumer and business marketing channels

Indirect marketing channel
Channel containing one or
more intermediary levels.

Singer sells its sewing machines through its own stores. The remaining channels in Figure 10-2A are **indirect marketing channels**. Channel 2 contains one intermediary level. In consumer markets, this level is typically a retailer. For example, the makers of televisions, cameras, tires, furniture, major appliances, and many other products sell their goods directly to large retailers such as Wal-Mart and Sears, which then sell the goods to final consumers. Channel 3 contains two intermediary levels, a wholesaler and a retailer. This channel is often used by small manufacturers of food, drugs, hardware, and other products. Channel 4 contains three intermediary levels. In the meatpacking industry, for example, jobbers usually come between wholesalers and retailers. The jobber buys from wholesalers and sells to smaller retailers who generally are not served by larger wholesalers. Distribution channels with even more levels are sometimes found, but less often. From the producer's point of view, a greater number of levels means less control and greater channel complexity.

Lands' End sells direct through mail order, telephone, and the Internet.

Figure 10-2B shows some common business distribution channels. The business marketer can use its own sales force to sell directly to business customers. It can also sell to industrial distributors, who in turn sell to business customers. It can sell through manufacturer's representatives or its own sales branches to business customers, or it can use these representatives and branches to sell through industrial distributors. Thus, business markets commonly include multilevel distribution channels.

All of the institutions in the channel are connected by several types of *flows*. These include the *physical flow* of products, the *flow of ownership*, the *payment flow*, the *information flow*, and the *promotion flow*. These flows can make even channels with only one or a few levels very complex.

Channel Behavior and Organization

Distribution channels are more than simple collections of firms tied together by various flows. They are complex behavioral systems in which people and companies interact to accomplish individual, company, and channel goals. Some channel systems consist only of informal interactions among loosely organized firms; others consist of formal interactions guided by strong organizational structures. Moreover, channel systems do not stand still—new types of intermediaries emerge and whole new channel systems evolve. Here we look at channel behavior and at how members organize to do the work of the channel.

Channel Behavior

A distribution channel consists of firms that have banded together for their common good. Each channel member is dependent on the others. For example, a Ford dealer depends on the Ford Motor Company to design cars that meet consumer needs. In turn, Ford depends on the dealer to attract consumers, persuade them to buy Ford cars, and service cars after the sale. The Ford dealer also depends on other dealers to provide good sales and service that will uphold the reputation of Ford and its dealer body. In fact, the success of individual Ford dealers depends on how well the entire Ford distribution channel competes with the channels of other auto manufacturers.

Each channel member plays a role in the channel and specializes in performing one or more functions. For example, Compaq's role is to produce personal computers that consumers will like and to create demand through national advertising. Best Buy's role is to display these Compaq computers in convenient locations, to answer buyers' questions, and to close sales. The channel will be most effective when each member is assigned the tasks it can do best.

Ideally, because the success of individual channel members depends on overall channel success, all channel firms should work together smoothly. They should understand and accept their roles, coordinate their goals and activities, and cooperate to attain overall channel goals. By cooperating, they can more effectively sense, serve, and satisfy the target market.

However, individual channel members rarely take such a broad view. They are usually more concerned with their own short-run goals and their dealings with those firms closest to them in the channel. Cooperating to achieve overall channel goals sometimes means giving up individual company goals. Although channel members are dependent on one another, they often act alone in their own short-run best interests. They often disagree on the roles each should play—on who should do what and for what rewards. Such disagreements over goals and roles generate **channel conflict** (see Marketing at Work 10-1).

Horizontal conflict occurs among firms at the same level of the channel. For instance, some Ford dealers in Chicago might complain about other dealers in the city who steal sales from them by being too aggressive in their pricing and advertising or by selling outside their assigned territories. Or Pizza Inn franchisees might complain about other Pizza Inn franchisees cheating on ingredients, giving poor service, and hurting the overall Pizza Inn image.

Vertical conflict, conflicts between different levels of the same channel, is even more common. For example, McDonald's came into conflict recently with some of its dealers when its aggressive expansion plans called for placing new stores in areas that took business from existing locations. Motorola created conflict with its distributors when it tried to enforce strict policies for marketing its popular StarTAC cellular phones. Motorola required that dealers set up StarTAC displays, sell the phones only within their own territories, and buy 75 percent of their phones from the company. Despite the phone's popularity with consumers, the restrictions angered dealers, many of whom refused to accept the terms. This conflict threatened to crimp StarTAC sales, harming both Motorola and its distributors.[3]

Some conflict in the channel takes the form of healthy competition. Such competition can be good for the channel—without it, the channel could become passive and

Channel conflict
Disagreement among marketing channel members on goals and roles—who should do what and for what rewards.

noninnovative. But sometimes conflict can damage the channel, as it did in the case of Motorola's StarTAC phone. For the channel as a whole to perform well, each channel member's role must be specified and channel conflict must be managed. Cooperation, role assignment, and conflict management in the channel are attained through strong channel leadership. The channel will perform better if it includes a firm, agency, or mechanism that has the power to assign roles and manage conflict.

Vertical Marketing Systems

Historically, distribution channels have been loose collections of independent companies, each showing little concern for overall channel performance. These *conventional distribution channels* have lacked strong leadership and have been troubled by damaging conflict and poor performance. One of the biggest recent channel developments has been the *vertical marketing systems* that have emerged to challenge conventional marketing channels. Figure 10-3 contrasts the two types of channel arrangements.

A **conventional distribution channel** consists of one or more independent producers, wholesalers, and retailers. Each is a separate business seeking to maximize its own profits, even at the expense of profits for the system as a whole. No channel member has much control over the other members, and no formal means exists for assigning roles and resolving channel conflict. In contrast, a **vertical marketing system (VMS)** consists of producers, wholesalers, and retailers acting as a unified system. One channel member owns the others, has contracts with them, or wields so much power that they must all cooperate. The VMS can be dominated by the producer, wholesaler, or retailer. Vertical marketing systems came into being to control channel behavior and manage channel conflict.

We look now at three major types of VMSs: *corporate*, *contractual*, and *administrative*. Each uses a different means for setting up leadership and power in the channel. We now take a closer look at each type of VMS.

Corporate VMS A **corporate VMS** combines successive stages of production and distribution under single ownership. Coordination and conflict management are attained through regular organizational channels. For example, Sears obtains more than 50 percent

Conventional distribution channel
A channel consisting of one or more independent producers, wholesalers, and retailers, each a separate business seeking to maximize its own profits even at the expense of profits for the system as a whole.

Vertical marketing system (VMS)
A distribution channel structure in which producers, wholesalers, and retailers act as a unified system. One channel member owns the others, has contracts with them, or has so much power that they all cooperate.

Corporate VMS
A vertical marketing system that combines successive stages of production and distribution under single ownership; channel leadership is established through common ownership.

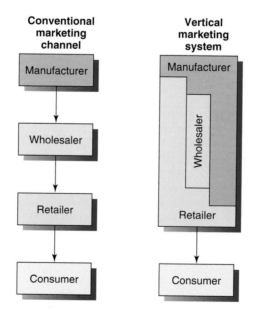

Figure 10-3
Comparison of conventional distribution channel with vertical marketing system

Goodyear Rolls, but over Its Dealers?

For more than 60 years, Goodyear Tire and Rubber Company sold replacement tires exclusively through its powerful network of independent Goodyear dealers. Both Goodyear and its 2,500 dealers profited from this partnership. Goodyear received the undivided attention and loyalty of its single-brand dealers, and the dealers gained the exclusive right to sell the highly respected Goodyear tire line. In mid-1992, however, Goodyear shattered tradition and jolted its dealers by announcing that it would now sell Goodyear-brand tires through Sears auto centers, placing Goodyear dealers in direct competition with the giant retailer. This departure from the previously sacred dealer network left many dealers shaken and angry. Said one Goodyear dealer: "You feel like after 35 years of marriage, your [spouse] is stepping out on you." Said another, "I feel like they just stabbed me in the back."

Channel conflict: Goodyear came into conflict with its independent dealers when it expanded its channels to meet changing consumer buying patterns.

Several factors forced the change in Goodyear's distribution system. During the late 1980s, massive international consolidation reshaped the tire industry, leaving only five competitors. Japan's Bridgestone acquired Firestone; Germany's Continental bought General Tire; Italy's Pirelli snapped up Armstrong; and France's Michelin acquired Uniroyal Goodrich. After six decades as the world's largest tire maker, Goodyear slipped to third behind Michelin and Bridgestone. As the only remaining U.S.-owned tire company, instead of having its way with smaller domestic rivals, Goodyear now found itself battling for U.S. market share against large and newly strengthened international competitors.

To add to Goodyear's woes, consumers were changing how and where they bought tires. Tires have become more of an impulse item, and value-minded tire buyers were increasingly buying from cheaper, multibrand discount outlets, department stores, and warehouse clubs. The market share of these outlets had grown 30 percent in the previous five years, while that of tire dealers had fallen 4 percent. By selling exclusively through its dealer network, Goodyear simply wasn't putting its tires where many consumers were going to buy them. The shifts in consumer buying were also causing problems for dealers. Although Goodyear offered an ample variety of premium lines, it provided its dealers with none of the lower-priced lines that many consumers were demanding.

Entering the 1990s, Goodyear was foundering. Although it remained number one in the United States, its share of the U.S. replacement-tire market had fallen 3 percent in only five years. Battling a prolonged recession and vicious price competition from Michelin and Bridgestone, Goodyear suffered its first money-losing year since the Great Depression. Drastic measures were needed.

Enter new management, headed by Stanley Gault, the

miracle-working manager who had transformed Rubbermaid from a sleepy Ohio rubber company into one of America's most-admired market leaders. Gault took the helm of Goodyear in mid-1991 and moved quickly to streamline the company, reducing its heavy debt, cutting costs, and selling off noncore businesses. But the biggest changes came in marketing. Under Gault, Goodyear speeded up new-product development and boosted ad spending. For example, in late 1991, it introduced four new tires simultaneously: the innovative, nonhydroplaning Aquatred, the Wrangler line for pickup trucks and vans, a fuel-efficient "green" tire, and a new high-performance Eagle model. In 1992, Goodyear brought out 12 more new tires, three times the usual number.

Gault also wasted little time in shaking up Goodyear's stodgy distribution system. In addition to selling its tires through Sears, the company began selling the Goodyear brand at Wal-Mart. Marketing research showed that one out of four Wal-Mart customers is a potential Goodyear buyer and that these buyers come from a segment unlikely to be reached by independent Goodyear dealers. The company also began drumming up new private-label business. Its Kelly-Springfield unit soon inked a deal to sell private-label tires through Wal-Mart, and agreements with Kmart, Montgomery Ward, and even the warehouse clubs also seem likely. Goodyear has since begun exploring other new distribution options as well. For example, it is now testing a no-frills, quick-serve discount store concept—Just Tires—designed to fend off low-priced competitors. In another test, it recently began selling Goodyear-brand tires to multibrand retailers in selected U.S. cities.

The expanded distribution system appeared to be a significant plus, at least in the short run. For example, by itself, Sears controls 10 percent of the U.S. replacement-tire market. Even a 20 percent share of Sears' business for Goodyear meant three million additional tires a year, enough to erase more than half of the company's previous market-share losses.

The marketing, distribution, and other changes got Goodyear rolling again. In its first year under Gault, Goodyear's sales and earnings soared, its market share increased 1 percent, and its stock price quadrupled. In 1993 and 1994, Goodyear made more profit than its nine direct competitors combined. By the time Gault stepped down in 1996, he'd delivered $4\frac{1}{2}$ years of heady profit gains. Gault became known around Goodyear as the man who saved the company, and his successor announced his intention to return Goodyear by the year 2000 to "its rightful position as the undisputed world leader."

In the long run, however, developing new channels risks eroding the loyalty and effectiveness of Goodyear's prized exclusive-dealer network, one of the company's major competitive assets. To be fully effective, Goodyear and its dealers must work together in harmony for their mutual benefit. But the agreements with Sears and other retailers has created hard feelings and conflict. Some disgruntled dealers have struck back by taking on and aggressively promoting cheaper, private-label brands that offer higher margins to dealers and more appeal to some value-conscious consumers. And U.S. dealers in California took Goodyear to court in a class action suit, causing Goodyear to somewhat restrict the tire lines sold through its new channels there. Such dealer actions could eventually weaken the Goodyear name and the premium price that it can command.

Goodyear has taken steps to bolster anxious dealers. For example, it is now supplying dealers with a much-needed line of lower-priced Goodyear-brand tires. Goodyear sincerely believes that expanded distribution will help its dealers more than harm them. In the end, selling through Sears means better visibility for the Goodyear name, the company contends, and the resulting expansion of business will mean more money for dealer support. However, many dealers remain skeptical. In the long run, dealer defections could lessen Goodyear's market power and offset sales gains from new channels. For example, shortly after the Sears announcement, one large Goodyear dealership in Florida adopted several lower-priced private brands, reducing its sales of Goodyear tires by 20 percent but increasing its profit margins. The defiant dealer notes, "We [now] sell what we think will give the customer the best value, and that's not necessarily Goodyear." Thus, although Goodyear may be rolling again, there are still many bumps in the road ahead.

Sources: Quotes from Dana Milbank, "Independent Tire Dealers Rebelling Against Goodyear," *Wall Street Journal*, July 8, 1992, p. B1; Schiller, "Goodyear Is Gunning Its Marketing Engine," *Business Week*, March 16, 1992, p. 42; Zachary Schiller, "Stan Gault's Designated Driver," *Business Week*, April 8, 1996; Charles Waltner, "Goodyear Rolls with the Market," *Advertising Age's Business Marketing*, January–February 1997, p. 58; and Al McGrath, "Managing Distribution Channels," *Business Quarterly*, Spring 1996, pp. 56–65. Also see Alex Taylor, "Goodyear Wants to Be No. 1 Again," *Fortune*, April 27, 1998, pp. 131–34.

Corporate vertical marketing systems: AT&T markets telephones and related equipment through its own chain of Phone Centers.

of its goods from companies that it partly or wholly owns. AT&T markets telephones and related equipment through its own chain of Phone Centers. Giant Food Stores operates an ice-making facility, a soft-drink bottling operation, an ice cream plant, and a bakery that supplies Giant stores with everything from bagels to birthday cakes. E. J. Gallo, the world's largest winemaker, grows its own grapes to produce wine which it pours into Gallo-made bottles topped with caps produced in Gallo's wholly owned Midcal Aluminum Co. plant. Gallo's Fairbanks Trucking Company hauls wine out of Gallo wineries and raw materials back in. The raw materials include lime from Gallo's quarry near Sacramento. Thus, Gallo participates in every aspect of producing and selling "short of whispering in the ear of each imbiber."

Contractual VMS

A vertical marketing system in which independent firms at different levels of production and distribution join together through contracts to obtain more economies or sales impact than they could achieve alone.

Contractual VMS A **contractual VMS** consists of independent firms at different levels of production and distribution who join together through contracts to obtain more economies or sales impact than each could achieve alone. Coordination and conflict management are attained through contractual agreements among channel members. There are three types of contractual VMSs: wholesaler-sponsored voluntary chains, retailer cooperatives, and franchise organizations.

In *wholesaler-sponsored voluntary chains*, wholesalers organize voluntary chains of independent retailers to help them compete with large chain organizations. The wholesaler develops a program in which independent retailers standardize their selling practices and achieve buying economies that let the group compete effectively with chain organizations. Examples include the Independent Grocers Alliance (IGA), Western Auto, and Sentry Hardware.

In *retailer cooperatives*, retailers organize a new, jointly owned business to carry on wholesaling and possibly production. Members buy most of their goods through the retailer co-op and plan their advertising jointly. Profits are passed back to members in proportion to their purchases. Examples include Certified Grocers, Associated Grocers, and Ace Hardware.

In **franchise organizations**, a channel member called a *franchisor* links several stages in the production-distribution process. The more than 500,000 franchise operations in the United States now account for nearly $760 billion in sales, about 40 percent of all U.S. retail sales.[4] Almost every kind of business has been franchised—from motels and fast-food restaurants to dental centers and dating services, from wedding consultants and maid services to funeral homes and fitness centers.

There are three forms of franchises. The first form is the *manufacturer-sponsored retailer franchise system*, as found in the automobile industry. Ford, for example, licenses dealers to sell its cars; the dealers are independent businesspeople who agree to meet various conditions of sales and service. The second type of franchise is the *manufacturer-sponsored wholesaler franchise system*, as found in the soft drink industry. Coca-Cola, for example, licenses bottlers (wholesalers) in various markets who buy Coca-Cola syrup concentrate and then carbonate, bottle, and sell the finished product to retailers in local markets. The third franchise form is the *service-firm-sponsored retailer franchise system*, in which a service firm licenses a system of retailers to bring its service to consumers. Examples are found in the auto-rental business (Hertz, Avis); the fast-food service business (McDonald's, Burger King); and the motel business (Holiday Inn, Ramada Inn).

The fact that most consumers cannot tell the difference between contractual and corporate VMSs shows how successfully the contractual organizations compete with corporate chains. Chapter 11 presents a fuller discussion of the various contractual VMSs.

Administered VMS An **administered VMS** coordinates successive stages of production and distribution not through common ownership or contractual ties but through the size and power of one of the parties. In an *administered VMS*, leadership is assumed by one or a few dominant channel members. Manufacturers of a top brand can obtain strong trade cooperation and support from resellers. For example, General Electric, Procter & Gamble, Kraft, and Campbell Soup can command unusual cooperation from resellers regarding displays, shelf space, promotions, and price policies. And large retailers like Wal-Mart and Toys 'Я' Us can exert strong influence on the manufacturers that supply the products they sell.

Horizontal Marketing Systems

Another channel development is the **horizontal marketing system**, in which two or more companies at one level join together to follow a new marketing opportunity. By working together, companies can combine their capital, production capabilities, or marketing resources to accomplish more than any one company could alone. Companies might join forces with competitors or noncompetitors. They might work with each other on a temporary or permanent basis, or they may create a separate company. For example, the Lamar Savings Bank of Texas arranged to locate its savings offices and automated teller machines in Safeway stores. Lamar gained quicker market entry at a low cost, and Safeway was able to offer in-store banking convenience to its customers.

Such channel arrangements also work well globally. For example, because of Nestlés excellent coverage of international markets, the Swiss Corporation and General Mills have funded a joint venture that manufactures and markets breakfast cereals under both Nestlé and General Mills brands outside of North America. Coca-Cola and Nestlé formed a joint venture to market ready-to-drink coffee and tea worldwide. Coke provides worldwide experience in marketing and distributing beverages, and Nestlé contributes two established brand names—Nescafé and Nestea. Similarly, Coca-Cola and Procter & Gamble have created distribution systems linking Coca-Cola soft drinks and Pringles potato crisps in global markets. Seiko Watch's distribution partner in Japan, K. Hattori,

Franchise organization
A contractual vertical marketing system in which a channel member, called a *franchisor*, links several stages in the production-distribution process.

Administered VMS
A vertical marketing system that coordinates successive stages of production and distribution, not through common ownership or contractual ties but through the size and power of one of the parties.

Horizontal marketing system
A channel arrangement in which two or more companies at one level join together to follow a new marketing opportunity.

Horizontal marketing systems: Nestlé jointly sells General Mills cereal brands in markets outside North America.

markets Schick's razors there, giving Schick the leading market share in Japan, despite Gillette's overall strength in many other markets.[5]

Hybrid Marketing Systems

In the past, many companies used a single channel to sell to a single market or market segment. Today, with the proliferation of customer segments and channel possibilities, more and more companies have adopted *multichannel distribution systems*—often called **hybrid marketing channels**. Such multichannel marketing occurs when a single firm sets up two or more marketing channels to reach one or more customer segments. The use of hybrid channel systems has increased greatly in recent years.

Hybrid marketing channel Multichannel distribution system in which a single firm sets up two or more marketing channels to reach one or more customer segments.

Figure 10-4 shows a hybrid channel. In the figure, the producer sells directly to consumer segment 1 using direct-mail catalogs and telemarketing and reaches consumer segment 2 through retailers. It sells indirectly to business segment 1 through distributors and dealers and to business segment 2 through its own sales force.

IBM uses such a hybrid channel effectively. For years, IBM sold computers only through its own sales force. However, when the market for small, low-cost computers

Figure 10-4
Hybrid marketing channel

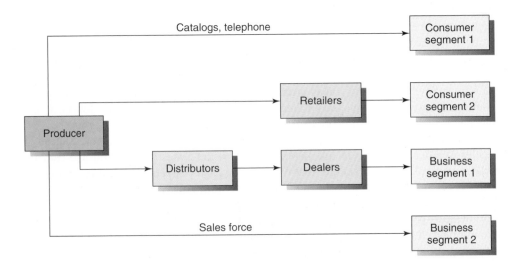

Hybrid channels: For years, IBM sold computers only through its salesforce. However, it now serves the rapidly fragmenting market through a wide variety of channels, including its IBM Direct catalog and telemarketing operation.

exploded, this single channel was no longer adequate. To serve the diverse needs of the many segments in the rapidly fragmenting computer market, IBM added 18 new channels in less than 10 years. For example, in addition to selling through the vaunted IBM sales force, the company now sells its complete line of computers and accessories through IBM Direct, its catalog and telemarketing operation. Consumers can also buy IBM personal computers from a network of independent IBM dealers or from any of several large retailers, including Wal-Mart, Circuit City, and Office Depot. IBM dealers and value-added resellers sell IBM computer equipment and systems to a variety of special business segments.[6]

Hybrid channels offer many advantages to companies facing large and complex markets. With each new channel, the company expands its sales and market coverage and gains opportunities to tailor its products and services to the specific needs of diverse customer segments. But such hybrid channel systems are harder to control, and they generate conflict as more channels compete for customers and sales. For example, when IBM began selling directly to customers at low prices through catalogs and telemarketing, many of its retail dealers cried "unfair competition" and threatened to drop the IBM line or to give it less emphasis.

Linking the Concepts

Stop here for a moment and apply the distribution channel concepts we've discussed so far.

- Compare the Caterpillar and Goodyear channels. Draw a diagram that shows the types of intermediaries in each channel. What kind of channel system does each company use?
- What are the roles and responsibilities of the members in each channel? How well do these channel members work together toward overall channel success?

Channel Design Decisions

We now look at several channel decisions facing manufacturers. In designing marketing channels, manufacturers struggle between what is ideal and what is practical. A new firm with limited capital usually starts by selling in a limited market area. Deciding on the *best* channels might not be a problem: The problem might simply be how to convince one or a few good intermediaries to handle the line.

If successful, the new firm might branch out to new markets through the existing intermediaries. In smaller markets, the firm might sell directly to retailers; in larger markets, it might sell through distributors. In one part of the country, it might grant exclusive franchises; in another, it might sell through all available outlets. In this way, channel systems often evolve to meet market opportunities and conditions. However, for maximum effectiveness, channel analysis and decision making should be more purposeful. Designing a channel system calls for analyzing consumer service needs, setting channel objectives and constraints, identifying major channel alternatives, and evaluating them.

Analyzing Consumer Service Needs

As noted previously, marketing channels can be thought of as *customer value-delivery systems* in which each channel member adds value for the customer. Thus, designing the distribution channel starts with finding out what targeted consumers want from the channel. Do consumers want to buy from nearby locations or are they willing to travel to more distant centralized locations? Would they rather buy in person, over the phone, through the mail, or via the Internet? Do they value breadth of assortment or do they prefer specialization? Do consumers want many add-on services (delivery, credit, repairs, installation) or will they obtain these elsewhere? The faster the delivery, the greater the assortment provided, and the more add-on services supplied, the greater the channel's service level.

But providing the fastest delivery, greatest assortment, and most services may not be possible or practical. The company and its channel members may not have the resources or skills needed to provide all the desired services. Also, providing higher levels of service results in higher costs for the channel and higher prices for consumers. The company must balance consumer service needs against not only the feasibility and costs of meeting these needs but against customer price preferences. The success of off-price and discount retailing shows that consumers are often willing to accept lower service levels if this means lower prices.

Setting Channel Objectives and Constraints

Channel objectives should be stated in terms of the desired service level of target consumers. Usually, a company can identify several segments wanting different levels of channel service. The company should decide which segments to serve and the best

Product characteristics affect channel decisions: Fresh flowers must be delivered quickly with a minimum of handling.

channels to use in each case. In each segment, the company wants to minimize the total channel cost of meeting customer service requirements.

The company's channel objectives are also influenced by the nature of the company, its products, marketing intermediaries, competitors, and the environment. For example, the company's size and financial situation determine which marketing functions it can handle itself and which it must give to intermediaries. Companies selling perishable products may require more direct marketing to avoid delays and too much handling. In some cases, a company may want to compete in or near the same outlets that carry competitors' products. In other cases, producers may avoid the channels used by competitors. Avon, for example, set up a profitable door-to-door selling operation rather than going head to head with other cosmetics makers for scarce positions in retail stores. Finally, environmental factors such as economic conditions and legal constraints may affect channel objectives and design. For example, in a depressed economy, producers want to distribute their goods in the most economical way, using shorter channels and dropping unneeded services that add to the final price of the goods.

Identifying Major Alternatives

When the company has defined its channel objectives, it should next identify its major channel alternatives in terms of *types* of intermediaries, *number* of intermediaries, and the *responsibilities* of each channel member.

Types of Intermediaries A firm should identify the types of channel members available to carry out its channel work. For example, suppose a manufacturer of test equipment has developed an audio device that detects poor mechanical connections in machines with moving parts. Company executives think this product would have a market in all industries in which electric, combustion, or steam engines are made or used. The company's current sales force is small, and the problem is how best to reach these different industries. The following channel alternatives might emerge from management discussion:

Company sales force: Expand the company's direct sales force. Assign salespeople to territories and have them contact all prospects in the area or develop separate company sales forces for different industries.

Manufacturer's agency: Hire manufacturer's agents—independent firms whose sales forces handle related products from many companies—in different regions or industries to sell the new test equipment.

Industrial distributors: Find distributors in the different regions or industries who will buy and carry the new line. Give them exclusive distribution, good margins, product training, and promotional support.

Number of Marketing Intermediaries Companies must also determine the number of channel members to use at each level. Three strategies are available: intensive distribution, exclusive distribution, and selective distribution.[7]

Producers of convenience products and common raw materials typically seek **intensive distribution**, a strategy in which they stock their products in as many outlets as possible. These goods must be available where and when consumers want them. For example, toothpaste, candy, and other similar items are sold in millions of outlets to provide maximum brand exposure and consumer convenience. Procter & Gamble, Campbell, Coca-Cola, and other consumer goods companies distribute their products in this way.

By contrast, some producers purposely limit the number of intermediaries handling their products. The extreme form of this practice is **exclusive distribution**, in which the producer gives only a limited number of dealers the exclusive right to distribute its products in their territories. Exclusive distribution is often found in the distribution of new automobiles and prestige women's clothing. For example, Rolls-Royce dealers are few and far between—even large cities may have only one or two dealers. By granting exclusive distribution, Rolls-Royce gains stronger distributor selling support and more control over dealer prices, promotion, credit, and services. Exclusive distribution also enhances the car's image and allows for higher markups.

Between intensive and exclusive distribution lies **selective distribution**—the use of more than one, but fewer than all, of the intermediaries who are willing to carry a company's products. Most television, furniture, and small-appliance brands are distributed in this manner. For example, Maytag, Whirlpool, and General Electric sell their major appliances through dealer networks and selected large retailers. By using selective distribution, they do not have to spread their efforts over many outlets, including many marginal

Intensive distribution
Stocking the product in as many outlets as possible.

Exclusive distribution
Giving a limited number of dealers the exclusive right to distribute the company's products in their territories.

Selective distribution
The use of more than one, but fewer than all, of the intermediaries who are willing to carry the company's products.

Exclusive distribution: Rolls-Royce sells exclusively through a limited number of dealerships. Such limited distribution enhances the car's image and generates stronger dealer support.

ones. They can develop good working relationships with selected channel members and expect a better-than-average selling effort. Selective distribution gives producers good market coverage with more control and less cost than does intensive distribution.

Responsibilities of Channel Members The producer and intermediaries need to agree on the terms and responsibilities of each channel member. They should agree on price policies, conditions of sale, territorial rights, and specific services to be performed by each party. The producer should establish a list price and a fair set of discounts for intermediaries. It must define each channel member's territory, and it should be careful about where it places new resellers. Mutual services and duties need to be spelled out carefully, especially in franchise and exclusive distribution channels. For example, McDonald's provides franchisees with promotional support, a recordkeeping system, training, and general management assistance. In turn, franchisees must meet company standards for physical facilities, cooperate with new promotion programs, provide requested information, and buy specified food products.

Evaluating the Major Alternatives

Suppose a company has identified several channel alternatives and wants to select the one that will best satisfy its long-run objectives. Each alternative should be evaluated against economic, control, and adaptive criteria.

Using *economic criteria*, a company compares the likely profitability of different channel alternatives. It estimates the sales that each channel would produce and the costs of selling different volumes through each channel. The company must also consider *control issues*. Using intermediaries usually means giving them some control over the marketing of the product, and some intermediaries take more control than others. Other things being equal, the company prefers to keep as much control as possible. Finally, the company must apply *adaptive criteria*. Channels often involve long-term commitments to other firms, making it hard to adapt the channel to the changing marketing environment. The company wants to keep the channel as flexible as possible. Thus, to be considered, a channel involving long-term commitment should be greatly superior on economic and control grounds.

Designing International Distribution Channels

International marketers face many additional complexities in designing their channels. Each country has its own unique distribution system that has evolved over time and changes very slowly. These channel systems can vary widely from country to country. Thus, global marketers must usually adapt their channel strategies to the existing structures within each country. In some markets, the distribution system is complex and hard to penetrate, consisting of many layers and large numbers of intermediaries. Consider Japan:

> The Japanese distribution system stems from the early seventeenth century when cottage industries and a [quickly growing] urban population spawned a merchant class. . . . Despite Japan's economic achievements, the distribution system has remained remarkably faithful to its antique pattern. . . . [It] encompasses a wide range of wholesalers and other agents, brokers, and retailers, differing more in number than in function from their American counterparts. There are myriad tiny retail shops. An even greater number of wholesalers supplies goods to them, layered tier upon tier, many more than most U.S. executives would think necessary.

The Japanese distribution system has remained remarkably traditional. A profusion of tiny retail shops are supplied by an even greater number of small wholesalers.

For example, soap may move through three wholesalers plus a sales company after it leaves the manufacturer before it ever reaches the retail outlet. A steak goes from rancher to consumers in a process that often involves a dozen middle agents. . . . The distribution network . . . reflects the traditionally close ties among many Japanese companies . . . [and places] much greater emphasis on personal relationships with users. . . . Although [these channels appear] inefficient and cumbersome, they seem to serve the Japanese customer well. . . . Lacking much storage space in their small homes, most Japanese homemakers shop several times a week and prefer convenient [and more personal] neighborhood shops.[8]

Many Western firms have had great difficulty breaking into the closely knit, tradition-bound Japanese distribution network.

At the other extreme, distribution systems in developing countries may be scattered and inefficient or altogether lacking. For example, China and India would appear to be huge markets, each with populations in the hundreds of millions. In reality, however, these markets are much smaller than the population numbers suggest. Because of inadequate distribution systems in both countries, most companies can profitably access only a small portion of the population located in each country's most affluent cities.[9]

Thus, international marketers face a wide range of channel alternatives. Designing efficient and effective channel systems between and within various country markets poses a difficult challenge. We discuss international distribution decisions further in chapter 15.

Channel Management Decisions

Once the company has reviewed its channel alternatives and decided on the best channel design, it must implement and manage the chosen channel. Channel management calls for selecting and motivating individual channel members and evaluating their performance over time.

Selecting Channel Members

Producers vary in their ability to attract qualified marketing intermediaries. Some producers have no trouble signing up channel members. For example, Toyota had no trouble attracting new dealers for its Lexus line. In fact, it had to turn down many would-be resellers. In some cases, the promise of exclusive or selective distribution for a desirable product will draw plenty of applicants.

At the other extreme are producers who have to work hard to line up enough qualified intermediaries. When Polaroid started, for example, it could not get photography stores to carry its new cameras, and it had to go to mass-merchandising outlets. Similarly, when the U.S. Time Company first tried to sell its inexpensive Timex watches through regular jewelry stores, most jewelry stores refused to carry them. The company then managed to get its watches into mass-merchandise outlets. This turned out to be a wise decision because of the rapid growth of mass merchandising.

When selecting intermediaries, the company should determine what characteristics distinguish the better ones. It will want to evaluate each channel member's years in business, other lines carried, growth and profit record, cooperativeness, and reputation. If the intermediaries are sales agents, the company will want to evaluate the number and character of other lines carried and the size and quality of the sales force. If the intermediary is a retail store that wants exclusive or selective distribution, the company will want to evaluate the store's customers, location, and future growth potential.

Motivating Channel Members

Once selected, channel members must be continuously motivated to do their best. The company must sell not only *through* the intermediaries but *to* them. Most companies see their intermediaries as first-line customers. Some use the carrot-and-stick approach: At times they offer *positive* motivators such as higher margins, special deals, premiums, cooperative advertising allowances, display allowances, and sales contests. At other times they use *negative* motivators, such as threatening to reduce margins, to slow down delivery, or to end the relationship altogether. A producer using this approach usually has not done a good job of studying the needs, problems, strengths, and weaknesses of its distributors.

More advanced companies try to forge long-term partnerships with their distributors to create a marketing system that meets the needs of both the manufacturer *and* the distributors. Thus, Procter & Gamble and Wal-Mart work together to create superior value for final consumers. They jointly plan merchandising goals and strategies, inventory levels, and advertising and promotion plans. Similarly, GE Appliances works closely with its independent dealers to help them be successful in selling the company's products (see Marketing at Work 10-2). In managing its channels, a company must convince distributors that they can make their money by being part of an advanced marketing system.[10]

Marketing at Work 10-2

Ge Appliances Forges Strong Partnerships with Dealers

Before the late 1980s, General Electric's appliance division worked at selling *through* its dealers rather than *to* them or *with* them. GE Appliances operated a traditional system of trying to load up the channel with its appliances on the premise that "loaded dealers are loyal dealers." Loaded dealers would have less space to feature other brands and would recommend GE appliances to reduce their high inventories. To load its dealers, GE Appliances would offer the lowest price when the dealer ordered a full truckload of products.

GE eventually realized that this approach created many problems, especially for smaller, independent appliance dealers who could ill afford to carry a large stock. These dealers were hard pressed to meet price competition from larger, multibrand dealers. Rethinking its strategy from the point of view of creating dealer satisfaction and profitability, GE created an alternative distribution system to serve its dealers—a system now called GE CustomerNet.

GE CustomerNet gives dealers instant on-line access to GE Appliances' distribution and order-processing system, 24 hours a day, seven days a week. By logging onto the GE CustomerNet Web site, dealers can obtain product specifications, photos, feature lists,

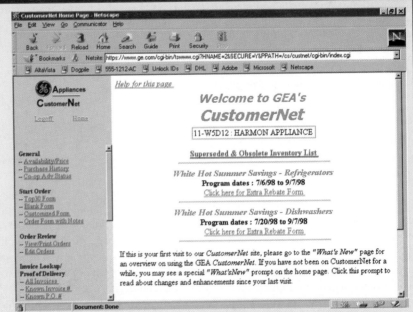

Creating dealer satisfaction and profitability: GE CustomerNet gives dealers instant on-line access to GE Appliances' distribution and order-processing system, 24 hours a day, seven days a week.

and side-by-side model comparisons for hundreds of GE appliance models. They can check on product availability and prices, place orders, review order status, and even download "advertising slicks"—professionally prepared GE appliance ads ready for insertion in local media. Says Brian Kelly, sales vice-president for GE Appliances, "With this system, we're putting all

our backroom capabilities right in the store with our [dealers]. We want [them] to get closer to us and have better access to our data."

GE CustomerNet yields substantial benefits to dealers. Instead of loading up dealers with big inventories, the system gives them a large "virtual inventory" from which to satisfy their customers' needs. GE promises next-day

Evaluating Channel Members

The producer must regularly check the channel member's performance against standards such as sales quotas, average inventory levels, customer delivery time, treatment of damaged and lost goods, cooperation in company promotion and training programs, and services to the customer. The company should recognize and reward intermediaries who are performing well. Those who are performing poorly should be assisted or, as a last

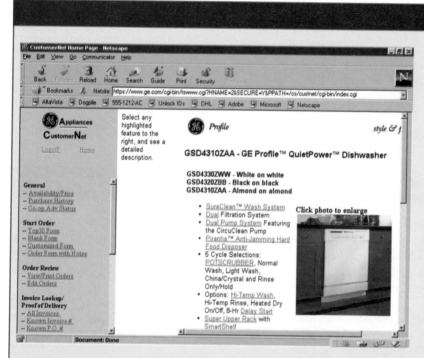

locations, so it can deliver appliances to 90 percent of the United States within 24 hours.

Perhaps the biggest benefit to GE Appliances, however, is that the system builds strong bonds between the company and its dealers and motivates dealers to put more push behind the company's products. Beyond its sales-support features, GE CustomerNet contains an on-line feedback system that lets dealers communicate promptly and regularly with GE Appliances about anything related to products, service, or the Web site. Notes Kelly, "We want to make it simple and easy for [dealers] who have questions, complaints, and suggestions. This helps us constantly enhance relationships with our customers."

The GE CustomerNet system now handles upwards of 50,000 transactions per week. As a result of the system, dealer profit margins have skyrocketed. Thus, over the past decade, GE Appliances has replaced the old "us-against-them" mentality with a passion for partnerships that benefits both the company and its dealers.

delivery on most appliance models, so dealers need carry only display models in their stores and can rely on the virtual inventory to fill orders. This greatly reduces inventory costs, making even small dealers more price competitive. GE CustomerNet also helps dealers to sell GE appliances more easily and effectively. A dealer can put a computer terminal on the showroom floor, where salespeople and customers together can use the system to dig through detailed product specifications and check availability for GE's entire line of appliances. As one dealer states, "You can quickly tell customers whether or not a product is available, and you can print them a great looking picture with the click of a button."

GE Appliances also benefits from the new system. GE CustomerNet dramatically decreases the volume of costly and time-consuming phone inquiries and orders, and the electronic order-entry system saves the company substantial clerical costs. GE Appliances now knows the actual sales of its goods at the retail level, which helps it to schedule production more accurately. It now can produce in response to demand rather than to meet inventory replenishment rules. And GE has been able to simplify its warehouse

Sources: Michael Treacy and Fred Wiersema, "Customer Intimacy and Other Discipline Values," *Harvard Business Review,* January–February 1993, pp. 84–93; Robert D. Buzzell and Gwen Ortmeyer, "Channel Partnerships Streamline Distribution," *Sloan Management Review,* Spring 1995, pp. 85–96; Cathy Ciccolella, "GE to Offer Online Dealer Support with CustomerNet," *Twice,* April 21, 1997, p. 88; Cathy Ciccolella, "GE Online Support Wins Dealers Over," *Twice,* February 9, 1998, p. 38; and information supplied by GE Appliances, August 1998.

resort, replaced. A company may periodically "requalify" its intermediaries and prune the weaker ones.

Finally, manufacturers need to be sensitive to their dealers. Those who treat their dealers lightly risk not only losing their support but also causing some legal problems. The next section describes various rights and duties pertaining to manufacturers and their channel members.

Linking the Concepts

Time for another break. This time, compare the Goodyear and GE Appliances channel systems.

- Diagram the Goodyear and GE Appliances systems. How do they compare in terms of channel levels, types of intermediaries, channel member roles and responsibilities, and other characteristics? How well is each system designed?
- Assess how well Goodyear and GE Appliances have managed and supported their channels. With what results?

Public Policy and Distribution Decisions

For the most part, companies are legally free to develop whatever channel arrangements suit them. In fact, the laws affecting channels seek to prevent the exclusionary tactics of some companies that might keep another company from using a desired channel. Most channel law deals with the mutual rights and duties of the channel members once they have formed a relationship.

Many producers and wholesalers like to develop exclusive channels for their products. When the seller allows only certain outlets to carry its products, this strategy is called *exclusive distribution*. When the seller requires that these dealers not handle competitors' products, its strategy is called *exclusive dealing*. Both parties can benefit from exclusive arrangements: The seller obtains more loyal and dependable outlets, and the dealers obtain a steady source of supply and stronger seller support. But exclusive arrangements also exclude other producers from selling to these dealers. This situation brings exclusive dealing contracts under the scope of the Clayton Act of 1914. They are legal as long as they do not substantially lessen competition or tend to create a monopoly and as long as both parties enter into the agreement voluntarily.

Exclusive dealing often includes *exclusive territorial agreements*. The producer may agree not to sell to other dealers in a given area or the buyer may agree to sell only in its own territory. The first practice is normal under franchise systems as a way to increase dealer enthusiasm and commitment. It is also perfectly legal—a seller has no legal obligation to sell through more outlets than it wishes. The second practice, whereby the producer tries to keep a dealer from selling outside its territory, has become a major legal issue.

Producers of a strong brand sometimes sell it to dealers only if the dealers will take some or all of the rest of the line. This is called *full-line forcing*. Such *tying agreements* are not necessarily illegal, but they do violate the Clayton Act if they tend to lessen competition substantially. The practice may prevent consumers from freely choosing among competing suppliers of these other brands.

Finally, producers are free to select their dealers, but their right to terminate dealers is somewhat restricted. In general, sellers can drop dealers "for cause." However, they cannot drop dealers if, for example, the dealers refuse to cooperate in a doubtful legal arrangement, such as exclusive dealing or tying agreements.[11]

Physical Distribution and Logistics Management

In today's global marketplace, selling a product is sometimes easier than getting it to customers. Companies must decide on the best way to store, handle, and move their products and services so that they are available to customers in the right assortments, at the right time, and in the right place. Logistics effectiveness has a major impact on both customer satisfaction and company costs. Here we consider the *nature and importance of marketing logistics, goals of the logistics system, major logistics functions*, and the need for *integrated logistics management*.

Nature and Importance of Physical Distribution and Marketing Logistics

To some managers, physical distribution means only trucks and warehouses. But modern logistics is much more than this. **Physical distribution (marketing logistics)** involves planning, implementing, and controlling the physical flow of materials, final goods, and related information from points of origin to points of consumption to meet customer requirements at a profit. In short, it involves getting the right product to the right customer in the right place at the right time.

> **Physical distribution (marketing logistics)**
> The tasks involved in planning, implementing, and controlling the physical flow of materials, final goods, and related information from points of origin to points of consumption to meet customer requirements at a profit.

Traditional physical distribution typically started with products at the plant and then tried to find low-cost solutions to get them to customers. However, today's marketers prefer *market logistics* thinking, which starts with the marketplace and works backward to the factory. Logistics addresses not only the problem of outbound distribution (moving products from the factory to customers) but also the problem of inbound distribution (moving products and materials from suppliers to the factory). It involves the management of entire *supply chains*, value-added flows from suppliers to final users, as shown in Figure 10-5. Thus, the logistics manager's task is to coordinate activities of suppliers, purchasing agents, marketers, channel members, and customers. These activities include forecasting, information systems, purchasing, production planning, order processing, inventory, warehousing, and transportation planning.

Companies today are placing greater emphasis on logistics for several reasons. First, customer service and satisfaction have become the cornerstones of marketing strategy, and distribution is an important customer service element. More and more, companies are finding that they can attract and keep customers by giving better service or lower prices through better physical distribution.

Second, logistics is a major cost element for most companies. According to one study, in a recent year American companies "spent $670 billion—a gaping 10.5 percent of Gross Domestic Product—to wrap, bundle, load, unload, sort, reload, and transport goods."[12] About 15 percent of an average product's price is accounted for by shipping and transport alone. Poor physical distribution decisions result in high costs. Improvements in physical distribution efficiency can yield tremendous cost savings for both the company and its customers.

Third, the explosion in product variety has created a need for improved logistics management. For example, in 1911 the typical A&P grocery store carried only 270 items. The store manager could keep track of this inventory on about 10 pages of notebook paper stuffed in a shirt pocket. Today, the average A&P carries a bewildering stock of more than 16,700 items.[13] Ordering, shipping, stocking, and controlling such a variety of products presents a sizable logistics challenge.

Finally, improvements in information technology have created opportunities for major gains in distribution efficiency. The increased use of computers, point-of-sale scanners, uniform product codes, satellite tracking, electronic data interchange (EDI), and electronic funds transfer (EFT) has allowed companies to create advanced systems for order processing, inventory control and handling, and transportation routing and scheduling.

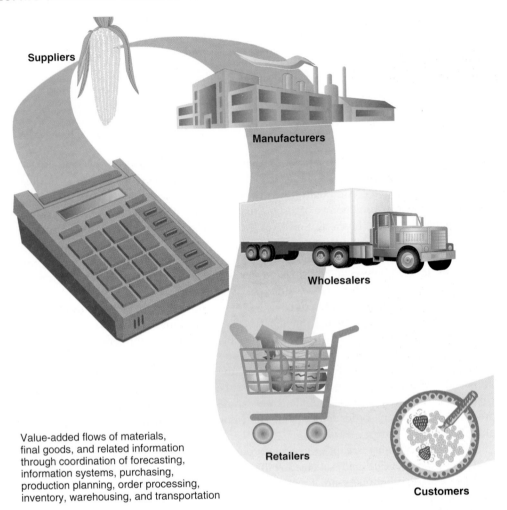

Figure 10-5
Marketing logistics:
managing supply
chains

Value-added flows of materials,
final goods, and related information
through coordination of forecasting,
information systems, purchasing,
production planning, order processing,
inventory, warehousing, and transportation

Goals of the Logistics System

Some companies state their logistics objective as providing maximum customer service at the least cost. Unfortunately, no logistics system can *both* maximize customer service *and* minimize distribution costs. Maximum customer service implies rapid delivery, large inventories, flexible assortments, liberal returns policies, and other services—all of which raise distribution costs. In contrast, minimum distribution costs imply slower delivery, smaller inventories, and larger shipping lots—which represent a lower level of overall customer service.

The goal of the marketing logistics system should be to provide a targeted level of customer service at the least cost. A company must first research the importance of various distribution services to its customers and then set desired service levels for each segment. The company normally will want to offer at least the same level of service as its competitors do. But the objective is to maximize *profits*, not sales. Therefore, the company must weigh the benefits of providing higher levels of service against the costs. Some companies offer less service than their competitors and charge a lower price. Other companies offer more service and charge higher prices to cover higher costs.

Major Logistics Functions

Given a set of logistics objectives, the company is ready to design a logistics system that will minimize the cost of attaining these objectives. The major logistics functions include *order processing, warehousing, inventory management,* and *transportation.*

Order Processing

Orders can be submitted in many ways: by mail or telephone, through salespeople, or via computer and electronic data interchange (EDI). In some cases, the suppliers might actually generate orders for their customers:

✧ One Kmart quick response program calls for selected suppliers to manage the retailer's inventory replenishment for their products. Kmart transmits daily records of product sales to the vendor, who analyzes the sales information, comes up with an order, and sends it back to Kmart through EDI. Once in Kmart's system, the order is treated as though Kmart itself created it. Says a Kmart executive, "We don't modify the order, and we don't question it. . . . Our relationship with those vendors is such that we trust them to create the type of order that will best meet our inventory needs."[14]

Once received, orders must be processed quickly and accurately. Both the company and its customers benefit when order processing is carried out efficiently. Most companies now use computerized order-processing systems that speed up the order-shipping-billing cycle. For example, General Electric operates a computer-based system that, on receipt of a customer's order, checks the customer's credit standing as well as whether and where the items are in stock. The computer then issues an order to ship, bills the customer, updates the inventory records, sends a production order for new stock, and relays the message back to the salesperson that the customer's order is on its way—all in less than 15 seconds.

Warehousing

Every company must store its goods while they wait to be sold. A storage function is needed because production and consumption cycles rarely match. For example, Snapper, Toro, and other lawn mower manufacturers must produce all year long and store up their product for the heavy spring and summer buying seasons. The storage function overcomes differences in needed quantities and timing.

A company must decide on *how many* and *what types* of warehouses it needs and *where* they will be located. The company might use either *storage warehouses* or *distribution centers.* Storage warehouses store goods for moderate to long periods. **Distribution centers** are designed to move goods rather than just store them. They are large and highly automated warehouses designed to receive goods from various plants and suppliers, take orders, fill them efficiently, and deliver goods to customers as quickly as possible. For example, Wal-Mart operates huge distribution centers. One center, which serves the daily needs of 165 Wal-Mart stores, contains some 28 acres of space under a single roof. Laser scanners route as many as 190,000 cases of goods per day along 11 miles of conveyer belts, and the center's 1,000 workers load or unload 310 trucks daily.[15]

Warehousing facilities and equipment technology have improved greatly in recent years. Older, multistoried warehouses with outdated materials-handling methods are facing competition from newer, single-storied *automated warehouses* with advanced materials-handling systems under the control of a central computer. In these warehouses, only a few employees are necessary. Computers read orders and direct lift trucks, electric hoists, or robots to gather goods, move them to loading docks, and issue invoices. These warehouses have reduced worker injuries, labor costs, theft, and breakage and have improved inventory control.

Distribution center
A large, highly automated warehouse designed to receive goods from various plants and suppliers, take orders, fill them efficiently, and deliver goods to customers as quickly as possible.

Inventory Inventory levels also affect customer satisfaction. The major problem is to maintain the delicate balance between carrying too much inventory and carrying too little. Carrying too much inventory results in higher-than-necessary inventory-carrying costs and stock obsolescence. Carrying too little may result in stock-outs, costly emergency shipments or production, and customer dissatisfaction. In making inventory decisions, management must balance the costs of carrying larger inventories against resulting sales and profits.

During the past decade, many companies have greatly reduced their inventories and related costs through *just-in-time* logistics systems. Through such systems, producers and retailers carry only small inventories of parts or merchandise, often only enough for a few days of operations. New stock arrives exactly when needed, rather than being stored in inventory until being used. Just-in-time systems require accurate forecasting along with fast, frequent, and flexible delivery so that new supplies will be available when needed. However, these systems result in substantial savings in inventory-carrying and handling costs.

Transportation Marketers need to take an interest in their company's *transportation* decisions. The choice of transportation carriers affects the pricing of products, delivery performance, and condition of the goods when they arrive—all of which will affect customer satisfaction. In shipping goods to its warehouses, dealers, and customers, the company can choose among five transportation modes: rail, water, truck, pipeline, and air.

Railroads are the nation's largest carrier, accounting for 26 percent of total cargo ton-miles moved.[16] They are one of the most cost-effective modes for shipping large amounts of bulk products—coal, sand, minerals, farm and forest products—over long distances. In recent years, railroads have increased their customer services by designing new equipment to handle special categories of goods, providing flatcars for carrying truck trailers by rail (piggyback), and providing in-transit services such as the diversion of shipped goods to other destinations en route and the processing of goods en route. Thus, after decades of losing out to truckers, railroads appear ready for a comeback.[17]

Trucks have increased their share of transportation steadily and now account for 24 percent of total cargo ton-miles (more than 52 percent of actual tonnage). They account for the largest portion of transportation *within* cities as opposed to *between* cities. Each year in the United States, trucks travel more than 600 billion miles—equal to nearly 1.3 million round trips to the moon—carrying 2.5 billion tons of freight.[18] Trucks are highly flexible in their routing and time schedules, and they can usually offer faster service than railroads. They are efficient for short hauls of high-value merchandise. Trucking firms have added many services in recent years. For example, Roadway Express now offers satellite tracking of shipments and sleeper tractors that move freight around the clock.

Water carriers transport large amounts of goods by ships and barges on U.S. coastal and inland waterways. Mississippi River barges alone account for 15 percent of the freight shipped in the United States. Although the cost of water transportation is very low for shipping bulky, low-value, nonperishable products such as sand, coal, grain, oil, and metallic ores, water transportation is the slowest mode and may be affected by the weather. *Pipelines* are a specialized means of shipping petroleum, natural gas, and chemicals from sources to markets. Most pipelines are used by their owners to ship their own products.

Although *air carriers* transport less than 1 percent of the nation's goods, they are becoming more important as a transportation mode. Air freight rates are much higher than rail or truck rates, but air freight is ideal when speed is needed or distant markets have to be reached. Among the most frequently air-freighted products are perishables (fresh fish, cut flowers) and high-value, low-bulk items (technical instruments, jewelry). Companies

Roadway and other trucking firms have added many services in recent years, such as satellite tracking of shipments and sleeper tractors that keep freight moving around the clock.

find that air freight also reduces inventory levels, packaging costs, and the number of warehouses needed.

Shippers increasingly are using **intermodal transportation**—combining two or more modes of transportation. *Piggyback* describes the use of rail and trucks; *fishyback*, water and trucks; *trainship*, water and rail; and *airtruck*, air and trucks. Combining modes provides advantages that no single mode can deliver. Each combination offers advantages to the shipper. For example, not only is piggyback cheaper than trucking alone but it also provides flexibility and convenience.

Intermodal transportation
Combining two or more modes of transportation.

In choosing a transportation mode for a product, shippers must balance many considerations: speed, dependability, availability, cost, and others. Thus, if a shipper needs speed, air and truck are the prime choices. If the goal is low cost, then water or pipeline might be best.

Integrated Logistics Management

Today, more and more companies are adopting the concept of **integrated logistics management**. This concept recognizes that providing better customer service and trimming distribution costs requires *teamwork*, both inside the company and among all the marketing channel organizations. Inside, the company's various functional departments must

Integrated logistics management
The logistics concept that emphasizes teamwork, both inside the company and among all the marketing channel organizations, to maximize the performance of the entire distribution system.

work closely together to maximize the company's own logistics performance. Outside, the company must integrate its logistics system with those of its suppliers and customers to maximize the performance of the entire distribution system.

Cross-Functional Teamwork Inside the Company In most companies, responsibility for various logistics activities is assigned to many different functional units: marketing, sales, finance, manufacturing, purchasing. Too often, each function tries to optimize its own logistics performance without regard for the activities of the other functions. However, transportation, inventory, warehousing, and order-processing activities interact, often in an inverse way. For example, lower inventory levels reduce inventory-carrying costs. But they may also reduce customer service and increase costs from stock-outs, back orders, special production runs, and costly fast-freight shipments. Because distribution activities involve strong trade-offs, decisions by different functions must be coordinated to achieve superior overall logistics performance.

The goal of integrated logistics management is to harmonize all of the company's distribution decisions. Close working relationships among functions can be achieved in several ways. Some companies have created permanent logistics committees made up of managers responsible for different physical distribution activities. Companies can also create management positions that link the logistics activities of functional areas. For example, Procter & Gamble has created supply managers, who manage all of the supply chain activities for each of its product categories. Many companies have a vice-president of logistics with cross-functional authority. The important thing is that the company coordinate its logistics and marketing activities to create high market satisfaction at a reasonable cost.

Building Channel Partnerships The members of a distribution channel are linked closely in delivering customer satisfaction and value. One company's distribution system is another company's supply system. The success of each channel member depends on the performance of the entire supply chain. For example, Wal-Mart can charge the lowest prices at retail only if its entire supply chain—consisting of thousands of merchandise suppliers, transport companies, warehouses, and service providers—operates at maximum efficiency.

Companies must do more than improve their own logistics. They must also work with other channel members to improve whole-channel distribution. Today, smart companies are coordinating their logistics strategies and building strong partnerships with suppliers and customers to improve customer service and reduce channel costs.

These channel partnerships can take many forms. Many companies have created *cross-functional, cross-company teams*. For example, Procter & Gamble has a team of almost 100 people living in Bentonville, Arkansas, home of Wal-Mart. The P&Gers work with their counterparts at Wal-Mart to jointly find ways to squeeze costs out of their distribution system. Working together benefits not only P&G and Wal-Mart but also their final consumers. Haggar Apparel Company has a similar system called "multiple points of contact," in which a Haggar team works with JCPenney people at corporate, divisional, and store levels. As a result of this partnership, JCPenney now receives Haggar merchandise within 18 days of placing an order—10 days fewer than its next-best supplier. Haggar ships the merchandise "floor ready"—hangered and pretagged—reducing the time it takes JCPenney to move the stock from receiving docks to the sales floor from four days to just one.[19]

Other companies partner through *shared projects*. For example, many larger retailers are working closely with suppliers on in-store programs. Home Depot allows key suppliers to use its stores as a testing ground for new merchandising programs. The suppliers spend time at Home Depot stores watching how their product sells and how customers relate to it. They then create programs specially tailored to Home Depot and its customers. Western Publishing Group, publisher of "Little Golden Books" for children, formed a similar partnership with Toys "Я" Us. Western and the giant toy retailer coordinated their marketing strategies to create minibookstore sections, called Books "Я" Us, within each Toys "Я" Us store. Toys "Я" Us provides the locations, space, and customers; Western serves as distributor, consolidator, and servicer for the Books "Я" Us program.[20] Clearly, both the supplier and customer benefit from such partnerships.

Channel partnerships may also take the form of *information sharing* and *continuous inventory replenishment* systems. Companies manage their supply chains through information. Suppliers link up with customers through electronic data interchange (EDI) systems to share information and coordinate their logistics decisions. Here are just two examples:

- ✦ Increasingly, high-performance retailers are sharing point-of-sale scanner data with their suppliers through electronic data interchange. Wal-Mart was one of the first companies to provide suppliers with timely sales data. With its Retail Link system, major suppliers have "earth stations" installed by which they are directly connected to Wal-Mart's information network. Now, the same system that tells Wal-Mart what customers are buying lets suppliers know what to produce and where to ship the goods. For example, Wal-Mart sells millions of Wrangler jeans each year. Every night, Wal-Mart sends sales data collected on its scanners directly to VF Corporation (which makes Wrangler jeans), which then restocks automatically. So if a Wal-Mart customer buys a pair of Wranglers on Tuesday morning, by the evening, records of the sales arrive in VF's central computer. If VF has a replacement pair in stock, it's shipped directly to the store the next day—and by Thursday, Wal-Mart's shelf is replenished. If not, VF's computers automatically order up a replacement—and a new pair of jeans is shipped within a week.[21]

- ✦ Bailey Controls, a manufacturer of control systems for big factories, from steel and paper mills to chemical and pharmaceutical plants, . . . treats some of its suppliers almost like departments of its own plants. Bailey has plugged two of its main electronics suppliers into itself. Future Electronics is hooked on through an electronic data interchange system. Every week, Bailey electronically sends Future its latest forecasts of what materials it will need for the next six months so that Future can stock up in time. Bailey itself stocks only enough inventory for a few days of operation, as opposed to the three or four months worth it used to carry. Whenever a bin of parts falls below a designated level, a Bailey employee passes a laser scanner over the bin's bar code, instantly alerting Future to send the parts at once. Arrow Electronics . . . is plugged in even more closely: It has a warehouse in Bailey's factory, stocked according to Bailey's twice-a-month forecasts. Bailey provides the space, Arrow the warehouseman and the $500,000 of inventory.[22]

Today, as a result of such partnerships, many companies have switched from *anticipatory-based distribution systems* to *response-based distribution systems*.[23] In anticipatory distribution, the company produces the amount of goods called for by a sales forecast. It builds and holds stock at various supply points, such as the plant, distribution centers, and retail outlets. A response-based distribution system, in contrast, is *customer triggered*. The producer continuously builds and replaces stock as orders arrive. It

Marketing at Work 10-3

Go Ryder, and Leave the Delivering to Us

Most big companies love to make and sell their products. But many loathe the associated logistics "grunt work"—the bundling, loading, unloading, sorting, storing, reloading, transporting, and tracking required to supply their factories and to get products out to customers. They hate it so much that more than half of the Fortune 500 now outsource some or all of these functions. Increasingly, companies are handing over their logistics to suppliers that specialize in helping them tighten up sluggish, overstuffed supply chains, slash inventories, and get products to customers more quickly and reliably. Below are some examples:

Saturn. Saturn's just-in-time production system allows for almost no parts inventory at the plant. Instead, it relies on a world-class logistics system to keep parts flowing into the factory at precisely the times they're needed. Saturn is so adroit in managing its supply chain that in four years it has had to halt production just once—for only 18 minutes—

because the right part failed to arrive at the right time. Most of the credit, however, goes to Ryder Integrated Logistics, the nation's largest logistics management firm. Ryder, best known for renting trucks, manages Saturn's far-ranging supply chain, moving the automaker's materials, parts, and products efficiently and reliably from supplier to factory to dealer showroom.

To keep Saturn's assembly lines humming, Ryder transports thousands of preinspected and presorted parts—more than 2,200 receiving dock transactions every day—hitting delivery windows as narrow as five minutes. Ryder keeps its parts, people, and trucks in a nearly constant blur of high-tech motion. For example, according to one account, when delivering service parts to Saturn dealerships, Ryder's long-haul drivers "plug a plastic key, loaded with electronic data, into an onboard computer. The screen tells them exactly where to go, which route to take, and how much time to spend getting there." Ryder's effective supply-chain

management results in lower costs, improved operations, more productive dealers, and—in the end—more-satisfied customers.

Cisco Systems. This vendor of computer networking equipment and network management software ships tons of routers to Europe daily. It needs to know where each box is at any given time and may have to reroute orders on short notice to fill urgent customer requests. Moreover, Cisco's customers need to know exactly when orders will arrive. When Cisco handled its own logistics, deliveries took up to three weeks. Now, the company contracts its complex distribution process to UPS Worldwide Logistics. Leveraging its knowledge of international plane, train, and trucking schedules, UPS Worldwide can speed routers to European customers in fewer than four days. If its own planes or trucks can't make the fastest delivery, UPS subcontracts the job to Lufthansa, KLM, or Danzas, a European trucking firm. Such superfast delivery saves Cisco Systems a bundle on inventories.

produces what is currently selling. For example, Japanese car makers take orders for cars, then produce and ship them within four days. Benetton, the Italian fashion house, uses a *quick-response system*, dyeing its sweaters in the colors that are currently selling instead of trying to guess far in advance which colors people will want. Producing for order rather than for forecast substantially cuts down inventory costs and risks.

Third-party logistics provider

An independent logistics provider that performs any or all of the functions required to get their clients' product to market.

Third-Party Logistics More than 90 percent of U.S. businesses perform their own logistics functions. However, a growing number of firms now outsource their logistics to **third-party logistics providers** such as Ryder Integrated Logistics, UPS Worldwide Logistics, FedEx Logistics, or Emory Global Logistics (see Marketing at Work 10-3). Such integrated logistics companies perform any or all of the functions required to get their clients' product to market. For example, Emory's Global Logistics unit provides clients with coordinated, single-source logistics services including supply-chain management, customized information technology, inventory control, warehousing, transportation

Soon, UPS Worldwide will begin installing custom software into Cisco's routers at its warehouse in the Netherlands, letting Cisco cut its inventories even more.

Cisco's reaps some additional advantages from the logistics partnership. For example, UPS Worldwide has extensive knowledge of local customs laws and import duties. It recently arranged with Dutch customs to aggregate Cisco's import duties into a monthly bill, paid once customers receive shipments instead of each time the routers land at the airport. The result: even more savings in time and paperwork.

National Semiconductor. In the early 1990s, National Semiconductor, whose chips end up inside everything from cars and computers to telecommunications gear, faced a logistics nightmare. National produced and assembled chips at 13 plants located in the United States, Britain, Israel, and Southeast Asia. Finished products were then shipped to an array of large customers—IBM, Toshiba, Compaq, Ford, Siemens—each with factories scattered around the globe.

On their way to customers, chips traveled any of 20,000 direct routes, mostly in the cargo holds of planes flown by 12 airlines, stopping along the way at 10 different warehouses. National's logistics performance left much to be desired: 95 percent of its products were delivered within 45 days of the order. The other 5 percent took as long as 90 days. Because customers never knew which 5 percent would be late, they demanded 90 days' worth of inventory in everything. "We had buffer stocks all along the line," comments a National executive. "The whole system was awash in inventory."

National's management set out to overhaul its global logistics network. It decided that all finished products would be transported to a central distribution center in Asia, where they would be sorted and air-freighted to customers. Although strategically sound, the plan created some big practical problems: National knew a lot about making chips but very little about air freight. "To do that," says the executive, "we would have had to make our company into FedEx." Instead, National *hired* FedEx to

handle its global distribution. FedEx Logistics now runs National's distribution center in Singapore, conducting all storage, sorting, and shipping activities. The results have been startling. Within two years, National's distribution costs fell 27 percent. At the same time, sales jumped by $584 million and delivery performance improved dramatically. National can now move products from the factory to customers in an average of four days or less, and it's well on its way toward its goal of a 72-hour turnaround. Thus, by outsourcing its distribution to a firm that specializes in efficient logistics, National Semiconductor has both cut its costs and improved its service to customers.

Sources: Quotes and other information from Ronald Henkoff, "Delivering the Goods," *Fortune,* November 28, 1994, pp. 64–77; Lisa H. Harrington, "Special Report on Contract Logistics," *Transportation & Distribution,* September 1996, pp. A–N; Scott Woolley, "Replacing Inventory with Information," *Forbes,* March 24, 1997, pp. 54–58; and Allen Allnoch, "Third-Party Logistics Industry Poised for Growth in U.S. and Abroad," *IIE Solutions,* January 1998, p. 10. Also see Harry L. Sink and C. John Langley Jr., "A Managerial Framework for the Acquisition of Third-Party Logistics Services," *Journal of Business Logistics,* vol. 18:2, 1997, pp. 163–89; Beth M. Schwartz, "Make TPL"s Earn Your Business," *Transportation & Distribution,* March 1998, pp. 89–94; Robert J. Bowman, "Musical Logistics Chairs," *World Trade,* January 1999, pp. 86–87; and Ira Sager, "Go Ahead, Farm Out Those Jobs," *Business Week,* March 22, 1999, p. EB35.

management, customer service and fulfillment, and freight auditing and control. Last year, U.S. manufacturers and distributors spent more than $25 billion on third-party logistics (also called *outsourced logistics* or *contract logistics*) services, and the market is expected to increase to $50 billion by the year 2000.[24]

Companies may use third-party logistics providers for several reasons. First, because getting the product to market is their main focus, these providers can often do it more efficiently and at lower cost than clients whose strengths lie elsewhere. According to one study, outsourcing warehousing alone typically results in 10 percent to 15 percent cost savings.[25] Second, outsourcing logistics frees a company to focus more intensely on its core business. Finally, integrated logistics companies understand increasingly complex logistics environments. This can be especially helpful to companies attempting to expand their global market coverage. For example, companies distributing their products across Europe face a bewildering array of environmental restrictions that affect logistics, including packaging standards, truck size and weight limits, and noise and emissions pollution

Third-party logistics: Many companies are now outsourcing logistics tasks to companies like Ryder Integrated Logistics. Here, Ryder promises: "By applying flow-through principles to your inbound and outbound distribution, we can help cut your . . . inventory investment."

controls. By outsourcing its logistics, a company can gain a complete Pan-European distribution system without incurring the costs, delays, and risks associated with setting up its own system.[26]

REST STOP   Reviewing the Concepts

So, what have you learned about distribution channels and integrated logistics management? Marketing channel decisions are among the most important decisions that management faces. A company's channel decisions directly affect every other marketing decision. Each channel system creates a different level of revenues and costs and reaches a

different segment of target consumers. Management must make channel decisions carefully, incorporating today's needs with tomorrow's likely selling environment. Some companies pay too little attention to their distribution channels, but others have used imaginative distribution systems to gain competitive advantage.

1. Explain why companies use distribution channels and explain the functions that these channels perform.

Most producers use intermediaries to bring their products to market. They try to forge a *distribution channel*, a set of interdependent organizations involved in the process of making a product or service available for use or consumption by the consumer or business user. Through their contacts, experience, specialization, and scale of operation, intermediaries usually offer the firm more than it can achieve on its own. Distribution channels perform many key functions. Some help *complete* transactions by gathering and distributing *information* needed for planning and aiding exchange; by developing and spreading persuasive *communications* about an offer; by performing *contact* work—finding and communicating with prospective buyers; by *matching*—shaping and fitting the offer to the buyer's needs; and by entering into *negotiation* to reach an agreement on price and other terms of the offer so that ownership can be transferred. Other functions help to *fulfill* the completed transactions by offering *physical distribution*—transporting and storing goods; *financing*—acquiring and using funds to cover the costs of the channel work; and *risk taking*—assuming the risks of carrying out the channel work.

2. Discuss how channel members interact and how they organize to perform the work of the channel.

The channel will be most effective when each member is assigned the tasks it can do best. Ideally, because the success of individual channel members depends on overall channel success, all channel firms should work together smoothly. They should understand and accept their roles, coordinate their goals and activities, and cooperate to attain overall channel goals. By cooperating, they can more effectively sense, serve, and satisfy the target market. In a large company, the formal organization structure assigns roles and provides needed leadership. But in a distribution channel made up of independent firms, leadership and power are not formally set. Traditionally, distribution channels have lacked the leadership needed to assign roles and manage conflict. In recent years, however, new types of channel organizations have appeared that provide stronger leadership and improved performance.

3. Identify the major channel alternatives open to a company.

Each firm identifies alternative ways to reach its market. Available means vary from direct selling to using one, two, three, or more intermediary *channel levels*. Marketing channels face continuous and sometimes dramatic change. Three of the most important trends are the growth of *vertical, horizontal*, and *hybrid marketing systems*. These trends affect channel cooperation, conflict, and competition. *Channel design* begins with assessing customer channel-service needs and company channel objectives and constraints. The company then identifies the major channel alternatives in terms of the *types* of intermediaries, the *number* of intermediaries, and the *channel responsibilities* of each. Each channel alternative must be evaluated according to economic, control, and adaptive criteria. Channel management calls for selecting qualified intermediaries and motivating them. Individual channel members must be evaluated regularly.

4. Discuss the nature and importance of physical distribution.

Just as firms are giving the marketing concept increased recognition, more business firms are paying attention to the *physical distribution* or *marketing logistics*. Logistics is an area of potentially high cost savings and improved customer satisfaction. Marketing logistics involves coordinating the activities of the entire *supply chain* to deliver maximum value to customers. No logistics system can both maximize customer service and minimize distribution costs. Instead, the goal of logistics management is to provide a *targeted* level of service at the least cost. The major logistics functions include *order processing, warehousing, inventory management*, and *transportation*.

5. Analyze integrated logistics, including how it may be achieved and its benefits to the company.

The *integrated logistics concept* recognizes that improved logistics requires teamwork in the form of close working relationships across functional areas inside the company and across various organizations in the supply chain. Companies can achieve logistics harmony among functions by creating cross-functional logistics teams, integrative supply manager positions, and senior-level logistics executives with cross-functional authority. Channel partnerships can take the form of cross-company teams, shared projects, and information-sharing systems. Through such partnerships, many companies have switched from *anticipatory-based distribution systems* to customer-triggered *response-based distribution systems*. Today, some companies are outsourcing their logistics functions to third-party logistics providers to save costs, increase efficiency, and gain faster and more effective access to global markets.

Navigating the Key Terms

For a detailed analysis of the meaning and importance of each of the following key terms, visit our Web site of **www.prenhall.com/kotler**.

Administered VMS
Channel conflict
Channel level
Contractual VMS

Conventional distribution channel
Corporate VMS
Direct marketing channel
Distribution center
Distribution channel
Exclusive distribution
Franchise organization
Horizontal marketing system
Hybrid marketing channel

Indirect marketing channel
Integrated logistics management
Intensive distribution
Intermodal transportation
Physical distribution (or marketing logistics)
Selective distribution
Third-party logistics provider
Vertical marketing system (VMS)

Travel Log

The following concept checks and discussion questions will help you to keep track of and apply the concepts you've studied in this chapter.

Concept Checks

1. A _____ is a set of interdependent organizations involved in the process of making a product or service available for use or consumption by the consumer or business user.

2. The key functions performed by members of the marketing channel include: _____, _____, _____, _____, _____, physical distribution, financing, and risk taking.

3. A _____ marketing channel has no intermediary levels.

4. McDonald's recently came into _____ channel conflict with some of its dealers when its aggressive expansion plans called for placing new stores in areas that took business from existing locations.

5. Three forms of vertical marketing systems (VMS) include _____, _____, and _____ VMSs.

6. Producers of convenience products and common raw materials typically employ _____ distribution—a strategy in which they stock their products in as many outlets as possible.

7. Another term used to describe physical distribution is _____.

8. The major logistics functions include _____, _____, _____, and _____.

9. With respect to common transportation modes, _____ are the nation's largest carrier, account for 26 percent of total cargo ton-miles moved, and are the most cost-effective modes for shipping bulk products over long distances.

10. Given the growing popularity of outsourcing, _____ logistics providers such as Ryder Systems, UPS Worldwide Logistics, and FedEx Logistics are providing more services for customers than ever before.*

Discussing the Issues

1. The Book-of-the-Month Club (BOMC) has been successfully marketing books by mail for over 50 years. (a) Why do few publishers sell books directly by mail? (b) How has BOMC survived competition from B. Dalton, Waldenbooks, Borders, and other large retail booksellers? (3) Do you think BOMC will compete well against on-line booksellers such as Amazon.com (see www.amazon.com)? Should BOMC's strategy focus on product, price, distribution, promotion, or market segmentation? Explain.

2. Describe the channel service needs of (a) consumers buying a computer for home use, (b) retailers buying computers to resell to individual consumers,

---

* *Concept check answers:* 1. distribution channel; 2. information, promotion, contact, matching, negotiation; 3. direct; 4. vertical; 5. corporate, contractual, administered; 6. intensive; 7. marketing logistics; 8. order processing, warehousing, inventory management, transportation; 9. railroads; 10. third-party.

and (c) purchasing agents buying computers for company use. What channels would a computer manufacturer need to design to satisfy these different service needs?

3. Decide which distribution strategies—intensive, selective, or exclusive—are used for the following products, and why: (a) Piaget watches, (b) Acura automobiles, and (c) Snickers candy bars.

4. Historically, distribution channels have consisted of loose collections of independent companies, each with its own policies, strategies, and objectives. In contrast, a vertical marketing system (VMS) acts as a unified system. Give an example of each of the three major VMS forms (different from those mentioned in the chapter) and comment on the effectiveness of each.

5. Outsourcing has allowed new business synergies and alliances that would have been unthinkable only a decade ago. (a) Why would a company choose to outsource its distribution activities? (b) What major factors contribute to successful outsourcing relationships? (c) What are the potential dangers of an outsource relationship? (d) Give an example of a company that you believe could benefit from outsourcing its logistics and suggest some practical outsourcing alternatives for that company. For additional information on outsourcing, see The Outsourcing Institute's Web site at www.outsourcing. com.

Traveling the Net

Point of Interest: Hybrid Marketing Systems

Marketers in many industries are constantly on the lookout for new ways to put their products into the hands of consumers. The goal is to surround the consumer with buying alternatives. Such is the case in the music industry. Multichannel distribution alternatives include retail stores of many types (department stores, specialty stores, discount stores), catalog merchants, mail-order clubs, and Internet Web sites (both for the company and those that carry the company's products). Music is one of the easiest items to buy on the Web, and purchasing music via the Web is gaining in popularity. In fact, it has become a major channel choice for many younger buyers (the chief market segment for the industry). Buyers have learned that they can often obtain better prices from Web retailers than from record stores, even after shipping and handling are added on. Examine the following Web sites for more information on purchasing music via the Web: (a) Web Amazon.com at www.amazon.com, (b) Music Boulevard at www.musicblvd.com, (c) Compact Disc Connection atwww.cd-connection.com, (d) CDNow at www.cdnow.com, and (e) Columbia House at www.columbiahouse.com.

For Discussion

1. What are the primary advantages of ordering music tapes or CDs via the Internet? The disadvantages?

2. How will Web music retailing affect the more traditional channels such as record stores and book-record combination stores?

3. In what ways can music producers handle the conflicts that are bound to arise when multichannel distribution alternatives are used.

4. After visiting each of the noted Web sites, compare marketing and distribution strategies each of the distributors seems to be using. (a) Prepare a grid (using variables of your choice) that compares the sites. (b) Which site do you find to be the most customer-friendly? Which seems to be the easiest to use? From which would you be most likely to order? Explain.

Application Thinking

What characteristics are most important in your choice of a place to purchase a tape or CD? In terms of importance, how would you rank such factors as price, location, selection, personal service, atmosphere, guarantees, and being able to take your selection home immediately? Companies that sell through Web sites are betting that price and selection (especially for those hard-to-find titles) will rank higher than location (such as a mall) or immediate possession. Most on-line music sellers guarantee shipment of a "top 100" title almost immediately and of most more obscure titles within 4 to 10 days. These on-line companies have access to 200,000 or more titles and can almost always obtain and ship hard-to-find titles more quickly than music stores using traditional ordering processes. Moreover, they typically offer lower prices, lots of discounts, and bonuses on volume purchases. Such price and access benefits, however, may be offset by membership requirements (as for Columbia

House), an inability to give the consumer immediate purchase gratification, or complicated ordering and return processes. Assume that you are the marketing manager for an on-line music service. Construct policies and strategies that will make you competitive with other types of music resellers. Profile the proposed target market for your service. Prepare a list of "musts" that your service will have to accomplish in order to attract consumer attention and purchasing. Evaluate your chances of success in your new endeavor.

MAP — Marketing Applications

MAP Stop 10

You know about the Internet, but have you ever heard of the "Extranet"? An "Extranet" occurs when a company opens its own internal network (or Intranet) to selected business partners. Trusted suppliers, distributors, and other special users can then link into the company's network without having to go through traditional bureaucratic and organizational "red-tape." The connecting companies can use the Internet or virtual private networks for communication. Once inside the company's Intranet, the outside company (or partner) can view whatever data the company makes available. What types of data? A supplier might analyze a customer's inventory needs (Boeing booked $100 million in spare parts from airline customers in one year). Partners might swap customer lists for interrelated products and services or share purchasing systems to gain savings through more efficient purchasing (General Electric claims that $500 million can be saved in purchasing costs by using the "Extranet" portion of the Internet). Imagine the strategic advantages that are created when "virtual" partners move information to one another in seconds about shifting supply and demand situations, customer requests and opportunities, and just-in-time inventory needs. Purchase processing times can be reduced from weeks to minutes at enormous cost savings that can be passed along to consumers.

Thinking Like a Marketing Manager

1. What role might the Extranet play in distribution decisions for (a) retailers, (b) wholesalers, and (c) manufacturers?
2. What are the potential dangers of an Extranet system?
3. What areas of a marketing organization's Intranet would be most interesting to a partner using the Extranet?
4. Assume that you are the marketing manager of Cisco Systems (investigate this master of E-commerce and networking at www.cisco.com). How could the Extranet help you to better assist resellers? How could costs be saved by using the Extranet? How does the Extranet work with an outsourcing concept (if at all)? After examining the advantages and disadvantages of using the Extranet, write a short position paper that outlines your thoughts on the subject and its future in marketing commerce.

Retailing and Wholesaling

> ROAD MAP:
> ## Previewing the Concepts
>
> In the previous chapter, you learned the basics of distribution channel design and management. Now, we'll look more deeply into the two major intermediary channel functions, retailing and wholesaling. You already know something about retailing—you're served every day by retailers of all shapes and sizes. However, you probably know much less about the hoard of wholesalers that work behind the scenes. In this chapter, we'll navigate through the characteristics of different kinds of retailers and wholesalers, the marketing decisions they make, and trends for the future. You'll see that the retailing and wholesaling landscapes are changing rapidly to match explosive changes in markets and technology.
>
> ▶ **After studying this chapter, you should be able to**
>
> 1. explain the roles of retailers and wholesalers in the distribution channel
> 2. describe the major types of retailers and give examples of each
> 3. identify the major types of wholesalers and give examples of each
> 4. explain the marketing decisions facing retailers and wholesalers
>
> To start the tour, we'll look in on Home Depot, the highly successful home improvement retailer. This "category killer's" rapid growth has resulted not from a focus on sales but from an obsession with building customer relationships. But to take care of customers, Home Depot must first take care of those who take care of customers. The Home Depot story will acquaint you with the dramatic changes taking place among channel institutions.

Home Depot, the giant do-it-yourself home improvement retail chain, is one of the world's hottest retailers. It's one of a breed of retailers called *category killers*. These giant retailers get their name from their marketing strategy: Carry a huge selection of merchandise in a single product category at such good prices that you destroy the competition. Category killers now operate in a wide range of industries, including home improvement, furniture, toys, music, sporting goods, housewares, and consumer electronics.

At first glance, a cavernous Home Depot store doesn't look like much. With its cement floors and drafty, warehouselike interior, the store offers all the atmosphere of an airplane hangar. But the chances are good that you'll find exactly what you're looking for, priced to make it a real value. Home Depot carries a huge assortment of more than 35,000 items—anything and everything related to home improvement. And its prices run 20 to 30 percent below those of local hardware stores.

Home Depot provides more than the right products at the right prices, however. Perhaps the best part of shopping at Home Depot is the high quality of its customer

service. Home Depot is more than just customer driven—it's customer *obsessed*. In the words of cofounder and chief executive Bernie Marcus, "All of our people understand what the Holy Grail is. It's not the bottom line. It's an almost blind, passionate commitment to taking care of customers." Arthur Blank, Home Depot's other cofounder and president, gives all new store managers the following six pieces of advice: "Serve the customer, serve the customer, serve the customer, serve the customer, serve the customer. And number 6, kick [butt]."

Bernie Marcus and Arthur Blank founded Home Depot with the simple mission of helping customers solve their home improvement problems. Their goal: "To take ham-handed homeowners who lack the confidence to do more than screw in a light bulb and transform them into Mr. and Ms. Fixits." Accomplishing this mission takes more than simply peddling the store's products and taking the customers' money. It means building lasting customer relationships.

Bernie and Arthur understand the importance of customer satisfaction. They calculate that a satisfied customer is worth more than $25,000 in customer lifetime value ($38 per store visit, times 30 visits per year, times about 22 years of patronage). Customer satisfaction, in turn, results from interactions with well-trained, highly motivated employees who consistently provide good value and high-quality service. "The most important part of our formula," says Arthur, "is the quality of caring that takes place in our stores between the employee and the customer." Thus, at Home Depot, taking care of customers begins with taking care of employees.

Home Depot attracts the best salespeople by paying above-average salaries; then it trains them thoroughly. All employees take regular "product knowledge" classes to gain hands-on experience with problems customers will face. When it comes to creating customer value and satisfaction, Home Depot treats its employees as partners. All full-time employees receive at least 7 percent of their annual salary in company stock. As a result, Home Depot employees take ownership in the business of serving customers. Each employee wears a bright orange apron that says, "Hello, I'm _____ , a Home Depot stockholder. Let me help you."

Bernie and Arthur have become energetic crusaders in the cause of customer service. For example, four Sundays a year at 6:30 A.M. the two don their own orange aprons and air *Breakfast with Bernie and Art*, a good old-fashioned revival broadcast live over closed-circuit TV to the company's more than 100,000 employees nationwide. According to one account, "Bernie regularly rouses his disciples with the following: 'Where do you go if you want a job?' They yell back: 'Sears . . . Lowe's . . . Builders Square.' 'Where do you go if you want a *career*?' 'HOME DEPOT!' they roar. At times, when the excitement becomes feverish, Marcus has been known to grab a resisting Blank, plant a noisy kiss on his cheek, and exclaim, 'Arthur, I love you!'"

Home Depot avoids the high-pressure sales techniques used by some retailers. Instead, it encourages salespeople to build long-term relationships with customers—to spend whatever time it takes, visit after visit, to solve customer problems. Home Depot pays employees a straight salary so that they can spend as much time as necessary with customers without worrying about making the sale. Bernie Marcus declares, "The day I'm dead with an apple in my mouth is the day we'll pay commissions." In fact, rather than pushing customers to *overspend*, employees are trained to help customers spend *less* than they expected. "I love it when shoppers tell me they were prepared to spend $150 and our people showed them how to do the job for four or five bucks," says Bernie.

Taking care of customers has made Home Depot one of today's most successful retailers. Founded in 1978, in little more than 20 years it has grown explosively to become the nation's largest do-it-yourself chain, with more than 600 stores reaping more than $30 billion in sales. Home Depot sales have grown 36 percent annually over the past decade, and earnings have risen 57 percent per year since 1990. The company's stock price has shot up 28,000 percent—yes, 28,000 percent—since the company went public in 1981! In fact, a current problem in some stores is too many customers—some outlets are generating an astounding $600 of sales per square foot (compared with Wal-Mart at $250 and Kmart at $150). This has created problems with clogged aisles, stockouts, too few salespeople, and long checkout lines. Although many retailers would welcome this kind of problem, it bothers Bernie and Arthur greatly, and they've quickly taken corrective action. Continued success, they know, depends on the passionate pursuit of customer satisfaction. Bernie will tell you, "Every customer has to be treated like your mother, your father, your sister, or your brother." And you certainly wouldn't want to keep your mother waiting in line.[1]

This chapter looks at *retailing* and *wholesaling*. In the first section, we look at the nature and importance of retailing, major types of store and nonstore retailers, the decisions retailers make, and the future of retailing. In the second section, we discuss these same topics as they relate to wholesalers.

Retailing

Retailing
All activities involved in selling goods or services directly to final consumers for their personal, nonbusiness use.

Retailer
Business whose sales come *primarily* from retailing.

What is retailing? We all know that Wal-Mart, Sears, and Kmart are retailers, but so are Avon representatives, the local Holiday Inn, and a doctor seeing patients. **Retailing** includes all the activities involved in selling goods or services directly to final consumers for their personal, nonbusiness use. Many institutions—manufacturers, wholesalers, and retailers—do retailing. But most retailing is done by **retailers**: businesses whose sales come *primarily* from retailing. Although most retailing is done in retail stores, in recent years nonstore retailing—selling by mail, telephone, door-to-door contact, vending machines, the Internet, and numerous electronic means—has grown tremendously. Finally, although many retail stores are independently owned, an increasing number are now banding together under some form of corporate or contractual organization.

Because store retailing accounts for most of the retail business, we discuss it first. Next, we look at nonstore retailing and then at various forms of retailer organizations.

Store Retailing

Retail stores come in all shapes and sizes, and new retail types keep emerging. The most important types of retail stores are described in Table 11-1 and discussed in the following sections. They can be classified in terms of several characteristics, including the *amount of service* they offer, the breadth and depth of their *product lines*, and the *relative prices* they charge.

Amount of Service Different products require different amounts of service, and customer service preferences vary. Retailers may offer one of three levels of service: self-service, limited service, and full service.

Self-service retailers serve customers who are willing to perform their own "locate-compare-select" process to save money. Self-service is the basis of all discount operations and is typically used by sellers of convenience goods (such as supermarkets) and nationally branded, fast-moving shopping goods (such as catalog showrooms like Service Merchandise).

Limited-service retailers, such as Sears or JCPenney, provide more sales assistance because they carry more shopping goods about which customers need information. Their increased operating costs result in higher prices. In *full-service retailers*, such as specialty stores and first-class department stores, salespeople assist customers in every phase of the shopping process. Full-service stores usually carry more specialty goods for which customers like to be "waited on." They provide more services resulting in much higher operating costs, which are passed along to customers as higher prices.

Specialty store
A retail store that carries a narrow product line with a deep assortment within that line.

Product Line Retailers also can be classified by the length and breadth of their product assortments. Some retailers, such as **specialty stores**, carry narrow product lines with deep assortments within those lines. Today, specialty stores are flourishing. The increasing use of market segmentation, market targeting, and product specialization has resulted in a greater need for stores that focus on specific products and segments.

Table 11-1 Major Types of Retailers

Type	Description	Examples
Specialty stores	Carry a narrow product line with a deep assortment within that line: apparel stores, sporting-goods stores, furniture stores, florists, and bookstores. Specialty stores can be subclassified by the degree of narrowness in their product line. A clothing store would be a *single-line store*; a men's clothing store would be a *limited-line store*; and a men's custom-shirt store would be a *superspecialty store*.	Athlete's Foot (sport shoes only); Tall Men (tall men's clothing); The Limited (women's clothing); The Body Shop (cosmetics and bath supplies)
Department stores	Carry several product lines—typically clothing, home furnishings, and household goods—with each line operated as a separate department managed by specialist buyers or merchandisers.	Sears, Saks Fifth Avenue, Marshall Fields, May's, JCPenney, Nordstrom, Macy's
Supermarkets	Relatively large, low-cost, low-margin, high-volume, self-service operations designed to serve the consumer's total needs for food, laundry, and household maintenance products.	Safeway, Kroger, A&P Winn-Dixie, Publix, Food Lion, Vons, Jewel
Convenience stores	Relatively small stores that are located near residential areas, open long hours seven days a week, and carry a limited line of high-turnover convenience products. Their long hours and their use by consumers mainly for "fill-in" purchases make them relatively high-price operations.	7-Eleven, Circle K, Stop-N-Go, White Hen Pantry
Superstores	Larger stores that aim at meeting consumers' total needs for routinely purchased food and nonfood items. They include *supercenters*, combined supermarket and discount stores, which feature cross-merchandising. They also include so-called *category killers* that carry a very deep assortment of a particular line. Another superstore variation is *hypermarkets*, huge stores that combine supermarket, discount, and warehouse retailing to sell routinely purchased goods as well as furniture, large and small appliances, clothing, and many other items.	*Supercenters:* Wal-Mart Supercenters and Super Kmart Centers; *Category killers:* Toys 'Я' Us (toys), Petsmart (pet supplies), Staples (office supplies), Home Depot (home improvement), Best Buy (consumer electronics); *Hypermarkets:* Carrefour (France); Pyrca (Spain); Meijer's (Netherlands)
Discount stores	Sell standard merchandise at lower prices by accepting lower margins and selling higher volumes. A true discount store *regularly* sells its merchandise at lower prices, offering mostly national brands, not inferior goods. Discount retailers include both general merchandise and specialty merchandise stores.	*General discount stores:* Wal-Mart, Kmart, Target; *Specialty discount stores:* Circuit City (electronics), Crown Book (books)
Off-price retailers	Sell a changing and unstable collection of higher-quality merchandise, often leftover goods, overruns, and irregulars obtained at reduced prices from manufacturers or other retailers. They buy at less than regular wholesale prices and charge consumers less than retail. They include three main types:	
Independent off-price retailers	Owned and run either by entrepreneurs or by divisions of large retail corporations.	T.J. Maxx, Filene's Basement, Loehmann's, and Hit or Miss

Table 11-1 *(continued)*

Type	Description	Examples
Factory outlets	Owned and operated by manufacturers and normally carry the manufacturer's surplus, discontinued, or irregular goods. Such outlets increasingly group together in *factory outlet malls*, where dozens of outlet stores offer prices as much as 50 percent below retail on a broad range of items.	Mikasa (dinnerware), Dexter (shoes), Ralph Lauren and Liz Claiborne (upscale apparel)
Warehouse clubs (or wholesale clubs)	Sell a limited selection of brand-name grocery items, appliances, clothing, and a hodgepodge of other goods at deep discounts to members who pay $25 to $50 annual membership fees. They serve small businesses and other club members out of huge, low-overhead, warehouselike facilities and offer few frills or services.	Wal-Mart-owned Sam's Club, Max Clubs, Price-Costco, BJ's Wholesale Club

Department store

A retail organization that carries a wide variety of product lines—typically clothing, home furnishings, and household goods; each line is operated as a separate department managed by specialist buyers or merchandisers.

In contrast, **department stores** carry a wide variety of product lines. In recent years, department stores have been squeezed between more focused and flexible specialty stores on the one hand, and more efficient, lower-priced discounters on the other. In response, many have added "bargain basements" and promotional events to meet the discount threat. Others have set up store brand programs, "boutiques" and "designer shops" (such as Tommy Hilfiger or Polo shops within department stores), and other store formats that compete with specialty stores. Still others are trying mail-order, telephone, and Web site selling. Service remains the key differentiating factor. Department stores such as Nordstrom, Saks, Neiman Marcus, and other high-end department stores are doing well by emphasizing high-quality service.

Supermarket

Large, low-cost, low-margin, high-volume, self-service store that carries a wide variety of food, laundry, and household products.

Supermarkets are the most frequently shopped type of retail store. Today, however, they are facing slow sales growth because of slower population growth and an increase in competition from convenience stores, discount food stores, and superstores. Supermarkets also have been hit hard by the rapid growth of out-of-home eating. Thus, most supermarkets are making improvements to attract more customers. In the battle for "share of stomachs," most large supermarkets have moved upscale, providing from-scratch bakeries, gourmet deli counters, and fresh seafood departments. Others are cutting costs, establishing more efficient operations, and lowering prices in order to compete more effectively with food discounters.[2]

Convenience store

A small store, located near a residential area, that is open long hours seven days a week and carries a limited line of high-turnover convenience goods.

Convenience stores are small stores that carry a limited line of high-turnover convenience goods. In the 1990s, the convenience store industry has suffered from overcapacity as its primary market of young, blue-collar men shrunk. As a result, many chains have redesigned their stores with female customers in mind. They are dropping the image of a "truck stop" where men go to buy beer, cigarettes, and magazines, and instead offer fresh, prepared foods and cleaner, safer environments. Many convenience chains also are experimenting with micromarketing—tailoring each store's merchandise to the specific needs of its surrounding neighborhood. For example, a Stop-N-Go in an affluent neighborhood carries fresh produce, gourmet pasta sauces, chilled Evian water, and expensive wines. Stop-N-Go stores in Hispanic neighborhoods carry Spanish-language magazines and other goods catering to the specific needs of Hispanic consumers.[3]

Superstores are much larger than regular supermarkets and offer a large assortment of routinely purchased food products, nonfood items, and services. Examples include Safeway's Pak 'N Pay and Pathmark Super Centers. Wal-Mart, Kmart, and other discount retailers are now opening *supercenters*, combination food and discount stores that emphasize cross-merchandising. For example, at a Super Kmart Center, toasters are above the fresh-baked bread, kitchen gadgets are across from produce, and infant centers carry everything from baby food to clothing. Supercenters are growing in the United States at an annual rate of 25 percent, compared with a supermarket industry growth rate of only 1 percent. Wal-Mart, which opened its first supercenter in 1988, had opened an estimated 530 such stores by 1998, capturing almost two-thirds of all supercenter volume. By 2005, the retailing giant will likely be operating 1,200 to 1,500 supercenters.[4]

Recent years have also seen the explosive growth of superstores that are actually giant specialty stores, the so-called **category killers**. They feature stores the size of airplane hangars that carry a very deep assortment of a particular line with a knowledgeable staff. Category killers are prevalent in a wide range of categories, including books, baby gear, toys, electronics, home improvement products, linens and towels, party goods, sporting goods, even pet supplies. Another superstore variation, *hypermarkets*, are huge superstores, perhaps as large as *six* football fields. Although hypermarkets have been very successful in Europe and other world markets, they have met with little success in the United States.

Finally, for some retailers, the product line is actually a service. Service retailers include hotels and motels, banks, airlines, colleges, hospitals, movie theaters, tennis clubs, bowling alleys, restaurants, repair services, hair-care shops, and dry cleaners. Service retailers in the United States are growing faster than product retailers.

Superstore
A store almost twice the size of a regular supermarket that carries a large assortment of routinely purchased food products, nonfood items, and offers services.

Category killer
Giant specialty store that carries a very deep assortment of a particular line and is staffed by knowledgeable employees.

Category killers, such as Best Buy and SportMart, feature stores the size of airplane hangars that carry a very deep assortment of a particular line. They are prevalent in such categories as books, toys, electronics, home improvement products, linens and towels, sporting goods, even pet supplies.

Relative Prices Retailers can also be classified according to the prices they charge. Most retailers charge regular prices and offer normal-quality goods and customer service. Others offer higher-quality goods and service at higher prices. The retailers that feature low prices are discount stores, "off-price" retailers, and catalog showrooms (see Table 11-1).

Discount store
A retail institution that sells standard merchandise at lower prices by accepting lower margins and selling at higher volume.

DISCOUNT STORES A **discount store** sells standard merchandise at lower prices by accepting lower margins and selling higher volume. The early discount stores cut expenses by offering few services and operating in warehouselike facilities in low-rent, heavily traveled districts. In recent years, facing intense competition from other discounters and department stores, many discount retailers have "traded up." They have improved decor, added new lines and services, and opened suburban branches, which has led to higher costs and prices.

Off-price retailer
Retailer that buys at less-than-regular wholesale prices and sells at less than retail. Examples are factory outlets, independents, and warehouse clubs.

OFF-PRICE RETAILERS When the major discount stores traded up, a new wave of **off-price retailers** moved in to fill the low-price, high-volume gap. Ordinary discounters buy at regular wholesale prices and accept lower margins to keep prices down. In contrast, off-price retailers buy at less-than-regular wholesale prices and charge consumers less than retail. Off-price retailers can be found in all areas, from food, clothing, and electronics to no-frills banking and discount brokerages.

Independent off-price retailer
Off-price retailer that is either owned and run by entrepreneurs or is division of larger retail corporation.

The three main types of off-price retailers are *independents*, *factory outlets*, and *warehouse clubs*. **Independent off-price retailers** are either owned and run by entrepreneurs or are divisions of larger retail corporations. Although many off-price operations are run by smaller independents, most large off-price retailer operations are owned by bigger retail chains. Examples include Loehmann's (owned by Associated Dry Goods, owner of Lord & Taylor), Filene's Basement (Federated Department Stores), and T.J. Maxx (TJX Cos).

Factory outlet
Off-price retailing operation that is owned and operated by a manufacturer and that normally carries the manufacturer's surplus, discontinued, or irregular goods.

Factory outlets—such as the Burlington Coat Factory Warehouse, Manhattan's Brand Name Fashion Outlet, and the factory outlets of Levi Strauss, Carters, and Ship 'n' Shore—sometimes group together in *factory outlet malls* and *value-retail centers*, where dozens of outlet stores offer prices as low as 50 percent below retail on a wide range of items. Whereas outlet malls consist primarily of manufacturers' outlets, value-retail centers combine manufacturers' outlets with off-price retail stores and department store clearance outlets. Factory outlet malls have become one of the hottest growth areas in retailing.

The malls now are moving upscale, narrowing the gap between factory outlets and more traditional forms of retailers. As the gap narrows, the discounts offered by outlets are getting smaller. However, a growing number of factory outlets now feature brands such as Coach, Esprit, and Liz Claiborne, causing department stores to protest to the manufacturers of these brands. Given their higher costs, the department stores have to charge more than the off-price outlets. Manufacturers counter that they send last year's merchandise and seconds to the factory outlet malls, not the new merchandise that they supply to the department stores. The malls are also located far from urban areas, making travel to them more difficult. Still, the department stores are concerned about the growing number of shoppers willing to make weekend trips to stock up on branded merchandise at substantial savings.[5]

Warehouse club
Off-price retailer that sells a limited selection of brand-name grocery items, appliances, clothing, and a hodge-podge of other goods at deep discounts to members who pay annual membership fees.

Warehouse clubs (or *wholesale clubs*, or *membership warehouses*), such as Sam's and Costco, operate in huge, drafty, warehouselike facilities and offer few frills. Customers themselves must wrestle furniture, heavy appliances, and other large items to the checkout line. Such clubs make no home deliveries and accept no credit cards, but they

Factory outlet malls and value-retail centers have blossomed in recent years, making them one of retailing's hottest growth areas.

do offer rock-bottom prices. Warehouse clubs took the country by storm in the 1980s, but growth slowed considerably in the 1990s as a result of growing competition among warehouse store chains and effective reactions by supermarkets.[6]

Retail Organizations Although many retail stores are independently owned, an increasing number are banding together under some form of corporate or contractual organization. The major types of retail organizations—*corporate chain*, *voluntary chain* and *retailer cooperatives*, *franchise organizations*, *merchandising conglomerates*—are described in Table 11-2.

Chain stores are two or more outlets that are commonly owned and controlled. They have many advantages over independents. Their size allows them to buy in large quantities at lower prices. They can afford to hire corporate-level specialists to deal with areas such as pricing, promotion, merchandising, inventory control, and sales forecasting. And corporate chains gain promotional economies because their advertising costs are spread over many stores and over a large sales volume.

The great success of corporate chains caused many independents to band together in one of two forms of contractual associations. One is the *voluntary chain*, a wholesaler-sponsored group of independent retailers that engages in group buying and common merchandising. The other form of contractual association is the *retailer coop-*

Chain stores
Two or more outlets that are owned and controlled in common, have central buying and merchandising, and sell similar lines of merchandise.

Table 11-2 Major Types of Retail Organizations

Type	Description	Examples
Corporate chain stores	Two or more outlets that are commonly owned and controlled, employ central buying and merchandising, and sell similar lines of merchandise. Corporate chains appear in all types of retailing, but they are strongest in department stores, variety stores, food stores, drugstores, shoe stores, and women's clothing stores.	Tower Records, Fayva (shoes), Pottery Barn (dinnerware and home furnishings)
Voluntary chains	Wholesaler-sponsored groups of independent retailers engaged in bulk buying and common merchandising.	Independent Grocers Alliance (IGA), Sentry Hardwares, Western Auto, True Value
Retailer cooperatives	Groups of independent retailers who set up a central buying organization and conduct joint promotion efforts.	Associated Grocers (groceries), ACE (hardware)
Franchise organizations	Contractual association between a *franchiser* (a manufacturer, wholesaler, or service organization) and *franchisees* (independent businesspeople who buy the right to own and operate one or more units in the franchise system). Franchise organization are normally based on some unique product, service, or method of doing business, or on a trade name or patent, or on goodwill that the franchiser had developed.	McDonald's, Subway, Pizza Hut, Jiffy Lube, Meineke Mufflers, 7-Eleven
Merchandising conglomerates	A free-form corporation that combines several diversified retailing lines and forms under central ownership, along with some integration of their distribution and management functions.	Dayton-Hudson, F. W. Woolworth

erative, a group of independent retailers that bands together to set up a jointly owned, central wholesale operation and conducts joint merchandising and promotion efforts. These organizations give independents the buying and promotion economies they need to meet the prices of corporate chains.

Franchise
A contractual association between a manufacturer, wholesaler, or service organization (a franchisor) and independent businesspeople (franchisees) who buy the right to own and operate one or more units in the franchise system.

Another form of contractual retail organization is a **franchise**. The main difference between franchise organizations and other contractual systems (voluntary chains and retail cooperatives) is that franchise systems are normally based on some unique product or service; on a method of doing business; or on the trade name, goodwill, or patent that the franchiser has developed. Franchising has been prominent in fast foods, video stores, health/fitness centers, hair cutting, auto rentals, motels, travel agencies, real estate, and dozens of other product and service areas. Franchising is described in detail in Marketing at Work 11-1.

Finally, *merchandising conglomerates* are corporations that combine several different retailing forms under central ownership. Examples include Dayton-Hudson, JCPenney, and F.W. Woolworth. For example, Dayton-Hudson operates Target (discount stores), Mervyn's (lower-price clothing), B. Dalton (books), and many other chains in addition to its Dayton's, Hudson's, and other department stores. Woolworth, which no longer operates its variety stores, still owns numerous specialty chains, including Kinney Shoe Stores, Foot Locker, Champs Sports, Herald Square Stationers, Northern Reflections, Frame Scene, Afterthoughts (costume jewelry and handbags), and Face Fantasies (budget cosmetics). Diversified retailing, which provides superior management systems and economies that benefit all the separate retail operations, is likely to increase as we move into the next millennium.

Nonstore Retailing

Although most goods and services are sold through stores, nonstore retailing has been growing much faster than has store retailing. Traditional store retailers are facing increasing competition from nonstore retailers who sell through catalogs, direct mail, telephone, home TV shopping shows, on-line computer shopping services, home and office parties, and other direct retailing approaches. Nonstore retailing now accounts for more than 14 percent of all consumer purchases, and it may account for a third of all sales by 2000. Nonstore retailing includes *direct marketing*, *direct selling*, and *automatic vending*.

Direct Marketing **Direct marketing** consists of direct communications with carefully targeted individual consumers to obtain an immediate response. Mass marketing and advertising typically reach an unspecified number of people, most of whom are not in the market for a product or will not buy it until some future date. Direct marketing is used to obtain immediate orders directly from targeted consumers. Although direct marketing initially consisted mostly of direct mail and mail-order catalogs, it has taken on several additional forms in recent years, including telemarketing, direct radio and television marketing, and on-line and Internet shopping.

> **Direct marketing**
> Direct communications with carefully targeted individual consumers to obtain an immediate response.

Direct marketing has boomed in recent years, in both consumer and business-to-business markets. All kinds of organizations use direct marketing: manufacturers, retailers, service companies, catalog merchants, and nonprofit organizations, to name a few. The most rapidly growing area of direct marketing is *on-line marketing*, selling conducted through interactive on-line computer systems that link consumers with sellers electronically. We discuss direct marketing and the burgeoning field of on-line marketing fully in chapter 14.

Direct Selling **Door-to-door retailing**, which started centuries ago with roving peddlers, has grown into a huge industry. The pioneers in door-to-door selling are the Fuller Brush Company, vacuum cleaner companies such as Electrolux, and book-selling companies such as World Book and Southwestern. The image of door-to-door selling improved greatly when Avon entered the industry with its Avon representative—the homemaker's friend and beauty consultant. Tupperware and Mary Kay Cosmetics helped to popularize home sales parties, in which several friends and neighbors attend a party at a private home where products are demonstrated and sold.

> **Door-to-door retailing**
> Selling door to door, office to office, or at home sales parties.

The advantages of door-to-door selling are consumer convenience and personal attention. But the high costs of hiring, training, paying, and motivating the sales force result in higher prices. Although some door-to-door companies are still thriving, door-to-door selling has a somewhat uncertain future. The increase in the number of single-person and working-couple households decreases the chances of finding a buyer at home. Home party companies are having trouble finding nonworking women who want to sell products part time. And with recent advances in interactive direct marketing technology, the door-to-door salesperson may well be replaced in the future by the household telephone, television, or home computer.[7]

Automatic Vending **Automatic vending** is not new—in 215 B.C. Egyptians could buy sacrificial water from coin-operated dispensers. But this method of selling soared after World War II. There are now about 4.5 million vending machines in the United States—one machine for every 55 people. Vending machines are everywhere—in factories,

> **Automatic vending**
> Selling through vending machines.

Marketing at Work 11-1

Franchise Fever

Once considered upstarts among independent businesses, franchises now command 35 percent of all retail sales in the United States. These days, it's nearly impossible to stroll down a city block or drive on a suburban street without seeing a Wendy's, a McDonald's, a Jiffy Lube, or a 7-Eleven. One of the best-known and most successful franchisers, McDonald's, now has 21,000 stores worldwide and racks up more than $30 billion in systemwide sales. Gaining fast is Subway Sandwiches and Salads, one of the fastest-growing franchises, with more than 13,000 shops in 64 countries. Franchising is even moving into new areas such as education. For example, LearnRight Corporation, in State College, PA, franchises its methods for teaching students thinking skills.

How does a franchising system work? The individual franchises are a tightly knit group of enterprises whose systematic operations are planned, directed, and controlled by the operation's innovator, called a *franchiser.* Generally, franchises are distinguished by three characteristics:

1. *The franchiser owns a trade or service mark and licenses it to* franchisees in return for royalty payments.

2. *The franchisee is required to pay for the right to be part of the system.* Yet this initial fee is only a small part of the total amount that franchisees invest when they sign a franchising contract. Start-up costs include rental and lease of equipment and fixtures and sometimes a regular license fee. McDonald's franchisees may invest as much as $600,000 in initial start-up costs. The franchisee then pays McDonald's a service fee and a rental charge that equal 11.5 percent of the franchisee's sales volume. Subway's success is partly

Franchising fever: Most of us encounter dozens of franchised businesses each day, from familiar fast-food restaurants to franchised educational systems such as LearnRight.

due to its low start-up cost of just $100,000, which is lower than 70 percent of other franchise system start-up costs. However, Subway franchisees pay an 8 percent royalty on gross sales, highest in the food franchise industry, plus a 3.5 percent advertising fee.

3. *The franchiser provides its franchisees with a marketing and operations system for doing business.* McDonald's requires franchisees to attend its "Hamburger University" in Oak Brook, Illinois, for three weeks to learn how to manage the business. Franchisees must also adhere to certain procedures in buying materials.

In the best cases, franchising is mutually beneficial to both franchiser and franchisee. Franchisers can cover a new territory in little more than the time it takes the franchisee to sign a contract. They can achieve enormous purchasing power (consider the purchase order that Holiday Inn is likely to make for bed linens, for instance). Franchisers also benefit from the franchisees' familiarity with local communities and conditions and from the motivation and hard work of employees who are entrepreneurs rather than "hired hands." Similarly, franchisees benefit from buying into a proven business with a well-known and accepted brand name. And they receive ongoing support in areas ranging from marketing and advertising to site selection, staffing, and financing.

As a result of the franchise explosion in recent years, many types of franchisers (such as fast-food franchisers) are facing worrisome market saturation. One indication is the number of franchisee complaints filed with the Federal Trade Commission against parent companies, which has been growing by more than 50 percent annually since 1990. The most common complaint: Franchisers "encroach" on existing franchisees' territory by bringing in another store. For example, McDonald's franchisees in California and other states recently complained when the company decided to open new company-owned stores in their areas. Or franchisees may object to parent company marketing programs that may adversely affect their local operations. For instance, franchisees strongly resisted McDonald's "Campaign 55" promotion, in which the company reduced prices on Big Macs and Egg McMuffins to 55 cents in an effort to revive stagnant sales. Many franchisees believed that the promotion might cheapen McDonald's image and unnecessarily reduce their profit margins. Another complaint is higher-than-advertised failure rates. Subway, in particular, has been criticized for misleading its franchisees by telling them that it has only a 2 percent failure rate when the reality is much different. In addition, some franchisees feel that they've been misled by exaggerated claims of support, only to feel abandoned after the contract is signed and $100,000 is invested.

There will *always* be a conflict between the franchisers, who seek systemwide growth, and the franchisees, who want to earn a good living from their individual franchises. Some new directions that may deliver both franchiser growth and franchisee earnings are:

- *Strategic alliances with major outside corporations*: An example is the alliance between film company Fuji USA and Moto Photo, a one-hour photo developer. Fuji gained instant market penetration through Moto Photo's 400 locations, and Moto Photo franchisees enjoyed Fuji's brand-name recognition and advertising reach.
- *Expansion abroad*: Fast-food franchises have become very popular throughout the world. For example, Domino's has entered Japan with master franchisee Ernest Higa, who owns 106 stores in Japan with combined sales of $140 million. Part of Higa's success can be attributed to adapting Domino's product to the Japanese market, where food presentation is everything. Higa carefully charted the placement of pizza toppings and made cutmark perforations in the boxes for perfectly uniform slices.
- *Nontraditional site locations*: Franchises are opening in airports, sports stadiums, college campuses, hospitals, gambling casinos, theme parks, convention halls, and even river boats.

Thus, it appears, franchise fever will not cool down soon. Experts expect that by 2000, franchises will capture 50 percent of all U.S. retail sales.

Sources: Norman D. Axelrad and Robert E. Weigand, "Franchising—A Marriage of System Members," in Sidney Levy, George Frerichs, and Howard Gordon, eds., *Marketing Managers Handbook,* 3d ed. (Chicago: Dartnell, 1994), pp. 919–34; Andrew E. Serwer, "McDonald's Conquers the World," *Fortune,* October 17, 1994, pp. 103–16; Roberta Maynard, "The Decision to Franchise," *Nation's Business,* January 1997, pp. 49–53; and Cliff Edwards, "'Campaign 55' Flop Shows Growing Power of Franchisees," *Marketing News,* July 7, 1997, p. 9; Richard Behar, "Why Subway Is the Biggest Problem in Franchising," *Fortune,* March 16, 1998, pp. 126–34; and Patrick J. Kaufmann and Sevgin Eroglu, "Standardization and Adaptation in Business Format Franchising," *Journal of Business Venturing,* January 1999, pp. 69–85.

Door-to-door and in-home selling provide customers with convenience and personal attention, but higher costs result in higher prices.

offices, lobbies, retail stores, gasoline stations, airports, and train and bus terminals. Today's automatic vending uses space-age and computer technology to sell a wide variety of convenience and impulse goods: beverages, candy, newspapers, foods and snacks, hosiery, cosmetics, paperback books, T-shirts, insurance policies, pizza, CDs and video-cassettes, and even shoeshines and fishing worms. Vending machines are even more popular in Japan, where they dispense everything from $100 Armani ties (gift-wrapped), boxer shorts, beer, and sausages to pearls, stuffed animals, and $8 health drinks.[8]

Compared to store retailing, vending machines offer consumers greater convenience (available 24 hours, self-service) and fewer damaged goods. But the expensive equipment and labor required for automatic vending make it a costly channel, and prices of vended goods are often 15 to 20 percent higher than are those in retail stores. Customers also must put up with annoying machine breakdowns, out-of-stock items, and the fact that merchandise cannot be returned.

Linking the Concepts

Slow down and think about all the different kinds of retailers you deal with regularly, many of which overlap in the products they carry.

🗓 Pick a familiar product: a camera, microwave oven, hand tool, or something else. Shop for this product at two very different store types, say a discount store or category killer on the one hand, and a department store or smaller specialty store on the other. Compare the stores on product assortment, services, and prices. If you were going to buy the product, where would you buy it and why?

🗓 What does your shopping trip suggest about the futures of the competing store formats that you sampled?

Retailer Marketing Decisions

Retailers are searching for new marketing strategies to attract and hold customers. In the past, retailers attracted customers with unique products, more or better services than their competitors offered, or credit cards. Today, national-brand manufacturers, in their drive for volume, have placed their branded goods everywhere. Thus, stores offer more similar assortments—national brands are found not only in department stores but also in mass-merchandise and off-price discount stores. As a result, stores are looking more and more alike.

Service differentiation among retailers has also eroded. Many department stores have trimmed their services, whereas discounters have increased theirs. Customers have become smarter and more price sensitive. They see no reason to pay more for identical brands, especially when service differences are shrinking. For all these reasons, many retailers today are rethinking their marketing strategies.

As shown in Figure 11-1, retailers face major marketing decisions about their *target markets* and *positioning*, *product assortment and services*, *price*, *promotion*, and *place*.

Target Market and Positioning Decision Retailers first must define their target markets and then decide how they will position themselves in these markets. Should the store focus on upscale, midscale, or downscale shoppers? Do target shoppers want variety, depth of assortment, convenience, or low prices? Until they define and profile their markets, retailers cannot make consistent decisions about product assortment, services, pricing, advertising, store decor, or any of the other decisions that must support their positions.

Too many retailers fail to define their target markets and positions clearly. They try to have "something for everyone" and end up satisfying no market well. In contrast, successful retailers define their target markets well and position themselves strongly. For example, in 1963, Leslie H. Wexner borrowed $5,000 from his aunt to create The Limited, which started as a single store targeted to young, fashion-conscious women. All aspects of the store—clothing assortment, fixtures, music, colors, personnel—were orchestrated to match the target consumer. He continued to open more stores, but a decade later his original customers were no longer in the "young" group. To catch the new "youngs," he started the Limited Express. Over the years, he has started or acquired other highly targeted store chains, including Lane Bryant, Victoria's Secret, Lerner, Express, Structure, Limited Too, Abercrombie & Fitch, Bath & Body Works, and others to reach new segments. Today The Limited, Inc. operates more than 4,000 stores in several different segments of the market, with sales of more than $9 billion.[9]

Even large stores such as Wal-Mart, Kmart, and Sears must define their major target markets in order to design effective marketing strategies. In fact, in recent years, thanks to strong targeting and positioning, Wal-Mart has zoomed past Sears and Kmart to become the world's largest retailer (see Marketing at Work 11-2).

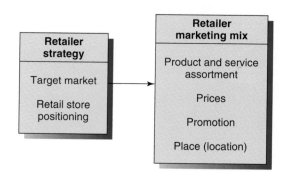

Figure 11-1
Retailer marketing decisions

Marketing at Work 11-2

Wal-Mart: The World's Largest Retailer

In 1962, Sam Walton and his brother opened the first Wal-Mart discount store in small-town Rogers, Arkansas. It was a big, flat, warehouselike store that sold everything from apparel to automotive supplies to small appliances at very low prices. Experts gave the fledgling retailer little chance; conventional wisdom suggested that discount stores could succeed only in large cities. Yet, from these modest beginnings, the chain expanded rapidly, opening new stores in one small southern town after another.

By the mid-1980s, Wal-Mart had exploded onto the national retailing scene. Incredibly, by 1998, Wal-Mart's annual sales exceeded $120 billion—more than those of Sears, Kmart, JCPenney, and Target combined—making it the world's largest retailer and the nation's fourth largest company. Last year in the United States, Wal-Mart sold one out of every four quarts of motor oil, one out of every five deodorants, and one out of every

four replacement toilet seats. It sold a Timex watch every 7.4 seconds and a Barbie Doll every 2 seconds. Wal-Mart's phenomenal growth shows few signs of slowing. The company is now well established in larger cities and has expanded into Central and South America, Canada, Europe, and Asia. Such sparkling performance has rewarded investors handsomely. An investment of $1,650 in Wal-Mart stock in 1970 would be worth a whopping $3 million today!

What are the secrets behind this spectacular success? Wal-Mart listens to and takes care of its customers, treats employees as partners, and keeps a tight rein on costs.

Listening to and Taking Care of Customers

Wal-Mart positioned itself strongly in a well-chosen target market. Initially, Sam Walton focused on value-conscious consumers in small-

town America. The chain built a strong everyday low-price position long before it became fashionable in retailing. It grew rapidly by bringing the lowest possible prices to towns ignored by national discounters—towns such as Van Buren, Arkansas, and Idabel, Oklahoma.

Wal-Mart knows its customers and takes good care of them. As one analyst puts it, "The company gospel . . . is relatively simple: Be an agent for customers, find out what they want, and sell it to them for the lowest possible price." Thus, the company listens carefully; for example, each top Wal-Mart executive spends at least two days a week visiting stores, talking directly with customers and getting a firsthand look at operations. Then, Wal-Mart delivers what customers want: a broad selection of carefully selected goods at unbeatable prices. Concludes Wal-Mart's current president and chief executive, "We're obsessed with delivering value to customers."

A Wal-Mart "people greeter" lends a helping hand.

But the right merchandise at the right price isn't the only key to Wal-Mart's success; Wal-Mart also provides the kind of service that keeps customers satisfied. A sign reading "Satisfaction Guaranteed" hangs prominently at each store's entrance. Another sign inside the store reads "At Wal-Mart, our goal is: You're always next in line!" Customers are often welcomed by "people greeters" eager to lend a helping hand or just to be friendly. And, sure enough, the store opens extra checkout counters to keep waiting lines short.

Treating Employees as Partners

Wal-Mart believes that, in the final accounting, the company's people are what really make it better. Thus, it works hard to show employees that it cares about them. Wal-Mart calls employees "associates," a practice now widely copied by competitors. The associates work as partners, become deeply involved in operations, and share rewards for good performance.

> Everyone at Wal-Mart [is] an associate—from [the CEO] . . . to a cashier named Janet at the Wal-Mart on Highway 50 in Ocoee, Florida. "We," "us," and "our" are the operative words. Wal-Mart department heads, hourly associates who look after one or more of 30-some departments ranging from sporting goods to electronics, see figures that many companies never show general managers: costs, freight charges, profit margins. The company sets a profit margin for each store, and if the store exceeds it, then the hourly associates share part of the additional profit.

The partnership concept is deeply rooted in the Wal-Mart corporate culture. Wal-Mart's concern for its employees translates into high employee satisfaction, which in turn translates into greater customer satisfaction.

Keeping a Tight Rein on Costs

Wal-Mart has the lowest cost structure in the industry. Thus, Wal-Mart can charge lower prices but still reap higher profits, allowing it to offer better service. Wal-Mart's lower prices and better service attract more shoppers, producing more sales, making the company more efficient, and enabling it to lower prices even more.

Wal-Mart's low costs result in part from superior management and more sophisticated technology. Its Bentonville, Arkansas headquarters contains a computer communications system that the Defense Department would envy, giving managers around the country instant access to sales and operating information. And its huge, fully automated distribution centers employ the latest technology to supply stores efficiently. Wal-Mart also spends less than competitors on advertising—only 0.5 percent of sales, compared to 2.5 percent at Kmart and 3.8 percent at Sears. Because Wal-Mart has what customers want at the prices they'll pay, its reputation has spread rapidly by word of mouth. It has not needed more advertising.

Finally, Wal-Mart keeps costs down through good old "tough buying." Whereas the company is known for the warm way it treats customers, it is equally well known for the cold, calculated way it wrings low prices from suppliers.

The following passage describes a visit to Wal-Mart's buying offices:

> Don't expect a greeter and don't expect friendly. . . . Once you are ushered into one of the spartan little buyers' rooms, expect a steely eye across the table and be prepared to cut your price. "They are very, very focused people, and they use their buying power more forcefully than anyone else in America," says the marketing vice president of a major vendor. "All the normal mating rituals are [forbidden]. Their highest priority is making sure everyone at all times in all cases knows who's in charge, and it's Wal-Mart. They talk softly, but they have piranha hearts, and if you aren't totally prepared when you go in there, you'll have your [head] handed to you."

Some observers wonder whether Wal-Mart can be so big and still retain its focus and positioning. They wonder if an ever-larger Wal-Mart can stay close to its customers and employees. The company's managers are betting on it. No matter where it operates, Wal-Mart's announced policy is to take care of customers "one store at a time." Says one top executive: "We'll be fine as long as we never lose our responsiveness to the consumer."

Sources: Quoted material from Bill Saporito, "Is Wal-Mart Unstoppable?" *Fortune*, May 6, 1991, pp. 50–59; and John Huey, "Wal-Mart: Will It Take Over the World?" *Fortune*, January 30, 1998, pp. 52–61; and Jay L. Johnson, "A Borderless Wal-Mart," *Discount Merchandiser*, April 1998, p. 43. Also see Bill Saporito, "And the Winner Is Still . . . Wal-Mart," *Fortune*, May 2, 1994, pp. 62–70; Nelson D. Schwartz, "Why Wall Street's Buying Wal-Mart Again," *Fortune*, February 16, 1998, pp. 92–94; Wendy Zellner, "A Grand Reopening of Wal-Mart," *Business Week*, February 9, 1998, pp. 86–88; and Gene Hoffman, "Beware the Steamroller," *Progressive Grocer*, January 1999, p. 104.

Product Assortment and Services Decision Retailers must decide on three major product variables: *product assortment*, *services mix*, and *store atmosphere*.

The retailer's *product assortment* should match target shoppers' expectations. In its quest to differentiate itself from competitors, a retailer can use any of several product-differentiation strategies. For one, it can offer merchandise that no other competitor carries—its own private brands or national brands on which it holds exclusives. For example, The Limited designs most of the clothes carried by its store and Saks gets exclusive rights to carry a well-known designer's labels. Second, the retailer can feature blockbuster merchandising events—Bloomingdale's is known for running spectacular shows featuring goods from a certain country, such as India or China. Or the retailer can offer surprise merchandise, as when Loehmann's offers surprise assortments of seconds, overstocks, and closeouts. Finally, the retailer can differentiate itself by offering a highly targeted product assortment—Lane Bryant carries goods for larger women; Brookstone offers an unusual assortment of gadgets in what amounts to an adult toy store.

Retailers also must decide on a *services mix* to offer customers. The old mom-and-pop grocery stores offered home delivery, credit, and conversation—services that today's supermarkets ignore. The services mix is one of the key tools of nonprice competition for setting one store apart from another.

The *store's atmosphere* is another element in its product arsenal. Every store has a physical layout that makes moving around in it either hard or easy. Each store has a "feel"; one store is cluttered, another charming, a third plush, a fourth somber. The store must have a planned atmosphere that suits the target market and moves customers to buy.

Increasingly, retailers are turning their stores into theaters that transport customers into unusual, exciting shopping environments. For example, Barnes & Noble uses atmospherics to turn shopping for books into entertainment. It has found that, "to consumers, shopping is a social activity. They do it to mingle with others in a prosperous-feeling crowd, to see what's new, to enjoy the theatrical dazzle of the display, to treat themselves to something interesting or unexpected." Thus, Barnes & Noble stores are designed with "enough woody, traditional, soft-colored library to please book lovers; enough sophisticated modern architecture and graphics, sweeping vistas, and stylish displays to satisfy fans of the theater of consumption. And for everyone, plenty of space, where they can meet other people and feel at home. . . . [Customers] settle in at heavy chairs and tables to browse through piles of books; they fill the cafes [designed] to increase the festivities. . . . " As one Barnes & Noble executive notes: "The feel-good part of the store, the quality of life contribution, is a big part of the success."[10]

Perhaps the most dramatic conversion of stores into theatre is the Mall of America near Minneapolis. Containing more than 400 specialty stores, the mall is a veritable playground. Under a single roof, it shelters a seven-acre Knott's Berry Farm amusement park featuring 23 rides and attractions, an ice-skating rink, an Underwater World featuring hundreds of marine specimens and a dolphin show, and a two-story miniature golf course. One of the stores, Oshman Supersports USA, features a basketball court, a boxing gym, a baseball batting cage, a 50-foot archery range, and a simulated ski slope.[11]

All of this confirms that retail stores are much more than simply assortments of goods. They are environments to be experienced by the people who shop in them. Store atmospheres offer a powerful tool by which retailers can differentiate their stores from those of competitors.

Price Decision A retailer's price policy is a crucial positioning factor and must be decided in relation to its target market, its product and service assortment, and its competition. All retailers would like to charge high markups and achieve high volume, but the two seldom go together. Most retailers seek *either* high markups on lower volume (most specialty stores) *or* low markups on higher volume (mass merchandisers and discount stores). Thus, Bijan's on Rodeo Drive in Beverly Hills prices men's suits starting at $1,000 and shoes at $400; it sells a low volume but makes a hefty profit on each sale. At the other extreme, T.J. Maxx sells brand-name clothing at discount prices, settling for a lower margin on each sale but selling at a much higher volume.

Promotion Decision Retailers use the normal promotion tools—advertising, personal selling, sales promotion, and public relations—to reach consumers. They advertise in newspapers, magazines, radio, and television. Advertising may be supported by newspaper inserts and direct-mail pieces. Personal selling requires careful training of salespeople in how to greet customers, meet their needs, and handle their complaints. Sales promotions may include in-store demonstrations, displays, contests, and visiting celebrities. Public relations activities, such as press conferences and speeches, store openings, special events, newsletters, magazines, and public service activities, are always available to retailers.

Place Decision Retailers often cite three critical factors in retailing success: *location*, *location*, and *location*! A retailer's location is key to its ability to attract customers. And the costs of building or leasing facilities have a major impact on the retailer's profits. Thus, site-location decisions are among the most important the retailer makes. Small retailers may have to settle for whatever locations they can find or afford. Large retailers usually employ specialists who select locations using advanced methods. Two of the savviest location experts in recent years have been the off-price retailer T.J. Maxx and toy-store giant Toys 'Я' Us. Both put the majority of their new locations in rapidly growing areas where the population closely matches their customer base. The undisputed winner in the "place race" has been Wal-Mart, whose strategy of being the first mass-merchandiser to locate in small and rural markets was one of the key factors in its phenomenal early success.

Most stores today cluster together to increase their customer pulling power and to give consumers the convenience of one-stop shopping. *Central business districts* were the main form of retail cluster until the 1950s. Every large city and town had a central business district with department stores, specialty stores, banks, and movie theaters. When people began to move to the suburbs, however, these central business districts, with their traffic, parking, and crime problems, began to lose business. Downtown merchants opened branches in suburban shopping centers, and the decline of the central business districts continued. In recent years, many cities have joined with merchants to try to revive downtown shopping areas by building malls and providing underground parking.

A **shopping center** is a group of retail businesses planned, developed, owned, and managed as a unit. A *regional shopping center*, the largest and most dramatic shopping center, contains from 40 to over 200 stores. It is like a covered minidowntown and attracts customers from a wide area. A *community shopping center* contains between 15 and 40 retail stores. It normally contains a branch of a department store or variety store, a supermarket, specialty stores, professional offices, and sometimes a bank. Most shopping centers are *neighborhood shopping centers* or *strip malls* that generally contain between 5 and 15 stores. They are close and convenient for consumers. They usually contain a supermarket, perhaps a discount store, and several service stores: dry cleaner, self-service laundry, drugstore, video-rental outlet, barber or beauty shop, hardware store, or other stores.

Shopping center
A group of retail businesses planned, developed, owned, and managed as a unit.

Combined, all shopping centers now account for about one-third of all retail sales, but they may have reached their saturation point. Recent studies show that consumers are spending less time in traditional shopping malls. Observes one retail consultant, "You and I are going less often, we're staying a shorter period of time, and we're visiting fewer stores while we're there. That's bad news for the malls."[12]

Shopping centers: The spectacular Mall of America near Minneapolis contains more than 800 stores, 45 restaurants, 7 theaters, and a 7-acre indoor theme park. It attracts 35 million visitors a year.

Why are people using shopping malls less? First, with more women in the work-force and the baby boomers spending more time with their children, people have less time to shop. Second, shoppers appear to be tiring of traditional malls, which are too big, too crowded, and too much alike. Today's large malls offer great selection but are less comfortable and convenient. Finally, today's consumers have many alternatives to traditional malls, ranging from online shopping to so-called *power centers*. These huge unenclosed shopping centers consist of a long strip of retail stores, including large, free-standing anchors such as Wal-Mart, Home Depot, Best Buy, Michaels, OfficeMax, and CompUSA. Each store has its own entrance with parking directly in front for shoppers who wish to visit only one store. Power centers have increased rapidly during the past few years to challenge traditional indoor malls. Thus, despite the recent development of many new "megamalls," such as the spectacular Mall of America, the current trend is toward value-oriented outlet malls, power centers, and smaller malls located in medium-size and smaller cities in fast-growing areas such as the Southwest.[13]

The Future of Retailing

Retailers operate in a harsh and fast-changing environment, which offers threats as well as opportunities. For example, the industry suffers from chronic overcapacity. There is too much retail space—about 18 square feet for every man, woman, and child, more than double that of 30 years ago—resulting in fierce competition for customer dollars.

Consumer demographics, lifestyles, and shopping patterns are changing rapidly, as are retailing technologies. Moreover, quickly rising costs make more efficient operation and smarter buying essential. To be successful, then, retailers will have to choose target segments carefully and position themselves strongly. They will have to take the following retailing developments into account as they plan and execute their competitive strategies.

New Retail Forms and Shortening Retail Lifecycles

New retail forms continue to emerge to meet new situations and consumer needs, but the life cycle of new retail forms is getting shorter. Department stores took about 100 years to reach the mature stage of the life cycle; more recent forms, such as catalog showrooms and furniture warehouse stores, reached maturity in about 10 years. In such an environment, seemingly solid retail positions can crumble quickly. Of the top 10 discount retailers in 1962 (the year that Wal-Mart and Kmart began), not one still exists today.[14]

Consider the Price Club, the original warehouse store chain. When Sol Price opened his first warehouse store outside San Diego in 1976, he launched a retailing revolution. Selling everything from tires and office supplies to five-pound tubs of peanut butter at superlow prices, his store chain was generating $2.6 billion a year in sales within 10 years. But Price refused to expand beyond its California base. And as the industry quickly matured, Price ran headlong into wholesale clubs run by such retail giants as Wal-Mart and Kmart. Only 17 years later, in a stunning reversal of fortune, a faltering Price sold out to competitor Costco. Price's rapid rise and fall "serves as a stark reminder to mass-market retailers that past success means little in a fiercely competitive and rapidly changing industry."[15] Thus, retailers can no longer sit back with a successful formula. To remain successful, they must keep adapting.

Many retailing innovations are partially explained by the **wheel of retailing concept**.[16] According to this concept, many new types of retailing forms begin as low-margin, low-price, low-status operations. They challenge established retailers that have become "fat" by letting their costs and margins increase. The new retailers' success leads them to upgrade their facilities and offer more services. In turn, their costs increase, forcing them to increase their prices. Eventually, the new retailers become like the conventional retailers they replaced. The cycle begins again when still-newer types of retailers evolve with lower costs and prices. The wheel of retailing concept seems to explain the initial success and later troubles of department stores, supermarkets, and discount stores, and the recent success of off-price retailers.

Wheel of retailing concept A concept of retailing that states that new types of retailers usually begin as low-margin, low-price, low-status operations but later evolve into higher-priced, higher-service operations, eventually becoming like the conventional retailers they replaced.

Growth of Nonstore Retailing

Although most retailing still takes place the old-fashioned way across countertops in stores, consumers now have an array of alternatives, including mail order, television, phone, and online shopping (see Marketing at Work 11-3). "Some Americans never face a single crowd at holiday time; they do all of their gift shopping via phone or computer. A few may never even talk to a human being; they can punch in their order and credit card numbers on a Web site and have gifts delivered to recipients. This might remove some of the personal touch from the process, but it sure saves time."[17] Although such advances may threaten some traditional retailers, they offer exciting opportunities for others. Most store retailers are now actively exploring direct retailing channels.

Increasing Intertype Competition

Today's retailers increasingly face competition from many different forms of retailers. For example, a consumer can buy CDs at specialty music stores, discount music stores, electronics superstores, video-rental outlets, and through dozens of Web sites. They can buy books at stores ranging from independent

Marketing at Work 11-3
Retailing Goes On-Line

Most of us still make the majority of our purchases the old-fashioned way: We go to the store, find what we want, wait patiently in line to plunk down our cash or credit card, and bring home the goods. However, a growing number of on-line retailers are providing an attractive alternative—one that lets us browse, select, order, and pay with little more effort than it takes to apply an index finger to a mouse button. They sell a rich variety of goods ranging from flowers, CDs, books, and food to stereo equipment, kitchen appliances, airplane tickets, auto parts, and bags of cement. Here are just a few examples.

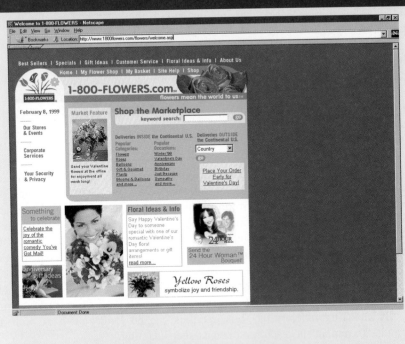

Music: CDNow's cyberstore (www.cdnow.com) offers Web shoppers more than 165,000 CD titles, including every jazz album in the United States and 20,000 imports. Customers place their orders on-line, CDNow contacts the distributor, and customers receive their music within 24 hours. It site is so popular, CDNow is making money from other companies that advertise on its site—something the traditional music store cannot do. The best news: CDNow spent only $2,500 to build its Web site, but the site earned more than $25 million last year. On average, more than 120,000 shoppers visit the Web site daily.

Books: Amazon.com, (www.amazon.com) offers 3.1 million books on-line—more than 14 times the number carried by the largest superstore—and discounts bestsellers up to 30 percent. Amazon has attracted

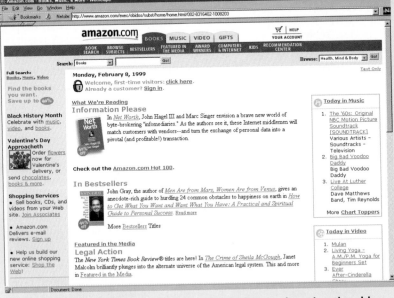

On-line retailers provide an attractive alternative to shopping the old fashioned way.

local bookstores to discount stores such as Wal-Mart, superstores such as Barnes & Noble or Borders Books and Music, or Web sites such as www.amazon.com. And when it comes to brand-name appliances, department stores, discount stores, off-price retailers, or

more than 120 million customers and has annual sales of more than $400 million and growing fast. The company orders books from publishers and has no store, no inventory. Most customers receive books two to three days after ordering. Though Amazon.com can't offer couches and coffee, it has authors post comments on their books, encourages customers to share opinions on books, and recommends titles to individual customers based on each customer's profile. The company even tracks down hard-to-find books. "Businesses can do things on the Web that simply cannot be done any other way," says founder and CEO Jeff Bezos. "We are changing the way people buy books."

Flowers: One-fourth of all flowers sold in the United States are now ordered on the Internet. 1-800-FLOWERS.com is one of the most successful on-line retailers doing business today. 1-800-FLOWERS (www.1-800-flowers.com) president and owner Jim McCann, who created a $300-million company from one that was $7 million in debt in 1987, started selling flowers on-line in 1992. Now customers can find 1-800-FLOWERS on interactive services such as America Online, eWorld, and the Plaza on the Microsoft Network. They can choose from some 150 different gift arrangements, from roses and daisies to balloons and fruit baskets, with same-day delivery in most locations. In Arthur Andersen's latest *International Trends in Retailing*, McCann discusses taking the shopping experience on-line. "For many businesses—for flowers, certainly—"he writes, "moving that [shopping] experience to an electronic medium is a bear. It just doesn't translate that directly. . . . We learned that to achieve the result we want, we would have to think about marketing in a new way. . . . Where we [used to have] actual conversations, we now would have to provide a constant, changing stream of relevant information and entertainment. What has to happen, in other words, is that retailers must learn how to re-create the physical retail experience on-line."

Apparel: Many basic apparel items already move like wildfire via catalogs. And most catalog retailers—L.L. Bean, Lands' End, and others—have already put their catalogs on-line. However, other noncatalog specialty retailers are also setting up to sell on-line. For example, Gap now uses its Web site (www.gap.com) to sell a wide range of products, from jeans and khakis, T-shirts, socks, and sweaters to accessories and fragrances. Since launching its Web site, Gap has mapped visitor usage patterns and found that, on average, people stayed 50 percent longer at the Gap site than at other sites. This statistic bodes well for the chain's chances at on-line retailing. Gap's entry into on-line retail is a natural, asserts one industry analyst. "It's about time," says the analyst. "The Gap is a marquee brand and an excellent demographic fit" with Web users. The challenge will be to develop ways to spark impulse buys, which often add significantly to sales.

Food: Consumers could buy most of their groceries without touching them. Half of European food retailers surveyed recently by the *Financial Times* believe that home delivery will represent 20 percent of volume by 2005. A few on-line food retailers have already sprung up in the United States. Peapod (www.peapod.com), which has teamed with supermarkets in Atlanta, Boston, Chicago, Dallas, Houston, San Francisco, and Columbus, Ohio, has attracted 75,000 members. The supermarkets receive orders by fax or over Peapod's software. They pack the orders and Peapod makes the delivery. Food Express in New Hampshire plans to cut grocery stores from the process by setting up warehouses where it will pack orders for customers to pick up. It believes it can serve the same number of customers as supermarkets with one-third of the space.

Still, succeeding on-line is anything but a given. "The on-line success stories in retail are few and far between," cautions another analyst. Those who fair well tend to be catalog companies with internal structures and staff to deal with orders. However, he admits, with each passing day, technological advances make it a bit easier for retailers to make their bottom lines on-line.

Source: Portions adapted from Jay A. Scansaroli and Vicky Eng, "Interactive Retailing: Marketing Products," *Chain Store Age*, January 1997, pp. 9A–10A. Gap example and quotes from Alice Z. Cuneo, "The Gap Readies Electronic Commerce Plan for Web Site," *Advertising Age*, June 23, 1997, p. 18. Also see Anya Sacharow, "Kind of Green," *Adweek*, March 23, 1998, p. IQ6; Clint Willis, "Does Amazon.com Really Matter?" *Forbes*, April 6, 1998, pp. 55–58; "Future Shop: Groceries," *Forbes*, April 6, 1998, p. 43; and Kate Maddox, "My Flower Shop Blooms at Modified 1-800-Flowers", *Advertising Age*, November 9, 1998, p. 70; George Anders, "Amazon.com Sales more than Triple," *Wall Street Journal*, January 6, 1999, p. B7; and Erika Rasmusson, "The Death of Retailing?" *Sales & Marketing Management*, March 1999, p. 17.

electronics superstores all compete for the same customers. Suggests one industry expert, "What we're seeing is cross-shopping—consumers buying one item at Neiman Marcus and another at Wal-Mart or General Dollar."[18]

The competition between chain superstores and smaller, independently owned stores has become particularly heated. Because of their bulk buying power and high sales volume, chains can buy at lower costs and thrive on smaller margins. The arrival of a superstore can quickly force nearby independents out of business. For example, the decision by Best Buy, the electronics superstore, to sell CDs as loss leaders at rock-bottom prices pushed a number of specialty record store chains into bankruptcy.[19] Yet the news is not all bad for smaller companies. Many small, independent retailers are thriving. Independents are finding that sheer size and marketing muscle are often no match for the personal touch small stores can provide or the specialty niches that small stores fill for a devoted customer base.

The Rise of Megaretailers The rise of huge mass-merchandisers and specialty superstores, the formation of vertical marketing systems and buying alliances, and a rash of retail mergers and acquisitions have created a core of superpower megaretailers. Through their superior information systems and buying power, these giant retailers are able to offer better merchandise selections, good service, and strong price savings to consumers. As a result, they grow even larger by squeezing out their smaller, weaker competitors. The megaretailers also are shifting the balance of power between retailers and producers. A relative handful of retailers now controls access to enormous numbers of consumers, giving them the upper hand in their dealings with manufacturers. For example, in the United States, Wal-Mart's revenues are more than three times those of Procter & Gamble. Wal-Mart can, and often does, use this power to wring concessions from P&G and other suppliers.[20]

Growing Importance of Retail Technology Retail technologies are becoming critically important as competitive tools. Progressive retailers are using computers to produce better forecasts, control inventory costs, order electronically from suppliers, send e-mail between stores, and even sell to customers within stores. They are adopting checkout scanning systems, on-line transaction processing, electronic funds transfer, electronic data interchange, in-store television, and improved merchandise-handling systems.

One innovative scanning system now in use is the shopper scanner, a radarlike system that counts store traffic. When a New Jersey Saks Fifth Avenue used one such system, ShopperTrak, it learned that there was a shopper surge between the hours of 11 A.M. and 3 P.M. To better handle the shopper flow, the store varied lunch hours for its counter clerks. Pier One Imports uses the same system to test, among other things, the impact of newspaper ads on store traffic. By combining traffic and sales data, retailers say they can find out how well the store converts browsers into buyers.[21]

Global Expansion of Major Retailers Retailers with unique formats and strong brand positioning are increasingly moving into other countries. Many are expanding internationally to escape mature and saturated home markets. Over the years, several giant U.S. retailers—McDonald's, Gap, Toys 'Я' Us—have become globally prominent as a result of their great marketing prowess. Others, such as Wal-Mart and Kmart, are rapidly establishing a global presence. Wal-Mart, which now operates more than 300 stores in 6 countries, sees exciting potential abroad. For example, here's what happened when it recently opened two new stores in Shenzhen, China:

> [Customers came] by the hundreds of thousands—up to 175,000 on Saturdays alone—to China's first Wal-Mart Supercenter and Sam's Club. They broke the display glass to snatch out chickens at one store and carted off all the big-screen TVs before the other store had been open an hour. The two outlets . . . were packed on Day One and have been bustling ever since.[22]

Store atmosphere: Like many book retailers today, Tattered Cover Bookstores in Denver provide plenty of space where customers hang out, browse, meet others, and feel at home.

However, U.S retailers are still significantly behind Europe and Asia when it comes to global expansion. Only 18 percent of the top U.S. retailers operate globally, compared to 40 percent of European retailers and 31 percent of Asian retailers. Among foreign retailers that have gone global are Britain's Marks and Spencer, Italy's Benetton, France's Carrefour hypermarkets, Sweden's Ikea home furnishings stores, and Japan's Yaohan supermarkets.[23] Marks and Spencer, which started out as a penny bazaar in 1884, grew into a chain of variety stores over the decades and now has a thriving string of 150 franchised stores around the world, which sell mainly its private-label clothes. It also runs a major food business. Ikea's well-constructed but fairly inexpensive furniture has proven very popular in the United States, where shoppers often spend an entire day in an Ikea store.

Retail Stores as "Communities" or "Hangouts" With the rise in the number of people living alone, working at home, or living in isolated and sprawling suburbs, there has been a resurgence of establishments that, regardless of the product or service they offer, also provide a place for people to get together. These places include cafes, tea shops, juice bars, bookshops, superstores, children's play spaces, brew pubs, and urban greenmarkets. Denver's two Tattered Cover Bookstores host more than 250 events annually, from folk dancing to women's meetings. Brew pubs such as New York's Zip City Brewing and Seattle's Trolleyman Pub (run by Red Hook Brewery) offer tastings and a place to pass the time. The Discovery Zone, a chain of children's play spaces, offers indoor spaces where kids can go wild without breaking anything and stressed-out parents can exchange stories. And, of course, there are the now-ubiquitous coffee houses and espresso bars, such as Starbucks, whose numbers have grown from 2,500 in 1989 to an estimated 10,000 by 1999.[24]

Linking the Concepts

Time out! So-called experts have long predicted that nonstore retailing eventually will replace store retailing as our primary way to shop. What do you think?

- Shop for a good book at the Web site of on-line bookseller Amazon.com (www.Amazon. com), taking time to browse the site and see what it has to offer. Next, shop at Barnes & Noble, Borders Books, or another local bookstore. Compare the two shopping experiences. Where would you rather shop? On what occasions? Why?
- Barnes & Noble creates an ideal "community" where people can "hang out." How does Amazon.com compare on this dimension?

Wholesaling

Wholesaling
All activities involved in selling goods and services to those buying for resale or business use.

Wholesaler
A firm engaged *primarily* in wholesaling activity.

Wholesaling includes all activities involved in selling goods and services to those buying for resale or business use. A retail bakery is engaging in wholesaling when it sells pastry to the local hotel. We call **wholesalers** those firms engaged *primarily* in wholesaling activity.

Wholesalers buy mostly from producers and sell mostly to retailers, industrial consumers, and other wholesalers. But why are wholesalers used at all? For example, why would a producer use wholesalers rather than selling directly to retailers or consumers? Quite simply, wholesalers are often better at performing one or more of the following channel functions:

- *Selling and promoting:* Wholesalers' sales forces help manufacturers reach many small customers at a low cost. The wholesaler has more contacts and is often more trusted by the buyer than the distant manufacturer.
- *Buying and assortment building:* Wholesalers can select items and build assortments needed by their customers, thereby saving the consumers much work.
- *Bulk-breaking:* Wholesalers save their customers money by buying in carload lots and breaking bulk (breaking large lots into small quantities).
- *Warehousing:* Wholesalers hold inventories, thereby reducing the inventory costs and risks of suppliers and customers.
- *Transportation:* Wholesalers can provide quicker delivery to buyers because they are closer than the producers.
- *Financing:* Wholesalers finance their customers by giving credit, and they finance their suppliers by ordering early and paying bills on time.
- *Risk bearing:* Wholesalers absorb risk by taking title and bearing the cost of theft, damage, spoilage, and obsolescence.
- *Market information:* Wholesalers give information to suppliers and customers about competitors, new products, and price developments.
- *Management services and advice:* Wholesalers often help retailers train their sales-clerks, improve store layouts and displays, and set up accounting and inventory control systems.

Types of Wholesalers

Merchant wholesaler
Independently owned business that takes title to the merchandise it handles.

Broker
A wholesaler who does not take title to goods and whose function is to bring buyers and sellers together and assist in negotiation.

Agent
A wholesaler who represents buyers or sellers on a relatively permanent basis, performs only a few functions, and does not take title to goods.

Wholesalers fall into three major groups (see Table 11-3): *merchant wholesalers, brokers and agents,* and *manufacturers' sales branches and offices.* **Merchant wholesalers** are the largest single group of wholesalers, accounting for roughly 50 percent of all wholesaling. Merchant wholesalers include two broad types: full-service wholesalers and limited-service wholesalers. *Full-service wholesalers* provide a full set of services, whereas the various *limited-service wholesalers* offer fewer services to their suppliers and customers. The several different types of limited-service wholesalers perform varied specialized functions in the distribution channel.

Brokers and *agents* differ from merchant wholesalers in two ways: They do not take title to goods, and they perform only a few functions. Like merchant wholesalers, they generally specialize by product line or customer type. A **broker** brings buyers and sellers together and assists in negotiation. **Agents** represent buyers or sellers on a more permanent basis. *Manufacturers' agents* (also called *manufacturers' representatives*) are the most common type of agent wholesaler. The third major type of wholesaling is that done

Merchant wholesalers: A typical Fleming Companies, Inc. wholesale food distribution center. The average Fleming warehouse contains 500,000 square feet of floor space (with 30-foot high ceiling), carries 16,000 different food items, and serves 150 to 200 retailers within a 500-mile radius.

in **manufacturers' sales branches and offices** by sellers or buyers themselves rather than through independent wholesalers.

Manufacturers' sales branches and offices Wholesaling by sellers or buyers themselves rather than through independent wholesalers.

Wholesaler Marketing Decisions

Wholesalers have experienced mounting competitive pressures in recent years. They have faced new sources of competition, more demanding customers, new technologies, and more direct-buying programs on the part of large industrial, institutional, and retail buyers. As a result, they have had to improve their strategic decisions on target markets and positioning and on the marketing mix—product assortments and services, price, promotion, and place (see Figure 11-2).

Target Market and Positioning Decision Like retailers, wholesalers must define their target markets and position themselves effectively; they cannot serve everyone. They can choose a target group by size of customer (only large retailers), type of customer

Figure 11-2
Wholesaler marketing decisions

Table 11-3 Major Types of Wholesalers

Type	Description
Merchant Wholesalers	Independently owned businesses that take title to the merchandise they handle. In different trades they are called *jobbers,* distributors, *or mill supply houses.* Include full-service wholesalers and limited-service wholesalers:
Full-service wholesalers	Provide a full line of services: carrying stock, maintaining a sales force, offering credit, making deliveries, and providing management assistance. There are two types:
Wholesale merchants	Sell primarily to retailers and provide a full range of services. *General-merchandise wholesalers* carry several merchandise lines, whereas *general-line wholesalers* carry one or two lines in great depth. *Specialty wholesalers* specialize in carrying only part of a line. (Examples: health food wholesalers, seafood wholesalers.)
Industrial distributors	Sell to manufacturers rather than to retailers. Provide several services, such as carrying stock, offering credit, and providing delivery. May carry a broad range of merchandise, a general line, or a specialty line.
Limited-service wholesalers	Offer fewer services than full-service wholesalers. Limited-service wholesalers are of several types:
Cash-and-carry wholesalers	Carry a limited line of fast-moving goods and sell to small retailers for cash. Normally do not deliver. Example: A small fish store retailer may drive to a cash-and-carry fish wholesaler, buy fish for cash, and bring the merchandise back to the store.
Truck wholesalers (or truck jobbers)	Perform primarily a selling and delivery function. Carry a limited line of semiperishable merchandise (such as milk, bread, snack foods), which they sell for cash us they make their rounds to supermarkets, small groceries, hospitals, restaurants, factory cafeterias, and hotels.
Drop shippers	Do not carry inventory or handle the product. On receiving an order, they select a manufacturer, who ships the merchandise directly to the customer. The drop shipper assumes title and risk from the time the order is accepted to its delivery to the customer. They operate in bulk industries, such as coal, lumber, and heavy equipment.
Rack jobbers	Serve grocery and drug retailers, mostly in nonfood items. They send delivery trucks to stores, where the delivery people set up toys, paperbacks, hardware items, health and beauty aids, or other items. They price the goods, keep them fresh, set up point-of-purchase displays, and keep inventory records. Rack jobbers retain title to the goods and bill the retailers only for the goods sold to consumers.
Producers' cooperatives	Owned by farmer members and assemble farm produce to sell in local markets. The co-op's profits are distributed to members at the end of the year. They often attempt to improve product quality and promote a co-op brand name, such as Sun Maid raisins, Sunkist oranges, or Diamond walnuts.
Mail-order wholesalers	Send catalogs to retail, industrial, and institutional customers featuring jewelry, cosmetics, specialty foods, and other small items. Maintain no outside sales force. Main customers are businesses in small outlying areas. Orders are filled and sent by mail, truck, or other transportation.
Brokers and agents	Do not take title to goods. Main function is to facilitate buying and selling, for which they earn a commission on the selling price. Generally specialize by product line or customer types.
Brokers	Chief function is bringing buyers and sellers together and assisting in negotiation. They are paid by the party who hired them and do not carry inventory, get involved in financing, or assume risk. Examples: food brokers, real estate brokers, insurance brokers, and security brokers.

Table 11-3   (continued)

Type	Description
Agents	Represent either buyers or sellers on a more permanent basis than brokers do. There are several types:
Manufacturers' agents	Represent two or more manufacturers of complementary lines. A formal written agreement with each manufacturer covers pricing, territories, order-handling, delivery service and warranties, and commission rates. Often used in such lines as apparel, furniture, and electrical goods. Most manufacturers' agents are small businesses, with only a few skilled salespeople as employees. They are hired by small manufacturers who cannot afford their own field sales forces and by large manufacturers who use agents to open new territories or to cover territories that cannot support full-time salespeople.
Selling agents	Have contractual authority to sell a manufacturer's entire output. The manufacturer either is not interested in the selling function or feels unqualified. The selling agent serves as a sales department and has significant influence over prices, terms, and conditions of sale. Found in product areas such as textiles, industrial machinery and equipment, coal and coke, chemicals, and metals.
Purchasing agents	Generally have a long-term relationship with buyers and make purchases for them, often receiving, inspecting, warehousing, and shipping the merchandise to the buyers. They provide helpful market information to clients and help them obtain the best goods and prices available.
Commission merchants	Take physical possession of products and negotiate sales. Normally, they are not employed on a long-term basis. Used most often in agricultural marketing by farmers who do not want to sell their own output and do not belong to producers' cooperatives. The commission merchant takes a truckload of commodities to a central market, sells it for the best price, deducts a commission and expenses, and remits the balance to the producers.
Manufacturers' and retailers' branches and offices	Wholesaling operations conducted by sellers or buyers themselves rather than through independent wholesalers. Separate branches and offices can be dedicated to either sales or purchasing.
Sales branches and offices	Set up by manufacturers to improve inventory control, selling, and promotion. *Sales branches* carry inventory and are found in industries such as lumber and automotive equipment and parts. *Sales offices* do not carry inventory and are most prominent in dry-goods and notions industries.
Purchasing offices	Perform a role similar to that of brokers or agents but are part of the buyer's organization. Many retailers set up purchasing offices in major market centers such as New York and Chicago.

(convenience food stores only), need for service (customers who need credit), or other factors. Within the target group, they can identify the more profitable customers, design stronger offers, and build better relationships with them. They can propose automatic reordering systems, set up management-training and advising systems, or even sponsor a voluntary chain. They can discourage less-profitable customers by requiring larger orders or adding service charges to smaller ones.

Marketing-Mix Decisions Like retailers, wholesalers must decide on product assortment and services, prices, promotion, and place. The wholesaler's "product" is the assortment of *products and services* that it offers. Wholesalers are under great pressure to carry a full line and to stock enough for immediate delivery. But this practice can damage profits.

Wholesalers today are cutting down on the number of lines they carry, choosing to carry only the more profitable ones. Wholesalers are also rethinking which services count most in building strong customer relationships and which should be dropped or charged for. The key is to find the mix of services most valued by their target customers.

Price is also an important wholesaler decision. Wholesalers usually mark up the cost of goods by a standard percentage—say, 20 percent. Expenses may run 17 percent of the gross margin, leaving a profit margin of 3 percent. In grocery wholesaling, the average profit margin is often less than 2 percent. Wholesalers are trying new pricing approaches. They may cut their margin on some lines in order to win important new customers. They may ask suppliers for special price breaks when they can turn them into an increase in the supplier's sales.

Although *promotion* can be critical to wholesaler success, most wholesalers are not promotion minded. Their use of trade advertising, sales promotion, personal selling, and public relations is largely scattered and unplanned. Many are behind the times in personal selling—they still see selling as a single salesperson talking to a single customer instead of as a team effort to sell, build, and service major accounts. Wholesalers also need to adopt some of the nonpersonal promotion techniques used by retailers. They need to develop an overall promotion strategy and to make greater use of supplier promotion materials and programs.

Finally, *place* is important—wholesalers must choose their locations and facilities carefully. Wholesalers typically locate in low-rent, low-tax areas and tend to invest little money in their buildings, equipment, and systems. As a result, their materials-handling and order-processing systems are often outdated. In recent years, however, large and progressive wholesalers are reacting to rising costs by investing in automated warehouses and online ordering systems. Orders are fed from the retailer's system directly into the wholesaler's computer, and the items are picked up by mechanical devices and automatically taken to a shipping platform where they are assembled. Most large wholesalers use computers to carry out accounting, billing, inventory control, and forecasting. Modern wholesalers are adapting their services to the needs of target customers and finding cost-reducing methods of doing business.

Trends in Wholesaling

As the thriving wholesaling industry moves into the twenty-first century, it faces considerable challenges. The industry remains vulnerable to one of the most enduring trends of the 1990s: fierce resistance to price increases and the winnowing out of suppliers based on cost and quality. Progressive wholesalers constantly watch for better ways to meet the changing needs of their suppliers and target customers. They recognize that, in the long run, their only reason for existence comes from adding value by increasing the efficiency and effectiveness of the entire marketing channel. To achieve this goal, they must constantly improve their services and reduce their costs.

McKesson, the nation's leading wholesaler of pharmaceuticals, health and beauty care, and home health-care products, provides an example of progressive wholesaling. To survive, McKesson had to remain more cost effective than manufacturers' sales branches. Thus, the company automated its 36 warehouses, established direct computer links with 225 drug manufacturers, designed a computerized accounts-receivable program for pharmacists, and provided drugstores with computer terminals for ordering inventories. Retailers can even use the McKesson computer system to maintain medical profiles on their customers. Thus, McKesson has delivered better value to both manufacturers and retail customers.

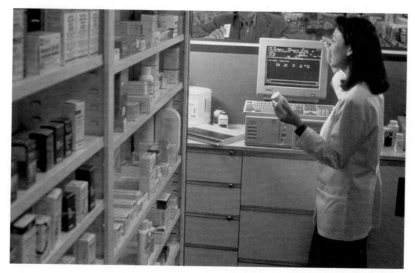

To improve both efficiency and service, drug wholesaler McKesson set up direct computer links with drugstores. Retailers can order merchandise directly and even use the McKesson computer system to maintain medical profiles on their customers.

One study predicts several developments in the wholesaling industry.[25] Geographic expansion will require that distributors learn how to compete effectively over wider and more diverse areas. Consolidation will significantly reduce the number of wholesaling firms. Surviving wholesalers will grow larger, primarily through acquisition, merger, and geographic expansion. The trend toward vertical integration, in which manufacturers try to control their market share by owning the intermediaries that bring their goods to market, remains strong. In health care, for instance, drug makers have purchased drug-distribution and pharmacy-management companies. This trend began in 1993 when drug-industry giant Merck acquired Medco Containment Services, a drug-benefits manager and mail-order distributor. The surviving wholesaler-distributors in this sector and in others will be bigger and will provide more services for their customers.[26]

The distinction between large retailers and large wholesalers continues to blur. Many retailers now operate formats such as wholesale clubs and hypermarkets that perform many wholesale functions. In return, many large wholesalers are setting up their own retailing operations. SuperValu and Flemming, both leading food wholesalers, now operate their own retail outlets. In fact, almost 30 percent of SuperValu's $16.6 billion in sales comes from its Cub Foods, Shop 'n Save, Save-A-Lot, Laneco, and Scott's supermarket operations.[27]

Wholesalers will continue to increase the services they provide to retailers: retail pricing, cooperative advertising, marketing and management information reports, accounting services, on-line transactions, and others. Rising costs on the one hand, and the demand for increased services on the other, will put the squeeze on wholesaler profits. Wholesalers who do not find efficient ways to deliver value to their customers will soon drop by the wayside. However, the increased use of computerized and automated systems will help wholesalers to contain the costs of ordering, shipping, and holding inventory, boosting their productivity. By 1990, more than three-fourths of all wholesalers were using on-line order systems.

Finally, facing slow growth in their domestic markets and such developments as the North American Free Trade Agreement, many large wholesalers are now going global. For example, in 1991, McKesson bought out its Canadian partner, Provigo. The company now receives about 13 percent of its total revenues from Canada.

REST STOP Reviewing the Concepts

Pull in here and reflect back on this retailing and wholesaling chapter, the last of two chapters on distribution channels. Although most retailing is conducted in retail stores, in recent years, nonstore retailing has increased enormously. In addition, although many retail stores are independently owned, an increasing number are now banding together under some form of corporate or contractual organization. Wholesalers, too, have experienced recent environmental changes, most notably mounting competitive pressures. They have faced new sources of competition, more demanding customers, new technologies, and more direct-buying programs on the part of large industrial, institutional, and retail buyers.

1. Explain the roles of retailers and wholesalers in the distribution channel.

Retailing and wholesaling consist of many organizations bringing goods and services from the point of production to the point of use. *Retailing* includes all activities involved in selling goods or services directly to final consumers for their personal, nonbusiness use. *Wholesaling* includes all the activities involved in selling goods or services to those who are buying for the purpose of resale or for business use. Wholesalers perform many functions, including selling and promoting, buying and assortment building, bulk-breaking, warehousing, transporting, financing, risk bearing, supplying market information, and providing management services and advice.

2. Describe the major types of retailers and give examples of each.

Retailers can be classified as *store retailers* and *nonstore retailers*. Store retailers can be further classified by the *amount of service* they provide (self-service, limited service, or full service); *product line sold* (specialty stores, department stores, supermarkets, convenience stores, superstores, and service businesses); and *relative prices* (discount stores, off-price retailers, and catalog showrooms). Today, many retailers are banding together in corporate and contractual *retail organizations* (corporate chains, voluntary chains and retailer cooperatives, franchise organizations, and merchandising conglomerates).

Although most goods and services are sold through stores, nonstore retailing has been growing much faster than store retailing. *Nonstore retailers* now account for more than 14 percent of all consumer purchases, and they may account for a third of all sales by the end of the century. Nonstore retailing consists of *direct marketing*, *direct selling*, and *automatic vending*.

3. Identify the major types of wholesalers and give examples of each.

Wholesalers fall into three groups. First, *merchant wholesalers* take possession of the goods. They include *full-service wholesalers* (wholesale merchants, industrial distributors) and *limited-service wholesalers* (cash-and-carry wholesalers, truck wholesalers, drop shippers, rack jobbers, producers' cooperatives, and mail-order wholesalers). Second, *brokers* and *agents* do not take possession of the goods but are paid a commission for aiding buying and selling. Finally, *manufacturers' sales branches and offices* are wholesaling operations conducted by nonwholesalers to bypass the wholesalers.

4. Explain the marketing decisions facing retailers and wholesalers.

Each retailer must make decisions about its target markets, product assortment and services, price, promotion, and place. Retailers need to choose target markets carefully and position themselves strongly. Today, wholesaling is holding its own in the economy. Progressive wholesalers are adapting their services to the needs of target customers and are seeking cost-reducing methods of doing business. Faced with slow growth in their domestic markets and developments such as the North American Free Trade Association, many large wholesalers are also now going global.

Navigating the Key Terms

For a detailed analysis of the meaning and importance of each of the following key terms, visit our Web page at **www.prenhall.com/kotler.**

Agent
Automatic vending
Broker
Category killer
Chain stores
Convenience store

Department store
Direct marketing
Discount store
Door-to-door retailing
Factory outlets
Franchise
Independent off-price retailer
Manufacturers' sales branches and offices
Merchant wholesaler
Off-price retailer

Retailers
Retailing
Shopping center
Specialty store
Supermarkets
Superstore
Warehouse club
Wheel of retailing concept
Wholesaler
Wholesaling

Travel Log

The following concept checks and discussion questions will help you to keep track of and apply the concepts you've studied in this chapter.

Concept Checks

1. _____ includes all the activities involved in selling goods or services directly to final consumers for their personal, nonbusiness use.

2. Retailers can be classified by the length and breadth of their product assortments. _____ stores carry narrow product lines with deep assortments within those lines.

3. Superstores the size of airplane hangars that carry a deep assortment of a particular line with a knowledgeable staff are called _____.

4. The major types of retail organizations include corporate chains, _____, _____, and _____.

5. _____ consists of direct communications with carefully targeted individual consumers to obtain an immediate response.

6. When establishing themselves, retailers must decide on three major product variables: _____, _____, and _____.

7. Retailers often cite three critical factors in retailing success: _____, _____, and _____!

8. _____ includes all activities involved in selling goods and services to those buying for resale or business use.

9. Typical functions performed by wholesalers include: (a) selling and promoting, (b) _____, (c) _____, (d) _____, (e) _____, (f) _____, (g) risk bearing, (h) market information, and (i) management services and advice.

10. _____ are the largest single group of wholesalers, accounting for roughly 50 percent of all wholesaling.*

Discussing the Issues

1. Warehouse clubs such as Costco and Sam's Wholesale are restricted to members only and are growing rapidly. They offer a very broad but shallow line of products, often in institutional packaging, at very low prices. Some members buy for resale, others buy to supply a business, and still others buy for personal use. Are such store chains wholesalers or retailers? Explain.

2. Off-price retailers provide tough price competition to other types of retailers. How do you think the growing power of other large retailers will affect the willingness of manufacturers to sell to off-price retailers at or below regular wholesale rates? What policy should Sony establish for selling the following products to off-price retailers: (a) big-screen

televisions, (b) HDTV televisions, (c) regular televisions, (d) stereo sound systems, (e) VCRs, and (f) Walkman cassette players? Explain.
3. According to Marketing At Work 11-3, retailing has gone on-line. (a) How will going on-line change the competitive balance between store retailers, direct marketers, catalog marketers, wholesalers, and direct purchasing from manufacturers? (b) What are the potential pitfalls of on-line retailing? (c) What do you think will be the future of this practice?

4. Compare the fundamental marketing decisions made by retailers, wholesalers, and manufacturers. Give examples that show the similarities and differences in decisions made by the three groups.
5. Take a retail form in your immediate market area and describe how it has gone through the stages of the "wheel of retailing." What will be the next stage for the retail form?

* *Concept check answers:* 1. retailing; 2. specialty; 3. category killers; 4. voluntary chains and retailer cooperatives, franchise organizations, merchandising conglomerates; 5. direct marketing; 6. product assortment, services mix, store atmosphere; 7. location, location, location; 8. wholesaling; 9. buying and assortment building, bulk-breaking, warehousing, transportation, financing; 10. merchant wholesalers.

Traveling the Net

Point of Interest: Virtual Retailing

As American consumers demand increasing service and customization from retailers and manufacturers, virtual retailing seems to have an ever-brighter future. Exactly what is virtual retailing? It is the ability of a seller to come directly into your home, at your convenience, and allow you to participate in designing your own personalized product and shopping experience. Sound great? Many think so. Imagine—no more ill-fitting bathing suits, and no greeting cards that seem like they were written for someone else, no more high-pressure salespeople, no more congested shopping mall parking lots. And, at virtual retail sites, you can spend as much or as little time as you need to make up your mind. Through the wonders of virtual retailing, mass customization is now a reality. All you have to do is point and click. Examine the following Web sites for more information on customized clothes buying: (a) Gap (www.gap.com), (b) Interactive Custom Clothes (www.ic3d.com), (c) Callabay (www.Callabay.com), and (d) QVC's Fashion Advisor (www.QVC.com).

For Discussion

1. How does virtual retailing compare with more traditional shopping formats? What are the primary advantages of virtual retailing for consumers? The disadvantages?

2. What target markets would be most interested in virtual retailing? Do the Web sites you just visited appear to be appealing to those segments? Explain.
3. Based on your visits to the preceding Web sites, compare the marketing strategies of the various Web retailers.
4. Pick one of the Web sites and design your own article of clothing. (a) Discuss the pros and cons of your experience. (b) How was this experience different from buying in a retail store? (c) Would you be willing to purchase the item you designed?

Application Thinking

Today, the virtual retail store seems to be limited to clothing and fashion, greeting cards, automobiles, photographic communication, and computers and associated technologies. Popularity, familiarity, and advanced security will change this rapidly. Assume that you are the marketing manager for Toys 'Я' Us and that you've begun losing sales to on-line marketers such as eToys (www.etoys.com). Devise a virtual retailing plan for Toys 'Я' Us. Be certain to identify target markets, potential competitors, potential advantages, potential disadvantages, and keys to success. After you finish, evaluate your effort and discuss the future of virtual retailing on the Internet.

MAP—Marketing Applications

MAP Stop 11

If people had told you a few years ago that you would willingly stand in line to pay $2 for a cup of coffee, you'd have thought they were nuts. Not so any more. Consumers do it every day at the counters of the some 1,800 Starbuck's locations across the country. Daily espresso has become an expensive must for millions of Americans. However, as with all retailing trends, success may be fleeting without constant change. Starbuck's success has drawn an explosion of competitors from "look-a-likes," to grocery stores (and their sophisticated coffee aisles), to ice cream distributors, and even restaurants. Starbucks is at a crossroads. How can it maintain its phenomenal 42 percent earnings growth rate? The company has decided on expansion as the best course of action. Current expansion strategies include new product development (for example, Tiazzi—an icy concoction of tea and juice), expansion of past new product stars (Frappuccino—a cold-blended drink), and joint ventures (partnering with Pepsi to bottle Frappuccino and with Dreyers Grand Ice Cream to bottle coffee ice cream). Also in the works are expansions in traditional retail endeavors (such as more stores and more partnerships with retail giants such as Barnes & Noble booksellers), and moves into untested waters (opening several Cafe Starbucks and expansion into international markets).

Thinking Like a Marketing Manager

1. Assess Starbucks' retail strategy so far. Why has it been so successful? What appear to be its major strengths and weaknesses? From a competitive standpoint, how is Starbucks vulnerable?

2. How dependent does Starbucks' growth seem be on direct retail sales? Do you see any potential problems with the company's aggressive expansion plans? Will cannibalization among stores and formats be a problem?

3. Assume that you are the marketing manager for Starbucks. Design a growth strategy for the company for the next two years. Considering the company's current situation, look for new growth possibilities that will avoid cannibalism among existing outlets. What partnerships, alliances, and new-product alternatives seem to be "naturals" for the company? What forms of new competition do you think will emerge? How are competitors and other distribution forms likely to react to your plan? What will you do about this? Report your findings.

chapter 12

Integrated Marketing Communications: Advertising and Public Relations

ROAD MAP:
Previewing the Concepts

We'll forge ahead now into the last of the marketing mix tools—promotion. You'll find that promotion is not a single tool but rather a mix of several tools. Ideally, under the concept of *integrated marketing communications*, the company will carefully coordinate these promotion elements to deliver a clear, consistent, and compelling message about the organization and its products. We'll begin by introducing you to the various promotion mix tools and to the importance of integrated marketing communications. Then, we'll look more carefully at two of the tools—advertising and public relations. In the next two chapters, we'll visit personal selling, sales promotion, and direct and on-line marketing.

▶ After reading this chapter, you should be able to

1. discuss the process and advantages of integrated marketing communications
2. define the five promotion tools and discuss the factors that must be considered in shaping the overall promotion mix
3. describe and discuss the major decisions involved in developing an advertising program
4. explain how companies use public relations to communicate with their publics

First stop: Southwest Airlines. In an industry plagued by uneven sales and large losses, Southwest has experienced steady profitability for more than two decades. How? As you'll see, this rapidly growing airline offers its customers low fares, dependable service, and plenty of wacky fun. As importantly, it knows how to communicate these benefits to customers.

Founded 27 years ago at Love Field in Dallas, Southwest Airlines sees itself as the "love" airline. The company even uses LUV as its New York Stock Exchange symbol. Southwest showers most of this love on its passengers in the form of shockingly low prices for highly dependable, no-frills service. In 1992, Southwest received the U.S. Department of Transportation's first-ever Triple Crown Award for best on-time service, best baggage handling, *and* best customer service. Southwest rated first in customer satisfaction among the nation's nine major airlines. It repeated this feat in the years 1993 through 1996.

Customers have returned Southwest's love by making it the industry's most profitable airline. In an industry plagued by huge losses—$12.8 billion between 1990 and 1994 alone—Southwest has experienced 25 straight years of profits. In 1992, when the industry lost $3 billion, Southwest *made* $91 million. Over the past 10 years, its revenues have grown 388 percent and net earnings by 1,490 percent. Southwest has successfully beaten off determined challenges from several major competitors who have tried to copy

the Southwest formula, including Continental Lite, Delta Express, and Shuttle by United. In 1998, Southwest was recognized by *Fortune* magazine as one of the nation's six most admired companies. All this from an airline only one-quarter the size of industry leader American Airlines.

Southwest's amazing success results from two factors: a superior marketing strategy and outstanding marketing communications. The marketing strategy is a simple one: Southwest knows its niche and stays with it. It has positioned itself firmly as *the* short-haul, no-frills, low-price airline. Its average flight time is one hour; its average one-way fare just $75. In fact, its prices are so low that when it enters a new market, it actually increases total air traffic by attracting customers who might otherwise travel by car or bus. For example, when Southwest began its Louisville-Chicago flight at a one-way rate of $49 versus competitors' $250, total weekly air passenger traffic between the two cities increased from 8,000 to 26,000.

To these practical benefits, Southwest adds one more key positioning ingredient—lots of good fun. With its happy-go-lucky CEO, Herb Kelleher, leading the charge, Southwest refuses to take itself seriously. For example, when an aviation company once confronted Southwest for using its slogan, "Just Plane Smart," Kelleher challenged the company's CEO to a public arm-wrestling match, with the slogan going to the winner. Kelleher was quickly pinned, but the CEO showdown became a national media event, winning Southwest lots of publicity. Southwest was later allowed to continue using the slogan.

In another instance, Northwest Airlines ran ads claiming that it ranked number one in customer satisfaction among the nation's eight largest airlines. Southwest, which at the time rated number one among the *nine* largest airlines, responded in classic Southwest fashion. Print ads boldly proclaimed, "After lengthy deliberation at the highest levels, and extensive consultation with our legal department, we have arrived at an official corporate response to Northwest Airlines' claim to be number one in customer satisfaction. Liar, liar. Pants on fire."

As the arm wrestling and "Liar, liar" incidents suggest, Southwest has little trouble communicating with consumers in a very memorable way. But beyond these special cases, the airline dispenses a carefully coordinated flow of marketing communications, ranging from media advertising, special events, and public relations to direct marketing and personal selling.

Entering a new city presents the greatest communications challenge. For example, when Southwest entered Baltimore in 1993, East Coast consumers knew almost nothing about the airline. The Baltimore campaign began with public relations and community affairs events. Says the president of Southwest's advertising agency, "We always start out with the public relations side. . . . Then we integrate government relations, community affairs, service announcements, special events, and advertising and promotions. By the time Southwest comes into the market, the airline already is part of the community."

Five weeks before the first flight, CEO Kelleher and the Maryland's Governor William Schaefer held a news conference to announce Southwest's entry into Baltimore. The governor gave Kelleher a basket of products made in Maryland; Kelleher gave the governor a flotation device—a "lifesaver" from high airfares for the people of Baltimore. Southwest next dramatized its $49 fare between Baltimore and Cleveland by flying 49 school children to Cleveland for a day to visit the Rain Forest at Cleveland Metroparks Zoo. This event garnered substantial media coverage in both Baltimore and Cleveland.

A week later, Southwest employees took to Baltimore's streets, handing out fliers on street corners promoting Southwest's "Just Plane Smart" slogan. At about the same time, Southwest sent direct mail to frequent short-haul travelers in the Baltimore area offering a special promotion to join its Rapid Rewards frequent-flier program. The public relations and community affairs efforts set the stage. Next, the company began running "Just Plane Smart" television and print commercials, and outdoor ads shouted "Hello, Baltimore, Goodbye High Fares." The integrated communications campaign was incredibly successful. In all, 90,000 Baltimore passengers purchased tickets before the start of service—a company record for advance bookings.

When the introductory fanfare had settled down, Southwest set up a Baltimore marketing office to continue working on local advertising, promotions, and community events. And now, of course, Baltimore travelers will be treated to the unique brand of more personal communication dispensed by Southwest's cheerful employees.

Southwest workers often go out of their way to amuse, surprise, or somehow entertain passengers. During delays at the gate, ticket agents will award prizes to the passenger with the largest hole in his or her sock. Flight attendants have been known to hide in overhead luggage bins and then pop out when passengers start filing onboard. Veteran Southwest fliers looking for a few yuks have learned to listen up to announcements over the intercom. A recent effort: "Good morning ladies and gentlemen. Those of you who wish to smoke will please file out to our lounge on the wing, where you can enjoy our feature film, *Gone With the Wind*." On that same flight, an attendant later made this announcement: "Please pass all plastic cups to the center aisle so that we can wash them out and use them for the next group of passengers."

Southwest owes much of its success to its ability to deliver dependable no-frills, low-cost service to its customers. But success also depends on Southwest's skill at blending all of its promotion tools—advertising, sales promotion, public relations, personal selling, and direct marketing—into an integrated marketing communications program that communicates the Southwest story.[1]

Modern marketing calls for more than just developing a good product, pricing it attractively, and making it available to target customers. Companies must also *communicate* with current and prospective customers, and what they communicate should not be left to chance.

The Marketing Communications Mix

A modern company manages a complex marketing communications system (see Figure 12-1). The company communicates with its intermediaries (retailers and wholesalers), consumers, and various publics. In turn, the intermediaries communicate with their consumers and publics. Consumers have word-of-mouth communication with each other and with other publics. Meanwhile, each group provides feedback to every other group.

A company's total **marketing communications mix**, also called its **promotion mix**, consists of the specific blend of advertising, personal selling, sales promotion, public relations, and direct marketing tools that the company uses to pursue its advertising and marketing objectives. Definitions of the five major promotion tools follow:[2]

Advertising: Any paid form of nonpersonal presentation and promotion of ideas, goods, or services by an identified sponsor.

Personal selling: Personal presentation by the firm's sales force for the purpose of making sales and building customer relationships.

Sales promotion: Short-term incentives to encourage the purchase or sale of a product or service.

Public relations: Building good relations with the company's various publics by obtaining favorable publicity, building up a good corporate image, and handling or heading off unfavorable rumors, stories, and events.

Direct marketing: Direct communications with carefully targeted individual consumers to obtain an immediate response—the use of mail, telephone, fax, e-mail, and other nonpersonal tools to communicate directly with specific consumers or to solicit a direct response.

Each category involves specific tools. For example, advertising includes print, broadcast, outdoor, and other forms. Personal selling includes sales presentations, trade shows, and incentive programs. Sales promotion includes point-of-purchase displays, premiums,

Marketing communications mix (promotion mix)
The specific mix of advertising, personal selling, sales promotion, public relations, and a direct marketing tool a company uses to pursue its advertising and marketing objectives.

Advertising
Any paid form of nonpersonal presentation and promotion of ideas, goods, or services by an identified sponsor.

Personal selling
Personal presentation by the firm's sales force for the purpose of making sales and building customer relationships.

Sales promotion
Short-term incentives to encourage the purchase or sale of a product or service.

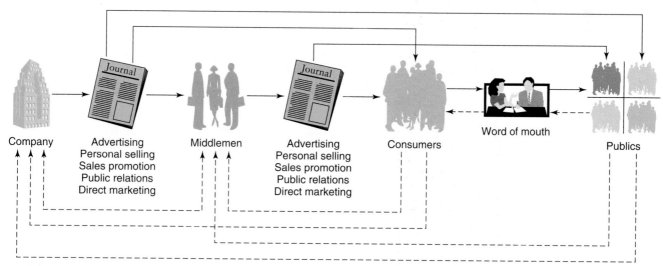

Figure 12-1
The marketing communications systems

Public relations
Building good relations with the company's various publics by obtaining favorable publicity, building up a good "corporate image," and handling or heading off unfavorable rumors, stories, and events.

Direct marketing
Direct communications with carefully targeted individual consumers to obtain an immediate response.

discounts, coupons, specialty advertising, and demonstrations. Direct marketing includes catalogs, telemarketing, fax, the Internet, and more. Thanks to technological breakthroughs, people can now communicate through traditional media (newspapers, radio, telephone, television), as well as through newer media forms (fax machines, cellular phones, pagers, and computers). The new technologies have encouraged more companies to move from mass communication to more targeted communication and one-to-one dialogue.

At the same time, communication goes beyond these specific promotion tools. The product's design, its price, the shape and color of its package, and the stores that sell it—*all* communicate something to buyers. Thus, although the promotion mix is the company's primary communication activity, the entire marketing mix—promotion *and* product, price, and place—must be coordinated for greatest communication impact.

In this chapter, we begin by examining the rapidly changing marketing communications environment, the concept of integrated marketing communications, and the marketing communication process. Next, we discuss the factors that marketing communicators must consider in shaping an overall communication mix. Finally, we look at the two mass-communication tools, *advertising* and *public relations*, in greater detail. Chapter 13 examines two more communication and promotion tools, *personal selling* and *sales promotion*. Chapter 14 reviews recent developments in *direct* and *on-line marketing*.

Integrated Marketing Communications

During the past several decades, companies around the world have perfected the art of mass marketing—selling highly standardized products to masses of customers. In the process, they have developed effective mass-media advertising techniques to support their mass-marketing strategies. These companies routinely invest millions of dollars in the mass media, reaching tens of millions of customers with a single ad. However, as we move into the twenty-first century, marketing managers face some new marketing communications realities.

The Changing Communications Environment

Two major factors are changing the face of today's marketing communications. First, as mass markets have fragmented, marketers are shifting away from mass marketing. More and more, they are developing focused marketing programs designed to build closer relationships with customers in more narrowly defined micromarkets. Second, vast improvements in information technology are speeding the movement toward segmented marketing. Today's information technology helps marketers to keep closer track of customer needs—more information about consumers at the individual and household levels is available more than ever before. New technologies also provide new communications avenues for reaching smaller customer segments with more tailored messages.

The shift from mass marketing to segmented marketing has had a dramatic impact on marketing communications. Just as mass marketing gave rise to a new generation of mass-media communications, the shift toward one-to-one marketing is spawning a new generation of more specialized and highly targeted communications efforts.[3]

Given this new communications environment, marketers must rethink the roles of various media and promotion mix tools. Mass-media advertising has long dominated the promotion mixes of consumer product companies. However, although television, magazines, and other mass media remain very important, their dominance is now declining. *Market* fragmentation has resulted in *media* fragmentation, in an explosion of more focused media that better match today's targeting strategies. For example, in 1975 what used to be the three major TV networks (ABC, CBS, and NBC) attracted 82 percent of the 24-hour viewing audience. By 1995 that number had dropped to only 35 percent, as cable television and satellite broadcasting systems offered advertisers dozens or even hundreds of alternative channels that reach smaller, specialized audiences. And it's expected to drop even further, down to 25 percent by the year 2005.[4] Similarly, the relatively few mass magazines of the 1940s and 1950s—*Look*, *Life*, *Saturday Evening Post*—have been replaced by more than 11,000 special-interest magazines reaching more focused audiences. Beyond these channels, advertisers are making increased use of new, highly targeted media, ranging from video screens on supermarket shopping carts to CD-ROM catalogs and Web sites on the Internet.

More generally, advertising appears to be giving way to other elements of the promotion mix. In the glory days of mass marketing, consumer product companies spent the lion's share of their promotion budgets on mass-media advertising. Today, media advertising captures only about 23 percent of total promotion spending.[5] The rest goes to various sales promotion activities, which can be focused more effectively on individual consumer and trade segments. They are using a richer variety of focused communication tools in an effort to reach their diverse target markets. In all, companies are doing less *broadcasting* and more *narrowcasting*.

The Need for Integrated Marketing Communications

The shift from mass marketing to targeted marketing, and the corresponding use of a richer mixture of communication channels and promotion tools, poses a problem for marketers. Consumers are being exposed to a greater variety of marketing communications from and about the company from a broader array of sources. However, customers don't distinguish between message sources the way marketers do. In the consumer's mind, advertising messages from different media such as television, magazines, or on-line sources blur into one. Messages delivered via different promotional approaches—such as advertising, personal selling, sales promotion, public relations, or direct marketing—all become part of a single message about the company. Conflicting messages from these different sources can result in confused company images and brand positions.

All too often, companies fail to integrate their various communications channels. The result is a hodgepodge of communications to consumers. Mass advertisements says one thing, a price promotion sends a different signal, a product label creates still another message, company sales literature says something altogether different, and the company's Web site seems out of sync with everything else.

The problem is that these communications often come from different company sources. Advertising messages are planned and implemented by the advertising department or advertising agency. Personal-selling communications are developed by sales management. Other functional specialists are responsible for public relations, sales promotion, direct marketing, on-line sites, and other forms of marketing communications.

In the past, no one person was responsible for thinking through the communication roles of the various promotion tools and coordinating the promotion mix. Today, however, more companies are adopting the concept of **integrated marketing communications (IMC)**. Under this concept, as illustrated in Figure 12-2, the company carefully integrates and coordinates its many communications channels to deliver a clear, consistent, and compelling message about the organization and its products.[6] As one marketing executive puts it, "IMC builds a strong brand identity in the marketplace by tying together and reinforcing all your images and messages. IMC means that all your corporate messages, positioning and images, and identity are coordinated across all [marketing communications]

Integrated marketing communications (IMC) The concept under which a company carefully integrates and coordinates its many communications channels to deliver a clear, consistent, and compelling message about the organization and its products.

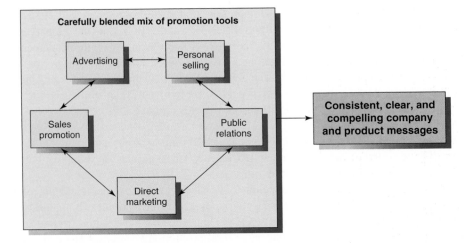

Figure 12-2
Integrated Marketing
Communications (IMC)

Marketing at Work 12-1

Integrated Marketing Communications at Hewlett-Packard

An ever-increasing number of companies are learning that carefully integrated marketing communications can pay big dividends. Hewlett-Packard is a good example. HP puts integrated marketing communications (IMC) to work in all of its business-to-business markets.

For example, HP's workstation division uses a closely coordinated mix of advertising, event marketing, direct and on-line marketing, and personal selling to sell workstations to high-level corporate buyers. At the broadest level, corporate image television ads, coupled with targeted ads in trade magazines, position HP as a supplier of high-quality solutions to customers' workstation problems. Overall, HP rates as one of the nation's top 10 media advertising spenders among technology companies. But beneath this broad advertising umbrella, HP then uses direct and Internet marketing to polish its image, update its customer database, and generate leads for the sales force.

IMC: Hewlett-Packard uses a closely coordinated mix of advertising, event marketing, direct marketing, and personal selling to sell its products to corporate buyers. To achieve coordination, HP assigns cross-functional teams made up of representatives from sales, advertising, marketing, production, and information systems to oversee its integrated communications efforts.

Finally, company sales reps follow up to close sales and build customer relationships.

True IMC involves more than a company's marketing department and ad agency, and it goes far beyond casually coordinating graphic design elements and key messages. HP managers warn that integrated marketing requires great dedication and practical rigor. It requires a whole-company effort

venues. It means that your PR materials say the same thing as your direct mail campaign, and your advertising has the same 'look and feel' as your Web site."[7]

To help implement integrated marketing communications, some companies appoint a marketing communications director, or *marcom manager*, who has overall responsibility for the company's communications efforts. Integrated marketing communications produces better communications consistency and greater sales impact. It places the responsibility in someone's hands, where none existed before, to unify the company's image as it is shaped by thousands of company activities. It leads to a total marketing communication strategy aimed at showing how the company and its products can help customers solve their problems (see Marketing at Work 12-1).

A View of the Communication Process

Integrated marketing communications involves identifying the target audience and shaping a well-coordinated promotional program to elicit the desired audience response. Too often, marketing communications focus on overcoming immediate awareness, image, or

and a strong customer focus. Perhaps the toughest challenge necessary to success is the intense and detailed coordination of the efforts of many company departments. To achieve coordination, HP assigns cross-functional teams made up of representatives from sales, advertising, marketing, production, and information systems to oversee its integrated communications efforts.

HP's software systems engineering division (SSED) began its IMC process with a cross-functional workshop aimed at developing a better understanding of customers' problems. "As we went through the workshop, we discovered that each group—sales, product marketing, engineering, customer support—understood a different aspect of our customers' needs," says SSED's marketing manager. She continues, "By integrating all these perspectives, we were able to really think constructively about how our product addressed these [needs]." Out of all this, SSED developed an integrated communications strategy centered on the theme "We understand," which emphasized HP's understanding of the issues, pressures, and con-

straints that software developers and their managers face. This theme was communicated throughout the division's marketing communications program, beginning with an advertising campaign, reinforced in three direct-mail pieces and a trade show handout, and finally on its Web site.

HP's highly successful program of "interactive audio teleconferences" illustrates the company's mastery of integrated communications. These teleconferences are like mammoth conference calls in which HP workstation representatives discuss key industry issues and HP practices with current and potential customers. To garner participation in the program, HP employs a five-week, seven-step "registration process." First, four weeks before a teleconference, HP mails out an introductory direct-mail package, complete with a toll-free number and business reply cards. One or two days after the mail package is received, HP telemarketers call prospects to register them for the conference, and registrations are confirmed immediately by direct mail. A week before the teleconference, HP mails out detailed briefing

packages, and three days before the event, calls are made again to confirm participation. A final confirmation call is made the day before the teleconference. Finally, one week after the event, HP uses follow-up direct mail and telemarketing to qualify sales leads and develop account profiles for sales reps.

What is the result of this integrated marketing communications effort? A response rate of 12 percent, as compared with just 1.5 percent using a traditional mail and telemarketing approach. Moreover, 82 percent of those who say they'll participate actually take part, as compared with only 40 percent for past, nonsynchronized efforts. The program has generated qualified sales leads at 200 percent above the forecasted level, and the average workstation sale has increased 500 percent.

Sources: Portions based on Mark Suchecki, "Integrated Marketing: Making It Pay," *Direct,* October 1993, p. 43; and P. Griffith Lindell, "You Need Integrated Attitude to Develop IMC," *Marketing News,* May 26, 1997, p. 6. Also see Erika Rasmusson, "The Channels to Watch," *Sales & Marketing Management,* March 1998, pp. 54–56; Kathryn Dennis, "Who's Spending What and Where?" *MC Technology Marketing Intelligence,* April 1998, pp. 32–38; and Bradley Johnson, "Hewlett-Packard Takes Step to Consolidation," *Advertising Age,* April 26, 1999, p. 2.

preference problems in the target market. But this approach to communication is short-sighted. Today, marketers are moving toward viewing communications as the *management of the customer buying process over time*, during the preselling, selling, consuming, and postconsumption stages. Because customers differ, communications programs need to be developed for specific segments, niches, and even individuals. And, given the new interactive communications technologies, companies must ask not only "How can we reach our customers?" but also "How can we find ways to let our customers reach us?"

Thus, the communications process should start with an audit of all the potential interactions target customers may have with the product and company. For example, someone purchasing a new computer may talk to others, see television ads, read articles and ads in newspapers and magazines, visit various Web sites, and try out computers in the store. The marketer needs to assess the influence that each of these communications experiences will have at different stages of the buying process. This understanding will help marketers allocate their communication dollars more efficiently and effectively.

Setting the Overall Communication Mix

The concept of integrated marketing communications suggests that the company must blend the promotion tools carefully into a coordinated *promotion mix*. But how does the company determine what mix of promotion tools it will use? Companies within the same industry differ greatly in the design of their promotion mixes. For example, Avon spends most of its promotion funds on personal selling and direct marketing, whereas Revlon spends heavily on consumer advertising. Compaq Computer relies on advertising and promotion to retailers, whereas Dell Computer uses only direct marketing. We now look at factors that influence the marketer's choice of promotion tools.

The Nature of Each Promotion Tool

Each promotion tool has unique characteristics and costs. Marketers must understand these characteristics in selecting their tools.

Advertising Advertising can reach masses of geographically dispersed buyers at a low cost per exposure, and it enables the seller to repeat a message many times. Large-scale advertising says something positive about the seller's size, popularity, and success. Because of advertising's public nature, consumers tend to view advertised products as more legitimate. Advertising is also very expressive—it allows the company to dramatize its products through the artful use of visuals, print, sound, and color. On the one hand, advertising can be used to build up a long-term image for a product (such as Coca-Cola ads). On the other hand, advertising can trigger quick sales (as when Sears advertises a weekend sale).

Advertising also has some shortcomings. Although it reaches many people quickly, advertising is impersonal and cannot be as directly persuasive as company salespeople. For the most part, advertising can carry on only a one-way communication with the audience, and the audience does not feel that it has to pay attention or respond. In addition, advertising can be very costly. Although some advertising forms, such as newspaper and radio advertising, can be done on smaller budgets, other forms, such as network TV advertising, require very large budgets.

With personal selling, the customer feels a greater need to listen and respond, even if the response is a polite "no thank you."

Personal Selling Personal selling is the most effective tool at certain stages of the buying process, particularly in building up buyers' preferences, convictions, and actions. It involves personal interaction between two or more people, so each person can observe the other's needs and characteristics and make quick adjustments. Personal selling also allows all kinds of relationships to spring up, ranging from a matter-of-fact selling relationship to personal friendship. The effective salesperson keeps the customer's interests at heart in order to build a long-term relationship. Finally, with personal selling the buyer usually feels a greater need to listen and respond, even if the response is a polite "no thank you."

These unique qualities come at a cost, however. A sales force requires a longer-term commitment than does advertising—advertising can be turned on and off, but sales force size is harder to change. Personal selling is also the company's most expensive promotion tool, often costing companies well over $200 per sales call. U.S. firms spend up to three times as much on personal selling as they do on advertising.

Sales Promotion Sales promotion includes a wide assortment of tools—coupons, contests, cents-off deals, premiums, and others—all of which have many unique qualities. They attract consumer attention, offer strong incentives to purchase, and can be used to dramatize product offers and to boost sagging sales. Sales promotions invite and reward quick response; whereas advertising says, "Buy our product," sales promotion says, "Buy it now." Sales-promotion effects are often short-lived, however, and often are not as effective as advertising or personal selling in building long-run brand preference.

Public Relations Public relations is very believable: News stories, features, and events seem more real and believable to readers than ads do. Public relations can also reach many prospects who avoid salespeople and advertisements: The message gets to the buyers as "news" rather than as a sales-directed communication. And, as with advertising, public relations can dramatize a company or product. Marketers tend to underuse public relations or to use it as an afterthought. Yet a well-thought-out public relations campaign used with other promotion-mix elements can be very effective and economical.

Direct Marketing Although there are many forms of direct marketing—direct mail, telemarketing, electronic marketing, on-line marketing, and others—they all share four distinctive characteristics. Direct marketing is *nonpublic*: The message is normally addressed to a specific person. Direct marketing also is *immediate* and *customized*: Messages can be prepared very quickly, and they can be tailored to appeal to specific consumers. Finally, direct marketing is *interactive*: It allows a dialogue between the marketing and the consumer, and messages can be altered depending on the consumer's response. Thus, direct marketing is well suited to highly targeted marketing efforts and to building one-to-one customer relationships.

Promotion-Mix Strategies

Push strategy
A promotion strategy that calls for using the sales force and trade promotion to push the product through channels.

Pull strategy
A promotion strategy that calls for spending a lot on advertising and consumer promotion to build up consumer demand.

Marketers can choose from two basic promotion-mix strategies—*push* promotion or *pull* promotion. Figure 12-3 contrasts the two strategies. The relative emphasis on the specific promotion tools differs for push and pull strategies. A **push strategy** involves "pushing" the product through distribution channels to final consumers. The producer directs its marketing activities (primarily personal selling and trade promotion) toward channel members to induce them to carry the product and to promote it to final consumers. Using a **pull strategy**, the producer directs its marketing activities (primarily advertising and consumer promotion) toward final consumers to induce them to buy the product. If the pull strategy is effective, consumers will then demand the product from channel members, who will in turn demand it from producers. Thus, under a pull strategy, consumer demand "pulls" the product through the channels.

Some small, industrial goods companies use only push strategies; some direct-marketing companies use only pull. However, most large companies use some combination of both. For example, Frito-Lay uses mass-media advertising to pull its products, and a large sales force and trade promotions to push its products through the channels. In recent years, consumer goods companies have been decreasing the pull portions of their promotion mixes in favor of more push.

Companies consider many factors when developing their promotion-mix strategies, including *type of product/market* and the *product life-cycle stage*. For example, the importance of different promotion tools varies between consumer and business markets.

Figure 12-3
Push versus pull promotion strategy

Consumer goods companies usually "pull" more, putting more of their funds into advertising, followed by sales promotion, personal selling, and then public relations. In contrast, business-to-business marketers tend to "push" more, putting more of their funds into personal selling, followed by sales promotion, advertising, and public relations. In general, personal selling is used more heavily with expensive and risky goods and in markets with fewer and larger sellers.

The effects of different promotion tools also vary with stages of the product life cycle. In the introduction stage, advertising and public relations are good for producing high awareness, and sales promotion is useful in promoting early trial. Personal selling must be used to get the trade to carry the product. In the growth stage, advertising and public relations continue to be powerful influences, whereas sales promotion can be reduced because fewer incentives are needed. In the mature stage, sales promotion again becomes important relative to advertising. Buyers know the brands, and advertising is needed only to remind them of the product. In the decline stage, advertising is kept at a reminder level, public relations is dropped, and salespeople give the product only a little attention. Sales promotion, however, might continue strong.

Socially Responsible Marketing Communication

In shaping its promotion mix, a company must be aware of the large body of legal and ethical issues surrounding marketing communications. Most marketers work hard to communicate openly and honestly with consumers and resellers. Still, abuses may occur, and public policy makers have developed a substantial body of laws and regulations to govern advertising, sales-promotion, personal-selling, and direct-marketing activities. In this section, we discuss issues regarding advertising, sales promotion, and personal selling. Issues regarding direct marketing are addressed in chapter 14.

Advertising and Sales Promotion By law, companies must avoid false or deceptive advertising. Advertisers must not make false claims, such as suggesting that a product cures something when it does not. They must avoid ads that have the capacity to deceive, even though no one actually may be deceived. An automobile cannot be advertised as getting 32 miles per gallon unless it does so under typical conditions, and a diet bread cannot be advertised as having fewer calories simply because its slices are thinner.

Sellers must avoid bait-and-switch advertising that attracts buyers under false pretenses. For example, a large retailer advertised a sewing machine at $179. However, when consumers tried to buy the advertised machine, the seller downplayed its features, placed faulty machines on showroom floors, understated the machine's performance, and took other actions in an attempt to switch buyers to a more expensive machine. Such actions are both unethical and illegal.

A company's trade promotion activities also are closely regulated. For example, under the Robinson-Patman Act, sellers cannot favor certain customers through their use of trade promotions. They must make promotional allowances and services available to all resellers on proportionately equal terms.

Beyond simply avoiding legal pitfalls, such as deceptive or bait-and-switch advertising, companies can use advertising to encourage and promote socially responsible programs and actions. For example, State Farm joined with the National Council for Social Studies, National Science Teachers Association, and other national teachers' organizations to create a Good Neighbor Award to recognize primary and secondary teachers for innovation, leadership, and involvement in their profession. State Farm promotes the award through a series of print advertisements. Similarly, Caterpillar is one of several companies and environmental groups forming the Tropical Forest Foundation, which is

Social responsibility: State Farm encourages and promotes social responsibility with its Good Neighbor Award ads.

working to save the great Amazon rain forest. It uses advertising to promote the cause and its involvement.

Personal Selling A company's salespeople must follow the rules of "fair competition." Most states have enacted deceptive sales acts that spell out what is not allowed. For example, salespeople may not lie to consumers or mislead them about the advantages of buying a product. To avoid bait-and-switch practices, salespeople's statements must match advertising claims.

Different rules apply to consumers who are called on at home versus those who go to a store in search of a product. Because people called on at home may be taken by surprise and may be especially vulnerable to high-pressure selling techniques, the Federal Trade Commission (FTC) has adopted a *three-day cooling-off rule* to give special protection to customers who are not seeking products. Under this rule, customers who agree in their own homes to buy something costing more than $25 have 72 hours in which to cancel a contract or return merchandise and get their money back, no questions asked.

Much personal selling involves business-to-business trade. In selling to businesses, salespeople may not offer bribes to purchasing agents or to others who can influence a sale. They may not obtain or use technical or trade secrets of competitors through bribery or industrial espionage. Finally, salespeople must not disparage competitors or competing products by suggesting things that are not true.[8]

We now examine each major communication and promotion tool in more detail. The remaining sections of this chapter cover advertising and public relations. Subsequent chapters deal with personal selling, sales promotion, and direct and on-line marketing.

Linking the Concepts

Stop here for a moment. Flip back through and try to link the parts of the chapter you've read so far.

- How do the *integrated marketing communications* and *promotion-mix* concepts relate to one another?
- Describe the promotion mix of a company like Kellogg, Coca-Cola, Campbell, or some other consumer goods producer. What pull promotion elements does the company use? What push elements? Are the company's communications well integrated?

Advertising

Advertising can be traced back to the very beginnings of recorded history. Archaeologists working in the countries around the Mediterranean Sea have dug up signs announcing various events and offers. The Romans painted walls to announce gladiator fights, and the Phoenicians painted pictures promoting their wares on large rocks along parade routes. Modern advertising, however, is a far cry from these early efforts. U.S. advertisers now run up an annual advertising bill of more than $175 billion; worldwide ad spending exceeds $414 billion. Procter & Gamble, the world's leading advertiser, last year spent $2.8 billion on U.S. advertising. It spent a whopping $5.1 billion globally.[9]

Although advertising is used mostly by business firms, it also is used by a wide range of nonprofit organizations, professionals, and social agencies that advertise their causes to various target publics. In fact, the fortieth largest advertising spender is a nonprofit organization, the U.S. government. Advertising is a good way to inform and persuade, whether the purpose is to sell Coca-Cola worldwide or to get consumers in a developing nation to drink milk or use birth control.

Marketing management must make five important decisions when developing an advertising program (see Figure 12-4): *setting advertising objectives, setting advertising budgets, developing advertising strategy (message decisions and media decisions)*, and *evaluating advertising campaigns*.

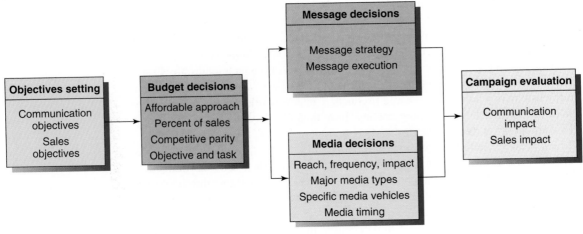

Figure 12-4
Major decisions in advertising

Setting Advertising Objectives

The first step is to set *advertising objectives*. These objectives should be based on past decisions about the target market, positioning, and marketing mix, which define the job that advertising must do in the total marketing program.

An **advertising objective** is a specific communication *task* to be accomplished with a specific *target* audience during a specific period of *time*. Advertising objectives can be classified by primary purpose: whether the aim is to *inform*, *persuade*, or *remind*. Table 12-1 lists examples of each of these objectives.

Informative advertising is used heavily when introducing a new product category. In this case, the objective is to build primary demand. Thus, producers of compact-disk players first informed consumers of the sound and convenience benefits of CDs. *Persuasive advertising* becomes more important as competition increases. Here, the company's

Advertising objective
A specific communication *task* to be accomplished with a specific *target* audience during a specific period of *time*.

Table 12-1 Possible Advertising Objectives

Informative advertising	Telling the market about a new product	Describing available services
	Suggesting new uses for a product	Correcting false impressions
	Informing the market of a price change	Reducing consumers' fears
	Explaining how the product works	Building a company image
Persuasive advertising	Building brand preference	Persuading customer to purchase now
	Encouraging switching to your brand	Persuading customer to receive a sales call
	Changing customer's perception of product attributes	
Reminder advertising	Reminding consumer that the product may be needed in the near future	Keeping it in customer's mind during off-seasons
	Reminding consumer where to buy it	Maintaining its top-of-mind awareness

objective is to build selective demand. For example, once compact-disk players were established, Sony began trying to persuade consumers that its brand offered the best quality for their money.

Some persuasive advertising has become *comparison advertising*, in which a company directly or indirectly compares its brand with one or more other brands. Comparison advertising has been used for products ranging from soft drinks and computers to batteries, pain relievers, long-distance telephone services, car rentals, and credit cards. For example, in its classic comparison campaign, Avis positioned itself against market-leading Hertz by claiming, "We're number two, so we try harder." More recently, Visa advertised, "American Express is offering you a new credit card, but you don't have to accept it. Heck, 7 million merchants don't." American Express responded with ads bashing Visa, noting that AmEx's green card offers benefits not available with Visa's regular card, such as rapid replacement of lost cards and higher credit limits. As often happens with comparison advertising, both sides complain that the other's ads are misleading.[10]

Reminder advertising is important for mature products; it keeps consumers thinking about the product. Expensive Coca-Cola ads on television are designed primarily to remind people about Coca-Cola, not to inform or persuade them.

Setting the Advertising Budget

After determining its advertising objectives, the company next sets its *advertising budget* for each product and market. Deciding how much to spend on advertising is one of the hardest marketing decisions facing a company. John Wanamaker, the department store magnate, once said, "I know that half of my advertising is wasted, but I don't know which half. I spent $2 million for advertising, and I don't know if that is half enough or twice too much." Thus, it is not surprising that companies vary widely in how much they spend on promotion. Even within a given industry, both low and high spenders can be found.

How does a company decide on its promotion budget? We look at four common methods used to set the total budget for advertising: the *affordable method*, the *percentage-of-sales method*, the *competitive-parity method*, and the *objective-and-task method*.[11]

Affordable Method Some companies use the **affordable method**: They set the promotion budget at the level they think the company can afford. Small businesses often use this method, reasoning that the company cannot spend more on advertising than it has. They start with total revenues, deduct operating expenses and capital outlays, and then devote some portion of the remaining funds to advertising.

Affordable method
Setting the promotion budget at the level management thinks the company can afford.

Unfortunately, this method of setting budgets completely ignores the effects of promotion on sales. It tends to place advertising last among spending priorities, even in situations in which advertising is critical to the firm's success. It leads to an uncertain annual promotion budget, which makes long-range market planning difficult. Although the affordable method can result in overspending on advertising, it more often results in underspending.

Percentage-of-Sales Method Other companies use the **percentage-of-sales method**, setting their promotion budget at a certain percentage of current or forecasted sales. Or they budget a percentage of the unit sales price. The percentage-of-sales method has advantages. It is simple to use and helps management think about the relationships between promotion spending, selling price, and profit per unit.

Percentage-of-sales method
Setting the promotion budget at a certain percentage of current or forecasted sales or as a percentage of the unit sales price.

Despite these claimed advantages, however, the percentage-of-sales method has little to justify it. It wrongly views sales as the *cause* of promotion rather than as the *result*. "A study in this area found good correlation between investments in advertising and the strength of the brands concerned—but it turned out to be effect and cause, not cause and effect. . . . The strongest brands had the highest sales and could afford the biggest investments in advertising!"[12] Thus, the percentage-of-sales budget is based on availability of funds rather than on opportunities. It may prevent the increased spending sometimes needed to turn around falling sales. Because the budget varies with year-to-year sales, long-range planning is difficult. Finally, the method does not provide any basis for choosing a *specific* percentage, except what has been done in the past or what competitors are doing.

Competitive-parity method
Setting the promotion budget to match competitors' outlays.

Competitive-Parity Method Still other companies use the **competitive-parity method**, setting their promotion budgets to match competitors' outlays. They monitor competitors' advertising or get industry promotion spending estimates from publications or trade associations and then set their budgets based on the industry average.

Two arguments support this method. First, competitors' budgets represent the collective wisdom of the industry. Second, spending what competitors spend helps prevent promotion wars. Unfortunately, neither argument is valid. There are no grounds for believing that the competition has a better idea of what a company should be spending on promotion than does the company itself. Companies differ greatly, and each has its own special promotion needs. Finally, there is no evidence that budgets based on competitive parity prevent promotion wars.

Objective-and-task method
Developing the promotion budget by (1) defining specific objectives, (2) determining the tasks that must be performed to achieve these objectives, and (3) estimating the costs of performing these tasks. The sum of these costs is the proposed promotion budget.

Objective-and-Task Method The most logical budget-setting method is the **objective-and-task method**, whereby the company sets its promotion budget based on what it wants to accomplish with promotion. This budgeting method entails (1) defining specific promotion objectives, (2) determining the tasks needed to achieve these objectives, and (3) estimating the costs of performing these tasks. The sum of these costs is the proposed promotion budget.

The objective-and-task method forces management to spell out its assumptions about the relationship between dollars spent and promotion results. But it is also the most difficult method to use. Often, it is hard to figure out which specific tasks will achieve specific objectives. For example, suppose Sony wants 95 percent awareness for its latest camcorder model during the six-month introductory period. What specific advertising messages and media schedules should Sony use to attain this objective? How much would these messages and media schedules cost? Sony management must consider such questions, even though they are hard to answer.

No matter what method is used, setting the advertising budget is no easy task. Measuring the results of advertising spending remains an inexact science. How does a company know if it is spending the right amount? Some critics charge that large consumer packaged-goods firms tend to spend too much on advertising and business-to-business marketers generally underspend on advertising. They claim that, on the one hand, the large consumer companies use lots of image advertising without really knowing its effects. They overspend as a form of "insurance" against not spending enough. On the other hand, business advertisers tend to rely too heavily on their sales forces to bring in orders. They underestimate the power of company and product image in preselling industrial customers. Thus, they do not spend enough on advertising to build customer awareness and knowledge.

Developing Advertising Strategy

Advertising strategy consists of two major elements: creating advertising *messages* and selecting advertising *media*. In the past, companies often viewed media planning as secondary to the message-creation process. The creative department first created good advertisements, then the media department selected the best media for carrying these advertisements to desired target audiences. This often caused friction between creatives and media planners.

Today, however, media fragmentation, soaring media costs, and more focused target marketing strategies have promoted the importance of the media-planning function. In some cases, an advertising campaign might start with a great message idea, followed by the choice of appropriate media. In other cases, however, a campaign might begin with a good media opportunity, followed by advertisements designed to take advantage of that opportunity. Increasingly, companies are realizing the benefits of planning these two important elements *jointly*. Messages and media should blend harmoniously to create an effective overall advertising campaign (see Marketing at Work 12-2).

Creating the Advertising Message No matter how big the budget, advertising can succeed only if commercials gain attention and communicate well. Good advertising messages are especially important in today's costly and cluttered advertising environment. The average number of television channels beamed into U.S. homes has skyrocketed from 3 in 1950 to 47 today, and consumers have 11,500 magazines from which to choose.[13] Add the countless radio stations and a continuous barrage of catalogs, direct-mail and on-line ads, and out-of-home media, and consumers are being bombarded with ads at home, at work, and at all points in between.

Until recently, television viewers were pretty much a captive audience for advertisers. Viewers had only a few channels from which to choose. But with the growth in cable

These award-winning ads broke through advertising clutter by putting milk mustaches on familiar faces.

Marketing at Work 12-2
The Medium and the Message: A New Harmony

There's a creative revolution taking place in ad agencies today, but it isn't necessarily coming from the creatives. More and more, creative directors are turning to the media departments to make their best ideas work harder. Media planning is no longer an after-the-fact complement to a new ad campaign. Media planners are now working more closely than ever with creatives to allow media selection to help shape the creative process, often before a single ad is written. In some cases, media people are even initiating ideas for new campaigns.

Among the more noteworthy ad campaigns based on tight media-creative partnerships is the one for Absolut vodka, marketed by Seagram. The Absolut team and TBWA, its New York ad agency, meet once each year with a slew of magazines to set Absolut's media schedule. The schedule consists of up to 100 magazines, ranging from consumer and business magazines to theater playbills. The agency's creative department is charged with creating media-specific ads.

The result is a wonderful assortment of very creative ads for Absolut, tightly targeted to audiences of the media in which they appear. For example, an "Absolut Bravo" ad in playbills has roses adorning a clear bottle, while business magazines contain an "Absolut Merger" foldout. Los Angeles-area magazines carry "Absolut LA" ads featuring an LA-style swimming pool in the shape of

Media planners for Absolut Vodka work with creatives to design ads targeted to specific media audiences. "Absolut Bravo" appears in theater playbills. "Absolut Chicago" targets consumers in the Windy City.

an Absolut bottle. In New York-area magazines, "Absolut Manhattan" ads feature a satellite photo of

Manhattan, with Central Park assuming the distinctive outline of an Absolut bottle. In Chicago, the

TV, VCRs, and remote-control units, today's viewers have many more options. They can avoid ads by watching commercial-free cable channels. They can "zap" commercials by pushing the fast-forward button during taped programs. With remote control, they can instantly turn off the sound during a commercial or "zip" around the channels to see what else is on.

ABSOLUT CHICAGO.

TO SEND A GIFT OF ABSOLUT VODKA (EXCEPT WHERE PROHIBITED BY LAW) CALL 1-800-243-3787
PRODUCT OF SWEDEN. 40 AND 50% ALC/VOL (80 AND 100 PROOF). 100% GRAIN NEUTRAL SPIRITS. © 1998 CARILLON IMPORTERS, LTD., TEANECK, N.J.

expect, the creative content of the brand's award-winning Web site (www.absolutvodka.com) nicely matches the medium. It contains an interactive history of experimental animation, including works by the world's best contemporary animators. This theme advances the brand's involvement with contemporary art, which began in 1985 when artist Andy Warhol said that he would like to paint the Absolut bottle. Since then, Absolut has commissioned more than 600 artists to create their versions of the icon, many of which have been featured in Absolut ads.

At a time of soaring media costs and cluttered communication channels, increased creative-media harmony can pay big dividends. The Absolut experience has had a positive impact on TBWA's approach to the advertising creative process. Says the agency's CEO, "What [Absolut] has done for us is to give us a more open mind and put more demand on all departments to be creative in their ideas than might be the case otherwise." And closer cooperation between creative and media people has paid off handsomely for Absolut. Largely as a result of its breakthrough advertising, Absolut now captures a 63 percent share of the imported vodka market.

windy city, ads show an Absolut bottle with the letters on the label blown askew. An "Absolut Primary" ad run during the political season featured the well-known bottle spattered with mud. In some cases, the creatives even developed ads for magazines not yet on the schedule, as was the case with a clever "Absolut Centerfold" ad for Play-boy magazine. The ad portrayed a clear, unadorned Playmate bottle ("11-inch bust, 11-inch waist, 11-inch hips").

In all, Absolut has developed more than 500 ads for the almost two-decade-old campaign. The company has now taken its message-media creative passions onto the Internet. As you might

Sources: Information from Gary Levin, "'Meddling in Creative More Welcome," Advertising Age, April 9, 1990, pp. S4, S8; Todd Pruzan, "Beer, Liquor Marketers in Voting Spirits," Advertising Age, April 1, 1996, p. 21; Glen Fest, "Absolut Vodka," Mediaweek, January 27, 1997, p. 52; Laura Rich, "Nothing but Red Sky: Agency Wins Absolut Vodka Business," Adweek, January 5, 1998, p. 24; Lynne Roberts, "New Media Choice: Absolut Vodka," Marketing, April 9, 1998, p. 12; and the Q&A section at www.absolutvodka.com, July 1998.

Thus, just to gain and hold attention, today's advertising messages must be better planned, more imaginative, more entertaining, and more rewarding to consumers. "Today we have to entertain and not just sell, because if you try to sell directly and come off as boring or obnoxious, people are going to press the remote on you," points out one advertising executive. "When most TV viewers are armed with remote channel switchers, a commercial has to cut through the clutter and seize the viewers in one to three seconds, or they're gone," comments another.[14]

MESSAGE STRATEGY The first step in creating effective advertising messages is to decide what general message will be communicated to consumers—to plan a *message strategy*. The purpose of advertising is to get consumers to think about or react to the product or company in a certain way. People will react only if they believe that they will benefit from doing so. Thus, developing an effective message strategy begins with identifying customer *benefits* that can be used as advertising appeals. Ideally, advertising message strategy will follow directly from the company's broader positioning strategy.

Message strategy statements tend to be plain, straightforward outlines of benefits and positioning points that the advertiser wants to stress. The advertiser must next develop a compelling *creative concept*, or *"big idea"*, that will bring the message strategy to life in a distinctive and memorable way. At this stage, simple message ideas become great ad campaigns. Usually, a copywriter and art director will team up to generate many creative concepts, hoping that one of these concepts will turn out to be the big idea. The creative concept may emerge as a visualization, a phrase, or a combination of the two.

The creative concept will guide the choice of specific appeals to be used in an advertising campaign. *Advertising appeals* should have three characteristics. First, they should be *meaningful*, pointing out benefits that make the product more desirable or interesting to consumers. Second, appeals must be *believable*—consumers must believe that the product or service will deliver the promised benefits. However, the most meaningful and believable benefits may not be the best ones to feature. Appeals should also be *distinctive*—they should tell how the product is better than the competing brands. For example, the most meaningful benefit of owning a wristwatch is that it keeps accurate time, yet few watch ads feature this benefit. Instead, based on the distinctive benefits they offer, watch advertisers might select any of a number of advertising themes. For years, Timex has been the affordable watch that "Takes a lickin' and keeps on tickin.'" In contrast, Swatch has featured style and fashion, and Rolex stresses luxury and status.

MESSAGE EXECUTION The advertiser now has to turn the big idea into an actual ad execution that will capture the target market's attention and interest. The creative people must find the best style, tone, words, and format for executing the message. Any message can be presented in different *execution styles*, such as the following:

- *Slice of life:* This style shows one or more "typical" people using the product in a normal setting. For example, two mothers at a picnic discuss the nutritional benefits of Jif peanut butter.
- *Lifestyle:* This style shows how a product fits in with a particular lifestyle. For example, an ad for Mongoose mountain bikes shows a serious biker traversing remote and rugged but beautiful terrain and states, "There are places that are so awesome and so killer that you'd like to tell the whole world about them. But please, *don't.*"
- *Fantasy:* This style creates a fantasy around the product or its use. For instance, many ads are built around dream themes. Gap even introduced a perfume named Dream. Ads show a woman sleeping blissfully and suggests that the scent is "the stuff that clouds are made of." In another example, an ad for I Can't Believe It's Not Butter spray features a daydreaming sculptress whose work comes to life as romance-novel hunk Fabio. The company claims the campaign helped boost sales 17 percent.[15]
- *Mood or image:* This style builds a mood or image around the product, such as beauty, love, or serenity. No claim is made about the product except through suggestion. Bermuda tourism ads create such moods.

- *Musical:* This style shows one or more people or cartoon characters singing a song about the product. For example, one of the most famous ads in history was a Coca-Cola ad built around the song "I'd like to teach the world to sing."
- *Personality symbol:* This style creates a character that represents the product. The character might be *animated* (the Jolly Green Giant, Cap'n Crunch, Garfield the Cat) or *real* (the Marlboro man, Ol' Lonely the Maytag repairman, Betty Crocker, Morris the 9-Lives Cat).
- *Technical expertise:* This style shows the company's expertise in making the product. Thus, Maxwell House shows one of its buyers carefully selecting coffee beans, and Gallo tells about its many years of wine-making experience.
- *Scientific evidence:* This style presents survey or scientific evidence that the brand is better or better liked than one or more other brands. For years, Crest toothpaste has used scientific evidence to convince buyers that Crest is better than other brands at fighting cavities.
- *Testimonial evidence or endorsement:* This style features a highly believable or likable source endorsing the product. It could be ordinary people saying how much they like a given product ("My doctor said Mylanta") or a celebrity presenting the product. Many companies use actors or sports celebrities as product endorsers (see Marketing at Work 12-3).

The advertiser also must choose a *tone* for the ad. Procter & Gamble always uses a positive tone: Its ads say something very positive about its products. P&G also avoids humor that might take attention away from the message. In contrast, Taco Bell ads use humor, in the form of an odd but cute little Chihuahua that has put the phrase "Yo quiero Taco Bell," along with millions of tacos, on the tongues of U.S. consumers.

The advertiser must use memorable and attention-getting *words* in the ad. For example, rather than claiming simply that "a BMW is a well-engineered automobile," BMW uses more creative and higher-impact phrasing: "The ultimate driving machine." Instead of stating plainly that Hanes socks last longer than less-expensive ones, Hanes suggests, "Buy cheap socks and you'll pay through the toes."

Finally, *format* elements make a difference on an ad's impact as well as on its cost. A small change in ad design can make a big difference in its effect. The *illustration* is the first thing the reader notices; it must be strong enough to draw attention. Next, the *headline* must effectively entice the right people to read the copy. Finally, the *copy*, the main block of text in the ad, must be simple but strong and convincing. Moreover, these three elements must effectively work *together*.

Selecting Advertising Media The major steps in media selection are (1) deciding on *reach, frequency,* and *impact*; (2) choosing among major *media types*; (3) selecting specific *media vehicles*; and (4) deciding on *media timing*.

DECIDING ON REACH, FREQUENCY, AND IMPACT To select media, the advertiser must decide what reach and frequency are needed to achieve advertising objectives. *Reach* is a measure of the *percentage* of people in the target market who are exposed to the ad campaign during a given period of time. For example, the advertiser might try to reach 70 percent of the target market during the first three months of the campaign. *Frequency* is a measure of how many *times* the average person in the target market is exposed to the message. For example, the advertiser might want an average exposure frequency of three. The advertiser also must decide on the desired *media impact*, the *qualitative value* of a message exposure through a given medium. For example, for products that need to be demonstrated, messages on television may have more impact than messages on radio

Marketing at Work 12-3

Athletes as Endorsers: Nice Guys Finish First

Companies today are paying big bucks to have their products associated with big-name athletes. U.S. companies this year spent more than $1 billion for endorsement deals and licensing rights with perhaps 2000 athletes—10 times the spending of just a decade ago. With so much money riding on athletes as pitchpersons, companies are taking great care to put their money on endorsers with the right stuff. Consider the following example from *Forbes*:

"Kid, you've got the talent, but you've got a problem," barks Bill Laimbeer, one of basketball's all-time dirtiest players, at young superstar Grant Hill during a commercial for Fila. "You're too nice." A series of drills follows in which Laimbeer tries to teach Hill elbowing, tripping, referee abuse, cameraman pushing, nose

piercing—all the skills needed for today's modern athletes to make big money off the court and playing field. But the joke is on Laimbeer. A follow-up spot shows Hill calling his mom, asking her to rescue him. The next commercial in the series depicts Hill finally breaking free of Laimbeer's hold, despite 52 days of brainwashing at "Camp Tough Guy." "I've got to play with decency, honesty," he says as a ray of light dawns upon him. "I've got to play clean." Clean is now cool. Clean is also lucrative. For endorsing Fila's sneakers, Hill will get about $25 million over 5 years.

Thus, despite what Dennis Rodman, Charles Barkley, Deion Sanders, and a rogues' gallery of other thuggish professional athletes might have you believe, it's the nice guys who are finishing first. In fact, of the $203 million earned in

endorsements and licensing income by *Forbes* magazine's Super 40 list of top-earning athletes last year, $175 million went to athletes with sterling reputations.

Picking the wrong spokesperson can result in embarrassment and a tarnished image. Hertz found this out when it entrusted its good name to the care of O. J. Simpson. Pepsi and Kodak faced similar embarrassment when their spokesperson, boxer Mike Tyson, was accused of beating his wife and was later jailed for rape. The risks are even greater for small companies. According to *Forbes*:

When Dallas Cowboys star Michael Irvin was caught in a motel with go-go dancers and drugs, it was a blip on the radar screen at [sponsor] Nike, . . . which alone spends perhaps $100 million a year on endorsement contracts. But 13

Athletes as endorsers: Michael Jordan, Tiger Woods, and Pete Sampras. Clean is now cool. Clean is also lucrative.

because television uses sight *and* sound. The same message in one magazine (say, *Newsweek*) may be more believable than in another (say, *The National Enquirer*). In general, the more reach, frequency, and impact the advertiser seeks, the higher the advertising budget will have to be.

Toyota dealerships that had paid Irvin $120,000 to do a series of commercials had little choice but to pull the ads—swallowing $400,000 in production costs. . . . Rather than hire another athlete, the dealers created a cartoon monkey—no unpleasant surprises that way.

Manufacturers and advertisers seek an endorser's "halo effect," the positive association that surrounds a product after a popular sports celebrity has pitched it. *Forbes* notes:

The trend toward nice is very good news for good guys like baseball's iron man, Cal Ripken, Jr. . . . Ripken is a known quantity, a safe bet. . . . Throughout his 16-year career, Ripkin has taken only endorsement deals that would create and reinforce the image he desired. In his rookie year Ripken turned down a chance to make big money endorsing Jockey underwear with his then-teammate Jim Palmer. "I couldn't see myself (promoting) under-wear," says Ripken. "I chose a milk radio spot instead because that's the kind of person I am." Now the image is paying off. Ripken's endorsement fees have taken off, jetting from $1 million to $6 million in three years.

Another sports nice guy cashing in on the trend is Pete Sampras, one of the world's top tennis players, who pulled down $8 million in endorsements this year, twice his haul of four years ago. "You don't have to be a jerk," Sampras advises. The latest beneficiary is super nice-guy phenom Tiger Woods, whom many have tabbed as heir apparent to Air Jordan. To go with his tremendous talent, Woods has "brains, cover-boy style, a smile to die for, and charm for days," notes one sports journalist. After winning the 1997 Masters, the charismatic Woods landed sponsorship contracts with Nike, Titleist, American Express, and other companies totaling close to $100 million over five years.

Nice plays well overseas, too—increasingly important as brand names are marketed globally.

Chinese American tennis star Michael Chang has emerged as the most popular athlete in Asia by far. Reebok is basing its entire Asian strategy around him, as is Procter & Gamble's Rejoice (Pert Plus) shampoo line. What makes Asia so Chang crazy? It's not just his heritage. It's his persona, as well. On a continent where family is considered paramount, Chang is coached by his brother, and they travel frequently with their parents. He's properly humble and soft-spoken as well. "We've always been a very close-knit family, and I think that's pretty characteristic of Asian families, period," says Chang.

Few embody the new breed of superstar nice guy better than Grant Hill. His father played football at Yale, then with the Dallas Cowboys. Growing up, Grant practiced basketball, then the piano. Hill's idols back then included nice guys Michael Jordan, Julius Erving, and Arthur Ashe. That was the profile Fila was looking for in 1994. Says Howe Burch, Fila's vice-president for advertising, "We don't care if they're the best athlete in the world if he or she isn't a solid citizen." Hill's impact?

With Hill as spokesperson, Fila has become the third-largest sneaker maker domestically. Sales shot up 37 percent [last year] and another 40 percent this year, to $750 million. Hill's namesake shoe trails only Nike's Air Jordans in sales. . . . "He's played a big role in our success," says Burch.

Perhaps the ultimate advantage of having a likable personality is that it extends beyond the athlete's career. Arnold Palmer hasn't played golf seriously in 20 years, but sponsors still pay $15 million a year for his good-guy aura. And even after retirement from his long and venerable career, Michael Jordan, the granddaddy of celebrity endorsers, still pulls down more than $42 million a year from endorsements for such blue-chip sponsors as Nike, McDonald's, Quaker Oats, Sara Lee, and Wilson Sporting Goods. Jordan's enduring wholesomeness and universal appeal have made him a "superbrand" in his own right. His appeal will extend well into his retirement—most of his endorsement contracts extend 5 to 10 years into the future. Says one analyst, "He's another Arnold Palmer and Jack Nicklaus. He'll be around forever."

Sources: Extracts from Lane Randall, "Nice Guys Finish First," *Forbes,* December 16, 1996, pp. 236–42. Also see Susan Chandler, "Michael Jordan's Full Corporate Press," *Business Week,* April 7, 1997; Roy S. Johnson, "Tiger!" *Fortune,* May 12, 1997, pp. 73–84; Kellee Harris, "Athlete Endorsers Can Equal Net Worth," *Sporting Goods Business,* January 6, 1998, p. 14; and; Roy S. Johnson, "The Jordan Effect," *Fortune,* July 22, 1998, pp. 124–34; and Wayne Friedman, "Jordan the Star Athlete Retires, Jordan the Band Comes to Life," *Advertising Age,* January 18, 1999, p. 3.

CHOOSING AMONG MAJOR MEDIA TYPES The media planner has to know the reach, frequency, and impact of each of the major media types. As summarized in Table 12-2, the major media types are newspapers, television, direct mail, radio, magazines, outdoor, and on-line. Each medium has advantages and limitations.

Table 12-2   Profiles of Major Media Types

Medium	Advantages	Limitations
Newspapers	Flexibility; timeliness; good local market coverage; broad acceptability; high believability	Short life; poor reproduction quality; small pass-along audience
Television	Good mass-market coverage; low cost per exposure; combines sight, sound, and motion; appealing to the senses	High absolute costs; high clutter; fleeting exposure; less audience selectivity
Direct mail	High audience selectivity; flexibility; no ad competition within the same medium; allows personalization	Relatively high cost per exposure; "junk mail" image
Radio	Good local acceptance; high geographic and demographic selectivity; low cost	Audio only, fleeting exposure; low attention ("the half-heard" medium); fragmented audiences
Magazines	High geographic and demographic selectivity; credibility and prestige; high-quality reproduction; long life and good pass-along readership	Long ad-purchase lead time; high cost; no guarantee of position
Outdoor	Flexibility; high repeat exposure; low cost; low message competition; good positional selectivity	Little audience selectivity; creative limitations
On-line	High selectivity; low cost; immediacy; interactive capabilities	Small, demographically skewed audience; relatively low impact; audience controls exposure

Media planners consider many factors when making their media choices. The *media habits of target consumers* will affect media choice—advertisers look for media that reach target consumers effectively. So will the *nature of the product*; for example, fashions are best advertised in color magazines, and automobile performance is best demonstrated on television. Different *types of messages* may require different media. A message announcing a major sale tomorrow will require radio or newspapers; a message with a lot of technical data might require magazines, direct mailings, or an on-line ad and Web site. *Cost* is another major factor in media choice. For example, network television is very expensive—advertisers regularly pay $200,000 or more for 30 seconds of advertising time during a popular prime-time program, even more if it's an especially popular program such as *ER* ($565,000 per 30-second spot), *Frasier* ($475,000 per spot), or a megaevent such as the Super Bowl (more than $1.6 million).[16] Newspaper or radio advertising cost much less but also reach fewer consumers. The media planner looks at both the total cost of using a medium and at the cost per thousand exposures—the cost of reaching 1,000 people using the medium.

Media impact and cost must be reexamined regularly. For a long time, television and magazines have dominated in the media mixes of national advertisers, with other media often neglected. Recently, however, the costs and clutter of these media have gone up, audiences have dropped, and marketers are adopting strategies beamed at narrower segments. As a result, advertisers are increasingly turning to alternative media, ranging from cable TV and outdoor advertising to parking meters and shopping carts, that cost

Marketers have discovered a dazzling array of "alternative media."

less and target more effectively:

Tiny billboards on shopping carts, ads on shopping bags, and even advertising tiles on supermarket floors urge you to buy Jell-O Pudding Pops or Pampers. Signs atop parking meters hawk everything from Jeeps to Recipe dog food. A city bus rolls by, fully painted as a traveling ad for the Cezanne exhibit at your local art museum. You escape to the ballpark, only to find billboard-size video screens running Budweiser ads while a blimp with an electronic message board circles lazily over-head. You pay to see a movie at your local theater, but first you view a two-minute science fiction fantasy that turns out to be an ad for General Electric portable stereo boxes. Then the movie itself is full of not-so-subtle promotional plugs for Pepsi, Domino's Pizza, Fritos, or Ray Ban sunglasses. How about a quiet trip in the coun-try? Sorry—you find an enterprising farmer using his milk cows as four-legged billboards mounted with ads for Ben & Jerry's ice cream. At the airport its CNN Airport Network; at the local rail station, it's the Commuter Channel. Boats cruise along public beaches flashing advertising messages for Sundown Sunscreen or Gatorade as sunbathers spread their towels over ads for Skippy peanut butter pressed into the sand. Even church bulletins carry ads for Campbell's soup. All of this may leave you wondering if there are any commercial-free havens remaining for ad-weary consumers. The back seat of a taxi, perhaps, or public elevators, or stalls in a public restroom? Forget it! Each has already been invaded by innovative marketers.[17]

Some of these alternative media seem a bit farfetched, and they sometimes irritate consumers. But for many marketers, these media can save money and provide a way to hit selected consumers where they live, shop, work, and play.

SELECTING SPECIFIC MEDIA VEHICLES The media planner now must choose the best *media vehicles*, specific media within each general media type. For example, television vehicles include *ER*, and *ABC World News Tonight*. Magazine vehicles include *Newsweek*, *People*, and *Sports Illustrated*.

Media planners must compute the cost per thousand persons reached by a vehicle. For example, if a full-page, four-color advertisement in *Newsweek* costs $155,000 and *Newsweek*'s readership is 3.1 million people, the cost of reaching each group of 1,000 persons is $50. The same advertisement in *Business Week* may cost only $81,000 but reach only 875,000 persons—at a cost per thousand of about $93. The media planner ranks each magazine by cost per thousand and favor those magazines with the lower cost per thousand for reaching target consumers.[18]

The media planner must also consider the costs of producing ads for different media. Whereas newspaper ads may cost very little to produce, flashy television ads may cost millions. On average, U.S. advertisers pay $278,000 to produce a single 30-second television commercial. A few years ago, Nike paid a cool $2 million to make a single ad called "The Wall."[19]

In selecting media vehicles, the media planner must balance media cost measures against several media impact factors. First, the planner should balance costs against the media vehicle's *audience quality*. For a baby lotion advertisement, for example, *New Parents* magazine would have a high-exposure value; *Gentlemen's Quarterly* would have a low-exposure value. Second, the media planner should consider *audience attention*. Readers of *Vogue*, for example, typically pay more attention to ads than do *Newsweek* readers. Third, the planner should assess the vehicle's *editorial quality*: *Time* and the *Wall Street Journal* are more believable and prestigious than *The National Enquirer*.

DECIDING ON MEDIA TIMING The advertiser must also decide how to schedule the advertising over the course of a year. Suppose sales of a product peak in December and drop in March. The firm can vary its advertising to follow the seasonal pattern, to oppose the seasonal pattern, or to be the same all year. Most firms do some seasonal advertising. Some do *only* seasonal advertising: For example, Hallmark advertises its greeting cards only before major holidays.

Finally, the advertiser has to choose the pattern of the ads. *Continuity* means scheduling ads evenly within a given period. *Pulsing* means scheduling ads unevenly over a given time period. Thus, 52 ads could either be scheduled at one per week during the year or pulsed in several bursts. The idea is to advertise heavily for a short period to build awareness that carries over to the next advertising period. Those who favor pulsing feel that it can be used to achieve the same impact as a steady schedule but at a much lower cost. However, some media planners believe that although pulsing achieves minimal awareness, it sacrifices depth of advertising communications.

Recent advances in technology have had a substantial impact on the media planning and buying functions. Today, for example, new computer software applications called *optimizers* allow media planners to evaluate vast combinations of television programs and prices. Such programs help advertisers to make better decisions about which mix of networks, programs, and dayparts will yield the highest reach per ad dollar.[20]

Evaluating Advertising

The advertising program should evaluate both the communication effects and the sales effects of advertising regularly. Measuring the *communication effects* of an ad, *copy testing*, tells whether the ad is communicating well. Copy testing can be done before or after an ad is printed or broadcast. Before the ad is placed, the advertiser can show it to consumers, ask how they like it, and measure recall or attitude changes resulting from it. After the ad is run, the advertiser can measure how the ad affected consumer recall or product awareness, knowledge, and preference.

But what *sales* are caused by an ad that increases brand awareness by 20 percent and brand preference by 10 percent? The *sales effects* of advertising are often harder to measure than the communication effects. Sales are affected by many factors besides advertising, such as product features, price, and availability.

One way to measure the sales effect of advertising is to compare past sales with past advertising expenditures. Another way is through experiments. For example, to test the effects of different advertising spending levels, Pizza Hut could vary the amount it spends on advertising in different market areas and measure the differences in the resulting sales levels. It could spend the normal amount in one market area, half the normal amount in another area, and twice the normal amount in a third area. If the three market areas are similar, and if all other marketing efforts in the area are the same, then differences in sales in the three areas could be related to advertising level. More complex experiments could be designed to include other variables, such as difference in the ads or media used.

Other Advertising Considerations

In developing advertising strategies and programs, the company must address two additional questions. First, how the company will organize its advertising function—who will perform which advertising tasks? Second, how will the company adapt its advertising strategies and programs to the complexities of international markets?

Organizing for Advertising Different companies organize in different ways to handle advertising. In small companies, advertising might be handled by someone in the sales department. Large companies set up advertising departments whose job it is to set the advertising budget, work with the ad agency, and handle direct-mail advertising, dealer displays, and other advertising not done by the agency. Most large companies use outside advertising agencies because they offer several advantages.

How does an **advertising agency** work? Advertising agencies were started in the mid-to-late 1800s by salespeople and brokers who worked for the media and received a commission for selling advertising space to companies. As time passed, the salespeople began to help customers prepare their ads. Eventually, they formed agencies and grew closer to the advertisers than to the media. Today's agencies employ specialists who can often perform advertising tasks better than the company's own staff. Agencies also bring an outside point of view to solving the company's problems, along with lots of experience from working with different clients and situations. Thus, today, even companies with strong advertising departments of their own use advertising agencies.

> **Advertising agency**
> A marketing services firm that assists companies in planning, preparing, implementing, and evaluating all or portions of their advertising programs.

Some ad agencies are huge; the largest U.S. agency, J. Walter Thompson, has annual billings (the dollar amount of advertising placed for clients) of more than $2.7 billion. In recent years, many agencies have grown by gobbling up other agencies, thus creating huge agency holding companies. The largest of these agency "mega-groups," Omnicom Group, includes several large advertising, public relations, and promotion agencies—DDB Needham, BBDO, TBWA, and several others—with combined billings approaching $32 billion.[21] Most large advertising agencies have the staff and resources to handle all phases of an advertising campaign for even the largest of clients, from creating a marketing plan to developing ad campaigns and preparing, placing, and evaluating ads.

International Advertising Decisions International advertisers face many complexities not encountered by domestic advertisers. The most basic issue concerns the degree to which global advertising should be adapted to the unique characteristics of various country markets. Some large advertisers have attempted to support their global brands with highly standardized worldwide advertising, with campaigns that work as well in Bangkok as they do in Baltimore. For example, Jeep has created a worldwide brand image of ruggedness and reliability; Coca-Cola's Sprite brand uses standardized appeals to target the world's youth; and Nike urges Americans, Africans, Asians, and Europeans alike to think "I can." Standardization produces many benefits: lower advertising costs, greater global advertising coordination, and a more consistent worldwide image.

Standardization also has drawbacks. Most importantly, it ignores the fact that country markets differ greatly in their cultures, demographics, and economic conditions. Thus, most international advertisers "think globally but act locally." They develop global advertising *strategies* that make their worldwide advertising efforts more efficient and consistent. Then they adapt their advertising *programs* to make them more responsive to consumer needs and expectations within local markets.

Companies adapt their global advertising to varying degrees. Kellogg's Frosted Flakes commercials are almost identical worldwide, with only minor adjustments for local cultural differences. For example, one campaign uses a tennis theme that has worldwide appeal and features teenage actors with generic good looks—neither too Northern European nor too Latin American. Of course, Kellogg translates the commercials into different languages. In the English version, Tony growls, "They're Gr-r-reat!" whereas in the German version it's "Gr-r-rossartig!" Other adaptations are more subtle. In the

Gillette Sensor Excel for Women ads are almost identical worldwide, with only minor adjustments to suit the local culture.

American ad, after winning the match, Tony leaps over the net in celebration. In other versions, he simply "high fives" his young partner. The reason: Europeans do not jump over the net after winning at tennis.[22]

In contrast, Parker Pen Company changes its advertising substantially from country to country. In Germany, ads show a hand holding a Parker pen writing the headline, "This is how you write with precision." In the United Kingdom, where Parker is the brand leader, ads emphasize the exotic processes used to make pens, such as gently polishing the gold nibs with walnut chips. In the United States, ads stress status and image, with headlines such as, "Here's how you tell who's boss," and "There are times when it has to be Parker." In this way, the company creates different images that match customer motives in each market.[23]

Global advertisers face several additional problems. For instance, advertising media costs and availability differ vastly from country to country. Countries also differ in the extent to which they regulate advertising practices. Many countries have extensive systems of laws restricting how much a company can spend on advertising, the media used, the nature of advertising claims, and other aspects of the advertising program. Such restrictions often require advertisers to adapt their campaigns from country to country. Consider the following example:

> A 30-second Kellogg commercial produced for British TV would have to have [several] alterations to be acceptable [elsewhere] in Europe: Reference to iron and vitamins would have to be deleted in the Netherlands. A child wearing a Kellogg's T-shirt would be edited out in France where children are forbidden from endorsing products on TV. In Germany, the line "Kellogg makes cornflakes the best they've ever been" would be cut because of rules against making competitive claims. After alterations, the 30-second commercial would be [only] about five seconds long.[24]

Thus, although advertisers may develop global strategies to guide their overall advertising efforts, specific advertising programs must usually be adapted to meet local cultures and customs, media characteristics, and advertising regulations.

Linking the Concepts

Think about what goes on behind the scenes for the ads we all tend to take for granted.

- Pick a favorite print or television ad. Why do you like it? Do you think that it's effective? Can you think of an ad that people like that may not be effective?
- Dig a little deeper and learn about the campaign *behind* your ad. What are the campaign's objectives? What is its budget? Assess the campaign's message and media strategies. Looking beyond your own feelings about the ad, is the campaign likely to be effective?

Public Relations

Another major mass-promotion tool is *public relations*—building good relations with the company's various publics by obtaining favorable publicity, building up a good corporate image, and handling or heading off unfavorable rumors, stories, and events. Public relations departments may perform any or all of the following functions:[25]

- *Press relations or press agentry:* Creating and placing newsworthy information in the news media to attract attention to a person, product, or service.
- *Product publicity:* Publicizing specific products.
- *Public affairs:* Building and maintaining national or local community relations.
- *Lobbying:* Building and maintaining relations with legislators and government officials to influence legislation and regulation.
- *Investor relations:* Maintaining relationships with shareholders and others in the financial community.
- *Development:* Public relations with donors or members of nonprofit organizations to gain financial or volunteer support.

Public relations is used to promote products, people, places, ideas, activities, organizations, and even nations. Trade associations have used public relations to rebuild interest in declining commodities such as eggs, apples, milk, and potatoes. New York City turned its image around when its "I ♥ New York!" campaign took root, bringing millions more tourists to the city. Johnson & Johnson's masterly use of public relations played a major role in saving Tylenol from extinction after its product-tampering scare. Nations have used public relations to attract more tourists, foreign investment, and international support.

Marketing at Work 12-4
Public Relations: Stretching the Marketing Budget

Italian sports-car maker Lamborghini sells less than 100 of its cars each year in the United States. Marketing Lamborghinis is no simple matter. The car is pure poetry in motion, but at a steep price. The Diablo VT's 492-horsepower engine delivers a top speed of 202 MPH and goes from 0 to 60 MPH in just 4.1 seconds. The price: $239,000. Just to lease a Diablo VT runs $2,999 a month with a $52,000 down payment. Moreover, because so few Lamborghinis are sold, most people rarely see one. Thus, to gain exposure and persuade would-be buyers, the company must invest its modest $600,000 U.S. marketing budget carefully.

Lamborghini's eventual goal is to sell 1,500 to 2,000 units a year in the United States. This goal is based partly on expanding its product lineup to include a sport utility vehicle priced in the $75,000-to-$100,000 range. To reach this ambitious sales goal, however,

the car maker will need to increase its exposure and awareness. It currently advertises in several selective business, travel, and lifestyle magazines, emphasizing the car's speed and sensual beauty. In addition, the company recently fielded a direct-mail campaign to 50,000 prospective buyers with median household incomes of $1.5 million.

When it comes to advertising, however, $600,000 doesn't go far. So Lamborghini stretches its limited marketing budget with an assortment of less-expensive public relations efforts. The company actively courts the press. For example, it makes the car available to auto journalists for test drives. This resulted in a recent *New York Times* review describing the car as "kinetic sculpture, proof of affluence, and amusement park ride wrapped into one." After a test drive, a *Fortune* journalist wrote, "On the beauty meter, the screaming lemon-yellow

Diablo rates right up there with a roomful of Matisse originals. . . . Neighbors I have never met come rushing out of their homes to get a closer look." And after riding with Lamborghini's chief U.S. test driver, another journalist reported, "He fired up the engine and shot out of Lamborghini's vast and immaculate garage. He slammed the car sideways through the parking lot [and] a split second later straightened the Diablo out with a snap and hammered ahead. No swaying, no rolling, no hesitation, just unadulterated energy. It was an all-sensory extravaganza." Lamborghini also sponsors tasteful public relations events. For example, it recently held a cocktail party for 200 people at a Georgio Armani store in Boston, with an invitation list put together by the store and *The Robb Report*, a publication devoted to the lifestyles of the wealthy. Lamborghini is constantly seeking new ways to expose the car to its affluent audience. As

Public relations can have a strong impact on public awareness at a much lower cost than advertising (see Marketing at Work 12-4). The company does not pay for the space or time in the media. Rather, it pays for a staff to develop and circulate information and to manage events. If the company develops an interesting story, it could be picked up by several different media, having the same effect as advertising that would cost millions of dollars. And it would have more credibility than advertising. Public relations results can sometimes be spectacular.

✧ Georgia-Pacific developed a World's Fastest Roofer contest to give its roofing-contractor target market hands-on experience with Summit, a new high-quality shingle whose key feature was its ease of installation. Contestants installed 100 square feet of shingles, and judges chose the winner based on roofing speed and job quality. First prize was an all-expenses-paid trip to Hawaii for two. The contest began with eight regional eliminations held at G-P distribution centers around the country. Months in advance, each distribution center promoted the contest to area roofers using direct-mail promotional materials furnished by the G-P public relations department. In all, more than 150 roofers competed in the local contests. The eight regional winners were flown to Atlanta to compete in the national contest, timed to coincide with National Roofing Week. Tie-ins with a home-oriented

dealers to give prospective buyers a ride around the track in the days before a race. Says a Lamborghini executive, "We sold three cars by doing that last year at the Detroit Grand Prix." Also, for the first time, Lamborghini is making a demonstrator available to its 19 U.S. dealers so that prospects can test-drive the car without the dealer worrying about mileage and insurance costs.

Lamborghini's total annual U.S. *sales* of $22 million amount to only a tiny fraction of the *advertising budgets* of the major car makers. However, through the innovative use of public relations, the company successfully stretches its modest marketing budget to gain exposure among affluent buyers.

The $239,000 Lamborghini Diablo VT moved one journalist to say that "on the beauty meter . . . it rates right up there with a roomful of Matisse originals. . . . Neighbors I have never met come rushing out of their homes to get a closer look."

a result of good public relations efforts, the Lamborghini Diablo VT was designated as a pace car for the 1995 PPG Indy Car World Series. This gave Lamborghini exposure at 15 race sites and allowed local

Sources: Quotes from Raymond Serafin, "Even Lamborghini Must Think Marketing," *Advertising Age*, May 1, 1995, p. 4; Faye Rice, "Lamborghini's Sales Drive," *Fortune*, June 12, 1995, p. 13; and Sue Zesiger, "Driving with the Devil," *Fortune*, February 17, 1997, pp. 170–1. Also see Jean Halliday, "Ultraluxury Cars Avoid Traditional Marketing Path," *Advertising Age*, April 27, 1998, p. 27; and "Prestige Brands Such as Ferrari, Rolls, Lambo Spend Little on Ads," *Automotive News*, May 11, 1998, p. 8B.

Atlanta radio station resulted in widespread on-air promotion and raised several thousand dollars for an Atlanta children's hospital. The mayor of Atlanta issued a proclamation recognizing roofers, National Roofing Week, and Georgia-Pacific. Caps, T-shirts, and posters were used to merchandise the event both locally and nationally. After the contest, G-P sent a print and video media kit to key national media and media in the hometowns of contest participants. The budget: only $50,000 to $75,000. The results: The promotion generated more than 2.5 million media impressions and increased sales in Georgia-Pacific's targeted markets by 90 percent.

Despite its potential strengths, public relations is often described as a marketing stepchild because of its limited and scattered use. The public relations department is usually located at corporate headquarters. Its staff is so busy dealing with various publics—stockholders, employees, legislators, city officials—that public relations programs to support product marketing objectives may be ignored. And marketing managers and public relations practitioners do not always talk the same language. Many public relations practitioners see their job as simply communicating. In contrast, marketing managers tend to be much more interested in how advertising and public relations affect sales and profits.

This situation is changing, however. Many companies now want their public relations departments to manage all of their activities with a view toward marketing the company and improving the bottom line. Some companies are setting up special units called *marketing public relations* to support corporate and product promotion and image making directly. Many companies hire marketing public relations firms to handle their PR programs or to assist the company public relations team.

Major Public Relations Tools

Public relations professionals use several tools. One of the major tools is *news*. PR professionals find or create favorable news about the company and its products or people. Sometimes news stories occur naturally, and sometimes the PR person can suggest events or activities that would create news. *Speeches* can also create product and company publicity. Increasingly, company executives must field questions from the media or give talks at trade associations or sales meetings, and these events can either build or hurt the company's image.

Another common PR tool is *special events*, ranging from news conferences, press tours, grand openings, and fireworks displays to laser shows, hot-air balloon releases, multimedia presentations and star-studded spectaculars, or educational programs designed to reach and interest target publics. Here's an example of an interesting public relations program launched by Levi Strauss & Company:

✧   In the increasingly more casual business world, as companies relax their dress codes, they are often dismayed to find employees showing up at the office in anything from sweatsuits to torn jeans. Where can they turn for a little fashion advice? Levi Strauss & Company to the rescue! The world's largest apparel maker has put together an elaborate and stealthy program to help companies advise their people on how to dress casually without being sloppy. To promote the program initially, Levi mailed a newsletter to 65,000 human resource managers and sent videos to some 7,000 companies. During the past three years, the company has visited or advised more than 22,000 corporations, including Charles Schwab & Company, IBM, Nynex, and Aetna Life & Casualty. Through the program, Levi offers snazzy brochures and videos showing how to dress casually. Other activities range from putting on fashion shows and manning a toll-free number for employees who have questions about casual wear to holding seminars for human resource directors. Levi also created a Web page from which human resource managers can obtain advice and Levi's Casual Businesswear Kit, a detailed guide for starting and maintaining company dress policies. Levi's avoids outright product pitches. Instead, the company explains, it's simply "trying to create a dress code for dress-down wear." Of course, it wouldn't hurt if that wear had the Levi label attached.[26]

Public relations people also prepare *written materials* to reach and influence their target markets. These materials include annual reports, brochures, articles, and company newsletters and magazines. *Audiovisual materials*, such as films, slide-and-sound programs, and video- and audiocassettes, are being used increasingly as communication tools. *Corporate identity* materials can also help create a corporate identity that the public immediately recognizes. Logos, stationery, brochures, signs, business forms, business cards, buildings, uniforms, and company cars and trucks—all become marketing tools when they are attractive, distinctive, and memorable. Finally, companies can improve public goodwill by contributing money and time to *public service activities*.

A company's Web site can be a good public relations vehicle. Consumers and members of other publics can visit the site for information and entertainment. Such sites can be extremely popular. For example, Butterball's site (www.butterball.com), which features cooking and carving tips, received 550,000 visitors in one day during Thanksgiving week last year. Web sites can also be ideal for handling crisis situations. For example, when several bottles of Odwalla apple juice sold on the West Coast were found to contain

A company's Web site can be a good public relations vehicle. Butterball's site, which features cooking and carving tips, received 550,000 visitors in one day during Thanksgiving week last year.

E. coli bacteria, Odwalla initiated a massive product recall. Within only three hours, it set up a Web site laden with information about the crisis and Odwalla's response. Company staffers also combed the Internet looking for newsgroups discussing Odwalla and posted links to the site. In another example, American Home Products quickly set up a Web site to distribute accurate information and advice after a model died reportedly after inhaling its Primatene Mist. The Primatene site, up less than 12 hours after the crisis broke, remains in place today (www.primatene.com).[27]

As with the other promotion tools, in considering when and how to use product public relations, management should set PR objectives, choose the PR messages and vehicles, implement the PR plan, and evaluate the results. The firm's publics relations should be blended smoothly with other promotion activities within the company's overall integrated marketing communications effort.

REST STOP Reviewing the Concepts

In this chapter, you've learned in general about available promotion tools, promotion-mix strategies, and the concept of integrated marketing communications. We've also explored two of the promotion mix elements, advertising and public relations, more deeply. Before moving on to other promotion tools, let's briefly review the important concepts. Modern marketing calls for more than just developing a good product, pricing it attractively, and making it available to target customers. Companies also must *communicate* with current and prospective customers to inform them about product benefits and carefully position products in consumers' minds. To do this, they must blend five promotion-mix tools, guided by a well-designed and implemented integrated marketing communications strategy.

1. Discuss the process and advantages of integrated marketing communications.

Recent shifts toward targeted or one-to-one marketing, coupled with advances in information technology, have had a dramatic impact on marketing communications. As marketing communicators adopt richer but more fragmented media and promotion mixes to reach their diverse markets, they risk creating a communications hodgepodge for consumers. To prevent this, more companies are adopting the concept of *integrated marketing communications (IMC)*. Guided by an overall IMC strategy, the company works out the roles that the various promotional tools will play and the extent to which each will be used. It carefully coordinates the promotional activities and the timing of when major campaigns take place. Finally, to help implement its integrated marketing strategy, the company appoints a marketing communications director who has overall responsibility for the company's communications efforts.

2. Define the five promotion tools and discuss factors that must be considered in shaping the overall promotion mix.

A company's total *marketing communications mix*, also called its *promotion mix*, consists of the specific blend of *advertising*, *personal-selling*, *sales promotion*, *public relations*, and *direct-marketing* tools that the company uses to pursue its advertising and marketing objectives. Advertising includes any paid form of nonpersonal presentation and promotion of ideas, goods, or services by an identified sponsor. In contrast, public relations focuses on building good relations with the company's various publics by obtaining favorable unpaid publicity. Personal selling is any form of personal presentation by the firm's sales force for the purpose of making sales and building customer relationships. Firms use sales promotion to provide short-term incentives to encourage the purchase or sale of a product or service. Finally, firms seeking immediate response from targeted individual customers use nonpersonal direct-marketing tools to communicate with customers.

The company wants to create an integrated *promotion mix*. It can pursue a *push* or a *pull* promotional strategy, or a combination of the two. The best specific blend of promotion tools depends on the type of product/market and the product life-cycle stage. People at all levels of the organization must be aware of the many legal and ethical issues surrounding marketing communications.

3. Describe and discuss the major decisions involved in developing an advertising program.

Advertising—the use of paid media by a seller to inform, persuade, and remind about its products or organization—is a strong promotion tool that takes many forms and has many uses. *Advertising decision making* involves decisions about the objectives, the budget, the message, the media, and, finally, the evaluation of results. Advertisers should set clear *objectives* as to whether the advertising is supposed to inform, persuade, or remind buyers. The advertising *budget* can be based on what is affordable, on sales, on competitors' spending, or on the objectives and tasks. The *message decision* calls for planning a message strategy and executing it effectively. The *media decision* involves defining reach, frequency, and impact goals; choosing major media types; selecting media vehicles; and deciding on media timing. Message and media decisions must be closely coordinated for maximum campaign effectiveness. Finally, *evaluation* calls for evaluating the communication and sales effects of advertising before, during, and after the advertising is placed.

4. Explain how companies use public relations to communicate with their publics.

Public relations involves building good relations with the company's various publics. Its functions include *press agentry*, *product publicity*, *public affairs*, *lobbying*, *investor relations*, and *development*. Public relations can have a strong impact on public awareness at a much lower cost than advertising; and public relations results can sometimes be spectacular. Despite its potential strengths, however, public relations sometimes gets only limited and scattered use. Public relations tools include *news*, *speeches*, *special events*, *written materials*, *audiovisual materials*, *corporate identity materials*, and *public service activities*. A company's Web site can be a good public relations vehicle. In considering when and how to use product public relations, management should set PR objectives, choose the PR messages and vehicles, implement the PR plan, and evaluate the results. Publics relations should be blended smoothly with other promotion activities within the company's overall integrated marketing communications effort.

Navigating the Key Terms

For a detailed analysis of the meaning and importance of each of the following key terms, visit our Web page at **www.prenhall.com/kotler.**

Advertising
Advertising agency
Advertising objective

Affordable method
Competitive-parity method
Direct marketing
Integrated marketing communications
Marketing communications mix (promotion mix)
Objective-and-task method

Percentage-of-sales method
Personal selling
Public relations
Pull strategy
Push strategy
Sales promotion

Travel Log

The following concept checks and discussion questions will help you to keep track of and apply the concepts you've studied in this chapter.

Concept Checks

1. A company's promotion mix consists of a blend of _____, _____, _____, _____, and _____.

2. _____ is any paid form of nonpersonal presentation and promotion of ideas, goods, or services by an identified sponsor.

3. _____ builds strong brand identity in the marketplace by tying together and reinforcing all your images and messages.

4. _____ can reach masses of geographically dispersed buyers at a low cost per exposure, and it enables the seller to repeat a message many times.

5. Using a _____ promotion strategy, the producer directs its marketing activities (primarily advertising and consumer promotion) toward final consumers to induce them to buy the product.

6. Advertising objectives can be classified by primary purpose, whether the aim is to _____, _____, or _____.

7. There are four common methods used to set the total budget for advertising: the affordable method, the _____ method, the _____ method, and the _____ method.

8. Any advertising message can be presented in different execution styles. Under the _____ style, one or more "typical" people are shown using the product in normal setting (such as two mothers at a picnic discussing the nutritional benefits of JIF peanut butter).

9. _____ is a measure of the percentage of people in the target market who are exposed to the ad campaign during a given period of time.

10. Public relations departments perform many functions. Through _____, the department builds and maintains relations with legislators and government officials to influence legislation and regulation.*

Discussing the Issues

1. The shift from mass marketing to targeted marketing, and the corresponding use of a richer mixture of promotion tools and communication channels, poses problems for many marketers. Using all of the promotion-mix elements suggested in the chapter, propose a plan for integrating marketing communications at one of the following: (a) your university or college, (b) McDonald's, (c) Burton Snow

Boards, (d) a local zoo, museum, theater, or civic event. Discuss your findings in class.

2. Advertising objectives can be classified by primary purpose: to inform, persuade, or remind. Using your local newspaper, find examples of ads that address each of these objectives. Using Table 12.1, discuss why your examples fit the chosen objective.

3. Surveys show that many Americans are skeptical of advertising claims. (a) Do you mostly trust or mistrust advertising? Explain. (b) What type of advertising do you trust the most? the least? (c) Suggest some things the advertising industry could do to increase advertising credibility.

4. What factors call for more *frequency* in an advertising media schedule and what factors call for more *reach*? Can you increase one without sacrificing the other or increasing the advertising budget?

5. The latest public relations frontier is the Internet. Cyberspace travelers can now post their problems with goods and services on electronic bulletin boards and in company chat rooms, putting pressure on companies to respond. Customers regularly share their experiences with product design flaws, service difficulties, prices, warranties, and other problems. What kinds of special public relations problems and opportunities does cyberspace present to today's companies? How should companies change their company policies and Web sites to deal with these problems and opportunities? Find an example of a company that uses its Web site as a proactive public relations tool.

Concept check answers: 1. advertising, personal selling, sales promotion, public relations, and direct marketing; 2. advertising; 3. integrated marketing communications (IMC); 4. advertising; 5. pull; 6. inform, persuade, or remind; 7. percentage-of-sales, competitive-parity, and objective-and-task; 8. slice-of-life; 9. reach; 10. lobbying.

Traveling the Net

Point of Interest: Advertising Technological Products

The manufacturers of today's highly complicated computer products face a difficult task in figuring out how to advertise them effectively. Consumers do not appear to respond well to the detailed descriptions that are often needed to describe technological features and differences found in competing products. To make matters worse, the explosion in computer technology continues, and consumers face an ever more-bewildering selection of computer options from which to choose. How do you tell consumers in "plain terms" what they

need to know about this new generation of products without boring them with the details? Good question. The answer may be as close as the computer company's Web site. Experts predict that more and more consumers will be surfing the Internet for the product information they need rather than relying on traditional information sources. Examine the following Web sites for more information on new PC products: (a) Sharp (www.sharp-usa.com), (b) IBM (www.ibm.com), (c) NEC Computer Systems (www. nec.com), (d) Casio (www.casio.com), and (e) Sony (www.sony.com).

For Discussion

1. How is the marketing communication at these Web sites different from that found in traditional advertising media? Develop a grid that compares and critiques the two forms of marketing communication. Assess the advantages and disadvantages of each form.

2. Which of the companies listed above seems to be the most effective Web marketer for personal computer products? Explain.

3. After reviewing each of the preceding sites, pick a type of product that you might like to own (such as a laptop or handheld computer). (a) Based solely on the Web sites that you visited, which company and product most grabs your attention and purchasing interest? (b) Critique your information-gathering experience: What information was most useful? What features (such as price or warranty) caught your eye? How could the communications be improved? (c) Would you be willing to purchase the product via the Internet? Why or why not?

Application Thinking

The past few years have seen the emergence of a new generation of electronic and information products. Consumers can now carry electronic books in their palms, libraries on their laps, and their offices strapped over their shoulders. Marketers are under increasing pressure to provide better information products and better information about these products. Product costs do not seem to be the primary selection variable for such products. Of primary importance are dependability and the fulfillment of personal and business needs. Assume that you are the marketing manager for Casio (see www.casio.com for more information on the company). You plan to expand your product line into more expensive laptop versions of your traditionally smaller handheld products. Devise an advertising strategy to accompany this expansion. In preparing your plan, consider potential target markets, old and new competitors, potential distribution outlets, communications messages, and media choices. How much of your strategy will be based on your existing Web site? How will you set your advertising budget? Present your findings.

MAP—Marketing Applications

MAP Stop 12

One of the best recent examples of competitive integrated marketing communications warfare occurred in the fall of 1998 when DreamWorks's *Antz* went head-to-head against Disney/Pixar's *A Bug's Life*. These were not just superbly animated features designed to capture consumer dollars at the box office. They were all-out marketing efforts between two of the industry's giants. "Thou shalt not undermarket" became the battle cry. Both companies developed massive media blitzes, merchandise licensing (everything from toothbrushes and toys to bedsheets), public relations and sales promotion efforts directed at influential media (always with an eye toward Oscar nominations), and tie-ins of every imaginable description (such as McDonald's and Beanie Babies). The initial promotion budgets of the competitors were estimated at $75 and $100 million dollars each. And these initial expenditures were only the opening salvo in a longer-term battle between the two studios—their head-to-head competitive projects are expected through the year 2000. An additional wrinkle is speculation that Steve Jobs (the mastermind behind Apple Computer and Pixar) will use the success of *Toy Story* (1995) and *A Bug's Life* to form his own studio.

Thinking Like a Marketing Manager

1. Evaluate the integrated marketing communications strategies being used by DreamWorks and Disney/Pixar. From a competitive standpoint, which group do you believe to be the winner? Explain.

2. Explain how advertising for *A Bug's Life* through tie-ins (such as McDonald's and Ty's Beanie Babies) benefits both the movie company and the tie-in partner.

3. Assume that you are the marketing manager for either DreamWorks or Disney/Pixar. (a) Design an integrated communications strategy that goes beyond what has already been done. Focus on other possible tie-ins, the Internet, and licenses for products. Additional ideas can be obtained for your strategy by reading news stories about two companies and their movie products. (b) What can be learned about integrated marketing communications from this example?

Integrated Marketing Communications: Personal Selling and Sales Promotion

---

ROAD MAP:
Previewing the Concepts

In the previous chapter, you learned about integrated marketing communication (IMC) and two specific elements of the marketing communications mix—advertising and publicity. In this chapter, your journey continues with two new IMC stops—personal selling and sales promotion. Personal selling is the interpersonal arm of marketing communications in which the sales force interacts with customers and prospects to make sales and build relationships. Sales promotion is a collection of short-term incentives used to encourage purchase or support of a product or service. As you read on, remember that although this chapter examines personal selling and sales promotion as separate tools in the marketer's workshop, these tools must be carefully coordinated with other elements of the marketing communication mix.

▶ **After studying this chapter, you should be able to:**

1. discuss the role of a company's salespeople in creating value for customers and building customer relationships
2. identify and explain the six major sales force management steps
3. discuss the personal selling process, distinguishing between transaction-oriented marketing and relationship marketing
4. explain how sales promotion campaigns are developed and implemented

We'll begin this journey with a look at Lear Corporation's sales force. Although you may never have heard of Lear, the chances are good that you've spent lots of time in one or more of the car interiors that it supplies to the world's major automotive manufacturers. Before you read on, close your eyes for a moment and envision a typical salesperson. If what you see is a stereotypical glad-hander out to lighten your wallet or purse by selling you something that you don't really need, you might be in for a surprise.

When someone says "salesperson," what image comes to mind? Perhaps it's the stereotypical "traveling salesman"—the fast-talking, ever-smiling peddler who travels his territory foisting his wares on reluctant customers. Such stereotypes, however, are sadly out of date. Today, most professional salespeople are well educated, well trained men and women who work to build long-term, value-producing relationships with their customers. They succeed not by taking customers in but by helping them out, by assessing customer needs and solving customer problems.

Consider Lear Corporation, one of the largest, fastest-growing, and most successful automotive suppliers in the world. Each year, Lear produces more than $7.3 billion worth of automotive interiors—seat systems, instrument panels, door panels, floor and acoustic systems, and headliners. Its customers include most of the world's leading automotive companies, from Ford, General Motors, Fiat, and Volvo to Mercedes, Ferrari, Rolls-Royce,

and more than a dozen others. Lear now operates 190 facilities in 28 countries around the globe. During the past few years, Lear has achieved record-breaking sales and earnings growth. Last year, sales increased 18 percent; earnings surged 28 percent. Lear's sales during the past five years have more than tripled, and its "average content per car" in North America has increased more than fourfold since 1990.

Lear Corporation owes its success to many factors, including a strong customer orientation and a commitment to continuous improvement, teamwork, and customer value. But perhaps more than any other part of the organization, it's Lear's outstanding sales force that makes the company's credo, "Consumer driven. Customer focused," ring true. In fact, Lear's sales force was recently rated by *Sales & Marketing Management* magazine as number six among "America's Best Sales Forces." What makes this an outstanding sales force? Lear knows that good selling these days takes much more than just a sales rep covering a territory and convincing customers to buy the product. It takes teamwork, relationship building, and doing what's best for the customer. Lear's sales force excels at these tasks.

Lear's sales depend completely on the success of its customers. If the automakers don't sell cars, Lear doesn't sell interiors. So the Lear sales force strives to create not just sales but customer success. In fact, Lear salespeople aren't "sales reps," they're "account managers" who function more as consultants than order getters. "Our salespeople don't really close deals," says Lear's Pat Burke, vice-president of sales and business development, "they consult and work with customers to learn exactly what's needed and when."

To more fully match up with customers' needs, Lear has diversified its product line to become a kind of "one-stop shopping" source. Until a few years ago, Lear supplied only seats; now it sells almost everything for a car's interior. Providing complete interior solutions for customers also benefits Lear. "It used to be that we'd build a partnership and then get only a limited amount of revenue from it," Burke says. "Now we can get as much as possible out of our customer relationships."

Lear is heavily customer focused, so much so that it's broken up into separate divisions dedicated to specific customers. For example, there's a Ford division and a General Motors division, and each operates as its own profit center. Within each division, high-level "platform teams" made up of salespeople, engineers, and program managers work closely with their customer counterparts. These platform teams are closely supported by divisional manufacturing, finance, quality, and advanced technology groups. Lear's limited customer base, consisting of only a few dozen customers in all, allows Lear's sales teams to get very close to their customers. "Our teams don't call on purchasers; they're linked to customer operations at all levels," Burke says. "We try to put a system in place that creates continuous contact with customers." In fact, Lear often locates its sales offices in customers' plants. For example, the team that handles GM's light truck division works at GM's truck operation campus. "We can't just be there to give quotes and ask for orders," Burke says. "We need to be involved with customers every step of the way—from vehicle concept through launch."

Lear's average customer is worth more than $250 million in annual sales to the company. Maintaining profitable relationships with such large customers takes much more than a nice smile and a firm handshake. And certainly there's no place for the "smoke and mirrors" or "flimflam" sometimes mistakenly associated with personal selling. Success in such a selling environment requires careful teamwork among well-trained, dedicated sales professionals who are bent on profitably taking care of their customers.[1]

In this chapter, we examine two more communication and promotion tools: *personal selling* and *sales promotion*.

Personal Selling

Robert Louis Stevenson once noted that "everyone lives by selling something." We are all familiar with the sales forces used by business organizations to sell products and services to customers around the world. But sales forces are also found in many other kinds of organizations. For example, colleges use recruiters to attract new students, and churches use membership committees to attract new members. Hospitals and museums use fundraisers to contact donors and raise money. Even governments use sales forces. The U.S. Postal Service, for instance, uses a sales force to sell Express Mail and other services to corporate customers, and the Agricultural Extension Service sends agricultural specialists to sell farmers on new farming methods. In this section, we examine the role of personal selling in the organization, sales force management decisions, and basic principles of personal selling.

There are many types of personal selling jobs, and the role of personal selling can vary greatly from one company to another. Here, we look at the nature of personal selling positions and at the role the sales force plays in modern marketing organizations.

The Nature of Personal Selling

Selling is one of the oldest professions in the world. The people who do the selling go by many names: *salespeople*, *sales representatives*, *account executives*, *sales consultants*, *sales engineers*, *agents*, *district managers*, and *marketing representatives*, to name just a few.

People hold many stereotypes of salespeople, including some unfavorable ones. "Salesman" may bring to mind the image of Arthur Miller's pitiable Willy Loman in *Death of a Salesman*. Or you might think of Meredith Willson's cigar-smoking, back-slapping, joke-telling Harold Hill in *The Music Man*. Both examples depict salespeople as loners, traveling their territories trying to foist their wares on unsuspecting or unwilling buyers.

The term "salesperson" covers a wide range of positions, from the clerk selling in a retail store to the engineering salesperson who consults with client companies.

However, modern salespeople are a far cry from these unfortunate stereotypes. Today, most salespeople build and maintain long-term customer relationships by listening to their customers, assessing customer needs, and organizing the company's efforts to solve customer problems. Consider Boeing, the aerospace giant that dominates the worldwide commercial aircraft market with a 55 percent market share. It takes more than a friendly smile and a firm handshake to sell expensive airplanes:

Selling high-tech aircraft at $70 million or more a copy is complex and challenging. A single big sale can easily run into the billions of dollars. Boeing salespeople head up an extensive team of company specialists—sales and service technicians, financial analysts, planners, engineers—all dedicated to finding ways to satisfy airline customer needs. The salespeople begin by becoming experts on the airlines, much like Wall Street analysts would. They find out where each airline wants to grow, when it wants to replace planes, and details of its financial situation. The team runs Boeing and competing planes through computer systems, simulating the airline's routes, cost per seat, and other factors to show that their planes are most efficient.

Then the high-level negotiations begin. The selling process is nerve-rackingly slow—it can take two or three years from the first sales presentation to the day the sale is announced. Sometimes top executives from both the airline and Boeing are brought in to close the deal. After getting the order, salespeople then must stay in almost constant touch to keep track of the account's equipment needs and to make certain the customer stays satisfied. Success depends on building solid, long-term relationships with customers, based on performance and trust. According to one analyst, Boeing's salespeople "are the vehicle by which information is collected and contacts are made so all other things can take place."[2]

Salesperson
An individual acting for a company by performing one or more of the following activities: prospecting, communicating, servicing, and information gathering.

The term **salesperson** covers a wide range of positions. At one extreme, a salesperson might be largely an *order taker*, such as the department store salesperson standing behind the counter. At the other extreme are *order getters*, whose positions demand the *creative selling* of products and services ranging from appliances, industrial equipment, or airplanes to insurance, advertising, or consulting services. Other salespeople engage in *missionary selling*: These salespeople are not expected or permitted to take an order but only build goodwill or educate buyers. An example is a salesperson for a pharmaceutical company who calls on doctors to educate them about the company's drug products and to urge them to prescribe these products to their patients. Here, we focus on the more creative types of selling and on the process of building and managing an effective sales force.

The Role of the Sales Force

Personal selling is the interpersonal arm of the promotion mix. Advertising consists of one-way, nonpersonal communication with target consumer groups. In contrast, personal selling involves two-way, personal communication between salespeople and individual customers, whether face to face, by telephone, through video conferences, or by other means. Personal selling can be more effective than advertising in more complex selling situations. Salespeople can probe customers to learn more about their problems. They can adjust the marketing offer to fit the special needs of each customer and can negotiate terms of sale. They can build long-term personal relationships with key decision makers.

The role of personal selling varies from company to company. Some firms have no salespeople at all; for example, companies that sell only through mail-order catalogs or companies that sell through manufacturer's reps, sales agents, or brokers. In most firms, however, the sales force plays a major role. In companies that sell business products, such as Xerox or DuPont, the company's salespeople work directly with customers. In fact, to many customers, salespeople may be the only contact. To these customers, the sales force *is* the company. In consumer product companies such as Procter & Gamble or Nike that sell through intermediaries, final consumers rarely meet salespeople or even know about them. Still, the sales force plays an important behind-the-scenes role. It works with wholesalers and retailers to gain their support and to help them be more effective in selling the company's products.

The sales force serves as a critical link between a company and its customers. In many cases, salespeople serve both masters—the seller and the buyer. First, they *represent the company to customers*. They find and develop new customers and communicate information about the company's products and services. They sell products by approaching customers, presenting their products, answering objections, negotiating prices and terms, and closing sales. In addition, salespeople provide services to customers, carry out market research and intelligence work, and fill out sales call reports.

At the same time, salespeople *represent customers to the company*, acting inside the firm as "champions" of customers' interests. Salespeople relay customer concerns about company products and actions back to those who can handle them. They learn about customer needs and work with others in the company to develop greater customer value. Thus, the salesperson often acts as an "account manager" who manages the relationship between the seller and buyer.

As companies move toward a stronger market orientation, their sales forces are becoming more market focused and customer oriented. The old view was that salespeople should worry about sales and the company should worry about profit. However, the current view holds that salespeople should be concerned with more than just producing *sales*—they also must know how to produce *customer satisfaction* and *company profit*.

Managing the Sales Force

We define **sales force management** as the analysis, planning, implementation, and control of sales force activities. It includes designing sales force strategy and structure and recruiting, selecting, training, compensating, supervising, and evaluating the firm's salespeople. These major sales force management decisions are shown in Figure 13-1 and are discussed in the following sections.

Sales force management
The analysis, planning, implementation, and control of sales force activities. It includes setting and designing sales force strategy and recruiting, selecting, training, supervising, compensating, and evaluating the firm's salespeople.

Designing Sales Force Strategy and Structure

Marketing managers face several sales force strategy and design questions. How should salespeople and their tasks be structured? How big should the sales force be? Should salespeople sell alone or work in teams with other people in the company? Should they sell in the field or by telephone? We address these issues over the next few pages.

Sales Force Structure A company can divide up sales responsibilities along any of several lines. The decision is simple if the company sells only one product line to one industry with customers in many locations. In that case the company would use a *territorial sales force structure*. However, if the company sells many products to many types of customers, it might need either a *product sales force structure*, a *customer sales force structure*, or a combination of the two.

TERRITORIAL SALES FORCE STRUCTURE In the **territorial sales force structure**, each salesperson is assigned to an exclusive geographic area and sells the company's full line of products or services to all customers in that territory. This organization has many advantages. It clearly defines the salesperson's job, and because only one salesperson works the territory, he or she gets all the credit or blame for territory sales. The territorial structure also increases the salesperson's desire to build local business relationships that, in turn, improve selling effectiveness. Finally, because each salesperson travels within a limited geographic area, travel expenses are relatively small.

Territorial sales force structure
A sales force organization that assigns each salesperson to an exclusive geographic territory in which that salesperson sells the company's full line.

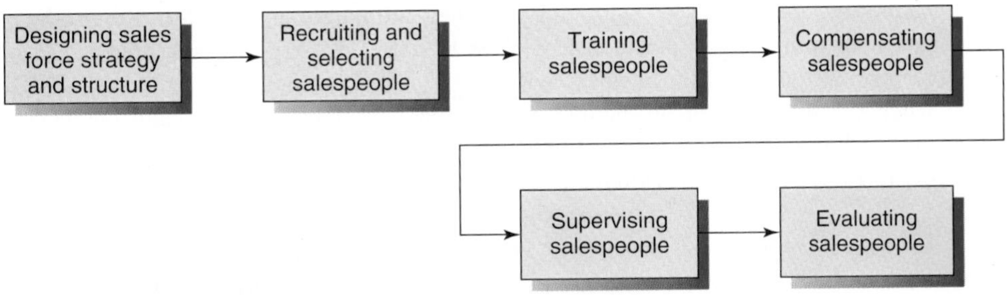

Figure 13-1
Major sales force management decisions

A territorial sales organization is often supported by many levels of sales management positions. For example, Campbell Soup uses a territorial structure in which each salesperson is responsible for selling all Campbell Soup products. Starting at the bottom of the organization, sales merchandisers report to sales representatives, who report to retail supervisors, who report to directors of retail sales operations, who report to 1 of 22 regional sales managers. Regional sales managers, in turn, report to 1 of 4 general sales managers (West, Central, South, and East), who report to a vice-president and general sales manager.

PRODUCT SALES FORCE STRUCTURE Salespeople must know their products, especially when the products are numerous and complex. This need, together with the growth of product management, has led many companies to adopt a **product sales force structure**, in which the sales force sells along product lines. For example, Kodak uses different sales forces for its film products than for its industrial products. The film products sales force deals with simple products that are distributed intensively, whereas the industrial products sales force deals with complex products that require technical understanding.

Product sales force structure
A sales force organization under which salespeople specialize in selling only a portion of the company's products or lines.

The product structure can lead to problems, however, if a single large customer buys many different company products. For example, Baxter International, a hospital supply company, has several product divisions, each with a separate sales force. Several Baxter salespeople might end up calling on the same hospital on the same day. This means that they travel over the same routes and wait to see the same customer's purchasing agents. These extra costs must be compared with the benefits of better product knowledge and attention to individual products.

Customer sales force structure
A sales force organization under which salespeople specialize in selling only to certain customers or industries.

CUSTOMER SALES FORCE STRUCTURE More and more companies are now using a **customer sales force structure**, in which they organize the sales force along customer or industry lines. Separate sales forces may be set up for different industries, for serving current customers versus finding new ones, and for major accounts versus regular accounts.

Organizing the sales force around customers can help a company to become more customer focused and build closer relationships with important customers. For example, giant ABB, the $29-billion-a-year Swiss-based industrial equipment maker, recently changed from a product-based to a customer-based sales force. The new structure resulted in a stronger customer orientation and improved service to clients:

> Until four months ago, David Donaldson sold boilers for ABB. . . . After 30 years, Donaldson sure knew boilers, but he didn't know much about the broad range of other products offered by ABB's U.S. Power Plant division. Customers were frustrated because as many as a dozen ABB salespeople called on them at different times to peddle their products. ABB's bosses decided that this was a poor way to run a sales force. So [recently], David Donaldson and 27 other power plant salespeople began new jobs. [Donaldson] now also sells turbines, generators, and three other product lines. He handles six major accounts . . . instead of a [mixed batch] of 35. His charge: Know the customer intimately and sell him the products that help him operate productively. Says Donaldson: "My job is to make it easy for my customers to do business with us. . . . I show them where to go in ABB whenever they have a problem." The president of ABB's power plant businesses [adds]: "If you want to be a customer-driven company, you have to design the sales organization around individual buyers rather than around your products."[3]

IBM recently made a similar shift from a product-based structure to a customer-based one. Before the shift, droves of salespeople representing different IBM software, hardware, and services divisions might call on a single large client, creating confusion and frustration. Such large customers wanted a "single face," one point of contact for all of IBM's vast array of products and services. Now, following the restructuring, a single IBM "client executive" works with each large customer and manages a team of IBMers— product reps, systems engineers, consultants, and others—who work with the customer. The client executive becomes an expert in the customer's industry. Greg Buseman, a client executive in the distribution industry who spends most of his time working with a major consumer packaged-goods customer, describes his role this way: "I am the owner of the business relationship with the client. If the client has a problem, I'm the one who pulls together software or hardware specialists or consultants. At the customer I work most closely with, we usually have 15 to 20 projects going at once, and I have to manage them."[4] Such an intense focus on customers is widely credited for IBM's dramatic turnaround in recent years.

COMPLEX SALES FORCE STRUCTURES   When a company sells a wide variety of products to many types of customers over a broad geographic area, it often combines several types of sales force structures. Salespeople can be specialized by customer and territory, by product and territory, by product and customer, or by territory, product, and customer. No single structure is best for all companies and situations. Each company should select a sales force structure that best serves the needs of its customers and fits its overall marketing strategy.

Sales Force Size

Once the company has set its structure, it is ready to consider *sales force size*. Salespeople constitute one of the company's most productive—and most expensive—assets. Therefore, increasing their number will increase both sales and costs.

Many companies use some form of **workload** **approach** to set sales force size. Using this approach, a company first groups accounts into different classes according to size, account status, or other factors related to the amount of effort required to maintain them. It then determines the number of salespeople needed to call on each class of accounts the desired number of times. The company might think as follows: Suppose we have 1,000 Type-A accounts and 2,000 Type-B accounts. Type-A accounts require 36 calls a year and Type-B accounts require 12 calls a year. In this case, the sales force's workload—the number of calls it must make per year—is 60,000 calls [(1,000 × 36) + (2,000 × 12) = 36,000 + 24,000 = 60,000]. Suppose our average salesperson can make 1,000 calls a year. Thus, the company needs 60 salespeople (60,000 ÷ 1,000).

> **Workload approach**
> An approach to setting sales force size in which the company groups accounts into different size classes and then determines how many salespeople are needed to call on them the desired number of times.

Other Sales Force Strategy and Structure Issues

Sales management must also decide who will be involved in the selling effort and how various sales and sales support people will work together.

OUTSIDE AND INSIDE SALES FORCES   The company may have an **outside sales force** (or *field sales force*), an **inside sales force**, or both. Outside salespeople travel to call on customers. Inside salespeople conduct business from their offices via telephone or visits from prospective buyers.

To reduce time demands on their outside sales forces, many companies have increased the size of their inside sales forces. Inside salespeople include technical support people, sales assistants, and telemarketers. *Technical support people* provide technical information and answers to customers' questions. *Sales assistants* provide clerical backup for outside salespeople. They call ahead and confirm appointments, conduct credit checks, follow up on deliveries, and answer customers' questions when outside salespeople cannot be reached. *Telemarketers* use the phone to find new leads and qualify prospects for the field sales force or to sell and service accounts directly.

> **Outside sales force (or field sales force)**
> Outside salespeople who travel to call on customers.
>
> **Inside sales force**
> Inside salespeople who conduct business from their offices via telephone or visits from prospective buyers.

The inside sales force frees outside salespeople to spend more time selling to major accounts and finding major new prospects. Depending on the complexity of the product and customer, a telemarketer can make from 20 to 33 decision-maker contacts a day, compared to the average of 4 that an outside salesperson can make. And for many types of products and selling situations, **telemarketing** can be as effective as a personal call but much less expensive. For example, whereas the average personal sale costs about $110, a routine industrial telemarketing call costs only about $5 and a complex call about $20.[5] Telemarketing can be used successfully by both large and small companies:

Telemarketing
Using the telephone to sell directly to customers.

◇ DuPont uses experienced former field salespeople as telemarketing reps to help sell the company's complex chemical products. Housed in DuPont's state-of-the-art Corporate Telemarketing Center, the telemarketers handle technical questions from customers, smooth out product and distribution problems, and alert field sales reps to hot prospects. The teamwork pays off—80 percent of the leads passed on to the field force are converted into sales. Notes one DuPont telemarketer: "I'm more effective on the phone. [When you're in the field], if some guy's not in his office, you lose an hour. On the phone, you lose 15 seconds. . . . Through my phone calls, I'm in the field as much as the rep is." There are other advantages, quips the rep. "Customers can't throw things at you, . . . and you don't have to outrun dogs."[6]

Experienced telemarketers sell complex chemical products by phone at DuPont's Customer Telecontact Center. Quips one: "I'm more effective on the phone . . . and you don't have to outrun dogs."

✧ Climax Portable Machine Tools has proven that a small company can use tele-marketing to save money and still lavish attention on buyers. Under the old system, Climax sales engineers spent one-third of their time on the road, training distributor salespeople and accompanying them on calls. They could make about four contacts a day. Now, each of five sales engineers on Climax's telemarketing team calls about 30 prospects a day, following up on leads generated by ads and direct mail. Because it takes about five calls to close a sale, the sales engineers update a prospect's computer file after each contact, noting the degree of commitment, requirements, next call date, and personal comments. "If anyone mentions he's going on a fishing trip, our sales engineer enters that in the computer and uses it to personalize the next phone call," says Climax's president, noting that's just one way to build good relations. Another is that the first mailing to a prospect includes the sales engineer's business card with his picture on it. Of course, it takes more than friendliness to sell $15,000 machine tools over the phone (special orders may run $200,000), but the telemarketing approach is working well. When Climax customers were asked, "Do you see the sales engineer often enough?" the response was overwhelmingly positive. Obviously, many people didn't realize that the only contact they'd had with Climax had been on the phone.[7]

TEAM SELLING The days when a single salesperson handled a large and important customer are vanishing rapidly. Today, as products become more complex, and as customers grow larger and more demanding, one person simply cannot handle all of a large customer's needs anymore. Instead, most companies now are using **team selling** to service large, complex accounts. Sales teams might include people from sales, marketing, engineering, finance, technical support, and even upper management. For example, Procter & Gamble assigns teams consisting of salespeople, marketing managers, technical service people, and logistics and information-systems specialists to work closely with large retail customers such as Wal-Mart, Kmart, and Target. In such team-selling situations, salespeople become "orchestrators" who help coordinate a whole-company effort to build profitable relationships with important customers (see Marketing at Work 13-1).[8]

> **Team selling**
> Using teams of people from sales, marketing, engineering, finance, technical support, and even upper management to service large, complex accounts.

Yet companies recognize that just asking their people for teamwork does not produce it. They must revise their compensation and recognition systems to give credit for work on shared accounts, and they must set up better goals and measures for sales force performance. They must emphasize the importance of teamwork in their training programs while at the same time honoring the importance of individual initiative.

Recruiting and Selecting Salespeople

At the heart of any successful sales force operation is the recruitment and selection of good salespeople. The performance difference between an average salesperson and a top salesperson can be substantial. In a typical sales force, the top 30 percent of the salespeople might bring in 60 percent of the sales. Thus, careful salesperson selection can greatly increase overall sales force performance. Beyond the differences in sales performance, poor selection results in costly turnover. When a salesperson quits, the costs of finding and training a new salesperson—plus the costs of lost sales—can run as high as $50,000 to $75,000. And a sales force with many new people is less productive.[9]

What Makes a Good Salesperson?
Selecting salespeople would not be a problem if the company knew what traits to look for. If it knew that good salespeople were outgoing, aggressive, and energetic, for example, it could simply check applicants for these characteristics. But many successful salespeople are bashful, soft-spoken, and laid back.

Marketing at Work 13-1

Team Selling: From "Soloists" to "Orchestrators"

For years, the customer has been solely in the hands of the salesperson. The salesperson identified the prospect, arranged the call, explored the customer's needs, created and proposed a solution, closed the deal, and turned cheerleader as others delivered what he or she promised. For selling relatively simple products, this approach can work well. But if the products are more complex and the service requirements greater, the salesperson simply can't go it alone. Consider the following example:

This was Michael Quintano's big chance. The 23-year-old, up-and-coming MCI sales rep had only called on customers billing less than $2,000 a month. Then, from out of the blue, he hit upon Nat Schwartz and Company (NS&C), a china and crystal retail-telemarketer with monthly telephone billings exceeding $7,000. In over his head, he offered MCI veteran Al Rodriguez a split on the commission in return for some help. When the pair visited NS&C headquarters, they found a store filled with nothing but china and crystal. "No way does this store bill $7,000. We'll close this deal in one or two calls," Quintano thought. However, when they were led to a bustling back room filled with telemarketers working the phones, their visions of a quick close were swiftly put on hold. Quintano and Rodriguez realized they would have to expand their sales team. They called on sales manager Stephen Smith and MCI Telecommunications consultant Tom Mantone, who during two meetings with NS&C cleared up questions about technical details such as phone line installations. That smoothed the way for Quintano and Rodriguez to close the deal. Thus, by relying on team selling, Michael Quintano landed the largest account of his career.

More and more, companies are finding that sales teams can unearth problems, solutions, and sales opportunities that no individual salesperson could. Such teams might include experts from any area or level of the selling firm—sales, marketing, technical and support services, R&D, engineering, operations, finance, and others. In team selling situations, the salesperson shifts from "soloist" to "orchestrator." One such salesperson puts it in sports terms: "It's my job to be the quarterback. [Taking care of a large customer] gets farmed out to different areas of the company, and different questions have to be answered by different people. We set up a game plan and then go in and make the call."

In many cases, the move to team selling mirrors similar changes in customers' buying organizations. According to the director of sales education at Dow Chemical, by 2000 more than 80 percent of purchasing decisions will be made by multifunctional buying teams, including purchasing, engineering, and financial management staff. To sell effectively to such selling teams, he states, "Our sellers will have to captain selling teams. There are no more lone wolves."

Some companies, like IBM and Xerox, have used teams for a long time. Others have only recently reorganized to adopt the team concept. John Hancock, for example, recently set up sales-and-service

Still, the search continues for the magic list of traits that spells sure-fire sales success. One survey suggests that good salespeople have a lot of enthusiasm, persistence, initiative, self-confidence, and job commitment. They are committed to sales as a way of life and have a strong customer orientation. Another study suggests that good salespeople are independent and self-motivated and are excellent listeners. Still another study advises that salespeople should be a friend to the customer as well as persistent, enthusiastic, attentive, and—above all—honest. They must be internally motivated, disciplined, hard working, and able to build strong relationships with customers. Finally, studies show that good salespeople are team players rather than loners.[10]

How can a company find out what traits salespeople in its industry should have? Job *duties* suggest some of the traits a company should look for. Does the job require a lot of planning and paperwork? Does it call for much travel? Will the salesperson face a lot of rejections? Will the salesperson be working with high-level buyers? The successful

teams in six territories. Each team is led by a director of sales who acts as a mini-CEO, managing all aspects of customer contact: sales, service, and technical support. The result is an informed, dedicated team that is closer to the customer.

When a customer's business becomes so complex that a single company's sales organization can't provide a complete solution, firms might even create multicompany sales teams. For example, teams from MCI, IBM, and Rohm recently joined forces in an effort to provide solutions to a large customer that was setting up a complex data-application network. MCI's team provided information on data communication, IBM's on computer hardware and software, and Rohm's on switching equipment. "The meeting provided the customer with one point of contact to solve a variety of needs," said an MCI sales executive.

Some companies have even opened special sites for team sales meetings, called *executive briefing centers*. Xerox runs six of these centers. Xerox sales teams invite key people from important accounts to one of the centers, where center staff conduct briefings, arrange video conferences with experts in

other parts of the country, and provide other services that help the team build business and improve customer service.

Team selling does have some pitfalls. For example, selling teams can confuse or overwhelm customers who are used to working with only one salesperson. Salespeople who are used to having customers all to themselves may have trouble learning to work with and trust others on a team. Finally, difficulties in evaluating individual contributions to the team selling effort can create some sticky compensation issues.

Still, team selling can produce dramatic results. For example, Dun & Bradstreet, the world's largest marketer of business information and related services, recently established sales teams made up of representatives from its credit, collection, and marketing business units, which up to then had worked separately. Their mission was to work as a team to call on higher-ups in customer organizations, learn about customer needs, and offer solutions. The teams concentrated on D&B's top 50 customers. When one of the D&B sales teams asked to meet with the chief financial officer of a

major telecommunications company, the executive responded, "I'm delighted you asked, but why talk?" He found out after a one-hour meeting. The D&B team listened as he discussed problems facing his organization, and by the end of the information-seeking session, the team had come up with several solutions for the executive and had identified $1.5 million in D&B sales opportunities from what had been a $700,000 customer. More teams met with more clients, creating more opportunities. About a year after the program started, D&B's marketing department had targeted $200 million in sales opportunities, about half of which would not have been found under the old system. Now these teams are getting together with D&B's top 200 customers.

Sources: Portions adapted from Joseph Conlin, "Teaming Up," *Sales & Marketing Management*, October 1993, pp. 98–104; Richard C. Whiteley, "Orchestrating Service," *Sales & Marketing Management*, April 1994, pp. 29–30; and Rick Mullin, "From Lone Wolves to Team Players," *Chemical Week*, January 14, 1998, pp. 33–34. Also see Christopher Meyer, "How the Right Measures Help Teams Excel," *Harvard Business Review*, May–June 1994, pp. 95–103; Geoffrey Brewer, "Brain Power," *Sales and Marketing Management*, May 1997, pp. 39–48; Michele Marchetti, "Why Teams Fail," *Sales & Marketing Management*, June 1997, p. 91, and Melinda Ligos, "On with the Show," *Sales & Marketing Management*, November 1998, pp. 70–76.

salesperson should be suited to these duties. The company also should look at the characteristics of its most successful salespeople for clues to needed traits.

Recruiting Procedures After management has decided on needed traits, it must *recruit* salespeople. The human resources department looks for applicants by getting names from current salespeople, using employment agencies, placing classified ads, and contacting college students. Until recently, companies sometimes found it hard to sell college students on selling. Many thought that selling was a job and not a profession, that salespeople had to be deceitful to be effective, and that selling involved too much insecurity and travel. In addition, some women believed that selling was a man's career. To counter such objections, recruiters now offer high starting salaries and income growth and note that more than one-fourth of the presidents of large U.S. corporations started out in marketing and sales. They point out that more than 23 percent of all professional salespeople in the United States are women. Women account for a much higher percentage of the sales force in some industries, such as lodging (63 percent), banking and financial services (53 percent), and health services (52 percent).[11]

Selecting Salespeople Recruiting will attract many applicants from whom the company must select the best. The selection procedure can vary from a single informal interview to lengthy testing and interviewing. Many companies give formal tests to sales applicants. Tests typically measure sales aptitude, analytical and organizational skills, personality traits, and other characteristics. Test results count heavily in companies such as IBM, Prudential, Procter & Gamble, and Gillette. Gillette claims that tests have reduced turnover by 42 percent and that test scores have correlated well with the later performance of new salespeople. But test scores provide only one piece of information in a set that includes personal characteristics, references, past employment history, and interviewer reactions.[12]

Training Salespeople

Many companies used to send their new salespeople into the field almost immediately after hiring them. They would be given samples, order books, and general instructions ("sell west of the Mississippi"). To many companies, a training program translated into high expense for instructors, materials, space, and salary for a person who was not yet selling, and a loss of sales opportunities because the person was not in the field.

Today's new salespeople, however, may spend anywhere from a few weeks or months to a year or more in training. The average training period is four months. In all, U.S. companies spend more than $7 billion annually on training salespeople and devote more than 33 hours per year to the average salesperson.[13] Although training can be expensive, it can also yield dramatic returns on the training investment. For example, Nabisco recently did an extensive analysis of the return on investment of its two-day Professional Selling Program, which teaches sales reps how to plan for and make professional presentations to their retail customers. Although it cost about $1,000 to put each sales rep through the program, the training resulted in additional sales of more than $122,000 per rep and yielded almost $21,000 of additional profit per rep.[14]

Training programs have several goals. Salespeople need to know and identify with the company, so most training programs begin by describing the company's history and objectives, its organization, its financial structure and facilities, and its chief products and markets. Salespeople also need to know the company's products, so sales trainees are shown how products are produced and how they work. They also need to know customers' and competitors' characteristics, so the training program teaches them about competitors' strategies and about different types of customers and their needs, buying motives, and buying habits. Because salespeople must know how to make effective presentations, they are trained in the principles of selling. Finally, salespeople need to understand field procedures and responsibilities. They learn how to divide time between active and potential accounts and how to use an expense account, prepare reports, and route communications effectively.

Compensating Salespeople

To attract salespeople, a company must have an appealing compensation plan. These plans vary greatly both by industry and by companies within the same industry. The level of compensation must be close to the "going rate" for the type of sales job and needed skills. To pay less than the going rate would attract too few quality salespeople; to pay more would be unnecessary.

Compensation is made up of several elements: a fixed amount, a variable amount, expenses, and fringe benefits. The fixed amount, usually a salary, gives the salesperson some stable income. The variable amount, which might be commissions or bonuses based on sales performance, rewards the salesperson for greater effort. Expense allowances, which repay salespeople for job-related expenses, let salespeople undertake needed and desirable selling efforts. Fringe benefits, such as paid vacations, sickness or accident benefits, pensions, and life insurance, provide job security and satisfaction.

Management must decide what *mix* of these compensation elements makes the most sense for each sales job. Different combinations of fixed and variable compensation give rise to four basic types of compensation plans: straight salary, straight commission, salary plus bonus, and salary plus commission. A study of sales force compensation plans showed that 70 percent of all companies surveyed use a combination of base salary and incentives. The average plan consisted of about 60 percent salary and 40 percent incentive pay.[15]

The sales force compensation plan can both motivate salespeople and direct their activities. For example, if sales management wants salespeople to emphasize new account development, it might pay a bonus for opening new accounts. Thus, the compensation plan should direct the sales force toward activities that are consistent with overall marketing objectives.

Table 13-1 illustrates how a company's compensation plan should reflect its overall marketing strategy. For example, if the overall strategy is to grow rapidly and gain market share, the compensation plan should reward high sales performance and encourage salespeople to capture new accounts. This might suggest a larger commission component coupled with new-account bonuses. In contrast, if the marketing goal is to maximize profitability of current accounts, the compensation plan might contain a larger base-salary component, with additional incentives based on current account sales or customer satisfaction. In fact, more and more companies are moving away from high commission plans that may drive salespeople to make short-term grabs for business. Notes one sales force expert, "The last thing you want is to have someone ruin a customer relationship because they're pushing too hard to close a deal." Instead, companies are designing compensation plans that reward salespeople for building customer relationships and growing the long-run value of each customer.[16] (See Marketing at Work 13-2.)

Table 13-1   The Relationship between Overall Marketing Strategy and Sales Force Compensation

	Strategic Goal		
	To Rapidly Gain Market Share	**To Solidify Market Leadership**	**To Maximize Profitability**
Ideal salesperson	✳ An independent self-starter	✳ A competitive problem solver	✳ A team player ✳ A relationship manager
Sales focus	✳ Deal making ✳ Sustained high effort	✳ Consultative selling	✳ Account penetration
Compensation role	✳ To capture accounts ✳ To reward high performance	✳ To reward new and existing sales	✳ To manage the product mix ✳ To encourage team selling ✳ To reward account management

Source: Adapted from Sam T. Johnson, "Sales Compensation: In Search of a Better Solution," *Compensation & Benefits Review,* November–December 1993, pp. 53–60.

Marketing at Work 13-2

Paying for Customer Value

For years, companies have paid their salespeople based on sales volume and dollar sales. Both are worthy goals, as long as the primary objective is selling the product. However, as the emphasis shifts to adding customer value, retaining customers and building strong relationships, and building "share-of-customer" (percentage of the customer's total business captured), companies are adding a new set of measures to their sales compensation equations. More and more, salespeople are being evaluated and compensated based on the following kinds of measures:

Long-term customer satisfaction: This requires a salesperson to not oversell customers in the short run in order to satisfy a sales quota but to look out for customers' best interests and focus on helping them to achieve their goals.

Full customer service: This requires that the salesperson provide whatever customers need by working within the firm as well as building alliances with other companies that offer complementary products and services needed by customers. The goal: Never send a customer out the door to become someone else's customer.

Retention rates: The salesperson's goal becomes making sure that once a customer buys from the company, the customer doesn't buy from anyone else.

Growth of customer value: This involves increasing each customer's value to the company by increasing the customer's overall volume of business and capturing a greater share of that business. To make this happen, the salesperson must build strong relationships based on real value and customer success.

To see how including such measures in the compensation formula might affect a salesperson's performance, imagine rewarding a car salesperson differently. Most car dealerships reward salespeople for selling cars; each car sale results in a commission. Once the commission is paid, the salesperson turns to finding a new customer for the next sale. But what if, in addition to a token commission, the dealership rewarded the sales associate for long-term customer satisfaction, such as high 18-month satisfaction scores? Such rewards would motivate the salesperson to follow up with the customer, to make sure the service department was handling the customer well, and to identify and resolve a host of other problems that might upset the customer.

Suppose the dealership further rewarded the sales associate for share-of-customer. The associate would then find out what else is in the customer's garage and concentrate on ways to use the dealership's products to build "share-of-garage." If rewarded for such smart selling, the associate would find service, repair, and accessories for a customer and get them all under the dealership's roof. The dealership would know what the customer wanted next, and when. In addition, the sales associate would feed customer information into the dealership's database so that the customer would be served well even when the associate was on a well-earned vacation. Then, the dealership and the associate could work together to track customer needs electronically.

Most importantly, suppose that the dealership rewarded this salesperson for increasing long-term customer value to the dealership, perhaps by paying a tiny percentage of every dollar ever spent at the dealership by the customer on cars, financing, insurance, service, and repair. The salesperson would thus be motivated not just to make the sale but to make sure that each customer came back to this dealership for everything, forever.

To be sure, reaching this level of sophistication in sales force compensation will not be easy. Such measures are difficult to track and apply. However, salespeople usually do what they are rewarded for doing. Sales compensation plans can help motivate salespeople to build real relationships between customers and the company, increasing the value of each customer to the company.

Source: Adapted from Don Peppers and Martha Rogers, "The Money Trap," *Sales & Marketing Management*, May 1997, pp. 58–60. Also see James Champy, "Taking Sales to New Heights," *Sales & Marketing Management*, July 1998, p. 26.

Supervising Salespeople

New salespeople need more than a territory, compensation, and training—they need *supervision*. Through supervision, the company *directs* and *motivates* the sales force to do a better job.

Directing Salespeople How much should sales management be involved in helping salespeople manage their territories? It depends on everything from the company's size to the experience of its sales force. Thus, companies vary widely in how closely they supervise their salespeople.

Many companies help their salespeople to identify customer targets and set call norms. In addition, companies may specify how much time their sales forces should spend prospecting for new accounts. Companies may also direct salespeople in how to use their time efficiently. One tool is the *annual call plan* that shows which customers and prospects to call on in which months and which activities to carry out. Activities include taking part in trade shows, attending sales meetings, and carrying out marketing research. Another tool is *time-and-duty analysis*. In addition to time spent selling, the salesperson spends time traveling, waiting, eating, taking breaks, and doing administrative chores.

Figure 13-2 shows how salespeople spend their time. On average, actual face-to-face selling time accounts for less than 30 percent of total working time! If selling time could be raised from 30 percent to 40 percent, this would be a 33 percent increase in the time spent selling. Companies always are looking for ways to save time: using phones instead of traveling, simplifying record-keeping forms, finding better call and routing plans, and supplying more and better customer information.

Many firms have adopted *sales force automation systems*, computerized sales force operations for more efficient order-entry transactions, improved customer service, and better salesperson decision-making support. Salespeople use computers to profile customers and prospects, analyze and forecast sales, manage accounts, schedule sales calls, enter orders, check inventories and order status, prepare sales and expense reports, process correspondence, and carry out many other activities. Sales force automation not only

Figure 13-2
How salespeople spend their time

Source: Dartnell Corporation; 30th Sales Force Compensation Survey. © 1998 Dartnell Corporation.

Sales force automation: Owens-Corning's FAST sales force automation system makes working directly with customers easier than ever.

lowers sales force costs and improves productivity, it also improves the quality of sales management decisions. Here is an example of successful sales force automation:[17]

✧   Owens-Corning recently put its sales force on-line with FAST—its newly developed Field Automation Sales Team system. FAST gives Owens-Corning salespeople a constant supply of information about their company and the people they're dealing with. Using laptop computers, each salesperson can access three types of programs. First, FAST gives them a set of *generic tools*, everything from word processing to fax transmission to creating presentations on-line. Second, it provides *product information*—tech bulletins, customer specifications, pricing information, and other data that can help close a sale. Finally, it offers up a wealth of *customer information*—buying history, types of products ordered, and preferred payment terms. Reps previously stored such information in loose-leaf books, calendars, and account cards. FAST makes working directly with customers easier than ever. Salespeople can prime themselves on backgrounds of clients; call up prewritten sales letters; transmit orders and resolve customer-service issues on the spot during customer calls; and have samples, pamphlets, brochures, and other materials sent to clients with a few keystrokes.

Perhaps the fastest-growing sales force technology tool is the Internet. In a survey by Dartnell Corporation of 1,000 salespeople, 61 percent reported using the Internet regularly in their daily selling activities. The most common uses include gathering competitive information, monitoring customer Web sites, and researching industries and specific customers. As more and more companies provide their salespeople with Web access, experts expect continued growth in sales force Internet usage.[18]

Motivating Salespeople Some salespeople will do their best without any special urging from management. To them, selling may be the most fascinating job in the world. But selling can also be frustrating. Salespeople often work alone, and they must sometimes travel away from home. They may face aggressive competing salespeople and difficult customers. They sometimes lack the authority to do what is needed to win a sale and may thus lose large orders they have worked hard to obtain. Therefore, salespeople often need special encouragement to do their best.

Management can boost sales force morale and performance through its organizational climate, sales quotas, and positive incentives. *Organizational climate* describes the feeling that salespeople have about their opportunities, value, and rewards for a good performance within the company. Some companies treat salespeople as if they are not very important. Other companies treat their salespeople as their prime movers and allow virtually unlimited opportunity for income and promotion. Not surprisingly, in companies that hold their salespeople in low esteem, there is high turnover and poor performance. Where salespeople are held in high esteem, there is less turnover and higher performance.

Many companies motivate their salespeople by setting *sales quotas*—standards stating the amount they should sell and how sales should be divided among the company's

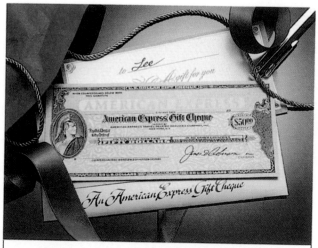

Sales force incentives: Many companies award cash, merchandise, trips, or other gifts as incentives for outstanding sales performance.

products. Compensation is often related to how well salespeople meet their quotas. Companies also use various *positive incentives* to increase sales force effort. *Sales meetings* provide social occasions, breaks from routine, chances to meet and talk with "company brass," and opportunities to air feelings and to identify with a larger group. Companies also sponsor *sales contests* to spur the sales force to make a selling effort above what would normally be expected. Other incentives include honors, merchandise and cash awards, trips, and profit-sharing plans.

Evaluating Salespeople

We have thus far described how management communicates what salespeople should be doing and how it motivates them to do it. This process requires good feedback. And good feedback means getting regular information from salespeople to evaluate their performance.

Management gets information about its salespeople in several ways. The most important source is *sales reports*, including weekly or monthly work plans and longer-term territory marketing plans. Salespeople also write up their completed activities on *call reports* and turn in *expense reports* for which they are partly or wholly repaid. Additional information comes from personal observation, customer surveys, and talks with other salespeople.

Using various sales force reports and other information, sales management evaluates members of the sales force. It evaluates salespeople on their ability to "plan their work and work their plan." Formal evaluation forces management to develop and communicate clear standards for judging performance. It also provides salespeople with constructive feedback and motivates them to perform well.

Linking the Concepts

Take a break and reexamine your thoughts about salespeople and sales management.

- As you did at the start of the chapter, close your eyes and envision a typical salesperson. Have your perceptions of salespeople changed after what you've just read? How? Be specific. (In Marketing at Work 13-3, you'll journey further into this territory.)
- Apply each of the steps in sales force management shown in Figure 13-1 to the Lear Corporation example.
- Find and talk with someone employed in professional sales. Ask about and report on how this salesperson's company designs its sales force and recruits, selects, trains, compensates, supervises, and evaluates its salespeople. Would you like to work as a salesperson for this company?

Principles of Personal Selling

We now turn from designing and managing a sales force to the actual personal selling process. Personal selling is an ancient art that has spawned a large body of literature and many principles. Effective salespeople operate on more than just instinct—they are highly trained in methods of territory analysis and customer management.

The Personal Selling Process

Most companies take a *customer-oriented approach* to personal selling. They train salespeople to identify customer needs and to find solutions. This approach assumes that customer needs provide sales opportunities, that customers appreciate good suggestions, and that customers will be loyal to salespeople who have their long-term interests at heart. The problem-solver salesperson fits better with the marketing concept than does a hard-sell salesperson or the glad-handing extrovert. Buyers today want solutions, not smiles; results, not razzle-dazzle. They want salespeople who listen to their concerns, understand their needs, and respond with the right products and services.

Steps in the Selling Process

Most training programs view the **selling process** as consisting of several steps that the salesperson must master (see Figure 13-3). These steps focus on the goal of getting new customers and obtaining orders from them. However, most salespeople spend much of their time maintaining existing accounts and building long-term customer *relationships*. We discuss the relationship aspect of the personal selling process in a later section.

Selling process
The steps that the salesperson follows when selling, which include prospecting and qualifying, preapproach, approach, presentation and demonstration, handling objections, closing, and follow-up.

Prospecting and Qualifying The first step in the selling process is **prospecting**— identifying qualified potential customers. Approaching the right potential customers is crucial to selling success. As one expert puts it: "If the sales force starts chasing anyone who is breathing and seems to have a budget, you risk accumulating a roster of expensive-to-serve, hard-to-satisfy customers who never respond to whatever value proposition you have." He continues, "The solution to this isn't rocket science. [You must] train salespeople to actively scout the right prospects. If necessary, create an incentive program to reward proper scouting."[19]

Prospecting
The step in the selling process in which the salesperson identifies qualified potential customers.

The salesperson must often approach many prospects to get just a few sales. Although the company supplies some leads, salespeople need skill in finding their own. They can ask current customers for referrals. They can build referral sources, such as suppliers, dealers, noncompeting salespeople, and bankers. They can join organizations to which prospects belong or can engage in speaking and writing activities that will draw attention. They can search for names in newspapers or directories and use the telephone and mail to track down leads. Or they can drop in unannounced on various offices (a practice known as "cold calling").

Salespeople also need to know how to *qualify* leads, that is, how to identify the good ones and screen out the poor ones. Prospects can be qualified by looking at their financial ability, volume of business, special needs, location, and possibilities for growth.

Preapproach Before calling on a prospect, the salesperson should learn as much as possible about the organization (what it needs, who is involved in the buying) and its buyers (their characteristics and buying styles). This step is known as the **preapproach**. The salesperson can consult standard sources (*Moody's, Standard & Poor's, Dun & Bradstreet*), acquaintances, and others to learn about the company. The salesperson should set *call objectives*, which may be to qualify the prospect, to gather information, or to make an immediate sale. Another task is to decide on the best approach, which might

Preapproach
The step in the selling process in which the salesperson learns as much as possible about a prospective customer before making a sales call.

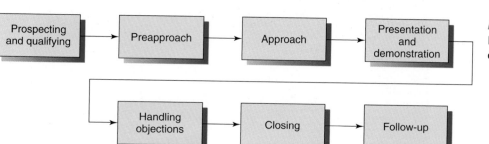

Figure 13-3
Major steps in effective selling

be a personal visit, a phone call, or a letter. The best timing should be considered carefully because many prospects are busiest at certain times. Finally, the salesperson should give thought to an overall sales strategy for the account.

Approach
The step in the selling process in which the salesperson meets and greets the buyer to get the relationship off to a good start.

Approach During the **approach** step, the salesperson should know how to meet and greet the buyer and get the relationship off to a good start. This step involves the salesperson's appearance, opening lines, and the follow-up remarks. The opening lines should be positive, such as "Mr. Johnson, I am Chris Bennett from the Alltech Company. My company and I appreciate your willingness to see me. I will do my best to make this visit profitable and worthwhile for you and your company." This opening might be followed by some key questions to learn more about the customer's needs or by showing a display or sample to attract the buyer's attention and curiosity.

Presentation
The step in the selling process in which the salesperson tells the product "story" to the buyer, showing how the product will make or save money for the buyer.

Presentation and Demonstration During the **presentation** step of the selling process, the salesperson tells the product "story" to the buyer, showing how the product will make or save money. The salesperson describes the product features but concentrates on presenting customer benefits. Using a *need-satisfaction approach*, the salesperson starts with a search for the customer's needs by getting the customer to do most of the talking.

This approach calls for good listening and problem-solving skills. "I think of myself more as a . . . well, psychologist," notes one experienced salesperson. "I listen to customers. I listen to their wishes and needs and problems, and I try to figure out a solution. If you're not a good listener, you're not going to get the order." Another salesperson suggests, "It's no longer enough to have a good relationship with a client. You have to understand their problems. You have to feel their pain."[20]

The qualities that purchasing agents *dislike most* in salespeople include being pushy, late, and unprepared or disorganized. The qualities they *value most* include empathy, honesty, dependability, thoroughness, and follow-through.[21] Sales presentations can be improved with demonstration aids, such as booklets, flip charts, slides, videotapes or videodiscs, and product samples. If buyers can see or handle the product, they will better remember its features and benefits.

Handling objections
The step in the selling process in which the salesperson seeks out, clarifies, and overcomes customer objections to buying.

Handling Objections Customers almost always have objections during the presentation or when asked to place an order. The problem can be either logical or psychological, and objections are often unspoken. In **handling objections**, the salesperson should use a

In the sales presentation, the salesperson tells the product story to the buyers.

positive approach, seek out hidden objections, ask the buyer to clarify any objections, take objections as opportunities to provide more information, and turn the objections into reasons for buying. Every salesperson needs training in the skills of handling objections.

Closing After handling the prospect's objections, the salesperson now tries to close the sale. Some salespeople do not get around to **closing** or do not handle it well. They may lack confidence, feel guilty about asking for the order, or fail to recognize the right moment to close the sale. Salespeople should know how to recognize closing signals from the buyer, including physical actions, comments, and questions. For example, the customer might sit forward and nod approvingly or ask about prices and credit terms. Salespeople can use one of several closing techniques. They can ask for the order, review points of agreement, offer to help write up the order, ask whether the buyer wants this model or that one, or note that the buyer will lose out if the order is not placed now. The salesperson may offer the buyer special reasons to close, such as a lower price or an extra quantity at no charge.

Closing
The step in the selling process in which the salesperson asks the customer for an order.

Follow-up The last step in the selling process, **follow-up**, is necessary if the salesperson wants to ensure customer satisfaction and repeat business. Right after closing, the salesperson should complete any details on delivery time, purchase terms, and other matters. The salesperson then should schedule a follow-up call when the initial order is received to make sure there is proper installation, instruction, and servicing. This visit would reveal any problems, assure the buyer of the salesperson's interest, and reduce any buyer concerns that might have arisen since the sale.

Follow-up
The last step in the selling process in which the salesperson follows up after the sale to ensure customer satisfaction and repeat business.

Relationship Marketing

The principles of personal selling as just described are *transaction oriented*; their aim is to help salespeople close a specific sale with a customer. But in many cases, the company is not seeking simply a sale, it has targeted a major customer that it would like to win and keep. The company would like to show that it has the capabilities to serve the customer over the long haul in a mutually profitable *relationship*.

Most companies today are moving away from transaction marketing, with its emphasis on making a sale. Instead, they are practicing **relationship marketing**, which emphasizes maintaining profitable long-term relationships with customers by creating superior customer value and satisfaction. They are realizing that when operating in maturing markets and facing stiffer competition, it costs a lot more to wrest new customers from competitors than to keep current customers.

Relationship marketing
The process of creating, maintaining, and enhancing strong, value-laden relationships with customers and other stakeholders.

Today's customers are large and often global. They prefer suppliers who can sell and deliver a coordinated set of products and services to many locations. They favor suppliers who can quickly solve problems that arise in their different parts of the nation or world and who can work closely with customer teams to improve products and processes. For these customers, the sale is only the beginning of the relationship.

Unfortunately, some companies are not set up for these developments. They often sell their products through separate sales forces, each working independently to close sales. Their technical people may not be willing to lend time to educate a customer. Their engineering, design, and manufacturing people may have the attitude that "it's our job to make good products and the salesperson's to sell them to customers." However, other companies are recognizing that winning and keeping accounts requires more than making good products and directing the sales force to close lots of sales. It requires a carefully coordinated whole-company effort to create value-laden, satisfying relationships with important customers.

Marketing at Work 13-3

Great Salespeople—Drive, Discipline, and Relationship-Building Skills

What sets great salespeople apart from all the rest? What separates the masterful from the merely mediocre? In an effort to profile top sales performers, Gallup Management Consulting, a division of the well-known Gallup polling organization, has interviewed as many as half a million salespeople. Its research suggests that the best salespeople possess four key talents: intrinsic motivation, disciplined work style, the ability to close a sale, and perhaps most important, the ability to build relationships with customers.

Intrinsic Motivation

"Different things drive different people—pride, happiness, money, you name it," says one expert. "But all great salespeople have one thing in common: an unrelenting drive to excel." This strong, internal drive can be shaped and molded, but it can't be taught. The source of the motivation varies: Some are driven by money, some by hunger for recognition, some by a yearning to build relationships.

The Gallup research revealed four general personality types, all high performers, but all with different sources of motivation. *Competitors* are people who not only want to win but crave the satisfaction of beating specific rivals—other companies *and* their fellow salespeople. They'll come right out and say to a colleague, "With all due respect, I know you're salesperson of the year, but I'm going after your title." The *ego-driven* are salespeople who just want to experience the glory of winning. They want to be recognized as being the best, regardless of the competition. *Achievers* are a rare breed who are almost completely self-motivated. They like accomplishment and routinely set goals that are higher than what is expected of them.

They often make the best sales managers because they don't mind seeing other people succeed, as long as the organization's goals are met. Finally, *service-oriented* salespeople are those whose strength lies in their ability to build and cultivate relationships. They are generous, caring, and empathetic. "These people are golden," says the national training manager of Minolta Corporation's business equipment division. "We need salespeople who will take the time to follow up on the 10 questions a customer might have, salespeople who love to stay in touch."

No one is purely a competitor, an achiever, ego driven, or service driven. There's at least some of each in most top performers. "A *competitor* with a strong sense of *service* will probably bring in a lot of business while doing a great job of taking care of customers," observes the managing director of the Gallup Management

Relationship marketing is based on the premise that important accounts need focused and ongoing attention. Studies have shown that the best salespeople are those who are highly motivated and good closers, but more than this, they are customer problem solvers and relationship builders (see Marketing at Work 13-3). Good salespeople working with key customers do more than call when they think a customer might be ready to place an order. They also study the account and understand its problems. They call or visit frequently, work with the customer to help solve the customer's problems and improve its business, and take an interest in customers as people.

Sales Promotion

Sales promotion
Short-term incentives to encourage the purchase or sale of a product or service.

Advertising and personal selling often work closely with another promotion tool, sales promotion. **Sales promotion** consists of short-term incentives to encourage purchase or sales of a product or service. Whereas advertising and personal selling offer reasons to buy a product or service, sales promotion offers reasons to buy *now*.

Consulting Group. "Who could ask for anything more?"

Disciplined Work Style

Whatever their motivation, if salespeople aren't organized and focused, and if they don't work hard, they can't meet the ever-increasing demands customers are making these days. Great salespeople are tenacious about laying out detailed, organized plans then following through in a timely, disciplined way. There's no magic here, just solid organization and hard work. "Our best sales reps never let loose ends dangle," says the president of a small-business equipment firm. "If they say they're going to make a follow-up call on a customer in six months, you can be sure that they'll be on the doorstep in six months." Top sellers rely on hard work, not luck or gimmicks. "Some people say it's all technique or luck," notes one sales trainer. "But luck happens to the best salespeople when they get up early, work late, stay up till two in the morning working on a proposal, or keep making calls when everyone is leaving at the end of the day."

The Ability to Close the Sale

Other skills mean little if a seller can't ask for the sale. No close, no sale. Period. So what makes for a great closer? For one thing, an unyielding persistence, say managers and sales consultants. Claims one, "Great closers are like great athletes. They're not afraid to fail, and they don't give up until they close." Part of what makes the failure rate tolerable for top performers is their deep-seated belief in themselves and what they are selling. Great closers have a high level of self-confidence and believe that they are doing the right thing. And they've got a burning need to make the sale happen, to do whatever it takes within legal and ethical standards to get the business.

The Ability to Build Relationships

Perhaps most important in today's relationship-marketing environ-ment, top salespeople are customer problem solvers and relationship builders. They have an instinctive understanding of their customers' needs. Talk to sales executives and they'll describe top performers in these terms: Empathetic. Patient. Caring. Responsive. Good listeners. Even *honest*. Top sellers can put themselves on the buyer's side of the desk and see the world through their customers' eyes. Today, customers are looking for business partners, not golf partners. "At the root of it all," says a Dallas sales consultant, "is an integrity of intent. High performers don't just want to be liked, they want to add value." High-performing salespeople, he adds, are "always thinking about the big picture, where the customer's organization is going, and how they can help them get there."

Source: Adapted from Geoffrey Brewer, "Mind Reading: What Drives Top Salespeople to Greatness?" *Sales & Marketing Management*, May 1994, pp. 82–88. Also see Barry J. Farber, "Success Stories for Salespeople," *Sales & Marketing Management*, May 1995, pp. 30–31; and Roberta Maynard, "Finding the Essence of Good Salespeople," *Nation's Business*, February 1998, p. 10.

Examples of sales promotions are found everywhere. A freestanding insert in the Sunday newspaper contains a coupon offering 50 cents off on Folger's coffee. The end-of-the-aisle display in the local supermarket tempts impulse buyers with a wall of Coke cartons. An executive buys a new Compaq laptop computer and gets a free carrying case, or a family buys a new Taurus and receives a rebate check for $500. A hardware store chain receives a 10 percent discount on selected Black & Decker portable power tools if it agrees to advertise them in local newspapers. Sales promotion includes a wide variety of promotion tools designed to stimulate earlier or stronger market response.

Rapid Growth of Sales Promotion

Sales promotion tools are used by most organizations, including manufacturers, distributors, retailers, trade associations, and nonprofit institutions. They are targeted toward final buyers (*consumer promotions*), business customers (*business promotions*), retailers and wholesalers (*trade promotions*), and members of the sales force (*sales force promotions*). Today, in many consumer packaged-goods companies, sales promotion accounts for 75 percent or more of all marketing expenditures.[22]

Several factors have contributed to the rapid growth of sales promotion, particularly in consumer markets. First, inside the company, product managers face greater pressures to increase their current sales, and promotion is viewed as an effective short-run sales tool. Second, externally, the company faces more competition, and competing brands are less differentiated. Increasingly, competitors are using sales promotion to help differentiate their offers. Third, advertising efficiency has declined because of rising costs, media clutter, and legal restraints. Finally, consumers have become more deal oriented, and retailers are demanding more deals from manufacturers.

The growing use of sales promotion has resulted in *promotion clutter*, similar to advertising clutter. Consumers are increasingly tuning out promotions, weakening their ability to trigger immediate purchase. In fact, the extent to which U.S. consumers have come to take promotions for granted was illustrated dramatically by the reactions of Eastern European consumers when Procter & Gamble gave out samples of a newly introduced shampoo. To P&G, the sampling campaign was just business as usual. To consumers in Poland and Czechoslovakia, however, it was little short of a miracle:

> With nothing expected in return, Warsaw shoppers were being handed free samples of Vidal Sassoon Wash & Go shampoo. Just for the privilege of trying the new product; no standing in line for a product that may not even be on the shelf. Some were so taken aback that they were moved to tears. In a small town in Czechoslovakia, the head of the local post office was so pleased to be part of the direct-mail sampling program, he sent the P&G staffer roses to express his thanks. The postmaster told the P&G'er: "This is the most exciting thing that's ever happened in this post office—it's a terrific experience to be part of this new market economy that's coming."[23]

Although no sales promotion is likely to create such excitement among promotion-prone consumers in the United States and other Western countries, manufacturers are now searching for ways to rise above the clutter, such as offering larger coupon values or creating more dramatic point-of-purchase displays.

In developing a sales promotion program, a company must first set sales promotion objectives and then select the best tools for accomplishing these objectives.

Sales Promotion Objectives

Sales promotion objectives vary widely. Sellers may use *consumer promotions* to increase short-term sales or to help build long-term market share. Objectives for *trade promotions* include getting retailers to carry new items and more inventory, getting them to advertise the product and give it more shelf space, and getting them to buy ahead. For the *sales force*, objectives include getting more sales force support for current or new products or getting salespeople to sign up new accounts. Sales promotions are usually used together with advertising or personal selling. Consumer promotions must usually be advertised and can add excitement and pulling power to ads. Trade and sales force promotions support the firm's personal selling process.

In general, sales promotions should be *consumer relationship building*. Rather than creating only short-term sales or temporary brand switching, they should help to reinforce the product's position and build long-term relationships with consumers. Increasingly, marketers are avoiding "quick fix," price-only promotions in favor of promotions designed to build brand equity. For example, in France, Nestlé set up roadside Relais Bébé centers, where travelers can stop to feed and change their babies. At each center, Nestlé hostesses provide free disposable diapers, changing tables, high chairs, and free samples of Nestlé baby food. Each summer, 64 hostesses welcome 120,000 baby visits and dispense 6,000,000 samples of baby food. This ongoing promotion provides real value to parents and an ideal opportunity to build relationships with customers. At key mealtime moments, Nestlé hostesses are in direct contact with mothers in a unique, brand-related relationship. Nestlé also provides a toll-free phone number for free baby-nutrition counseling.[24]

Even price promotions can be designed to help build customer relationships. Examples include all of the frequency marketing programs and clubs that have mushroomed in recent years (see Marketing at Work 13-4). If properly designed, every sales promotion tool has the potential to build consumer relationships.

Major Sales Promotion Tools

Many tools can be used to accomplish sales promotion objectives. Descriptions of the main consumer and trade promotion tools follow.

Consumer Promotion Tools The main consumer promotion tools include samples, coupons, cash refunds, price packs, premiums, advertising specialties, patronage rewards, point-of-purchase displays and demonstrations, and contests, sweepstakes, and games.

Samples are offers of a trial amount of a product. Some samples are free; for others, the company charges a small amount to offset its cost. The sample might be delivered door-to-door, sent by mail, handed out in a store, attached to another product, or featured in an ad. Sampling is the most effective, but most expensive, way to introduce a new product. Sometimes, samples are combined into sample packs, which can then be used to promote other products and services. An example is Blockbuster Video's "Bonus Box" promotion, in which customers who rent at least three movies receive a box containing samples of Triples and other General Mills cereals, Hawaiian Punch from Procter and Gamble, Hidden Valley dip from Clorox, and Lever 2000 soap from Lever Brothers. Blockbuster hands out more than four million of these boxes over a typical July Fourth weekend.[25]

Sample
Offers to consumers of a small amount of a product for trial.

Point-of-sale couponing: Using Checkout Direct technology, marketers can dispense personalized coupons to carefully targeted buyers at the checkout counter. This avoids the waste of poorly targeted coupons delivered through FSIs (coupon pages inserted into newspapers).

Marketing at Work 13-4

Promoting Customer Relationships: Frequency Marketing Programs and Clubs

Many companies have developed sales promotion programs that build long-term relationships with customers rather than creating only short-term sales volume. The most common efforts are *frequency marketing programs* and *club marketing programs*, which give select customers special privileges and awards that keep them coming back, buying more, and staying loyal.

Frequency Marketing Programs

Frequency marketing programs (FMP) reward customers who buy frequently or in large amounts. Such programs capture more lifetime value from a company's best customers by developing long-term, interactive, value-added relationships with them.

American Airlines was one of the first companies to pioneer a frequency marketing program. In the early 1980s, it offered the AAdvantage program through which frequent flyers could accumulate credits for miles flown with American and redeem them for free airline tickets, seat upgrades, or other benefits. Hotels soon adopted FMPs. Marriott took the lead with its Honored Guest Program, quickly followed by Hyatt (with its Gold Passport Program) and other hotel chains. Frequent guests receive room upgrades or free rooms after earning enough points. Next, car rental firms sponsored FMPs, and credit card companies began to offer points based on their cards' usage level. For example, Shell Oil card users can earn free gasoline and the American Express Custom Extras program automatically awards account holders deals and discounts based on frequency of purchases at participating retailers.

Typically, the first company to introduce an FMP gains the most benefit. However, after competitors respond, FMPs can become a burden to all the offering companies. Soon, many customers belong to several competing FMPs, and companies may find that they are giving away many flights, rooms, and merchandise without gaining much advantage. Despite these problems, frequency marketing programs remain an important tool for building long-term relationships with customers.

Club Marketing Programs

Many companies have created club concepts around their products. Club membership may be offered automatically on purchase of a product or by paying a fee. Some clubs have been very successful:

The Valley View Center Mall in Dallas sponsors the Smart Shoppers Club, a program that rewards customers who tap onto their computerized interactive touch-screen kiosks. To obtain a membership and personal identification number, mallgoers fill out a short application that asks simple demographic and psychographic questions. Then, each time members visit the mall, they input their ID number into one of the mall's three touch-screen kiosks and receive daily discount retail coupons, prizes awarded randomly each week, and a calendar of events. While customers reap discounts and prizes, Valley View retailers get valuable marketing information about their customers. The shopping center is one of only about 10 of the nation's 35,000 malls to use this high-tech consumer loyalty program.

Norwegian Cruise Lines sponsors a loyalty program called *Latitudes*, a co-branding effort with Visa. The program includes a two-for-one cruise offer and a Latitudes Visa card that rewards users with points redeemable for discounts on NCL cruises.

Waldenbooks sponsors a Preferred Reader Program that has attracted over four million members, each paying $5 to receive mailings about new books, a 10 percent discount on book purchases, toll-free ordering, and many other services.

Lladro, maker of fine porcelain figurines, sponsors a Collectors Society with an annual membership fee of $35. Members receive a free subscription to a quarterly

---

Coupon
Certificate that gives buyers a saving when they purchase a specified product.

Coupons are certificates that give buyers a saving when they purchase specified products. Some 290 billion coupons are distributed in the United States each year. Consumers redeem 5.3 billion of these coupons, for a redemption rate of about 2 percent. Coupons can stimulate sales of a mature brand or promote early trial of a new brand. As a result of coupon clutter, redemption rates have been declining in recent years. Thus,

Club marketing: for a $45 annual membership fee, Lladro's "Collectors Society" members receive a subscription to *Expressions* magazine, a bisque plaque, free enrollment in the Lladro Museum of New York, and other relationship building benefits.

magazine, a bisque plaque, free enrollment in the Lladro Museum of New York, and member-only tours to visit the company and Lladro family in Valencia, Spain.

Gateway Federal, a Cincinnati thrift bank, sponsors The Stateman's Club for customers who maintain a minimum deposit of $10,000. Its 10,000 members receive over 26 benefits including free checking, money orders, and

traveler's checks; social gatherings and guest lecturers; and complimentary refreshments. Members have access to IBM computers and other equipment, and they can reserve the Club room for private receptions after regular hours.

Harley-Davidson sponsors the Harley Owners Group (HOG) that now numbers 330,000 members, about a third of all Harley owners. The first-time buyer of a Harley-

Davidson motorcycle gets a free one-year membership with annual renewal costing $40. HOG benefits include a magazine (*Hog Tales*), a copy of the *H.O.G. Touring Handbook*, a complete *H.O.G. World Atlas*, an emergency pickup service, a specially designed insurance program, theft reward service, discount hotel rates, and a *Fly & Ride* program enabling members to rent Harleys while on vacation.

Well-executed clubs and frequency marketing programs can produce significant results. For example, when Sears found that it was losing too many of its best customers to competitors, it launched its Best Customer Program. It defined its best customers as those who shop at Sears frequently and in a variety of departments and who spend a large amount of money annually at the store. About 7.2 million Sears customers fit this definition, and the retailer estimates that each is worth about six times more to Sears than the average new customer. Best Customers receive special benefits and privileges, such as guaranteed response to a service call within 24 hours. The program has improved Sears's customer retention rate by 11 percent and increased sales from best customers by 9 percent.

Sources: See Cyndee Miller, "Rewards for the Best Customers," *Marketing News*, July 5, 1993, pp. 1,6; Louise O'Brien and Charles Jones, "Do Rewards Really Create Loyalty?" *Harvard Business Review*, May–June 1995, pp. 75–82; Grahame R. Dowling and Mark Uncles, "Do Customer Loyalty Programs Really Work?" *Sloan Management Review*, Summer 1997, pp. 71–82; "Harley Owners Journey to Meet Their Maker . . . Again and Again," *Colloquy*, vol. 5, issue 4, 1997, pp. 13–14; and "Building Brand Loyalty," *Advertising Age's Business Marketing*, May 1998, pp. S1–S3.

major consumer goods companies, led by Procter & Gamble, are issuing fewer coupons and targeting them more carefully.

In the past, marketers have relied almost solely on mass-distributed coupons delivered through the mail or on freestanding inserts or ads in newspapers and magazines. Today, however, they are increasingly distributing coupons through shelf dispensers at the point of sale, by electronic point-of-sale coupon printers, or through "paperless coupon systems." An example is Catalina Marketing Network's Checkout Direct system, which dispenses personalized discounts to targeted buyers at the checkout counter in stores.[26] Some companies are now offering coupons on their Web sites or through on-line coupon services such as Interactive Coupon Network's CoolSavings site (www.coolsavings.com) and Money Mailer's H.O.T. Coupons site (www.hotcoupons.com). Participants in Cool-Savings include JCPenney, Toys 'Я' Us, Boston Market, Domino's Pizza, and H&R Block.[27]

Cash refund offer (rebate)
Offer to refund part of the purchase price of a product to consumers who send a "proof of purchase" to the manufacturer.

Cash refund offers (or **rebates**) are like coupons except that the price reduction occurs after the purchase rather than at the retail outlet. The consumer sends a "proof of purchase" to the manufacturer, who then refunds part of the purchase price by mail. For example, Toro ran a clever preseason promotion on some of its snow blower models, offering a rebate if the snowfall in the buyer's market area turned out to be below average. Competitors were not able to match this offer on such short notice, and the promotion was very successful.

Price pack (cents-off deal)
Reduced price that is marked by the producer directly on the label or package.

Price packs (also called **cents-off deals**) offer consumers savings off the regular price of a product. The reduced prices are marked by the producer directly on the label or package. Price packs can be single packages sold at a reduced price (such as two for the price of one), or two related products banded together (such as a toothbrush and toothpaste). Price packs are very effective—even more so than coupons—in stimulating short-term sales.

Premium
Good offered either free or at low cost as an incentive to buy a product.

Premiums are goods offered either free or at low cost as an incentive to buy a product, ranging from toys included with kid's products to phone cards, compact discs, and computer CD-ROMs. In its "Treasure Hunt" promotion, for example, Quaker Oats inserted $5 million worth of gold and silver coins in Ken-L Ration dog food packages. In another premium promotion, Cutty Sark offered a brass tray with the purchase of one bottle of its scotch and a desk lamp with the purchase of two. And Pepsi mounted an extremely successful "Pepsi Stuff" campaign through which customers can order sports-related merchandise by collecting Pepsi points.[28] A premium may come inside the package (in-pack), outside the package (on-pack), or through the mail.

Advertising specialty
Useful article imprinted with an advertiser's name, given as a gift to consumers.

Advertising specialties are useful articles imprinted with an advertiser's name given as gifts to consumers. Typical items include pens, calendars, key rings, matches, shopping bags, T-shirts, caps, nail files, and coffee mugs. Such items can be very effective. In a recent study, 63 percent of all consumers surveyed were either carrying or wearing an ad specialty item. More than three-quarters of those who had an item could recall the advertiser's name or message before showing the item to the interviewer.[29]

Patronage reward
Cash or other award for the regular use of a certain company's products or services.

Patronage rewards are cash or other awards offered for the regular use of a certain company's products or services. For example, airlines offer frequent-flier plans, awarding points for miles traveled that can be turned in for free airline trips. Marriott Hotels has adopted an honored-guest plan that awards points to users of their hotels. Baskin-Robbins offers frequent-purchase awards—for every 10 purchases, customers receive a free quart of ice cream.

Point-of-purchase (POP) promotion
Display and demonstration that takes place at the point of purchase or sale.

Point-of-purchase (POP) promotions include displays and demonstrations that take place at the point of purchase or sale. An example is a five-foot-high cardboard display of Cap'n Crunch next to Cap'n Crunch cereal boxes. Unfortunately, many retailers do not like to handle the hundreds of displays, signs, and posters they receive from manufacturers each year. Manufacturers have responded by offering better POP materials, tying them in with television or print messages, and offering to set them up.

Contests, sweepstakes, games
Promotional events that give consumers the chance to win something—such as cash, trips, or goods—by luck or through extra effort.

Contests, **sweepstakes**, and **games** give consumers the chance to win something, such as cash, trips, or goods, by luck or through extra effort. A *contest* calls for consumers to submit an entry—a jingle, guess, suggestion—to be judged by a panel that will select the best entries. A *sweepstakes* calls for consumers to submit their names for a drawing. A *game* presents consumers with something—bingo numbers, missing letters—every time they buy, which may or may not help them win a prize. A sales contest urges dealers or the sales force to increase their efforts, with prizes going to the top performers.

Trade Promotion Tools More sales promotion dollars are directed to retailers and wholesalers (69 percent) than to consumers (31 percent). Trade promotion can persuade retailers or wholesalers to carry a brand, give it shelf space, promote it in advertising, and push it to consumers. Shelf space is so scarce these days that manufacturers often have to offer price-offs, allowances, buy-back guarantees, or free goods to retailers and wholesalers to get products on the shelf and, once there, to stay on it.

Manufacturers use several trade promotion tools. Many of the tools used for consumer promotions—contests, premiums, displays—can also be used as trade promotions. Or the manufacturer may offer a straight **discount** off the list price on each case purchased during a stated period of time (also called a *price-off*, *off-invoice*, or *off-list*). The offer encourages dealers to buy in quantity or to carry a new item. Dealers can use the discount for immediate profit, for advertising, or for price reductions to their customers.

Manufacturers also may offer an **allowance** (usually so much off per case) in return for the retailer's agreement to feature the manufacturer's products in some way. An *advertising allowance* compensates retailers for advertising the product. A *display allowance* compensates them for using special displays.

Manufacturers may offer *free goods*, which are extra cases of merchandise, to resellers who buy a certain quantity or who feature a certain flavor or size. They may offer *push money*—cash or gifts to dealers or their sales force to "push" the manufacturer's goods. Manufacturers may give retailers free *specialty advertising items* that carry the company's name, such as pens, pencils, calendars, paperweights, matchbooks, memo pads, ashtrays, and yardsticks.

Business Promotion Tools Companies spend billions of dollars each year on promotion to industrial customers. These business promotions are used to generate business leads, stimulate purchases, reward customers, and motivate salespeople. Business promotion includes many of the same tools used for consumer or trade promotions. Here, we focus on two additional major business-promotion tools: conventions and trade shows, and sales contests.

Many companies and trade associations organize *conventions and trade shows* to promote their products. Firms selling to the industry show their products at the trade show. More than 4,300 trade shows take place every year, drawing as many as 85 million people. Vendors receive many benefits, such as opportunities to find new sales leads, contact customers, introduce new products, meet new customers, sell more to present customers, and educate customers with publications and audiovisual materials. Trade shows also help companies reach many prospects not reached through their sales forces. About 90 percent of a trade show's visitors see a company's salespeople for the first time at the show. Business marketers may spend as much as 35 percent of their annual promotion budgets on trade shows.[30]

A *sales contest* is a contest for salespeople or dealers to motivate them to increase their sales performance over a given period. Sales contests motivate and recognize good company performers, who may receive trips, cash prizes, or other gifts. Some companies award points for performance, which the receiver can turn in for any of a variety of prizes. Sales contests work best when they are tied to measurable and achievable sales objectives (such as finding new accounts, reviving old accounts, or increasing account profitability).

Discount
A straight reduction in price on purchases during a stated period of time.

Allowance
Promotional money paid by manufacturers to retailers in return for an agreement to feature the manufacturer's products in some way.

More than 5,800 trade shows take place every year, giving sellers chances to introduce new products and meet new customers. At this consumer electronics trade show, 2,000 exhibitors attracted more than 91,000 professional visitors.

Developing the Sales Promotion Program

The marketer must make several other decisions in order to define the full sales promotion program. First, the marketer must decide on the *size of the incentive*. A certain minimum incentive is necessary if the promotion is to succeed; a larger incentive will produce more sales response. The marketer also must set *conditions for participation*. Incentives might be offered to everyone or only to select groups.

The marketer must decide how to *promote and distribute the promotion* program itself. A 50-cents-off coupon could be given out in a package, at the store, by mail, or in an advertisement. Each distribution method involves a different level of reach and cost. Increasingly, marketers are blending several media into a total campaign concept. The *length of the promotion* is also important. If the sales promotion period is too short, many prospects (who may not be buying during that time) will miss it. If the promotion runs too long, the deal will lose some of its "act now" force.

Evaluation is also very important. Yet many companies fail to evaluate their sales promotion programs, and others evaluate them only superficially. Manufacturers can use one of many evaluation methods. The most common method is to compare sales before, during, and after a promotion. Suppose a company has a 6 percent market share before the promotion, which jumps to 10 percent during the promotion, falls to 5 percent right after, and rises to 7 percent later on. The promotion seems to have attracted new triers and more buying from current customers. After the promotion, sales fell as consumers used up their inventories. The long-run rise to 7 percent means that the company gained some new users. If the brand's share had returned to the old level, then the promotion would have changed only the *timing* of demand rather than the *total* demand.

Consumer research would also show the kinds of people who responded to the promotion and what they did after it ended. *Surveys* can provide information on how many consumers recall the promotion, what they thought of it, how many took advantage of it, and how it affected their buying. Sales promotions also can be evaluated through *experiments* that vary factors such as incentive value, length, and distribution method.

Clearly, sales promotion plays an important role in the total promotion mix. To use it well, the marketer must define the sales promotion objectives, select the best tools, design the sales promotion program, implement the program, and evaluate the results. Moreover, sales promotion must be coordinated carefully with other promotion mix elements within the integrated marketing communications program.

REST STOP Reviewing the Concepts

Hit the brakes, pull over, and revisit this chapter's key concepts. The chapter is the second of three chapters covering the final marketing-mix element, promotion. The previous chapter dealt with advertising and public relations; this one investigates personal selling and sales promotion. In the next chapter, you'll learn about the final promotion-mix element, direct and on-line marketing.

Personal selling and sales promotion are two additional tools for communicating with and persuading current and prospective customers. Selling is one of the world's oldest professions and people who do the selling are called by a variety of names. Regardless of their titles, members of the sales force play a key role in modern marketing organizations. To be successful in personal selling, a company must first build and then manage an effective sales force. Sales promotion consists of short-term incentives to encourage purchase or sales of a product or service. Whereas advertising and personal selling offer reasons to buy a product or service, sales promotion offers reasons to buy *now*.

1. Discuss the role of a company's salespeople in creating value for customers and building customer relationships.

Most companies use salespeople, and many companies assign them an important role in the marketing mix. For companies selling business products, the firm's salespeople work directly with customers. Often, the sales force is the customer's only direct contact with the company and therefore may be viewed by customers as representing the company itself. In contrast, for consumer product companies that sell through intermediaries, consumers usually do not meet salespeople or even know about them. The sales force works behind the scenes, dealing with wholesalers and retailers to obtain their support and helping them become effective in selling the firm's products.

As an element of the promotion mix, the sales force is very effective in achieving certain marketing objectives and carrying out such activities as prospecting, communicating, selling and servicing, and information gathering. But with companies becoming more market oriented, a market-focused sales force also works to produce both *customer satisfaction* and *company profit*. To accomplish these goals, the sales force needs skills in marketing analysis and planning in addition to the traditional selling skills.

2. Identify and explain the six major sales force management steps.

High sales force costs necessitate an effective *sales management process* consisting of six steps: *designing sales force strategy and structure*, *recruiting and selecting*, *training*, *compensating*, *supervising*, and *evaluating* salespeople.

In designing a sales force, sales management must address issues such as what type of sales force structure will work best (territorial, product, customer, or complex structured); how large the sales force should be; who will be involved in the selling effort and how its various sales and sales support people will work together (inside or outside sales forces and team selling).

To hold down the high costs of hiring the wrong people, salespeople must be *recruited* and *selected* carefully. In recruiting salespeople, a company may look to job duties and the characteristics of its most successful salespeople to suggest the traits it wants in its salespeople and then look for applicants through recommendations of current salespeople, employment agencies, and classified ads and by contacting college students. In the selection process, the procedure can vary from a single informal interview to lengthy testing and interviewing. After the selection process is complete, *training* programs familiarize new salespeople not only with the art of selling but with the company's history, its products and policies, and the characteristics of its market and competitors.

The sales force *compensation* system helps to reward, motivate, and direct salespeople. In compensating salespeople, companies try to have an appealing plan, usually close to the going rate for the type of sales job and needed skills. In addition to compensation, all salespeople need *supervision*, and many need continuous encouragement because they must make many decisions and face many frustrations. Periodically, the company must *evaluate* their performance to help them do a better job. In evaluating salespeople the company relies on getting regular information gathered through sales reports, personal observations, customers' letters and complaints, customer surveys, and conversations with other salespeople.

3. Discuss the personal selling process, distinguishing between transaction-oriented marketing and relationship marketing.

The art of selling involves a seven-step *selling process*: *prospecting and qualifying, preapproach, approach, presentation and demonstration, handling objections, closing,* and *follow-up.* These steps help marketers close a specific sale and as such are *transaction oriented.* However, a seller's dealings with customers should be guided by the larger concept of *relationship marketing.* The company's sales force should help to orchestrate a whole-company effort to develop profitable long-term relationships with key customers based on superior customer value and satisfaction.

4. Explain how sales promotion campaigns are developed and implemented.

Sales promotion covers a wide variety of short-term incentive tools—coupons, premiums, contests, buying allowances—designed to stimulate final and business consumers, the trade, and the company's own sales force. Sales promotion spending has been growing faster than advertising spending in recent years. A sales promotion campaign first calls for setting sales promotions objectives (in general, sales promotions should be *consumer relationship building*). It then calls for developing and implementing the sales promotion program by using consumer promotion tools (*samples, coupons, cash refunds or rebates, price packs, premiums, advertising specialties, patronage rewards,* and others); trade promotion tools (*discounts, allowances, free goods, push money*); and business promotion tools (*conventions, trade shows, sales contests*). The sales promotion effort should be coordinated carefully with the firm's other promotion efforts.

Navigating the Key Terms

For a detailed analyses of the meaning and importance of each of the following key terms, visit our Web page at **www.prenhall.com/kotler.**

Advertising specialty
Allowance
Approach
Cash refund offer (rebate)
Closing
Contests, sweepstakes, games
Coupon

Customer sales force structure
Discount
Follow-up
Handling objections
Inside sales force
Outside sales force
Patronage reward
Point-of-purchase promotion (POP)
Preapproach
Premium
Presentation
Price pack (cents-off deal)

Product sales force structure
Prospecting
Relationship marketing
Sales force management
Sales promotion
Salesperson
Sample
Selling process
Team selling
Telemarketing
Territorial sales force structure
Workload approach

Travel Log

The following concept checks and discussion questions will help you to keep track of and apply the concepts you've studied in this chapter.

Concept Checks

1. Robert Louis Stevenson once noted that "everyone lives by _____ something."

2. In the _____ structure, each salesperson is assigned to an exclusive geographic area and sells the company's full line of products or services to all customers in that area.

3. Sales force compensation includes several elements: a _____, a _____, _____, and _____.

4. Through supervision, the company _____ and _____ the sales force to do a better job.

5. According to Figure 13-3, the selling process consists of the following steps: _____, _____, approach, presentation and demonstration, _____, _____, and follow-up.

6. The first step in the selling process is _____—identifying qualified potential customers.

7. Most companies today are moving away from _____ marketing, with its emphasis on making a sale, and are moving toward _____ marketing, which emphasizes maintaining profitable long-term relationships with customers by creating superior customer value and satisfaction.

8. _____ consists of short-term incentives to encourage purchase or sales of a product or service.

9. Sales promotion tools can be targeted toward _____, business customers, _____, and _____.

10. One form of a consumer promotion tool is the _____, which offers a trial amount of a product.*

Discussing the Issues

1. What did Robert Louis Stevenson mean when he said "everyone lives by selling something"? De-scribe all the various positions and roles the modern salesperson might be required to fill or play.

2. Many people feel they do not have the ability to be a successful salesperson. Suggest what role training plays in helping someone develop selling ability.

3. Marketing managers face several sales force strat-egy and design questions. One of the most pressing is how to structure salespeople and their tasks. Evaluate the methods described in the text. For each method (a) provide a brief description of its chief characteristics, (b) an example of how its used, and (c) a critique of its effectiveness.

4. Most companies today are moving away from trans-action marketing and toward relationship marketing. Explain the meaning of relationship marketing. Next, describe how relationship marketing might be used in (a) selling a computer to a consumer, (b) selling a new car, (c) providing a student with a college education, and (d) selling a consumer season tickets to a local drama theater.

5. Which of the sales promotion tools described in the chapter would be best for stimulating sales of the fol-lowing products or services: (a) a dry cleaner that wishes to emphasize low prices on washed and pressed dress shirts, (b) Gummy Bears new Black Cherry fla-vor, (c) Procter & Gamble's efforts to bundle laundry detergent and fabric softer together in a combined mar-keting effort, and (d) a company that wants its cus-tomers to help in developing a new advertising jingle.

Concept check answers: 1. selling; 2. territorial sales force; 3. fixed amount, variable amount, expenses, and fringe benefits; 4. directs and motivates; 5. prospecting and qualifying, preapproach, handling objections, closing; 6. prospecting; 7. transaction, relationship; 8. sales promo-tion; 9. final buyers, retailers and wholesalers, members of the sales force; 10. samples.

Traveling the Net

Point of Interest: On-line Selling

Being a stockbroker can be an exciting and challenging occupation. In past years, young broker trainees received extensive training on technical workings of the stock market and characteristics of potential clients. One of the most difficult tasks for new brokers was learning how to find and develop clients. The learning process in-volved long hours spent on the telephone "cold-calling" and "prospecting" potential clients. Through this difficult and often discouraging process, young brokers "paid their dues" in the brokerage business. Today, however, things have begun to change. New investing and information alternatives are making the broker's job dif-ferent in more challenging ways. Most major brokerage organizations are on-line, and brokers of investment services can now help information-hungry investors in ways that would have been unimaginable only a few years ago. Visit the following Web sites for more information on buying and selling stocks and bonds on-line: (a) E-TRADE (www.etrade.com), (b) Fidelity Investments (www.fidelity.com), (c) Merrill Lynch (www.ml.com), (d) Charles Schwab (www.schwab.com), and (e) T. Rowe Price (www.troweprice.com).

For Discussion

1. How have such Web sites changed the brokerage business? How is the selling function in the bro-kerage business changing?

2. How can on-line brokerage services help the average broker to be a more effective salesperson (if at all)? What sales strategies appear to be most appropriate for the broker who wishes to use personal contact and on-line connections to do business?

3. Which of the preceding Web sites seems to be the most "user friendly"? Why? Which of the sites (if any) makes it easiest for you to get in touch with a broker in your local area? How could a broker in your local area find out that you had been using his or her company's on-line service?

4. Review each of the preceding sites and prepare an analysis grid that compares the sites with respect to sales stimulation, information services, costs, graphic design, responsiveness, security, and relationship marketing. Which site is best? Explain.

Application Thinking

Will on-line marketing eventually replace the human contact that has been an essential ingredient of sales relationships? On-line stock and bond trading provides a good case in point. On-line investment trading differs from ordering merchandise, designing custom clothing, or playing with computer design options. Quick response, security, expert advice and the latest information, trend analysis, and low cost per transaction appear to be much more important than the normal services provided by the average on-line retailer. In the past, stockbrokers served as a link between the trader and the vast information services provided by the brokerage company. On-line trading now appears to be altering this relationship. Assume that you are an on-line trader about to invest $20,000 in the stock market. (a) Which of the Web sites and the associated brokerage companies would you feel most comfortable with? Why? (b) If you used this site, what would be the nature of your relationship with the brokerage? Did personal selling associated with your chosen site influence your decision? (c) How could local brokers use their company's Web site to improve their selling function and skills? Present your findings.

MAP — Marketing Applications

MAP Stop 13

Showman P.T. Barnum would have been proud of Richard Branson. Branson is the founder and president of Virgin Atlantic Airways/Virgin Entertainment Group. He considers himself to be in the same league with Barnum. His empire includes airlines, trains, financial services, music stores, cinemas, and even a cola product. Branson is almost as skilled at developing new ideas as he is at selling and sales promotion. Even though his outward image is that of a flamboyant showman, he is a skilled negotiator, businessman, and brand developer. Recently, Branson introduced Virgin Cola in the United States, competing head-to-head with giants Coca-Cola and Pepsi. To get media attention for the launch of his new product (and to secure much-needed distribution and bottling networks), he rode a tank covered with Virgin Cola cans through Times Square. Instead of traditional commercials for his cola product, Branson's Virgin Cola commercials invited viewers to come on the air and talk about whatever was on their minds. Ringmaster Branson claims that his company is committed to the new product and that Coca-Cola and Pepsi haven't seen anything yet when it comes to unconventional promotion.

Thinking Like a Marketing Manager

1. Evaluate Richard Branson's approach to new product promotion. Do you think that Branson has a sound strategy in pursuing Coca-Cola and Pepsi head-to-head? Explain.

2. What additional sales promotion devices can you suggest to help Virgin Cola establish good relations with dealers? With consumers? How would you tie these promotions in with advertising for the new product?

3. Assume that you are the marketing manager for Virgin Cola. Design a full sales promotion strategy that would allow the brand to expand from the East Coast to the West Coast, and then to the Midwest. What factors would be critical to the success of your venture? Can you use the flamboyance of the company's founder as an advantage? What do you think of your company's chances of success in the United States market?

Direct and On-line Marketing

chapter 14

ROAD MAP:
Previewing the Concepts

Movin' on down the road, it's time to visit the final element of the marketing communications mix: direct and on-line marketing. Actually, direct and on-line marketing can be viewed as more than just communications tools. In many ways, they constitute an overall marketing *approach*—a blend of communications and distribution channels all rolled into one. We'll look first at direct marketing in general: what it is, its benefits and rapid growth, and its many forms. Then we'll travel more deeply into the exciting new world of on-line marketing.

▶ **After studying this chapter, you should be able to**

1. **discuss the benefits of direct marketing to customers and companies and the trends fueling its rapid growth**
2. **define a customer database and outline the ways companies use databases in direct marketing**
3. **identify the major forms of direct marketing**
4. **compare the two types of on-line marketing channels and explain the effect of the Internet on electronic commerce**
5. **identify the benefits of on-line marketing to consumers and marketers and the ways marketers can conduct on-line marketing**
6. **discuss the public policy and ethical issues facing direct marketers**

To start, let's look in on Dell Computer Corporation. In only 15 years, this company has grown explosively from little more than a gleam in Michael Dell's eye into a direct-marketing powerhouse. As you read on, ask yourself this: Has Dell's spectacular success resulted from a breakthrough marketing strategy, from changes in the marketing environment, or from some combination of the two?

When 19-year-old Michael Dell began selling personal computers out of his college dorm room in 1984, few would have bet on his chances for success. In those days, most computer makers sold their PCs through an extensive network of all-powerful distributors and resellers. Even as the fledgling Dell Computer Corporation began to grow, competitors and industry insiders scoffed at the concept of mail-order computer marketing. PC buyers, they contended, needed the kind of advice and hand-holding that only full-service channels could provide. Mail-order PC sales, like mail-order clothing, would never amount to more than 15 percent of the market.

Yet young Michael Dell has proved the skeptics wrong—way wrong. In little more than a decade, he has turned his dorm-room mail-order business into a burgeoning, $18 billion computer empire. Dell computer is now the world's largest direct marketer of computer systems and the world's fastest-growing computer manufacturer. Over the past

473

three years, Dell's sales have increased at an average of 53 percent per year, twice as fast as any competitor and five times the industry average. Profits have skyrocketed 89 percent per year. Since 1990, Dell's stock has risen an incredible 29,600 percent! Direct buyers now account for nearly a third of all PC sales, and Dell's once-skeptical competitors are now scrambling to build their own direct-marketing systems.

What's the secret to Dell's stunning success? Dell's direct-marketing approach delivers greater customer value through an unbeatable combination of product customization, low prices, fast delivery, and award-winning customer service. A customer can talk by phone with a Dell representative on Monday morning; order a fully customized, state-of-the-art PC to suit his or her special needs; and have the machine delivered to his or her doorstep by Wednesday—all at a price that's 10 to 15 percent below competitors' prices. Dell backs its products with high-quality service and support. As a result, Dell consistently ranks among the industry leaders in product reliability and service, and its customers are routinely among the industry's most satisfied.

Dell customers get exactly the machines they need. Michael Dell's initial idea was to serve individual buyers by letting them customize machines with the special features they wanted at low prices. However, this one-to-one approach also appeals strongly to corporate buyers, because Dell can so easily preconfigure each computer to precise requirements. Dell routinely preloads machines with a company's own software and even undertakes tedious tasks such as pasting inventory tags onto each machine so that computers can be delivered directly to a given employee's desk. As a result, about 90 percent of Dell's sales now come from large corporate, government, and educational buyers.

Direct selling results in more efficient selling and lower costs, which translate into lower prices for customers. Because Dell builds machines to order, it carries barely any inventory. Dealing one-to-one with customers helps the company react immediately to shifts in demand, so Dell doesn't get stuck with PCs no one wants. Finally, by selling directly, Dell has no dealers to pay. As a result, on average, Dell's costs are 12 percent lower than those of Compaq, its leading PC competitor.

Dell knows that time is money, and the company is obsessed with "speed." For example, Dell has long been a model of just-in-time manufacturing and efficient supply-chain management. It has also mastered the intricacies of today's lightning-fast electronic commerce. The combination makes Dell a lean and very fast operator. According to one account, "Dell calls it 'velocity'—squeezing time out of every step in the process—from the moment an order is taken to collecting the cash. [By selling direct, manufacturing to order, and] tapping credit cards and electronic payment, Dell converts the average sale to cash in less than 24 hours. By contrast, Compaq Computer Corp., which sells primarily through dealers, takes 35 days, and even mail-order rival Gateway 2000 takes 16.4 days." Such blazing speed results in more satisfied customers and still lower costs. For example, customers are often delighted to find their new computers arriving within as few as 36 hours of placing an order. And because Dell doesn't order parts until an order is booked, it can take advantage of ever-falling component costs. On average, its parts are 60 days newer than those in competing machines and, hence, 60 days farther down the price curve. This gives Dell a 6 percent profit advantage from parts costs alone.

Flush with success, Dell is taking its direct-marketing formula a step further. It is again doing what once seemed impossible: selling PCs on the Internet. Now, by simply clicking the "Buy a Dell" icon at Dell's Web site (www.dell.com), customers can design and price customized computer systems electronically. Then, with a click on the "purchase" button, they can submit an order, choosing from on-line payment options that include a credit card, company purchase order, or corporate lease. Dell dashes out a digital confirmation to customers within five minutes of receiving the order. After receiving confirmation, customers can check the status of the order on-line at any time.

The Internet is a perfect extension of Dell's direct-marketing model. Customers who are already comfortable buying direct from Dell now have an even more powerful way to do so. "The Internet," says Michael Dell, "is the ultimate direct model. . . . [Customers] like the immediacy, convenience, savings, and personal touches that the [Internet] experience provides. Not only are some sales done completely on-line, but people who call on the phone after having visited Dell.com are twice as likely to buy."

If initial sales are any indication, it looks as though Dell has once again rewritten the book on successful direct marketing. The direct-marketing pioneer now sells more than $10 million worth of computers daily from its Web site, and Internet sales are growing at 20 percent each month. Some 225,000 browsers visit Dell's site each week, and buyers range from individuals purchasing home computers to large business users buying high-end $30,000 servers. Michael Dell sees on-line marketing as the next great conquest in the company's direct-marketing crusade. "The Internet is like a booster rocket on our sales and growth," he proclaims. "Our vision is to have *all* customers conduct *all* transactions on the Internet, globally."

This time, competitors aren't scoffing at Michael Dell's vision of the future. It's hard to argue with success, and Michael Dell has been very successful. By following his hunches, at the tender age of 32 he has built one of the world's hottest computer companies. In the process, he's amassed a personal fortune exceeding $13 billion.[1]

Many of the marketing tools we examined in previous chapters were developed in the context of *mass marketing*: targeting broadly with standardized messages and marketing offers. Today, however, with the trend toward more narrowly targeted or one-to-one marketing, more and more companies are adopting *direct marketing* as a primary marketing approach or as a supplement to other approaches. Increasingly, companies are turning to direct marketing in an effort to reach carefully targeted customers more efficiently and to build stronger, more personal, one-to-one relationships with them.

In this chapter, we examine the nature, role, and growing applications of direct marketing and its newest form, on-line marketing. We address the following questions: What is direct marketing? What are its benefits to companies and their customers? How do customer databases support direct marketing? What channels do direct marketers use to reach individual prospects and customers? What marketing opportunities do on-line channels provide? How can companies use integrated direct marketing for competitive advantage? What public and ethical issues are raised by direct and on-line marketing?

What Is Direct Marketing?

Mass marketers have typically sought to reach millions of buyers with a single product and a standard message delivered through the mass media. Thus, Procter & Gamble originally launched Crest toothpaste in one version with a single message ("Crest fights cavities"), hoping that 270 million Americans would get the message and buy the brand. P&G did not need to know its customers' names or anything else about them, only that they wanted to take good care of their teeth. Most marketing communications consisted of one-way communication directed *at* consumers, not two-way communication *with* them.

Direct Marketing
Direct communications with carefully targeted individual consumers to obtain an immediate response.

In contrast, **direct marketing** consists of direct communications with carefully targeted individual consumers to obtain an immediate response. Thus, direct marketers communicate directly with customers, often on a one-to-one, interactive basis. They closely match their marketing offers and communications to the needs of narrowly defined segments or even individual buyers. And beyond brand and image building, they usually seek a direct, immediate, and measurable consumer response. For example, Dell Computer interacts directly with customers, by telephone or through its Web site, to design systems that meet their individual needs. Buyers order directly from Dell, and Dell quickly and efficiently delivers the new computers to their homes or offices.

Early direct marketers—catalog companies, direct mailers, and telemarketers—gathered customer names and sold their goods mainly through the mail and by telephone. Today, improved database technologies and new media—computers, modems, fax machines, e-mail, the Internet, and on-line services—permit more sophisticated direct marketing. Their availability and reasonable costs have greatly enlarged direct-marketing opportunities.

Today, most direct marketers see direct marketing as playing an even broader role than simply selling products and services. They see it as an effective tool for interacting with customers to build long-term customer relationships. Thus, catalog companies send birthday cards, information on special events, or small gifts to select members of their customer bases. Airlines, hotels, and other businesses build strong customer relationships through frequency award programs and club programs. Company Web sites provide ways for customers to "visit" companies, learn about their products and services, interact with company personnel, and participate in entertaining events and activities. In this way, direct marketing becomes *direct-relationship marketing*.

Growth and Benefits of Direct Marketing

Reflecting the trend toward more targeted and one-to-one marketing, direct marketing is now the fastest-growing form of marketing. In this section, we discuss the benefits of direct marketing to customers and sellers and the reasons for its rapid growth.

The Benefits of Direct Marketing

Direct marketing benefits customers in many ways. Consumers report that home shopping is fun, convenient, and hassle-free. It saves time and introduces them to a larger selection of merchandise. They can do comparative shopping by browsing through mail catalogs and on-line shopping services, then order products for themselves or others. Industrial customers can learn about available products and services without waiting for and tying up time with salespeople.

Sellers also benefit. Direct marketers can buy mailing lists containing names of almost any group: millionaires, new parents, left-handed people, or recent college graduates. They can then personalize and customize their messages. With today's technology, a direct marketer can select small groups or even individual consumers, customize offers to their special needs and wants, and promote these offers through individualized communications.

The direct marketer can build an ongoing relationship with each customer. For example, Nestlé's baby food division maintains a database of new parents and mails them six personalized packages of gifts and advice at key stages in the baby's life. P&G's Pampers Parenting Institute Web site (www.pampers.com) offers parents of young children more than just product information. It offers ongoing advice on baby development, health, and safety; a newsletter; a resource library; and an "ask our experts" feature where they can get answers to personal parenting questions.

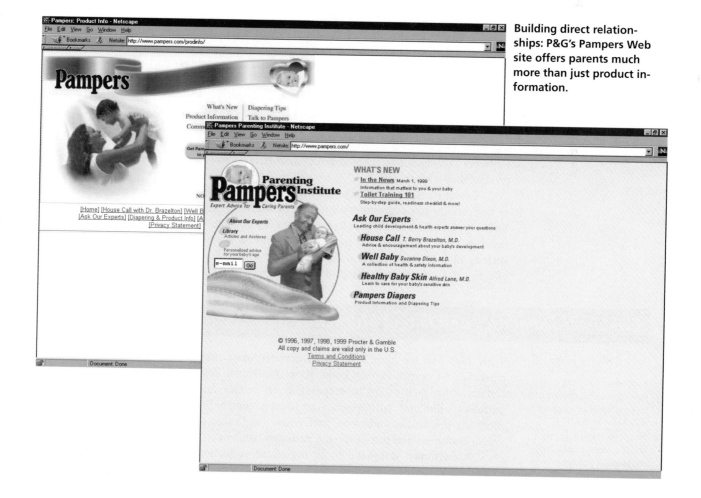

Building direct relationships: P&G's Pampers Web site offers parents much more than just product information.

Direct marketing can also be timed to reach prospects at just the right moment. Because they reach more interested consumers at the best times, direct-marketing materials receive higher readership and response. Direct marketing also permits easy testing of alternative media and messages. Finally, direct marketing provides privacy—the direct marketer's offer and strategy are less visible to competitors.

The Growth of Direct Marketing

Sales through traditional direct-marketing channels (catalogs, direct mail, and telemarketing) have been growing rapidly. Whereas U.S. retail sales grow about 3 percent annually, catalog and direct-mail sales are growing at about 7 percent. These sales include sales to the consumer market (50 percent), business-to-business sales (29 percent), and fund raising by charitable institutions (21 percent).[2]

While direct marketing through traditional channels is growing rapidly, on-line marketing is growing explosively. Today, more than 50 percent of the 97 million U.S. households have a PC, and one recent survey found that 23 percent of U.S. adults had been on-line during the past 30 days.[3] We will examine on-line marketing more closely later in this chapter.

In the consumer market, the extraordinary growth of direct marketing is a response to the new marketing realities discussed in previous chapters. Market "demassification" has resulted in an ever-increasing number of market niches with distinct preferences. Direct marketing allows sellers to focus efficiently on these minimarkets with offers that better match specific consumer needs.

Other trends have also fueled the rapid growth of direct marketing in the consumer market. Higher costs of driving, traffic congestion, parking headaches, lack of time, a shortage of retail sales help, and lines at checkout counters all encourage at-home shopping. Consumers are responding favorably to direct marketers' toll-free phone numbers, their willingness to accept telephone orders 24 hours a day, seven days a week, and their growing commitment to customer service. The growth of 24-hour and 48-hour delivery via Federal Express, Airborne, UPS, DHL, and other express carriers has made direct shopping fast as well as easy. Finally, the growth of affordable computer power and customer databases has enabled direct marketers to single out the best prospects for any product they wish to sell.

Direct marketing has also grown rapidly in business-to-business marketing, partly in response to the ever-increasing costs of reaching business markets through the sales force. When personal sales calls cost $200 per contact, they should be made only when necessary and to high-potential customers and prospects. Lower cost-per-contact media such as telemarketing, direct mail, and the newer electronic media often prove more cost-effective in reaching and selling to more prospects and customers.

Customer Databases and Direct Marketing

Customer database
An organized collection of comprehensive data about individual customers or prospects, including geographic, demographic, psychographic, and behavioral data.

Table 14-1 lists the main differences between mass marketing and so-called *one-to-one marketing*.[4] Companies that know about individual customer needs and characteristics can customize their offers, messages, delivery modes, and payment methods to maximize customer value and satisfaction. And today's companies have a very powerful tool for accessing the names, addresses, preferences, and other pertinent information about individual customers and prospects: the customer database.

A **customer database** is an organized collection of comprehensive data about individual customers or prospects, including geographic, demographic, psychographic,

Table 14-1   Mass Marketing vs. One-to-One Marketing

Mass Marketing	One-to-One Marketing
Average customer	Individual customer
Customer anonymity	Customer profile
Standard product	Customized market offering
Mass production	Customized production
Mass distribution	Individualized distribution
Mass advertising	Individualized message
Mass promotion	Individualized incentives
One-way message	Two-way messages
Economies of scale	Economies of scope
Share of market	Share of customer
All customers	Profitable customers
Customer attraction	Customer retention

Source: Adapted from Don Peppers and Martha Rogers, *The One-to-One Future* (New York: Doubleday/Currency, 1993).

and behavioral data. The database can be used to locate good potential customers, tailor products and services to the special needs of targeted consumers, and maintain long-term customer relationships. *Database marketing* is the process of building, maintaining, and using customer databases and other databases (products, suppliers, resellers) for the purpose of contacting and transacting with customers.

Many companies confuse a customer mailing list with a customer database. A customer mailing list is simply a set of names, addresses, and telephone numbers. A customer database contains much more information. In business-to-business marketing, the salesperson's customer profile might contain the products and services the customer has bought; past volumes and prices; key contacts (and their ages, birthdays, hobbies, and favorite foods); competitive suppliers; status of current contracts; estimated customer expenditures for the next few years; and assessments of competitive strengths and weaknesses in selling and servicing the account. In consumer marketing, the customer database might contain a customer's demographics (age, income, family members, birthdays), psychographics (activities, interests, and opinions), and buying behavior (past purchases, buying preferences), and other relevant information. For example, the catalog company Fingerhut maintains a database containing some 1,300 pieces of information about each of 30 million households (see Marketing at Work 14-1). And Ritz-Carlton's database holds more than 500,000 individual customer preferences.

Database marketing is most frequently used by business-to-business marketers and service retailers (hotels, banks, and airlines). Increasingly, however, consumer packaged-goods companies and retailers are also employing database marketing. A recent survey found that almost two-thirds of all large consumer products companies are currently using or building such databases for targeting their marketing efforts.[5] Armed with the information in their databases, these companies can identify small groups of customers to receive fine-tuned marketing offers and communications. Procter & Gamble uses its database to market Pampers disposable diapers, using tactics such as "individualized" birthday cards for babies and reminder letters to move up to the next size. Kraft Foods has amassed a list of more than 30 million users of its products who have responded to coupons or other Kraft promotions. Based on their interests, the company sends these customers tips on issues such as nutrition and exercise, as well as recipes and coupons for specific Kraft brands. Blockbuster, the massive entertainment company, uses its database

Marketing at Work 14-1

Database Marketing: Fingerhut Builds Strong Customer Relationships

As Betty Holmes of Detroit, Michigan, sifts through the day's stack of mail, one item in particular catches her eye. It's only a catalog but it's speaking directly to her. A laser-printed personal message on the catalog's cover states: "Thank you, Mrs. Holmes, for your recent purchase of women's apparel. To show our thanks, we are offering you up to 5 free gifts, plus deferred payment until July 31st." The note goes on, with amazing accuracy, to refer Betty to specific items in the catalog that will likely interest her.

The catalog is from Fingerhut, the giant direct-mail retailer and master database marketer. A typical Fingerhut catalog offers products ranging from $20 toy phones to $2,000 big-screen TVs. Fingerhut operates on a *huge* scale: It sends out some 558 million mailings each year, more than 1.5 million per day. When new customers first respond to a direct-mail offer, Fingerhut asks them to fill out a questionnaire about the kinds of products that interest them. Using information from this questionnaire and from other sources, along with information about later purchases, Fingerhut has built an impressive marketing database. The database contains some 1,300 pieces of information on each of 30 million active and potential customers. It's filled to the brim with the usual

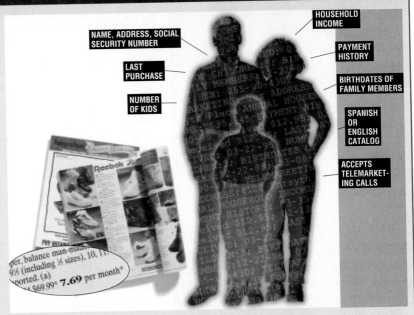

Fingerhut's database stores scores of facts on tens of millions of consumers. Catalogs list monthly payments in bold type and actual prices in fine print.

demographic details such as address, age, marital status, and number of children but also tracks hobbies, interests, birthdays, and other seemingly obscure facts.

The database allows Fingerhut to target the most likely buyers with products that interest them most. Instead of sending out the same catalogs and letters to all of its customers, Fingerhut tailors its offers based on what each

customer is likely to buy. Moreover, promotions such as the Birthday Club provide opportunities to create special offers that sell more products. A month before a child's birthday, Birthday Club customers receive a free birthday gift for their child if they agree to try any one of the products Fingerhut offers in an accompanying mailing. A customer who responds to these and other offers might become one of

of 36 million households and 2 million daily transactions to help its video-rental customers select movies and to steer them to other Blockbuster subsidiaries. Lands' End uses a technique known as "data mining" to identify different groups of catalog clothing purchasers; at last count, it had identified 5,200 different segments! And American Express uses its database to tailor offers to cardholders. In Belgium, it is testing a system that links cardholder spending patterns with postal-zone data. If a new restaurant opens, for

millions of "promotable" customers who receive Fingerhut mailings. As a result of such skillful use of its database, Fingerhut achieves direct-mail response rates that are three times the industry average. Says one retailing consultant, "Fingerhut is one of those pioneering companies that is making intense knowledge of their customer a core competency."

Fingerhut uses its database to build long-term customer relationships that go well beyond its merchandise. It stays in continuous touch with preferred customers through regular special promotions: an annual sweepstakes, free gifts, a deferred-billing promotion, and others. These special offers are all designed with one goal in mind: to create a reason for Fingerhut to be in the customer's mailbox. Once in the mailbox, the personalized messages and targeted offers get attention.

Credit is an important cornerstone of Fingerhut's relationship with customers. The average Fingerhut customer has a household income of just $25,000. Whereas many retailers and credit companies are reluctant to extend credit to this moderate-income group, Fingerhut encourages credit. Catalogs list monthly payments in bold type and actual prices in fine print. Customers can spread a $40 sneaker purchase over 13 months with payments of just $4.79 per month. Thus, Fingerhut regularly extends credit to people who would

otherwise have to pay cash. "When I started out, Fingerhut was the only place that would give me credit," says Marilyn Gnat from Eagle River, Wisconsin, a loyal Fingerhut customer who raised nine children on a modest income.

Despite selling to consumers of modest means, Fingerhut turns credit into a competitive advantage by using its huge database to effectively control credit risks. Some 40 percent of Fingerhut customers have had so little credit that they don't even have credit reports. Thus, the company's extensive database helps it to do a better job than its competitors can of predicting customers' creditworthiness. Fingerhut further controls credit risks by what it offers to whom. When a new customer makes a first order, the amount of credit allowed may be limited to $50. If the customer pays promptly, the next mailing offers higher-ticket items. Good customers who pay their bills regularly get cards and rewards to reinforce this behavior. For example, an award envelope cheers "Congratulations! You've been selected to receive our 'exceptional customer award!'" and contains a certificate suitable for framing.

Recently, Fingerhut has begun applying its database touch to the Internet. Customers can now log onto the Fingerhut On-line Web site (www.fingerhut.com) and order products from the catalog using an online order form. The company's

popular Andy's Garage Sale site (www.andysgarage.com) even customizes its interactions with Web customers. "If you are repeatedly buying golf equipment and I'm buying boat supplies, it'll show you golf bags, and it'll show me life jackets," explains Fingerhut's vice-president of marketing.

The skillful use of database marketing and relationship building has made Fingerhut one of the nation's largest direct-mail marketers. Founded in 1948 by brothers Manny and William Fingerhut, it now sells more than $2 billion worth of mail-order merchandise each year, making it the nation's second-largest consumer catalog company behind JCPenney. In fact, one in every six U.S. households has *bought* something from the company. Fingerhut's success is no accident. "Most of our competitors use a full catalog; they could care less about what the individuals want," notes a Fingerhut executive. "Fingerhut finds out what each customer wants and builds an event around each promotion."

Sources: Quotes from Eileen Norris, "Fingerhut Gives Customers Credit," *Advertising Age*, March 6, 1986, p. 19; Susan Chandler, "Data Is Power: Just Ask Fingerhut," *Business Week*, June 3, 1996, p. 69; and Mitch Wagner, "Repeat Traffic Is Goal of Customerized Web Sites," *Computer World*, November 25, 1996, p. 48. Also see David Pearson, "Marketing for Survival," *CIO*, April 15, 1998, pp. 44–48; Thomas Hoffman, "Too Many IT Duties? Hire a Second CIO," *Computerworld*, March 16, 1998, p. 10; Gene G. Marcial, "Fingerhut Gets a Grip on the Net," *Business Week*, December 14, 1998, p. 128; and "Retailer Buys Fingerhut Marketing Company," *Marketing News*, March 15, 1999, p. 15.

example, the company might offer a special discount to cardholders who live within walking distance and who eat out a lot.[6]

Companies use their databases in four ways:

1. *Identifying prospects:* Many companies generate sales leads by advertising their products or offers. Ads generally have some sort of response feature, such as a business

reply card or toll-free phone number. The database is built from these responses. The company sorts through the database to identify the best prospects, then reaches them by mail, phone, or personal calls in an attempt to convert them into customers.

2. *Deciding which customers should receive a particular offer:* Companies identify the profile of an ideal customer for an offer. Then they search their databases for individuals most closely resembling the ideal type. By tracking individual responses, the company can improve its targeting precision over time. Following a sale, it can set up an automatic sequence of activities: one week later, send a thank-you note; five weeks later, send a new offer; ten weeks later (if the customer has not responded), phone the customer and offer a special discount.

3. *Deepening customer loyalty:* Companies can build customers' interest and enthusiasm by remembering their preferences and by sending appropriate information, gifts, or other materials. For example, Mars, a market leader in pet food as well as candy, maintains an exhaustive pet database. In Germany, the company has compiled the names of virtually every German family that owns a cat. It obtained these names by contacting veterinarians and by offering the public a free booklet titled "How to Take Care of Your Cat." People who request the booklet fill out a questionnaire, providing their cat's name, age, birthday, and other information. Mars then sends a birthday card to each cat in Germany each year, along with a new cat food sample and money-saving coupons for Mars brands. The result is a lasting relationship with the cat's owner.

4. *Reactivating customer purchases:* The database can help a company make attractive offers of product replacements, upgrades, or complementary products just when customers might be ready to act. For example, a General Electric customer database contains each customer's demographic and psychographic characteristics along with an appliance purchasing history. Using this database, GE marketers assess how long specific customers have owned their current appliances and which past customers might be ready to purchase again. They can determine which customers need a new GE video recorder, compact disc player, stereo receiver, or something else to go with other recently purchased electronics products. Or they can identify the best past GE purchasers and send them gift certificates or other promotions to apply against their next GE purchases. A rich customer database allows GE to build profitable new business by locating good prospects, anticipating customer needs, cross-selling products and services, and rewarding loyal customers.[7]

Like many other marketing tools, database marketing requires a special investment. Companies must invest in computer hardware, database software, analytical programs, communication links, and skilled personnel. The database system must be user friendly and available to various marketing groups, including those in product and brand management, new-product development, advertising and promotion, direct mail, telemarketing, field sales, order fulfillment, and customer service. A well-managed database should lead to sales gains that will more than cover its costs. Miami-based Royal Caribbean cruises has had success in this area. Database marketing allows it to offer spur-of-the-moment cruise packages that help to fill all the berths on its ships. Fewer unbooked rooms mean maximized profits for the cruise line.

As more companies move into database marketing, the nature of marketing will change. Mass marketing and mass retailing will continue, but their prevalence and power may diminish as more buyers turn to nonretail shopping. More consumers will use electronic shopping to search for the information and products they need. On-line services will provide more objective information about the comparative merits of different brands. Marketers will need to think of new ways to create effective on-line messages as well as new channels for delivering products and services efficiently.

Forms of Direct Marketing Communication

The major forms of direct marketing, as shown in Figure 14-1, include *face-to-face selling*, *direct-mail marketing*, *catalog marketing*, *telemarketing*, *direct-response television marketing*, *kiosk marketing*, and *on-line marketing*.

Face-to-Face Selling

The original and oldest form of direct marketing is the sales call, which we examined in the previous chapter. Today, most business-to-business marketers rely heavily on a professional sales force to locate prospects, develop them into customers, build lasting relationships, and grow the business. Or they hire manufacturers' representatives and agents to carry out the direct selling task. In addition, many consumer companies use a direct-selling force to reach final consumers: insurance agents, stockbrokers, and salespeople working part- or full-time for direct-sales organizations such as Avon, Amway, Mary Kay, and Tupperware.

Direct-Mail Marketing

Direct-mail marketing involves sending an offer, announcement, reminder, or other item to a person at a particular address. Using highly selective mailing lists, direct marketers send out millions of mail pieces each year: letters, ads, samples, foldouts, and other "salespeople with wings." Direct mail is well suited to direct, one-to-one communication. It permits high target-market selectivity, can be personalized, is flexible, and allows easy measurement of results. Whereas the cost per thousand people reached is higher than with mass media such as television or magazines, the people who are reached are much better

> **Direct-mail marketing**
> Direct marketing through single mailings that include letters, ads, samples, foldouts, and other "salespeople with wings" sent to prospects on mailing lists.

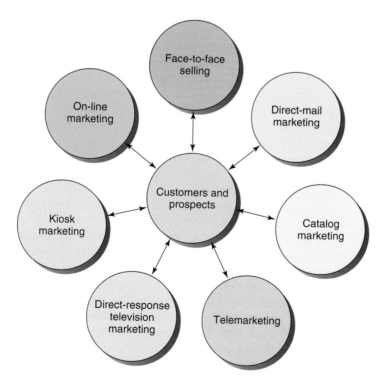

Figure 14-1
Forms of direct marketing

New direct mail approaches: To introduce its Donkey Kong Country video game, Nintendo sent this 13-minute MTV-style video to 2 million avid video game players, helping it sell 6.1 million units of the game in only 45 days.

prospects. Direct mail has proved successful in promoting all kinds of products, from books, magazine subscriptions, and insurance to gift items, clothing, gourmet foods, and industrial products. Direct mail is also used heavily by charities to raise billions of dollars each year.

The direct-mail industry constantly seeks new methods and approaches. For example, videocassettes have become one of the fastest-growing direct-mail media. With VCRs now in 85 percent of American homes, marketers mailed out an estimated 85 million tapes in 1995. For instance, to introduce its Donkey Kong Country video game, Nintendo of America created a 13-minute MTV-style video and sent 2 million copies to avid video game players. This direct-mail video helped Nintendo sell 6.1 million units of the game in only 45 days, making it the fastest-selling game in industry history.[8] Some direct marketers even mail out computer diskettes. For example, Ford sends a computer diskette called "Disk Drive Test Drive" to consumers responding to its ads in computer publications. The diskette's menu provides technical specifications and attractive graphics about Ford cars and answers frequently asked questions.

Until recently, all mail was paper based and handled by the U.S. Post Office, telegraphic services, or for-profit mail carriers such as Federal Express, DHL, or Airborne Express. Recently, however, three new forms of mail delivery have become popular:

- *Fax mail:* Fax machines allow delivery of paper-based messages over telephone lines. Fax mail has one major advantage over regular mail: The message can be sent and received almost instantaneously. Marketers now routinely send fax mail announcing offers, sales, and other events to prospects and customers with fax machines. Fax numbers of companies and individuals are now available through published directories. However, some prospects and customers resent receiving unsolicited fax mail, which ties up their machines and consumes their paper.
- *E-mail:* E-mail (short for *electronic mail*) allows users to send messages or files directly from one computer to another. Messages arrive almost instantly and are stored until the receiving person retrieves them. Many marketers now send sales announcements, offers, product information, and other messages to e-mail addresses—sometimes to a few individuals, sometimes to large groups. As people begin to receive more e-mail

messages, including unimportant ones, they may look for an "agent" software program to sort out the more important messages from those that can be ignored or discarded.

- *Voice mail:* Voice mail is a system for receiving and storing oral messages at a telephone address. Telephone companies sell this service as a substitute for answering machines. The person with a voice-mail account can check messages by dialing into the voice-mail system and entering a personal code. Some marketers have set up programs that will dial a large number of telephone numbers and leave the selling messages in the recipients' voice mail boxes.

These new forms deliver direct mail at incredible speeds compared to the post office's "snail mail" pace. Yet, much like mail delivered through traditional channels, they may be resented as "junk mail" if sent to people who have no interest in them. For this reason, marketers must carefully identify appropriate targets so as not waste their money and recipients' time.

Catalog Marketing

Catalog marketing involves selling through catalogs mailed to a select list of customers or made available in stores. Some huge general-merchandise retailers, such as JCPenney and Spiegel, sell a full line of merchandise through catalogs. But recently, the giants have been challenged by thousands of specialty catalogs that serve highly specialized market niches. Over 14 billion copies of more than 8,500 different consumer catalogs are mailed out annually, and the average household receives some 50 catalogs a year. Last year, catalog sales accounted for more than $86 billion in sales, almost 4 percent of total retail sales.[9] Consumers can buy just about anything from a catalog. Sharper Image sells $2,400 jet-propelled surf boards. The Banana Republic Travel and Safari Clothing Company features everything you would need to go hiking in the Sahara or the rain forest. And each year Lillian Vernon sends out 33 editions of its catalogs with total circulation of 178 million copies to its 20-million-person database, selling everything from shoes to decorative lawn birds and monogrammed oven mitts.[10]

Specialty department stores, such as Neiman Marcus, Bloomingdale's, and Saks Fifth Avenue, send catalogs to cultivate upper-middle-class markets for high-priced, often exotic, merchandise. Several major corporations have also developed or acquired mail-order divisions. For example, Avon now issues 10 women's fashion catalogs along with catalogs for children's and men's clothes. The Walt Disney Company mails out over 6 million catalogs each year featuring videos, stuffed animals, and other Disney items.

Most consumers enjoy receiving catalogs and will sometimes even pay to get them. Many catalog marketers are now even selling their catalogs at bookstores and magazine stands. Some companies, such as Royal Silk, Neiman Marcus, Sears, and Spiegel, are also experimenting with videotape, computer diskette, CD-ROM, and Internet catalogs. Royal Silk sells a 35-minute video catalog to its customers for $5.95. The tape contains a polished presentation of Royal Silk products, tells customers how to care for silk, and provides ordering information. Most major direct retailers have also put their catalogs on the World Wide Web. For example, L.L. Bean shoppers can visit www.llbean.com and browse a more current and complete catalog than they are likely to receive by mail.

Many business-to-business marketers also rely heavily on catalogs. Whether in the form of a simple brochure, three-ring binder, book, or encoded videotape or computer disk, catalogs remain one of today's hardest-working sales tools. For some companies, in fact, catalogs have even taken the place of salespeople. In all, companies mail out more than 1.1 *billion* business-to-business catalogs each year, reaping more than $50 billion worth of catalog sales.[11]

Catalog marketing
Direct marketing through catalogs that are mailed to a select list of customers or made available in stores.

Telemarketing

Telemarketing
Using the telephone to sell directly to customers.

Telemarketing, using the telephone to sell directly to consumers, has become the major direct-marketing communication tool. Marketers use *outbound* telephone marketing to sell directly to consumers and businesses. *Inbound* toll-free 800 numbers are used to receive orders from television and radio ads, direct mail, or catalogs. The use of 800 numbers has taken off in recent years as more and more companies have begun using them and as current users have added new features such as toll-free fax numbers. Residential use has also grown. To accommodate this rapid growth, new toll-free area codes (888, 877, 866) have been added. After the 800 area code was established in 1967, it took almost 30 years before its 8 million numbers were used up. In contrast, 888 area code numbers, established in 1996, were used up in only two years.[12]

Other marketers use 900 numbers to sell consumers information, entertainment, or the opportunity to voice an opinion on a pay-per-call basis. For example, for a charge, consumers can obtain weather forecasts from American Express (900-WEATHER—75 cents a minute); pet care information from Quaker Oats (900-990-PETS—95 cents a minute); advice on snoring and other sleep disorders from Somnus (900-USA-SLEEP—$2 for the first minute, then $1 a minute); golf lessons from *Golf Digest* (900-454-3288—95 cents a minute); or individual answers to nutrition questions from a registered dietician sponsored by the American Dietetic Association (900-CALL-AN-RD—$1.95 for the first minute, then 95 cents a minute). In addition to its 800 number and Internet site, Nintendo offers a 900 number, for $1.50 per minute, for game players wanting assistance with the company's video games. Ronald McDonald House Charities uses a 900 number to raise funds. Each call to 900-CALL-RMHC results in a $15.00 contribution, which is simply charged to the caller's local phone bill. Overall, the use of 900 numbers has grown by more than 10 percent a year over the past five years.[13]

Business-to-business marketers use telemarketing extensively. In fact, more than $115 billion worth of business products were marketed by phone last year. For example, General Electric uses telemarketing to generate and qualify sales leads and to manage small accounts. Raleigh Bicycles uses telemarketing to reduce the amount of personal selling needed for contacting its dealers; in the first year, sales force travel costs were reduced 50 percent, and sales in a single quarter increased 34 percent.[14]

Many consumers appreciate many of the offers they receive by telephone. Properly designed and targeted telemarketing provides many benefits, including purchasing convenience and increased product and service information. However, the recent explosion in unsolicited telephone marketing has annoyed many consumers who object to the almost daily "junk" phone calls that pull them away from the dinner table or fill their answering machines. Lawmakers around the country are responding with legislation ranging from banning unsolicited telemarketing calls during certain hours to letting households sign up for a national "Don't Call Me" list. Most telemarketers support some action against random and poorly targeted telemarketing. As a Direct Marketing Association executive notes, "We want to target people who want to be targeted."[15]

Direct-Response Television Marketing

Direct-response television marketing
Direct marketing via television, including *direct-response television advertising* or *infomercials* and *home shopping channels.*

Direct-response television marketing takes one of two major forms. The first is *direct-response advertising*. Direct marketers air television spots, often 60 or 120 seconds long, that persuasively describe a product and give customers a toll-free number for ordering. Television viewers often encounter 30-minute advertising programs, or *infomercials*, for a single product. Such direct-response advertising works well for magazines, books, small appliances, tapes and CDs, collectibles, and many other products.

Some successful direct-response ads run for years and become classics. For example, Dial Media's ads for Ginsu knives ran for seven years and sold almost three million sets of knives worth more than $40 million in sales; its Armourcote cookware ads generated more than twice that much. For years, infomercials have been associated with somewhat questionable pitches for juicers, get-rich-quick schemes, and nifty ways to stay in shape without working very hard at it. Recently, however, a number of top marketing companies—GTE, Johnson & Johnson, MCA Universal, Sears, Procter & Gamble, Revlon, Apple Computer, Toyota, Anheuser Busch, and others—have begun using infomercials to sell their wares over the phone, refer customers to retailers, or send out coupons and product information. In all, infomercials produce almost $1.6 billion in sales each year.[16]

Home shopping channels, another form of direct-response television marketing, are television programs or entire channels dedicated to selling goods and services. Some home shopping channels, such as the Quality Value Channel (QVC) and the Home Shopping Network (HSN), broadcast 24 hours a day. On HSN, the program's hosts offer bargain prices on products ranging from jewelry, lamps, collectible dolls, and clothing to power tools and consumer electronics—usually obtained by the home shopping channel at closeout prices. The show is upbeat, with the hosts honking horns, blowing whistles, and praising viewers for their good taste. Viewers call an 800 number to order goods. At the other end of the operation, 400 operators handle more than 1,200 incoming lines, entering orders directly into computer terminals. Orders are shipped within 48 hours. QVC sells more than $1.6 billion worth of merchandise each year and averages 113,000 orders per day. Sears, Kmart, JCPenney, Spiegel, and other major retailers are now looking into the home shopping industry.[17]

Beyond infomercials, home shopping channels, and other direct-response television marketing approaches, many experts think that advances in two-way, interactive television and linkages with Internet technology will one day make television shopping one of the major forms of direct marketing.[18]

Kiosk Marketing

Some companies place information and ordering machines, called *kiosks* (in contrast to vending machines, which dispense actual products), in stores, airports, and other locations. Hallmark and American Greetings use kiosks to help customers create and purchase personalized greeting cards. Lee jeans stores use a kiosk called Fit Finder to provide women with a quick way to determine the size and style of Lee jeans to match their personal preference. Tower Records has listening kiosks that let customers listen to the music before purchase. Kiosks in the do-it-yourself ceramics stores of California-based Color Me Mine Inc. contain clip-art images that customers can use to decorate the ceramic pieces they purchase in the store. At Car Max, the used-car superstore, customers use a kiosk with a touch-screen computer to get information about its vast inventory of as many as 1,000 cars and trucks. Customers can choose a handful and print out photos, prices, features, and location on the store's lot. The use of such kiosks is expected to increase fivefold during the next three years.[19]

Business marketers also use kiosks. For example, Dow Plastics places kiosks at trade shows to collect sales leads and to provide information on its 700 products. The kiosk system reads customer data from encoded registration badges and produces technical data sheets that can be printed at the kiosk or faxed or mailed to the customer. The system has resulted in a 400 percent increase in qualified sales leads.[20]

Linking the Concepts

Hold up a moment and think about the impact of direct marketing on your life.

- When was the last time that you *bought* something via direct marketing? What did you buy and why did you buy it direct? When was the last time that you *rejected* a direct-marketing offer? Why did you reject it? Based on these experiences, what advice would you give to direct marketers?
- For the next week, keep track of all the direct-marketing offers that come your way via direct mail and catalogs, telephone, and direct-response television. Then analyze the offers by type, source, and what you liked or disliked about each offer and the way it was delivered. Which offer best hit its target (you)? Which missed by the widest margin?

On-line Marketing and Electronic Commerce

On-line marketing
Marketing conducted through interactive on-line computer systems, which link consumers with sellers electronically.

Commercial on-line services
Services that offer on-line information and marketing services to subscribers who pay a monthly fee, such as America Online, CompuServe, and Prodigy.

On-line marketing is conducted through interactive on-line computer systems, which link consumers with sellers electronically. A modem connects the consumer's computer or TV set-top "Web machine" with various services through telephone lines. There are two types of on-line marketing channels: commercial on-line services and the Internet.

Commercial on-line services offer on-line information and marketing services to subscribers who pay a monthly fee. The best-known on-line services are America Online, CompuServe, Prodigy, and MicroSoft Network.[21] These on-line services provide subscribers with information (news, libraries, education, travel, sports, reference), entertainment (fun and games), shopping services, dialogue opportunities (bulletin boards, forums, chat boxes), and e-mail. With a few clicks of the mouse button at their home PCs, subscribers can order thousands of products and services electronically from dozens of major stores and catalogs. They can also do their banking with local banks; buy and

Commercial on-line services—like America Online—offer information and marketing services to subscribers who pay a monthly fee.

sell investments through discount brokerage services; book airline, hotel, and car-rental reservations; play games, quizzes, and contests; check *Consumer Reports* ratings of various products; receive the latest sports scores and statistics; obtain weather forecasts; and exchange e-mail messages with other subscribers around the country.

After growing rapidly through the mid-1990s, the commercial on-line services are now being overtaken by the **Internet** as the primary on-line marketing channel. In fact, all of the on-line service firms now offer Internet access as a primary service. The Internet is a vast and burgeoning global web of computer networks. The Internet evolved from a network created by the Defense Department during the 1960s, initially to link government labs, contractors, and military installations. Today, this huge, public computer network links computer users of all types all around the world. Anyone with a PC, a modem, and the right software can browse the Internet to obtain or share information on almost any subject and to interact with other users.[22]

> **Internet (or the Net)**
> The vast and burgeoning global web of computer networks that links computers around the world.

Internet usage has surged with the recent development of the user-friendly **World Wide Web** and Web browser software such as Netscape Navigator, Microsoft Internet Explorer, and Mosaic. Now, even novices can surf the Net and experience fully integrated text, graphics, images, and sound. Users can send e-mail, exchange views, shop for products, and access news, food recipes, art, and business information. The Internet itself is free, although individual users usually must pay a commercial access provider to be hooked up to it.

> **World Wide Web (or the Web)**
> The user-friendly Internet access standard.

Rapid Growth of On-line Marketing

Although still in their infancy, Internet usage and on-line marketing are growing explosively. By 1998, some 60 million people in the U.S. were dialing into the Internet, up from just 1 million in 1994. The U.S. Internet population is expected to swell to some 320 million by the year 2002. Total worldwide Internet purchasing on the Web is expected to skyrocket from zero in 1994 and $9 billion in 1998 to as much as one trillion by 2005.[23]

This explosion of Internet usage heralds the dawning of a new world of *electronic commerce*. **Electronic commerce** is the general term for a buying and selling process that is supported by electronic means. *Electronic markets* are "marketspaces" in which sellers offer their products and services electronically and buyers search for information, identify what they want, and place orders using a credit card or other means of electronic payment.

> **Electronic commerce**
> The general term for a buying and selling process that is supported by electronic means.

The electronic commerce explosion is all around us. Here are just a few examples:

◇ A reporter wants to buy a 35-mm camera. She turns on her computer, logs onto the Shopper's Advantage Web site, clicks on cameras, then clicks on 35-mm cameras. A list of all the major brands appears, along with information about each brand. She can retrieve a photo of each camera and reviews by experts. Finding the camera she wants, she places an order by typing in her credit card number, address, and preferred shipping mode.

◇ An affluent investor decides to do his own banking and investing. He signs onto discount brokerage Charles Schwab Company's SchwabNOW Web site (www.schwab.com), checks the current status of his investment account, and obtains reports on several stocks he is considering buying. After completing his research, he reviews current stock prices and places his buy and sell orders.

◇ An executive is planning a trip to London and wants to locate a hotel that meets her needs. She signs onto the Travelocity Web site (www.travelocity.com) and inputs her criteria (rate, location, amenities, safety). The computer produces a list of appropriate hotels, and she can book a room once she has made her choice. Eventually, videos giving a "guided tour" of each hotel will be included in the program.

Electronic commerce is all around us—the SchwabNOW Web site allows Schwab clients to check the status of their accounts, research stocks, review current stock prices, and place buy and sell orders.

A recent study found that 39 percent of all Net users have searched for product information on-line prior to making a purchase. Fifteen percent of Net users have purchased a product or service on-line, and the percentage is growing daily.[24]

The On-line Consumer

When people envision the typical Internet user, many mistakenly envision a pasty-faced computer nerd or "cyberhead." Others envision a young, techy, upscale male professional. Although such stereotypes are sadly outdated, the Net population does differ demographically from the general population.

As a whole, Internet users remain an elite group. By and large, the Net population is younger (median age of 38), more affluent (median household income around $66,000), better educated (50 percent are college graduates), and more male (54 percent) than the general population.[25] However, as more and more people find their way onto the Net, the cyberspace population is becoming more mainstream and diverse. Increasingly, the Internet provides on-line marketers with access to a broad range of demographic segments. For example, the proportion of female Net users has doubled in the past two years. And although more than half of all users are professionals or managers, this percentage is decreasing.

Net users come from all age groups. For example, the population of more than 4 million "Net kids" (predicted to reach almost 20 million by the year 2000) has attracted a host of on-line marketers. America On-line offers a Kids Only area featuring homework help and on-line magazines along with the usual games, software, and chat rooms. The Microsoft Network site carries Disney's Daily Blast, which offers kids games, stories, comic strips with old and new Disney characters, and current events tailored to preteens.

Internet users come from all age groups: "Net kids"—expected to reach almost 20 million in number by the year 2000—are likely to use the Internet for entertainment and socializing. Older Net surfers go online for more serious matters.

And Nickelodeon (www.nick.com) offers Natalie's Backseat Traveling Web Show, which includes games based on a Nickelodeon character named Natalie.[26]

Although Internet users are younger on average than the population as a whole, 45 percent are 40 years of age or older. Whereas younger groups are more likely to use the Internet for entertainment and socializing, older Net surfers go on-line for more serious matters. For example, 24 percent of people aged 50 to 64 years old use the Net for investment purposes, compared with only 3 percent of those 25 to 29. And although only 5 percent of consumers over 65 use the Internet, 42 percent of those users have purchased something on-line.

Internet users also differ psychographically from the general consumer population. SRI, creator of the VALS 2 lifestyle typology discussed in chapter 5, is now developing an iVALS typology, which focuses on the attitudes, preferences, and behaviors of on-line service and Internet users. SRI's Web site (www.future.sri.com/VALS/survey/html) allows visitors to take the VALS 2 questionnaire and get immediate feedback on their VALS 2 type. Fully 50 percent of those who have visited this site so far are Actualizers, the typical upscale, technically oriented academics and professionals. Only 10 percent of the general population belongs to this segment.[27]

Finally, Internet consumers differ in their approaches to buying and in their responses to marketing. They are empowered consumers who have greater control over the marketing process.[28] People who use the Net place greater value on information and tend to respond negatively to messages aimed only at selling. Whereas traditional marketing targets a somewhat passive audience, on-line marketing targets people who actively select which Web sites they will visit and which ad banners they will click on. They decide what marketing information they will receive about which products and services and under what conditions. Thus, in on-line marketing, the consumer controls more of the interaction.

Internet search engines, such as Yahoo, Infoseek, and Excite give consumers access to varied information sources, making them better informed and more discerning shoppers. In fact, on-line buyers are increasingly creators of product information, not just consumers of it. As greater numbers of consumers join Internet interest groups that share product-related information, "word of Web" is joining "word of mouth" as an important buying influence. Thus, the new world of electronic commerce will require new marketing approaches.

The Benefits of On-line Marketing

Why have on-line services become so popular? On-line marketing yields benefits to both consumers and marketers.

Benefits to Consumers On-line buying provides the same basic benefits to consumers as other forms of direct marketing. It is *convenient*: Customers don't have battle traffic, find a parking space, and walk through seemingly countless stores and aisles to find and examine products. They can compare brands, check out prices, and order merchandise 24 hours a day from any location. On-line buying is *easy* and *private*: Customers face fewer buying hassles and don't have to face salespeople or open themselves up to persuasion and emotional pitches.

On-line buying offers consumers some additional advantages. The commercial on-line services and the Internet give consumers access to an abundance of comparative *information*, information about companies, products, and competitors. In addition, on-line buying is *interactive* and *immediate*. Consumers often can interact with the seller's site to find exactly the information, products, or services they desire, then order or download them on the spot.

Benefits to Marketers On-line marketing also yields many benefits to marketers. Because of its one-to-one, interactive nature, on-line marketing is a good tool for *customer relationship building*. It brings companies and their customers closer together. Companies can interact with customers to learn more about specific customer needs and wants and to build customer databases. In turn, on-line customers can ask questions and volunteer feedback. Based on this ongoing interaction, companies can increase customer value and satisfaction through product and service refinements. They can also tailor their communications and offers to the requirements of specific customers. George Fisher, CEO of Eastman Kodak Company, sums it up this way: "On-line activity gives us a way to meet customer needs and desires that is unparalleled since the days of the door-to-door salesman."[29]

On-line marketing can *reduce costs* and *increase efficiency*. On-line marketers avoid the expense of maintaining a store and the accompanying costs of rent, insurance, and utilities. Because customers deal directly with sellers, on-line marketing often results in lower costs and improved efficiencies for channel and logistics functions such as order processing, inventory handling, delivery, and trade promotion. Finally, communicating electronically often costs less than communicating on paper through the mail. For instance, a company can produce digital catalogs for much less than the cost of printing and mailing paper ones. The relatively low costs of setting up an on-line marketing operation mean that both small and large firms can afford it. For example, it generally costs less to set up an effective Web site than it does to purchase 30 seconds of commercial time on prime-time network TV.

On-line marketing also offers greater *flexibility*, allowing the marketer to make ongoing adjustments to its offers and programs. For example, once a paper catalog is mailed, the products, prices, and other catalog features are fixed until the next catalog is sent. However, an on-line catalog can be adjusted daily or even hourly, adapting product assortments, prices, and promotions to match changing market conditions.

Finally, the Internet is a truly *global* medium that allows buyers and sellers to click from one country to another in seconds. A Web surfer from Paris or Istanbul can access a Lands' End catalog as easily as someone living on 1 Lands' End Lane in Dodgeville, Wisconsin, the direct retailer's hometown. Thus, even small on-line marketers find that they have ready access to global markets.

Despite these many benefits, however, on-line marketing is not for every company nor for every product. Careful thought has to be given to if, when, and how it should be undertaken.

On-line Marketing Channels

Marketers can conduct on-line marketing in four ways: by creating an electronic storefront; placing ads on-line; participating in Internet forums, news groups, or "Web communities"; or using on-line e-mail or Webcasting.

Creating an Electronic Storefront In opening an electronic storefront, a company has two choices: It can buy space on a commercial on-line service or it can open its own Web site. Buying a location on a commercial on-line service involves either renting storage space on the on-line service's computer or establishing a link from the company's own computer to the on-line service's shopping mall. JCPenney, for example, has links to America Online, CompuServe, and Prodigy, gaining access to the millions of consumers who subscribe to these services. The on-line services typically design the storefront for the company and introduce it to their subscribers. For these services, the company pays the on-line service an annual fee plus a small percentage of the company's on-line sales.

In addition to buying a location on an on-line service, or as an alternative, thousands of companies have now created their own Web sites. These sites vary greatly in purpose and content. The most basic type is a **corporate Web site**.[30] These sites are designed to handle interactive communication *initiated by the consumer*. They seek to build customer goodwill and to supplement other sales channels rather than to sell the company's products directly (see Marketing at Work 14-2). Corporate Web sites typically offer a rich variety of information and other features in an effort to answer customer questions, build closer customer relationships, and generate excitement about the company. Corporate Web sites generally provide information about the company's history, its mission and philosophy, and the products and services that it offers. They might also tell about current events, company personnel, financial performance, and employment opportunities. Many corporate Web sites also provide exciting entertainment features to attract and hold visitors. Finally, the site might also provide opportunities for customers to ask questions or make comments through e-mail before leaving the site.

Corporate Web site Web sites that seek to build customer goodwill and to supplement other sales channels rather than to sell the company's products directly.

Marketing at Work 14-2

Pillsbury Central: Information and a Whole Lot More to Keep Customers Coming Back

Pillsbury Central (www.pillsbury.com) does everything that a good corporate Web site should do. No, you can't use the site to order up products bearing one of the company's familiar brands—Pillsbury, Green Giant, Hungry Jack, LeSueur, Progresso, Old El Paso, Totino's, Häagen-Dazs, or one of a dozen others. *Pillsbury Central* isn't designed to be a direct-selling channel. Instead, it's meant to be a one-to-one communication tool for enhancing Pillsbury's relationships with consumers.

Pillsbury Central provides interesting and useful information—*lots* of information—that keeps consumers coming back again and again. A click on the Pillsbury Story icon provides access to detailed information on everything from the company's history, mission, and values; to its environmental and community involvement efforts; to it products, brand logos, and facts about familiar characters such as Poppin' Fresh, the Pillsbury Doughboy, and the Jolly Green Giant. For example, did you know that the Green Giant brand was originally named for the company's new "Green Giant" pea hybrid and that the giant was originally white? When the company's trademark attorney suggested a switch to

the more distinctive green, management responded with the argument, "Who ever heard of a green giant?" Obviously, everyone has by now.

For fun, click on the Doughboy.com icon and you'll be treated to "games, giggles, and other goodies from our lovable little guy," including the opportunity to send a DoughMail greeting to a friend. Tap the Bake-Off Contest icon and you'll find out all you ever wanted to know about the Pillsbury Bake-Off: history, winning recipes, rules,

tips, even an on-line entry form. The Mealtime Ideas icon provides a gateway to recipes and entertaining ideas—hundreds of them—for every season. Feeding a group? Try the Casual Gatherings icon to see plans for a patio party, backyard summer social, or football fiesta open house. Preparing a meal for a special occasion? Try Dazzling Do-Able Feasts for tips on how to host an event plus meal plans for a celebration ham dinner or an elegant asparagus eggs-Benedict brunch. Looking for meals on the

Pillsbury Central does all that a good corporate Web site should do. No, you can't use it to order one of the company's familiar brands. However, as these Web pages suggest, it's a good means of enhancing Pillsbury's relationships with consumers.

Marketing Web site
Web sites designed to engage consumers in an interaction that will move them closer to a purchase or other marketing outcome.

Other companies create a **marketing Web site**. These sites are designed to engage consumers in an interaction that will move them closer to a purchase or other marketing outcome. With a marketing Web site, communication and interaction are *initiated by the marketer*. Such a site might include a catalog, shopping tips, and promotional features such as coupons, sales events, or contests. Companies aggressively promote their marketing Web sites in print and broadcast advertising and through "banner-to-site" ads that pop up on other Web sites. Consumers can find a Web site for buying almost anything: clothing from Lands' End or JCPenney, books from Prentice Hall, or flowers from Grant's Flowers to be sent anywhere in the world.

fly? Visit Busy Day Meals to get plans for meals fitting today's fast-paced lifestyles. Or you can browse the Pillsbury recipe box using the Recipe Search feature to locate specific recipes by course (appetizers, salads, main dishes, snacks, . . .), ingredient (almonds, beans, . . .), Pillsbury product (Pet milk, LeSueur peas, Progresso soups, . . .), or key word (for instance, try "low fat" or "pasta dishes"). If you still don't have enough particulars, you can use the site to request a free recipe book from Green Giant or to get the latest research on the nutritional value of frozen or canned vegetables.

Pillsbury Central contains a bulletin board that lets you interact with other site surfers to post and share cooking shortcuts, tips on saving time and money, or requests for long-lost recipes. For example, a visitor named Sonya recently posted: "Please help me! I lost a favorite recipe for Hungry Jack Biscuits Coffee Cake Dessert that Pillsbury printed about 10 years ago on those little 3 × 5 cards they used to put out. Has anyone got this recipe? Please post ASAP." Another visitor posted the requested recipe the very next day.

The *Pillsbury Central* Web site also offers visitors an opportunity to subscribe to *Pillsbury's Digital Dispatch*, a periodic e-mail bulletin sent automatically to subscribers containing cooking and entertaining tips, recipes, and time-saving ideas to make life easier. To receive the bulletins, you fill out an on-line form with your name and address, age, and other demographic information, and indicate your cooking interests and the kinds of information you'd like to receive. Providing this information is optional—"You don't have to answer every question . . . for instance, if you're worried that we're going to pester you or send you a bunch of junk mail (we won't)." However, the company explains, the information will help them build a better site. In fact, using this information, Pillsbury has built an impressive consumer database. It uses the database to prepare individualized e-mail dispatches tailored to the specific demographics and expressed interests of these self-selected and very receptive consumers. For example, this past fall, Pillsbury sent a dispatch to parents of school-age children containing recipes for easy-to-prepare school-day meals and instructions on how to receive e-mailed recipes for "Snacks to Pack: Portable Munchies for Kids of All Ages." The dispatch also contained links to Pillsbury Web sites filled with menu ideas and quick-to-make recipes suited for the busy family's back-to-school schedule.

According to Michael Lundeby, president of Creative Resource Center, the marketing communications agency that created and manages the site, *Pillsbury Central* has been a huge success. The site draws millions of hits each month, and Pillsbury's digital dispatch has attracted tens of thousands of subscribers whose demographics closely match Pillsbury's target market. Whereas the majority of Web users are male, digital dispatch subscribers are predominantly females who cook more than five times per week. E-mail responses to the newsletter suggest that members appreciate not only the information it contains but also the personal interaction with Pillsbury. As an additional benefit, by tracking which recipes visitors access most frequently, Pillsbury obtains valuable information about current consumer desires and cooking habits. All of these benefits come at a surprisingly low cost. The annual budget for the site totals less than the amount the company spends for a single advertisement on prime-time television.

According to Lundeby, Web technology is changing rapidly, as are consumer usage and buying patterns. Thus, *Pillsbury Central* remains a work in constant process. "That's the beauty of the Internet as a communication form," says Lundeby. "As our audience—and what they want—change, so will the site."

Toyota operates a marketing Web site at www.toyota.com. Once a potential customer clicks in, the car maker wastes no time trying to turn the inquiry into a sale. The site offers plenty of entertainment and useful information, from cross-country trip guides and tips for driving with kids to a tour of Jay Leno's garage and events such as a Golf Skills Challenge and a Bike Express. But the site is also loaded with more serious selling features, such as detailed descriptions of current Toyota models and information on dealer locations and services, complete with maps and dealer Web links. Visitors who want to go further can fill out an on-line order form (supplying name, address, phone number, and e-mail address) for brochures and a free, interactive CD-ROM that shows off the features of Toyota models. The chances are good that before the CD-ROM arrives, a local dealer will call to invite the prospect in for a test drive. Toyota's Web site has now replaced its 800 number as the number one source of customer leads.[31]

Business-to-business marketers also make good use of marketing Web sites. For example, corporate buyers can visit Sun Microsystems' Web site (www.sun.com), select detailed descriptions of Sun's products and solutions, request sales and service information, and interact with staff members. Customers visiting GE Plastics' Web site can draw on more than 1,500 pages of information to get answers about the company's products any time and from anywhere in the world. And FedEx's Web site (www.fedex.com) allows customers to schedule their own shipments, request a courier, and track their packages in transit.

Electronics components supplier AMP Inc. knows the value of maintaining a marketing Web site. Its AMPemerce Internet Solutions site interacts with both large and small customers, but in different ways:

> Large customers use a password to obtain customized pricing and product information. Smaller customers as well as new visitors and prospects can view AMP's catalog; browse articles on company and product news, industry news, and technical instruction; and get information on joining AMP's preferred customer program, ACES. Select customers can order a number of AMP's 9,000 products on-line. . . . The site receives 130,000 hits a day from its 132,000 registered users in 144 countries. [The site] has put a big dent in AMP's annual $15 million printed catalog budget, as well as its $800,000 fax-back service. [Moreover,] customers can get up-to-the-minute product information from the Web site whenever they need it, and, consequently, AMP reps gain more time to build relationships—and sales. . . . Says [one AMP customer], "The site is user friendly and just keeps getting better."[32]

Marketing Web site: AMP's customers can get up-to-the-minute product information from the Web site whenever they need it, allowing AMP reps to gain more time to build relationships— and sales. The site receives 130,000 hits a day from its 132,000 registered users in 144 countries.

Creating a Web site is one thing; getting people to *visit* the site is another. The key is to create enough value and excitement to get consumers to come to the site, stick around, and come back again. This means that companies must constantly update their sites to keep them fresh and exciting. Doing so involves time and expense, but the expense is necessary if the on-line marketer wishes to cut through the increasing on-line clutter.

For some types of products, attracting visitors is easy. Consumers buying new cars, computers, or financial services will be open to information and marketing initiatives from sellers. Marketers of lower-involvement products, however, may face a difficult challenge in attracting Web site visitors. As one veteran notes, "If you're shopping for a computer and you see a banner that says, 'We've ranked the top 12 computers to purchase,' you're going to click on the banner. [But] what kind of banner could encourage any consumer to visit dentalfloss.com."[33] For such low-interest products, the company should create a corporate Web site to answer customer questions and build goodwill, using it only to supplement selling efforts through other channels.

Placing Advertisements On-line Companies can place on-line advertisements in any of four ways. First, they can place *classified ads* in special sections offered by the major commercial on-line services. The ads are listed according to when they arrived, with the latest ones heading the list. Second, ads can be placed in certain Internet *newsgroups* that are set up for commercial purposes. Third, the company can buy **on-line ads** that pop up while subscribers are surfing on-line services or Web sites. Such ads include banner ads, pop-up windows, "tickers" (banners that move across the screen), and "roadblocks" (full-screen ads that users must pass through to get to other screens they wish to view). For example, a Web user or America Online subscriber who is looking up airline schedules or fares might find a flashing banner on the screen exclaiming, "Rent a car from Alamo and get up to 2 days free!" To attract visitors to its own Web site, Toyota sponsors Web banner ads on other sites, ranging from ESPN SportZone (www.espn.com) to Parent Soup (www.parentsoup.com), a kind of on-line coffee klatch through which moms and dads exchange views. A final form of Web advertising is *content sponsorships*. For example, Advil sponsors ESPN Sportzone's Injury Report and Oldsmobile sponsors AOL's Celebrity Circle.

On-line ads Ads that appear while subscribers are surfing on-line services or Web sites, including banners, pop-up windows, "tickers," and "roadblocks."

Web advertising is on the increase. However, many marketers still question its value as an effective tool. Costs are reasonable compared with those of other advertising media. For example, Web advertising on ESPNet SportsZone, which attracts more than 500,000 Web surfers and 20 million "hits" (the number of times the site is accessed) per week, costs about $300,000 per year. Netscape, the popular Web browser site, charges about $360,000 per year and delivers an estimated 1 million impressions. Still, Web surfers can easily ignore these banner ads and often do. Ad Web locations that sell advertising space are still working to develop good measures of advertising impact. Thus, although many firms are experimenting with Web advertising, it still plays only a minor role in their promotion mixes. In 1998, U.S. firms spent only $1.5 billion on Web advertising, compared with more than $40 billion each in ad spending for newspapers and broadcast television. However, on-line advertising revenues are expected to hit $9 billion by 2002.[34]

Participating in Forums, Newsgroups, and Web Communities Companies may decide to participate in or sponsor Internet forums, newsgroups, and bulletin boards that appeal to specific special-interest groups. Such activities may be organized for commercial or noncommercial purposes. *Forums* are discussion groups located on commercial on-line services. A forum may operate a library, a "chat room" for real-time message exchanges, and even a classified ad directory. For example, America Online boasts some

14,000 chat rooms, which account for a third of its members' on-line time. It recently introduced "buddy lists," which alert members when friends are on-line, allowing them to exchange instant messages.[35] Most forums are sponsored by special interest groups. Thus, as a major musical instruments manufacturer, Yamaha might start a forum on classical music.

Newsgroups are the Internet version of forums. However, such groups are limited to people posting and reading messages on a specified topic, rather than managing libraries or conferencing. Internet users can participate in newsgroups without subscribing. There are thousands of newsgroups dealing with every imaginable topic, from healthful eating and caring for your Bonsai tree to collecting antique cars or exchanging views on the latest soap opera happenings.

Bulletin board systems (BBSs) are specialized on-line services that center on a specific topic or group. There are over 60,000 BBSs originating in the United States, dealing with topics such as vacations, health, computer games, and real estate. Marketers might want to identify and participate in newsgroups and BBSs that attract subscribers who fit their target markets. However, newsgroups and BBS users often resent commercial intrusions on their Net space, so the marketer must tread carefully, participating in subtle ways that provide real value to participants.

The popularity of forums and newsgroups has resulted in a rash of commercially sponsored Web sites called *Web communities*. Such sites allow members to congregate on-line and exchange views on issues of common interest. They are "the cyberspace equivalent to the bar at TV's *Cheers*, where everybody knows your e-mail address."[36] For example, Women's Wire is a Web community in which career-oriented women can engage in discussion forums and celebrity chats on women's issues. Tripod is an on-line hangout for twentysomethings, offering chat rooms and free home pages for posting job resumes. And Parent Soup is an on-line community of more than 200,000 parents who spend time on-line gathering parenting information, chatting with other parents about kid-related issues, and linking with other related sites.

Visitors to these Net neighborhoods develop a strong sense of community. Such communities are attractive to advertisers because they draw consumers with common interests and well-defined demographics. For example, Parent Soup provides an ideal environment for the Web ads of Johnson and Johnson, Gerber's, and other makers of children's products. Moreover, cyberhood consumers visit frequently and stay on-line longer, increasing the chance of meaningful exposure to the advertiser's message.

Web communities can be either social or work related. One successful work-related community is Agriculture Online (or @agriculture Online). This site offers commodity prices, recent farm news, and chat rooms of all types. Rural surfers can visit the Electronic Coffee Shop and pick up the latest down-on-the-farm joke or join a hot discussion on controlling soybean cyst nematodes. @agriculture Online has been highly successful, attracting as many as 5 million hits per month.[37]

Using E-mail and Webcasting A company can encourage prospects and customers to send questions, suggestions, and even complaints to the company via e-mail. Customer service representatives can quickly respond to such messages. The company may also develop Internet-based electronic mailing lists of customers or prospects. Such lists provide an excellent opportunity to introduce the company and its offerings to new customers and to build ongoing relationships with current ones. Using the lists, on-line marketers can send out customer newsletters, special product or promotion offers based on customer purchasing histories, reminders of service requirements or warranty renewals, or announcements of special events.

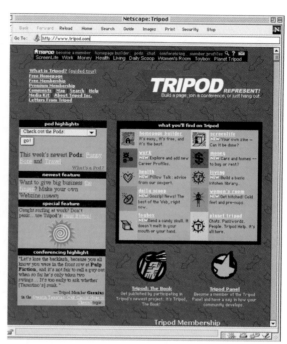

Web communities: Tripod is an on-line hangout for twentysomethings, offering chat rooms and free home pages for posting job resumes.

3Com Corporation, a manufacturer of high-tech computer hardware, made good use of e-mail to generate and qualify customer leads for its Network Interface Cards. The company used targeted e-mail and banner ads on 18 different computer-related Web sites to attract potential buyers to its own Web site featuring a "3Com Classic" sweepstakes, where by filling out the entry form, visitors could register to win a 1959 Corvette. The campaign generated 22,000 leads, which were further qualified using e-mail and telemarketing. "Hot" leads were passed along to 3Com's inside sales force. "[Sales reps] were very skeptical," says a 3Com marketing manager, "but they were blown away by how well the contest did." Of the 482 leads given to reps, 71 turned into actual sales that totaled $2.5 million. What's more, states the manager, "Now I've got 22,000 names in my e-mail database that I can go back and market to."[38]

Companies can also sign on with any of a number of **"Webcasting"** services, which automatically download customized information to recipients' PCs. For a monthly fee, subscribers to these services can specify the channels they want—news, company information, entertainment, and others—and the topics they're interested in. Then, rather than spending hours scouring the Internet, they can sit back while the Webcaster automatically delivers information of interest to their desktops.[39]

Webcasting, also known as "push" programming, affords an attractive channel through which on-line marketers can deliver their Internet advertising or other information content. Webcasting services such as PointCast and Ifusion are growing fast and attracting an ever-increasing number of advertisers. The major commercial on-line services are also beginning to offer Webcasting to their members. For example, America Online has added a feature called Driveway that will fetch information, Web pages, and e-mail based on members' preferences and automatically deliver it to their PCs. However, as with other types of on-line marketing, companies must be careful that they don't cause

Webcasting
The automatic downloading of customized information of interest to recipients' PCs, affording an attractive channel for delivering Internet advertising or other information content.

resentment among Internet users who are already overloaded with "junk e-mail." Warns one analyst, "There's a fine line between adding value and the consumer feeling that you're being intrusive."[40]

The Promise and Challenges of On-line Marketing

On-line marketing offers great promise for the future. Its most ardent apostles envision a time when the Internet and electronic commerce will replace magazines, newspapers, and even stores as sources for information and buying. Yet despite all the hype and promise, on-line marketing may be years away from realizing its full potential. And even then, it is unlikely to fulfill such sweeping predictions. Instead, eventually, on-line marketing will become another important tactical tool that works alongside other tactical elements in a fully integrated marketing mix.

Although novel and exhilarating, on-line marketing has yet to carve out a central role in consumers' lives. As one analyst comments, "The Web is hip. The Web is cool. And increasingly, the Web is way frustrating," for both marketers and the Internet users they wish to reach. For most marketers, the Web is still not a money-making proposition; according to one report, less than half of today's Webs sites are profitable.[41] Here are just some of the challenges that on-line marketers face:

- *Limited consumer exposure and buying:* Although expanding rapidly, on-line marketing still reaches only a limited marketspace. Moreover, Web users appear to do more window browsing than actual buying. Only an estimated 18 percent of Web surfers actually use the Web regularly for shopping or to obtain commercial services such as travel information.[42]
- *Skewed user demographics and psychographics:* Although the Web audience is broadening, on-line users still tend to be more upscale and technically oriented than the general population. This makes on-line marketing ideal for marketing computer hardware and software, consumer electronics, financial services, and certain other classes of products. However, it makes on-line marketing less effective for selling mainstream products.
- *Chaos and clutter:* The Internet offers up millions of Web sites and a staggering volume of information. Thus, navigating the Internet can be frustrating, confusing, and time consuming for consumers. In this chaotic and cluttered environment, many Web ads and sites go unnoticed or unopened. Even when noticed, marketers will find it difficult to hold consumer attention. One study found that a site must capture Web surfers' attention within eight seconds or lose them to another site. That leaves very little time for marketers to promote and sell their goods.
- *Security:* Consumers worry that unscrupulous snoopers will eavesdrop on their on-line transactions or intercept their credit card numbers and make unauthorized purchases. In turn, companies doing business on-line fear that others will use the Internet to invade their computer systems for the purposes of commercial espionage or even sabotage. On-line marketers are developing solutions to such security problems. However, there appears to be a "never-ending competition between the technology of security systems and the sophistication of those seeking to thwart them."[43]
- *Ethical concerns:* Privacy is a primary concern. Marketers can easily track Web site visitors, and many consumers who participate in Web site activities provide extensive personal information. This may leave consumers open to information abuse if companies make unauthorized use of the information in marketing their products or exchanging electronic lists with other companies. There are also concerns about seg-

mentation and discrimination. The Internet currently serves upscale consumers well. However, poorer consumers have less access to the Net, leaving them increasingly less informed about products, services, and prices.[44]

Despite these challenges, companies large and small are quickly integrating on-line marketing into their marketing mixes. More than the latest fad, on-line marketing will prove to be a powerful tool for building customer relationships, improving sales, communicating company and product information, and delivering products and services more efficiently and effectively.

Linking the Concepts

Take a brief detour and have some fun exploring the Web.

- Find a good *corporate* Web site. Find a good *marketing* Web site. Then find poor sites of each kind. For each, explain its purpose and why you think it's good or poor.
- While you're surfing, find two examples of good Internet advertisements. Find two poor advertisements. Describe each ad's design and placement and explain why you think the ad is good or poor.

Integrated Direct Marketing

Although direct marketing and on-line marketing have boomed in recent years, many companies still relegate them to minor roles in their marketing and promotion mixes. And too many direct marketers use only a "one-shot" effort to reach and sell a prospect or a single vehicle in multiple stages to trigger purchases. For example, a magazine publisher might send a series of four direct-mail notices to a household to get a subscriber to renew before giving up. A more powerful approach is **integrated direct marketing**, which involves using multiple-vehicle, multiple-stage campaigns. Such campaigns can greatly improve response. Whereas a direct-mail piece alone might generate a 2 percent response, adding a toll-free phone number can raise the response rate by 50 percent. A well-designed outbound telemarketing effort might lift response by an additional 500 percent. Suddenly, a 2 percent response has grown to 15 percent or more by adding interactive marketing channels to a regular mailing.[45]

More elaborate integrated direct-marketing campaigns can be used. Consider the multimedia, multistage campaign shown in Figure 14-2. Here, the paid ad creates product awareness and stimulates inquiries. The company immediately sends direct mail to those who inquire. Within a few days, the company follows up with a phone call seeking an order. Some prospects will order by phone; others might request a face-to-face sales call. In such a campaign, the marketer seeks to improve response rates and profits by adding media and stages that contribute more to additional sales than to additional costs (see Marketing at Work 14-3).

Integrated direct marketing Direct-marketing campaigns that use mutiple vehicles and multiple stages to improve response rates and profits.

Figure 14-2
An integrated direct-marketing campaign

Marketing at Work 14-3

American Standard's Integrated Direct Marketing: Anything but Standard

You probably haven't thought much about your bathroom—it's not something that most of us get all that inspired about. But as it turns out, you probably have a relationship with your bathroom unlike that with any other room in your house. It's where you start and end your day, primp and preen and admire yourself, escape from the rigors of everyday life, and do some of your best thinking. The marketers at American Standard, the plumbing fixtures giant, understand this often-overlooked but special little room. And they've set out upon a mission to help people design bathrooms worthy of their finest moments.

Working with its ad agency, Carmichael Lynch, American Standard has created a wonderfully warm and highly effective but not-so-standard integrated marketing campaign. The campaign, called "We want you to love your bath-room," targets men and women aged 25 to 54 from households planning to remodel bathrooms or replace fixtures. The campaign employs a carefully integrated mix of brand-image and direct-response media ads, direct mailings, and personal contacts to create a customer database, generate sales leads, gently coax customers into its retail showrooms, and build sales and market share.

The campaign begins with a series of humorous, soft-sell brand-image ads in home and shelter magazines such as *Home*, *House Beautiful*, and *Country Living*, which have a high percentage of readers undertaking remodeling

projects. Featuring simple but artistic shots of ordinary bathroom fixtures and scenes, the ads position American Standard as a company that understands the special relationships we have with our bathrooms. For example, one ad shows a white toilet and a partially unwound roll of toilet paper, artfully arranged in a corner against plain blue-gray walls. "We're not in this business for the glory," proclaims the headline. "Designing a toilet or sink may not be as glamorous as, say, designing a Maserati. But to us, it's every bit as important. After all, more people will be sitting on our seats than theirs."

Another ad shows the feet of a man standing on a white tile bathroom floor wearing his goofy-looking floppy-eared dog slippers. "The rest of the world thinks you're a genius," notes the ad. But "after

a long day of being brilliant, witty, and charming, it's nice just to be comfortable. The right bathroom understands. And accepts you unconditionally." Each simple but engaging ad includes a toll-free phone number and urges readers to call for a free guidebook

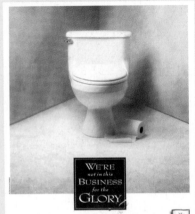

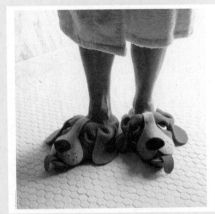

American Standard has created a wonderfully warm and highly effective but not-so-standard integrated marketing campaign. It all starts with ads like these.

"overflowing with products, ideas, and inspiration."

Whereas the brand-image ads position American Standard and its products, when it comes to generating inquiries, the real workhorses are the one-third-page, couponlike direct-response ads that run in the same magazines. One such ad notes, "You will spend seven years of your life in the bathroom. You will need a good book." Readers can obtain the free guidebook by mailing in the coupon or calling the toll-free number listed in the ad.

Consumers who respond find that they've taken the first step in a carefully orchestrated relationship-building venture. First, they receive the entertaining, highly informative, picture-filled 30-page guidebook *We Want You To Love Your Bathroom*, along with a folksy letter thanking them for their interest and noting the locations of nearby American Standard dealers. The guidebook's purpose is straightforward: "Walk into your bathroom, turn the knob and suddenly, for a moment or an hour, the world stops turning. You should love the place. If you don't, well, American Standard wants to further your relationship. Thumb through this book. In the bathroom, perhaps . . . ."

The guidebook is chock-full of helpful tips on bathroom design, starting with answers to some simple questions: What kind of lavatory—what color? The bathtub—how big; big enough for two? The toilet—sleek one-piece or familiar two-piece? The faucet? "You'll fumble for it every morning, so be particular about how it operates." To spice things up, the guidebook also contains loads of entertaining facts and trivia. An example: Did you know that "you will spend seven years in your bathroom . . . here's hoping your spouse doesn't sneak in first!" Another example: "During the Middle Ages, Christianity preached that to uncover your skin, even to bathe it, was an invitation to sin. Thank heavens for perfume. These days, we average about 4 baths or 7.5 showers a week." And, of course, the booklet contains plenty of information on American Standard products, along with a tear-out card that prospective customers can return to obtain more detailed guides and product catalogs.

In addition to the guidebook, customers receive a carefully coordinated stream of communications from American Standard, starting with a series of "Bathroom Reading" bulletins, each containing information on specific bathroom design issues. For example, one issue contains information and tips on how to make a bathroom safer; another issue offers "ten neat ways to save water."

Meanwhile, information about prospective customers and their remodeling projects collected by the 1-800 operator or from the coupon goes into American Standard's customer database. The database generates leads for salespeople at American Standard's showrooms around the country. The company markets the program to key distributors and kitchen and bath dealers, motivating them to follow up on leads and training them how to do it effectively. The key is to get customers who've made inquiries to come into the showroom. Not long after making their inquiries, prospective customers typically receive a handwritten postcard, or perhaps even a phone call, from a local dealer's showroom consultant, who extends a personal invitation to visit, see American Standard products firsthand, and discuss bathroom designs. Thus, the integrated direct marketing program builds relationships not just with buyers but with dealers as well.

American Standard's integrated direct marketing campaign has done wonders for the company's positioning and performance. Since the campaign began, American Standard's plumbing division has experienced steady increases in sales and earnings—earnings last year tripled those of the previous year. The campaign generates tens of thousands of qualified leads per year for local showrooms—more than a half million qualified leads so far. Research confirms significant shifts in consumer perceptions of American Standard and its products—from "boring and institutional" to well designed and loaded with "personal spirit." According to Bob Srenaski, group vice-president of marketing at American Standard, the campaign has "totally repositioned our company and established a momentum and winning spirit that is extraordinary." Says Joe Summary, an account manager at Carmichael Lynch, "the campaign has been incredible. It's given American Standard and its products a more personal face, one that's helped us to build closer relationships with customers and dealers. From the first ad to the last contact with our dealers, the campaign is designed to help customers create bathrooms they'll love."

Public Policy and Ethical Issues in Direct Marketing

Direct marketers and their customers usually enjoy mutually rewarding relationships. Occasionally, however, a darker side emerges. The aggressive and sometimes shady tactics of a few direct marketers can bother or harm consumers, giving the entire industry a black eye. Abuses range from simple excesses that irritate consumers to instances of unfair practices or even outright deception and fraud. During the past few years, the direct-marketing industry has also faced growing concerns about invasion-of-privacy issues.[46]

Irritation, Unfairness, Deception, and Fraud

Direct-marketing excesses sometimes annoy or offend consumers. Most of us dislike direct-response TV commercials that are too loud, too long, and too insistent. Especially bothersome are dinnertime or late-night phone calls. Beyond irritating consumers, some direct marketers have been accused of taking unfair advantage of impulsive or less sophisticated buyers. TV shopping shows and program-long "infomercials" seem to be the worst culprits. They feature smooth-talking hosts, elaborately staged demonstrations, claims of drastic price reductions, "while they last" time limitations, and unequaled ease of purchase to inflame buyers who have low sales resistance.

Worse yet, so-called heat merchants design mailers and write copy intended to mislead buyers. Political fundraisers, among the worst offenders, sometimes use gimmicks such as "look-alike" envelopes that resemble official documents, simulated newspaper clippings, and fake honors and awards. Other direct marketers pretend to be conducting research surveys when they are actually asking leading questions to screen or persuade consumers. Fraudulent schemes, such as investment scams or phony collections for charity, have also multiplied in recent years. Crooked direct marketers can be hard to catch: Direct-marketing customers often respond quickly, do not interact personally with the seller, and usually expect to wait for delivery. By the time buyers realize that they have been bilked, the thieves are usually somewhere else plotting new schemes.

Invasion of Privacy

Invasion of privacy is perhaps the toughest public policy issue now confronting the direct-marketing industry. These days, it seems that almost every time consumers order products by mail or telephone, enter a sweepstakes, apply for a credit card, or take out a magazine subscription, their names are entered into some company's already bulging database. Using sophisticated computer technologies, direct marketers can use these databases to "microtarget" their selling efforts.

Consumers often benefit from such database marketing: they receive more offers that are closely matched to their interests. However, many critics worry that marketers may know *too* much about consumers' lives and that they may use this knowledge to take unfair advantage of consumers. At some point, they claim, the extensive use of databases intrudes on consumer privacy. For example, they ask, should AT&T be allowed to sell marketers the names of customers who frequently call the 800 numbers of catalog companies? Is it right for credit bureaus to compile and sell lists of people who have recently applied for credit cards—people who are considered prime direct-marketing targets because of their spending behavior? Or is it right for states to sell the names and addresses of driver's license holders, along with height, weight, and gender information, allowing apparel retailers to target tall or overweight people with special clothing offers?

In their drives to build databases, companies sometimes get carried away. For example, Microsoft caused substantial privacy concerns when it introduced its Windows 95 software. It used a "Registration Wizard," which allowed users to register their new software on-line. However, when users went on-line to register, Microsoft took the opportunity, without their knowledge, to "read" the configurations of their PCs. Thus, the company gained instant knowledge of the major software products running on each customer's system. When users learned of this invasion, they protested loudly and Microsoft abandoned the practice. However, such actions have spawned a quiet but determined "privacy revolt" among consumers and public policy makers.[47]

In one survey of consumers, 79 percent of respondents said that they were concerned about threats to their personal privacy. In another survey, *Advertising Age* asked advertising industry executives how they felt about database marketing and the privacy issue. The responses of two executives show that even industry insiders have mixed feelings about these issues:[48]

> There are profound ethical issues relating to the marketing of specific household data—financial information, for instance. . . . For every household in the United States, the computer can guess with amazing accuracy . . . things like credit use, net worth, and investments, the kind of information most people would never want disclosed, let alone sold to any marketer.

> It doesn't bother me that people know I live in a suburb of Columbus, Ohio, and have X number of kids. It [does] bother me that these people know the names of my wife and kids and where my kids go to school. They . . . act like they know me when the bottom line is they're attempting to sell me something. I do feel that database marketing has allowed companies to cross the fine line of privacy. . . . [And] in a lot of cases, I think they know they have crossed it.

The direct-marketing industry is addressing issues of ethics and public policy. Direct marketers know that, left untended, such problems will lead to increasingly negative consumer attitudes, lower response rates, and calls for more restrictive state and federal legislation. More importantly, most direct marketers want the same things that consumers want: honest and well-designed marketing offers targeted only toward consumers who will appreciate and respond to them. Direct marketing is just too expensive to waste on consumers who don't want it.

REST STOP Reviewing the Concepts

You've earned a rest! With this chapter, you've completed your study of the marketing mix. Before moving along to the last leg of the journey, let's review some key concepts concerning direct and online marketing.

Mass marketers have typically tried to reach

millions of buyers with a single product and a standard message communicated via the mass media. Consequently, most mass-marketing communications were one-way communications directed *at* consumers rather than two-way communications *with* consumers. Today, many companies are turning to direct marketing in an effort to reach carefully targeted customers more efficiently and to build stronger, more personal, one-to-one relationships with them.

1. Discuss the benefits of direct marketing to customers and companies and the trends fueling its rapid growth.

Customers benefit from direct marketing in many ways. For consumers, home shopping is fun, convenient, hassle-free, saves time, and gives them a bigger selection of merchandise. It allows them to comparison shop using mail catalogs and on-line shopping services, then order products and services without dealing with salespeople. Sellers also benefit. Direct marketers can target almost any group, customize offers to special wants and needs, and then use individualized communications to promote these offers. Direct marketers can also build an ongoing relationship with each customer; time offers to reach prospects at the right moment, thereby receiving higher readership and response; and easily test alternative media and messages. Finally, direct marketers gain privacy because their offer and strategy is less visible to competitors.

Various trends have led to the rapid growth of direct marketing. Market "demassification" has produced a constantly increasing number of market niches with specific preferences. Direct marketing enables sellers to focus efficiently on these minimarkets with offers that better match particular consumer wants and needs. Other trends encouraging at-home shopping include higher costs of driving, traffic and parking congestion, lack of time, a shortage of retail sales help, and long lines at checkout counters. Consumers like the convenience of direct marketers' toll-free phone numbers, their acceptance of orders round the clock, and their commitment to customer service. The growth of quick delivery via express carriers has also made direct shopping fast and easy. The increased affordability of computers and customer databases has allowed direct marketers to single out the best prospects for each of their products. Finally in business-to-business marketing, lower cost-per-contact media has proven more cost-effective in reaching and selling to more prospects and customers than using a sales force.

2. Define a customer database and list the four ways companies use databases in direct marketing.

A *customer database* is an organized collection of comprehensive data about individual customers or prospects, including geographic, demographic, psychographic, and behavioral data. Companies use databases to identify prospects, decide which customers should receive a particular offer, deepen customer loyalty, and reactivate customer purchases.

3. Identify the major forms of direct marketing.

The main forms of direct marketing include *face-to-face selling*, *direct-mail marketing*, *catalog marketing*, *telemarketing*, *direct-response television marketing*, *kiosk marketing*, and *on-line marketing*. Most companies today continue to rely heavily on *face-to-face* selling through a professional sales force, or they hire manufacturers' representatives and agents. *Direct-mail marketing* consists of the company sending an offer, announcement, reminder, or other item to a person at a specific address. Recently, three new forms of mail delivery have become popular: *fax mail*, *e-mail*, and *voice mail*. Some marketers rely on *catalog marketing*, or selling through catalogs mailed to a select list of customers or made available in stores. *Telemarketing* consists of using the telephone to sell directly to consumers. *Direct-response television marketing* has two forms: *direct-response advertising* or *infomercials* and *home shopping channels*. *Kiosks* are information and ordering machines that direct marketers place in stores, airports, and other locations. *On-line marketing* involves online channels and electronic commerce and is usually conducted through interactive online computer systems, which electronically link consumers with sellers.

4. Compare the two types of on-line marketing channels and explain the effect of the Internet on electronic commerce.

The two types of on-line marketing channels are *commercial on-line services* and the *Internet*. *Commercial on-line services* provide on-line information and marketing services to subscribers for a monthly fee. The *Internet* is a vast global and public web of computer networks. In contrast to commercial on-line services, use of the Internet is free—anyone with a PC, a modem, and the right software can browse the Internet to obtain or share information on almost any subject and to interact with other users. The explosion of Internet usage has created a new world of *electronic commerce*, a term that refers to the buying and selling process that is supported by electronic means. In this process, *electronic markets* become "marketspaces" in which sellers offer products and services electronically, while buyers search for information, identify their wants and needs, and then place orders using a credit card or other form of electronic payment.

5. Identify the benefits of on-line marketing to consumers and marketers and the four ways marketers can conduct on-line marketing.

For consumers, on-line marketing is beneficial for many reasons. It is *interactive, immediate,* and provides access to an abundance of comparative *information* about products, companies, and competitors. Marketers also benefit from on-line marketing. For them, it helps *consumer relationship building, reduces costs, increases efficiency,* provides more *flexibility,* and is, in the form of the Internet, a *global* medium that enables buyers and sellers in different countries to interact with each other in seconds. Marketers can conduct on-line marketing by creating an electronic storefront; placing ads on-line; participating in Internet forums, news groups, or "Web communities"; or by using on-line e-mail or Webcasting.

6. Discuss the public policy and ethical issues facing direct marketers.

Direct marketers and their customers have typically forged mutually rewarding relationships. However, there remains a potential for customer abuse, ranging from irritation and unfair practices to deception and fraud. In addition, there have been growing concerns about invasion of privacy, perhaps the most difficult public policy issue currently facing the direct-marketing industry.

Navigating the Key Terms

For a detailed analysis of the meaning and importance of each of the following key terms, visit our Web page at **www.prenhall.com/kotler**.

Catalog marketing
Commercial on-line services

Corporate Web site
Customer database
Direct marketing
Direct-mail marketing
Direct-response television marketing
Electronic commerce
Integrated direct marketing

Internet (or the Net)
Marketing Web site
On-line ads
On-line marketing
Telemarketing
Webcasting
World Wide Web (or the Web)

Travel Log

The following concept checks and discussion questions will help you to keep track of and apply the concepts you've studied in this chapter.

Concept Checks

1. _____ consists of direct communications with carefully targeted individual consumers to obtain an immediate response.

2. A _____ is an organized collection of comprehensive data about individual customers or prospects, including geographic, demographic, psychographic, and behavioral data.

3. Companies use their databases in four ways: _____, deciding which customers should receive a particular offer, _____, and _____.

4. According to Figure 14-1, the major forms of direct marketing include: face-to-face selling, _____, _____, _____, direct-response television marketing, _____, and _____.

5. _____ involves sending an offer, announcement, reminder, or other item to a person at a particular address.

6. According to the chapter, the three newest forms of mail delivery are: _____, _____, and _____.

7. Unlike vending machines (which dispense actual products), _____ are information and ordering machines.

8. _____ is conducted through interactive on-line computer systems, which link consumers with sellers electronically.

9. _____ are "marketspaces" in which sellers offer their products and services electronically, and buyers search for information, identify what they want, and place orders using a credit card or other means of electronic payment.

10. Companies interested in doing on-line marketing can sign on with any number of _____ services, which automatically download customized information to recipients' PCs.*

Discussing the Issues

1. Contact one of the personal computer direct marketers (such as Dell Computer at www.dell.com). Answer the following questions about your contact: (a) How does the company make it easy to order their products? (b) What differentiates it from traditional retailers or manufacturers? (c) What are its chief marketing advantages and disadvantages? (d) How is security provided (or not)? (e) Based on this experience, what is your opinion of on-line marketers?

2. Direct marketing benefits the customers in many ways. Provide three examples of direct marketers that demonstrate strong marketing benefits for their customers. Describe and explain the benefits fully.

3. Companies that know about individual customer needs and characteristics can customize their offers, messages, delivery modes, and payment methods to maximize customer value and satisfaction. Pick two of these organizations and answer the following questions about them: (a) State Farm Insurance, (b) IBM, (c) New York Metropolitan Opera, (d) American Cancer Society, and (e) Lexus. What information should these companies keep in their customer databases? Where would they get this information? How much would it cost to build such a database? How might they use the databases?

4. Direct-mail marketing used to mean sending an offer, announcement, reminder, or item to a person through the mail. Today, however, we are fast becoming a paperless society and new forms of direct communication are emerging. Critique (a) fax mail, (b) e-mail, and (c) voice mail as forms of direct mail. Be sure to discuss the advantages, disadvantages, customer profiles, costs, and futures of the forms.

5. On-line marketing offers great promise for the future. Assume that you are the sales manager for a local travel agency. Make a case that would persuade your superiors that going "on-line" would be a good investment. Cite both the positive and negative potential outcomes.

 Traveling the Net

Point of Interest: On-line Shopping and E-commerce

In the past, many consumers have dreaded anniversaries, birthdays, Mother's Day, Valentine's Day, and seemingly countless other "memorable" occasions because of the responsibility and associated hassles of trying to find the "perfect" gift or floral arrangement for loved ones or significant others. E-commerce is beginning to change all of that. Today, when you need to send flowers or small gifts at the last minute, the Internet is definitely the

---

* *Concept check answers:* 1. direct marketing; 2. customer database; 3. identifying prospects, deepening customer loyalty, and reactivating customer purchases; 4. direct-mail marketing, catalog marketing, telemarketing, kiosk marketing, and on-line marketing; 5. direct-mail marketing; 6. fax, e-mail, and voice mail; 7. kiosks; 8. on-line marketing; 9. electronic markets; 10. Webcasting.

way to go. A fast-growing number of florist Web sites provide the e-shopper with a convenient way to search by price, occasion, or types of flowers. Forgetful gift-givers no longer have to rely on a florist's judgment about what flowers to send. They don't even have to visit the florist to pick them out. The numerous florist Web sites allow them to make their own selection without having to leave home or the office. Most of these Web retailers also offer an event reminder service (via e-mail) so that buyers will never again forget important dates and occasions. Visit the following Web sites for more information on buying floral arrangements and gifts via the Internet: (a) 1-800-Flowers (www.1800flowers.com), (b) PC Flowers and Gifts (www.pcflowers.com), (c) 2G Roses (www.freshroses.com), (d) GiftTree (www.gifttree.com), and (e) Gourmet Gift Net (www. gourmetgift.com).

For Discussion

1. How does purchasing floral arrangements via the Internet compare with buying them by telephone or in person? Compare these channels in terms of cost, speed of delivery, selection of merchandise, freshness, dependability, ease of ordering, and ability to personalize requests.

2. What are the difficulties in using the Internet for this type of purchasing? How could these difficulties be overcome?

3. Which of the Web sites above seem to be the most "user friendly"? Why? Which site would you be most willing to use to order flowers or gifts? Why?

4. What future do you see for marketing flowers and gifts via the Internet? If you were a local florist, would you invest in a Web page? Why or why not? If you were to invest in a Web page, how would you get old and new customers to use it?

Application Thinking

With the explosive growth of the Internet, many companies are vying to become the main "portal" or starting point through which individuals access the Web. In a scramble to become the world's portal of choice, companies ranging from on-line service providers (such as America Online) and computer hardware and software makers (Microsoft, Dell, Compaq) to news and entertainment firms (Disney, Warner Communications, NBC) are snapping up or forming alliances with browser and portal companies such as Netscape, Yahoo!, Infoseek, and Snap!. General-purpose portals are even beginning to give way to niche portals such as in sports (ESPN and Sportline) and health (Intelihealth and Dr. Koop). Assume that you are a marketing manager for 1-800-Flowers (see www.1800flowers.com) and would like to ensure access to as many consumers as possible. Even though you are using traditional advertising media to reach consumers, you want to secure broader exposure through alliances with various Internet portal providers. Develop a plan for gaining such exposure. Specify which portal providers you would be most interested in and why. Be sure to consider what market segments you are pursuing.

MAP — Marketing Applications

MAP Stop 14

"Danger, Will Robinson, Danger!" This familiar cry from the robot of *Lost In Space* fame may soon be more a reality than just a futuristic fantasy. Designers are now very close to true voice recognition and speech transfer between computer and man. Consumers will most likely see the first evidences of computer voice recognition and speech technology applied in some rather low-tech ways (such as Samsung's voice-activated cell phones). However, for those with the right equipment, voice-

automated mortgage brokers, stock trading, yellow pages information, seat reservation services, and voice-based Web browsing are already a reality. Cost savings is a major factor driving this new technology. For example, voice recognition is now widely used for collect calls (such as "Will you accept? Yes or No?") and other human-assisted functions, saving millions of dollars each year. Organizations serving the disabled and handicapped, the toy industry, and the personal computer and software industries are just a few of the likely winners from advances in this technology and its applications. So, in the future, remember to speak up—your computer wants to hear from you.

Thinking Like a Marketing Manager

1. Thinking as a marketing manager, what applications appear to be naturals for this newly emerging technology? What companies will be most interested in the technology?

2. What applications will this new technology have in the on-line and direct-marketing industries?

3. Assume that you are the marketing manager for a personal computer company that is considering adding voice-recognition hardware and software to its existing product line. Devise a plan for this introduction. What critical factors must be addressed for success to occur? Who will be the most likely customers? How will you educate target consumers about this new technology and persuade them to make the investment needed to purchase it? How will you deal with older technologies that will now become obsolete?

The Global Marketplace

ROAD MAP:
Previewing the Concepts

You've come a long way on your marketing journey. You've now learned the fundamentals of how companies develop marketing strategies and marketing mixes to build lasting customer relationships by creating superior customer value. In the final two chapters, we'll extend these fundamentals to two special areas: global marketing, and social responsibility and marketing ethics. Although we've visited these topics regularly in each previous chapter, because of their special importance, we will focus exclusively on them here at the end of your journey. We'll look first at special considerations in global marketing. As we move into the new millennium, advances in communication, transportation, and other technologies have made the world a much smaller place. Today, almost every firm, large or small, faces international marketing issues. In this chapter, we will examine six major decisions marketers make in going global.

▶ **After studying this chapter, you should be able to**

1. **discuss how the international trade system and the economic, political-legal, and cultural environments affect a company's international marketing decisions**
2. **describe three key approaches to entering international markets**
3. **explain how companies adapt their marketing mixes for international markets**
4. **identify the three major forms of international marketing organization**

Buckle up and let's get going! Our first stop is the National Basketball Association (NBA). You probably think of professional basketball as an exclusively all-American passion. Not so! During the past decade, the NBA has become a world-class global powerhouse. Read on and learn why and how.

What could be more American than basketball? The sport was invented in the United States, and each year tens of millions of excited fans crowd their local gyms or huddle around their television sets to cheer on their favorite rec league, high school, college, or pro teams. But basketball is rapidly becoming a worldwide craze. For example, a recent *New York Times* survey of more than 45,000 teenagers on five continents asked, "What are your favorite entertainment pursuits?" The answers: (1) watching television, (2) basketball.

No organization is doing more to promote worldwide basketball than the National Basketball Association (NBA). During the past decade, the NBA has become a truly global marketing enterprise. NBA games are televised in 190 countries throughout the world, and worldwide sales of NBA-licensed basketballs, backboards, T-shirts, and other merchandise topped $3 billion last year. The NBA is now a powerful worldwide brand. A recent *Fortune* article summarizes:

Forget about going to Disneyland. Now that the NBA season is over, basketball's big stars are headed for more exotic locales: Shaquille O'Neal to South Korea, Karl Malone to Hong Kong, Allen Iverson to Chile, and all the Chicago Bulls—including chief luminary Michael Jordan—to France. Deployed by global sponsors Coca-Cola, Reebok, and McDonald's, these well-paid traveling salesmen will hawk soda, sneakers, burgers, and basketball to legions of mostly young fans. That they are recognized from Santiago to Seoul says a lot about the soaring worldwide appeal of hoops—and about the marketing juggernaut known as the NBA. After watching their favorite stars swoop in and slam-dunk on their local TV stations, fans of the league now cheer the *mate* in Latin America, the *trofsla* in Iceland, and the *smash* in France. Care to guess the most popular basketball team in China? Why, it's the "Red Oxen" from Chicago, of course.

Basketball has even become a diplomatic tool. Last summer, the U.S. Secretary of State, in an effort to preserve a fragile peace in Bosnia, requested that the NBA allow the broadcast of basketball games in the war-torn country. As a result, this year the NBA finals were aired in Bosnia for the first time ever. According to a State Department official, NBA broadcasts are "the most popular program there. The Bosnians are very big basketball buffs."

Like many other businesses, the NBA's primary motive for going global is growth. The league now sells out most of its games, and domestic licensing revenues have flattened in recent years. According to NBA Commissioner David Sterns, "There are just so many seats in an arena and so many hours of television programming, period. The domestic business is becoming mature. That's why we're moving internationally." Compared with the NBA's overall yearly revenues of $1.5 billion, current international revenues are modest—estimated at a little more than $60 million from TV rights fees, sponsorships, and the league's share of licensing sales. But worldwide potential is huge, and the league is investing heavily to build its popularity and business abroad. For example, its international staff of 105 is nearly double the number of people who ran the entire league back in the early 1980s.

Thanks to skillful marketing, and to the growing worldwide popularity of basketball itself, the NBA's investment appears to be paying off. According to *Fortune*, the NBA enjoys huge natural advantages over football, baseball, and other rivals:

It's selling a sport, basketball, that's played nearly everywhere and easily understood. (Try explaining a nickel defense to a Swede.) Pro and amateur leagues have been thriving for years in Europe and Asia, and basketball has been an Olympic sport since 1936. The U.S. "Dream Team" in 1992 was a worldwide sensation, sparking even greater interest in pro basketball in the U.S. . . . By then the groundwork had been laid for the NBA's global growth. Two men deserve much of the credit: David Stern and Michael Jordan, with a big assist from Nike. [The NBA and Nike] turned Jordan into a worldwide celebrity, known not just for his gravity-defying skills but also for his winning personality and competitive zeal. . . . In China, which has its own professional basketball leagues, boys on the streets of Beijing and Shanghai wear Bulls gear because they want to be like Mike. . . . A survey of 28,000 teenagers in 45 countries by [a global ad agency] found that [even after retirement] Jordan was the world's favorite athlete by far.

Broader historical forces also helped to promote the league's efforts to go global: the collapse of communism and the growth of market economies, the globalization of American consumer companies, and a revolution in worldwide television. Most recent is the explosion of the global Internet. The NBA's site (www.NBA.com) offers programming in several languages and draws 35 percent of its visitors from outside the United States.

However, beyond these natural forces, the NBA's success abroad results in large part from the league's strong marketing efforts. To exploit international opportunities:

The NBA rolled out a marketing machine that's been fine-tuned for a decade in the United States. Television programming leads the way—not just broadcasts of games but an array of NBA-produced programs, mostly targeted at kids and teenagers, that promote the league and its players. Two weekly programs, a highlights show called *NBA Action* and a teen show called *NBA Jam* that features music, fashion, and player profiles, are produced solely for the international marketplace. . . . Once television has pried open a market, the NBA and its partners move in with an array of live events, attractions, and grassroots activities. The Bulls, for instance, will go to Paris in October to play teams from Spain, Greece, Argentina, Italy, and France in this year's McDonald's Championship, which will be telecast worldwide—and promoted in 500 McDonald's restaurants in France. McDonald's and the NBA also sponsor a program called 2Ball that teaches basic basketball skills to thousands of kids outside the U.S. Coca-Cola, meanwhile, targets basketball-crazed teenagers by putting NBA and team logos on Sprite soft drink cans sold in 30 countries. "We're using the NBA and their players to help sell Sprite, but at the same time it does a lot for the NBA," says [Coca-Cola's] director for worldwide sports.

Yet another factor driving the NBA's global appeal is the increased presence of foreign-born players. Almost every team roster includes one: Toni Kukoc from Croatia, Luc Longley from Australia, Georghe Muresan from Romania, Arvydas Sabonis from Lithuania, or Detlef Shrempf from Germany. Such players attract large followings in their home countries. As *Fortune* concludes:

Imagine, then, the impact in China if a promising 18-year-old, 7-foot-1 center named Wong Zhizhi, who played for that country's 1996 Olympic team, develops into an NBA star. Basketball's popularity is already exploding in China, one of the very few nations where the NBA gives away its TV programming because [it] is determined to make inroads there. Nearly all of China's 250 million TV households get the *NBA Action* highlights show and a game of the week on Saturday mornings;

this year China Central TV broadcast the NBA All-Star game live for the first time. Winning the loyalty of two billion Chinese won't be a *kou qui*—a slam-dunk—but Stern is, well, bullish. "The upside is tremendous," he says. Can Ping-Pong survive an NBA invasion? Stay tuned.[1]

In the past, U.S. companies paid little attention to international trade. If they could pick up some extra sales through exporting, that was fine. But the big market was at home, and it teemed with opportunities. The home market was also much safer. Managers did not need to learn other languages, deal with strange and changing currencies, face political and legal uncertainties, or adapt their products to different customer needs and expectations. Today, however, the situation is much different.

Global Marketing into the Twenty-First Century

The world is shrinking rapidly with the advent of faster communication, transportation, and financial flows. Products developed in one country—Gucci purses, Mont Blanc pens, McDonald's hamburgers, Japanese sushi, Pierre Cardin suits, German BMWs—are finding enthusiastic acceptance in other countries. We would not be surprised to hear about a German businessman wearing an Italian suit meeting an English friend at a Japanese restaurant who later returns home to drink Russian vodka and watch *Home Improvement* on TV.

True, many companies have been carrying on international activities for decades. Coca-Cola, IBM, Kodak, Nestlé, Bayer, Sony, and other companies are familiar to most consumers around the world. But today global competition is intensifying. Foreign firms are expanding aggressively into new international markets, and home markets are no longer as rich in opportunity. Domestic companies that never thought about foreign competitors suddenly find these competitors in their own backyards. The firm that stays at home to play it safe not only might lose its chance to enter other markets but also risks losing its home market.

In the United States, names such as Sony, Toyota, Nestlé, Norelco, Mercedes, and Panasonic have become household words. Other products and services that appear to be American are in fact produced or owned by foreign companies: Bantam books, Baskin-Robbins ice cream, GE and RCA televisions, Firestone tires, Carnation milk, Pillsbury food products, Universal Studios, and Motel 6, to name just a few. Few U.S. industries are now safe from foreign competition.

Although some companies would like to stem the tide of foreign imports through protectionism, in the long run this would only raise the cost of living and protect inefficient domestic firms. The better way for companies to compete is to continuously improve their products at home and expand into foreign markets. Many U.S. companies have been successful at international marketing: IBM, Xerox, Corning, Coca-Cola, McDonald's, Gillette, Colgate, General Electric, Caterpillar, Ford, Kodak, 3M, Boeing, Motorola, and dozens of other American firms have made the world their market. But there are too few such firms. In fact, just five U.S. companies account for 12 percent of all exports; 1,000 manufacturers (out of 300,000) account for 60 percent.[2]

The longer companies delay taking steps toward internationalizing, the more they risk being shut out of growing markets in Western Europe, Eastern Europe, the Pacific Rim, and elsewhere. Domestic businesses that thought they were safe now find companies from neighboring countries invading their home markets. All companies will have to answer some basic questions: What market position should we try to establish in our country, in our economic region, and globally? Who will our global competitors be, and

Many American companies have made the world their market.

what are their strategies and resources? Where should we produce or source our products? What strategic alliances should we form with other firms around the world?

Ironically, although the need for companies to go abroad is greater today than in the past, so are the risks. Companies that go global confront several major problems. High debt, inflation, and unemployment in many countries have resulted in highly unstable governments and currencies, which limits trade and exposes U.S. firms to many risks. Governments are placing more regulations on foreign firms, such as requiring joint ownership with domestic partners, mandating the hiring of nationals, and limiting profits that can be taken from the country. Moreover, foreign governments often impose high tariffs or trade barriers in order to protect their own industries. Finally, corruption is an increasing problem—officials in several countries often award business not to the best bidder but to the highest briber.

Marketing at Work 15-1

The Internet: A Whole New World

As the Internet and on-line services attract ever more users around the world, many marketers are taking advantage of the Internet's global reach. Major global marketers already on the Net range from automakers (General Motors) to direct-mail companies who put their catalogs on-line (L.L. Bean) to global wine shippers (Virtual Vineyards) to compact disk marketers (CDNow). All are taking advantage of cyberspace's trivialization of national boundaries.

Whether or not they intend it, companies that sell or promote on the Internet have the whole world for a market. For some of these companies, the global market has largely been a hit-or-miss affair. They put their content up in English for the American market, and if any international users stumble across it and end up buying something, so much the better. Such orders can be gravy for U.S.-focused marketers. CompuServe's Electronic Mall, for instance, reports that 40 percent of some merchants' sales come from CompuServe's overseas members, who are largely attracted to merchandise that previously had been available only in the United States.

Other marketers have made a more strategic decision to dive into the global market. They're using the Web and on-line services to reach new customers outside their home countries, support existing customers who reside abroad, and build global brand awareness. Some of these companies adapt their Web sites to provide country-specific content and services to their best potential international markets, ideally in the local language. They may also provide local sales support and, where applicable, bill in local currencies. Other marketers go with an on-line service such as CompuServe, Europe On-line, America Online, Microsoft Network in Europe, or services such as Nifty-Serve or PC Van in Japan. Such on-line services can form "partnerships" with the marketer, helping to perform transactions and other services abroad.

For the most part, marketers have zeroed in on the countries or regions with the largest potential on-line populations. Europe and Japan are prime targets. International Data Corporation, a European market research firm, estimates that by the year 2000 in Europe alone some 35 million users—both businesses and consumers—will be logging onto the Web, buying more than $3 billion worth of goods and services.

Despite these encouraging numbers, Internet marketers sometimes get caught up in the hype and overstate the Web's seemingly sure-fire global opportunities. The reality of the global Internet market depends on each country's economic, technical, cultural, political, and regional dynamics. Many countries remain technologically underdeveloped and have a low-income citizenry lacking PCs or even phone connections. Other countries have acceptable phone and PC penetrations, but high connection costs sharply restrict casual uses such as surfing on the Internet. For example, even in advanced countries such as the United Kingdom, connection rates can run over $3.50 per hour, with long-distance calling and data surcharges in rural areas running as high as $16 per hour.

In addition, depending on the country, the global marketer may also run up against governmental restrictions on electronic commerce. France, for instance, has laws against providing encrypted content. In Germany, it is against the law for credit-card companies and direct-marketing firms to gather certain types of data on potential applicants—a precaution taken by the country to prevent the massive abuses of centralized information experienced during the Nazi era. Such restrictions, sometimes combined with underdeveloped banking systems, have limited credit-card and direct-mail usage in many countries. Subsequently, marketers outside the United States sometimes have to find alternative marketing and collection approaches.

Finally, there is the problem faced by any new medium in any country—just getting recognition. Given the cyberspace hype in the United States, many marketers are surprised to learn that familiarity with the Internet among the masses overseas is still very low. Affluent, information-intensive residents are catching on to the Internet, but mainstream consumers remain clueless.

Despite these barriers, global Internet enterprise is growing rapidly.

Global firm
A firm that, by operating in more than one country, gains R&D, production, and marketing advantages in its costs and reputation that are not available to purely domestic competitors.

Still, companies selling in global industries have no choice but to internationalize their operations. A *global industry* is one in which the competitive positions of firms in given local or national markets are affected by their global positions. A **global firm** is one that, by operating in more than one country, gains marketing, production, R&D, and financial advantages that are not available to purely domestic competitors. The global company

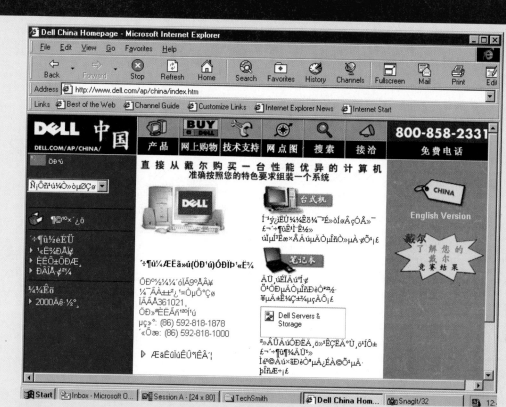

Many marketers are taking advantage of the Internet's global reach. For example, Dell Computer offers dozens of different Web site choices tailored to the languages and situations of specific countries, here China.

In fact, a whopping 83 percent of managers surveyed recently by consulting firm KPMG Peat Marwick said that electronic commerce will be a major export vehicle by the year 2000. For companies that wish to go global, the Internet and on-line services can represent an easy way to get started, or to reinforce other efforts. For large companies, casting an international Web is a natural. For example, Hewlett-Packard uses a Web site to deal with its resellers Europe-wide, offering information in many languages. Dell Computer offers dozens of different Web site choices tailored to the languages and situations of specific countries. And Texas Instruments' European Semiconductor group uses an English-only "TI & Me" site to sell and support its signal processors, logic devices, and other chips across the European continent. TI receives between 100 and 150 inquiries per day over the Web.

But small companies can also market globally on the Web. Take compact disk marketer CDNow. Although only a few years old, this virtual company now has a global market and multimillion dollar revenues. More than 30 percent of its $60 million in sales comes from outside North America. And it exists *only* on the Web.

Source: Portions adapted from Peter Krasilovsky, "A Whole New World," Marketing Tools supplement, *American Demographics*, May 1996, pp. 22–25. Also see Richard N. Miller, "The Year Ahead," *Direct Marketing*, January 1997, pp. 42–44; Jack Gee, "Parlez-Vous Inter-Net?" *Industry Week*, April 21, 1997, pp. 78–79; Donald N. Thompson, "The Winner Is . . . ," *Ivey Business Quarterly*, Spring 1998, pp. 39–45; Chris Lydgate, "Cutting Out the Middleman," *Asian Business*, May 1998, pp. 12–13; and Michael Dell, "Maximum Speed," *Executive Excellence*, January 1999, pp. 15–16.

sees the world as one market. It minimizes the importance of national boundaries and raises capital, obtains materials and components, and manufactures and markets its goods wherever it can do the best job. For example, Ford's "world truck" sports a cab made in Europe and a chassis built in North America. It is assembled in Brazil and imported to the United States for sale. Otis Elevator gets its elevators' door systems from France, small

Figure 15-1
Major international
marketing decisions

geared parts from Spain, electronics from Germany, and special motor drives from Japan.[3] It uses the United States only for systems integration. Thus, global firms gain advantages by planning, operating, and coordinating their activities on a worldwide basis.

Because firms around the world are globalizing at a rapid rate, domestic firms in global industries must act quickly before the window closes. This does not mean that small and medium-size firms must operate in a dozen countries to succeed. These firms can practice global niching. In fact, companies marketing on the Internet may find themselves going global whether they intend it or not (see Marketing at Work 15-1). But the world is becoming smaller, and every company operating in a global industry—whether large or small—must assess and establish its place in world markets.

As shown in Figure 15-1, a company faces six major decisions in international marketing. Each decision will be discussed in detail in this chapter.

Looking at the Global Marketing Environment

Before deciding whether to operate internationally, a company must thoroughly understand the international marketing environment. That environment has changed a great deal in the last two decades, creating both new opportunities and new problems. The world economy has globalized. World trade and investment have grown rapidly, with many attractive markets opening up in Western and Eastern Europe, China and the Pacific Rim, Russia, and elsewhere. There has been a growth of global brands in automobiles, food, clothing, electronics, and many other categories. The number of global companies has grown dramatically. Meanwhile, the United States's dominant position has declined. Other countries, such as Japan and Germany, have increased their economic power in world markets. The international financial system has become more complex and volatile, and U.S. companies face increasing trade barriers erected to protect domestic markets from outside competition.

Tariff
A tax levied by a government against certain imported products.

Quota
A limit on the amount of goods that an importing country will accept in certain product categories.

Embargo
A ban on the import of a certain product.

The International Trade System

The U.S. company looking abroad must start by understanding the international *trade system*. When selling to another country, the U.S. firm faces various trade restrictions. The most common is the **tariff**, which is a tax levied by a foreign government against certain imported products. The tariff may be designed either to raise revenue or to protect domestic firms. The exporter also may face a **quota**, which sets limits on the amount of goods the importing country will accept in certain product categories. The purpose of the quota is to conserve on foreign exchange and to protect local industry and employment. An **embargo**, or boycott, which totally bans some kinds of imports, is the strongest form of quota.

American firms may face **exchange controls** that limit the amount of foreign exchange and the exchange rate against other currencies. The company also may face **nontariff trade barriers**, such as biases against U.S. company bids or restrictive product standards or other rules that go against American product features:

> One of the cleverest ways the Japanese have found to keep foreign manufacturers out of their domestic market is to plead "uniqueness." Japanese skin is different, the government argues, so foreign cosmetics companies must test their products in Japan before selling there. The Japanese say their stomachs are small and have room for only the *mikan*, the local tangerine, so imports of U.S. oranges are limited. Now the Japanese have come up with what may be the flakiest argument yet: Their snow is different, so ski equipment should be too.[4]

At the same time, certain forces *help* trade between nations. Examples include the General Agreement on Tariffs and Trade and various regional free trade agreements.

The World Trade Organization and GATT The General Agreement on Tariffs and Trade (GATT) is a 50-year-old treaty designed to promote world trade by reducing tariffs and other international trade barriers. Since the treaty's inception in 1948, member nations (currently numbering more than 120) have met in eight rounds of GATT negotiations to reassess trade barriers and set new rules for international trade. The first seven rounds of negotiations reduced the average worldwide tariffs on manufactured goods from 45 percent to just 5 percent.

The most recent GATT negotiations, dubbed the Uruguay Round, dragged on for seven long years before concluding in 1993. The benefits of the Uruguay Round will be felt for many years, as the accord promotes long-term global trade growth. It reduces the world's remaining merchandise tariffs by 30 percent, which could boost global merchandise trade by up to 10 percent, or $270 billion in current dollars, by the year 2002. The new agreement also extends GATT to cover trade in agriculture and a wide range of services, and it toughens international protection of copyrights, patents, trademarks, and other intellectual property.[5]

Beyond reducing trade barriers and setting international standards for trade, the Uruguay Round established the World Trade Organization (WTO) to enforce GATT rules. One of the WTO's first major tasks was to host negotiations on the General Agreement on Trade in Services, which deals with worldwide trade in banking, securities, and insurance services. In general, the WTO will act as an umbrella organization, overseeing GATT, the General Agreement on Trade in Services, and a similar agreement governing intellectual property. In addition, the WTO mediates global disputes and imposes trade sanctions, authorities that the previous GATT organization never possessed.

Regional Free Trade Zones Certain countries have formed *free trade zones* or **economic communities**, groups of nations organized to work toward common goals in the regulation of international trade. One such community is the *European Union (EU)*. Formed in 1957, the European Union—then called the Common Market—set out to create a single European market by reducing barriers to the free flow of products, services, finances, and labor among member countries and developing policies on trade with nonmember nations. Today, the European Union represents one of the world's single largest markets. Its 15 member countries contain more than 370 million consumers and account for 20 percent of the world's exports. During the next decade, as more European nations seek admission, the EU could contain as many as 450 million people in 28 countries.

Exchange controls
A government's limits on the amount of its foreign exchange with other countries and on its exchange rate against other currencies.

Nontariff trade barriers
Nonmonetary barriers to foreign products, such as biases against a foreign company's bids or restrictive product standards.

Economic community
A group of nations organized to work toward common goals in the regulation of international trade.

Wal-Mart and other companies are expanding rapidly in Mexico and Canada to take advantage of the many opportunities presented by NAFTA. The trade agreement establishes a single market of 360 million people in Mexico, Canada, and the United States.

European unification offers tremendous trade opportunities for U.S. and other non-European firms. However, it also poses threats. As a result of increased unification, European companies will grow bigger and more competitive. Perhaps an even bigger concern, however, is that lower barriers *inside* Europe will only create thicker *outside* walls. Some observers envision a "Fortress Europe" that heaps favors on firms from EU countries but hinders outsiders by imposing obstacles such as stiffer import quotas, local content requirements, and other nontariff barriers.

Progress toward European unification has been slow—many doubt that complete unification will ever be achieved. Even if the European Union does manage to standardize its general trade regulations, from a marketing viewpoint, creating an economic community will not create a homogeneous market. With many different languages and distinctive national customs, it is unlikely that the EU will ever become the "United States of Europe." Although economic and political boundaries may fall, social and cultural differences will remain, and companies marketing in Europe will face a daunting mass of local rules. Still, even if only partly successful, European unification will make a more efficient and competitive Europe a global force with which to reckon.[6]

In North America, the United States and Canada phased out trade barriers in 1989. In January 1994, the *North American Free Trade Agreement (NAFTA)* established a free trade zone among the United States, Mexico, and Canada. The agreement created a single market of 360 million people who produce and consume $6.7 trillion worth of goods and services. As it is implemented over a 15-year period, NAFTA will eliminate all trade barriers and investment restrictions among the three countries. Prior to NAFTA, tariffs on American products entering Mexico averaged 13 percent, while U.S. tariffs on Mexican goods averaged 6 percent.

Other free trade areas are forming in Latin America and South America. For example, MERCOSUL now links Brazil, Colombia, and Mexico; and Chile and Mexico have formed a successful free trade zone. Venezuela, Colombia, and Mexico—the "Group of Three"—are negotiating a free trade area as well. It is likely that NAFTA will eventually merge with this and other arrangements to form an all-Americas free trade zone.

Although the recent trend toward free trade zones has caused great excitement and new market opportunities, this trend also raises some concerns. For example, in the United States, unions fear that NAFTA will lead to the further exodus of manufacturing jobs to Mexico where wage rates are much lower. Environmentalists worry that companies that are unwilling to play by the strict rules of the U.S. Environmental Protection Agency will relocate in Mexico where pollution regulation has been lax.[7]

Each nation has unique features that must be understood. A nation's readiness for different products and services and its attractiveness as a market to foreign firms depend on its economic, political legal, and cultural environments.

Economic Environment

The international marketer must study each country's economy. Two economic factors reflect the country's attractiveness as a market: the country's industrial structure and its income distribution.

The country's *industrial structure* shapes its product and service needs, income levels, and employment levels. The four types of industrial structures are as follows:

- *Subsistence economies:* In a subsistence economy, the vast majority of people engage in simple agriculture. They consume most of their output and barter the rest for simple goods and services. They offer few market opportunities.
- *Raw material exporting economies:* These economies are rich in one or more natural resources but poor in other ways. Much of their revenue comes from exporting these resources. Examples are Chile (tin and copper), Zaire (copper, cobalt, and coffee), and Saudi Arabia (oil). These countries are good markets for large equipment, tools and supplies, and trucks. If there are many foreign residents and a wealthy upper class, they are also a market for luxury goods.
- *Industrializing economies:* In an industrializing economy, manufacturing accounts for 10 to 20 percent of the country's economy. Examples include Egypt, the Philippines, India, and Brazil. As manufacturing increases, the country needs more imports of raw textile materials, steel, and heavy machinery, and fewer imports of finished textiles, paper products, and automobiles. Industrialization typically creates a new rich class and a small but growing middle class, both demanding new types of imported goods.
- *Industrial economies:* Industrial economies are major exporters of manufactured goods and investment funds. They trade goods among themselves and also export them to other types of economies for raw materials and semifinished goods. The varied manufacturing activities of these industrial nations and their large middle class make them rich markets for all sorts of goods.

The second economic factor is the country's *income distribution*. Countries with subsistence economies may consist mostly of households with very low family incomes. In contrast, industrialized nations may have low-, medium-, and high-income households. Still other countries may have only households with either very low or very high incomes. However, even people in low-income countries may find ways to buy products that are important to them, or sheer population numbers can counter low average incomes. Also, in many cases, poorer countries may have small but wealthy segments of upper-income consumers:

Recall that in the U.S. the first satellite dishes sprang up in the poorest parts of Appalachia. . . . The poorest slums of Calcutta are home to 70,000 VCRs. In Mexico, homes with color televisions outnumber those with running water. Remember

Income distribution: Even poorer countries may have small but wealthy segments. Although citizens of Budapest, Hungary have relatively low annual incomes, well-dressed shoppers flock to elegant stores like this one, stocked with luxury goods.

also that low average-income figures may conceal a lively luxury market. In Warsaw (average annual income: $2,500) well-dressed shoppers flock to elegant boutiques stocked with Christian Dior perfume and Valentino shoes. . . . In China, where per capita annual income is less than $600, the Swiss company Rado is selling thousands of its $1,000 watches.[8]

Thus, international marketers face many challenges in understanding how the economic environment will affect decisions about which global markets to enter and how.

Political-Legal Environment

Nations differ greatly in their political-legal environments. At least four political-legal factors should be considered in deciding whether to do business in a given country: attitudes toward international buying, government bureaucracy, political stability, and monetary regulations.

In their *attitudes toward international buying*, some nations are quite receptive to foreign firms and others are quite hostile. For example, India has bothered foreign businesses with import quotas, currency restrictions, and limits on the percentage of the management team that can be nonnationals. As a result, many U.S. companies left India. In contrast, neighboring Asian countries such as Singapore, Thailand, Malaysia, and the Philippines court foreign investors and shower them with incentives and favorable operating conditions.[9]

A second factor is *government bureaucracy*—the extent to which the host government runs an efficient system for helping foreign companies: efficient customs handling, good market information, and other factors that aid in doing business. A common shock to Americans is how quickly barriers to trade disappear in some countries if a suitable payment (bribe) is made to some official.

Political stability is another issue. Governments change hands, sometimes violently. Even without a change, a government may decide to respond to new popular feelings. The foreign company's property may be taken, its currency holdings may be blocked, or import quotas or new duties may be set. International marketers may find it profitable to do business in an unstable country, but the unstable situation will affect how they handle business and financial matters.

Finally, companies must also consider a country's *monetary regulations.* Sellers want to take their profits in a currency of value to them. Ideally, the buyer can pay in the seller's currency or in other world currencies. Short of this, sellers might accept a blocked currency—one whose removal from the country is restricted by the buyer's government—if they can buy other goods in that country that they need themselves or can sell elsewhere for a needed currency. Besides currency limits, a changing exchange rate also creates high risks for the seller.

Most international trade involves cash transactions. Yet many nations have too little hard currency to pay for their purchases from other countries. They may want to pay with other items instead of cash, which has led to a growing practice called **countertrade**. Countertrade may account for more than one-half of all international trade by the year 2000. It takes several forms: *Barter* involves the direct exchange of goods or services, as when Australian cattlemen swapped beef on the hoof for Indonesian goods including beer, palm oil, and cement. Another form is *compensation* (or *buyback*), whereby the seller sells a plant, equipment, or technology to another country and agrees to take payment in the resulting products. Thus, Goodyear provided China with materials and training for a printing plant in exchange for finished labels. Another form is *counterpurchase*, in which the seller receives full payment in cash but agrees to spend some portion of the money in the other country within a stated time period. For example, Pepsi sells its cola syrup to Russia for rubles and agrees to buy Russian-made Stolichnaya vodka for sale in the United States.

Countertrade deals can be very complex. For example, Daimler-Benz recently agreed to sell 30 trucks to Romania in exchange for 150 Romanian jeeps, which it then sold to Ecuador for bananas, which were in turn sold to a German supermarket chain for German currency. Through this roundabout process, Daimler-Benz finally obtained payment in German money. In another case, when Occidental Petroleum Company wanted to sell oil to Yugoslavia, it hired a trading firm, SGD International, to arrange a countertrade. SGD arranged for a New York City automobile dealer-distributor, Global Motors Inc., to import more than $400 million worth of Yugoslavian Yugo automobiles, paid for by Occidental oil. Global then paid Occidental in cash. SGD, however, was paid in Yugos, which it peddled piecemeal by trading them for everything from cash to Caribbean resort hotel rooms, which it in turn sold to tour packagers and travel agencies for cash.[10]

Countertrade
International trade involving the direct or indirect exchange of goods for other goods instead of cash.

Cultural Environment

Each country has its own folkways, norms, and taboos. The seller must examine the ways consumers in different countries think about and use certain products before planning a marketing program. There are often surprises. For example, the average French man uses almost twice as many cosmetics and beauty aids as his wife. The Germans and the French eat more packaged, branded spaghetti than do Italians. Italian children like to eat chocolate bars between slices of bread as a snack. Women in Tanzania will not give their children eggs for fear of making them bald or impotent.

Companies that ignore such differences can make some very expensive and embarrassing mistakes. Here's an example:

✧ McDonald's and Coca-Cola managed to offend the entire Muslim world by putting the Saudi Arabian flag on their packaging. The flag's design includes a passage

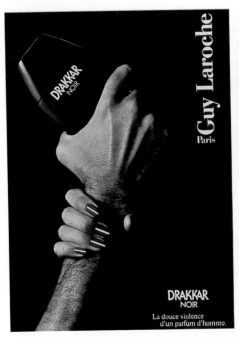 

Adapting to the cultural environment: Compared with the European version of this ad (left), Guy Laroche tones down the sensuality in the Arab version (right); the man is clothed and the woman barely touches him.

from the Koran (the sacred text of Islam), and Muslims feel very strongly that their Holy Writ should never be wadded up and tossed in the garbage.[11]

Business norms and behavior also vary from country to country. American business executives need to be briefed on these factors before conducting business in another country. Here are some examples of different global business behavior:[12]

- South Americans like to sit or stand very close to each other when they talk business—in fact, almost nose-to-nose. The American business executive tends to keep backing away as the South American moves closer. Both may end up being offended.
- Fast and tough bargaining, which works well in other parts of the world, is often inappropriate in Japan and other Asian countries. Moreover, in face-to-face communications, Japanese business executives rarely say no. Thus, Americans tend to become impatient with having to spend time in polite conversation about the weather or other such topics before getting down to business. And they become frustrated when they don't know where they stand. However, when Americans come to the point quickly, Japanese business executives may find this behavior offensive.
- In France, wholesalers don't want to promote a product. They ask their retailers what they want and deliver it. If an American company builds its strategy around the French wholesaler's cooperation in promotions, it is likely to fail.
- When American executives exchange business cards, each usually gives the other's card a cursory glance and stuffs it in a pocket for later reference. In Japan, however, executives dutifully study each other's cards during a greeting, carefully noting company affiliation and rank. They hand their card to the most important person first.

Thus, each country and region has cultural traditions, preferences, and behaviors that the marketer must study.

Deciding Whether to Go International

Not all companies need to venture into international markets to survive. For example, many companies are local businesses that need to market well only in the local marketplace. Operating domestically is easier and safer. Managers need not learn another country's language and laws, deal with volatile currencies, face political and legal uncertainties, or redesign their products to suit different customer needs and expectations. However, companies that operate in global industries, where their strategic positions in specific markets are affected strongly by their overall global positions, must compete on a worldwide basis if they are to succeed.

Any of several factors might draw a company into the international arena. Global competitors might attack the company's domestic market by offering better products or lower prices. The company might want to counterattack these competitors in their home markets to tie up their resources. Or the company might discover foreign markets that present higher profit opportunities than the domestic market does. The company's domestic market might be stagnant or shrinking, or the company might need an enlarged customer base in order to achieve economies of scale. The company might want to reduce its dependence on any one market so as to reduce its risk. Finally, the company's customers might be expanding abroad and require international servicing.

Before going abroad, the company must weigh several risks and answer many questions about its ability to operate globally. Can the company learn to understand the preferences and buyer behavior of consumers in other countries? Can it offer competitively attractive products? Will it be able to adapt to other countries' business cultures and deal effectively with foreign nationals? Do the company's managers have the necessary international experience? Has management considered the impact of regulations and the political environments of other countries?

Because of the risks and difficulties of entering international markets, most companies do not act until some situation or event thrusts them into the global arena. Someone—a domestic exporter, a foreign importer, a foreign government—may ask the company to sell abroad. Or the company may be saddled with overcapacity and must find additional markets for its goods.

Deciding Which Markets to Enter

Before going abroad, the company should try to define its international *marketing objectives and policies*. It should decide what *volume* of foreign sales it wants. Most companies start small when they go abroad. Some plan to stay small, seeing international sales as a small part of their business. Other companies have bigger plans, seeing international business as equal to or even more important than their domestic business.

The company must also choose *how many* countries it wants to market in. Generally, it makes sense to operate in fewer countries with deeper commitment and penetration in each. The Bulova Watch Company decided to operate in many international markets and expanded into more than 100 countries. As a result, it spread itself too thin, made profits in only two countries, and lost around $40 million. In contrast, although consumer product company Amway is now breaking into markets at a furious pace, it is doing so only after decades of gradually building up its overseas presence. Known for its neighbor-to-neighbor direct-selling networks, Amway expanded into Australia in 1971, a country

Marketing at Work 15-2

The Last Marketing Frontiers: China, Vietnam, and Cuba

As communist and formerly communist countries reform their markets, and as the United States continues to dismantle its trade barriers, U.S. companies are eagerly anticipating the profits that await them. Here are "snapshots" of the opportunities and challenges that marketers face in three of the world's global marketing frontiers.

China: 1.2 Billion Consumers

In Guangdong province, Chinese "yuppies" walk department store aisles to buy $95 Nike or Reebok sneakers or think nothing of spending $4 on a jar of Skippy peanut butter in the supermarket section. Although consumers here might make as little as $130 a month, they still have plenty of spending money because of subsidized housing and health care and lots of savings under the mattress. In Shenzen, Guangdong's second-largest city, consumers have the highest disposable income in all of China—$3,900 annually. With purchasing power like this, a population of 1.2 billion, and the fastest-growing economy in the world, China is encouraging companies from around the planet to set up shop there. Instead of the communist propaganda of yore, modern Chinese billboards exclaim, "Give China a chance."

Yet for all the market potential, there are many hurdles to clear in establishing businesses in China and marketing to the Chinese. For one, China is not one market but many, and regional governments may discriminate against certain goods. Distribution channels are undeveloped, consisting of thousands of tiny mom-and-pop stores that can afford to stock only a few bottles or packages at a time. And China's dismal infrastructure can turn a rail shipment traveling from Guanzhou to Beijing into a month-long odyssey. Smart firms, such as Allied Signal and Kodak, try to jump these hurdles by partnering with Chinese government bodies—in some regions doing so is a must for establishing a business. Others acquire Chinese business partners who can help them penetrate distribution channels and hire experienced personnel.

A major concern to some U.S. businesses has been China's distressing human rights record. Levi Strauss has turned its back on China's vast market for blue jeans because of such concerns. But other U.S. firms counter that industry can be part of the solution. "Supporting the business section will result in economic and political freedoms for the Chinese people," says a 3M spokesperson.

Vietnam: An Untapped Market

Vietnam seems like a marketer's dream: 72 million consumers, 80 percent of whom are younger than 40; loads of natural resources, including oil, gold, gas, and timber; and a coastline of pristine beaches that could turn out to be the hot new tourist spots. Vietnam is the world's twelfth most populous nation and Southeast Asia's second-largest market. With the ending of the U.S. trade embargo against Vietnam, this marketer's dream has become a reality for many U.S. companies. While European and Asian companies have been taking advantage of the Vietnamese market reforms that began in 1986, their foothold doesn't faze many U.S. marketers, who are banking on the popularity of American brands.

Amid all the excitement, however, there are some notes of caution. The per capita income of most Vietnamese is $200 a year, and like China, Vietnam's transportation and communication systems rank among the world's worst. While the country and its markets develop, marketers are spending their money cautiously. Because most consumers are seeing products for the first time ever, companies are investing most of their marketing dollars in very simple advertising campaigns. For this reason radio and billboards are

far away but similar to the U.S. market. Then, in the 1980s, Amway expanded into 10 more countries, and the pace increased rapidly from then on. By 1994 Amway was firmly established in 60 countries, including Hungary, Poland, and the Czech Republic, and boasted worldwide sales of $5 billion.[13]

Next, the company needs to decide on the *types* of countries to enter. A country's attractiveness depends on the product, geographical factors, income and population, political climate, and other factors. The seller may prefer certain country groups or parts of the world. In recent years, many major new markets have emerged, offering both substantial opportunities and daunting challenges (see Marketing at Work 15-2).

fruitful venues for advertising. One billboard in Ho Chi Minh City boasts a single word: Sony.

Cuba: Watching and Waiting

While the United States is tightening the screws on Havana by extending its Cuban trade embargo, other countries are tightening their grip on the Cuban market. U.S. policy makers hope the embargo will pressure Fidel Castro to liberalize his repressive regime. The drawback, however, is that other nations have refused to participate in the embargo. For example, at Havana In-Bond, a quasi-free trade zone on the capital's outskirts, warehouses are packed with Mexican goods entering Cuba. Cuba is one of the lushest Caribbean islands, so the biggest influx has been the boom in hotels built or managed by Spanish, Canadian, and Mexican operators. Some 800,000 tourists crammed Cuba's shores last year, and tourism overtook sugar exports as Cuba's top hard-currency earner.

While U.S. companies are currently losing out on a potentially lucrative market, many are preparing for Castro's imminent fall and the subsequent lifting of the embargo. "Here we have a consumer market of 11 million that is a 32 minute flight away with 30 years of pent-up demand. Is that not exciting?" says Ana Maria Fernandez Haar, a Cuban-American who is president

With 72 million consumers, Vietnam seems like a marketer's dream. However, the country's communication and transportation systems rank among the world's worst.

of the IAC Advertising Group. Procter & Gamble, United Airlines, American Airlines, and Sprint are just a few of the marketers interested in serving a free Cuban market. For now, though, foreign companies will continue to make inroads in Cuba, and U.S. marketers will simply watch and wait.

As with the emerging markets of China and Vietnam, Cuba's infrastructure needs years of rebuilding. Some places have no running water, gasoline, sewer systems, and energy sources. "They'll have to take care of the basic concept of survival before

they can think about pizza and Pepsi," says Joe Zubizarreta, a Cuban-born advertising executive.

Sources: Marlene Piturro, "Capitalist China?" *Brandweek,* May 16, 1994, pp. 22–27; Mark L. Clifford, "How You Can Win in China," *Business Week,* May 26, 1997, pp. 66–68; Louis Tong, "Consumerism Sweeps the Mainland," *Marketing Management,* Winter 1998, pp. 32–35; Cyndee Miller, "U.S. Firms Rush to Claim Share of Newly Opened Vietnam Market," *Marketing News,* March 14, 1994, p. 11; Thomas A. Kissane, "What Are We Doing in Vietnam?" *Sales & Marketing Management,* May 1996, pp. 96–97; Christy Fisher, "U.S. Marketers Wait for Opening in Cuba," *Advertising Age,* August 29, 1994, pp. 1, 6; Sean Mehegan, "Is Castro Convertible?" *Restaurant Business,* May 1, 1996, pp. 36–38; Jim Carrier, "Marxist Cuba Beckons, and U.S. Capitalists Champ at the Bit," *New York Times,* April 22, 1998, p. 1; and James C. McKinley Jr., "In Cuba's New Dual Economy, Have-Nots Far Exceed Haves," *New York Times,* January 11, 1999, p. 1.

After listing possible international markets, the company must screen and rank each one. Consider the following example:

✧ Many mass marketers dream of selling to China's more than 1.2 billion people. For example, Colgate is waging a pitched battle in China, seeking control of the world's largest toothpaste market. Colgate now holds a 7 percent share of the $350 million dollar Chinese market, where local brands dominate. Yet, this country of infrequent brushers offers great potential. Only 20 percent of China's rural dwellers brush daily, so Colgate and its competitors are aggressively pursuing promotional and

Table 15-1   Indicators of Market Potential

Demographic characteristics	Size of population Rate of population growth Degree of urbanization Population density Age structure and composition of the population
Geographic characteristics	Physical size of a country Topographical characteristics Climate conditions
Economic factors	GNP per capita Income distribution Rate of growth of GNP Ratio of investment to GNP
Technological factors	Level of technological skill Existing production technology Existing consumption technology Education levels
Sociocultural factors	Dominant values Lifestyle patterns Ethnic groups Linguistic fragmentation
National goals and plans	Industry priorities Infrastructure investment plans

Source: Susan P. Douglas, C. Samuel Craig, and Warren Keegan, "Approaches to Assessing International Marketing Opportunities for Small and Medium-Sized Business," *Columbia Journal of World Business,* Fall 1982, pp. 26–32.

educational programs, from massive ad campaigns to visits to local schools to sponsoring oral care research.[14]

Colgate's decision to enter the Chinese market seems fairly simple and straightforward: China is a huge market without established competition. Given the low rate of brushing, this already huge market can grow even larger. Yet we still can question whether market size *alone* is reason enough for selecting China. Colgate also must consider other factors: Will the Chinese government remain stable and supportive? Does China provide for the production and distribution technologies needed to produce and market Colgate's products profitably? Will Colgate be able to overcome cultural barriers and convince Chinese consumers to brush their teeth regularly? Can Colgate compete effectively with dozens of local competitors?

Possible global markets should be ranked on several factors, including market size, market growth, cost of doing business, competitive advantage, and risk level. The goal is to determine the potential of each market, using indicators such as those shown in Table 15-1. Then the marketer must decide which markets offer the greatest long-run return on investment.

General Electric's appliance division uses what it calls a "smart bomb" strategy for selecting global markets to enter. GE appliance executives examine each potential country microscopically, measuring factors such as strength of local competitors, market growth potential, and availability of skilled labor. Then they target only markets in which they can earn more than 20 percent on their investment. The goal: "To generate the best returns possible on the smallest investment possible." Once targets are selected, GE Appliances zeros in with marketing smart bombs—products and programs tailored to yield the best performance in each market. As a result of this strategy, GE is trouncing competitors Whirlpool and Maytag in Asian markets.[15]

Linking the Concepts

Slow down, stretch your legs, and think for a minute about the difficulties of assessing and selecting international markets.

- Assess China as a market for McDonald's. What factors make it attractive? What factors make it less attractive?
- Assess Canada as a market for McDonald's. In what ways is Canada more attractive than China? In what ways is it less attractive?
- If McDonald's could operate in only one of these countries, which one would you choose and why?

Deciding How to Enter the Market

Once a company has decided to sell in a foreign country, it must determine the best mode of entry. Its choices are *exporting*, *joint venturing*, and *direct investment*. Figure 15-2 shows three market entry strategies, along with the options each one offers. As the figure shows, each succeeding strategy involves more commitment and risk, but also more control and potential profits.

Exporting

The simplest way to enter a foreign market is through **exporting**. The company may passively export its surpluses from time to time, or it may make an active commitment to expand exports to a particular market. In either case, the company produces all its goods in its home country. It may or may not modify them for the export market. Exporting involves the least change in the company's product lines, organization, investments, or mission.

Companies typically start with *indirect exporting*, working through independent international marketing intermediaries. Indirect exporting involves less investment because the firm does not require an overseas sales force or set of contacts. It also involves less risk. International marketing intermediaries—domestic-based export merchants or agents, cooperative organizations, and export-management companies—bring know-how and services to the relationship, so the seller normally makes fewer mistakes.

Exporting
Entering a foreign market by sending and selling products through international marketing middlemen (indirect exporting) or the company's own department, branch, or sales representatives or agents (direct exporting).

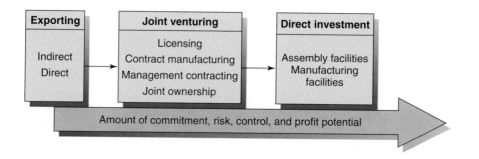

Figure 15-2
Market-entry
strategies

Sellers may eventually move into *direct exporting*, whereby they handle their own exports. The investment and risk are somewhat greater in this strategy, but so is the potential return. A company can conduct direct exporting in several ways: It can set up a domestic export department that carries out export activities. It can set up an overseas sales branch that handles sales, distribution, and perhaps promotion. The sales branch gives the seller more presence and program control in the foreign market and often serves as a display center and customer service center. The company can also send home-based salespeople abroad at certain times in order to find business. Finally, the company can do its exporting either through foreign-based distributors who buy and own the goods or through foreign-based agents who sell the goods on behalf of the company.

Joint Venturing

Joint venturing
Entering foreign markets by joining with foreign companies to produce or market a product or service.

A second method of entering a foreign market is **joint venturing**—joining with foreign companies to produce or market products or services. Joint venturing differs from exporting in that the company joins with a host country partner to sell or market abroad. It differs from direct investment in that an association is formed with someone in the foreign country. There are four types of joint ventures: licensing, contract manufacturing, management contracting, and joint ownership.

Licensing
A method of entering a foreign market in which the company contracts with a licensee in the foreign market, offering the right to use a manufacturing process, trademark, patent, trade secret, or other item of value for a fee or royalty.

Licensing Licensing is a simple way for a manufacturer to enter international marketing. The company enters into an agreement with a licensee in the foreign market. For a fee or royalty, the licensee buys the right to use the company's manufacturing process, trademark, patent, trade secret, or other item of value. The company thus gains entry into the market at little risk; the licensee gains production expertise or a well-known product or name without having to start from scratch.

Coca-Cola markets internationally by licensing bottlers around the world and supplying them with the syrup needed to produce the product. In Japan, Budweiser beer flows from Kirin breweries, Lady Borden ice cream is churned out at Meiji Milk Products dairies, and Marlboro cigarettes roll off production lines at Japan Tobacco, Inc. Tokyo Disneyland is owned and operated by Oriental Land Company under license from the Walt Disney Company. The 45-year license gives Disney licensing fees plus 10 percent of admissions and 5 percent of food and merchandise sales. In Mexico, Wal-Mart is joining with Cifra, the country's top retailer, to open Wal-Mart Supercenters and Sam's Clubs.[16]

Licensing has potential disadvantages, however. The firm has less control over the licensee than it would over its own production facilities. Furthermore, if the licensee is very successful, the firm has given up these profits, and if and when the contract ends, it may find it has created a competitor.

Contract manufacturing
A joint venture in which a company contracts with manufacturers in a foreign market to produce a product.

Contract Manufacturing Another option is **contract manufacturing**—the company contracts with manufacturers in the foreign market to produce its product or provide its service. Sears used this method in opening up department stores in Mexico and Spain, where it found qualified local manufacturers to produce many of the products it sells. The drawbacks of contract manufacturing are decreased control over the manufacturing process and loss of potential profits on manufacturing. The benefits are the chance to start faster, with less risk, and the later opportunity either to form a partnership with or to buy out the local manufacturer.

Management contracting
A joint venture in which the domestic firm supplies the management know-how to a foreign company that supplies the capital.

Management Contracting Under **management contracting**, the domestic firm supplies management know-how to a foreign company that supplies the capital. The domestic firm exports management services rather than products. Hilton uses this arrangement in managing hotels around the world.

夜がきれい、君もきれい、スターライト★デート。

Licensing: Tokyo
Disneyland is owned
and operated by the
Oriental Land Co., Ltd.
(a Japanese develop-
ment company), under
license from Walt
Disney Company.

Management contracting is a low-risk method of getting into a foreign market, and it yields income from the beginning. The arrangement is even more attractive if the contracting firm has an option to buy some share in the managed company later on. The arrangement is not sensible, however, if the company can put its scarce management talent to better uses or if it can make greater profits by undertaking the whole venture. Management contracting also prevents the company from setting up its own operations for a period of time.

Joint Ownership **Joint ownership** ventures consist of one company joining forces with foreign investors to create a local business in which they share joint ownership and control. A company may buy an interest in a local firm, or the two parties may form a new business venture. Joint ownership may be needed for economic or political reasons. The firm may lack the financial, physical, or managerial resources to undertake the venture alone. Or a foreign government may require joint ownership as a condition for entry.

Joint ownership has certain drawbacks. The partners may disagree over investment, marketing, or other policies. Whereas many U.S. firms like to reinvest earnings for growth, local firms often prefer to take out these earnings; and whereas U.S. firms emphasize the role of marketing, local investors may rely on selling.

Joint ownership
A joint venture in which a company joins investors in a foreign market to create a local business in which the company shares joint ownership and control.

Direct Investment

The biggest involvement in a foreign market comes through **direct investment**—the development of foreign-based assembly or manufacturing facilities. If a company has gained experience in exporting and if the foreign market is large enough, foreign production facilities offer many advantages. The firm may have lower costs in the form of cheaper labor or raw materials, foreign government investment incentives, and freight savings. The firm may improve its image in the host country because it creates jobs. Generally, a firm develops a deeper relationship with government, customers, local suppliers, and distributors, allowing it to better adapt its products to the local market. Finally, the

Direct investment
Entering a foreign market by developing foreign-based assembly or manufacturing facilities.

firm keeps full control over the investment and therefore can develop manufacturing and marketing policies that serve its long-term international objectives.

The main disadvantage of direct investment is that the firm faces many risks, such as restricted or devalued currencies, falling markets, or government changes. In some cases, a firm has no choice but to accept these risks if it wants to operate in the host country.

Deciding on the Global Marketing Program

Standardized marketing mix
An international marketing strategy for using basically the same marketing mix in all of the company's international markets.

Adapted marketing mix
An international marketing strategy for adjusting the marketing mix elements to each international target market, bearing more costs but hoping for a larger market share and return.

Companies that operate in one or more foreign markets must decide how much, if at all, to adapt their marketing mixes to local conditions. At one extreme are global companies that use a **standardized marketing mix** worldwide. Proponents of global standardization claim that it results in lower production, distribution, marketing, and management costs, letting companies offer consumers higher quality and more reliable products at lower prices. This is the thinking behind Coca-Cola's decision that Coke should taste about the same around the world and Ford's production of a "world car" that suits the needs of most consumers in most countries.

At the other extreme is an **adapted marketing mix**. In this case, the producer adjusts the marketing-mix elements to each target market, bearing more costs but hoping for a larger market share and return. Nestlé, for example, varies its product line and its advertising in different countries. Proponents argue that consumers in different countries vary greatly in their geographic, demographic, economic, and cultural characteristics, resulting in different needs and wants, spending power, product preferences, and shopping patterns. Therefore, companies should adapt their marketing strategies and programs to fit unique consumer needs in each country.

The question of whether to adapt or standardize the marketing mix has been much debated in recent years. However, global standardization is not an all-or-nothing proposition but rather a matter of degree. Companies should look for more standardization to help keep down costs and prices and to build greater global brand power. But they must not replace long-run marketing thinking with short-run financial thinking. Although standardization saves money, marketers must make certain that they offer what consumers in each country want.[17]

Many possibilities exist between the extremes of standardization and complete adaptation. For example, Coca-Cola sells virtually the same Coke beverage worldwide, and it pulls advertisements for specific markets from a common pool of ads designed to have cross-cultural appeal. However, the company sells a variety of other beverages created specifically for the tastebuds of local markets, and it modifies its distribution channels according to local conditions. Similarly, McDonald's uses the same basic operating formula in its restaurants around the world but adapts its menu to local tastes. For example, in India, where cows are considered sacred, McDonald's serves chicken, fish, vegetable burgers, and the Maharaja Mac—two all-mutton patties, special sauce, lettuce, cheese, pickles, onions on a sesame-seed bun. And although Whirlpool ovens, refrigerators, clothes washers, and other major appliances share the same interiors worldwide, their outer styling and features are designed to meet the preferences of consumers in different countries.[18]

Product

Five strategies allow for adapting product and promotion to a foreign market (see Figure 15-3).[19] We first discuss the three product strategies and then turn to the two promotion strategies.

Marketing mix adaptation: In India, McDonald's serves chicken, fish, vegetable burgers, and the Maharaja Mac—two all-mutton patties, special sauce, lettuce, cheese, pickles, onions on a sesame-seed bun.

Straight product extension means marketing a product in a foreign market without any change. Top management tells its marketing people: "Take the product as is and find customers for it." The first step, however, should be to find out whether foreign consumers use that product and what form they prefer.

Straight extension has been successful in some cases and disastrous in others. Coca-Cola, Kellogg cereals, Heineken beer, and Black & Decker tools are all sold successfully in about the same form around the world. But General Foods introduced its standard powdered Jell-O in the British market only to find that British consumers prefer a solid wafer or cake form. Likewise, Philips began to make a profit in Japan only after it reduced the size of its coffee makers to fit into smaller Japanese kitchens and its shavers to fit smaller Japanese hands. Straight extension is tempting because it involves no additional product-development costs, manufacturing changes, or new promotion. But it can be costly in the long run if products fail to satisfy foreign consumers.

Product adaptation involves changing the product to meet local conditions or wants. For example, Procter & Gamble's Vidal Sassoon shampoos contain a single fragrance worldwide but the amount of scent varies by country: less in Japan, where subtle scents are preferred, and more in Europe. General Foods blends different coffees for the British (who drink their coffee with milk), the French (who drink their coffee black), and Latin Americans (who prefer a chicory taste). In Japan, Mister Donut serves coffee in smaller and lighter cups that better fit the fingers of the average Japanese consumer; even the doughnuts are a little smaller. Gerber serves the Japanese baby food fare that might

Straight product extension
Marketing a product in a foreign market without any change.

Product adaptation
Adapting a product to meet local conditions, wants, or needs in foreign markets.

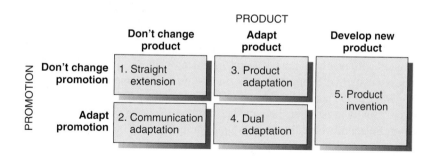

Figure 15-3
Five international product and promotion strategies

turn the stomachs of many western consumers; local favorites include flounder and spinach stew, cod roe spaghetti, mugwort casserole, and sardines ground up in white radish sauce. Similarly, Campbell serves up soups that match unique tastes of consumers in different countries. For example, it sells duck-gizzard soup in the Guangdong Province of China; in Poland, it features *flaki*, a peppery tripe soup. In Brazil, Levi's developed its Femina jeans featuring curvaceous cuts that provide the ultratight fit traditionally favored by Brazilian women. IBM must make dozens of different keyboards—20 for Europe alone—to match different languages.[20]

In some instances, products must also be adapted to local superstitions or spiritual beliefs. In Asia, the supernatural world often relates directly to sales. Hyatt Hotels' experience with the concept of *feng shui* is a good example:

✧   A practice widely followed in China, Hong Kong, and Singapore (and which has spread to Japan, Vietnam, and Korea), *feng shui* means "wind and water." Practitioners of *feng shui*, or geomancers, will recommend the most favorable conditions for any venture, particularly the placement of office buildings and the arrangement of desks, doors, and other items within. To have good *feng shui*, a building should face the water and be flanked by mountains. However, it should not block the view of the mountain spirits. The Hyatt Hotel in Singapore was designed without *feng shui* in mind, and as a result had to be redesigned to boost business. Originally the front desk was parallel to the doors and road, and this was thought to lead to wealth flowing out. Furthermore, the doors were facing northwest, which easily let undesirable spirits in. The geomancer recommended design alterations so that wealth could be retained and undesirable spirits kept out.[21]

Product invention
Creating new products or services for foreign markets.

Product invention consists of creating something new for the foreign market. This strategy can take two forms. It might mean reintroducing earlier product forms that happen to be well adapted to the needs of a given country. For example, the National Cash Register Company reintroduced its crank-operated cash register at half the price of a modern cash register and sold large numbers in Asia, Latin America, and Spain. Or a company might create a new product to meet a need in another country. For example, an enormous need exists for low-cost, high-protein foods in less-developed countries. Companies such as Quaker Oats, Swift, Monsanto, and Archer Daniels Midland are researching the nutrition needs of these countries, creating new foods, and developing advertising campaigns to gain product trial and acceptance. Product invention can be costly but the payoffs are worthwhile.

Promotion

Companies can either adopt the same promotion strategy they used in the home market or change it for each local market. Consider advertising messages. Some global companies use a standardized advertising theme around the world. Exxon used "Put a Tiger in Your Tank," which gained international recognition. Of course, the copy may be varied in minor ways to adjust for language differences. In Japan, for instance, where consumers have trouble pronouncing "snap, crackle, pop," the little Rice Crispies critters say "patchy, pitchy, putchy." Colors also are changed sometimes to avoid taboos in other countries. Purple is associated with death in most of Latin America; white is a mourning color in Japan; and green is associated with jungle sickness in Malaysia. Even names must be changed. In Sweden, Helene Curtis changed the name of its Every Night Shampoo to Every Day because Swedes usually wash their hair in the morning. Kellogg also had to rename Bran Buds cereal in Sweden, where the name roughly translates as "burned farmer." (See Marketing at Work 15-3 for more on language blunders in international marketing.)

Marketing at Work 15-3

Watch Your Language!

Many global companies have had difficulty crossing the language barrier, with results ranging from mild embarrassment to outright failure. Seemingly innocuous brand names and advertising phrases can take on unintended or hidden meanings when translated into other languages. Careless translations can make a marketer look downright foolish to foreign consumers.

We've all run across examples when buying products from other countries. Here's one from a firm in Taiwan attempting to instruct children on how to install a ramp on a garage for toy cars: "Before you play with, fix waiting plate by yourself as per below diagram. But after you once fixed it, you can play with as is and no necessary to fix off again." Many U.S. firms are guilty of such atrocities when marketing abroad.

The classic language blunders involve standardized brand names that do not translate well. When Coca-Cola first marketed Coke in China in the 1920s, it developed a group of Chinese characters that, when pronounced, sounded like the product name. Unfortunately, the characters actually translated to mean "bite the wax tadpole." Now, the characters on Chinese Coke bottles translate as "happiness in the mouth."

Several U.S. car makers have had similar problems when their brand names crashed into the language barrier. Chevy's Nova translated into Spanish as *no va*—"it doesn't go." GM changed the name to Caribe and sales increased. Ford introduced its Fiera truck only to discover that the name means "ugly old woman" in Spanish. And it introduced its Comet car in Mexico as the Caliente—slang for "street-walker." Rolls-Royce avoided the name Silver Mist in German markets, where *mist* means "manure." Sunbeam, however, entered the German market with its Mist Stick hair curling iron. As should have been expected, the Germans had little use for a "manure wand." A similar fate awaited Colgate when it introduced a toothpaste in France called Cue, the name of a notorious porno magazine.

One well-intentioned firm sold its shampoo in Brazil under the name Evitol. It soon realized it was claiming to sell a "dandruff contraceptive." An American company reportedly had trouble marketing Pet milk in French-speaking areas. It seems that the word *pet* in French means, among other things, "to break wind." Interbrand of London, the firm that created household names such as Prozac and Acura, recently developed a brand-name "hall of shame" list, which contained these and other foreign brand names you're never likely to see inside the local A&P: Krapp toilet paper (Denmark), Crapsy Fruit cereal (France), Happy End toilet paper (Germany), Mukk yogurt (Italy), Zit lemonade (Germany), Poo curry powder (Argentina), and Pschitt lemonade (France).

Travelers often encounter well-intentioned advice from service firms that takes on meanings very different from those intended. The menu in one Swiss restaurant proudly stated: "Our wines leave you nothing to hope for." Signs in a Japanese hotel pronounced: "You are invited to take advantage of the chambermaid." At a laundry in Rome, it was: "Ladies, leave your clothes here and spend the afternoon having a good time." The brochure at a Tokyo car rental offered this sage advice: "When passenger of foot heave in sight, tootle the horn. Trumpet him melodiously at first, but if he still obstacles your passage, tootle him with vigor."

Advertising themes often lose—or gain—something in the translation. The Coors beer slogan "get loose with Coors" in Spanish came out as "get the runs with Coors." Coca-Cola's "Coke adds life" theme in Japanese translated into "Coke brings your ancestors back from the dead." In Chinese, the KFC slogan "finger-lickin' good" came out as "eat your fingers off." And Frank Perdue's classic line, "It takes a tough man to make a tender chicken," took on added meaning in Spanish: "It takes a sexually stimulated man to make a chicken affectionate." Even when the language is the same, word usage may differ from country to country. Thus, the British ad line for Electrolux vacuum cleaners—"Nothing sucks like an Electrolux"—would capture few customers in the United States.

Such classic boo-boos are soon discovered and corrected, and they may result in little more than embarrassment for the marketer. But countless other, more subtle blunders may go undetected and damage product performance in less obvious ways. The multinational company must carefully screen its brand names and advertising messages to guard against those that might damage sales, make it look silly, or offend consumers in specific international markets.

Sources: See David A. Ricks, "Products that Crashed into the Language Barrier," *Business and Society Review,* Spring 1983, pp. 46–50; David A. Ricks, "Perspectives: Translation Blunders in International Business," *Journal of Language for International Business,* vol. 7, no. 2, 1996, pp. 50–55; David W. Helin, "When Slogans Go Wrong," *American Demographics,* February 1992, p. 14; "But Will It Sell in Tulsa," *Newsweek,* March 17, 1997, p. 8; "What You Didn't Learn in Marketing 101," *Sales & Marketing Management,* May 1997, p. 20; and Ken Freidenreich, "The Lingua Too France," *World Trade,* April 1998, p. 98.

Communication adaptation
A global communication strategy of fully adapting advertising messages to local markets

Other companies follow a strategy of **communication adaptation**, fully adapting their advertising messages to local markets. The Schwinn Bicycle Company might use a pleasure theme in the United States and a safety theme in Scandinavia. Kellogg ads in the United States promote the taste and nutrition of Kellogg's cereals versus competitors' brands. In France, where consumers drink little milk and eat little for breakfast, Kellogg's ads must convince consumers that cereals are a tasty and healthful breakfast. In India, where many consumers eat heavy, fried breakfasts, Kellogg's advertising convinces buyers to switch to a lighter, more nutritious breakfast diet.[22]

Media also need to be adapted internationally because media availability varies from country to country. TV advertising time is very limited in Europe, for instance, ranging from four hours a day in France to none in Scandinavian countries. Advertisers must buy time months in advance, and they have little control over airtimes. Magazines also vary in effectiveness. For example, magazines are a major medium in Italy and a minor one in Austria. Newspapers are national in the United Kingdom but are only local in Spain.

Price

Companies also face many problems in setting their international prices. For example, how might Black & Decker price its power tools globally? It could set a uniform price all around the world, but this amount would be too high a price in poor countries and not high enough in rich ones. It could charge what consumers in each country would bear, but this strategy ignores differences in the actual costs from country to country. Finally, the company could use a standard markup of its costs everywhere, but this approach might price Black & Decker out of the market in some countries where costs are high.

Regardless of how companies go about pricing their products, their foreign prices probably will be higher than their domestic prices. A Gucci handbag may sell for $60 in Italy and $240 in the United States. Why? Gucci faces a *price escalation* problem. It must add the cost of transportation, tariffs, importer margin, wholesaler margin, and retailer margin to its factory price. Depending on these added costs, the product may have to sell for two to five times as much in another country to make the same profit. For example, a pair of Levi's jeans that sells for $30 in the United States typically fetches $63 in Tokyo and $88 in Paris. A computer that sells for $1,000 in New York may cost £1,000 in the United Kingdom. A Chrysler automobile priced at $10,000 in the United States sells for more than $47,000 in South Korea.

Another problem involves setting a price for goods that a company ships to its foreign subsidiaries. If the company charges a foreign subsidiary too much, it may end up paying higher tariff duties even while paying lower income taxes in that country. If the company charges its subsidiary too little, it can be charged with *dumping*. Dumping occurs when a company either charges less than its costs or less than it charges in its home market. Thus, Harley-Davidson accused Honda and Kawasaki of dumping motorcycles on the U.S. market. The U.S. International Trade Commission agreed and responded with a special five-year tariff on Japanese heavy motorcycles, starting at 45 percent in 1983 and gradually dropping to 10 percent by 1988. Various governments are always watching for dumping abuses, and they often force companies to set the price charged by other competitors for the same or similar products.[23]

Whole-channel view
Designing international channels that take into account all the necessary links in distributing the seller's products to final buyers.

Distribution Channels

The international company must take a **whole-channel view** of the problem of distributing products to final consumers. Figure 15-4 shows the three major links between the seller and the final buyer. The first link, the *seller's headquarters organization*, supervises

| Seller | → | Seller's headquarters organization for international marketing | → | Channels between nations | → | Channels within nations | → | Final user or buyer |

Figure 15-4
Whole-channel concept for international marketing

the channels and is part of the channel itself. The second link, *channels between nations*, moves the products to the borders of the foreign nations. The third link, *channels within nations*, moves the products from their foreign entry point to the final consumers. Some U.S. manufacturers may think their job is done once the product leaves their hands, but they would do well to pay more attention to its handling within foreign countries.

Channels of distribution within countries vary greatly from nation to nation. First, there are the large differences in the *numbers* and *types of intermediaries* serving each foreign market. For example, a U.S. company marketing in China must operate through a frustrating maze of state-controlled wholesalers and retailers. Chinese distributors often carry competitors' products and frequently refuse to share even basic sales and marketing information with their suppliers. Hustling for sales is an alien concept to Chinese distributors, who are used to selling all they can obtain. Working with or getting around this system sometimes requires substantial time and investment.

When Coke first entered China, for example, customers bicycled up to bottling plants to get their soft drinks. Many shopkeepers still don't have enough electricity to run soft drink coolers. Now, Coca-Cola is setting up direct-distribution channels, investing heavily in refrigerators and trucks, and upgrading wiring so that more retailers can install coolers.[24] Moreover, its always on the lookout for innovative distribution approaches:

> Stroll through any residential area in a Chinese city and sooner or later you'll encounter a senior citizen with a red arm band eyeing strangers suspiciously. These are the pensioners who staff the neighborhood committees, which act as street-level watchdogs for the ruling Communist Party. In Shanghai, however, some of these socialist guardians have been signed up by the ultimate symbol of American capitalism, Coca Cola. As part of its strategy to get the product to the customer, Coke approached 14 neighborhood committees . . . with a proposal. The head of Coke's Shanghai division outlines the deal: "We told them, 'You have some old people who aren't doing much. Why don't we stock our product in your office? Then you can sell it, earn some commission, and raise a bit of cash.' Done. So . . . how are the party snoops adapting to the market? Not badly, reports the manager. "We use the neighborhood committees as a sales force," he says. Sales aren't spectacular, but since the committees supervise housing projects with up to 200 families, they have proved to be useful vehicles for building brand awareness.[25]

A "neighborhood committee" member sells Coke in Shanghai.

Another difference lies in the *size* and *character of retail units* abroad. Whereas large-scale retail chains dominate the U.S. scene, much retailing in other countries is done by many small, independent retailers. In India, millions of retailers operate tiny shops or sell in open markets. Their markups are high, but the actual price is lowered through haggling. Supermarkets could offer lower prices, but supermarkets are difficult to build and open because of many economic and cultural barriers. Incomes are low, and people prefer to shop daily for small amounts rather than weekly for large amounts. They also lack storage and refrigeration to keep food for several days. Packaging is not well developed because it would add too much to the cost. These factors have kept large-scale retailing from spreading rapidly in developing countries.

Linking the Concepts

Slow down here and think again about McDonald's global marketing issues.

- To what extent can McDonald's standardize for the Chinese market? What marketing strategy and program elements can be similar to those used in the United States and other parts of the Western world? Which ones must be adapted? Be specific.
- To what extent can McDonald's standardize its products and programs for the Canadian market? What elements can be standardized and which must be adapted?

Deciding on the Global Marketing Organization

Companies manage their international marketing activities in at least three different ways: Most companies first organize an export department, then create an international division, and finally become a global organization.

A firm normally gets into international marketing by simply shipping out its goods. If its international sales expand, the company organizes an export department with a sales manager and a few assistants. As sales increase, the *export department* can expand to include various marketing services so that it can actively go after business. If the firm moves into joint ventures or direct investment, the export department will no longer be adequate.

Many companies get involved in several international markets and ventures. A company may export to one country, license to another, have a joint ownership venture in a third, and own a subsidiary in a fourth. Sooner or later it will create an *international division* or subsidiary to handle all its international activity.

International divisions are organized in a variety of ways. The international division's corporate staff consists of marketing, manufacturing, research, finance, planning, and personnel specialists. They plan for and provide services to various operating units, which can be organized in one of three ways. They can be *geographical organizations*, with country managers who are responsible for salespeople, sales branches, distributors, and licensees in their respective countries. Or the operating units can be *world product groups*, each responsible for worldwide sales of different product groups. Finally, operating units can be *international subsidiaries*, each responsible for its own sales and profits.

Several firms have passed beyond the international division stage and become truly *global organizations*. They stop thinking of themselves as national marketers who sell abroad and start thinking of themselves as global marketers. The top corporate management and staff plan worldwide manufacturing facilities, marketing policies, financial flows, and logistical systems. The global operating units report directly to the chief executive or executive committee of the organization, not to the head of an international division. Executives are trained in worldwide operations, not just domestic *or* international. The company recruits management from many countries, buys components and supplies where they cost the least, and invests where the expected returns are greatest.

Moving into the twenty-first century, major companies must become more global if they hope to compete. As foreign companies successfully invade their domestic markets, companies must move more aggressively into foreign markets. They will have to change from companies that treat their international operations as secondary, to companies that view the entire world as a single borderless market.[26]

REST STOP Reviewing the Concepts

It's time to stop and think back about the global marketing concepts you've covered in this chapter. In the past, U.S. companies paid little attention to international trade. If they could pick up some extra sales through exporting, that was fine. But the big market was at home, and it teemed with opportunities. Companies today can no longer afford to pay attention only to their domestic market, regardless of its size. Many industries are global industries, and firms that operate globally achieve lower costs and higher brand awareness. At the same time, *global marketing* is risky because of variable exchange rates, unstable governments, protectionist tariffs and trade barriers, and several other factors. Given the potential gains and risks of international marketing, companies need a systematic way to make their international marketing decisions.

1. Discuss how the international trade system, economic, political-legal, and cultural environments affect a company's international marketing decisions.

A company must understand the *global marketing environment*, especially the international trade system. It must assess each foreign market's *economic, political-legal,* and *cultural characteristics*. The company must then decide whether it wants to go abroad and consider the potential risks and benefits. It must decide on the volume of international sales it wants, how many countries it wants to market in, and which specific markets it wants to enter. This decision calls for weighing the probable rate of return on investment against the level of risk.

2. Describe three key approaches to entering international markets.

The company must decide how to enter each chosen market—whether through *exporting, joint venturing,* or *direct investment*. Many companies start as exporters, move to joint ventures, and finally make a direct investment in foreign markets. In *exporting*, the company enters a foreign market by sending and selling products through international marketing intermediaries (indirect exporting) or the company's own department, branch, or sales representative or agents (direct exporting). When establishing a *joint venture*, a company enters foreign markets by joining with foreign companies to produce or market a product or service. In *licensing*, the company enters a foreign market by contracting with a licensee in the foreign market, offering the right to use a manufacturing process, trademark, patent, trade secret, or other item of value for a fee or royalty. Many companies start as exporters, move to joint ventures, and finally make a direct investment in foreign markets.

3. Explain how companies adapt their marketing mixes for international markets.

Companies must also decide how much their products, promotion, price, and channels should be adapted for each foreign market. At one extreme, global companies use a *standardized marketing mix* worldwide. Others use an *adapted marketing mix*, in which they adjust the marketing mix to each target market, bearing more costs but hoping for a larger market share and return.

4. Identify the three major forms of international marketing organization.

The company must develop an effective organization for international marketing. Most firms start with an *export department* and graduate to an *international division*. A few become *global organizations*, with worldwide marketing planned and managed by the top officers of the company. Global organizations view the entire world as a single, borderless market.

Navigating the Key Terms

For a detailed analysis of the meaning and importance of each of the following key terms, visit our Web page at **www.prenhall.com/kotler.**

Adapted marketing mix
Communication adaptation
Contract manufacturing
Countertrade

Direct investment
Economic community
Embargo
Exchange controls

Exporting
Global firm
Joint ownership
Joint venturing
Licensing

Management contracting
Nontariff trade barriers
Product adaptation
Product invention
Quota

Standardized marketing mix
Straight product extension
Tariff
Whole-channel view

Travel Log

The following concept checks and discussion questions will help you to keep track of and apply the concepts you've studied in this chapter.

Concept Checks

1. A _____ is one that, by operating in more than one country, gains marketing, production, R&D, and financial advantages that are not available to purely domestic competitors. It sees the world as one market.

2. The most common trade restriction is the _____, which is a tax levied by a foreign government against certain imported products.

3. The _____ treaty is a 50-year-old treaty designed to promote world trade by reducing tariffs and other international trade barriers.

4. The four types of industrial structures are as follows: _____, _____, _____, and industrial economies.

5. When a nation seeking to trade is cash poor, it may choose to pay with other items instead of cash. This is called _____.

6. Once a company has decided to sell in a foreign country, it must decide the best mode of entry. Its choices are _____, _____, and _____.

7. When a company pays a fee or royalty in order to use another company's manufacturing process, trademark, patent, trade secret, or other item of value, the company is using _____ as a means to enter an international market.

8. Coca-Cola uses pretty much the same product, pricing, communication, and distribution system worldwide. This is called a _____ marketing mix.

9. _____ involves changing the product to meet local conditions or wants.

10. Problems often occur in international marketing when a company ships to its foreign subsidiaries. _____ occurs when a company either charges less than its costs or less than it charges in its home market.*

Discussing the Issues

1. When exporting goods to a foreign country, a marketer may be faced with various trade restrictions. Discuss the effects these restrictions might have on an exporter's marketing mix: (a) tariffs, (b) quotas, and (c) embargoes.

2. With all the problems facing companies that "go global," explain why so many companies are choosing to expand internationally. What are the advantages of expanding beyond the domestic market?

3. Before going abroad, a company should try to define its international marketing objectives, policies, and modes of entry. Assume that you are a product manager for Nike. Outline a plan for expanding your operations and marketing efforts into Africa.

4. "Dumping" leads to price savings to the consumer. Determine why governments make dumping illegal. What are the *disadvantages* to the consumer of dumping by foreign firms?

5. Which type of international marketing organization would you suggest for the following companies: (a) eToys (a new Internet company) that sells toys online worldwide, (b) a European perfume firm that plans to expand its operation into the United States, and (c) Daimler-Chrysler planning to sell its full line of products in the Middle East?

---

* *Concept check answers:* 1. global firm; 2. tariff; 3. general agreement on tariffs and trade (GATT); 4. subsistence economies, raw material exporting economies, industrializing economies; 5. countertrade; 6. exporting, joint venturing, direct investment; 7. licensing; 8. standardized; 9. product adaptation; 10. dumping.

Traveling the Net

Point of Interest: Researching the International Market

One of the most difficult tasks facing the company that wishes to enter into the international marketplace is how to obtain accurate and relevant data on the various markets around the globe. At one time, the only alternatives for obtaining this needed data were to pay expensive consultants, hire researchers in the foreign market, or make attempts domestically through existing library and government sources. Today, the interested manager can use the ever-expanding World Wide Web and its vast resource databank alternatives. There is a catch, however. The manager must know how to navigate the Web and where to look for the needed data. Luckily, there currently exist many excellent general international business Web sites that offer the manager entry into more specific sites which often hold the answers to the manager's most important questions concerning international markets and sales potential. Examine the following research Web sites: (a) Center for International Business Education and Research—Michigan State University (ciber.bus.msu.edu/busres.htm), (b) International Trade Association (www.ita.doc.gov), (c) The 1997 World Fact Book—CIA publication (www.odci.gov/cia/publications/factbook/index.html), and (d) The World Bank (www.worldbank.org).

For Discussion

1. How could a manager seeking information on an international market use the above reference sites to find needed data?
2. Does the World Wide Web seem to be a better source for information than traditional sources of information? What problems occur when attempting to use the reference sources cited above? Can you think of alternatives for overcoming these problems?

3. Using these sites, put together an information fact profile for a manager who plans to distribute a new digital watch (approximate cost $50 US) in South America. Based on this fact profile: (a) Which country or countries seem to hold the most promise for the new watch? How did you determine this? (b) What critical information is missing from your fact profile? Where might you find this information? (c) Evaluate your information search process using the Internet. What did you learn?

Application Thinking

Critics in other countries sometimes accuse the United States and U.S. companies of being "cultural imperialists"—of exporting the U.S. culture with the same competitiveness and determination with which they export its products and services. They point to entertainment (movies, television programs, music, magazines), business practices, language, legal interpretations, moral views, and behavioral practices (such as sex, religion, and customs) as major areas in which the United States, through its sheer marketing and other muscle, is attempting to dominate other world cultures. Some Canadians, for example, are concerned that Canadian culture is in serious danger of being absorbed by their neighbor to the south. Assume that you are a marketing executive for Prentice Hall, a publishing company. You have decided that, in the future, all marketing textbooks will be more global in nature. Based on information obtained from the Web sites mentioned above, make a list of general cultural statements that will help the sales of your company's products in the culturally sensitive Canadian market. What specific actions would you take to avoid "cultural imperialism?"

MAP — Marketing Applications

MAP Stop 15

During the past few years, many pillars of the Japanese economy appear to have weakened. Once hailed as the very foundations of Japan's dramatic successes in past decades, institutions and practices such as keiretsus (alliances between multilayers of businesses including banks, manufacturers, and distributors), lifelong employment for the labor force, and close oversight by government ministries seem now to be blamed as major contributors to Japan's economic difficulties in the late 1990s.

With the proper reforms, and by building on its many existing strengths (including world-class manufacturing and marketing capabilities, well-funded research, and a highly educated and motivated labor force), Japan will no doubt recover much of its former economic prowess. In the meantime, however, Japan's economic distress has spilled over into the rest of Asia and to other parts of the world.

Thinking Like a Marketing Manager

1. As a marketing manager, what lessons can be learned from the difficulties that have plagued Japan in recent years?

2. If the Japanese economy performs poorly, should you as a U.S. marketing manager be pleased, worried, or some of both? Explain.

3. Assume that you are the marketing manager for a U.S. cellular phone company that does business in both the United States and Asia. (a) What strategies would you consider for taking advantage of Japan's economic difficulties in your U.S. and other Western markets? (b) What strategies might you employ to dampen the effects of Japan's economic difficulties in your Japanese and Asian markets? (c) Are the two sets of strategies linked? Explain.

Marketing and Society: Social Responsibility and Marketing Ethics

> ⊕ **ROAD MAP:**
> ### Previewing the Concepts
>
> You've almost completed your introductory marketing travels. In this final chapter, we'll focus on marketing as a social institution. First, we'll look at some common criticisms of marketing as it impacts individual consumers, other businesses, and society as a whole. Then, we'll examine consumerism, environmentalism, and other citizen and public actions to keep marketing in check. Finally, we'll see how companies themselves can benefit from proactively pursuing socially responsible and ethical practices. You'll see that social responsibility and ethical actions are more than just the right thing to do, they're also good for business.
>
> ▶ **After studying this chapter, you should be able to**
>
> 1. identify the major social criticisms of marketing
> 2. define *consumerism* and *environmentalism* and explain how they affect marketing strategies
> 3. describe the principles of socially responsible marketing
> 4. explain the role of ethics in marketing
>
> Before traveling on, let's stop off at one of Ben & Jerry's scoop shops. Ben & Jerry's prides itself on being a "values-led" business, one that places social and environmental responsibility above profits. But as you read on, ask yourself: *Can* a company successfully serve a "double bottom line"—values *and* profits?

When Ben Cohen and Jerry Greenfield first met in the seventh grade, they were, by their own admission, the "two slowest kids round the track." However, in 1978, after staring a life of mediocrity full in the face, the two friends decided to try something different. They took a $5 correspondence course on making ice cream, borrowed $12,000, and started their own scoop shop, Ben & Jerry's Homemade, in an abandoned gas station in Burlington, Vermont. The rest, as they say, is history. Two decades later, despite many growing pains, Ben & Jerry's has become the nation's number-two super premium ice cream brand, with a 39 percent market share that trails only Häagen-Dazs's 43 percent share. Last year, Ben & Jerry's sold more than $208 million worth of ice cream, frozen yogurt, and sorbet products through supermarkets, convenience stores, and 180 Ben & Jerry's scoop shops around the country.

Why the strong appeal? For one thing, Ben & Jerry's is a master at creating innovative flavors such as Cherry Garcia, Chocolate Chip Cookie Dough, Phish Food, Chunky Monkey, Chubby Hubby, and S'mores. Moreover, the company has taken on the appealing, laid-back personality of its founders, who beam at you from the sides of the company's cartons. "If you passed [Ben and Jerry] in the street," notes one industry observer, "with their sloppy T-shirts and portly figures . . . , you'd probably think they were a couple

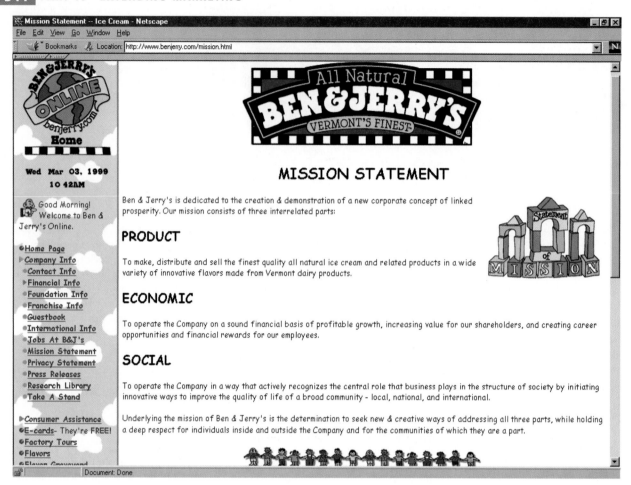

of Grateful Dead roadies. [Ben & Jerry's] markets its products with a combination of down-home hippie folksiness and 'right-on' credibility."

But behind the creative flavors and folksy image, Ben & Jerry's is a company that cares deeply about its social responsibilities. The company's mission statement challenges all employees, from top management to ice cream scoopers in each store, to include concern for individual and community welfare in their day-to-day decisions. It reads as follows:

> Ben & Jerry's is dedicated to the creation and demonstration of a new corporate concept of *linked prosperity*. Our mission consists of three interrelated parts: *Product:* To make, distribute and sell the finest quality all natural ice cream and related products in a variety of innovative flavors made from Vermont dairy products. *Economic:* To operate the company on a sound financial basis of profitable growth, increasing value for shareholders, and creating career opportunities and financial rewards for our employees. *Social:* To operate the company in a way that actively recognizes the central role that business plays in the structure of society by initiating innovative ways to improve the quality of life of the broad community—local, national, and international. Underlying the mission of Ben & Jerry's is the determination to seek new and creative ways of addressing all three parts, while holding a deep respect for the individuals, inside and outside the company, and for the communities of which they are a part.

The notion of linked prosperity—also called *values-led business* or *caring capitalism*—forms the heart and soul of the company. Ben & Jerry's aims to do well *while also* doing good.

Ben & Jerry's does more than just pay lip service to social and environmental concerns—the mission also translates into specific company policies and actions. For example, whereas the average U.S. corporation earmarks less than 2 percent of pretax profits to philanthropy, Ben & Jerry's has a set policy to donate a whopping 7.5 percent to a variety of social and environmental causes. The funds are dispensed through the Ben & Jerry's employee led Foundation, and community action teams, and corporate grants made by the company's director of social mission development. Each supports projects that exhibit "creative problem solving and hopefulness . . . relating to children and families, disadvantaged groups, and the environment."

The company routinely assesses the environmental and social impact of almost everything it does. For example, it buys only hormone-free milk and cream. Closer to home, Ben & Jerry's recently created a flavor called Phish Food, a tribute to the rock band Phish, the royalties of which will be used to clean up Lake Champlain.

Ben & Jerry's also goes to great lengths to buy from minority and disadvantaged suppliers. For example, even though it raises ingredient prices a few cents a pint, Ben & Jerry's buys the brownies for its Chocolate Fudge Brownie ice cream from a nonprofit New York bakery that trains and employs disadvantaged workers. To use the brownies, it had to devise a new ice cream recipe and change its production process. Similarly, to support Vermont farmers and their causes, Ben & Jerry's buys its hormone-free milk and cream exclusively from Vermont dairies, an action which cost the company an extra $375,000 last year.

Ben & Jerry's obeys its social conscience in other ways as well. For example, it used to make a popular ice cream called Oreo Mint but discontinued the flavor because company stockholders didn't like doing business with tobacco merchant RJR Nabisco, which supplied the Oreos. The company changed recipes and started making a new flavor called Mint Chocolate Cookie. Finally, the mission helps shape internal as well as external policies. For example, Ben & Jerry's offers its employees insurance benefits for domestic partners.

Such caring capitalism has earned Ben & Jerry's a measure of respect and the loyal patronage of many consumers. However, there is a downside—having a double bottom line of values and profits is not easy. Such policies cost money, which some critics claim is "wasted on righteousness." In the words of one especially harsh critic, "Ben and Jerry want to use ice cream to solve the world's problems. They call it running a values-led business; I call it a mess. What makes it a mess are its conflicting objectives. Operating a business is tough enough. Once you add social goals to the demands of serving customers, making a profit, and returning value to shareholders, you tie yourself up in knots. [Ben and Jerry's] ideas are simplistic, and partly as a result their company has been hurt."

For sure, it's sometimes difficult to take good intentions to the bank. Over the years, the company has at times found it difficult to live up to the title of the founders' recent book *Ben & Jerry's Double Dip: Lead with Your Values and Make Money Too*. It's done fine with the values part but has produced less-than-stellar financial returns. Over the past several years, its once-meteoric sales growth has slowed, its profits have wavered, and its stock price has languished. The company reported 20 percent sales growth in 1998, as well as an increase in net income of 60 percent. Notes the critic: "As for dividends, to date they have been entirely spiritual."

However, such spiritual returns appear to satisfy Ben & Jerry's owners, still mostly small shareholders from Vermont rather than large institutions. "According to Jerry, [shareholder meetings] are incredibly well attended by the locals in a carnival-type atmosphere," states an industry analyst. "The shareholders who do ask questions . . . ask the board why it isn't being more progressive and radical." They appear to agree with Alan Parker, Ben & Jerry's one-time director of investor relations and social accounting, who said, "We . . . desire to be the kind of company that measures its success as much by its social contribution as by its financial success."[1]

Responsible marketers discover what consumers want and respond with the right products, priced to give good value to buyers and profit to the producer. The *marketing concept* is a philosophy of customer service and mutual gain. Its practice leads the economy by an invisible hand to satisfy the many and changing needs of millions of consumers.

Not all marketers follow the marketing concept, however. In fact, some companies use questionable marketing practices, and some marketing actions that seem innocent in themselves strongly affect the larger society. Consider the sale of cigarettes. On the face of it, companies should be free to sell cigarettes, and smokers should be free to buy them. But this transaction affects the public interest. First, the smoker is harming his or her health and may be shortening his or her own life. Second, smoking places a financial burden on the smoker's family and on society at large. Third, other people around the smoker may suffer discomfort and harm from secondhand smoke. Finally, marketing cigarettes to adults might also influence young people to begin smoking. Thus, the marketing of tobacco products has sparked substantial debate and negotiation in recent years.[2] This example shows that private transactions may involve larger questions of public policy.

This chapter examines the social effects of private marketing practices. We examine several questions: What are the most frequent social criticisms of marketing? What steps have private citizens taken to curb marketing ills? What steps have legislators and government agencies taken to curb marketing ills? What steps have enlightened companies taken to carry out socially responsible and ethical marketing? We examine how marketing affects and is affected by each of these issues.

Social Criticisms of Marketing

Marketing receives much criticism. Some of this criticism is justified; much is not. Social critics claim that certain marketing practices hurt individual consumers, society as a whole, and other business firms.

Marketing's Impact on Individual Consumers

Consumers have many concerns about how well the American marketing system serves their interests. Surveys usually show that consumers hold mixed or even slightly unfavorable attitudes toward marketing practices.[3] Consumers, consumer advocates, government agencies, and other critics have accused marketing of harming consumers through high prices, deceptive practices, high-pressure selling, shoddy or unsafe products, planned obsolescence, and poor service to disadvantaged consumers.

High Prices Many critics charge that the American marketing system causes prices to be higher than they would be under more "sensible" systems. They point to three factors: *high costs of distribution*, *high advertising and promotion costs*, and *excessive markups*.

HIGH COSTS OF DISTRIBUTION A longstanding charge is that greedy intermediaries mark up prices beyond the value of their services. Critics charge that there are too many intermediaries, that intermediaries are inefficient and poorly run, or that they provide unnecessary or duplicate services. As a result, distribution costs too much, and consumers pay for these excessive costs in the form of higher prices.

How do resellers answer these charges? They argue that intermediaries do work that would otherwise have to be done by manufacturers or consumers. Markups reflect services that consumers themselves want: more convenience, larger stores and assortment, longer store hours, return privileges, and others. Moreover, the costs of operating stores keep rising, forcing retailers to raise their prices. In fact, they argue, retail competition is so intense that margins are actually quite low. For example, after taxes, supermarket chains are typically left with barely 1 percent profit on their sales. If some resellers try to charge too much relative to the value they add, other resellers will step in with lower prices. Low-price stores such as Wal-Mart, Best Buy, and other discounters pressure their competitors to operate efficiently and keep their prices down.

HIGH ADVERTISING AND PROMOTION COSTS Modern marketing is also accused of pushing up prices to finance heavy advertising and sales promotion. For example, a dozen tablets of a heavily promoted brand of aspirin sell for the same price as 100 tablets of less-promoted brands. Differentiated products—cosmetics, detergents, toiletries—include promotion and packaging costs that can amount to 40 percent or more of the manufacturer's price to the retailer. Critics charge that much of the packaging and promotion adds only psychological value to the product rather than functional value. Retailers use additional promotion—advertising, displays, and sweepstakes—that add several cents more to retail prices.

Marketers respond that consumers can usually buy functional versions of products at lower prices. However, they *want* and are willing to pay more for products that also provide psychological benefits—that make them feel wealthy, attractive, or special. Brand-name products may cost more, but branding gives buyers confidence. Heavy advertising adds to product costs but is needed to inform millions of potential buyers of the merits of a brand. If consumers want to know what is available on the market, they must expect manufacturers to spend large sums of money on advertising. Also, heavy advertising and promotion may be necessary for a firm to match competitors' efforts—the business would lose "share of mind" if it did not match competitive spending. At

A heavily promoted brand of antacid sells for much more than a virtually identical nonbranded or store-branded product. Critics charge that promotion adds only psychological value to the product rather than functional value.

the same time, companies are cost-conscious about promotion and try to spend their money wisely.

EXCESSIVE MARKUPS Critics also charge that some companies mark up goods excessively. They point to the drug industry, where a pill costing 5 cents to make may cost the consumer $2 to buy. They point to the pricing tactics of funeral homes that prey on the confused emotions of bereaved relatives and to the high charges for television repair and auto repair.

Marketers respond that most businesses try to deal fairly with consumers because they want repeat business. Most consumer abuses are unintentional. When shady marketers do take advantage of consumers, they should be reported to Better Business Bureaus and to state and federal agencies. Marketers also respond that consumers often don't understand the reason for high markups. For example, pharmaceutical markups must cover the costs of purchasing, promoting, and distributing existing medicines plus the high research and development costs of formulating and testing new medicines.

Deceptive Practices Marketers are sometimes accused of deceptive practices that lead consumers to believe they will get more value than they actually do. Deceptive practices fall into three groups: deceptive pricing, promotion, and packaging. *Deceptive pricing* includes practices such as falsely advertising "factory" or "wholesale" prices or a large price reduction from a phony high retail list price. *Deceptive promotion* includes practices such as overstating the product's features or performance, luring the customer to the store for a bargain that is out of stock, or running rigged contests. *Deceptive packaging* includes exaggerating package contents through subtle design, not filling the package to the top, using misleading labeling, or describing size in misleading terms.

Deceptive practices have led to legislation and other consumer protection actions. For example, in 1938 Congress reacted to such blatant deceptions as Fleischmann's Yeast's claim to straighten crooked teeth by enacting the Wheeler-Lea Act giving the Federal Trade Commission (FTC) power to regulate "unfair or deceptive acts or practices." The FTC has published several guidelines listing deceptive practices. The toughest problem is defining what is "deceptive." For example, some years ago, Shell Oil advertised that Super Shell gasoline with platformate gave more mileage than did the same gasoline without platformate. Now, this was true but what Shell did not say is that almost *all* gasoline includes platformate. Its defense was that it had never claimed that platformate was found only in Shell gasoline. But even though the message was literally true, the FTC felt that the ad's *intent* was to deceive.

Marketers argue that most companies avoid deceptive practices because such practices harm their business in the long run. If consumers do not get what they expect, they will switch to more reliable products. In addition, consumers usually protect themselves from deception. Most consumers recognize a marketer's selling intent and are careful when they buy, sometimes to the point of not believing completely true product claims. One noted marketing thinker, Theodore Levitt, claims that some advertising puffery is bound to occur—and that it may even be desirable: "There is hardly a company that would not go down in ruin if it refused to provide fluff, because nobody will buy pure functionality. . . . Worse, it denies . . . man's honest needs and values. Without distortion, embellishment, and elaboration, life would be drab, dull, anguished, and at its existential worst."[4]

High-Pressure Selling Salespeople are sometimes accused of high-pressure selling that persuades people to buy goods they had no thought of buying. It is often said that encyclopedias, insurance, real estate, cars, and jewelry are *sold*, not *bought*. Salespeople are trained to deliver smooth, canned talks to entice purchase. They sell hard because sales contests promise big prizes to those who sell the most.

Marketers know that buyers often can be talked into buying unwanted or unneeded things. Laws require door-to-door and telephone salespeople to announce that they are selling a product. Buyers also have a "three-day cooling-off period" in which they can cancel a contract after rethinking it. In addition, consumers can complain to Better Business Bureaus or to state consumer protection agencies when they feel that undue selling pressure has been applied. But in most cases, marketers have little to gain from high-pressure selling. Such tactics may work in the short run but will damage the marketer's long-run relationships with customers.

Shoddy or Unsafe Products Another criticism is that products lack the quality they should have. One complaint is that many products are not made well and services not performed well. A second complaint is that many products deliver little benefit. For example, some consumers are surprised to learn that many of the "healthy" foods being marketed today, such as cholesterol-free salad dressings, low-fat frozen dinners, and high-fiber bran cereals, may have little nutritional value. In fact, they may even be harmful.

> [Despite] sincere efforts on the part of most marketers to provide healthier products, . . . many promises emblazoned on packages and used as ad slogans continue to confuse nutritionally uninformed consumers and . . . may actually be harmful to that group. . . . [Many consumers] incorrectly assume the product is "safe" and eat greater amounts than are good for them. . . . For example, General Foods USA's new Entenmann's "low-cholesterol, low-calorie" cherry coffee cake . . . may confuse some consumers who shouldn't eat much of it. While each serving is only 90 calories, not everyone realizes that the suggested serving is tiny [one-thirteenth of the small cake]. Although eating half an Entenmann's cake may be better than eating half a dozen Dunkin Donuts, . . . neither should be eaten in great amounts by people on restrictive diets.[5]

A third complaint concerns product safety. Product safety has been a problem for several reasons, including manufacturer indifference, increased production complexity, poorly trained labor, and poor quality control. For years, Consumers Union, the organization that publishes *Consumer Reports*, has reported various hazards in tested products: electrical dangers in appliances, carbon monoxide poisoning from room heaters, injury risks from lawn mowers, and faulty automobile design, among many others. The organization's testing and other activities have helped consumers make better buying decisions and encouraged businesses to eliminate product flaws (see Marketing at Work 16-1).

However, most manufacturers *want* to produce quality goods. The way a company deals with product quality and safety problems can damage or help its reputation. Companies selling poor-quality or unsafe products risk damaging conflicts with consumer groups and regulators. Moreover, unsafe products can result in product liability suits and large awards for damages. More fundamentally, consumers who are unhappy with a firm's products may avoid future purchases and talk other consumers into doing the same. Today's marketers know that customer-driven quality results in customer satisfaction, which in turn creates profitable customer relationships.

Planned Obsolescence Critics also have charged that some producers follow a program of planned obsolescence, causing their products to become obsolete before they actually should need replacement. For example, critics charge that some producers continually

Marketing at Work 16-1
When *Consumer Reports* Talks, Buyers Listen

For more than 60 years, *Consumer Reports* has given buyers the lowdown on everything from sports cars to luggage to lawn sprinklers. Published by Consumers Union, the nonprofit product-testing organization, the magazine's mission can be summed up by CU's motto: Test, Inform, Protect. With more than five million subscribers and several times that many borrowers, as dog-eared library copies will attest, *Consumer Reports* is one of the nation's most-read magazines. It's also one of the most influential. In 1988, when its car testers rated Suzuki's topple-prone Samurai as "not acceptable"— meaning don't even take one as a gift—sales plunged 70 percent the following month. Last year, when it raved about Saucony's Jazz 3000 sneaker, sales doubled, leading to nationwide shortages.

Although nonreaders may view *Consumer Reports* as a deadly dull shopper's guide to major household appliances, the magazine does a lot more than rate cars and refrigerators. In recent issues, it has looked at mutual funds, prostate surgery, home mortgages, retirement communities, and public health policies. In the 1930s, Consumers Union was one of the first organizations to urge a boycott of products imported from Nazi Germany, and it's been calling for nationalized health care since 1937. In the 1950s, it warned the nation that fallout from nuclear tests was contaminating milk supplies. In the 1960s and

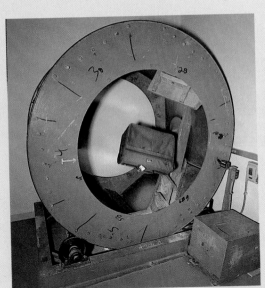 

Consumers Union carries out its testing mission: Suitcases bang into one another inside the huge "Mechanical Gorilla," and a staffer coats the interiors of self-cleaning ovens with a crusty concoction called "Monster Mash."

change consumer concepts of acceptable styles to encourage more and earlier buying. An obvious example is constantly changing clothing fashions. Other producers are accused of holding back attractive functional features, then introducing them later to make older models obsolete. Critics claim that this occurs in the consumer electronics and computer industries. For example, Intel and Microsoft have been accused in recent years of holding back their next-generation computer chips or software until demand is exhausted for the current generation. Still other producers are accused of using materials and components that will break, wear, rust, or rot sooner than they should.

1970s, it prodded car makers to install seat belts, then air bags.

Yet the magazine is rarely harsh or loud. Instead, it's usually understated, and it can even be funny. The very first issue in 1936 noted that Lifebuoy soap was itself so smelly that it simply overwhelmed your B.O. with L.O. And what reader didn't delight to find in a 1990 survey of soaps that the most expensive bar, Eau de Gucci at 31 cents per handwashing, wound up dead last in a blind test.

Consumer Reports readers clearly appreciate CU and its magazine. It is unlikely that any other magazine in the world could have raised $17 million toward a new building simply by asking readers for donations. To avoid even the appearance of bias, CU has a strict no-ads, no-freebies policy. It buys all of its product samples on the open market and anonymously.

A visit to CU's maze of labs confirms the thoroughness with which CU's testers carry out their mission. A chemist performs a cholesterol extraction test on a small white blob in a beaker: a ground-up piece of turkey enchilada, you are told. Elsewhere you find the remains of a piston-driven machine called Fingers that added 1+1 on pocket calculators hundreds of thousands of times or until the calculators failed, whichever came first. You watch suitcases bang into one another inside a huge contraption—

affectionately dubbed the "Mechanical Gorilla"—that looks like an eight-foot-wide clothes dryer.

Down the hall in the appliance department, a pair of "food soilers" will soon load 20 dishwashers with identical sets of dirty dishes. A sample dinner plate is marked off with scientific precision into eight wedge-shaped sections, each with something different caked to it—dried spaghetti, spinach, chipped beef, or something else equally difficult to clean. Next door, self-cleaning ovens are being tested, their interiors coated with a crusty substance—called "Monster Mash" by staffers—that suggests month-old chili sauce. The recipe includes tapioca, cheese, lard, grape jelly, tomato sauce, and cherry pie filling—mixed well and baked one hour at 425 degrees. If an oven's self-cleaning cycle doesn't render the resulting residue into harmless-looking ash, five million readers will be so informed.

Some of the tests that CU runs are standard tests, but many are not. Several years ago, in a triumph of low-tech creativity, CU's engineers stretched paper towels across embroidery hoops, moistened the center of each with exactly ten drops of water, then poured lead shot into the middle. The winner held seven pounds of shot; the loser, less than one. Who could argue with that? There is an obvious logic to such

tests, and the results are plainly quantifiable.

From the start, Consumers Union has generated controversy. The second issue dismissed the Good Housekeeping Seal of Approval as nothing more than a fraudulent ploy by publisher William Randolph Hearst to reward loyal advertisers. *Good Housekeeping* responded by accusing CU of prolonging the depression. To the business community, *Consumer Reports* was at first viewed as a clear threat to the American way of doing business. During its early years, more than 60 advertising-dependent publications, including the *New York Times, Newsweek*, and the *New Yorker*, refused to accept CU's subscription ads.

In 1939, in a move that would seem ludicrous today, Congress' new House UnAmerican Activities Committee (then known as the Dies Committee) branded CU a subversive organization. And through the years, many manufacturers have filed suit against CU, challenging findings unfavorable to their products. However, the controversy has more often helped than hurt subscriptions, and to this day Consumers Union has never lost or settled a libel suit.

Source: Adapted from Doug Stewart, "To Buy or Not To Buy, That Is the Question at *Consumer Reports*," *Smithsonian*, September 1993, pp. 34–43. Additional information obtained from the Consumers Union Web site, accessed on-line at www.consunion.org, February 1999.

Marketers respond that consumers *like* style changes; they get tired of the old goods and want a new look in fashion or a new design in cars. No one has to buy the new look, and if too few people like it, it will simply fail. Companies frequently withhold new features when they are not fully tested, when they add more cost to the product than consumers are willing to pay, and for other good reasons. But they do so at the risk that a competitor will introduce the new feature and steal the market. Moreover, companies often put in new materials to lower their costs and prices. They do not design their products to break down earlier, because they do not want to lose customers to other brands.

The American Association of Advertising Agencies runs ads to counter common advertising criticisms.

Instead, they implement total quality programs to ensure that products will consistently meet or exceed customer expectations. Thus, much of so-called planned obsolescence is the working of the competitive and technological forces in a free society—forces that lead to ever-improving goods and services.[6]

Poor Service to Disadvantaged Consumers

Finally, the American marketing system has been accused of poorly serving disadvantaged consumers. For example, critics claim that the urban poor often have to shop in smaller stores that carry inferior goods and charge higher prices. A Consumers Union study compared the food-shopping habits of low-income consumers and the prices they pay relative to middle-income consumers in the same city. The study found that the poor do pay more for inferior goods. The results suggested that the presence of large national chain stores in low-income neighborhoods made a big difference in keeping prices down. However, the study also found evidence of "redlining," a type of economic discrimination in which major chain retailers avoid placing stores in disadvantaged neighborhoods. Similar redlining charges have been leveled at the home insurance and consumer lending industries.[7]

Clearly, better marketing systems must be built in low-income areas; one hope is to get large retailers to open outlets in low-income areas. Moreover, low-income people clearly need consumer protection. The FTC has taken action against merchants who advertise false values, sell old merchandise as new, or charge too much for credit. The commission is also trying to make it harder for merchants to win court judgments against low-income people who were wheedled into buying something.

Linking the Concepts

Hit the brake for a moment and cool down. Few marketers want to abuse or anger consumers—it's simply not good business. Instead, as you know well by now, most marketers work to build long-term relationships with customers based on real value and caring. Yet, some marketing abuses do occur.

- Think back over the past three months or so and list the instances in which you've suffered a marketing abuse such as those just discussed. Analyze your list: What kinds of companies were involved? Were the abuses intentional? What did the situations have in common?
- Pick one of the instances you listed and describe it in detail. How might you go about righting this wrong? Write out an action plan, then do something to remedy the abuse. If we all took such actions when wronged, there would be far fewer wrongs to right!

Marketing's Impact on Society as a Whole

The American marketing system has been accused of adding to several "evils" in American society at large. Advertising has been a special target—so much so that the American Association of Advertising Agencies launched a campaign to defend advertising against what it felt to be common but untrue criticisms.

False Wants and Too Much Materialism Critics have charged that the marketing system urges too much interest in material possessions. People are judged by what they *own* rather than by who they *are*. To be considered successful, people must own a large home, two cars, and the latest consumer electronics. This drive for wealth and possessions hit new highs in the 1980s, when phrases such as "greed is good" and "shop 'til you drop" seem to characterize the times. As we enter the new millennium, even though many social scientists have noted a reaction against the opulence and waste of the previous decades and a return to more basic values and social commitment, our infatuation with material things continues. For example, when asked in a poll what they value most in their lives, subjects listed enjoyable work (86 percent), happy children (84 percent), a good marriage (69 percent), and contributions to society (66 percent). However, when asked what most symbolizes success, 85 percent said money and the things it will buy.[8]

The critics do not view this interest in material things as a natural state of mind but rather as a matter of false wants created by marketing. Businesses hire Madison Avenue to stimulate people's desires for goods, and Madison Avenue uses the mass media to create materialistic models of the good life. People work harder to earn the necessary money. Their purchases increase the output of American industry, and industry in turn uses Madison Avenue to stimulate more desire for the industrial output. Thus, marketing is seen as creating false wants that benefit industry more than they benefit consumers.

These criticisms overstate the power of business to create needs, however. People have strong defenses against advertising and other marketing tools. Marketers are most effective when they appeal to existing wants rather than when they attempt to create new ones. Furthermore, people seek information when making important purchases and often do not rely on single sources. Even minor purchases that may be affected by advertising messages lead to repeat purchases only if the product performs as promised. Finally, the high failure rate of new products shows that companies are not able to control demand.

On a deeper level, our wants and values are influenced not only by marketers but also by family, peer groups, religion, ethnic background, and education. If Americans are highly materialistic, these values arose out of basic socialization processes that go much deeper than business and mass media could produce alone.[9]

Too Few Social Goods Business has been accused of overselling private goods at the expense of public goods. As private goods increase, they require more public services that are usually not forthcoming. For example, an increase in automobile ownership (private good) requires more highways, traffic control, parking spaces, and police services (public goods). The overselling of private goods results in "social costs." For cars, the social costs include traffic congestion, air pollution, and deaths and injuries from car accidents.

A way must be found to restore a balance between private and public goods. One option is to make producers bear the full social costs of their operations. For example, the government could require automobile manufacturers to build cars with even more safety features and better pollution control systems. Automakers would then raise their prices to cover extra costs. If buyers found the price of some cars too high, however, the producers of these cars would disappear, and demand would move to those producers that could support the sum of the private and social costs. A second option is to make consumers pay the social costs. For example, a number of highway authorities around the world are starting to charge "congestion tolls" in an effort to reduce traffic congestion:

> Already, in Southern California, drivers are being charged premiums to travel in underused car pool lanes; Singapore, Norway, and France are managing traffic with varying tolls; peak surcharges are being studied for roads around New York, San Francisco, Los Angeles, and other cities. [Economists] point out that traffic jams are caused when drivers are not charged the costs they impose on others, such as delays. The solution: Make 'em pay.[10]

If the costs of driving are high enough, consumers will travel at nonpeak times or find alternative transportation modes.

Cultural Pollution Critics charge the marketing system with creating *cultural pollution*. Our senses are being constantly assaulted by advertising. Commercials interrupt serious programs; pages of ads obscure printed matter; billboards mar beautiful scenery. These interruptions continually pollute people's minds with messages of materialism, sex, power, or status. Although most people do not find advertising overly annoying (some even think it is the best part of television programming), some critics call for sweeping changes.

Marketers answer the charges of "commercial noise" with these arguments: First, they hope that their ads reach primarily the target audience. But because of mass-communication channels, some ads are bound to reach people who have no interest in the product and are therefore bored or annoyed. People who buy magazines addressed to

Making consumers pay the social costs: On this private highway in California, consumers pay "congestion tolls" to drive in the fast—and unclogged—lane.

their interests—such as *Vogue* or *Fortune*—rarely complain about the ads because the magazines advertise products of interest. Second, ads make much of television and radio free to users and keep down the costs of magazines and newspapers. Many people think commercials are a small price to pay for these benefits. Finally, todays' consumers have alternatives; for example, they can zip and zap TV commercials or avoid them altogether on many cable or satellite channels. Thus, advertisers are making their ads more entertaining and informative.

Too Much Political Power Another criticism is that business wields too much political power. "Oil," "tobacco," "auto," and "pharmaceuticals" senators support an industry's interests against the public interest. Advertisers are accused of holding too much power over the mass media, limiting their freedom to report independently and objectively. One critic has asked: "How can *Life* . . . and *Reader's Digest* afford to tell the truth about the scandalously low nutritional value of most packaged foods . . . when these magazines are being subsidized by such advertisers as General Foods, Kellogg's, Nabisco, and General Mills? . . . The answer is *they cannot and do not*."[11]

American industries do promote and protect their own interests. They have a right to representation in Congress and the mass media, although their influence can become too great. Fortunately, many powerful business interests once thought to be untouchable have been tamed in the public interest. For example, Standard Oil was broken up in 1911, and the meatpacking industry was disciplined in the early 1900s after exposures by Upton Sinclair. Ralph Nader caused legislation that forced the automobile industry to build more safety into its cars, and the Surgeon General's Report resulted in cigarette companies putting health warnings on their packages. More recently, giants such as AT&T, Microsoft, Intel, and R. J. Reynolds have felt the impact of regulators seeking to balance the interests of big business against those of the public. Moreover, because the media receive advertising revenues from many different advertisers, it is easier to resist the influence of one or a few of them. Too much business power tends to result in counterforces that check and offset these powerful interests.

Marketing's Impact on Other Businesses

Critics also charge that a company's marketing practices can harm other companies and reduce competition. Three problems are involved: acquisitions of competitors, marketing practices that create barriers to entry, and unfair competitive marketing practices.

Critics claim that firms are harmed and competition reduced when companies expand by acquiring competitors rather than by developing their own new products. The large number of acquisitions and rapid pace of industry consolidation over the past two decades have caused concern that vigorous young competitors will be absorbed and that competition will be reduced. In virtually every major industry—banking, electric utilities, railroads, telecommunications, health care, aircraft manufacturing—the number of major competitors is shrinking.[12]

Acquisition is a complex subject. Acquisitions can sometimes be good for society. The acquiring company may gain economies of scale that lead to lower costs and lower prices. A well-managed company may take over a poorly managed company and improve its efficiency. An industry that was not very competitive might become more competitive after the acquisition. But acquisitions can also be harmful and, therefore, are closely regulated by the government.

Critics have also charged that marketing practices bar new companies from entering an industry. Large marketing companies can use patents and heavy promotion spending and can tie up suppliers or dealers to keep out or drive out competitors. Those concerned with antitrust regulation recognize that some barriers are the natural result of the economic advantages of doing business on a large scale. Other barriers could be challenged by existing and new laws. For example, some critics have proposed a progressive tax on advertising spending to reduce the role of selling costs as a major barrier to entry.

Finally, some firms have in fact used unfair competitive marketing practices with the intention of hurting or destroying other firms. They may set their prices below costs, threaten to cut off business with suppliers, or discourage the buying of a competitor's products. Various laws work to prevent such predatory competition. It is difficult, however, to prove that the intent or action was really predatory. For example, in recent years, Wal-Mart and American Airlines have been accused of predatory pricing—setting prices that could not be profitable in order to drive out smaller or weaker competitors. The question is whether this was unfair competition or the healthy competition of a more efficient company against the less efficient.[13]

Citizen and Public Actions to Regulate Marketing

Because some people view business as the cause of many economic and social ills, grassroots movements have arisen from time to time to keep business in line. The two major movements have been *consumerism* and *environmentalism*.

Consumerism

American business firms have been the target of organized consumer movements on three occasions. The first consumer movement took place in the early 1900s. It was fueled by rising prices, Upton Sinclair's writings on conditions in the meat industry, and scandals in the drug industry. The second consumer movement, in the mid-1930s, was sparked by an upturn in consumer prices during the Great Depression and another drug scandal.

The third movement began in the 1960s. Consumers had become better educated, products had become more complex and potentially hazardous, and people were unhappy with American institutions. Ralph Nader appeared on the scene to force many issues, and other well-known writers accused big business of wasteful and unethical practices. President John F. Kennedy declared that consumers had the right to safety and to be informed, to choose, and to be heard. Congress investigated certain industries and proposed consumer-protection legislation. Since then, many consumer groups have been organized, and several consumer laws have been passed. The consumer movement has spread internationally and has become very strong in Europe.[14]

Consumerism
An organized movement of citizens and government agencies to improve the rights and power of buyers in relation to sellers.

But what is the consumer movement? **Consumerism** is an organized movement of citizens and government agencies to improve the rights and power of buyers in relation to sellers. Traditional *sellers' rights* include:

- The right to introduce any product in any size and style, provided it is not hazardous to personal health or safety, or, if it is, to include proper warnings and controls.
- The right to charge any price for the product, provided no discrimination exists among similar kinds of buyers.
- The right to spend any amount to promote the product, provided it is not defined as unfair competition.
- The right to use any product message, provided it is not misleading or dishonest in content or execution.
- The right to use any buying incentive schemes, provided they are not unfair or misleading.

Nutrition Information

Ingredients

Consumer desire for more information led to putting ingredients, nutrition, and dating information on product labels.

Traditional *buyers' rights* include:

- The right not to buy a product that is offered for sale.
- The right to expect the product to be safe.
- The right to expect the product to perform as claimed.

Comparing these rights, many believe that the balance of power lies on the sellers' side. True, the buyer can refuse to buy. But critics feel that the buyer has too little information, education, and protection to make wise decisions when facing sophisticated sellers. Consumer advocates call for the following additional consumer rights:

- The right to be well informed about important aspects of the product.
- The right to be protected against questionable products and marketing practices.
- The right to influence products and marketing practices in ways that will improve the "quality of life."

Each proposed right has led to more specific proposals by consumerists. The right to be informed includes the right to know the true interest on a loan (truth in lending), the true cost per unit of a brand (unit pricing), the ingredients in a product (ingredient labeling), the nutritional value of foods (nutritional labeling), product freshness (open dating), and the true benefits of a product (truth in advertising). Proposals related to consumer protection include strengthening consumer rights in cases of business fraud, requiring greater product safety, and giving more power to government agencies. Proposals relating to quality of life include controlling the ingredients that go into certain products (detergents) and packaging (soft-drink containers), reducing the level of advertising "noise," and putting consumer representatives on company boards to protect consumer interests.

Consumers have not only the *right* but also the *responsibility* to protect themselves instead of leaving this function to someone else. Consumers who believe they got a bad deal have several remedies available, including contacting the company or the media; contacting federal, state, or local agencies; and going to small-claims courts.

Environmentalism

Whereas consumerists consider whether the marketing system is efficiently serving consumer wants, environmentalists are concerned with marketing's effects on the environment and with the costs of serving consumer needs and wants. **Environmentalism** is an organized movement of concerned citizens, businesses, and government agencies to

Environmentalism
An organized movement of concerned citizens and government agencies.

protect and improve people's living environment. Environmentalists are not against marketing and consumption; they simply want people and organizations to operate with more care for the environment. The marketing system's goal, they assert, should not be to maximize consumption, consumer choice, or consumer satisfaction but rather to maximize life quality. And "life quality" means not only the quantity and quality of consumer goods and services but also the quality of the environment. Environmentalists want environmental costs included in both producer and consumer decision making.

The first wave of modern environmentalism in the United States was driven by environmental groups and concerned consumers in the 1960s and 1970s. They were concerned with damage to the ecosystem caused by strip mining, forest depletion, acid rain, loss of the atmosphere's ozone layer, toxic wastes, and litter. They also were concerned with the loss of recreational areas and with the increase in health problems caused by bad air, polluted water, and chemically treated food.

The second environmentalism wave was driven by government, which passed laws and regulations during the 1970s and 1980s governing industrial practices impacting the environment. This wave hit some industries hard. Steel companies and utilities had to invest billions of dollars in pollution control equipment and costlier fuels. The auto industry had to introduce expensive emission controls in cars. The packaging industry had to find ways to reduce litter. These industries and others have often resented and resisted environmental regulations, especially when they have been imposed too rapidly to allow companies to make proper adjustments. Many of these companies claim they have had to absorb large costs which have made them less competitive.

As we move into the twenty-first century, the first two environmentalism waves are merging into a third and stronger wave in which companies are accepting responsibility for doing no harm to the environment. They are shifting from protest to prevention, and from regulation to responsibility. More and more companies are adopting policies of **environmental sustainability**—developing strategies that both sustain the environment and produce profits for the company. According to one strategist, "The challenge is to develop a *sustainable global economy*: an economy that the planet is capable of supporting indefinitely. . . . [It's] an enormous challenge—and an enormous opportunity."[15]

Figure 16-1 shows a grid that companies can use to gauge their progress toward environmental sustainability.[16] At the most basic level, a company can practice *pollution prevention*. This involves more than pollution control—cleaning up waste after it has been created. Pollution prevention means eliminating or minimizing waste before it is created. Companies emphasizing prevention have responded with "green marketing" programs—developing ecologically safer products, recyclable and biodegradable packaging, better pollution controls, and more energy-efficient operations (see Marketing at Work 16-2). They are finding that they can be both green *and* competitive. Consider how the Dutch flower industry has responded to its environmental problems:

Environmental sustainability
A management approach that involves developing strategies that both sustain the environment and produce profits for the company.

> Intense cultivation of flowers in small areas was contaminating the soil and groundwater with pesticides, herbicides, and fertilizers. Facing increasingly strict regulation, . . . the Dutch understood that the only effective way to address the problem would be to develop a closed-loop system. In advanced Dutch greenhouses, flowers now grow in water and rock wool, not in soil. This lowers the risk of infestation, reducing the need for fertilizers and pesticides, which are delivered in water that circulates and is reused. The . . . closed-loop system also reduces variation in growing conditions, thus improving product quality. Handling costs have gone down because the flowers are cultivated on specially designed platforms. . . . The net result is not only dramatically lower environmental impact but also lower costs, better product quality, and enhanced global competitiveness.[17]

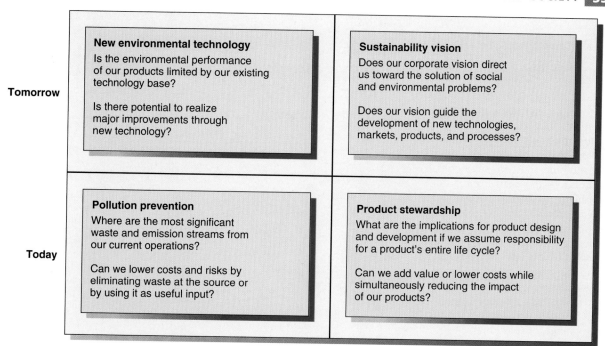

Figure 16-1
The environmental sustainability grid

Source: Reprinted by permission of *Harvard Business Review*. From "Beyond Greening: Strategies for a Sustainable World," by Stuart L. Hart, January–February 1997, p. 74. Copyright © 1997 by the President and Fellows of Harvard College; all rights reserved.

At the next level, companies can practice *product stewardship*—minimizing not just pollution from production but all environmental impacts throughout the full product life cycle. Many companies are adopting *design for environment (DFE)* practices, which involve thinking ahead in the design stage to create products that are easier to recover, reuse, or recycle. DFE not only helps to sustain the environment, it can be highly profitable:

> Consider Xerox Corporation's Asset Recycle Management (ARM) program, which uses leased Xerox copiers as sources of high-quality, low-cost parts and components for new machines. A well-developed [process] for taking back leased copiers combined with a sophisticated remanufacturing process allows . . . components to be reconditioned, tested, and then reassembled into "new" machines. Xerox estimates that ARM savings in raw materials, labor, and waste disposal in 1995 alone were in the $300-million to $400-million range. . . . By redefining product-in-use as part of the company's asset base, Xerox has discovered a way to add value and lower costs. It can continually provide lease customers with the latest product upgrades, giving them state-of-the-art functionality with minimum environmental impact.[18]

At the third level of environmental sustainability, companies look to the future and plan for *new environmental technologies*. Many organizations that have made good headway in pollution prevention and product stewardship are still limited by existing technologies. To develop fully sustainable strategies, they will need to develop new technologies. Monsanto is doing this by shifting its agricultural technology base from bulk

Marketing at Work 16-2
The New Environmentalism and "Green Marketing"

On Earth Day 1970, a newly emerging environmentalism movement made its first large-scale effort to educate people about the dangers of pollution. This was a tough task: At the time, most folks weren't all that interested in environmental problems. These days, however, environmentalism has broad public support. People hear and read daily about a growing list of environmental problems—global warming, acid rain, depletion of the ozone layer, air and water pollution, hazardous waste disposal, the buildup of solid wastes—and they are calling for solutions.

The new environmentalism has caused many consumers to rethink what products they buy and from whom. Many consumers are now willing to pay a premium to support truly environmentally friendly products and companies. For example, when the Massachusetts utility market was opened to competition recently, more than 25 percent of customers chose to pay more by signing up with a utility employing "green" sources such as wind, geothermal, and solar power. More broadly, the Green Gauge Report by Roper Starch Worldwide, a major marketing research firm, divides American consumers into groups according to their environmental knowledge and concerns. The company's recent study found that the most concerned group—True-Blue Greens, which makes up 10 percent of the U.S. adult population—is willing to pay 7 percent more for ecologically friendly products. Another group—Greenback Greens, the 5 percent

Corporate environmentalism: Enlightened companies are taking action not because someone is forcing them to, but because it is the right thing to do.

of the population who are both concerned and reasonably well off—will pay 20 percent more for green products. Such consumer attitudes have sparked a major marketing thrust—*green marketing*—the movement by companies to develop and market environmentally responsible products. Committed "green" companies pursue not only environmental cleanup but also pollution prevention. True "green" work requires companies to practice the three Rs of waste management: reducing, reusing, and recycling waste.

McDonald's provides a good example of green marketing. It used to purchase Coca-Cola syrup in plastic bags encased in cardboard, but now the syrup is delivered as gasoline is, pumped directly from tank trucks into storage vats at restaurants. The change saved 68 million pounds of packaging a year. All napkins, bags, and tray liners in McDonald's restaurants are made from recycled paper, as are its carry-out drink trays and even the stationery used at headquarters. For a company the size of McDonald's, even small changes can make a big difference. For example, just making its drinking straws 20 percent lighter saved the company 1 million pounds of waste per year. Beyond turning its own products green, McDonald's purchases recycled materials for building and remodeling its restaurants, and it challenges its suppliers to furnish and use recycled products.

Producers in a wide range of industries are responding to

chemicals to biotechnology. By controlling plant growth and pest resistance through bioengineering rather through the application of pesticides or fertilizers, it hopes to find an environmentally sustainable path to increased agricultural yields.[19]

environmental concerns. For example, 3M runs a Pollution Prevention Pays program, which has led to substantial pollution and cost reduction. Xerox now remanufactures its copy machines and markets them as "proven workhorses" under names such as "Eco-series," "Renaissance," and "Green Line." Hoover doubled its market share in Germany by introducing a recyclable washing machine that creates less pollution and waste during production and reduces water, detergent, and energy consumption during use. Dow built a new ethylene plant in Alberta that uses 40 percent less energy and releases 97 percent less waste water. Herman Miller, a large office-furniture manufacturer, set a trend in the furniture industry when it began using tropical woods from sustainably managed sources, altering even its classic furniture lines. But it went even further by reusing packaging, recapturing solvents used in staining, and burning fabric scraps and sawdust to generate energy for its manufacturing plant. These moves not only help the environment, they also save Herman Miller $750,000 per year on energy and landfill costs.

Even retailers are jumping onto the "green" bandwagon. For example, Grow Biz International has developed a $100 million business selling used equipment through retail chains such as Play It Again, Once Upon a Child, Computer Renaissance, Music Go Round, and Disk Go Round. Wal-Mart is pressuring its 7,000 suppliers to provide it with more recycled products. In its stores, Wal-Mart runs videos to help educate customers, and the retailer has set up more than 900 recycling drop-off bins in store parking lots around the nation. It's even opening "eco-friendly" stores. In these stores, the air conditioning systems use nonozone-depleting refrigerant, rainwater is collected from parking lots and rooftops for landscaping, skylights supplement fluorescent lighting adjusted by photo sensors, and the road sign is solar powered.

During the early phase of the new environmentalism, promoting environmentally improved products and actions ballooned into a big business. In fact, environmentalists and regulators became concerned that companies were going overboard with their use of terms like *recyclable*, *degradable*, *compostable*, and *environmentally responsible*. Perhaps of equal concern was that, as more and more marketers used green marketing claims, more and more consumers would view them as little more than gimmicks. In 1992, as a result of such concerns, the Federal Trade Commission issued a set of voluntary guidelines for green marketing terms to help guide marketers making environmental claims for their products. Revisions of the guidelines were finalized in 1998.

As we move into the next century, environmentalism appears to be moving into a more mature phase. Gone are the hastily prepared environmental pitches and products designed to capitalize on, or even exploit, growing public concern. The new environmentalism is now going mainstream—broader, deeper, and more sophisticated. In the words of one analyst:

Dressing up ads with pictures of eagles and trees will no longer woo an environmentally sophisticated audience. People want to know that companies are incorporating environmental values into their manufacturing processes, products, packaging, and the very fabric of their corporate cultures. They . . . want to know that companies will not compromise the ability of future generations to enjoy the quality of life that we enjoy today. . . . As a result, we're seeing the marriage of performance benefits and environmental benefits . . . one reinforces the other.

In all, some companies have responded to consumer environmental concerns by doing only what is required to avert new regulations or to keep environmentalists quiet. Others have rushed to make money by catering to the public's mounting concern for the environment. But enlightened companies are taking action not because someone is forcing them to, or to reap short-run profits, but because it is the right thing to do. They believe that environmental farsightedness today will pay off tomorrow—for both the customer and the company.

Sources: Quotes from Robert Rehak, "Green Marketing Awash in Third Wave," *Advertising Age*, November 22, 1993, p. 22; and Jacquelyn Ottman, "Green Consumers not Consumed by 'Eco-anxiety,'" *Marketing News*, July 29, 1996, p. 13. Also see Eric Wieffering, "Wal-Mart Turns Green in Kansas," *American Demographics*, December 1993, p. 23; Ottman, "What Sustainability Means to Marketers," *Marketing News*, July 21, 1997, p. 4; Tibbett L. Speer, "Growing the Green Market," *American Demographics*, August, 1997, pp. 45–49; Ottman, "Innovative Marketers Give New Products the Green Light," *Marketing News*, March 30, 1998, p. 10; and "FTC Finalizes Green Marketing Guidelines," *Environmental Manager*, July 1998, p. 2.

Finally, companies can develop a *sustainability vision*, which serves as a guide to the future. It shows how the company's products and services, processes, and policies must evolve and what new technologies must be developed to get there. This vision of sustainability provides a framework for pollution control, product stewardship, and environmental technology.

Most companies today focus on the lower-left quadrant of the grid in Figure 16-1, investing most heavily in pollution prevention. Some forward-looking companies practice product stewardship and are developing new environmental technologies. Few companies have well-defined sustainability visions. However, emphasizing only one or a few cells in the environmental sustainability grid in Figure 16-1 can be shortsighted. For example, investing in only the bottom half of the grid puts a company in a good position today but leaves it vulnerable in the future. In contrast, a heavy emphasis on the top half suggests that a company has good environmental vision but lacks the skills needed to implement it. Thus, companies should work at developing all four dimensions of environmental sustainability.

Environmentalism creates some special challenges for global marketers. As international trade barriers come down and global markets expand, environmental issues are having an ever-greater impact on international trade. Countries in North America, Western Europe, and other developed regions are developing stringent environmental standards. In the United States, for example, more than two dozen major pieces of environmental legislation have been enacted since 1970, and recent events suggest that more regulation is on the way. A side accord to the North American Free Trade Agreement (NAFTA) set up a commission for resolving environmental matters. And the European Union's Eco-Management and Audit Regulation provides guidelines for environmental self-regulation.[20]

However, environmental policies still vary widely from country to country, and uniform worldwide standards are not expected for another 15 years or more.[21] Although countries such as Denmark, Germany, Japan, and the United States have fully developed

Figure 16-2
Major marketing decision areas that may be called into question under the law

Selling decisions
Bribing?
Stealing trade secrets?
Disparaging customers?
Misrepresenting?
Disclosure of customer rights?
Unfair discrimination?

Advertising decisions
False advertising?
Deceptive advertising?
Bait-and-switch advertising?
Promotional allowances and services?

Channel decisions
Exclusive dealing?
Exclusive territorial distributorships?
Tying agreements?
Dealer's rights?

Product decisions
Product additions and deletions?
Patent protection?
Product quality and safety?
Product warranty?

Packaging decisions
Fair packaging and labeling?
Excessive cost?
Scarce resources?
Pollution?

Price decisions
Price fixing?
Predatory pricing?
Price discrimination?
Minimum pricing?
Price increases?
Deceptive pricing?

Competitive relations decisions
Anticompetitive acquisition?
Barriers to entry?
Predatory competition?

environmental policies and high public expectations, major countries such as China, India, Brazil, and Russia are in only the early stages of developing such policies. Moreover, environmental factors that motivate consumers in one country may have no impact on consumers in another. For example, PVC soft-drink bottles cannot be used in Switzerland or Germany. However, they are preferred in France, which has an extensive recycling process for them. Thus, international companies are finding it difficult to develop standard environmental practices that work around the world. Instead, they are creating general policies and then translating these policies into tailored programs that meet local regulations and expectations.

Public Actions to Regulate Marketing

Citizen concerns about marketing practices will usually lead to public attention and legislative proposals. New bills will be debated—many will be defeated, others will be modified, and a few will become workable laws.

Many of the laws that affect marketing are listed in chapter 3. The task is to translate these laws into the language that marketing executives understand as they make decisions about competitive relations, products, price, promotion, and channels of distribution. Figure 16-2 illustrates the major legal issues facing marketing management.

Business Actions Toward Socially Responsible Marketing

At first, many companies opposed consumerism and environmentalism. They thought the criticisms were either unfair or unimportant. But by now, most companies have grown to accept the new consumer rights, at least in principle. They might oppose certain pieces of legislation as inappropriate ways to solve specific consumer problems, but they recognize the consumer's right to information and protection. Many of these companies have responded positively to consumerism and environmentalism in order to serve consumer needs better.

Enlightened Marketing

The philosophy of **enlightened marketing** holds that a company's marketing should support the best long-run performance of the marketing system. Enlightened marketing consists of five principles: *consumer-oriented marketing*, *innovative marketing*, *value marketing*, *sense-of-mission marketing*, and *societal marketing*.

Consumer-Oriented Marketing **Consumer-oriented marketing** means that the company should view and organize its marketing activities from the consumer's point of view. It should work hard to sense, serve, and satisfy the needs of a defined group of customers. Consider the following example:

✧ Barat College, a women's college in Lake Forest, Illinois, published a college catalog that openly spelled out Barat College's strong and weak points. Among the weak points it shared with applicants were the following: "An exceptionally talented student musician or mathematician . . . might be advised to look further for a college with top faculty and facilities in that field. . . . The full range of advanced specialized courses offered in a university will be absent. . . . The library collection is average for a small college, but low in comparison with other high-quality institutions."

Enlightened marketing
A marketing philosophy holding that a company's marketing should support the best long-run performance of the marketing system.

Consumer-oriented marketing
A principle of enlightened marketing that holds that the company should view and organize its marketing activities from the consumers' point of view.

"Telling it like it is" is intended to build confidence so that applicants really know what they will find at Barat College and to emphasize that Barat College will strive to improve its consumer value as rapidly as time and funds permit.

Innovative marketing
A principle of enlightened marketing that requires that a company seek real product and marketing improvements.

Innovative Marketing The principle of **innovative marketing** requires that the company continuously seek real product and marketing improvements. The company that overlooks new and better ways to do things will eventually lose customers to another company that has found a better way. An excellent example of an innovative marketer is Colgate-Palmolive:

✧ Last year, the American Marketing Association (AMA) named Colgate-Palmolive its new-product marketer of the year. Colgate took the honors by launching an abundance of innovative and highly successful new consumer products, including three AMA Edison "Best New Product" Award winners—Colgate Total toothpaste, the Colgate Wave toothbrush, and Softsoap Aquarium Series Liquid Soap. In all, more than a third of Colgate-Palmolive's current sales comes from products launched during the past five years. Perhaps the best example of the company's passion for continuous improvement is its recently introduced Total toothpaste. Marketing research showed shifts in consumer demographics and concerns—a growing population of aging, health-conscious, and better-educated consumers. For these consumers, Colgate-Palmolive came up with Total, a breakout brand that provides a combination of benefits, including cavity prevention, tartar control, fresh breath, and long-lasting effects. The company also launched an innovative marketing program for the new product, which included advertising in health magazines targeting educated consumers who have high involvement in the health of their mouth and teeth. The new brand helped revitalize the mature toothpaste category. Consumers responded by making Colgate-Palmolive the toothpaste market leader for the first time since 1962, with a 32 percent share versus Procter & Gamble's 25 percent.[22]

Value marketing
A principle of enlightened marketing that holds that a company should put most of its resources into value-building marketing investments.

Value Marketing According to the principle of **value marketing**, the company should put most of its resources into value-building marketing investments. Many things marketers do—one-shot sales promotions, minor packaging changes, advertising puffery—may raise sales in the short run but add less *value* than would actual improvements in the product's quality, features, or convenience. Enlightened marketing calls for building long-run consumer loyalty by continually improving the value consumers receive from the firm's marketing offer.

Sense-of-mission marketing
A principle of enlightened marketing that holds that a company should define its mission in broad social terms rather than narrow product terms.

Sense-of-Mission Marketing **Sense-of-mission marketing** means that the company should define its mission in broad *social* terms rather than narrow *product* terms. When a company defines a social mission, employees feel better about their work and have a clearer sense of direction. For example, defined in narrow product terms, Ben & Jerry's mission might be "to sell ice cream and frozen yogurt." However, as discussed at the beginning of the chapter, the company states its mission more broadly as one of "linked prosperity," including product, economic, and social missions. Reshaping the basic task of selling consumer products into the larger mission of serving the interests of consumers, employees, and others in the company's various "communities" gives Ben & Jerry's a vital sense of purpose. Like Ben & Jerry's, many companies today are undertaking socially responsible actions or even building social responsibility into their underlying missions (see Marketing at Work 16-3).

Societal Marketing Following the principle of **societal marketing**, an enlightened company makes marketing decisions by considering consumers' wants and interests, the company's requirements, and society's long-run interests. The company is aware that neglecting consumer and societal long-run interests is a disservice to consumers and society. Alert companies view societal problems as opportunities.

A societally oriented marketer wants to design products that are not only pleasing but also beneficial. The difference is shown in Figure 16-3. Products can be classified according to their degree of immediate consumer satisfaction and long-run consumer benefit. **Deficient products**, such as bad-tasting and ineffective medicine, have neither immediate appeal nor long-run benefits. **Pleasing products** give high immediate satisfaction but may hurt consumers in the long run. An example is cigarettes. **Salutary products** have low appeal but benefit consumers in the long run, for instance seat belts and air bags. **Desirable products** give both high immediate satisfaction and high long-run benefits—a tasty *and* nutritious breakfast food.

An example of a desirable product is Archer Daniels Midland's Harvest Burgers:

✧ Archer Daniels Midland (ADM) is the country's largest agricultural commodities processor. Asked by Mother Teresa to develop a product that would help her feed the world, ADM perfected a soy product which, when mixed with water and cooked, tastes like hamburger. But the soy product costs much less than real meat. Claims an ADM executive, "You can feed 30 times as many people off an acre of land by raising soy alone, than by growing soy and feeding it to an animal and then eating the animal." The soy product is also more nutritious—it has 75 percent less fat, 40 percent fewer calories, and less than 30 percent of the cholesterol found in a typical hamburger. Thus, the product promises to have enormous economic and nutritional impact. While doing good, it appears that ADM will also do well. It is now selling the meatlike product in Italy, Finland, Hungary, and Russia, and the United States. In Kiev, where meat shortages are a major problem, officials ordered $100 million worth. They calculate that the purchase would eliminate the need for 13 million cows. Sales are also brisk in U.S. and other consumer markets, where ADM sells the product as Harvest Burgers, aimed at a health-conscious, vegetarian niche.[23]

The challenge posed by pleasing products is that they sell very well but may end up hurting the consumer. The product opportunity, therefore, is to add long-run benefits without reducing the product's pleasing qualities. For example, Sears developed a phosphate-free laundry detergent that was also very effective. The challenge posed by salutary products is to add some pleasing qualities so that they will become more desirable in the consumers' minds. For example, synthetic fats and fat substitutes, such as NutraSweet's Simplesse, have improved the appeal of more healthful low-calorie and low-fat foods.

Societal marketing
A principle of enlightened marketing that holds that a company should make marketing decisions by considering consumers' wants, the company's requirements, consumers' long-run interests, and society's long-run interests.

Deficient products
Products that have neither immediate appeal nor long-run benefits.

Pleasing products
Products that give immediate satisfaction but may hurt consumers in the long run.

Salutary products
Products that have low appeal but may benefit consumers in the long run.

Desirable products
Products that give both high immediate satisfaction and high long-run benefits.

Linking the Concepts

Pause here, hold your place with your finger, and go way back and take another look at the "Societal Marketing Concept" section in chapter 1.

☐ How does Figure 1-4 apply to the "Enlightened Marketing" section in this chapter?
☐ Use the five principles to assess the actions of a company that you believe exemplifies socially responsible marketing. (If you can't think of one, use Johnson & Johnson, Ben & Jerry's, or one of the companies discussed in Marketing at Work 16-3.)
☐ Use the principles of enlightened marketing to assess the actions of a company that you believe falls short of socially responsible marketing.

Marketing at Work 16-3
Mission: Social Responsibility

In a recent poll, 92 percent of consumers said they believe it's important for marketers to be good corporate citizens. More than three-quarters responded that they would switch brands and retailers when price and quality are equal for a product associated with a good cause. Companies have responded to this call for social responsibility with actions ranging from supporting worthwhile causes to writing social responsibility into the underlying mission statements.

Today, acts of good corporate citizenship abound. For example, over the past four years, American Express's Charge Against Hunger program, through which the company donates 3 cents from every transaction made during the traditional holiday season, has raised more than 20 million dollars for hunger relief in the United States. Maxwell House, a division of Kraft Foods, recently created a partnership with Habitat for Humanity to build 100 homes in as many days, while working to raise awareness for the organization.

And Post Cereal recently celebrated its 100th anniversary in unique fashion by donating to Second Harvest, the nation's largest network of hunger-relief charities, enough cereal to feed more than one million people. In addition, Post partnered with grocery retailers to sponsor a 100-day food drive across the United States, supported by national and local ads to increase hunger awareness and to encourage consumer participation in the drive.

It seems that almost every company has a pet cause. Alarm company ADT gives away personal-security systems to battered women. Avon Products helps fund the fight against breast cancer. Coca-Cola sponsors local Boys and Girls Clubs, and Barnes & Noble promotes literacy. There are some 800 companies belonging to a San Francisco-based group called Business for Social Responsibility.

In the chapter-opening example, we examined the socially responsible mission of Ben & Jerry's. Here are two more examples

of companies working to better their communities:

Saturn. From its inception, Saturn Corporation has worked to distinguish itself as a unique car company. As its slogan states, Saturn is "A different kind of company. A different kind of car." The company claims to focus more on its employees, customers, and communities than on revenues and bottom lines. Saturn President and Chairman Don Hudler notes that "a part of Saturn's business philosophy is to meet the needs of our neighbors." An example of this philosophy in action is Saturn Playgrounds, a company program for employee involvement and community betterment. The goal of the program is to provide young children in poor communities with a safe, fun environment during nonschool hours as an alternative to gangs, drugs, and crime. Backed by Saturn dollars, local Saturn employees and customers join with community members to build a community

Marketing Ethics

Conscientious marketers face many moral dilemmas. The best thing to do is often unclear. Because not all managers have fine moral sensitivity, companies need to develop *corporate marketing ethics policies*—broad guidelines that everyone in the organization must follow. These policies should cover distributor relations, advertising standards, customer service, pricing, product development, and general ethical standards.

Figure 16-3
Societal classification
of products

The "Saturn Playgrounds" program: Backed by local Saturn retailers, Saturn retail team members and Saturn owners join with community members to build a community playground in a single day.

playground in a single day. So far, the Saturn Playgrounds project has built 58 playgrounds across the country. Joe Rypkowski, president of a local United Auto Workers union, commented that "the Saturn Playgrounds project is a perfect example of the partnership we've built at Saturn. Working together can bring powerful results, not just in our jobs, but in our communities."

The Body Shop: In 1976, Anita Roddick opened The Body Shop in Brighton, England, a tiny storefront selling beauty products out of specimen bottles. Now the company and its franchisees operate nearly 1,500 stores in 47 countries. Fundamental to this rapid growth, Roddick advocates including social responsibility alongside financial performance as a measure of company success. The Body Shop's mission is "to dedicate our business to the pursuit of social and environmental change." In keeping with that mission, the company manufactures and sells natural-ingredient-based cosmetics in simple and appealing recyclable packaging. All the products are formulated without any animal testing and supplies are often sourced from developing countries. Each franchise is required to participate in annual projects designed to better its community. In addition to these projects, The Body Shop is committed to continuous activism. For example, to promote AIDS awareness, the company has handed out condoms and pamphlets about safe sex at its over 290 U.S. stores. In addition, The Body Shop donates a certain percentage of profits each year to animal-rights groups, homeless shelters, Amnesty International, Save the Rainforest, and other social causes. As The Body Shop grows, however, it now appears to be moving from rebel to mainstream. And as its markets are being invaded by other retailers not shackled by The Body Shop's "principles before profits" mission, the retailer's sales growth and profits are flattening. Still, says Roddick, "Business innovation is no longer just about product [and profits]. It's about the very role of business itself."

Sources: Quotes from Anat Arkin, "Open Business Is Good for Business," *People Management*, January 1996, pp. 24–27; David Lennon, "Roddick Isn't Finished Yet," *Europe*, March 1997, pp. 39–40; and "Saturn Dealers Build Six New Playgrounds in One Weekend," *PR Newswire*, June 4, 1997. Also see Daniel Kadlec, "The New World of Giving," *Time*, May 5, 1997, pp. 62–64; Heather Salerno, "From Selling Cars to Building Playgrounds," *The Washington Post*, June 9, 1997, p. F11; "Can Doing Good Be Good for Business?" *Fortune*, February 2, 1998, pp. 148G–J; Jacquelyn Ottman, "Innovative Marketers Give New Product Green Light," *Marketing News*, March 30, 1998, p. 10; Ernest Beck, "Body Shop Founder Roddick Steps Aside as CEO," *Wall Street Journal*, May 13, 1998, p. B14; and information from the Body Shop Web site, accessed on-line at www.bodyshop.com, February 2, 1999.

The finest guidelines cannot resolve all the difficult ethical situations the marketer faces. Table 16-1 lists some difficult ethical situations marketers could face during their careers. If marketers choose immediate sales-producing actions in all these cases, their marketing behavior might well be described as immoral or even amoral. If they refuse to go along with *any* of the actions, they might be ineffective as marketing managers and unhappy because of the constant moral tension. Managers need a set of principles that will help them figure out the moral importance of each situation and decide how far they can go in good conscience.

But *what* principle should guide companies and marketing managers on issues of ethics and social responsibility?[24] One philosophy is that such issues are decided by the free market and legal system. Under this principle, companies and their managers are not responsible for making moral judgments. Companies can in good conscience do whatever the system allows.

A second philosophy puts responsibility not in the system but in the hands of individual companies and managers. This more enlightened philosophy suggests that a company should have a "social conscience." Companies and managers should apply high standards of ethics and morality when making corporate decisions, regardless of

Table 16-1 Some Morally Difficult Situations in Marketing

1. You work for a cigarette company and up to now have not been convinced that cigarettes cause cancer. However, recent public policy debates now leave no doubt in your mind about the link between smoking and cancer. What would you do?

2. Your R&D department has changed one of your products slightly. It is not really "new and improved," but you know that putting this statement on the package and in advertising will increase sales. What would you do?

3. You have been asked to add a stripped-down model to your line that could be advertised to pull customers into the store. The product won't be very good, but salespeople will be able to switch buyers up to higher-priced units. You are asked to give the green light for this stripped-down version. What would you do?

4. You are thinking of hiring a product manager who just left a competitor's company. She would be more than happy to tell you all the competitor's plans for the coming year. What would you do?

5. One of your top dealers in an important territory has recently had family troubles, and his sales have slipped. It looks like it will take him awhile to straighten out his family trouble. Meanwhile you are losing many sales. Legally, you can terminate the dealer's franchise and replace him. What would you do?

6. You have a chance to win a big account that will mean a lot to you and your company. The purchasing agent hints that a "gift" would influence the decision. Your assistant recommends sending a fine color television set to the buyer's home. What would you do?

7. You have heard that a competitor has a new product feature that will make a big difference in sales. The competitor will demonstrate the feature in a private meeting at the annual trade show. You can easily send a snooper to this meeting to learn about the new feature. What would you do?

8. You have to choose between three ad campaigns outlined by your agency. The first (a) is a soft-sell, honest information compaign. The second (b) uses sex-loaded emotional appeals and exaggerates the product's benefits. The third (c) involves a noisy, irritating commercial that is sure to gain audience attention. Pretests show that the campaigns are effective in the following order: c, b, and a. What would you do?

9. You are interviewing a capable female applicant for a job as salesperson. She is better qualified than the men just interviewed. Nevertheless, you know that some of your important customers prefer dealing with men, and you will lose some sales if you hire her. What would you do?

10. You are a sales manager in an encyclopedia company. Your competitor's salespeople are getting into homes by pretending to take a research survey. After they finish the survey, they switch to their sales pitch. This technique seems to be very effective. What would you do?

"what the system allows." History provides an endless list of examples of company actions that were legal and allowed but were highly irresponsible. Consider the following example:

✧ Prior to the Pure Food and Drug Act, the advertising for a diet pill promised that a person taking this pill could eat virtually anything at any time and still lose weight. Too good to be true? Actually the claim was quite true; the product lived up to its billing with frightening efficiency. It seems that the primary active ingredient in this "diet supplement" was tapeworm larvae. These larvae would develop in the intestinal tract and, of course, be well fed; the pill taker would in time, quite literally, starve to death.[25]

Each company and marketing manager must work out a philosophy of socially responsible and ethical behavior. Under the societal marketing concept, each manager must look beyond what is legal and allowed and develop standards based on personal integrity, corporate conscience, and long-run consumer welfare. A clear and responsible philosophy will help the marketing manager deal with the many knotty questions posed by marketing and other human activities.

As with environmentalism, the issue of ethics provides special challenges for international marketers. Business standards and practices vary a great deal from one country to the next. For example, whereas bribes and kickbacks are illegal for U.S. firms, they are standard business practice in many South American countries. The question arises as to whether a company must lower its ethical standards to compete effectively in countries with lower standards. In a recent study, two researchers posed this question to chief executives of large international companies and got a unanimous response: No.[26] For the sake of all of the company's stakeholders—customers, suppliers, employees, shareholders, and the public—it is important to make a commitment to a common set of shared standards worldwide.

For example, John Hancock Mutual Life Insurance Company operates successfully in Southeast Asia, an area that by Western standards has widespread questionable business and government practices. Despite warnings from locals that Hancock would have to bend its rules to succeed, Hancock Chairman Stephen Brown notes:

> We faced up to this issue early on when we started to deal with Southeast Asia. We told our people that we had the same ethical standards, same procedures, same policies in these countries that we have in the United States, and we do. . . . We just felt that things like payoffs were wrong—and if we had to do business that way, we'd rather not do business. Our employees would not feel good about having different levels of ethics. There may be countries where you have to do that kind of thing. We haven't found that country yet, and if we do, we won't do business there.[27]

Many industrial and professional associations have suggested codes of ethics, and many companies are now adopting their own codes. For example, the American Marketing Association, an international association of marketing managers and scholars, developed the code of ethics shown in Table 16-2. Companies are also developing programs to teach managers about important ethics issues and help them find the proper responses. They hold ethics workshops and seminars and set up ethics committees.

Further, more than 200 major U.S. companies have appointed high-level ethics officers to champion ethics issues and to help resolve ethics problems and concerns facing employees. For example, in 1991 Nynex created a new position of vice-president of ethics, supported by a dozen full-time staff and a million-dollar budget. Since then, the new department has trained some 95,000 Nynex employees. Such training includes sending 22,000 managers to full-day workshops that include case studies on ethical actions in marketing, finance, and other business functions. One workshop deals with the use of improperly obtained competitive data, which, managers are instructed, is not permitted.[28]

Many companies have developed innovative ways to educate employees about ethics:

Table 16-2 American Marketing Association Code of Ethics

Members of the American Marketing Association are committed to ethical, professional conduct. They have joined together in subscribing to this Code of Ethics embracing the following topics:

Responsibilities of the Marketer

Marketers must accept responsibility for the consequences of their activities and make every effort to ensure that their decisions, recommendations, and actions function to identify, serve, and satisfy all relevant publics: customers, organizations, and society.

Marketers' professional conduct must be guided by:

1. The basic rule of professional ethics: not knowingly to do harm.
2. The adherence to all applicable laws and regulations.
3. The accurate representation of their education, training, and experience.
4. The active support, practice, and promotion of this Code of Ethics.

Honesty and Fairness

Marketers shall uphold and advance the integrity, honor, and dignity of the marketing profession by:

1. Being honest in serving consumers, clients, employees, suppliers, distributors, and the public.
2. Not knowingly participating in conflict of interest without prior notice to all parties involved.
3. Establishing equitable fee schedules including the payment or receipt of usual, customary, and/or legal compensation for marketing exchanges.

Rights and Duties of Parties in the Marketing Exchange Process

Participants in the marketing exchange process should be able to expect that:

1. Products and services offered are safe and fit for their intended uses.
2. Communications about offered products and services are not deceptive.
3. All parties intend to discharge their obligations, financial and otherwise, in good faith.
4. Appropriate internal methods exist for equitable adjustment and/or redress of grievances concerning purchases.

It is understood that the above would include, but are not limited to, the following responsibilities of the marketer:

* Disclosure of all substantial risks associated with product or service usage.
* Identification of any product component substitution that might materially change the product or impact on the buyer's purchase decision.

* Identification of extra cost-added features.

In the area of promotions,

* Avoidance of false and misleading advertising.
* Rejection of high-pressure manipulations, or misleading sales tactics.
* Avoidance of sales promotions that use deception or manipulation.

In the area of distribution,

* Not manipulating the availability of a product for purpose of exploitation.
* Not using coercion in the marketing channel.
* Not exerting undue influence over the reseller's choice to handle a product.

In the area of pricing,

* Not engaging in price fixing.
* Not practicing predatory pricing.
* Disclosing the full price associated with any purchase.

In the area of marketing research,

* Prohibiting selling or fundraising under the guise of conducting research.
* Maintaining research integrity by avoiding misrepresentation and omission of pertinent research data.
* Treating outside clients and suppliers fairly.

Organizational Relationships

Marketers should be aware of how their behavior may influence or impact on the behavior of others in organizational relationships. They should not demand, encourage, or apply coercion to obtain unethical behavior in their relationships with others, such as employees, suppliers, or customers.

1. Apply confidentiality and anonymity in professional relationships with regard to privileged information.
2. Meet their obligations and responsibilities in contracts and mutual agreements in a timely manner.
3. Avoid taking the work of others, in whole, or in part, and representing this work as their own or directly benefitting from it without compensation or consent of the originator or owner.
4. Avoid manipulations to take advantage of situations to maximize personal welfare in a way that unfairly deprives or damages the organization of others.

Any AMA member found to be in violation of any provision of this Code of Ethics may have his or her Association membership suspended or revoked.

Citicorp has developed an ethics board game, which teams of employees use to solve hypothetical quandaries. General Electric employees can tap into specially designed software on their personal computers to get answers to ethical questions. At Texas Instruments, employees are treated to a weekly column on ethics over an electronic news service. One popular feature: a kind of Dear Abby mailbag, answers provided by the company's ethics officer, . . . that deals with the troublesome issues employees face most often.[29]

Still, written codes and ethics programs do not ensure ethical behavior. Ethics and social responsibility require a total corporate commitment. They must be a component of the overall corporate culture. According to David R. Whitman, chairman of the board of Whirlpool Corporation, "In the final analysis, 'ethical behavior' must be an integral part of the organization, a way of life that is deeply ingrained in the collective corporate body. . . . In any business enterprise, ethical behavior must be a tradition, a way of conducting one's affairs that is passed from generation to generation of employees at all levels of the organization. It is the responsibility of management, starting at the very top, to both set the example by personal conduct and create an environment that not only encourages and rewards ethical behavior, but which also makes anything less totally unacceptable."[30]

The future holds many challenges and opportunities for marketing managers as they move into the new milennium. Technological advances in solar energy, personal computers, interactive television, modern medicine, and new forms of transportation, recreation, and communication provide abundant marketing opportunities. However, forces in the socioeconomic, cultural, and natural environments increase the limits under which marketing can be carried out. Companies that are able to create new values in a socially responsible way will have a world to conquer.

REST STOP Reviewing the Concepts

Well—here you are at the end of your introductory marketing travels! In this chapter, we've closed with many important concepts involving marketing's sweeping impact on individual consumers, other businesses, and society as a whole. You learned that responsible marketers discover what consumers want and respond with the right products, priced to give good value to buyers and profit to the producer. A marketing system should sense, serve, and satisfy consumer needs and improve the quality of consumers' lives. In working to meet consumer needs, marketers may take some actions that are not to everyone's liking or benefit. Marketing managers should be aware of the main *criticisms of marketing*.

1. Identify the major social criticisms of marketing.
Marketing's *impact on individual consumer welfare* has been criticized for its high prices, deceptive practices, high-pressure selling, shoddy or unsafe products, planned obsolescence, and poor service to disadvantaged consumers. Marketing's *impact on society* has been criticized for creating false wants and too much materialism, too few social goods, cultural pollution, and too much political power. Critics have also criticized marketing's *impact on other businesses* for harming competitors and reducing competition through acquisitions, practices that create barriers to entry, and unfair competitive marketing practices.

2. Define *consumerism* and *environmentalism* and explain how they affect marketing strategies.
Concerns about the marketing system have led to *citizen-action movements*. *Consumerism* is an organized social movement intended to strengthen the rights and power of consumers relative to sellers. Alert marketers view it as an opportunity to serve consumers better by

providing more consumer information, education, and protection. *Environmentalism* is an organized social movement seeking to minimize the harm done to the environment and quality of life by marketing practices. The first wave of modern environmentalism was driven by environmental groups and concerned consumers, whereas the second wave was driven by government, which passed laws and regulations governing industrial practices impacting the environment. Moving into the twenty-first century, the first two environmentalism waves are merging into a third and stronger wave in which companies are accepting responsibility for doing no environmental harm. Companies now are adopting policies of *environmental sustainability*—developing strategies that both sustain the environment and produce profits for the company.

3. Describe the principles of socially responsible marketing.

Many companies originally opposed these social movements and laws, but most of them now recognize a need for positive consumer information, education, and protection. Some companies have followed a policy of *enlightened marketing*, which holds that a company's marketing should support the best long-run performance of the marketing system. Enlightened marketing consists of five principles: *consumer-oriented marketing, innovative marketing, value marketing, sense-of-mission marketing*, and *societal marketing*.

4. Explain the role of ethics in marketing.

Increasingly, companies are responding to the need to provide company policies and guidelines to help their managers deal with questions of *marketing ethics*. Of course, even the best guidelines cannot resolve all the difficult ethical decisions that individuals and firms must make. But there are some principles that marketers can choose among. One principle states that such issues should be decided by the free market and legal system. A second, and more enlightened principle, puts responsibility not in the system but in the hands of individual companies and managers. Each firm and marketing manager must work out a philosophy of socially responsible and ethical behavior. Under the societal marketing concept, managers must look beyond what is legal and allowable and develop standards based on personal integrity, corporate conscience, and long-term consumer welfare.

Because business standards and practices vary from country to country, the issue of ethics poses special challenges for international marketers. The growing consensus among today's marketers is that it is important to make a commitment to a common set of shared standards worldwide.

Now that you've completed this marketing journey, we hope that it will be only the first of many enjoyable marketing excursions. Whether you continue your marketing studies in later marketing classes, in pursuit of your career, or simply as a consumer, you'll be starting out on a solid footing.

Navigating the Key Terms

For a detailed analysis of the meaning and importance of each of the following key terms, visit our Web page at **www.prenhall.com/kotler**.

Consumerism
Consumer-oriented marketing

Deficient products
Desirable products
Enlightened marketing
Environmental sustainability
Environmentalism
Innovative marketing
Pleasing products

Salutary products
Sense-of-mission marketing
Societal marketing
Value marketing

Travel Log

The following concept checks and discussion questions will help you to keep track of and apply the concepts you've studied in this chapter.

Concept Checks

1. Consumers, consumer advocates, government agencies, and other critics have accused marketing

of harming consumers through high prices, deceptive practices, _____, _____, _____, and poor service to disadvantaged consumers.

2. If the American marketing system causes prices to be higher than necessary, this probably occurs because of the high costs of _____, _____, and _____.

3. The _____ Act gave the Federal Trade Commission (FTC) the power to regulate "unfair or deceptive acts or practices."

4. Critics have charged that some producers follow a program of _____, causing their products to become obsolete before they actually should need replacement.

5. Common criticisms against modern advertising practice include indictments that advertising has or creates: _____, _____, _____, and too much political power.

6. _____ is an organized movement of citizens and government agencies to improve the rights and power of buyers in relation to sellers.

7. _____ is an organized movement of concerned citizens, businesses, and government agencies to protect and improve people's living environment.

8. Enlightened marketing consists of five principles: consumer-oriented marketing, _____, _____, _____, and societal marketing.

9. _____ marketing means that the company should define its mission in broad social terms rather than narrow product terms.

10. Products can be classified according to their degree of immediate consumer satisfaction and long-run consumer benefit. _____ products have low appeal but benefit consumers in the long run, for instance seat belts and air bags.*

Discussing the Issues

1. You have been invited to appear along with an economist on a panel assessing marketing practices in the soft-drink beverage industry. You are somewhat surprised when the economist opens the discussion with a long list of criticisms (focusing especially on unnecessarily high marketing costs and deceptive promotional practices). Abandoning your prepared comments, you feel the need to defend marketing in general and the beverage industry in particular. How would you respond to the economist's attack?

2. Discuss which of the following firms (if any) practice the principle of enlightened marketing: (a) McDonald's, (b) Procter & Gamble, (c) General Motors, and (d) Johnson & Johnson.

3. Knowing that you have studied consumerism and issues of seller's and buyer's rights, a consumer group has hired you to write a "Car Buyer's Bill of Rights." The group plans to use this document to lobby for improvement in how car buyers are treated by the automobile industry and by government regulators. (a) Draft such a bill of rights. (b) If adopted, how would your bill of rights benefit car buyers? (c) If you were an auto industry marketing executive, how would you react to such a bill of rights?

4. Compare the marketing concept with the principle of societal marketing. Do you think all marketers should adopt the societal marketing concept? Why or why not?

5. You are the marketing manager for a small kitchen appliance firm. While conducting field tests, you discover a design flaw in one of your most popular appliances that could potentially be harmful to a small number of customers. However, a product recall would likely bankrupt your company and cause all of the employees (including yourself) to lose their jobs. What would you do? Explain.

Concept check answers: 1. high-pressure selling, shoddy or unsafe products, planned obsolescence; 2. distribution, advertising and promotion, excessive markups; 3. Wheeler-Lea; 4. planned obsolescence; 5. false wants and too much materialism, too few social goods, cultural pollution; 6. consumerism; 7. environmentalism; 8. innovative marketing, sense-of-mission marketing; 9. sense-of-mission; 10. salutary.

Traveling the Net

Point of Interest: Marketing and the Law

As business and marketing become more complicated, judging what is fair and honest becomes more difficult for consumers and marketers alike. In some industries and areas of practice, rules and regulations governing marketing are reasonably well established and understood. However, this is not the case with respect to marketing on the Internet, where there appears to be little or no established regulation. The wide-open spaces of the Internet have been characterized as the "old West" of the 1990s, where self-rule seems to abound. This will all change, but when and to what extent remains uncertain. However, understanding current laws and regulations pertaining to Internet practices, and anticipating future regulatory issues and actions, are extremely important for today's modern marketing manager. Take a look at the following Web sites: (a) Federal Trade Commission (www.ftc.gov), (b) Federal Communications Commission (www.fcc.gov), (c) FedWorld Information Network (www.fedworld.gov), (d) Consumer Information Center (www.pueblo.gsa.gov), and (e) National Archives and Records Administration (www.nara.gov).

For Discussion

1. How easy is it to find information about laws and regulations relating to marketing on the Internet? (a) If you were an entrepreneur wishing to set up a Web marketing site, where could you go to find out what laws govern what you could put on your Web site? (b) Based on your visits to the preceding sites, give illustrations of things you could not do on your Web site. (c) Describe the problems you encountered during your search for information.

2. Find at least one other Web site that provides information useful for establishing a Web site. Explain the site to your class.

3. The Internet offers consumers great opportunities but also potential difficulties, frustrations, and dangers. Offsetting its wonders, the World Wide Web is flooded with less-desirable elements such as spam mail (unsolicited and often unwanted e-mail distributed indiscriminately in bulk), pornography, and unscrupulous offers and schemes. As marketing manager of a firm that sells via the Internet, you want to interact with your consumers in a positive and uncluttered environment. (a) What organizations should be involved in regulating Internet usage and commerce? (b) What types of regulations would you propose? (c) What difficulties do you see in attempting to implement such regulations?

Application Thinking

The "greening of America" has much more to do with lifestyles than with forestry. Adopting a "green" lifestyle means that the consumer demands products and services that are more environmentally responsible. As consumers turn greener, companies respond with environmentally responsible products and programs. McDonald's, Wal-Mart, and Procter & Gamble are just a few of the companies that now cater to a more "green" way of thinking and consuming. (See the "Community" section of the McDonald's Web site (www.mcdonalds.com) and the Internet Green Marketplace Web site (www.envirolink.org). Assume that you are a marketing manager for Crayola Crayons (www.crayola.com) and formulate a "green policy" that will make your product both environmentally responsible and competitive. As you formulate this policy, consider the product itself, packaging, distribution, promotion, and merchandising with distributors. Explain your policy to the class.

MAP—Marketing Applications

MAP Stop 16

Few business cases have captured as much media and public attention as the Microsoft antitrust case. The case involves complex issues and the outcome likely will have a far-reaching future impact on how firms conduct their business and consumers conduct their lives. Like it or not, Microsoft affects everyone's daily life. The question becomes: "Is that good or bad?" Competitors and the federal government claim that Microsoft's uses of its massive marketplace muscle constitute predatory practices that damage competition and long-run consumer welfare. Microsoft Chairman and CEO Bill Gates believes that no firm can become a monopolist in the highly charged and ever-changing computer software industry and that his company is doing nothing more than competing aggressively, effectively, and fairly. Most consumers love the company's products and do not seem to mind living in a "Microsoft world," as long as that world works well for them. The fact that Microsoft's success has helped to make the United States a world leader in computer software technology presents a dilemma for U.S. regulators. To what extent should they tamper with one of the country's most successful and competitive companies? Whatever the answer, it will have a substantial impact on our economy and lives.

Thinking Like a Marketing Manager

1. Thinking like a marketing manager, what lessons can be learned from the Microsoft trial? What are

the major issues? Which of these issues seem to be the most important?

2. After researching the issues in the Microsoft case, take a stand. Do you side with Microsoft or its competitors? Explain and justify your position.

3. Assume that you are the marketing manager for Amazon.com, the large on-line bookseller. How might the outcome of the Microsoft case affect your company and its marketing efforts? How will it affect competition in the computer software industry? In the server and browser industry? For the Internet and e-commerce in general? Present any views you might have on large mergers and acquisitions in this industry.

Marketing Arithmetic

One aspect of marketing not discussed within the text is marketing arithmetic. The calculation of sales, costs, and certain ratios is important for many marketing decisions. This appendix describes three major areas of marketing arithmetic: the *operating statement, analytic ratios,* and *markups* and *markdowns.*

Operating Statement

The operating statement and the balance sheet are the two main financial statements used by companies. The **balance sheet** shows the assets, liabilities, and net worth of a company at a given time. The **operating statement** (also called **profit-and-loss statement** or **income statement**) is the more important of the two for marketing information. It shows company sales, cost of goods sold, and expenses during a specified time period. By comparing the operating statement from one time period to the next, the firm can spot favorable or unfavorable trends and take appropriate action.

Table A1-1 shows the 1999 operating statement for Dale Parsons Men's Wear, a specialty store in the Midwest. This statement is for a retailer; the operating statement for a manufacturer would be somewhat different. Specifically, the section on purchases within the "cost of goods sold" area would be replaced by "cost of goods manufactured."

The outline of the operating statement follows a logical series of steps to arrive at the firm's $25,000 net profit figure:

Net sales	$300,000
Cost of goods sold	−175,000
Gross margin	$125,000
Expenses	−100,000
Net profit	$ 25,000

The first part details the amount that Parsons received for the goods sold during the year. The sales figures consist of three items: *gross sales, returns and allowances,* and *net sales.* **Gross sales** is the total amount charged to customers during the year for merchandise purchased in Parsons's store. As expected, some customers returned merchandise because of damage or a change of mind. If the customer gets a full refund or full credit on another purchase, we call this a *return.* Or the customer may decide to keep the item if Parsons will reduce the price. This is called an *allowance.* By subtracting returns and allowances from gross sales, we arrive at net sales—what Parsons earned in revenue from a year of selling merchandise:

Gross sales	$325,000
Returns and allowances	−25,000
Net sales	$300,000

Table A1-1   Operating Statement: Dale Parsons Men's Wear
Year Ending December 31, 1999

Gross sales			$325,000
Less: Sales returns and allowances			25,000
Net sales			$300,000
Cost of goods sold			
Beginning inventory, January 1, at cost		$60,000	
Gross purchases	$165,000		
Less: Purchase discounts	15,000		
Net purchases	$150,000		
Plus: Freight-in	10,000		
Net cost of delivered purchases		$160,000	
Cost of goods available for sale		$220,000	
Less: Ending inventory, December 31, at cost		$ 45,000	
Cost of goods sold			$175,000
Gross margin			$125,000
Expenses			
Selling expenses			
Sales, salaries, and commissions	$ 40,000		
Advertising	5,000		
Delivery	5,000		
Total selling expenses		$ 50,000	
Administrative expenses			
Office salaries	$ 20,000		
Office supplies	5,000		
Miscellaneous (outside consultant)	5,000		
Total administrative expenses		$ 30,000	
General expenses			
Rent	$ 10,000		
Heat, light, telephone	5,000		
Miscellaneous (insurance, depreciation)	5,000		
Total general expenses		$ 20,000	
Total expenses			$100,000
Net profit			$ 25,000

The second major part of the operating statement calculates the amount of sales revenue Dale Parsons retains after paying the costs of the merchandise. We start with the inventory in the store at the beginning of the year. During the year, Parsons bought $165,000 worth of suits, slacks, shirts, ties, jeans, and other goods. Suppliers gave the store discounts totaling $15,000, so that net purchases were $150,000. Because the store is located away from regular shipping routes, Parsons had to pay an additional $10,000 to get the products delivered, giving the firm a net cost of $160,000. Adding the beginning inventory, the cost of goods available for sale amounted to $220,000. The $45,000 ending inventory of clothes in the store on December 31 is then subtracted to come up with the $175,000 **cost of goods sold**. Here again, we have followed a logical series of steps to figure out the cost of goods sold:

Amount Parsons started with (beginning inventory)	$60,000
Net amount purchased	+150,000
Any added costs to obtain these purchases	+10,000
Total cost of goods Parsons had available for sale during year	$220,000
Amount Parsons had left over (ending inventory)	−45,000
Cost of goods actually sold	$175,000

The difference between what Parsons paid for the merchandise ($175,000) and what he sold it for ($300,000) is called the **gross margin** ($125,000).

In order to show the profit Parsons "cleared" at the end of the year, we must subtract from the gross margin the *expenses* incurred while doing business. *Selling expenses* included two sales employees, local newspaper and radio advertising, and the cost of delivering merchandise to customers after alterations. Selling expenses totaled $50,000 for the year. *Administrative expenses* included the salary for an office manager, office supplies such as stationery and business cards, and miscellaneous expenses including an administrative audit conducted by an outside consultant. Administrative expenses totaled $30,000 in 1999. Finally, the general expenses of rent, utilities, insurance, and depreciation came to $20,000. Total expenses were therefore $100,000 for the year. By subtracting expenses ($100,000) from the gross margin ($125,000), we arrive at the net profit of $25,000 for Parsons during 1999.

Analytic Ratios

The operating statement provides the figures needed to compute some crucial ratios. Typically these ratios are called **operating ratios**, the ratio of selected operating statement items to net sales. They let marketers compare the firm's performance in one year to that in previous years (or with industry standards and competitors in the same year). The most commonly used operating ratios are the *gross margin percentage*, the *net profit percentage*, the *operating expense percentage*, and the *returns and allowances percentage*.

Ratio		Formula	Computation From Table A1-1
Gross margin percentage	=	$\dfrac{\text{gross margin}}{\text{net sales}}$	$= \dfrac{\$125,000}{\$300,000} = 42\%$
Net profit percentage	=	$\dfrac{\text{net profit}}{\text{net sales}}$	$= \dfrac{\$25,000}{\$300,000} = 8\%$
Operating expense percentage	=	$\dfrac{\text{total expenses}}{\text{net sales}}$	$= \dfrac{\$100,000}{\$300,000} = 33\%$
Returns and allowances percentage	=	$\dfrac{\text{returns and allowances}}{\text{net sales}}$	$= \dfrac{\$25,000}{\$300,000} = 8\%$

Another useful ratio is the *stockturn rate* (also called *inventory turnover rate*). The stockturn rate is the number of times an inventory turns over or is sold during a specified time period (often one year). It may be computed on a cost, selling price, or units basis. Thus the formula can be:

$$\text{Stockturn rate} = \frac{\text{cost of goods sold}}{\text{average inventory at cost}}$$

or

$$\text{Stockturn rate} = \frac{\text{selling price of goods sold}}{\text{average selling price of inventory}}$$

or

$$\text{Stockturn rate} = \frac{\text{sales in units}}{\text{average inventory in units}}$$

We will use the first formula to calculate the stockturn rate for Dale Parsons Men's Wear:

$$\frac{\$175,000}{(\$60,000 + \$45,000)/2} = \frac{\$175,000}{\$52,500} = 3.3$$

That is, Parsons's inventory turned over 3.3 times in 1999. Normally, the higher the stockturn rate, the higher the management efficiency and company profitability.

Return on investment (ROI) is frequently used to measure managerial effectiveness. It uses figures from the firm's operating statement and balance sheet. A commonly used formula for computing ROI is:

$$\text{ROI} = \frac{\text{net profit}}{\text{sales}} \times \frac{\text{sales}}{\text{investment}}$$

You may have two questions about this formula: Why use a two-step process when ROI could be computed simply as net profit divided by investment? And what exactly is "investment"?

To answer these questions, let's look at how each component of the formula can affect the ROI. Suppose Dale Parsons Men's Wear has a total investment of $150,000. Then ROI can be computed as follows:

$$\text{ROI} = \frac{\$25,000\ (\text{net profit})}{\$300,000\ (\text{sales})} \times \frac{\$300,000\ (\text{sales})}{\$150,000\ (\text{investment})}$$

$$= 8.3\% \times 2$$

$$= 16.6\%$$

Now suppose that Parsons had worked to increase his share of market. He could have had the same ROI if his sales doubled while dollar profit and investment stayed the same (accepting a lower profit ratio to get higher turnover and market share):

$$\text{ROI} = \frac{\$25,000\ (\text{net profit})}{\$600,000\ (\text{sales})} \times \frac{\$600,000\ (\text{sales})}{\$150,000\ (\text{investment})}$$

$$= 4.16\% \times 4$$

$$= 16.6\%$$

Parsons might have increased its ROI by increasing net profit through more cost cutting and more efficient marketing:

$$\text{ROI} = \frac{\$50,000 \text{ (net profit)}}{\$300,000 \text{ (sales)}} \times \frac{\$300,000 \text{ (sales)}}{\$150,000 \text{ (investment)}}$$

$$= 16.6\% \times 2$$

$$= 33.2\%$$

Another way to increase ROI is to find some way to get the same levels of sales and profits while decreasing investment (perhaps by cutting the size of Parsons's average inventory):

$$\text{ROI} = \frac{\$25,000 \text{ (net profit)}}{\$300,000 \text{ (sales)}} \times \frac{\$300,000 \text{ (sales)}}{\$75,000 \text{ (investment)}}$$

$$= 8.3\% \times 4$$

$$= 33.2\%$$

What is "investment" in the ROI formula? *Investment* is often defined as the total assets of the firm. But many analysts now use other measures of return to assess performance. These measures include *return on net assets (RONA), return on stockholders' equity (ROE),* or *return on assets managed (ROAM)*. Because investment is measured at a point in time, we usually compute ROI as the average investment between two time periods (say, January 1 and December 31 of the same year). We can also compute ROI as an "internal rate of return" by using discounted cash flow analysis (see any finance textbook for more on this technique). The objective in using any of these measures is to determine how well the company has been using its resources. As inflation, competitive pressures, and cost of capital increase, such measures become increasingly important indicators of marketing and company performance.

Markups and Markdowns

Retailers and wholesalers must understand the concepts of **markups** and **markdowns**. They must make a profit to stay in business, and the markup percentage affects profits. Markups and markdowns are expressed as percentages.

There are two different ways to compute markups—on *cost* or on *selling price*:

$$\text{Markup percentage on cost} = \frac{\text{dollar markup}}{\text{cost}}$$

$$\text{Markup percentage on selling price} = \frac{\text{dollar markup}}{\text{selling price}}$$

Dale Parsons must decide which formula to use. If Parsons bought shirts for $15 and wanted to mark them up $10, his markup percentage on cost would be $10/$15 = 67.7%. If Parsons based markup on selling price, the percentage would be $10/$25 = 40%. In figuring markup percentage, most retailers use the selling price rather than the cost.

Suppose Parsons knew his cost ($12) and desired markup on price (25%) for a man's tie, and wanted to compute the selling price. The formula is:

$$\text{Selling price} = \frac{\text{cost}}{1 - \text{markup}}$$

$$\text{Selling price} = \frac{\$12}{.75} = \$16$$

As a product moves through the channel of distribution, each channel member adds a markup before selling the product to the next member. This "markup chain" is shown for a suit purchased by a Parsons customer for $200:

		$ Amount	% of Selling Price
Manufacturer	Cost	$108	90%
	Markup	12	10
	Selling price	120	100
Wholesaler	Cost	120	80
	Markup	30	20
	Selling price	150	100
Retailer	Cost	150	75
	Markup	50	25
	Selling price	200	100

The retailer whose markup is 25 percent does not necessarily enjoy more profit than a manufacturer whose markup is 10 percent. Profit also depends on how many items with that profit margin can be sold (stockturn rate) and on operating efficiency (expenses).

Sometimes a retailer wants to convert markups based on selling price to markups based on cost, and vice versa. The formulas are:

$$\text{Markup percentage on selling price} = \frac{\text{markup percentage on cost}}{100\% + \text{markup percentage on selling cost}}$$

$$\text{Markup percentage on cost} = \frac{\text{markup percentage on selling price}}{100\% - \text{markup percentage on selling price}}$$

Suppose Parsons found that his competitor was using a markup of 30 percent based on cost and wanted to know what this would be as a percentage of selling price. The calculation would be:

$$\frac{30\%}{100\% + 30\%} = \frac{30\%}{130\%} = 23\%$$

Because Parsons was using a 25 percent markup on the selling price for suits, he felt that his markup was suitable compared with that of the competitor.

Near the end of the summer Parsons still had an inventory of summer slacks in stock. Therefore, he decided to use a *markdown*, a reduction from the original selling price. Before the summer he had purchased 20 pairs at $10 each, and he had since sold 10 pairs at $20 each. He marked down the other pairs to $15 and sold 5 pairs. We compute his *markdown ratio* as follows:

$$\text{Markdown percentage} = \frac{\text{dollar markdown}}{\text{total net sales in dollars}}$$

The dollar markdown is $25 (5 pairs at $5 each) and total net sales are $275 (10 pairs at $20 + 5 pairs at $15). The ratio, then, is $25/$275 = 9%.

Larger retailers usually compute markdown ratios for each department rather than for individual items. The ratios provide a measure of relative marketing performance for each department and can be calculated and compared over time. Markdown ratios can also be used to compare the performance of different buyers and salespeople in a store's various departments.

Key Terms

Balance sheet
Cost of goods sold
Gross margin
Gross sales

Markdown
Markup
Operating ratios

Operating statement (or profit-and-loss statement or income statement)
Return on investment (ROI)

Careers in Marketing

Now that you have completed this course in marketing, you have a good idea of what the field entails. You may have decided you want to pursue a marketing career because it offers constant challenge, stimulating problems, the opportunity to work with people, and excellent advancement opportunities. But you still may not know which part of marketing best suits you—marketing is a very broad field offering a wide variety of career options. This appendix helps you discover what types of marketing jobs best match your special skills and interests, shows you how to conduct the kind of job search that will get you the position you want in the company of your choice, describes marketing career paths open to you, and suggests other information resources.

Marketing Careers Today

The field of marketing boomed during the 1990s, with nearly a third of all Americans now employed in marketing-related positions. As we move into the twenty-first century, job growth in marketing will likely accelerate.

Marketing salaries may vary by company, position, and region, and salary figures change constantly. In general, entry-level marketing salaries usually are only slightly below those for engineering and chemistry but equal or exceed starting salaries in economics, finance, accounting, general business, and the liberal arts. Moreover, if you succeed in an entry-level marketing position, it's likely that you will be promoted quickly to higher levels of responsibility and salary. In addition, because of the consumer and product knowledge you will gain in these jobs, marketing positions provide excellent training for the highest levels in an organization. A recent study by an executive recruiting firm found that more top executives come out of marketing than any other functional group.

This appendix can be used alone, but to aid you in your job search, you may also want to consult some of the supplements to the first edition of *Marketing: An Introduction.* The *Career Paths* CD-ROM guides you through a self-test to identify the marketing paths that suit your skills and interests and describes the main types of marketing jobs. The Prentice Hall Web site (www.prenhall.com) also provides regularly updated information on marketing careers. Click Business Publishing, scroll to the bottom of the page, and click PHLIP.

Overall Marketing Facts and Trends

In conducting your job search, consider the following facts and trends that are changing the world of marketing.

> *Technology:* Technology is changing the way marketers work. For example, price coding allows instantaneous retail inventorying. Software for marketing training, forecasting, and other functions is changing the ways we market. And the Internet is creating new jobs and new recruiting rules. For example, consider the explosive growth in new media marketing. Whereas advertising firms have tradi-

tionally recruited "generalists" in account management, "generalist" has now taken on a whole new meaning — advertising account executives must now have both broad and specialized knowledge.

Diversity: The number of women and minorities in marketing continues to rise. Traditionally, women were mainly in retailing. Now, women and minorities are rapidly moving into all industries. They also are rising rapidly into marketing management. For example, women now outnumber men by nearly two to one as advertising account executives. As marketing becomes more global, the need for diversity in marketing positions will continue to increase, opening new opportunities.

Global: Companies such as Coca-Cola, McDonald's, MTV, and Procter & Gamble have become multinational, with offices and manufacturing operations in hundred of countries. Indeed, such companies often make more profit from sales outside the United States than from within. And it's not just the big companies that are involved in international marketing. Organizations of all sizes have moved into the global arena. Many new marketing opportunities and careers will be directly linked to the expanding global marketplace. The globalization of business also means that you will need more cultural, language, and people skills in the marketing world of the twenty-first century.

Not-for-profit organizations: Increasingly, colleges, arts organizations, libraries, hospitals, and other not-for-profit organizations are recognizing the need for effectively marketing their "products" and services to their various publics. This awareness has led to new marketing positions — with these organizations hiring their own marketing directors and marketing vice-presidents or using outside marketing specialists.

Looking for a Job in Today's Marketing World

To choose and find the right job, you will need to apply the marketing skills you've learned in this course, especially marketing analysis and planning. Follow these nine steps for marketing yourself: (1) conduct a self-assessment and seek career counseling; (2) examine job descriptions; (3) develop job search objectives; (4) explore the job market and assess opportunities; (5) develop search strategies; (6) prepare a resume; (7) write a cover letter and assemble supporting documents; (8) interview for jobs; and (9) follow up.

Conduct a Self-Assessment and Seek Career Counseling

If you're having difficulty deciding what kind of marketing position is the best fit for you, start out by doing some self-testing or get some career counseling. Self-assessments require that you honestly and thoroughly evaluate your interests, strengths, and weaknesses. What do you do well (your best and favorite skills) and not so well? What are your favorite interests? What are your career goals? What makes you stand out from other job seekers? The answers to such questions may suggest which marketing careers you should seek or avoid. For help in making an effective self-assessment, look at the following books in your local bookstore: Richard Bolles, *What Color Is Your Parachute?* (Berkeley, CA: Ten Speed Press, published annually) and Tom Jackson, *Guerrilla Tactics in the Job Market* (New York: Bantam Books, Second edition, 1991).

For help in finding a career counselor to guide you in making a career assessment, Richard Bolles, *What Color Is Your Parachute?* contains a useful state-by-state sampling. (Some counselors can help you in your actual job search, too.) You can also consult the career counseling, testing, and placement services at your college or university.

Career Counseling on the Internet

Today an increasing number of colleges, universities, and commercial career counselors offer career guidance on the Internet. In general, college and university sites are by far the best. But one useful commercial site you might look at is JobSmart (jobsmart.org/tools/resume/index.htm).

Examine Job Descriptions

After you have identified your skills, interests, and desires, you need to see which marketing positions are the best match for them. Two U.S. Labor Department publications in your local library, the *Occupation Outlook Handbook* and the *Dictionary of Occupational Titles*, describe the duties involved in various occupations, the specific training and education needed, the availability of jobs in each field, possibilities for advancement, and probable earnings.

Your initial career shopping list should be broad and flexible. Look for different ways to achieve your objectives. For example, if you want a career in marketing management, consider the public as well as the private sector, and regional as well as national firms. Be open initially to exploring many options, then focus on specific industries and jobs, listing your basic goals as a way to guide your choices. Your list might include: "a job in a start-up company, near a big city, on the West Coast, doing new product planning, with a computer software firm."

Explore the Job Market and Assess Opportunities

At this stage, you need to look at the market and see what positions are actually available. You do not have to do this alone. Any of the following may assist you.

College Placement Centers

Your college placement center is an excellent place to start. Besides posting specific job openings, placement centers have the current edition of the *College Placement Annual*, which lists job openings in hundreds of companies seeking college graduates for entry-level positions, as well as openings for people with experience or advanced degrees. More and more, schools are also going on the Internet. For example, the Web site of the career center of Emory University in Atlanta, Georgia, has a list of career links (www.emory.edu/CAREER/Links.html).

In addition, find out everything you can about the companies that interest you by consulting business magazines, annual reports, business reference books, faculty, career counselors, and others. Try to analyze the industry's and the company's future growth and profit potential, advancement opportunities, salary levels, entry positions, travel time, and other factors of significance to you.

Job Fairs

College placement offices often work with corporate recruiters to organize on-campus job fairs. You might also use the Internet to check on upcoming career fairs in your region. The site Career Fairs has such listings (www.cyberplex.com/hitech).

Networking and the Yellow Pages

Networking, or asking for job leads from friends, family, people in your community, and career centers, is one of the best ways to find a marketing job. An estimated 33 percent of jobs are found through networking. The idea is to spread your net wide, contacting anybody and everybody.

The phone book's yellow pages are another effective way to job search. Check out employers in your field of interest in whatever region you want to work, then call and ask if they are hiring for the position of your choice.

Summer Jobs and Internships

In some parts of the country one in seven students gets a job where they interned. *The Back Door Guidebook* (Berkeley, CA: Ten Speed Press, 1997) lists 1,000 short-term work experiences around the world. On the Internet, look at the National Internship Directory (www.tripod.com/work/internships). In addition, the major job listing sites, such as the Monster Board (www.monster.com), have separate areas for internships. If you know a company for which you wish to work, go to that company's corporate Web site, enter the personnel area, and check for internships. If there are none listed, try e-mailing the personnel department, asking if internships are offered.

The Internet

A constantly increasing number of sites on the Internet deal with job hunting. You can also use the Internet to make contacts with people who can help you gain information on companies and research companies that interest you. The Riley Guide offers a great introduction to what jobs are available (www.jobtrak.com/jobguide). In addition, Job Search and Employment Opportunities: Best Bets on the Net provides a very comprehensive listing (http:/asa.ugl.lib.umich.edu/chdocs/employment/). Other helpful sites are Employment Opportunities for People with Disabilities (www.disserv.stu.umn.edu/TC/Grants /COL/listing/disemp/) and The Global Village: Resources for Minorities on the Internet (www.vjf.com/pub/docs/jobsearch.html), which contains information on opportunities for African Americans, Hispanic Americans, Asian Americans, and Native Americans.

Most companies have their own Web sites upon which they post job listings. This may be helpful if you have a specific and fairly limited number of companies that you are keeping your eye on for job opportunities. But if this is not the case, remember that to find out what interesting marketing jobs the companies themselves are posting, you may have to visit hundreds of corporate sites.

Develop Search Strategies

Once you've decided which companies you are interested in, you need to contact them. One of the best ways is through on-campus interviews. But not every company you are interested in will visit your school. In such instances, you can write (this includes e-mail) or phone the company directly or ask marketing professors or school alumni for contacts.

Prepare Resumes

A resume is a concise yet comprehensive written summary of your qualifications, including your academic, personal, and professional achievements, that showcases why you are the best candidate for the job. Many organizations use resumes to decide which candidates to interview.

In preparing your resume, remember that all information on it must be accurate and complete. Resumes typically begin with the applicant's full name, telephone and fax numbers, and traditional mail and e-mail addresses. A simple and direct statement of career objectives generally appears next, followed by work history and academic data (including awards and internships), and then by personal activities and experiences applicable to the job sought. The resume usually ends with a list of references the employer may contact. If your work or internship experience is limited, nonexistent, or irrelevant, then it is a good idea to emphasize your academic and nonacademic achievements, showing skills related to those required for excellent job performance.

There are three types of resumes. *Chronological* resumes, which emphasize career growth, are organized in reverse chronological order, starting with your most recent job. They focus on job titles within organizations, describing the responsibilities required for each job. *Functional* resumes focus less on job titles and work history and more on assets and achievements. This format works best if your job history is scanty or discontinuous. *Mixed*, or *combined*, resumes take from each of the other two formats. First, the skills used for a specific job are listed, then the job title is stated. This format works best for applicants whose past jobs are in other fields or seemingly unrelated to the position.

Your local bookstore or library has many books that can assist you in developing your resume. Two popular guides are Tom Jackson, with Ellen Jackson, *The New Perfect Resume* (Garden City, NY: Anchor Press/Doubleday, revised, 1996) and Yana Parker, *The Damn Good Resume Guide* (Berkeley, CA: Ten Speed Press, 1996). Computer software programs such as *WinWay Resume*, provides hundreds of sample resumes and ready-to-use phrases while guiding you through the resume preparation process.

On-line Resumes

Today more and more job seekers are posting their resumes on the Internet. Preparing an electronic resume is somewhat different from preparing a traditional resume. For example, you need to know the relevant rules about scanning (including that your computer will be unable to scan the attractive fonts you used in your original resume) and keywords. Moreover, if you decide to post your resume in a public area like a Web site, then for security purposes you might not want to include your street or business address or the names of previous employers or references. (This information can be mailed later to employers after you have been contacted by them.) The following sites might assist you in writing your on-line resume: Job Smart (jobsmart.org/tools/resume/index.htm) and ResumixResumeBuilder (www.resumix.com/resume-form.html1). In addition, placement centers usually assist you in developing a resume. (Placement centers can also help with your cover letter and provide job-interview workshops.

After you have written your resume, you need to post it. The following sites may be good locations to start: Online Career Center, the biggest job bank in the world (www.occ.com); The World Wide Web Employment Center, an international listing of sites by occupation (www.harbornet.com/biz/office/annex.html); and Yahoo! Resume Services, a listing narrowed to business and economy companies (www.yahoo.com/Business_and_Economy/Companies/Employment/resume_services/)

Resume Tips

- Communicate your worth to potential employers in a concrete manner, citing examples whenever possible.
- Be concise and direct.
- Use active verbs to show you are a doer.
- Do not skimp on quality or use gimmicks. Spare no expense in presenting a professional resume.
- Have someone critique your work. A single typo can eliminate you from being considered.
- Customize your resume for specific employers. Emphasize your strengths as they pertain to your targeted job.
- Keep your resume compact, usually one page.

☐ Format the text to be attractive, professional, and readable. Avoid too much "design" or gimmicky flourishes.

Write Cover Letter and Assemble Supporting Documents

Cover Letter

You should include a cover letter informing the employer that a resume is enclosed. But a cover letter does more than this. It also serves to summarize in one or two paragraphs the contents of the resume and explains why you think you are the right person for the position. The goal is to persuade the employer to look at the more detailed resume. A typical cover letter is organized as follows: (1) the name and position of the person you are contacting; (2) a statement identifying the position you are applying for, how you heard of the vacancy, and the reasons for your interest; (3) a summary of your qualifications for the job; (4) a description of what follow-ups you intend to make, such as phoning in two weeks to see if the resume has been received; (5) an expression of gratitude for the opportunity of being a candidate for the job.

Letters of Recommendation and Other Supporting Documents

Letters of recommendation are written references by professors, former and current employers, and others that testify to your character, skills, and abilities. A good reference letter tells why you would be an excellent candidate for the position. In choosing someone to write a letter of recommendation, be confident that the person will give you a good reference. In addition, do not assume the person knows everything about you or the position you are seeking. Rather, provide the person with your resume and other relevant data. As a courtesy, allow the reference writer at least a month to complete the letter and enclose a stamped, addressed envelope with your materials.

In the packet containing your resume, cover letter, and letters of recommendation, you may also want to attach other relevant documents that support your candidacy, such as academic transcripts, graphics, portfolios, and samples of writing.

Interview for Jobs

As the old saying goes, "The resume gets you the interview; the interview gets you the job." The job interview offers you an opportunity to gather more information about the organization, while at the same time allowing the organization to gather more information about you. You'll want to present your best self. The interview process consists of three parts: before the interview, the interview itself, and after the interview. If you successfully pass through these stages, you will be called back for the follow-up interview.

Before the Interview

In preparing for your interview, do the following:

1. Understand that interviewers have diverse styles, including the "chitchat," let's-get-to-know-each-other style; the interrogation style of question after question; and the tough-probing "why, why, why" style, among others. So be ready for anything.
2. With a friend, practice being interviewed and then ask for a critique. Or, videotape yourself in a practice interview so that you can critique your own performance. Your college placement service may also offer "mock" interviews to help you.
3. Prepare at least five good questions whose answers are not easily found in the company literature, such as, "What is the future direction of the firm?" "How does the firm differentiate itself from competitors?" "Do you have a new-media division?"

4. Anticipate possible interview questions, such as "Why do you want to work for this company?" or "Why should we hire you?" Prepare solid answers before the interview. Have a clear idea of why you are interested in joining the company and the industry to which it belongs.
5. Avoid back-to-back interviews—they can be exhausting and it is unpredictable how long they will last.
6. Dress conservatively and professionally. Be neat and clean.
7. Arrive 10 minutes early to collect your thoughts and review the major points you intend to cover. Check your name on the interview schedule, noting the name of the interviewer and the room number. Be courteous and polite to office staff.
8. Approach the interview enthusiastically. Let your personality shine through.

During the Interview

During the interview, do the following:

1. Shake hands firmly in greeting the interviewer. Introduce yourself, using the same form of address the interviewer uses. Focus on creating a good initial impression.
2. Keep your poise. Relax, smile when appropriate, be upbeat throughout.
3. Maintain eye contact, good posture, and speak distinctly. Don't clasp your hands or fiddle with jewelry, hair, or clothing. Sit comfortably in your chair. Do not smoke, even if asked.
4. Carry extra copies of your resume with you. Bring samples of your academic or professional work along
5. Have your story down pat. Present your selling points. Answer questions directly. Avoid one-word or too-wordy answers.
6. Let the interviewer take the initiative but don't be passive. Find an opportunity to direct the conversation to things about yourself that you want the interviewer to hear.
7. To end on a high note, make your most important point or ask your most pertinent question during the last part of the interview.
8. Don't hesitate to "close." You might say, "I'm very interested in the position, and I have enjoyed this interview."
9. Obtain the interviewer's business card or address and phone number so that you can follow up later.

A tip for acing the interview: Before you open your mouth, find out *what it's like* to be a brand manager, sales representative, market researcher, advertising account executive, or other position for which you're interviewing.

After the Interview

After the interview, do the following:

1. After leaving the interview, record the key points that arose. Be sure to note who is to follow up and when a decision can be expected.
2. Analyze the interview objectively, including the questions asked, the answers to them, your overall interview presentation, and the interviewer's responses to specific points.
3. Immediately send a thank-you letter, mentioning any additional items and your willingness to supply further information.
4. If you do not hear within the specified time, write or call the interviewer to determine your status.

Follow-Up

If you are successful, you will be invited to visit the organization. The in-company interview will probably run from several hours to an entire day. The organization will examine your interest, maturity, enthusiasm, assertiveness, logic, and company and functional knowledge. You should ask questions about issues of importance to you. Find out about the working environment, job role, responsibilities, opportunity for advancement, current industrial issues, and the company's personality. The company wants to discover if you are the right person for the job, whereas you want to find out if it is the right job for you. The key is to determine if the right fit exists between you and the company.

Marketing Jobs

This section describes some of the key marketing positions.

Advertising

Advertising is one of today's hottest fields in marketing. In fact, *Money* magazine lists a position in advertising as among the 50 best jobs in America.

Job Descriptions

Key advertising positions include copywriter, art director, production manager, account executive, and media planner/buyer. *Copywriters* write advertising copy and help find the concepts behind the written words and visual images of advertisements. *Art directors*, the other part of the creative team, help translate the copywriters' ideas into dramatic visuals called "layouts." Agency artists develop print layouts, package designs, television layouts (called "storyboards"), corporate logotypes, trademarks, and symbols. *Production managers* are responsible for physically creating ads, in-house or by contracting through outside production houses. *Account executives* serve as liaisons between clients and agencies. They coordinate the planning, creation, production, and implementation of an advertising campaign for the account. *Media planners* determine the best mix of television, radio, newspaper, magazine, and other media for the advertising campaign.

Skills Needed, Career Paths, and Typical Salaries

Work in advertising requires strong people skills in order to interact closely with an often difficult and demanding client base. In addition, advertising attracts people with high skills in planning, problem solving, creativity, communication, initiative, leadership, and presentation. Advertising involves working under high levels of stress and pressure created by unrelenting deadlines. Advertisers frequently have to work long hours to meet deadlines for a presentation. But work achievements are very apparent, with the results of creative strategies observed by thousands or even millions of people.

Because they are so sought after, positions in advertising sometimes require an MBA. But there are many jobs open for business, graphic arts, and liberal arts undergraduates. Advertising positions often serve as gateways to higher-level management. Moreover, with large advertising agencies opening offices all over the world, there is the possibility of eventually working on global campaigns.

Starting advertising salaries are relatively low compared to some other marketing jobs because of strong competition for entry-level advertising jobs. You may even want to consider working for free to break in. Compensation will increase quickly as you move into account executive or other management positions. For more facts and figures, see the

Web pages of *Advertising Age*, a key ad industry publication (www.adage.com, click on the Job Bank button) and the American Association of Advertising Agencies (www.commercepark.com/AAAA/).

Brand and Product Management

Brand and product managers plan, direct, and control business and marketing efforts for their products. They are involved with research and development, packaging, manufacturing, sales and distribution, advertising, promotion, market research, and business analysis and forecasting.

Job Descriptions

A company's brand management team consists of people in several positions. The *brand manager* guides the development of marketing strategies for a specific brand. The *assistant brand manager* is responsible for certain strategic components of the brand. The *product manager* oversees several brands within a product line or product group. The *product category manager* directs multiple product lines in the product category. The *market analyst* researches the market and provides important strategic information to the project managers. The *project director* is responsible for collecting market information on a marketing or product project. The *research director* oversees the planning, gathering, and analyzing of all organizational research.

Skills Needed, Career Paths, and Typical Salaries

Brand and product management requires high problem-solving, analytical, presentation, communication, and leadership skills, as well as the ability to work well in a team. Product management requires long hours and involves the high pressure of running large projects. In consumer goods companies, the newcomer, who usually needs an MBA, joins a brand team as an assistant and learns the ropes by doing numerical analyses and watching senior brand people. This person eventually heads the team and later moves on to manage a larger brand, then several brands. Many industrial goods companies also have product managers. Product management is one of the best training grounds for future corporate officers. Product management also offers good opportunities to move into international marketing. Product managers command relatively high salaries. Because this job category encourages or requires a master's degree, starting pay tends to be higher than in other marketing categories such as advertising or retailing.

Sales, Sales Management

Sales and sales management opportunities exist in a wide range of profit and nonprofit organizations and in product and service organizations, including financial, insurance, consulting, and government organizations.

Job Descriptions

Key jobs include consumer sales, industrial sales, national account manager, service support, sales trainers, sales management, and teleseller. *Consumer sales* involves selling consumer products and services through retailers. *Industrial sales* includes selling products and services to other businesses. *National account managers (NAM)* oversee a few very large accounts. *Service support* personnel support salespeople during and after the sale of a product. *Sales trainers* train new hires and provide refresher training for all sales personnel. *Sales management* includes a sequence of positions ranging from district manager to vice-president of sales. The *teleseller* (not to be confused with the home consumer telemarketer) offers service and support to field salespeople.

Salespeople enjoy active professional lives, working outside the office and interacting with others. They manage their own time and activities. Competition for top jobs can be intense. Every sales job is different, but some positions involve extensive travel, long work days, and working under pressure, which can negatively impact personal life. You can also expect to be transferred more than once between company headquarters and regional offices.

Skills Needed, Career Paths, and Typical Salaries

Selling is a people profession in which you will work with people every day, all day long. Besides people skills, sales professionals need sales and communication skills. Most sales positions also require high problem-solving, analytical, presentation, and leadership ability as well as creativity and initiative. Teamwork skills are increasingly important.

Career paths lead from salesperson to district, regional, and higher levels of sales management and, in many cases, to the top management of the firm. Today, most entry-level sales management positions require a college degree. Increasingly, people seeking selling jobs are acquiring sales experience in an internship capacity or from a part-time job before graduating. Although there is a high turnover rate (one in four people leave their jobs in a year), sales positions are great springboards to leadership positions, with more CEOs starting in sales than in any other entry-level position. Possibly this explains why competition for top sales jobs is intense.

Starting base salaries in sales may be moderate, but compensation is often supplemented by significant commission, bonus, or other incentive plans. In addition, many sales jobs include a company car or car allowance. Successful salespeople are among most companies' highest paid employees.

Other Marketing Jobs

Retailing

Retailing provides an early opportunity to assume marketing responsibilities. Key jobs include store manager, regional manager, buyer, department manager, and salesperson. *Store managers* direct the management and operation of an individual store. *Regional managers* manage groups of stores across several states and report performance to headquarters. *Buyers* select and buy the merchandise that the store carries. The *department manager* acts as store manager of a department, such as clothing, but on the department level. The *salesperson* sells merchandise to retail customers. Retailing can involve relocation, but generally there is little travel, unless you are a buyer. Retailing requires high people and sales skills because retailers are constantly in contact with customers. Enthusiasm, willingness, and communication skills are very helpful for retailers, too. Retailers work long hours, but their daily activities are often more structured than some types of marketing positions. Starting salaries in retailing tend to be low, but pay increases as you move into management or some retailing specialty job.

Marketing Research

Marketing researchers interact with managers to define problems and identify the information needed to resolve them. They design research projects, prepare questionnaires and samples, analyze data, prepare reports, and present their findings and recommendations to management. They must understand statistics, consumer behavior, psychology, and sociology. A master's degree helps. Career opportunities exist with manufacturers, retailers, some wholesalers, trade and industry associations, marketing research firms, advertising agencies, and governmental and private nonprofit agencies.

New-Product Planning

People interested in new-product planning can find opportunities in many types of organizations. They usually need a good background in marketing, marketing research, and sales forecasting; they need organizational skills to motivate and coordinate others; and they may need a technical background. Usually, these people work first in other marketing positions before joining the new-product department.

Marketing Logistics (Physical Distribution)

Marketing logistics, or physical distribution, is a large and dynamic field, with many career opportunities. Major transportation carriers, manufacturers, wholesalers, and retailers all employ logistics specialists. Increasingly, marketing teams include logistics specialists, and marketing managers' career paths include marketing logistics assignments. Coursework in quantitative methods, finance, accounting, and marketing will provide you with the necessary skills for entering the field.

Public Relations

Most organizations have a public relations staff to anticipate problems with various publics, handle complaints, deal with media, and build the corporate image. People interested in public relations should be able to speak and write clearly and persuasively, and they should have a background in journalism, communications, or the liberal arts. The challenges in this job are highly varied and very people oriented.

Not-for-Profit Services

The key jobs in not-for-profit include marketing director, director of development, event coordinator, publication specialist, and intern/volunteers. The *marketing director* is in charge of all marketing activities for the organization. The *director of development* organizes, manages, and directs the fund-raising campaigns that keep a not-for-profit in existence. An *event coordinator* directs all aspects of fund-raising events, from initial planning through implementation. The *publication specialist* oversees publications designed to promote awareness of the organization. Although typically an unpaid position the *intern/volunteer* performs various marketing functions, and this work can be an important step to gaining a full-time position. The not-for-profit sector is typically not for someone who is money driven. Rather, most not-for-profits look for people with a strong sense of community spirit and the desire to help others. So starting pay is usually lower than in other marketing fields. However, the bigger the not-for-profit, the better your chance of rapidly increasing your income when moving into upper management.

Other Resources

Professional marketing associations and organizations are another source of information about careers. Marketers belong to many such societies. You may want to contact some of the following in your job search:

American Advertising Federation, 1101 Vermont Avenue, NW, Suite 500, Washington, D.C. 2005. (202) 898-0089.

American Marketing Association, 250 South Wacker Drive, Suite 200, Chicago, IL 60606. (312) 648-0536 (www.ama.org)

Council of Sales Promotion Agencies, 750 Summer Street, Stamford,CT 06901. (203) 325-3911.

Market Research Association, 2189 Silas Deane Highway, Suite 5, Rocky Hill, CT 06067. (860) 257-4008

National Council of Salesmen's Organizations, 389 Fifth Avenue, Room 1010, New York, NY 10016. (718) 835-4591

National Management Association, 2210 Arbor Boulevard, Dayton, OH 45439. (513) 294-0421

National Retail Federation, 701 Pennsylvania Avenue NW, Suite 710, Washington, D.C. 20004. (202) 783-7971

Product Development and Management Association, 401 North Michigan Avenue, Chicago, IL 60611. (312) 527-6644

Public Relations Society of America, 33 Irving Place, Third Floor, New York, NY 10003. (212) 995-2230. (www.prsa.org)

Sales and Marketing Executives International, Statler Office Tower, Number 977, Cleveland, OH 44115. (216) 771-6650.

Women in Advertising and Marketing, 4200 Wisconsin Avenue NW, Suite 106-238, Washington, D.C. 20016. (301) 369-7400

Women Executives in Public Relations, P.O. Box 609, Westport, CT, 06881. (203) 226-4947

Glossary

Adapted marketing mix An international marketing strategy for adjusting the marketing-mix elements to each international target market, bearing more costs but hoping for a larger market share and return.

Administered VMS A vertical marketing system that coordinates successive stages of production and distribution, not through common ownership or contractual ties but through the size and power of one of the parties.

Adoption process The mental process through which an individual passes from first hearing about an innovation to final adoption.

Advertising Any paid form of nonpersonal presentation and promotion of ideas, goods, or services by an identified sponsor.

Advertising agency A marketing services firm that assists companies in planning, preparing, implementing, and evaluating all or portions of their advertising programs.

Advertising objective A specific communication *task* to be accomplished with a specific *target* audience during a specific period of *time*.

Advertising specialty Useful article imprinted with an advertiser's name, given as a gift to consumers.

Affordable method Setting the promotion budget at the level management thinks the company can afford.

Age and life-cycle segmentation Dividing a market into different age and life-cycle groups.

Agent A wholesaler who represents buyers or sellers on a relatively permanent basis, performs only a few functions, and does not take title to goods.

Allowance Promotional money paid by manufacturers to retailers in return for an agreement to feature the manufacturer's products in some way.

Attitude A person's consistently favorable or unfavorable evaluations, feelings, and tendencies toward an object or idea.

Automatic vending Selling through vending machines.

Baby boom The major increase in the annual birthrate following World War II and lasting until the early 1960s. The "baby boomers," now moving into middle age, are a prime target for marketers.

Balance sheet A financial statement that shows assets, liabilities, and net worth of a company at a given time.

Behavioral segmentation Dividing a market into groups based on consumer knowledge, attitude, use, or response to a product.

Belief A descriptive thought that a person holds about something.

Benefit segmentation Dividing the market into groups according to the different benefits that consumers seek from the product.

Brand A name, term, sign, symbol, or design, or a combination of these, intended to identify the goods or services of one seller or group of sellers and to differentiate them from those of competitors.

Brand equity The value of a brand, based on the extent to which it has high brand loyalty, name awareness, perceived quality, strong brand associations, and other assets such as patents, trademarks, and channel relationships.

Brand extension Using a successful brand name to launch a new or modified product in a new category.

Break-even pricing (target-profit pricing) Setting price to break even on the costs of making and marketing a product, or setting price to make a target profit.

Broker A wholesaler who does not take title to goods and whose function is to bring buyers and sellers together and assist in negotiation.

Business analysis A review of the sales, costs, and profit projections for a new product to find out whether these factors satisfy the company's objectives.

Business buyer behavior The buying behavior of organizations that buy goods and services for use in the production of other products and services that are sold, rented, or supplied to others. It also includes buying of goods by retailers and wholesalers for the purpose of reselling or renting them.

Business portfolio The collection of businesses and products that make up the company.

Buyer The person who makes an actual purchase.

Buyer-readiness stages The stages consumers normally pass through on their way to purchase, including awareness, knowledge, liking, preference, conviction, and purchase.

Buying center All the individuals and units that participate in the business buying decision process.

Byproduct pricing Setting a price for byproducts in order to make the main product's price more competitive.

Captive-product pricing Setting a price for products that must be used along with a main product, such as blades for a razor and film for a camera.

Cash discount A price reduction to buyers who pay their bills promptly.

Cash refund offer (rebate) Offer to refund part of the purchase price of a product to consumers who send a "proof of purchase" to the manufacturer.

Catalog marketing Direct marketing through catalogs that are mailed to a select list of customers or made available in stores.

Category killer Giant specialty store that carries a very deep assortment of a particular line and is staffed by knowledgeable employees.

Causal research Marketing research to test hypotheses about cause-and-effect relationships.

Chain stores Two or more outlets that are owned and controlled in common, have central buying and merchandising, and sell similar lines of merchandise.

Channel conflict Disagreement among marketing channel members on goals and roles—who should do what and for what rewards.

Channel level A layer of intermediaries that performs some work in bringing the product and its ownership closer to the final buyer.

Closing The step in the selling process in which the salesperson asks the customer for an order.

Co-branding The practice of using the established brand names of two different companies on the same product.

Cognitive dissonance Buyer discomfort caused by postpurchase conflict.

Commercial on-line services Services that offer on-line information and marketing services to subscribers who pay a monthly fee, such as America Online, CompuServe, and Prodigy.

Commercialization Introducing a new product into the market.

Communication adaptation A global communication strategy of fully adapting advertising messages to local markets.

Competition-base pricing Setting prices based on the prices that competitors charge for similar products

Competitive advantage An advantage over competitors gained by offering consumers greater value, either through lower prices or by providing more benefits that justify higher prices.

Competitive-parity method Setting the promotion budget to match competitors' outlays.

Concentrated marketing A market-coverage strategy in which a firm goes after a large share of one or a few submarkets.

Concept testing Testing new-product concepts with a group of target consumers to find out if the concepts have strong consumer appeal.

Consumer buyer behavior The buying behavior of final consumers—individuals and households who buy goods and services for personal consumption.

Consumer market All the individuals and households who buy or acquire goods and services for personal consumption.

Consumer-oriented marketing A principle of enlightened marketing that holds that the company should view and organize its marketing activities from the consumers' point of view.

Consumer product Product bought by final consumer for personal consumption.

Consumerism An organized movement of citizens and government agencies to improve the rights and power of buyers in relation to sellers.

Contests, sweepstakes, games Promotional events that give consumers the chance to win something—such as cash, trips, or goods—by luck or through extra effort.

Contract manufacturing A joint venture in which a company contracts with manufacturers in a foreign market to produce the product.

Contractual VMS A vertical marketing system in which independent firms at different levels of production and distribution join together through contracts to obtain more economies or sales impact than they could achieve alone.

Convenience product Consumer product that the customer usually buys frequently, immediately, and with a minimum of comparison and buying effort.

Convenience store A small store, located near a residential area, that is open long hours seven days a week and carries a limited line of high-turnover convenience goods.

Conventional distribution channel A channel consisting of one or more independent producers, wholesalers, and retailers, each a separate business seeking to maximize its own profits even at the expense of profits for the system as a whole.

Corporate VMS A vertical marketing system that combines successive stages of production and distribution under single ownership; channel leadership is established through common ownership.

Corporate Web site Web sites that seek to build customer goodwill and to supplement other sales channels rather than to sell the company's products directly.

Cost of goods sold The net cost to the company of goods sold.

Cost-plus pricing Adding a standard markup to the cost of the product.

Countertrade International trade involving the direct or indirect exchange of goods for other goods instead of cash. Forms include barter, compensation (buyback), and counterpurchase.

Coupon Certificate that gives buyers a saving when they purchase a specified product.

Cultural environment Institutions and other forces that affect society's basic values, perceptions, preferences, and behaviors.

Culture The set of basic values, perceptions, wants, and behaviors learned by a member of society from family and other important institutions.

Customer-centered company A company that focuses on customer developments in designing its marketing strategies and on delivering superior value to its target customers.

Customer database An organized collection of comprehensive data about individual customers or prospects, including geographic, demographic, psychographic, and behavioral data.

Customer sales force structure A sales force organization under which salespeople specialize in selling only to certain customers or industries.

Customer satisfaction The extent to which a product's perceived performance matches a buyer's expectations. If the product's performance falls short of expectations, the buyer is dissatisfied. If performance matches or exceeds expectations, the buyer is satisfied or delighted.

Customer value The difference between the values the customer gains from owning and using a product and the costs of obtaining the product.

Decline stage The product life-cycle stage in which a product's sales decline.

Deficient products Products that have neither immediate appeal nor long-run benefits.

Demand curve A curve that shows the number of units the market will buy in a given time period at different prices that might be charged.

Demands Human wants that are backed by buying power.

Demarketing Marketing to reduce demand temporarily or permanently—the aim is not to destroy demand but only to reduce or shift it.

Demographic segmentation Dividing the market into groups based on demographic variables such as age, sex, family size, family life cycle, income, occupation, education, religion, race, and nationality.

Demography The study of human populations in terms of size, density, location, age, gender, race, occupation, and other statistics.

Department store A retail organization that carries a wide variety of product lines—typically clothing, home furnishings, and household goods; each line is operated as a separate department managed by specialist buyers or merchandisers.

Derived demand Business demand that ultimately comes from (derives from) the demand for consumer goods.

Descriptive research Marketing research to better describe marketing problems, situations, or markets, such as the market potential for a product or the demographics and attitudes of consumers.

Desirable products Products that give both high immediate satisfaction and high long-run benefits.

Differentiated marketing A market-coverage strategy in which a firm decides to target several market segments and designs separate offers for each.

Direct investment Entering a foreign market by developing foreign-based assembly or manufacturing facilities.

Direct marketing Direct communications with carefully targeted individual consumers to obtain an immediate response.

Direct marketing channel A marketing channel that has no intermediary levels.

Direct-mail marketing Direct marketing through single mailings that include letters, ads, samples, foldouts, and other "salespeople with wings" sent to prospects on mailing lists.

Direct-response television marketing Direct marketing via television, including *direct-response television advertising* or *infomercials* and *home shopping channels*.

Discount A straight reduction in price on purchases during a stated period of time.

Discount store A retail institution that sells standard merchandise at lower prices by accepting lower margins and selling at higher volume.

Distribution center A large, highly automated warehouse designed to receive goods from various plants and suppliers, take orders, fill them efficiently, and deliver goods to customers as quickly as possible.

Distribution channel A set of interdependent organizations involved in the process of making a product or service available for use or consumption by the consumer or business user.

Diversification A strategy for company growth by starting up or acquiring businesses outside the company's current products and markets.

Door-to-door retailing Selling door to door, office to office, or at home sales parties.

Economic community A group of nations organized to work toward common goals in the regulation of international trade.

Economic environment Factors that affect consumer buying power and spending patterns.

Electronic commerce The general term for a buying and selling process that is supported by electronic means.

Embargo A ban on the import of a certain product.

Engel's laws Differences noted over a century ago by Ernst Engel in how people shift their spending across food, housing, transportation, health care, and other goods and services categories as family income rises.

Enlightened marketing A marketing philosophy holding that a company's marketing should support the best long-run performance of the marketing system; its five principles include consumer-oriented marketing, innovative marketing, value marketing, sense-of-mission marketing, and societal marketing.

Environmental management perspective A management perspective in which the firm takes aggressive actions to affect the publics and forces in its marketing environment rather than simply watching and reacting to them.

Environmental sustainability A management approach that involves developing strategies that both sustain the environment and produce profits for the company.

Environmentalism An organized movement of concerned citizens and government agencies to protect and improve people's living environment.

Exchange The act of obtaining a desired object from someone by offering something in return.

Exchange controls Government limits on the amount of foreign exchange with other countries and on the exchange rate against other currencies.

Exclusive distribution Giving a limited number of dealers the exclusive right to distribute the company's products in their territories.

Experimental research The gathering of primary data by selecting matched groups of subjects, giving them different treatments, controlling related factors, and checking for differences in group responses.

Exploratory research Marketing research to gather preliminary information that will help define problems and suggest hypotheses.

Factory outlet Off-price retailing operation that is owned and operated by a manufacturer and that normally carries the manufacturer's surplus, discontinued, or irregular goods.

Fads Fashions that enter quickly, are adopted with great zeal, peak early, and decline very fast.

Fashion A currently accepted or popular style in a given field.

Fixed costs Costs that do not vary with production or sales level.

Focus group interviewing Personal interviewing that involves inviting six to ten people to gather for a few hours with a trained interviewer to talk about a product, service, or organization. The interviewer "focuses" the group discussion on important issues.

Follow-up The last step in the selling process in which the salesperson follows up after the sale to ensure customer satisfaction and repeat business.

Forecasting The art of estimating future demand by anticipating what buyers are likely to do under a given set of conditions.

Franchise A contractual association between a manufacturer, wholesaler, or service organization (a franchiser) and independent businesspeople (franchisees) who buy the right to own and operate one or more units in the franchise system.

Franchise organization A contractual vertical marketing system in which a channel member, called a *franchiser*, links several stages in the production-distribution process.

Gender segmentation Dividing a market into different groups based on sex.

Geographic segmentation Dividing a market into different geographical units such as nations, states, regions, counties, cities, or neighborhoods.

Global firm A firm that, by operating in more than one country, gains R&D, production, marketing, and financial advantages in its costs and reputation that are not available to purely domestic competitors.

Gross margin The difference between net sales and cost of goods sold.

Gross sales The total amount that a company charges during a given period of time for merchandise.

Group Two or more people who interact to accomplish individual or mutual goals.

Growth-share matrix A portfolio-planning method that evaluates a company's strategic business units in terms of their market growth rate and relative market share. SBUs are classified as stars, cash cows, question marks, or dogs.

Growth stage The product life-cycle stage in which a product's sales start climbing quickly.

Handling objections The step in the selling process in which the salesperson seeks out, clarifies, and overcomes customer objections to buying.

Horizontal marketing system A channel arrangement in which two or more companies at one level join together to follow a new marketing opportunity.

Hybrid marketing channel Multichannel distribution system in which a single firm sets up two or more marketing channels to reach one or more customer segments.

Idea generation The systematic search for new-product ideas.

Idea screening Screening new-product ideas in order to spot good ideas and drop poor ones as soon as possible.

Income segmentation Dividing a market into different income groups.

Independent off-price retailer Off-price retailer that is either owned and run by entrepreneurs or is division of larger retail corporation.

Indirect marketing channel Channel containing one or more intermediary levels.

Individual marketing Tailoring products and marketing programs to the needs and preferences of individual customers—also labeled "markets-of-one marketing," "customized marketing," and "one-to-one marketing."

Industrial product Product bought by individuals and organizations for further processing or for use in conducting a business.

Innovative marketing A principle of enlightened marketing that requires that a company seek real product and marketing improvements.

Inside sales force Inside salespeople who conduct business from their offices via telephone or visits from prospective buyers.

Institutional market Schools, hospitals, nursing homes, prisons, and other institutions that provide goods and services to people in their care.

Integrated direct marketing Direct-marketing campaigns that use multiple vehicles and multiple stages to improve response rates and profits.

Integrated logistics management The logistics concept that emphasizes teamwork, both inside the company and among all the marketing channel organizations, to maximize the performance of the entire distribution system.

Integrated marketing communications (IMC) The concept under which a company carefully integrates and coordinates its many communications channels to deliver a clear, consistent, and compelling message about the organization and its products.

Intensive distribution Stocking the product in as many outlets as possible.

Interactive marketing Marketing by a service firm that recognizes that perceived service quality depends heavily on the quality of buyer-seller interaction.

Intermarket segmentation Forming segments of consumers who have similar needs and buying behavior even though they are located in different countries.

Intermodal transportation Combining two or more modes of transportation.

Internal databases Computerized collections of information obtained from data sources within the company.

Internal marketing Marketing by a service firm to train and effectively motivate its customer-contact employees and all the supporting service people to work as a team to provide customer satisfaction.

Internet (or the Net) The vast and burgeoning global web of computer networks that links computers around the world.

Introduction stage The product life-cycle stage in which the new product is first distributed and made available for purchase.

Joint ownership A joint venture in which a company joins investors in a foreign market to create a local business in which the company shares joint ownership and control.

Joint venturing Entering foreign markets by joining with foreign companies to produce or market a product or service.

Learning Changes in an individual's behavior arising from experience.

Licensing A method of entering a foreign market in which the company enters into an agreement with a licensee in the foreign market, offering the right to use a manufacturing process, trademark, patent, trade secret, or other item of value for a fee or royalty.

Lifestyle A person's pattern of living as expressed in his or her activities, interests, and opinions.

Line extension Using a successful brand name to introduce additional items in a given product category under the same brand name, such as new flavors, forms, colors, added ingredients, or package sizes.

Macroenvironment The larger societal forces that affect the microenvironment—demographic, economic, natural, technological, political, and cultural forces.

Management contracting A joint venture in which the domestic firm supplies the management know-how to a foreign company that supplies the capital; the domestic firm exports management services rather than products.

Manufacturers' sales branches and offices Wholesaling by sellers or buyers themselves rather than through independent wholesalers.

Markdown A percentage reduction from the original selling price.

Market The set of all actual and potential buyers of a product or service.

Market development A strategy for company growth by identifying and developing new market segments for current company products.

Market penetration A strategy for company growth by increasing sales of current products to current market segments without changing the product.

Market-penetration pricing Setting a low price for a new product in order to attract a large number of buyers and a large market share.

Market positioning Arranging for a product to occupy a clear, distinctive, and desirable place relative to competing products in the minds of target consumers. Formulating competitive positioning for a product and a detailed marketing mix.

Market potential The upper limit of market demand.

Market segment A group of consumers who respond in a similar way to a given set of marketing efforts.

Market segmentation Dividing a market into distinct groups of buyers on the basis of needs, characteristics, or behavior who might require separate products or marketing mixes.

Market-skimming pricing Setting a high price for a new product to skim maximum revenues layer by layer from the segments willing to pay the high price; the company makes fewer but more profitable sales.

Market targeting The process of evaluating each market segment's attractiveness and selecting one or more segments to enter.

Marketing A social and managerial process by which individuals and groups obtain what they need and want through creating and exchanging products and value with others.

Marketing audit A comprehensive, systematic, independent, and periodic examination of a company's environment, objectives, strategies, and activities to determine problem areas and opportunities and to recommend a plan of action to improve the company's marketing performance.

Marketing communications mix (promotion mix) The specific mix of advertising, personal selling, sales promotion, and public relations a company uses to pursue its advertising and marketing objectives.

Marketing concept The marketing management philosophy that holds that achieving organizational goals depends on determining the needs and wants of target markets and delivering the desired satisfactions more effectively and efficiently than competitors do.

Marketing control The process of measuring and evaluating the results of marketing strategies and plans and taking corrective action to ensure that marketing objectives are achieved.

Marketing environment The actors and forces outside marketing that affect marketing management's ability to develop and maintain successful transactions with its target customers.

Marketing implementation The process that turns marketing strategies and plans into marketing actions in order to accomplish strategic marketing objectives.

Marketing information system (MIS) People, equipment, and procedures to gather, sort, analyze, evaluate, and distribute needed, timely, and accurate information to marketing decision makers.

Marketing intelligence Everyday information about developments in the marketing environment that helps managers prepare and adjust marketing plans.

Marketing intermediaries Firms that help the company to promote, sell, and distribute its goods to final buyers; they include resellers, physical distribution firms, marketing service agencies, and financial intermediaries.

Marketing management The analysis, planning, implementation, and control of programs designed to create, build, and maintain beneficial exchanges with target buyers for the purpose of achieving organizational objectives.

Marketing mix The set of controllable tactical marketing tools—product, price, place, and promotion—that the firm blends to produce the response it wants in the target market.

Marketing process The process of (1) analyzing marketing opportunities; (2) selecting target markets; (3) developing the marketing mix; and (4) managing the marketing effort.

Marketing research The systematic design, collection, analysis, and reporting of data relevant to a specific marketing situation facing an organization.

Marketing strategy The marketing logic by which the business unit hopes to achieve its marketing objectives.

Marketing strategy development Designing an initial marketing strategy for a new product based on the product concept.

Marketing Web site Web sites designed to engage consumers in an interaction that will move them closer to a purchase or other marketing outcome.

Markup The percentage of the cost or price of a product added to cost in order to arrive at a selling price.

Maturity stage The stage in the product life cycle in which sales growth slows or levels off.

Merchant wholesaler Independently owned business that takes title to the merchandise it handles.

Microenvironment The forces close to the company that affect its ability to serve its customers— the company, suppliers, marketing channel firms, customer markets, competitors, and publics.

Micromarketing The practice of tailoring products and marketing programs to suit the tastes of specific individuals and locations; includes *local marketing* and *individual marketing*.

Mission statement A statement of the organization's purpose—what it wants to accomplish in the larger environment.

Modified rebuy A business buying situation in which the buyer wants to modify product specifications, prices, terms, or suppliers.

Motive (drive) A need that is sufficiently pressing to direct the person to seek satisfaction of the need.

Natural environment Natural resources that are needed as inputs by marketers or that are affected by marketing activities.

Need A state of felt deprivation.

New product A good, service, or idea that is perceived by some potential customers as new.

New-product development The development of original products, product improvements, product modifications, and new brands through the firm's own R&D efforts.

New task A business buying situation in which the buyer purchases a product or service for the first time.

Niche marketing Focusing on subsegments or niches with distinctive traits that may seek a special combination of benefits.

Nontariff trade barriers Nonmonetary barriers to foreign products, such as biases against a foreign company's bids or product standards that go against a foreign company's product features.

Objective-and-task method Developing the promotion budget by (1) defining specific objectives, (2) determining the tasks that must be performed to achieve these objectives, and (3) estimating the costs of performing these tasks. The sum of these costs is the proposed promotion budget.

Observational research The gathering of primary data by observing relevant people, actions, and situations.

Occasion segmentation Dividing the market into groups according to occasions when buyers get the idea to buy, actually make their purchase, or use the purchased item.

Off-price retailer Retailer that buys at less-than-regular wholesale prices and sells at less than retail. Examples are factory outlets, independents, and warehouse clubs.

Oligopolistic competition A market in which there are few sellers, all of whom are highly sensitive to each other's pricing and marketing strategies.

On-line ads Ads that appear while subscribers are surfing on-line services or Web sites, including banners, pop-up windows, "tickers," and "roadblocks."

On-line databases Computerized collections of information available from on-line commercial sources or via the Internet.

On-line marketing Marketing conducted through interactive on-line computer systems, which link consumers with sellers electronically.

On-line (Internet) marketing research Collecting primary data through Internet surveys and on-line focus groups.

Operating ratios Ratios of selected operating statement items to net sales that allow marketers to compare the firm's performance in one year with that in previous years (or with industry standards and competitors in the same year).

Operating statement (or profit-and-loss statement or income statement) A financial statement that shows company sales, cost of goods sold, and expenses during a given period of time.

Opinion leader Person within a reference group who, because of special skills, knowledge, personality, or other characteristics, exerts influence on others.

Optional-product pricing The pricing of optional or accessory products along with a main product.

Outside sales force (or field sales force) Outside salespeople who travel to call on customers.

Packaging The activities of designing and producing the container or wrapper for a product.

Patronage reward Cash or other award for the regular use of a certain company's products or services.

Percentage-of-sales method Setting the promotion budget at a certain percentage of current or forecasted sales or as a percentage of the unit sales price.

Perception The process by which people select, organize, and interpret information to form a meaningful picture of the world.

Personal selling Personal presentation by the firm's sales force for the purpose of making sales and building customer relationships.

Physical distribution (marketing logistics) The tasks involved in planning, implementing, and controlling the physical flow of materials, final goods, and related information from points of origin to points of consumption to meet customer requirements at a profit.

Pleasing products Products that give high immediate satisfaction but may hurt consumers in the long run.

Point-of-purchase (POP) promotion Display and demonstration that takes place at the point of purchase or sale.

Political environment Laws, government agencies, and pressure groups that influence and limit various organizations and individuals in a given society.

Portfolio analysis A tool by which management identifies and evaluates the various businesses that make up the company.

Preapproach The step in the selling process in which the salesperson learns as much as possible about a prospective customer before making a sales call.

Premium Good offered either free or at low cost as an incentive to buy a product.

Price The amount of money charged for a product or service, or the sum of the values that consumers exchange for the benefits of having or using the product or service.

Price elasticity A measure of the sensitivity of demand to changes in price.

Price pack (cents-off deal) Reduced price that is marked by the producer directly on the label or package.

Primary data Information collected for the specific purpose at hand.

Primary demand The level of total demand for all brands of a given product or service; for example, the total demand for motorcycles.

Private brand (or store brand) A brand created and owned by a reseller of a product or service.

Product Anything that can be offered to a market for attention, acquisition, use, or consumption that might satisfy a want or need. It includes physical objects, services, persons, places, organizations, and ideas.

Product adaptation Adapting a product to meet local conditions or wants in foreign markets.

Product bundle pricing Combining several products and offering the bundle at a reduced price.

Product concept The idea that consumers will favor products that offer the most quality, performance, and features and that the organization should therefore devote its energy to making continuous product improvements. A detailed version of the new-product idea stated in meaningful consumer terms.

Product development A strategy for company growth by offering modified or new products to current market segments. Developing the product concept into a physical product in order to ensure that the product idea can be turned into a workable product.

Product invention Creating new products or services for foreign markets.

Product life cycle (PLC) The course of a product's sales and profits over its lifetime. It involves five distinct stages: product development, introduction, growth, maturity, and decline.

Product line A group of products that are closely related because they function in a similar manner, are sold to the same customer groups, are marketed through the same types of outlets, or fall within given price ranges.

Product line pricing Setting the price steps between various products in a product line based on cost differences between the products, customer evaluations of different features, and competitors' prices.

Product/market expansion grid A portfolio-planning tool for identifying company growth opportunities through market penetration, market development, product development, or diversification.

Product mix (or product assortment) The set of all product lines and items that a particular seller offers for sale.

Product position The way the product is defined by consumers on important attributes; the place the product occupies in consumers' minds relative to competing products.

Product quality The ability of a product to perform its functions; it includes the product's overall durability, reliability, precision, ease of operation and repair, and other valued attributes.

Product sales force structure A sales force organization under which salespeople specialize in selling only a portion of the company's products or lines.

Production concept The philosophy that consumers will favor products that are available and highly affordable and that management should therefore focus on improving production and distribution efficiency.

Promotional pricing Temporarily pricing products below the list price, and sometimes even below cost, to increase short-run sales.

Proposal solicitation The stage of the business buying process in which the buyer invites qualified suppliers to submit proposals.

Prospecting The step in the selling process in which the salesperson identifies qualified potential customers.

Psychographic segmentation Dividing a market into different groups based on social class, lifestyle, or personality characteristics.

Psychological pricing A pricing approach that considers the psychology of prices and not simply the economics; the price is used to say something about the product.

Public Any group that has an actual or potential interest in or impact on an organization's ability to achieve its objectives.

Public relations Building good relations with the company's various publics by obtaining favorable publicity, building up a good "corporate image," and handling or heading off unfavorable rumors, stories, and events. Major PR tools include press relations, product publicity, corporate communications, lobbying, and public service.

Pull strategy A promotion strategy that calls for spending a lot on advertising and consumer promotion to build up consumer demand. If the strategy is successful, consumers will ask their retailers for the product, the retailers will ask the wholesalers, and the wholesalers will ask the producers.

Push strategy A promotion strategy that calls for using the sales force and trade promotion to push the product through channels. The producer promotes the product to wholesalers, the wholesalers promote to retailers, and the retailers promote to consumers.

Quota A limit on the amount of goods that an importing country will accept in certain product categories; it is designed to conserve on foreign exchange and to protect local industry and employment.

Reference prices Prices that buyers carry in their minds and refer to when they look at a given product.

Relationship marketing The process of creating, maintaining, and enhancing strong, value-laden relationships with customers and other stakeholders.

Reminder advertising Advertising used to keep consumers thinking about a product.

Retailer Business whose sales come *primarily* from retailing.

Retailing All activities involved in selling goods or services directly to final consumers for their personal, nonbusiness use.

Return on investment (ROI) A common measure of managerial effectiveness—the ratio of net profit to investment.

Sales force management The analysis, planning, implementation, and control of sales force activities. It includes setting and designing sales force strategy and recruiting, selecting, training, supervising, compensating, and evaluating the firm's salespeople.

Sales promotion Short-term incentives to encourage the purchase or sale of a product or service.

Salesperson An individual acting for a company by performing one or more of the following activities: prospecting, communicating, servicing, and information gathering.

Salutary products Products that have low appeal but may benefit consumers in the long run.

Sample Offers to consumers of a small amount of a product for trial.

Secondary data Information that already exists somewhere, having been collected for another purpose.

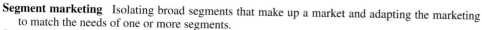

Segment marketing Isolating broad segments that make up a market and adapting the marketing to match the needs of one or more segments.

Segmented pricing Selling a product or service at two or more prices, where the difference in prices is not based on differences in costs.

Selective distribution The use of more than one, but fewer than all, of the intermediaries who are willing to carry the company's products.

Selling concept The idea that consumers will not buy enough of the organization's products unless the organization undertakes a large-scale selling and promotion effort.

Selling process The steps that the salesperson follows when selling, which include prospecting and qualifying, preapproach, approach, presentation and demonstration, handling objections, closing, and follow-up.

Sense-of-mission marketing A principle of enlightened marketing that holds that a company should define its mission in broad social terms rather than narrow product terms.

Sequential product development A new-product development approach in which one company department works to complete its stage of the process before passing the new product along to the next department and stage.

Service Any activity or benefit that one party can offer to another that is essentially intangible and does not result in the ownership of anything.

Service inseparability A major characteristic of services—they are produced and consumed at the same time and cannot be separated from their providers, whether the providers are people or machines.

Service intangibility A major characteristic of services—they cannot be seen, tasted, felt, heard, or smelled before they are bought.

Service perishability A major characteristic of services—they cannot be stored for later sale or use.

Service-profit chain The chain that links service firm profits with employee and customer satisfaction.

Service variability A major characteristic of services—their quality may vary greatly, depending on who provides them and when, where, and how.

Shopping center A group of retail businesses planned, developed, owned, and managed as a unit.

Shopping product Consumer good that the customer, in the process of selection and purchase, characteristically compares on such bases as suitability, quality, price, and style.

Simultaneous (or team-based) product development An approach to developing new products in which various company departments work closely together, overlapping the steps in the product-development process to save time and increase effectiveness.

Single-source data systems Electronic monitoring systems that link consumers' exposure to television advertising and promotion (measured using television meters) with what they buy in stores (measured using store checkout scanners).

Slotting fees Payments demanded by retailers before they will accept new products and find "slots" for them on the shelves.

Social classes Relatively permanent and ordered divisions in a society whose members share similar values, interests, and behaviors.

Social marketing The design, implementation, and control of programs seeking to increase the acceptability of a social idea, cause, or practice among a target group.

Societal marketing A principle of enlightened marketing that holds that a company should make marketing decisions by considering consumers' wants, the company's requirements, consumers' long-run interests, and society's long-run interests.

Societal marketing concept The idea that the organization should determine the needs, wants, and interests of target markets and deliver the desired satisfactions more effectively and efficiently than do competitors in a way that maintains or improves the consumer's and society's well-being.

Specialty product Consumer product with unique characteristics or brand identification for which a significant group of buyers is willing to make a special purchase effort.

Specialty store A retail store that carries a narrow product line with a deep assortment within that line.

Standardized marketing mix An international marketing strategy for using basically the same product, advertising, distribution channels, and other elements of the marketing mix in all the company's international markets.

Straight product extension Marketing a product in a foreign market without any change.

Straight rebuy A business buying situation in which the buyer routinely reorders something without any modifications.

Strategic business unit (SBU) A unit of the company that has a separate mission and objectives and that can be planned independently from other company businesses. An SBU can be a company division, a product line within a division, or sometimes a single product or brand.

Strategic planning The process of developing and maintaining a strategic fit between the organization's goals and capabilities and its changing marketing opportunities. It involves defining a clear company mission, setting supporting objectives, designing a sound business portfolio, and coordinating functional strategies.

Style A basic and distinctive mode of expression.

Subculture A group of people with shared value systems based on common life experiences and situations.

Supermarket Large, low-cost, low-margin, high-volume, self-service store that carries a wide variety of food, laundry, and household products.

Superstore A store almost twice the size of a regular supermarket that carries a large assortment of routinely purchased food and nonfood items and offers services such as dry cleaning, post offices, photo finishing, check cashing, bill paying, lunch counters, car care, and pet care.

Survey research The gathering of primary data by asking people questions about their knowledge, attitudes, preferences, and buying behavior.

Systems selling Buying a packaged solution to a problem from a single seller thus avoiding all the separate decisions involved in a complex buying situation.

Target costing Pricing that starts with an ideal selling price, then targets costs that will ensure that the price is met.

Target market A set of buyers sharing common needs or characteristics that the company decides to serve.

Tariff A tax levied by a government against certain imported products. Tariffs are designed to raise revenue or to protect domestic firms.

Team selling Using teams of people from sales, marketing, engineering, finance, technical support, and even upper management to service large, complex accounts.

Technological environment Forces that create new technologies, creating new product and market opportunities.

Telemarketing Using the telephone to sell directly to customers.

Territorial sales force structure A sales force organization that assigns each salesperson to an exclusive geographic territory in which that salesperson sells the company's full line.

Test marketing The stage of new-product development in which the product and marketing program are tested in more realistic market settings.

Third-party logistics provider An independent logistics provider that performs any or all of the functions required to get their clients' product to market.

Total quality management (TQM) Programs designed to constantly improve the quality of products, services, and marketing processes.

Transaction A trade between two parties that involves at least two things of value, agreed-upon conditions, a time of agreement, and a place of agreement.

Undifferentiated marketing A market-coverage strategy in which a firm decides to ignore market segment differences and go after the whole market with one offer.

Unsought product Consumer product that the consumer either does not know about or knows about but does not normally think of buying.

Value analysis An approach to cost reduction in which components are studied carefully to determine if they can be redesigned, standardized, or made by less costly methods of production.

Value-based pricing Setting price based on buyers' perceptions of value rather than on the seller's cost.

Value delivery network The network made up of the company, suppliers, distributors, and ultimately customers who "partner" with each other to improve the performance of the entire system.

Value marketing A principle of enlightened marketing that holds that a company should put most of its resources into value-building marketing investments.

Value pricing Offering just the right combination of quality and good service at a fair price.

Vertical marketing system (VMS) A distribution channel structure in which producers, wholesalers, and retailers act as a unified system. One channel member owns the others, has contracts with them, or has so much power that they all cooperate.

Want The form taken by a human need as shaped by culture and individual personality.

Warehouse club Off-price retailer that sells a limited selection of brand-name grocery items, appliances, clothing, and a hodgepodge of other goods at deep discounts to members who pay annual membership fees.

Webcasting The automatic downloading of customized information of interest to recipients' PCs, affording an attractive channel for delivering Internet advertising or other information content.

Wheel of retailing concept A concept of retailing that states that new types of retailers usually begin as low-margin, low-price, low-status operations but later evolve into higher-priced, higher-service operations, eventually becoming like the conventional retailers they replaced.

Whole-channel view Designing international channels that take into account all the necessary links in distributing the seller's products to final buyers, including the seller's headquarters organization, channels among nations, and channels within nations.

Wholesaler A firm engaged *primarily* in wholesaling activity.

Wholesaling All activities involved in selling goods and services to those buying for resale or business use.

Word-of-mouth influence Personal communication about a product between target buyers and neighbors, friends, family members, and associates.

Workload approach An approach to setting sales force size in which the company groups accounts into different size classes and then determines how many salespeople are needed to call on them the desired number of times.

World Wide Web (or the Web) The user-friendly Internet access standard.

Chapter 1

1. Quotes from Bill Saporito, "Can Nike Get Unstuck?" *Time*, March 30, 1998, pp. 48–53; and Jolie Solomon, "When Cool Goes Cold," *Newsweek*, March 30, 1998, pp. 36–37. Also see Linda Himelstein, "The Swoosh Heard 'Round the World," *Business Week*, May 12, 1997, p. 76; Gary Hamel, "Killer Strategies that Make Shareholders Rich," *Fortune*, June 23, 1997, pp. 70–83; Dottie Enrico, "Nike Hopes to Regain Sales Footing with New Ads," *USA Today*, December 29, 1997, p. 3B; Patricia Sellers, "Four Reasons Nike's Not Cool," *Fortune*, March 30, 1998, pp. 26–27; and Nike's Web page at www.nike.com.

2. See Theodore Levitt's classic article, "Marketing Myopia," *Harvard Business Review*, July–August 1960, pp. 45–56; and Dhananjayan Kashyap, "Marketing Myopia Revisited: "A Look through the 'Colored Glass of a Client,'" *Marketing and Research Today*, August 1996, pp. 197–201.

3. See Andy Cohen, "Federal Express," *Sales & Marketing Management*, November 1996, p. 50. For good discussions of defining and measuring customer value, see Howard E. Butz Jr. and Leonard D. Goodstein, "Measuring Customer Value: Gaining Strategic Advantage," *Organizational Dynamics*, Winter 1996, pp. 63–77; and Robert B. Woodruff, "Customer Value: The Next Source of Competitive Advantage," *Journal of the Academy of Marketing Science*, Spring 1997, pp. 139–153.

4. For more on customer satisfaction, see Jaclyn Fierman, "Americans Can't Get No Satisfaction," *Fortune*, December 11, 1995, p. 186; Richard. A. Spreng, Scott B. MacKenzie, and Richard W. Olshavsky, "A Reexamination of the Determinants of Customer Satisfaction," *Journal of Marketing*, July 1996, pp. 15–32; and Thomas A. Stewart, "A Sat-

isfied Customer Isn't Enough," *Fortune*, July 21, 1997, pp. 112–113.

5. See Claes Fornell, Michael D. Johnson, Eugene W. Anderson, Jaesung Cha, and Barbara Everitt Bryant, "The American Customer Satisfaction Index: Nature, Purpose, and Findings," *Journal of Marketing*, October 1996, pp. 7–18; Becky Ebenkamp, "Can't Get No (Customer) Satisfaction," *Brandweek*, February 2, 1998, p. 21; and Ronald B. Lieber, "Now Are You Satisfied? The 1998 American Customer Satisfaction Index," *Fortune*, February 16, 1998, pp. 161–164.

6. Thomas O. Jones and W. Earl Sasser Jr. "Why Satisfied Customers Defect," *Harvard Business Review*, November–December 1995, pp. 88–99; and Steve Lewis, "All or Nothing: Customers Must Be 'Totally Satisfied,'" Marketing News, March 2, 1998, pp. 11–12. For other examples, see Roger Sant, "Did He Jump or Was He Pushed?" *Marketing News*, May 12, 1997, pp. 2, 21.

7. Thomas E. Caruso, "Got a Marketing Topic? Kotler Has an Opinion," *Marketing News*, June 8, 1992, p. 21.

8. Lois Therrien, "Motorola and NEC: Going for Glory," *Business Week*, special issue on quality, 1991, pp. 60–61. For more on quality, see Roland T. Rust, Anthony J. Zahorik, and Timothy L. Keiningham, "Return on Quality (ROQ): Making Service Quality Financially Accountable," *Journal of Marketing*, April 1995, pp. 58–70; Martha T. Moore, "Is TQM Dead?" *USA Today*, October 17, 1995, pp. B1–B2; and Lakshmi U. Tatikonda and Rao J. Tatikonda, "Measuring and Reporting Costs of Quality," *Production and Inventory Management Journal*, Issue 2, 1996, pp. 1–7.

9. See Cyndee Miller, "TQM Out; 'Continuous Process Improvement' In," *Marketing News*," May 9, 1994, pp. 5, 10; Roland T. Rust, Anthony J. Zahorik, and

Timothy L. Keiningham, "Return on Quality (ROQ): Making Service Quality Financially Accountable," *Journal of Marketing*, April 1995, pp. 58–70; Martha T. Moore, "Is TQM Dead?" *USA Today*, October 17, 1995, pp. B1–B2; and Lakshmi U. Tatikonda and Rao J. Tatikonda, "Measuring and Reporting Costs of Quality," *Production and Inventory Management Journal*, issue 2, 1996, pp. 1–7; and George Thorne, "TQM Connects All Segments of Marketing," *Advertising Age's Business Marketing*, March 1998, p 34.

10. See James C. Anderson, Hakan Hakansson, and Jan Johanson, "Dyadic Business Relationships within a Business Network Context," *Journal of Marketing*, October 15, 1994, pp. 1–15. For more discussion of relationship marketing, see Thomas W. Gruen, "Relationship Marketing: The Route to Marketing Efficiency and Effectiveness," *Business Horizons*, November–December 1997, pp. 32–38; and John V. Petrof, "Relationship Marketing: The Emperor in Used-Clothes," *Business Horizons*, March–April 1998, pp. 79–82.

11. Edwin McDowell, "Ritz-Carlton's Keys to Good Service," *New York Times*, March 31, 1993, p. 1; Don Peppers, "Digitizing Desire," *Forbes*, April 10, 1995, p. 76; and Ginger Conlon, "True Romance," *Sales & Marketing Management*, May 1996, pp. 85–89.

12. Andy Cohen, "It's Party Time for Saturn," *Sales & Marketing Management*, June 1994, p. 19; and T. L. Stanley, Betsy Spethman, Terry Lefton, and Karen Benezra, "Brand Builders," *Brandweek*, March 20, 1995, p. 20.

13. For example, see Bill Stoneman, "Banking on Customers," *American Demographics*, February 1997, pp. 37–41.

14. For more discussion on demand states, see Philip Kotler, *Marketing Management: Analysis, Planning, Implementa-*

tion, and Control, 10th ed. (Upper Saddle River, NJ: Prentice Hall, 2000), chapter 1.

15. See Kevin J. Clancy and Robert S. Shulman, "Breaking the Mold," *Sales & Marketing Management*, January 1994, pp. 82–84; James R. Rosenfield, "Plugging the Leaky Bucket," *Sales and Marketing Management*, October 1994, pp. 34–36; Douglas Pruden, "Retention Marketing Gains Spotlight," *Brandweek*, February 6, 1995, p. 15; Thomas O. Jones and W. Earl Sasser Jr., "Why Satisfied Customers Defect," *Harvard Business Review*, November–December 1995, pp. 88–99; and Susan Fournier, Susan Dobscha, and David Glen Mick, "Preventing the Premature Death of Relationship Marketing," *Harvard Business Review*, January–February 1998, pp. 42–50.

16. For more on assessing customer value, see Gordon A. Wyner, "Customer Valuation: Linking Behavior and Economics," *Marketing Research*, Summer 1996, pp. 36–38; Wyner, "Which Customers Will Be Valuable in the Future?" *Marketing Research*, Fall 1996, pp. 44–46; Bill Stoneman, "Banking on Customers," *American Demographics*, February 1997.

17. Barry Farber and Joyce Wycoff, "Customer Service: Evolution and Revolution," *Sales & Marketing Management*, May 1991, p. 47. Also see Jaclyn Fierman, "Americans Can't Get No Satisfaction," *Fortune*, December 11, 1995, pp. 186–194.

18. See Don E. Schultz, "Traditional Marketers Have Become Obsolete," *Marketing News*, June 6, 1994, p. 11.

19. Howard Schlossberg, "Customer Satisfaction: Not a Fad, but a Way of Life," *Marketing News*, June 10, 1991, p. 18. Also see Bernard J. Jaworski and Ajay K. Kohli, "Market Orientation: Antecedents and Consequences," *Journal of Marketing*, July 1993, pp. 53–70; and E. K. Valentin, "The Marketing Concept and the Conceptualization of Market Strategy," *Journal of Marketing Theory and Practice*, Fall 1996, pp. 16–27.

20. See "Leaders of the Most Admired," *Fortune*, January 29, 1990, pp. 40–54; and Thomas A. Stewart, "America's

Most Admired Companies," *Fortune*, March 2, 1998, pp. 70–82.

21. Ibid., p. 54.

22. For other examples, and for a good review of nonprofit marketing, see Philip Kotler and Alan R. Andreasen, *Strategic Marketing for Nonprofit Organizations*, 5th ed. (Upper Saddle River, NJ: Prentice Hall, 1996); and William P. Ryan, "The New Landscape for Nonprofits," *Harvard Business Review*, January–February 1999, pp. 127–136. Also see Rachel Zoll, "Hospitals Offer Hotel-Style Perks to Fill Maternity Beds," *Marketing News*, May 12, 1997, p. 11.

23. See Cyndee Miller, "Churches Turn to Research for Help in Saving New Souls," *Marketing News*, April 11, 1994, pp. 1, 2; and Marc Spiegler, "Scouting for Souls," *American Demographics*, March 1996, pp. 42–50.

24. Jeff Smyth, "Non-Profits Get Market-Savvy," *Advertising Age*, May 29, 1995, pp. 1, 7.

25. For more examples, see Philip Kotler and Karen Fox, *Strategic Marketing for Educational Institutions* (Upper Saddle River, NJ: Prentice Hall, 1985); Norman Shawchuck, Philip Kotler, Bruce Wren, and Gustave Rath, *Marketing for Congregations: Choosing to Serve People More Effectively* (Nashville, TN: Abingdon Press, 1993); and Joanne Scheff and Philip Kotler, "How the Arts Can Prosper," *Harvard Business Review*, January–February 1996, pp. 52–62.

26. See Cyndee Miller, "U.S. Postal Service Discovers the Merits of Marketing," *Marketing News*, February 1, 1993, pp. 9, 18; and "USPS Targets Coupons to Change-of-Address Set," *Advertising Age*, March 3, 1997, p. 34.

27. Don Peppers and Martha Rogers, *The One-to-One Future* (New York: Doubleday, 1993), p. 315.

28. For more on the basics of using the Internet, see Raymond D. Frost and Judy Strauss, *The Internet: A New Marketing Tool—1998* (Upper Saddle River, NJ: Prentice Hall, 1998).

29. "International Data Corp.—Report: Global Market Forecast for Internet Usage and Commerce," *CIO*, April 1, 1998, p. 46. Internet usage statistics obtained from various CommerceNet reports (see www.commerce.net/nielsen/),

June 1998. Consult this site for the most recent statistics. Also see Ted Bridis, "Report: Internet Growing Exponentially," *The Durham Herald-Sun*, April 16, 1998, p. A1.

30. Robert D. Hof, "The 'Click Here' Economy," *Business Week*, June 22, 1998, pp. 122–128.

31. Wallys W. Conhaim, "E-Commerce," *Link-Up*, March–April 1998, pp. 8–10.

32. Peter H. Lewis, "Getting Down to Business on the Net," *The New York Times*, June 19, 1994, 3, 1:2. Also see John Deighton, "The Future of Interactive," *Harvard Business Review*, November–December 1996, pp. 151–162; Debora Spar and Jeffrey Bussgang, "The Net," *Harvard Business Review*, May–June 1996, pp. 125–133; and Andy Reinhardt, "Zooming Down the I-Way," *Business Week*, April 7, 1997, pp. 76–87.

33. See William S. Stavropoulos, "Environmentalism's Third Wave," *Executive Speeches*, August/September 1996, pp. 28–30; and Stuart L. Hart, "Beyond Greening: Strategies for a Sustainable World," *Harvard Business Review*, January–February 1997, pp. 67–76.

34. Richard C. Whitely, *The Customer-Driven Company* (Reading, MA: Addison-Wesley, 1991); Charles Sewell; *Customers for Life: How to Turn the One-Time Buyer into a Lifetime Customer* (New York: Pocket Books, 1990); Joan K. Cannie, *Turning Lost Customers into Gold: And the Art of Achieving Zero Defections* (New York: Amacom, 1993); Ron Zemke and Thomas K. Connellan, *Sustaining Knock Your Socks Off Service* (New York: Amacom, 1993); Richard Cross and Janet Smith, *Customer Bonding: The Five-Point System for Maximizing Customer Loyalty* (Chicago: NTC Business Books, 1994); and Frederick F. Reichheld, *The Loyalty Effect* (Boston: Harvard Business School Press, 1996).

Chapter 2

1. Quotes from David Kirkpatrick, "Intel's Amazing Profit Machine," *Fortune*, February 17, 1997, pp. 60–72; and Damon Darlin, "Intel's Palace," *Forbes*, September 9, 1996, pp. 42–43. Also see Andy Reinhardt, "Pentium: The Next Generation," *Business Week*, May 12,

1997, pp. 42–43; "The Fortune 500 Largest Firms," *Fortune*, April 22, 1998, pp. F1–F2; and Brent Schlender, "The New Man Inside Intel," May 11, 1998, pp. 161–162.

2. For a more detailed discussion of corporate and business-level strategic planning as they apply to marketing, see Philip Kotler, *Marketing Management: Analysis, Planning, Implementation, and Control*, 10th ed. (Upper Saddle River, NJ: Prentice Hall, 2000), chapter 3.

3. The above examples are from Romauld A. Stone, "Mission Statements Revisited," *SAM Advanced Management Journal*, Winter 1996, pp. 31–37; and Rhymer Rigby, "Mission Statements," *Management Today*, March 1998, pp. 56–58.

4. Romauld A. Stone, "Mission Statements Revisited," p. 33.

5. See Bradley Johnson, "Bill Gates' Vision of Microsoft in Every Home," *Advertising Age*, December 19, 1994, pp. 14–15. For more on mission statements, see J. W. Graham and W. C. Havlick, *Mission Statements: A Guide to the Corporate and Nonprofit Sectors* (New York: Garland Publishing, 1994); P. Jones and L. Kahaner, *Say It and Live It: The 50 Corporate Mission Statements That Hit the Mark* (New York: Doubleday, 1995); and Thomas A. Stewart, "A Refreshing Change: Vision Statements That Make Sense," *Fortune*, September 30, 1996, pp. 195–196.

6. Gilbert Fuchsberg, " 'Visioning' Mission Becomes Its Own Mission," *The Wall Street Journal*, January 7, 1994, B1, 3.

7. See Linda Grant, "Monsanto's Bet: There's Gold in Going Green," *Fortune*, April 14, 1997, pp. 116–118.

8. For an interesting discussion of assessing the business portfolio, see John O. Whitney, "Strategic Renewal of Business Units," *Harvard Business Review*, July–August 1996, pp. 84–98.

9. See John A. Byrne, "Strategic Planning," *Business Week*, August 26, 1996, pp. 46–51; Pete Bogda, "Fifteen Years Later, the Return of 'Strategy,' " *Brandweek*, February 1997, p. 18; and Diane Sanchez, "Now That's Customer Focus," *Sales & Marketing Management*, April 1998, p. 24.

10. H. Igor Ansoff, "Strategies for Diversifi-cation," *Harvard Business Review*, September–October 1957, pp. 113–24. Also see Philip Kotler, *Kotler on Marketing* (New York: The Free Press, 1999), pp. 46–48.

11. Michael E. Porter, *Competitive Advantage: Creating and Sustaining Superior Performance* (New York: Free Press, 1985); and Michel E. Porter, "What Is Strategy?" *Harvard Business Review*, November–December 1996, pp. 61–78.

12. John C. Narver and Stanley F. Slater, "The Effect of a Market Orientation on Business Profitability," *Journal of Marketing*, October 1990, pp. 20–35. Also see Susan Foreman, "Interdepartmental Dynamics and Market Orientation," *Manager Update*, Winter 1997, pp. 10–19.

13. Myron Magnet, "The New Golden Rule of Business," *Fortune*, February 21, 1994, pp. 60–63.

14. Leslie Brokaw, "The Secrets of Great Planning," *Inc.*, October 1992, p. 152; and Philip Kotler, *Marketing Management: Analysis, Planning, Implementation, and Control*, 10th ed. (Upper Saddle River, NJ: Prentice Hall, 2000), chapter 3.

15. Bradford McKee, "Think Ahead, Set Goals, and Get out of the Office," *Nation's Business*, May 1993, p. 10. For more on small business strategic planning, see Nancy Drozdow, "Tools for Strategy Development in Family Firms," *Sloan Management Review*, Fall 1997, pp. 75–88; and Wendy M. Beech, "In It for the Long Haul," *Black Enterprise*, March 1998, p. 25.

16. The four P classification was first suggested by E. Jerome McCarthy, *Basic Marketing: A Managerial Approach* (Homewood, IL: Irwin, 1960). For more discussion of this classification scheme, see Walter van Waterschoot and Christophe Van den Bulte, "The 4P Classification of the Marketing Mix Revisited," *Journal of Marketing*, October 1992, pp. 83–93; and Michael G. Harvey, Robert F. Lusch, and Branko Cavarkapo, "A Marketing Mix for the 21st Century," *Journal of Marketing Theory and Practice*, Fall 1996, pp. 1–15.

17. For more on marketing plans, see Jay Winchester, "What's the Plan?" *Sales &*

Marketing Management, October 1997, pp. 73–78.

18. For a good discussion of gaining advantage through implementation effectiveness versus strategic differentiation, see Michael E. Porter, "What Is Strategy," *Harvard Business Review*, November–December 1996, pp. 61–78.

19. Brain Dumaine, "Why Great Companies Last," *Business Week*, January 16, 1995, p. 129. See James C. Collins and Jerry I. Porras, *Built to Last: Successful Habits of Visionary Companies* (New York: HarperBusiness, 1995); and Geoffrey Brewer, "Firing Line: What Separates Visionary Companies from All the Rest?" *Performance*, June 1995, pp. 12–17.

20. Joseph Winski, "One Brand, One Manager," *Advertising Age*, August 20, 1987, p. 86. Also see Jack Neff, "P&G Redefines the Brand Manager," *Advertising Age*, October 13, 1997, pp. 1, 18; Alan J. Bergstrom, "Brand management Poised for Change," *Marketing News*, July 7, 1997, p. 5; and James Bell, Brand management for the Next Millennium," *The Journal of Business Strategy*, March–April 1998, p. 7.

21. For more complete discussions of marketing organization approaches and issues, see Robert W. Ruekert, Orville C. Walker Jr., and Kenneth J. Roering, "The Organization of Marketing Activities: A Contingency Theory of Structure and Performance," *Journal of Marketing*, Winter 1985, pp. 13–25; Ravi S. Achrol, "Evolution of the Marketing Organization: New Forms for Turbulent Environments," *Journal of Marketing*, October 1991, pp. 77–93; and Geoffrey Brewer, "Love the Ones You're With," *Sales & Marketing Management*, February 1997, pp. 38–45.

22. For details, see Kotler, *Marketing Management: Analysis, Planning, Implementation, and Control*.

Chapter 3

1. Quotes from James R. Rosenfield, "Millennial Fever," *American Demographics*, December 1997, pp. 47–51; Keith Naughton and Bill Vlasic, "The Nostalgia Boom: Why the Old Is New Again," *Business Week*, March 23, 1998, pp. 58–64, and "New Beetles:

Drivers Wanted," accessed on-line at www.vw.com/cars/newbeetle/main.html August 11, 1998. Also see Greg Farrell, "Getting the Bugs Out," *Brandweek*, April 6, 1998, pp. 30–40; and "Beetle Mania," *Adweek*, July 13, 1998, p. 24.

2. World POPClock, U.S. Census Bureau, www.census.gov, May 1998. This Web site provides continuously updated projections of the world population.

3. Sally D. Goll, "Marketing: China's (Only) Children Get the Royal Treatment," *Wall Street Journal*, February 8, 1995, pp. B1, B3.

4. See Diane Crispell, "Generations to 2025," *American Demographics*, January 1995, p. 4; and POPClock Projection, U.S. Census Bureau, www.census.gov, May 1998.

5. Crispell, "Generations to 2025," p. 4; and Brad Edmondson, "Children in 2001," *American Demographics*, March 1997, pp. 14–15.

6. See Diane Crispell, "Married Couples Endure," *American Demographics*, January 1998, p. 39; and www.census.gov/population/projections/nation/hh-fam/table5n.txt.

7. Judith Waldrop, "What Do Working Women Want?" *American Demographics*, September 1994, pp. 36–38; Patricia Braus, "Sorry Boys—Donna Reed Is Still Dead," *American Demographics*, September 1995, pp. 13–14; and "Just Why Do Wives Work?" *Business Week*, June 15, 1998, p. 30.

8. Dan Fost, "Americans on the Move," *American Demographics*, Tools Supplement, January/February 1997, pp. 10–13.

9. See Kevin Heubusch, "Small Is Beautiful," *American Demographics*, January 1998, pp. 43–49.

10. See Thomas Moore, "Different Folks, Different Strokes," *Fortune*, September 16, 1985, pp. 65–68; and "Looking at Expansion?" *Home Textiles Today*, April 6, 1998, p. 172.

11. See Fabian Linden, "In the Rearview Mirror," *American Demographics*, April 1984, pp. 4–5; Peter Francese, "America at Mid-Decade," *American Demographics*, February 1995, pp. 23–29; Rebecca Piirto Heath, "The New Working Class," *American Demographics*, January 1998, pp. 51–55; and *Digest of Education Statistics 1997*, National Center for Educa-

tion Statistics, January 1998, at http://nces01.ed.gov/pubs/digest97/.

12. See "A True Melting Pot," *Advertising Age*, February 17, 1997, p. S2; "Foreign-Born Diversity," *American Demographics*, July 1997, p. 33; Nancy Coltun Webster, "Multicultural," *Advertising Age*, November 17, 1997, pp. S1–S2; and "Diversity," *Advertising Age*, February 16, 1998, pp. S1, S14.

13. Dan Frost, "The Fun Factor: Marketing Recreation to the Disabled," *American Demographics*, February 1998, pp. 54–58; and Michelle Wirth Fellman, "Selling IT Goods to Disabled End-Users," *Marketing News*, March 15, 1999, pp. 1, 17.

14. James W. Hughes, "Understanding the Squeezed Consumer," *American Demographics*, July 1991, pp. 44–50.

15. See U.S. Census Bureau, Income Inequity—Table 2, February 25, 1997, at www.census.gov/hes/income/incineq/p60tb2.html.

16. David Leonhardt, "Two-Tier Marketing," *Business Week*, March 17, 1997, pp. 82–90.

17. For more discussion, see the "Environmentalism" section. Also see Michael E. Porter and Claas van der Linde, "Green and Competitive: Ending the Stalemate," *Harvard Business Review*, September–October 1995, pp. 120–134; William S. Stavropoulos, "Environmentalism's Third Wave," *Executive Speeches*, August/September 1996, pp. 28–30; Stuart L. Hart, "Beyond Greening: Strategies for a Sustainable World," *Harvard Business Review*, January–February 1997, pp. 67–76; and Jacquelyn Ottman, "Environment Winners Show Sustainable Strategies," *Marketing News*, April 27, 1998, p. 6.

18. See M. F. Wolff, "Real R&D Spending Increase Forecast for 1998," *Research Technology Management*, March–April, 1998, p. 6.

19. For a summary of U.S. legal developments in marketing, see Louis W. Stern and Thomas L. Eovaldi, *Legal Aspects of Marketing Strategy: Antitrust and Consumer Protection Issues* (Upper Saddle River, NJ: Prentice Hall, 1984); and Robert J. Posch, Jr., *The Complete Guide to Marketing and the Law* (Upper Saddle River, NJ: Prentice Hall, 1988).

For more on the study of public policy and marketing issues, see Michael B. Mazis, "Marketing and Public Policy: Prospects for the Future," *Journal of Public Policy and Marketing*, Spring 1997, pp. 139–143.

20. For more on today's shifting values, see Chip Walker and Elissa Moses, "The Age of Self-Navigation," *American Demographics*, September 1996, pp. 36–42; and Paul H. Ray, "The Emerging Culture," *American Demographics*, February 1997, pp. 29–34.

21. See Cyndee Miller, "Trendspotters: 'Dark Ages' Ending; So Is Cocooning," *Marketing News*, February 3, 1997, pp. 1, 16.

22. Rebecca Piirto Heath, "The Frontier of Psychographics," *American Demographics*, July 1996, pp. 38–43.

23. Also see V. Kasturi Rangan, Sohel Karim, and Sheryl K. Sandberg, "Do Better at Doing Good," *Harvard Business Review*, May–June 1996, pp. 42–54; Julie Garrett and Lisa Rochlin, "Cause Marketers Must Learn to Play by Rules," *Marketing News*, May 12, 1997, p. 4; and Sarah Lorge, "Is Cause-Related Marketing Worth It?" *Sales & Marketing Management*, June 1998, p. 72.

24. Bill McDowell, "New DDB Needham Report: Consumers Want It All," *Advertising Age*, November 1996, pp. 32–33.

25. Jennifer Harrison, "Advertising Joins the Journal of the Soul," *American Demographics*, June 1997, pp. 22–28; and David B. Wolfe, "The Psychological Center of Gravity," *American Demographics*, April 1998, pp. 16–19.

26. See Carl P. Zeithaml and Valerie A. Zeithaml, "Environmental Management: Revising the Marketing Perspective," *Journal of Marketing*, Spring 1984, pp. 46–53.

27. Howard E. Butz Jr. and Leonard D. Goodstein, "Measuring Customer Value: Gaining the Strategic Advantage," *Organizational Dynamics*, Winter 1996, pp. 66–67.

Chapter 4

1. Quotes from Susan Caminiti, "A Star Is Born," *Fortune*, special issue on "The Tough New Consumer," Autumn/Winter 1993, pp. 44–47. Also see Terry Lefton, "B&D Retools with Quantum," *Brandweek*, July 5, 1993, p. 4; Roy Furchgott,

"Opening Up Europe," *Business Week,* June 3, 1996, p. 82; Ken Miller, "Where You Really Hear Consumers," *Brandweek,* January 20, 1998, p. 17; and Amy Barrett, "Home Improvement at Black & Decker," *Business Week,* May 11, 1998, pp. 54–55.

2. "Harnessing the Data Explosion," *Sales & Marketing Management,* January 1987, p. 31; Joseph M. Winski, "Gentle Rain Turns into Torrent," *Advertising Age,* June 3, 1991, p. 34; David Shenk, *Data Smog: Surviving the Information Glut* (San Francisco: HarperSanFrancisco, 1997); Nancy Doucette, "Relieving Information Overload," *Rough Notes,* February 1998, pp. 26–27; and Diane Trommer, "Information Overload—Study Finds Intranet Users Overwhelmed with Data," *Electronic Buyers' News,* April 20, 1998, p. 98.

3. Alice LaPlante, "Still Drowning!" *Computer World,* March 10, 1997, pp. 69–70.

4. See Thomas A. Stewart, "What Information Costs," *Fortune,* July 10, 1995, pp. 119–121.

5. See Jeffrey Rotfeder and Jim Bartimo, "How Software Is Making Food Sales a Piece of Cake," *Business Week,* July 2, 1990, pp. 54–55; and Terence P. Pare, "How to Find Out What They Want," *Fortune,* special issue on "The Tough New Consumer," Autumn/Winter 1993, pp. 39–41; and Geoffrey Brewer, "The Customer Stops Here," *Sales & Marketing Management,* March 1998, pp. 31–36.

6. For good discussions of marketing intelligence systems, see David B. Montgomery and Charles Weinberg, "Toward Strategic Intelligence Systems," *Marketing Management,* Winter 1998, pp. 44–52; and Morris C. Attaway, Sr., "A Review of Issues Related to Gathering and Assessing Competitive Intelligence," *American Business Review,* January 1998, pp. 25–35.

7. For a review of marketing models, see Gary Lilien, Philip Kotler, and Sridhar Moorthy, *Marketing Models* (Upper Saddle River, NJ: Prentice Hall, 1992); and Gary Lilien and Arvind Rangaswamy, *Marketing Engineering: Marketing Analysis and Planning in an Information Age* (Addison Wesley Longman, 1998).

8. For more on research firms that supply marketing information, see Jack Honomichl, "Honomichl 50," special section, *Marketing News,* June 8, 1998, pp. H1–H33; and Honomichl, "Honomichl Global 25," special section, *Marketing News,* August 17, 1998, pp. H1–H23.

9. "Researching Researchers," *Marketing Tools,* September 1996, pp. 35–36.

10. See Marydee Ojala, "The Daze of Future Business Research," *Online,* January–February 1998, pp. 78–80; and Guy Kawasaki, "Get Your Facts Here," *Forbes,* March 23, 1998, p. 156.

11. Justin Martin, "Ignore Your Customer," *Fortune,* May 1, 1995, pp. 121–126; and "Even Executives Are Losing Their Offices," *HR Magazine,* March 1998, p. 77. Also see William B. Helmreich, "Louder Than Words: On-Site Observational Research," *Marketing News,* March 1, 1999, p. 16.

12. Justin Martin, "Ignore Your Customers," p. 126.

13. See James C. Raymondo, "Confession of a Nielsen Household," *American Demographics,* March 1997, pp. 24–31; and Brad Edmondson, "TV Execs to Nielsen: Get SMART," *American Demographics,* October 1997, pp. 10–15.

14. Rebecca Piirto Heather, "Future Focus Groups," *American Demographics,* January 1994, p. 6. For more on focus groups, see Thomas L. Greenbaum, "Focus Group by Video Next Trend of the '90s," *Marketing News,* July 29, 1996, p. 4; Howard Furmansky, and "Debunking the Myths about Focus Groups," *Marketing News,* June 23, 1997, p. 2; and Judith Langer, "15 Myths of Qualitative Research: It's Conventional, but Is It Wisdom?" *Marketing News,* March 1, 1999, p. 13.

15. Diane Crispell, "People Talk, Computers Listen," *American Demographics,* October 1989, p. 8; Peter J. DePaulo and Rick Weitzer, "Interactive Phones Technology Delivers Survey Data Quickly," *Marketing News,* June 6, 1994, pp. 33–34; Peter Francese, "Managing Marketing Information," *American Demographics,* September 1995, pp. 56–62; Emil E. Becker, "Automated Interviewing Has Advantages," *Marketing News,* January 2, 1995, p. 9; and

Thomas Kiely, "Wired Focus Groups," *Harvard Business Review,* January–February 1998, pp. 12–16.

16. For a discussion of the importance of the relationship between market researchers and research users, see Christine Moorman, Gerald Zaltman, and Rohit Deshpande, "Relationships between Providers and Users of Market Research: The Dynamics of Trust within and between Organizations," *Journal of Marketing Research,* August 1992, pp. 314–328; Christine Moorman, Rohit Deshpande, and Gerald Zaltman, "Factors Affecting Trust in Market Research Relationships," *Journal of Marketing,* January 1993, pp. 81–101; Arlene Farber Sirkin, "Maximizing the Client-Researcher Partnership," *Marketing News,* September 13, 1994, p. 38; Pippa Considine, "Divided by a Common Cause," *Campaign,* September 19, 1997, p. 43; and Kevin P. Lonnie, "Researchers Must Show Their Findings to Clients," *Marketing News,* May 11, 1998, p. 4.

17. See Nancy Levenburg and Tom Dandridge, "Can't Afford Research? Try Miniresearch," *Marketing News,* March 31, 1997, p.19.

18. Jack Honomichl, "Honomichl Global 25," special section, *Marketing News,* August 17, 1998, pp. H1–H23; Cyndee Miller, "Research Firms Go Global to Make Revenue Grow," *Marketing News,* January 6, 1997, pp. 1, 22; and "International Expansion Slows to 7% Gain," *Advertising Age,* May 25, 1998, p. S3.

19. Many of the examples in this section, along with others, are found in Subhash C. Jain, *International Marketing Management,* 3rd ed. (Boston: PWS-Kent Publishing Company, 1990), pp. 334–39. Also see Jack Honomichl, "Research Cultures Are Different in Mexico, Canada," *Marketing News,* May 5, 1993, pp. 12–13; Naghi Namakforoosh, "Data Collection Methods Hold Key to Research in Mexico," *Marketing News,* August 29, 1994, p. 28; Thomas L. Greenbaum, "Understanding Focus Group Research Abroad," *Marketing News,* June 3, 1996, pp. H14, H36; and Jack Edmonston, "U.S., Overseas Differences Abound," *Advertising Age's Business Marketing,* January 1998, p. 32.

20. Jain, *International Marketing Management*, p. 338.

21. "MRA Study Shows Refusal Rates Are Highest at Start of Process," *Marketing News*, August 16, 1993, p. A15; and "Private Eyes," *Marketing Tools*, January–February 1996, pp. 31–32. Also see John Hagel III and Jeffrey F. Rayport, "The Coming Battle for Consumer Information," *Harvard Business Review*, January–February 1997, pp. 53–65.

22. Cynthia Crossen, "Studies Galore Support Products and Positions, but Are They Reliable?" *Wall Street Journal*, November 14, 1991, pp. A1, A9. Also see Betsy Spethmann, "Cautious Consumers Have Surveyers Wary," *Advertising Age*, June 10, 1991, p. 34.

23. For example, see Betsy Peterson, "Ethics Revisited," *Marketing Research*, Winter 1996, pp. 47–48. For discussion of a framework for ethical marketing research, see Naresh K. Malhotra and Gina L. Miller, "An Integrated Model of Ethical Decisions in Marketing Research," *Journal of Business Ethics*, February 1998, pp. 263–280.

Chapter 5

1. Quotes from Richard A. Melcher, "Tune-Up Time for Harley," *Business Week*, April 8, 1997, pp. 90–94; Ian P. Murphy, "Aided by Research, Harley Goes Whole Hog," *Marketing News*, December 2, 1996, pp. 16, 17; and Dyan Machan, "Is the Hog Going Soft?" *Forbes*, March 10, 1997, pp. 114–119. Also see "Harley-Davidson Announces Record Fourth Quarter Earnings and 12th Consecutive Year of Record Earnings," *Harley-Davidson News*, accessed at www.harley-davidson.com, January 22, 1998; and Sarah Lorge, "Revving Up Customers," *Sales & Marketing Management*, June 1998, p. 15.

2. For current population estimates, see the U.S. and world POP clocks at www.census.gov.

3. Several models of the consumer buying process have been developed by marketing scholars. For a summary, see Leon G. Schiffman and Leslie Lazar Kanuk, *Consumer Behavior*, 6th ed. (Upper Saddle River, NJ: Prentice Hall, 1997), pp. 560–564.

4. Nancy Coltun Webster, "Multicultural," *Advertising Age*, November 17, 1997, pp. S1–S2.

5. Jacquelyn Lynn, "Tapping the Riches of Bilingual Markets," *Management Review*, March 1995, pp. 56–61. Also see "Targeting the Hispanic Market," *Advertising Age*, special section, March 31, 1997, pp. A1–A12; Meredith Lockard, "Hispanics Seek Respect for Culture," *Target Marketing*, May 1998, p. 14; and Jeff Jensen, "Marketing to Hispanics," *Advertising Age*, August 24, 1998, pp. S1–S2.

6. Webster, "Multicultural," p. S1.

7. See Christy Fisher, "Black, Hip, and Primed (to Shop)," *American Demographics*, September 1996, pp. 52–58; Cliff Edwards, "Study Says Blacks Spend More on Big Ticket Items Than Whites," *Marketing News*, September 23, 1996, p. 27; and Alice Z. Cuneo, "New Sears Label Woos Black Women," *Advertising Age*, May 5, 1997, p. 6.

8. Webster, "Multicultural," p. S1; and Saul Gitlin, "A Yen for Brands," January 5, 1998, p. 17.

9. See Christy Fisher, "Marketers Straddle Asian-America Curtain," *Advertising Age*, November 7, 1994; John Steere, "How Asian-Americans Make Purchasing Decisions," *Marketing News*, March 13, 1995, p. 9; "Asian Demographics," *Media Week*, April 17, 1995, p. S1; and Brad Edmondson, "Asian Americans in 2001," *American Demographics*, February 1997, pp. 16–17.

10. See Rick Adler, "Stereotypes Won't Work with Seniors Anymore," *Advertising Age*, November 11, 1996, p. 32; Richard Lee, "The Youth Bias in Advertising," *American Demographics*, January 1997, pp. 47–50; Cheryl Russell, "The Ungraying of America," *American Demographics*, July 1997, pp. 12–15; and D. Allen Kerr, "Where There's Gray, There's Green," *Marketing News*, May 25, 1998, p. 2.

11. For more on social class, see Schiffman and Kanuk, *Consumer Behavior*, chapter 13; David Leonhardt, "Two-Tier Marketing," *Business Week*, March 17, 1997, p. 82; and Rebecca Piirto Heath, "The New Working Class," *American Demographics*, January 1998, pp. 51–55.

12. Patricia Sellers, "The Best Way to Reach Your Buyers," *Fortune*, special issue on "The Tough New Consumer,"

Autumn/Winter, 1993, pp. 14–17. Also see, Chip Walker, "Word of Mouth," *American Demographics*, July 1995, pp. 38–43.

13. For these and other examples, see Schiffman and Kanuk, *Consumer Behavior*, chapter 17.

14. Debra Goldman, "Spotlight Men," *Adweek*, August 13, 1990, pp. M1–M6; Nancy Ten Kate, "Who Buys the Pants in the Family?" *American Demographics*, January 1992, p. 12; and Laura Zinn, "Real Men Buy Paper Towels, Too," *Business Week*, November 9, 1992, pp. 75–76.

15. Jeffery Zbar, "Hardware Builds Awareness among Women," *Advertising Age*, July 11, 1994, p. 18.

16. David Leonhardt, "Hey Kids, Buy This," *Business Week*, June 30, 1997, pp. 62–67. Also see Kay M. Palan and Robert E. Wilkes, "Adolescent-Parent Interaction in Family Decisions," *Journal of Consumer Research*, September 1997, pp. 159–169; Chankon Kim and Hanjoon Lee, "Development of Family Triadic Measures for Children's Purchase Influence," *Journal of Marketing Research*, August 1997, pp. 307–321; and Judann Pollack, "Foods Targeting Children Aren't Just Child's Play," *Advertising Age*, March 1, 1999, p. 16.

17. See Rebecca Piirto, "VALS the Second Time," *American Demographics*, July 1991, p. 6; and Rebecca Piirto, "The Frontier of Psychographics," *American Demographics*, July 1996, pp. 38–43.

18. This and other examples of companies using VALS 2 can be found in Rebecca Piirto, "Measuring Minds in the 1990s," *American Demographics*, December 1990, pp. 35–39; and Piirto, "VALS the Second Time," p. 6. For good discussions of other lifestyle topics, see Basil G. Englis and Michael Solomon, "To Be or Not to Be: Lifestyle Imagery, Reference Groups, and the Clustering of America," *Journal of Advertising*, March 1995, p. 13; and Tom Miller, "Global Segments from 'Strivers' to 'Creatives,'" *Marketing News*, July 20, 1998, p. 11.

19. Myron Magnet, "Let's Go for Growth," *Fortune*, March 7, 1994, p. 70. Also see Timothy R. Graeff, "Consumption Situations and the Effects of Brand Image

on Consumers' Brand Evaluations," *Psychology and Marketing*, January 1997, pp. 49–70; and Dun Gifford, Jr., "Moving Beyond Loyalty," *Harvard Business Review*, March–April 1997, pp. 9–10.

20. See Barbara Marx Hubbard, "Seeking Our Future Potentials," The *Futurist*, May 1998, pp. 29–32.

21. See Leon Festinger, *A Theory of Cognitive Dissonance* (Stanford, CA: Stanford University Press, 1957); and Schiffman and Kanuk, *Consumer Behavior*, pp. 271–272.

22. See Frank Rose, "Now Quality Means Service Too," *Fortune*, April 22, 1991, pp. 97–108; Chip Walker, "Word of Mouth," *American Demographics*, July 1995, p. 40; Thomas O. Jones and W. Earl Sasser, Jr., "Why Satisfied Customers Defect," *Harvard Business Review*, November–December 1995, pp. 88–99; and Roger Sant, "Did He Jump or Was He Pushed?" *Marketing News*, May 12, 1997, pp. 2, 21.

23. The following discussion draws heavily from Everett M. Rogers, *Diffusion of Innovations*, 3rd ed. (New York: Free Press, 1983). Also see Hubert Gatignon and Thomas S. Robertson, "A Propositional Inventory for New Diffusion Research," *Journal of Consumer Research*, March 1985, pp. 849–867; and Rogers, *Diffusion of Innovations*, 4th ed. (New York: Free Press, 1995).

24. Mir Maqbool Alam Khan, "Kellogg Reports Brisk Cereal Sales in India," *Advertising Age*, November 14, 1994, p. 60.

25. Sarah Lorge, "Purchasing Power," *Sales & Marketing Management*, June 1998, pp. 43–46.

26. Patrick J. Robinson, Charles W. Faris, and Yoram Wind, *Industrial Buying Behavior and Creative Marketing* (Boston: Allyn & Bacon, 1967). Also see Erin Anderson, Weyien Chu, and Barton Weitz, "Industrial Purchasing: An Empirical Exploration of the Buyclass Framework," *Journal of Marketing*, July 1987, pp. 71–86; Cynthia Webster, "Buying Involvement in Purchasing Success," *Industrial Marketing Management*, August 1993, p. 199; and Edward G. Briety, Robert W. Eckles, and Robert R Reeder, *Business Marketing*, 3rd ed. (Upper Saddle River, NJ: Prentice Hall, 1998), pp. 74–82.

27. See Philip Kotler, *Marketing Management: Analysis, Planning, Implementation, and Control*, ninth edition (Upper Saddle River, NJ: Prentice Hall, 1997), pp. 208–209.

28. See John Huey, "The Absolute Best Way to Fly," *Fortune*, May 30, 1994, pp. 121–128; and Anthony Bianco, "Gulfstream's Pilot," *Business Week*, April 14, 1997, pp. 64–76. For more on influence strategies within buying centers, see R. Venkatesh, Ajay K. Kohli, and Gerald Zaltman, "Influence Strategies in Buying Centers," *Journal of Marketing*, October 1995, pp. 71–82; David I. Gilliland and Wesley J. Johnson, "Toward a Model of Business-to-Business Marketing Communications Effects," *Industrial Marketing Management*, January 1997, pp. 15–29; and Philip L. Dawes, Don Y. Lee, and Grahame R. Dowling, "Information Control and Influence in Emergent Buying Centers," *Journal of Marketing*, July 1998, pp. 55–68.

29. Al Ries, "One and the Same," *Sales & Marketing Management*, February 1996, pp. 22–23.

30. Frederick E. Webster, Jr., and Yoram Wind, *Organizational Buying Behavior* (Upper Saddle River, NJ: Prentice hall, 1972), pp. 33–37. Also see Brierty, Eckles, and Reeder, *Business Marketing*, chap. 3.

31. Bonoma, "Major Sales," p. 114. Also see Ajay Kohli, "Determinants of Influence in Organizational Buying: A Contingency Approach," *Journal of Marketing*, July 1989, pp. 50–65.

32. Robinson, Faris, and Wind, *Industrial Buying Behavior*, p. 14.

33. See "Xerox Multinational Supplier Quality Survey," *Purchasing*, January 1995, p. 112.

34. See "What Buyers Really Want," *Sales & Marketing Management*, October 1989, p. 30; "Purchasing Managers Sound Off," *Sales & Marketing Management*, February 1995, pp. 84–85; Thomas Y. Choi and Janet L. Hartley, "An Exploration of Supplier Selection Practices Across the Supply Chain," *Journal of Operations Management*, November 1996, pp. 333–343; and Graig M. Gustin, Patricia J. Daugherty, and Alexander E. Ellinger, "Supplier Selection Decisions in Systems/Software,"

International Journal of Purchasing and Materials Management, Fall 1997, pp. 41–46.

Chapter 6

1. See Kerri Walsh, "Soaps and Detergents," *Chemical Week*, January 28, 1998, pp. 27–29.

2. Regis McKenna, "Real-Time Marketing," *Harvard Business Review*, July–August 1995, p. 87.

3. Edward Baig, "Platinum Cards: Move Over AmEx," *Business Week*, August 19, 1996, p. 84; and "AmEx's No-Frills Snob Card," *Credit Card Management*, April 1997, pp. 12–14.

4. Laurel Cutler, quoted in "Stars of the 1980s Cast Their Light," *Fortune*, July 3, 1989, p. 76.

5. Robert E. Linneman and John L. Stanton Jr., *Making Niche Marketing Work: How to Grow Bigger by Acting Smaller* (New York: McGraw-Hill, Inc., 1991).

6. See Don Peppers and Martha Rogers, *The One-to-One Future: Building Relationships One Customer at a Time* (New York: Currency/Doubleday, 1993); Tom Andel, "Mass Customization for Markets of One," *Transportation & Distribution*, November 1997, pp. 59–64; and Don Peppers, Martha Rogers, and Bob Dorf, "Is Your Company Ready for One-to-One Marketing?" *Harvard Business Review*, January–February 1999, pp. 151–160.

7. See B. Joseph Pine II, *Mass Customization* (Boston: Harvard Business School Press, 1993); B. Joseph Pine II, Don Peppers, and Martha Rogers, "Do You Want to Keep Your Customers Forever?" *Harvard Business Review*, March–April 1995, pp. 103–114; Christopher W. Hart, "Made to Order," *Marketing Management*, Summer 1996, pp. 11–22; and James H. Gilmore and B. Joseph Pine II, "The Four Faces of Customization," *Harvard Business Review*, January–February 1997, pp. 91–101; and "Toffler: Change—or Else," *Inc*, May 1998, p. 23.

8. See Sarah Schafer, "Have It Your Way," *Inc*, November 18, 1997, pp. 56–64.

9. McKenna, "Real-Time Marketing," p. 87.

10. Jennifer Lawrence, "Don't Look for P&G to Pare Detergents," *Advertising Age*, May 31, 1993, pp. 1, 3.

11. Bruce Hager, "Podunk Is Beckoning," *Business Week*, December 2, 1991, p. 76; and David Greisling, "The Boonies are Booming," *Business Week*, October 9, 1995, pp. 104–110.

12. Leah Nathans Spiro, "Saks Tries on a Petite," *Business Week*, October 7, 1997, p. 8.

13. Pat Sloan and Jack Neff, "With Aging Baby Boomers in Mind, P&G, Den-Mat Plan Launches," *Advertising Age*, April 13, 1998, pp. 3, 38.

14. Alice Z. Cuneo, "Advertisers Target Women, but Market Remains Elusive," *Advertising Age*, November 10, 1997, pp. 1, 24.

15. "Automakers Learn Better Roads to Women's Market," *Marketing News*, October 12, 1992, p. 2; and Jean Halliday, "GM Taps Harris to Help Lure Women," *Advertising Age*, February 17, 1997, pp. 1, 37.

16. Raymond Serafin, "I Am Woman, Hear Me Roar . . . In My Car," *Advertising Age*, November 7, 1994, pp. 1, 8. Also see, Gerry Myers, "Selling to Women," *American Demographics*, April 1996, pp. 36–41; and Mary Louis Quinlin, "Women: We've Come a Long Way, Maybe," *Advertising Age*, February 13, 1999, p. 46.

17. See "The Wealthy," *Advertising Age*, April 3, 1995, p. S28; David Leonhardt, "Two-Tiered Marketing," *Business Week*, March 17, 1997, pp. 82–90; and Rebecca Piirto Heath, "Life on Easy Street," *American Demographics*, April 1997, pp. 33–37.

18. Brian Bremner, "Looking Downscale without Looking Down," *Business Week*, October 8, 1990, pp. 62–67; Cyndee Miller, "The Have-Nots: Firms with the Right Products and Services Succeed among Low-Income Consumers," *Marketing News*, August 1, 1994, pp. 1, 2; Wendy Zellner, "Leave the Driving to Lentzsch," *Business Week*, March 18, 1996, pp. 66–67; and Anne Faircloth, "Value Retailers Go Dollar for Dollar," *Fortune*, July 6, 1998, pp. 164–166.

19. For a detailed discussion of personality and buyer behavior, see Leon G. Schiffman and Leslie Lazar Kanuk, *Consumer Behavior*, 6th ed. (Upper Saddle River, NJ: Prentice Hall, 1997), chapter 5.

20. See Laurie Freeman and Cleveland Horton, "Spree: Honda's Scooters Ride the Cutting Edge," *Advertising Age*, September 5, 1985, pp. 3, 35; and Honda's Web site at www.hondamotorcycle.com/scooter/, June 1998.

21. Mark Maremont, "The Hottest Thing since the Flashbulb," *Business Week*, September 7, 1992. Also see Laura Loro, "Single-Use Cameras Snap the Photo Industry," *Advertising Age*, September 28, 1994, p. 28; and Bruce Nussbaum, "A Camera in a Wet Suit," *Business Week*, June 2, 1997, p. 109.

22. Stowe Shoemaker, "Segmenting the U.S. Travel Market according to Benefits Realized," *Journal of Travel Research*, Winter 1994, pp. 8–21.

23. See Ronald E. Goldsmith, Leisa Reinecke, and Mark Bonn, "An Empirical Study of Heavy Users of Travel Agencies," *Journal of Travel Research*, Summer 1994, pp. 38–43; and Warren Thayer, "Target Heavy Buyers!" *Frozen Food Age*, March 1998, pp. 22–24.

24. See Norton Paley, "Cut out for Success," *Sales & Marketing Management*, April 1994, pp. 43–44. Quote from Erick Schonfeld, "Paging Investors for a Smart Call," *Fortune*, January 15, 1996, p. 117. Also see Lesley Alderman, "Buy a Messaging System That's Right for You—at the Right Price," *Money*, March 1997, pp. 168–170; Christopher Palmeri, "Brand-New Message," *Forbes*, February 9, 1998, pp. 49–50, and Michael J. Himowitz, "A Pager that Talks," *Fortune*, May 11, 1998, pp. 168–170.

25. Daniel S. Levine, "Justice Served," *Sales & Marketing Management*, May 1995, pp. 53–61.

26. V. Kasturi Rangan, Rowland T. Moriarty, and Gordon S. Swartz, "Segmenting Customers in Mature Industrial Markets," *Journal of Marketing*, October 1992, pp. 72–82. Also see "Penetrating Purchaser Personalities," *Marketing Management*, Spring 1995, p. 22.

27. For more on segmenting business markets, see John Berrigan and Carl Finkbeiner, *Segmentation Marketing: New Methods for Capturing Business* (New York: Harper-Business, 1992); Rodney L. Griffith and Louis G. Pol,

"Segmenting Industrial Markets," *Industrial Marketing Management*, no. 23, 1994, pp. 39–46; Sally Dibb and Lyndon Simkin, "Implementation Problems in Industrial Market Segmentation," *Industrial Marketing Management*, No. 23, 1994, pp. 55–63; and Stavros P. Kalafatis and Vicki Cheston, "Normative Models and Practical Applications of Segmentation in Business Markets," *Industrial Marketing Management*, November 1997, pp. 519–530.

28. Marlene L. Rossman, "Understanding Five Nations of Latin America," *Marketing News*, October 11, 1985, p. 10; as cited in Subhash C. Jain, *International Marketing Management*, 3rd ed. (Boston: PWS-Kent Publishing Company, 1990), p. 366.

29. For example, see Philemon Oyewole, "Country Segmentation of the International Market Using ICP-Based Consumption Patterns," *Journal of Global Marketing*, vol. 11, issue 4, 1998, pp. 75–94.

30. Cyndee Miller, "Teens Seen as the First Truly Global Consumer," *Advertising Age*, March 27, 1995, p. 9.

31. Shawn Tully, "Teens: The Most Global Market of All," *Fortune*, May 16, 1994, pp. 90–97. Also see Matthew Klein, "Teen Green," *American Demographics*, February 1998, p. 39.

32. See Joe Schwartz, "Southpaw Strategy," *American Demographics*, June 1988, p. 61; "Few Companies Tailor Products for Lefties," *Wall Street Journal*, August 2, 1989, p. 2; Kate Bertrand, "New-Product Design: Shape of the Future," *Advertising Age's Business Marketing*, July 1991, p. 18; and Greg Cebrzynski, "Burger King: Nation Ready for Left-Handed Whopper," *Nation's Restaurant News*, April 13, 1998, p. 16.

33. See Michael Porter, *Competitive Advantage* (New York: Free Press, 1985), pp. 4–8 and pp. 234–236.

34. Philip Kotler, Gary Armstrong, John Saunders, and Veronica Wong, *Principles of Marketing: The European Edition* (Prentice Hall Europe, 1996), p. 333; and Stephen J. Mraz, "Stealth Stalks the High Seas," *Machine Design*, May 22, 1997, pp. 40–44.

35. Christopher Power, "How to Get Closer to Your Customers," *Business Week*, spe-

cial issue on economies of scale, 1993, pp. 42–45.

36. For an interesting discussion of finding ways to differentiate marketing offers, see Ian C. MacMillan and Rita Gunther McGrath, "Discovering New Points of Differentiation," *Harvard Business Review*, July–August 1997, pp. 133–145.

37. See Tom Peters, *Thriving on Chaos* (New York: Knopf, 1987), pp. 56–57; "Pushing to Improve Quality," *Research and Technology Management*, May–June 1990, pp. 19–23; and Bruce Whitehall, "How Milliken's Action Teams Involve Clients in Quality," *Business Marketing Digest*, first quarter, 1992, pp. 11–17.

38. "Big Flops," *American Demographics*, February 1995, pp. 1, 6.

39. Tim Triplett, "Consumers Show Little Taste for Clear Beverages," *Marketing News*, May 23, 1994, pp. 1, 11.

Chapter 7

1. See "What Lies Behind the Sweet Smell of Success," *Business Week*, February 27, 1984, pp. 139–43; S. J. Diamond, "Perfume Equals Part Mystery, Part Marketing," *Los Angeles Times*, April 22, 1988, section 4, p. 1; Pat Sloan, "Revlon Plans Fragrance Turnaround," *Advertising Age*, February 10, 1997, p. 6; and "Revlon Records Record Full Year and Fourth Quarter Results," press release, www.revlon.com, January 22, 1998. Charlie brand positionings from www.revlon.com/fragrances/, June 1998.

2. Check out the tourism Web pages of these states at www.TravelTex.com, www.michigan.org, and www.iloveny.state.ny.us.

3. See V. Rangan Kasturi, Sohel Karim, and Sheryl K. Sandberg, "Do Better at Doing Good," *Harvard Business Review*, May–June 1996, pp. 42–54; Alan R. Andreasen, Marketing Social Change: Changing Behavior to Promote Health, Social Development, and the Environment (San Francisco: Jossey-Bass Publishers, 1995); and Rance Crain, "Ruth Wooden Wheels and Deals to Lure Ad Council Sponsors," *Advertising Age*, March 9, 1998, p. 34.

4. See Roland T. Rust, Anthony J. Zahorik, and Timothy L. Keiningham, "Return on Quality (ROQ): Making Service Quality Financially Accountable," *Journal of Marketing*, April 1995, pp. 58–70; Valerie A. Zeithaml, Leonard L. Berry, and A. Parasuraman, "The Behavioral Consequences of Service Quality," *Journal of Marketing*, April 1996, pp. 31–46; Otis Port, "The Baldrige's Other Reward," *Business Week*, March 10, 1997, p. 75; and George Thorne, "TQM Connects All Segments of Marketing," *Advertising Age*'s *Business Marketing*, March 1998, p 34.

5. Joseph Weber, "A Better Grip on Hawking Tools," *Business Week*, June 5, 1995, p. 99; Norman C. Remich, Jr., "A Prize Winner," Appliance Manufacturing," August 6, 1996, p. 48; and Craig Levitt, "Keeping the Lights On," *Discount Merchandiser*, September 1997, pp. 73–77. For more on product design, see Peter H. Bloch, "Seeking the Ideal Form: Product Design and Consumer Response," *Journal of Marketing*, July 1995, pp. 16–29.

6. Kurt Badenhausen, "Blind Faith," *Financial World*, July 8, 1996, pp. 51–65. Also see David A. Aaker, *Managing Brand Equity* (New York: The Free Press, 1991); Terry Lefton and Weston Anson, "How Much Is Your Brand Worth?" *Brandweek*, January 26, 1996, pp. 43–44; and David Kiley, "Q&A: Brand Value Rx," *Brandweek*, March 23, 1998, pp. 36–40.

7. Emily DeNitto, "They Aren't Private Labels Anymore—They're Brands," *Advertising Age*, September 13, 1993, p. 8; Warren Thayer, "Loblaws Exec Predicts: Private Labels to Surge," *Frozen Food Age*, May 1996, p. 1; and "President's Choice Continues Brisk Pace," *Frozen Food Age*, March 1998, pp. 17–18.

8. See Patrick Oster, "The Erosion of Brand Loyalty," *Business Week*, July 19, 1993, p. 22; Marcia Mogelonsky, "When Stores Become Brands," *American Demographics*, February 1995, pp. 32–38; John A. Quelch and David Harding, "Brands versus Private Labels: Fighting to Win," *Harvard Business Review*, January–February 1996, pp. 99–109; Stephanie Thompson, "Private Lable Marketers Getting Savvier to Consumption Trends," *Brandweek*, No-

vember 24, 1997, p. 9; and David Dunne and Chakravarthi Narasimham, "The New Appeal of Private Labels," *Harvard Business Review*, May–June 1999, pp. 41–52.

9. See Silvia Sansoni, "Gucci, Armani, and . . . John Paul II?" *Business Week*, May 13, 1996, p. 61; Cyndee Miller, "Seuss Characters Leap From Page into Licensing World," *Marketing News*, April 14, 1997, p. 2; Andrew E. Serwer, "Who Gets What in the Star Wars Toy Deal?" *Fortune*, August 18, 1997, pp. 29–30; and Bart A. Lazar, "Licensing Gives Known Brands New Life," *Advertising Age*, February 16, 1998, p. 8.

10. Terry Lefton, "Warner Brothers' Not Very Looney Path to Licensing Gold," *Brandweek*, February 14, 1994, pp. 36–37; and Robert Scally, "Warner Builds Brand Presence, Strengthens 'Tunes' Franchise," *Discount Store News*, April 6, 1998, p. 33.

11. Phil Carpenter, "Some Cobranding Caveats to Obey," *Marketing News*, November 7, 1994, p. 4; Karen Benezra, "Coke, Mattel Ink Pact for Collectable Barbie," *Brandweek*, October 14, 1996, p. 5; Tobi Elkin, "Brand Builders," *Brandweek*, February 2, 1998, pp. 16–18; and Stenhanie Thompson, "Brand Buddies," *Brandweek*, February 23, 1998, pp. 22–30.

12. David Aaker, "Should You Take Your Brand to Where the Action Is?" *Harvard Business Review*, September–October 1997, pp. 135–145.

13. For more on the use of line and brand extensions and consumer attitudes toward them, see David A. Aaker and Kevin L. Keller, "Consumer Evaluations of Brand Extensions," *Journal of Marketing*, January 1990, pp. 27–41; Susan M. Broniarczyk and Joseph W. Alba, "The Importance of Brand in Brand Extension," *Journal of Marketing Research*, May 1994, pp. 214–228; Srinivas K. Reddy, Susan L. Holak, and Subodh Bhat, "To Extend or Not to Extend: Success Determinants of Line Extensions," *Journal of Marketing Research*, May 1994, pp. 243–262; and Deborah Roedder John, Barbara Loken, and Christopher Joiner, *Journal of Marketing*, January 1998, pp. 19–32.

14. See Bill Abrams, "Marketing," *Wall Street Journal*, May 20, 1982, p. 33; Bernice Kanner, "Package Deals," New York, August 22, 1988, pp. 267–268; and Joan Holleran, "Packaging Speaks Volumes," *Beverage Industry*, February 1998, p. 30.

15. Robert M. McMath, "Chock Full of (Pea)nuts," *American Demographics*, April 1997, p. 60.

16. See Marilyn Stern, "Is This the Ultimate in Recycling?" *Across the Board*, May 1993, pp. 28–31; Peter Sibbald, "Manufacturing for Reuse," *Fortune*, February 6, 1995, pp. 102–112; "Plastics Waste: Germany Beats Recycling Targets," *Chemical Week*, June 5, 1996, p. 22; and Peter L. Grogan, "European Influence," *BioCycle*, September 1997, p. 86.

17. Bro Uttal, "Companies That Serve You Best," *Fortune*, December 7, 1987, p. 116. For an excellent discussion of support services, see James C. Anderson and James A. Narus, "Capturing the Value of Supplementary Services," *Harvard Business Review*, January–February 1995, pp. 75–83.

18. See Paula Mergenbagen, "Product Liability: Who Sues?" *American Demographics*, June 1995, p. 48; "Support Urged for Product Liability Reform," *Industrial Distribution*, April 1997, p. SA3; and Owen Ullmann, "Product Liability Deadlock," *Business Week*, January 12, 1998, p. 51.

19. John Templeman, "A Mercedes in Every Driveway?" *Business Week*, August 26, 1996, pp. 38–40; and Sam Pickens and Dagmar Mussey, "Swatch Taps Zurich Shop to Develop Euro Car Ads," *Advertising Age*, May 19, 1997, p. 32.

20. See Ronald Henkoff, "Service Is Everybody's Business," *Fortune*, June 27, 1994, pp. 48–60; Adrian Palmer and Catherine Cole, *Services Marketing: Principles and Practice* (Upper Saddle River, NJ: Prentice Hall, 1995), pp. 56–60; Valerie Zeithaml and Mary Jo Bitner, Services Marketing (New York: McGraw Hill, 1996), pp. 8–9; and Michael van Biema and Bruce Greenwald, "Managing Our Way to Higher Service-Sector Productivity," *Harvard Business Review*, July–August 1997, pp. 87–95.

21. "Presto! The Convenience Industry: Making Life a Little Simpler," *Business Week*, April 27, 1987, p. 86; also see Ronald Henkoff, "Piety, Profits, and Productivity," *Fortune*, June 1992, pp. 84–85.

22. See James L. Heskett, Thomas O. Jones, Gary W. Loveman, W. Earl Sasser, Jr., and Leonard A. Schlesinger, "Putting the Service-Profit Chain to Work," *Harvard Business Review*, March–April, 1994, pp. 164–174; and James L. Heskett, W. Earl Sasser, Jr., and Leonard A. Schlesinger, *The Service Profit Chain: How Leading Companies Link Profit and Growth to Loyalty, Satisfaction, and Value* (New York: Free Press, 1997). Also see Anthony J. Rucci, Steven P. Kirn, and Richard T. Quinn, "The Employee-Customer-Profit Chain at Sears," *Harvard Business Review*, January–February 1998, pp. 83–97.

23. For excellent discussions of service quality, see A. Parasuraman, Valerie A. Zeithaml, and Leonard L. Berry, "A Conceptual Model of Service Quality and Its Implications for Future Research," *Journal of Marketing*, Fall 1985, pp. 41–50; J. Joseph Cronin, Jr. and Steven A. Taylor, "Measuring Service Quality: A Reexamination and Extension," *Journal of Marketing*, July 1992, pp. 55–68; Parasuraman, Zeithaml, and Berry, "Reassessment of Expectations as a Comparison Standard in Measuring Service Quality: Implications for Further Research," *Journal of Marketing*, January 1994, pp. 111–124; Zeithaml, Berry, and Parasuraman, "The Behavioral Consequences of Service Quality," *Journal of Marketing*, April 1996, pp. 31–46; and Service Competitiveness: An Anglo-US Study," *Business Strategy Review*, Vol. 8, No. 1, 1997, pp. 7–22.

24. See Erika Rasmusson, "Winning Back Angry Customers," *Sales & Marketing Management*, October 1997, p. 131; and Stephen S. Tax, Stephen W. Brown, and Murali Chandrashekaran, "Customer Evaluations of Service Complaint Experiences: Implications for Relationship Marketing," *Journal of Marketing*, April 1998, pp. 60–76.

25. Ronald Henkoff, "Finding and Keeping the Best Service Workers," *Fortune*, October 3, 1994, pp. 110–122.

26. See James L. Heskett, W. Earl Sasser, Jr., and Christopher W. L. Hart, Service Breakthroughs (New York: The Free Press, 1990).

27. Nilly Landau, "Are You Being Served?" *International Business*, March 1995, pp. 38–40; and Omar A El Sawy, "Redesigning the Customer Support Process for the Electronic Economy: Insights from Storage Dimensions," *MIS Quarterly*, December 1997, pp. 457–483. Also see Michael van Biema and Bruce Greenwald, "Managing Our Way to Higher Service-Sector Productivity," *Harvard Business Review*, July–August 1997, pp. 87–95.

28. Philip Cateora, *International Marketing*, 8th ed. (Homewood, IL: Irwin, 1993), p. 270.

29. See Carla Rapoport, "Retailers Go Global," *Fortune*, February 20, 1995, pp. 102–108; "Top 200 Global Retailers," *Stores*, January 1998, pp. S5–S12; and Jeffery Adler, "The Americanization of Global Retailing," *Discount Merchandiser*, February 1998, p. 102.

30. Lee Smith, "What's at Stake in the Trade Talks," *Fortune*, August 27, 1990, pp. 76–77.

Chapter 8

1. Quotes from Lawrence Ingrassia, "Taming the Monster: How Big Companies Can Change," *Wall Street Journal*, December 10, 1992, pp. A1, A6; William H. Miller, "Gillette's Secret to Sharpness," *Industry Week*, January 3, 1994, pp. 24–30; Linda Grant, "Gillette Knows Shaving—and How to Turn Out Hot New Products," *Fortune*, October 14, 1996, pp. 207–210; and Leslie Gevirtz, "Focus—Gillette Posts Record Results in Quarter," *Reuters Financial Service* release, April 17, 1997. Also see William C. Symonds, "Gillette's Edge," *Business Week*, January 19, 1998, pp. 70–77; Symonds, "Would You Spend $1.50 for a Razor Blade?" *Business Week*, April 27, 1998, p. 46; and James Heckman, "Razor Sharp: Adding Value, Making Noise with Mach3 Intro,' *Marketing News*, March 29, 1999, pp. E4, E13.

2. See Kevin J. Clancy and Robert S. Shulman, *The Marketing Revolution: A Radical Manifesto for Dominating the*

Marketplace (New York: Harper Business, 1991), p. 6; Robert G. Cooper, "New Product Success in Industrial Firms," Industrial *Marketing Management*, 1992, pp. 215–223; Christopher Power, "Flops," *Business Week*, August 16, 1993, pp. 76–82, here p. 77; William Bolding, Ruskin Morgan, and Richard Staelin, "Pulling the Plug to Stop the New Product Drain," *Journal of Marketing* Research, February 1997, pp. 164–176; and Constance Gustke, "Built to Last," *Sales & Marketing Management*, August 1997, pp. 78–83.

3. See Robert G. Cooper and Elko J. Kleinschmidt, *New Product: The Key Factors in Success* (Chicago: American Marketing Association, 1990); X. Michael Song and Mark E. Perry, "A Cross-National Comparative Study of New Product Development Processes: Japan and the United States," *Journal of Marketing*, April 1997, pp. 1–18; Jerry Wind and Vijay Mahajan, "Issues and Opportunities in New Product Development," *Journal of Marketing* Research, February 1997, pp. 1–12; Jean-Marie Martino, "Not Only to Succeed but to Endure," *Across the Board*, January 1998, p. 55; and Don H. Lester, "Critical Success Factors for New Product Development," *Research Technology Management*, January–February 1998, pp. 36–43.

4. See Linda Grant, "Gillette Knows Shaving—and How to Turn Out Hot New Products," *Fortune*, October 14, 1996, pp. 207–210; Rosabeth Moss Kanter, "Don't Wait to Innovate," *Sales & Marketing Management*, February 1997, pp. 22–24; and Greg A. Stevens and James Burley, "3,000 Raw Ideas Equals 1 Commercial Success!" *Research-Technology Management*, May/June 1997, pp. 16–27.

5. See Tim Stevens, "Idea Dollars," *Industry Week*, February 16, 1998, pp. 47–49.

6. Constance Gustke, "Built to Last," *Sales & Marketing Management*, August 1997, pp. 78–83.

7. For this and other examples, see Jennifer Reese, "Getting Hot Ideas from Customers," *Fortune*, May 18, 1992, pp. 86–87; and Ken Miller, "Where You Really Need to Hear Customers," *Brandweek*, January 20, 1998, p. 17.

8. Pam Weisz, "Avon's Skin-So-Soft Bugs Out," *Brandweek*, June 6, 1994, p. 4.

9. Russell Mitchell, "How Ford Hit the Bullseye with Taurus," *Business Week*, June 30, 1986, pp. 69–70; and Jeremy Main, "How to Steal the Best Ideas Around," *Fortune*, October 19, 1992, pp. 102–106.

10. Brian O'Reilly, "New Ideas, New Products," *Fortune*, March 3, 1997, pp. 61–64.

11. See David Woodruff, "The Hottest Thing in 'Green' Wheels," *Business Week*, April 28, 1997, p. 42; and Stuart F. Brown, "The Automaker's Big-Time Bet on Fuel Cells," *Fortune*, March 30, 1998, pp. 122C–122P.

12. See Raymond R. Burke, "Virtual Reality Shopping: Breakthrough in Marketing Research," *Harvard Business Review*, March–April 1996, pp. 120–131; and Brian Silverman, "Get 'Em While They're Hot," *Sales & Marketing Management*, February 1997, pp. 47–52.

13. Adrienne Ward Fawcett, "Oreo Cones Make Top Grade in Poll," *Advertising Age*, June 14, 1993, p. 30; and "Fat-Free Cupcakes? Ok; Frozen Icetea Bars? Nope." *Marketing News*, February 12, 1996, p. 14.

14. See Faye Rice, "Secrets of Product Testing," *Fortune*, November 28, 1994, pp. 172–174.

15. Judann Pollack, "Baked Lays," *Advertising Age*, June 24, 1996, p. S2.

16. Laurel Wentz, "Unilever's Power Failure a Wasteful Use of Haste," *Advertising Age*, March 6, 1995, p. 42; Philip Kotler, Gary Armstrong, John Saunders, and Veronica Wong, *Principles of Marketing: The European Edition* (London: Prentice Hall Europe, 1996), pp. 129–133; and Robert McMath, "To Test or Not to Test," *Advertising Age*, June 1998, p. 64.

17. Jennifer Lawrence, "P&G Rushes on Global Diaper Rollout," *Advertising Age*, October 14, 1991, p. 6; Bill Saporito, "Behind the Tumult at P&G," *Fortune*, March 7, 1994, pp. 75–82; and George M. Chryssochoidis, "Rolling Out New Products Across Country Markets: An Empirical Study of Causes of Delays," *The Journal of Product Innovation Management*, January 1998, pp. 16–41.

18. See Hirotaka Takeuchi and Ikujiro Nonaka, "The New New-Product Development Game," *Harvard Business Review*, January–February 1986, pp. 137–46; Craig A. Chambers, "Transforming New Product Development," *Research-Technology Management*, November–December 1996, pp. 32–38; and Srikant Datar, C. Clark Jordan, Sunder Kekre, Surendra Rajiv, and Kannan Srinivasan, "Advantages of Time-Based New Product Development in a Fast-Cycle Industry," *Journal of Marketing Research*, February 1997, pp. 36–49. For a good review of research on new-product development, see Shona L. Brown and Kathleen M. Eisenhardt, "Product Development: Past Research, Present Findings, and Future Directions," *Academy of Management Review*, April 1995, p. 343–378; Jerry Wind and Vijay Mahajan, "Issue and Opportunities in New Product Development," *Journal of Marketing Research*, February 1997, pp. 1–12; Durward K. Sobek, II, Jeffrey K. Liker, and Allen C. Ward, "Another Look at How Toyota Integrates Product Development," *Harvard Business Review*, July–August 1998, pp. 36–49; and Susanne Willsey, "Taking These 7 Steps Will Help You Launch a New Product," *Marketing News*, March 29, 1999, p. 17.

19. See Martin G. Letscher, "How to Tell Fads from Trends," *American Demographics*, December 1994, pp. 38–45; John Grossmann, "A Follow-up on Four Fabled Frenzies," *Inc.*, October 1994, pp. 66–67; and David Stipp, "The Theory of Fads," *Fortune*, October 14, 1996, pp. 49–52.

20. See George S. Day, "The Product Life Cycle: Analysis and Applications Issues," *Journal of Marketing*, Fall 1981, pp. 60–67; Chuck Ryan and Walter E. Riggs, "Redefining the Product Life Cycle: The Five-Element Product Wave," *Business Horizons*, September–October 1996, pp. 33–40; and Carole R. Hedden, "The Circle of (Product) Life," *American Demographics*, September 1996, pp. 26–30.

21. For a more comprehensive discussion of marketing strategies over the course of the product life cycle, see Philip Kotler, *Marketing Management*, 10th ed. (Up-

per Saddle River, NJ: Prentice Hall, 2000), chap. 12.

Chapter 9

1. Thomas T. Nagle and Reed K. Holden, *The Strategy and Tactics of Pricing*, 2nd ed. (Upper Saddle River, NJ: Prentice Hall, 1995), p. 1. Also see Philip Kotler, *Kotler on Marketing* (New York: The Free Press, 1999), pp. 142–48.

2. Portions adapted from Valerie Reitman, "Retail Resistance: Eliminated Discounts on P&G Goods Annoy Many Who Sell Them," *Wall Street Journal*, August 11, 1992, pp. A1, A3. Also see Zachary Schiller, "Not Everyone Loves a Supermarket Special," *Business Week*, February 17, 1992, pp. 64–68; Karen Benezra, "Beyond Value," *Brandweek*, October 7, 1996, pp. 14–16; Dagmar Mussey, "Heat's on Value Pricing," *Advertising Age International*, January 1997, pp. i21–i22; and Cathy Bond, "P&G's Gamble: Price or Promotion?" *Marketing*, February 13, 1997, pp. 30–33.

3. See David J. Schwartz, *Marketing Today: A Basic Approach*, 3rd ed. (New York: Harcourt Brace Jovanovich, 1981), pp. 270–273.

4. For an excellent discussion of factors affecting pricing decisions, see Thomas T. Nagle and Reed K. Holden, *The Strategy and Tactics of Pricing*, 2nd ed. (Upper Saddle River, NJ: Prentice Hall, 1995), chapter 1.

5. Norton Paley, "Fancy Footwork," *Sales & Marketing Management*, July 1994, pp. 41–42; and "About Pitney Bowes: Office Systems," at www.pitneybowes.com/pbi/pbinc/about/aboutpb.htm, June 1998.

6. See Timothy M. Laseter, "Supply Chain Management: the Ins and Outs of Target Costing," *Purchasing*, March 12, 1998, pp. 22–25. Also, check out the Swatch Web page at www.swatch.com.

7. Brian Dumaine, "Closing the Innovation Gap," *Fortune*, December 2, 1991, pp. 56–62.

8. Joshua Rosenbaum, "Guitar Maker Looks for a New Key," *The Wall Street Journal*, February 11, 1998, p. B1.

9. See Nagle and Holden, *The Strategy and Tactics of Pricing*, chap. 4.

10. Melissa Campanelli, "The Price to Pay," *Sales & Marketing Management*, September 1994, pp. 96–102.

11. See Stephen J. Hoch, Xavier Dr'ze, and Mary E. Purk, "EDLP, Hi-Lo, and Margin Arithmetic," *Journal of Marketing*, October 1994, pp. 16–27.

12. For a comprehensive discussion of pricing strategies, see Thomas T. Nagle and Reed K. Holden, *The Strategy and Dynamics of Pricing*, 2nd ed. (Upper Saddle River, NJ: Prentice Hall, 1995). Also see Joshua D. Libresco, "The Pricing Game, Have I Got a Deal for You," *Marketing News*, December 8, 1997, p. 10.

13. Andy Reinhardt, "Pentium: The Next Generation," *Business Week*, May 12, 1997, pp. 42–43.

14. See David Kirkpatrick, "Intel's Amazing Profit Machine," *Fortune*, February 17, 1996, pp. 60–72; and Kelly Spang, "Intel Alters Price Cut Plans," *Computer Reseller News*, March 9, 1998, pp. 1, 8.

15. See Eryn Brown, "Could the Very Best PC Maker Be Dell Computer?" *Fortune*, April 14, 1997, pp. 26–27; and "Michael Dell Rocks," *Fortune*, May 11, 1998, pp. 58–66.

16. Seanna Browder, "Nintendo: At the Top of Its Game," *Business Week*, June 9, 1997, pp. 72–73.

17. Susan Krafft, "Love, Love Me Doo," *American Demographics*, June 1994, pp. 15–16; and Damon Darlin, "Zoo Doo," *Forbes*, May 22, 1995, p. 92.

18. See Nagle, The Strategy and Tactics of Pricing, pp. 225–228; and Manjit S. Yadav and Kent B. Monroe, "How Buyers Perceive Savings in a Bundle Price: An Examination of a Bundle's Transaction Value," *Journal of Marketing Research*, August 1993, pp. 350–358.

19. Gary M. Erickson and Johnny K. Johansson, "The Role of Price in Multi-Attribute Product Evaluations," *Journal of Consumer Research*, September 1985, pp. 195–199.

20. For more reading on reference prices and psychological pricing, see K. N. Rajendran and Gerard J. Tellis, "Contextual and Temporal Components of Reference Price," *Journal of Marketing*, January 1994, pp. 22–34; Richard A. Briesch, Lakshman Krishnamurthi, Tridib Mazumdar, and S. P. Raj, "A Comparative Analysis of Reference Price Models," *Journal of Consumer Research*, September 1997, pp. 202–214; John Huston and Nipoli Kamdar, "$9.99: Can 'Just-Below' Pricing Be Reconciled with Rationality?" *Eastern Economic Journal*, Spring 1996, pp. 137–145; Robert M. Schindler and Patrick N. Kirby, "Patterns of Right-Most Digits Used in Advertised Prices: Implications for Nine-Ending Effects," *Journal of Consumer Research*, September 1997, pp. 192–201; and Dhruv Grewal, Kent B. Monroe, and R. Krishnan, "The Effects of Price-Comparison Advertising on Buyers' Perceptions of Acquisition Value, Transaction Value, and Behavioral Intentions," *Journal of Marketing*, April 1998, pp. 46–59.

21. Philip R. Cateora, International Marketing, 7th ed. (Homewood, IL: Irwin, 1990), p. 540. Also see S. Tamer Cavusgil, "Pricing for Global Markets," *Columbia Journal of World Business*, Winter 1996, pp. 66–78.

22. For more on price cutting and its consequences, see Erika Rasmusson, "The Pitfalls of Price Cutting," *Sales & Marketing Management*, May 1997, p. 17; David R. Henderson, "What Are Price Wars Good For? Absolutely Nothing," *Fortune*, May 12, 1997, p. 156; and Kevin J. Clancy, "At What Profit Price?" *Brandweek*, June 23, 1997, pp. 24–28.

23. Jonathon Berry and Zachary Schiller, "Attack of the Fighting Brands," *Business Week*, May 2, 1994, p. 125; and Jeff Ansell, "Luvs," *Advertising Age*, June 30, 1997, p. s16.

24. For more on public policy and pricing, see Louis W. Stern and Thomas L. Eovaldi, *Legal Aspects of Marketing Strategy* (Upper Saddle River, NJ: Prentice Hall, 1984), chapter 5; Robert J. Posch, *The Complete Guide to Marketing and the Law* (Upper Saddle River, NJ: Prentice Hall, 1988), chapter 28; Thomas T. Nagle and Reed K. Holden, *The Strategy and Tactics of Pricing* (Upper Saddle River, NJ: Prentice Hall, 1995), chapter 14; Joseph P. Guiltinan and Gregory Gunlach, "Aggressive and Predatory Pricing: A Framework for Analysis," *Journal of Marketing*, July 1996, pp. 87–102; and Bruce Upbin, "Vindication," *Forbes*, November 17, 1997, pp. 52–56.

Chapter 10

1. Quotes from Donald V. Fites, "Make Your Dealers Your Partners," *Harvard Business Review*, March–April 1996, pp. 84–95; and De Ann Weimer, "A New Cat on the Hot Seat," *Business Week*, March 1998, pp. 56–62. Also see Peter Elstrom, "This Cat Keeps on Purring," *Business Week*, January 20, 1997, pp. 82–84; Carl Quintanilla, "Caterpillar Posts Record Earnings as U.S. Demand Remains Strong," *The Wall Street Journal*, April 20, 1998, p. A6; and Caterpillar's Web page at www.cat.com.

2. See Louis Stern, Adel I. El-Ansary, and Anne Coughlin, *Marketing Channels*, 5th ed. (Upper Saddle River, NJ: Prentice Hall, 1996), p. 3.

3. Peter Elstrom, "Motorola Goes for the Hard Cell," *Business Week*, September 23, 1996, p. 39; Greg Burns, "Fast-Food Fight," *Business Week*, June 2, 1997, pp. 34–36; and Roger O. Crockett, "How Motorola Lost Its Way," *Business Week*, May 4, 1998, pp. 140–148.

4. See Stern, El-Ansary, and Coughlin, *Marketing Channels*, p. 251.

5. See Allan J. Magrath, "Collaborative Marketing Comes of Age—Again," *Sales & Marketing Management*, September 1991, pp. 61–64; Andrew E. Serwer, "What Price Loyalty?" *Fortune*, January 10, 1995, pp. 103–104; and Judann Pollack and Louise Kramer, "Coca-Cola and Pringles Eye Global Brand Linkup," *Advertising Age*, June 15, 1998, pp. 1, 73.

6. See Rowland T. Moriarity and Ursula Moran, "Managing Hybrid Marketing Systems," *Harvard Business Review*, November–December 1990, pp. 146–155; Frank V. Cespedes and E. Raymond Corey, "Managing Multiple Channels," *Business Horizons*, July–August 1990, pp. 67–77; and Mark J. Ryan, "Big Blue Walks the Talk," Reseller Management, June 1997, pp. 88–89.

7. For an interesting discussion of distribution intensity, see Gary L. Frazier and Walfried M. Lassar, "Determinants of Distribution Intensity," *Journal of Marketing*, October 1996, pp. 39–51.

8. Subhash C. Jain, International *Marketing Management*, 3rd ed. (Boston, MA: PWS-Kent Publishing, 1990), pp. 489–91. Also see Emily Thronton, "Revolution in Japanese Retailing," *Fortune*, February 7, 1994, pp. 143–47; and "Ever-Shorter Channels—Wholesale Industry Restructures," *Focus Japan*, July–August 1997, pp. 3–4.

9. For examples, see Philip Cateora, International Marketing, 7th ed. (Homewood, IL: Irwin, 1990), pp. 570–571; and Dexter Roberts, "Blazing Away at Foreign Brands," *Business Week*, May 12, 1997, p. 58.

10. See James A. Narus and James C. Anderson, "Turn Your Industrial Distributors into Partners," *Harvard Business Review*, March–April 1986, pp. 66–71; Jan B. Heide, "Interorganizational Governance in Marketing Channels," *Journal of Marketing*, January 1994, pp. 71–85; Nirmalya Kumar, The Power of Trust in Manufacturer-Retailer Relationships," *Harvard Business Review*, November–December 1996, pp. 92–106; James A. Narus and James C. Anderson, "Rethinking Distribution," *Harvard Business Review*, July–August 1996, pp. 112–120; and Jakki J. Mohr and Robert E. Spekman, "Several Characteristics Contribute to Successful Alliances Between Channel Members," *Marketing Management*, Winter/Spring 1996, pp. 35–42.

11. For a full discussion of laws affecting marketing channels, see Stern, El-Ansary, and Coughlan, *Marketing Channels*, Chapter 8.

12. Ronald Henkoff, "Delivering the Goods," *Fortune*, November 18, 1994, pp. 64–78. Also see Shlomo Maital, "The Last Frontier of Cost Reduction," *Across the Board*, February 1994, pp. 51–52.

13. Maital, "The Last Frontier of Cost Reduction," p. 52.

14. See "Linking with Vendors for Just-in-Time Service," *Chain Store Age Executive*, June 1993, pp. 22A–24A; Ken Cottrill, "Reforging the Supply Chain," *The Journal of Business Strategy*, November–December 1997, pp. 35–39; and "Kmart to Outsource Most EDI Tasks," *Chain Store Age*, April 1998, pp. 74–76.

15. John Huey, "Wal-Mart: Will It Take Over the World?" *Fortune*, January 30, 1989, pp. 52–64. Also see "Distribution Centers," *Chain Store Age*, October 1996, pp. 4–10.

16. For statistics on freight shipments, see Transportation Statistics Annual Report 1997, U.S. Department of Transportation, Bureau of Transportation Statistics, Washington, DC, 1997. A copy can be obtained from www.fedstats.gov.

17. Shawn Tully, "Comeback Ahead for Railroads," *Fortune*, June 17, 1991, pp. 107–113; and Joseph Weber, "High-balling Toward Two Big Railroads," *Business Week*, March 17, 1997, pp. 32–33.

18. See "Trucking Deregulation: A Ten-Year Anniversary," *Fortune*, August 13, 1990, pp. 25–35; and Brian O'Reilly and Alicia Hills Moore, "On the Road Again," *Fortune*, April 27, 1998, pp. 182–195.

19. See Sandra J. Skrovan, "Partnering with Vendors: The Ties that Bind," *Chain Store Age Executive*, January 1994, pp. 6MH–9MH; Robert D. Buzzell and Gwen Ortmeyer, "Channel Partnerships Streamline Distribution," *Sloan Management Review*, March 22, 1995, p. 85; and Ken Cottrill, "Reforging the Supply Chain," *The Journal of Business Strategy*, November–December 1997, pp. 35–39.

20. Skrovan, "Partnering with Vendors," p. 6MH; and Susan Caminiti, "After You Win, the Fun Begins," *Fortune*, May 2, 1994, p. 76.

21. See Joseph Weber, "Just Get It to the Store on Time," *Business Week*, March 6, 1995, pp. 66–67; and Gary Robbins, "Pushing the Limits of VMI (Vendor Managed Inventory)," *Stores*, March 1995, p. 42.

22. Myron Magnet, "The New Golden Rule of Business," *Fortune*, February 21, 1994, pp. 60–64. For a related example, see Justin Martin, "Are You as Good as You Think You Are?" *Fortune*, September 1996, pp. 145–146.

23. Based on an address by Professor Donald J. Bowersox at Michigan State University on August 5, 1992. For a general discussion of improving supply chain performance, see Marshall L. Fisher, "What Is the Right Supply Chain for Your Product?" *Harvard Business Review*, March–April 1997, pp. 105–116.

24. Francis J. Quinn, "Logistics' New Customer Focus," *Business Week*, March 10, 1997, pp. 53–71. Also see Stern, et. al., *Marketing Channels*, 5th ed., pp. 158–160.

25. Ibid., p. 68; and Gail DeGeorge, "Ryder Sees the Logic of Logistics," *Business Week*, August 5, 1996, p. 56.

26. See Stern, et. al., Marketing Channels, 5th ed., p. 160; Patrick Byrne, "A New Roadmap for Contract Logistics," *Transportation & Distribution*, April 1993, pp. 58–62; Ronald Henkoff, "Delivering the Goods," *Fortune*, November 18, 1994, pp. 64–77); and Scott Wooley, "Replacing Inventory with Information," *Forbes*, March 24, 1997, pp. 54–58.

Chapter 11

1. Quotes in this Home Depot tale are from Patricia Sellers, "Companies That Serve You Best," *Fortune*, May 31, 1993, pp. 74–88; and Patricia Sellers, "Can Home Depot Fix Its Sagging Stock?" *Fortune*, March 4, 1996, pp. 139–146. Also see Graham Button, "The Man Who Almost Walked Out on Ross Perot," *Forbes*, November 22, 1993, pp. 68–76; Charles Butler, "The Magnificant Seven," *Performance*, November 1994, pp. 41–50; Gretchen Morgenson, "Too Much of a Good Thing?" *Forbes*, June 3, 1996, pp. 115–119; "Home Depot," *Sales & Marketing Management*, October 1997, pp. 65–66, "Business Brief: Home Depot, Inc.," The Wall Street Journal, April 27, 1998, B4; and "The Fortune 500 Largest Corporations," *Fortune*, April 27, 1998, p. F-2.

2. See Kimberly D. Lowe, "The Supermarket Challenge," *Restaurants and Institutions*, March 1, 1997, pp. 32–44; and Cyndee Miller, "It's Not Take-Out; It's Now 'Home Meal Replacement,'" *Marketing News*, June 9, 1997, pp. 2, 8.

3. See "Stop-N-Go Micromarkets New Upscale Mix," *Chain Store Age Executive*, January 1990, p. 145; Matt Nannery, "Convenience Stores Get Fresh," *Chain Store Age*, August 1996, pp. 18A–19A; Wendy Zellner, "How Classy Can 7-Eleven Get?" *Business Week*, September 1, 1997, pp. 74–75; and "Convenience Stores," *Chain Store Age*, January 1998, pp. 8A–9A.

4. Laura Liebeck, "The 'Killer' Supermerchants," *Discount Store News*, March 18, 1996, pp. F5–F6; "Traditional Discount Stores Take a Back Seat to Supercenters," *Discount Store News*, March 3, 1997, p. 43; and Daniel T. Spindel, "Supercenters: Wal-mart's Massive but Quiet Evolution," *Discount Merchandiser*, April 1998, pp. 34–35.

5. See Duke Ratliff, "Evolution of Off-Price Retailers," *Discount Merchandising*, March 1996, pp. 22–30; Roberta Maynard, "A Growing Outlet for Small Firms," *Nation's Business*, August 1996, pp. 45–48; and Charles V. Bagli, "Discount Mania," *New York Times*, April 5, 1998, p. 12.

6. Ronald Henkoff, "Why Every Red-Blooded Consumer Owns a Truck, and a Five-Pound Jar of Peanut Butter, . . . ," *Fortune*, May 29, 1995, pp. 86–100; and "Warehouse Clubs Experience Renewed Sales Growth," *Discount Store News*, March 9, 1998, pp. 7, 10.

7. For an excellent summary of direct selling, see Robert A. Peterson and Thomas R. Wotruba, "What Is Direct Selling?" *Journal of Personal Selling and Sales Management*, Fall 1996, pp. 1–16.

8. See "Vending Your Way," *Training and Development*, September 1996, p. 72; and Maxim Lenderman, "Vending Machines: Hot, Hot, Hot," *Beverage World*, February 1997, pp. 58–62.

9. Dyan Machan, "Knowing Your Limits," *Forbes*, June 5, 1995, p. 128; "25 VIPs: Leslie Wexner," *Chain Store Age*, September 1997, p. 118: and Marianne Wilson, "Unlimited Potential," *Chain Store Age*, March 1998, p. 164.

10. Myron Magnet, "Let's Go for Growth," *Fortune*, March 7, 1994, pp. 60–72. Also see Dierdre Donahue, "Bookstores: A Haven for the Intellect," *USA Today*, July 10, 1997, pp. D1, D2.

11. Kenneth Labich, "What Will It Take to Keep Them Hanging Out at the Mall?" *Fortune*, May 29, 1995, pp. 102–106; Sarah Hoban, "Retail Entertainment," *Commercial Real Estate Investment Journal*, March 1997, pp. 24–29; "It's Not Just a Mall. It's Mallville, U.S.A.," *New York Times Magazine*, February 8, 1998, p. 19; and "The History of Mall of America," www.mallofamerica.com, June 1998.

12. Tim Cavanaugh, "Mall Crawl Palls," *American Demographics*, September 1996, pp. 14–16.

13. See Kate Fitzgerald, "Mega Malls: Built for the '90s, or the '80s?" *Advertising Age*, January 27, 1992, pp. S1, S8; Gretchen Morgenson, "The Fall of the Mall," *Forbes*, May 24, 1993, pp. 106–1112; Kenneth Labich, "What Will It Take to Keep Them Hanging Out at the Mall?" *Fortune*, May 29, 1995, pp. 102–105; and Allison Lucus, "The Fall of the Mall," *Sales & Marketing Management*, April 1996, pp. 13–14; and "Welcome to the 'Powerhood,'" *Chain Store Age*, November 1997, pp. 152–154.

14. Bill Saporito, "Is Wal-Mart Unstoppable?" *Fortune*, May 6, 1991, pp. 50–59.

15. Amy Barrett, "A Retailing Pacesetter Pulls Up Lame," *Business Week*, July 12, 1993, pp. 122–23.

16. See Malcolm P. McNair and Eleanor G. May, "The Next Revolution of the Retailing Wheel," *Harvard Business Review*, September–October 1978, pp. 81–91; Stephen Brown, "The Wheel of Retailing: Past and Future," *Journal of Retailing*, Summer 1990, pp. 143–47; Stephen Brown, "Variations on a Marketing Enigma: The Wheel of Retailing Theory," The *Journal of Marketing* Management, vol. 7, no. 2, 1991, pp. 131–155; and Stanley C. Hollander, "The Wheel of Retailing," reprinted in *Marketing Management*, Summer 1996, pp. 63–66.

17. Diane Crispell, "Retailing's Next Decade," *American Demographics*, May 1997, p. 9.

18. Stephanie Anderson Forest and Keith Naughton, "I'll Take That and That and That and . . .", *Business Week*, June 22, 1998, p. 38.

19. Tim Carvell, "The Crazy Record Business: These Prices Really Are Insane," *Fortune*, August 4, 1997, pp. 109–116.

20. See Nirmalya Kumar, "The Power of Trust in Manufacturer-Retailer Relationships," *Harvard Business Review*, November–December 1996, pp. 92–106.

21. "Business Bulletin: Shopper Scanner," *Wall Street Journal*, February 18, 1995, p. A1, A5.

22. James Cox, "Red-Letter Day as East Meets West in the Aisles," *USA Today*, September 11, 1996, p. B1. Also see

Wendy Zellner, Louisa Shepard, Ian Katz, and David Lindorff, "Wal-Mart Spoken Here," *Business Week*, June 23, 1997, pp. 138–143.

23. Shelby D. Coolidge, "Facing Saturated home Markets, Retailers Look to Rest of World," *Christian Science Monitor*, February 14, 1994, 7:1; Carla Rapoport, "Retailers Go Global," *Fortune*, February 20, 1995, pp. 102–108; and Joseph H. Ellis, "Global Retailing's Winners and Losers," *Chain Store Age*, December 1997, pp. 27–29.

24. See Gherry Khermouch, "Third Places," *Brandweek*, March 13, 1995, pp. 36–40; and Dierdre Donahue, "Bookstores: A Haven for the Intellect," *USA Today*, July 10, 1997, pp. D1, D2.

25. See Arthur Andersen & Co., *Facing the Forces of Change: Beyond Future Trends in Wholesale Distribution* (Washington, D.C.: Distribution Research and Education Foundation, 1987), p. 7. Also see Joseph Weber, "Its 'Like Somebody Had Shot the Postman,'" *Business Week*, January 13, 1992, p. 82; and Michael Mandel, "Don't Cut Out the Middleman," *Business Week*, September 16, 1996, p. 30.

26. Richard A. Melcher, "The Middlemen Stay on the March," *Business Week*, January 9, 1995, p. 87.

27. *SuperValu Distribution and Retailing Handbook*, SuperValu, Inc., Minneapolis, MN, November, 1993; and "SuperValu Inside: Company Profile," at www.supervalu.com/inside/inside_sv.htm, June 1998.

28. Joseph Weber, "On a Fast Boat to Anywhere," *Business Week*, January 11, 1993, p. 94.

Chapter 12

1. Extract from Kenneth Labich, "Is Herb Kelleher America's Best CEO?" *Fortune*, May 2, 1994, pp. 44–52. Other information from Charles Butler, "General Excellence: Southwest Airlines," *Sales & Marketing Management*, August 1993, p. 38; Jennifer Lawrence, "Integrated Mix Makes Expansion Fly," *Advertising Age*, November 8, 1993, pp. S10, S12; Jackie and Kevin Freiberg, "Is This Company Completely Nuts?" *Executive Excellence*, September 1996, p. 20; Wendy Zellner, "Southwest's Love Fest at Love Field," *Business Week*, April 28, 1997, p. 12E4; Thomas A. Stewart, "America's Most Admired Companies," *Fortune*, March 2, 1998, pp. 70–73; Stephanie Gruner, "Have Fun, Make Money," Inc, May 1998, p. 123; and Chad Kaydo, "Riding High," *Sales & Marketing Management*, July 1998, pp. 64–69. Also see Southwest Airlines Fact Sheet—May 1999 at www.southwest.com.

2. The first four of these definitions are adapted from Peter D. Bennett, *Dictionary of Marketing Terms* (Chicago: American Marketing Association, 1995).

3. For more discussion, see Don E. Schultz, Stanley I. Tannenbaum, and Robert F. Lauterborn, *Integrated Marketing Communication* (Chicago, IL: NTC Publishing, 1992), pp. 11, 17.

4. Michael Kubin, "Simple Days of Retailing on TV Are Long Gone," *Marketing News*, February 17, 1997, pp. 2, 13; Elizabeth Lesly Stevens and Ronald Glover, "The Entertainment Glut," *Business Week*, February 16, 1998, pp. 88–95; and Ronald Glover, "If These Shows Are Hits, Why Do They Hurt So Much?" *Business Week*, April 13, 1998, p. 36.

5. Judann Pollack, "Trade Promotion Luster Dims for Marketers, Retailers." *Advertising Age*, April 7, 1997, p. 18.

6. See Schultz, Tannenbaum, and Lauterborn, *Integrated Marketing Communication*, chapters 3 and 4; Don E. Schultz and Philip J. Kitchen, "Integrated Marketing Communications in U.S. Advertising Agencies: An Exploratory Study," *Journal of Advertising Research*, September–October 1997, pp. 7–18; and George E. Balch and Michael A. Balch, *Advertising and Promotion: An Integrated Marketing Communications Perspective*, 4th ed. (Irwin/McGraw Hill, 1998), pp. 9–13.

7. P. Griffith Lindell, "You Need Integrated Attitude to Develop IMC," *Marketing News*, May 26, 1997, p. 6; and Don E. Schultz, "New Media, Old Problem: Keeping Marcom Integrated," *Marketing News*, March 29, 1999, p. 11.

8. For more on the legal aspects of promotion, see Louis W. Stern and Thomas I. Eovaldi, *Legal Aspects of Marketing Policy* (Upper Saddle River, NJ: Prentice Hall, 1984), chapters 7 and 8; Robert J. Posch, *The Complete Guide to Marketing and the Law* (Upper Saddle River, NJ: Prentice Hall, 1988), chapters 15 to 17; and William Wells, John Burnett, and Sandra Moriarty, *Advertising Principles and Practice*, 4th ed. (Upper Saddle River, NJ: Prentice Hall, 1998), chapter 2.

9. See Mark Gleason and Keith J. Kelly, "Ad Growth Expected to Slow in 1997," *Advertising Age*, December 16, 1996, p. 6; Robert J. Coen, "Advertising Spending Beats Expectations in '97," *USA Today*, December 9, 1997, p. 2B; and Rebecca A. Fannin, "Top Global Marketers See Ad Spending Rise by 3.1%," *Advertising Age*, November 10, 1997, p. 20.

10. See James B. Arndorfer, "AmEx Takes Another Swipe at Visa in New Commercials," *Advertising Age*, June 16, 1997, p. 59; and Dhruv Grewel, Sukumar Kavanoor, Edward F. Fern, Carolyn Costley, and James Barnes, "Comparative Versus Noncomparative Advertising: A Meta-Analysis," *Journal of Marketing*, October 1997, pp. 1–15.

11. For a more comprehensive discussion on setting promotion budgets, see J. Thomas Russell and W. Ronald Lane, *Kleppner's Advertising Procedure* (Upper Saddle River, NJ: Prentice Hall, 1996), chapter 6; and Balch and Balch, *Advertising and Promotion*, chapter 4.

12. David Allen, "Excessive Use of the Mirror," *Management Accounting*, June 1966, p. 12. Also see Laura Petrecca, "4A's Will Study Financial Return on Ad Spending," *Advertising Age*, April 7, 1997, pp. 3, 52; and Dana W. Hayman and Don E. Schultz, "How Much Should You Spend on Advertising," *Advertising Age*, April 26, 1999, p. 32.

13. "Swimming the Channels," *American Demographics*, June 1998, p. 37.

14. Edward A. Robinson, "Frogs, Bears, and Orgasms: Think Zany If You Want to Reach Today's Consumers," *Fortune*, June 9, 1997, pp. 153–156. Also see Marc Gunther, "What's Wrong with This Picture?" *Fortune*, January 12, 1998, pp. 107–114; and John Consoli, "A Crescendo of Clutter," *Mediaweek*, March 16, 1998, pp. 4–5.

15. Leah Haran, "Madison Avenue Visits Dreamland," *Advertising Age*, March 18, 1996, p. 12.

16. Ronald Glover, "If These Shows Are Such Hits, Why Do They Hurt So Much?" *Business Week*, April 13, 1998, p. 36; Ellen Neuborne, "More Bang for the Super Bowl Bucks," *Business Week*, February 2, 1998, p. 70; Chuck Ross, "Super Sein-Off," *Advertising Age*, May 11, 1998, pp. 1, 62; and Ronald Glover, "And Now, a Few Costly Words from Our Sponsor," *Business Week*, March 29, 1999, p. 96.

17. For these and other examples, see Kathy Martin, "What's Next? Execs Muse Over Boundless Ad Possibilities," *Advertising Age*, August 27, 1990; John P. Cortez, "Ads Head for the Bathroom," *Advertising Age*, May 18, 1992, p. 24; and Cristina Merrill, "Alternative Reality," *Adweek*, February 3, 1997, pp. 23–30; Jeff Jensen, "High Hopes for 'Men in Black' and Ray Bans," *Advertising Age*, April 14, 1997, pp. 1, 52; Ellen Neuborne, "Saturday Night at the Ads," *Business Week*, September 15, 1997, pp. 63–64; Andy Fry, "Choose Your Weapon," *Marketing*, April 16, 1998, pp. 31–34; and "Advertising's New Beachhead," *Advertising Age*, July 13, 1998, p. 44.

18. For current magazines rates and circulations, see SRDS's Web site at www.srds.com.

19. See Television Production Cost Survey (New York: American Association of Advertising Agencies, 1997).

20. See Gary Schroeder, "Behavioral Optimization," *American Demographics*, August 1998, pp. 34–36.

21. "Agency Report: Omnicom Storms Past WWP," *Advertising Age*, April 27, 1998, pp. S1, S40; and "Top 25 Advertising Organizations," *Advertising Age*, April 27, 1998, p. S22.

22. Michael Lev, "Advertisers Seek Global Messages," *New York Times*, November 18, 1991, p. D9. Also see Jay Schulberg, "Successful Global Ads Need Simplicity, Clarity," *Advertising Age*, June 30, 1997, p. 17.

23. Philip R. Cateora, *International Marketing*, 7th ed. (Homewood, IL: Irwin, 1990), p. 462. Also see Marcio M. Moreira, "The Idea's the Thing for Good Global Ads," *Advertising Age*, November 11, 1996, p. 34; and Kip D. Cassino, "A World of Advertising," *American Demographics*, November 1997, pp. 57–60.

24. Cateora, *International Marketing*, pp. 466–467. For other examples and more on international advertising, see Dexter Roberts, "Winding up for the Big Pitch," *Business Week*, October 23, 1995, p. 52; and Balch and Balch, *Advertising and Promotion*, chap. 20.

25. Adapted from Scott Cutlip, Allen Center, and Glen Broom, *Effective Public Relations*, 8th ed. (Upper Saddle River, NJ: Prentice Hall, 1999), chap. 1.

26. Linda Himelstein, "Levi's vs. the Dress Code," *Business Week*, April 1, 1996, pp. 57–58; "Dressing for Success," IAB *Online Advertising Guide*, Spring 1998, p. 29A, and www.levistrauss.com/ casual_wear.html.

27. Mark Gleason, "Edelman Sees Niche in Web Public Relations," *Advertising Age*, January 20, 1997, p. 30.

Chapter 13

1. Quotes from Andy Cohen, "Top of the Charts: Lear Corporation," *Sales & Marketing Management*, July 1998, p. 40. Also see Sarah Lorge, "Better Off Branded," *Sales & Marketing Management*, March 1998, pp. 39–42; Tony DeLorenzo, "International Growth Fuels Lear's Record First Quarter," press release, accessed on-line at www.lear.com/e/e1ll/htm, April 21, 1998; and "This Is Lear," accessed on-line at www.lear.com/d.htm, July 20, 1998.

2. See Bill Kelley, "How to Sell Airplanes, Boeing-Style," *Sales & Marketing Management*, December 9, 1985, pp. 32–34. Also see Tim Smart, "Finally, We Have Ignition," *Business Week*, September 16, 1996, p. 45; and Andy Cohen, "Boeing," *Sales & Marketing Management*, October 1997, p. 68.

3. Patricia Sellers, "How to Remake Your Sales Force," *Fortune*, May 4, 1992, pp. 96–103, here p. 96. Also see Melissa Campanelli, "Reshuffling the Deck," *Sales & Marketing Management*, June 1994, pp. 83–89.

4. Geoffrey Brewer, "Love the Ones You're With," *Sales & Marketing Management*, February 1997, pp. 38–45.

5. See Dartnell's 30th Sales Force Compensation Survey, Dartnell Corporation, August 1998.

6. See Martin Everett, "Selling by Telephone," *Sales & Marketing Management*, December 1993, pp. 75–79.

7. See "A Phone Is Better Than a Face," *Sales & Marketing Management*, October 1987, p. 29. Also see Brett A. Boyle, "The Importance of the Industrial Inside Sales Force: A Case Study," Industrial *Marketing Management*, September 1996, pp. 339–348; Victoria Fraza, "Upgrading Inside Sales," *Industrial Distribution*, December 1997, pp. 44–49; and Michele Marchetti, "Look Who's Calling," *Sales & Marketing Management*, May 1998, pp. 43–46.

8. See Frank V. Cespedes, Stephen X. Doyle, and Robert J. Freedman, "Teamwork for Today's Selling," *Harvard Business Review*, March–April 1989, pp. 44–54, 58; Joseph Conlin, "Teaming Up," *Sales & Marketing Management*, October 1993, pp. 98–104; Richard C. Whiteley, "Orchestrating Service," *Sales & Marketing Management*, April 1994, pp. 29–30; and Mark A. Moon and Susan Forquer Gupta, "Examining the Formation of Selling Centers: A Conceptual Framework," *Journal of Personal Selling and Sales Management*, Spring 1997, pp. 31–41.

9. See George H. Lucas Jr., A. Parasuraman, Robert A. Davis, and Ben M. Enis, "An Empirical Study of Sales Force Turnover," *Journal of Marketing*, July 1987, pp. 34–59; Lynn G. Coleman, "Sales Force Turnover Has Managers Wondering Why," *Marketing News*, December 4, 1989, p. 6; Thomas R. Wotruba and Pradeep K. Tyagi, "Met Expectations and Turnover in Direct Selling," *Journal of Marketing*, July 1991, pp. 24–35; and Chad Kaydo, "Overturning Turnover," *Sales & Marketing Management*, November 1997, pp. 50–60.

10. See Geoffrey Brewer, "Mind Reading: What Drives Top Salespeople to Greatness?" *Sales & Marketing Management*, May 1994, pp. 82–88; Barry J. Farber, "Success Stories for Salespeople," *Sales & Marketing Management*, May 1995, pp. 30–31; and Roberta Maynard, "Finding the Essence of Good Sales-

people," *Nation's Business*, February 1998, p. 10.

11. "23 Percent of U.S. Salespeople Are Women," *American Salesman*, April 1995, p. 8. Also see Nancy Arnott, "It's a Woman's World," *Sales & Marketing Management*, March 1995, pp. 55–59; and "Selling Sales to Students," *Sales & Marketing Management*, January 1998, p. 15.

12. See "To Test or Not to Test," *Sales & Marketing Management*, May 1994, p. 86.

13. Sarah Lorge, "Getting into Their Heads," *Sales & Marketing Management*, February 1998, pp. 58–67.

14. Robert Klein, "Nabisco Sales Soar After Sales Training," *Marketing News*, January 6, 1997, p. 23.

15. Christen P. Heide, "All Levels of Sales Reps Post Impressive Earnings," press release, www.dartnellcorp.com, May 5, 1997; and Dartnell's 30th Sales Force Compensation Survey, Dartnell Corporation, August 1998.

16. Geoffrey Brewer, "Brain Power," *Sales & Marketing Management*, May 1997, pp. 39–48; Don Peppers and Martha Rogers, "The Money Trap," *Sales & Marketing Management*, May 1997, pp. 58–60; and Michele Marchetti, "No Commissions? Are You Crazy?" *Sales & Marketing Management*, May 1998, p. 83.

17. Tony Seideman, "Who Needs Managers?" *Sales & Marketing Management*, part 2, June 1994, pp. 15–17. Also see Tim McCollum, "High-Tech Marketing Hits the Target," *Nation's Business*, June 1997, pp. 39–42; Lon Orenstein and Kenneth Leung, "The Dos and Don'ts of Sales Force Automation," *Marketing News*, November 10, 1997, p. 14; and Mary E. Boone, "When Reps Resist Automation," *Sales & Marketing Management*, April 1998, pp. 30–31.

18. Christen Heide, "Rep Use of the Internet Up 226 Percent in 2 Years," *Sales & Marketing Executive Report*, August 19, 1998, pp. 8–9.

19. Bob Donath, "Delivering Value Starts with Proper Prospecting," *Marketing News*, November 10, 1997, p. 5. Also see Sarah Lorge, "The Best Way to Prospect," *Sales & Marketing Management*, January 1998, p. 80.

20. David Stamps, "Training for a New Sales Game," *Training*, July 1997, pp. 46–52.

21. Brewer, "Brain Power," p. 42; and Rosemay P. Ramsey and Ravipreet S. Sohi, "Listening to Your Customers: The Impact of Perceived Salesperson Listening Behavior on Relationship Outcomes," *Journal of the Academy of Marketing Science*, Spring 1997, pp. 127–137.

22. 18th Annual Survey of Promotional Practices, Carol Wright Promotions, Inc., Naperville, IL, May 1996, p. 9. Also see, Judann Pollack, "Trade Promotion Luster Dims for Marketers, Retailers," *Advertising Age*, April 7, 1997, p. 18.

23. Jennifer Lawrence, "Free Samples Get Emotional Reception," *Advertising Age*, September 30, 1991, p. 10.

24. "Nestlé Banks on Databases," *Advertising Age*, October 25, 1993, pp. 16.

25. Terry Lefton, "Blockbuster Re-Ups 'Bonus Box,'" *Brandweek*, August 9, 1994, p. 3. Also see "Free for All," *Brandweek*, March 13, 1995, p. S5; and Kate Fitzgerald, "Sampels Go on Tour," *Advertising Age*, May 5, 1997, pp. 37, 57.

26. Larry Armstrong, "Coupon Clippers, Save Your Scissors," *Business Week*, June 20, 1994, pp. 164–166; "Targeted Couponing Slows Redemption Slide," *Marketing News*, February 12, 1996, p. 11; Ginger Conlon, "Still Clipping Away," *Sales & Marketing Management*, March 1997, pp. 74–75; and "Loyal Shoppers Can Score by Using In-Store Kiosks," *Advertising Age*, May 1998, p. S4.

27. Kate Fitzgerald, "Coupons Expand on Web," *Advertising Age*, March 31, 1997, p. 24; and Gregg Cebrzyski, "Domino's to Join Other Chains in Testing Internet Coupons," *Nation's Restaurant News*, May 25, 1998, p. 12.

28. See Judann Pollack, "Huge Promotion Key as Soft Drinks Enter Summer Season," *Advertising Age*, May 12, 1997, p. 89; Laurie Freeman, "Premium Giveaway Products Pass Cost-Benefit Analysis," *Advertising Age*, March 17, 1997, p. 2; and Kate Bertrand, "Premiums Prime the Market," *Advertising Age's Business Marketing*, May 1998, p. S6.

29. See "Power to the Key Ring and T-Shirt," *Sales & Marketing Management*, December 1989, p. 14; and Chad Kaydo, "Your Logo Here," *Sales & Marketing Management*, April 1998, pp. 65–70.

30. See Richard Szathmary, "Trade Shows," *Sales & Marketing Management*, May 1992, pp. 83–84; Srinath Gopalakrishna, Gary L, Lilien, Jerome D. Williams, and Ian Sequeira, "Do Trade Shows Pay Off?" *Journal of Marketing*, July 1995, pp. 75–83; Robyn Griggs, "How to Succeed at Trade Shows," *Sales & Marketing Management*, July 1997, pp. 83–84; and Allen Konopacki, "Seven Hot Trends in Trade Shows This Year," *Agency Sales*, June 1998, p. 34.

Chapter 14

1. Quotes from Gary McWilliams, "Whirlwind on the Web," *Business Week*, April 7, 1997, pp. 132–136; and Bill Robbins and Cathie Hargett, "Dell Internet Sales Top $1 Million a Day," press release, Dell Computer Corporation, March 4, 1997. Also see Eryn Brown, "Could the Very Best PC Maker Be Dell Computer?" *Fortune*, April 14, 1997, pp. 26–27; Joan Magretta, "The Power of Virtual Integration: An Interview with Dell Computer's Michael Dell," *Harvard Business Review*, March–April 1998, pp. 73–84; Andrew E. Serwer, "Michael Dell Rocks," *Fortune*, May 11, 1998, pp. 58–66; Erick Schonfeld, "The Customized, Digitized, Have-It-Your-Way Economy," *Fortune*, September 28, 1998, pp. 115–124; "Nerdy Like a Fox," *Business Week*, January 1999, p. 74.

2. See Arnold Fishman's *1994 Guide to Mail Order Sales* (Highland Park, IL: Market Logistics); and "1994 Mail Order Overview," *Direct Marketing*, August 1994, pp. 26–28).

3. James Champy, "The Cyber-Future Is Now," *Sales & Marketing Management*, September 1997, p. 28; Melanie Berger, "It's Your Move," *Sales & Marketing Management*, March 1998, pp. 45–54; Ted Bridis, "Report: Internet Growing Exponentially," *The Durham Herald-Sun*, April 16, 1998, p. A1; and Cheryl Russell, "The Haves and the Want-Nots," *American Demographics*, April 1998, pp. 10–12.

4. See Don Peppers and Martha Rogers, *The One-to-One Future* (New York: Doubleday/Currency, 1993).

5. *18th Annual Survey of Promotional Practices*, Carol Wright Promotions, Inc., Naperville, IL, 1996, p. 36.

6. See Jonathan Berry, "A Potent New Tool for Selling: Database Marketing," *Business Week*, September 4, 1994, pp. 56–62; "How to Turn Junk Mail into a Gold Mine," *The Economist*, April 1, 1995, p. 51; Weld F. Royal, "Do Databases Really Work?" *Sales & Marketing Management*, October 1995, pp. 66–74; and Daniel Hill, "Love My Brand," *Brandweek*, January 19, 1998, pp. 26–29.

7. See Joe Schwartz, "Databases Deliver the Goods," *American Demographics*, September 1989, pp. 23–25; Gary Levin, "Database Draws Fevered Interest," *Advertising Age*, June 8, 1992, p. 31; Jonathan Berry, "A Potent New Tool for Selling: Database Marketing," *Business Week*, September 5, 1994, pp. 56–62; Richard Cross and Janet Smith, "Customer Bonding and the Information Core," *Direct Marketing Magazine*, February, 1995, p. 28; Frederick Newell, *The New Rules of Marketing* (New York: McGraw-Hill, 1997); and R. M. Gordon, "Consumer Guidance," *Marketing Management*, Spring 1998, pp. 59–60.

8. Junu Bryan Kim, "Marketing with Video: The Cassette Is in the Mail," *Advertising Age*, May 22, 1995, p. S1. Also see, Albert Fried-Cassorla, "The Bright Future of Direct Mail: (Yes, Even in the Online Era!)," *Direct Marketing*, March 1998, pp. 40–42.

9. Jane Hodges, "Direct Marketing Tackles Benefits of New Media," *Advertising Age*, November 4, 1996, p. 22.

10. "Lillian Vernon Announces New Catalog Title," *Direct Marketing*, April 1998, pp. 15–16.

11. Bristol Voss, "Calling All Catalogs!" *Sales & Marketing Management*, December 1990, pp. 32–37; Thayer C. Taylor, "Catalogs Come of Age," *Sales & Marketing Management*, December 1993, pp. 39–41; and "15 Tips from Catalog Experts," *Catalog Age*, April 1, 1998, pp. 47–48.

12. Matthew L. Wald, "Third Area Code Is Added In the Land of the Toll-Free," *New York Times*, April 4, 1998, p. 10.

13. Kevin R. Hopkins, "Dialing in to the Future," *Business Week*, July 28, 1997, p. 90; and Holly McCord, "1-900-CALL-AN-RD," *Prevention*, August 1997, p. 54.

14. See Richard L. Bencin, "Telefocus: Telemarketing Gets Synergized," *Sales & Marketing Management*, February 1992, pp. 49–57; Martin Everett, "Selling by Telephone," *Sales & Marketing Management*, December 1993, pp. 75–79; and John F. Yarbrough, "Dialing for Dollar$," *Sales & Marketing Management*, January 1997, pp. 61–67.

15. See Judith Waltrop, "The Business of Privacy," *American Demographics*, October 1994, pp. 46–55; Ira Teinowitz, "FTC's Revised Rules Calm Telemarketers," *Advertising Age*, June 5, 1995, p. 8; and Chad Ruebl, "Stiffer Rules for Telemarketers as U.S. Cracks Down on Fraud," *Marketing News*, February 26, 1996, pp. 1, 8.

16. Timothy R. Hawthorne, "Opening Doors to Retail Sales," *Direct Marketing*, January 1998, pp. 48–51. Also see Jacqueline M. Graves, "The Fortune 500 Opt for Infomercials," *Fortune*, March 6, 1995, p. 20; "Infomercials," *Advertising Age*, September 8, 1997, pp. A1–A2.

17. See Dale D. Buss, "Capturing Customers with TV Retailing," *Nation's Business*, February 1997, pp. 29–32; "Shopping from the Sofa," *American Demographics*, April 1997, pp. 31–32; and Doreen Carvajal, "Publishers Find New Market Through Television Shopping Network," *New York Times*, February 14, 1998, p. D1.

18. See Frank Rose, "The End of TV as We Know It," *Fortune*, December 23, 1996, pp. 58–68; Elizabeth Lesly and Robert D. Hof, "Is Digital Convergence for Real?" *Business Week*, June 23, 1997, pp. 42–43; Amy Cortese, "Not @ Home Alone: Bill Comes Knocking," *Business Week*, July 14, 1997, p. 24; B. G. Yovovich, "Webbed Feet: Marketing Opportunities Emerge from Interactive Television Applications and Services," *Marketing News*, January 19, 1998, pp. 1, 18; and Horst Stipp, "Should TV Marry PC?" *American Demographics*, July 1998, pp. 16–18.

19. DeAnn Weimer, "Can You Keep 'Em Down on the Mall?" *Business Week*, December 15, 1997, pp. 66–70; "Lining Up for Interactive Kiosks," *Nation's Business*, February 1998, p. 46; Warren S. Hersch, "Kiosks Poised to Be A Huge Growth Market," *Computer Reseller News*, May 18, 1998, p. 163; and Catherine Yang, "No Web Is an Island, *Business Week*, March 22, 1999, p. EB38.

20. "Interactive: Ad Age Names Finalists," *Advertising Age*, February 27, 1995, pp. 12–14.

21. See Catherine Yang, "AOL: The Right Kind of Busy Signals," *Business Week*, February 23, 1998, pp. 34–35; David Bank, "Microsoft Plans to Cut Back on Its Online Services," *Wall Street Journal*, February 27, 1998, p. B6; and Christopher Peacock, "A Look at the Pioneers," *Money*, Summer 1998, pp. 54–60.

22. For more on the basics of using the Internet, see Raymond D. Frost and Judy Strauss, *The Internet: A New Marketing Tool—1999* (Upper Saddle River, NJ: Prentice Hall, 1999).

23. Internet usage statistics obtained from various CommerceNet reports (see www.commerce.net/nielsen/), June 1998; Robert D. Hof, "Amazon.com: The Wild World of E-commerce," *Business Week*, December 14, 1998, pp. 106–119; and Rochelle Garner, "The E-commerce Connection," *Sales & Marketing Management*, January 1999, pp. 40–46.

24. "'Startling Increase' in Internet Shopping Reported in New CommerceNet/Nielsen Media Research Survey," CommerceNet press release, www.commerce.net/nielsen/press-97.html, March 12, 1997.

25. Lynn Branigan, "The Internet: The Emerging Premier Direct Marketing Channel," *Direct Marketing*, May 1998, pp. 46–48; J. D. Mosley-Matchett, "Marketers: There's a Feminine Side to the Web," *Marketing News*, February 16, 1998, p. 6; and Roger O. Crockett, "A Web That Looks Like the World," *Business Week*, March 22, 1999, pp. EB46–EB47.

26. See Paul M. Eng, "Cybergiants See the Future—and It's Jack and Jill," *Busi-

ness Week, April 14, 1997, p. 44; Jeffrey H. Epstein, "The Net Generation Is Changing the Marketplace," *The Futurist*, April 1998, p. 14; and "Web Nets the Masses," *American Demographics*, December 1998, pp. 18–19.

27. See Rebecca Piirto Heath, "The Frontiers of Psychographics," *American Demographics*, July 1996, pp. 38–43.

28. See Philip Kotler, Gary Armstrong, Peggy H. Cunningham, and Robert Warren, *Principles of Marketing*, Third Canadian Edition (Scarborough, Ontario: Prentice Hall Canada: 1996), pp. 526–527.

29. John Deighton, "The Future of Interactive Marketing," *Harvard Business Review*, November–December 1996, pp. 151–162.

30. *Ibid.*, p. 154.

31. See Kathy Rebello, "Making Money on the Net," *Business Week*, September 23, 1996, pp. 104–118.

32. Melanie Berger, "It's Your Move," *Sales & Marketing Management*, March 1998, pp. 45–53.

33. John Deighton, "The Future of Interactive Marketing, p. 154.

34. "Advertising Age Teams with eMarketer for Research Report," *Advertising Age*, May 3, 1999, p. s24.

35. Robert D. Hof, "Internet Communities," *Business Week*, May 5, 1997, pp. 64–80.

36. *Ibid.*, p. 66.

37. *Ibid.*, p. 67. Also see Ian P. Murphy, "Web 'Communities' a Target Marketer's Dream," *Advertising Age*, July 7, 1997, p. 2; Patricia Riedman, "Web Communities Offer Shopping Options for Users," *Advertising Age*, October 26, 1998, p. S10; and Neil Cross, "Building Global Communities," *Business Week*, March 22, pp. EB42–EB43.

38. Erika Rasmusson, "Tracking Down Sales," *Sales & Marketing Management*, June 1998, p. 19.

39. See Mary J. Cronin, "Using the Web to Push Key Data to Decision Makers," *Fortune*, September 19, 1997, p. 254; and Tim McCollum, "All the News That's Fit to Print," *Nation's Business*, June 1998, pp. 59–61.

40. Amy Cortese, "It's Called Webcasting, and It Promises to Deliver the Info You Want, Straight to Your PC," *Business Week*, February 24, 1997, pp. 95–104. Also see Kenneth Leung, "Marketing with Electronic Mail without Spam," *Marketing News*, January 19, 1998, p. 11; and Philip M. Perry, "E-mail Hell: The Dark Side of the Internet Age," *Folio: The Magazine for Magazine Management*, June 1998, pp. 74–75.

41. Heather Green, "Cyberspace Winners: How They Did It," *Business Week*, June 22, 1998, pp. 154–160. Also see Michael D. Donahue, "Adapting the Internet to the Needs of Business," *Advertising Age*, February 2, 1998, p. 26; and Shikhar Ghosh, "Making Business Sense of the Internet," *Harvard Business Review*, March–April 1998, pp. 126–135.

42. John Deighton, "The Future of Interactive Marketing," p. 156; and Kate Maddix, "Information Still Killer App on the Internet," *Advertising Age*, October 6, 1997, p. 42.

43. *Ibid.*, p. 158.

44. See Heather Green, "A Little Privacy, Please," *Business Week*, March 16, 1998, pp. 98–102; and Rebecca Quick, "Privacy: On-Line Groups Are Offering Up Privacy Plans," *Wall Street Journal*, June 22, 1998, p. B1.

45. See Ernan Roman, *Integrated Direct Marketing* (New York: McGraw-Hill, 1988), p. 108; and Mark Suchecki, "Integrated Marketing: Making It Pay," *Direct*, October 1993, p. 43.

46. Portions of this section are based on Terrence H. Witkowski, "Self-Regulation Will Suppress Direct Marketing's Downside," *Marketing News*, April 24, 1989, p. 4. Also see Katie Muldoon, "The Industry Must Rebuild Its Image," *Direct*, April 1995, p. 106; Jim Castelli, "How to Handle Personal Information," *American Demographics*, March 1996, pp. 50–57; and Elyssa Yoon-Jung Lee, "How Do You Say 'Leave Me Alone!'" *Money*, June 1998, p. 140.

47. John Hagel III and Jeffrey F. Rayport, "The Coming Battle for Customer Information," *Harvard Business Review*, January–February 1997, pp. 53–65.

48. Melanie Rigney, "Too Close for Comfort, Execs Warn," *Advertising Age*, January 13, 1992, p. 31. Also see "Summary of '1992 Harris-Equifax Consumer Privacy Survey,'" *Marketing News*, August 16, 1993, p. A18; Laura Hanson, "A Short List of Telemarketing No-Nos," *Marketing Tools*, January/February 1997, p. 50; and Joshua Cho, "DMA Mandates Use of Opt-Out List," *Catalog Age*, March 1998, p. 33.

Chapter 15

1. Extracts and quotes from Marc Gunther, "They All Want to Be Like Mike," *Fortune*, July 21, 1997, pp. 51–53: (1997 Time, Inc., all rights reserved; and Warren Cohen, "Slam-Dunk Diplomacy," *U.S. News & World Report*, June 8, 1998, p. 7. Also see Bob Ryan, "Hoop Dreams," *Sales & Marketing Management*, December 1996, pp. 48–53; Jeff Jensen, "'Experiential Branding' Makes It to the Big Leagues," *Advertising Age*, April 14, 1997, pp. 20, 14; William Echikson, "Michael, the NBA, and the Slam-Dunking of Paris," *Paris*, November 3, 1997, p. 82; and Stefan Fatsis, "NBA Bravely Plans for Post-Jordan Era," *Wall Street Journal*, February 6, 1998, p. B1.

2. See "Top 50 U.S. Industrial Exporters," *Fortune*, August 22, 1994, p. 132; Edmund Faltermayer, "Competitiveness: How U.S. Companies Stack Up Now," *Fortune*, April 18, 1994, pp. 52–64; and "The Fortune Global 5 Hundred," *Fortune*, August 4, 1997, p. F1.

3. See Philip Kotler, *Marketing Management: Analysis, Planning, Implementation, and Control*, 9th ed. (Upper Saddle River, NJ: Prentice Hall, 1997), p. 403.

4. "The Unique Japanese," *Fortune*, November 24, 1986, p. 8. For more on nontariff and other barriers, see Warren J. Keegan and Mark C. Green, *Principles of Global Marketing* (Upper Saddle River, NJ: Prentice Hall, 1997), pp. 200–203.

5. Douglas Harbrecht and Owen Ullmann, "Finally GATT May Fly," *Business Week*, December 29, 1993, pp. 36–37; and Ping Deng, "Impact of GATT Uruguay Round on Various Industries," *American Business Review*, June 1998, pp. 22–29. Also see Charles W. L. Hill, *International Business* (Chicago: Irwin, 1997), pp. 165–168; and "Special Article: World Trade: Fifty Years On," *The Economist*, May 16, 1998, pp. 21–23.

6. For more on the European Union, see Andrew Hilton, "Mythology, Markets, and the Emerging Europe," *Harvard Business Review*, November–December 1992, pp. 50–54; "Around Europe in 40 Years," The Economist, May 31, 1997, p. S4; "European Union to Begin Expansion," *New York Times*, March 30, 1998, p. A5; and Joan Warner, "Mix Us Culturally? It's Impossible," *Business Week*, April 27, 1998, p. 108.

7. For more reading on free-trade zones, see Hilton, "Mythology, Markets, and the Emerging Europe;" William C. Symonds, "Meanwhile, to the North, NAFTA Is a Big Smash," *Business Week*, February 27, 1995, p. 66; Paul Magnusson, "NAFTA: Where's That Giant Sucking Sound?" *Business Week*, July 7, 1997, p. 45; and David M. Gould, "Has NAFTA Changed North American Trade?" *Economic Review— Federal Reserve Bank of Dallas*, first quarter, 1998, pp. 12–23.

8. Bill Saporito, "Where the Global Action Is," *Fortune*, special issue on "The Tough New Consumer," Autumn–Winter 1993, pp. 62–65. Also see Keegan and Green, *Principles of Global Marketing*, pp. 39–44; and "Income Distribution, Capital Accumulation, and Growth," *Challenge*, March–April 1998, pp. 61–80.

9. Manjeet Kripalani, "As the Politicians Squabble, India Stagnates," *Business Week*, May 5, 1997, p. 58; and Amy Louise Kazmin, "Why New Delhi Is Picking on Pepsi," *Business Week*, May 18, 1998, p. 54.

10. For these and other examples, see Louis Kraar, "How to Sell to Cashless Buyers," *Fortune*, November 7, 1988, pp. 147–154; Nathaniel Gilbert, "The Case for Countertrade," *Across the Board*, May 1992, pp. 43–45; Kwanena Anyane-Ntow and Santhi C. Harvey, "A Countertrade Primer," *Management Accounting (USA)*, April 1995, p. 47; and Darren McDermott and S. Karen Witcher, "Bartering Gains Currency," *Wall Street Journal*, April 6, 1998, p. A10.

11. Rebecca Piirto Heath, "Think Globally," *Marketing Tools*, October 1996, pp. 49–54.

12. For other examples, see Sergey Frank, "Global Negotiating," *Sales & Marketing Management*, May 1992, pp. 64–

69; Andrea L. Simpson, "Doing Business in Asia Pacific Requires New Skills," *Marketing News*, August 4, 1994, p. 4; "The Way We Live," *Advertising Age*, January 16, 1995, p. I3; and Sak Onkvisit and John J. Shaw, *International Marketing: Analysis and Strategy* (Upper Saddle River, NJ: Prentice Hall, 1997), chapter 6.

13. Charles A. Coulombe, "Global Expansion: The Unstoppable Crusade," *Success*, September 1994, pp. 18–20.

14. See "Crest, Colgate Bare Teeth in Competition for China," *Advertising Age International*, November 1996, p. I3; and Mark L. Clifford, "How You Can Win in China," *Business Week*, May 26, 1997, pp. 66–68.

15. Linda Grant, "GE's 'Smart Bomb' Strategy," *Fortune*, July 21, 1997, pp. 109–110.

16. Robert Neff, "In Japan, They're Goofy about Disney," *Business Week*, March 12, 1990, p. 64; and Geri Smith, "NAFTA: A Green Light for Red Tape," *Business Week*, July 25, 1994, p. 48.

17. See See Theodore Levitt, "The Globalization of Markets," *Harvard Business Review*, May–June 1983, pp. 92–102; David M. Szymanski, Sundar G. Bharadwaj, and Rajan Varadarajan, "Standardization versus Adaptation of International Marketing Strategy: An Empirical Investigation," *Journal of Marketing*, October 1993, pp. 1–17; Ashish Banerjee, "Global Campaigns Don't Work; Multinationals Do," *Advertising Age*, April 18, 1994, p. 23; Cyndee Miller, "Chasing Global Dream," *Marketing News*, December 2, 1996, pp. 1, 2; and Jeryl Whitelock and Carole Pimblett, "The Standardization Debate in International Marketing," *Journal of Global Marketing*, 1997, p. 22.

18. See Patrick Oster and John Rossant, "Call It Worldpool," *Business Week*, November 28, 1994, pp. 98–99; "In India, Beef-Free Mickie D," *Business Week*, April 7, 1995, p. 52; Miller, "Chasing Global Dream;" and Jeff Walters, "Have Brand Will Travel," *Brandweek*, October 6, 1997, pp. 22–26.

19. See Warren J. Keegan, *Global Marketing Management*, 4th ed. (Upper Saddle River, NJ: Prentice Hall, 1989), pp. 378–381; and Warren J. Keegan and

Mark C. Green, *Principles of Global Marketing* (Upper Saddle River, NJ: Prentice Hall, 1997), pp. 294–298.

20. For these and other examples, see Andrew Kupfer, "How to Be a Global Manager," *Fortune*, March 14, 1988, pp. 52–58; Maria Shao, "For Levi's: A Flattering Fit Overseas," *Business Week*, November 5, 1990, 76–77; Joseph Weber, "Campbell: Now It's M-M-Global," *Business Week*, March 15, 1993, pp. 52–53; Zachary Schiller, "Make It Simple," *Business Week*, September 9, 1996, p. 102; and Chester Dawson, "Gerber Feeding Booming Japanese Baby Food Market," *Durham Herald-Sun*, February 21, 1998, p. C10.

21. J. S. Perry Hobson, "Feng Shui: Its Impacts on the Asian Hospitality Industry," *International Journal of Contemporary Hospitality Management*, vol. 6, no. 6, 1994, pp. 21–26; Bernd H. Schmitt and Yigang Pan, "In Asia, the Supernatural Means Sales," *New York Times*, February 19, 1995, 3, 11:2; and Sally Taylor, "Tackling the Curse of Bad Feng Shui," *Publishers Weekly*, April 27, 1998, p. 24.

22. Mir Maqbool Alam Khan, "Kellogg Reports Brisk Cereal Sales in India," *Advertising Age*, November 14, 1994, p. 60. For more on international advertising and promotion, see George E. Belch and Michael A. Belch, *Advertising and Promotion* (New York: Irwin/McGraw Hill, 1998), pp. 625–632.

23. See Michael Oneal, "Harley-Davidson: Ready to Hit the Road Again," *Business Week*, July 21, 1986, p. 70; and "EU Proposes Dumping Change," *East European Markets*, February 14, 1997, pp. 2–3.

24. See Maria Shao, "Laying the Foundation for the Great Mall of China," *Business Week*, January 25, 1988, pp. 68–69; and Mark L. Clifford and Nicole Harris, "Coke Pours into China," *Business Week*, October 28, 1996, p. 73.

25. Richard Tomlinson, "The China Card," *Fortune*, May 25, 1998, p. 82.

26. See Kenichi Ohmae, "Managing in a Borderless World," *Harvard Business Review*, May–June 1989, pp. 152–161; William J. Holstein, "The Stateless Corporation," *Business Week*, May 14, 1990, pp. 98–105; and John A. Byrne and Kathleen Kerwin, "Borderless Man-

agement," *Business Week*, May 23, 1994, pp. 24–26.

Chapter 16

1. Quotes and extracts from Rhymer Rigby, "Tutti-Frutti Management," *Management Today*, February 1998, pp. 54–56; Alex Taylor III, "Yo, Ben! Yo Jerry! It's Just Ice Cream," *Fortune*, April 28, 1997, p. 374; and "Ben & Jerry's Mission Statement," accessed on-line at www.benjerry.com/mission.html. Also see Tom McInerney, "Double Trouble: Combining Business and Ethics," *Business Ethics Quarterly*, January 1998, pp. 187–189; and "Everything You Ever Wanted to Know about Ben & Jerry's," accessed on-line at www.benjerry.com/aboutbj.html, July 21, 1998.

2. See Jeffrey H. Birnbaum, "Tobacco's Can of Worms," *Fortune*, July 21, 1997, pp. 58–60; John McCain and Robert Pitofsky, "Sorting Through Tobacco Dilemma," *Advertising Age*, March 16, 1998, p. 24; and Krik Davidson, "Up in Smoke: For Tobacco, There's No Turing Back," *Marketing News*, May 25, 1998, pp. 6, 21.

3. See Faye Rice, "How to Deal with Tougher Customers," *Fortune*, December 3, 1990, pp. 38–48; Richard W. Pollay and Banwari Mittal, "Here's the Beef: Factors, Determinants, and Segments in Consumer Criticism of Advertising," *Journal of Marketing*, July 1993, pp. 99–114; and Leah Rickard, "Ex-Soviet States Lead World in Ad Cynicism," *Advertising Age*, June 5, 1995, p. 3.

4. Excerpts from Theodore Levitt, "The Morality (?) of Advertising," *Harvard Business Review*, July–August 1970, pp. 84–92. Also see Joel J. Davis, "Ethics in Advertising Decision Making," *Journal of Consumer Affairs*, December 22, 1994, p. 380; and Chuck Ross, "Marketers Fend off Shift in Rules for Ad Puffery," *Advertising Age*, February 19, 1996, p. 41. For a good review of advertising regulation and self-regulations, see John McDonough, "25 Years of Self-Regulation," *Advertising Age*, December 2, 1996, pp. C1, C2.

5. Sandra Pesmen, "How Low Is Low? How Free Is Free?" *Advertising Age*, May 7, 1990, p. S10. For other exam-

ples, see "Feeding Frenzy," *Marketing Week*, April 16, 1998, p. 28.

6. For a thought-provoking short case involving planned obsolescence, see James A. Heely and Roy L. Nersesian, "The Case of Planned Obsolescence," *Management Accounting*, February 1994, p. 67. Also see Joel Dryfuss, "Planned Obsolescence Is Alive and Well," *Fortune*, February 15, 1999, p. 192.

7. See Judith Bell and Bonnie Maria Burlin, "In Urban Areas: Many More Still Pay More for Food," *Journal of Public Policy and Marketing*, Fall 1993, pp. 268–270; Alan R. Andreasen, "Revisiting the Disadvantages: Old Lesson and New Problems," *Journal of Public Policy and Marketing*, Fall 1993, pp. 270–275; Laura Mazzuca Toops, "Multicultural Marketing," *Rough Notes*, January 1998, pp. 30–32; Tony Attrino, "Nationwide Settles Redlining Suit in Ohio," *National Underwriter*, April 27, 1998, p. 4; and Angelo B. Henderson, "First Chicago Unit Agrees to Lend $3 Billion in Detroit," *Wall Street Journal*, June 26, 1998.

8. See Anne B. Fisher, "A Brewing Revolt Against the Rich," *Fortune*, December 17, 1990, pp. 89–94; and Norval D. Glenn, "What Does Family Mean?" *American Demographics*, June 1992, pp. 30–37.

9. For more on materialism, see Leon G. Schiffman and Leslie Lazar Kanuk, *Consumer Behavior*, 6th ed. (Upper Saddle River, NJ: Prentice Hall, 1997), pp. 132–133; and James A. Muncy and Jacqueline K. Eastman, "Materialism and Consumer Ethics: An Exploratory Study," *Journal of Business Ethics*, January 1998, pp. 137–145.

10. Kim Clark, "Real-World-O-Nomics: How to Make Traffic Jams a Thing of the Past," *Fortune*, March 31, 1997, p. 34.

11. From an advertisement for Fact magazine, which does not carry advertisements.

12. See Shaifali Puri, "Deals of the Year," *Fortune*, February 17, 1997, pp. 102–103; and Michael J. Mandel, "A Pack of 800-Lb. Gorillas," *Business Week*, February 3, 1997, pp. 34–35.

13. Nancy Arnott, "Drugstore Cowboys Shoot It Out," *Sales & Marketing Man-

agement*, August 1994, p. 15; Glenn Snyder, "Wal-Mart Wins Pricing Case—Or Did It?" *Progressive Grocer*, February 1995, p. 11; "Conditions that Trigger Probes Are Defined," *Aviation Week & Space Technology*, April 13, 1998, p. 24; and James E. Meeks, "Predatory Behavior as an Exclusionary Device in the Emerging Telecommunications Industry," *Wake Forest Law Review*, Spring 1998, p. 21.

14. For more details, see Paul N. Bloom and Stephen A. Greyser, "The Maturing of Consumerism," *Harvard Business Review*, November–December 1981, pp. 130–139, Robert J. Samualson, "The Aging of Ralph Nader," *Newsweek*, December 16, 1985, p. 57; Douglas A. Harbrecht, "The Second Coming of Ralph Nader," *Business Week*, March 6, 1989, p. 28; and George S. Day and David A. Aaker, "A Guide to Consumerism," *Marketing Management*, Spring 1997, pp. 44–48.

15. Stuart L. Hart, Beyond Greening: Strategies for a Sustainable World," *Harvard Business Review*, January–February 1997, pp. 66–76. Also see Jacquelyn Ottman, "What Sustainability Means to Marketers," *Marketing News*, July 21, 1997, p. 4;

16. Ibid., p. 74.

17. Michael E. Porter and Claas van der Linde, "Green and Competitive: Ending the Stalemate," *Harvard Business Review*, September–October 1995, pp. 120–134.

18. Hart, "Beyond Greening," p. 72. For other examples, see Jacquelyn Ottman, "Environmental Winners Show Sustainable Strategies," *Marketing News*, April 27, 1998, p. 6.

19. Hart, "Beyond Greening," p. 73; and Linda Grant, "Monsanto's Bet: There's Gold in Going Green," *Fortune*, April 14, 1997, pp. 116–118.

20. "Transnational Corporations and Global Environmental Policy," *Prizm*, Arthur D. Little, Inc., Cambridge, MA, first quarter, 1994, pp. 51–63.

21. Ibid., p. 56.

22. Michelle Wirth Fellman, "New Product Marketer of 1997," *Marketing News*, March 30, 1998, pp. E2, E12.

23. See Mollie Neal, "Reaping the Rewards of Skillful Marketing . . . While Help-

ing Humanity," *Direct Marketing*, September 1993, p. 24; and James R. Norman, "With or Without the Ketchup?" *Forbes*, March 14, 1995, p. 107.

24. For more discussion of basic ethics philosophies, see Carolyn Wiley, "The ABCs of Business Ethics: Definitions, Philosophies, and Implementation," *Industrial Management*, January 1995, p. 22.

25. Dan R. Dalton and Richard A. Cosier, "The Four Faces of Social Responsibility," *Business Horizons*, May–June 1982, pp. 19–27.

26. John F. Magee and P. Ranganath Nayak, "Leaders' Perspectives on Business Ethics," Prizm, Arthur D. Little, Inc., Cambridge, MA, first quarter, 1994, pp. 65–77.

27. Ibid., pp. 71–72. Also see Thomas Donaldson, "Values in Tension: Ethics away from Home," *Harvard Business Review*, September–October 1996, pp. 48–62.

28. Mark Hendricks, "Ethics in Action," *Management Review*, January 1995, pp. 53–55.

29. Kenneth Labich, "The New Crisis in Business Management," *Fortune*, April 20, 1992, pp. 167–76, here p. 176.

30. From "Ethics as a Practical Matter," a message from David R. Whitman, Chairman of the Board of Whirlpool Corporation, as reprinted in Ricky E. Griffin and Ronald J. Ebert, *Business* (Upper Saddle River, NJ: Prentice Hall, 1989), pp. 578–579. For more on marketing ethics, see Lynn Sharp Paine, "Managing for Organizational Integrity," *Harvard Business Review*, March–April 1994, pp. 106–117; Tom McInerney, "Double Trouble: Combining Business and Ethics," *Business Ethics Quarterly*, January 1998, pp. 187–189; and Robert B. Reich, "The New Meaning of Corporate Responsibility," *California Management Review*, Winter 1998, pp. 8–17.

Airline Alliances: Winging Their Way to Disaster?

Suppose you lived in Chicago and needed to fly on business to Atlanta, then to Seattle, and home again. How many times would you enter Chicago's O'Hare Airport? In the past, the answer would have been three times—you'd have flown directly from United's hub in Chicago to Atlanta but returned to Chicago for a layover before traveling on to Seattle. Under the new United-Delta alliance, however, the answer now is twice. You'd still fly United to Atlanta but now you'd fly Delta directly to Seattle and then fly United back to Chicago.

Try the same math for a complicated round-the-world business trip. Let's say you had to fly from Chicago to Stockholm and then on to Germany, Thailand, and Brazil before returning to Chicago. Ticketing that trip could be a nightmare. You'd have to travel several airlines with very long delays and stopovers between flights. Further, unless you have frequent flyer cards for all of the airlines involved, you would not be able to accumulate frequent flyer miles for most of the trip. Now, however, thanks to the global Star Alliance—which consists of United, Air Canada, Lufthansa of Germany, Scandinavian Airlines System, Thai Airways, and Varig Brazilian—ticketing can be a breeze, layovers can be minimized, and you can put all the air miles on your United frequent flyer card.

Such alliances are the latest wave in airline services. These cooperative arrangements between airlines allow for code sharing (each airline can sell tickets on the other's flights) and combining frequent flyer miles into the program of the customer's choice. Beyond the obvious services that customers are likely to see, the alliances provide numerous other benefits. When two or more airlines enter an alliance, they can rearrange their schedules to minimize layovers between connecting flights, and they can provide more convenient and efficient service to more airports.

For example, Bush Field in Augusta, Georgia, is one of 14 airports receiving United's and Delta's "first competitive service." Thanks to the new alliance, travelers in Augusta can fly either Delta or United depending on their destination. "You can buy a United ticket at Augusta, if it's cheaper, and take the Delta flight to your destination," said Peggy Estes, Delta spokeswoman. "Or you could be buying a seat on Delta and sitting on a United plane." For Augusta travelers, the result could be cheaper tickets and more direct flights because they can now fly not only where Delta goes but where United goes as well.

This United-Delta alliance combines the country's biggest and third-biggest airlines. In 1997, United and Delta had 1,174 jets and combined revenues of $31.3 billion. The nation's other four major airlines (American, US Airways, Northwest, and Continental) had 1,760 jets and combined revenues of $44.5 billion. With the alliance, United and Delta control more than 34 percent of all U.S. flights. That worries consumer advocates such as Ralph Nader, who believes that alliances will shrink competition in the industry and ultimately result in higher fares.

Advocates for both business travelers and final consumers are concerned about the alliances. "While these mergers may create avenues of seamless travel for consumers and marketing economies of scale for the carriers, we do not anticipate that these alliances will alleviate the high cost of air fares that business travelers experience," says Mark Johnson, president of the National Business Travel Association. As the global economy grows, international business travel has mushroomed and business travelers who cannot plan their travel well in advance sometimes find themselves paying as much as 10 times the fare of the leisure traveler sitting next to them.

Supporting this concern over higher prices is the Brussels–New York route example. Three years ago, three airlines were competing on the route, offering corporate discounts of 20 percent or more to fill seats. But when Delta and Sabena gained antitrust immunity for their alliance in 1996 and the ability to coordinate marketing and fares, American dropped out of the market. As a result, corporate discounts were cut nearly in half and average fares paid between New York and Brussels have risen 23 percent, versus an 18 percent jump in all international fares. In the United States, airline alliances will not have the ability to coordinate fares, which may alleviate the problem somewhat. But the basic point that airline alliances, especially among large airlines, can put nonaligned airlines at a disadvantage in terms of economies of scale remains valid.

"But these alliances are not about fares, they're about convenience," maintains Kenneth P. Quinn, an aviation lawyer and former chief counsel for the Federal Aviation Administration. "Any airline can get you to a connection, if you don't mind how long you wait in the airport. But partners in an alliance time their flights for the convenience of connecting passengers." However, how much is such convenience worth? Is it worth fare hikes of 5 percent, 10 percent, or 25 percent? Because airline fares are no longer regulated, a decrease in competition will likely result in higher fares as so many airlines struggle to generate profits.

Passengers are not the only ones leery of airline alliances—labor is also concerned. Pilots fear that such deals will limit a carrier's growth and pilot earning potential. Labor leaders worry that alliances will lead to the lowest-common-denominator contracts. "You've certainly set yourself up to be whipsawed, one labor contract versus another," says Allied Pilots Association President Richard T. LaVoy at American. Could disgruntled labor result in more lost or misplaced bags, or in work stoppages? What happens to an alliance if one of the partner's labor force goes on strike?

Others argue that higher fares, lack of competition, or labor issues may not be the most important concern about alliances. The biggest issue might be safety. Many international alliances tie U.S. airlines with foreign carriers that have much higher accident rates. For example, United is allied with Thai airlines, which has a fatal accident rate eight times that of United. Delta is partnered with AeroPeru which has significantly higher fatality rates, and Continental's alliance includes Aserca Airlines of Venezuela, which fails to meet FAA air safety standards. Even alliances with well-respected airlines can create legal problems when accidents occur. In the first lawsuit arising out of an international code-sharing deal, Delta was sued by several survivors of Delta ticket holders aboard Swissair flight 111 that crashed off the coast of Nova Scotia in September 1998. Although Swissair had one of the industry's best safety records, the suits allege that Delta was responsible for its passengers' safety. If the suit is successful, the ruling could cause major turbulence throughout the airline industry.

Currently, there is no means by which U.S. FAA standards can be enforced in other countries. The only solution at present would be for airlines to demand higher standards from their partners, but partners from third-world countries may be unable or unwilling to meet those standards. And even if U.S. airlines stick to their guns, such a strategy would still not absolve a U.S. airline from responsibility. Although it might reduce crashes, the U.S. airline could still be sued. One observer offers some cheap legal advice to U.S. airlines: "Safety should never take a back seat to profits. Demand higher safety standards from your partners."

Not all airlines are eager to enter into alliances. An American Airlines spokesman comments that American's pact with US Airways is simply a response to what's going on in the marketplace, not a sign of American's support for these domestic pairings. But most airlines appear determined not to be left out of these "virtual mergers," which appear to be defensive strategies rather than offensive ones.

The fears of monopoly power implicit in these alliances may be legitimate given the proposed merger of Continental and Northwest. Whereas most alliances are sharing arrangements that don't involve any ownership, the Continental-Northwest merger would involve cross-ownership. Continental would gain Northwest Airlines' strengths in Asia while Northwest would gain Continental's Latin American network. The result would be the creation of a fourth truly national and international player in the airline industry. However, as Continental is learning, mergers present more risks than alliances do. Although Northwest was the on-time airline for much of the nineties, its recent labor and service problems have set Continental to rethinking this marriage.

If the Continental-Northwest merger fails to get off the ground, leisure and business travelers may breathe a sigh of relief that other mergers are less likely to follow. In the meantime, the Justice Department is still scrutinizing proposed alliances, and the legal repercussions of the Swissair crash may cause U.S. airlines to rethink alliances.

Questions for Discussion

1. What are the plusses and minuses of airline alliances for consumers and the airlines?
2. How do the alliances add value to the airlines' offerings? For which target market—leisure or business travelers—would alliances have the strongest positive impact? The strongest negative impact?
3. How would you determine whether the benefits of alliances outweigh the disadvantages for air travelers?
4. Explain how alliances could affect airline pricing.
5. If you were the Justice Department, how would you rule on alliances? Would you allow them? Why or why not?

Sources: Damon Cline, "Some Airports Will Get Competition Between United, Delta in Merger," *Knight-Ridder Tribune Business News*, April 30, 1998; Scott McCartney, "Airline Agreements Encounter Some Turbulence," *Wall Street Journal*, August 24, 1998, p. B1; Edwin McDonald, "For Corporate Fliers, Airlines' Alliances May Mean More Convenience, but Higher Fares," *New York Times*, April 29, 1998, p. D5; Lorraine Woellert, "U.S. Airlines: Make Sure Your Partners Are Safe," *Business Week*, October 19, 1998, p. 132; Wendy Zellner, "Where Are All Those Airline Tie-Ups Headed?" *Business Week*, May 11, 1998, pp. 32–33.

Video Case 2
Nike: Running over the Competition

Nobody takes the admonition to "Just do it" more seriously than Nike, the company for whom the slogan was written. Whether it's entering a new sport, moving into a new geographic market, or developing a new product, Nike approaches its mission with the dedication and single-mindedness of an athlete training for competition. And whatever the task, the goal is always the same: To turn in a peak performance, one that leaves no doubt as to who the best is. That's because at Nike, winning isn't merely a corporate philosophy—it's the company's business.

"This brand is all about building products for athletes, high-performance products, very authentic products, innovative products, bringing new technology to athletes so they can perform better—at a higher level in their sport," says Bill Zeitz, global director of advertising development at Nike.

Liz Dolan, the company's marketing director, puts it in even more basic terms. "We have a really incredibly simple mission, which is, 'serve the athlete.' If you're in product development that means you have to make sure that the products really work, that they're really great for whatever sport you are assigned to. If you're in the communications area, it means that you have to communicate with an authenticity about the sports experience, what athletes know to be true of what it feels like to win a basketball game, or run a marathon, or whatever."

This near-obsession with authentic athletic performance comes naturally to the Beaverton, Oregon company. It was started in the 1960s by Phil Knight, a sports enthusiast and runner who believed the needs of serious athletes were being neglected by Adidas and Puma, the German companies that dominated the athletic shoe industry. With the help of Bill Bowerman, his former track coach at the University of Oregon, Knight set out to develop a shoe that would make a difference in a runner's performance.

The rest, as they say, is history. Nike has become a dominant player in sports apparel. With track, basketball, tennis, and other traditional sports in the "win" column, Nike recently has turned its attention to building its franchise in soccer, cricket, rugby, hockey, and in-line skating, among others. After all, Dolan explains, being a global sports brand requires an intensely local focus.

Being a global brand is extremely important to Nike as its home market, the United States, is nearing saturation. According to John Horan of newsletter *Sporting Goods Intelligence*, sporting goods chains have overexpanded and profit margins are threatened. Nike's first-ever quarterly loss in the second quarter of 1998 underscores the company's need to grow international markets, where it has only a 27 percent share of the athletic shoe market compared to a 43 percent share in the United States.

Going global is not a sure win for Nike. "Understanding what sports the people in a country play, and then being great at those sports . . . that's always the challenge. In the U.K., for instance, we are a really good basketball brand, but they don't play that there. And we are a really good tennis brand, but they kept telling us, 'Other than the two weeks during Wimbledon, nobody in the U.K. really cares about tennis.' So in the U.K. soccer is what they play. Rugby is what they play. So we had to really concentrate on being great at two sports that were not really something that came from our American tradition at all. That took years of product development and talking to consumers about, 'What does this sport really mean to you when you play it and what does it really mean to you when you watch it?' The brand attributes for Nike in the U.K. are the same—we really want to be the authentic sports brand—but the sports that are the building blocks for that are very different in the U.K. than they would be in the United States or than they would be in Japan."

Outside the United States, soccer is the main sport, with sales of $5 billion, and Nike has pursued the soccer player and fan with a vengeance. In the United States, it has signed a multiyear contract with Major League Soccer that calls for it to spend $3.75 million a year to sponsor 5 of the league's 10 teams. The contract contains a clause that allows Nike to retain sponsorship of half of the league's teams as the league expands.

But the real action is overseas and Nike has gone after that market aggressively. First, it has spent money—lots of it. It spent $20 million in a sealed-bid process to sponsor the Italian National team. During the 1997 European championships, it bought up all the billboards around stadiums where matches were held, effectively undermining the event's official sponsor, Umbro. In the spring of 1997, it sponsored a worldwide soccer tour that featured top teams. It has also spent millions on global advertising and signed leading national soccer stars such as Eric Cantona (captain of the national champion Manchester United soccer team in the U.K.) to highly lucrative contracts.

Nike's biggest money deal is its sponsorship agreement with the Confederacao Brasil de Futebol, Brazil's soccer federation, which cost Nike a breathtaking $200 million. Why Brazil? It won the 1994 World Cup soccer tournament. The Brazil contract represents a 10-year deal that includes appearances in Nike-produced exhibition matches and community events. Nike will supply Brazil's national teams with sports kits and, in return, the teams will participate in five friendly soccer games that Nike is arranging annually and to which Nike retains the television rights. Nike also will have access to training clinics in Brazil and to the infrastructure of the game.

Second, Nike has used its classic "in-your-face" marketing approach, even though it has generated much criticism of "the brash Americans from Nike." In 1996, Nike flew eight of soccer's hottest players to Tunisia to film an advertisement in which the athletes competed against the devil. Not surprisingly, this ad drew a spate of angry letters from offended fans. Signing bad boy Eric Cantona generated criticism and infuriated sports bureaucrats in the U.K. Even the Brazil deal has been roundly criticized. As part of that deal, Nike had to pay Umbro an undisclosed amount to cover the remaining two years of its contract with the Brazilian federation. "Nike is going in and almost encouraging teams to break contracts," says James R. Gorman, president of Puma North America. At the 1998 World Cup, Nike was relegated to the outskirts of Paris in the giant Grand Arche de la Defense building, which the company touted as the Popular Republic of Football — a slur on the "sporteaucrats," the guys in gray suits who tightly control international athletics. Le Mouvement Contre le Racisme et Pour l'Amitié Entre les Peuples (Movement Against Racism and for Friendship between Peoples) accused Nike of fascist imagery in ads such as the one featuring a dictatorlike athlete staring into the distance with the tagline, "Youth of the world, football is calling you! Join us." In response, Nike took down the ad.

To succeed, Nike will have to outdistance Adidas-Salomon AG, the traditional sponsor of international soccer. Although Nike's annual sales of $9 billion far outpace Adidas' $3 billion, Adidas commands much loyalty in the soccer market. It retains sponsorship of many top players and top teams, including the national teams of Germany, Spain, and France. It sponsored World Cup 1998, with the rights to sell official soccer balls and sports apparel, and it will sponsor the Women's World Cup in 1999. Further, Adidas has invaded Nike's home turf by sponsoring three U.S. teams and featuring players from those teams in U.S. advertising. "We don't think that anybody can get near to us on the product side," says Peter Csandai, an Adidas spokesman.

The big matchup between Nike and Adidas came in the 1998 World Cup in Paris. Although Nike bid to become the official supplier of uniforms, it never had a chance against Adidas, which controls 40 percent of soccer sales and is tight with the FIFA officials who control World Cup Soccer. Its fan park was across from the Eiffel Tower, whereas Nike's was on the outskirts of Paris. All the branded advertising in official stadiums said Adidas. The company spent close to $100 million on this World Cup and is expected to sponsor the 2002 and 2006 cups. Nike, on the other hand, sponsored Tour de Foot, a grassroots effort in which marketing people held soccer camps at various cities in France.

The two teams in the championship were Nike's Brazilian team, the favorite, and Adidas' French team. For the first time in history, the French team won the World Cup. So, temporarily, Adidas is ahead with the winning team. But this has not blunted Nike's enthusiasm for soccer. It still aims to be the top-selling soccer shoe by 2002.

Does it have a chance? Well, the U.S. team's poor showing in the 1998 World Cup did not enhance Nike's (or any other U.S. firm's) image in soccer. In 1994, Nike used a soccer shoe with low-quality cleats, but it has since improved the technology of its shoes. As a consequence, there were a lot of swoosh symbols seen on the field and in the stands at the last World Cup. One youthful fan was even spotted sporting a swoosh nose ring. Nike's low-keyed Tour de Foot was successful at targeting *young* soccer fans, who will be supporting the sport in the future. And any soccer fan knows that Brazil is a soccer pow-erhouse—far more likely to be in World Cup 2002 than the French team. Finally, Nike is the biggest player in the game. Its spending of $680 million on soccer in 1998 far outdistances Adidas, Umbro, or Reebok. With such free spending, Nike would appear to have changed the economics of the game, but it has a long way to go before it scores a match-winning goal in the global soccer market.

Questions for Discussion

1. What is Nike's mission and how does the company accomplish it?
2. Explain Nike's businesses in portfolio terms. Using the Boston Consulting Group matrix approach, how would you characterize its basketball, running, and soccer businesses?
3. What kinds of growth strategies is Nike using?
4. What are Nike's markets? How does it reach these markets?
5. What is Nike's proposed positioning in the global soccer market? Describe its marketing mix in global soccer.
6. Is Nike likely to be successful in global soccer?

Sources: "In the Vanguard: Trainers, Sneakers and Shoes," *The Economist*, June 7, 1997, p. 62; Geoff Dyer, "Nike Puts Its Hands on Ultimate Trophy," *The Financial Times*, December 14, 1996, p. 9; Stefan Fatsis, "Nike Tackles Soccer, Nicely," *Wall Street Journal*, July 2, 1998, p. A12; Patrick Harverson, "Putting Their Shirts on Soccer Deals", *The Financial Times*, November 1, 1997, p. 15; Linda Himelstein, "The Swoosh Heard Round the World," *Business Week*, May 12, 1997, pp. 76–80; Daniel Tilles, "Nike Pulls 'Totalitarian' World Cup Billboards," *ADWEEK Eastern Edition*, June 22, 1998, p. 3.

Video Case 3
Levi Strauss & Co.: Aiming at the Echo Boomers

In 1986, Levi Strauss & Co. found that the best way to stay true blue to its customers was to change its colors. Riding high on the results of a recent marketing campaign to return the company's flagship 501 jeans "back to basics," Levi Strauss & Co. was enjoying rein-vigorated sales of its denim pants. But the good news was followed by bad. Research showed that baby boomers, the core of the company's customer franchise, were buying only one or two pairs of jeans annually compared to the four to five pairs purchased each year by 15- to 24-year-olds.

Born between 1946 and 1964, the postwar baby boomers had adopted jeans as a symbol of their break from the tastes and traditions of their parents. They had, in the words of Steve Goldstein, vice-president of marketing and research for Levi's, helped turn the company into an "international global colossus" in the apparel industry. But now they were looking for a different kind of pant. They still wanted clothing that was com-fortable and made from natural fabrics, but fashion had become more important to them. Many worked in environments with relaxed dress codes, so they sought a pant that com-bined style and versatility—something that would be appropriate for both professional and leisure activities.

"We set ourselves out to answer the big question," Goldstein says. "How do we keep the baby boomer generation in Levi's brands when they weren't wearing so many pairs of Levi's jeans? And the answer was Dockers—something between the jean that they loved and a dress pant that their parents expected them to wear when they got their first job."

Dockers essentially created a product category—new casuals. Blue denim was out; cotton khaki in brown, green, black, and navy, but mostly in traditional tan, was in. Positioned as more formal than jeans and more casual than dress slacks, Dockers satisfied an unfulfilled need in the market. They were the right pant for a variety of occasions, an unpretentious alternative to dressy, tailored slacks.

The challenge in marketing Dockers was to leverage the Levi name and heritage while establishing the independence of the new brand, and to do so without detracting from Levi's core jeans focus. Goldstein says the company briefly considered not using the Levi name at all but realized that would be "sort of like trying to put a space shuttle up without any launch rockets." So the original tagline on the pants was "Levi's 100 percent cotton Dockers. If you're not wearing Dockers, you're just wearing pants."

Response from retailers and from the target market of 25- to 49-year-olds was everything Levi Strauss & Co. hoped for. All the top menswear accounts across the country placed Dockers in their stores and, in only five years, it had become a $1 billion consumer brand. Brand awareness among men 25 and older was 98 percent, and 70 percent of the target market had at least one pair of Dockers in their closets.

As Dockers began to mature, Levi Strauss & Co. brought out Slates, an extensive line of wool polyester microfiber and fine-gauge cotton dress pants. "We thought there was room in a man's closet for a third brand," says Jann Westfall, president of the Slates division. "That's why Slates was created to drive those options between khakis and suits."

A year later, everyone agreed that Slates was a dynamite brand. It had turned the Dockers customer onto dress slacks and appeared just when corporate casual started to dress up. Notes Zanella vice-president Tom Cohan, "Slates and other labels have pushed the envelope. This has created a tremendous consumer awareness for slacks in general." Some retailers found that their tailored business was up 15 to 20 percent.

But just like the good news about the "back-to-basics" move, the good news about Slates was followed by bad news—plummeting market share. Whereas Levi Strauss & Co. had a 31 percent of U.S. blue jeans business in 1990, it had only 19 percent seven years later. Worse yet, Levi's sales to teens—the core blue jeans buyer—had dropped from 33 percent in 1993 to 26 percent in 1997. Once the darling of the 15-to-24-year-old buyer, Levi Strauss & Co. now confronted indifference and an attitude that Levis are your dad's pants. The bottom line message: Levis are uncool.

Male teenagers increasingly prefer brands like Tommy Hilfiger and Old Navy. Even girls, who are more likely to buy Levis, like brands such as Calvin Klein, Gap, and Guess. Levi's was being squeezed on one end by upscale brands such as Tommy Hilfiger and Ralph Lauren and on the other by private label or store brands.

It's a classic marketing goof. Levi Strauss & Co. lost sight of the market that launched it to success. By concentrating on Dockers and, more recently, Slates, executives were distracted from the threat to their core jeans business. "They missed all the kids and those are your future buyers," says Bob Levi, owner of Dave's Army & Navy Store in New York. "It's very important that you attract this age group," says Gordon Hart, vice-president of the Lee brand at VF Corp. "By the time they're 24, they've adopted brands that they will use for the rest of their lives." The mistake was costly: falling sales and share forced Levi Strauss to lay off 1,000 salaried workers in February 1997 and to shutdown 11 plants and lay off one-third of its North American workforce in November of that year.

So, what is Levi Strauss & Co. doing about this? First, it brought in TBWA Chiat/Day to reposition Levi's image. It wanted to capitalize on Levi's heritage while turning around the "uncool" image through advertising and brand promotion aimed at multiple target markets. For the younger market, Levi Strauss is pumping up the Silver Tab brand, an eight-year-old jeans line that is considered more stylish among young consumers. Silver Tab has a baggier fit and uses nondenim fabrics. The median age of a Silver Tab buyer is 18 compared to 25 for Levi's other products. Levi's plans to expand the line to include more tops, more trendy styles, and new khaki pants. The company also plans to boost Silver Tab promotional spending fivefold for events such as concerts in New York and San Francisco, tie-ins to the music this age group listens to from retro to hip-hop, and outfitting players on hot television shows such as *Friends* and *Beverly Hills 90210*. In late August 1998, Levi's line launched an urban art campaign consisting of outdoor ads, transit posters, and magazine ads depicting the entire line of SilverTab apparel on cartoonlike drawings of kids with exotic hair and skin colors.

To appeal to those young female customers, Levi's sponsored Lilith Fair—one of the biggest musical tours among female teens. In addition, it bought a spread in Vogue magazine that features Lilith performers such as Sarah McLachlan and Liz Phair wearing Levi's. "When you are a 14-year-old girl and you know your favorite singer wears Levi's, somewhere in your head it's imprinted that Levi's is cool," says Jimmy Hanrahan, wardrobe stylist for MTV.

Levi Strauss & Co. also wanted to build on its heritage as the original, American jean. "We are the original jean," says Mark Hogan, Levi's director of consumer marketing. "We need to reclaim that." Doing so won't be easy. "When brands that start out very special, very pure, and very focused become a huge brand, it is the hugeness that homogenizes it and makes it less potent and powerful," says Lee Clow, TBWA Chiat/Day's chairman and chief creative officer.

Levi's decided to go back to its roots—the original dark-blue jean made of coarse fabric (the same fabric it had spent the last decade stone washing and bleaching to make it soft) using deep indigo-dying. These are Levi's "Hard" jeans—the original Levi's of the forties and fifties. Therefore, some of the first ads featured Marlon Brando (of the Wild Ones) and Marilyn Monroe in classic Levi's. Updating that image slightly, TBWA Chiat/Day ran a series of ads staging "Calvin wore them" and "Tommy wore them"—clearly an attempt to attack Klein and Hilfiger by associating them with Levi's roots.

Then came a series of ads more strident in tone that pushed the "Hard" image. In one commercial, a pair of rigid, bodiless jeans pivot around against a stark, white background. "Deep. Dark. Stiff as cheap plywood. Hard as old pipes," says the voice-over. "Just to wear them once, you gotta' learn to walk all over again." The jeans tip over and crash with a metallic clang. "Levi's Hard jeans. You break these in, you've got something." Other ads show the jeans deflecting cannons and being shot by a firing squad because they are "stiff with a vengeance." TV spots for the hard jeans ran on network prime time, Fox, ESPN, MTV, WB, Comedy Central, and other syndicated programming, which gives some indication of how varied Levi's and TBWA Chiat/Day think the market for these jeans is.

To be "continuously surprising," the ads change constantly. Instead of relying on one all-encompassing image campaign, with an overarching tagline, the agency replaces the ads regularly. "The overall message is about the brand's originality," says Hogan. "You can be the first and say it, but you have to continue to prove it by doing things that are new and original."

And speaking of new and original, Levi Strauss & Co. is now introducing a retroinspired line called "Red" aimed at "opinion-leading" consumers who set fashion trends. This is a premium product (in contrast to the hard jeans) aimed at older men and women. Because these consumers do not want to be targeted, Levi Strauss & Co. is using a series of teaser posters to build interest in the brand. These are usually black and white with one red object. Examples are one red bandage, one red spool of thread, or one red rectangle. There's no mention of the brand (or company) and no ad copy. "The entire concept behind this business unit is to have a brand that evolves and is discovered by the consumer" says Julia Hansen, director of the Red Line. "The purpose is to have the (Red) story unfold to each consumer," she said.

Not all of the changes at Levi Strauss & Co. are obvious to consumers. Accompanying the bold new look of Levi's is an internal transformation. Previously, individual departments such as design, marketing, and merchandising functioned relatively autonomously in three buildings. This meant that marketing and advertising might figure out a campaign for a product without checking with the designers about what was likely to be hot that season. As a result, Levi's was slow to market with new styles and fits. It didn't have enough novel products like wide-leg jeans at the right time. Now all of these personnel work under one roof. Presumably, the result will be faster market response and better coordinated advertising and merchandising efforts.

Levi Strauss & Co. is also taking action on the retail front. In 1998, Levi Strauss will come out with jazzier, more colorful packaging aimed at giving its products a more exciting, youthful look. It has ditched plans to open 100 new stores in malls across the country in favor of NikeTown-type stores, which will serve as the company's flagship stores in large cities. And it has re-vamped its Internet site to include a matchmaking service and profiles of emerging musical bands.

Will the new strategy work? Many industry insiders think that Levi Strauss has the money and market clout to pull it off. It's important that the company is facing the problem and taking action. But didn't we just read that some of those trendy new styles for Silver Tab include khakis? Doesn't that sound like Dockers? And speaking of Dockers, Levi Strauss may have a problem making that brand relevant to the next generation of young men. Baby boomers who are aging out of the Dockers' target market have refused to leave the brand behind. Consequently, the brand that has been positioned for consumers just moving out of their core jeans-wearing years may now be thought of by the next generation of young men moving into this segment as "my dad's brand." Thus, the "dad's brand" problem that hit Levi's in the blue jeans segment now threatens the Dockers market. Even as Levi's is working to get its core jeans business back on track, it will have to contend with a similar problem with Dockers.

The irony is that the "new" hard jeans are very, very reminiscent of dad's original brand of jeans. Levi Strauss may not be avoiding the "dad's brand" problem with "hard" jeans. Will today's youth see "hard" jeans as something different and exciting, or as the jeans that their dad (or even granddad) wore? Will they be sold on a product attribute of coarseness?

And, finally, what about Red? Suppose the story just doesn't unfold for some consumers? Will they really believe that they are not being marketed to by posters and ads that don't have copy, brand names, and selling points? In short, will this repositioning of Levis work? Has TBWA Chiat/Day come up with a new position or just a new way of talking about the old position?

Questions for Discussion

1. What forces in Levi's microenvironment and macroenvironment have affected its marketing position? How has Levi Strauss responded to changes in its marketing environment?
2. Why was Levi Strauss so successful in designing products for the baby boomers?
3. Evaluate Levi's strategy for Silver Tab brand. Is this likely to be successful? How does Silver Tab compare with the competition? Does it meet the criticisms of teenagers?
4. Evaluate Levi's strategy for "Hard" jeans. Is this likely to be successful? To whom are the Hard jeans likely to sell? How does the brand meet the competition from Klein and Hilfiger?

5. Evaluate Levi's strategy with Red. Is this likely to be successful?

6. In all, are Levi's repositioning efforts likely to be successful?

Sources: "Denim Dish: Dream Jeans for Teens," *Women's Wear Daily*, December 11, 1997, p. 12; Wendy Bounds, "Inside Levi's Race to Restore a Tarnished Brand," *Wall Street Journal*, August 4, 1998, p. B1: Becky Ebenkamp, "Slates Speaks Directly to Men," *Adweek*, September 8, 1997, p. 5; Stan Gellers, "Tailored Slacks Follow the Mainfloor Leader: Slates Boom Trickles-Up to Better Makers in Casual Fabrics and Golfwear," *Daily News Record*, September 24, 1997, p. 3; Linda Himelstein, "Levi's Is Hiking Up Its Pants," *Business Week*, December 1, 1997, p. 70, 75; Molly Knight, "Levi's Goes for the Hard Sell, Pushes Product to the Fore," *Daily News Record*, June 19, 1998, p. 4; Eleftheria Parpis, "Reborn to be Wild," *ADWEEK Western Advertising News*, August 3, 1998, p. 15; Mike Socha, "Levi's Posters Signal Launch of New Line," *WWD*, August 11, 1998, p. 16; Elaine Underwood, "Levi's New Dress Code," *Brandweek*, August 19, 1996, p. 22.

Video Case 4
Sputnik: Insights from the Streets

If Levi Strauss & Co. wants to know what jeans 17-year-olds want, they commission a big market research firm to do a survey. Right? Wrong. Instead, they call Sputnik, a New York research firm. Sputnik then sends its teenaged and twenty-something correspondents into city streets, clubs, coffeehouses, parks, cafes, and other hangouts, where they videotape the trendsetters—today's alternative youth—themselves.

These are not the usual depth interviews or focus groups. Sputnik's founders, Janine Lopiano-Misdom and Joanne De Luca, disdain such approaches because having conversations with interviewers doesn't get at the reality of consumers in their natural environment. As Lopiano-Misdom and De Luca ask in their book, *Street Trends*, "how insightful can a focus group be when everyone in the room knows they are being paid to answer questions for a corporation?"

Instead, Sputnik correspondents strive for intimacy to uncover the personal quirks, desires, and interests of individuals, their circles of friends, and the influences around them. They go after the trendsetters, not the followers. Followers can tell you what's happening now, but for the future you have to find the imaginative youth who think independently about how they want their jeans, shoes, skateboards, and other possessions to look, feel, and perform. To reach these trendsetters, Sputnik's interviewers go not to consumer labs or rented focus group rooms but directly to trendsetter environments, wherever they might be.

Sputnik videotapes conversations to pick up the body language as well as what respondents are saying about their likes and dislikes. To understand youth's styles, fashions, fads, colors, and the ways they view the world, these things have to be seen. Because seeing and hearing, in this case, are believing, a Sputnik report includes not only a written document but also an edited videotape. Many of the trendsetters are heavy viewers of videos, so Sputnik is actually videotaping the video watchers.

The videotaping technique won't work well if done by a homemaker looking for part-time work conducting interviews. It takes someone who understands the youth culture; someone who respects youth and who can connect with them; someone who can enter their scene, engage in intimate conversations, and uncover on videotape deeper insights than are found in surveys, magazines, and TV shows. In short, it takes another member of the youth culture, but one with a journalistic bent—someone who is able to probe responses and get at the "story." That's why Sputnik's peer interviewers are called correspondents. They explore respondents' lifestyles to determine how they relate to the product.

Where does Sputnik find its correspondents? Usually through a "snowballing" technique. Once it finds one good correspondent, he or she frequently suggests other possible correspondents. When first hired, correspondents are given a brief training session in which they are shown a sample of a tape and given pointers about what was done well and poorly. Because correspondents are freelancers, often working on other non-Sputnik projects, Sputnik usually contacts them by telephone concerning new assignments. Once briefed about the client's general problem, they are turned loose. Sputnik rarely tells interviewers exactly what problem the firm is trying to solve. Doing so would unduly constrain their questioning. Instead, correspondents are given general problem areas that they must explore on their own.

Sputnik's correspondents find respondents anywhere they think appropriate. For example, they might go to skateboard contests to film interviews for an athletic shoe manufacturer, or poetry readings to check out makeup for a cosmetics manufacturer. For fashion brands, they might find respondents in groups near high schools or at clubs. The respondents and interviewing locations depend on the type of product being investigated. Interviewers rarely have problems with owners and managers at clubs and other interview locations. They usually get permission in advance, and the owners and managers don't mind as long as the respondents are having fun with the interviews.

Given the length of most videotapes (for example, a whole evening in a club), Sputnik samples tend to be much smaller than those used with other research approaches. The company makes a trade-off between sample size and depth of information.

Most Sputnik interviews occur in big cities such as New York, Atlanta, Miami, and Chicago, or in cities with large student populations such as Austin, Texas and San Diego—that's where the trendsetters are located. For some clients, Sputnik will conduct interviews outside the United States in locations such as London, Berlin, Paris, Tokyo, and São Paulo. However, going outside the United States poses language problems. Videotapes must be translated if done in a foreign language or must be translated simultaneously with the interview. Because the videotapes are Sputnik's "data," translation may impair the quality of the insights attainable in the interviews. Thus, Sputnik generally prefers to operate domestically.

The videotapes are important not only for their stories but also as a quality control measure. They reveal the quality of the interviewer's work, which is frequently not ascertainable from the interviewer's written comments. Unlike written reports and audiotapes, videotapes allow Sputnik and its clients to check the research environments and the appearance and types of respondents. Additionally, the videotapes give the full story—comments are not condensed according to what the interviewer thinks is important.

By watching the videos, De Luca and Lopiano-Misdom can tell whether correspondents are interviewing the right types of respondents, asking the right questions, and working in the right environments. To help them improve, new correspondents are given extensive feedback about their performance. If the interview is very short, or if respondents on tape appear uncomfortable or give a series of yes-no answers, the correspondent is not doing a good job. According to Lopiano-Misdom, correspondents must ask relentlessly Why? Why? Why? Knowing the whats, whens, and wheres does not uncover motivations and needs. To get at that, they must continually ask the whys.

Sputnik was founded in 1994 by Janine Lopiano-Misdom and Joanne De Luca, each of whom had 14 years working in research and marketing. Realizing that surveys and focus groups were not the answer to understanding youth, they wanted to start a "grassroots" marketing research firm that would use today's tools to search out tomorrow's trends.

To understand a trend, they maintain, you first have to understand the culture that produces the trend and why it emerged. To understand the culture, you have to get into it, experience it, and be able to think like members of the culture. Then, you might be able to analyze where fashion or food is heading with this group. This is a "bubble up" theory of fashion and style rather than the "trickle down" approach. "Now we're watching kids, whereas we used to watch designers," says Ruth A. Davis, a product director at Sputnik client Reebok International Ltd.

Every research project produces miles of videotape, which Lopiano-Misdom, De Luca, and their staff pore through carefully, looking for commonalties, themes, or ideas that span interviews. Once these are identified, Lopiano-Misdom and De Luca use them to point clients in the right direction. An example is product development research done for Burlington Industries in which club kids said they would like to have plastic jeans (it sounds strange, but this is a group that likes reflective materials and shiny things). Would people really wear plastic jeans? Probably not, but Sputnik suggested that Burlington use materials that resemble plastic. The result—laminated jeans popular among high schoolers.

Sputnik deals with more than product development topics, however. It can help clients build brand images, prepare ad messages, and develop marketing strategies to create insider brands that remain relevant to youthful consumers. Through assessments of videotapes, Sputnik staff can explain to clients how they are viewed by the youth market and where they should be headed. PepsiCo's Mountain Dew used Sputnik research to develop promotions. Finding that pagers were still considered cool, Mountain Dew developed a successful promotion through which young consumers could obtain low-priced pagers if they did enough Dew.

Is research based on small samples of alternative youth valid? Should corporations pour millions into product development or promotion based on such touchy-feely research results? Reebok's Ms. Davis cautions that although it's important to follow cutting-edge trends, they shouldn't be relied on totally. According to Christopher Ireland, a principal in Cheskin + Maasten/Imagenet, alternative kids may experiment with 10 trends, only one of which crosses over to the mainstream culture. The trick is to identify *which* one trend.

Does this concern bother Lopiano-Misdom and De Luca? Not at all. They are too busy keeping up with the demand for their research services from firms such as Reebok, Burlington Industries, PepsiCo, Asics Tiger, Keds, BOSS, AVIA Group, Sam & Libby, Gap, and Converse.

Questions for Discussion

1. What type of research does Sputnik conduct? Causal, descriptive, or exploratory? Explain.
2. What are the advantages and disadvantages of Sputnik's research techniques?
3. For each of the following, compare the Sputnik approach with more standard mail survey, personal survey, and focus group approaches: sample selection, selection and training of interviewers, data collection, data analysis, report writing.
4. Suppose you worked for a toiletries firm making products such as shampoo, conditioner, and hair spray. Would it make sense for your firm to hire Sputnik to research product areas such as hair color? Who might be interviewed and what might you learn?
5. Suppose you worked for a cellular telephone company such as Nokia. Would it make sense for your firm to hire Sputnik? Who might be interviewed and what might you learn?

Sources: An interview with Janine Lupiano-Misdom of Sputnik, December 1998, and other materials supplied by the company.

Video Case 5
DuPont: Shaping up the World

Imagine how tough it would be to market a "disappearing" product. That's the challenge faced by a group of marketers at DuPont, a company with a portfolio of brands that, for the most part, reach final consumers only as ingredients in finished products. Teflon non-stick coating, Lycra fibers, Freon refrigerant, Kevlar bullet-resistant fabric, Stainmaster carpet—these well-known DuPont products share the distinction of being used in the manufacture of products that ultimately bear some other company's brand.

However, Jamie Murray, the person in charge of managing what people think of the overall DuPont brand, doesn't mind marketing products that can't be found on store shelves or ordered from catalogs. "We are the youngest 200-year-old company you will ever meet. We are always out there searching for those needs that we can invent something to satisfy."

The company's slogan, "Better things for better living," hints broadly at the variety of needs DuPont has satisfied over the years. When the computer industry required new forms of insulation for smaller and smaller electrical components, or the aerospace program needed stronger material for satellite tethers, or firefighters wanted fire-retardant suits, DuPont researchers headed to the laboratory. The company owns almost 2,000 trademarks and markets them in 200 countries around the world.

The challenges DuPont faces in marketing its ingredient brands are no less daunting than the challenges it faces in inventing them, so the company has developed five key principles to guide its actions. The first is *personality management*—controlling what the brand stands for and means to consumers. Gary Johnston, national marketing communications manager for nylon furnishings, says that, for DuPont, it's "science, business savvy, and a moral core." The second principle is *visibility management*, which entails creating awareness and familiarity for the invisible ingredients through integrated marketing communications.

The third is *target management*, which Johnston says involves "very clearly defining who it is that you need to connect with." For a brand such as DuPont, that includes not only the end consumer but also the many constituencies who are backstream in the manufacturing or value chain. The fourth principle is *marketing management*, which has to do with understanding the dynamics of the marketplace so the company can fashion the best connections with its target. Finally, there is *reputation management*, which is a proactive approach to helping people understand who the company is and what it is about.

All of these principles are evident in DuPont's marketing of Lycra. To connect with consumers worldwide, Lycra management started a global campaign in 1994 to make customers familiar with the Lycra name and icon. To emphasize what the product does, the company used the tagline "Nothing moves like Lycra," which it updated in 1996 with the line "Clothes that move the way you do." As a result, more than 50 percent of consumers recognize the brand name and, more importantly, ask for garments made with Lycra. It's rare when customers ask for a fiber by name.

Understanding the dynamics of the marketplace has led DuPont to invest in research to develop a newer, softer Lycra product. As the baby boomer market ages, it also gains a few pounds, sags a little, and moves up to larger sizes despite diets and exercise. Consequently, these consumers are looking for more support, lift, and control in bodywear, undergarments, and activewear, which is exactly what the new Lycra products offer.

By developing new products such as Lycra Soft, DuPont not only helps its own profit line but also that of its immediate customers. Firms such as Wacoal Japan, a Kyoto-based innerwear giant, have begun using Lycra Soft in the Far East in a control brief called "Magic Pants." According to Alan Fisher, vice-president of merchandising at the

Wacoal America unit, "It's a premium fiber . . . (and) it certainly has the stretch advantages of all-over fit and function, and less yardage is used. Prettier, more feminine-looking shapewear items can be made."

Firms in the United States are not missing out on this opportunity. Maidenform is already into wear-test trials with it, so U.S. women may soon be using these same soft undergarments with superior support.

New Lycra products are also helping manufacturers in other product lines. One industry that finds Lycra attractive is the hosiery industry. With the casualization of America, fewer pairs of hose are sold. Therefore, hosiery manufacturers are looking for products that women will want to wear even when they don't need hose for looks. One example of such a product is No Nonsense's Renew Age-Defying sheers that provide support that will leave the wearer's legs less tired. "People are on their feet all day; their feet get tired. This will help them feel better, even if they are wearing slacks," comments Diane Warren, director of marketing for Kayser Roth. Another industry benefiting from Lycra technology advances is the swimwear industry. In 1998, DuPont introduced Lycra products that provide superior chlorine resistance and completely resist mildew.

Some manufacturers are even willing to tie their names to that of Lycra. Liz Claiborne, a giant in women's clothing, launched a program called Liz and Lycra which includes leggings, pants, turtlenecks, a crewneck, an A-line dress, an A-line wrap skirt, and two jackets. All pieces will have a special Liz and Lycra hangtag.

The decision to launch Liz and Lycra was made based on trends from Europe, which showed stretch items increasing in popularity, and on market research in which the company found that women wanted versatility, comfort, and durability in a garment. The products were wear tested by staff at Claiborne headquarters, who found that Lycra eliminated the bagging that generally occurs at the knees on leggings and stretch pants.

Given these good results, the new line kicked off in Macy's Herald Square in March 1996 with in-store events, following a *New York Times* ad on Sunday. The ad and in-store visuals featured American Ballet Theater principal dancer Julie Kent photographed by Jose Picayo. Thus, creation of Liz and Lycra benefited not only Liz Claiborne and DuPont but also Macy's, which is considering adding its own products that include Lycra. Association with the American Ballet Theater is also a plus for all parties. The ABT adds cachet to the Liz, Lycra, and Macy's brands and also creates a positive association between each brand and the ballet—a sort of good-citizenship status. The ballet gains promotion at no charge.

One of the more interesting uses for Lycra is in making wool supple and flexible. For example, Lycra management teamed with the International Wool Secretariat to produce woven fabrics made with wool and Lycra known as Wool Plus. The venture gives wool a new value-added feature by leveraging recognition of products off the well-known Lycra name, and DuPont can market Lycra beyond its traditional markets in areas where it has little expertise.

What market would you target with this new wool product? Think of products in which a lot of wool is used. If you guessed men's suits, you were correct—lots of men's suits and slacks contain wool. But will men wear Lycra? Because it's usually associated with women's wear (and underwear at that), you might suspect that men would be resistant to the idea of wool with Lycra suits. "When you say 'stretch' to a guy, he's thinking men-in-tights. He's thinking Batman and Robin. He's thinking, 'This is not for me,'" concedes Brian Gallagher, Dupont marketing manager.

So, how do Brian and DuPont sell suits with stretch? First, Brian and his staff work out of offices in New York's fashion district, where they can keep in touch with the latest happenings in the fashion market. Second, his company sponsors fashion shows that illustrate the advantages of DuPont's products. In spring 1997, DuPont and the Fashion Association held a show featuring 60 ways to dress a man in spandex. Models wore tailored suits, golf slacks, and sports jackets. After the show, Brian knew he had a hit when several members of the audience asked to try the garments on.

Between shows, Brian spends his days making presentations to retailers and clothing manufacturers, where he frequently encourages them to try on his suit jacket. For this product, trying it is believing. So far, his efforts are slowly paying off—15 percent of the men's wool suits sold in the United States in 1997 contained Lycra. Still, it's tough going. One of his most recent clients looked at the suit and asked, "Does it come with a cape?"

High standards are required of all the partners with whom DuPont enters arrangements. "One of the most serious challenges any ingredient brand faces is [that] when your brand becomes very popular and very strong, lots of companies want to use it," says Mary Kopf, brand manager for Kevlar and Nomex. "Unfortunately, not all of those companies have high ethical standards, so you might run into what we call counterfeiters. These are companies who either don't buy any of your product at all, or companies who may use a tiny bit of it, or use it sometimes and other times not. But they label the product as if it contains our ingredient, and what we have to do as responsible trademark owners is make sure that we pursue those counterfeiting situations." Enforcing the proper use of its ingredient brands is well worth the cost to DuPont, which sees those brands as the source of the company's success during its almost 200-year history.

To protect the Lycra name, DuPont has a toll-free number in the United States (1-800-64-LYCRA) for customers and final consumers to report any suspected infringement or counterfeiting. It also runs campaigns stating that Lycra is trademarked, and its staff worldwide continually tests garments for Lycra brand authenticity. When labeled products that do not contain the Lycra brand are identified, the company takes steps—frequently legal steps.

"Your competition may try to imitate you technically, they may try to imitate you with service, but one thing they can't imitate is your brand," Kopf says. In this case, the appropriate use of the Lycra brand protects not only DuPont but also Liz Claiborne, the International Wool Secretariat, Macy's, Maidenform, and any of DuPont's hundreds of partners. All benefit from the value added by the Lycra name.

Questions for Discussion

1. What are the markets for Lycra?
2. How does the "selling-buying" relationship that occurs when Liz Claiborne wants to team up with Lycra differ from that in which a final consumer purchases a garment that contains Lycra?
3. What type of buying situation occurs when Liz Claiborne wants to team with DuPont to obtain Lycra for the Liz and Lycra line?
4. Why would Liz Claiborne want to use Lycra rather than some other elastic-type product that would be less expensive?
5. If you were Brian Gallagher, what types of brands would you try to sell the men's suits to—designer brands, midprice brands such as Joseph Banks, or house brands such as JCPenny?
6. DuPont spends tens of millions of dollars for consumer advertising for Lycra and for tracking down counterfeiters. Does it make sense profitwise for the company to spend money advertising to a market that it does not sell to directly? Does it make sense to track down counterfeiters?

Sources: "Can Stepped-up Products Shore up Sheers?" *Discount Store News*, September 21, 1998, p. A14–A18; "DuPont Launches Lycra Spandex," *Women's Wear Daily*, January 26, 1996, p. 15; Elizabeth Gladfelter, "Liz Stretches Out," *Wind*, March 6, 1996, p. 9; Chris McEvoy, "DuPont Swims in with New Lycras," *Sporting Goods Business*, Nov. 10, 1997, p. 23; Michael McNamara, "DuPont, IWS Expanding Wool Plus Lycra Program," *Women's Wear Daily*, October 2, 1995, p. 2; Karyn Monget, "Next Generation of Lycra Targets Aging Baby Boomers," *Women's Wear Daily*, January 29, 1996, p. 6; and Susan Warren, "Fashion: Updating a Classic: 'The Man in the Gray Spandex Suit,'" *Wall Street Journal*, January 27, 1998, p. B1.

Video Case 6
House of Blues: Singing the Blues?

When Isaac Tigrett founded the House of Blues in 1992, he was on a mission to "create a profitable, principled, global entertainment company that would encourage racial and spiritual harmony." Born in the South and immersed in the fertile Southern and African American cultures of the region, Tigrett wanted to expose Americans to the rich cultural heritage of the blues. He believed he could use both the blues and folk art as a bridge to racial harmony in our increasingly multicultural environment.

As a first step, Tigrett established the initial House of Blues restaurant in Cambridge, Massachusetts. He followed quickly with Houses of the Blues restaurants in New Orleans, Los Angeles, Orlando, Myrtle Beach, Chicago, and the newest House of Blues in Las Vegas. Each of these themed restaurants features such Southern specialties as crispy catfish nuggets for appetizers, The Elwood—a blackened chicken sandwich—and white chocolate banana bread pudding with whipped cream. However, each restaurant is also free to adapt its menu to local tastes. For example, the Los Angeles House of Blues offers tempura chicken tenders, a spicy swordfish sandwich, and seared ahi tuna with a shiso leaf dressing. The Cambridge House of Blues treats guests to a roasted portobello mushroom sandwich served with a watercress-jicama salad. The House of Blues in Myrtle Beach features New Orleans style seafood gumbo, pizza, and southern pecan pie.

Each restaurant also has different decor and facilities. The Orlando House of Blues is covered with corrugated Mississippi tin and nestled in a voodoo garden and Louisiana-style bayou. It boasts a state-of-the-art, 2,000-person concert hall, complete with a 30-foot-tall hydraulic stage. The plaster and clay ceiling of its 500-seat restaurant displays such traditional blues greats as B.B. King and Robert Johnson. The House of Blues restaurant in Chicago is smaller—only 300 seats—but is divided into two dining halls. One hall features bas-reliefs of Chicago blues legends; the other hall features Delta blues legends. Each is decorated with pieces from Tigrett's extensive folk-art collection. Tigrett claims to have created a "juke-joint" opera house to showcase blues and blues-influenced music, which he claims is America's authentic "opera."

The Chicago House of Blues is part of the Marina City renovation complex. Marina City was designed in the mid-1960s as one of the first urban high-rise residential developments. Containing both apartments and commercial buildings, it forms a kind of city within a city. Tigrett renovated 55,000 square feet of the commercial property to house television production, multimedia, and radio broadcast facilities along with a 1,500-person concert venue that includes a multimedia restaurant, a classically designed music hall, and a bilevel foundation room enhanced with opera sky boxes—all this plus a House of Blues hotel with 400 rooms and 30 guest suites.

House of Blues also attempts to nurture local music groups. According to Jim Mallonee, who books acts at the Myrtle Beach House of Blues, "If we can give a local band an opportunity to showcase themselves—if they've got a buzz that's beneficial for both sides—then why not make it work on occasion? Any good promoter would do that." By booking acts into the Myrtle Beach HOB, which attracts large tourist crowds, Mallonee is also fulfilling HOB's goal of supporting new music groups. At a tourist location, the band may be seen by people from many states who would not normally be exposed to the group. "So the band is not only appealing to the local crowd they help to draw, but they are also exposing themselves to people from 10 states in one fell swoop" says Mallonee.

The House of Blues markets itself to business firms as well as individual restaurant/concertgoers. In Chicago, corporations can rent the opera sky boxes, enabling their guests to watch shows at the restaurant. In Myrtle Beach, corporate executives can use the multimedia and internet connections found in all rooms and booths at the House of Blues to participate more efficiently and effectively in business presentations, executive conferences, and trade shows.

To continue its growth and spread the word about the blues culture, House of Blues has entered a number of other ventures. According to Tigrett, "The House of Blues is a brand that is into new media, books, CDs, records, television, and concerts. It's not about restaurants anymore. It's about zones of entertainment." From themed specialty restaurants, the jump to selling recordings and books about the blues was obvious. Other equally obvious endeavors include operating radio broadcasts, such as the *House of Blues Radio Hour* and *Elwood's House of Blues Revue*, and television shows such as *Gumbo TV* (a weekly series focusing on music and pop culture trends) and *Mojo TV* (a miniseries about the roots of blues.) A retail store selling recordings, books, videos, T-shirts, mugs, and other merchandise with the HOB logo also followed naturally.

Less obvious were Tigrett's ventures with the Internet. "Music and art transcend all cultural barriers," says Tigrett "and now the World Wide Web and the Internet are providing the means to bridge any communication gap that may separate us." HOB teamed with Sun MicroSystems to create the HOB web site (www.hob.com) and HOB New Media, an interactive entertainment and electronic publishing division. New Media will produce HOB Software about art and music education, video games, and HOB screensavers. It is also responsible for HOB Online which sponsors a series of issue-oriented conferences and special events such as a live gospel concert performed over the Internet to commemorate Dr. Martin Luther King's birthday. Through New Media, HOB will netcast concerts from HOB venues and rebroadcast performances filmed at HOB sites.

In 1996, under the direction of Marc Schiller, New Media developed LiveConcerts.com—an Internet site specifically dedicated to live concerts. "Usually the people that were putting up concerts—including ourselves—weren't doing it on a regular basis," Schiller comments. "It would be once every couple of months, and if you didn't happen to log on, you'd miss the concert. So we decided that we were going to create a destination on the Internet specifically for live concerts."

LiveConcerts.com is only one of HOB's Web sites. Another is HOBTours.com, which features information about HOB-produced tours, including itineraries, artist biographies, merchandise, and sound clips. HOB partnered with Adventure Vacations and Frontier Vacations to launch a nationwide "meal inclusion" program on January 1, 1999. Participating HOB locations will be featured in every Adventure Vacation and Frontier Vacation package purchased by travelers coming to a HOB location. In addition, Adventure Tours, Inc. provides thousands of vacation packages to House of Blues locations each year. Again, HOB tries to include corporations in their marketing of HOB sites as travel destinations. HOB Entertainment, Inc. tries to sell its special-event and party capabilities to corporate purchasers looking for conference and seminar sites.

In addition, Tigrett and the HOB have put together temporary blues entertainment and dining parties for the Super Bowls in San Diego and New Orleans. In 1996, Tigrett transformed the 93-year-old "Baptist Tabernacle" church at 145 Nassau St. into a House of Blues for the duration of the Atlanta Olympics.

Despite all this activity, the HOB has been criticized as not moving fast enough in opening new restaurants, which constitute the personal, up-close sales center of the firm. Although it continues to look for new sites, the company has opened only six restaurants in six years—not a blistering pace. One reason is that HOB is a privately held corporation that does not franchise its restaurants. Opening a new HOB, however, takes a lot of money—the Chicago restaurant cost $20 million. Part of that expense results from the unique designs of each restaurant and the use of expensive art. Costs could be lowered through a standardized decor used in multiple sites. To date, however, the HOB has resisted efforts to "package" its restaurants.

Tigrett has stated that he isn't interested in attracting massive audiences to HOB venues. "Eventually, if we are successful, we're going to have bus loads of grandparents and kids and families flocking to our places," he says. "But now that is not the demographic I want. I want the hip and the cool, and the more I can hold back that family demographic, the greater will be our ability to leverage the (HOB) brand in the future." In the meantime, Tigrett managed to raise over $65 million from the likes of Harvard Management Co., Aerosmith, Walt Disney, and entertainers Dan Aykroyd and John Goodman.

But Tigrett's time at the head of HOB finally ran its course. Despite his close association with board member Dan Aykroyd, Tigrett was ousted last year as CEO of HOB. The board wanted to rein in his free-spending habits and perhaps bring in that family demographic a little sooner than planned. As a result of excessive spending on the Atlanta Olympics site, other publicity stunts, and aggressive diversification efforts, HOB was losing money, and corporate investors wanted their house on a much more solid footing.

To achieve faster growth, HOB is now broadening its music appeal. Chris Stevenson, vice-president of marketing at HOB, says the blues part of the brand's name has hindered the company's efforts to be recognized as a broad-based music brand. "It's a complex brand. House of Blues is about a whole portfolio of music, not just blues. That's what we need to communicate to consumers," he says. This echoes Tigrett's contention that the blues is the basis for most other American musical forms. But widening the appeal appears to be at odds with the name House of Blues and the company's founding mission to spread the Southern culture of the blues.

Questions for Discussion

1. How does Tigrett's vision of the House of Blues represent segmentation of the music market?
2. How does House of Blues segment its market? What kind of segmentation does the local adaptation of each House of Blues represent?
3. Is the House of Blues brand strongly positioned? Does broadening the types of music promoted by House of Blues blur the meaning of the brand?
4. Should House of Blues franchise its operation? Why or why not?

Sources: "Diversity, Not Airplay, the Key for House of Blues' Booker Mallonee," *Amusement Business*, March 24, 1997, p. 6; Jeff Jensen, "House of Blues Ventures Woo a Broader Musical Base," *Advertising Age*, December 15, 1996, p. 16; Jill Krueger, "Striking a Different Chord: Blues Man Meets House," *Orlando Business Journal*, August 29, 1997, p. 12; Kathleen Morris, "Oh Yeah, They Also Serve Food," *Business Week*, February 24, 1997, p. 60; and "For Its Founder, House of Blues Indeed," *Business Week*, October 13, 1997, p. 6; and numerous press releases from the House of Blues Web site, December 1998.

Video Case 7
Starbucks: Stirring Up a Stormy Brew

To say that Starbucks Corp. has stirred up the coffee industry would be an understatement. In 1987, the Seattle-based company's sales were $10 million; today, they're $1 billion. Its more than 1,000 stores serve almost 5.5 million customers a week, many of whom visit twice a day, some as often as 18 times a month. Not bad for a company that charges four to five times as much for a cup of coffee as the competition and doesn't advertise much.

So what is Starbucks' secret? Howard Schultz, company founder, believes the brand is so strong because it was built from within. "I am concerned about the customers who pay for the coffee, but my primary concern is for the people who serve it," he says. "We built the brand by putting them in a position to win by recognizing that we wanted to build a company in which they were not left behind. We want to exceed the expectations every single day of the customer buying coffee at Starbucks. But we could not do that if we didn't first try, every single day, to exceed the expectations of our people."

Starbucks employs 25,000 people, each of whom—even part-timers—receives equity in the company in the form of stock options and comprehensive health care plus a free pound of coffee each week. The health care plan is so novel that President Clinton invited Schultz to the White House for a private lunch to talk about it.

The general philosophy of business at Starbucks emphasizes respect for employees, customers, and especially coffee. Whereas other firms might use artificially flavored coffee brews, Starbucks uses only genuine coffee beans for a rich flavor. Although Schultz admits that Starbucks could probably increase business by using artificial brews, he is adamant about sticking to the integrity of the Starbucks product. "I couldn't possibly face our people and say we're diluting the integrity of the company by going down that track and growing the business with that kind of coffee," he comments.

Besides employees, coffee, and customers, Starbucks also demonstrates a lot of respect for the cities and towns in which the company operates. Before opening a new store, Starbucks develops added-value programs that give something back to the local community, such as the establishment of a hospice, food bank, or AIDS foundation. On a national level, in 1997 the company inaugurated the Starbucks Foundation, which will provide financial and other support for children in need and children-related causes. These grass-roots efforts take the place of more conventional forms of marketing at Starbucks. The company has spent more money on employee training in the last 10 years than it has spent on advertising.

The low media spending was fine as long as Starbucks continued to grow at its phenomenal clip, but growth began to slow in 1997. By mid-1998, the company's stock had plunged 50 percent, with growth for the rest of the year forecast to be 2 percent. Expected earnings fell from 42 percent to 30 percent. Clearly, Starbucks had to take action.

With more than 1,500 coffee shops worldwide, Starbucks faced the classic struggle of restaurants and retailers—how to attract new users and extend business into new offerings to lift individual store and company sales. For Starbucks, this is a particularly acute question as the company tends to "cluster" its coffee shops by putting many shops in the same geographic area. As a consequence, new shops can cannibalize as much as 30 percent of old stores' sales. The company believes, however, that savings on marketing and distribution make up for the cannibalized sales.

To attract new users, Starbucks rolled out a new television advertising campaign in the spring of 1997. The tagline of the campaign—"Purveyors of coffee, tea and sanity"—was chosen because of its simple, upscale nature. Starbucks and the ad agency wanted something simple and unassuming that evokes images of the neighborhood coffee house where friends meet to relax and unwind. The image should be that of a friendly, intimate, neighborhood sort of place. The advertising campaign used simple stick figures that were almost crudely drawn so as not to detract from the central focus on the coffee. In these ads, it's the coffee that performs.

Starbucks also served as a sponsor of Lilith Fair in 1998. To exploit its sponsorship, to raise awareness of the music festival, and to raise funds for women's organizations around the country, the company showcased Lilith Fair artists, such as Tara MacLean from Vancouver, in its coffee shops. In-shop appearances gave some customers a chance to see artists when they couldn't get tickets to the Fair and offered others an opportunity to see the same artists in a different setting. For the tour locations, Starbucks created Starbucks Traveling Cafes, which served refreshments, camaraderie, and an exclusive album, "1998 Lilith Fair—A Starbucks Blend CD." About 10 percent of the CD's sales will go to Wider Opportunities for Women in the United States and the YWCA in Canada. "Starbucks has built a reputation for encouraging new and emerging artists," says Lilith Fair partner Terry McBride. "We're very proud to have such a dedicated partner."

Starbucks opted to broaden its product line by introducing Frappuccino in 1996, broadening its flavors in 1997, and selling it in grocery stores. Frappuccino is a joint venture with Pepsi-Cola, whose clout in the supermarket business helped get shelf placement. In 1998, the shrink-wrapped Frappuccino bottle was replaced by a clear glass bottle with minimal decoration. "The overriding rationale was, gee, let those flavors be seen," said a Pepsi spokesman. Power Frappuccino, a vitamin-enriched version, debuted in 1998. By mid-1998, Frappuccino led the $101.4 million ready-to-drink coffee category with more than $65 million in sales. Following the success of Frappuccino, to expand in-store sales, Starbucks introduced a coffee-flavored ice cream in conjunction with Dreyer's Ice Cream and Tiazzi, a made-to-order juice and tea drink.

To stretch its business further into the day and evening, in September 1998 Starbucks opened Café Starbucks, a full-service restaurant in Seattle. Three more restaurants were scheduled to open by the end of the year. Café Starbucks offers hot meals and a bar with coffee liqueur drinks. This venture is both more costly and more complex than serving a shot of java. "It makes me nervous," says Harvey G. Bateman, principal portfolio manager for Sirach Capital Management, which trimmed its Starbucks holdings from 1 million to 700,000 shares. "It defies the simplicity of the Starbucks model."

Complicating the model further, Starbucks has entered new markets ranging from the supermarket to the Internet market. In the summer of 1997, Starbucks test marketed six varieties of ground- and whole-bean coffees in Chicago supermarkets. Sales were good enough to merit an expansion into 12 major markets in the United States in mid-1998. To kick off the expansion, Starbucks gave away almost $800,000 worth of coffee with morning newspapers in a three-city promotion. The giveaway, to 400,000 targeted newspaper subscribers who matched Starbucks' customer demographics, included a 2.5-ounce bag of ground coffee and a coupon for 50 cents off Starbucks coffee. When customers cashed in those coupons, they found that prices in the grocery store are the same as at a Starbucks coffee house. This equi-pricing strategy helps decrease the probability that customers will shop at grocery stores rather than coffee houses.

Starbucks' test market revealed that customers don't like to carry a bag of beans away from the coffee shop; they prefer to buy their bag coffee in supermarkets. As a result, Starbucks can use its coffee shops as test sites for products such as Frappuccino that later wind up on grocery store shelves. In grocery stores, however, Starbucks will encounter much larger, freer spending competition in the form of P&G, Welch's, Coca-Cola (Fruitopia), and Nestlé. That's risky for a brand that spent only $12 million on media in 1997.

In the fall of 1998, Starbucks launched its Internet site, where coffee lovers could purchase coffee and related products, find out where coffee is grown, learn what affects its flavor, and get tips for brewing coffee. "We want to create a space where people feel comfortable, where it has value, where they can be educated about things," said Jonathan Nelson, chief executive officer of Organic Inc. of San Francisco, which created the Starbucks site.

In addition to the Internet site, Starbucks is making a beer with Redhook Ale Brewery and plans to design "cybercafes" (cafes that rent time on computers). So far, these new ideas haven't yielded any profits.

Finally, Starbucks has plans to expand internationally. It already has coffee shops in Japan, where the lines snake out the doors of those establishments in spite of the Asian financial crisis. Starbucks has also opened shops in Thailand, and it snatched up London-based Seattle Coffee Co., giving it shops in the U.K. that can be used as a base to expand into Europe. Howard Schultz, Starbuck's chief executive officer, plans to open 500 stores in Asia and Europe over the next five years.

If all goes as planned, Starbucks will become an umbrella brand under which coffee will be one of the lesser items. Schultz argues that Starbucks' new investments in brand extensions are necessary to maintain the company's impressive growth. "We have to keep pushing the envelope and reinventing ourselves," he says. But others argue that Starbucks is diluting its brand. According to Al Ries of Ries & Ries consultants, "The problem down the road a piece is invariably going to be the line-extension problem. They are getting into too many things," he said. "Initially, it doesn't hurt you. But from a longer point of view, it destroys the mystique of going into a Starbucks and having a cup of coffee."

Questions for Discussion

1. In terms of its service and product line, how would you classify Starbucks?
2. As a corporate chain, what advantages does Starbucks enjoy?
3. What are Starbucks target market(s) and how has the company tried to appeal to them?
4. How has Starbucks positioned itself? Describe all the actions that Starbucks has taken to support its positioning.
5. Describe Starbucks' line extensions and explain how they relate to one another. How do they support or detract from the overall brand image?
6. Which of Starbucks' new ventures are most likely to succeed? Why? Which ventures are likely to fail? Why?

Sources: Seanna Browder, "Reheating Starbucks," *Business Week*, September 28, 1998, pp. 66, 68; Alice Cuneo and Louise Kramer, "Starbucks Chain Unwraps Summer Marketing Plans: New Look for Frappuccino; New Ads from BBDO," *Advertising Age*, June 8, 1998; Donna Hood Crecca, "Coffee Klatch," *Restaurants and Institutions*, January 15, 1997, pp. 64–68; Robert Goldrich, "Starbucks Chooses Simple Spots for Simple Pleasures," *Shoot*, June 20, 1997, pp. 22–23; Adrienne Mand, "Starbucks.com Will Let Coffee Drinkers Get Wired," *ADWEEK Western Advertising News*, April 27, 1998, p. 23; John Simons, "A Case of the Shakes: As Starbucks Cafes Multiply, So Do the Growing Pains," *U.S. News & World Report*, July 14, 1997, pp. 42–45; Steve Traiman, "Starbucks, Lilith Link with CD, Café," *Billboard*, July 4, 1998, p. 1; Richard Turcsik, "Starbucks to Test Lines in Chicago Supermarkets," *Supermarket News*, July 14, 1997, p. 38.

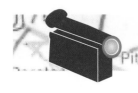

Video Case 8
Kodak: Taking Pictures—Further

Where are your Kodak moments? In a shoebox, an album, or a drawer somewhere? Or are you not entirely sure? If you keep them in albums, when was the last time you took an album from the shelf, blew off the dust, and paged through it? For many Americans, those Kodak moments lie forgotten in unopened boxes, albums, or drawers.

Suppose, however, that you could upload those Kodak moments onto your computer, rotate them, crop or resize them, and add captions. When finished, you could send them via the Internet to a friend at another university or to your parents at home. Or you could store them on a CD and use them in slide shows—maybe for a class presentation—or put them on a T-shirt, baseball cap, or mug. Would that stretch your Kodak moments and make them more meaningful?

Kodak hopes that you will say yes. Its goal is to change the clarity, usability, and life of Kodak moments—to make them bigger, better, and more enduring. Carl Gustin, chief marketing officer at Kodak says, "Over 82 billion pictures are taken every year and only about 2 percent are used. The rest are in an album, drawer, or shoe box somewhere." Kodak wants to take your memories out of that shoebox and bring them to life. How? Through digital imaging. Gustin sees digitization as the future of photography. He points out that there have been three significant innovations in the photography business. The first was silver halide photography that brought us black-and-white pictures. The second was color photography. The third, he believes, is digital imaging and digitization.

Prior to the fall of 1998, to get digital pictures, photographers had to use a digital camera, which cost from $300 to $20,000. In 1996, Kodak entered this market with its Digital Photography Kit. The kit gave home users everything they needed to take and share digital pictures, including a Kodak DC20 Digital Camera, easy-to-use software packages, and paper for making great prints. After processing, consumers received a CD, called PhotoCD, which contained pictures that could then be loaded onto a computer. Sales of digital cameras and PhotoCD, however, were disappointing. Digital photography was expensive and involved behavior that consumers simply didn't associate with picture taking. Consumers were reluctant to replace their highly familiar and functional, far-from-worn-out traditional cameras. Going digital also required that consumers be wired (have a computer) and computer literate.

To overcome those obstacles, Kodak teamed with Intel to merge traditional photography with digital imaging. The result is "digitization," the ability to convert traditional film to digital format through the standard photographic processing method that consumers have used for decades. By checking Picture CD on the envelope containing a regular roll of film to be developed, consumers can receive their prints and a CD containing digital images. The CD also contains all the software necessary for viewing and altering the images. Consumers need only pop the CD into their computer and the software takes over. The processing cost? A mere $8.95 to $10.95.

Kodak and Intel developed the new Picture CD technology after hundreds of one-on-one interviews with consumers in 10 cities around the country. Then, to fine-tune the Picture CD marketing program before rolling it out nationally, Kodak test marketed the service in Salt Lake City and Indianapolis. These cities were chosen because they do not overlap with other market areas and their demographics match those of the picture-taking public at large.

Both Kodak and Intel developed advertising and promotional campaigns for Picture CD. Kodak's television advertising showed the benefits of digital imaging and emphasized that people did not have to change their picture-taking habits. The introductory campaign included 30-second television commercials, radio spots, outdoor advertising, and print ads. It featured a new Kodak tagline, "Take Pictures. Further." Intel's advertising, in contrast, focused on computer users and promoted the Intel Pentium II processor.

"The intent of the collaborative advertising is to communicate the simplicity of digital imaging by using Kodak Picture CD as an example and to establish a strong connection between the product and high-performance PCs" said Rory Gumina, worldwide marketing manager for Kodak's Digital and Applied Imaging. "First, Kodak's ad will show how Kodak Picture CD lets people do innovative things with their pictures on computers, followed by Intel Pentium II advertisements promoting Kodak Picture CD as a feature application."

What kinds of innovative things can users do with their pictures and their computers? Lots. They can rotate images, add names and captions, and sharpen colors. They can copy images to a hard drive, e-mail them, and print single or multiple prints. They can create slide shows, use images as wallpaper on their computer screens, or upload them to Kodak PhotoNet Online. Advanced users can remove red-eye and adjust brightness, contrast, and sharpness. They can also stylize pictures, create artistic looks, and apply visual effects. Soon, they'll be able to send their pictures through AOL's "You've Got Pictures," a graphic form of e-mail. In short, users can adjust, modify, glamorize, and send their pictures and have a lot of fun doing it.

In moving to digitization, Kodak has extended well beyond its initial core competencies in cameras and film. Few consumers connect the Kodak brand with computers and computer technology. Thus, Kodak linked up with computer hardware and software firms, such as Intel, Microsoft, Adobe Systems, and Hewlett-Packard. The new digitization product is not just a Kodak product or an Intel product, it's Kodak + Intel or Kodak + Microsoft. This creates a whole new product category in the consumer's mind, and combining the Kodak brand with those of its computer technology partners lends digital credibility and forges a quality image.

Managing its brand name has become a major issue at Kodak. The mid-1990s have not been kind to Kodak's bottom line. Competition has increased dramatically as Japanese rival Fuji has aggressively pursued the U.S. market, primarily through price cutting. Fuji started a film price war that cut Kodak's margins at the same time that Kodak was investing heavily in digital imaging and digitization, resulting in a lot of red ink. Kodak reacted by cutting costs. CEO George Fisher slashed more than 7,600 jobs and reduced costs by $350 million, which boosted Kodak's operating profit margin from 14.3 percent of sales to 18.5 percent. This increased second-quarter 1998 earnings to $495 million, far exceeding Wall Street's expectations. That was the good news. The bad news is that the red ink kept flowing in the digital imaging division, where Kodak suffered a 5 percent sales decline in the quarter and a $64 million loss, following a $400 million loss in 1997. To withstand the continuing onslaught by Fuji, Fisher intends to cut another 12,300 jobs and reduce costs by another $1 billion.

Cost reductions, however, will carry the firm only so far. To increase revenues, Kodak is betting on the digital imaging business. To make it there, Kodak will have to sell consumers on digital imaging and digitization. Picture CD is a major step in making digital images available to everyone. However, folks without PCs can't do anything with the digital images once they receive them. To reach nonwired consumers, beginning in 1999, Kodak is converting its photo kiosks to digitization technology so that all consumers can have the fun of remaking their photographs.

That is not the end of the digitization process, however. Digital images can be uploaded to Kodak PhotoNet Online, a Kodak service where consumers can see their pictures online and over the Internet. Pictures can be loaded on PhotoNet by the developer or by the PC user. Once the images are online, consumers can order reprints, enlargements, and photo gifts such as aprons and mugs. Kodak PhotoNet Online not only helps consumers do more with their pictures, it provides greater revenue opportunities for Kodak.

"More importantly," notes Carl Gustin, "it provides Kodak with the opportunity to get to know and establish a relationship with consumers." At present, Kodak makes the camera, the film, some of the developing equipment, and the paper upon which pictures are printed, but retailers have the face-to-face contact with consumers. Through PhotoNet Online and similar services, Kodak can track customer purchases and determine who its consumers are, what types of pictures they take, what sorts of services they use. This will give Kodak an opportunity to make various offers and promotions available to carefully selected households, to provide advice to picture takers, and to send them information.

Kodak has targeted a number of market segments that could benefit from using digital photography and digitization. Its Digital Science DVC 300 digital video camera, which captures both high-quality still pictures and motion video, can be used by news and photojournalists as well as by businesses. For schools, Kodak has developed the Photo Verification System, by which photos can be generated in seconds for use in searching for and identifying children. For criminologists and law enforcement programs, Kodak has developed the Point and Shoot Camera System 50 for use in situations such as accidents where "instant" photography is required. For web designers, real estate professionals, news-gathering organizations, and the travel and tourism industries, Kodak has developed the Digital Science DC200 zoom lens, which lets photographers develop 360×360-degree photographic images.

Kodak CEO George Fisher envisions far-reaching future applications for new digital-imaging technology from Kodak and Intel, in industries ranging from consumer electronics to banking. "Imagine if your palm PC could scan a credit card," contemplates Fisher, "and could simultaneously take your picture and imprint it on the card for verification at the checkout counter, if you could 'see' everyone in an electronic chat room, easily and inexpensively . . . if you could attach a set of 'smart eyeballs' to consumer products, and turn them into machines that see. These are the kinds of 'killer apps' our emerging joint technologies could help define as we move forward." To appeal to trade and business audiences, the combined companies have come up with a new slogan, "Cool Technology. Warm Moments." In the future, they may even use a new, joint brand for upcoming technology-related products.

Kodak is positioning itself for the future with digital imaging, digitization, and partnerships with technology firms. In the meantime, however, it has to protect its core picture and camera business from the likes of Fuji. At the retail level, things have not gone as Kodak hoped. Pricing pressures in 1997 caught Kodak off guard and led to price differentials of as much as 30 percent between Kodak and Fuji. As a result, Kodak had to lower prices, eliminate less-profitable product items, and make strong price promotion offers. Kodak appears to have realized that it cannot lose sight of Fuji and plans aggressive new marketing programs in the United States to counteract Fuji's actions.

In emphasizing digital, Kodak has been criticized for not paying enough attention to such basic problems in its core camera and film businesses. Fisher disagrees. "Digital imaging will supplement, and I emphasize that—supplement, not supplant—silver halide imaging," he says. "The goal for Kodak is help people take pictures," he says, "then to remake them, access them, digitize them, and make it easy to display them, recompose them, share them, and communicate them around the world. Products such as those we are developing with Intel will fuel our growth by providing consumers with exciting new ways to use their pictures." It seems that the original Kodak slogan, "You push the button and we'll do the rest," has been updated for the new millennium as "You click on the icon and we'll do the rest."

To make its gamble on digital imaging pay, Kodak has to attract the millions of households using traditional photography. In doing so, it is moving to the next frontier in photography and redefining Kodak's meaning and mission. But like microwaves and central air conditioning, some innovations tend to take a long time to catch on. Kodak is trying to speed up adoption of digital and digitization products before the red ink overwhelms it.

Questions for Discussion

1. What types of innovation are digital photography and digitization? What implications does this have for marketing-mix elements such as price, promotion, and distribution? How has Kodak planned for these?

2. What factors in the consumer market explain the slow adoption of digital photography? What business market factors explain the faster adoption of digital photography? Does Picture CD overcome the consumer market factors?

3. Do digital photography and digitization change Kodak's business definition and mission?

4. How does the emphasis on digital photography and digitization affect Kodak's relationship with consumers? How does digital imaging add value for the consumer and business markets? In which market does it add greater value?

5. How does Kodak's move to digital affect its competitive situation against Fuji? How should it counter Fuji's price cuts?

6. In your opinion, is digital photography and digitization the right route for Kodak to take or should it retrench to focus on its core business?

Sources: "Kodak Sees $300 Digital Camera," *Television Digest*, April 3, 1995, p. 13; "Momentous Shifts," *Brandweek*, June 1, 1998, p. 26; William Symonds, "Finally, a Good Kodak Moment," *Business Week*, July 27, 1998, p. 34; numerous press releases from the Kodak Web site, and an interview with Carl Gustin Jr., senior vice-president, Eastman Kodak Company.

Video Case 9
The New Products Showcase: A Museum of Losers

Eighty percent of all new products fail. How can a company ensure that *its* new product is among the 20 percent that succeed? "Research, research, research," according to Bob Mc-Math of the New Products Showcase in Ithaca, New York. And one way that you might do research is to visit his museum of new product losers (and occasional winners).

Fascinated with new products, Bob has been collecting examples of new-product flops for thirty years—ever since he left Colgate-Palmolive, where he learned one of his first lessons about managing new products. Not all failures result from marketplace factors. After shepherding a deodorant through a new-packaging design process, Bob saw it shot down by a boss who simply didn't like the color blue—anywhere—including on Bob's new deodorant packaging. "He was a brown suit kind of guy," muses Bob.

In the New Products Showcase, Bob and his staff have collected over 60,000 once-new consumer products, some of which are 30 years old. There are products in five categories: foods, beverages, health and beauty care, household, and pet items. They are neatly arranged on shelves and wall units in a 6,500-square-foot warehouse, where you can wander around inspecting items at your leisure. Bob and his staff entertain a continuous flow of representatives from prestigious companies who come to Showcase to search for new-product and packaging ideas, review what's been done in the past, track trends, and evaluate current product development projects. Bob preaches that most companies have a kind of "corporate Alzheimer's." Most don't know much about past new-product activities—their own, let alone those of competitors. They need to browse his showcase to avoid repeating past mistakes.

Bob and his staff hold workshops for company new-product groups to help stimulate creativity in generating new-product ideas and to critique the proposed new-product positioning plans. They can often point out mistakes in a new product's name, packaging, proposed positioning, or labeling that might save millions of dollars in development costs as well as possible embarrassment over a new-product flop. For example, if Gillette had first checked with Bob several years ago, it might not have marketed its new shampoo under the name For Oily Hair Only. Although the product was sound, Bob predicted that the name would create problems. What consumer wants to advertise to other shoppers, check-out clerks, and whoever else might be looking on that he or she is plagued by oily hair?

To date, firms such as Bausch & Lomb, General Mills, Kellogg, Sara Lee, Kimberly Clark, Scott Paper, Kraft General Foods, Nabisco, Procter & Gamble, and Mitsubishi Corporation have stopped by Bob's place in Ithaca to inspect the results of over $12 billion in product development costs—mostly spent by other firms. While there, they can listen to Bob expound on "Why Products Fail: Principles for Success"; listen to Marilyn Raymond, staff consumer behaviorist and home economist, talk about "Preparing for 2000 and Beyond: Emerging Trends and Consumer Hot Buttons"; or participate in "Shop the Showcase," a series of directed exercises using the products on display as stimuli for new-product, packaging, and positioning ideas.

Those who can't make it to Ithaca can read Bob's book, *What Were They Thinking?*, in which he discusses many of the reasons that new products fail. One major reason is that a new product doesn't offer the consumer a clear benefit. Rather than focusing on *benefits*, or what consumers want, the company focuses on *features*, what the lab people like to talk about. However, successful new-product marketers know that features are not nearly as powerful as benefits in selling products. As an example, Bob points out that year in and year out Coca-Cola offers consumers refreshment through a series of ever-changing advertisements. "Suppose," Bob contends "that Coke's advertising slogan had been 'The pause that's cold and wet' rather than 'The pause that refreshes.'"

Miller and Pepsi could have learned from Coca-Cola. For example, when Miller introduced Clear Beer from Miller, what benefits was it offering the consumer? None, really. The new product tasted about the same as previous products but looked like water, suggesting that it might be watered down. Needless to say, the product flopped. Pepsi had the same problems with Clear Pepsi. Not only did these products fail, they damaged each company's flagship brand by cannibalizing sales of regular Pepsi and Miller beer and by tarnishing the equity of the main brands. As Bob asks in his book, "What were they thinking?"

Sometimes, new-product developers fail to adequately consider how consumers use and think about products. For example, Nabisco brought us Oreo Little Fudgies, which were Oreos with a chocolate coating. But this line extension simply didn't fit consumers' fancies. For decades, cookie munchers have been pulling their Oreos apart and going for the good stuff inside. When they tried pulling apart the little fudgies, all they got was a big mess.

Another product that violated consumer behavior and familiarity patterns was Sweater Fresh, a sweater freshener and deodorizer. Instead of sending a dirty sweater to the dry cleaners or putting it in the laundry, consumers could simply spray it with Sweater Fresh and put it in the dryer for a few minutes. It all sounds great, but the idea didn't wash with consumers. According to Bob, consumers associate odor with dirt. Although Sweater Fresh did eliminate odors, consumers still viewed the sweaters as too dirty to wear.

Bob also warns that companies can't trust consumers to read labels. His classic example involves Heublein's Wine and Dine, a kind of upscale Hamburger Helper. This new product was attractively packaged in a box that showed a bottle of chianti on one side of the box and pasta on the other. How did typical consumers use this product? Most cooked up the pasta, chilled the wine, and sat down to dine in style. Unfortunately, this behavior brought an unexpected and unpleasant result. It turns out that the wine was for cooking, not for drinking—it was laced with salt and herbs. "Yuck, phooey" might be a good way to describe a consumer's response to the first sip. Of course, *if* consumers stopped to read the label, they learned that the wine was to be used to spice up the pasta. But few consumers—mostly harried working women anxious to get dinner on the table—bother to read the details on a box.

Bob also believes that you can't fool the customer. Take cause-related marketing, for example. A firm such as Ben & Jerry's has been very successful in selling its Rain Forest Crunch and donating part of the proceeds to save the Brazilian rain forest. The product tastes good and it's made with plenty of nuts from the rain forest. However, when Wegman's supermarkets tried selling a private label rain forest snack line, consumers weren't buying it, literally. The product flopped when consumers realized that it contained too few rain forest products to be credible.

Other products that failed to fool consumers include those gourmet TV dinners you once saw in your grocer's freezer section. On the assumption that Americans were tiring of the standard TV dinner fare of mashed potatoes and green beans with fried chicken or salisbury steak, producers tried to jazz up their dinners with ingredients such as grilled eggplant and ratatouille. Unfortunately, many consumers—especially children—didn't like these more exotic sides. As a result, 25 percent to 33 percent of the average gourmet TV dinner ended up in the trash. People quit buying them because they didn't like paying more for something they didn't eat. Bob notes that you simply can't fool consumers' taste buds. "If you've ever tasted sugar-free Jell-O Pudding," he concludes, "you know that the proof of the pudding is in the eating. It's awful. That's not just my opinion. Most people agree, which is why sales are so poor."

With these examples in mind, what questions do Bob, his staff, and the thousands of failed products at the New Products Showcase suggest? To be certain that their new products are truly innovative and likely to succeed, companies should ask the following questions:

1. Is the new product positioned to create new users or new usage?
2. Is there new packaging that provides a consumer benefit?
3. Is value added through a new formulation?
4. Is there a technological introduction?
5. Does the product open up a new market for the category?

Companies that stop to ask such questions may avoid the dubious distinction of having their new products one day appear in Bob McMath's museum of losers.

Questions for Discussion

1. How do Bob McMath's "don'ts," as discussed in the case, mesh with the new-product development process outlined in the text?
2. Explain why the five questions at the end of the case are important in determining the success of new products.
3. How would Bob's guidelines for new products explain the success of Mentadent, cell phones, and Snackwell cookies?
4. How would you explain the failure of these products: rabbit jerky, Gerber's baby food for adults, and Dr. Care toothpaste (a toothpaste for kids that came in an aerosol can)?

Sources: "Shelf Centered," *People*, March 23, 1998, p. 166; Michael J. McCarthy, "Food Companies Hunt for a Next Big Thing but Few Can Find One," *Wall Street Journal*, May 6, 1997, pp. A1, A6; Robert M. McMath and Thom Forbes, *What Were They Thinking?* (New York: Times Business Press, Random House, 1998); Heather Pauly, "Flipping Over Flops," *Chicago Sun-Times*, June 29, 1998, pp. 1, 45; and materials from the New Product Showcase.

Video Case 10
Intel Inside: But Only If the Price Is Right?

What's in a name? Ask Dennis Carter and he'll tell you it's the not-so-secret ingredient to his company's success in the computer industry. Carter is vice-president and director of sales and marketing for Intel, which became the third most valuable brand in the world by convincing consumers that, when it comes to computers, it's what's inside that counts.

Prior to the 1980s, few but the most sophisticated computer users knew what kind of microprocessing chip their machines contained, let alone who made it. However, all that changed in 1989, when Intel, one of the world's largest makers of semiconductors, took the cover off of what many consumers thought of as a black box and gave them a look around. The company's decision to focus on end users was based on its recognition that the pace of technological change and the rate of sales growth in the consumer market were both accelerating. Intel realized that, in order to stay ahead of the competition, it had to begin talking to consumers in the mass market.

Intel initiated it's now widely acclaimed "Intel Inside" logo and advertising campaign to educate users about its chips. "From very early on," says Carter, ". . . we've used our advertising to take the consumer inside the computer, . . . de-mystify it a little bit, show them the technology, [and] explain what the microprocessor does—the fact that it may run their software faster, or that it [runs] a greater range of software . . . whatever the particular benefit of that particular processor is." In the process of explaining the benefits of Intel's microprocessors, says Carter, the company "accidentally created a brand."

The Intel Inside campaign consists of a two-pronged push and pull effort to enlist the support of computer producers. At the heart of the pull strategy was the need to make it easy for consumers to identify, at the point of purchase, computers that contained Intel microprocessors. Consequently, producers who included the Intel Inside logo on their machines and in their advertising received rebates from the company. The more familiar the Intel Inside logo became, the more eager producers were to join the program.

Intel's heavy investment in building the brand name has paid off in high brand recognition, insistence, and loyalty. Today, the Intel brand is one of the most valuable in the world—right behind such other consumer brands as Marlboro and Coca-Cola. Intel hopes to use this brand strength as a springboard to inclusion in a variety of other extended and new products.

Starting in early 1997, however, the Intel brand began to face some serious challenges. Major computer makers announced intentions to enter the below-$1,000 computer market segment, a segment in which chip price was more important to many than brand reputation. Intel had typically avoided the low-end market because of the low margin it yielded. However, with the rapid growth of the low-price segment, Intel has now moved to make it a top priority. Why? Because of *volume*. In a single year, sales in this segment surged from 7 percent of market volume to 25 percent, and these sales are expected to grow another 55 percent before cooling. In contrast, sales of $1,000-plus computers are expected to grow only 10 percent annually. By 1998, although it maintained a mind-blowing 99 percent lock on the $1,500-plus segments, Intel had only a 45 percent share of the sub-$1,000 segment.

In mid-1998, to maintain its position in the industry, Intel hastily introduced the Celeron chip, a stripped-down version of the Pentium II processor. However, in its rush to get a low-priced product on the market, Intel overlooked one of its heritage success factors—quality. Unfortunately, the initial Celeron was about 20 percent slower than comparable low-cost chips from competitors AMD and National Semiconductor. As a result, these rivals sold four of their faster chips for every Celeron chip Intel managed to sell. "The Celeron has been somewhat of a disaster," declares one industry analyst. Partly as a result of Intel's low-end difficulties, its sales fell off slightly in 1998 and profits fell off significantly. Intel moved quickly to produce an improved Celeron chip, but analysts expect that AMD will continue to gain share in the low-price segment.

Entering 1998, Intel faced competition only in the consumer PC market. But by midyear, it was facing similar competitive threats in its business markets. One survey of business buyers revealed that 34 percent were willing to buy chips from AMD or National Semiconductor. Worse yet, 27 percent were "highly interested" in switching. "The thinking has been that businesses would not be willing to consider anything beyond Intel, but this disproves that," says the market analyst.

How did Intel react to maintain its market dominance? In the consumer market, Intel has begun cutting chip prices more dramatically and more frequently than in the past.

It recently dropped the 266-MHz Celeron price from $106 to $86 and the 300 MHz Celeron from $159 to $112. To hold onto its business markets, Intel also has cut prices on its Pentium II processors, the chips that power $1,500 to $2,000 computers. It recently dropped prices on the 350-MHz Pentium II from $423 to $299, on the 300-MHz Pentium II from $305 to $209, and on the 266-MHz Pentium II with MMX technology from $240 to $160.

In addition, Intel planned to launch a version of its Celeron processor for "basic" notebook computers, enabling notebook makers to build systems for around $1,500 without skimping on technology. Beyond their lower prices, the new chips are contained in a much thinner tape carrier package, which will enable producers (especially Southeast Asian producers) to build notebooks from standardized designs. Such standardized designs could stimulate a further decrease in notebook computer prices, resulting in more value for mobile users.

Price cuts are only part of Intel's changing marketing strategy. To counterbalance the loss of margins on stripped-down chips, Intel plans to sell lots of high-priced Pentium IIs and highly promoted 64-bit Merced chips, expected in late 1999, both of which are used in workstations and servers. At present, Intel has a large share of the under-$25,000 server market but is only a small player in the $25,000-to-$250,000 server market. The Merced is Intel's entry ticket to the high end of the workstation and server market. It was designed with radically different technology that speeds software by running multiple tasks simultaneously. Merced will cost $1,200 or more and could help Intel grab 41 percent of the high-end server market. However, competition in this market will be tough—Intel will be battling such giants as Sun Microsystems and Hewlett-Packard.

The workstation market could become another cash cow for Intel because it slipstreams behind Microsoft's Windows NT software. Intel's share of the workstation market is expected to grow from 50 percent to 86 percent by the year 2000, and workstation revenues could total as much as $26 billion, going a long way to offset the lower margins of cheaper chips.

At the same time that Intel is going upscale in the workstation and server markets, it is going downscale in non-PC markets, such as set-top boxes for televisions. At present, companies such as Hitachi and MIPS Technologies crank out processors for this market that cost as little as $15. These companies also dominate the market for handheld PCs, smart phones, and digital cameras. To compete, Intel abandoned one of its most strongly held policies. Rather than developing its own technology, it uses an embedded chip that it neither designed nor completely controls, the StrongARM made by ARM Ltd. of England. Although StrongARM has only a tiny share of market today, with Intel's backing and a new version of Microsoft's Windows CE software for ARM, it could become a frontrunner with handheld devices. The StrongARM has blazing speed, uses very little power, and costs only $30 in comparison with the cheapest Celeron at $86. "It's an incredibly fast piece of technology," says Albert E. Montross, CEO of Mylex Corp., which makes computer storage devices using StrongARM.

Intel also has its eye on "information appliances." The explosive growth of the Internet, along with falling component prices, could boost sales of Web phones and other handheld devices from fewer than 5 million units in 1998 to 43 million by 2001. "Intel is going to need new opportunities," notes an analyst, "and appliances could be one of them." So far, this market is looking good for Intel, as digital telephone giants Nokia and L. M. Ericsson are committed to using the StrongARM chip.

However, the appliance market opportunity is far from a sure thing for Intel; there are significant differences in serving the PC markets and the information appliance markets. In PC markets, chips often become obsolete in six months or less. However, for lower-priced appliances, such as telephones, manufacturers want a customized chip that won't be obsolete quickly, and they care little about the ability to run reams of software. Whereas Intel has a big advantage in the PC market, "in [the information appliance market], Intel is like anybody else," says an engineering executive for competitor MIPS Technologies.

Intel has had incredible success in building a strong brand that commands respect and customer preference. However, if Intel begins to compete more in markets where price, not quality, is the key sales driver, Dennis Carter might begin to wonder whether building that strong brand image was so important after all.

Questions for Discussion

1. What is the value of the Intel brand? What does it mean to consumers?
2. How will placing Intel components in lower-priced PCs affect buyer perceptions of Intel? How would placing them in products such as set-top boxes and information appliances affect perceptions? Does it matter whether Intel designs and controls the chips used in these applications?
3. Compare the markets for the set-top boxes, information appliances, lower-priced PCs, higher-priced PCs, notebook computers, and workstations and servers? Where is each market in its life cycle? Where are the various Intel chips in their product life cycles?
4. Where is Intel in the new-product development process for each market?
5. What are Intel's advantages and disadvantages relative to competitors such as AMD and Sun Microsystems in each market that buys products that may have Intel inside? Which markets should Intel emphasize?
6. What marketing strategy and mix would you suggest for each market?

References: "Intel Chopping Chip Prices Again," *Greensboro News and Record*, September 16, 1998, p. B10; Jim Carlton, "Many Firms Would Switch From Intel to Rival Chip Makers, Survey Finds," *Wall Street Journal*, August 5, 1998, p. B2; Peter Coffee, "Embedded Chips Deliver Invisible Software," *PC Week*, October 13, 1997, p. 45; Tom Quinlan, "Intel, Digital Seek to Resolve Trademark Battle," *Knight-Ridder/Tribune Business News*, October 7, 1997, p. 100; Andy Reinhardt, "Intel," *Business Week*, December 22, 1997, pp. 70–77; Reinhardt, "It's Not Easy Being Cheap", *Business Week*, August 17, 1998, pp. 62–63; and materials from Intel's Web site (www.Intel.com).

Video Case 11
DHL: More Global than Local

Since the early 1970s, DHL has been the leading or only overnight carrier in many international markets. Started in 1969 by Adrian Dalsey, Larry Hillblom, and Robert Lynn (DH & L) to transport letters of credit across the Pacific, DHL expanded rapidly in Asia and Europe (the early 1970s), the Middle East (1976), Latin America (1977), Africa (1978), Eastern Europe (early 1980s), the People's Republic of China (1986), and Albania and the Baltic States (1992). Today, DHL provides service to more than 675,000 destinations worldwide; has more than 53,000 employees; serves 227 countries; and has 209 aircraft, 2,381 stations, 12,203 vehicles, and 32 hubs and subhubs around the globe. In one year, it handles 95 million shipments—not bad for a company approaching its thirtieth birthday!

To handle all those shipments, DHL uses a worldwide hub-and-spoke system. It collects packages, documents, and letters locally from individual businesses and offices and sends them to the nearest service center. From there, each service center sends the parcels to a hub that serves a larger geographic area (such as Australia or the Middle East). At the hubs, items are sorted according to destination and transported to service centers in each country, from whence they are resorted by destination and begin the last leg of their journey.

The Brussels hub is a prime example of the system. Each night, starting at 10:30 P.M., more than 120,000 documents and packages begin arriving at the hub. As they are unloaded, workers throw them onto $15 million worth of sorting machines, resembling a crazy amusement-park ride. Dozens of conveyor belts whisk the parcels away. As many as 400 people sort packages and put them on other belts, hurrying to get them loaded on trucks and airplanes before 3:30 A.M.

In another room, more than 50 people frantically read paperwork in dozens of languages so that all the parcels can clear customs. Without them, delivery of packages would be delayed. In-house translators and customs clearance services are among DHL's distinguishing characteristics. Another is that DHL hires its own people to deliver documents and packages abroad, in contrast to most other carriers, which hire local agencies.

Another difference in DHL's service is that it doesn't always use its own airplanes, as FedEx and UPS do. Instead, DHL buys lift capability from international carriers where possible, establishing its own air service only when it must. The logic behind this is that DHL can find flights at all times between locations rather than relying on one or two flights of its own. This gives DHL greater flexibility not only in timing but also in capacity.

Flexibility is important in serving today's distribution customers. One important form of flexibility is the timing of delivery and pickups. To provide multiple times for these services, DHL is experimenting with mobile collections. In Dublin, DHL launched the Super Bus, which follows a set route throughout the city to pick up and deliver parcels. From the bus, walking couriers deliver and collect shipments from businesses. By replacing multiple trucks or vans following numerous routes through Dublin's city center to a collection center with one large bus, DHL has reduced congestion and, more importantly, improved service through earlier delivery and later pickups.

The same principle is at work in DHL's floating express-distribution center in Amsterdam. The center is actually a canal boat that follows a preset route through Amsterdam's canals and uses bicycle couriers rather than walking ones to handle parcels. The boat will not only relieve congestion and improve service, it will also reduce pollution in one of Europe's most crowded cities.

Another important customer service is provided through DHLNET, a high-speed data network developed jointly by DHL and IBM. DHL employees enter shipment information when packages enter the system. Each package's airway bill has a unique barcoded number that is scanned into DHL's information network at each stage of its journey. The system provides DHL management with information on routing, delivery times, and volumes. DHL also created a system called EasyShip, which lets customers prepare their own shipping documents and maintain databases of customer addresses in-house. DHL will install the EasyShip computer and software free of charge in the customer's office or provide software that can be used on the customer's computer system.

Recently, DHL and AT&T introduced the industry's most comprehensive automated international shipment notification system, which enables U.S. shippers to alert recipients electronically that a delivery is on its way. Recipients are provided with the shipment airbill number for easy tracking along with other critical shipment information.

When preparing a shipment with DHL's shipping software, customers are given an option of sending their recipients an e-mail message or fax describing the shipment's contents and other information. Because the shipment airbill number is provided, the shipment's progress can be traced through DHL's Web site (DHL.com), DHL's Global-TrackSM Software, or by calling DHL's automated GlobalTrack telephone service. With certain e-mail applications, customers can even link from the Electronic Shipment Advisory e-mail message directly to the tracking page on the DHL Web site. In some countries, the message is translated automatically from English to the local language. "As DHL is the leader in international air express delivery, Electronic Shipment Advisory is designed with the international shipper in mind, offering 10 language options," says Alan Boehme, director of customer access for DHL Airways.

"Confirming the trend of the growing importance of information to international and domestic shippers, our customers indicated that there was demand for a system that automatically advises a recipient that a shipment is coming their way," said Patrick Foley, chairman and chief executive officer of DHL. "Shippers can now eliminate extra phone calls, faxes, and paperwork associated with informing a recipient of an inbound shipment."

In addition to its traditional services, such as overnight mail for documents and parcels, same-day service between locations in the United States and to some foreign countries, and international air freight, DHL has become a provider of logistics services. As corporations downsize and attempt to reduce costs, they have begun to reduce their investment in inventories and warehouses by outsourcing logistics functions. An example is DHL's experience with Japan's Kubota. DHL warehouses spare parts for Kubota computers. When customers call the Kubota service number, they actually reach DHL, which immediately ships needed parts through the DHL system.

Another example is Bendon, Ltd., a New Zealand manufacturer of women's lingerie. In the past, it took 10 days for Bendon to ship goods to Australia. However, through its alliance with DHL, Bendon can now accept orders until 1:00 P.M. for next morning delivery in Australia. By using DHL's information system, Bendon knows that all its shipments have cleared customs, and it receives delivery reports on all shipments. As a result, Bendon can invoice customers more quickly, improving its cash flow and reducing inventories.

More recently, DHL Worldwide Express formalized a multimillion-dollar agreement with Roche Logistics, a division of the international healthcare company, F. Hoffman-La Roche Ltd. DHL will act as Roche's logistics partner, with responsibility for the storage, pick-and-pack distribution, and inventory management of parts for diagnostic analytical systems. All routine deliveries will be dispatched from the DHL Strategic Parts Center in Hoofddorp, the Netherlands, whereas consignments will be delivered door-to-door using DHL's air express capabilities.

This partnership with DHL will enable Roche Diagnostics to stockpile fewer spare parts around the world, provide speedier and more reliable response to customer requests, and provide a value-added emergency service that will set Roche apart from its competitors in the worldwide logistics market.

Although DHL has captured the leading share of the international air express market, it lags competitors FedEx and UPS in the United States with a less than 2 percent market share. But Patrick Lupo, chairman and CEO of DHL Worldwide Express, comments, "It (DHL's share) may be less than 2 percent of the intra-U.S. market, but from the United States to a foreign point, DHL's share would be in the 22 percent to 25 percent range. That's a statement about our management focus on export shipments. . . . As the large U.S. couriers (FedEx and UPS) are launching expensive fleets of aircraft, they're saddled with high fixed costs. DHL's U.S. position is that it can buy uplift on an as-needed basis to match customer requirements. This gives us a lot of flexibility."

His comments highlight the heightened competition in the air express business. FedEx, with 30 percent of U.S. shipments overseas, spends millions on advertising and touts its image of speed and reliability. UPS, with only 10 percent of U.S. exports, also spends heavily on advertising that emphasizes speed and diversified services to more than 200 international territories. How do they stack up against DHL? Well, when FedEx and UPS announced same-day delivery in 1995, they found that DHL was already providing such a service.

Is DHL worried about the competition? "DHL has always had a very good reputation," says Foley. "We find that international customers have a proclivity to stay with their service provider much more than in the United States. In the United States, if you misship one shipment out of 400 or even 4,000 . . . your customer may lose patience and make a change. Internationally, that isn't so. We were the first in the international field, and we service the international field very professionally and efficiently. Because of that, we rarely lose customers."

Another asset is that DHL does not have a single national identity. It is a truly global corporation. "If you look at our main competition, FedEx and UPS, their (international) focus has always been into and out of the United States. That's where they advertise and that's where they specialize," comments Foley. "But its a big world and DHL goes everyplace." Perhaps so, but some critics wonder if DHL can keep its international market-share lead without more market share in the United States.

Questions for Discussion

1. When DHL assumes the logistics function for Kubota, Bendon, and Roche, what type of marketing system does this represent? What advantages does each party gain from the partnership?
2. Explain how DHL helps its partners Kubota, Bendon, and Roche with (a) order processing, (b) warehousing, (c) inventory, (d) transportation.
3. Explain how DHL helps its other customers with (a) order processing, (b) warehousing, (c) inventory, (d) transportation.
4. What are DHL's primary competitive advantages in the air express service business? What are the competitive advantages of FedEx and UPS?
5. Why would obtaining a large share of the U.S. market be important to DHL? How could it get a larger share?

Sources: Lisa Coleman, "Overnight Isn't Fast Enough," *Brandweek*, July 31, 1995, pp. 26–27; Douglas W. Nelms, "Holding Its Own," *Air Transport World*, June, 1996, pp. 151–4; Andrew Tausz, "DHL Is Delivering on Courier Challenges," *Distribution*, September 1997, p. 22; Mitch Wagner, "Apps Gather Diverse Data from the Web," *Computerworld*, April 14, 1997, p. 61; and company-supplied materials and information from the DHL Web site, January 1999.

Video Case 12
Forum Shops: Entertainment Retailing

Why do people go to Las Vegas? To gamble? Surprisingly, the answer is no. Most people today visit Las Vegas to *shop*. A study of 8,000 leisure travelers to Las Vegas, conducted by Plog Research of Reseda, California, revealed that 67 percent listed shopping as their major activity, whereas only 18 percent listed gambling. However, it's not ordinary retailing that attracts folks to shop in Las Vegas—it's entertainment retailing. And the Forum Shops at Caesar's are leading the way.

Although the Forum Shops at Caesar's is not a huge shopping complex—only 250,000 square feet initially—it is certainly one of the most dramatic shopping spots in the United States. It's a prime example of the themed shopping centers that are cropping up across the nation. Based on the Forum in Rome, the entire shopping center attempts to recreate the vias, the marketplaces, and piazzas that might have been found in ancient Rome. These avenues are ideal for strolling and window shopping 24 hours a day, or for just sitting at a table enjoying a cappuccino and perhaps thinking about how unfortunate the old Romans were that they hadn't yet discovered coffee.

At the intersections of major shopping streets in the mall are fountains and statues of Roman gods and goddesses. Prime among these is the Festival Fountain, featuring a seven-minute special-effects fantasy spectacular. As the spectacular begins, Bacchus, the god of merriment and wine, awakens and decides to host a party for himself and the Forum shoppers gathered in his domed rotunda. Apollo, the god of music, plays his lyre and entices an appearance from Venus, the goddess of love. Plutus, the god of wealth, provides the spectacle by bringing the fountain to life with cascades of jewel-like effects in the waters. Through music, sound effects, animatronics, computer-controlled waterscape effects, theatrical lighting, and special scenic projections on the dome, these marble gods come to life, talk, laugh, sing, and, in the end, invite shoppers to enjoy the pleasures of the Forum Shops at Las Vegas. Just imagine the impact of this spectacular on a first-time visitor who just stepped out of the Nevada sun into the neoclassical world of a latter-day Rome!

Following the main thoroughfare of quarried stone from Festival Fountain, visitors pass two-story shops with burnt orange facades, entered through carved and grilled doorways and topped with statues of Roman senators. In the main piazza is the Fountain of the Gods, which features a rushing-waters fountain, the Temple of Neptune, beneath a 52-foot-high dome. Eventually, shoppers pass the 25-foot statue of Fortuna to enter the Caesar's Palace gaming casino. The entire shopping center resides under a curved ceiling painted to represent a surprisingly realistic Mediterranean sky. Through special effects, the lighting of the ceiling changes every 20 minutes from a rosy dawn to a bright afternoon, a glorious golden sunset, and a darkened evening sky complete with stars.

"The Forum Shops is entertainment," says Terry Dougall of Dougall Design, which created the interior of Forum Shops. "It transports the visitor into something totally unique," he continues, referring to a "journey" through ancient Rome, spanning the period from 300 B.C. to 1700 A.D. The streetscape traverses time through architecture and replication of materials, textures, and design details of each period.

Moreover, Dougall contends, "merchandise is secondary. It's not the product but the environment that has to be on display," he says. "You have to do something inside to get people in front of the product." New York architect Christopher Barriscale says, "The design of a retail store is of the utmost importance. There's a lot of competition out there. The lifestyle retailers are targeting goes beyond product to the environment it's displayed in." These comments reinforce the idea that outside of location, the proper tenants and the environment they create are the most important factor in shopping center retailing. Michael P. McCarty, senior vice-president and director of market research for the Simon DeBartolo Group, which developed the Forum Shops, states, "Entertainment cannot overcome a poor tenant mix in the balance of a mall."

"Every weekend here is like Christmas at other malls," comments Forum Shops General Manager Thomas A. Roberts. When the shopping complex first opened, management anticipated that 10 million visitors annually would wander the streets of this Rome, but these estimates were off. Instead, more than 20 million shoppers visited in 1998. To support this extravagant shopping experience, the rents are high at the Forum Shops—in excess of $250 to $300 per square foot. That means that the 4,000-square-foot Bernini unit at Forum Shops pays more than a million dollars in rent per year. Does this make good business sense? It does when the Bernini unit at Forum (the top-grossing unit of Bernini) rings up $1,700 in *sales* per square foot a year. President Manny Mashouf of Bebe comments that his shop at Forum is also his top-grossing unit, bringing in sales of about $1,500 per square foot annually. Not all shops do this well, but sales per square foot for Forum shops average more than $1,200 per square foot, compared with a national average of $350. It seems that entertainment retailing really does work.

For most buyers, shopping while on vacation is entirely different from shopping at home. Shoppers are relaxed and have more time to stroll, browse, be entertained, drink coffee, and chat. Even though tourists are going to the same stores and buying the same goods that are available at home, they tend to spend more at the Forum Shops. It's the experience that matters. Comments one tired Forum Shops visitor, "It's just a better experience to shop when I'm away. I'm more focused on shopping."

From the retailer's point of view, tourists are wonderful customers. They spend four to ten times more than local shoppers and rarely return anything. Frequently, shops carry only the higher ends of their lines at the Forum because, as CEO Larry Hansel says, "Price is no object in this center."

Indeed, the Forum is known for its upscale tenants, which include Christian Dior, Gucci, Fendi, Bulgari, Salvatore Ferragamo, Stuart Weitzman, Hugo Boss, DKNY, Emporio Armani, The Polo Store/Ralph Lauren, FAO Schwartz, and Lalique. However, the store mix includes everyday stores as well, such as Banana Republic, Gap, Victoria's Secret, The Disney Store, Swatch, Brookstone, and Footworks. But even the Disney Store at the Forum Shops is different. Here, a "Goofy" Zeus sends down bolts of lighting from a perch high atop a store column, causing fiber optics in the floor to swirl around Mickey's head and run along a path to a giant torch, lighting its flame. By the way, Mickey is a bronze-gilded sculpture, in keeping with the Romanesque theme. Entertainment doesn't end when you leave the street to enter a shop.

To capitalize on its success, the Forum Shops expanded in 1997 by adding another 283,000 square feet. The centerpiece of the new addition is the Roman Great Hall, which is 160 feet in diameter and 85 feet high. The major attraction is "Atlantis," an enormous fountain which "comes to life" every hour from 10 A.M. to 11 P.M., unleashing the wrath of the gods on the city of Atlantis. Fire, water, smoke, and special effects combine in this extravaganza, as animatronic characters Atlas, Gadrius, and Alia struggle to rule Atlantis. Surrounded by a 50,000-gallon saltwater aquarium, the mythical sunken continent rises and falls before the very eyes of spectators.

As if they can't grow fast enough, in 1998 the Forum Shops announced the recreation of the Pantheon, one of the greatest architectural masterpieces in Roman history. The Pantheon will add 240,000 more square feet of multilevel specialty retail, restaurant, and entertainment space connecting to the existing Forum Shops. Construction began in the last quarter of 1998 and will be completed in mid-2000.

Recalling the comments of McCarty, it's important for the Forum Shops to begin considering what stores they would like to include in the Pantheon. For example, the current Forum Shops has only one bookstore. What about adding a larger Barnes & Noble type of store? What about a candy store—perhaps a Godiva or Brach's specialty store? Although the mall contains many upscale shoe outlets, how about adding a moderate-priced shoe store, such as a Nine West, or a woman's specialty shop, such as The Limited, to go with the designer shops? Or perhaps the Forum Shops should add an Imposters store, which makes copies of Bulgari-type jewelry. With regard to new tenants, Rick Sokolov, president and chief operating officer of Simon DeBartolo, says, "Obviously, it's (the Forum Shops) so successful that we can bring in who we want. It's a who's who." However, the question of which right "who's who" tenants to invite will occupy Forum Shops management for the next few years.

Questions for Discussion

1. Compare the Forum Shops to a shopping mall in your area in terms of (a) use of a theme for the shopping center, (b) entertainment value of the shopping center, (c) types of retail tenants, and (d) types of shoppers.

2. Why are retail sales per square foot so high at the Forum Shops?

3. Would a mall like the Forum Shops do well in a city of a million people that is not a tourist destination? Why or why not? Would the same Roman theme, with its fountains and statues of gods and goddesses be as enticing to shoppers in other cities as it is to Las Vegas? Why or why not?

4. If you were going to add a book retailer to the Forum Shops store mix, which one would you add—a large Barnes & Noble store or a smaller specialty store? Which candy store would you add—Godiva or Brach's? Would you add the Nine West Store? The Imposters Store? Explain your choices.

Sources: Teena Hammond, "Las Vegas Retailing on a Roll," *WWD*, April 29, 1997, p. 15; Teena Hammond, "Second Expansion Set for Las Vegas Forum Shops," *WWD*, May 26, 1998, p. 3; Sarah Hoban, "Retail Entertainment," *Commercial Investment Real Estate Journal*, March/April 1997, pp. 24–29; Laurie MacDonald, "Under Renovation," *Footwear News*, August 5, 1995, p. 8; Michael Marlow, "Caesars' Forum Shops Conquers New Territory," *Daily News Record*, September 5, 1997, p. 17; Marianne Wilson, "Disney's One-Two Punch," *Chain Store Age Executive with Shopping Center Age*, July 1995, p. 92; and materials supplied by the Forum Shops, December 1998.

Video Case 13
Got Milk?

What would you do if you were in charge of marketing a product that people only noticed when it was all gone? If you were Jeff Manning, you wouldn't be depressed by research indicating that consumers took your product for granted—you'd milk the news for all it was worth.

As the executive director of the newly formed California Milk Processing Board (CMPB), Manning faced the challenge of reinvigorating sales of a staple in American households that had been declining steadily in consumption for more than 15 years. In 1993, the year the CMPB was established, per capita consumption of milk was 23 gallons, down from 29 gallons in 1980. In contrast, per capita consumption of soft drinks had increased 80 percent over roughly the same period. "And there was really no reason to believe that it wouldn't continue to go down to some base level of 15 or 18 gallons because you had this incredible influx of, obviously, the sodas, but then the New Age beverages, the Snapples, the isotonics, the Gatorades, and then all of this bottled water stuff," Manning says.

According to a survey by *Beverage Industry* magazine, 1,805 new beverages were introduced in 1991 alone. However, a consumer research study commissioned in 1992 by the United Dairy Industry Association revealed that the proliferation of beverage alternatives wasn't the only factor behind milk's decline. People also cited milk's lack of portability and flavor variety, the belief that milk is not thirst-quenching or refreshing, and the fact that milk is "forgettable" because of low spending on advertising.

Although these research results were useful, it was a different kind of finding that especially caught the eye of Manning and representatives of the CMPB's advertising agency, Goodby Silverstein and Partners in San Francisco. In the minds of consumers, drinking milk is closely tied to the consumption of other types of food, such as cereal and cookies. This perceived link was important because it opened up a completely new direction for a marketing communications campaign. At the time, the dominant advertising strategy for milk around the world was "Milk is good for you." But, as Manning points out, "The problem is, was, remains, that 92 or 93 percent of the people already believed milk was good for you. So what do you have to say? It's white? It comes in cartons? We had no news whatsoever."

The connection between milk and food gave the CMPB something new and different to talk about, but it was only half the glass. The other half—the truly compelling portion of the story—was based on Goodby Silverstein's insight that the time milk was most important to people was when they ran out. "[Consumers] pour their Cheerios, they slice the banana, and they reach in [the refrigerator for] the carton [of milk]. They bring the carton [out], and it's got about two ounces of backwash from their teenagers from the night before. They're out of milk," Manning says. "Milk suddenly becomes very, very important to them. And nothing else wins. You can't take Snapple and put it on there; you can't take orange juice or tea or coffee. Only milk is important at that moment."

To help develop the concept of "milk deprivation," a group of consumers was asked to live without milk for one week. They couldn't have milk in their coffee, in their cereal, with meals or desserts, or in any recipes. After seven days without milk, Manning says, they were "insane" because they realized how much they took the beverage for granted. "I keep saying it's like air. You know, we don't walk around [inhaling], saying 'Whoa, good air.' Take it away for about a minute and see how you feel about air. That's kind of how it is with milk deprivation, because without it you realize, 'I can't live without this product.'"

Jeff Goodby, a principal with the advertising agency, believed that the best way to execute the milk deprivation idea was not to lecture consumers about keeping enough of the beverage on hand but to ask them to think about it and answer the question for themselves. Hence was born "Got milk?" The campaign was launched in November 1993 and produced spectacular results, both in terms of the attention it garnered among consumers and its impact on consumption. The *Los Angeles Times* reported that the ads had a "near-cult following." More importantly, the number of individuals who reported consuming milk at least "several times a week" jumped from 72 percent at the start of the campaign to 78 percent a year later. The total turnaround in first-year sales volume was $31 million, in contrast to the rest of the country, where consumption continued to decline. This shake-up was accomplished on a budget of only $23 million in a product category where total competitive media spending tops $2 billion annually.

In 1995, the CMPB licensed the hugely successful campaign to the National Dairy Board. Television advertisements depicting people in frustrating situations without milk are the keystone of the integrated marketing communications campaign, which also includes billboards, print ads, sales promotions, joint promotions with major brands, and public relations. One popular "Got milk?" advertisement features Oscar the Grouch from Sesame Street looking at a big pile of chocolate chip cookies with a more-than-usual disgruntled look on his face. The slogan "Got milk?" appears above his right shoulder. He's obviously unhappy about no milk.

What's next? "The key challenge is, how do you nurture 'Got milk?'" How do you make "Got milk?" stronger and bigger and more influential in people's lives, which is exactly the challenge that any good advertising campaign has? One idea is to cross-promote milk with other, but associated, products. So, think for a moment. What other brands of products do you use with milk? What about bananas? Ever eaten bananas and milk and cereal? Most of us have. So, Jeff Manning, executive director of the California Milk Processor Board, contacted the marketing folks at Dole and the result was 100 million bananas with Got Milk? stickers on them. What especially appeals to Jeff is the lack of competing brands and commercial messages in the highly generic produce section of the grocery store.

By now, you've probably realized that Got Milk could be used with cereal. Who would you associate with "Got milk?" in the cereal section? Maybe Snap, Crackle, and Pop? Just imagine how unexciting they would be without milk. Kellogg thought it would improve with "Got Milk?" and used the milk slogan on billboards with its cereal characters. Kellogg is hoping that the "Got Milk?" campaign can work the same magic for Rice Krispies, which has recently lost 18 percent of its market share, that it did for milk.

Probably the most interesting comarketing effort came about when the "Got Milk?" and the "Where's your mustache?" campaigns merged. The milk mustache ads were produced by Dairy Management Inc., a national organization of milk producers. Both of these popular ad campaigns had probably merged in the consumer's mind long before they merged in actuality.

This merger represents the first producer-processor supported advertising campaign in milk's history. "The most important thing about this announcement (about the blending of the two campaigns) is that we will now have one campaign theme for the entire milk industry," said Jeff Manning. It also brings a host of celebrity endorsements to the "Got Milk?" campaign. Amy Heineman, director of marketing for the International Dairy Foods Association, which administered the milk mustache campaign, believes that the merger is good because it eliminates the redundancy of the "Where's your mustache?" campaign. Clearly, the mustache can be seen, so why ask about it. The result is a stronger ad campaign.

At least it would appear that way, as a slew of imitators have used the campaigns. A Disney ad for *George of the Jungle* showed star Brendan Fraser with a white mustache and a "Got coconut milk?" caption, and an HBO ad for *The Larry Sanders Show* depicted a mustachioed Garry Shandling and a "Got Milk of Magnesia?" tagline. The award for the most unusual takeoff on the "Got Milk?" campaign may go to Pocket Books. It used a campaign with the slogan "Got books?" in which a little boy had a paper strip of words glued to his face. Unlike other imitators, Pocket Books sought permission from Manning's and Heineman's offices. Both gave their permission because, as Heineman says, "In this case, it's not a competitive product, and it doesn't disparage milk in any way, so if they can use our campaign to further a good, educational message, we're happy to help." That cannot be said for imitators such as the Combat insecticide ad that asked, "Got Death?" or the adult bookstore with a "Got Porn?" ad in the window. Manning says he's even seen panhandlers with "Got Work?" and "Got Change?" signs.

Although all of this is very flattering, the important issue is whether the ads are working, and the answer to that is not clear. Even though the two organizations spent a combined $367 million in 1996 and 1997, per capita milk consumption inched up 0.2 percent in 1996, then fell 1.3 percent in 1997. In the first six months of 1998, consumption was off nearly another 1 percent. The question is whether the "Got Milk?" campaign needs a new shot in the arm—new ads—or needs to be replaced entirely. However, although consumption may be down slightly, one could argue that it would be down much more without these successful ad campaigns.

If the industry opts for new ads, the campaign might be changed to stress consumption of milk away from home. Today, nearly 90 percent of all milk is consumed in the home, but U.S. citizens are spending more and more time away from home. Therefore, consumption should rise with increased consumption in restaurants and at work. But how can the industry increase consumption away from home? The answer may lie in milk-based drinks or soups that could be heated and eaten in the office. However, would the "Got Milk?" campaign work in those situations?

So, maybe it's time to replace the "Got milk?" campaign. After all, it's been running for over five years and consumers may be tired of the slogan. Perhaps the campaign is worn out, especially in California, where consumers have been exposed to it even longer. Knowing when to replace an ad campaign is important—advertisers don't want to bore consumers or risk zapping when ads come on during commercial breaks. Even Nike has replaced its famous "Just do it" slogan. Consumers are exposed to hundreds of promotional messages every day, and they learn to unconsciously screen out ads that are overly familiar, focusing instead on the new and unusual. So, Manning and associates may find that they have been too successful, that everyone knows about "Got milk?" and no longer pays close attention to the message.

Questions for Discussion

1. Why has the "Got Milk?" campaign been so successful?
2. What are the current objectives of the "Got Milk?" campaign? What audiences does the campaign target?
3. What are the advantages and disadvantages of combining the "Got Milk?" and "Where's your mustache?" campaigns?
4. What products besides bananas and cereal could be used to copromote milk? What are the pros and cons of attempting to stimulate milk usage in situations away from the home?
5. Does it weaken the "Got Milk?" campaign to be so widely imitated? Why or why not?
6. Should the "Got Milk?" campaign be replaced? What information would the CMPB and its agency need to make that decision? How could they get this information?
7. Suppose the CMPB decides to replace the campaign and you are in charge of developing a new theme and slogan. Develop at least two new ideas. Be certain to specify the target audiences, campaign objectives, message themes, and appropriate media to use.

Sources: "Bananas Provide a Rip Billboard To Boost Milk Sales and 'Anastasia'," *Wall Street Journal*, November 24, 1997, p. B14; "Got Milk?—California Fluid Milk Processors Advisory Board," *Adweek*, August 5, 1996, p. A6; "Milk Ads Shaking Up Sales," *Supermarket News*, August 12, 1996, p. 39; Jerry Dryer, "Milk's About Face," *Dairy Foods*, February 1997, p. 28; Dave Fusaro, "Got Milk . . . Cooperation?," *Dairy Foods*, September 1998, p. 9; Donna Hemmila, "Award-Winning 'Got Milk?' Ads Promote Healthy Sales," *Power Marketing*, July 18–24, 1997, pp. 4A–5A; Paul Lukas, "Got Milk? Got books? Got a clue?" *Fortune*, September 7, 1998, pp. 40–41; Charlie McCollum, "Milk Industry Combines 'Got Milk?' and Mustache Ad Campaigns," *Knight-Ridder/Tribune Business News*, June 26, 1998; Stephanie Thompson, "Kellogg Gets Krispies Guys into 'Got Milk?'," *Brandweek*, August 4, 1997, p. 12; and Kathy Tyrer, "Goodby's Got More Milk," *Adweek*, March 25, 1996, p. 4.

Video Case 14
NASCAR: Racing for Sponsorships

With pedal-to-the-metal growth, stock car racing has roared out of the dirt tracks of the Southeast and into second place among American sports. Although football is currently more popular, NASCAR racing is growing faster. Annual revenues for NASCAR exceed $2 billion. More than six million fans attend races each year, with another 123 million watching on television. Attendance at Winston Cup races (the top level of NASCAR racing) is rising at a phenomenal 65.5 percent rate annually. Each one of the 32 Winston Cup races held annually brings in between $60 million and $80 million in revenues. For the region in which the race track is located, hosting a Winston Cup race is roughly equivalent to hosting the Super Bowl. Sales of NASCAR licensed products alone have grown from $80 million in 1990 to over $900 million in 1998.

Why is stock car racing so popular? One of the most frequently given answers is that it's family-oriented. At any race, you will find plenty of families, sitting together in the stands or camped out in the infield where they can get close to the action. Far from the early days of dusty, dirty tracks, primitive facilities, and beer-drinking, tobacco-spitting, brawling fans, stock car racing has now cleaned up its act. Today's tracks are clean and comfortable, featuring air-conditioned suites with gourmet meals, hospitality tents with linen-covered tables, and waiters anxious to deliver the requested food. It's a suitable environment for any family.

The stars of stock car racing are also a different breed. In NASCAR racing, there are no strikes and the drivers and crews are well behaved. More importantly, NASCAR and its participants are responsive to fans. At every race, you will find smiling drivers patiently autographing programs. Fans can attend qualifying trials, camp in the infield before a race, and mingle with the drivers and pit crews—no other sport offers such close contact. A few years back, when Richard Petty was still racing, over 1,000 fans showed up at his home in Level Cross, North Carolina, on his birthday and stood in line for hours to wish him well. Petty sat on the front porch all day and into the evening to personally thank everyone who came to see him. Few other star athletes would do that. NASCAR intends to keep the image of drivers clean and the sport fan-friendly. It strongly encourages interaction between fans and drivers, and it quickly fines any drivers, no matter how popular, who are found violating the rules.

NASCAR also keeps racing exciting through parity, safety, and low cost. To make races fair, NASCAR requires a series of vehicle inspections. To make it safe, it devotes more than half of the pages in the NASCAR rule book to safety. To contain costs, NASCAR limits the types of cars that can be used and the adjustments that can be made to them. The cars you see on the track start out like the cars you could buy in a dealership. They are standard American cars, not exotic sports or formula one models. The engines are standard V8s with a maximum displacement of 358 cubic inches. Every feature of each car—cylinder compression, carburetors, height, weight, aerodynamic design—is regulated by NASCAR, with the result that many cars are not that much different.

To determine winners, NASCAR uses a point system that ensures close racing. Points are allocated so that a steady driver who finishes in the top five consistently throughout the season will garner more points than one who wins a dozen races but doesn't finish a dozen other races. To be a grand champion, drivers must enter all the major races in their circuit, and they must finish. This means that whether you go to Talledega, Darlington, Phoenix, or Watkins Glen, you will get to see the top drivers.

One difference between stock car racing and other sports is that driving teams are sponsored by corporations, not cities. Each driver's car and uniform are covered with decals denoting various sponsors. After winning a race, the driver and pit crew engage in the "hat dance"—changing hats for photos so that *all* of their sponsors will be pictured in the winners' circle. Any spot on a car can be used for advertising, except the roof and the doors, where the team's number is located. Teams can sell the hood, trunk, and bumpers for anywhere from $250,000 to several million dollars. Corporations with smaller budgets can buy 26-inch decals for a mere $62,000. Says Bill France Jr., CEO of NASCAR, "We have the biggest uniform in professional sports."

Sponsorship does not stop with the driving teams. Firms can also sponsor individual races such as the Mountain Dew Southern 500, racing circuits such as the Winston Cup Series, and awards such as the Anheuser-Busch Pole Award. In addition, firms can advertise at a race or become an official NASCAR sponsor. For example, Coca-Cola is the official drink of NASCAR and Goodyear is the official tire.

Sponsorship is necessary because stock car racing is so expensive. Purchase of a standard American car is just the beginning. It takes drivers, pit crews, mechanics, and increasing technology to adjust, maintain, and refine cars within NASCAR standards, and teams frequently need several cars. In addition, race tracks are expensive. The new Texas Motor Speedway near Dallas cost $120 million and the California Speedway cost $105 million. Team owners use their winnings to cover these costs, but winnings cannot be counted on. They also rely on sponsorships to foot the bill.

But why would 250 corporations, including more than 70 Fortune 500 companies, want to pour millions of dollars into stock car sponsorships? The answer is the nature of the fans. As already noted, families attend races, which means that corporate sponsors can reach both women and children at races in addition to men. More than 38 percent of stock racing fans are women, which is why you see all those P&G detergents advertised on race cars. It's a relatively affluent crowd: more than 29 percent of fans have incomes above $50,000 per year. Stock car racing also appeals to the 25–44 age group, which most advertisers and corporations are trying to reach.

Most importantly, NASCAR fans are very brand loyal. When Kodak surveyed fans, it found that 95 percent of them buy Kodak film. According to Performance Research, a marketing research firm in Newport, Rhode Island, more than 70 percent of NASCAR fans consciously choose NASCAR sponsors' products over other brands. Only half of tennis fans and golf fans have that same kind of loyalty, and only one in three fans of football, baseball, and basketball buy sponsors' products. More astonishingly, more than 40 percent of NASCAR fans said they purposely switched to sponsors' brands. Finally, fans know that drivers are supported by sponsors and that without the sponsors there would be no racing. According to Ardy Arani, director at Championship Group/Atlanta, "when you see Joe Montana holding a candy bar, you know he has been paid to do a commercial. When you see Bill Elliott, you know McDonald's has paid for him to race. So you better go to McDonald's or Elliott might not race."

For corporations, association with the fast, tough, exciting, innovative, and aggressive sport of stock car racing carries over to their corporate images. Somehow being a NASCAR sponsor breathes new life into old products such as cereal brands and makes them more exciting to today's customers. But a sponsorship is only as good as the use that the firm makes of it. To leverage its investment in a sponsorship, a company needs to devise promotional tie-ins that enable it to deepen its relationship with NASCAR fans or reach a broader audience.

Examples of successful sponsorship efforts abound. Heilig-Meyers, a Charlotte, North Carolina, furniture retailer, offered a 10 percent discount on purchases to customers who brought in a ticket stub from a Charlotte race. Thorn Apple Valley meats ran a "mega meat sale" at a Super Kmart in Canton, Michigan, that featured five NASCAR show cars in the store's parking lot, a live on-location broadcast by a popular hard-rock radio station, ticket giveaways for the circuit race nearby, and a sweepstakes for a go-car replica of the company's NASCAR vehicle.

In 1998, the Coca-Cola company featured nine members of the Coca-Cola Racing Family on eight-ounce classic bottles, along with Coca-Cola Racing Family graphics and drivers' images on six-pack carriers for the bottles. McDonald's gave away different die-cast NASCAR cars in Happy Meals in September of 1998. McDonalds and Service Merchandise cosponsored a promotion. Service Merchandise offered a set of racing models plus stand that included a food offer from McDonald's, while McDonald's bags promoted the exclusive collection available at Service Merchandise and included a $3 coupon toward purchase of the set. RJ Reynolds has a Winston Cup fan club in which members get reduced-cost Winston merchandise, such as calendars, baseball caps and T-shirts, along with the latest news on drivers, races, and NASCAR for a small entry fee. Reynolds uses the resulting database to promote its other products, as well as cigarettes.

George Pyne, VP of marketing for NASCAR, has the major responsibility for developing sponsorships tied to NASCAR itself, and right now he would like to find a hotel or motel chain(s) to be a NASCAR sponsor(s). After all, NASCAR fans travel on average more than 200 miles to get to a race. Once there, they spend $126 per person per race on tickets, food, lodging, and souvenirs. On average, that totals $604 for a family of four, and many families will spend more. Statistics indicate that there are many affluent NASCAR fans who would stay in more upscale lodgings. Of course, less affluent families would opt for more budget-priced motels or hotels. Thus, many hotel or motel chains should be glad to become NASCAR sponsors.

According to George, "It is important for any sponsor to have a clear-cut set of goals for their sponsorship. They should think about whether they want to sponsor a car or event. Sponsoring a car will get them media exposure at the track and can be used for retail events; whereas sponsoring an event will generate regional appeal, provide them with signage at the event, and provide them an opportunity for hospitality at the event." In addition, George stresses that NASCAR wants sponsors that will leverage their sponsorships in interesting ways to broaden the appeal of NASCAR to potential fans in order to maintain the growth of both stock car racing and NASCAR.

Questions for Discussion

1. If you were George Pyne, what specific hotel or motel chains would you seek as sponsors? List the criteria that each should have and relate those criteria to characteristics of the NASCAR market.
2. If you were a marketing manager for the hotel or motel chain you selected above, would you be interested in such a sponsorship? Why or why not? If so, what type of sponsorship would you agree to? Why?
3. What specific types of promotional tie-ins could a hotel or motel chain create to exploit its NASCAR sponsorship?

Sources: "Driving NASCAR," *Discount Store News*, May 15, 1995, p. A46; "NASCAR Bottled Up," *Beverage World*, September 15, 1998, p. 34; "Numbers Reflect NASCAR's Growth," *Knight-Ridder/Tribune Business News*, April 6, 1998, p. 406B; "Service Merchandise, McDonald's Celebrate NASCAR's 50th," *Discount Store News*, p. 2; Dale Buss, "Retailers, Start Your Engines," *Supermarket News*, September 14, 1998, p. 80; Adam Cohen, "Blowing the Wheels Off Bubba," *Time*, February 26, 1996, pp. 56–57; Robert G. Hagstrom, *The NASCAR Way* (New York: John Wiley and Sons, 1998); Suzanne Oliver, "A Fan-friendly Sport," *Forbes*, July 3, 1995, pp. 10 ff.; Donna Seiling, "West Mifflin Firm Seeks Sweet Taste of Success with NASCAR Candy Bar," *Pittsburgh Business Times*, June 5, 1998, p. 5; plus an interview with George Pyne at NASCAR, November 1998.

Video Case 15
Yahoo!-ing the World!!

Do you Yahoo!? If so, you are one of many millions of daily Yahoo!-viewing Netizens who are making it the fastest-growing, most popular, and first-to-be-profitable portal on the Internet. If you aren't, you are a target for Yahoo! and competitors such as Warner Online, Infoseek (Disney), Snap! (NBC), and archrival AOL, all of whom are scrambling to become the nation's, and maybe the world's, portal of choice.

Market share growth is the name of the game in this industry, where experts expect a shakeout during the next two years to only a handful of survivors. Right now, Yahoo! is doing very well. It records more than 95 million page viewings per month from more than 40 million people. One survey found that 51 percent of Net surfers at work and 42 percent of those at home now use Yahoo!. More than 18 million registered users have given the company personal data in order to use the wide range of services Yahoo! offers. By the end of 1998, riding record sales and profits, Yahoo's stock price had risen eight-fold in just the past year.

Yahoo! is the number-one portal for users at work, and many home users log onto the Internet through AOL but then shift to Yahoo!. Why? For the answer, compare the two home pages (AOL.com and Yahoo.com) and decide for yourself. Which is more interesting and informative? Which offers more services? Which looks like more fun? While many observers would attribute Yahoo!'s success to its wide array of services, the folks at Yahoo and a lot of users would tell you it's more what Yahoo! stands for—its brand image. According to Karen Edwards, vice-president for brand marketing, Yahoo! stands for "fun, friendly, human, and accessible."

What makes Yahoo! fun? Well, the name is kinda' funky and cool—not some technospeak like InfoSeek or technobabble like Lycos. Yahoo! suggests something to the user. "It reinforces the idea that when I go to Yahoo!, I'll be so pleased that I'll be Yahooing afterwards," says one industry analyst. The name, which is an acronym for "Yet Another Hierarchical Officious Oracle," connotes pleasure, happiness, and having a good time. This appears to be just what Net-surfing consumers want—to have fun exploring the Internet, to find unusual services (a hamster camp?), to spot unusual sites that zero in on their interests.

How does Yahoo! live up to this name? To start with, its colors are an unusual purple and yellow, and it advertises in unlikely places such as on tins of breath mints, Slinkys, parachutes, skateboards, sailboats, yo-yos, and kazoos. If advertising media tell us something about a company and its audience, what do the media listed above tell you about Yahoo! and its audience? The audience is young and active, interested in the unusual, and likes to have a good time and, well, this has to be an unusual company. Where will you see Yahoo! ads next? On shoes, music CDs, the *ER* show, the Ron Howard movie *Ed tv*, and in product placements on *Ally McBeal* and *Caroline in the City*.

The real value of the fun may be that it eliminates an intimidating technological image. Yahoo! is perceived as entertaining and easy to use (but not simple). As Internet companies try to increase market share, they will have to attract more and more households with older or less computer-literate consumers. That will be a harder sell than attracting young people or office workers who long ago conquered their computer and Internet fears.

In a growth industry like the Internet and its affiliated services, innovation is critical. Innovation, in turn, requires motivated employees, an entrepreneurial spirit, and a creative environment. At Yahoo!, the company motto is: "Do what's crazy, but not stupid." Lots of work is done around the coffee table, interrupted by office antics such as bouncing balloons over the walls of cubicles. Employees preserve the casual atmosphere in dress—there aren't many places where you can wear your baseball cap at work, and backwards at that. Executives meet in rooms named "Decent" and "Consistent," just so people will be forced to say "Oh, they're in Decent" or "They're in Consistent." All of this keeps employees thinking and on their toes, but it doesn't intimidate. It eliminates stress from watching computer screens and hunching over terminals. People are relaxed and able to let their ideas flow.

Lots of ideas are needed to create the many services that Yahoo! provides. Just look at the Yahoo! home page for the long list of subjects you can search on the net. Yahoo! can take you to a ton of other sites (that's why it's called a *portal*—you go through the Yahoo! door to these other sites). In addition, Yahoo! offers a long list of special services. There's a travel service where you can find lodgings, research cruises, or book airline travel. The site has a great news service, with links to sources such as Reuters, Associated Press, and *Hollywood Reporter*. There's shopping in stores, such as Gap, and there are auctions if you want to bid on a painting, a set of dishes, or computer parts. The site can even help you find a house online, complete with a mortgage.

Yahoo! offers these services to convert surfers into loyal Yahoo! customers. Although the company earns advertising revenue from other firms, Yahoo! would like to be more than just the doorway to other sites. To build its own revenue stream, it provides services such as My Yahoo!, through which registered customers shop at various sites with Yahoo! tracking their purchases and transferring them to the user's Visa card. The user gets one bill instead of separate ones for each purchase and Yahoo earns a little revenue. Through programs such as My Yahoo!, the company learns about customers: who they are, where they live, what they do, and what their interests are. Yahoo! can profile customers and send them suggestions about items that they might want to buy, sites they might want to visit, information they might be interested in, trips they might like to take, or events they might like to catch, such as the World Series. "I can picture Yahoo! as a big depository for people's preferences and consumption patterns," explains Timothy Koogle, Yahoo!'s CEO. "We'll have the ability to notify people of things they should tune into."

Such services afford a major opportunity for Yahoo! to build strong customer relationships. Relationships translate into loyalty, which in turns translates into spending more time (and money) with Yahoo! than with the competition. At this time, relationship building is particularly important for Yahoo! because its customers spend an average of only nine minutes per visit on the site, while AOL users spend significantly longer.

To connect with customers, Yahoo! tries to tailor some of the events it sponsors to local communities. In San Francisco, it may participate in the Gay/Lesbian parade, whereas in Washington, DC, it has worked with the Smithsonian to produce an educational display that explains what the Internet is and where it came from, the milestones in its history, and how to use it. The goal is to make each local market think "that's for me — it's my Yahoo!."

On-line selling, or e-commerce, is growing rapidly, and in the future such sales will have to generate a bigger share of Yahoo!'s revenue. E-commerce is expected to bring in about $42 million or 25 percent of Yahoo's 1998 income. Such sales revenues are important because Internet advertising revenues may decline. Some advertisers aren't convinced that Internet advertising is worth the investment versus traditional media. At an August 1998 on-line conference, several executives said that they wouldn't increase Web advertising spending until electronic ads become more consumer-friendly and interactive and until their effectiveness can be measured better. At present, even big advertising spenders allocate only modest funds to Internet advertising. For example, P&G allocates only $10 million of its $3 billion annual ad budget to the Internet.

While things appear to be going very well for Yahoo! now, the company faces some well-financed dark clouds on the cyberspace horizon. Lured by expectations that 328 million people around the globe will be using the Internet and that on-line shopping will balloon to $37.5 billion by 2002, firms such as AOL, NBC, Microsoft, and Disney are getting on the Net and improving their services. Mighty AOL is expected to launch a new Web portal based on its recently purchased instant messaging service, ICQ (I seek you). ICQ has nearly 7.5 million users and is wildly popular for its mix of e-mail and chat, called *instant messaging*. This service appears to hold strong appeal for younger users. NBC talks of making its portal, Snap!, a household name and of "building a search engine as big as the Web itself."

Technology heavyweights such as Microsoft, Intel, and the major PC makers are currently of less concern to Yahoo!. Such competitiors are not known for particularly appealing sites. According to Karen Edwards, their sites are too "techy" for many users; they are bland in comparison to Yahoo! and don't communicate the same sense of friendliness and fun.

However, one competitor with the potential to really cut into Yahoo's market is Disney. It has teamed with Infoseek (one of those techy portals). With Disney's imagination and resources, both financial and human, it could produce some very exciting content. And Disney's clean-cut family image will hold definite appeal for much of the market. In addition to television, Disney plans to use its movies, theme parks, and cruise ships to raise Infoseek's profile. Given the loyalty tens of millions of households around the globe feel toward Disney, Infoseek may not have to build loyalty so much as to exploit the potential of the already existing loyalty to Disney.

Another way that Yahoo! can expand is internationally. Currently, the site is available in 14 countries in native languages as well as English: Australia and New Zealand, Canada, Taiwan, Denmark, France, Germany, Italy, Japan, Korea, Norway, Spain, Sweden, the UK, and Ireland. Is it the same Yahoo!? Not exactly. Much of it is the same, but it's localized for things such as weather, travel, news, and fashion. Some subjects can be used anywhere in the world, with many of the same sites attached. And Yahoo! tries to create the same fun, friendly, human, and accessible image worldwide, which isn't always easy. Not everyone has the same idea of what is fun and what is human. Even so, Yahoo! has been successful internationally, with 30 percent of its revenues coming from outside the United States. In Japan, Yahoo! is the number-one Web site with more than 10 million people on-line.

Whereas Yahoo! has been successful in Europe and Asia, it has yet to enter Latin and South America. This is a very large block of more than 700 million consumers, almost all of whom speak some form of Spanish (except Brazilians, who speak Portuguese). However, income and education levels are lower in this market than in Europe and many parts of Asia, and many Latin and South American countries are smaller than Germany, France, and Japan, for which Yahoo! localizes its format. A good start might be Yahoo! in Spanish, but even that would have to be adapted because the Spanish spoken in different Latin and South American countries is not the same.

What is Yahoo! doing to extend its appeal in current markets? It is trying to make Yahoo! accessible through as many outlets as possible—through telephones, televisions, pagers, handheld organizers, and others. "We want to build the biggest company we can," says Tim Koogle, "We've taken the lid off." But does everyone want Yahoo! everywhere? Will older users be comfortable with all this technology? Is accessing Web sites a good experience on the small screen of an electronic organizer, which for many doesn't come in color? Can so much information be made to fit into devices such as handheld telephones, which will continue to decrease in size? Will small screens affect readability? Will they force the quantity of information to be reduced? These are just some of the questions that face the clever folks at Yahoo! as they approach the twenty-first century.

Co-branding offers Yahoo! a means of responding to the many threats it faces. For example, it recently concluded a deal with AT&T Worldnet Service. "This combination provides Yahoo! On-line users with what they would expect from two Internet leaders—rapid, easy access to the best of the Net," says Dan Schulman, president of AT&T WorldNet Service. "Now, Yahoo!'s members can get connected to a wide array of AT&T communications from one Web location." Yahoo! has also signed a deal with on-line bookseller Amazon.com in which Amazon will become the premier book merchant throughout many of Yahoo!'s World sites, including international ones. This expands Yahoo!'s offerings and Amazon's markets, and the good brand images of both companies serve to reinforce one another.

On a lighter note, Yahoo! has also opened the Yahoo! Internet surfing station in New York's Times Square Visitors Center. This is an interactive kiosk featuring six computer terminals with high-speed Internet access giving tourists an opportunity to surf the Web, find lodgings and other tourist information, and send video postcards to their friends and themselves as a reminder of their trip.

While all of these efforts are aimed at final consumers, Yahoo! is not overlooking the business market. Its Yahoo! Small Business site is a comprehensive on-line resource to help small business professionals and entrepreneurs compete better. The site provides industry news and small business information about products and services such as those provided by Airborne Express, FedEx, and UPS. Small business leaders can meet at this site to share ideas, discuss business issues, and improve their communication skills.

However you look at it, Yahoo! seems to have cast its net widely to capture as many Internet users as possible. Even with all of the competition, "Yahoo! has the potential to emerge as the first pure Internet giant," says one analyst. Another comments that banking on Yahoo! is a no-brainer. "It's like playing Double Jeopardy," he says. "You place your biggest bets on the squares that will give you the best return. And Yahoo! is the Double Jeopardy Square on the Internet."

Questions for Discussion

1. What does Yahoo! sell — a product or a service? How does it add value to its marketing offering?
2. How has Yahoo! segmented its markets? What products has it aimed at each segment? How can Yahoo! serve both older and younger markets?
3. Explain how Yahoo! creates its image of fun, friendliness, humanness, and accessibility.
4. Evaluate the handheld devices, televisions, and pagers as potential access devices for Yahoo!.
5. Compare the Yahoo! and AOL pages in terms of excitement, interest, attractiveness, ease of use, and communication of brand image. Which do you think is the better product? What are Yahoo!'s best means of responding to the competition?
6. Should Yahoo! be standardized or localized in various global markets? Would Latin and South America make a good market for Yahoo!? Why or why not?

Sources: Amy Cortese, "Portals: A Golden Door for PC Makers," *Business Week*, October 12, 1998, p. 90; Steve Hamm, "Yahoo! The Company, The Strategy, The Stock," *Business Week*, September 7, 1998, pp. 66–76; Kara Swisher, "Yahoo's Profit Beats Forecasts as Traffic Swells", *Wall Street Journal*, April 9, 1998, p. B6; numerous press releases from the Yahoo! Web site and an interview with Karen Edwards, vice-president of brand marketing at Yahoo!.

Video Case 16
Nivea: Softening and Standardizing Global Markets

Just as healthy skin requires the proper pH balance to flourish, a strong global brand must find the right balance between marketing efforts that build consistency in the overall brand's worldwide positioning and the need to appeal to specific geographical and cultural markets. Beiersdorf (BDF), the German manufacturer of Nivea skin care products, seems to have mastered that balancing act with all the skill of an Olympic gymnast.

Introduced in 1912, Nivea Creme was a unique water-in-oil emulsion, a formulation that set it apart from the fat-only creams available at the time. The brand's positioning also made it distinct from other products on the market: It was a multipurpose cream sold at a price that made it attainable to the masses, rather than to only upper-class women who comprised the competition's target market.

Over the years, Nivea's positioning strategy has remained as simple and steadfast as the now-familiar blue-and-white package. Despite all the technological developments the company has introduced in skin care products, and all the markets it has sold in, Nivea's marketing always focuses on key brand benefits: high quality, reasonable price, straightforward approach, and mild skin care.

This commitment to the mainstream market and focus on multipurpose applications means that every product introduced under the Nivea name has to conform to guidelines established to ensure that everyone working on the brand around the world would know what it stands for. Nivea's marketing strategy is well stated by Rolf Kunish, chairman of the Beiersdorf Group: "The strategy of concentration on exploiting market potentials and regional growth opportunities is to be continued. The same applies to moves into new market segments and to increased investment in research and development."

Exploiting market potentials means constantly introducing new products that meet current market needs and the needs of newly targeted market segments. One example of this strategy from the past is Nivea's emphasis on the health and active lifestyles of women as more women went to work in the 1920s. Others include the introduction of sunscreen, skin protection, and tanning products to match the more active, outdoor lifestyles in vogue from the 1960s to today; and products for every skin type and need, consistent with the multiplicity of product choices available in most products today. To meet the needs of new market segments, Nivea expanded its lines of products for children and men. All of these new products were guided by the constant Nivea standards that each product must meet a basic need, be simple and uncomplicated, refrain from offering to solve only one specific problem, be a quality leader, and be priced such that consumers perceive a balanced cost–benefit relationship.

BDF's new-product strategy was honed in the 1970s when competitive challenges prompted the company to take steps to revitalize the brand using a two-pronged approach. First, to counteract perceptions that Nivea had an older, less dynamic image than other brands, the company for the first time described specific product benefits in its advertising, instead of focusing on the variety of settings in which each product could be used. Second, BDF introduced additional products that would leverage the recognition and reputation of the Nivea name in growing segments of the market. These are subbrands, such as Nivea Shower and Bath, Nivea for Men, Nivea Sun, Nivea Hair Care, Nivea Body, Nivea Visage, and the recently introduced Nivea Baby.

During the 1980s, new products were supported by separate ad campaigns that helped build individual personalities and associations for each subbrand, while linking them to each other and to Nivea Creme through the use of the word "care" in all headlines. The subbrands helped establish Nivea as a broad skin and personal care brand, but their success was both pleasing and problematic for BDF. The company worried that the proliferation of products bearing the Nivea name might leave consumers confused about what the brand represented and that the image of Nivea Creme, the heart of the brand, might be weakened or diluted.

A recent example of this was the introduction of Nivea Visage Anti-Wrinkle Cream Q10 in 1998. This new treatment contains a restructuring coenzyme, Q10, that functions as an antioxidant and stimulates cell renewal, thereby leaving skin toned and smooth. Tests indicate that it will reduce signs of aging by 43 percent within 10 weeks when used regularly. Given the aging of markets around the world, a wrinkle-reducing cream poses enormous market share and revenue potential. Although Q10 was discovered by a U.S. scientist, Beiersdorf holds the exclusive world patent to use it in beauty fields. Naturally, the company plans to exploit this opportunity.

But where should the new cream be positioned in the company's product mix? It has a very different formula from the original Nivea Creme, and its specific consumer benefits are quite different. Therefore, Nivea's marketers decided to include it in the Visage subbrand line. Visage is a more upscale product aimed at mostly urban consumers between the ages of 18 and 54. In these age ranges, wrinkle reduction is more likely to be effective and the appeal of the product would be greatest. Although Visage is a more upscale product for Beiersdorf, the price of the Anti-Wrinkle cream is still under $10, which gives it strong appeal for the mass market.

By the 1990s, Beiersdorf had developed a global positioning strategy for its product mix. All ads for the core brand, Nivea Creme, had to incorporate its underlying values of timelessness and agelessness, motherhood and a happy family, honesty and trustworthiness, and the product benefits of mildness and quality. Ads for the subbrands had to reflect elements of these values as well as those that were uniquely their own. This strategy was supported by the creation of a worldwide name for each product category and common packaging on a global basis. Moreover, all ads, regardless of the country in which they ran, had to evoke common emotion, use the same typeface, incorporate aspirational people, and employ a uniform Nivea logo.

The result is a highly standardized approach to global marketing. Rather than focusing on the individual differences in peoples around the globe, the firm focuses on the similarities. After all, as one company official notes, all people have skin and many people have the same needs and ideas.

When a firm operates in as many markets as BDF, consistency, simplicity, and focus on the same benefits not only create a universal brand image, they also reduce headaches because fewer decisions have to be made. Standardized advertising campaigns need be adapted only slightly by translation into the local language. Because the costs can be spread around the globe, it's much less expensive to run a single global campaign, and marketing control is much simpler and easier. Packaging costs are reduced and product recognition is very high when people encounter the product in other countries.

The second element of the BDF strategy, exploiting regional growth opportunities, may necessitate some tempering of the standardized global approach. Because Nivea Creme is a European product, its appeal and marketing approach can be very similar in many parts of the globe such as the United States, Canada, Latin America, and South America, which were settled primarily by Europeans. The result is commonality in cultural backgrounds and light skin types, so that many products developed for the German market can be sold in these markets with little or no product or marketing adaptation. The appeal of skin care products in these markets is the same—a healthy, glowing skin.

As Nivea moves away from this common European cultural base, its products may be less well suited to the market. This is particularly true in African nations, where a majority of people have much darker skin and may require different sorts of moisturizers and sunscreen products. In between the European and African markets are the Asian markets, which are characterized by yellow and frequently more pale complexions. Although Nivea sells well in some Asian markets, such as Indonesia and Thailand, it sells less well in Japan. The difference in sales is attributable to both market and cultural conditions.

In the past, Japanese markets were strongly protected and had relatively little competition from nondomestic manufacturers. Unfortunately for Japanese merchants, the resulting high prices lured foreign producers, and BDF was no exception. As more companies entered the Japanese market, competition increased, price maintenance was abolished, and prices have fallen. As a result, BDF has reduced the number of products sold there, focusing on the more profitable ones.

Besides differences in market conditions, there are cultural differences between European, U.S., and Japanese markets. Europe and the United States are "low-context countries," which means that ads should explicitly state what the product will do. Japan, in contrast, is a "high-context" country, in which product claims do not need to be explicitly stated. Instead, the Japanese consumer wants to know about the company and form a relationship with it. Once satisfied about the company, then they will buy the company's products. Thus, Japanese and German advertising are quite different—an advertising campaign prepared for Germany requires more than just a little tweaking in order to successfully promote products in Japan.

All of these differences might argue for more adaptation of Nivea products and marketing outside Germany and the European market. However, as economies develop, they tend to acquire many of the same tastes as developed economies. An example is Russia, where men—especially younger men—are beginning to spend more on cosmetics. They are buying many of the same brands as their Western European counterparts: Gillette, Nivea for Men, Old Spice, and a few designer brands such as Christian Dior, Armani, Aramis, Guy Laroche, Gucci, and Paco Rabanne. Price is not the only crucial variable in the purchase decision. These men are interested in product characteristics such as fragrance. The bottom line in selling to these markets seems to be the increasing homogenization of markets, which favors the standardized global approach.

Taking this into account, Beiersdorf decided in 1997 to expand its product line for men, particularly with skin care products. "Men are becoming more aware of looking after their skin," says Thomas Ingelfinger, a marketing director for Nivea, but he admits that it will take some time to educate men. "There is a significant inertia which won't go away in one or two years, " he comments.

The quest to convince men of the need to take better care of their skin has led Nivea into some interesting comarketing ventures. One is its alliance with Norelco to produce the new Advantage Razor. To use it, men press the razor's side buttons to squeeze a moisturizing lotion onto their faces. Although you might think this would cause a goopy mess, amazingly enough, it doesn't. Although the shave isn't much closer, your skin feels softer and you don't have to wash your face. For men with a five o'clock shadow, a quick, no-water shave could be a real plus as they rush out of the office to meet a date or attend a social function. Of course, the razor costs $200, but that contains five lotion inserts, each of which lasts about eight shaves. A refill of five inserts costs about $8.

Questions for Discussion

1. How do economic, legal, and cultural factors affect the worldwide marketing of Nivea products?
2. Describe Beiersdorf's product and promotion strategies for Nivea. Is BDF engaging in product adaptation, dual adaption, or something else? What are the arguments for and against this strategy?
3. Would you say that Beiersdorf engages in global rather than international marketing? Explain your answer.
4. Find a Nivea ad and try to adapt it for the Japanese market. Should Beiersdorf continue with its fairly rigid standardized marketing strategy?
5. How would you market the new line of men's skin products from Nivea? Would you use a standardized or customized approach? Why?
6. From a marketing viewpoint, is the homogenization of global markets good or bad? From a nationalism viewpoint, is this homogenization good or bad?

Sources: "Nivea Launches Anti-Wrinkle Cream in Italy," *Drug & Cosmetic Industry*, May 1998, p. 22; "Nivea to Test UK Men," *Marketing*, May 15, 1997, p. 9; "Men's Lines Grow in Russia," *Cosmetics International*, March 25, 1997, p. 2; "Beiersdorf Beauty Sales Get a Boost from Nivea," *Womens' Wear Daily*, March 1, 1996, p. 11; "Sales Indicate Global Direction of Beiersdorf," *Cosmetics International*, July 10, 1997, p. 12; "Beiersdorf Increases Profits as Nivea Sees Continued Success," *Cosmetics International*, June 25, 1996, pp. 12–14; Melissa Drier, "Beiersdorf's Growth Bolstered by Nivea," *Women's Wear Daily*, February 28, 1997, p. 11; Ron Geraci, "The Electric Glide," *Men's Health*, May 1998, p. 70; and information from the Nivea Web site (www.nivea.com).

When Senda Berenson Abbott adapted James Naismith's basketball rules for women to play at Smith College, she had no idea what she was starting. Within a decade, women across the United States were playing basketball—at Tulane, the University of California-Berkeley, Stanford, the North Carolina College for Women, and at Ivy League schools for women such as Smith and Mt. Holyoke. The rules kept changing, making the game more like men's basketball, until Dr. Anna Norris published the *Official BasketBall Guide for Women*.

In 1924, the International Women's Sports Federation was formed and hosted its own version of the Olympics, which included basketball for women, who were excluded from the men's Olympics. Women's basketball continued to grow at the high school and college levels but with only sporadic attempts to take it to the professional level. In 1996, however, the American Basketball League was formed. The Women's National Basketball Association (WNBA) followed in 1997.

As the name suggests, the WNBA is affiliated with the men's National Basketball Association (NBA). Partly because of this affiliation, and partly to avoid competing in the crowded winter sports schedule, the WNBA chose to play a shorter schedule of 28 summer games in 1997. The WNBA's initial eight teams quickly expanded to ten for the 1998 season, divided into two conferences of five teams each. The Eastern Conference consisted of the Charlotte Sting, the Cleveland Rockers, the Detroit Shock, the New York Liberty, and the Washington Mystics. The Western Conference consisted of the Houston Comets, the Los Angeles Sparks, the Phoenix Mercury, the Sacramento Monarchs, and the Utah Starzz. The league expanded further to twelve teams for the 1999 season. The 1999 season will be expanded to a 32 game regular season schedule.

The WNBA's rules differ from those followed by the NBA. Its 3-point line is 19'9" from the basket compared with the NBA's 22', and the lane is 12' wide compared to the NBA's 16'. Although the WNBA ball is smaller (28.5" instead of 29.5"), it is the same size as that used in high school and college. Games consist of two 20-minute halves and the league uses a 30-second shot clock instead of the NBA's 24-second clock.

In its first season, WNBA attendance averaged more than 9,500 per game—far exceeding forecasts—and televised games scored a respectable average rating of 2 on NBC. Each rating point equals 980,000 television households. Thus, on average, some 2 million households tuned in to televised WNBA games. The WNBA's clout was evident in its ability to sign TV deals, not only with NBC but also with ESPN and Lifetime, giving the league hefty exposure. The WNBA also has attracted a host of prestigious sponsors, including the likes of American Express, Anheuser-Busch, Champion, Coca-Cola, General Motors, Kellogg, Lady Foot Locker, Lee Jeans, McDonald's, Nike, Sears, and Spalding. Licensees include Accessory Network (duffel bags), Aminco (jewelry), Bulova, ESPN Video, HarperCollins, Huffy (backboards), Mattel (WNBA Barbie), Hunter Manufacturing (mugs, ceramics), and Pinnacle (trading cards). WNBA-licensed merchandise has been flying off shelves at games, making it difficult for vendors to keep adequate merchandise supplies. The WNBA also has three marketing partners: Adidas, FILA USA, and Reebok.

Although it took a long time to establish professional womens' basketball in the United States, the sport now seems to be on secure footing. According to some sports pundits, the WNBA offers more benefits than even the NBA. First, it's more affordable.

Tickets average $13 dollars, much lower than the NBA's sky-high prices. Rosie O'Don-nell pays only $150 for a courtside seat to see the New York Liberty; an equivalent seat to watch the New York Knicks costs Spike Lee $1,000. Families constitute a prime market for womens' basketball. The Charlotte Sting offers a $25 "Valupak" for families consist-ing of four tickets, four hot dogs, four sodas, and popcorn.

The second WNBA benefit is the level of competition. According to John Wooden, UCLA's legendary coach, women's basketball is more watchable than men's basketball. It's more structured and team-oriented than the helter-skelter men's games. A third attrac-tion is player accessibility. Whereas NBA fans often must settle for brief off-court glimpses of haughty millionaire superstars, WNBA players frequently mix and mingle with their fans. For example, after a recent game with New York, Charlotte Sting star Vicky Bullett signed autographs on everything put in front of her and then asked "Have I missed anyone?" Few fans ever get that close to Patrick Ewing or Michael Jordan.

Less obvious but equally important, the WNBA also has a strong sense of "give-back." It has adopted two causes that all teams in the league support. The first is a com-mitment to breast cancer awareness. Because breast cancer affects one in every nine U.S. women, it is an issue for all women, according to WNBA president Val Ackerman. She states, "We are pleased that the WNBA, our players, our partners, and our fans have formed a team to make an impact in the fight against breast cancer."

In 1997, the WNBA produced two breast cancer awareness public service an-nouncements featuring Cynthia Cooper of the Houston Comets and Pam McGee of the Sacramento Monarchs. WNBA marketing partner General Motors donated 50 cents for every fan who attended a WNBA game to the National Alliance of Breast Cancer Organi-zations (NABCO). GM's Buick Division also contributed $32,000 to NABCO ($1,000 for every Buick Regal Player of the Game on nationally televised WNBA games). In all, GM's contributions totaled $575,000. Lee Jeans also got into the act with its "Shoot for the Cure" program. At half times during televised games, a randomly selected fan was in-vited onto the court to "shoot for the cure" by making as many baskets as possible, each worth a certain dollar amount, during a 30-second time period. Another WNBA market-ing partner, Champion (maker of WNBA uniforms), contributed $25,000 from the sales of its licensed merchandise.

In the fight against breast cancer, the WNBA, NABCO, and GM sponsor in-arena breast health awareness nights at games. On these evenings, materials are distributed in the arena and announcements and video messages about breast health awareness are broadcast during the games. The WNBA also sponsors breast health awareness seminars, scheduled in conjunction with local games. Finally, the WNBA also distributes a breast health guide, obtainable at seminars, on awareness nights, and through mail order from the WNBA.

In addition to the breast awareness program, the WNBA and Sears jointly sponsor a "Be Active" program aimed at children. This program, aligned with the President's Coun-cil on Physical Fitness and Sports attempts to teach youngsters aged 11 to 14 how to be-come fit and stay in shape through proper nutrition and exercise. The focus of the pro-gram is to reduce the growing obesity among American children. The program travels to 13 sites including all 12 WNBA cities plus Philadelphia and San Jose. At a "Be Active" clinic, WNBA stars talk to children and their parents about the importance of fitness, ex-ercise, and eating right. These ideas are reinforced through a series of drills. The WBNA team selects the youth organization that will be participating in the clinic. The program has been promoted through public service announcements featuring Ruthie Bolton-Holifield, the Sacramento Monarchs all-WNBA guard. Another public service announce-ment was created which featured Tamecka Dixon (Los Angeles Sparks), Suze McConnell Serio (Cleveland Rockers), and Tina Thompson (Houston Comets).

Not all of the give-back occurs at the league level, however. Washington Mystics' forward Heidi Burge developed "Heidi's Hoops for Hope," a not-for-profit organization that includes clinics and camps emphasizing life skills as well as basketball skills. According to Heidi, "I did this thing in inner city D.C. because I know there are places where the basketball is really good, but they don't have the resources." The program includes raising money for uniforms and equipment as well as camps and clinics. Heidi reasons that if young people are busy playing basketball and learning life skills, they are kept off the streets.

Through efforts such as these, the WNBA has attracted a very loyal following of fans and families. One of the most vocal supporters is Rosie O'Donnell, who says, "One of the great things about the WNBA is that it has allowed women to be dreamers. I caught the fever big. . . ." The same goes for all those mothers and fathers taking their daughters to games, where the girls can not only dream of being basketball players, they can also learn valuable lessons about responsibility to the community and society.

Questions for Discussion

1. How does the WNBA's support of breast cancer awareness illustrate socially responsible marketing?
2. Are breast cancer awareness and children's physical fitness appropriate causes for the WNBA to support? Explain. Should the WNBA support additional causes? Why or why not? If so, which other national causes might make sense?
3. What sorts of local causes should individual WNBA teams support? Think of the WNBA team nearest you and outline a plan for creating community support for the WNBA through community involvement.
4. Is it a good idea for individual players to form foundations such as Heidi Burge has done? Do these efforts enhance or reduce support for the WNBA-supported causes?

Sources: Marianne Bhonslay, "Born to be Rivals," *Sporting Goods Business*, July 10, 1998, pp. 40–42; Dan Crawford, "Rival Women's Basketball Leagues Slug It Out for Supremacy On and Off Court," *Business First-Columbus*, October 31, 1997, pp. 1–2; Steve Wulf, "The NBA's Sister Act," *Time*, August 4, 1997, pp. 41–44; interview with Mark Pray of the WNBA, December 1998; and numerous press releases from the WNBA Web site.

Credits

Chapter 1 **2** Reprinted with permission of Nike, Inc.; **7 (all)** Courtesy of State of Health Products; **12** Reprinted with permission of Ford Motor Company; **16** Copyright Taco Bell Corporation; **20** Courtesy of L. L. Bean; **22** Courtesy of Johnson & Johnson; **26** Copyright Arthur Meyerson/Reproduced with permission of The Coca-Cola Company; **29** Reprinted with permission of ITT.

Chapter 2 **35** Reprinted by permission of Intel Corporation, Copyright 1999 Intel Corporation; **38** Courtesy of 3M; **40** Courtesy of Monsanto; **46** Reprinted with permission of The Clorox Company; **48** Courtesy of Campbell Soup Company; **52 (left)** AP/Wide World Photos; **52 (middle and right)** © Melvyn Calderon/Gamma-Liaison, Inc.; **54 (left)** Reprinted with permission of Red Roof Inns, Inc.; **54 (right)** Reprinted with permission of Four Seasons Hotels; **57** Copyright M. Osterreicdher/Black Star and Courtesy DuPont; **60** © Mark Seliger/Campbell Soup Company.

Chapter 3 **68** Courtesy of Volkswagen of America, Inc. and Arnold Communications; **72** Courtesy of Credit Suisse; **74** Reprinted with permission of Wal-Mart; **77** © Jonathan Nourok/Tony Stone Images; **78** Courtesy of Sports Illustrated Kids; **81** Copyright General Motors Corporation. Used with permission; **83** Reprinted with the permission of Business Week; **85** Reprinted with permission of Daimler-Chrysler Corporation; **86** © Sally Wiener Grotta/The Stock Market; **92** Courtesy of Seattle Chocolates; **94** Courtesy of Johnson & Johnson.

Chapter 4 **102 (all)** Courtesy of Black & Decker; **108** Reprinted with the permission of Porsche Cars North America, Inc.; **112** © Roger Ressmeyer/Copyright

Corbis; **116** Reprinted with the permission of LEXIS-NEXIS, a division of Reed Elsevier, Inc. LEXIS-NEXIS are registered trademarks of Reed Elsevier Properties, Inc.; **118** © Steelcase Personal Harbor® Workspace. Photo courtesy of Steelcase, Inc.; **120** © Information Resources Inc.; **122** © Focus Vision Network, Inc.; **127 (both)** Twin Vision Productions, Inc.; **129** Courtesy of U.S. Small Business Association; **131** © Jane Lewis/Tony Stone Images.

Chapter 5 **139** Courtesy of Harley-Davidson, Inc.; **143 (both)** Reprinted with permission of McDonald's Corp.; **146** Reprinted with permission of Chevrolet; **148** Reprinted with permission of Lee Apparel Co., Inc. and Fallon McElligott; **149** © Bachmann/PhotoEdit; **150** © McCann Erikson Worldwide, Inc.; **154** Courtesy of Bell Sports & Goodby, Silverstein & Partners; **159** Photo courtesy of Gerber Products Company; **162** ©1997 Compaq Computer Corporation, Art Director: John Morten. Copywriter: Don Glassman. Artist: William Lowe.; **166** Courtesy of International Business Machines Corporation. Unauthorized use not permitted.; **171** Courtesy of GE Information Services.

Chapter 6 **178** © Richard Megna/Fundamental Photographs; **182 (both)** © Courtesy of Marriott Hotels; **185** © Steve Woit; **190** Reprinted with permission of Duck Head Apparel Company, Inc.; **192** Courtesy of Reddi-Wip; **197** © Claritas, Inc.; **198** © Shonna Valeska; **204** © Vosper Thornycroft (UK) Limited; **207** Reprinted with the permission of Porsche Cars North America, Inc.; **211** Reprinted with permission of Schott Corporation.

Chapter 7 **218** © Ed Quinn/SABA Press Photo, Inc.; **221** Reprinted with permis-

sion of Aaron Jones Studio; **223** Reprinted with permission of Service-Master; **225** © Ad Council; **228** Courtesy of Motorola, Inc.; **231 (top left)** Reproduced with permission of The Coca-Cola Company; **231 (top right)** Courtesy of International Business Machines Corporation. Unauthorized use not permitted.; **231 (bottom)** KODAK is a trademark of Eastman Kodak Company; **233** Courtesy of Warner Bros.; **235** © Martha Stanitz Photography; **236** Courtesy of Swiss Army Brand Sunglasses; **239 (both)** © Regis Bossu/Sygma; **242** © Mercedes-Benz of North America, Inc.; **245 (left)** © Robert Holmgren; **245 (right)** © The Service-Master Company; **248** Reprinted with the permission of Ritz–Carlton Hotel Company, L.L.C.; **250** Reprinted with permission of British Airways; **254** © Mushi Ahmed Photography.

Chapter 8 **260** © Ed Quinn/SABA Press Photo, Inc.; **264** Courtesy of U.S. Surgical Corp.; **265** © Toyota Motor Sales, USA, Inc.; **266** Courtesy of WD-40 Company; **270** © Shaw Industries, Inc.; **272** © Alternate Realities Corporation; **274** Reprinted with permission of Colgate International; **275** Courtesy Black & Decker; **280** © Frank Siteman/Stock Boston.

Chapter 9 **288** © Terry Wild Studio 1998; **291** Courtesy of Hewlett-Packard; **294** © Ann States/SABA Press Photos, Inc.; **296** Courtesy of Bicks Pickles; **302** Courtesy of Parker Pen Company. **305 (left)** © Rolex Watch USA, Inc.; **305 (right)** Reprinted with permission of Timex Corp. and Mitch Sondreaal, Ripsaw, Inc.; **307** Reprinted with permission of Infinity Systems, Inc.; **309 (both)** Courtesy of Zoo Doo Compost Company, Inc.; **312** © Blair Seitz/Photo Researchers, Inc.; **317** Courtesy of JEAN

PATOU, INC; **319** Reprinted with permission of Leo Burnett Company, Inc. and The Procter & Gamble Company.

Chapter 10 **327 (all)** Courtesy of Caterpillar® Inc.; **333** Reprinted with permission of Land's End, Inc.; **336** © Will Crocker; **338** Courtesy of AT&T; **340** © Cereal Partners U.K.; **341** Reprinted with permission of IBM Corporation; **343 (left)** © Lee Lockwood/Black Star; **343 (right)** © Michael Rizza/Stock Boston; **344** © Dan Rubin Medichrome The Stock Shop, Inc.; **346** © Charles Gupton/Stock Boston; **348, 349** Courtesy of GE Appliances; **355** Courtesy of Roadway Express; **360** Courtesy of Ryder Systems, Inc.

Chapter 11 **366 (both)** Courtesy Home Depot; **371 (both)** © Churchill & Klehr Photography; **373** © John Coletti/Stock Boston; **376 (left)** © Bill Horsman/Stock Boston; **376 (right)** © LearnRight Corporation; **378** © Tom McCarthy/Unicorn Stock Photos; **380 (left)** © Bradley Johnson/Advertising Age; **380 (right)** © Katherine Lambert; **384** © Owen Franken/Stock Boston; **386 (top)** © 800-Flowers, 1999; **386 (bottom)** Courtesy of Amazon.com, Inc.; **389** © Ernie Leyba; **391 (both)** Courtesy of Fleming Companies, Inc.; **395** Courtesy of McKesson Corp.

Chapter 12 **401** © Pam Francis/Southwest Airlines Co. **406** Photo courtesy of Hewlett-Packard Company and Microsoft Corporation; **409** © Jon Feingersh/Stock Boston; **412** Courtesy of State Farm In-surance Companies; **417 (both)** Courtesy of Bozell Worldwide, Inc.; **418, 419** Reprinted with permission of TBWA; **422 (left)** © Mark Elias/AP/World Wide Photos; **422 (center)** © Jamie Squire/Allsport Photography (USA), Inc.; **422 (right)** © Bill Kostroun/AP/World Wide Photos; **425 (top left)** © Rosenthal, Lynn, "Wrapped Cezanne Bus at West Facade," Philadelphia Museum of Art; **425 (bottom left)** © Jodi Buren/Woodfin Camp & Associates; **425 (right)** © George Rose/GammaLiaison, Inc.; **428** © 1997 The Gillette Company (USA), Inc.; **431** © GammaLiaison, Inc.; **433** Courtesy of Butterball Turkey Company.

Chapter 13 **439** Courtesy of Lear Corporation; **441 (top)** © Tony Stone Images; **441 (bottom left)** © Gabe Palmer/Stock Market; Page **446** Courtesy of DuPont; **454** © Rob Nelson/Black Star; **455** Courtesy of American Express; **458** © Jose Palaez Photography/The Stock Market; **463** Courtesy of Catalina Marketing Association; **465** © Lladro Collectors Society; **468** © Jeff Scheid/Gamma-Liaison, Inc.

Chapter 14 **474** Photograph courtesy of Dell Computer Corp. Photography by Wyatt McSpadden, Austin, TX; **477** © The Procter & Gamble Company. Used with permission; **480** Ted Morrison/Still Life Stock, Inc. Reprinted from June 3, 1996 issue of Business Week by special permission, copyright © 1996 by The McGraw-Hill Companies, Inc.; **484** © Churchill & Klehr Photography; **488** © Churchill & Klehr Photography; **490** © Charles Schwab & Company, Inc.; **491 (top)** © David Young Wolff/PhotoEdit; **491 (bottom)** © David Young Wolff/Tony Stone Images; **494** Courtesy of Pillsbury Corporation; **499** Courtesy of Tripod, Inc.; **502** Courtesy of American Standard.

Chapter 15 **512 (left)** © Jeffrey Aaronson/Network Aspen; **512 (right)** © Mark Peterson/SABA Press Photos, Inc.; **515 (top left)** © Jeffrey Aaronson/Network Aspen; **515 (top right)** AP/Wide World Photos; **515 (bottom left)** © Margot Granitsas/Photo Researchers, Inc.; **515 (bottom right)** © Greg Davis/Stock Market; **517** Courtesy of Dell; **520** © Wesley Bocxe/The Image Works; **522** © R. Lord/The Image Works; **524** © Prestige & Collections; **527** © Shelia Nardulli/Gamma-Liaison, Inc.; **531** © The Walt Disney Company; **533** © Douglas E. Curran/Agence France-Presse; **537** © Fritz Hoffman.

Chapter 16 **544** © Ben & Jerry's Homemade Holdings, Inc. 1998. Ben & Jerry's is trademark of Ben & Jerry's Homemade Holdings, Inc. Used with permission of Ben & Jerry's Homemade Holdings, Inc. 1999; **547** © Churchill & Klehr Photography; **550 (both)** © Enrico Ferorelli; **552 (both)** Courtesy of American Association of Advertising Agencies; **554** © California Private Transportation Company; **557** Courtesy of Campbell Soup Company; **560 (top)** Reprinted with permission of Church & Dwight Co., Inc.; **560 (bottom)** Reprinted with permission of McDonald's Corporation.; **567** © Saturn Corporation.

Company/Brand Name Index

Author Index

Subject Index